VISUAL COMPUTING FOR MEDICINE

VISUAL COMPUTING FOR MEDICINE

THEORY, ALGORITHMS, AND APPLICATIONS

SECOND EDITION

BERNHARD PREIM

CHARL BOTHA

ELSEVIER

AMSTERDAM • BOSTON • HEIDELBERG • LONDON
NEW YORK • OXFORD • PARIS • SAN DIEGO
SAN FRANCISCO • SINGAPORE • SYDNEY • TOKYO
Morgan Kaufmann is an imprint of Elsevier

MK MORGAN KAUFMANN

Acquiring Editor: Meg Dunkerley
Editorial Project Manager: Heather Scherer
Project Manager: Priya Kumaraguruparan
Designer: Mark Rogers

Morgan Kaufmann is an imprint of Elsevier
225 Wyman Street, Waltham, MA, 02451, USA

Library of Congress Cataloging-in-Publication Data
Application submitted

British Library Cataloguing-in-Publication Data
A catalogue record for this book is available from the British Library.

ISBN: 978-0-12-415873-3

Contents

PART II VISUALIZATION AND EXPLORATION OF MEDICAL VOLUME DATA

Acknowledgments

This book was only possible with substantial support from a number of people. First, we want to thank Meg Dunkerley, Heather Scherer, Laura Lewin, and Lauren Mattos from Elsevier for the kind and intensive cooperation starting from the draft of a book proposal to the final stages of writing. Timo Ropinski provided the chapter on advanced volume rendering, making his long-term experience in that area available to the readers. The CAS chapter is based on the significant foundations laid by Thomas Kroes, and is considered to be joint work with him.

Petra Schumann, Petra Specht, and Steffi Quade did proof-reading, improved images, and helped with the generation of indices. We are grateful to all members, past and present, of the (Medical) Visualization group of the Delft University of Technology, who have formed an effective and especially pleasant platform for stimulating research on a number of the topics discussed in this book. We are grateful to the whole visualization group in Magdeburg, in particular Alexandra Baer, Steven Birr, Rocco Gasteiger, Sylvia Glaßer, Kerstin Kellermann, Paul Klemm, Christoph Kubisch, Arno Krüger, Kai Lawonn, Jeanette and Tobias Mönch, Konrad Mühler, Steffen Oeltze, Zein Salah, and Christian Tietjen. Jana and Lars Dornheim as well as Ivo Rössling carried out most of the developmental work described in the chapter on ENT surgery. Simon Adler (Fraunhofer IFF Magdeburg) contributed to surgery simulation. A number of Master students did extraordinary work that is partially reflected in this book: Roland Pfisterer, Daniel Proksch, and Christoph Russ.

The book is largely based on their research; they helped to focus and streamline the discussion of their research results. A number of people from other institutions helped to improve the book primarily by carefully commenting on individual chapters: Christian Rössl and Holger Theisel from the Visual Computing Group (Univ. of Magdeburg), Sebastian Schäfer and Klaus D. Toennies (Image Processing group, Univ. of Magdeburg), Raimund Dachselt (User Interface group, Univ. of Magdeburg), Oliver Speck and Daniel Stucht (Biomedical Magnetic Resonance group, Univ. of Magdeburg), Axel Böse and Georg Rose (Medical Technology group, Univ. of Magdeburg), Philipp Berg, Gabor Janiga and Dominique Thevenin (Fluid Simulation group, Univ. of Magdeburg), Oliver Großer (Radiology group, University of Magdeburg), Werner Korb (University of Applied Sciences, Leipzig), Tobias Isenberg (INRIA-Saclay) and Stefan Schlechtweg (Univ. of Applied Sciences, Koethen), Volker Diehl, Volker Dicken, Christian Hansen, Anja Hennemuth, Jan Klein, and Felix Ritter from Fraunhofer MEVIS Bremen, Ragnar Bade, Tobias Boskamp, and Olaf Konrad from MeVis Medical Solutions, Julian Ang and Alf Ritter from Brainlab, Roy van Pelt and Anna Vilanova (TU Eindhoven), Ralph Brecheisen (Arcus Solutions), Christian Dick (TU Munich), Heinz Handels (Univ. of Luebeck), Stefan Weber (Univ. of Bern), Claes Lindström, (University Linköping), Nigel W. John (Bangor University).

Finally, we want to acknowledge our long-term medical collaborators that provided the motivation for the research described in this book: Andreas Böhm, Andreas Dietz, Stefan Müller, and Gero Strauß (University hospital), Christoph Arens, Oliver Beuing, Jörg Franke, Martin Skalej, Christian and Ulrich

Vorwerk (University hospital Magdeburg), Karl Oldhafer (Asklepios hospital Hamburg). We would also like to thank all our colleagues in The Netherlands, both medical and technical, from the Image Processing Division (LKEB), and the departments of Orthopedics, Radiology, Anatomy, and Surgery of the Leiden University Medical Center, and from the departments of Ophthalmology and of Neuroscience and Anatomy of the Erasmus Medical Center in Rotterdam, for the fruitful collaboration over the years.

A special and tender thanks to Uta Preim for providing feedback on all medical issues discussed in this book and for her complementary research, in particular on perfusion imaging.

Foreword to the Second Edition

Visual Computing for Medicine is an excellent textbook for students, researchers, and practitioners in the field of medical visualization. It is an authoritative resource for medical experts and technical personnel as well.

The book is the sequel to the highly successful first edition which immediately established itself as the reference work in this rather new and vibrant research topic in medical informatics. Dirk Bartz as one of the co-authors of the first edition unfortunately and untimely passed away in 2010. This left a sorely felt void in our community and prevented him from collaborating on the second edition.

This second edition provides a substantially updated, restructured, and extended view on the current state of the field. In a recent talk Donald Knuth, the preeminent computer scientist, was asked about relevant open research directions in computer science. After some reflections, he said that medical visualization was one of the important topics in this respect. This was good to hear, though he quickly (and regrettably) added that according to his opinion not many problems have been solved yet. I take the liberty to slightly disagree and put this textbook forward as compelling and written evidence to the contrary. And what an evidence it is! On over one-thousand pages the authors survey the intensive and rapid developments in our area. The relatively short period between first and second edition and the considerable amount of added material in extent and volume are very clear indications of the fast-paced evolution of visualization in medicine.

The book is concerned with diagnosis, treatment, and therapy planning with a focus on the currently most prevalent 2D and 3D imaging modalities. It thoroughly discusses the elaborate pipeline from data acquisition, analysis, and interpretation to advanced volume visualization and exploration techniques. Human computer interaction in the context of medical visualization has been covered in detail and encompasses significant topics like volume interaction, labeling, and measurement. Important application areas and advanced visualization techniques for blood vessels, virtual endoscopy, ENT surgery planning, perfusion, and diffusion data are extensively dealt with.

The book is very well structured, where the 22 chapters are grouped into five focal themes. The authors primarily organize the book according to techniques as most of these are applicable to a variety of medical tasks. Some of the material has been combined into completely new chapters like the one on projection-based medical visualization techniques. Hints at further readings at the end of each chapter point the interested reader to additional useful material not discussed within the chapter. Various advanced topics, which are of interest to the software engineer but are maybe too detailed for the general audience, are included in clearly marked break-out sections. The substantial reference list is another eloquent testimony of the breadth and depth of the topic.

The authors are highly recognized experts in the field of medical visualization. They have achieved the impressive feat of comprehensively covering a dynamic and rapidly emerging subject. The book provides informative, broad, and didactically well-organized information for specialists from diverse areas of expertise. The book will be the standard guide to medical visualization for years to come.

Dr. Eduard Gröller
Vienna University of Technology

Preface to the Second Edition

This second edition of "Visualization in Medicine" reflects the dynamic development of medical imaging, algorithmic processing and applications in medical research and clinical use after 2006. After the tragic passing of Dirk Bartz in March 2010, Charl Botha stepped in to prepare this new edition. In addition to careful rewriting of all chapters, we added a number of completely new chapters and reorganized and updated others significantly. Advances in imaging technology, e.g., hybrid devices, ultra high field MRI, intraoperative imaging, and the trend towards interventional procedures, are reflected in various parts of the book.

Since more and more advanced applications, e.g., in processing the complex multi-modal data of cardiac or neuroradiological MRI, have entered the stage of routine clinical use, human-computer interaction is becoming increasingly important. A comprehensive chapter was added to introduce HCI concepts with applications in medicine, incorporating recent interaction styles and technology. Also the chapter related to clinical practice was strongly extended by discussing also nuclear medicine, radiation treatment and medical team meetings in addition to the classical diagnostic settings.

Another essential trend is the combination of biomedical simulations with advanced visual exploration. As a consequence, we prepared a chapter that introduces basic techniques, such as the generation of simulation grids from medical imaging data and flow visualization, to explore the results. We study a number of specific applications, such as the simulation of blood flow to better predict the success of treatment options.

While the first edition of this book was focused on visual exploration, we have added discussions of data analysis techniques and their integration in what is widely called "visual analytics". This relates, e.g., to cluster analysis and dimension reduction. We discuss these techniques in relation to high-dimensional data, such as perfusion data and diffusion tensor imaging data. They are, however, also relevant for volume classification, the basic process of assigning transfer functions to medical volume data.

Computer-assisted surgery (CAS), one of the most essential applications for medical visualization technology, has matured in the last decade. We use experiences gained in the design and evaluation of such systems to prepare a general introductory chapter on CAS, followed by chapters treating selected application areas, such as orthopedics. Intraoperative imaging and intraoperative guidance have grown in importance in the last years. The chapter devoted to this topic was significantly extended, e.g., with techniques developed for soft-tissue surgery. Even the chapters discussing basic medical visualization techniques, such as surface and direct volume rendering, deserved a careful revision.

Among others, GPU-based techniques play a more prominent role now. GPU-based rendering enables a huge step in improving image quality without compromising performance. We discuss how these improvements are employed, e.g., in virtual endoscopy—another chapter that could be improved by taking advantage of many new and refined techniques.

The increasing size and complexity of medical image data motivated the development of visualization techniques that radically differ from the classical surface and volume rendering techniques. To convey the complex information of medical flow data along with the relevant anatomy, for example, benefits from illustrative techniques that render the anatomy sparsely. Thus, illustrative rendering plays a more prominent role in this second edition discussing the extraction of various features from medical volume data and related meshes as a basis for rendering.

A second radically new class of visualization techniques are map-based techniques. While some isolated techniques, such as stretched curved planar reformations of vascular structures, have been introduced more than a decade ago, we can now discuss this topic in a more general fashion in a separate chapter. DTI was rather new when the first edition was prepared. It is meanwhile a mature technique that is discussed in a wider scope as one out of several techniques to understand *brain connectivity*.

Medical education in anatomy, interventional radiology and surgery remains an important use case of visual computing. One comprehensive chapter is dedicated to such applications with a focus on recent trends, such as web-based training platforms, and (automatic) skills assessment.

Companion Website

Visit this book's companion website for this work: http://medvisbook.com/

Author Biography

PROF. DR.-ING. BERNHARD PREIM was born in 1969 in Magdeburg, Germany. He received the diploma in computer science in 1994 (minor in mathematics) and a Ph.D. in 1998 from the Otto-von-Guericke University of Magdeburg (Ph.D. thesis "Interactive Illustrations and Animations for the Exploration of Spatial Relations"). In 1999 he finished work on a German textbook on Human Computer Interaction which appeared at Springer. He then moved to Bremen where he joined the staff of MeVis (Center for Medical Diagnosis and Visualization Systems, Bremen). In close collaboration with radiologists and surgeons he directed the work on "computer-aided planning in liver surgery" focusing on virtual resection, automatic resection proposals, visualization of vascular structures, and the integration of measurements in 3D visualizations. This work was largely influenced by Prof. Heinz-Otto Peitgen, the founder and director of MEVIS. In June 2002 Bernhard Preim received the post-doctoral lecture qualification for computer science from the University of Bremen. Since Mars 2003 he is full professor for "Visualization" at the computer science department at the Otto-von-Guericke-University of Magdeburg, heading a research group which is focussed on medical visualization and applications in surgical education and surgery planning. The focus of this research is illustrative medical visualization, visual exploration of blood flow, virtual endoscopy, and in particular surgery in the ear, nose, throat region. These developments are summarized in a textbook Visualization in Medicine (Co-author Dirk Bartz). His continuous interest in HCI lead to another textbook "Interaktive Systeme" (Co-author: R. Dachselt) (Springer, 2010). His regular teaching activities include "Medical Visualization", "Computer-Assisted Diagnosis and Treatment" as well as the introductory courses on "Visualization" and "Interactive Systems".

Bernhard Preim founded the working group Medical Visualization in the German Society for Computer Science in 2003 and acted as speaker until 2012. He is also a long-term member of CURAC, the German society for computer-assisted surgery, where he became board member in 2007, and vicepresident in 2009. He was Co-Chair and Co-Organizer of the first and second Eurographics Workshop on Visual Computing in Biology and Medicine (VCBM, together with Charl Botha) and is now member of the steering committee of that workshop. He is the chair of the scientific advisory board of ICCAS (International Competence Center on Computer-Assisted Surgery, since 2010), member of the advisory boards of Fraunhofer Heinrich-Hertz-Institute, Berlin and the Institute for Innovative Surgical Training Technologies (ISTT), Leipzig. He is also regularly a Visiting Professor at the University of Bremen where he closely collaborates with Fraunhofer MEVIS. At the University of Magdeburg, Bernhard Preim is member of the Board (since 2008). Bernhard Preim is married with the radiologist Uta Preim (Medical Doctor), born Hahn and has two children.

DR. CHARL P. BOTHA graduated from the University of Stellenbosch, South Africa, in 1997 with a degree in electronics engineering, followed by an M.Sc. in digital signal processing, in 1999, and finally a Ph.D. in medical visualization from the Delft University of Technology (TU Delft) in the Netherlands, under the supervision of Frits Post, one of the pioneers of scientific visualization in Europe.

After completing his Ph.D., he was appointed (2006) and soon after tenured (2007) as an assistant professor of Visualization at the TU Delft, where he started and headed the medical visualization lab. He also had an appointment at LKEB, the medical image processing section of the Department of Radiology at the Leiden University Medical Center (LUMC), in order to cultivate and expand the fruitful research collaboration between the technical university and the academic hospital.

His research focused on surgical planning and guidance, and visual analysis for medical research. He has published on, among other topics, anatomical modeling, virtual colonoscopy, shoulder replacement, and diffusion tensor imaging. Together with Bernhard Preim he initiated the Eurographics Workshop series on Visual Computing for Biology and Medicine, acted as co-chair in 2008 and 2010, and served as editor together with Prof. Preim of the Computers and Graphics special issue on VCBM.

Prior to his Ph.D. he worked in industry designing embedded image processing systems and algorithms for two different companies. Shortly after the Ph.D., he co-founded Treparel Information Solutions, a company specializing in data mining, and he acts as science advisor to Clinical Graphics, a spin-off company founded by an ex-Ph.D. student to commercialize surgical planning research results. He recently also decided to make the move back into industry full-time, where he has started a company that focuses on bringing computer science, imaging, and visualization research into real-world practice. He remains actively involved with the medical visualization community through the MedVis.org website and its related resources. Charl is married to Stella Botha-Scheepers, MD, Ph.D., a rheumatologist and internist, with whom he has two children.

Chapter 01

Introduction

Visualization refers to the use of computer graphics techniques to create interactive visual representations of data, with the goal of amplifying human cognition. When visualization is applied to medical data, it is called *visualization in medicine*, or *medical visualization* for short.

Most medical data has an inherent spatial embedding. For this reason, medical visualization is seen as a special area of *scientific visualization*. The start of scientific visualization as a research field is considered by many to be the publication of the 1987 report of the NSF on Visualization in Scientific Computing [McCormick *et al.*, 1987]. However, literature reveals instances of medical visualization, following the definition we have set in the first paragraph, as far back as the 1960s.

In an early radiotherapy planning example, patient contours were acquired from line drawings with a mechanical digitizer, and then shown on an oscilloscope display combined with calculated isodose distributions, using a computer especially designed for this purpose [Cox *et al.*, 1966, Holmes, 1970]. Already then this system was put into clinical use. Sunguroff and Greenberg [1978] demonstrated the extraction and visualization of smooth 3D surfaces from CT data. By the end of the 1970s, McShan *et al.* [1979] had demonstrated the use of 3D graphics for radiotherapy planning. In the early 1980s, 3D visualization was being used clinically for the computer-based preoperative planning of craniofacial surgery [Vannier *et al.*, 1983b].

On the one hand, the long tradition of scientists that illustrate their work by carefully crafted graphics laid the foundation for both scientific and medical visualization. Anatomical illustration, starting with da Vinci's work, is a prominent example. On the other hand, medical visualization is based on computer graphics that provide algorithms for the efficient rendering of data, with additional influences coming from the world of image processing and medical image analysis.

1.1 VISUALIZATION IN MEDICINE AS A SPECIALTY OF SCIENTIFIC VISUALIZATION

Scientific visualization deals primarily with the visualization, exploration, and analysis of datasets arising from measurements or simulation of real world phenomena. The investigation of air flow around planes and cars is a well-known example. The underlying datasets of scientific visualizations are often very large, which makes it necessary to consider the efficiency and hence the time and space complexity of algorithms. Important goals and research scenarios of scientific visualization are:

- to explore data (undirected search without a specific hypothesis),
- to test a hypothesis based on measurements or simulations and their visualization, and
- the presentation of results.

There are many relevant examples in medical visualization that address these general visualization goals. Whether or not a patient is suffering from a certain disease is a hypothesis to be tested through clinical investigations and medical imaging. If a physician cannot sufficiently assess a disease based on the symptoms described by the patient and by clinical examinations, radiological image data might be

Visual Computing for Medicine, Second Edition. http://dx.doi.org/10.1016/B978-0-12-415873-3.00001-8

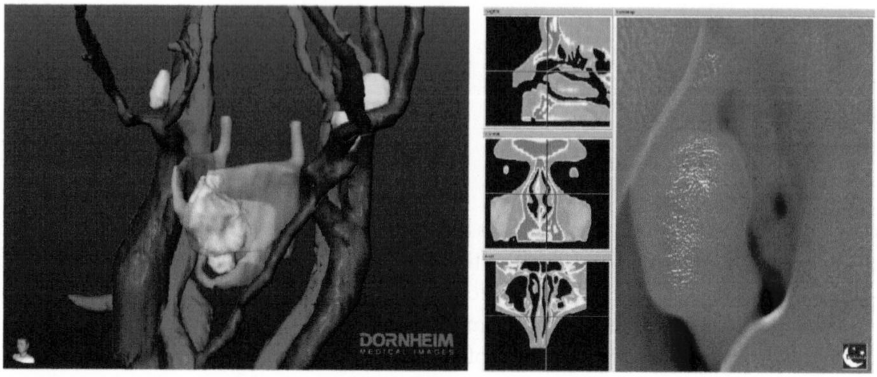

FIGURE 1.1 **Left:** *A 3D visualization of a neck tumor close to the larynx helps to decide on the resection strategy. A possible larynx infiltration is essential to decide whether the larynx can be preserved.* **Right:** *Virtual endoscopy of the paranasal sinus for preparing an endoscopic intervention aiming at polyp removal. With current graphics hardware, realistic rendering may be performed in real time (Courtesy of Dornheim Medical Images and Christoph Kubisch, University of Magdeburg).*

acquired without a specific hypothesis. Computer support, in particular image processing, quantitative image analysis, and visualization, may improve the radiologist's diagnosis.

Finally, if a radiologist has performed a diagnosis, specifying the stage and severity of a disease, certain visualizations are generated to present the diagnosis to the referring physician. Such visualization might include measurements, e.g., the extent of a pathological structure, and annotations, e.g., encircled regions or arrows, to enhance their interpretation. The ultimate goal of such visualizations and the attached report is to support *treatment decisions*. The presentation goal is also relevant for medical visualizations. Visualizations are generated to be discussed among colleagues, e.g., in a tumor board meeting, to employ them for educational purposes or as part of a publication. Figure 1.1 shows images which have been generated for surgical planning in ear, nose, and throat surgery.

There are several lessons from scientific visualization literature that are inspiring for the design of medical visualization systems. The most important is to consider visualization as a *process* directed at the understanding of data. "The purpose of visualization is insight, not pictures," as McCormick *et al.* [1987] state in their field-defining report on scientific visualization. Thus, it is essential to understand what kind of "insight" particular users want to achieve. For medical visualization systems, an in-depth understanding of diagnostic processes, therapeutic decisions, and of intraoperative information needs, is indispensable to provide dedicate computer support. It is also essential to consider organizational and technical constraints, such as sterility and space restrictions in an operating room.

Another consequence is that *interaction* plays a crucial role in the design of medical visualization systems. Interaction facilities should support the user in navigating within the data, in selecting relevant portions during exploration, in comparing data from different regions or different datasets, in the adjustment and fine-tuning of visualization parameters that define after all the optical properties observable by a human. The whole exploration process should support the interpretation and classification of the data. Examples for this classification in the medical domain are statements such as "The patient suffers from a certain disease in a particular stage," "The patient can be treated by a certain intervention. A particular surgical strategy was selected." Medical visualization is primarily based on 3D volume data. Our discussion of interaction facilities therefore has a focus on 3D interaction techniques that enable the flexible and efficient exploration of 3D data.

Regarding scientific and medical visualization as an analysis process leads to the conclusion that image generation and visual exploration are not the only way to get "insight." Equally important are tools to analyze the data, for example, to characterize the distribution of numerical values in certain regions of the data. Radiological workstations and therapy planning software systems therefore integrate functionality to derive quantitative information concerning the underlying data.

One important aspect that we should keep always in mind are the *limitations* of the data. These limitations define conditions for interpretation and analysis. Specific structures (i.e., tumors) may not show up at their full size. Other structures are so small, that their analysis might lead to a high error rate, or is highly subjective. Being aware of such limitations is therefore an important key to the successful application of the methods.

1.2 COMPUTERIZED MEDICAL IMAGING

Medical visualization deals with the analysis, visualization, and exploration of medical image data. The main application areas are:

- *Diagnosis.* The diagnosis of radiological data benefits from interactive 2D and 3D visualizations. In particular, if the situation of a particular patient is very unusual (complex fractures, defective positions), 3D visualizations are useful to get an overview of the morphology. More and more, functional and dynamic image data are employed to assess effects, such as blood perfusion or contrast agent enhancement, and metabolism. Various measures are derived from these image data. Appropriate visualizations depict the spatial correlation between these measurements.
- *Treatment planning.* Interactive 3D visualizations of the relevant anatomical and pathological structures may enhance the planning of surgical interventions, radiation treatment, and minimally-invasive interventions. The spatial relations between pathological lesions and life-critical structures at risk may be evaluated better with 3D visualizations. Starting with early work on craniofacial surgery planning [Vannier *et al.*, 1985], the visualization of anatomical structures has been steadily improved due to the progress in image acquisition, graphics and computing hardware, and better rendering. Visualizations may also include information which is not present in radiological data, such as the simulated dose distribution for radiation treatment planning and simulated territories of vascular supply. Treatment planning systems have found their way to many applications, for instance in orthopedic surgery, neurosurgery, abdominal surgery, and craniofacial surgery.
- *Intraoperative support.* Medical visualization based on 3D data is finding increasing application in the operating room. Preoperatively acquired images and intraoperative images are integrated to provide support during an intervention. Flexible and smart displays are needed for such applications (see Fig. 1.4 and Hansen [2012]).
- *Documentation.* Reporting and other documentation tasks benefit from the incorporation of representative visualizations. These visualizations are often annotated with labels and measurements to provide the necessary information to interpret the images. Quantitative analysis of image features, such as tumor extent, may help to fill data necessary for documentation.
- *Educational purposes.* Visualization techniques are the core of anatomy and surgery education systems. As an example, the VoxelMan, an advanced anatomy education system, combines high-quality surface and volume rendering with 3D interaction facilities and a knowledge base to support anatomy education [Höhne *et al.*, 2003]. More recently surgical simulators were developed on top of these 3D renderings. They support the acquisition and rehearsal of specific skills using tactile input devices

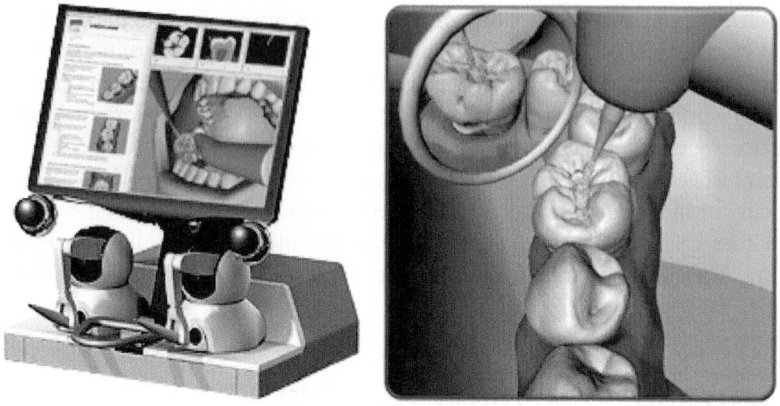

FIGURE 1.2 **Left:** 3D visualizations of the dental anatomy as a basis for training drilling procedures. **Right:** Tactile input devices are employed to provide an experience that is similar to real treatment. With the VoxelMan dental simulator, it is also possible to automatically assess the skills of the trainee (Courtesy Institute for Mathematics and Computer Science, University Hospital Hamburg-Eppendorf).

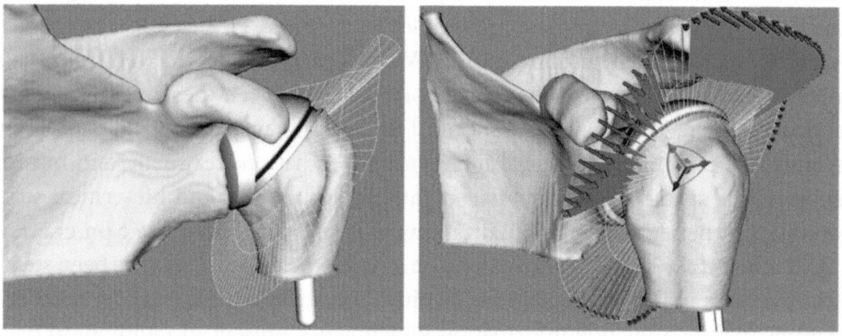

FIGURE 1.3 **Left:** The patient's shoulder anatomy is reconstructed from CT data and shown along with a joint implant and the simulated range of motion after treatment. **Right:** The range of motion corresponding to the current implant position is compared with the pretreatment range of motion. The comparative visualization highlights the sign and the extent of the changes (Courtesy of Peter Krekel, Clinical Graphics).

and appropriate models of tissue deformation (see Fig. 1.2) More and more, surgical training is performed in special institutions that employ physical and virtual models (see Fig. 1.6).

- *Medical research.* While some kinds of medical image data, e.g., 4D measured blood flow, are (still) too complex for regular clinical use, they are crucial for medical research. In research settings, time is not that strongly limited. Flexible exploration of the data is more important than strict guidance along a workflow. Moreover, in new kinds of applications, there is no defined clinical workflow, (e.g., in studying biomechanical parameters, see Fig. 1.3).

The computer support described above is not intended to replace medical doctors. Instead, physicians should be supported and assisted to perform their tasks more efficiently and/or with increased quality.

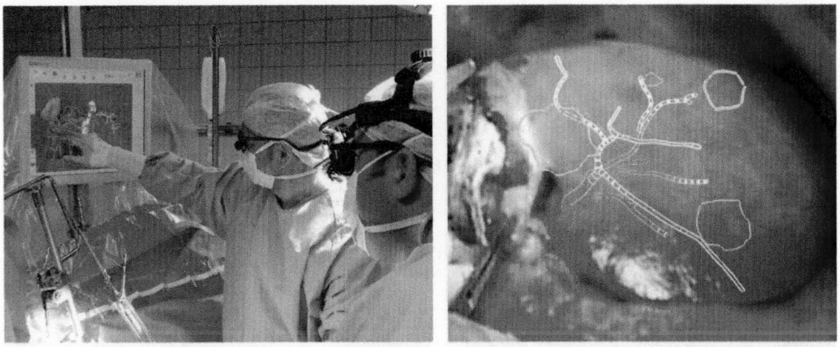

FIGURE 1.4 **Left:** *Preoperative planning information is provided in the operating room.* **Right:** *With appropriate image registration, essential planning data may be overlaid on current intraoperative images. In the specific example, hepatic vasculature is shown in an illustrative style on top of the liver surface (Courtesy of Christian Hansen, Fraunhofer MEVIS Bremen).*

Medical Image Data The data, on which medical visualization methods and applications are based, are acquired with scanning devices, such as computed tomography (CT) and magnetic resonance imaging (MRI). These devices have experienced an enormous development in the last 20 years. Although other imaging modalities, such as 3D ultrasound, positron emission tomography (PET), and imaging techniques from nuclear medicine are available, CT and MRI dominate due to their high resolution and their good signal-to-noise-ratio. The image resolution has increased considerably, with the introduction of Multislice CT devices in 1998. Also, the acquisition times have decreased—this development contributes to the quality of medical volume data because motion and breathing artifacts are reduced considerably. The acquisition of time-dependent volume data, which depict dynamic processes in the human body, has been improved with respect to spatial and temporal resolution. Today, also intraoperative imaging becomes a common practice to support difficult interventions, for example, in neurosurgery. Moreover, radiology interventions involving catheters, needles, applicators, and stents, crucially depend on frequent or even real-time imaging to control the position of these instruments and monitor treatment. With the improved quality and wide availability of medical volume data, new and better methods to extract information from such data are feasible and needed.

MRI data experienced a similar development. With improved motion correction and artifact reduction techniques, image quality increased strongly. High-field MRI, such as 7 or even 9.4 Tesla scanners, are expensive and rather rare research installations, but they enable the investigation of future routine possibilities. Figure 1.5 shows images of neurovascular structures that benefit from the high signal-to-noise-ratio of a 7 Tesla MRI scanner (compared to similar images acquired with a 3 Tesla scanner).

Today, a radiologist uses software instead of conventional lightboxes and films to establish a diagnosis. The development of monitors with a sufficient resolution in terms of gray values and spatial resolution was an essential prerequisite for the clinical application of image analysis and visualization techniques. Contrast and brightness may be adjusted with digital image data. This often allows the interpretation of images in a convenient manner even if the data acquisition process was not optimal. More convenient handling, such as touch-based interaction, is further increasing widespread acceptance.

With the increased resolution of the image data, reliable measurements can be derived. For instance, cross-sectional areas and volumes of certain structures can be determined with a reasonable amount of certainty. Measurements of cross-sectional areas are valuable in the diagnosis of vascular diseases (detection of stenosis and aneurysms). Volume measurements of pathological structures are of high relevance to assess

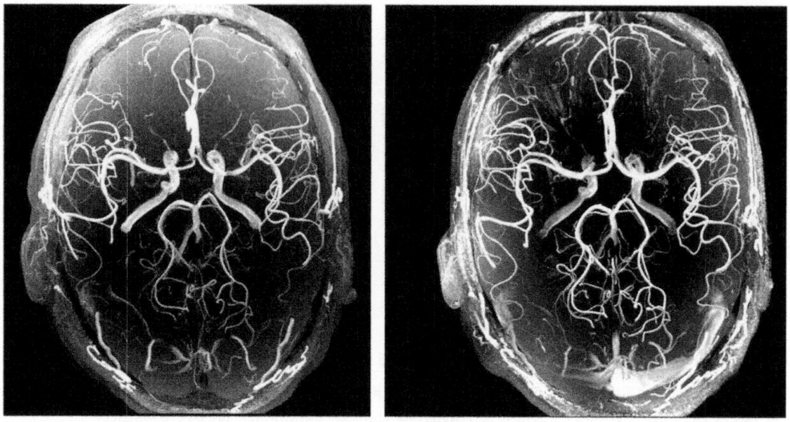

FIGURE 1.5 *A maximum-intensity projection of MRI data with a protocol that emphasizes vascular structures.* **Left:** *Data are acquired with a 3 Tesla scanner.* **Right:** *Data of the same patient acquired with a 7 Tesla scanner and similar settings for the visualization. The data acquired with the 7 Tesla scanner exhibit a better signal-to-noise-ratio but include also venous structures which is often not desired (Courtesy of Daniel Stucht, Biomedical Magnetic Resonance Group, University of Magdeburg).*

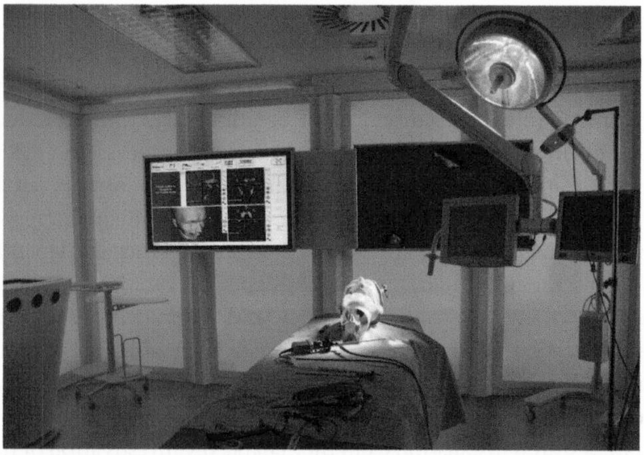

FIGURE 1.6 *The surgical planning unit supports the immediate preparation as well as the training of a surgical intervention. High-resolution displays enable a precise rehearsal of preoperatively acquired data (Courtesy of ICCAS Leipzig and KARL STORZ GmbH & Co. KG Tuttlingen).*

the success of a therapy. However, the quality of these measurements depends heavily on the quality of the image data. Specific artifacts (i.e., flow artifacts in MR angiography) may reduce the accuracy significantly.

Note that image analysis and visualization may provide comprehensible views of the data, but the results strongly depend on the original data. Physicians tend to overestimate what can be achieved by processing data with sophisticated algorithms. It is important to cultivate realistic expectations in users. If physicians complain about the results of medical visualization, the problem is often due to deficiencies in the image acquisition process. Structures with a 2 mm diameter cannot be reliably displayed with data that exhibits a 2 mm slice thickness, for example. It is essential that the requirements are stated precisely and that the scanning parameters of the image acquisition are adapted to these requirements.

The increased resolution and improved quality of medical image data also has a tremendous effect on therapy planning. With high-quality data, smaller structures—for example blood vessels and nerves, whose locations are often crucial in the treatment—can be reliably detected. In some cases, this can lead to a better decision of whether or not a particular disease can be successfully treated through surgery, for example whether or not a malignant tumor can be removed entirely. Still, too often such decisions have to be made intraoperatively. In so-called *explorative resections*, the body is opened and surgery starts to expose the relevant structure to determine whether or not the intervention is feasible. If a resection needs to be cancelled, the patient has been needlessly subjected to a potentially risky intervention. Visualization and computer support for treatment planning aim at reducing such unfavorable situations.

Improvements in Software Support Within the last years, the number of toolkits that directly support medical image analysis and visualization applications has increased significantly. Also the quality of these toolkits has improved, in terms of robustness, functionality, and performance. Among these toolkits are open source software systems, such as DeVIDE (http://graphics.tudelft.nl/Projects/DeVIDE) and Voreen (http://www.voreen.org/), and freely available closed-source systems such as MeVisLab (http://www.mevislab.de/), that enable, e.g., students and academic researchers to make rapid progress and focus on the problems of specific application areas [Botha and Post, 2008, Meyer-Spradow *et al.*, 2009, Ritter *et al.*, 2011].

1.3 2D AND 3D VISUALIZATIONS

Medical imaging started with X-ray imaging at the end of the 19th century. Since that time, diagnosis has been performed by inspecting X-ray films, or more recently, digital X-ray images. With the advent of computed tomography, many slices showing X-ray absorption in a particular region of the body have to be inspected. Slice-by-slice inspection of medical volume data is still common practice. Despite all the efforts to accelerate volume rendering, to employ high-quality reconstruction filters and to ease the adjustment of the necessary parameters, the inspection of 2D slices in radiology is still dominant. A typical explanation of this phenomenon is the assumed ability of a radiologist to mentally fuse the 2D slices in a 3D representation. This ability, however, is not generally accepted and is disputed even between radiologists. In particular, in the case of complex anatomical structures, such as the ear, and in the case of severe fractures or pathological abnormalities, a pure slice-based analysis is probably not adequate [Rodt *et al.*, 2002].

The dominant use of slice data is often attributed to radiological tradition. Well-established techniques are preferred despite obvious disadvantages compared to more recent techniques. However, a thorough analysis of radiological workflows reveals that there are still real benefits of using slice-by-slice inspection. In 2D views of the slices, each and every voxel can be seen and selected (for example to inquire the density value). 2D slice views support precise exploration and analysis of the data. Therefore, radiologists are also legally obliged to inspect every slice. Volume rendering or other 3D visualization, on the other hand, provide an *overview*. Radiologists use such overviews, for example, if very unfamiliar spatial relations occur, for example, to assess complex fractures. While radiologists rarely rely on 3D visualizations, physicians who carry out interventions (radiation therapy, surgery) strongly benefit from interactive and dynamic 3D visualizations. On the one hand, they do not have the radiological training to mentally imagine complex structures based on a stack of cross-sectional views. On the other hand, they have to understand the 3D spatial relations better than radiologists. While radiologists "only" describe the data the surgeon actually intervenes in the spatial relations with all the consequences this might have.

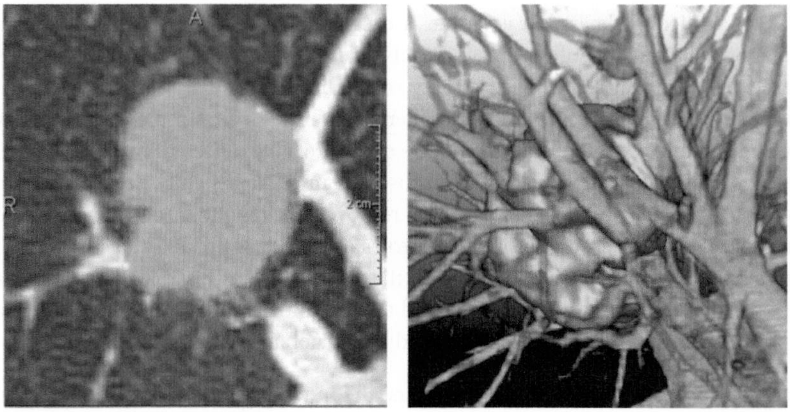

FIGURE 1.7 **Left:** *A lung nodule was segmented and is emphasized as overlay in a slice-based visualization. The quality of the segmentation and the relation between the tumor and the surroundings in this slice are clearly visible.* **Right:** *The same lung nodule is shown in a 3D rendering which provides an overview of the nodule's shape and its location in relation to the surrounding bronchial tree (Courtesy of Jan-Martin Kunigk, Fraunhofer MEVIS Bremen).*

Integration of 2D and 3D Visualizations In summary, 2D and 3D visualization techniques are needed. They should be considered independent presentations of radiology data, but should be connected closely, e.g., by synchronizing interaction facilities and display parameters, such as colors. While 3D techniques often provide a more comprehensible overall picture, 2D slice-oriented techniques typically allow a more accurate examination, and hence processing. The integration of slices or parts thereof in a 3D visualization may provide a reference to better understand the 3D spatial relations [Rodt *et al.*, 2002]. An example of a simultaneous employment of 2D and 3D visualizations is shown in Figure 1.7.

1.4 FURTHER INFORMATION

This book hopefully provides the reader with much useful information. However, at least for the in-depth practical or research problems, further information is certainly essential. We provide a paragraph "Further Reading" at the end of each chapter pointing to relevant publications not discussed within the chapter. The selection of these publications is based on relevance, quality, and availability.

To obtain information that is more recent than this book, we shall give some general hints. The leading visualization conferences *IEEE Visualization*, *EuroVis* and more recently *IEEE PacificVis* usually contain one or two "Medical Visualization" sessions. The journals *IEEE Transactions on Visualization and Graphics* and *Computer Graphics Forum* also contain high-quality research results in medical visualization. Medical imaging conferences, such as MICCAI, CARS, and SPIE Medical imaging have a focus on image analysis and medical applications but not on medical visualization algorithms and technology. Occasionally, intraoperative treatment support is covered there.

In the last decade, a small but coherent medical visualization community arose. Its most notable achievement is the Eurographics workshop series *Visual Computing in Biology and Medicine*[1] that was initiated in 2008. Even before that, two prizes were initiated that are awarded bi-annually. The EUROGRAPHICS Medical price was initiated in 2003 and is now named the Dirk Bartz Medical Prize to honor the co-author

1 http://vcbm.org/.

of the first edition of this book. The Karl-Heinz Höhne Award for Medical Visualization, honoring the pioneer of medical visualization, was initiated in 2004. Both competitions attract a reasonable spectrum of high-quality medical visualization research that is available online and worth looking at. Finally, we recommend the MedVis blog[2] that provides event reports, links to recent papers and videos. This blog will be used to inform our readers of new research related to the book, and to classify such new research according to the book's structure.

Finally, *datasets* are essential for evaluating medical visualization algorithms. There are various repositories where data may be downloaded via the internet, e.g., http://www.osirix-viewer.com/datasets/and http://www.volvis.org/. The Osirix-repository is more recently updated and contains even combined PET/CT datasets.

1.5 ORGANIZATION

A book on medical visualization may be structured primarily according to medical disciplines and tasks, e.g., diagnostic and treatment processes or according to analysis, visualization and interaction techniques. We chose an organization primarily guided by techniques, since most techniques are applicable to a large variety of tasks in medicine. Selected application areas are discussed within several chapters to discuss how the techniques contribute to these specific problems. As an example, we describe the peculiarities of cardiovascular imaging in the medical imaging chapter. Later we discuss, image analysis techniques, such as segmentation and registration, for these specific image data. Based on this discussion, we explain how advanced rendering techniques may be applied to reveal important features of the morphology of cardiac vessels and in further chapters, we discuss how the perfusion in such vessels is measured, analyzed, and visualized and how blood flow is investigated and interpreted as a further essential information for diagnosis diseases of the cardiovascular system. In a similar way, the diagnosis and treatment of tumor diseases plays an essential role in many chapters. The selection of these application areas is not only based by didactic criteria, but primarily by their socio-economic importance, that is by the prevalence and severity of diseases.

This book is structured into five parts.

Part I starts with an introduction into the characteristics of discrete data organized in (uniform) Cartesian grid datasets with scalar values, which is the typical structure of medical image data. In Chapter 2 we introduce the imaging modalities with a focus on computed tomography (CT) and magnetic resonance imaging (MRI) and an overview on other modalities, such as PET, SPECT, and Ultrasound. Chapter 3 deals with the clinical use of medical image data in radiology, radiation treatment planning, and surgery. The software used for the analysis of medical volume data must be carefully integrated in the information processing environment in hospitals and dedicated to usage scenarios, such as patient consult, tumor board discussions, diagnosis, treatment planning, treatment monitoring, and documentation.

This chapter is followed by an overview of medical image analysis (Chap. 4). It illustrates selected image analysis tasks and results. Image segmentation, the identification, and delineation of relevant structures is the focus of this chapter since visualization and many interaction techniques benefit from image segmentation.

We continue with an introduction to human computer interaction (HCI) focusing on the analysis of tasks in a user-centered way, on prototyping solutions and on 3D interaction including a discussion of

2 http://medvis.org/.

3D input devices (Chap. 5). The recent trend toward mobile computing and gesture-based interaction is essential for medical applications, e.g., for bedside use of medical image data. Thus, we carefully discuss the basics and medical applications of this technology.

Part II is devoted to the visualization of medical volume data and to basic interactions with them. Hardware and software aspects, quality, and speed of algorithms are discussed. Volume data can be visualized by directly projecting the data to the screen (direct volume rendering, DVR) or by generating an intermediate representation, which is subsequently rendered (indirect volume rendering). Chapter 6 is devoted to surface-based visualization. Isosurfaces are based on an isovalue selected by the user and display the surface that connects all elements of a volume dataset where this isovalue occurs. Chapter 7 provides an introduction to direct volume rendering including different rendering pipelines and compositing techniques. Chapter 8 describes advanced volume rendering techniques, in particular volume illumination and other techniques that enable an improved shape and depth perception.

After the introduction of volume visualization techniques, we discuss *volume interaction* (Chap. 9). This includes advanced transfer function design for volume rendering. Without dedicated support, users have to experiment with many possible transfer function settings before an appropriate specification is found. We also discuss clipping and virtual resection. Clipping, virtual resection, and transfer function design are often combined to specify which parts of the data should be displayed.

As another area that deals with the interactive use of medical volume data, we consider labeling and measurement techniques in Chapter 10. Labels and measurements are special kinds of annotations that enhance medical visualizations for diagnosis and particularly for documentation. The integration of these components raises issues of visual design, e.g., appropriate use of layout strategies, color, fonts, and line styles to provide a clear representation of medical image data and related annotations. The qualitative analysis of spatial relations is added through measurements that may directly support treatment decisions. The size and extent of a tumor strongly influences applicable therapies. The angle between bony structures may influence whether the anatomy is regarded as normal or whether treatment is necessary. Interactive measurements and automatic measurements which employ segmentation information are covered.

Part III "Advanced visualization techniques" starts with the visualization of anatomical tree structures, such as vascular structures (Chap. 11). We describe different methods that produce comprehensible visualizations at different levels of detail and accuracy. While this chapter was restricted to surface-based visualizations in the first edition, we shortened their treatment and provide instead more detail on volume rendering techniques, tailored, e.g., for the diagnosis of vascular diseases.

In Chapter 12, illustrative rendering and emphasis techniques are described. These techniques are essential for medical education and for therapy planning. One scenario is that the user selects an object via its name from a list and this object will be highlighted in the related visualization. In general, emphasis is difficult to carry out because most objects are at least partially occluded.

Chapter 13 is devoted to virtual endoscopy. Virtual endoscopy is inspired by real endoscopic procedures that are carried out for diagnosis (e.g., detection of polyps in the colon) or as minimally-invasive intervention. In real endoscopy, a small camera is inserted in the human body through small incisions or anatomical openings (e.g., the colon) and it is moved to inspect vascular structures or structures filled with air. In virtual endoscopy, similar images are produced through 3D visualization, on the basis of medical volume data. Virtual endoscopy has a great potential for surgery training and treatment planning, as well as for diagnosis and intraoperative navigation, because it has less restrictions than real endoscopy (the virtual camera can go everywhere) and is more comfortable for the patient. Visualization and navigation techniques in the virtual human are the issues which are discussed in this chapter.

In the next chapter, we discuss "Projection-based Medical Visualization Techniques" (Chap. 14). This chapter is another completely new chapter compared to the first edition and it is motivated by a variety of successful applications that incorporate map-like projections. Vessel flattening, brain and colon flattening, tumor maps, Bull's Eye plots in cardiology are just some of the examples, where 3D geometries are transformed to map projections to give an overview. Such projections from a higher to a lower dimensional space are related with distortions and a loss of information. We carefully discuss different strategies and their limitations.

Part IV discusses the visualization of high-dimensional medical image data. Thus, in this part we consider time-dependent data, and 3D vector and tensor data.

A special variation of MRI is Diffusion Tensor Imaging (DTI). With this modality, the inhomogeneity of the direction of (water) diffusion can be non-invasively determined. Strongly directed diffusion occurs for example in the whiter matter of the human brain, and thus indicates the direction and location of fiber tracks. This information is highly relevant, in particular in neuroradiology and neurosurgery. The analysis and visualization of DTI data poses many challenges, which are discussed in Chapter 15. In contrast to the first edition, we extend the scope here and consider DTI just one method to explore brain connectivity.

Chapter 16 describes techniques to explore and analyze perfusion data, a special instance of time-dependent volume data. These data have a great potential for medical diagnosis, e.g., for the assessment of tumors, where malignant tumors exhibit a stronger vascularization than benign tumors. This effect cannot be observed in static images. Techniques for the efficient visualization and analysis of such data are important, because the huge amount of dynamic volume data cannot be evaluated without dedicated software support.

Part V "Treatment planning, guidance and training" covers specific application areas and case studies related to ear-, nose-, and throat surgery. In Chapter 17, we discuss general requirements and solution strategies for computer-assisted surgery. Chapter 18 is dedicated to intraoperative visualization, image-guided surgery, and augmented reality in surgery. Here we will discuss how medical image data is integrated with an intervention itself. We discuss simple techniques that just provide access to medical image data intraoperatively and more advanced techniques combining pre and intraoperative imaging data similar to a car navigation system. The constraints of intraoperative use, interaction techniques appropriate in these settings and limitations with respect to setup times and accuracy will be carefully considered. We go on and discuss the visual exploration of medical flow data, resulting from measurements or simulations (Chap. 19) with a focus on blood flow data, a very active research area in recent years that also is relevant for medical treatment planning, e.g., neurovascular intervention and surgery.

In Chapter 20, we discuss image analysis and visualization for ENT surgery planning (neck dissection, endoscopic sinus surgery). Task analysis and evaluation are carefully described to provide orientation for the development of similar systems. In Chapter 21, the use of medical visualization techniques for educational purposes, in particular for anatomy and surgery education is discussed. Besides describing application areas, this chapter introduces some new techniques, such as labeling and animation of medical volume data, collision detection, and soft tissue deformation for surgical simulation.

Part I

Acquisition, Analysis, and Interpretation of Medical Volume Data

The first part contains introductory chapters for all most topics treated in this book.

In Chapter 2, we introduce the imaging modalities with a focus on computed tomography (CT) and magnetic resonance imaging (MRI) and an overview on other modalities, such as PET, SPECT, and Ultrasound. We aim at a balance between basic aspects of medical imaging and recent developments, such as Dual Source CT, ultra high field MRI, and integrated PET/CT devices. We also discuss intraoperative imaging, a topic that becomes increasingly important to support interventions and minimally-invasive surgery. This chapter should make the reader familiar with the data that serve as input for all kinds of medical visualization.

Chapter 3 deals with the clinical use of medical image data in radiology, radiation treatment planning, and surgery. As background, we describe the conventional reading process of radiologists and later how *soft-copy reading* may enhance the classic process. The software used for the analysis of medical volume data must be carefully integrated in the information processing environment in hospitals and dedicated to usage scenarios such as patient consult, tumor board discussions, diagnosis, treatment planning, treatment monitoring, and documentation. We use this chapter also to introduce some 3D visualization techniques, not to discuss how they work, but to discuss their value as an addition to slice-based viewing.

This chapter is followed by an overview of medical image analysis (Chap. 4). It illustrates selected image analysis tasks and results starting with noise reduction and other preprocessing techniques. Image segmentation, the identification and delineation of relevant structures is the focus of this chapter since visualization and many interaction techniques benefit from image segmentation. We also discuss *registration*, the process that aligns different datasets in one coordinate system. Registration is needed to integrate image data from different modalities, or different points in time, e.g., pre- and intraoperative images. Validation is a crucial aspect in image analysis.

We continue with an introduction to human computer interaction (HCI) focusing on the analysis of tasks in a user-centered way, on prototyping solutions, and on 3D interaction including a discussion of 3D input devices (Chap. 5). Scenario descriptions and workflow analysis represent the core of task analysis. Analysis of users is also discussed with a focus on *Personas*. The recent trend toward mobile computing and gesture-based interaction is essential for medical applications, e.g., for bedside use of medical image data. Thus, we carefully discuss the basics and medical applications of this technology.

Visual Computing for Medicine, Second Edition. http://dx.doi.org/10.1016/B978-0-12-415873-3.00030-4

Chapter 02

Acquisition of Medical Image Data

2.1 INTRODUCTION

Medical image data are acquired for different purposes, such as diagnosis, therapy planning, intraoperative navigation, post-operative monitoring, and biomedical research. Before we start with the description of medical imaging modalities, we briefly discuss major requirements that guide the selection of imaging modalities in practice:

- the relevant anatomy must be depicted completely,
- the resolution of the data should be *sufficient* to answer specific diagnostic and therapeutic questions,
- the image quality with respect to contrast, signal-to-noise ratio (SNR) and artifacts must be *sufficient* to interpret the data with respect to diagnostic and therapeutic questions,
- exposure and burden to the patient and to the medical doctor should be minimized, and
- costs should be limited.

Thus, neither optimum spatial resolution nor optimum image quality are relevant goals in clinical practice. As an example, a CT examination with high radiation dose in very high spatial resolution optimizes imaging with respect to resolution and image quality but fails to meet the minimum exposure criterion and may lead to higher costs, since a large dataset has to be archived and transferred over a network with often only moderate bandwidth.

In this chapter we focus on tomographic imaging modalities, in particular on CT and MRI data. Hybrid PET/CT and PET/MRI scanners are an exciting development of the last decade. We discuss them as examples for the potential of the complementary use of imaging data and the necessity to fuse the resulting information.

We will discuss examples where the image data are applied. Thus, it becomes obvious that a variety of imaging modalities is required to "answer" various diagnostic questions. The discussion includes recent developments, such as High-field MRI. We explain what is technically feasible along with the clinical motivation and use for these developments.

Organization We start with a general discussion of medical image data and their properties (§ 2.2) and continue with basic signal processing relevant for medical image acquisition (§ 2.3). The discussion of medical imaging modalities starts with an overview on X-ray imaging (§ 2.4). X-ray images were the first medical image data exposing information about inner structures inside the human body and it is still by far the most used image modality in modern health care. We will also discuss various flavors of X-ray imaging, such as angiography and rotational X-ray. We continue with a description of CT data acquisition, which is based on the same physical principle, but represents a tomographic modality generating volume data (§ 2.5). The second widespread tomographic modality is Magnetic Resonance Imaging (MRI), which is described in § 2.6. This versatile imaging modality exploits the different characteristics of human tissue in magnetic fields. Although most of the applications and algorithms presented in this book are based on CT and MRI data, we also introduce other modalities, which have a great importance in clinical practice and might be used more intensively in the future in computer-assisted diagnosis and therapy planning systems.

Visual Computing for Medicine, Second Edition. http://dx.doi.org/10.1016/B978-0-12-415873-3.00002-X

In § 2.7, we describe the principle of ultrasound generation. Finally, Positron Emission Tomography (PET) and Single Photon Emission Computed Tomography (SPECT) as the most wide-spread imaging modalities in nuclear medicine are described (§ 2.8).

2.2 MEDICAL IMAGE DATA

Medical image data is usually represented as a stack of individual images. A *modality* is a specific image acquisition technique, such as CT or MRI. Each image of a volume dataset represents a thin slice of the scanned body part and is composed of individual *pixels* (picture elements). These pixels are arranged on a 2D grid, where the distance between two pixels is typically constant in each direction. For most medical image modalities the horizontal (x) and vertical (y) directions have identical distances, which are called the *pixel distance*. A constant pixel distance allows the calculation of the actual position by multiplying the respective distance value with the respective pixel index i. If we assume that i is indexing the horizontal x position and j is indexing the vertical y position, the position of pixel $P_{i,j}$ is determined. Figure 2.1 (left) describes the 2D image grid arrangement.

Volumetric data combines images into a 3D grid (see Fig. 2.1, right). The data elements are called *voxels* (volume elements) and are located on the grid points. In addition to the horizontal and vertical dimensions, we also have a dimension representing the depth. The distance between two neighboring images (slices) is called *slice distance*. The three distances in every direction are also called *voxel spacing*. The position of a voxel $V_{i,j,k}$ is determined by the distance values and the voxel index (i, j, k) (Fig. 2.2).

If the pixel distance is identical to the slice distance, we speak of an *isotropic* grid or dataset. If this is not the case, we speak of an *anisotropic* grid. Most datasets in medical imaging are anisotropic and in many cases the slice distance is several times larger than the pixel distance (Fig. 2.2). Eight neighboring voxels which form a cuboid (see Fig. 2.1, right) are called a *volume cell* or short a *cell*.

This grid type is also called *cartesian* or *uniform* grid. Its special features are:

- constant or regular spacing in each dimension,
- regular geometry that can be computed by the grid index and the spacing,
- regular topology (it has the same connectivity for all grid points), and
- it is only composed of cuboid (volume) cells.

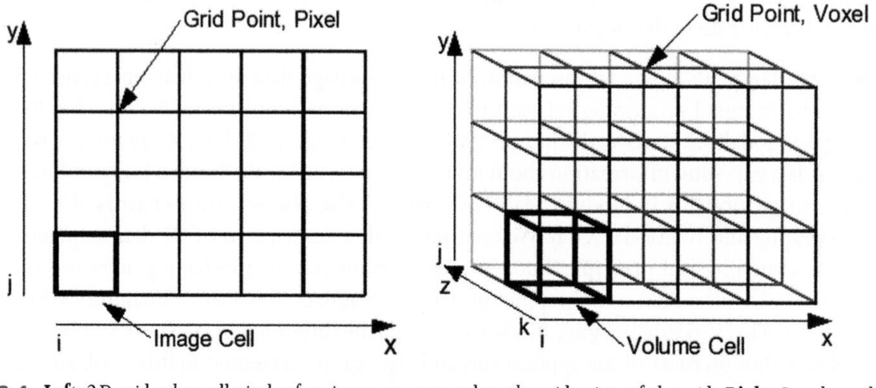

FIGURE 2.1 **Left:** *2D grid, where all pixels of an image are arranged on the grid points of the grid.* **Right:** *In volume datasets, the voxels are arranged on a 3D grid (Courtesy of Dirk Bartz, University of Leipzig).*

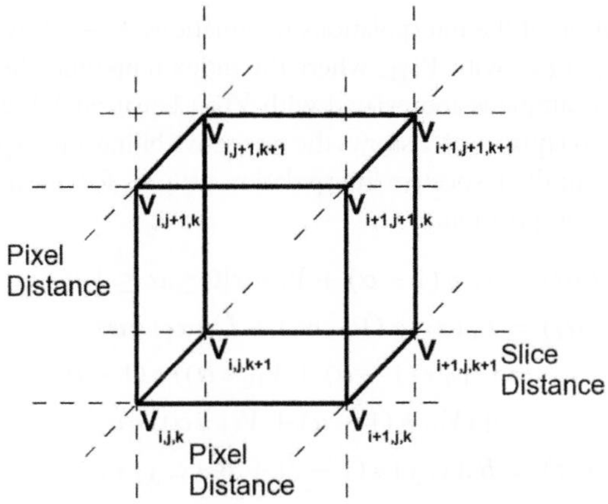

FIGURE 2.2 *Volume Cell: The indices i,j,k indicate the voxels that span the volume cell. Pixel distances are the spaces between the voxels that are indexed via i and j (within one image slice), and slice distance is the space between the voxels indexed via k (between image slices) (Courtesy of Dirk Bartz, University of Leipzig).*

While most medical image data are defined on such grid types, it is important to be aware that there are other grid types with varying spacing, geometry, and topology [Schroeder *et al.*, 2001].

A volume dataset is defined only at the discrete grid positions. However, we often need to calculate sample points within a volume cell. In the early days of volumetric data processing, this was achieved by *nearest-neighbor interpolation*, where a sample point within a volume cell was assigned the voxel value of the voxel with the smallest distance from that sample point. While nearest-neighbor interpolation is fast, the visual quality is low due to the discontinuous interpolation results in the middle between neighboring voxels, resulting in a blocky appearance of reconstructed surfaces.

Today, the most popular interpolation scheme is trilinear interpolation (Fig. 2.3).

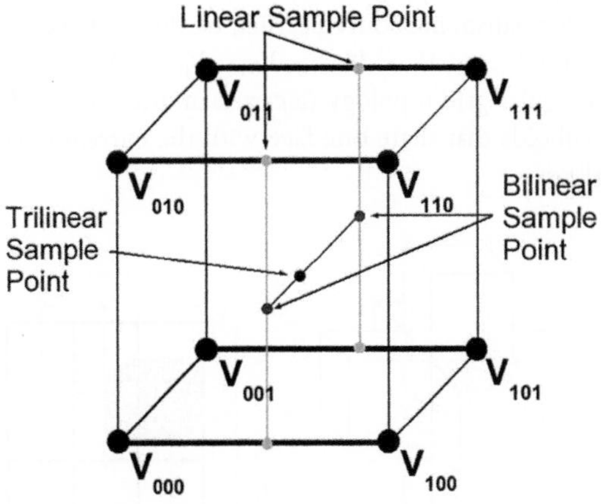

FIGURE 2.3 *Trilinear interpolation: Linear sample points are computed on the frontal and backward edges of the volume cell. Based on these points, bilinear interpolation is computed by linear interpolation. Finally, the trilinear sample point is computed by linear interpolation between the bilinear sample points (Courtesy of Dirk Bartz, University of Leipzig).*

For a simpler representation of the interpolations in Equations 2.1–2.3, we will abbreviate terms like $V_{i,j,k}$ with V_{000} and $V_{i+1,j+1,k+1}$ with V_{111}, where the index represents the increment of the position indices i, j, k. $V_{i+1,j,k}$ for example is abbreviated with V_{100}. Equation 2.1 shows a linear interpolation between two voxel values, and Equation 2.2 shows the respective bilinear interpolation between four voxel values. α, α_1, and α_2 represent the respective interpolation weights for linear and bilinear interpolation, and x, y, z for the trilinear interpolation.

$$L(\alpha) = V_0 * (1-\alpha) + V_1 * \alpha | 0 \leq \alpha \leq 1 \tag{2.1}$$

$$\begin{aligned} B(\alpha_1, \alpha_2) &= L_0(\alpha_1) * (1-\alpha_2) + L_1(\alpha_1) * \alpha_2 \\ &= (V_{00} * (1-\alpha) + V_{10} * \alpha)) * (1-\alpha_2) \\ &\quad +(V_{01} * (1-\alpha) + V_{11} * \alpha)) * \alpha_2 \end{aligned} \tag{2.2}$$

$$\begin{aligned} T(x,y,z) &= B_0(x,y) * (1-z) + B_1(x,y) * z \\ &= ((L_0(x) * (1-y) + L_1(x) * y)) * (1-z) \\ &\quad +((L_2(x) * (1-y) + L_3(x) * y)) * z \\ &= (((V_{000} * (1-x) + V_{100} * x)) * (1-y) \\ &\quad +((V_{010} * (1-x) + V_{110} * x)) * y) * (1-z) \\ &\quad +(((V_{001} * (1-x) + V_{101} * x)) * (1-y) \\ &\quad +((V_{011} * (1-x) + V_{111} * x)) * y) * z \end{aligned} \tag{2.3}$$

Trilinear interpolation involves only the immediate voxel neighborhood of a sample point, which are the voxels of the enclosing volume cell (Fig. 2.3). Other schemes involve higher-order interpolation functions, such as tricubic spline functions, which take a larger voxel neighborhood into account. Alternatively, the sample value can be reconstructed by convolving the voxel values with a Gaussian filter kernel.

Finally, we introduce the concept of *neighborhood*. This concept will be employed throughout the various chapters of this book, since it defines the *support* or area of influence for many operations. In some contexts, it will be also called *connectivity*, e.g., for region growing segmentation (see § 4.3.4). If, for example, only the voxels on the left/right, top/bottom, front/back of the current voxel are considered, we speak of a *6-neighborhood*. According to our formalism introduced earlier, we denote the current voxel with V_{000} and the voxels in the 6-neighborhood as V_{-100}, V_{100}, V_{0-10}, V_{010}, V_{00-1}, V_{001}. In other words, we selected the neighborhood according to regular grid topology (a cartesian grid) of our dataset. The 6-neighborhood represents all neighboring cuboids that share one face with the current cuboid (see Fig. 2.4, left). This also motivates the term *6-adjacent*.

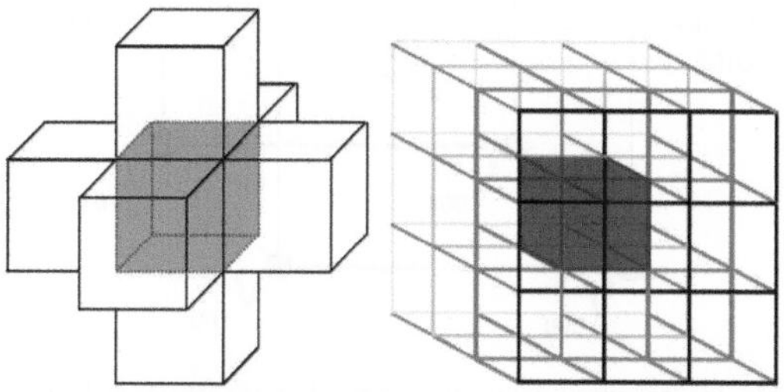

FIGURE 2.4 **Left:** *6-neighborhood—every face of the current cuboid (red) has a neighbor.* **Right:** *26-neighborhood—every face, every edge, every vertex of the current cuboid (red) has a neighbor (Courtesy of Dirk Bartz, University of Leipzig).*

The other frequently used neighborhood is the 26-*neighborhood*, which includes a neighborhood of 26 voxels. Next to the original six neighboring voxels, the 26-neighborhood also adds the voxels on the major and minor diagonals from the current voxel. In our formalism to enumerate voxels, this includes all index combinations with negative and positive index offsets, except 000 (the current voxel). With the cuboid analogon, we also include cuboids that connect to the current cuboid through shared edges (12) and shared vertices (8) (see Fig. 2.4, right). In other words, we have a 26-*adjacent* neighborhood.

2.3 DATA ARTIFACTS AND SIGNAL PROCESSING

Data artifacts are a phenomenon that is virtually omni-present in medical imaging. Medical image acquisition techniques have their theoretical roots in digital signal processing, and therefore, artifacts can be explained by the foundations of signal processing. In this section, we provide an introduction into the sampling theorem and its influence on medical imaging.

Important concepts for the discussion of artifacts are the *spatial domain* and the *frequency domain*. So far, we only examined datasets represented in the spatial domain, where the data is arranged as voxels or pixels on a spatial 3D or 2D grid.

The frequency domain is a representation of spatial data, which have been Fourier transformed. Now the data (or signals) are represented by a band of different frequencies, hence the name frequency domain. To transform the signals from the frequency domain to the spatial domain, we need to apply the Inverse Fourier transformation.

2.3.1 SAMPLING THEOREM

The main basis in signal theory is the sampling theorem that is credited to Nyquist [1924] —who first formulated the theorem in 1928.

The sampling theorem essentially says that a signal has to be sampled at least with twice the frequency of the original signal. Since signals and their respective speed can be easier expressed by frequencies, most explanations of artifacts are based on their representation in the frequency domain. The sampling frequency required by the sampling theorem is called the *Nyquist frequency*.

The transformation of signals into the frequency domain (Fig. 2.5) is performed by the Fourier transformation, which essentially reformulates the signal into a cosine function space. If, for example, we

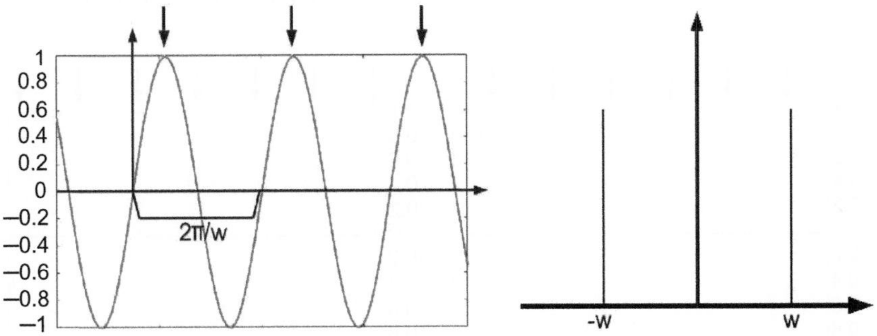

FIGURE 2.5 Sine -function is sampled (arrows) at same speed as sine periodicity of $T = 2\pi/w$. **Left:** spatial domain representation, **right:** frequency domain representation, where the frequency is represented by two symmetric peaks at $-w$ and w (Courtesy of Dirk Bartz, University of Leipzig).

transform the sine function into the frequency domain, this results in a peak at the frequency of the sine function (Fig. 2.5, right). Due to the symmetry of the Fourier transform for real values, there are two peaks on both sides of the ordinate (y) axis. More details on the frequency-domain-based interpretation can be found in Glassner [1995].

As all image data can be interpreted as a spatial or Fourier-transformed signal, we base our discussion on a simple example of an 1D signal, the sine function. This function has a straightforward representation in the spatial and the frequency domain. Figure 2.5 (left) shows a section of the sine function around the origin. If we transform this continuous representation into a discrete representation, we need to take samples of the continuous sine function to measure its characteristics. Figure 2.5 (left) demonstrates what happens if we take the samples at the same frequency as our original function. Since the sine function has the periodicity $T = 2\pi/w$ (or the frequency of $w/2\pi$), this sampling frequency would be also T. As Figure 2.5 (left) shows, sampling the sine function at the same speed would recover always the same sine value in different periods, thus pretending that it is a constant function.

If we increase the sampling speed to half of the periodicity of the continuous function, the minimum demand of the sampling theorem, we can recover the correct characteristics of the sine function, as it can be seen in Figure 2.6 (left). However, depending on what exact position in the period T of the original function we take the sample, we recover different amplitudes of the original signal. In an unfortunate case, we always sample the zero crossing of the sine function, as shown in Figure 2.6 (right). In this case, the characteristics could be correctly recovered, but the amplitude of the signal was recovered in an unfortunate way, so we are back with a constant signal. Overall, sampling at a rate satisfying the sampling theorem does not guarantee that the full signal strength is reconstructed, although higher sampling rates usually approach the original strength.

In the frequency domain, sampling of the original signal is described as the convolution of the original signal with a comb function (with peaks repeating at the sampling frequency). Due to the periodicity of the comb function (we take samples at regular positions), the convolved signal also exposes a replicating pattern. Since exactly one of these signal patterns is used, we need to select one copy of it with a low-pass filter, a technique that is explained in the next section. If the sampling rate is not high enough, it will result in an overlap of the replicating patterns, and hence in the inability to select one copy of the pattern.

Note that medical image data does consist of a full spectrum of frequencies, which are revealed once the Fourier transform of the data is calculated. Therefore, the respective limiting cut-off frequency of this spectrum should be taken into account, when estimating the correct sampling frequency.

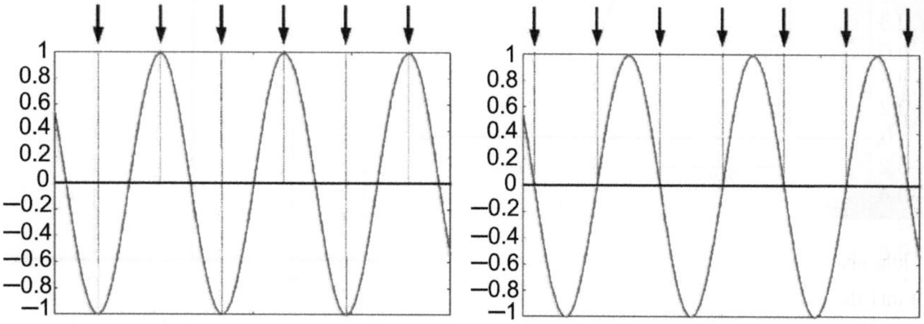

FIGURE 2.6 *Sine-function is sampled (arrows) at Nyquist rate.* **Left:** *Sampling at optimal position (detects peaks and valleys),* **right:** *Sampling phase shift—only a constant (zero) amplitude is sampled (Courtesy of Dirk Bartz, University of Leipzig).*

2.3.2 UNDERSAMPLING AND ALIASING

Aliasing is a phenomenon that is directly related to sampling. Essentially, it is caused by an incorrectly reconstructed signal, due to insufficient sampling. Therefore, the signal is mistaken for another signal, its *alias*. A typical visual result of aliasing is the Moiré artifact pattern, which can also be observed in our daily environment, e.g., when looking through two fences while we are moving. The top row of Figure 2.7 shows examples of the Moiré artifact, where the surface of the scanned phantom object is sampled at a speed below the Nyquist rate. This insufficient sampling is also called undersampling. Another undersampling artifact is shown in the middle row of Figure 2.7, where an insufficient slice distance is not able to recover the full geometry of the scanned object.

There are basically two solutions to overcome undersampling; first of all, the sampling rate can be increased until we satisfy the Nyquist rate. Figure 2.7 shows in the top row how the Moiré artifacts

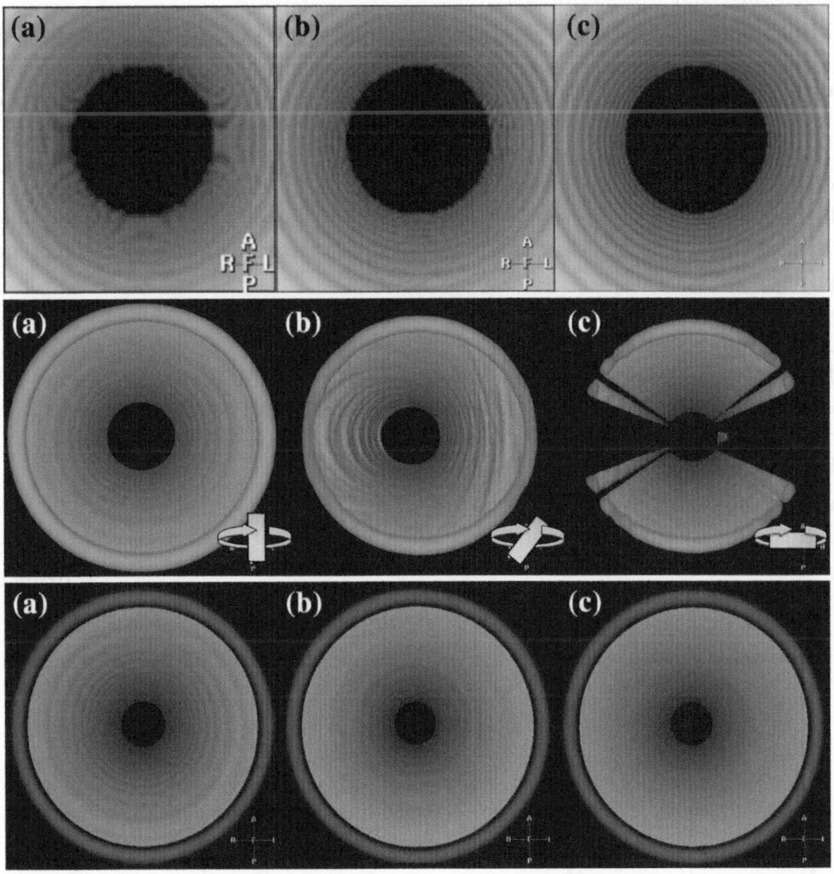

FIGURE 2.7 *Tube phantom with perspective projection from an endoscopic viewpoint.* **Top row:** *The sampling rate is increased from the left to right and the Moiré artifacts are reduced.* **Middle row:** *Different slice and pixel distance in anisotropic datasets can lead to insufficient sampling, if the object orientation is changed.* **Bottom row:** *If too many frequencies are removed by a low-pass filter, details disappear (the number of removed frequencies is increasing from left to right) (Courtesy of Florian Dammann, University Hospital Tübingen).*

are reduced by increasing the sampling rate. The other solution is to *band-limit* the signal by performing a low-pass filtering. As mentioned above, a signal will be represented by a spectrum of frequencies in the frequency domain. If this spectrum extends into a higher frequency range that we cannot correctly reconstruct, we remove those frequencies from the spectrum by convolving the original signal with a low-pass filter (removing higher frequencies, keeping lower frequencies, hence it is called a low-pass filter).

In the spatial domain, this results in a smoothed or blurred signal (or image). It depends on the size and quality of the low-pass filter how much the new signal is blurred. The bottom row of Figure 2.7 demonstrates what happens if too many high frequencies are removed.

The choice which low-pass filter to use is also important. Typically, three different low-pass filter are considered:

- a box filter,
- a triangle filter, and
- a Gaussian filter.

The box filter owes its name to its frequency domain representation as a rectangle (Fig. 2.8, left). If it is convolved with the spectrum of the original signal, only the frequencies covered by the box are kept in the convolved signal. The triangle filter introduces different weights for frequencies off-center of the triangle filter. Both filters have one common drawback. While they have a simple representation in the frequency domain, their representation in the spatial domain is the sinc function whose oscillating infinite extent must be truncated (Fig. 2.8, right). This truncation however, leads to an imperfect box filter representation in the frequency domain.

This situation is less difficult with the Gaussian low-pass filter, which essentially is a Gaussian function in the frequency and the spatial domain. The Gaussian has a better weighting cut-off than the triangle filter. While it still has an infinite extent that needs to be truncated, it lacks the oscillating behavior and has only positive weighting values. More information on filtering can be found in Glassner [1995].

2.3.3 INTERPOLATION ARTIFACTS

Many visual representations use interpolation schemes to compute data at positions between defined grid points. A popular scheme is trilinear interpolation (Eq. 2.3) for position and normal computation.

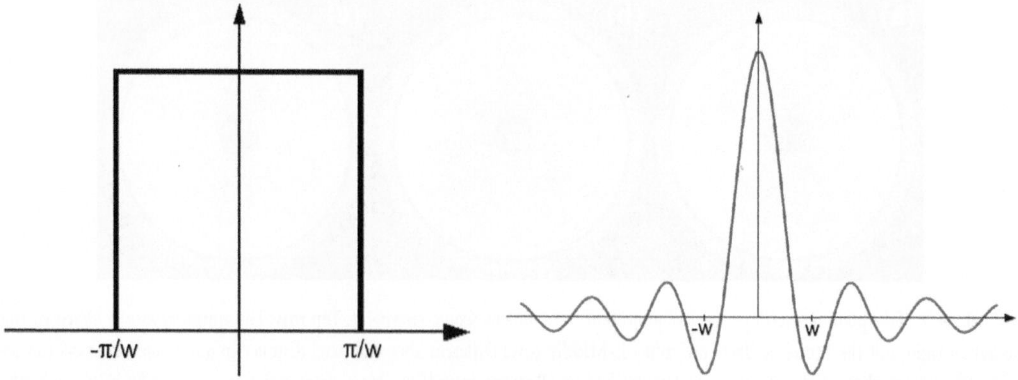

FIGURE 2.8 *The (1d) box filter has the shape of a rectangle in the frequency domain (left) and is a sinc function (right) with infinite support in the spatial domain (Courtesy of Dirk Bartz, University of Leipzig).*

The normals in volume datasets are usually approximated by gradients using central differences Höhne and Bernstein [1986]. Assuming a uniform grid with the distance h between voxels in x-, y- and z-direction central differences, compute the gradient at $p(x_i, y_i, z_i)$ as the difference between adjacent voxels in all 3D according to Equation 2.4

$$\nabla f(x_i, y_j, z_k) = \left(\frac{x_{i+1} - x_{i-1}}{2h}, \frac{y_{j+1} - y_{j-1}}{2h}, \frac{z_{k+1} - z_{k-1}}{2h} \right)^T \tag{2.4}$$

Unfortunately, central differences will cause artifacts, if the intensity differences are large, or the grid spacing is anisotropic.

In the case of binary segmentation, individual voxels are labeled as part of the segment (on) or not part of the segment (off). If the respective isosurface representing the material interface between the segment and its neighborhood is computed, large intensity differences on the material interface (all off-voxels are set to zero, all on-voxels contain the original voxel value) occur. In these situations, the positions of the isosurface and in particular their normals will experience the above-mentioned artifacts and result in a blocky appearance (Fig. 2.9).

Fortunately, there are several remedies for these interpolation artifacts, if the original data is used for isosurface computation and the label volume is only used as a map to indicate the voxels of the segments. The first remedy adds a layer of off-voxels around the segment voxels. This additional off-layer allows smoother local gradients on the material interface of the segment, since the intensity differences are significantly smaller than to zero intensities, due to the partial volume effect [Höhne and Bernstein, 1986]. Another possible remedy changes the original data values. Here, the material interface in the voxel values is processed by a low-pass volume filter, which generates a smooth transition between the segment and the off-voxels. However, this also changes the resulting isosurface and must hence be applied with great care.

A related interpolation issue arises also with the normal estimation based on central differences on anisotropic grids. Typically, the normal at a computed sample point within a volume cell is based on the trilinear interpolation of normals approximated by central differences at the surrounding voxels of this volume cell. This gradient estimation scheme, however, assumes an isotropic grid, since all three vector components are computed the same way. Since anisotropic datasets have different voxel distances in the three different spatial orientations, these differences are not properly addressed in most rendering

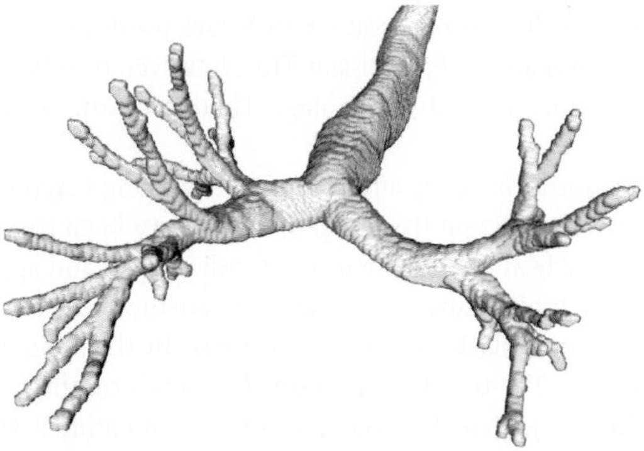

FIGURE 2.9 *Binary segmentation block artifacts. The image shows the block artifacts of an isosurface reconstruction of the label volume of a bronchial tree (Courtesy of Tobias Mönch, University of Magdeburg).*

approaches. The normals at the computed sample points are distorted in the different spacing direction. There are several solutions that reduce staircasing artifacts [Möller *et al.*, 1997]. More recently, Neumann *et al.* [2000] suggested to use linear regression to estimate better gradients.

2.4 X-RAY IMAGING

The discovery of X-rays by Wilhelm Conrad Röntgen in 1895 was the birth of medical imaging. For the first time, interior parts of a body could be visualized without actually cutting into it. The name X-rays was coined in Röntgen's original paper [Röntgen, 1895], where it denotes a new unknown ("X") kind of radiation. X-ray images are based on the attenuation of X-ray quanta traveling through the scanned object. The attenuation is based on two processes:

- X-ray quanta are *absorbed* by the object that is hit, and
- X-ray quanta are *scattered* due to the so-called Compton effect.

The Compton effect occurs if photons arrive at an atom with high energy and cause electrons from the outer hull of that atom to be detached and moved in a certain angle to the direction of the incoming photon. The Compton effect actually limits the contrast and quality of X-ray images. The denser the current part of that object is (e.g., bone or metal), the more the X-ray quanta are absorbed. The absorption also depends on the thickness of the object to be passed.

The X-ray quanta are generated by electrons that are accelerated through an electric field. When these electrons hit the target material (the anode), the kinetic energy is transformed into heat due to collisions with ions (approximately 99%) and X-ray quanta [Lehmann *et al.*, 1997]. The X-ray spectrum is dominated by the Bremsstrahlung, in particular for shorter wave length. The materials that are passed by X-rays lead to additional spikes in the spectrum. The target material of X-ray tubes is often tungsten, which exhibits characteristic X-ray energies that are appropriate for imaging bones. For other applications, such as mammography where soft tissue is imaged, other target materials are required, for example molybdenum.

The speed (and hence the energy) of the electrons depends on the strength of the electric field that accelerates the electrons. If the generating voltage is larger than 80 kV, we speak of *hard beam X-rays*. *Soft beam X-rays* are generated by a voltage of 20–40 kV. The limits are not generally agreed on, but mammography, e.g., with 30 kV is considered as an application of soft X-rays.

If hard beam X-rays are used, the scattering effect dominates the interaction with the object. Consequently, the quanta are only absorbed in very dense material. In medical imaging, this is exploited for the representation of bone structures. In contrast, soft beam X-rays result predominately in absorption, and hence can be used for the representation of soft tissue. This, however, results in more energy intake of the tissue itself, which in turn leads to more tissue damage. Therefore, soft beam X-rays are more harmful than hard beam X-rays.

A film behind the patient records the X-ray attenuation. The varying brightness of the film is a result of the interactions of X-rays with the different tissue types, which have been passed. Tissue types that absorb a large fraction of X-ray intensity lead to a low density of radiographs and appear bright.

Skeletal structures exhibit the highest absorption rates and are therefore the brightest structures. Tissue with lower absorption rate appears dark or even black areas. In the human body, air has the lowest absorption rate and appears black. The resulting intensity I depends on the thickness of the material that is passed as well as on a coefficient μ, which characterizes the attenuation S. The initial intensity I_o drops exponentially with increasing distance d (Eq. 2.5).

$$I(d) = I_0 * e^{-\mu * d} \tag{2.5}$$

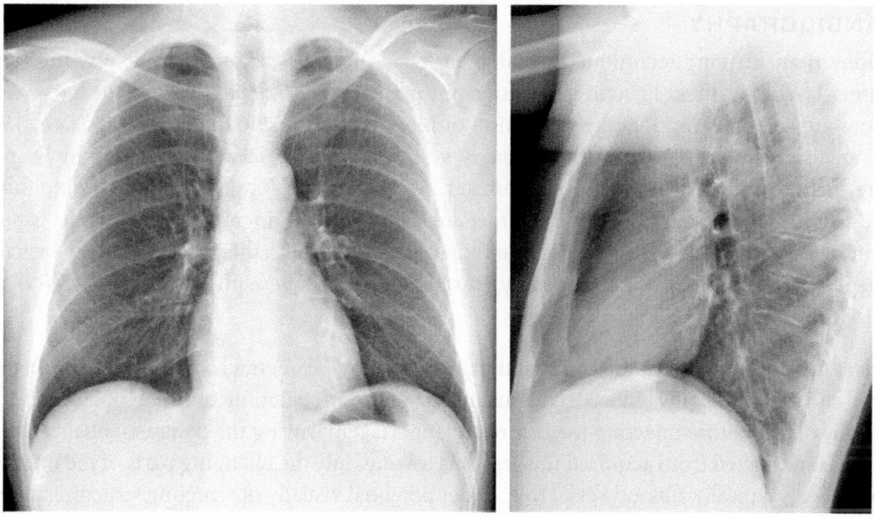

FIGURE 2.10 *A frontal and a lateral view of a thorax where no pathologies were detected* (Courtesy of Hans-Holger Jend, Hospital Bremen-Ost Germany).

The product $\mu * d$ characterizes the attenuation S. Usually, different tissue types are involved, which leads to the approximation of the attenuation S as a sum of different materials with individual attenuation coefficients μ_i and a certain distance d_i (Eq. 2.6).

$$S = \sum_{i=1}^{n} \mu_i * d_i \tag{2.6}$$

Note that the elements of an X-ray image characterize the whole pass of the radiation through the body and produce a weighted average value of X-ray attenuation. Thus, primarily the silhouettes of objects and structures are recognizable. Therefore, individual X-ray images cannot be used to accurately localize structures. As a consequence, X-ray images are often generated in two different imaging planes (see Fig. 2.10). Today, X-ray images are typically recorded digitally by a detector array ("direct radiograph").

Digital Mammography A special variant is *digital mammography* where digital X-ray images of the female breast are acquired. Similar to conventional mammography, the breast needs to be compressed to fixate it, to reduce motion artifacts and move the breast as close as possible to the detector thus reducing the necessary dose. Mammography requires an excellent image quality, where small structures (>100 μm) need to be sharply displayed.

Because of the epidemiological importance of breast cancer, digital mammography has experienced an enormous development, which lead to dedicated workstations aiming at an improved diagnosis of mammographic images. While reading mammographies, it is often essential to detect small features that could be early signs of breast cancer. Thus, monitors with high spatial and gray value resolution are required. It is often essential to compare the current mammography (from two viewing angles) with previous images to evaluate the progress of suspicious regions over time. Since these mammography images are available in a digital form, they can be processed algorithmically to improve their interpretation.

2.4.1 ANGIOGRAPHY

Angiography is an imaging technique in which an X-ray picture is acquired to display the inner open space (lumen) of blood-filled structures. Angiography is employed to depict arteries; the most widespread applications are cerebral angiography (depiction of blood vessels inside the brain) [Osborn, 1999] and coronary angiography (depiction of the coronary vessels around the heart). Angiography is an invasive procedure that requires the insertion of a catheter. A catheter is a long, thin, and flexible tube that is employed to administer contrast agent in a target area. Coronary angiography, for example, is performed by inserting a catheter in an artery in the arm and then advancing the catheter into a major coronary artery. The concept of angiography was developed by EGAS MONIZ, a Portuguese physician, in 1927 (documented in [Moniz, 1940]).

Digital Subtraction Angiography Digital Subtraction Angiography (DSA) tracks the blood flow through contrast agent-enhanced imaging. In order to maximize the representation of the blood vessels, a "mask image" of the object before injecting the contrast agent is taken. During the contrast-enhanced phase, this mask image is subtracted from acquired images, thus leaving only the changing parts of the images, which in case of a DSA is typically a blood vessel tree. Other potential visually obstructing structures are removed with the mask image (see Fig. 2.11). There are many applications of this principle to guide neurosurgical procedures, such as the treatment of cerebral aneurysms (enlargements of vascular structures with a high risk for rupture).

2.4.2 ROTATIONAL X-RAY

Rotational X-ray is based on DSA. Hence, most of the associated applications are angiography applications and this technique is frequently referred to as *rotational angiography* (Fig. 2.12) [Koppe *et al.*, 1995, Fahrig, 1999]. Rotational X-ray acquires a series of X-ray images while rotating around the subject to be scanned. The images can be rotated in any direction. Since the rotation of the emitter/detector system is performed

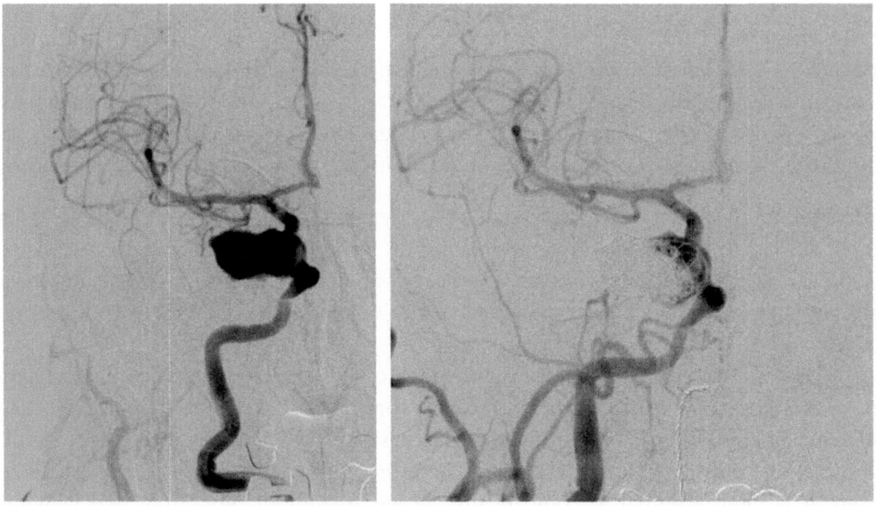

FIGURE 2.11 Digital subtraction angiography. **Left:** bleeding as a consequence of aneurysm rupture. **Right:** after successful treatment with a coil of wire, thrombosis occurred and the aneurysm is cured (Courtesy of Martin Skalej, University Hospital Magdeburg).

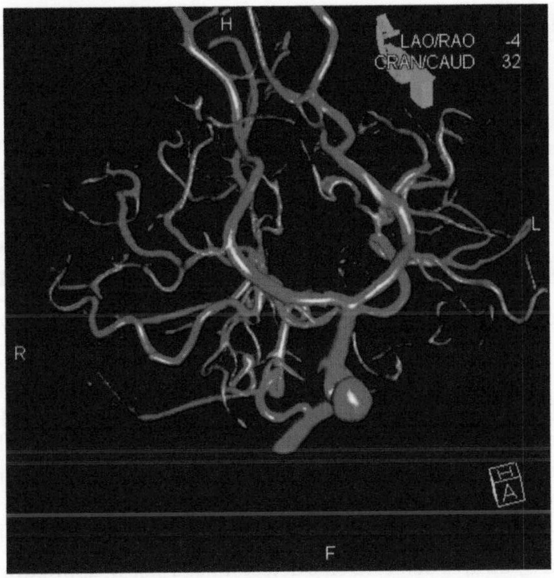

FIGURE 2.12 *Rotational angiography of cerebral arteries. With the used reconstruction algorithm, only bones and contrast-enhanced blood vessels can be represented well. Here, the display of bones is suppressed. The image contains a large cerebral aneurysm (Courtesy of Martin Skalej, University Hospital Magdeburg).*

on a C-shape mounting, it is also called C-arm X-ray. Many systems consist of a pair of emitter/detector systems to acquire two projections at a time. These systems are named rotational bi-planar X-ray.

To generate volumetric datasets, a series of up to 132 X-ray projections are taken from a rotation range of 200 degrees around the scanning object. In contrast to CT, rotational X-ray is using a full array of up to 1024^2 detectors, which allow the measurement of a full cone of rays. To account for reconstruction errors, a modified back-projection algorithm is used [Feldkamp *et al.*, 1984, Kalender, 2000]. Additionally, special filter kernels are used to further reduce potential artifacts. Current rotational angiography systems provide very high resolution, isotropic datasets, good reconstruction quality (for selected organs, such as bones and contrast-enhanced blood vessels), and a high data acquisition speed.

The image quality that is achieved with this modality is similar to CT and thus some product names may lead to confusion, e.g., SIEMENS DynaCT or Philips xperCT. Compared to "real" CT data (§ 2.5), the contrast resolution is lower. However, the spatial resolution is even better. The acquisition lasts slightly longer but the whole volume is acquired within one rotation.

Digital Volume Tomography Digital volume tomography (DVT), also called *cone-beam* CT, is based on the same principles as rotational angiography and delivers a similar image quality. DVT is frequently used in implant dentistry and orthodontics, for both diagnosis and treatment planning. It is a smaller and cheaper device optimized for the use cases in dentistry. The name *cone-beam* CT was coined, since the X-rays diverge leading to a cone-shaped area.

An *orthopantomogram* (OPG) is a dental X-ray of the upper and lower jaw that is usually acquired for diagnosis of caries, peridontioditis, and peridontal abscess. Also, diagnosis and treatment planning in case of fractures relies on OPGs. The X-ray source is rotated around the head (from ear to ear) imaging a half-cycle panoramic view that depicts all teeth and the maxillary sinuses.

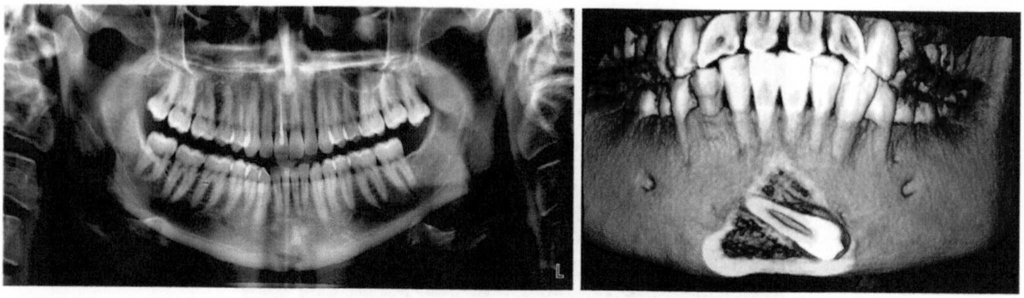

FIGURE 2.13 *Imaging in dentistry.* **Left:** *an orthopantomogram,* **right:** *digital volume tomography.*

Flat-Panel Volume CTs A promising development of X-ray technology is the flat-panel volume CT (which is actually not a CT scanner, but a C-arm) that allows to scan a whole organ within one rotation. Instead of axial slices, arbitrary reformatting of the data is possible with volume CT scanners. The terms flat panel volume CT and 3D rotation angiography are in fact synonyms.

Gupta *et al.* [2008] explain the flat-panel volume CT scanners as a conventional multislice CT where the detector rows are replaced by an area detector. This detector has a size of approximately 40×30 cm divided into 2048×1536 detector elements and facilitates an isotropic spatial resolution of about 150 μm. Despite a lower contrast resolution and the need for a higher dose rate for the same flat panel SNR, flat panel detectors have a number of applications, e.g., for intraoperative use and angiography. With continuous movements of the detector, flat panel volume CT enables dynamic data acquisition in a good quality, which is essential for intraoperative use. Other applications include placement of electrodes in cochlear implants, atherosclerotic plaque characterization, and assessment of endovascular stents where the high spatial resolution is essential. For explanations of reconstruction and data processing algorithms, see Gupta *et al.* [2008] (see Fig. 2.13).

2.4.3 DISCUSSION

2D X-ray imaging provides only a projection image of the scanned object. Hence, the representation of positional relationships is difficult. In most cases, X-ray images from two different viewing directions (bi-planar imaging) are acquired to provide a better spatial understanding of the different anatomical structures and to ensure that no pathologies are missed as a consequence of being obscured in one projection. Despite the availability of many 3D modalities, 2D X-ray imaging is still a standard image acquisition method in clinical practice.

A general problem of X-rays is their potential to impair the genetic material, which may contribute to the development of cancer. The danger for the patient depends on the dose of radiation (measured in Sievert). In general, there is a trade-off between image quality (high SNR) and the dose of radiation. Lower doses of radiation tend to compromise image quality. Despite of this relation the image quality has improved considerably while reducing the necessary radiation.

2.4.4 CURRENT AND FUTURE DEVELOPMENTS OF X-RAY IMAGING

While the explanation of X-ray variants above was focused on developments that have already proven their clinical value, we briefly discuss in the following developments that have the potential of clinical progress in the near future. While currently used X-ray scanners employ only the absorption of X-rays leading to an attenuation of the intensity according to Equation 2.6, there are further effects when X-rays pass tissue that enable to more sensitively discriminate different tissue types, e.g., by evaluating diffraction properties. The amplitude of the intensity decreases and the phase is shifted. The latter effect is much larger when hard X-rays are employed [Momose and Fukuda, 1995]. To employ this phase shift for diagnosis in biomedical imaging requires to convert the phase shift into a change of the X-ray intensity that is recorded with current X-ray scanners (see [Yoneyama *et al.*, 2011] for an overview over *Phase contrast X-ray imaging* approaches toward this conversion). *Interferometry* detects the phase shift directly, whereas other methods use indirect information, such as derivatives. Momose *et al.* [2000] and Takeda *et al.* [2002] discuss the use phase contrast X-ray for vessel imaging discussing appropriate contrast agents.

2.5 COMPUTED TOMOGRAPHY

The introduction of X-ray Computed Tomography (CT) in 1968 by Godfrey Hounsfield and Allan McLeod Cormack provided for the first time a volumetric representation of objects. It was first applied to get cross-sectional images of the brain in order to evaluate a lesion, which turned out to be a cyst [Hounsfield, 1973]. The invention of the CT is the hour of birth for the modern tomographic imaging modalities and was recognized with the Nobel prize for "Physiology or Medicine" in 1979.

In essence, CT data represents a series of individual X-ray images that are composed into one volume dataset. These X-ray images are acquired by an emitter/detector system that is rotating around the object to be scanned (Fig. 2.14, left). Each X-ray image represents an intensity profile measured by the detectors. From the intensity profiles of a full rotation, the slice image of the scanned object is computed based on the filtered backprojection. Afterwards, a table on which the scanned object is positioned will be moved forward and the next image slice of the object will be acquired.

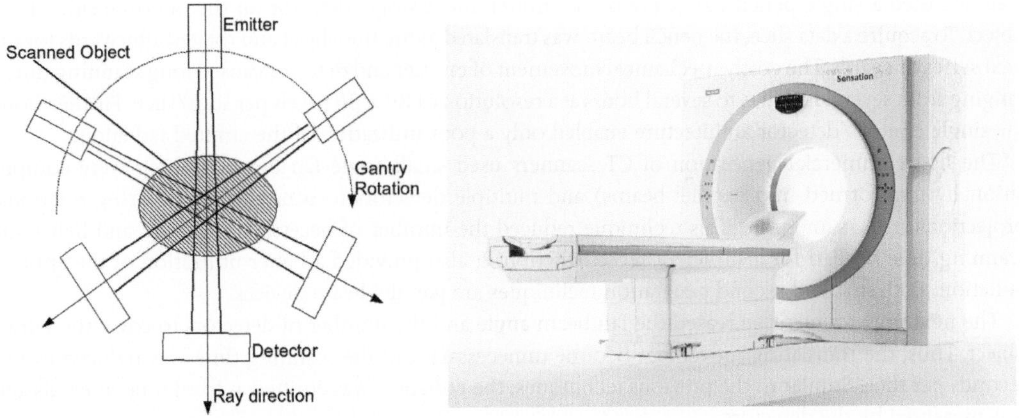

FIGURE 2.14 **Left:** *A series of measurements from different angles are reconstructed to a 2D cross-sectional image.* **Right:** *A photo of a modern CT scanner (Copyright SIEMENS Medical Solutions, Somatom Sensation).*

2.5.1 COMPUTED TOMOGRAPHY COMPARED TO X-RAY IMAGING

CT has a variety of advantages as imaging modality compared to the conventional use of X-rays [Hounsfield, 1980]. These are:

- **Localization of anatomical structures.** Most notably, CT can provide accurate localization of objects in depth. While X-ray images superimpose the X-ray absorption values of many tissues along a ray, CT records X-ray attenuation for small volume elements independently.
- **Sensitivity.** CT data are two orders of magnitude more sensitive than X-ray images. X-ray images are not able to distinguish different soft tissues, such as liver and pancreas, whereas CT image data discriminate these tissues. The contrast between soft tissues, however, is small with CT data.
- **Quantitative measurements.** Since the X-ray absorption is computed with high accuracy for individual volume elements, it is possible to analyze CT data quantitatively. For example, the mean X-ray absorption in a selected region can be used as an indicator for the severity of a disease, such as osteoporosis, fibrosis, or emphysema.

In general, CT produces detailed anatomical information and allows to discriminate pathological variations from healthy tissue. It was soon recognized that the precise anatomical localization is crucial for diagnosis as well as for therapy planning. Craniofacial surgery planning [Vannier *et al.*, 1983a] was the first application area, primarily since bones, that are essential for these interventions, could be discriminated well with CT data from the surroundings. Precise craniofacial surgery planning is important, since functional and esthetic aspects are involved. Later, many other application areas, such as radiation treatment planning followed. CT data, therefore, also fostered the cooperation between medical doctors from different disciplines.

2.5.2 PRINCIPLE OF CT DATA GENERATION

The major differences between the development stages of CT are projection reconstruction algorithms and the emitter and detector architecture (data acquisition) [Kalender, 2000]. The first generation of CT scanners used a single pencil-like X-ray beam emitter and a single detector on the opposite side of the object. To acquire a data slice, the pencil beam was translated along the object and rotated afterwards for the next series of beams. The costly mechanical movement of emitter and detector caused long scanning times, ranging from several minutes to several hours at a resolution of 80×80 pixels per scan/slice. Furthermore, the single emitter/detector architecture enabled only a poor utilization of the emitted radiation.

The first commercial generation of CT scanners used small angle fan beams (which were computationally transformed into parallel beams) and multiple detectors to scan two neighboring rotational projections at the same time. This technique reduced the number of necessary rotations, and hence the scanning time needed for a sufficient reconstruction. It also provided a better utilization of the emitted radiation. Both first and second generation techniques are parallel beam devices.

The next improvement increased the fan beam angle and the number of detectors to cover the whole object. Thus, the translating movement became unnecessary and the scanning time was reduced to five seconds per slice. Similar to the previous techniques, the radiation was emitted at fixed time intervals and was measured by the detectors.

In the fourth generation, the rotating detector was replaced by a fixed circular ring detector, which reduced the technical effort of moving the larger mass of emitter and detector. Here, the radiation was permanently emitted and only the detectors were enabled at certain intervals. However, several problems of ring detectors led to further developments. Besides the higher costs for the detector ring, X-ray scattering

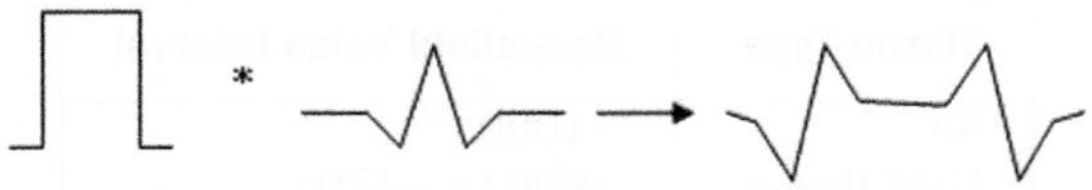

FIGURE 2.15 Principles of CT reconstruction filters. The original signal (left) is modified according to the filter (middle) to produce the reconstructed signal (right). Reconstruction filters change the amplitude of the signal and the form of edges. In general, the output signal exhibits more contrast than the input image. These filters are applied in all three dimensions in the actual image acquisition process.

problems reduced the image quality of these systems while collimator technology could reduce the scattering problems with a rotating emitter/detector system of the third generation.

Currently, the state-of-the-art are spiral or helical CT where the emitter/detector system is rotating permanently around the object, while the object is moving continuously in the perpendicular direction to acquire a full data volume. This technique allows faster scans, due to the continuous rotating movement of the emitter/detector system. This saves time previously required to accelerate and slow down these heavy parts of the scanner. Since 1999, multiple layers of emitters and detectors are combined to create multislice CT scanners, realizing fast and near-isotropic scanning of large object areas. The introduction of multislice CTs required advanced reconstruction algorithms since the emitted X-rays are no longer restricted to one plane. Today (mid 2013), the state-of-the-art in multislice CT scanners acquire up to 320 slices (actually spirals) at a time (Fig. 2.14, right). Reconstruction filters are designed to enhance differences in signal intensity (see Fig. 2.15).

Besides the architectural development, different volume/slice reconstruction algorithms are used in the various systems and generations. In the beginning of CT, *algebraic reconstruction techniques* (ART) were used to solve the inverse problem. However, the high computational costs of iteratively solving the large matrices[1] rendered this approach as not feasible for standard applications [Kalender, 2000]. The standard method today is *filtered back-projection* (parallel beam [Shepp and Logan, 1974] and cone-beam [Feldkamp *et al.*, 1984] reconstruction), where each projection is composed according to the measured direction. While there are parallel and fan beam methods to perform this back-projection, the current fan beam methods for CT are more complex and less efficient than state-of-the-art parallel beam reconstruction algorithms. Hence, the projections of today's fan-beam scanners are re-sorted in parallel beams before the actual reconstruction. Another modification is required to address the continuously moving object tray of modern spiral CT scanners where a z-interpolation corrects the measured projections according to the tray movement [Kalender, 2000].

2.5.3 STANDARDIZATION WITH HOUNSFIELD UNITS

The computed intensity values represent the densities of the scanned object. In medical imaging, these intensity values are normalized into Hounsfield Units (HU). This normalization maps the data range into a 12 bit range where the intensity of water is mapped to zero, and air is mapped to -1000. This normalization is formalized in Equation 2.7, where μ_{H_2O} represents the intensity value of water. Note that while only 12 bits are occupied by the dynamic range of the intensity values, they are typically packed into two bytes (16 bits) to provide easy voxel data access.

$$HU = \frac{\mu - \mu_{H_2O}}{\mu_{H_2O}} * 1000 \qquad (2.7)$$

Table 2.1 lists Hounsfield values for different organs and tissue types. The table indicates that parenchymatous organs, such as heart and liver, have similar or even overlapping intensity values.

1 The size of a reconstruction matrix is equal to the resolution of the slice.

Tissue Type	Hounsfield Value Interval
Air	−1000
Lung tissue	−900 to −170
Fat tissue	−220 to −30
Water (H_2O)	0
Pancreas	10–40
Liver	20–60
Heart	20–50
Kidney	30–50
Bones	45–3000

TABLE 2.1 *Hounsfield values for selected tissue types* (From [Lehmann et al., 1997]).

2.5.4 PARAMETERS OF CT SCANNING

In the following, we describe major parameters of CT image acquisition and their interaction. The first set of parameters relates to the resolution of CT data:

- the *number of slices*,
- the *number of pixels per slice*,
- the *voxel distances*,
- the *pitch*, and
- the *table increment*, also known as *table feed*.

The number of pixels in one slice is also referred to as *image matrix*. If we have a CT dataset with an image matrix of 512 × 512 and 300 slices, this corresponds to a volume dataset with the resolution 512 × 512 × 300. The distances between the voxels are differentiated into the slice (out-of-plane) and pixel distance (in-plane) (recall § 2.2).

The *table increment* specifies how much the table (where the object to be scanned is positioned) is advanced through the scanner during one rotation of the gantry. The *pitch* p defines the ratio between the table increment d and the *total slice collimation*, which is the factor of number of slices per rotation M, e.g., four for a four-slice multislice CT scanner and the slice thickness S. Therefore, we can compute the pitch as $p = d/(M \cdot S)$. If, for example, we have a 16-slice CT scanner (M = 16), a slice thickness of S = 0.5 mm, and a table increment of d = 6 mm, the pitch is p = 0.75. With a pitch larger than 1, we have gaps in the data, whereas a pitch $p < 1$ indicates that the slices overlap.

Resolution and Signal-to-Noise Ratio The resolution of the data has an influence on the noise level: data with higher resolution are more noisy if the radiation dose remains the same (see Fig. 2.16). With higher dose of radiation a better SNR ratio is achieved. The trade-off between the desired image quality and the negative effects of radiation has to be resolved such that the image quality is just sufficient to answer the diagnostic question at hand.

Gantry Tilt The rotating emitter/detector system of a CT scanner—through which the table with the scanned object is moved—is called the *gantry* (Fig. 2.14, left). The tilt of the gantry also defines the tilt of the image slices. Since most CT datasets are anisotropic, it can be useful to adapt the tilt gantry to the target organ of an examination, e.g., to ensure optimal sampling of the respective organ structures. Therefore, the *gantry tilt* is an additional parameter of CT scanning. If data are processed with a non-zero gantry tilt,

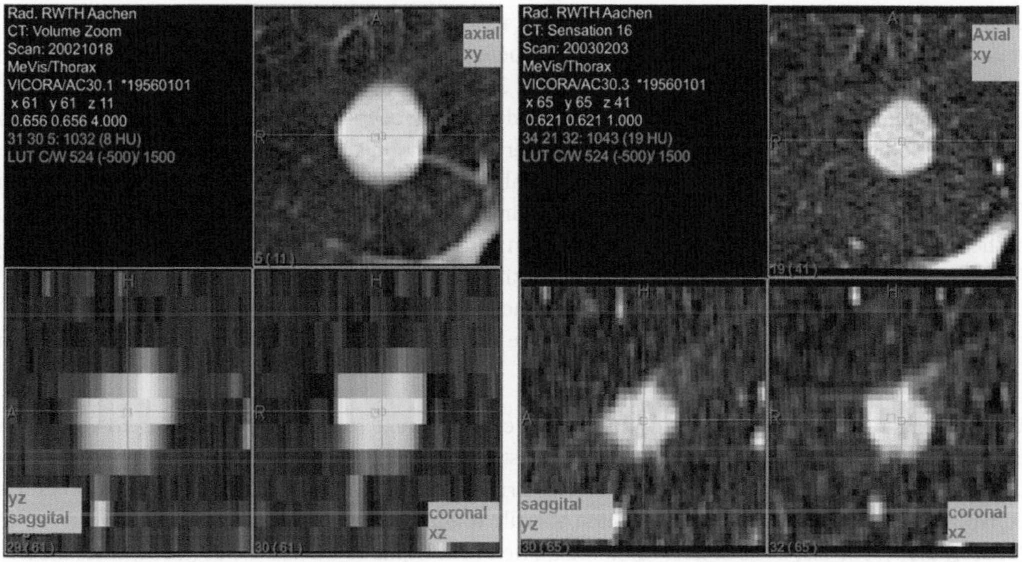

FIGURE 2.16 *Portion of a CT slice.* ***Left:*** *With a slice distance of 4 mm, a lung nodule exhibits a strong partial volume effect in the coronal and sagittal view.* ***Right:*** *A slice distance of 1 mm enables a precise evaluation of the nodule's shape in all directions. For volumetry, the higher spatial resolution is essential (Courtesy of Berthold Wein, Aachen).*

they should be warped to compensate for the gantry tilt in order to generate correct 3D visualizations. However, in contrast to rotational angiography, the angular flexibility is strongly limited (the gantry may be tilted at most by a few degrees).

When X-rays are casted from the emitter, they usually diverge like a fan from the emitter. Since these diverging X-rays will influence neighboring signal acquisition, it is useful to focus the rays along the main direction of the emitter. This is achieved by an aperture that limits the fan-out of the X-rays and is called *collimation*. The related collimation parameter specifies how open the aperture is.

Radiation Dose CT exposes a patient to a moderate or high radiation, which is a serious problem in special cases, for example in children. Also, if the success of a treatment needs to be regularly controlled, the radiation of CT data is particularly critical. The radiation efficiency has been considerably improved in the development of CT scanning devices. However, some new and complex scanning techniques as well as the goal to provide high resolution images have compensated this effect—leading to an increased radiation dose. This is considered as a serious problem, especially in cardiac imaging. In a recent survey article Sun and Ng [2011] state that the focus of research in cardiac CT has shifted from improving image quality to dose reduction, listing numerous dose-saving strategies. In cardiac imaging, ECG triggering is probably the most essential of these strategies—the coupling of CT acquisition with the patients' ECG enables to turn on the X-ray tube only when images in a high quality may be acquired according to the position in the cardiac cycle. In general, patients with a low risk for a severe disease and patients with a long life expectancy should be imaged with low dose protocols.

Contrast Enhancement Many CT examinations concern the blood vessel system. The blood vessels are difficult to detect and delineate in standard (native) CT scans. Therefore, a contrast agent (usually iodine) is injected into the venous system to enhance the representation of the arteries (and later during the venous cycle, the respective veins). Important parameters to consider for a contrast-enhanced CT scan are quantity of contrast agent (typically iodine between 300 and 400 mg I/ml) and the injection parameters that determine how the contrast agent is administered (as bolus, continuously, or in a varying distribution). Depending on how long the scan is performed after the injection and what kind of injection parameter was chosen, the visual representation of the arterial (high iodine flow of 3–4 ml/s) or venous system (low iodine flow of 2 ml/s) will be enhanced by an increased image intensity. For cardiac imaging an even higher flow of 6 ml/s is typically used and leads to an enhancement to 300–350 HU [Hennemuth, 2012]. To enable an optimum timing, automatic bolus tracking is often used. Thus, when the image intensity at a certain position reaches a predefined value, image acquisition is triggered. Note that the image intensity of adjacent organs can also be slightly increased due to the contrast agent, which has a positive effect on the segmentation of this organ (see Chap. 4).

Bi- and Triphasic CT Data Image acquisition with a contrast agent requires careful timing to ensure that the contrast agent is just in the relevant vascular system. The contrast agent is applied intravenously and thus reaches venous structures first and arterial structures later. Biphasic datasets capture the contrast enhancement at two different points in time, usually to emphasize both venous and arterial structures (see Fig. 2.17). For diagnosis of liver carcinoma, often even triphasic CT data are acquired, since the liver contains arteries, portal veins, and hepatic veins.

When bi- or triphasic data are used for the reconstruction of a 3D model, some structures are extracted from one phase, e.g., the arterial phase, and others from the second, e.g., the venous phase. At least slight movements occur in between. Therefore, it might be necessary to transform one of the datasets to better match the other.

Smooth and Hard Reconstruction Filters The intensity profiles of the projection images are subject to a filter process at data reconstruction, which may enhance or soften boundaries. Figure 2.18 shows the effect of two different reconstruction filters applied to the same CT dataset. The user can choose one of these filters (actually there are more than two).

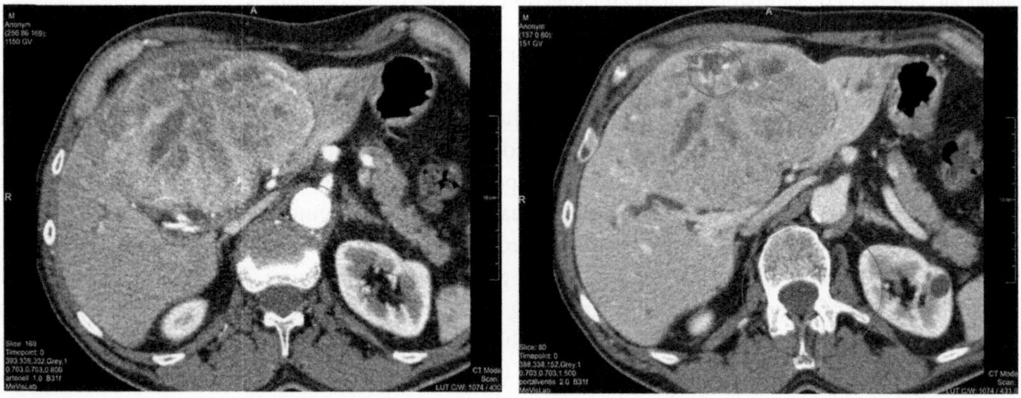

FIGURE 2.17 Portion of a CT slice in a biphasic abdominal dataset. In both images, selected regions where the contrast is enhanced, are encircled. **Left:** The contrast agent reaches the arterial structures. **Right:** Venous phase of the biphasic dataset (Courtesy of Jeanette Mönch, University of Magdeburg).

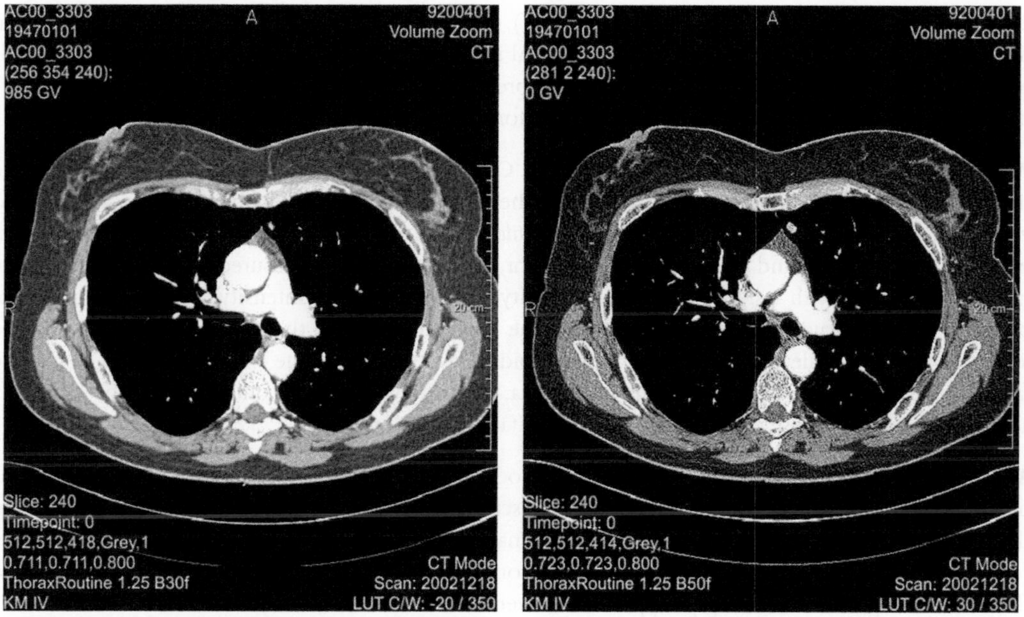

FIGURE 2.18 *A portion of a slice through the thorax is shown. Different reconstruction filters were employed in CT imaging.* ***Left:*** *a soft (smoothing) filter.* ***Right:*** *an edge-enhancing filter (Courtesy of Berthold Wein, Aachen).*

2.5.5 ARTIFACTS IN CT IMAGE ACQUISITION

Correct interpretation of CT data requires an understanding of the most severe artifacts. An artifact is a systematic difference between the measured Hounsfield units and actual attenuation coefficients [Barrett and Keat, 2004]. Due to the complex reconstruction process, CT exhibits more diverse artifacts than X-ray that degrade image quality and can make them even diagnostically unusable. Artifacts are due to

- the physical processes of data acquisition,
- patient-related factors, and
- imperfections in the scanner [Barrett and Keat, 2004].

Imperfections in the scanner, of course, should be avoided. Regularly, CT scanners are checked and calibrated using phantoms of different size and shape. Despite ongoing developments on reduction or avoidance of artifacts, still a number of artifacts has to be considered [Barrett and Keat, 2004, Yazdi and Beaulieu, 2008]. In the following, we briefly describe the following selected artifacts:

- beam hardening artifacts,
- partial volume artifacts,
- artifacts from metallic implants,
- scattering artifacts,
- motion artifacts.

Beam Hardening Artifacts These artifacts are physics-based. Beam hardening refers to the fact that an X-ray beam increases its energy after passing through a dense object. This artifact is illustrated in

Barrett and Keat [2004] by means of a (uniform) cylindrical phantom. The attenuation decreases in the center of the cylinder, leading to a higher signal intensity compared to beams passing a smaller volume of the cylinder. Various techniques exist to suppress these artifacts, e.g., flat metal pieces "pre-harden" the beams to remove lower energy components before the beam enters the human body.

Partial Volume Artifacts The limited resolution of a CT scanner leads to an averaging effect if multiple tissues occur in a volume element. This is called the *partial volume effect* and hampers image analysis and visualization of small structures. The *partial volume artifact* is due to strong changes in the X-ray absorption within one volume cell and disturbs the signal. If for example a bone is measured with a CT scanner, the neighboring tissue with a significantly lower density will create a steep intensity difference that cannot properly be reconstructed. Hence, the voxels on the boundary between the two tissue materials will be low-pass filtered. While this low-pass filtering avoids aliasing artifacts, the smoothed intensities create false connections or holes in the resulting image data. Partial volume artifacts must therefore be taken into account for segmentation, classification, and quantitative image analysis.

Artifacts from Metallic Implants These artifacts are another variant of beam hardening artifacts. They occur in case of non-removable metallic elements in the scanner, such as dental or vascular implants. Without dedicate correction algorithms they hamper the image interpretation seriously in a rather large image region. Correction algorithms may not reliably reconstruct the interface between metallic implants and the surrounding, but they strongly suppress the adverse effects in a distance. Since this kind of artifacts is particularly severe (see Fig. 2.19), it gained widespread attention and many correction algorithms have been devised [Kalender *et al.*, 1987, Watzke and Kalender, 2004].

Scattering Artifacts occur primarily in multi slice CT scanners with a wide and rapid coverage in the longitudinal direction. Scattering artifacts are caused by scattered photons [Zbijewski and Beekman, 2006]. Scattering artifacts appear as dark shadows between bones. Various software correction techniques were suggested, e.g., [Sabo-Napadensky and Amir, 2005].

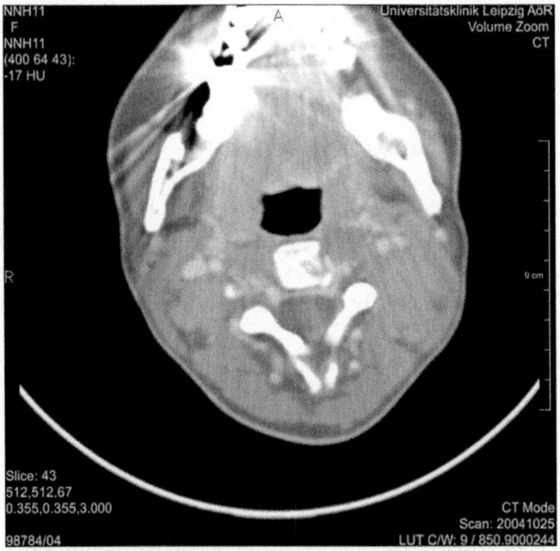

FIGURE 2.19 *A CT slice where metallic implants in the teeth severely hamper diagnosis.*

Motion *Artifacts* These artifacts belong to the patient-related artifacts and are due to movement of the scanned object, e.g., movement of the patient, breathing, heartbeat, or muscle relaxation. They appear as blurred regions where the anatomy is not sharply depicted. Motion blurring might be reduced by a number of techniques, such as ECG-triggered data acquisition of coronary CT data. Obviously, fast imaging during breathhold reduces motion artifacts.

A further limitation of CT data is noise resulting in grain. This problem is particularly severe in case of thin slice CT data with a low to moderate dose. As a consequence, data may be resampled at a lower resolution or, better, should be acquired in a lower resolution on the first place.

Streak Artifacts These artifacts summarize artifacts represented by dark or bright streaks in CT image data. Thus, they are not single artifacts, as the artifacts discussed before. Streak artifacts result from beam hardening and occur in strongly heterogenous regions between two dense objects, such as bone, contrast-enhanced vasculature, or metal. The artifact leads to streaks and dark bands in the image. These streaks can be caused by undersampling, photon starvation, motion, beam hardening, or scatter. This type of artifact commonly occurs in the posterior fossa of the brain, or if there are metal implants.

Streak artifacts and other beam hardening artifacts may be suppressed by adapting the scanned anatomy to avoid larger skeletal structures. The gantry tilt and the patient position influence beam hardening artifacts. In addition, manufacturers use beam hardening correction software.

Discussion Experienced radiologists recognize artifacts often by sudden changes of anatomical shape, such as vessels that no longer have a plausible cross section. In their education, radiologists get trained on the assessment of anatomical and pathological structures in case of artifacts. Whole books describe and illustrate these issues with large series of case studies. The complexity of knowledge involved in correctly assessing medical image data in case of artifacts explains why automatic solutions are so hard to develop.

2.5.6 CURRENT AND FUTURE DEVELOPMENTS OF CT SCANNERS

New CT devices are currently under development and in first clinical trials. We briefly discuss recent developments in CT reconstruction and multislice CT development, including dual source CT scanners. Most of these recent developments are primarily motivated by the peculiarities of cardiac imaging. To visualize the morphology of the beating heart, even in the presence of a fast and irregular heart beat is particularly challenging and relevant for the diagnosis of severe pathologies, such as the coronary heart disease (CHD).

256 and 320 Slice CT The recent improvements in detector technology with further miniaturized detector elements resulted in CT scanners that acquire 256 or even 320 slices simultaneously. While some scanners indeed comprise 256 rows or detector elements, others, e.g., the Brilliance iCT from Philips healthcare, contain 128 rows but use two alternating focal spots and are also referred to as 256-slice CT [Hsiao *et al.*, 2010]. A CT scanner with 320 detector rows was introduced by Toshiba Medical systems. These developments are particularly relevant for coronary CT, since the reduced examination times favor the acquisition of high-quality image data of the beating heart. As an example, one of the first case reports on using the 320 slice CT technology from Dewey *et al.* [2008] describes the use for evaluating severe coronary heart disease. The improved image quality in cardiac imaging enables a better discrimination of various plaque types, which is essential for risk assessment and treatment planning. The 320 slice technology in cardiac imaging is also used to capture the heart over several heart cycles, leading to four-dimensional CT data (with time being the fourth dimension). A recent survey on coronary CT angiography [Sun and Ng, 2011] lists numerous studies confirming that the severity of stenosis in coronary vessels as well as the assessment of plaque morphology strongly benefits from 256 to 320 slice CT scanners. The resulting datasets are rather large, comprising volumes of $512 \times 512 \times 400$ slices with isotropic voxels of 0.4–0.5^3 mm [Hennemuth, 2012].

Dual Source CT An essential line of development is the dual source CT where two detector units are placed in the scanner, with a 90 degree displacement against each other [Flohr *et al.*, 2006]. The main advantage of these devices is the improved temporal resolution (the detector array system needs to rotate only half of the angle compared to single source CT) [Hsiao *et al.*, 2010]. With the second generation of these devices a rotation is performed within 0.28 seconds. Dual source CTs were introduced by SIEMENS, but meanwhile other manufacturers, such as General Electric, also enables dual source CT imaging. While the spatial resolution is not changed, the acquisition times are reduced by a factor of two.

A further significant advantage is that the two sources may be operated at two different energy levels, e.g., at 140 and 100 kV. This *dual energy* mode results in two energy spectra and enables a detailed characterization of tissues and a better discrimination of different tissue types. This potential was recognized early [Genant and Boyd, 1977], but only recently it was technically feasible to exploit it and a variety of applications were described, e.g., the analysis of kidney stones, ligaments, and the discrimination between bones and vasculature [Johnson *et al.*, 2007]. In particular, if combined with contrast agents, this enables a range of new applications, since the detectors are operated simultaneously, allowing dual energy acquisition with lower dose and reduced motion artifacts compared to a conventional protocol. The differentiation of bones and vessels, especially in case of imaging neurovascular diseases, was investigated by Zhang *et al.* [2010b]. Basically, they achieved the same diagnostic quality that was previously possible with dedicated bone subtraction techniques [Tomandl *et al.*, 2006], a protocol where CT data are acquired with and without contrast agent, like a Digital Subtraction Angiography. However, less than half of the radiation dose was necessary with dual energy CT scanners.

The increased spatial and temporal resolution of these devices is important for a variety of complex diagnostic and therapeutic processes. The diagnosis of coronary heart disease, in particular the detection and classification of calcifications in coronary arteries, is a major field of application. In general, the dual energy mode enables to reliably discriminate structures that are rare in the human body, e.g., iodine. Thus, iodine uptake in a tumor after administering a contrast-agent with iodine may be clearly depicted and enables to assess malignancy. Also gout is diagnosed this way. The following series of images (Figs. 2.20–2.22) illustrates the potential of dual energy CTs. They are all acquired with a Siemens SOMATOM Definition Flash scanner. The spatial resolution equals 0.33 mm, and the energy levels of 100 and 140 kV have been used with a scan time of about 15 s.

While image reconstruction is primarily performed by means of filtered back projection, iterative techniques enable the same image quality with some less radiation at the expense of significantly longer computation time [Hara *et al.*, 2009]. In 2009, GE pioneered the commercial use of the "Adaptive Statistical Iterative Reconstruction" algorithm in a commercial product and reduced the average dose from 3.8 to 2.6 mSv.[2] Similar approaches are meanwhile used in related products. The dose-saving potential of iterative techniques is discussed, e.g., in Sun and Ng [2011]. It is likely that with further enhanced processing power a further (slight) decrease of average dose is possible.

Further improvements are possible with future detectors that do not only sum up radiation but register individual photons and measure their energy. Such detectors along with improved image reconstruction techniques will enable more diagnostic applications and reduced ionizing radiation.

Besides these developments, many attempts try to adapt the exposure to the body region and thus to further limit radiation. Mulkens *et al.* [2005] investigated 200 patients and analyzed five body regions,

2 Source: Wikipedia (accessed: 20/7/2012).

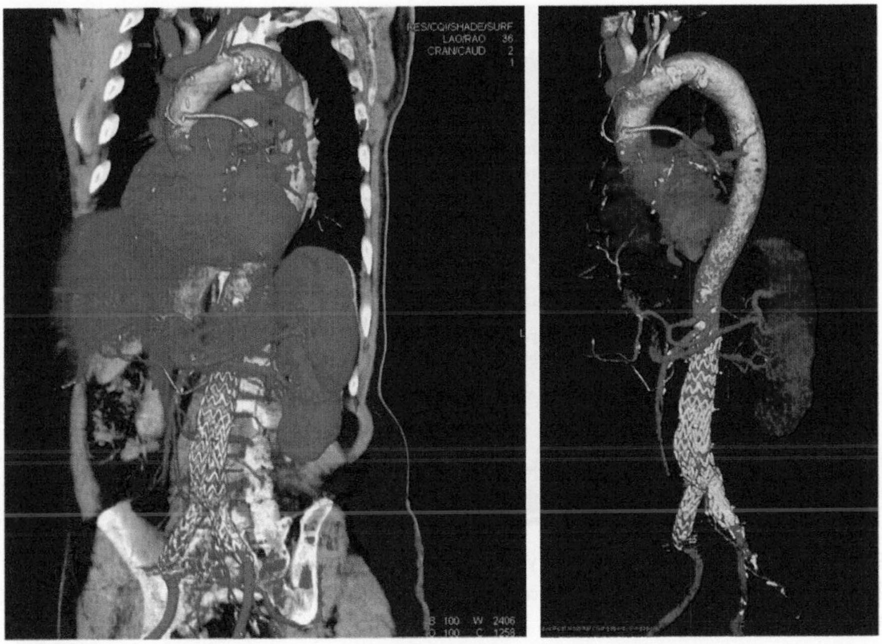

FIGURE 2.20 *Volume renderings made from dual energy CT of an aortic stent and its surroundings. On the left an overview showing more of the anatomical context, and on the right a rendering showing only the aorta and stent (Images courtesy of Khoo Teck Puat Hospital, Singapore, acquired with a Siemens SOMATOM Definition Flash).*

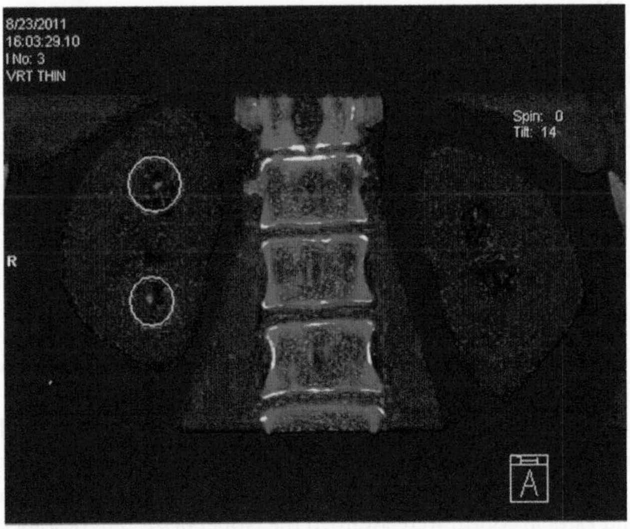

FIGURE 2.21 *Color-coded slice showing two kidney stones (Images courtesy of Manila Doctors Hospital, Philippines, acquired with a Siemens SOMATOM Definition Flash).*

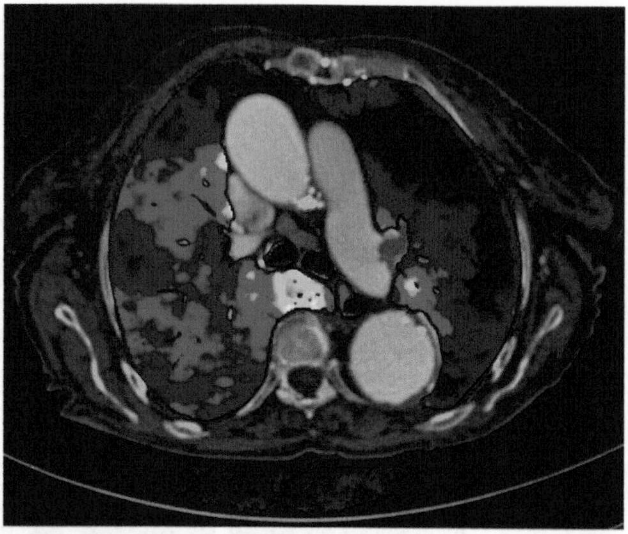

FIGURE 2.22 *Color-coded slice showing the density of the parenchyma in the lungs. After inhalation of Xenon gas, the density indicates the severity of a lung emphysema (Images courtesy of Hospital do Coracao, Sao Paulo, Brazil, acquired with a Siemens SOMATOM Definition Flash).*

e.g., the thorax and the spine, and reported on a decrease of tube current between 15% and 35% without quality degradation. Even more effective is, of course, a very careful selection of patients that undergo CT examinations. Thus, the justification of CT examination will likely be discussed more critical in the future.

2.5.7 DISCUSSION

CT data are frequently acquired and represent a huge advantage over X-ray imaging in its ability to localize pathologies and represent their shape. However, it is more expensive and the in-plane resolution is rather low. Thus, CT will not replace X-ray. CT data, in general, are rather easy to interpret, despite some artifacts that need to be considered. Due to its wide availability and the fast image acquisition, it is widely used, e.g., in emergency cases, to detect bleedings, to diagnose fractures and diseases related to skeletal structures. CT data with a high spatial resolution are required for planning surgery or radiation treatment.

2.6 MAGNETIC RESONANCE IMAGING

The dependency of the resonance frequency of protons on the magnetic field strength has been well-known for a long time. In the 1950s, it was also known that this dependency may be used to distinguish their localization. MR as imaging modality in medicine has been suggested by Lauterbur [1973] and was later refined. Most notably, extremely fast echo-planar image acquisition was developed by Mansfield [1977]. Lauterbur suggested that magnetic field gradients could be used to determine the spatial distribution of protons in water by different frequencies. Later, he became known for his work on contrast agents for MRI. Paul Lauterbur and Peter Mansfield were awarded the Nobel prize "Physiology or Medicine" in 2003 for these inventions. Finally, John Mallard should be mentioned because he headed the development of the first practical human MR scanner [Hennig, 2003].

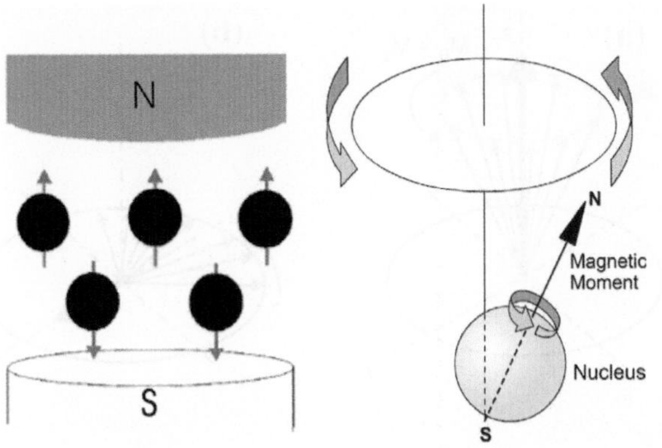

FIGURE 2.23 **Left:** The protons are aligned according to the external magnetic field. Some protons are aligned parallel to the magnetic field, while others are aligned anti-parallel. **Right:** Spin and precession of the protons. Next to their self-rotation (spin), they perform an additional precession movement around the direction of the magnetic field (Courtesy of Ragnar Bade, University of Magdeburg).

2.6.1 PRINCIPLES OF MRI

Magnetic resonance imaging (MRI) is based on different properties of human tissue in a (strong) magnetic field. In particular, the occurrence of Hydrogen nuclei in human tissue is exploited for image generation. They can be considered as small dipole magnets aligning themselves either parallel or anti-parallel along a strong external magnetic field. While aligned in that field, the Hydrogen protons (a Hydrogen nucleus only consists of one proton) spin arbitrarily around the axis of the field. There is a slight difference in the number of parallel and anti-parallel aligned protons (see Fig. 2.23, left).

In MRI a strong magnetic field is applied over the subject that is to be scanned. Unpaired protons, mostly those in the nuclei of the hydrogen atoms that form part of water molecules, precess about the magnetic field direction at the Larmor frequency[3] ω, an angular frequency that is related to the strength of the magnetic field B at that point by the gyromagnetic ratio γ. This precession is analogous to that of a spinning top in the gravity field.

When a radio frequency pulse is applied with a certain frequency, all protons precessing at exactly that frequency will resonate and precess in the plane orthogonal to the magnetic field (see Fig. 2.23, right). When the radio frequency pulse is switched off, these protons return to their lower energy state precessing around the magnetic field. In doing this, they release the energy difference as photons which are detected by the scanner as an electromagnetic signal. The speed at which protons regain their lower energy state, or the *relaxation time*, is related to the type of material they find themselves in.

A 90 degree RF pulse moves the protons perpendicular to the magnetic field, resulting in a zero z-component (along the magnetic field). After the stimulation of the protons they slowly release the received energy, *de-phase*, and re-align with the magnetic field. This *relaxation* is described as *free induction decay* (FID) and is divided into the transverse and longitudinal relaxation. The first relaxation of the transverse magnetization—also called spin-spin relaxation—describes the de-phasing of the x/y-component of the precession (see Fig. 2.24). The transversal relaxation is an exponential decay. The time required for a 63% decay $(1 - 1/e)$ relaxation is called T2 and is in the order of a few milliseconds. The longitudinal, or

3 The *Larmor* frequency can be described as the resonance frequency of the protons in a magnetic field. It is determined by the *gyromagnetic ratio* of the protons (which is constant for the respective protons, e.g., Hydrogen protons) and the strength of the magnetic field.

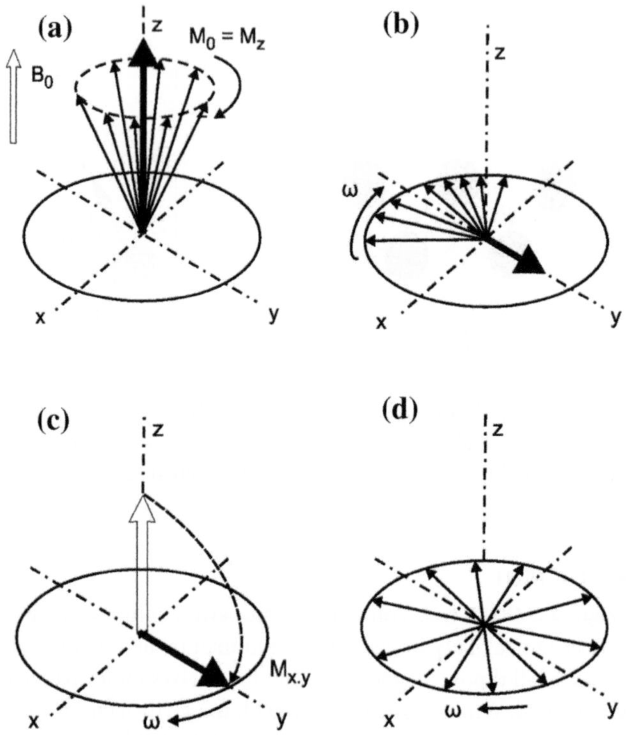

FIGURE 2.24 *Spin-spin relaxation. The protons are aligned in the magnetic field (a). In (b), they are moved due to a 90 degree RF impulse. In (c) and (d), protons de-phase (Courtesy of Petra Schumann, University of Magdeburg).*

spin-lattice (or spin-grid) relaxation describes the re-alignment according to the magnetic field, thus the restoring of the z-component (Fig. 2.25). This relaxation has a logarithmic increase. The time until 63% of the original magnetization is restored is called T1 and is in the order of 1 second. T1 largely depends on the material (tissue), its structure, and its surrounding tissue. Since water has a long T1 and T2 relaxation time, tissue that contains a large ratio of water will also have a long T1 and T2 time. The actual measured volumetric information is the proton density σ, which needs to be reconstructed at the specific voxels. In Figures 2.26 and 2.27, the relaxation curve for different brain tissue and the corresponding T1 and T2 times are shown. The different times are due to different densities of hydrogen protons in different tissue types; cerebrospinal fluid has the highest water content (97%). Gray matter and white matter have an 84% and 71% water content, respectively.

To reconstruct the spatial information of the measured signal, two additional gradient magnetic fields are applied [Lehmann *et al.*, 1997]. The first field selects the slice in z-direction of the volume, since only one layer of protons suffices the Larmor frequency for the main and gradient magnetic fields. An additional gradient field in x-direction selects a y-slab. By rotating the gradient fields, other projection directions are measured. This feature is very useful, since the slice direction can be adapted to the medical exam. This is not possible with a CT scan (always axial).

MR imaging is performed in a ring magnet, which is large enough to enclose the whole patient. Inside this magnet, gradient coils are embedded such that magnetic field gradients in three orthogonal directions

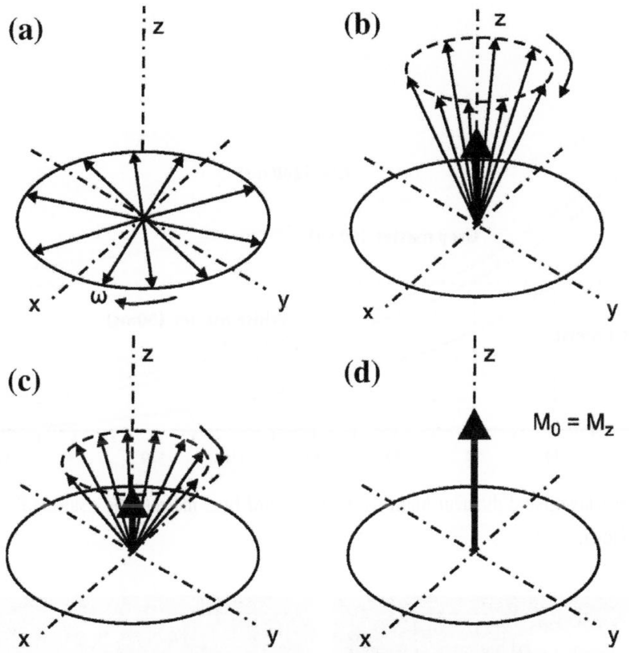

FIGURE 2.25 Spin-grid relaxation. In the upper left image, protons move in the transversal plane. In the upper right, lower left, and the lower right image, protons are again re-aligned according to the magnetic field—the transversal magnetization decreases (Courtesy of Petra Schumann, University of Magdeburg).

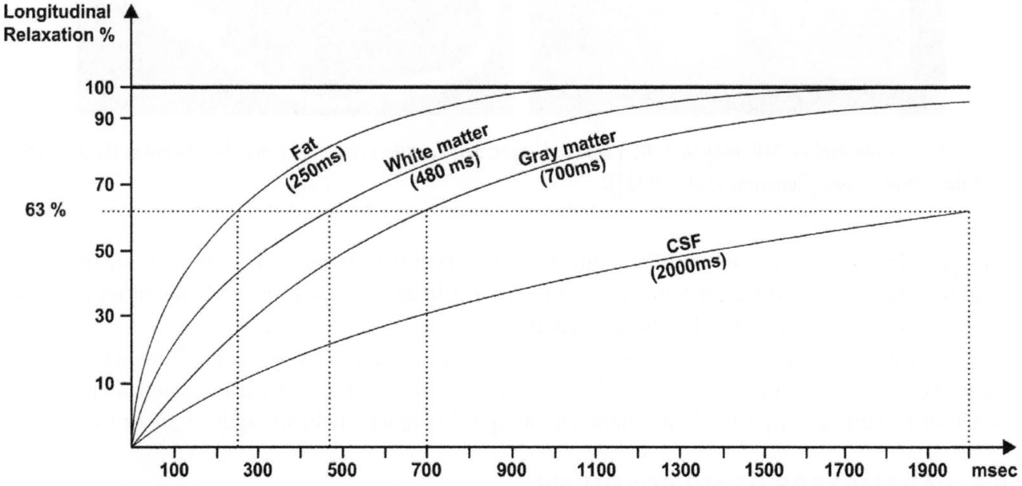

FIGURE 2.26 Longitudinal relaxation of different brain tissue. The dotted lines indicate the resulting T1 time (Courtesy of Ragnar Bade, University of Magdeburg).

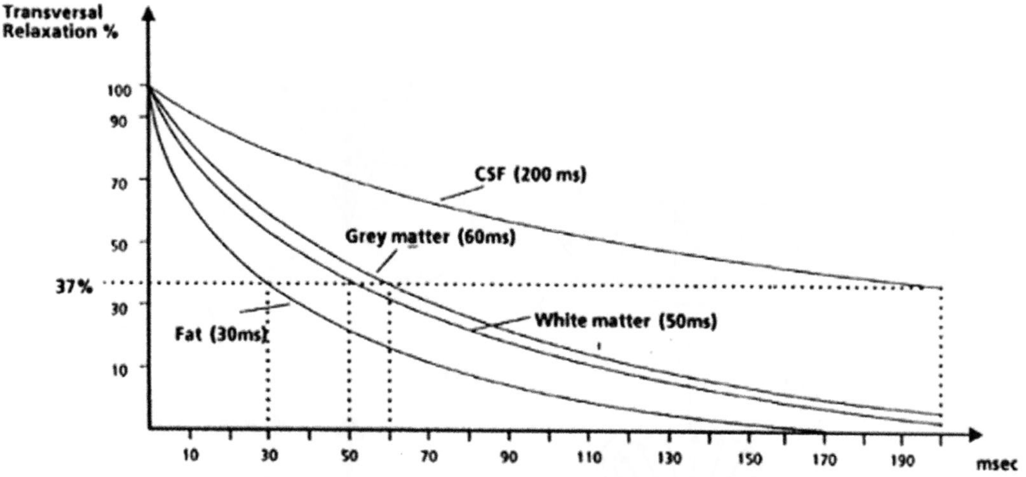

FIGURE 2.27 Transversal relaxation of different brain tissue. The dotted lines indicate the resulting T2 time (Courtesy of Ragnar Bade, University of Magdeburg).

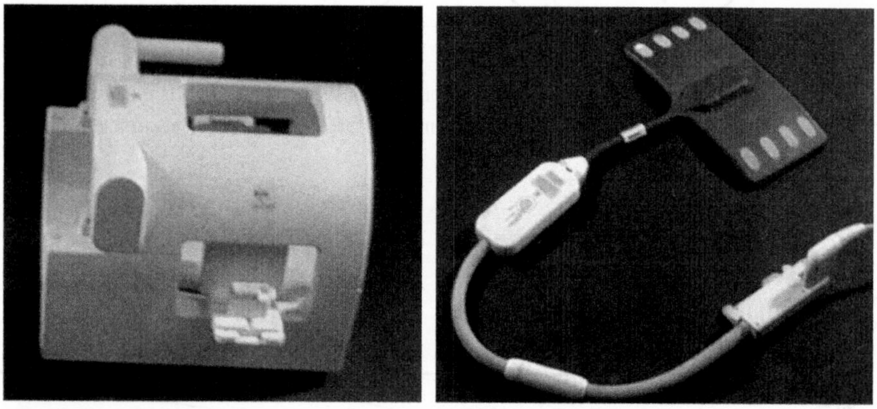

FIGURE 2.28 Coils used for MR imaging. **Left:** *A head coil,* **right:** *flexible surface coils which may be attached at the stomach and back of the patient (From: [Rummeny et al., 2002]).*

can be generated. The coils used for MRI acquisition are very different depending on the body region that should be imaged. In Figure 2.28, some frequently used coils are depicted. The coils are either integrated sender and receiver (such as head coils) or separate sender and receiver coils.

Depending on the strength of the magnetic field, MRI scanners are characterized as "low field" scanners with a magnetic field strength of up to 0.8 T (Tesla), as "full field" scanners with a magnetic field strength of 1.5 T, or recently as "high-field" scanners with a typical magnetic field strength of 3 T or more.

2.6.2 PARAMETERS OF MR SCANNING

MR acquisition itself is characterized by a huge parameter space. In general, 90 degree pulses as well as additional 180 degree pulses are applied to the magnetic field. The additional pulses compensate for inhomogeneities in the magnetic field and lead to more reliable results than would be achieved by directly measuring the FID. The common MR sequences composed of 90–180 degree impulses are referred to as *Spin echo* sequences. The signal intensity (SI) in these sequences is computed according to Equation 2.8 [Rummeny *et al.*, 2002].

$$SI \sim PDe^{\frac{-TE}{T2}}\left(1 - e^{\frac{-TR}{T1}}\right) \tag{2.8}$$

PD is the proton density, T1 and T2 the relaxation times of the specific material.

Different protocols describe sequences of various RF pulses and the actual measurement of the signal where the time between the initial stimulation and the measurement is called *echo time* T_E and the time between two (initial) stimulation cycles is called *repetition time* T_R. By varying T_E and T_R, different weight data can be achieved:

- with short echo (<25 ms) and short repetition times (<500 ms), the signal is dominated by the T1 relaxation time (T1-weighted),
- with long T_E (>1500 ms) and long T_R (>50 ms), the T2 relaxation time is dominating the signal (T2 weighting),
- with a long T_R and a short T_E (<25 ms), the signal is neither T1 nor T2 and can be seen as *the pure (proton) density function* (proton-weighted) [Cho *et al.*, 1993].

A frequent protocol is Echo Planar Imaging, or short EPI, which is a very fast acquisition method. EPI protocols are often used in functional MRI and Diffusion Tensor MRI discussed later. The drawback of EPI protocols is the increased geometric distortion.

Figure 2.29 compares T1- and T2-weighted images acquired for neuroradiological diagnosis. T1-weighted acquisition sequences emphasize tissue signals and suppress fluid signals with a very low

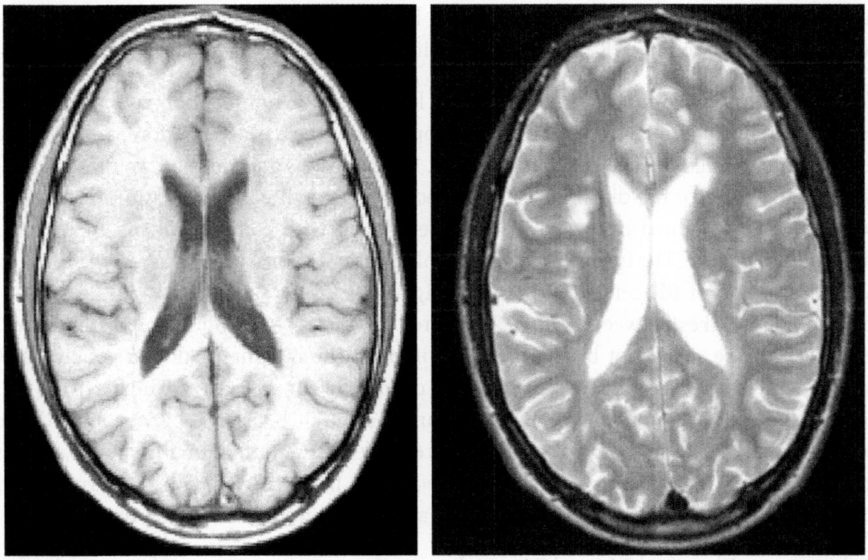

FIGURE 2.29 *Comparison of T1- and T2-weighted cerebral MRI data. In the left T1-weighted image (TR: 4000 ms, TE: 96 ms), the cerebrospinal fluid appears dark, whereas in the right image (TR: 500 ms, TE: 17 ms) the same region appears white. Also gray and white matter exhibit different intensity values in these images (Courtesy of Holger Bourquain, Fraunhofer MEVIS Bremen).*

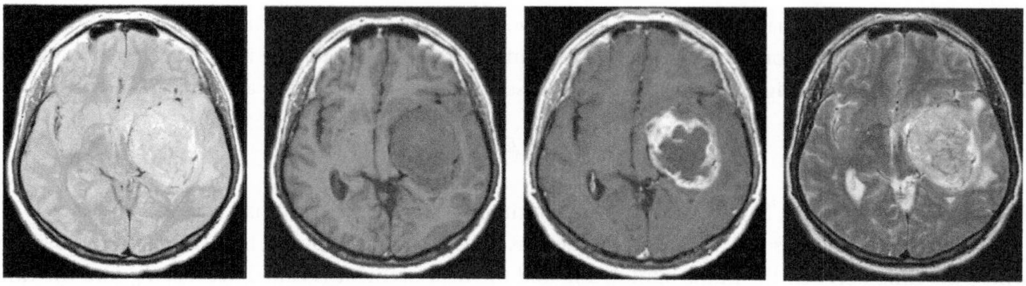

(a) PD-weighted **(b)** T1 native **(c)** T1 contrasted **(d)** T2

FIGURE 2.30 *A set of four MR sequences provides complementary information for the diagnosis of a brain tumor. (a) Proton density-weighted sequence, (b) T1-weighted native sequence, (c) contrast-enhanced T1-weighted sequence, and (d) T2-weighted sequence (Courtesy of Holger Bourquain, Fraunhofer MEVIS Bremen).*

image intensity. In contrast, T2-weighted acquisition sequences emphasize fluid signals with a high image intensity.

Orthogonal to the T1/T2 weighting, a variety of acquisition sequences are available. Each sequence puts emphasis on different optimization targets. An MRI FLASH (Fast Low Angle Shot) sequence for example enables a very rapid image acquisition. Combined with a T1-weighted image acquisition, it is often used for the acquisition of dynamic phenomena, e.g., the blood flow. Further sequences focus on different aspects of the metabolism. MR Angiography (MRA) is used for vascular imaging with or without a contrast enhancing agent. Typical examples of these (non-contrast agent) imaging protocols are Time-of-Flight (TOF) and Phase-Contrast-Angiography (PCA). Note that flow artifacts can reduce the quality and, in some cases of turbulent blood flows, lead to pseudo-stenosis.[4] New pulse sequences are also continuously developed by MR physicists to optimize for special diagnostic procedures.

Multimodal Imaging The large parameter space of MRI leads to a high number of imaging protocols that put emphasis on different functional or physiological properties of the tissue. Therefore, an MRI examination does often contain a variety of five or more different MRI scans. As an example, we present images from four sequences acquired for the diagnosis of an astrocytoma, a malignant brain tumor. The set of images comprise T1- and T2-weighted images, a T1-weighted image with contrast enhancement and a proton density-weighted sequence. The images provide complementary information to assess the location, extent, and possible infiltration of adjacent structures (see Fig. 2.30).

A typical MRI scan takes between 2 and 25 minutes. This relatively long scanning time is dominated by the relaxation of the spins, not by the time required for the measurements. In general, MRI data—acquired with a full-field MRI scanner—have a lower resolution compared to CT image data (the in-plane resolution/pixel distance is often between 1 and 2 mm and the slice distance between 2 and 5 mm). The resolution also depends on the acquisition time (more pulses are required for a higher spatial resolution, which leads to increased acquisition times). This, however, has changed with modern high-field MRI scanners, which acquire significantly higher (spatial and/or temporal) resolution image data.

Contrast Enhancement The usual T1- and T2-weighted images are often not sufficient to display the target structures adequately. As a consequence, either a sophisticated acquisition technique is used, e.g., to

4 A stenosis appears in the image data although it is not actually present.

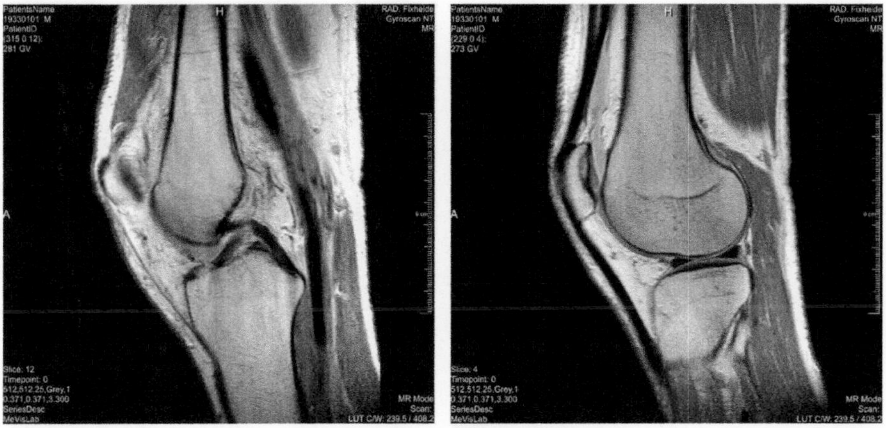

FIGURE 2.31 *Different slices of an MR examination of the knee. The high soft tissue contrast enables a good assessment of the ligaments and muscles (Courtesy of Holger Bourquain, Fraunhofer MEVIS Bremen).*

suppress structures such as fat, or a contrast agent is employed. Most commonly, contrast agents with special magnetic properties are employed. Gadolinium compounds are frequently used in connection with a T1-weighted image. Structures, which are enhanced by gadolinium, appear bright on T1-weighted images. Vascular structures or strongly vascularized tumors become clearly visible with contrast enhancement. In the CT section, we discussed cardiovascular imaging as an important application area. MR is also relevant in this area and plays an increasing role, since it enables a comprehensive analysis of morphology and functional parameters of myocardial tissue. Compared to CT data, however the spatial resolution is lower (often 1 mm^3) and image acquisition takes significantly longer increasing motion-related artifacts.

2.6.3 ARTIFACTS IN MRI DATA

MRI artifacts can be classified into

- artifacts by physiological causes (e.g., artifacts due to (body) motion or (blood) flow),
- hardware problems such as inhomogeneities of the magnetic field, and
- problems with the inherent physics (chemical shift, presence of metal, etc.).

Inhomogeneity, the most severe of these artifacts, strongly depends on the geometry of the coils employed in the scanner. Head coils only have one open end (near the shoulder), which leads to an intensity variation from the head toward the neck. Surface coils, which are used in abdominal imaging, for example, lead to stronger inhomogeneities. The intensity strongly depends on the distance to the coils.

Furthermore the partial volume artifact (recall § 2.5.5) has to be considered in MRI data as well. In Figure 2.32, a thin membrane located in the area indicated by the yellow oval is affected by that effect. Since the neighboring cavities, which are separated by this membrane, are represented with high intensities, the low intensity thin membrane could not be fully reconstructed. In Figure 2.32 the resolution of the MRI scanner is not sufficient to represent the (low intensity) septum between the (high intensity) upper cerebral ventricles, resulting in false connections between the upper ventricles.

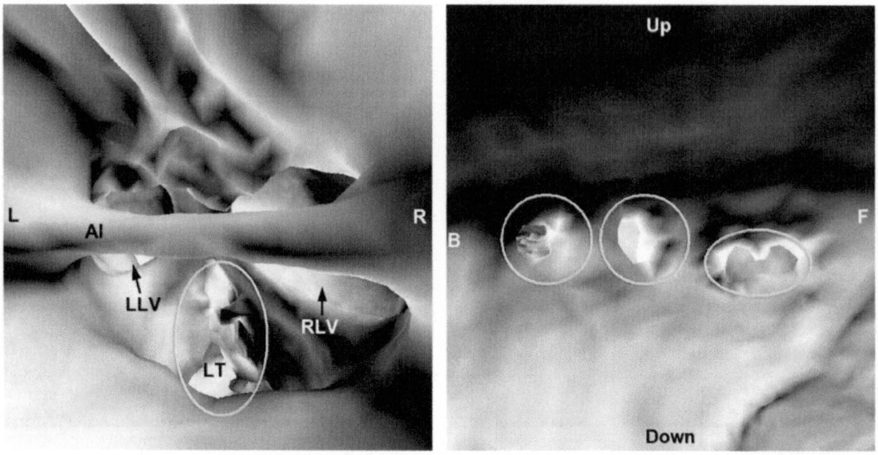

FIGURE 2.32 *Partial volume effect in an MRI scan of the cerebral ventricular system.* **Left:** *The thin membrane Lamina Terminalis (LT, yellow marking) at the floor of the third cerebral ventricle could not be fully reconstructed.* **Right:** *False connections (yellow markings) are due to the incompletely reconstructed septum between the upper lateral cerebral ventricles. "L" and "R" point to the left and right directions, "B" points to the back and "F" points to the frontal direction. "AI" depicts the Adhesio Interthalamica, and "LLV" and "RLV" to the entrance of the left and right cerebral ventricles (Foramen of Monro) (Courtesy of Dirk Bartz, University of Leipzig).*

2.6.4 FUNCTIONAL MRI

Functional MRI or short fMRI detects changes in cerebral blood flow and oxygen metabolism as a result of neural activation. These changes are recorded in time-intensity curves [Friston *et al.*, 1994]. The "blood oxygen level-dependent" (BOLD) effect is employed for image acquisition. Besides neuroanatomical studies, fMRI is clinically used to support access and resection planning in minimally-invasive epilepsy and brain tumor surgery [Gumprecht *et al.*, 2002].

fMRI data is acquired while the patient performs cognitive or behavioral tasks in an MR scanner, which leads to measurable changes of local blood flow and oxygenation. Sensorimotor and language regions, such as Wernicke's areal and the Broca's area, can be identified by tracking these changes. Significant research is dedicated to identify simple tasks that indicate the responsible brain region reliably. For the identification of the language region, for example, persons are asked to tell the names of the month, to generate words starting with a given character, or to fit words to a given noun [Prothmann *et al.*, 2005].

fMRI data are acquired along with anatomical MRI data. Activation signals are superimposed to MRI data in order to convey the anatomical location of certain regions (see Fig. 2.33). The correct mapping of functional data to the anatomy requires the *registration* of the two datasets. This challenging task is described in § 4.8 .

Most difficulties of the analysis of fMRI data are caused by long acquisition times and the complex nature of the recorded phenomena, which cause various artifacts. The visualization of activation patterns is guided by thresholds relating to

- the probability of an activation, and
- to the minimum size of a cluster, which is regarded as region.

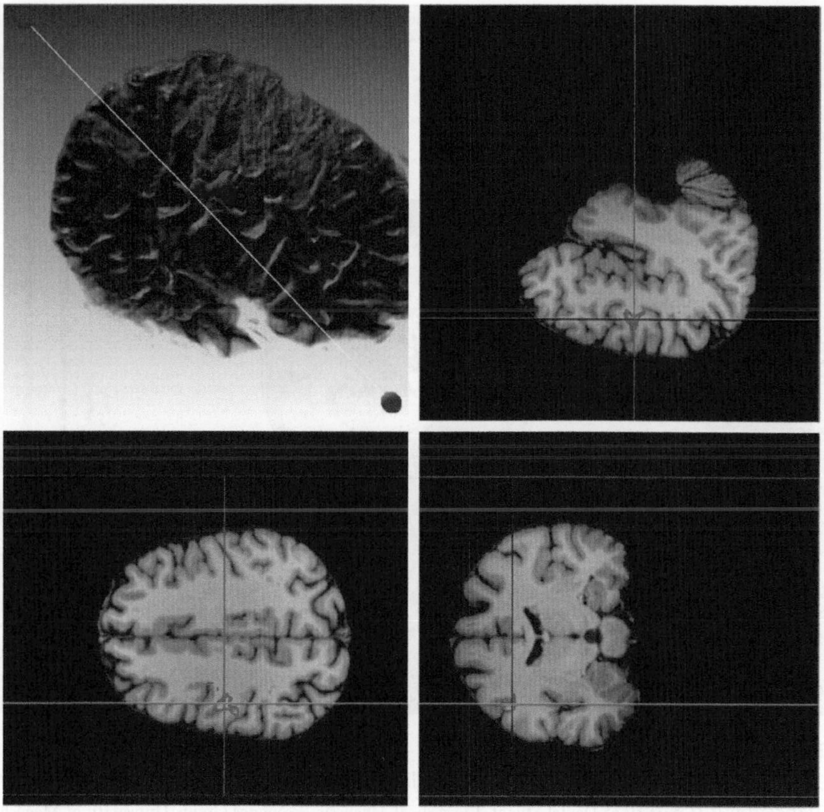

FIGURE 2.33 *Functional MRI data are acquired after auditory stimulation. The resulting activations are overlaid with anatomical MRI data. The integrated visualization of axial, sagittal, and coronal slices as well as a 3D volume rendering clearly reveal the location of the activation (Courtesy of David Kilias, Leibniz Institute for Neurobiology, Magdeburg).*

To address motion artifacts, modern MRI scanners provide motion correction. Various toolkits are common to analyze fMRI data. The BrainVoyager® [5] supports a retrospective motion correction and noise reduction, volume-based statistical analysis methods and a variety of visualization techniques. The second widespread software tool for the analysis of fMRI data is Statistical Parametric Mapping (SPM) provided by the Department of Imaging Neuroscience, University College of London. It provides even more advanced methods for the statistical analysis of fMRI data and supports other functional modalities, such as PET (see § 2.8). The fundamental text on SPM is the Human Brain Function book [Frackowiak *et al.*, 1997]. The SPM suite and associated theory was developed by Karl Friston for routine statistical analysis of functional neuroimaging data, primarily PET, and was released in 1991.

Before the advent of fMRI, activation patterns have been determined intraoperatively by stimulating the patient (with Electroencephalography (EEG) and Magnetoencephalography (MEG)). fMRI, in contrast, allows to map functional areas non-invasively to anatomical regions. Comparisons with the previous gold

5 http://www.brainvoyager.com/.

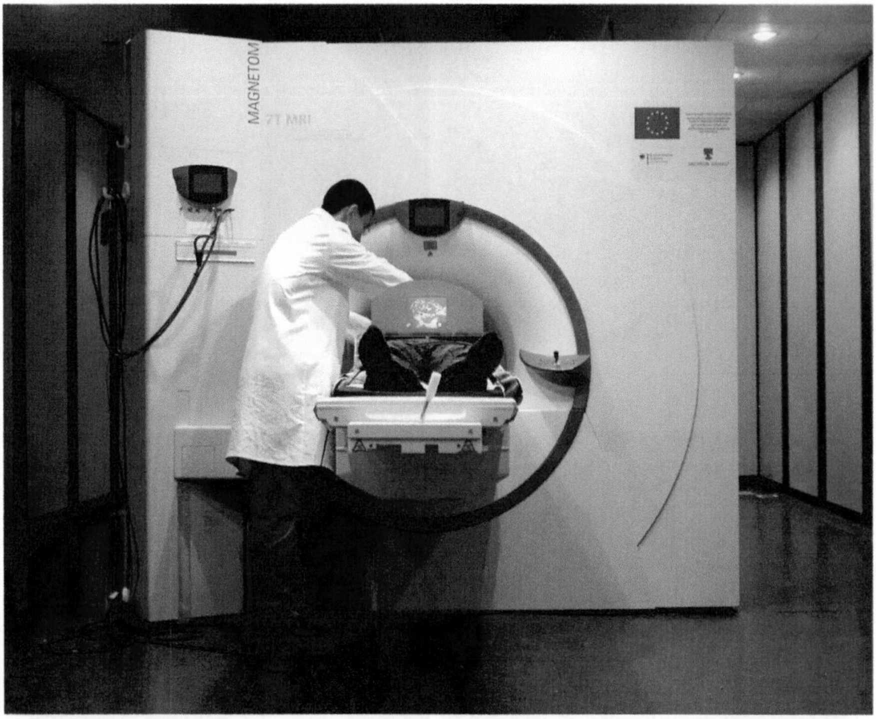

FIGURE 2.34 *A 7 Tesla scanner installed in 2004 that needs a substantial iron shield (240 tons). The magnet bore has a size of 3.4 m (3.8 m including external coverings). 1500 liters helium are required to cool the wire to the necessary temperature of 4 Kelvin (−269 °Celsius) (Courtesy of Daniel Stucht, Biomedical Magnetic Resonance Group, University of Magdeburg).*

standard, intraoperative activation, show a good correlation [Lurito *et al.*, 2000, Rutten *et al.*, 2002]. Therefore, fMRI is now widely used. A combination of intraoperative MRI and fMRI data to enhance neurosurgical interventions was proposed by Roux *et al.* [2001].

2.6.5 ULTRA-HIGH-FIELD MRI

While MR scanners with a field strength of 1.5 and high-field scanners with 3 Tesla represent the standard in clinical routine, in recent years ultra-high-field scanners with 7, 9.4 or even 11.7 Tesla field strength have been realized. These MR scanners are very expensive, both in the acquisition and installation stage and later during operation. A 7 Tesla MR scanner has a magnet that has a weight of more than 30 tons and an even larger metal shield around it is necessary to protect the environment from the fringe field (Fig. 2.34).

With these dimensions, the physical installation is a challenging endeavor. Usually, a new building is necessary to host an ultra-high-field MR scanner. Thus, they are primarily used for research purposes so far. Like conventional MR devices, neuroimaging is a major application area serving, e.g., a better understanding of neurodegenerative diseases [Schmierer *et al.*, 2010]. However, more and more studies indicate a potentially clinically relevant advantage of the image quality that can be obtained with these scanners. The higher field strength, in principle, enables an improved spatial resolution. However, geometric distortions and inhomogeneities also increase (see Fig. 2.35). Thus, a significant research effort from medical physics was necessary to optimize protocols and sequences to actually exploit the potential for improved image

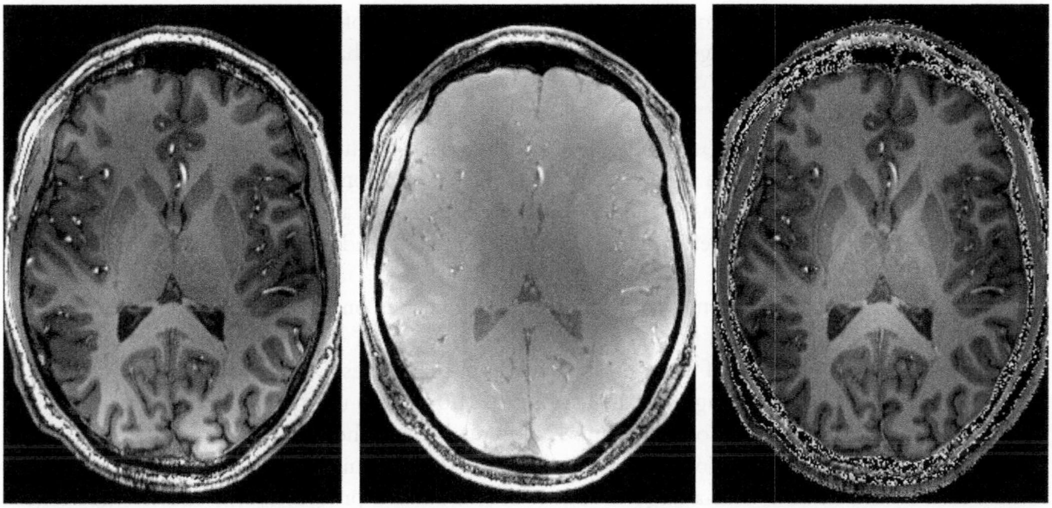

FIGURE 2.35 *MRI brain data from a 7 Tesla scanner deliver excellent soft tissue contrast. A T1-weighted MPRAGE protocol is used.* ***Left:*** *The original T1-weighted data exhibit strong inhomogeneities.* ***Middle:*** *For correction of these inhomogeneities, a 3D gradient echo sequence is applied.* ***Right:*** *Inhomogeneity correction is performed dividing the image intensities of the left image and the middle image leading to an improved image quality. However, the background gets very noisy and is removed here (Courtesy of Shan Yang, Biomedical Magnetic Resonance Group, University of Magdeburg).*

quality. Major applications of ultra-high-field MRI are fMRI, arterial spin labeling—a special kind of MR perfusion imaging—and angiography.

Clinical Applications In the following, we survey selected clinical application areas and the characteristics of the image data. MRI plays an essential role in the diagnosis of multiple sclerosis (MS). However, with conventional MRI only MS lesions in the white matter of the human brain can be detected. Schmierer *et al.* [2010] showed that this is also possible for gray matter lesions with ultra-high-field MRI. They employed a 9.4 Tesla scanner, which is not admitted for patients so far. Thus, their study is based on post-mortem data and therefore also longer acquisition times were possible, leading to a very good signal-to-noise ratio. The feasibility of gray matter lesion detection with 7 Tesla MRI was shown, e.g., by Kollia *et al.* [2009] and de Graaf *et al.* [2012]. They discuss protocols and the resulting imaging quality, in particular the lesion-to-white matter contrast and the lesion-to-gray matter contrast.

Another application area is the assessment of the meniscal structure. This is currently performed with light or electron microscopy requiring tissue samples. Wang *et al.* [2010] performed non-destructive imaging using a 9.4 Tesla scanner. Their study is based on porcine knee meniscal structures.

2.6.6 DIFFUSION TENSOR IMAGING

As another important MRI variant, MRI Diffusion Tensor Imaging (DTI) has become an image modality of high interest both in (neuroscience) research and clinical application, such as neurosurgery planning. DTI exploits the anisotropic nature of water diffusion to estimate the fiber direction of neural pathways and heart muscles. Water diffusion occurs primarily parallel to the fiber direction, since membranes act as barriers to a diffusion perpendicular to the fiber. At each voxel, diffusion is characterized as a diffusion tensor. An important aspect of the analysis of DTI data is the eigenanalysis of diffusion tensors, which allows to evaluate the major fiber orientation as well as the amount of anisotropy. This modality and the interpretation of the acquired images will be explained in detail in Chapter 15.

2.6.7 DISCUSSION

CT and MRI were introduced to overcome the limitations of X-ray imaging. Over and above advanced imaging, these modalities played a significant role in the collaboration between computer scientists and medical doctors. "For the first time, it seemed to scientists, engineers and doctors, that computers might have a genuine role in medicine, permitting the introduction of procedures that simply were not possible without them." [Young, 2003]

CT and MRI are rather complementary: MRI—since it depends on a sufficient water content—does not produce a good quality signal for skeletal structures, whereas CT is less appropriate to discriminate soft tissues due to the similarity of the X-ray attenuation in soft tissues.

Due to its ability to provide a high soft tissue contrast, MRI is often used in neuroimaging (to discriminate white and gray matter) and for the diagnosis of joints, such as the shoulder and the knee. Magnetic fields, such as those used in MRI, do not harm the patient (at least nothing is known about harmful effects so far). MRI is very flexible with a large variety of sequences and protocols. This enables experienced radiologists to generate appropriate data for specific diagnostic tasks. On the other hand, considerable experience is necessary to fully exploit the potential of MRI.

The disadvantages of using MRI data are the relatively high costs and the difficulties to interpret such data. CT data can often be understood by the referring physician, whereas MRI data are carefully commented by radiologists. In particular, except biphasic datasets, a CT examination results in only one image stack, whereas MRI examinations contain a number of stacks resulting from different sequences. Due to the lower price, CT scanners are more widely available.

For computer-supported analysis and visualization of medical data, the standardized Hounsfield units are an enormous help as they allow to predefine parameter values. With MRI data, one and the same structure can have very different intensity values even within one dataset (see the liver in Fig. 2.31). For the diagnosis of a radiologist a 10% variation of the gray value is not prohibitive; for the algorithmic selection of a threshold to discriminate a particular tissue it certainly is. In § 4.2.5 we discuss algorithmic corrections of inhomogeneities in MRI data.

As a summary, we cite Hounsfield for a comparison of the two kinds of image data. "At the present time, the two techniques should perhaps be seen not as potential competitors but rather as complementary techniques that can exist side by side [Hounsfield, 1980]." Although more than 30 years old, this assessment is still valid and probably will continue being valid in the foreseeable future.

2.7 ULTRASOUND

Ultrasound scanning is based on sound waves that are emitted at very high frequencies (more than 20 KHz, 1–15 MHz) from the ultrasound probe ("transducer") into the respective body part. The sound waves penetrate human tissue at a speed of 1450–1580 m/s [Sakas and Walter, 1995]. The waves are partially reflected if they hit an interface between two tissue types (Fig. 2.36). The reflected waves are recorded by sensors located next to the sound sources. Similar to a sonar, the reflections of these sound waves are received by the transducer and used to generate the respective images.

The efficient use of ultrasonic images requires in-depth knowledge on their typical problems to prevent that wrong conclusions are drawn [Sakas and Walter, 1995]. Typical problems are:

- a significant amount of noise and speckle,

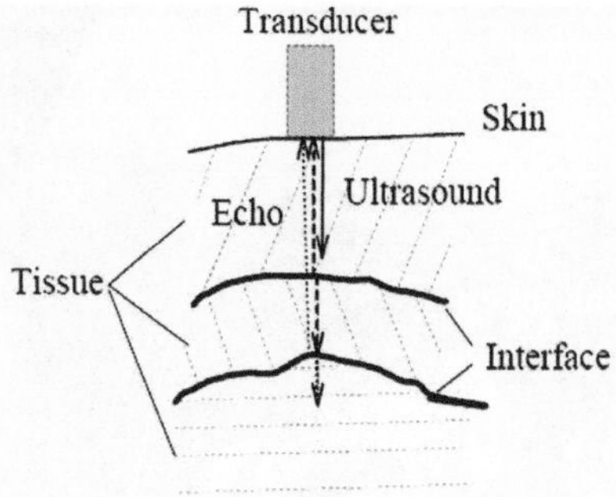

FIGURE 2.36 *Principle of ultrasound imaging. The acoustic waves are partially reflected by interfaces between different tissue types (Redrawn, inspired by [Sakas and Walter, 1995]).*

- a much lower intensity range, resulting in lower contrasts, compared to tomographic images,
- unsharp boundary regions,
- partially or completely shadowed surfaces from objects closer to and within the direction of the sound source, and
- boundaries with varying gray values due to variations of the surface orientation.

In the *B-mode* or *brightness mode*, the resulting pixels represent the echoes received by the transducer and show the respective body parts. Images generated by this mode typically show anatomical details. In contrast, the *A-mode* is only used to measure distances within the body, the *M-mode* to measure motion (e.g., of the heart), and finally, the *Doppler-mode* is used to measure velocities. Combined with the B-mode, the Doppler mode is typically employed to examine blood vessels, showing their anatomy and the blood flow simultaneously (Fig. 2.37). This is essential, e.g., to assess the neovascularization of a suspicious lymph node and thus to assess its potential malignancy.

In fluids the sound is transmitted without attenuation due to echoes. The fluids are hypoechogenic (black) and since there is no attenuation, increased echoes will occur behind it. Metastases are also hypoechogenic but do not show an increased signal behind it. Figure 2.38 depicts the kidney and the spleen in ultrasound data.

The major advantage of ultrasound is the real-time availability that is particularly important for intraoperative imaging. Ultrasound is used as navigation tool in traditional surgical interventions and in guided biopsies, such as biopsy of breast tumors [Fornage *et al.*, 1990]. Another advantage is that no ionizing radiation is employed.

Intravascular Ultrasound (IVUS) Similar to angiographic imaging, a catheter can be inserted into a vascular system to enable selective ultrasound imaging in a particular region. For this purpose, the catheter is attached with a tiny 1D transducer. With this device, a polar cross section image of the blood vessel may be generated. IVUS is used, for example, to depict the coronary arteries and has a high sensitivity in detecting plaques. Present day catheters are less than 1 mm in diameter and operate at 30–40 MHz frequencies. Mintz *et al.* [2001] describe standards for IVUS in cardiac diagnosis.

3D Ultrasound Some ultrasound scanning devices allow also three-dimensional image acquisition by acquiring and accumulating multiple scans, while tracking the movement of the ultrasound probe (performed by the physician). The most popular application is fetal examination. 3D ultrasound is acquired

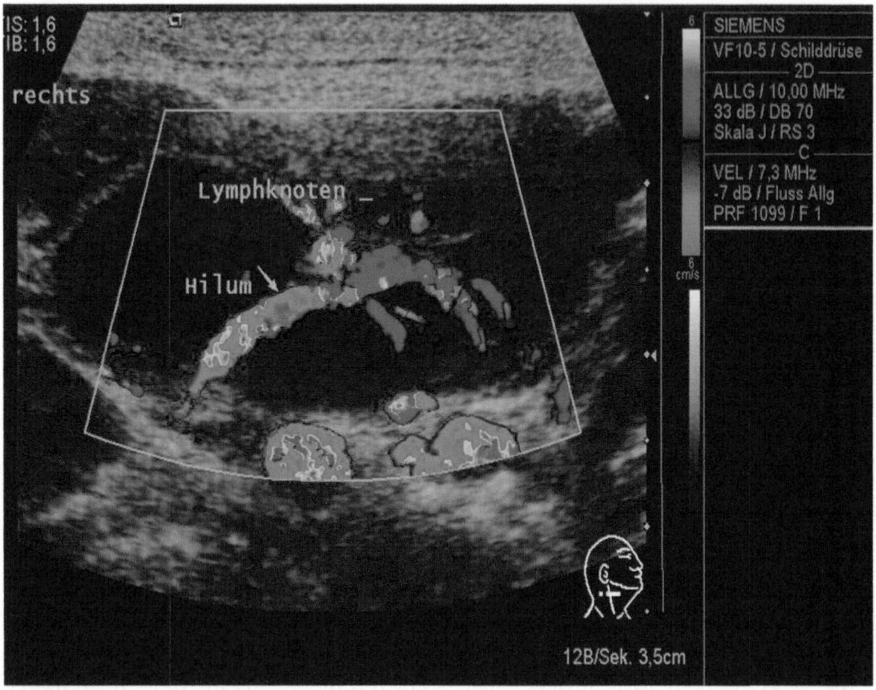

FIGURE 2.37 *The colored Doppler sonography of a suspicious neck lymph node reveals its vascularization. This information is essential to assess the potential malignancy of that lymph node (Courtesy of Christoph Arens, University Hospital Magdeburg).*

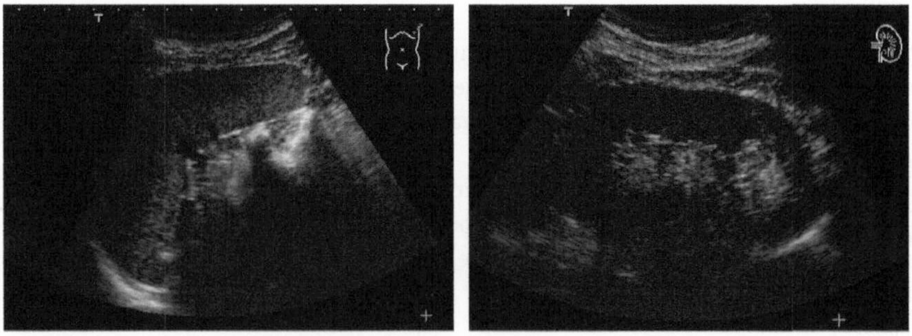

FIGURE 2.38 *Ultrasound images depicting the spleen (left) and the kidney (right). The outer portions of the kidney appear dark (low echo), whereas the fattier inner parts appear brighter. The dark stripes at the spleen represent the vessels in the hilum. The left portion of the left image appears black (acoustic shadow); the signal is strongly attenuated due to the air-filled lungs (Courtesy of Skadi Wilhelmsen, University Hospital Magdeburg).*

either by a parallel scanner—resulting in axis-aligned images—or by a rotation around a swivel. Depending on the chosen acquisition technique, different side effects must be considered; the rotational scan leads to a curvilinear organization of the data, while the parallel scan leads to an average gray value that differs from slice to slice.

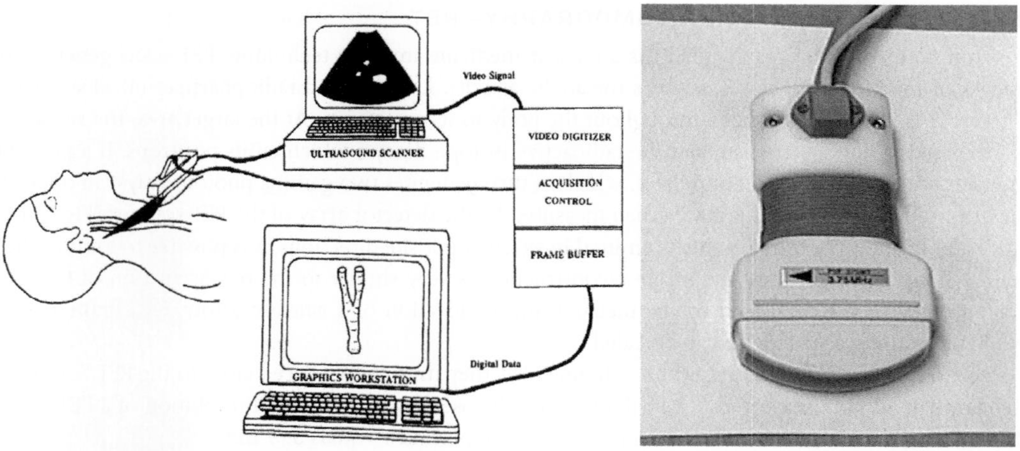

FIGURE 2.39 **Left:** *Block diagram of a 3D ultrasound display (From: [Nelson and Elvins, 1993]).* **Right:** *Mounting the magnetic receiver for tracking on the ultrasound transducer (Courtesy of Georgios Sakas and Stefan Walter, Fraunhofer Institute for Computer Graphics Research. See also [Sakas and Walter, 1995]).*

Freehand acquisition of 3D ultrasound data is an extension of 2D ultrasound, and it is hence feasible with most conventional devices [Richtscheid *et al.*, 1999]. In contrast, however, it acquires a volumetric dataset that can provide additional views, which are not available in 2D. In particular, the latter difference is similar to the difference between CT and X-ray.

Principle of 3D Ultrasound Acquisition and Processing Digital data acquisition in most cases requires a video framegrabber card in a computer that is connected with the video output of the ultrasound device [Richtscheid *et al.*, 1999] (see Fig. 2.39). During data acquisition, all B-scan images are digitized by the frame grabber. A magnetic receiver is attached to the ultrasound probe to record positional information (6 degrees of freedom: x, y and z-coordinate as well as $\theta_1, \theta_2, \theta_3$, which specify the orientation).

Discussion Ultrasound is frequently used for diagnosis and intraoperative navigation. Application areas include abdominal tumor diagnosis, artery plaque measurements, and fetal examinations. Compared to most other modalities, the interpretation of ultrasound images requires considerable experience.

3D ultrasound might also be employed for advanced diagnostic and therapy planning tasks. In particular for the localization of tumors and vascular structures in soft tissue, 3D ultrasound plays an essential role. However, widespread use of 3D ultrasound for computer-supported planning systems is currently hampered by technical problems. Whereas CT, MRI, and many other devices export their data in the DICOM standard (see § 3.4), the export of 3D ultrasound data remains a serious problem with a lack of accepted standards. The noisy and blurry nature of ultrasound data makes any kind of 3D visualization challenging. However, as we will see in later chapters, with appropriate filtering and noise removal expressive 3D visualizations may be generated.

2.8 IMAGING IN NUCLEAR MEDICINE

In this section, we describe PET and SPECT, the two essential modalities in nuclear medicine as well as their combination with the previously described modalities CT and MRI, leading to hybrid scanners, such as PET/CT.

2.8.1 POSITRON EMISSION TOMOGRAPHY—PET

Positron Emission Tomography (PET) is a nuclear medicine imaging technique. PET scans generate 3D images of functional processes, such as metabolic activity. A short-lived radiopharmaceutical substance ("tracer") is injected and traced throughout the body to its target area. At the target area, the substance is processed by the metabolism and the radioactive isotope decays, which emits positrons. If a positron interacts with an electron, it annihilates, which in turn generates two gamma photons (rays) in opposite directions (180°). These photons are then measured by the detector array of the PET scanner (Fig. 2.40). Since annihilation photons are always emitted in exactly opposite directions, it is possible to localize their source along a straight line. The image reconstruction is very similar to the reconstruction of CT data. Since the tracers are processed by the metabolism, the location of a *metabolic activity*, e.g., brain activity while performing a specific task, is revealed.

Due to the short-lived nature of the radionuclides, they must be produced close to the PET Scanner. A frequently used radionuclide is (18 F) fluorodeoxyglucose (FDG). The spatial resolution of a PET image dataset is significantly lower than CT and MRI data; the pixel size equals 3–4 mm.

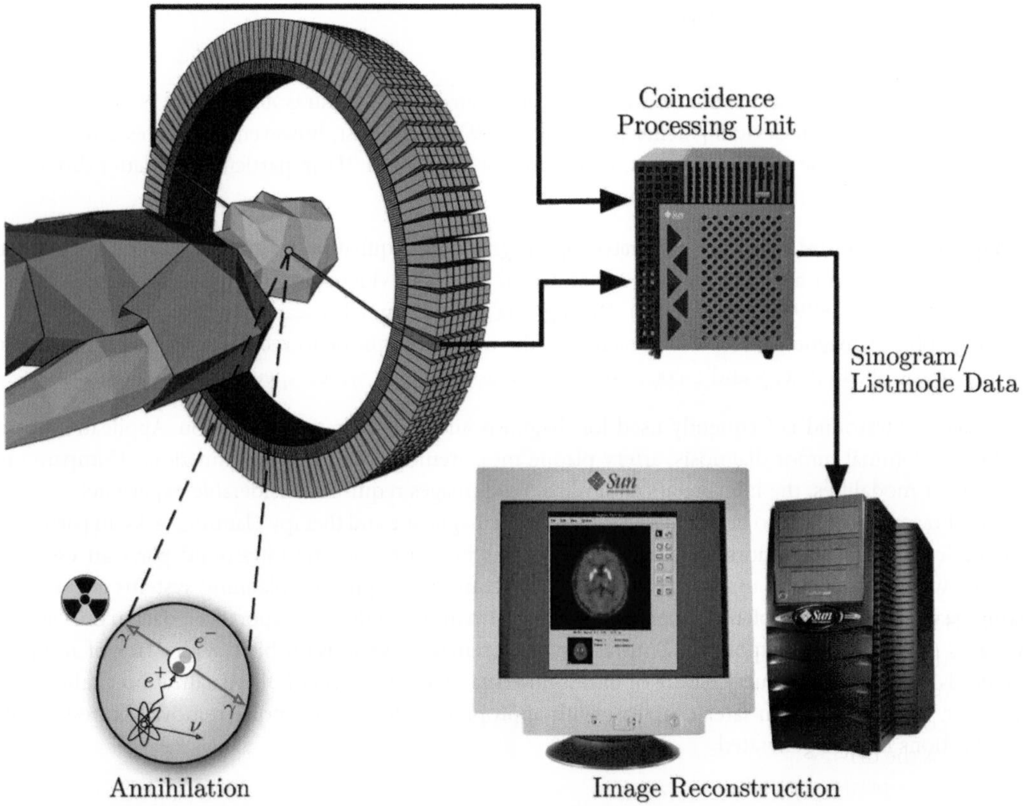

FIGURE 2.40 *In the annihilation process two photons are emitted in opposing directions and registered by the PET as they arrive at the detector ring. After that, the data is forwarded to a processing unit, which determines if two registered events represent a coincidence event. All coincidences are processed by the image processing unit where the final image data is produced (Courtesy of Jens Langner, Wikipedia).*

PET data is often combined with CT or MRI data to complement the low resolution functional data with high resolution morphological data of the respective body parts. This requires the alignment ("registration") of the generated volumetric datasets. This registration, however, is quite difficult, since the scanned patient has to be moved from one scanner to the other scanner. This movement will change the position and orientation of the body, and hence, it will complicate the matching of a set of landmarks. These obstacles are aggravated by the different resolutions of CT/MRI and PET image data, which renders the matching of properties difficult (this matching process is described in § 4.8).

PET and fMRI PET was developed prior to fMRI (first studies are reported in 1988) and had been the primary choice for neuroanatomical studies. PET data were employed to generate *parametric maps* that convey the amount of brain responses based on a per voxel statistical analysis. These parametric maps indicate the probability that an activation occurred in a particular region. The methodology and concepts of statistical parametric mapping were developed for PET data first [Friston *et al.*, 1990,1991] and later used and refined for the analysis of fMRI data, in particular with the SPM toolkit. In general, activations are modeled as Gaussian fields, a variant of stochastic processes, which allow to characterize the *significance* of an activation. The significance indicates the probability that the detected changes are indeed caused by an activation. The signals of PET data are spatially independent, whereas in fMRI data the signals are spatially dependent. As a consequence, PET data only require simpler models for the stochastic process to determine the significance of activations. The rigorous statistical analysis of activation patterns was necessary to make sure that the hot spots are really caused by activation patterns.

PET Applications Due to the ability of PET scanners to characterize metabolic activity, it plays a crucial role in the diagnosis of cancer and in the search for metastases. A special and important example is the search for primary tumor in case that only a metastasis is known so far (*cancer of unknown primary*). PET is also used to evaluate the success of a cancer therapy, e.g., a chemotherapy. Often PET reveals the success or failure of a therapy earlier compared to CT or MRI [Young *et al.*, 1999]. In follow-up examinations after radiation treatment, the representation of metabolic activity in PET data may help to discriminate a recurrent cancer from scar (resulting from the radiation). Oncology scans with FDG account for the large majority of all PET scans. In addition, PET is also essential in cardiology (to map heart function and contribute to the diagnosis of atherosclerosis) and neurology (to represent brain activity and thus to contribute to the diagnosis of neurodegenerative diseases).

Current and Future Developments Currently, several vendors develop TOF image reconstruction where the timing of annihilation events is registered and evaluated to precisely locate the positrons that caused these events. This development is already integrated in the Philips PET/MR scanner, whereas the first generation of SIEMENS PET/MR relies on the more established reconstruction process.

2.8.2 HYBRID PET/CT AND PET/MRI SCANNERS

To provide truly integrated information of metabolic activity and anatomy, hybrid scanners have been developed that integrate both modalities and thus strongly reduce the registration problem, since the patient's position has not changed between the two acquisition procedures. Also for the hybrid scanners, oncology is the driving application and it was soon realized that a hybrid PET/MRI scanner probably has the greatest potential. However, it was technically demanding to integrate PET and MRI. Thus, PET/CT scanners, suitable for regular examination of humans, arrived a decade earlier.

PET-CT Since their introduction in 2001, combined PET/CT scanners replace more and more the single PET devices. The spatial resolution increased from 5 to 8 mm with the single devices to

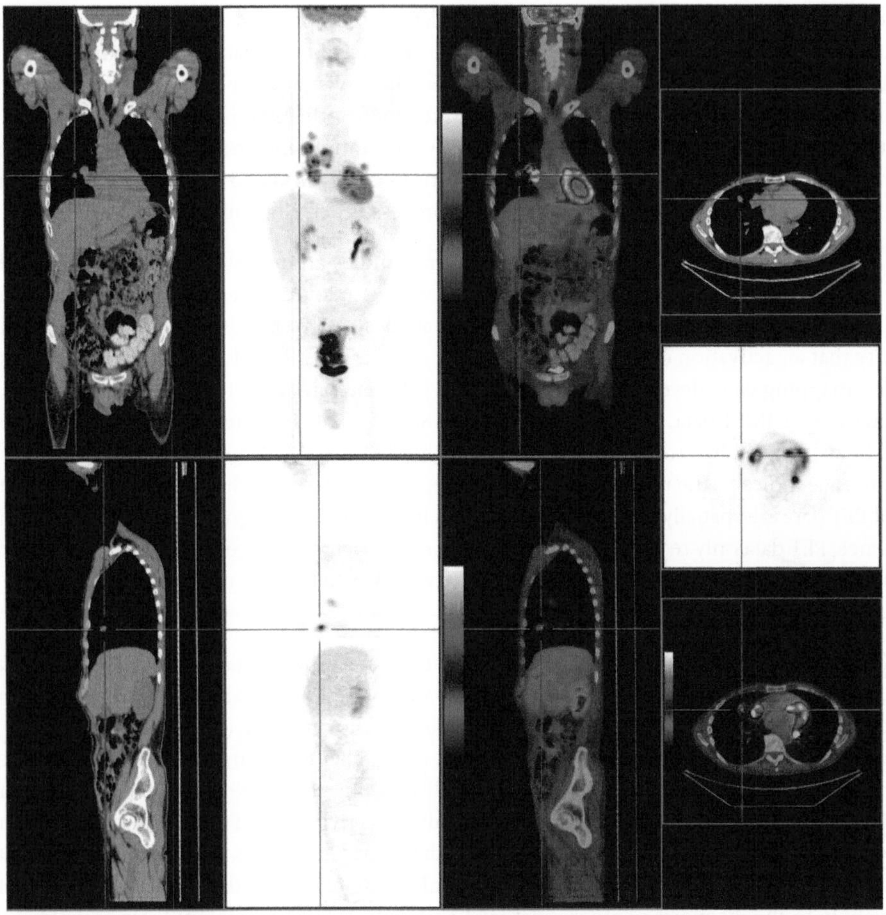

FIGURE 2.41 *CT and PET data are shown in isolation (left) and overlaid (right). The PET/CT of a staging exam of colon carcinoma reveals several lesions besides the primary tumor. On the current cursor position (see the cross-hair cursor), a lung nodule is shown. The images were acquired with a GE PET/CT Discovery 600 (Courtesy of Wikipedia).*

3–4 mm with the combined devices and the duration of the examinations could be drastically shortened. Figure 2.42 shows a modern device that is also used for intraoperative imaging.

Combined PET/CT examinations cause similar (high) costs like a single PET examination. Figure 2.41 shows an example of a combined PET/CT examination related to tumor staging. This is a second example of image overlays in this chapter after the discussion of an integrated visualization of fMRI activations and anatomical scans (recall § 2.6.4).

PET/MRI Hybrid PET/MR scanners have a great potential, in particular in oncology. When the high soft tissue contrast of MRI and the metabolic information provided by PET scanners are integrated without loss of information, the dignity of many tumors may be assessed more reliably than with other imaging modalities. Low-grade gliomas, for example, are often not correctly classified with conventional MRI [Boss *et al.*, 2010]. Although this potential was recognized early, only recently it was possible to actually build such scanners and make them commercially available. The major challenge was to construct a PET

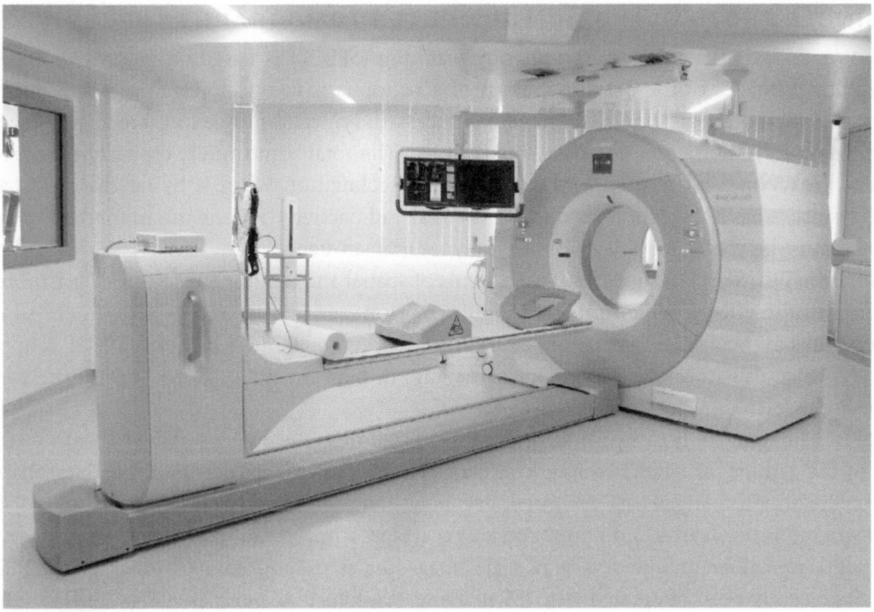

FIGURE 2.42 *A PET/CT from Siemens Health Care. The model mCT (molecular CT) contains a 64-slice CT scanner (in the frontal part of the gantry) and a PET scanner (in the rear part of the gantry). A laser installation (in the back part of the room above the gantry) supports radiation treatment planning. The dual monitor solution supports CT-guided interventions (Courtesy of Oliver Großer, University Hospital Magdeburg).*

scanner that is *MR compatible*. While hybrid PET/MR scanners for small animal imaging have been around since the 1990s, the first PET/MR scanner for patient care was developed by Siemens Healthcare and its technical specification is described in Schlemmer *et al.* [2008]. The system called BIOGRAPH was officially presented in late 2010 and got FDA clearance in 2011. A 3T whole body MR scanner was modified to be integrated with a PET detector based on MR compatible avalanche photodiodes. These diodes are highly sensitive semiconductors that employ the photoelectric effect. The PET scanner has an image matrix of 256×256 and an isotropic voxel size of 1.25 mm × 1.25 mm × 1.25 mm [Schwenzera *et al.*, 2012].

Applications The PET/MR scanner from SIEMENS is restricted to imaging the head and neck region and thus it is primarily used for the diagnosis and treatment monitoring of head and neck tumors. In addition, the treatment of further neurologic diseases may benefit from PET/MR imaging. A group of the University of Tübingen evaluated the BIOGRAPH research prototype. In a pilot study, ten patients with intracranial masses were examined [Boss *et al.*, 2010] and a number of parameters were determined to assess the image quality, e.g., the signal-to-noise ratio and, more specifically, tumor-to-reference tissues. These results were compared with the clinically indicated PET/CT examinations.

Later, Schwenzera *et al.* [2012] report on their experience with 50 patients and state that the MR quality is not degraded by the PET inset (only known artifacts arise and they are not more severe than in conventional MRI). Even advanced MR techniques, such as DTI and spectroscopy, were possible without quality problems. The quality of the PET images was comparable to PET imaging in PET/CT. However, the authors consider the PET component as still dynamically evolving. In particular streak artifacts were noted and compensated for with Gaussian filtering.

2.8.3 SINGLE PHOTON EMISSION COMPUTED TOMOGRAPHY—SPECT

Single Photon Emission Computed Tomography scanning (SPECT) is based on gamma cameras, which acquire multiple images of the 3D distribution of a radiopharmaceutical. A gamma ray camera reveals the location of the body part where the tracer is processed. Typically, projections are acquired every 3 or 6 degrees and a full 360 degree rotation is performed. The total scan time is typically between 15 and 20 minutes. Heavy metals are used as tracer elements. Technetium-99 m is by far the most frequently used tracer, since it has a low half period and only weak radioactivity. For the use in medical imaging, the heavy metal must be combined with a biologically neutral substance.

In contrast to PET, SPECT is more limited in terms of spatial and temporal resolution, and more limited with respect to the effects, which can be monitored. However, SPECT tracers decay more slowly than PET tracers, thus allowing the examination of longer lasting metabolic functions. SPECT is applied, for example, for diagnosis in oncology, for bone imaging, in neuroimaging, and to investigate myocardial perfusion in the left ventricle.

With SPECT imaging, only one gamma photon is emitted from the nucleus of the tracer that needs to be detected by the gamma camera. Therefore, collimators at the cameras are needed for path estimation. Due to these collimators less signals are recorded, and hence an even lower resolution is acquired. Typically, the voxel spacing is between 4 and 7 mm and a typical SPECT image slice consists of 64×64 or 96×96 pixels. Images are either provided as gray scale images or as pseudo-colored images. Like PET, SPECT imaging has recently been integrated with CT imaging in a hybrid scanner (see Fig. 2.43).

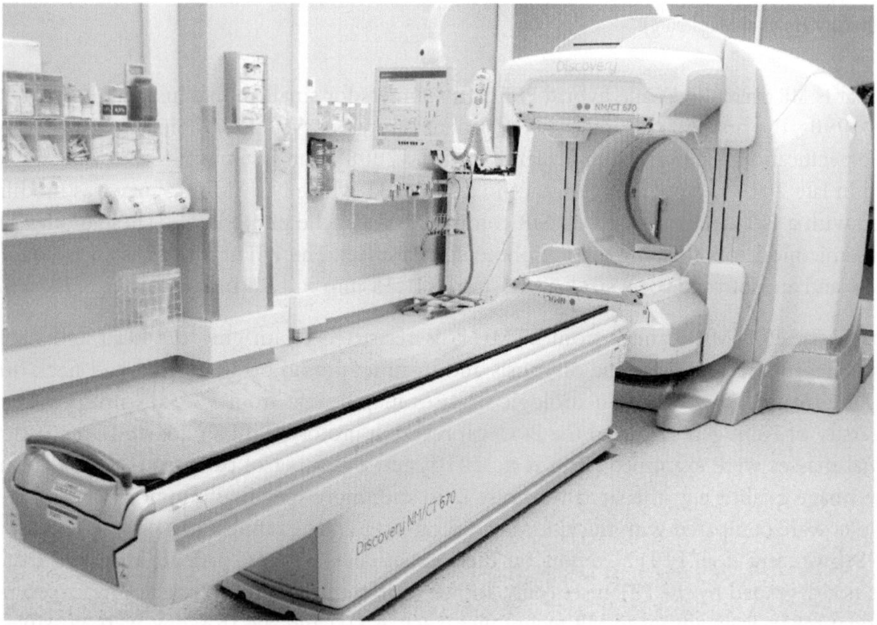

FIGURE 2.43 *Hybrid SPECT/CT scanner GE NM/CT 670 from General Electric. It contains a 16-slice CT scanner that can be used for all CT diagnosis tasks, but in a low-dose operation mode. The CT scanner is installed at the rear part, the two detector elements in the frontal part belong to the SPECT scanner (Courtesy of Oliver Großer, University Hospital Magdeburg).*

A more recent development is the free-hand acquisition of SPECT data that was first described by Wendler *et al.* [2007] and was developed since then into a viable and mature product that enables SPECT acquisition also during an intervention.

2.9 INTRAOPERATIVE IMAGING

While simple routine interventions are often performed solely based on preoperative imaging, for complex therapeutic interventions and operations intraoperative imaging provides useful guidance. Intraoperative imaging enables the localization of deep-seated tumors, e.g., in the brain, and to supervise interventions where a catheter or an applicator is inserted and should not damage vital structures. In particular endoscopic and other minimally-invasive operations benefit from intraoperative imaging, since the direct manual contact of the surgeon is missing. As an example, in abdominal surgery, the surgeon usually dissects vascular structures and employs their branchings for orientation. In neurosurgery, open surgery benefits from intraoperative imaging, since brain structures move significantly (the *brain shift* has an extent of up to 2 cm). The selection of an appropriate imaging modality depends on the structures that need to be displayed. In addition, intraoperative imaging should not hamper surgery strongly. Intraoperative imaging based on X-rays requires to carefully analyze the dose rate, since the patient but—to a smaller extent also the doctor and the nurses—are exposed to the radiation multiple times. As an example, in Figure 2.44, an angiography device is shown. It is primarily used for interventions of the peripheral vessels and for neuroradiological interventions such as coiling or stenting a cerebral aneurysm. This device is not only used intraoperatively, but provides also diagnostic imaging in high quality (recall § 2.4.2).

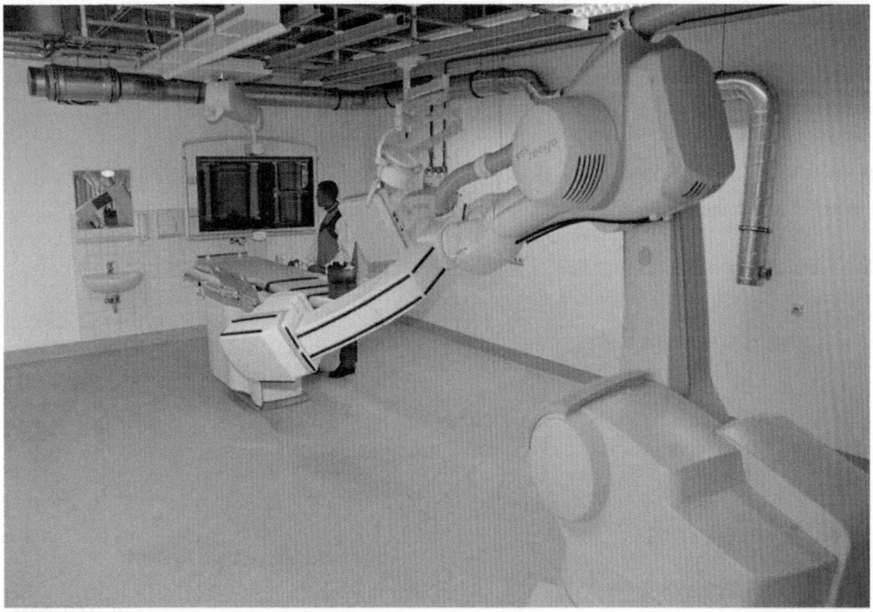

FIGURE 2.44 *A modern angiography unit with a flexible robot arm (Artis zeego). A large display is used for intraoperative guidance (Courtesy of Axel Böse, University of Magdeburg).*

2.9.1 CT- AND MR-GUIDED INTERVENTIONS

There is a large variety of interventions performed by radiologists for diagnosis or treatment that are performed under control of intraoperative guidance. Mahnken and Ricke [2008] provide a good survey of such procedures, necessary instruments, imaging techniques and case studies. We briefly discuss selected examples.

Biopsies Complex diagnostic procedures often require cytologic or histologic examination of tissue samples. The radiologist punctures the pathology, e.g., an abscess or a tumor to remove a small tissue sample. While for cytology small tissue samples are removed with a *fine needle biopsy*, for histologic examinations punch or drilled biopsies with larger needles are required [Begemann, 2008]. In general, larger biopsies involve a higher risk of bleeding and infections. For all kinds of biopsies, image guidance is needed to locate the biopsy needle and to ensure that no vital structures are hurt. CT and MR guidance are used for such biopsies.

Catheter-Based Interventions These interventions usually have a therapeutic intent. Catheters are used to administer medication, drain abscesses or place stents in the vascular system. Also the tumor therapies RFA, and LITT are based on catheters. Modern catheters are flexible and thus enable the insertion in curved anatomical structures. *Intelligent catheters* may be precisely controlled, e.g., to bend them accurately. Figure 2.45 presents a balloon catheter that is frequently used for cardiac interventions. Figure 2.46

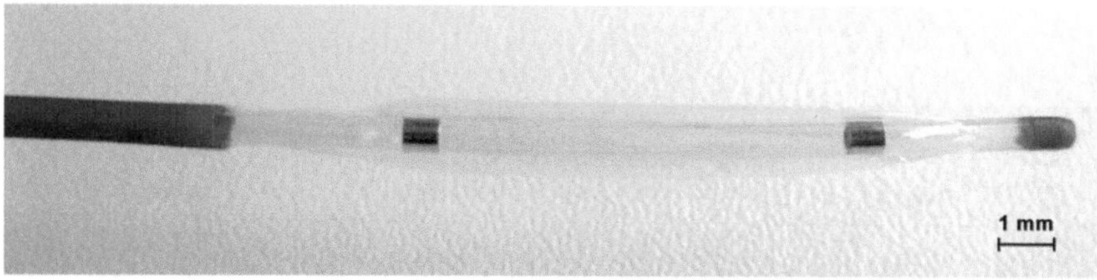

FIGURE 2.45 *A balloon catheter with markers visible in X-ray and CT data, that is employed, e.g., to transport a stent to the coronary arteries—the so-called balloon dilation (Courtesy of Axel Böse, University of Magdeburg).*

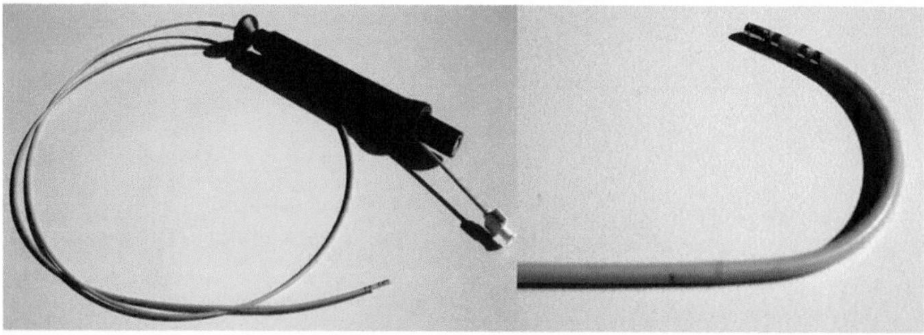

FIGURE 2.46 *A flexible catheter and the control unit to guide the catheter placement. This "intelligent" catheter is employed in CT-guided interventions (Courtesy of Axel Boese, University of Magdeburg).*

shows an "intelligent" catheter. During the intervention the position of the catheters needs to be carefully controlled.[6] Image analysis and visualization may be essential to track and emphasize catheters.

2.9.2 FLUOROSCOPY

Fluoroscopy is a special version of direct radiographs where the result can be immediately represented on a screen. Since the permanent exposure to X-radiation requires a significantly lower intensity, the overall image quality does not equal the quality of regular still X-ray images. However, the focus here is on dynamic processes that are visible over time. Typical examples are angiographies where an injected contrast agent is tracked while it travels through the respective blood vessels. Typically, fluoroscopy images are acquired intraoperatively by a C-arm[7] scanner.

2.9.3 INTRAOPERATIVE ULTRASOUND

Due to its real time capabilities, ultrasound is an attractive modality for intraoperative use. Also the flexibility of data acquisition and the fact that no radiation is involved are further advantages. Figure 2.47 shows an example where ultrasound is used for controlling biopsy placement. Other essential applications include various abdominal surgeries where ultrasound is primarily used to locate nearby vascular structures to avoid that they are hurt. In former times, radiologists used the ultrasound device occasionally, in the operating room. Meanwhile surgeons use ultrasound themselves.

Among the limitations for intraoperative use is the fact that ultrasound cannot penetrate thick bony structures. Thus, for most neurosurgical interventions ultrasound is not a viable option, since it may not penetrate the skull. An exception is a small region where the skull is thin and ultrasound is indeed used to provide intraoperative guidance [Lindner *et al.*, 2008, Müns *et al.*, 2011].

In this context, transcranial sonography (TCS) allows visualizing several brainstem structures, e.g., the substantia nigra and thus supports the diagnosis and differential diagnosis of various movement disorders,

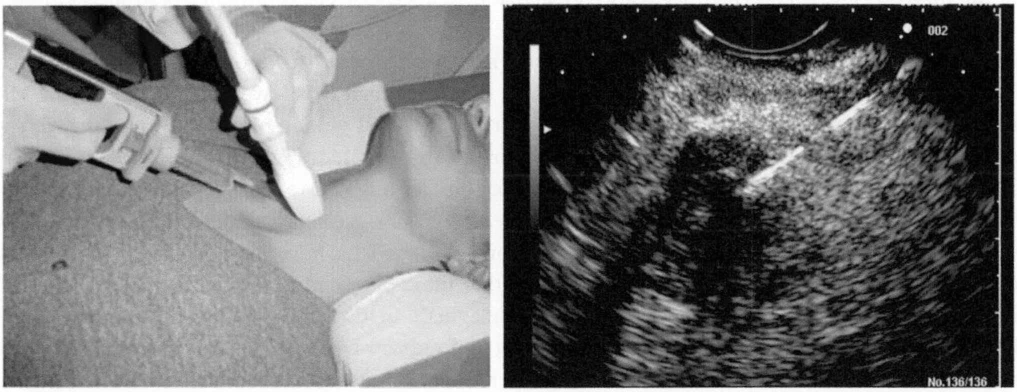

FIGURE 2.47 **Left:** *A biopsy needle is inserted in the neck to remove a tissue sample of a suspicious neck lymph node. The second hand controls the ultrasound probe.* **Right:** *The resulting ultrasound image is provided with an indication of the current position and orientation of the ultrasound probe (see the icon in the lower right corner) (Courtesy of Christoph Arens, University of Magdeburg).*

6 The research project Intelligent Catheters, http://www.inka-md.de, deals with the further development of such catheters.

7 The "C" characterizes the shape of the device.

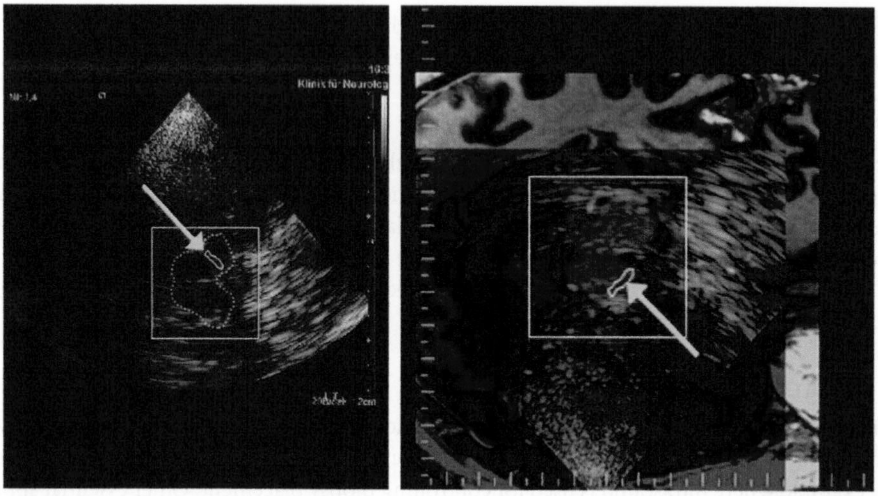

FIGURE 2.48 *Corresponding transcranial sonography and MRI tomographical sections showing different midbrain structures: the rectangle defines a region of interest, the dotted line delineates the Mesencephalon, the solid line, and the arrow mark the substantia nigra (Courtesy of Zein Salah, University of Magdeburg).*

especially in Parkinsonian syndromes. Figure 2.48 shows an example of a navigation-supported diagnosis relying on matching midbrain sonography and MRI data [Salah *et al.*, 2012].

2.9.4 INTRAOPERATIVE MRI

Because of the good soft tissue contrast and since no harmful radiation is involved, MRI is increasingly used intraoperatively. For this purpose, special devices were developed that provide access to the patient for the surgeon (Fig. 2.49). The images also reveal that patient access is not convenient and surgery in this environment involves an increased effort.

Intraoperative MRI is performed with lower magnetic field strength (0.5 or 1.0 Tesla) compared to the diagnostically used MRIs (1.5 or 3.0 Tesla). Thus, the image quality is lower with intraoperative MRI that is frequently used for biopsy removal and tumor surgery. MRI guided biopsies are performed, e.g., to remove small tissue samples from lesions in the breast or prostate to enable histologic examination. Open MRI scanners are also used to puncture suspicious lesions in breast tissue, for thermoablation (radio frequency ablation, Laser Induced Thermal Therapy (LITT). A crucial aspect of intraoperative MRI is the real-time visibility of the surgical or interventional devices. This, however, poses high requirements to these instruments. They have to be *MR compatible*; that means, they must not be ferromagnetic, since ferromagnetic materials are attracted by the strong magnetic field of the scanner. On the other hand, there must be an interaction between the instrument and radio waves to enable the visualization of the instrument. Moreover, instruments for use in intraoperative MRI must not be conductive, since conductive materials get heated and may cause damage to the patient.

While the open MR scanners of the first generation were restricted to the use for interventions, more recent devices can also be used diagnostically due to their improved image quality. This is essential, since the interventional use rarely is frequent enough to use an open MR scanner economically. Diagnostic use of an open MR scanner is particularly useful for claustrophobic patients that cannot tolerate the narrowness of a closed scanner.

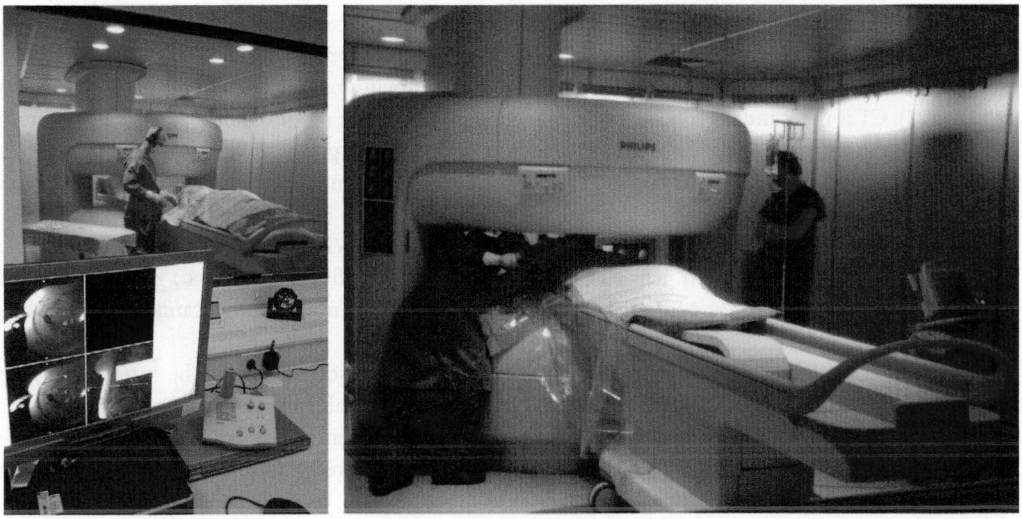

FIGURE 2.49 *A Philips Panorama MR scanner with 1.0 T field strength.* **Left:** *An overview with a screen showing intraoperative images. These images, however, are not directly visible to the operating doctor. Thus, intensive communication between a person observing the images and the operating doctor (in a second room) is necessary.* **Right:** *Patient access takes a lot of effort (Courtesy of Jens Ricke, University Hospital Magdeburg).*

Intraoperative MRI in Neurosurgery One of the phenomena that is targeted by intraoperative MRI is the brain shift effect in neurosurgery. This effect describes the local changes of location and shape of the brain after opening of the skull and dura mater [Nabavi *et al.*, 2001]. These changes render the preoperatively acquired image data (at least partially) useless, since it does not represent the current situation sufficiently accurate.

Full magnetic field MRI scanners (1.5 T, "full-field") have been introduced into the operating room (OR) [Nimsky *et al.*, 2003] a decade ago. However, these devices are very expensive and thus still rare. Since MR scanners are not open, the patient lying on the operating table has to be moved into the scanner for the image acquisition and moved back to the surgeons outside the area that is immediately influenced by the magnetic field. Next to the space required for the full-sized MRI, additional space in the OR is needed to operate in a safe distance to the scanner, and for the transportation of the patient. This renders full-field intraoperative MRI difficult to install, since regular ORs will not be able to accommodate the required space.

2.10 SUMMARY

Medical volume data, such as CT, MRI, and PET, are arranged on a cartesian voxel grid. Data values between the grid points are usually computed by trilinear interpolation within the voxel cells. Since this is a discrete representation of the data, all the datasets are subject to the sampling theorem, which specifies the boundary conditions for an alias-free representation. There are a number of other causes of artifacts, e.g., partial volume effect.

Medical data can be acquired through several different scanning modalities. The most typical are X-ray, Computed Tomography (CT), Magnetic Resonance Imaging (MRI), and ultrasound. While X-ray is used frequently for diagnosis and intraoperative navigation (through a C-arm X-ray scanner), it provides only a 2D projection image. For additional 3D cues, a second X-ray image is often acquired from an orthogonal direction. Typically, X-ray is employed for standard fracture diagnosis, mammography, and lung diagnosis.

CT is based on X-ray, but computes a volumetric image dataset from a series of X-rays acquired from different angles around the scanned body. Recent multislice CT scanners allow fast scanning at a very high resolution. Therefore, it is also used for the scanning of fast moving organs like the heart (synchronized with an ECG). CT is the standard modality for diagnostic purposes that require more spatial differentiation than an X-ray can provide. CT is also used for scanning in many emergency situations, in particular if the head must be scanned. While CT is well suited for the representation of (contrasted) blood vessels and skeletal structures, its soft tissue differentiation is limited.

MRI is based on the spin of protons in a strong magnetic field. While it is slower than CT and often provides only a coarser resolution, it is the standard modality if soft tissue needs to be discriminated. Furthermore, it is well suited for contrast agent-free blood vessel scanning and for scanning of functional information (fMRI).

Ultrasound is based on the penetration of human tissue with sound waves. The interpretation of ultrasound data with its various sources of artifacts requires considerable experience. On the other hand, ultrasound is a cheap real-time imaging modality that allows to represent soft tissue and vascular structures in high quality. The reconstruction of 3D volumes from freely acquired ultrasound slices is demanding, but represents a great potential.

This chapter served as an introduction to medical image data. Later, we will get to know more specialized modalities, such as CT and MRI perfusion data, phase contrast MRI data that are used for blood flow measurements and diffusion tensor imaging, used for representing fibrous structures, such as the white matter in the brain representing the communication network of the brain.

FURTHER READING

There are many books and other relevant sources of information on medical imaging. Kalra [2008] is a book that describes multislice CT data and its application. Also, [Buzug, 2008] is devoted to CT imaging. Cho *et al.* [1993] is a classical, signal theory-oriented book on data reconstruction. More recently, Suetens [2002] discussed various aspects of medical imaging and the related artifacts. Dhawan [2003] is an excellent book on medical imaging modalities. Most books on medical imaging relate to a single modality and its use for diagnostic questions, such as in pediatric radiology, neuroradiology, or in the diagnosis of vascular structures, for example [Osborn, 1999]. We cannot provide a comprehensive review on radiology teaching material. As an example, in cardiac imaging, a variety of books have been authored or edited in the last few years [Budoff, 2010, de Feyter, 2004, Halpern, 2011, Bogaert *et al.*, 2005]. These books provide an overview on the requirements and processes in image acquisition, present many examples of normal and pathological cases and discuss their interpretation. Jadvar and Parker [2005] and Workman and Coleman [2006] are dedicated to PET and PET/CT. Brown and Semelka [2010] and Hashemi *et al.* [2011] are updated books on MRI acquisition and application. Hennig and Speck [2011] describe principles and applications of high-field MRI.

Due to the importance of ultrasound in clinical medicine, dedicated conferences, journals, and books are available. A good and comprehensive introduction is provided by Meire *et al.* [1993]. A book with focus on the basics of physics, artifacts and instrument handling is Kremkau [2002]. The normal anatomy and physiology from an ultrasound perspective is described by Curry and Tempkin [2004].

Outlook New imaging techniques arise and develop further. As an example, Terahertz imaging employs wavelength between the microwave and infrared regions of the electromagnetic spectrum [Sun *et al.*, 2011]. This imaging technique is attractive, since it does not pose any ionization radiation to biological tissues. Biological materials yield unique absorption spectra due to intermolecular vibrations—a property that may be used, e.g., to characterize knee cartilage [Kan *et al.*, 2010].

Dual energy CT acquisition was discussed in some detail. In the future, there might be even acquisition techniques with more different energy levels. In his invited talk at the "Visual Computing in Biology and Medicine" workshop 2012, Anders Persson reported on trials with up to seven energy levels that turned out to be feasible and to increase the diagnostic power even further.

Chapter 03

An Introduction to Medical Visualization in Clinical Practice

3.1 INTRODUCTION

In this chapter, we introduce a number of use cases where medical image analysis and visualization play an essential role in clinical practice. We shall provide an introduction to the related clinical disciplines to enable the reader to analyze specific problems and communicate with physicians from related disciplines.

The acquisition of medical image data is usually not the first step in a diagnostic process; exceptions are urgent cases or severe accidents with unconscious patients. Usually, a patient describes his or her health-related problem to a medical doctor, who interprets these statements, taking into account also previous diseases or accidents, the habits of the patient and diseases that have occurred in the family. The information gained in this way is also called *anamnesis* or the medical history. As a second step, simple diagnostic procedures, such as palpation, auscultation with a stethoscope or blood pressure measurements, are carried out. As a further building block of diagnosis, clinical tests are performed, where liquids of the body, such as blood and urine, are analyzed.

Medical image data are acquired primarily when the previously described diagnostic steps raised the suspicion for a severe disease, such as a malignancy or heart diseases. In the large majority of cases where image data are acquired, a specific suspicion exists. The image acquisition and interpretation is dedicated to decide whether the suspicion can be confirmed or excluded. Therefore, it is essential that the relevant information of previous diagnostic steps are available to the radiologist. This situation is the motivation for developing electronic medical records and hospital information systems that represent this information and enable its sharing among all involved doctors. Important issues of hospital information systems, such as security, networking standards, and data protection, are beyond the scope of this book, but it is essential to understand that image data acquisition and interpretation cannot be regarded as an isolated problem. Instead, it is part of a complex process where information from previous diagnostic steps has to be integrated, and where results are produced that have to be made available to other medical doctors.

This whole discussion will provide a background on diagnostic, treatment planning, and monitoring processes. It should make the reader also familiar with terminology, recent changes in technology and guidelines for clinical practice, since these aspects are crucial for developing appropriate software support.

Organization Our focus is on the diagnostic use of medical volume data. As a consequence, we first describe general criteria for the quality of diagnostic processes (§ 3.2). We continue with a brief discussion of relevant aspects of visual perception, primarily the perception of contrasts in gray value images (§ 3.3). According to our focus on diagnostic processes, we carefully discuss *radiology*, where the large majority of medical image data are acquired. The discussion of radiology starts with an explanation of the storage of medical image data (§ 3.4) and continues with a description of conventional film-based diagnosis and soft-copy reading (§ 3.5 and 3.6). we also consider *nuclear medicine* (§ 3.7) and *radiation treatment* (§ 3.8). Radiation treatment is a special medical discipline, where image analysis and advanced 3D visualization is already a mandatory part of the clinical routine. Finally, we discuss how medical image data and derived

Visual Computing for Medicine, Second Edition. http://dx.doi.org/10.1016/B978-0-12-415873-3.00003-1

analysis results are used in medical team meetings (§ 3.9). Such meetings often involve physicians from different disciplines, discussing, e.g., combined treatment options for severe diseases.

3.2 DIAGNOSTIC ACCURACY

Diagnostic procedures, e.g., imaging procedures are evaluated with respect to their *diagnostic accuracy*. The diagnostic accuracy is high if every pathologic abnormality is correctly reported *and* all reported abnormalities are indeed pathologies (and not artifacts from the imaging process). The determination whether an abnormality was missed or incorrectly reported requires comparison to a method that is believed to be correct. This method is often referred to as the *gold standard*. The gold standard, however, might be limited in its correctness as well. Even an accepted and established gold standard does not replace a ground truth, which serves a reliable baseline for comparisons. With this in mind, it is clear that the comparison to a gold standard might be even misleading if a diagnostic procedure is introduced that is actually better than the (existing) gold standard.

If we consider the binary decision whether a patient has a certain disease, there are four possibilities: the patient may or may not suffer from this disease and the diagnostic procedure may or may not report this disease. Table 3.1 summarizes the different situations [Bowyer, 2000].

Definition 3.1. **Sensitivity** is the probability of correctly reporting an abnormality; it is defined as:

$$sensitivity = \frac{TP}{TP + FN} \tag{3.1}$$

Definition 3.2. **Specificity** is the probability of correctly reporting that no abnormality exists. It is defined as:

$$specificity = \frac{TN}{TN + FP} \tag{3.2}$$

Within this book, we restrict ourselves to these two terms of diagnostic accuracy. In particular, for cohort studies or for characterizing epidemic diseases, two more terms are frequently used: the positive and negative predictive value of a test.

$$ppv = \frac{TP}{TP + FP} \tag{3.3}$$

$$npv = \frac{TN}{TN + FN} \tag{3.4}$$

The *positive predictive value* (ppv) states how likely a disease is present when a positive test occurs. Similarly, the *negative predictive value* (npv) states the probability that a person is not ill when the test is negative. These predictive values strongly depend on the prevalence of a disease in this particular region and period.

If a diagnostic procedure has one parameter, the choice of this parameter determines the sensitivity and specificity. With a very low threshold for the size of detected colonic polyps (this example is explained in

	Disease Present	**Disease Not Present**
Disease present	true positive (TP)	false negative (FN)
Disease not present	false positive (FP)	true negative (TN)

TABLE 3.1 *Categories for the evaluation of diagnostic procedures.*

more detail in the following paragraphs), the sensitivity is very high but the specificity is low, since many persons have very small polyps that are not malignant. On the other hand, a higher threshold ensures that the specificity is increased at the expense of the sensitivity. Usually, the distribution of a parameter can be assumed to be normally distributed in healthy patients and (with different parameters) in sick persons, where both distributions overlap. The tradeoff is actually made by defining a threshold in that overlapping portion of the distributions (see Fig. 3.1)

This tradeoff is characterized in so-called receiver-operator curves (ROC, see Fig. 3.2). The area under the curve (AUC) is a measure for the quality of a diagnostic procedure. The imaging modalities, described

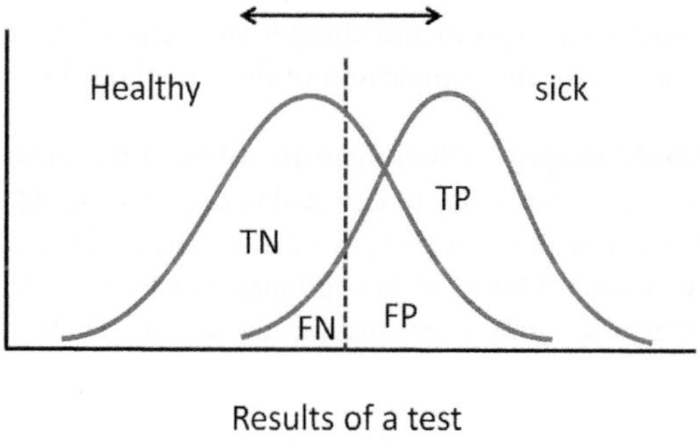

FIGURE 3.1 *A certain parameter, determined in a test, is assumed to be normally distributed among healthy and sick persons with a certain overlap. The vertical dotted line represents a threshold used to classify persons into "healthy" or "sick." The threshold selection determines the number of false positives (FP), false negatives (FN), true positives (TP), true negatives (TN), and as a consequence sensitivity and specificity.*

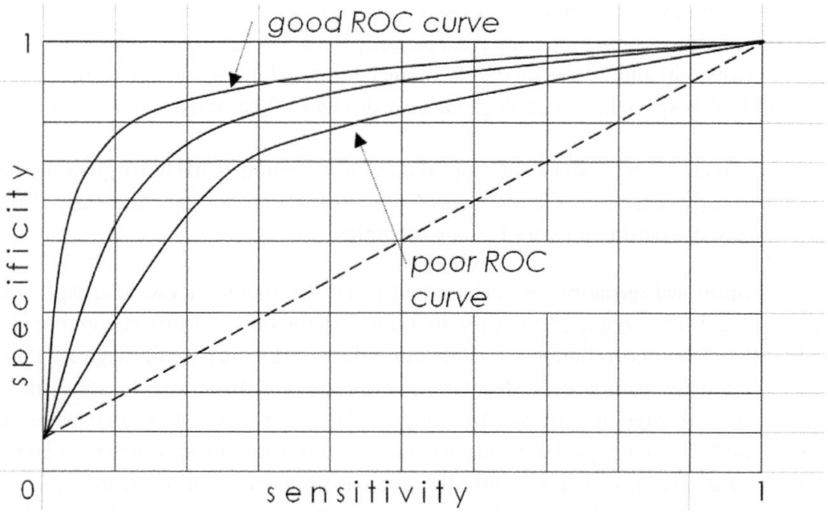

FIGURE 3.2 Examples of ROC curves. A "good" curve indicates that a diagnostic procedure has a high sensitivity and specificity at the same time. The dotted line represents a diagnostic procedure that is useless due to its poor diagnostic accuracy (Courtesy of Petra Specht, University of Magdeburg).

in the following, differ in their sensitivity and specificity for diagnostic questions, such as the detection of cancer, soft tissue abnormalities, or pathologic variations of vascular structures.

A Practical Example for the Diagnostic Accuracy As an example, we briefly discuss colonoscopy, a screening procedure to detect colon cancer in an early stage or even before a polyp converted to a malignant cancer. In this process, based on contrast-enhanced CT or MRI data, colonic polyps exceeding a certain size threshold are searched for and removed. The procedure is laborious and cumbersome for the patient, since the colon lumen must be cleaned before in order to avoid that residual material is interpreted as a colonic mass, such as a polyp. Colon cleansing is achieved by administering laxatives to the patient [Chen *et al.*, 2000]. Colonoscopy is not the only method for colon cancer screening: the fecal occult blood test and digital rectal examination are widespread and cheaper alternatives. The sensitivity and specificity of detecting significant polyps allows for the comparison of these methods [Kim *et al.*, 2007a].

Diagnostic Accuracy with Multimodal Imaging Often there are different diagnostic procedures to detect and characterize a disease, e.g., liver metastases may be detected with both CT and MRI data. Both have a certain sensitivity and specificity. The combined sensitivity is usually enhanced (in this particular example both modalities have a sensitivity of around 80% but in combination 85–90%). Whether a certain increase of sensitivity with combined diagnostic procedures justifies the additional effort depends primarily on the severity of the consequences.

Sensitivity and Specificity in Screening Determining the minimum sensitivity and specificity that a diagnostic procedure should attain in order to be accepted is a complicated issue. The requirements with respect to diagnostic accuracy are particularly high in *screening situations* where a large number of persons is involved. Usually, a certain age group of the population is invited for an examination to detect a severe disease, such as a certain type of cancer, at the earliest possible stage. On the one hand, the sensitivity must be very high to reliably detect the disease. On the other hand, the specificity must be high as well, since otherwise many persons would have to undergo further (expensive) diagnostics and would get unnecessarily alarmed. This explains why screening examinations are available only for a few diseases, such as breast cancer, where women aged between 50 and 70 are invited in many countries for X-ray mammography. With excellent technology and highly specialized radiologists, a sensitivity of 98% and a specificity of more than 90% is possible.

We mention screening here, since the importance of screening is likely to grow, in particular with respect to cancer. Early detection of colon cancer with virtual colonoscopy and early detection of lung cancer with CT thorax examinations are further examples.

Limitations of Sensitivity and Specificity While sensitivity and specificity are essential aspects for diagnostic procedures and enable their comparison, they are limited to the binary decision whether sick patients are correctly identified. To support therapeutic decisions, which is the purpose of diagnostic procedures, it is also essential to evaluate a pathology in detail, e.g., with respect to shape, size, location, and consequently to assess the severity or stage of a disease. The multimodal use of image data often serves these goals. As an example, while PET has a high diagnostic accuracy in detecting cancer, it needs to be complemented with anatomical image data, such as CT and MRI, as a basis for treatment decisions.

Furthermore, the selection of diagnostic procedures is affected by risks and adverse side-effects on the patient as well as by the associated effort in terms of time, money, and the demand for highly specialized physicians. If we consider screening examinations again, the adverse effects of an X-ray or a CT for the large majority of healthy persons is a serious argument for alternatives.

3.3 VISUAL PERCEPTION

Fundamental aspects of the human visual perception are relevant for clinical practice, since they explain why certain output devices are appropriate for diagnosis. Moreover, perceptual research explains why the illumination has an influence on the recognizability of features and thus on the diagnostic accuracy, and why certain interaction facilities, such as contrast and brightness adjustments as well as magnifying glasses, enable a more accurate diagnosis.

Our visual system perceives sensations in nature within a certain spectrum of frequencies (the visible light spectrum, comprising light with a wavelength between 380 and 780 nm). Thus, we perceive certain characteristics in our environment heavily filtered by cognitive processes, such as *visual attention*. This processing can be roughly divided into [Treisman, 1985]

- the *preattentive stage*, where objects, linear features, and textures are recognized without conscious attentions, and
- an *attentive stage*, where the low-level features are interpreted.

While the interpretation strongly depends on the experiences and knowledge of the observer, more general statements can be made with respect to the preattentive stage involving retinal image generation and processing.

We focus on gray values and their perception and discuss color perception more briefly. This is due to the fact that gray value images dominate in conventional diagnosis as well as in volume rendering. Although in the visualization community colors are used intensively also for visualization of medical volume data, this does not reflect the clinical use of medical volume data.

Visual perception is a scientific discipline in its own right. Readers with a stronger interest in perceptual processes, individual differences and in the design of experiments that investigate perceptual questions are referred to the classic book [Goldstein, 2006] as well as to a more recent book [Cunningham and Wallraven, 2011].

3.3.1 GRAY VALUE PERCEPTION

When we discuss gray value perception, we have to consider the physical parameter *luminance* (the amount of light intensity per unit area) and the perceived *brightness*. As one would expect, the relation is monotone: the more light intensity is applied to a CRT or LCD monitor, the brighter we perceive the image. However, this relation is distinctly non-linear. The human eye is relatively less sensitive in the brightest areas of an image. This variation in sensitivity makes it easier to see small relative changes in luminance in darker areas of an image.

Figure 3.3 shows the relation between image intensity and perceived brightness with a dark background. Note, however, that the measurement of perceived stimuli, in particular of the human visual system, is a complex task that requires a careful design of the experiments. The design of a gray scale such that adjacent perceived differences between gray values are similar, is called (perceptual) *linearization*.

3.3.1.1 Just Noticeable Differences

An important term in the discussion of visual perception is the *Just-Noticeable Difference* (JND). With respect to gray value perception, this term characterizes the smallest luminance difference of a given reference intensity that the average human observer can still perceive. The JND is not an absolute value, due to the non-linear characteristic of our visual perception. Instead, the JND for darker values is smaller than for brighter values. With this in mind, quantitative data, such as CT data, can be displayed such that

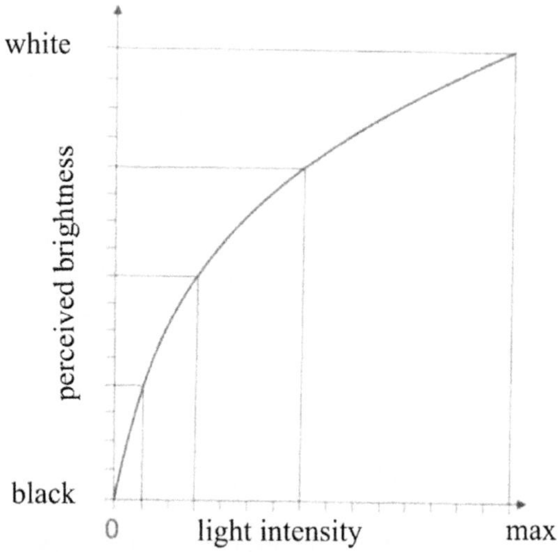

FIGURE 3.3 *When the light intensity (luminance) is increased, the perceived brightness increases quickly in the low intensity areas. Later, larger steps are necessary to achieve the same perceived brightness difference (Adapted from: [Ware, 2000]).*

humans can discriminate approximately 100 gray levels simultaneously [Rheingans, 1992].[1] The number of discernible gray values also depends on the type of display. Display systems with a wider luminance range are capable of presenting more just-noticeable luminance differences.

One hundred gray levels is a relatively small number: the CT scanner produces 4096 different intensity values, MR scanners may produce 256, 4096, or even 65,536 different intensity values. On the other hand, the gray level resolution of current display facilities is below 4096 (12 bit). Usually, 8 bit (256 gray values) are available in the graphics hardware. Only specialized monitors are able to reproduce 10 or 11 bits (1024 or 2048 gray values) [Stramare *et al.*, 2012]. Therefore, there is a need to map the gray level resolution of medical data to intensity values that can be reproduced on the screen. This mapping process should not be linear (cutting the least important bits), but instead consider the curve presented in Figure 3.3. Our discussion is based on a simplified view of visual perception; we ignore, for example, the influence of the image content and the viewer's visual capabilities.

For experts in perception, the non-linear visual perception is a special example of non-linear effects in the human perception in general. Also, our perception of sound is characterized by a distinctly non-linear relation to the underlying physical quantity. This is generally expressed in Weber's law that states: for each stimulus the JND is a constant proportion of the original stimulus.

3.3.1.2 Spatial Resolution

So far, we discussed perceivable gray level differences. Another important aspect for our ability to interpret image data is the spatial resolution of our visual system. To discuss this issue, it is essential to discuss some aspects of our retinal image processing. The incoming light is perceived at the retina that consists of many light sensitive cells (only at the blind spot, where the optical nerve starts, no such cells occur). Humans possess two kinds of light-sensitive cells, namely rods and cones. The cones are the smaller cells (width of about 3 μm) and respond very quickly to incoming light. Cones are responsible for color perception

1 Note that the JND is always a relative difference. If we select an arbitrary luminance intensity from a range that cannot be differentiated, the JND may point to a different intensity than for the intensity at the lower boundary of the range.

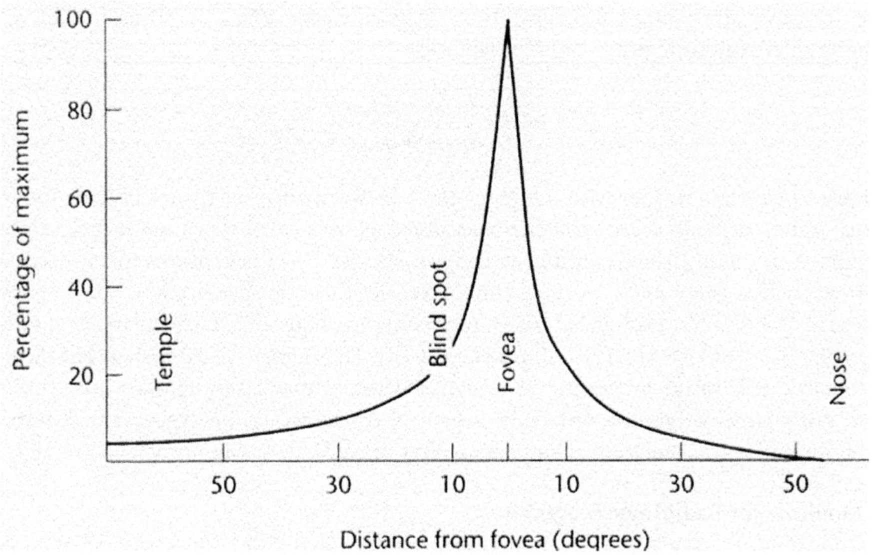

FIGURE 3.4 *Spatial resolution with varying distance from the fovea* (From: [Ware, 2000]).

(three classes of cones allow to perceive colors with different spectra of the visible light). Rods are the second type of light cells, which allow to perceive different gray values.

The spatial resolution of the retina is strongly different between a small central area where we can perceive small details and other regions on the retina where the spatial resolution is one order of magnitude lower. The *fovea* is the region where we have a high density of light-sensitive cells, primarily cones, which permits detailed perception (*foveatic vision*). The inspection of a pathology and its surrounding thus requires to bring this region in the area of foveatic vision. Inside the fovea, the spatial resolution is approximately one arc minute (measured as the visual angle between the borders of an object). The cells in the fovea are not aligned along a regular grid, but instead at a jittered grid. It is assumed that this distribution effectively avoids aliasing problems [Ware, 2000].

Outside the fovea, the density of the sensory cells is strongly reduced, which leads to *peripheral vision* (see Fig. 3.4). Whereas the cones are concentrated in the fovea, the rods occur in the periphery. The distribution of the cells is not perfectly symmetric. There are slightly more cells at the half where the blind spot occurs (probably to compensate for the missing cells there). If an image is interpreted, it takes some time to focus on an area that is relevant for diagnosis. For the development of software to support diagnostic processes, it is therefore highly desirable that interaction facilities for adjusting an image, for example the lightness and contrast, do not force the user to lose their focus. A bad user interface frequently requires the users to shift his or her visual attention, which not only takes more time but is also mentally more demanding and may cause errors. Therefore, a radiology workstation provides many adjustments that may be performed by just moving the mouse cursor over an image or additionally pressing a mouse button, instead of forcing the user to look to some control elements, such as sliders.

3.3.1.3 Contrast Perception

Another important aspect of visual perception relevant for reading medical data is the perceived *contrast*. As one would expect, the perceived contrast at the boundary of objects depends on the difference between gray values. However, the contrast also depends on image intensities (Eq. 3.5). Thus, to achieve a certain contrast in brighter regions requires larger differences.

$$C = \frac{I_{light} - I_{dark}}{I_{light} + I_{dark}} \tag{3.5}$$

It is desirable to generate images with a high contrast between adjacent tissues because the resolution of the visual system depends on the contrast: we can recognize smaller structures if they exhibit a good contrast to the surrounding. The contrast in an image is affected by a **transfer function** that maps data to optical properties, such as gray values. A simple kind of transfer function specification, called **windowing**, shall be discussed in § 3.6.2. More advanced image processing methods adaptively enlarge contrasts, e.g., in mammography data [Pizer *et al.*, 1987, Jin *et al.*, 2001b]. The human visual system enhances contrast through sophisticated "image processing." The signals detected at adjacent light-sensitive cells are combined such that a larger brightness difference is perceived than would be expected with respect to the actual intensity difference. Due to this, humans are very sensitive to aliasing problems (recall § 2.3.2).

3.3.1.4 Monitors for Radiologic Diagnosis

The properties of our visual processing system lead to requirements for monitors to be used for radiologic diagnosis. These requirements are related to

- the display size,
- the display resolution,
- the brightness of the display,
- the maximum contrast that may be displayed, and
- the gray value resolution.

In the following, we briefly discuss these characteristics for viewing CT and MRI data. The display size should provide a sufficient field of view for analyzing details and context. This size depends to a certain extent on the diagnostic task (viewing CT thorax data has particularly high requirements compared to other CT and MRI data).

Display Size Displays need to have at least 3 million pixels for medical diagnosis. The requirements are especially high if image data with high spatial resolution should be handled. An example is digital mammography where the typical size of the data is 4096 × 4096. Special monitors with a resolution of 2500 × 2000 pixels have been developed to support reading these images (see Fig. 3.5). However, even this resolution is below the original data resolution. Thus, some interpolation is required for image display.

Contrast and Gray Level Resolution The maximum contrast (recall Eq. 3.5) should be at least 40. The maximum brightness should be at least 200 cd/m^2. Conventional monitors with only 8 bit gray value resolution are admitted, although not optimal. Therefore, another special feature of display devices for soft-copy reading is an enhanced gray level resolution. It is not quite clear yet whether the enhanced gray-level resolution has a significant effect on the radiologist's performance. However, it is likely that an improved gray level resolution is favorable to detect, e.g., small signs of an early cancer.

LCD and CRT Monitors In general, LCD monitors are superior compared to CRT monitors for radiographic diagnosis based on some key physical properties [Krupinski *et al.*, 2004]. A high level of homogeneity, a brightness of about 700 cd/m^2, a high spatial resolution with 3–5 million pixels and a gray value resolution

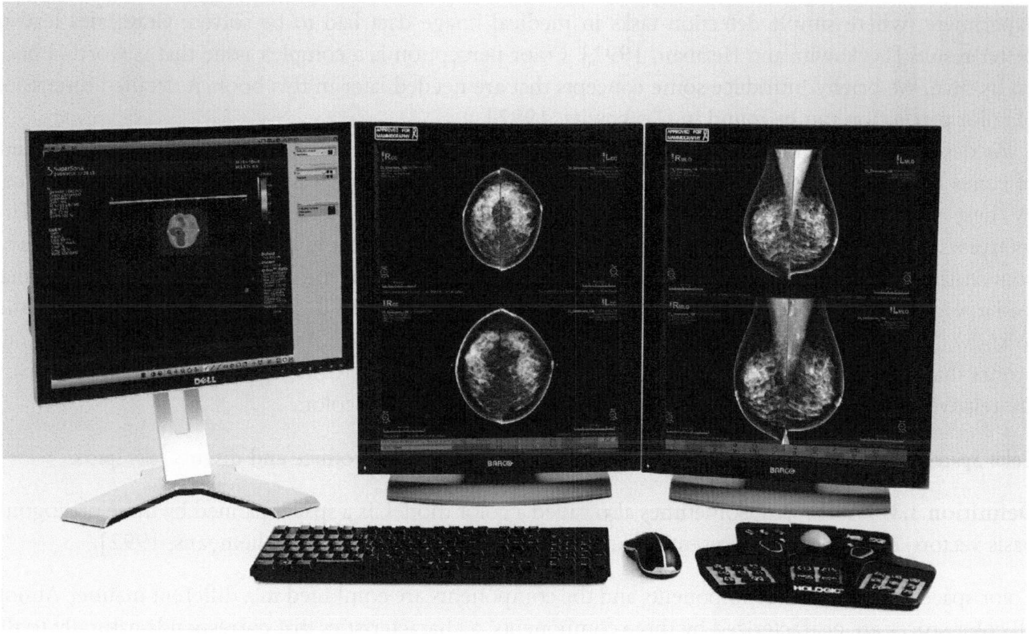

FIGURE 3.5 *Soft-copy reading of digital mammograms. The two vertical monitors support comparisons between the current images with previous images. The keypad on the right provides access to the most important functions such as changes of the layout (Screenshot Hologic's SecurView® diagnostic workstation that incorporates software developed by MeVis BreastCare Solutions GmbH & Co. KG).*

of 10 or 11 bits are characteristics of the best monitors for radiographic viewing. X-ray mammography poses the highest requirements. Double monitor solutions meanwhile dominate.

Quality Control Monitors need to be legally admitted for medical diagnosis, which involves a special test with respect to geometric distortion and the number of pixels that display erroneous values. Thus, such monitors frequently need to be tested with respect to their brightness and contrast and calibration is often necessary, since these properties change over time. Only very low geometric distortions and a low number of pixel defects are admitted.

Future Developments In current clinical practice, monitors without any support for stereoscopic perception and collaborative diagnosis prevail. However, in recent years first prototypes and commercial systems emerged that support stereoscopic viewing where users do not need to wear special hardware [Agus *et al.*, 2009]. The use of 3D visualizations may strongly benefit from such devices. Instead of operating complex 3D navigation, users may naturally move their heads to explore spatial relations.

3.3.2 COLOR SPACES, COLOR SCALES, AND COLOR PERCEPTION

In medical visualizations, color is frequently used to display complex information, for example in the diagnosis with diffusion tensor data (Chap. 15) and with dynamic image data (Chap. 16). The use of colors is primarily motivated by its higher dynamic range compared to gray scales. Despite the fact that the number of just noticeable differences can be considerably increased by means of appropriate color scales, color is not always a better choice compared to gray scales. This was shown for example in an experiment, where simple detection tasks in medical image data had to be solved: Grayscales lead to better results [Levkowitz and Herman, 1992]. Color perception is a complex issue that is worth a book on its own. We briefly introduce some concepts that are needed later in this book. A detailed discussion of color perception can be found in [Levkowitz, 1997].

As described above, humans possess three different kinds of light-sensitive cones. These three kinds of cones have different absorption maxima in the spectrum of visible wavelength. The light is absorbed by these cones and the color sensation is transmitted to the brain. There, it is interpreted as color. This interpretation is complex and not an easy translation. Instead, the color interpretation heavily depends on contextual information that could be shown in various experiments (the same physical wavelength may lead to very different color interpretations by the same person). For the design of color scales it is essential to know that the cones with an absorption maximum in the blue area of the spectrum are relatively rare (cones that perceive primarily green and red light occur 10 times more often). This explains why humans are relatively less sensitive to blue light and small changes in bluish colors.

Color Spaces Before we discuss the color scale, it is necessary to introduce and discuss *color spaces*.

Definition 3.3. A *color space*, sometimes also called a color model, is a space spanned by three orthogonal basis vectors, each of them representing one component of a color model [Rheingans, 1992].

Color spaces have different components and the components are combined in a different manner. Almost all color spaces are characterized by three components, a characteristics that corresponds naturally to the three kinds of cones on the retina. A color may be formed by three primary colors that are either added (to black) or subtracted (from white) to describe a particular color. The following categories of color spaces can be distinguished (see [Rheingans, 1992]):

- *device-oriented color spaces*, where color is defined in a way that corresponds to the physical realization of color output of that device, e.g., a printer or a computer monitor,
- *intuitive color spaces*, where color is defined in a way that adheres to natural properties of color, such as brightness, and
- *perceptually uniform color spaces*, where color is defined such that the Euclidean distance between a pair of colors corresponds to the perceived difference between these colors.

All three categories have their place. Device-oriented color spaces are necessary to control output devices. Intuitive color spaces make it easier to specify colors such that the expected result is achieved. Finally, perceptually uniform color spaces are useful if colors should be interpolated and if color scales should be designed. Since different color spaces are used, it is often necessary to transform a color specification from one space to another one. In the following, we briefly describe each category.

Device-Oriented Color Spaces The APIs of computer graphics libraries, such as OpenGL, usually require to specify colors as a triple with a red, green, and blue component. The RGB color space is based on an additive color model and motivated by the working principle of the cathode ray tube where a color is composed by adding red, green, and blue components. If the creator of a visualization considers appropriate colors, for example to highlight values in a critical range, the RGB-space is not well-suited, since no component of this space directly translates to emphasis.

Intuitive Color Spaces The most widespread intuitive color space is the HSV space that consists of a triplet of hue, saturation and value (see Fig. 3.6). Here, the saturation component directly translates to

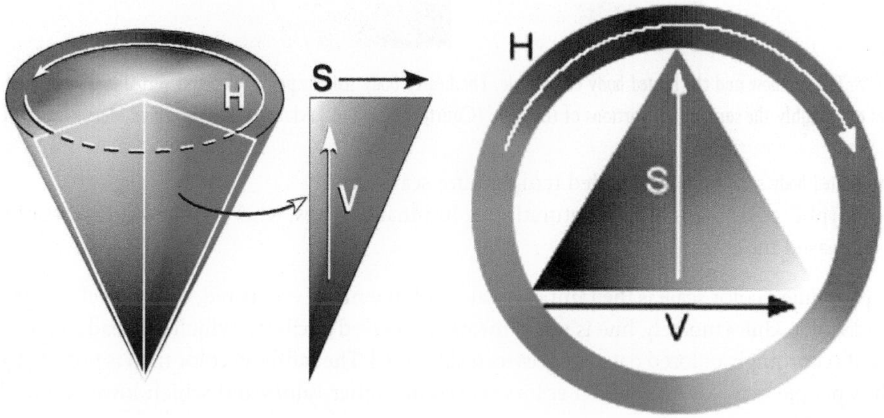

FIGURE 3.6 *The HSV color space has the shape of a cone. The angle between a point's connection to the center with a reference line denotes the hue component (see also the right image), the distance to the centerline denotes saturation (S), the height of a point in HSV space denotes darkness (V)* (Courtesy of Eric Pierce).

emphasis—strongly saturated colors direct attention. Hue interpolates between the six base colors, and it is modified with respect to saturation (0 represents a gray value and 1 a perfectly saturated color). The value component indicates the brightness. Geometrically, the HSV space has the shape of a cone. All saturated colors are represented along the base of the cone. The center line of the cone connects all gray values. Dark colors are therefore close to the apex. The hue is specified as an angle with 0 degrees representing red. In HSV space, for example, it is straightforward to specify a moderately saturated color. Closely related intuitive color spaces are HLS (Hue, Lightness, Saturation) and HSB (Hue, Saturation, Brightness).

Perceptually Uniform Color Spaces The design of a perceptually uniform color space is motivated by the goal that the perceived distance of two pairs of colors $pd(c_1, c_2)$ and $pd(c_3, c_4)$ should be exactly the same when the Euclidean distance between $dist(c_1, c_2)$ and $dist(c_3, c_4)$ in the color space is equal. None of the device-oriented and intuitive color spaces is—in this sense—perceptually uniform. The CIELUV color space, developed by the Commission Internationale de l'Eclairage [de l'Eclairage CIE] is specifically designed for this purpose. The first letters of CIELUV are related to the organization which defined it; LUV are the names for the components of the color space. The L values are always positive (range: 0–100), whereas the U and V values may be negative (range: -100 to 100). However, they have no intuitive meaning, in contrast to the HSV components. In general, it is agreed that for large distances between colors perceptual uniformity is not achieved. There is some debate whether the color space developed by Robertson and O'Callaghan [1986] is more perceptually uniform [Levkowitz and Herman, 1992].

Color Scales for Encoding Scalar Values Color is often used to encode a single scalar value. Color coding is controlled by color scales or color maps. A color scale is a one-dimensional parametric curve in a color space [Rheingans, 1992]. The concept of linearization is also known for color scales. It denotes that additional colors are inserted in the scale such that *perceived distances* between adjacent colors of the extended scale are as uniform as possible [Levkowitz and Herman, 1992]. At least, a color scale should be perceptually ordered such that intuitively, higher and lower values can be interpreted correctly.

In visualization libraries, a variety of color scales is usually provided:

- the *rainbow scale*, where the color spectrum of a rainbow is employed,

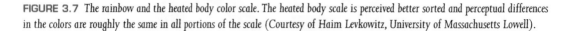

FIGURE 3.7 *The rainbow and the heated body color scale. The heated body scale is perceived better sorted and perceptual differences in the colors are roughly the same in all portions of the scale (Courtesy of Haim Levkowitz, University of Massachusetts Lowell).*

- the *heated body scale* or (often called temperature scale), and
- isomorphic color maps, such as saturation or luminance maps, where either saturation or luminance is increased monotonically.

The most prominent color scale is the rainbow scale with the major colors red, orange, yellow, green, blue, indigo, and violet. Unfortunately, hue is not a linearly perceived attribute, which can lead to interpretation problems of accordingly colored data [Rogowitz *et al.*, 1996]. The rainbow color map is not even *perceptually ordered*. Thus people may confuse which colors represent higher values and which lower values [Borland and Taylor, 2007].

Color scales with monotone behavior with respect to brightness or saturation also allow people with deficient color vision to recognize differences. The heated body scale [Levkowitz and Herman, 1992] is an example of a perceptually oriented color scale that uses primarily reddish and orange colors, where the sensitivity of humans is high (see Fig. 3.7). A good method is also to vary both hue and brightness to get a spiral color in the color space.

Isomorphic color maps include saturation and luminance maps. Such color scales also have a distinct and obvious start and endpoint, which is an essential aspect of perceptually oriented color scales [Levkowitz, 1997].

The design of color scales also has to consider predefined meanings of colors. In western countries, red is considered as signal for danger and thus for values in a critical range. Green on the other hand indicates that values are in a normal range. Yellow and orange are appropriate for values which are neither normal nor highly critical. In surgical planning, for example, this convention is often used to convey which structures are at high or moderate risk if a tumor in the surroundings should be removed. Thus, color may indicate distances.

The appropriateness of color scales, in particular if new color scales should be used, can only be assessed by means of a systematic user study. A user study should compare familiar images color-coded with different scales. The recognizability of differences needs to be assessed separately in different portions. Rogowitz and Kalvin [2001] carried out such a study to compare the most frequently used color scales. The experiment design may serve as orientation for similar experiments.

Discrete Color Scales Continuous color scales map scalar data in high precision. Often color is used instead to convey whether a value is in a certain interval. In such cases, *discrete color scales* consisting of clearly distinct colors are used. As an example, for surgery planning it is often essential to recognize whether a critical structure is close to a tumor or even infiltrated. To convey this information, a discrete scale with red representing distances below 2 mm, yellow representing distances between 2 and 5 mm and green representing more than 5 mm is appropriate. Discrete color scales are also referred to as *segmented color scales* [Tominski *et al.*, 2008]. Since color-coding is essential in medical visualization we will see many examples in the course of this book. The appropriateness of specific color scales depends on properties of the data, e.g., range, and frequency and on the tasks to be solved. For details of color mapping and their perceptual basis, see the task-oriented description of Tominski *et al.* [2008] which is restricted to 2D visualizations but some aspects may be generalized to 3D and [Borland and Taylor, 2007].

3.3.3 VISUAL PERCEPTION AND ATTENTION IN THE DIAGNOSIS OF MEDICAL VOLUME DATA

A number of research groups performed an in-depth analysis of factors influencing visual perception and attention on the performance of radiologists in specific diagnostic tasks, such as pulmonary nodule detection or diagnosis of early breast cancer in X-ray mammographies. As a stimulating overview Krupinski [2006] discussed perceptually relevant differences between environments based on the analog-light-box and the now prevailing digital display-based settings. This includes differences due to the different media (film vs. digital displays) but also differences arising from digital image processing. The need to perceptually optimize radiologic viewing was clearly described.

Wang *et al.* [2008] investigated *search patterns* of eight radiologists (reviewing 30 lung cancer screening exams) to understand the effectiveness of different display modes, such as slice-by-slice viewing and maximum-intensity projection. They examined the characteristics of wrong decisions, e.g., missed nodules or false positives. Krupinski *et al.* [2012a] demonstrated how the diagnostic accuracy in detecting lung nodules in CT data decreases after a long (usual) workday. In both experiments, ROC curves were determined to assess diagnostic accuracy (recall Fig. 3.2). The perceptual consequences of using compressed image data are crucial, since the large amount of image data motivates compressed storage. Perceptual studies were carried out to determine acceptable compression ratios using the hypotheses that only noticeable differences may influence diagnosis [Ringl *et al.*, 2007].

Erickson *et al.* [2010] examined slices of chest, abdomen and pelvis CT data that were compressed with different ratios in the JPEG 2000 format (8:1, 12:1, and 16:1 lossy compression). Radiologists with different levels of experience were asked whether they notice differences in the depiction of the pelvis as well as abdominal structures. Even in the lowest compression ratio, changes were noticeable and thus the compression *may* influence the time for diagnosis or even diagnostic decisions.

3.4 STORAGE OF MEDICAL IMAGE DATA

The following three sections are dedicated to the generation, storage and use of medical image data in radiology. Before, we discuss the image interpretation process (*reading*), we describe standardized methods of storing medical image data. Medical image data are physically stored together with information which is essential for the interpretation of the images. This information is highly standardized as a result of dedicated and long-term standardization activities. These led to the DICOM standard (Digital Imaging and Communications in Medicine) that has been established by the NEMA (National Electrical Manufacturers Association). The current version 3.0 was established in 1993. At the same time, publicly available software tools were presented that support the standard—this turned out to be essential for a widespread acceptance and support. DICOM is the industry standard for transferral of radiologic images and other medical information between computers and medical devices. In recent years, DICOM was further extended to capture also requirements from other medical disciplines including new types of image data, e.g., microscopy data acquired in pathology departments. These are primarily microscopy data, that are very large and DICOM also specifies how such data may be compressed. DICOM enables digital communication between diagnostic and therapeutic equipment and systems from various manufacturers. For example, workstations, CT and MR scanners, film digitizers, shared archives, laser printers, and host computers and mainframes made by multiple vendors can communicate by means of DICOM. Currently, most manufacturers of CT and MR scanners are officially accredited as being *DICOM conformant*, which means that their output meets the specification of the DICOM standard.

3.4.1 SCOPE OF DICOM

DICOM is continuously refined by the DICOM committee that includes 26 leading manufactures as well as several organizations, such as the American College of Radiology, which represent the users.

The standard is rather voluminous with 20 parts and more than 3000 pages (2012) that are constantly updated, e.g., by adding new supplements. In addition to the standard, many supplements reflect the current state of the discussion on enhancements and special solutions. Although not being a mandatory standard, many of these supplements contain useful recommendations for the design and development of software support. As an example, we discuss digital hanging protocols in § 3.6.3 based on a corresponding supplement to the DICOM standard.

There are different kinds of DICOM data. In case of Computed or Direct Radiography (CR, DR), individual images are represented as DICOM files (often two images per study). The results of a CT or MRI examination are series of DICOM files, each of which represents one slice. Usually, it is necessary to analyze such a stack of images to detect which of them belong together (forming a volume dataset). Only those data with identical image acquisition parameters, such as unique identifiers (study-id), are regarded as belonging together.

Working Groups In addition to the DICOM committee, 27 working groups deal with special topics, such as *Cardiac and Vascular Information*, *Dentistry*, *Nuclear Medicine*, *Pathology*, *Surgery*, and *Digital Mammography*. The most recently founded working group deals with *Web Technology* and might be of paramount importance in the future. These groups consist of representatives from industry, clinical practice and academia. The major results of a working group (WG) are *supplements* that provide a consensus of how a specific problem should be solved.

Surgical DICOM The DICOM working group 24 ("Surgical DICOM"), for example, elaborated on the efficient use of 3D surface meshes, that may result from segmentation, leading to the supplement 132 ("Polygonal surface description") that was accepted in 2008. This supplement is particularly important for medical 3D visualization and computer-assisted surgery, since it enables to store the results of surgical planning in a standardized manner. Further supplements of this working group are related to the definition of implants and implant plans (supplements 131 and 134, accepted in 2011). These supplements describe data structures and definitions, but no implementation details [Treichel *et al.*, 2011]. The development of new supplements is motivated by new and refined medical procedures and medical technology, such as more flexible imaging or new types of implants and surgical instruments. The three supplements developed in WG 24 are motivated by improved digital technology for planning implants, e.g., in total hip replacement [Treichel *et al.*, 2011, Viceconti, 2003].

3.4.2 STRUCTURE OF DICOM DATA

DICOM data contain information concerning a variety of aspects of medical image data. These are organized in a hierarchy with patients on the top. For each *patient* one or more *studies* are available; each study may contain several *series* and finally each series consists of *images*. For volume data, an image represents one two-dimensional slice.

In the following, we briefly mention some important parts of DICOM data. The official term of these parts is *group*. Each group consists of the elementary specification of DICOM tags.

- **Identification.** This section contains information essential to locate a series of image data in a database. This includes date and time of image acquisition. Some information is essential for the use of the results, for example, the name of the referring physician.

- **Acquisition parameters.** This section contains information concerning the imaging modality (CT, MRI, X-ray,...), the specific scanning parameters (sequence name, sequence variants) and the administration of a contrast agent. Also, the name of the manufacturer and its product are recorded. Finally, the position and orientation of the patient is stated. Some information is specific for a certain modality (and restricted to this modality), such as magnetic field strength, echo, and repetition time for MRI data. This section also includes information on the patient position relative to the imaging equipment, e.g., Feet First-Supine or Head First-Supine (eight default positions are represented).
- **Patient data.** The patient name, a unique patient id, the date of birth, and the sex (female, male) are part of this section. The weight and height of the patient are optional tags that are useful, for example, to relate certain findings to the patient weight.
- **Image data.** For the localization and evaluation of images, a variety of numbers is essential. The corresponding tags are part of the *image data* section. Examples are a study-id, a series number, an image group and an acquisition number.
- **Image presentation.** This section contains the slice distance and the *pixel spacing* that describes the in-plane resolution. The range of values (min, max) and the number of bits allocated are also represented in this section. Finally, a default configuration for the display of the data can be specified (*WindowWidth*, *WindowCenter*). In § 3.6, we discuss these parameters and their influence on image interpretation.

Some of these data have an immediate influence on image interpretation. It is therefore common practice in radiological workstations to include this information in a legend when the radiological data are viewed (on a CRT monitor or on a screen). In particular, patient data as well as some image interpretation data are usually displayed. Figure 3.8 shows image data and related information. The upper left corner presents patient-specific information. The name and the id of the patient were modified in the anonymization process. The third row represents the year of the patient's birth. The "voxel" entry indicates the coordinates of the currently selected voxel (represented by the mouse cursor) and the "value" entry represents the Hounsfield value at this location. The upper right corner refers to the institution where the images were acquired. The lower left corner shows which slice and which point in time is currently visible. The size of the dataset (number of voxels in x-, y- and z-direction) is also presented. The fourth row indicates the size of one voxel, the first two numbers (0.414, 0.414) represent the in-plane resolution, and the third number (2.0) represents the slice distance (in mm).

For medical visualization, part 14 of the DICOM standard is particularly important. It describes a *Grayscale Standard Display Function*. DICOM contains a model of the image acquisition process as well as a presentation chain, and the *Standardized Display System*. The Grayscale Standard Display Function describes the transformation of measured values to observable luminance values in a device-independent manner. The goal of the function is to transform measured values to be perceptually linear (taking into account that our visual perception is actually not linear, recall § 3.3). The purpose of defining this Grayscale Standard Display Function is to allow applications to know a priori how measured values are transformed to visible luminance values by a Standardized Display System.

3.5 CONVENTIONAL FILM-BASED DIAGNOSIS

The conventional way of reading image data is by means of transmissive films that are placed on a lightbox (see Fig. 3.9) where the radiologist inspects them. This way of reading images was also employed for 3D image data: a workstation was attached to the scanning devices (CT, MRI), and at this workstation images are preprocessed and a subset is selected to be printed on film to be read at the lightbox.

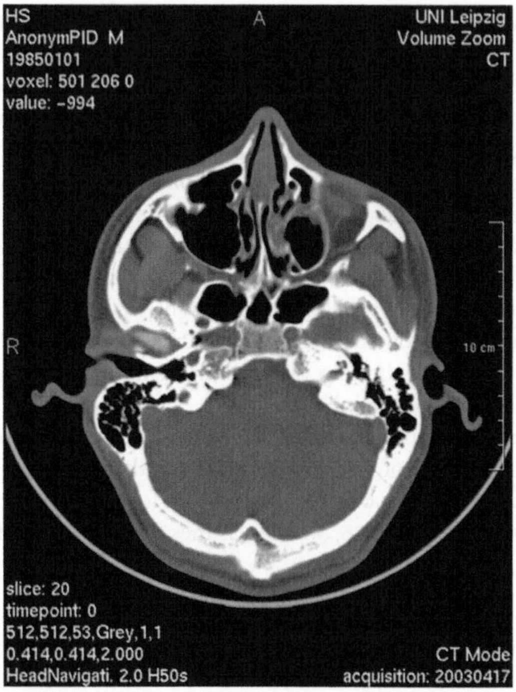

FIGURE 3.8 *A CT slice with additional information included in all four corners of the image.*

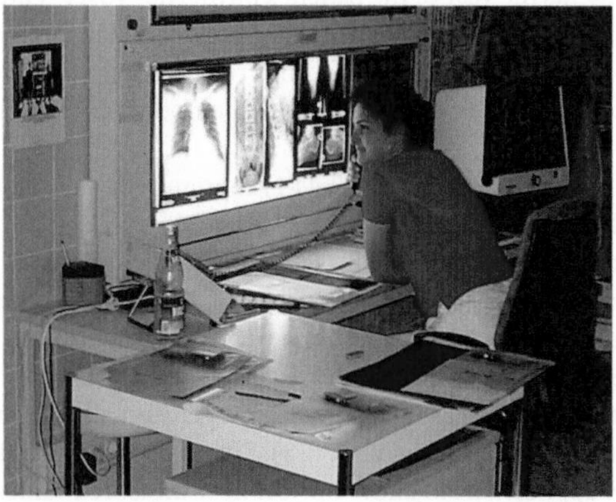

FIGURE 3.9 *The conventional lightbox as traditional work place of radiologists (Courtesy of Sebastian Meyer, MeVis Diagnostics Bremen).*

For the design of computer support it is essential to understand this process. On the one hand, experienced radiologists are accustomed to this kind of diagnosis. On the other hand, the lightbox is efficiently organized and thus the design of efficient software solutions strongly benefits from an understanding that organization.

3.5.1 COOPERATION OF RADIOLOGISTS AND RADIOLOGY TECHNICIANS

Diagnosis of medical image data is a cooperative process where radiologists (experienced medical doctors with a long-term postgraduate education) and radiology technicians are involved. The radiology technician education is much shorter—in several countries it is at the Bachelor level. This cooperation is designed such that the expert knowledge of the radiologist is used as effectively as possible. All tasks that involve the localization and initial arrangement of the images are carried out by a radiology technician. The preparation includes affixing images on the lightbox in such a way that a diagnostic process is supported in an optimal manner. This process is based on *hanging protocols* that define how images are arranged. Hanging protocols are neither formalized nor standardized. They differ from department to department and even from radiologist to radiologist. Hanging protocols are individual agreements between a radiologist and the radiology technician. They allow the radiologist to form a habit of inspecting images. With these hanging protocols, reporting of an examination is highly reproducible and very effective.

An example for a hanging protocol for X-ray thorax images is to use a lateral and a frontal image (this is actually the image acquisition protocol) to place the lateral image always on the left and the frontal image on the right. Hanging protocols differ from the body region to inspect, from the diagnostic question and from the modality (e.g., CT, X-ray).

3.5.2 TASKS IN CONVENTIONAL FILM-BASED DIAGNOSIS

There are some general and frequent tasks in film-based diagnosis.

- *Viewing* is the most essential task and involves getting an overview of the patient's anatomy and a local inspection of particularly relevant structures.
- Radiologists often *compare* current images with previous images.
- *Quantitative image analysis* is performed, e.g., to assess distances and angles.
- *Decision making* involved the evaluation of pathologies, recommendations further examinations or possible treatment options.
- *Documentation*. Finally, diagnostic findings are documented and supplied for further treatment.

In particular viewing of X-ray images, the detailed inspection of suspicious regions is necessary to detect the characteristics of an early stage of a disease. A magnifying glass is used for this purpose.

A comparison is facilitated if the image acquisition parameters are identical or at least very similar. Whether or not a pathologic lesion is regarded as malignant might depend on the difference to previous images. Whether or not a therapy with drugs is appreciated as effective depends on the comparison of pathologic lesions, in particular on the assessment of their volume. To locate the previous images for a particular patient, is often a tedious and error-prone process if no digital archive is available. It is estimated that only 80% of the required images could be found.

Quantitative image analysis is strongly limited with conventional diagnostics. Radiologists employ rulers to assess distances and protractors to assess angles. Distances are often essential for radiation treatment and surgery planning (distances between pathologic structures and vital structures), whereas angular measurements allow to assess the spatial relation between bones, which is crucial in orthopedics. The accuracy of these measurements is limited because they are carried out based on (axial) 2D slices. Other quantitative measurements such as cross-sectional areas, volumes of certain structures or mean gray values cannot be reliably assessed at all.

After viewing and analyzing, radiologists *make decisions* in the sense that they evaluate pathologies, recommend further examinations or possible treatment options. Finally, diagnostic findings are documented.

This *documentation* is often recorded with a voice recorder and later transformed to a written report (manually by a secretary or by employing voice recognition software). The diagnostic findings are often discussed with referring physicians in order to establish an appropriate treatment. Radiologists explain their findings by means of selected images and answer questions with respect to therapeutic decisions.

3.6 SOFT-COPY READING

Digitization of radiological departments and soft-copy reading was established to compensate for some of the obvious drawbacks of conventional film-based diagnosis. Within a completely digital radiology department, image data is stored in a database (a Picture Archiving and Communication System, PACS). The storage in a database is more reliable and allows faster access to image data. Also, the cost of developing and printing film is saved—on a longterm scale this is an enormous amount, which justifies the investment in software and infrastructure. Usually, the modalities (CT or MR scanners) send the image data (via DICOM) immediately to the PACS. From there, the data are distributed to the workplaces of the radiologists.

3.6.1 DIGITAL RADIOLOGY DEPARTMENTS

Before we discuss soft-copy reading, we describe the typical infrastructure and workflow in a digital radiological department that the reading process forms a part of based on [Breitenborn, 2004]. The process starts with an order of the referring physician that is registered in the *radiologic information system* (RIS). The RIS entry is either created manually or generated automatically if the referring physician and the radiology department share a common information system (such as a hospital information system, HIS).

By means of the RIS, a date and time is scheduled to carry out the examination and the referring physician is notified about this. Also, relevant prior image data are prefetched (from the PACS) and provided. The patient is welcomed by a radiology technician who knows from the RIS which examination should be carried out. The RIS submits relevant information to the imaging modality, such as patient name and patient id. This automatic process saves time and avoids confusion. These data are later part of the DICOM data that are transferred from the modality to the radiologist's workplace. After the image data acquisition, the RIS is notified about the completion of the procedure and the images are stored in the PACS. The images are retrieved at a diagnostic workstation, where a report is generated that is sent to a *report repository* and finally returned to the referring physician.

A RIS supports the management of different users with their permissions to read and write image data and reports. In particular, *task lists* for each individual radiologist and for each modality are created and managed to support the diagnostic processes within a department. The support provided by a RIS is valuable because there are orthogonal views on the orders and procedures, which are accomplished in a radiology department. On the one hand, there are workplaces where images from a certain modality are processed by one radiologist, on the other hand, there are referring physicians—the "customers"—who place orders to different modalities. The results of the diagnostic process are selected images and a written report. Such reports often follow a special structure that is dedicated to a particular anatomical region and diagnostic question, such as vascular anatomy in an organ in case of preoperative surgery planning. This structure may be defined by the head of a department or an experienced physician that has a long experience with this kind of examination. The reports contain links to selected images that are particularly relevant for the diagnosis. These images are often enhanced by annotations, such as arrows, encircled regions or labels.

The enhanced images are sent back to the PACS where again the DICOM format is employed to represent the information. RIS/PACS workplaces enable basic viewing of medical image data, but no advanced multimodal image analysis, as it is performed with radiology workstations.

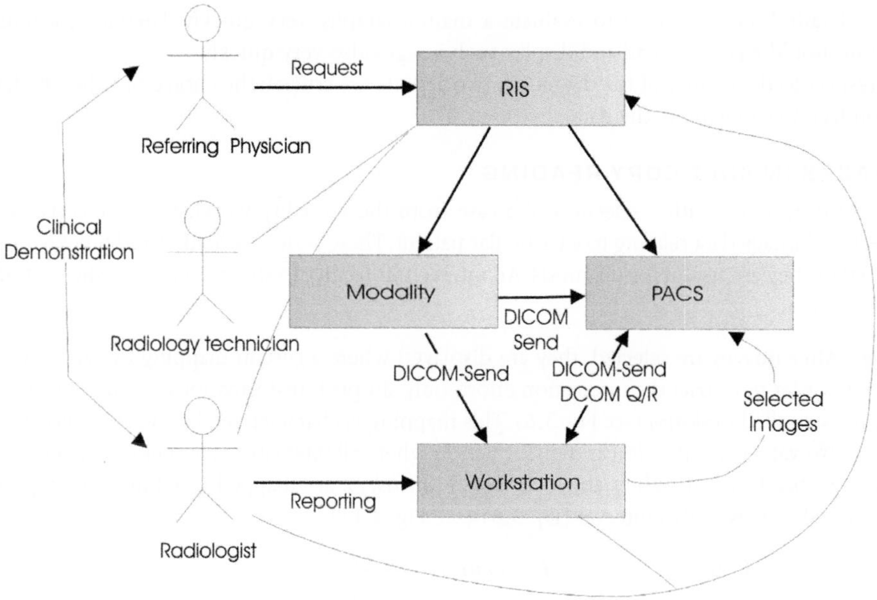

FIGURE 3.10 *Workflow in a digital radiology department (Adapted from: [Breitenborn, 2004]).*

Finally, radiologists demonstrate diagnostic results to the referring physicians. In university hospitals, for example, there is a regular demonstration for neurosurgeons, general surgeons, neurologists, and most of the other medical specialities (these demonstrations are often scheduled on a daily basis for operating specialities and on a weekly basis for others). These demonstrations start with a presentation of the diagnostic findings and provide room for questions from the referring physicians relating to therapeutic decisions. In a digital radiology department such demonstrations are carried out by means of a laptop and a video beamer. Figure 3.10 illustrates this process.

Structured Reporting Due to the importance of reporting, this process is explicitly supported by the DICOM standard, in particular by the *Structured report* entity [Hussein *et al.*, 2007a,b]. The standard defines a basic structure and the integration of image data. The basic structure consists of a heading, anamnesis, technical details of the examination, finding, and conclusions, e.g., recommendations for further treatment [Stramare *et al.*, 2012]. Also the integration of images and related measurements is defined in the *structured report* entity.

Despite this support, a structured report is in essence still a free-text document that is not always concise and may contain ambiguities. A lot of effort is spent on a further standardization. An essential aspect is a comprehensive database of radiology terms, called *RadLex* [Kundu *et al.*, 2009]. This database contains 7.500 words with generally accepted meanings [Stramare *et al.*, 2012]. These terms relate to imaging techniques, anatomical locations, and relationships. Due to the ongoing technical and medical development, RadLex will further evolve. To support daily clinical routine, RadLex needs to be integrated with diagnostic workstations.

Soft-copy reading became a viable alternative when the quality and speed of diagnostic procedures was similar (or better) than with conventional methods. Several iterations were necessary to achieve these requirements. With respect to speed, the enormous amount of data is a major problem. A digital mammography, for example, is represented as 4096×4096 image matrix with 12 bit gray values.

Experienced radiologists are able to evaluate a mammography very quickly. Therefore, a radiological workstation should enable to load and display such images also very quickly.

With respect to the quality of the diagnosis, two aspects are crucial: the choice of a display device and interaction facilities to explore the data.

3.6.2 TASKS IN SOFT-COPY READING

Soft-copy reading starts with a selection of a case from the modality worklist. A case consists often of several series of image data relating to a particular patient. These series are loaded and quickly browsed to assess whether they are useful for diagnosis. An interaction facility to step through the slices of 3D data is therefore essential.

Windowing After images are selected, they are displayed where a certain mapping of data to gray values is applied. In order to restrict the interaction effort, only simple transformations are offered. The simplest mapping is a so-called *windowing* (see Fig. 3.6). This mapping is characterized by a *window center* and a *window width*. These two values specify a linear transformation where all intensity values below $center - width/2$ are mapped to black and all values above $center + width/2$ are mapped to white. The gray values are employed for all values in this interval (Eq. 3.6) (see Fig. 3.11).

$$G = \begin{cases} 0 & I \leq center - \frac{width}{2} \\ \frac{I - center - \frac{width}{2}}{width} & I > center - \frac{width}{2} \text{ and } I \leq center + \frac{width}{2} \\ 1 & I > center + \frac{width}{2} \end{cases} \qquad (3.6)$$

The width of the window defines the steepness of the function and thus the contrast. The center defines the level of intensity values the user is interested in. Radiological workstations provide so-called presets for typical tasks. Presets are particularly useful for CT data where the standardized Hounsfield units are employed (recall Table 2.1).

The generalization of windowing is often called *adjusting a lookup table* (abbreviated as LUT). The LUT is in fact a table with two columns: one contains the intensity values and the second contains the associated

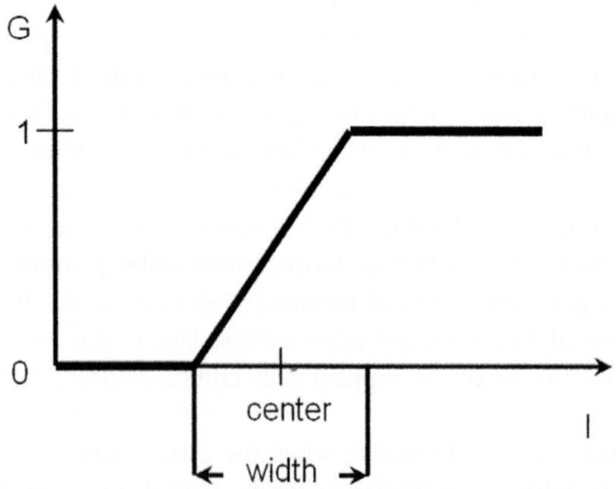

FIGURE 3.11 *Windowing as a simple transform from intensity values I to gray values G. For CT data, the Hounsfield values would be represented at the abscissa. The gray value "1" represents the brightest value that can be displayed (white), whereas "0" represents black.*

gray values defined by a mapping process. "Lookup" implies that the display system looks up the gray value associated with an intensity value.

Lookup tables are not directly edited. Instead, users define the graph of a function with an appropriate editor. This function is called *transfer function* and the LUT results from the discretization of the transfer function.

Browsing Slices An important interaction facility is to browse through the slices. The layout may consist of one large slice display or several slices shown simultaneously. If one slice is shown, the user should step forward and backward. If several slices are shown, either all slices are replaced when the user moves forward or backward or only one new slice is presented while the other slices move. The simultaneous view of several images is closer to conventional diagnosis with the lightbox. However, with CRT monitors, four or even more images are often too small to recognize small features reliably. Therefore, layouts with several images serve primarily as an overview.

A feature that is completely unknown from conventional diagnosis is to provide an animated movement through all slices (referred to as *cine mode*). The cine mode is effective because the continuous movement smoothly blends one cross-sectional slice with the next, which considerably reduces the cognitive effort to mentally integrate these images to form a 3D representation.

Evaluating Image Data in Different Orientations One of the advantages of soft-copy reading is the ability to reformat the stack of slice data. With this facility, the three orthogonal views (axial, coronal, or sagittal) as well as arbitrary oblique slices may be created. Radiology workstations often support the simultaneous display of the three orthogonal slicing directions (Fig. 3.12).

Quantitative Image Analysis A variety of features of radiologic workstations refer to the quantitative analysis. Distance measurements are accomplished by selecting the corresponding measurement mode and selecting two pixels. Figure 3.13 is an example, where different distances are measured to quantify spatial relations in cardiac CT data to support treatment planning. The pixels may be located in different slices, which allows to measure distances between positions that do not belong to the same (axial) slice. In a similar way, angular measurements are carried out. Here, a third position has to be selected. These measurements are more precise than those carried out in conventional diagnosis.

For specific diagnostic tasks, guidelines provide orientation as to what measures are essential and how they should be performed. As an example, in tumor diagnosis and follow-up studies evaluating treatment effects, tumors are assessed according to the RECIST (Response Evaluation Criteria In Solid Tumors) criteria. This includes to manually select the slice where a tumor appears to be largest and to determine the longest diameter. Although this measure cannot be determined very reliably, it is used to assess whether the disease is stable, progressing (increasing tumor size), or partially responding.

Another kind of quantitative analysis refers to the intensity distribution in a selected region. As a prerequisite for this analysis, the user must be able to define a region of interest (ROI). For this purpose, predefined shapes, such as circles, ellipsoids or rectangles are provided, which are scaled and translated by the user. In addition, it is often possible to create arbitrarily shaped ROIs by manually drawing on the slices. As feedback, the system presents how many pixels have been selected and which area is comprised by the ROI. In addition, the mean intensity value as well as the standard deviation are calculated. This information may be used to assess the severity of a disease, in particular when CT data are involved where intensity values are standardized. As a first example, the mean intensity value of a ROI in the bones—the vertebral mineral density—is an indicator for the severity of osteoporosis [Kalender *et al.*, 1989]. To further support the quantitative image analysis, algorithms that automatically place an appropriate ROI are promising in

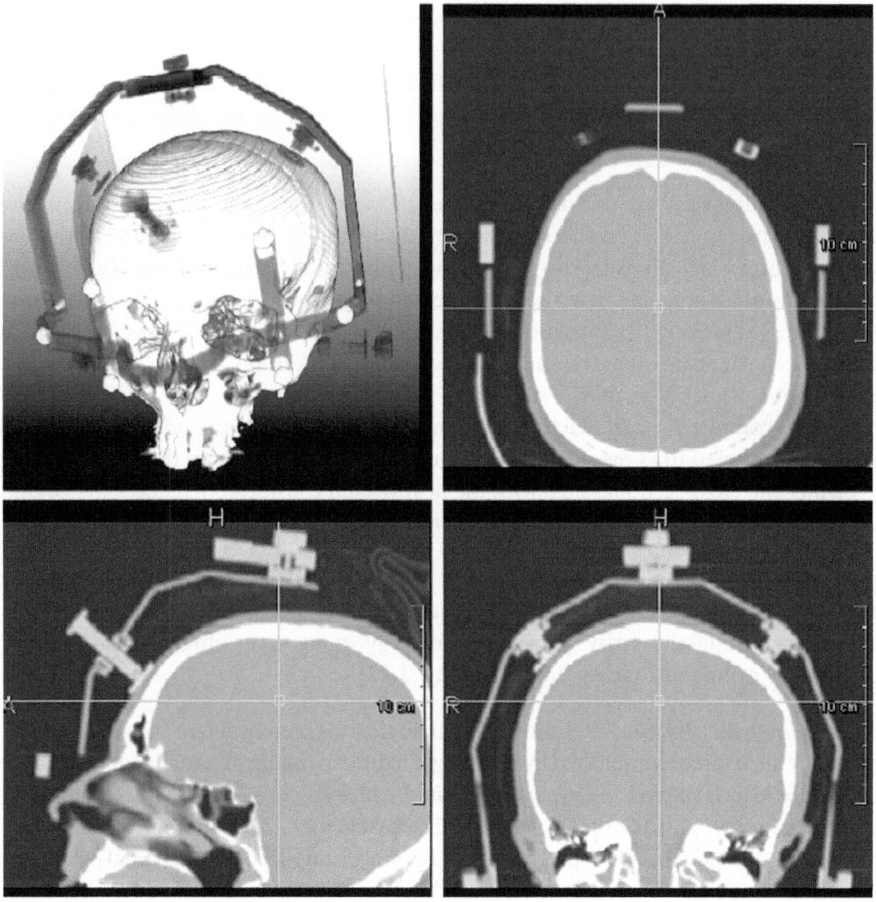

FIGURE 3.12 *Simultaneous display of three orthogonal views and a 3D view (upper left). The crosshair cursor is synchronized between these views. The ruler (on the right) is employed to roughly assess distances.*

order to increase the reproducibility. As an example, the determination of vertebral mineral density could be enhanced by automatic ROI definition [Louis *et al.*, 1988].

Example: Regional Lung Function Determination With respect to CT thorax data, the mean intensity value of a ROI in the thorax is related to functional defects of the lung [Hayhurst *et al.*, 1984], [Sakai *et al.*, 1987]. Under normal conditions, a value between −500 and −900 Hounsfield is expected [Wu *et al.*, 2002]. If the mean value is above this range, the patient probably suffers from a fibrosis. On the other hand, if the mean value is less than −900 Hounsfield, an emphysema is likely where lung tissue is degraded. An emphysema is characterized by a loss of elasticity in the lungs, resulting in increased breathing resistance and hence shortness of breath.

The severity of the disease is related to the mean value; the stronger it deviates from the normal interval the more severe the disease actually is. Figure 3.14 shows the ROI selection in a suspicious region of CT thorax data to derive the mean gray value. To assess the severity of an emphysema, not only the mean value but also the portion of voxels with HU values below −900 and −950 are registered [Park *et al.*, 1999].

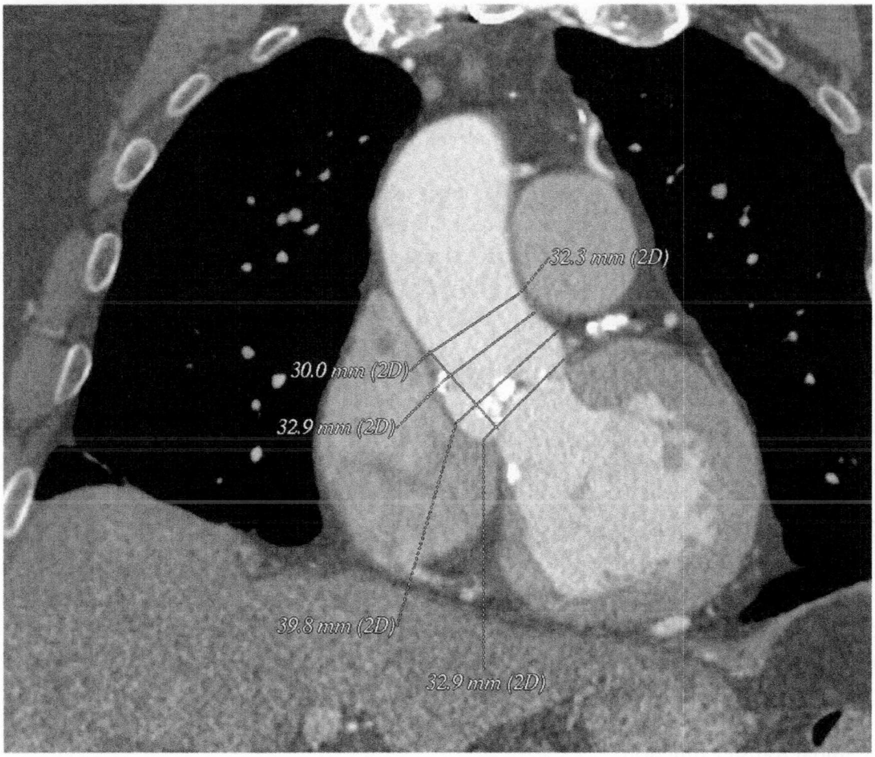

FIGURE 3.13 CT-Angiography showing a coronal 2D-plane with measurements performed prior to Transcatheter Aortic Valve Implantation (TAVI) (Courtesy of Hoen-Oh Shin, Medical School Hannover).

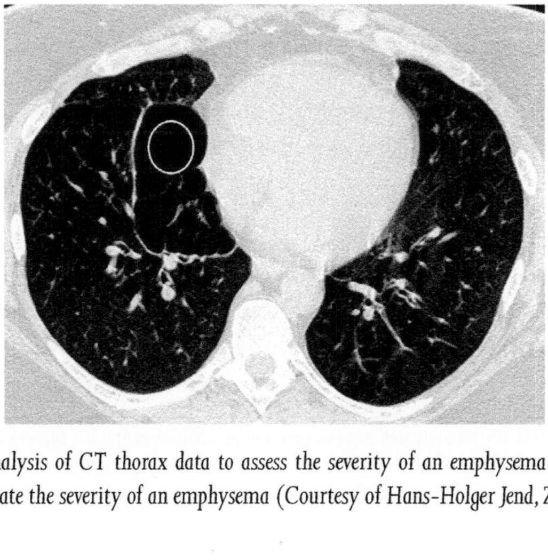

FIGURE 3.14 Quantitative analysis of CT thorax data to assess the severity of an emphysema. The mean intensity value in the encircled region is defined to evaluate the severity of an emphysema (Courtesy of Hans-Holger Jend, Zentralkrankenhaus Bremen-Ost).

The lung function may be also assessed with functional tests that are much faster to accomplish. However, these tests evaluate the global lung function. The quantitative CT analysis supports a regional analysis of the lung function that is essential for therapeutic decisions such as surgery planning. For surgery planning, the lung function in the remaining lung tissue is essential to evaluate the postoperative lung function and thus the feasibility of a surgical intervention.

Manual Segmentation For some advanced image analysis facilities, the identification and delineation of certain structures (*segmentation*) are a prerequisite. Facilities are provided to manually outline a structure. This is similar to the definition of an arbitrarily shaped ROI. However, the process has to be repeated in several slices. As feedback, it is common to overlay the segmented region onto the slice data as a semi-transparent colored region.

Annotation Annotation is the process of enhancing selected images with information to convey the findings. There are different kinds of information that can be added for this purpose. One example is the use of arrows that point to some pathologic variation. The arrow might be added by textual information which labels this region. Another annotation facility is to encircle a region.

3.6.3 DIGITAL HANGING PROTOCOL

The digital hanging protocol is the further development of hanging protocols for conventional diagnosis.[2] It is also targeted at an optimal cooperation between a radiologist and a radiology technician and aims at an automatic case preparation adapted to the specific disease. Digital hanging protocols include more information than conventional hanging protocols due to the extended capabilities of soft-copy reading. A digital hanging protocol may contain information with respect to

- the initial transfer function,
- the initially selected slice,
- the information presented in the legend, and
- synchronization specifications that define how one view is adapted if certain modifications occur in another view. Synchronization may refer to the presentation center/width specification of the presentation LUT and the selected slice. Such a synchronization supports the comparison between different visualizations.

Another crucial aspect of digital hanging protocols is the ability of the user to create such protocols or to refine existing protocols to tailor the diagnostic process to the diagnostic workflow in this particular department or to the personal habits of the radiologist. To further illustrate the spirit behind digital hanging protocols, we introduce a scenario elaborated in the DICOM Digital Hanging Protocol supplement (slightly modified):

> *"A physician sits at a workstation with two 1280 × 1024 screens and selects a chest CT case from the worklist. He decides to customize the viewing style and uses the viewing application to define what type of hanging protocol he prefers (layout style, interaction style) by pointing and clicking on graphical representations of the choices. He has chosen to define a 3 columns by 4 rows tiled presentation. He places the new exam on the left screen and the old exam on the right screen before he saves his preferences in a hanging protocol located at the DICOM server."*

2 The term digital hanging protocol is not formally defined and (currently) not part of the DICOM standard. There is a supplement to the standard, which discusses digital hanging protocols.

A large variety of digital hanging protocols is needed to adapt the diagnostic process to the imaging modality, to the characteristics of the display device, to image data characteristics, such as slice distance, and to the region of the body that is depicted. It is highly desirable that the most appropriate protocol is chosen automatically. This can be accomplished if image data are represented by means of the DICOM standard where appropriate tags represent these characteristics. Digital hanging protocols are particularly important to support

- multimodal image evaluation, such as CT, MRI, and PET, e.g., in oncology, and
- follow-up studies with a dedicated layout to facilitate comparisons.

In follow-up studies, findings from previous examinations may be automatically emphasized by presenting the related slices.

3.6.4 COMPUTER-AIDED DETECTION

In recent years, computer-aided detection (CAD) gained importance in clinical routine. CAD systems employ complex algorithms that search for suspicious findings in a dataset (*detection*) and analyze such findings in order to *classify* them and thus further support the diagnosis.

Here, it might be sufficient to mention that assumptions with respect to shape, size, and location of pathologies are incorporated. These features are combined to classify, e.g., a tumor, where most approaches are *supervised*. Thus, the possible classes are known before. Cluster analysis, artificial neural networks, support vector machines, and decision trees are among the basic techniques that are frequently employed for computer-aided detection.

These algorithms may not replace a human radiologist, but they may improve his or her efficiency and diagnostic accuracy by highlighting such findings, e.g., by encircling them or pointing with an arrow. Basically, there are two strategies how CAD algorithms may be incorporated in the diagnosis [Doi, 2007]:

- *Expert first*. The human expert makes a diagnosis based on the purely interactive exploration of the data. After the diagnosis is completed, the results of a CAD algorithm are displayed and the radiologist eventually refines his or her diagnosis.
- *Computer first*. The human expert uses the CAD results already in the initial diagnosis.

Obviously, an efficiency gain can only be achieved with the *computer first* strategy. There is, of course, some risk that the radiologist is biased toward the automatically determined result. However, as Doi [2007] point out, the diagnostic accuracy is very similar with both strategies. Thus, the more efficient *computer first* strategy is widely used. A particularly high sensitivity is required for CAD algorithms that are employed in the *computer first* mode. Successful examples include the search for suspicious masses in X-ray mammography, the search for polyps in the colon, and for fractures in case of osteoporosis.

Doi [2007] discussed a number of studies indicating that the combined sensitivity and specificity of a radiologist and a CAD algorithm improved indeed. In cases where the CAD algorithm erroneously considers a lesion as likely to be benign, the radiologists often correct this assessment. On the other hand, in cases where the radiologist missed a pathology or considered it erroneously as benign, he or she often changes the opinion if the CAD algorithm considers the lesion as very likely to be malignant. As an example, Jiang *et al.* [1999] was among the first larger studies on breast cancer diagnosis (104 histopathologically examined breast tumors) where the ROC analysis (recall Fig. 3.2) revealed an increase from 0.61 to 0.75.

In general, the development of CAD schemes have a number of common steps:

- *Feature selection.* In this step, features have to be determined that enable a discrimination between healthy and malignant tissue. As a general remark, it is rarely sufficient to use only very localized features. Often it is necessary to consider a spatial environment—like a physician would do—to discriminate real pathologies from artifacts, scars, or other similar features.
- *Feature extraction.* The relevant features need to be computed, e.g., length, diameters, surface areas, volume or more complex derived features, such as gradients and curvature-related information, is considered. In medical diagnosis, in particular *shape descriptors* play an essential role, e.g., compactness.
- *Classification.* Based on the extracted features, potential candidates are evaluated and graded as more or less suspicious. This includes the determination of weighting factors for the influence of individual features. A multidimensional feature space arises and a classifier is needed that optimally divides the distribution in that space in healthy and pathologic persons. Neural networks and other *machine learning* techniques are heavily used in the development of an appropriate classifier. The selection of a classifier is also (still) influenced by performance aspects: complex classification algorithms may take a long time to compute.
- *Integration in computer-assisted diagnosis.* Often, a CAD algorithm yields several suspicious findings, e.g., ten potential lung nodules or polyps. An overview of the occurrence of the CAD findings is necessary to convey the gross anatomical context and to enable to quickly locate the related slices. Each CAD finding needs to be emphasized, e.g., with an arrow, and labeled, e.g., with a computed likelihood for malignancy. Figure 3.15 gives an example.

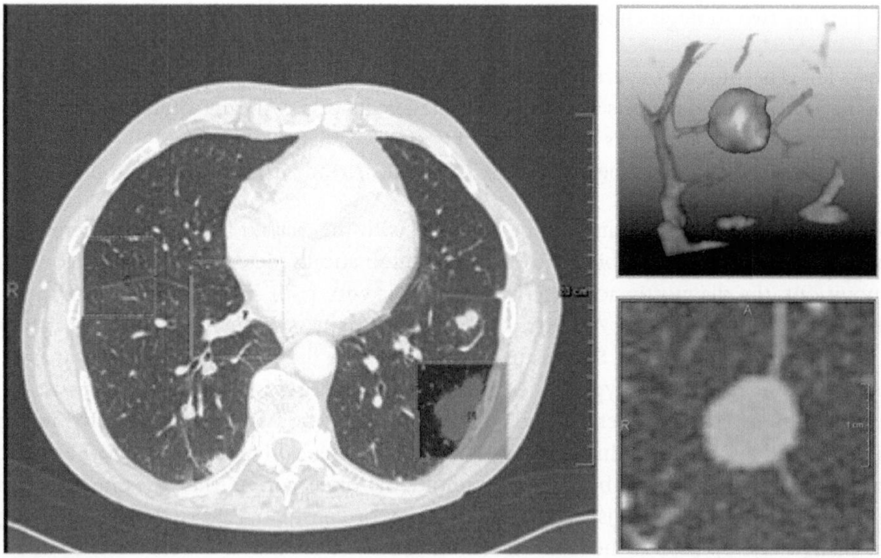

FIGURE 3.15 **Left:** In the slice view, all findings that are related to the current slice are shown and identified with a number. The small rectangular bar at the left of each finding indicates the range of slices to which the finding belongs and where the current slice is within that range. **Right:** For a selected finding, a close-up view in 2D and 3D is created (Courtesy of Volker Dicken and Jan-Martin Kunigk, Fraunhofer MEVIS).

The development and evaluation of CAD schemes requires a large data basis with a known ground truth to train classifiers on a subset to later evaluate them on the remaining cases. The collection of such data bases and the association with all relevant clinical data, e.g., results of further diagnosis and treatment, is a large effort. Fortunately, meanwhile such data bases exist for different clinical problems and may be used by algorithm developers.

3.6.4.1 CAD in Mammography Diagnosis

Suspicious regions in mammograms are either nodules or microcalcifications. These two target regions are very different and thus require separate features to detect and classify them. To assess the potential malignancy, the shape of nodules is essential, with round and lobulated shapes being less suspicious compared to microlobulated and stellate shapes. A feature that can be computed is the *compactness* of a nodule, that is the ratio between the circumference and the area. Figure 3.16 shows a benign and two malignant nodules in mammograms where the compactness strongly differs (the description is taken from [Wagner, 2009]). In general, features evaluating the margin of a lesion as well as features representing the density of a lesion are merged to yield a likelihood for malignancy [Huo *et al.*, 1998].

The detection and classification of pathologies in mammograms continues to evolve and lead the US Food and Drug Administration (FDA) to approve clinical use as second reader [Gur and Sumkin, 2006]. The detection rate increases by 2–10% according to a multitude of studies. In particular, smaller micro-calcification clusters are missed. As an example for a clinical study, Ko *et al.* [2006] employed the iCAD MammoReader to process 5.016 mammograms. The radiologist detected 43 of the total 48 malignancies, whereas the assistance of the CAD system helped to increase this number to 45.

The sensitivity of the best CAD algorithms improved from 87% in 1993 to 98% in 2007. In five large studies, involving in total more than 8000 women, the number of detected cancers increased by between 7% and 19%. The additionally detected cancers are often small (the number of small cancers <1 cm that were detected increased by 160%) and in these cases the cancer was diagnosed on average five years earlier. This improved diagnosis increases the chance of cure significantly, however, it comes at the expense of earlier anxiety among the involved women and despite earlier diagnosis, by far not all women get cured. Also, some of the additionally detected tumors might never cause problems to the affected women—thus, aggressive treatment would not be necessary.

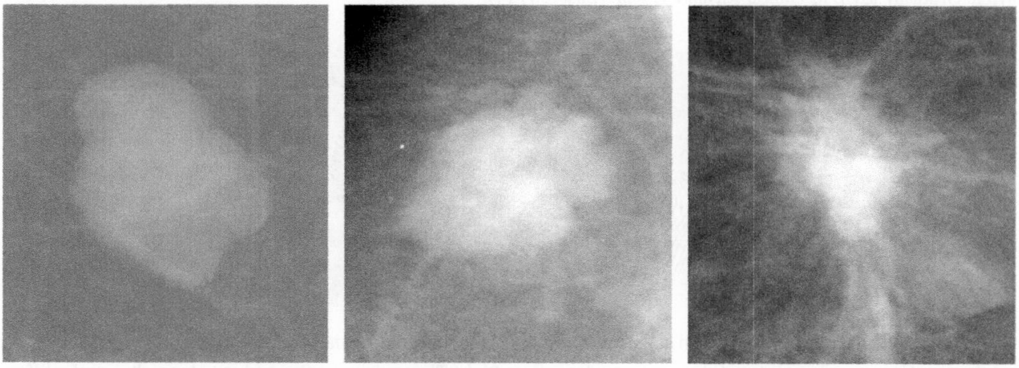

FIGURE 3.16 *Nodules in mammograms. The **left** benign nodule has a smooth boundary with a lobulated shape. Some features that are superimposed to the tumor are visible. In the **middle** image a malignant tumor is shown that has many small lobes. The malignant nodule in the **right** image is a stellar region with advanced spiculae. All tumors are part of the digital database for screening mammography (cases 305, 86, and 1262), described in: [Heath et al., 2001].*

3.6.4.2 CAD in Polyp Detection

A second important example where CAD was strongly advanced in recent years is polyp detection based on CT and MRI data. Polyps are protrusions of the colon wall, representing benign tumors that carry a risk to develop into colon cancer.[3] In contrast to mammography, 3D data are analyzed and a number of shape features are derived in order to detect and further evaluate polyp candidates (Fig. 3.17). Simple features may be evaluated when the polyp is segmented and decomposed in a (slim) polyp neck and the polyp cap, e.g., the size of the polyp neck and its height.

In addition to these simple features, curvature-related measures were investigated [Yoshida and Näppi, 2001, Yoshida *et al.*, 2002].[4] Obviously, minimum and maximum curvature change along the colon wall in case of a polyp. We will discuss curvature estimation and the use of curvature lines to characterize surface shapes later (§ 12.3). Here, we want to illustrate the use of curvature lines to characterize surface abnormalities (Fig. 3.18). The first step is to identify regions where the curvature changes strongly and

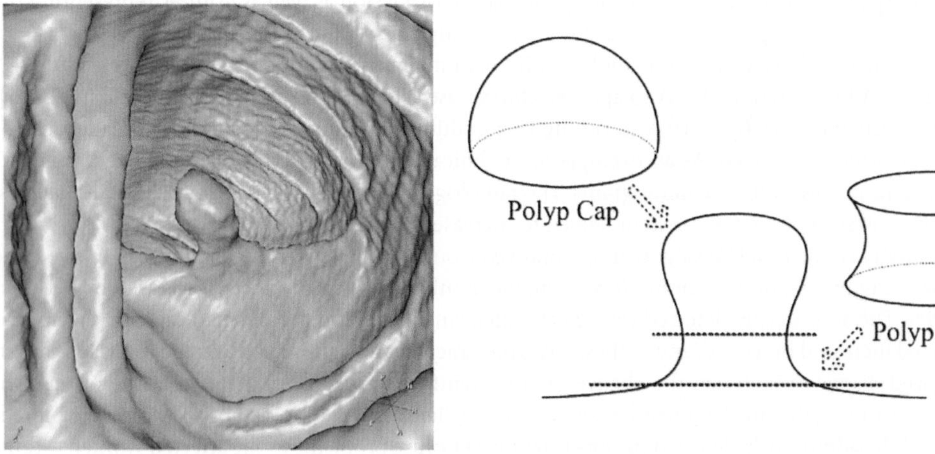

FIGURE 3.17 **Left:** *A polyp of the colon wall extracted from CT data.* **Right:** *Simple features that may be derived to characterize a polyp to eventually assess its clinical relevance (From: [Zhao 2011]).*

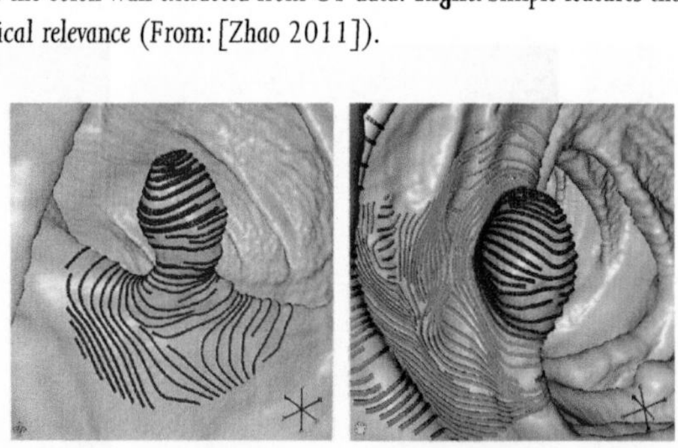

FIGURE 3.18 **Left:** *In a suspicious region of the colon, lines of maximum curvature are displayed. Actually, longer streamlines were created to provide a smooth rendition of the curvature information.* **Right:** *The suspicious region is clustered according to the different behavior of curvature and the cluster results are highlighted (From: [Zhao 2011]).*

3 We discuss the disease and its diagnosis later in more detail as an essential use case for virtual endoscopy (§ 13.6.1).

4 Curvature estimation is described in detail in Section 12.3.

to superimpose lines of maximum curvature along that (suspicious) region. A further support may be achieved by clustering these regions with respect to different curvature-related measures. Clustering will be discussed in § 9.2.2.1.

3.6.5 DIAGNOSIS WITH 3D VISUALIZATIONS

3D visualizations still play a minor role in radiologic diagnosis. As we have discussed in § 1.3, there are various reasons for the prevalence of slice-based reading. While 3D visualizations provide an overview of medical image data (only), the slices contain all details necessary for a diagnosis. One practical issue is that advanced 3D visualizations are still not convenient to generate and use on general diagnostics workstations. Instead, there are specialized "3D workstations." While the techniques described in the following *might* be available in general diagnostic workstations, they are rarely efficient and simple to handle. Thus, for generating advanced 3D visualizations, radiologists still have to transfer the data to a specialized workstation, such as the VITREA ADVANCED from VITAL or LEONARDO from SIEMENS. The limited availability of such (expensive) workstations and the more complex workflow hamper the widespread use of 3D visualizations for diagnosis. For selected diagnostic questions, clinical studies clearly show that an improved diagnostic accuracy may be provided with 3D visualizations. As an example, Remy-Jardin *et al.* [1998] could show that 3D renderings of patients with tracheobronchial stenosis provided relevant additional information in one third of 47 patients.

Meanwhile there is considerable evidence that 3D visualizations are useful for a variety of surgical planning tasks. Hu and Malthaner [2007] analyzed the use of 3D visualizations in six patients who were evaluated with respect to the surgical removal of lung cancer. Their study included 17 participants with varying degrees of experience. They found that resectability could be better predicted and the confidence of the prediction also increased. Lee *et al.* [2003] evaluated 3D display of CT data to preoperatively discuss laparoscopic gastric cancer surgery. 3D visualization provides "a vascular road map, which is critical for surgical guidance, and prevents the risks involved in surgery." Similarly, Shiozawa *et al.* [2009] found a benefit of 3D visualizations for planning treatment of adrenal tumors.

3D visualization techniques are explained in detail in Part III. In this subsection we briefly show which techniques are widespread and what can be achieved by using them. We start with *multiplanar reformatting*, which is actually a modified slicing through medical volume data and thus not a "true" 3D visualization technique. We go on with maximum-intensity projections which is a 3D visualization technique, but due to the image generation does not correctly represents depth relations. 3D visualization techniques that provide faithful depth perceptions follow. These are surface-shaded displays, volume rendering and virtual endoscopy.

3.6.5.1 Multiplanar Reformatting

Multiplanar reformatting (MPR) allows the user to define oblique slices through the volume data that might be useful, for example, to adapt a slice to the orientation of a relevant structure. MPRs might be defined automatically (based on segmentation and image analysis of certain objects) or interactively, as shown in Figure 3.19. The section of a rectangular plane with a parallelepiped is a plane with 3, 4, 5, or 6 vertices.

To use such visualizations that may have been generated at a radiology workstation for example, later in other settings, e.g., at the referring physician's desk where other software tools are employed. To enable this kind of interoperability, *persistent storage* of visualization options and parameters is necessary. This may be achieved if the tools adhere to the DICOM standard (recall § 3.4). The parameters of slice-based viewing, including slicing directions for MPR are part of the DICOM "Presentation State" that aims at an exact reproducibility of visualizations on different output devices. Parameters of more advanced 3D

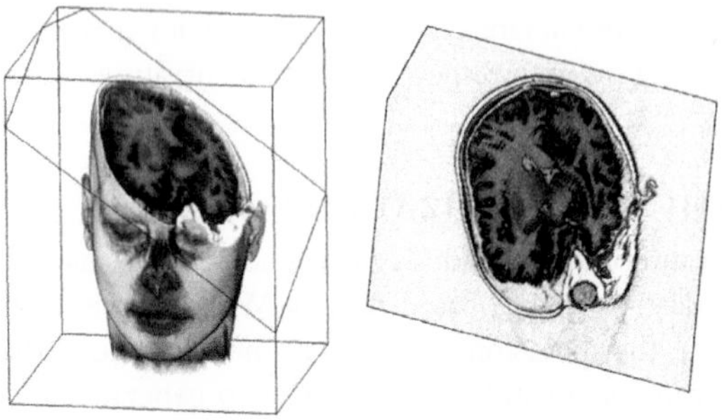

FIGURE 3.19 *Interactive definition of a multiplanar reformatting of cerebral MRI data. The 3D visualization on the left is used to define an oblique plane that is depicted undistorted on the right (Courtesy of Wolf Spindler, Fraunhofer MEVIS Bremen).*

visualization techniques, such as volume rendering, are not yet part of the accepted standard. At the time of this writing, the WG 11 is discussing these issues aiming at supplement 156 "multidimensional presentation states" [Burgert and Luszcz, 2012].

3.6.5.2 Maximum Intensity Projection

A frequently used technique is the maximum intensity projection (MIP). With this technique, images are generated by tracing rays from the viewing plane to the 3D volume data in the direction of the virtual camera. For each pixel of the viewplane, the voxel with maximum intensity is displayed. MIP images do not convey depth relations reliably, but they allow to assess contrast-enhanced vascular structures (these are often the voxels with highest intensity; other structures are therefore effectively suppressed). Hence, diagnosis of vascular structures is the most important application of MIP images. An advantage of the MIP display mode is that no user interaction is required.

3.6.5.3 Surface Shaded Display

Another visualization technique that is available in many diagnostic workstations is surface shaded display (SSD). Images are generated based on a threshold supplied by the user. 3D surfaces are created by generating polygonal meshes connecting adjacent voxels with the given threshold value (or a value very close to the threshold). Usually, some lighting is applied to produce shaded visualizations to convey depth relations well.

Visualization researchers have coined the term *isosurface visualization* for this visualization technique. SSD is a useful visualization option if surfaces of anatomical structures can be created based on an intensity-threshold that holds, for example, for bones in CT data. Surface generation is described in Chapter 6 (see Fig. 3.20).

3.6.5.4 Volume Rendering

In contrast to SSD where a binary decision classifies voxels as belonging to the surface, volume rendering produces semi-transparent renditions based on a transfer function. A transfer function is in principle the same as we have discussed in § 3.6.2 with respect to windowing. For volume rendering, two transfer functions are defined: one for the mapping of intensity values to gray values (as in 2D visualization) and one for the mapping of intensity values to transparency values. According to these transfer functions, voxels are overlaid from front to back. Opaque voxels block all voxels behind. If several semi-transparent voxels are encountered, which are projected to the same pixel, the gray value is determined as an

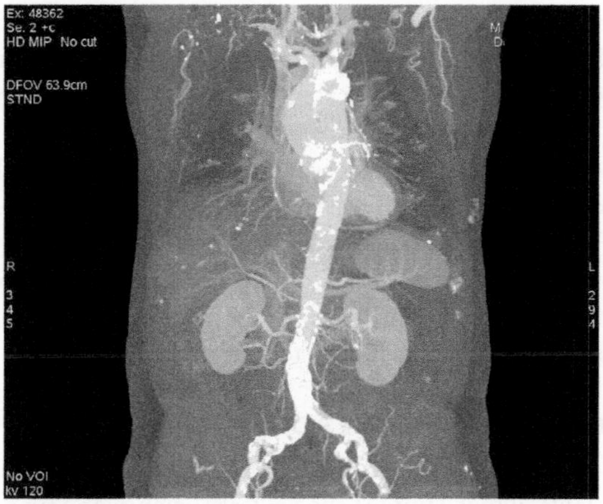

FIGURE 3.20 *Maximum intensity projection of abdominal CT data shows both, the contrast enhanced aortic lumen and strong calcifications since they exhibit high density. To get a 3D impression, the image needs to be rotated (automatic bone removal performed prior to MIP) (Courtesy of Hoen-Oh Shin, Medical School Hannover).*

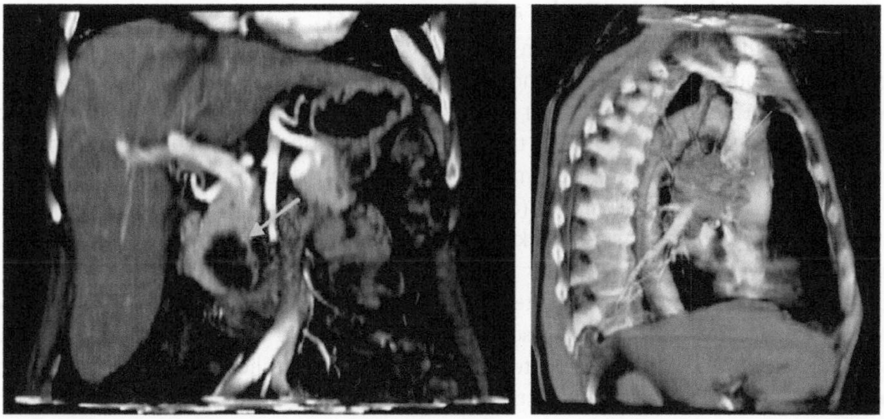

FIGURE 3.21 *Clinically relevant examples of direct volume rendering.* ***Left:*** *the location of a tumor in the pancreas (see the arrow) is evaluated.* ***Right:*** *a bronchial carcinoma (see the arrow) is assessed (Courtesy of Hoen-Oh Shin, Medical School Hannover).*

interpolation of the gray values of these voxels. Figure 3.21 gives two examples of volume renditions created for radiological diagnosis.

Volume rendering does not produce any intermediate representation such as polygonal meshes. To emphasize this property, volume rendering is often referred to as direct volume rendering (DVR), whereas SSD is an indirect method of rendering volume data. Volume rendering is discussed in detail in Chapter 7.

3.6.5.5 Virtual Endoscopy

Virtual endoscopy is a procedure inspired by real endoscopy where an endoscope is moved through air-filled or water-filled structures for diagnostic or therapeutic purposes. Virtual endoscopy is based on CT or MRI data and simulates the view through a real endoscope, providing internal views of cavities and walls that clearly improve the diagnosis with axial slices. The virtual camera is moved along a path in the center of the relevant structure. The calculation of this path requires segmentation and center-line extraction of the relevant structure (see § 11.4.2). The relevant structure may be visualized by means of SSD or volume rendering.

The most important application areas are virtual colonoscopy and virtual bronchoscopy. In virtual colonoscopy the virtual endoscope is moved through the colon in order to detect polyps (which are often a prestage of colon cancer). Virtual bronchoscopy aims at investigating the complex bronchial tree in a similar way than it is possible with a fiber endoscope. Computer support for virtual colonoscopy and bronchoscopy (path planning and navigation support) is provided by a number of manufacturers and has matured over the last years. Chapter 13 is dedicated to virtual endoscopy.

3.6.6 GUIDELINES FOR SOFT-COPY READING

In this subsection we give hints on user interface design for general radiological workstations as well as for dedicated software assistants, which support special tasks, such as thorax diagnosis. Since radiologists have to focus on the images. Software assistants have to provide as much space as possible to images and not to labels, pushbuttons, status bars and other interaction facilities. User interface facilities should be partitioned such that only a small subset is required in a special situation.

3.6.6.1 Interaction with Pointing Device and Function Keys

In order to support the focused observation of images, frequently required interaction tasks should be carried out using a mouse. Mouse buttons, modifier keys, and function keys may be employed to select the appropriate function. For the most important interaction tasks there are widespread interaction techniques available. As an example, browsing through the slices is accomplished with the middle mouse button or the mouse wheel. Windowing is often accomplished with the right mouse button. Movements from left to right control the width of the window (and thus the contrast); whereas movements in the vertical direction control the brightness. As feedback, the current values for window and center are included in the legend at the margin of the image view.

Radiologists use these functions very often and thus learn them quickly. If they would be forced to select slices or adjust contrast by means of some sliders, they would be heavily distracted and annoyed. The information in the legend, such as center/window and current slice, are crucial to allow others to reproduce the images. Other frequent interaction tasks, such as zooming or rotating, are also provided with mouse-based interaction in many radiologic workstations. Shift or Ctrl buttons are often employed to select the appropriate function. We discussed interaction tasks such as defining an ROI or selecting positions for distance measurements. Whenever objects (ROIs, distance lines, angular measures) are created, it should be possible to modify them. For this purpose, it is essential that the control points of such objects can be easily selected. This selection can be facilitated by rendering enlarged versions of the control points.

For special purpose workstations, even more functions might be provided by means of a keypad (see Fig. 3.5 where a special keypad accommodates functions for mammography reading).

3.6.6.2 Dedicated Support for Multimonitor Solutions

Typically, also this is not legally required, radiology workstations employ a 2- or even 3-monitor solution. In a 3-monitor solution, one monitor contains the worklist of the radiologist and the other two present medical image data. Such a setup enables a good support even for complex diagnostic tasks. To exploit this potential, hanging protocols should be provided that efficiently use the whole available space. Since display devices, even the high-quality devices for radiologic diagnosis, still get cheaper, it will be even more typical to have plenty of display space for viewing. The border of one display, of course, is slightly disturbing in the reading process. At the CARS conference 2012, a radiology workstation was presented, where a large horizontal monitor could replace two vertical monitors with a resolution of 1920 × 1280 pixels. Thus, one large monitor with an additional small display containing the worklist is an attractive option.

3.6.6.3 Dedicated Support for Report Generation

The major result of soft-copy reading is a written report that clearly describes the diagnosis, including the pathologies and contains precise answers to diagnostic questions leading to the exam. It also contains other aspects that might be relevant for deciding on the further treatment. The severity of a disease, the stage of a tumor disease or other relevant classifications should be considered. For many diseases, the structure and content of reports should adhere to official guidelines of professional societies. This report is often an essential document when physicians are sued for potential errors in diagnosis and treatment. Report generation often is considered a tedious and unwanted process. Thus, this process should be relieved as much as possible.

Report generation may be strongly supported by using administrative data from the RIS, by providing forms for frequent diagnostic questions and by integrating snapshots of (annotated) image data that show particularly relevant regions and diagnostic findings. Automatic emphasis of findings in follow-up studies or quantification of distances and diameters may support report generation.

3.7 MEDICAL VISUALIZATION IN NUCLEAR MEDICINE

In nuclear medicine, functional metabolic processes are investigated, in contrast to radiologic imaging that is focused on morphologic changes. PET and SPECT are two essential modalities in nuclear medicine. These imaging modalities employ radionuclide tracers. Since these tracers need to be carefully prepared and have a rather short radioactive half-life, no emergency cases are treated in nuclear medicine. The most essential development in recent years was the introduction of hybrid imaging, such as PET/CT, MR/PET, and SPECT/CT (recall § 2.8). These combined scanners can also be operated in a mode where only one modality is used, e.g., PET in isolation. With these capabilities, the hybrid devices tend to completely replace the isolated PET and SPECT scanners. PET data in isolation are primarily used for the diagnosis of diseases of the thyroid gland, such as hyperthyroidism. For these diseases, the precise location of a pathology is not essential. More frequently, the combined PET/CT mode is indeed essential.

Challenges of Hybrid Imaging The advantages of hybrid imaging are so obvious that it might seem straightforward to use them consequently for a large variety of tasks. In practice, this is challenging for a number of reasons:

- educational problems,
- organizational problems, and
- limited software support.

Educational problems are due to the fact that hybrid imaging requires in-depth knowledge of radiology and nuclear medicine, two distinct medical disciplines. Medical doctors who are at the same time board-certified in both disciplines, would be the ideal users but they are rare. At the very least, such systems can only be operated by doctors having a basic qualification in one discipline in addition to a full education in another discipline.

Organizational problems are related, since radiology and nuclear medicine historically are distinct departments of a hospital. The close cooperation required for an efficient use of hybrid imaging was only possible after a number of deep organizational changes, including questions of accounting. The necessary changes of organizational structures also enable to provide the necessary education.

Finally, widely available software support also aimed at either radiology or nuclear medicine and many adaptations were necessary to support streamlined reading of hybrid images. Primarily, powerful radiology workstations were enhanced with facilities to display PET or SPECT images, to overlay them with CT (or MRI) data and to record findings. Subtle problems still occur widely. The DICOM standard primarily supports the storage and communication of radiology data and later added nuclear medicine as a supplement, but hybrid imaging was added only recently. As an example of a practical problem, low resolution PET data are sometimes rendered as very blocky images when fused with high resolution CT data, because no appropriate interpolation scheme was implemented for upsampling the PET data. PET data is displayed in 2D and 3D where the maximum-intensity projection is the dominant 3D visualization technique, emphasizing regions with the most active metabolism.

Diagnosis and Treatment Planning with PET/CT An essential use case in nuclear medicine is to provide planning information for radiation treatment of malignant tumors (radiation treatment is discussed in § 3.8). To support this task in an optimal way, it is crucial that the patient lays on the table in a very similar way like during the actual radiation treatment. Thus, the same completely flat support plate (radio treatment table) is employed instead of a slightly bended plate that is more convenient and used for other patients. Moreover, these plates are associated with marks that enable to precisely record the patient position and thus to reproduce this position later in radiation treatment.

3.8 MEDICAL IMAGE DATA IN RADIATION TREATMENT PLANNING

Radiation treatment is an important treatment option, primarily in the case of tumors (benign but even more malignant tumors). Tumorous tissue is more sensitive to radiation than the surrounding normal tissue. Radiation treatment is often applied in combination with other therapies, such as surgery, chemotherapy, or hormonal therapy. It may be applied as an adjuvant therapy (simultaneously with other treatments) or as a neoadjuvant therapy preparing for another treatment. Radiation treatment planning is an essential use case for medical imaging, including image analysis, simulation and visualization. In fact, computer-assisted planning and optimization is widely considered a breakthrough that enabled 3D treatment planning with increasingly more complex beam configurations even adapted to complex-shaped target volumes [Bucci *et al.*, 2005]. With respect to cancer treatment, two parameters are essential:

- the *gross tumor volume* (GTV) indicate the tumor volume as it was determined in medical image data and
- the *clinical target volume* (CTV) is larger and comprises also areas at high risk for microscopic disease.

The exposure of a patient to strong radiation in order to destroy pathology is a treatment with severe risks and side effects. It is inevitable that also healthy tissue receives radiation and—depending on the type of tissue—upper limits for the radiation need to be considered carefully. As an example, the stomach should not receive a dose of more than 10 Gy because otherwise leaks (in the stomach) may be induced (Gy stands for gray, the standard unit for absorbed radiation dose). When patients with head and neck cancer are treated with radiation treatment, the salivary glands need to be preserved to avoid that patients suffer from a dry mouth and a reduction in health of teeth. Similar limits for basically all anatomical structures are part of guidelines for radiation treatment planning [Bucci *et al.*, 2005].

In solid tumors, a radiation of 60–80 Gy is required to reliably destroy the DNA of tumor cells. This is specified more precisely stating, e.g., at least 99% of the tumor volume should receive at least 93% of the prescribed dose and at least 95% should receive the prescribed dose of, e.g., 80 Gy

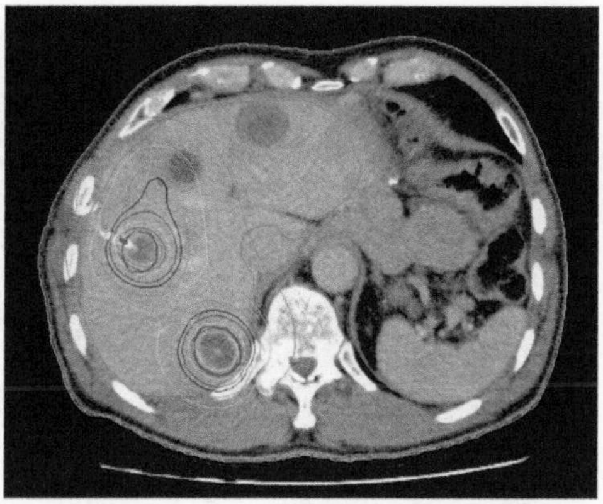

FIGURE 3.22 *Color-coded isolines convey the dose distribution along with the target anatomy in CT slices. The treatment of two liver metastasis is planned (Courtesy of Mathias Walke, Department of Radiation Treatment Planning, University of Magdeburg).*

[Men *et al.*, 2007]. Thus, radiation treatment is carefully planned and verified to ensure that the simulated dose calculations are correct. Figure 3.22 shows an example of a CT slice with the simulated dose distribution. The example shown in Figure 3.23 is more complex. However, in practice only the first step "Overview" in the verification of a treatment plan is accomplished with the BRAINLAB software IPLAN.

Radiation treatment planning is a particularly good example for trade-offs that are necessary in treatment decisions. Healthy tissue, in particular structures at risk, should be preserved. However, in the target region a high radiation is necessary to achieve the major treatment goal. Since the radiation must pass through a number of structures to treat the tumor, different sources of radiation are combined leading to radiation fields that intersect and reinforce each other in the target region. Thus, the target region is irradiated from several angles of exposure, resulting in a high cumulative dose in the target region and a comparably lower dose in the regions affected by only one of the sources. The standard is a treatment with three or four radiation sources.

Similar to tumor surgery planning, radiation therapy planning involves a security margin to account for uncertainties (actual tumor size may be larger than it appears in image data) and for movements, e.g., breathing. Usually, CT data are acquired as a basis for treatment planning. Only for a few tasks, such as defining the prostate anatomy, MRI is frequently used [Bucci *et al.*, 2005]. *Dose-volume histograms* are graphs that indicate how the resulting radiation in the target structure and in other structures at risk is related to the radiation in a source. These graphs are called *dose-volume histograms*, since they represent which percentage of a structure receives a certain amount of radiation, see Figure 3.24. This directly corresponds to the criteria used for specifying a treatment plan.

Although CT is by far the most essential modality for radiation treatment planning, also MRI data may be involved in case that essential structures are displayed more clearly in these data. In particular in cerebral data, the better soft-tissue contrast of MRI provides useful information (see Fig. 3.25). However, the planning process gets considerably more difficult, since these data need to be carefully registered before an integrated analysis is feasible.

Joint Responsibility of Medical Physicists and Physicians Like any treatment decision, a physician is responsible for the basic decision, for guidelines relating to the treatment plan and for actually delivering care. Unlike

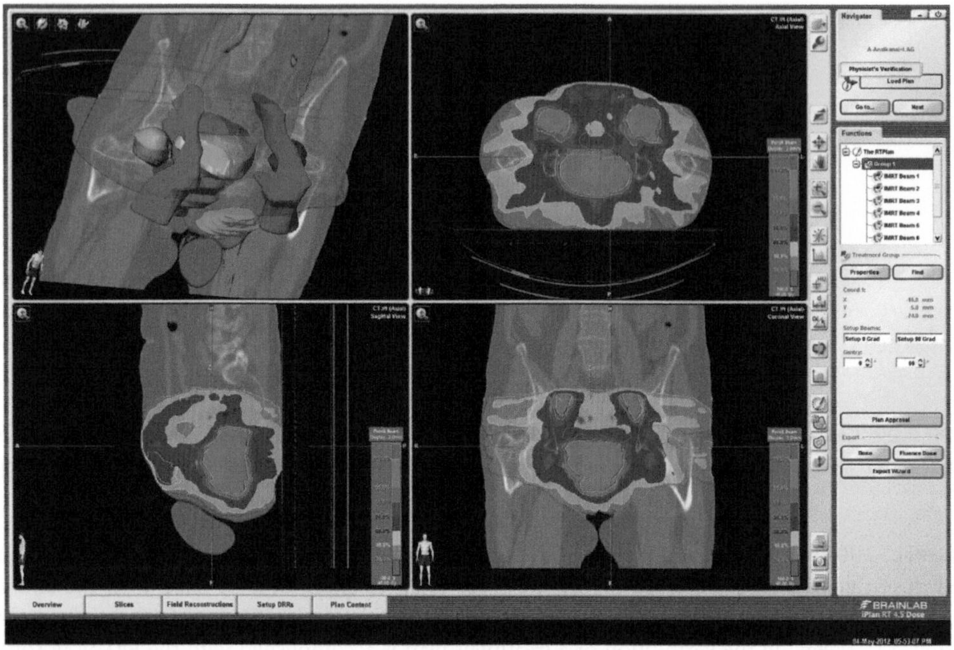

FIGURE 3.23 *Three axial slices and a 3D overview to evaluate the simulated dose distribution to treat prostate cancer. The 3D overview (upper left) shows the previously segmented anatomical structures along with the three orthogonal slices. The slice views employ isolines and colored regions to display the dose distribution as percentage of the target radiation in the tumor (Courtesy of Mathias Walke, Department of Radiation Treatment Planning, University of Magdeburg).*

other treatments, another person, namely a medical physicist, shares the responsibility for an efficient and successful treatment. He develops the precise treatment plan and discusses it on an equal footing with the physician. The physicist segments the target structures and employs planning and simulation software considering dose limits for risk structures as constraints. Discussions between medical physicists and physicians relate to the general state of the patient that may lead to less aggressive radiation therapy in case the patient is in bad state. A large display suitable for joint discussions of these complex visualizations is necessary. As an essential consequence, the development of new or the refinement of existing software should be carefully discussed with both user groups, medical physicists and physicians (see § 5.2).

Image Analysis and Visualization Radiation treatment planning requires the precise segmentation of the target structure and the risk structures. These segmentation results are used to define the desired levels of radiation. These data are put into the dose distribution simulation. The resulting visualization should integrate both the dose distribution and the anatomy. It should be interactive and enable the user to modify the dose distribution—leading to an optimization that defines new sources of radiation and the strength of radiation for these sources. This is also called *inverse planning*, radiation sources are not directly defined but are determined based on a desired distribution. Thus, in most systems, such as the IPLAN RT from Brainlab, isolines are visually dragged to change the distribution. Commercial products aim at strongly supporting a workflow using templates.

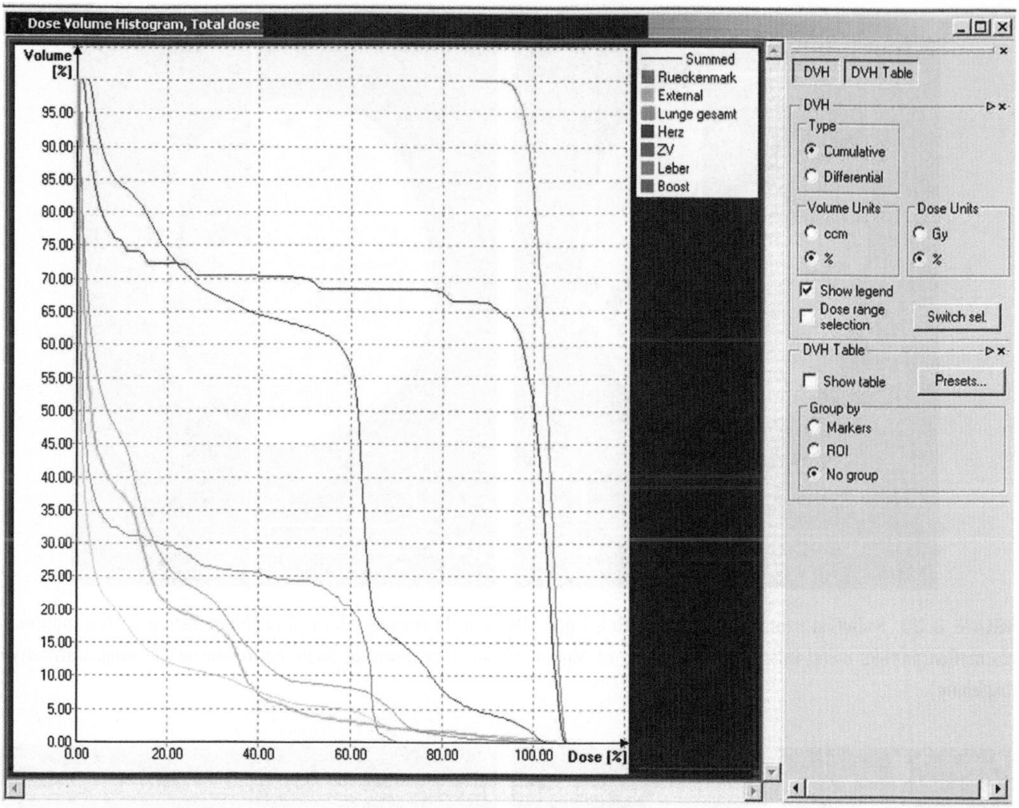

FIGURE 3.24 *The dose-volume histogram indicates which percentage of a structure receives a certain dose (x-axis) to treat an esophagus carcinoma. The orange curve relates to the tumor volume which indicates that 95% of its volume receive at least 95% of the target dose. In the lung, for example, only 13% receive at least 20% of the dose (Courtesy of Mathias Walke, Department of Radiation Treatment Planning, University of Magdeburg).*

3.8.1 CONFORMANT AND INTENSITY-MODULATED RADIATION TREATMENT

Many improvements in the last years enable better trade-offs. Most notably, conformant and intensity-modulated radiation treatment (IMRT) enables to define a dose distribution such that a high radiation is restricted to the target region.

Conformant Radiation Treatment In the 3D conformant radiation treatment the target region is in the center of the axis of radiation rays from different sources. Individual adaptations of apertures and modulations of the radiation fields with wedge filters enable a precise definition of the dose distribution. Treatment plans include two levels of target volumes that should be treated with a different amount of radiation.

Intensity-Modulated Radiation Treatment Intensity-modulated radiation treatment (IMRT) enables to define a dose distribution that is even more consistent with the target volume, in particular for concave-shaped target volumes or target volumes, such as tumors that are wrapped around vital structures. The challenge of preserving the salivary glands in the case of head and neck cancer motivated the development of IMRT that started around 1995 (see Fig. 3.26). With IMRT, not only arbitrary boundary volumes of

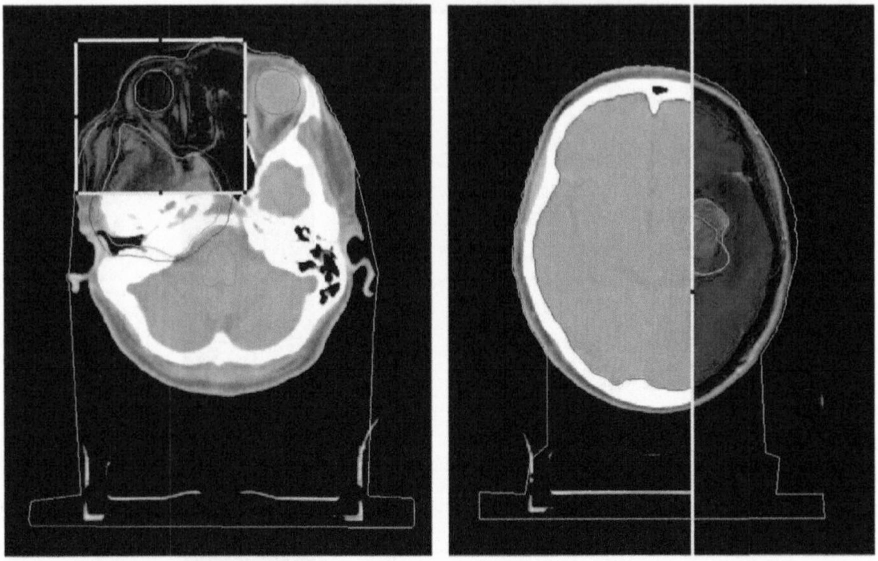

FIGURE 3.25 Radiation treatment planning with CT and MRI data. In particular for treating brain metastases, this multimodal information provides useful information (Courtesy of Mathias Walke, Department of Radiation Treatment Planning, University of Magdeburg).

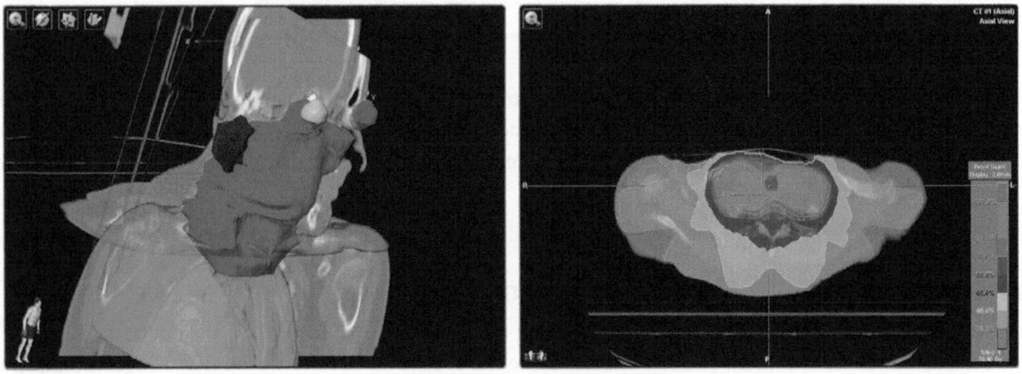

FIGURE 3.26 Intensity-modulated radiation treatment is particularly important for treating head and neck tumors. The left 3D visualization shows risk structures, e.g., the eye balls that need to be preserved, whereas the right visualization shows the simulated dose distribution (Courtesy of Mathias Walke, Department of Radiation Treatment Planning, University of Magdeburg).

the radiated tissue are possible but also the intensity along the rays can be flexibly modulated [Men *et al.*, 2007]. However, the planning process with IMRT has an enormous amount of decision variables. The selection of these variables affects not only the dose distribution but also the *beam-on time*, that is the total time the radiation treatment takes. Obviously, this time should be kept to the minimum. Fast and precise solutions to the underlying optimization problem are still an area of active research. The 3D geometry of the delineated target structures and the beams are discretized, similar to other biophysical simulation problems that we shall discuss in Chapter 19. The apertures of a multileaf collimator system are optimized to deliver the specified dose distribution. This whole process is carefully explained in a formal manner by Men *et al.* [2007]. A survey of solutions for this optimization problem is given in [Shepard *et al.*, 1999].

Limitations Computerized control of X-ray sources ensures that the treatment is delivered as planned. Bucci *et al.* [2005] cite various studies that demonstrate the value of online imaging. This rather new, refined therapy, however, is more difficult to plan and the delivery of the treatment to the patient takes more time. There are some further problems that may limit the effectiveness of IMRT. The accuracy of dose calculation is significantly higher than the ability to delineate microscopic tumor tissue. Also the successful realization of the precise treatment plan is very sensitive to movements of the patient or the tumor, e.g., to breathing and digestion. Even changes of the anatomy during a treatment period of several weeks (patients often loose weight) affect the precise IMRT plans more seriously. This gives rise to further research and development that actually considers temporal changes as well. Lung tumors may move considerably, depending on their position and the patient's type of breathing. The motion in cranio-caudal direction is most notably and can be quantified with a tumor tracking approach [Seppenwoolde *et al.*, 2002]. Considerable research aims at measuring and predicting the respiratory movement to adapt the treatment to the amount and direction of this movement, in particular in case of treating lung cancer [Seppenwoolde *et al.*, 2002, Ehrhardt *et al.*, 2008, 2011]. The adaptation of a breathing-controlled radiation is a natural consequence of such modeling.

The whole preparation time is about 2 hours in simple cases with the standard treatment and 4–5 hours with IMRT. In difficult cases with complex target shapes, e.g., concave shapes and more risk structures to consider, these times elongate considerably.

3.8.2 BRACHYTHERAPY

Besides irradiating human tissue from outside with the involved side effects, it is also possible to place radiation sources inside the pathology with strongly reduced exposition of healthy tissue and better treatment effect. For this purpose a catheter with short-range radiation sources is moved forward in the tumor (recall the discussion of catheters in angiography (§ 2.4.1) and in image-guided interventions (§ 2.9.1). This treatment is referred to as *brachytherapy* or *internal radiotherapy*. An essential advantage is that the radiation source takes part in all movements of the body, e.g., caused by breathing. In contrast, in standard radiation treatment, e.g., the lung moves significantly and the radiation targeted at a tumor may miss it for a large fraction of the breathing cycle. Moreover, brachytherapy is performed with shorter breaks between the cycles compared to radiation treatment which reduces the chance of tumor growth between the cycles.

Brachytherapy is now a standard option in prostate cancer treatment, but also increasingly used for other types of cancer such as hepatic metastases. The planning process, however, is complex, since the radiation source has to be precisely placed in the target. Usually, several sources are needed and their placement needs to be verified. For this purpose, sometimes open MR scanners are employed, since they enable arbitrary slicing orientations to better evaluate the catheter placement. However, on the other hand, MR compatibility of the catheters is required.

3.9 MEDICAL TEAM MEETINGS

The importance of medical team meetings is growing with advances in medical diagnosis and treatment that enable more complex treatment plans but require more decisions regarding the individual elements of such a treatment plan as well as their coordination and timing. In particular, *multidisciplinary* team meetings, where physicians from different disciplines participate, gain importance [Kane *et al.*, 2010]. Examples are:

- *tumor board meetings*, where all physicians participate that may contribute to cancer treatment,
- *decision meetings* in a stroke unit, where neurologists, neuroradiologists, and neurosurgeons discuss the treatment of patients with cerebral ischemic stroke,
- *preoperative meetings*, where a few surgeons prepare for surgery, and
- *postoperative meetings* to discuss the experience of the surgery and its results.

Such team meetings are based on diagnostic information, such as radiologic image data, nuclear medicine data and microscopy from biopsies. Therefore, medical team meetings represent an essential use case for interactive medical visualization. Although effectiveness is crucial in the way these meetings are organized, they also serve educational purposes. Thus, often younger medical doctors, who are not supposed to contribute essentially to decisions, participate passively.

Before we discuss the specific requirements of that use case, we briefly look at typical activities during such meetings. This discussion is based on a number of observations of the authors, in particular in tumor board meetings and on in-depth ethnographic research carried out over several years in two independent research groups [Kane and Luz, 2004, 2006, 2009, Olwal *et al.*, 2011]. We discuss such research methods later (§ 5.2). Here, it might be sufficient to state that observations, audio recordings, interviews and questionnaires are carefully analyzed to derive an understanding of the underlying processes and its structure.

Essential Aspects of Medical Team Meetings Medical team meetings take place regularly, e.g., a tumor board meeting is often scheduled weekly. Such a series of team meetings usually has a rather fixed participation, representing a number of clinical departments. As Kane *et al.* [2010] point out, there are various cultures, procedures that guide such meetings. So far, electronic meeting records are rarely used despite their potential, e.g., for quality control and audits. Instead, data are privately collected and used. Such a meeting has a key person that moderates the process and takes the major responsibility for the decision. A second person is primarily responsible for presenting image data (a pathologist presenting microscopy data from a biopsy or a radiologist presenting CT or MRI data). In most cases, projectors are employed to display the images the presentor prepares at a workstation to the audience.

A notorious problem is the desire for participants to express questions or comments that relate to a particular region in the data, e.g., asking to further zoom in or show related information. Without any technology support, this requires to verbally explain the location, which often turns out to be a mentally difficult task for the presenter and the inquiring participant. Sometimes, participants bring their own laser pointers to address this problem. Despite being cheap and portable, laser pointers are not ideal, since the presenter has to shift his or her attention from the workstation to the projection to recognize the pointing gesture.

Computer Support for Cooperative Activities Various technical solutions have been suggested to improve medical team meetings. Most notably, Olwal *et al.* [2011] presented a number of well-grounded ideas and concepts. These include shared mouse cursors and tablet PCs that each participant has available to interact with the presented data as well. In particular, pointing and annotating data should be supported. Among the possible options for remote control, also game controllers, such as the Nintendo Wii, remote should be considered [Agus *et al.*, 2009].

We do not want to discuss these concepts in detail, but want to emphasize that technology should fit in the process and not require to change the process drastically [Olwal *et al.*, 2011]. Thus, the consequences of technology support and workflow changes on collaboration, group dynamics, and individual roles must be carefully considered. As an example, giving *all* participants the opportunity to interact with the data may lead to a situation where participants no longer focus on the presentation of the radiologist who carefully prepared visualizations and explains them. In Chapter 5, we are going to discuss interaction techniques, such as multitouch input, that clearly have a potential to improve medical team meetings.

Cooperative Viewing of 3D Medical Visualizations The growing sizes of medical image data triggered many research projects to create effective and expressive 3D visualizations and explore them with appropriate (software) interaction techniques. An orthogonal research direction is the improvement of display technology. SPATIAL VIEW, for example, pioneered medical workstations equipped with an autostereoscopic monitor suitable for *collaborative* viewing in 2005. Thus, the restriction of most autostereoscopic monitors to only a single viewer that is rather fixed in space was overcome.

At the research front, Agus *et al.* [2009] presented a 3D medical visualization system for collaborative diagnosis that is based on a light field display [Jones *et al.*, 2007]. Such volumetric displays create light fields by projecting many light beams onto refractive or reflective media. They employ a large set of linearly arranged projectors each of which contributes to an image of a holographic screen (a 26 inch monitor from Holografika). At the time of writing, more tests are required to understand the benefits for specific clinical problems.

3.10 CONCLUDING REMARKS

In this chapter, we discussed application scenarios, such as diagnosis, tumor board, and other medical team meetings, to elaborate on requirements for technology support. We introduced the DICOM standard and current developments to extend it to enable interoperability in the heterogenous IT architectures of hospitals. The whole discussion was focused on diagnosis, radiation treatment planning and monitoring of treatment effects.

Computer Support for Surgery We will later get to know another essential aspect of "clinical practice": computer support for surgeons learning, planning, and performing surgical procedures (Chap. 17). Based on this chapter, we discuss selected applications in more detail. As an example, Chapter 20 is dedicated to the interpretation of CT neck data for the diagnosis of tumor diseases and the planning of therapies, such as radiation treatment and surgery, where many decisions are essential, such as access to the pathology and the amount of the planned resection.

Perceptual Aspects Visual perception was briefly explained to make the reader aware that aspects, such as calibration of a monitor and surrounding light, influence the performance of radiologists and other specialists that aim at detecting (small) pathologies. These aspects are particularly important in rather new use cases such as teleradiology and telepathology where medical doctors employ a laptop at their home to come up with an initial diagnosis. Color perception gains importance in medicine, e.g., in reading (digitized) microscopy data in pathology [Krupinski, 2010, Krupinski *et al.*, 2012b]. Perceptual aspects are also essential for designing image compression schemes, in case of large microscopy data for pathology [Johnson *et al.*, 2011]. We will discuss perceptual aspects more directly related to 3D visualizations later (Chaps. 8 and 12), where we focus on depth and shape perception.

FURTHER READING

We discussed perceptual issues in soft-copy reading with a focus on CT and MRI data. There are a number of studies that investigate luminance levels and contrast perception for X-ray images and various tasks, such as breast cancer diagnosis in mammograms [Apelt *et al.*, 2009, 2010]. O'Connell *et al.* [2008]

performed an experiment to verify the American College of Radiology (ACR) recommendation of a moderate increase of ambient lighting in mammography reading rooms. These studies are interesting since the basic design of the experimental studies can be transferred to the interpretation of medical volume data. With the increasing availability and better quality autostereoscopic displays and even stereoscopic endoscopes [Silvestri *et al.*, 2011] may become essential for clinical practice, e.g., to better understand spatial relations in 3D renderings [Abildgaard *et al.*, 2010].

Two use cases of medical visualization that are not (yet) widespread are virtual autopsy and *whole body imaging*. *Virtual autopsy* or *Virtopsy* refers to the use of medical imaging in forensics and serves to identify the cause of death, in particular if a crime is suspected. Primarily CT and MRI are employed [Thali *et al.*, 2003, Ehlert *et al.*, 2006]. Virtual autopsy is based on whole body imaging in high resolution and serves—in the absence of crimes—to better understand the source of death in addition to a classical autopsy or when the autopsy was refused. Bolliger *et al.* [2008] gives an overview and Persson *et al.* [2011] presents recent refinements. *Whole body imaging* is not only applied in forensics but also considered an option for preventive care, e.g., to detect vascular diseases in asymptomatic patients in an early stage. For this purpose, MR imaging is used, since the radiation of CT would not be justified. The preventive (screening) use of whole body MRI is discussed in [Ladd and Ladd, 2007] and [Ladd, 2009]. Whole body MRI is also used for specific diagnostic tasks in symptomatic patients. Schmidt *et al.* [2007] give an overview of whole body imaging of the musculoskeletal system. The same author discuss whole body imaging for tumor staging and follow-up examinations [Schmidt *et al.*, 2009]. The diagnosis of this large amount of data is challenging, careful selection of *hanging protocols* is essential and CAD algorithms are explored to efficiently diagnose such data. There is a continuous debate when whole body imaging is a meaningful diagnostic procedure.

Chapter 04

Image Analysis for Medical Visualization

4.1 INTRODUCTION

In this chapter, we discuss image analysis techniques which extract clinically relevant information from medical image data. Image analysis enables the generation of high-quality visualizations focused on selected anatomical structures and also supports quantitative analysis of pathologies and spatial relations, e.g., volumes of pathological structures or distances between anatomical structures. Image analysis is crucial for many diagnosis and therapy planning tasks. As an example, the identification and delineation of a tumor is often a prerequisite to determine its extent and volume and finally to select an optimal therapy.

The goal of this chapter is to provide an overview on important image analysis tasks. It is focused on *image segmentation*—a process which assigns labels (unique identifiers) of anatomical or pathological structures to parts of the image data. The overview includes validation aspects, because of the particular relevance of accuracy and reproducibility for medical applications.

We shall not only discuss algorithms which detect and analyze features in medical image data, but also *interaction techniques* which allow the user to guide an algorithm and to modify an existing result. Since medical doctors usually work under severe time pressure, it is preferable that no interaction at all is required. They prefer "one click" solutions, where the whole task is initiated with one mouse click and performed reliably and precisely in a fully automatic manner. In recent years, indeed such solutions were developed for some essential tasks. However, for typical image analysis problems this scenario is still not realistic. Medical image data, anatomical relations, pathological processes, image modalities, and biological variability exhibit such a large variety that automatic solutions for the detection and delineation of certain structures cannot cope with all such cases.

Image analysis is often carried out as a *pipeline* of individual steps. This pipeline starts with *preprocessing* and *filtering*, which is designed to support subsequent algorithms. The restriction of the image data to a relevant subset as well as methods to improve the signal-to-noise ratio (SNR) are examples for tasks to be carried out in this stage. Image segmentation usually represents the core of such pipelines.

Image segmentation is often a sophisticated time-consuming process. There are two basic strategies to address segmentation problems:

- the *edge-based approach* where discontinuities in the image data are located that probably belong to the border of the segmentation target structure, and
- the *region-based approach* where the target structure is regarded as a homogeneous region which is determined by a search process guided by appropriate criteria for homogeneity.

The two strategies can be combined with techniques that integrate assumptions related to the border of an anatomical structure and its internal region. Although this distinction is motivated by segmentation in 2D data, it can be translated to 3D data. Edge-based approaches in 3D data often operate on slices of a

Visual Computing for Medicine, Second Edition. http://dx.doi.org/10.1016/B978-0-12-415873-3.00004-3

volume dataset but some techniques also locate boundary surfaces in 3D space. Region-based approaches naturally extend to 3D. The terminology is not always consistent: a region-growing process in 3D space is referred to as *volume growing* by some but not all authors. At a technical level, adjacent voxels not only in the *x*- and *y*- but also in the *z*-direction are analyzed with respect to their similarity to an initial region.

Often, the results of the segmentation algorithm are enhanced by some kind of post-processing. A smoother boundary of segmentation results or the removal of small holes are among the post-processing tasks. Image segmentation results may be the input for a higher level of analysis. As an example, the shape of objects may be characterized in order to classify objects (benign or malignant tumor), or the skeleton of objects might be detected in order to assess its branching structure.

The discussion in this chapter is by no means complete; we refer to dedicated textbooks on medical image analysis, such as [Sonka and Fitzpatrick, 2000] and [Toennies, 2012] for further information. In particular, the recent book of [Toennies, 2012] can be recommended, since it provides a comprehensive review of image analysis algorithms and applications, including exercises.

Organization This chapter starts with a discussion of preprocessing and filtering (§ 4.2). The discussion of segmentation methods is subdivided into five sections: more general semi-interactive approaches, (§ 4.3) which do not require dedicated assumptions about the shape and appearance of objects and specialized methods. In § 4.4, we present three families of widely used segmentation techniques that are based on a graph representation of image data. These include livewire, random walker and graph cut segmentation. In § 4.5, we introduce advanced and model-based segmentation techniques, including level sets, active contours and statistical shape models. Interaction is an essential aspect of image segmentation. We discuss both general techniques for correcting pre-segmentations as well as selected examples of interaction techniques that are tailored to a specific segmentation method (§ 4.6). In the final segmentation section, we discuss the validation (§ 4.7).

The last section of this chapter is dedicated to the *registration* of medical image data as a prerequisite for comparing datasets of a patient acquired at different points in time and as a basis for image fusion, where, e.g., CT and MRI data of a patient are integrated in *one* view (§ 4.8).

4.2 PREPROCESSING AND FILTERING

Radiological image data exhibit artifacts, such as noise and inhomogeneities (recall § 2.5.5 and § 2.6.3 for discussions of artifacts in CT and MRI data). For image analysis as well as for direct visualization it is crucial to improve the quality of images. While some techniques, such as contrast enhancement, improve the visual quality only, other techniques also enhance the SNR and favor subsequent image analysis. Noise reduction leads to more homogeneous regions, which might be delineated with less interaction effort. On the other hand, noise reduction might compromise the detection of small relevant features. Preprocessing and filtering summarizes all aspects, which restrict the amount of data and enhances data for further processing.

We want to make the reader aware of some confusion with respect to the terms *preprocessing* and *post-processing*. In a radiology publication, all methods applied to image data *after* image acquisition including filtering, reformatting, segmentation and derived 3D visualization is referred to as *postprocessing*. Thus, the computer science term of preprocessing (pre to other more advanced algorithmic processing) translates to radiology term postprocessing. To make things worse, also in medical image analysis, postprocessing is a frequently used term, e.g., to enhance a segmentation result. Thus, preprocessing and postprocessing are terms that are potentially confusing in interdisciplinary discussions between medical doctors and computer scientists.

4.2.1 ROI SELECTION

Often, a first step is the definition of a region of interest (ROI) that comprises all relevant structures. The term ROI is usually applied to a region in 2D image data; in the context of 3D image data, volumes of interest (VOI) is also a common term. We use the term ROI for the selection of subimages in 2D data as well as for the selection of subvolumes in 3D data.

The ROI usually has the shape of a cuboid. Even if the ROI selection reduces the extent in each direction by 10% only, the overall amount of data is reduced by some 27%, which accelerates subsequent computations and enhances a visualization because irrelevant information is removed. Acceleration is an important aspect, since advanced segmentation and registration algorithms are still time-consuming. The interaction to accomplish ROI selection should be a combination of direct manipulation (drag the border lines of the ROI) in an appropriate visualization of the data and specification of numbers (precise input of ROI position and extent in each direction). The precise numerical specification of a ROI is useful when several datasets are compared. In such scenarios, often the same ROI should be selected, which is difficult to achieve with direct manipulation. As an example, to process a triphasic CT dataset of the abdomen, a corresponding ROI in each of the three datasets is needed.

It might be necessary for certain segmentation tasks to define further ROIs as a subset of the first ROI. These additional ROIs may serve as barriers, which reduce the search space for segmentation information. In contrast to the primary ROIs, these often have an irregular shape that might be defined by drawing in a few slices and interpolating between them.

4.2.2 RESAMPLING

As already pointed out in § 2.3, the anisotropic nature of many datasets can be a severe quality issue for image analysis and visualization techniques. Thus, a resampling step is often included in order to transform data to an isotropic grid. In this process, the accuracy of the data should not be degraded. Therefore, resampling is driven by the highest resolution (usually in-plane) and interpolates additional data in the dimension with lower resolution (usually the *z*-dimension). There are many interpolation algorithms. They differ in their quality and computational effort. Fast methods interpolate the value at a particular position by taking into account the neighboring voxels only, e.g., trilinear interpolation (recall § 2.2). Better results are achieved with triquadratic or tricubic interpolation. According to the reconstruction theory, the *Lanczos* filter based on the sinc-function has optimal properties but its infinite extent renders a practical implementation difficult. A detailed overview on image interpolation can be found in [Thévenaz *et al.*, 2000]. Since resampling increases the amount of data, it is carried out after ROI selection to increase the resolution only in relevant areas.

Resampling 3D Ultrasound Data Resampling is a challenging issue in 3D ultrasound processing (recall § 2.7). The slices acquired in freehand mode are neither parallel nor equidistant. Although 3D visualization techniques are available, which directly process data available at irregular grids, the general strategy is to convert the data to a regular grid (see Fig. 4.1). Without special care, gaps would result in the regular volume at places where the original slices were too far. Different interpolation schemes have been suggested to handle the resampling problem with 3D ultrasound: Lalouche *et al.* [1989] employ cubic spline filters, which incorporate many voxels in the neighborhood. Ohbuchi *et al.* [1992] proposed an adaptive interpolation scheme based on the Gaussian filter (see § 4.2.4). With this low-pass filter, smooth transitions of the data and their derivatives are achieved. The standard deviation of the Gaussian is adapted to the resolution of the Ultrasound data. In principle, the Gaussian has infinite support (all voxels contribute to the resampling at each point). For the computation, the filter is limited to a certain

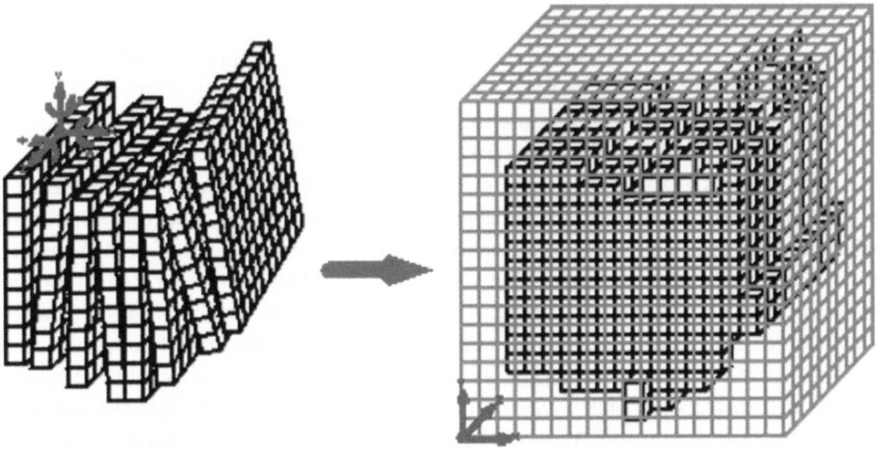

FIGURE 4.1 *Resampling the 3D ultrasound data into a regular three-dimensional grid (Courtesy of Georgios Sakas and Stefan Walter, Fraunhofer Institute for Computer Graphics Research. See also [Sakas and Walter, 1995]).*

size that is again adaptive with respect to an error term. However, it must be noted that all resampling schemes lead to problems with respect to the reliability of the results in case of irregularly sampled data.

4.2.3 HISTOGRAM AND HISTOGRAM TRANSFORMATION

For many operations applied to image data, we employ the *histogram* in order to select appropriate parameters. The term histogram inherently relates to discrete data (data that is sampled on a discrete grid and represented in a discrete range). Histograms indicate the frequency distribution of data values and indicate the probability that an image element exhibits a certain value. Therefore, a histogram represents a *discrete probability density function.*

Usually, histograms are presented as vertical bars over a horizontal axis of values. The height of the bars represents the frequency of a value or an interval of values. As an essential example in medical image processing, a histogram may represent the distribution of Hounsfield values in CT data. Formally, if we have a total number of N pixels or voxels, and values in the range $[0, \ldots, G-1]$, the probability of the occurrence of a particular value G_i is computed as:

$$p(G_i) = \frac{n_{G_i}}{N} \tag{4.1}$$

Histogram Analysis Histograms are analyzed, for example, with respect to their significant local maxima (or simply peaks). The precise definition of a *significant local maximum* is application-dependent. In general, a local maximum that strongly exceeds adjacent values and that is not too close to another significant local maximum is considered significant. In medical image data, a peak in the histogram is often related to one tissue type. Depending on the tissue types and the imaging modality, the tissue types may overlap each other in the histogram so that the number of peaks is lower than the number of actual tissue types. Figure 4.2 presents a slice of an MRI dataset of the shoulder region along with the histogram (of the whole dataset). Besides the global image histogram, the histogram within a local neighborhood is often used to derive parameters for filtering operations.

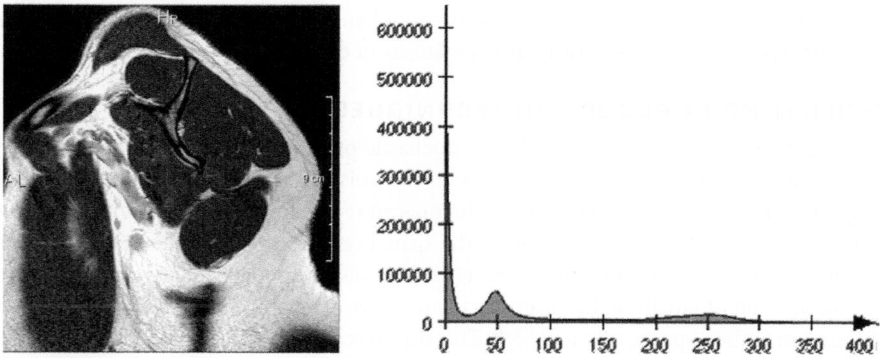

FIGURE 4.2 *A slice of an MRI dataset and the histogram of the whole 3D dataset. The large peak in the left portion of the histogram relates to background voxels, the second peak corresponds to muscles and the smaller third peak to soft tissue structures with higher image intensity. The large peak representing background voxels was cut to convey the remaining portions of the histogram better.*

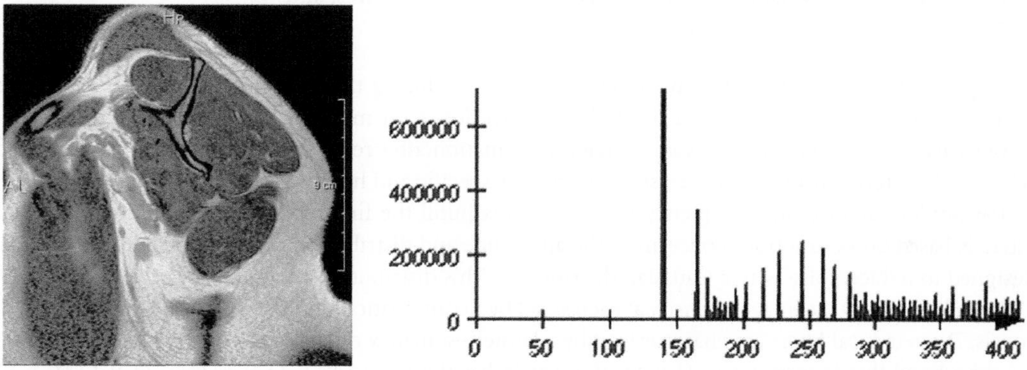

FIGURE 4.3 *Histogram equalization applied to the MRI shoulder dataset shown in Figure 4.2. The large peak in the left is cut again.*

Histogram Transformation The histogram equalization is the most common histogram transformation and is used to enhance the image contrast. This transformation T is used to transfer an image into a new histogram space with approximately constant brightness values. The precise computation of the output value G_o from the input value G_i is as follows:

$$G_{out} = T(G_{inp}) = \sum_{j=0}^{k} pG_j = \sum_{j=0}^{k} n_j N \quad (4.2)$$

Although the result is not a perfectly uniform histogram, the histogram of the output image is spread over a wider range of (gray) values (see Fig. 4.3).

T is a monotonically increasing function in the whole interval of intensity values. This property ensures that pixels which are darker in the original image remain darker in the processed image. Histogram transformations may strongly enhance the perception and interpretation of images. However, due to their strict monotonic behavior, image segmentation usually does not benefit from prior histogram transformations. Gonzales and Woods [1998] discuss histogram operations in detail.

4.2.4 GENERAL NOISE REDUCTION TECHNIQUES

Medical image data exhibits random noise due to stochastic processes in the image acquisition. Noise is characterized by a certain amplitude and distribution. The noise level is often measured as the SNR in the whole image. In fact, the noise level depends on the imaged tissue and on its mean gray value and is thus locally different. The noise level also depends on the spatial resolution of the data. High resolution data, such as CT data with 0.5 mm slice thickness, exhibit more noise. In X-ray and CT imaging, the noise level depends on the amount of radiation. To minimize the negative effects, the amount of ionizing radiation is kept at a minimum at the expense of a low SNR. This dose-saving aspect of X-ray and CT imaging gained attention in recent years and motivates efforts in improving image quality and enable a high diagnostic accuracy with limited radiation.

Ideally, noise reduction filters have the following properties [Schaap *et al.*, 2008]:

1. reduce the intensity variation in big anatomical structures, such as organs,
2. improve the detectability of edges between such big structures, and
3. preserve small scale structures.

In principle, noise reduction may either be performed during the image reconstruction process or, later, after image reconstruction. In the following, we focus on methods that are applied after image reconstruction for a pragmatic reason. Image representation after reconstruction is highly standardized, whereas the intermediate formats are strongly vendor-specific and hardly accessible.

Low pass filters reduce high-frequency noise and thus fulfill the first requirement. The design of such filters is based on assumptions concerning the amplitude and distribution of noise. A variety of filters is designed to reduce noise with a Gaussian distribution (this distribution occurs in X-ray in CT data).

Local filters modify the image intensity at each voxel by a combination of image intensities at neighboring voxels. Discrete local filters are characterized by a kernel—a matrix of elements with the same size as the neighborhood that is considered. Usually, the matrix has the size $(2N + 1) \times (2N + 1) \times (2M + 1)$. Typical values for N are 1, 2, or 3 and for M 0, 1, or 2 is typical. In case of isotropic data, M and N usually have the same value, whereas in (typical) anisotropic data M is chosen smaller to account for the larger extent in the z-direction. Odd numbers for the matrix size ensure that a central element exists.

With $M = 0$, the filter is applied to each slice separately and has no effect on other slices. This is the typical situation when data has a highly anisotropic voxel spacing. In such situations, the differences of the image intensities between adjacent slices are relatively large and these voxels should not be considered for filtering.

If the elements of the matrix are constant, the corresponding filter is *static*. Filters which adapt their content to local image characteristics are called *dynamic*. We will briefly discuss examples of both kinds of filters.

Static Noise Reduction Filters are scaled such that the sum of their elements is 1. Thus, the mean gray value of the image remains the same after the filter was applied. This normalization is important to maintain the overall image intensity.

Such filters are applied by iterating over all pixels and replacing the image intensity by a weighted average of neighboring pixels. The weights of the neighboring pixels are characterized by the filter matrix. The simplest filter is the average filter where each neighbor voxel has the same influence. Better results are achieved with a filter where the distance to the central voxel is taken into account. A frequent example is the Gaussian filter, which is optimal in case the noise follows a normal distribution.

Gaussian Filter The Gaussian filter kernel is represented by Equation 4.3, where μ represents the centroid of the function and σ represents the standard deviation and thus the width of the function. The Gaussian is appropriate for preprocessing CT data, which result from a weighted combination of X-ray projections. This acquisition process leads to a Gaussian probability distribution of intensity values of a particular tissue type [Gravel *et al.*, 2004].

$$G(x, \sigma, \mu) = \frac{1}{\sigma \cdot \sqrt{2 \cdot \pi}} \cdot exp\left(\frac{x - \mu}{\sigma^2}\right) \tag{4.3}$$

The Gaussian is an example of the general concept of filtering a function g with a filter F, which is often represented as a convolution (Eq. 4.4).

$$g'(x) = g(x) \otimes F(x) = \int_{-\infty}^{\infty} g(x) \cdot F(x - x_1) \cdot d_x \tag{4.4}$$

where $\otimes$ denotes the convolution operator.

For discrete image data, the convolution is expressed as a weighted sum of the signal g over the filter kernel F with $2N + 1$ elements (Eq. 4.5).

$$g'(u) = \sum_{i=-N}^{N} g(u) \cdot F(u - i) \tag{4.5}$$

To restrict the Gaussian filtering locally, the binomial filter is used. The binomial coefficients of that filter represent a discretization of the Gaussian function.[1] In Figure 4.6, the result of a 2D binomial filter with kernel size 5×5 is shown. In order to normalize the kernel elements, they are divided by the sum of all elements (256 for the 5×5 binomial filter) (see Table 4.1).

The 5×5 filter has the following kernel matrix:

Separable Filters For the efficient application of filters with larger kernels to large volume data, *separability* is an important issue. Separable filters with a two (or three)-dimensional kernel can be replaced by combining two (or three) one-dimensional filters. This way, the quadratic (cubic) complexity can be reduced to a linear one. The binomial filter is an example for a separable filter. The drawback of implementing a filter for n dimensions as a sequence of separable one-dimensional filters is the additional memory consumption to store intermediate results. Modern implementations using the GPU could handle this problem well.

Dynamic Noise Reduction Filters Local filters with a static matrix are not adaptive and, in general, fail to meet the second and third requirement stated in the beginning of this subsection. In particular, features, such as edges, are not preserved and appear washed out. Better results can be achieved with *dynamic* filters, which analyze and consider image intensities in the local neighborhood.

An important example is the *median filter*. With this filter, the voxels in the neighborhood of the current voxel are sorted according to their image intensity into bins, and the median (the middle bin of the

1 This filter is called *Gaussian* in many image processing systems.

1	4	6	4	1
4	16	24	16	4
6	24	36	24	6
4	16	24	16	4
1	4	6	4	1

TABLE 4.1 *5×5 binomial filter.*

sequence) is determined (intensity of the voxel that is in the middle of the sequence). The central voxel is then replaced by the median value. Since the median filter is based on a sorting process, it is considered as a *rank filter*. Other rank filters evaluate the local sequence in a different way and thus may also achieve different effects than noise reduction.

Compared to Gaussian filtering, extremely high and low outlier values do not significantly influence the result. The sorting stage however takes considerable time. Therefore, kernel sizes should not be too large. In general, dynamic filters are computationally more demanding but allow to adapt to features in the data.

σ-filter The σ-filter is a dynamic noise reduction filter that considers the *histogram* of image intensities in the local neighborhood [Lee, 1983]. If the current voxel has a very high or very low value compared to the average in its neighborhood, it remains unchanged. Thus, the σ-filter is restricted to voxels with an intensity that does not differ strongly from the local average (see Fig. 4.4).

σ is the parameter of the filter that quantifies how strongly the image intensity may deviate from the average (*avg*). With $\sigma = 1$, all voxels deviating less than one times the standard deviation from the average ($avg \pm \sigma$) are considered. If the central voxel has an intensity inside the specified interval, the image intensity is replaced by its local average. The σ-filter is also based on the assumption of Gaussian noise,

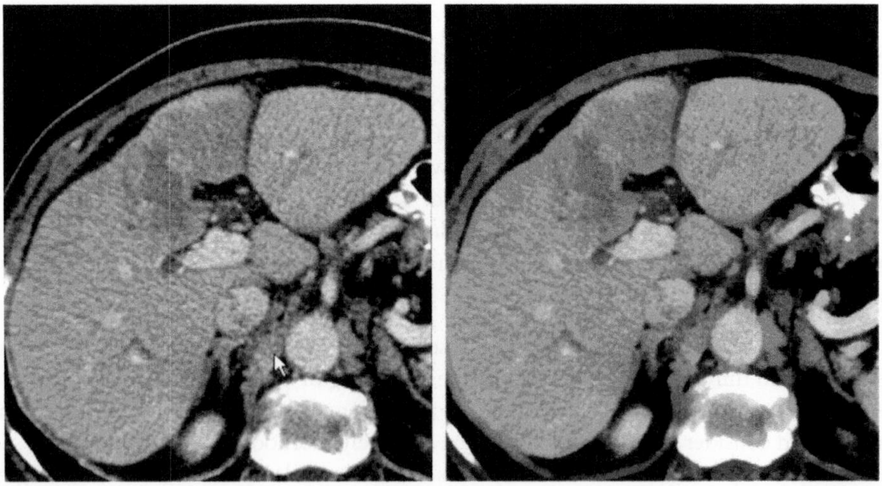

FIGURE 4.4 *The portion of a CT slice of an abdominal dataset (left) is processed with an $11 \times 11\sigma$ filter to reduce image noise (result image, right).*

like it occurs in CT data. It is better able to fulfill the requirements 2 and 3, since edges or very small structures are usually not modified with this noise-dependent averaging [Schaap *et al.*, 2008].

Diffusion Filtering There are more advanced feature-preserving filtering techniques. A family of such filter techniques is diffusion filtering, where diffusion is simulated. Diffusion filtering is one of many examples in image processing where a physical process, that exhibits the desired behavior, is determined empirically [Grady and Funka-Lea, 2006]. We will later get to know further examples of physical processes, e.g., in *image segmentation*. Often a partial differential equation (PDE) describes the physical process and has to be numerically solved.

Diffusion occurs between adjacent regions where for example concentrations of a liquid are different. These differences are adjusted in the diffusion process. As a result of diffusion, a stable balance arises that is characterized by FICK's law (Eq. 4.6):

$$j = -D\nabla(u) \tag{4.6}$$

Here, $\nabla(u)$ is the gradient of the concentration, D is the diffusion tensor (a symmetric matrix) and j is the energy flow that is necessary to achieve the balance.

The goal of advanced diffusion filtering techniques is to restrict the diffusion to areas without edges as well as along edges (see Fig. 4.5). To realize this behavior, an edge detector is included in the calculation of the diffusion tensor. In Figure 4.6, the results of diffusion filtering are compared with those of Gaussian and median filtering.

Non-linear anisotropic diffusion effectively reduces the noise level and preserves boundaries of different regions. In particular for the analysis of cerebral MRI data, diffusion filtering is a frequently used initial step [Gerig *et al.*, 1992]. An overview on diffusion filtering is given in [Weickert, 1997]. The original ideas underlying the simulation of diffusion processes in image smoothing go back to [Mumford and Shah, 1989, Perona and Malik (1990)]. While this filter is very popular in academic research, it is far less widespread in clinical practice for a simple reason: the computation is very time-consuming. In particular, the time step Δt influences both quality and performance and may be chosen such that computation times are moderate. Schaap *et al.* [2008] developed optimization techniques that increase the performance by a factor between 5 and 50 depending on the time step. GPU-based acceleration is also viable to spread the use of this high quality filter.

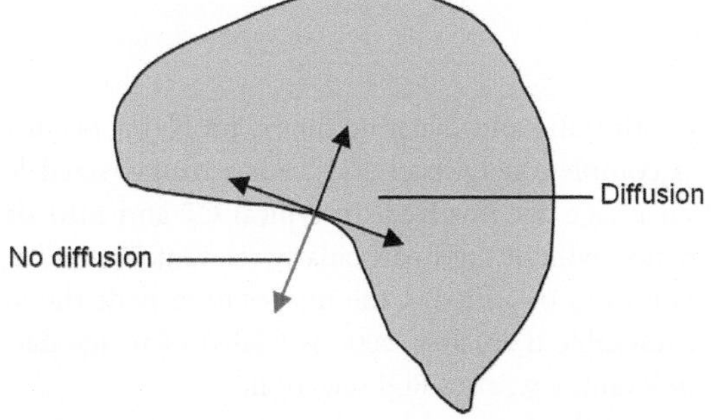

FIGURE 4.5 *Principle of non-linear anisotropic diffusion. Diffusion may occur along borders and inside of homogeneous regions. No diffusion is applied perpendicular to edges.*

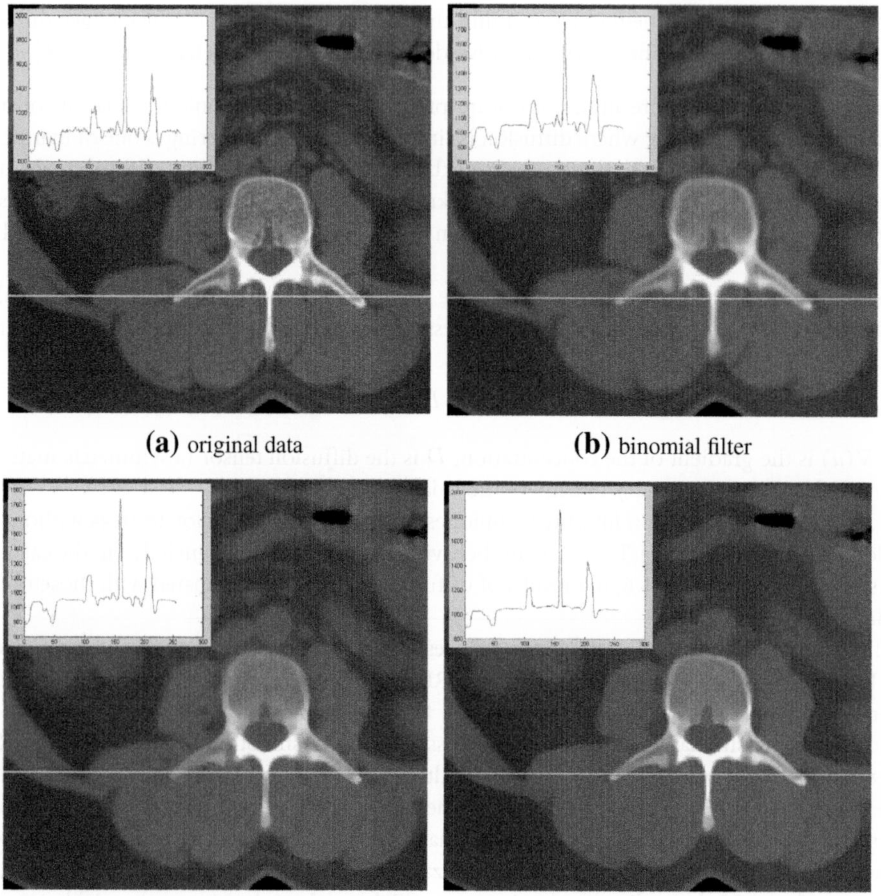

(a) original data (b) binomial filter

(c) median filter (d) diffusion filter

FIGURE 4.6 *Portion of a slice of a CT neck dataset processed with a 5 × 5 binomial filter (b), with a 5 × 5 median filter (c) and a diffusion filter (d) to reduce image noise. The intensity profile along the horizontal white lines are displayed in the upper left inset (Courtesy of Arno Krüger, University of Magdeburg).*

Filtering on Boundaries With both static and dynamic filters, problems occur at the boundary of images (where voxels do not have a complete neighborhood). For a matrix sized 5 × 5, the first and the last two rows and columns of an image are involved. In typical CT and MRI data, the border of the data contains background information which is not particularly relevant. Therefore, virtual rows and columns filled with the background color can be added to the images to provide the necessary neighborhood for filtering. This strategy is not resemble if smaller sections (slabs) of image data are acquired and also the border of the data is highly relevant, e.g., after ROI selection.

If 3D kernels are used, at least the first and last slice of the volume do not have the neighborhood information relevant for filtering. In such cases, it is more suitable to leave these slices unfiltered or to apply a reduced filter that only contains the non-zero elements for the available voxels. The implementation of such a filtering scheme is more complex because special variants of the filter have to be provided for each border and for each corner of the image data.

Multi-resolution Filtering The general problem of noise reduction is to prevent that relevant features are degraded. In particular, if large filter kernels are applied, the removal or degradation of features is a crucial problem. These problems may be alleviated by means of multi-resolution schemes. An image pyramid, for example, contains voxels at different levels, where each voxel at level n represents a low pass-filtered version of eight voxels at level $n - 1$. Such a data structure might be used to detect important features, such as larger surfaces at a higher level (coarser representation of the data). This information can be used to restrict or modify filtering at lower levels. As an example, Sakas and Walter [1995] employed a multi-resolution filtering scheme to enhance filtering of 3D ultrasound data.

We omit a discussion here how small features may be optimally preserved. We discuss this issue in the context of vessel visualization (§ 11.2), which is the major motivation for the development of such filters.

Physical Noise Modeling Obviously, noise reduction leads to optimum results if it fits to the noise characteristics in the image data to be processed. While the omnipresent assumption of a normal distribution of noise is correct in CT data, it is not in MRI or ultrasound data.

The intensity distribution in MRI data does not follow a Gaussian distribution, but a Rayleigh function. This is a simplified Rician function that is non-symmetric (see Fig. 4.7). MRI data are complex data and the intensity value represents the magnitude of a vector consisting of a real and imaginary part. The overall magnitude of a vector, e.g., wind speed, is a typical size that follows a Rician function [Hennemuth, 2012]. Roy *et al.* [2012] recently showed that a Rician distribution is superior to a Gaussian mixture model for classifying cerebral MRI data. It must be emphasized that the assumption of a certain probability distribution limits the applicability of a technique to situations where these assumptions are very likely to be true.

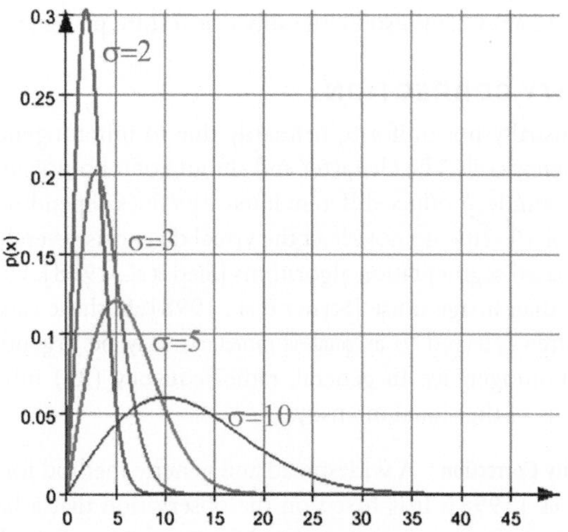

FIGURE 4.7 *Rician functions with different parameters that represent intensity values in MRI data. For larger parameters, the function becomes more symmetric and thus closer to a Gaussian function (From: [Hennemuth, 2012]).*

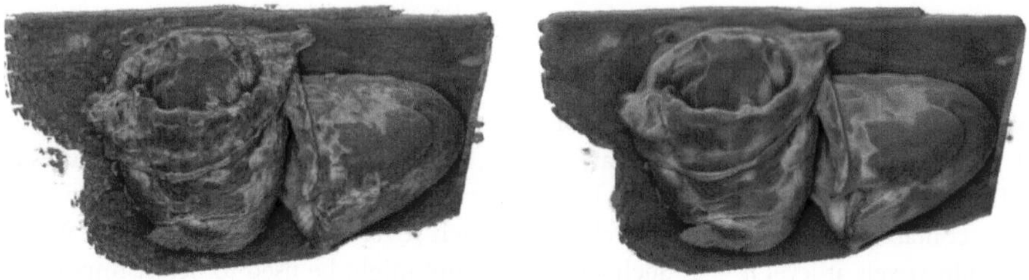

FIGURE 4.8 *Filtering ultrasound data (left) in the direction of the lowest local variance (right) preserves features very well. The method is demonstrated by means of a phantom* (*Courtesy of Veronika Šoltészová, Christian Michelsen Research AS, Norway. See also* [*Šoltészová et al.*, 2012]).

Diagnostic ultrasound is characterized by speckle noise. While the noise in CT and MRI data is *additive*, speckle noise in *multiplicative*. Thus, the amount of noise depends on the image intensity. The particular parameters of the noise distribution differ depending on the specific acquisition mode. Tenbrinck *et al.* [2012] showed that the application of the Loupas filter leads to very good results for B-scans of the heart. They carefully compared this filter with others and explain why the filter designed for suppressing multiplicative noise leads to optimum results.

Noise Reduction in Ultrasound Data Since the seminal work of Sakas and Walter [1995], the quality of ultrasound acquisition has improved and several attempts have been made to improve the filtering for both segmentation and visualization. A particularly important work was carried out in the framework of the "IllustraSound" project carried out at the University of Bergen.[2] As an example of this work Šoltészová *et al.* [2012] presented a method that analyzed the local distribution of variance and filtered the data in the direction of the lowest variance. This enables them to choose a filtering direction that is aligned with the underlying structure, similar to anisotropic diffusion. The authors provided several comparisons to other filtering methods and could demonstrate the superior feature preservation (see Fig. 4.8).

4.2.5 INHOMOGENEITY CORRECTION

MR signal intensities are usually not uniform, primarily due to inhomogeneities of the magnetic field induced by the radio frequency coils. The character and amount of inhomogeneity depends on the type of the coil. Surface coils, for example, produce different intensity values depending on the distance to the coil. While intensity variations of 10–20% do not affect the visual diagnosis severely, they strongly degrade the performance of intensity-based segmentation algorithms [Sled *et al.*, 1998]. For MRI data, inhomogeneity is a more serious problem than image noise [Styner *et al.*, 1998]. In those cases, an automatic correction of this inhomogeneity (often referred to as *gainfield correction*) may be urgently needed. This requires to provide models of the inhomogeneity. In general, radiofrequency (RF) inhomogeneity results in low spectral frequency variations of the signal intensity.

Histogram-based Inhomogeneity Correction A widespread and generic method for inhomogeneity correction was introduced by Sled *et al.* [1998]. It is based on the observation that a background distortion blurs the image histogram. Starting from assumptions on the smoothness of the background distortion and on the probability distribution of the background values, the image histogram is deconvolved with the

2 http://www.ii.uib.no/vis/projects/illustrasound/index.cgi.

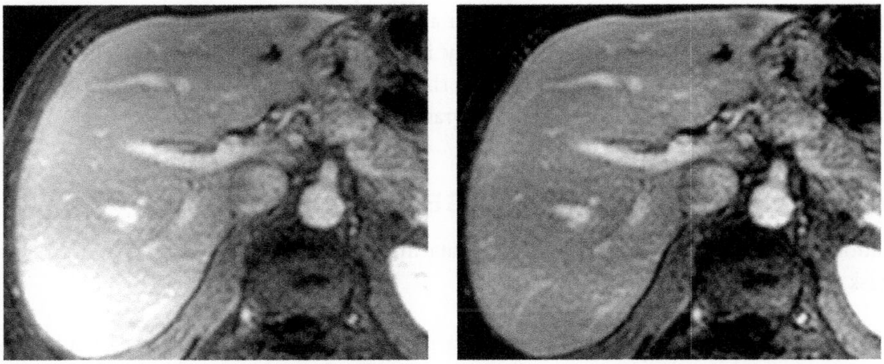

FIGURE 4.9 *Inhomogeneity correction for a slice of an abdominal MRI dataset (Courtesy of Andrea Schenk, Fraunhofer MEVIS Bremen).*

(modeled) background distribution. Subsequently, an intensity map is computed from the original and the deconvolved sharpened histogram. The difference between the mapped and the original image is smoothed according to the above mentioned assumptions, thus yielding an estimate of the background distortion. This procedure is iterated until convergence is achieved (see Fig. 4.9). This method has also been used as preprocessing step for the segmentation and analysis of vascular structures (see § 11.4 and [Boskamp *et al.*, 2004]).

Inhomogeneity Correction Based on Mixture Models Styner *et al.* [1998] presented a method, which relied on the image histogram only. This method is based on known statistics for the intensity distributions of the tissue classes in the image. The method is therefore more specialized, but produces better results if the necessary information can be provided. Application examples are breast MRI data and cerebral MRI data where statistical information concerning the distribution of gray matter, white matter, and cerebrospinal fluid are employed. This method is widely available as part of the Open Source software ITK (see www.itk.org and the related books [Ibanez and Schroeder, 2005; Yoo, 2004]).

4.2.6 GRADIENT FILTERING

Gradient filtering is a preprocessing operation that is particularly useful for subsequent edge detection and edge-based segmentation methods. The gradient of a function f is the vector consisting of the partial derivatives in each direction. The gradient has a direction (the direction of steepest descent) and a magnitude (mag) that is determined as the length of the gradient vector. For a two-dimensional function $f(x, y)$ the gradient's magnitude is computed according to Equation 4.7.

$$mag(\nabla f) = \sqrt{\left(\frac{\delta f}{\delta x}\right)^2 + \left(\frac{\delta f}{\delta y}\right)^2} \quad (4.7)$$

With respect to discrete image data, gradients have to be approximated by differences between neighboring voxels, e.g., with central differences (Eq. 2.4) Often, the gradient magnitude at each pixel location is essential for subsequent operations, such as segmentation with the watershed transform (§ 4.3.5). To yield an image with gradient magnitude per pixel, a suitable filter must be applied. The simplified denotation of such images is *gradient image*.

Widespread gradient filters are the Sobel operator and the Roberts-Cross operator (often 3×3-filters). Another variant is to calculate the average intensity in the local neighborhood in a first step and sum the absolute differences of all pixels in the neighborhood. This sum is a good indicator for the gradient magnitude. Gonzales and Woods [1998] describe gradient filtering in detail.

4.3 AN INTRODUCTION TO IMAGE SEGMENTATION

Segmentation is the task of decomposing image data into meaningful structures that are relevant for a specific task. Segmentation has two aspects:

- relevant objects should be identified, which means to recognize them as particular anatomical structures, and
- they should be delineated in the sense that their borders are precisely specified.

Recognition is a high-level task where humans usually perform better than computers. *Delineation*, on the other hand, is a task where accuracy is essential. Carefully designed algorithms may lead to excellent solutions for the delineation problem. A challenge for segmentation processes is therefore to combine the strength of the user with the potential of computer support.

Technically, a unique label is assigned to each voxel representing the membership to a particular structure. In medical applications, it is usually sufficient to only segment the relevant structures and not at all anatomical structures. We shall refer to the structure, which should be delineated as *target structure*. In contrast, *parcellation* refers to dividing data or a structure into a complete set of substructures. An example in medical image analysis is brain parcellation as an essential element of the analysis of cognitive processes.

Significance of Segmentation In the context of this book, we are primarily interested in segmentation as prerequisite for visualization. Segmentation information is required to selectively show certain (segmented) objects. On the other hand, segmentation is sometimes applied to suppress a structure that hampers the visualization. As a prominent example, bones in CT angiography data are often segmented to be removed from a visualization of contrast-enhanced vascular structures [Fiebich *et al.*, 1999].

Another application of segmentation is quantitative image analysis, for example, with respect to gray values, volumes, sizes, or shape parameters of relevant structures. In general, the required accuracy is larger for any kind of quantitative analysis. For visualization it is more important to support a comprehensible display of anatomical or pathological structures. A segmentation result, which favors a smooth (surface) visualization is essential for this process. Accuracy is of course also an issue in this application scenario to prevent misleading visualizations, but a sub-millimeter accuracy is often not necessary in particular in routine clinical tasks. Very high accuracy requirements occur in neuroscience where image acquisition is optimized for a precise understanding of functional regions.

Computer Support for Image Segmentation Much effort has been spent on the development of segmentation approaches. These rely on some homogeneity criteria, which are fulfilled for all voxels belonging to a certain structure. This criterion might be a certain range of intensity values, for example, with respect to the Hounsfield scale, if CT data are involved. Another example for such a criterion is the existence of a border line characterized by large gradient magnitude. We discuss first segmentation approaches, which rely on image features to delineate structures. It turns out that such approaches require substantial interaction effort. More advanced model-based approaches make use of assumptions concerning the shape, size, location, or gray level distribution of objects to identify a certain structure. These advanced methods may overcome situations where no reliable information is available, e.g., due to an artifact or a severe pathology.

4.3.1 REQUIREMENTS

Before we describe segmentation strategies, it is important to discuss essential requirements:

- **Robustness.** To be useful in the clinical routine, image analysis solutions have to be robust. They must work for a large variety of cases. It is acceptable that the interaction effort increases in difficult cases with abnormalities in the anatomy or in pathological structures, but there should be support even in those cases. Automatic solutions, which only work under certain circumstances might be part of a software system but must be complemented by a solution for other cases.
- **Accuracy.** Image segmentation and subsequent operations should provide results which are accurate. Validation studies are required to determine which accuracy is achieved with high certainty. Such studies are essential, although they have a limited scope, typically for one modality or even for a specialized imaging protocol.
- **Reproducibility.** This requirement is closely related to the previous one. Reproducibility means that a single user would get a very similar result if an algorithm is applied several times (intra-observer reproducibility) and different users would also produce very similar results (inter-observer reproducibility). This requirement is weaker than accuracy. However, it might be sufficient in some applications to demonstrate a reasonable reproducibility. This requirement is easier to prove because no correlation to some ground truth is necessary. As synonym for reproducibility, **precision** is often employed. We use the term reproducibility, because it is less likely to be confused with accuracy.
- **Speed.** There might be excellent solutions that are computationally extremely demanding. Sophisticated filtering or clustering techniques are among them. If it is not possible to accelerate these methods to a level where an interactive use is feasible, they should not be used. The growing power of computers alleviates the situation. However growing sizes of image data often compensate for the additional computing power.

While these requirements are general, the importance of each individual requirement differs strongly with respect to the application context. Speed might be the dominant requirement if image analysis is carried out under severe pressure of time, for example in the operating room. Reproducibility is crucial, if radiological data is analyzed for monitoring the progress of a disease (follow-up examinations). For radiation treatment planning (§ 3.8), however, accuracy is essential for the tumor segmentation as well as for the segmentation of structures at risk. Similar discussions of requirements can be found in [Hahn, 2005 and [Udupa and Herman, 2000].

4.3.2 MANUAL SEGMENTATION

The most general and easy to accomplish method for image segmentation is manual drawing in slices of radiological data—the user outlines the relevant structures with a pointing device. To modify the contour, it is often possible to redraw a particular portion that replaces the previously drawn portion of the contour. While the mouse is frequently used for manual segmentation, other pointing devices, such as a pen, better serve drawing tasks. Pointing devices and their use for segmentation will be discussed in § 5.7.

The manual segmentation is always applicable. However, it is time-consuming and neither reproducible nor precise because the user often deviates slightly from the desired contour. Despite of these problems, manual segmentation is widespread, in particular if objects are very difficult to delineate due to artifacts, low contrasts, or an unexpected shape. As an example, tumor segmentation is often performed manually, since the variable tumor biology hampers automatic support in many cases (we discuss semi-automatic tumor segmentation in § 4.5.6). The drawing facilities needed for manual segmentation should be provided in any segmentation tool for the correction of pre-segmentations and as a fallback method if other advanced techniques fail.

4.3.3 THRESHOLD-BASED SEGMENTATION

With a global threshold or an interval of a lower and upper threshold applied to the image intensity, a binary image is generated. Threshold-based segmentation can be extended to using multiple intensity intervals. Any kind of threshold-based segmentation may be supported by the presentation and analysis of the image histogram, which may support the selection of thresholds.

Usually, this will not produce a segmentation of the target structure immediately but it may serve as a starting point. In the next step, a *connected component analysis* may be carried out in order to detect connecting regions. Many segmentation workflows employ threshold-based segmentation either as a first step, or, to refine results obtained with other algorithms.

A typical application of threshold-based segmentation is the identification of bones in CT data, which can be characterized by large Hounsfield values. However, even in this application, the accuracy of threshold-based segmentation is limited, since thin bones usually are not correctly identified. This is due to the partial volume effect.

4.3.3.1 Threshold Selection

Threshold-based segmentation can be made more reproducible and faster if the threshold-selection is supported. There is a variety of methods to "suggest" meaningful threshold values. Most of these methods rely on the histogram of image intensities.

A local minimum in the histogram may represent the threshold that is optimal to distinguish two tissue types. The local minimum is a reasonable suggestion if the frequency at this position is low. If the image intensities of two tissue types strongly overlap, there might be no image intensity for which the histogram entry is small. A useful suggestion for a threshold might be derived by analyzing the approximated curvature of the image histogram. A popular threshold selection-method is introduced in [Otsu, 1979]. This method maximizes the separability between different threshold classes in the data, based on an initial guess of the thresholds. As an example, the initial guess may be $t_1 = max(V)/3$ and $t_2 = 2max(V)/3$, where $max(V)$ is the maximal voxel value in data volume V.

Since boundaries between different tissue types are typically represented by rising and falling edges of peaks in the histogram, the distinctness of these peaks is important for threshold-based segmentation. However, this distinctness is reduced by the partial volume effect and thus by the lack of sufficient spatial resolution. Small structures with a large portion of boundary voxels, tend to be blurred and loose this distinctness. With high spatial resolution and high SNR the histogram contains more clearly discernible peaks.

4.3.3.2 Probabilistic Models

If knowledge about the tissue types in the data and their distribution of gray values is available, threshold selection may be even further supported. While an ideal image acquisition system would generate a constant intensity for a particular tissue type, medical image data are far from being perfect in this sense. In § 4.2.4, we briefly explained that CT data follows a Gaussian distribution. Thus, if in a certain area, a low number of tissue types $t_1, \ldots, t_n$ may be expected, the two parameters μ and σ of a Gaussian distribution

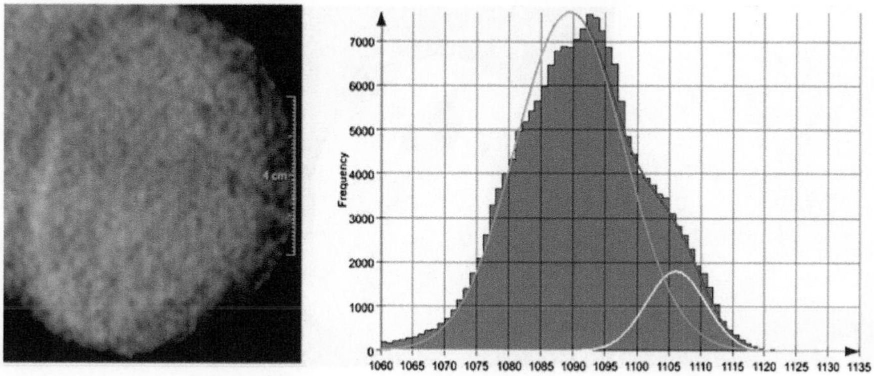

FIGURE 4.10 *Application of a Gaussian mixture model to CT data.* ***Left:*** *slice of CT late enhancement data.* ***Right:*** *Fitting two Gaussian distributions to the histogram of CT data shown on the left. The two parameters of the two tissue types (normal myocard and regions that exhibit a late enhancement behavior are determined by a least square fit. The red line indicates the cumulative Gaussian function that is close to the histogram (From: [Hennemuth, 2012]).*

may be estimated for each tissue type. Furthermore, weightings ω need to be determined that characterize the frequency of each tissue type and thus the corresponding height of a peak in the histogram. This process is referred to as fitting a *Gaussian mixture model* [Kainmueller *et al.*, 2007, Hennemuth, 2012]. In essence, the cumulative histogram is approximated by a weighted sum of Gaussians that provides the best fit. For determining the parameters of the Gaussians and their weights, *Expectation Maximization* algorithms are frequently used.

In Figure 4.10 a Gaussian mixture model is applied, to a special kind of cardiac CT data that may reveal defects of the myocardium where the contrast agent enhances the intensity late after contrast agent arrival.

4.3.3.3 Multidimensional Thresholding

The concept of threshold-based selection can be extended to derived information such as gradient magnitude. Such multidimensional thresholding can also be supported by presenting an appropriate histogram (a 2D histogram in this example). Instead of selecting rectangular regions in a 2D histogram, the user may also specify arbitrary polygons. With such a facility, threshold-based segmentation can be applied to more complex segmentation problems [Krekel *et al.*, 2006]. As another example, Seim *et al.* [2010] analyzed gradient histograms to derive a gradient magnitude threshold as parameter for the automatic segmentation of the knee from MRI data.

4.3.3.4 Connected Component Analysis

A connected component analysis (CCA) is based on binary images and initializes a first component with the first pixel. The algorithm recursively looks for adjacent pixels in the binary image and adds them to this component. If no more connected pixels are found and if there are still pixels that have not been visited, a new component is initialized. This process terminates when all pixels are processed and assigned to one region. These should be conveyed to the user, for example, by assigning individual colors. For some segmentation tasks the result basically corresponds to one of the regions. Minor corrections can be carried out in the post-processing stage (see § 4.6.3). The CCA is often employed in combination with thresholding, i.e., the user selects one component that results from a previous thresholding operation to

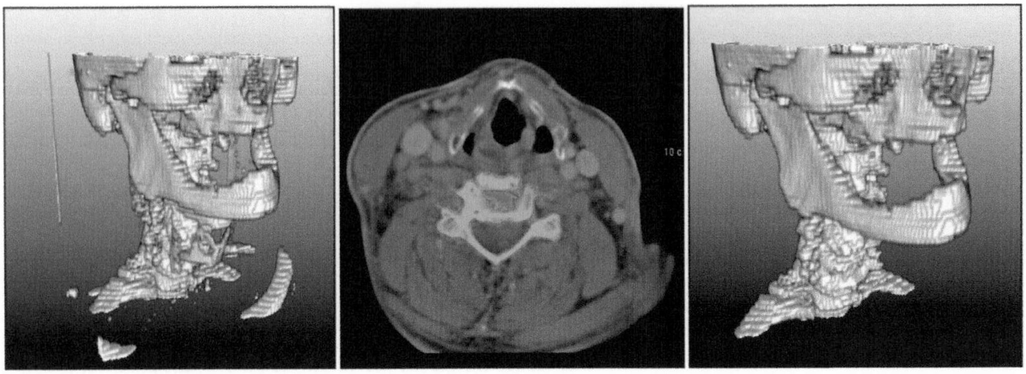

FIGURE 4.11 *Thresholding as input for a connected component analysis. The largest component (right) represents major parts of the skeletal structure (Courtesy of Jeanette Mönch, University of Magdeburg).*

segment a particular object (see Fig. 4.11 for bone segmentation by means of a CCA). The combination of threshold-based segmentation, connected component analysis and morphologic post-processing (see § 4.6.3) is powerful for segmentation tasks where the target objects are represented by homogeneous gray levels. Combined with immediate visual feedback, this concept was introduced and extensively used in the preparation of the VoxelMan [Höhne *et al.*, 1992].

4.3.4 REGION GROWING

A family of segmentation algorithms is based on the concept of growing a connected volumetric region. The standard approach of region growing is similar to threshold-based segmentation (again, a threshold determines which voxels belong to the segmentation result). The major difference to intensity-based thresholding is that *one* connected component is considered (that corresponds to the combination of thresholding and the selection of one connected component). We start the description with the simple region growing approach and later discuss refined homogeneity criteria.

The growing process is initiated by one or more seed points. These seed points are user-defined in most cases but may, in principle, also result from an automatic analysis. The growing process successively aggregates neighboring voxels until a user-selected inclusion criterion is no longer fulfilled (see Fig. 4.12). This inclusion criterion is usually a threshold for the intensity values (collect all voxels with an intensity lower or equal the seed point's intensity and above the threshold). With this approach, the user simply specifies seed points that belong to the target structure. Additionally, the user has to provide the threshold as additional parameter. The threshold selection is often a trial-and-error process: the segmentation is started with a certain threshold and then modified until a desired result is achieved.

Basic region growing is based on a fixed condition, usually one or two thresholds. For the interactive adjustment of these parameters, the basic strategy is too slow. Selle *et al.* [2002] introduced a progressive region growing in which the segmentation is performed for a whole range of thresholds in parallel. This can be effectively accomplished using the fact that the segmented voxel set for a higher (lower) threshold is completely included in the voxel set for a lower threshold. Region growing is often used for the segmentation of contrast-enhanced vascular structures [Selle *et al.*, 2002, Boskamp *et al.*, 2004]. Ideally, one seed point placed in the root of the vascular tree is sufficient to delineate the target structure. In practice, often several seed points have to be chosen and the segmentation results relating to each

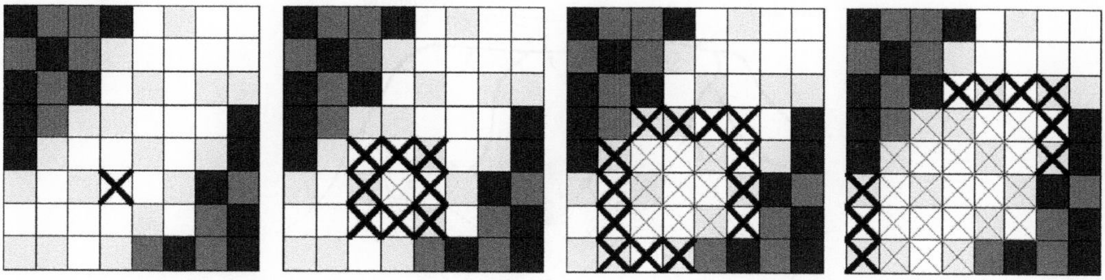

FIGURE 4.12 *Different stages of a region growing algorithm. Starting from one user-defined seed point (left), successively more voxels are aggregated, which fulfill an inclusion criterion. X marks the voxels of the current active wavefront (Courtesy of Dirk Selle. See also [Selle et al., 2002]).*

seed point are combined. After appropriate preprocessing the results are often acceptable. We shall discuss advanced region growing for vessel segmentation and visualization in § 11.4.1.

Advanced Region Growing Methods Region growing might be improved by combining different inclusion criteria. As an example, a lower and an upper threshold defining an intensity interval is used by Boskamp *et al.* [2004] to delineate contrast-enhanced vascular structures. The second (upper) threshold prevents leaking into bones, which appear even brighter in CT data. A limit to the gradient magnitude is incorporated as a second criterion. The concepts for threshold selection (recall § 4.3.3.1) may also be used for region growing. Instead of the global histogram, the local histogram in a region around the seed points is essential [Chang and Li, 1994, Pohle and Toennies, 2002, Salah *et al.*, 2003, Salah, 2006].

Adaptive Threshold Intervals Small inhomogeneities in image data can prevent correct segmentation of the target structure. In those cases, the threshold (interval) needs to adapt to the data. As Adams and Bischof [1994] suggest, an *adaptive average threshold* a_i may be used (Eq. 4.8).

$$t_i = \frac{t_{i-1}n_{i-1} + I(v)}{n_{i-1} + 1} \tag{4.8}$$

$I(v)$ is the currently added voxel. n_{i-1} is the number of voxels in the current segmentation before adding this voxel (step $i - 1$), and t_{i-1} is the respective average threshold before adding [Adams and Bischof, 1994].

There are situations where sophisticated criteria do not help to discriminate adjacent structures reliably. In such cases it is necessary to provide additional interaction facilities. As an example, the user may specify a direction of the growing process or specify barriers that should stop growing.

4.3.5 WATERSHED SEGMENTATION

Watershed segmentation is another region-based method that has its origins in mathematical morphology [Serra, 1982]. The general concept was introduced by [Digabel and Lantuejoul, 1978]. A break-through in applicability was achieved by Vincent and Soille [1991] who presented an algorithm that is orders of magnitudes faster and more accurate than previous ones (see also [Hahn, 2005] for a discussion of the "watershed segmentation history"). Since then, it has been widely applied to a variety of medical image segmentation tasks.

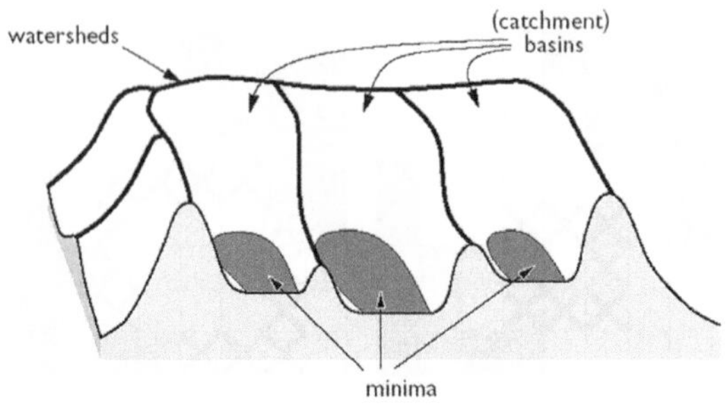

FIGURE 4.13 *Principle of the watershed transform where the intensity values define hills and basins. For segmentation purposes, basins may be flooded in order to combine corresponding regions (From: [Hahn, 2005]).*

In watershed segmentation an image is regarded as a topographic landscape with ridges and valleys. The elevation values of the landscape are typically defined by the gray values of the respective pixels or their gradient magnitude. Based on such a 3D representation the watershed transform decomposes an image into *catchment basins*. For each local minimum, a catchment basin comprises all points whose path of steepest descent terminates at this minimum (see Fig. 4.13). Watersheds separate basins from each other. The watershed transform decomposes an image completely and thus assigns each pixel either to a region or a watershed. With noisy medical image data, a large number of small regions arises. This is known as the "over-segmentation" problem (see Fig. 4.14).

The most widespread variant employs the gradient image (recall § 4.2.6) as the basis for the watershed transform. Gradient magnitude, however, is strongly sensitive to image noise. Therefore, appropriate filtering is essential. There are many variants how the watershed transform may be used as a basis for a general segmentation approach. The "over-segmentation" problem may be solved by some criteria for merging regions. The user must be provided with some facilities to influence the merging process. We describe the approach introduced by Hahn and Peitgen [2000] and later refined by Hahn and Peitgen [2003].

Merging Basins The decomposition of an image into regions is the basis for merging them. In the metaphorical sense of a landscape, catchment basins are merged at their watershed locations by flooding them.

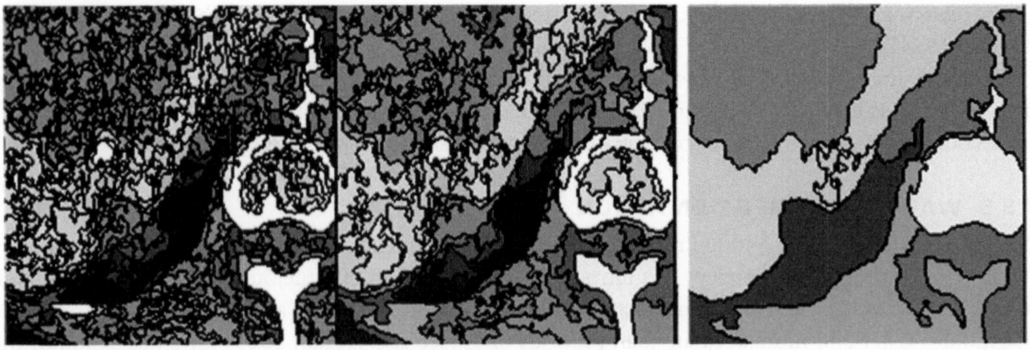

FIGURE 4.14 *Illustration of the over-segmentation problem of the watershed transform applied to an axial slice of a CT image. Individual basins are merged to form successively larger regions (Courtesy of Thomas Schindewolf, Fraunhofer MEVIS Bremen).*

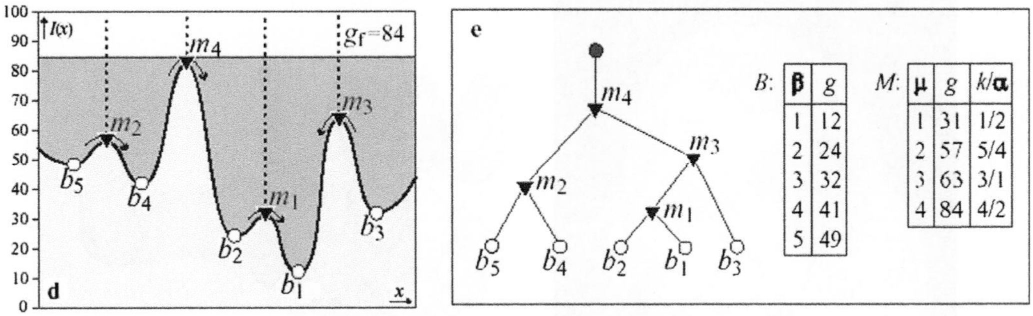

β	g
1	12
2	24
3	32
4	41
5	49

μ	g	k/α
1	31	1/2
2	57	5/4
3	63	3/1
4	84	4/2

FIGURE 4.15 *Principle of the watershed transform where the intensity values define hills and basins. For segmentation purposes, basins b_i may be flooded in order to combine corresponding regions. As result, a merge tree arises consisting of merge events m_i* (From: [Hahn and Peitgen, 2003]).

While some regions merge early (with low flooding level), other regions are merged later (see Fig. 4.15). In order to support interactive merging, Hahn and Peitgen [2003] introduced a *merge tree*. This tree consists of the original catchment basins as leafs and of intermediate nodes that represent *merging events*. A merging event is characterized by the nodes that are merged and by the flood level that is necessary for merging. As a first step, a certain amount of flooding may be applied ("pre-flooding" which may already be sufficient for segmenting the target structure [Hahn and Peitgen, 2000]).

Marker-based Watershed Often however, no examined flooding level is sufficient to segment target structures. Therefore, the user may specify image locations that belong to the target structure (include points), or that do not belong the target structure (exclude points). If the user specifies an include point and an exclude point, an additional watershed is constructed at the maximum level between them (see Fig. 4.16). The merge tree is traversed such that each region contains either include points or exclude points but not both. This interaction style is called *marker-based watershed segmentation*. There are many variants of the watershed transform. For example, merging may consider also gradient information or other criteria for homogeneity. A frequently used variant is to merge regions where the difference of the mean gray value is below a threshold. This process can be carried out iteratively and results also in a hierarchical merging tree.

Applications The watershed transform has been successfully applied to a variety of segmentation tasks. Hahn and Peitgen [2000] extracted the brain with a single watershed transform from MRI data. Also, the cerebral ventricles were reliably segmented with minimal interaction. Hahn and Peitgen [2003] demonstrated the application to the challenging problem of delineating individual bones in the human

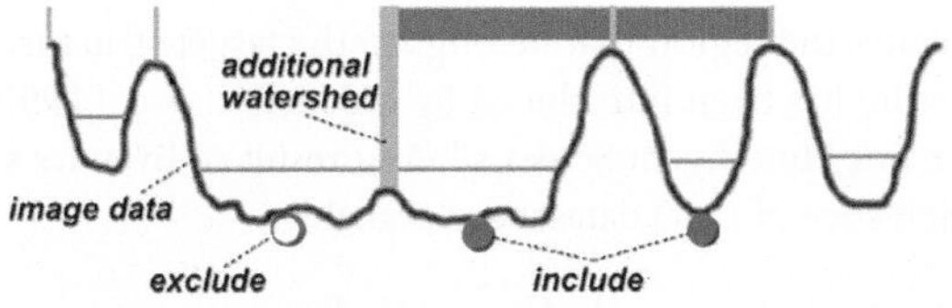

FIGURE 4.16 *The image data is considered as a landscape and flooded to merge small basins. To prevent merging, a watershed is erected between an include and an exclude point specified to the user (Courtesy of Horst Hahn, Fraunhofer MEVIS Bremen).*

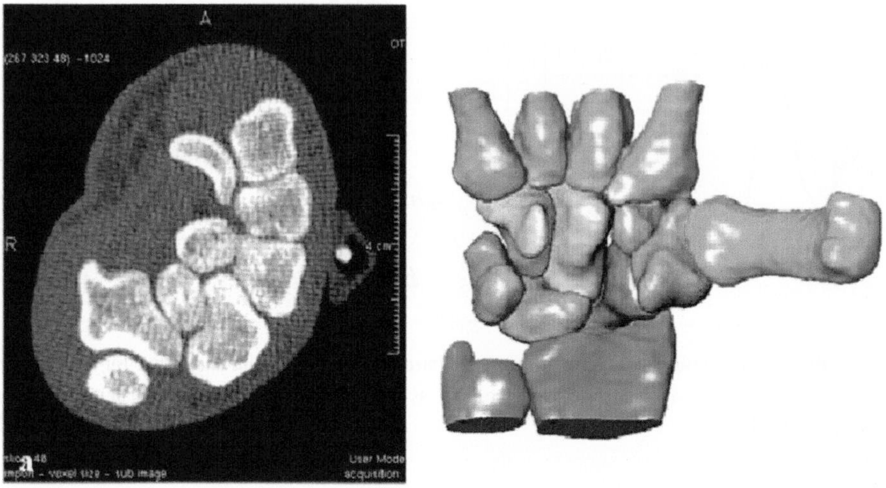

FIGURE 4.17 *Watershed segmentation was applied to segment individual bones from CT data. While bones are relatively easy to distinguish from other structures, the challenge is to delineate individual bones (From: [Hahn and Peitgen, 2003]).*

wrist (see Fig. 4.17). Kuhnigk *et al.* [2003] employed the above-described variant of the watershed segmentation to the delineation of lung lobes in CT data. Ray *et al.* [2008] used the iterative watershed transform for hepatic tumor segmentation (and volumetry).

4.4 GRAPH-BASED SEGMENTATION TECHNIQUES

In this section we discuss three segmentation techniques that have one important common aspect: they employ a graph representation of image data. The nodes or vertices V of this graph $G = (V, E)$ represent the pixels of the image data, and the edges E, connecting the nodes, represent the *costs* of moving between the related nodes. With all three approaches, segmentation is performed by searching paths in the graph representation that have a minimum cost according to a *cost function*. Thus, these segmentation approaches employ algorithms from discrete optimization to determine this minimum. In general, a cost function is designed such that a penalty is assigned for choosing edges where a strong discontinuity occurs, whereas edges in homogeneous regions are represented by low costs. The three methods differ considerably in the design and specific use of the cost function.

4.4.1 LIVEWIRE SEGMENTATION

While region growing generates the region that belongs to the target structure, livewire is an edge-based segmentation method. Livewire has been introduced by Mortensen *et al.* [1992] and Udupa *et al.* [1992]. It is also known under the name "Intelligent Scissors". As a result of livewire segmentation, the contours of the target structure in each slice of a 3D dataset are available.

Graph Construction Livewire employs a graph $G = (V, E)$ representation of an image. The vertices $v \in V$ represent image pixels and the edges $e \in E$ represent costs of connections between neighboring pixels. Simple cost functions employ image intensity and gradient information only, assigning low costs to connections with intensity values in a certain interval of expected values for that structure and to connections with low gradient magnitude.

In contrast to the other graph-based techniques the edges in most livewire implementations are directed and the orientation is opposite to each other. The "inside" of a directed edge is considered to be the left of this edge. Livewire selects paths with minimal costs (movements along boundaries with strong gradients in general have low costs) using Dijkstra's graph search algorithm [Dijkstra, 1959].

Costs are assigned to every directed edge [Kim and Horli, 2000]. Intensity to the left and to the right, gradient magnitude and direction as well as the Laplacian Zero-crossing (the approximated second order derivative of the image data) may be part of the cost function computation. Equation 4.9 is a general cost function for the computation of the local cost of an edge connecting the pixels p and q. It is a weighted sum of different components:

- the Laplacian zero crossing $f_z(q)$ that indicates proximity of the pixel q to an edge,
- $f_g(q)$ that represents the gradient magnitude at pixel q, and
- $f_D(p, q)$ that represents the gradient direction.

The gradient magnitude should be considered as a relative term, weighted with the maximum gradient in the image [Mortensen *et al.*, 1992]. The gradient direction is employed as a smoothness constraint: high costs are associated with sharp changes in the boundary direction. The weights w_z, w_g, and w_d can be adapted to the properties of the segmentation target object. Equation 4.9 does not consider an interval of expected intensity values, e.g., HU values in CT data. If the intensity interval is specific, an additional intensity-related term may be added.

$$l(p, q) = w_z \cdot f_z(q) + w_g \cdot f_g(q) + w_d \cdot f_D(p, q) \tag{4.9}$$

Figure 4.18 illustrates the traversal of the graph using the Dijkstra algorithm. Starting from seed point s minimal cost paths are searched. After four iterations, in which the costs to all local neighbors are considered, minimal cost paths to eight neighbors have been computed. This process can be repeated until all pixels have been processed and a *cost image* is computed. Since the computed connections in the graph are directed, it is essential that the user draws the contour in the same way as the cost function computation assumes (usually counterclockwise).

Costs are computed from a user-selected control point to the current mouse position. The contour that is associated with the lowest accumulated cost is highlighted. Ideally, the resulting path wraps around the target object. If the path deviates from the target object's boundary, the mouse is moved back until the suggested contour and the desired contour coincide and an additional control point is marked interactively. Thus, a first path segment is specified. The second control point becomes the new seed point and is used to define the next path segment. This process is repeated until the boundary is closed. The name "livewire" describes the appearance of a wire that trembles between a few possible paths if the mouse is moved.

Selection of the Cost Function The success of this segmentation method critically depends on the suitability of the cost function. In general, the cost function considers gray values of the relevant object (mean value and standard deviation), gray values of surrounding objects, strength of image gradients, and second order derivatives in the gradient direction. Each factor might be assigned with a certain weight that determines the influence of this factor. If the cost function perfectly fits to the target structure, the contour of an object might be defined with two mouse clicks (see Fig. 4.19). If the cost function is less suitable, the user must specify a larger number of control points. In worst case situations, livewire is not better than manual drawing. The choice of a good cost function can be supported by appropriate default values.

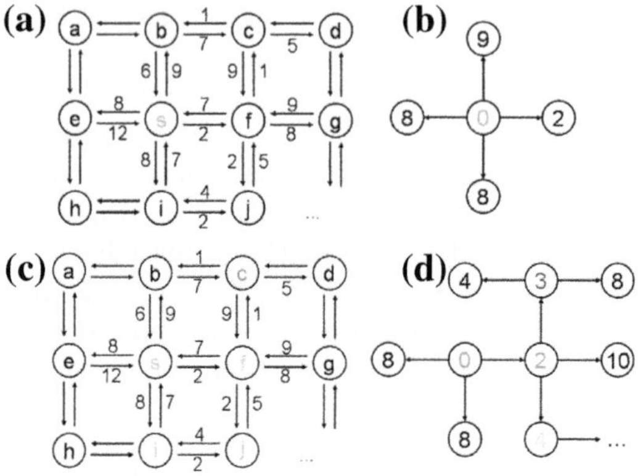

FIGURE 4.18 *Illustration of Dijkstra's algorithm for searching minimal paths in a directed graph. In each iteration, the local neighbors of all nodes, that have been processed, are considered with respect to their costs: (a) full cost graph, (b) portion of the cost graph related to the edges outgoing form s. After three iterations, it turned out that the path from s to b via f and c is associated with lower costs compared to the direct edge between s and b. Therefore, the edge from s to b was removed in (d), where the cumulative costs of a path from s to any other node is represented (Courtesy of Andrea Schenk, Fraunhofer MEVIS Bremen).*

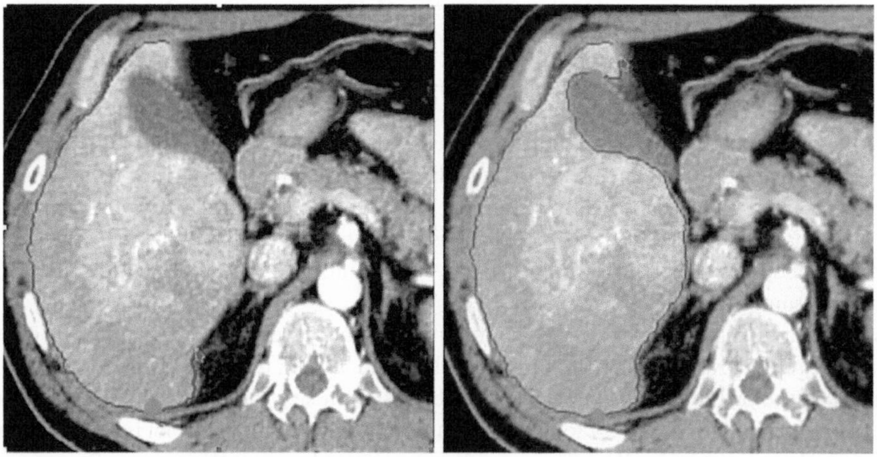

FIGURE 4.19 *Two stages in the segmentation of an organ with livewire. Two control points are necessary to precisely define the liver outline based on a suitable cost function (Courtesy of Andrea Schenk, Fraunhofer MEVIS Bremen).*

Using the Cost Image It is reasonable to compute the costs of all possible paths and to generate a *cost image* based on that information. An appropriate cost function would generate a cost image where the boundary of a target structure has a strong contrast to its surroundings, ideally in the whole image. If the user has to specify many control points, it should be attempted to change the cost function and to verify whether the cost image delineates the target object more clearly. In Figure 4.20 (left), the cost function is not suitable to efficiently segment the liver from CT data. The right cost image allows a faster segmentation, since the target object exhibits a clear boundary.

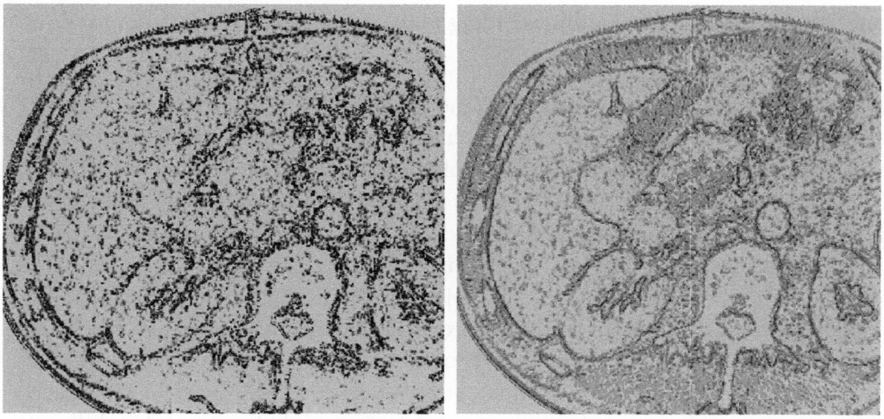

FIGURE 4.20 *Cost images related to livewire segmentation in CT data. The target object is the liver that is not clearly visible in the left cost image, whereas in the right image the liver is clearly delineated indicating that the corresponding cost function is appropriate (Courtesy of Andrea Schenk, Fraunhofer MEVIS Bremen).*

Livewire and Shape-based Interpolation Livewire is a slice-based segmentation approach. Since radiologists and their technical assistants are used to analyze and explore medical image data in a slice-oriented way, this approach is well-accepted.

However, the original livewire approach is rather laborious for the segmentation of larger 3D objects. Depending on the image resolution and the object size, an object might well be part of 100 or more slices. Therefore, the overall effort to segment an object with livewire may be 20 min, even with a suitable cost function. Another problem is the 3D slice consistency, since the defined contours of neighboring slices may deviate significantly.

To reduce the interaction effort and potential slice inconsistencies, livewire has been combined with interpolation methods [Schenk *et al.*, 2000]. Interpolation is employed to skip *intermediate slices* and to reduce the specification of control points to a subset of *key slices*. If the interpolation is carried out for intermediate slices S_1 and S_2, a binary image of the two slices is generated with "1" representing the pixels on the contour and "0" representing all other pixels. Based on these binary images, a distance-transformed image is computed (entries represent the Euclidean distance to the object contour with positive values for inside pixels and negative values for outside pixels). The interpolation is performed as a gray value interpolation of the distance values. In intermediate slices, the pixels with an assigned "0" are regarded as interpolated contours. Even better results are possible if the cost function is also employed for interpolated slices in order to pull the contour to the target structure [Schenk *et al.*, 2000].

For the segmentation of the liver in CT data, the overall segmentation effort could be considerably decreased by only minimally reduced accuracy. The number of slices that can be skipped depends on the image resolution. For CT liver data it turned out that it is sufficient to segment slices in a distance of 12 mm (for 2 mm slice distance, five slices are skipped). However, if the topology changes, for example, in case of branching structures, it is advisable to specify more contours [Schenk *et al.*, 2000].

Extrapolation of Boundary Contours A further support is possible by adding an *extrapolation step* that propagates a boundary contour not only between selected slices but also beyond. Without extrapolation, the user has to specify contours in the first and last slice of the target structure. With extrapolation, the first and last few examples may be omitted and the contour is determined automatically by propagating the contour from the nearest slice and adapt it locally according to the cost function. Thus, an organ does not have a *flat boundary surface* but a somehow rounded cap.

Discussion The result of livewire segmentation (and other edge-based methods) is a stack of contours represented as polygons or parametric curves. For a quantitative analysis as well as for visualization it is necessary to convert the contours to regions (sets of voxels, which represent the inner part of the target structure). The transformation of a (closed) contour to a region is carried out by a filling algorithm that is a basic algorithm in computer graphics [Foley *et al.*, 1995]. Since a livewire contour is a (possibly partial) directed line loop, the inside can be easily determined.

Livewire works best for compact and large objects without many indentations. The segmentation of highly folded areas, as they occur in the cortex of the brain, for example, would be a task where livewire is not appropriate—the user would have to set at least one seed point in every sulcus. Livewire is also less suited if the data are rather inhomogeneous, such as MRI data. In such data, even after inhomogeneity correction a completely different cost function might be required in different regions of an image [Schenk *et al.*, 2001]. Besides using livewire for the primary segmentation, it may also be used to correct segmentation results generated using other methods.

4.4.2 CONTOUR-BASED SEGMENTATION WITH VARIATIONAL INTERPOLATION

The segmentation with combining livewire and shape-based interpolation has two drawbacks that have recently been overcome:

- the resulting surfaces are only C^0 continuous, and
- all contours need to be defined in axial slicing direction.

Since anatomical surfaces, in general, are smooth, it is desirable that a reconstruction method generates at least C^1 continuous surfaces where no discontinuities in the surface normals occur. In particular, it would be desirable if a smooth cap is generated beyond the first and the last slice that is segmented by the user. With shape-based interpolation, the user has to carefully provide information in the first and last slices to avoid that the segmentation has large flat boundaries in the slicing direction.

It is sometimes also more appropriate to combine contours drawn in axial, sagittal, coronal or any other oblique orientation. With such a combination, a lower number of contours may be sufficient. The contours used as input may be generated with livewire, by manual drawing or by any other technique that produces closed contours.

A segmentation technique that provides these advantages has been presented by Heckel *et al.* [2011]. They consider the segmentation as an *energy minimization* problem where the user-drawn contours are transformed into a pointset (by sampling with an appropriate sampling rate) and using these points as constraints. In particular, they employ *thin plate splines*, which minimize the surface curvature by integrating along the sum of all (mixed) second order derivatives (Eq. 4.10).

$$E = \int_{\omega} \left[E_{int}\left(f_{xx}^2(x) + f_{yy}^2(x) + f_{zz}^2(x) + f_{xy}^2(x) + f_{xz}^2(x) + f_{yz}^2(x)\right)\right]dx \tag{4.10}$$

ω denotes the region of interest in which the interpolation is performed. The interpolation function $f(x)$ is expressed as a radial basis function, e.g., as a triharmonic spline, and incorporates the user-specified points. This kind of interpolation is known in computer graphics as *variational interpolation*. Figure 4.21 illustrates the application of this method for organ and tumor segmentation.

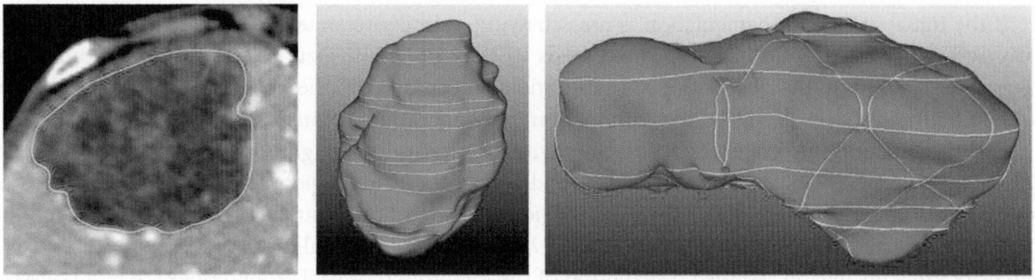

FIGURE 4.21 **Left:** *One of the contours used as input for tumor segmentation with variational interpolation.* **Middle:** *The result of variational interpolation is a smooth surface including a cap on top of the first and last user-specified contour.* **Right:** *14 contours specified in arbitrary orientations are used for liver segmentation (From: [Heckel et al., 2011]).*

Although the basic idea is rather straightforward, there are a number of specific problems, such as self-intersecting contours and performance issues [Heckel *et al.*, 2011].

In a follow up work, Heckel *et al.* [2012] focused on tumor segmentation and carefully discussed imperfections in user input during correction as well as heuristic to modify the segmentation result based on such input in one selected slice. An important issue is the *correction depth*, that is the number of slices that is adapted as a consequence of a modification. The choice of this value is a trade-off between the risk of changing region that were not intended to be changed versus a large effort if corrections have to be made in many slices. As a rule of thumb, the correction depth is derived from the size of the object (tumor) and clamped, if necessary, at the borders of the initial segmentation. Since the paper is based on a substantial evaluation, these correction techniques may be considered feasible for a wide range of tumors and imaging parameters.

4.4.3 GRAPH CUTS

The segmentation with graph cuts is another graph-based segmentation technique that employs seed points set by the user and a cost function. The seed points specify both foreground and background voxels and the graph cut segmentation searches for the best cut through the image that separates foreground from background voxels. More formally, the image data is represented as a graph with two sets of special nodes, called *terminals* that represent foreground and background seed voxels. A *cut* is a set of edges in the graph that completely separate the foreground from the background seeds, i.e., if the edges belonging to the cut are removed, there is no path between any foreground and background voxel. There are many sets of edges that exhibit this property. The selected cut is according to some criteria minimal. In the absence of any cost function, it would be just the cut with the minimum number of edges. Based on the cost function, the edges are weighted and the set of edges of the selected cut have the lowest overall weight. Graph cuts were introduced by Boykov and Jolly [2000], refined in [Boykov and Jolly, 2001] and described in more detail in [Boykov and Veksler, 2006]. It should be noted that graph cuts were used in computer vision even earlier. However, these early versions strongly favored short cuts.

From a theoretical point of view, one major difference to most other segmentation approaches is that a *global optimum* is searched for, instead of a local optimum. The seed points specified by the user serve as hard constraints, that is a boundary is searched in the whole volume data, but is has to separate foreground from background seeds.

If the initial graph cut segmentation is not satisfying—similar to watershed segmentation—the user may add either foreground or background seeds to steer the segmentation. The specific optimization technique is based on the observation that an optimal cut maximizes the flow between the foreground and background voxels. Therefore, algorithms from network optimization are used.

The cost functions integrate different factors with an appropriate weighting. These factors may incorporate both properties of the boundary edges and properties of the region, that is the internal parts of an object. In its most general form, the cost function is a sum of the boundary properties $B(A)$ and the regional properties $R(A)$ weighted with a factor λ. An essential regional property is how well a voxel's intensity value fits into an assumed distribution of the foreground or background object, e.g., a Gaussian (recall § 4.3.3.2). The boundary component of the cost functions is very similar to that of the livewire segmentation (§ 4.4.1), i.e., it may include gradient strength, gradient direction and features derived from approximated second order derivatives.

4.4.4 RANDOM WALKER SEGMENTATION

The random walker segmentation is initialized by the user with a few seeds that are labeled representing different objects. Based on these labels L_i, the random walker algorithm determines for each voxel the probability that a *random walker* reaches each label, and assigns it to the label L_k that has the highest probability (see Fig. 4.22 for an illustration of that strategy) [Grady, 2006]. The sum of these probabilities equals 1 for each voxel. Thus, with n labels, for each voxel the probabilities for $n - 1$ need to be computed and the last probability is just the difference to 1.

If the random walker algorithm cannot exploit any features of the image data, e.g., in case of a completely noisy image, a decomposition into a Voronoi diagram results. Thus, for each label L_i a segmentation is produced that contains all voxels with the lowest Euclidean distance to L_i. In a real medical image dataset, the probability that the random walker takes a particular path is modified by the gradient magnitude, since voxels with a high gradient magnitude are likely boundary voxels. Thus, the "random walker is biased to avoid crossing sharp boundaries" [Grady, 2006].

Graph Construction In contrast to the graph structure used for livewire segmentation, the edges in the graph underlying the random walker are undirected. Thus, the cost of moving from voxel v_i to voxel v_j is the same as vice versa. The random walker algorithm is based on an *affinity graph* that represents each voxel $v(x_i, y_j, z_k)$ of a dataset as a node and contains edges between all nodes and their direct neighbors, e.g., the six direct neighbors in x-, y-, and z-direction. Note that this is the same graph structure, as it is used for livewire segmentation. The edges are weighted with their *affinity*, i.e., by the difference between the

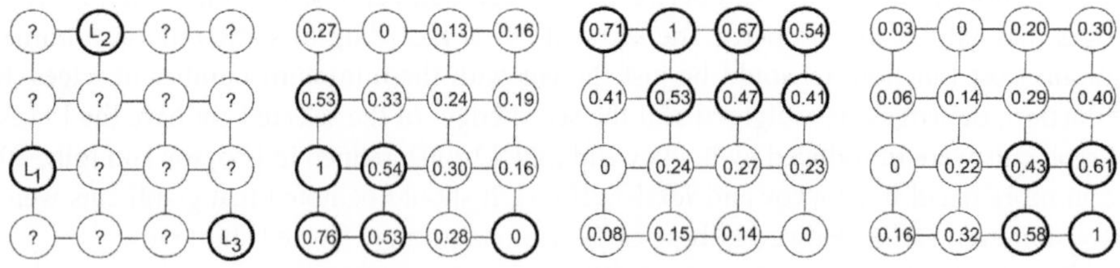

FIGURE 4.22 *Illustration of the random walker algorithm. The user provided the labels L_1, L_2 and L_3 (left image). The further images from left to right indicate the probability for each pixel to reach L_1, L_2 and L_3, respectively. The thick circle represents which label has the highest probability for each pixel (Adapted From: [Grady, 2006]).*

gray values g_i and g_j according to Equation 4.11. This equation was empirically determined by Grady [2006] who also tested other weightings.

$$\omega_{ij} = \exp(-\beta(g_i - g_j)^2) \tag{4.11}$$

Segmentation Algorithm The segmentation is internally realized as the solution of a sparse system of linear equations. This system has two favorable properties: it is symmetric and positive definite [Grady, 2006]. This particular class of equation systems can be solved very efficiently. However, direct solvers are not applicable, since their memory consumption is too high. The number of equations equals the number of voxels in the dataset, thus it is often more than 10 millions. Instead, iterative solvers are employed that may be easily parallelized, which enables efficient solutions on the GPU [Krüger and Westermann, 2003, Schiwietz, 2008]. There are also specific applications and adaptations of the random walker algorithm, e.g., for lesion segmentation in CT [Jolly and Grady, 2008].

4.5 ADVANCED AND MODEL-BASED SEGMENTATION METHODS

In this section, we give an overview of advanced and model-based approaches that provide a better support for highly specialized segmentation tasks. Model-based strategies employ knowledge of the size and shape of objects, or of gray level distributions. Shape knowledge may be represented as a single *template segmentation* of a *representative* instance [Montagnat and Delingette, 1997], but may also be derived from a statistical analysis of a larger series of segmentations that captures typical variances of an anatomical target structure (statistical shape models). As discussed in § 3.4, a number of relevant information on the acquisition process is stored along with the image data in the DICOM header. This information, e.g., the known position of the patient in the scanner relative to the imaging device, the reconstruction filter, the timings of an MR exam, and the specifics of contrast agent administration may be employed for automatic segmentation.

Characteristic anatomical landmarks, symmetry considerations, or typical orientations of the target structure may also be employed. In therapy planning applications, there is often a variety of segmentation target objects. With an appropriate sequence of the segmentation steps the relative location of these structures might also be employed for the segmentation.

Segmentation methods that rely on such kind of knowledge are referred to as *model-based segmentation*. Strictly speaking, livewire is also a model-based approach. Assumptions concerning gray value distributions and gradient characteristics are part of the cost function. We discussed it as a general method, since this knowledge is rather low-level and can be easily adapted to other structures.

Model-based segmentation is often a two-step process: In the first step, an initial contour is either manually supplied or automatically determined. In the second step, this initial contour is adapted to local features, often in an iterative optimization process to obtain the final segmentation. We discuss this second step in more detail, but it is essential to keep in mind that the final result may crucially depend on the initialization. While some approaches for the second step are rather robust against slight changes of the initial contour, others are very sensitive to such changes.

We start the discussion of model-based segmentation approaches with *active contour models*, which is a widespread variant of the general approach of fitting *deformable models* to the segmentation target structure (§ 4.5.1). We also discuss level set segmentation, a flexible region-based segmentation technique (§ 4.5.2), and statistical shape models (§ 4.5.3).

4.5.1 ACTIVE CONTOUR MODELS

Deformable models are based on a flexible geometric representation, such as B-splines, which provide the necessary degrees of freedom to adapt the model to a large variety of shapes. The process of fitting the model to the target structure is guided by physical principles and constraints which restrict, for example, the curvature along the boundary and thus favors smooth boundaries. The application of *deformable models* is guided by principles of elasticity theory, which describe how deformable bodies respond to forces. The resulting shape variations depend on some assumed stiffness properties of that body. Deformable models for image segmentation were suggested by Terzopoulos *et al.* [1988].

Active contour models or *snakes*—as they are often called—are a variant of deformable models, where initial contours are algorithmically deformed towards edges in the image [Kass *et al.*, 1988]. They are primarily used to approximate the shape of smooth object boundaries. The name *snake* is motivated by the behavior of such models, which adapt a contour between two control points like a snake.

The initial contour is either supplied by the user or derived from a priori knowledge (concerning geometric constraints, object shapes, and data constraints, such as range of expected gray level). Starting from the initial contour, an *energy functional* is minimized, based on contour deformation and external image forces. This optimization process cannot guarantee that a global minimum is found. Instead, a local minimum—based on the initial contour—is accepted.

Internal and External Energies The energy function with a parametric description of the curve $v(s) = (x(s), y(s))^T$, where $x(s)$ and $y(s)$ represent the coordinates along the curve $s \in [0, 1]$ is described by Equation 4.12

$$E_{contour} = \int_0^1 \left[E_{int}(v(s)) + E_{ext}(v(s))\right]ds \tag{4.12}$$

The inner energy E_{int} (Eq. 4.13) represents the smoothness of the curve and can be flexibly parameterized by α and β to encode expectations concerning the smoothness and elasticity of the target structure's contour. High α values, for example, contract the curve. Usually, α and β are constant [Lehmann *et al.*, 2003].

$$E_{int} = \alpha(s)\left|\frac{dv}{ds}\right|^2 + \beta(s)\left|\frac{d^2v}{ds^2}\right|^2 \tag{4.13}$$

The external energy E_{ext} counteracts the inner energy and is derived by the gray values and the gradient of the image according to Equation 4.14:

$$E_{ext} = w_1 f(x, y) - w_2|\nabla(G_\sigma(x, y) * f(x, y))|^2 \tag{4.14}$$

w_1 and w_2 are weights, which represent the influence of the gray value $f(x, y)$ and the gradient $\nabla(G)$. The gray values are assumed to be normally distributed with the standard deviation σ.

The curves are usually represented as (cubic) B-splines, which has the advantage that the resulting segmentation is smooth (continuous first order derivatives). The actual realization of the functional is very application-specific.

Balloon Segmentation as 3D Extension For 3D segmentation, active contour models are applied slice by slice, which is not only laborious, but also poses problems in the composition of a continuous surface based on a stack of contours. To better support 3D segmentation, the fitted contour in one slice may be used as initial contour in neighboring slices [Lin and Chen, 1989]. This process of *contour propagation* can be applied

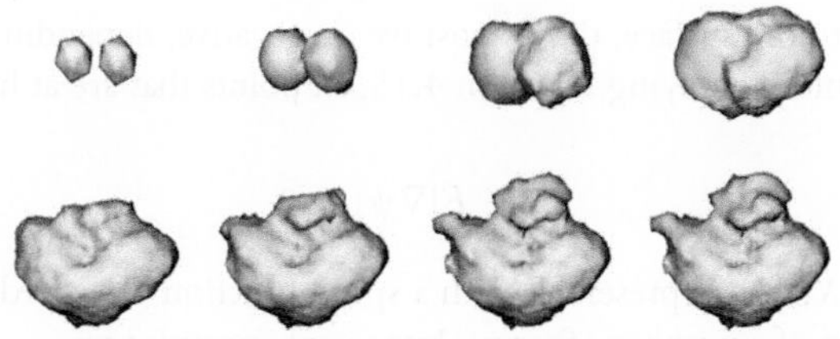

FIGURE 4.23 *Inflating balloon segmentation starting from the two small volumes in the upper left. After 40 iterations the final tumor segmentation is achieved (lower right image) (Courtesy of Olaf Konrad-Verse, Fraunhofer MEVIS Bremen).*

in a similar way than in livewire segmentation (recall § 4.4.1). Also, a combination with shape-based interpolation is feasible.

Active contour models have been extended to 3D, which is known as *balloon segmentation* [Terzopoulos et al., 1988]. Balloon segmentation is based on deforming surfaces instead of contours. This is accomplished by interactively fitting a polygonal representation of the initial shape to the target structure. There are two approaches how the segmentation process is initiated: either the user selects small volumes that are iteratively inflated until the forces converge, or enclosing volumes are specified by the user and iteratively deflated. Figure 4.23 illustrates the inflation with an application to tumor segmentation.

These 3D extensions bear a great potential. However, they pose some challenging user-interface problems (3D interaction with 2D input and output devices).

Discussion The internal energy constraints of active contour models restrict their flexibility and prevent that they represent tube-like shapes, branching structures or objects with strong protrusions [McInerney and Terzopoulos, 1996]. Therefore, they are generally not applied for the segmentation of vascular or bronchial trees. A problem of active contours (and their 3D extensions) is the strong dependence on a proper initialization; the contour might otherwise be attracted by a "wrong" edge in an image. A "wrong" edge is usually a part of the border of a nearby image but can also be an artifact. Although nice results can be presented in many publications, active contour models are (still) not widespread in clinical applications due to their difficult parameterization.

4.5.2 LEVEL SETS AND FAST MARCHING METHODS

If region growing is considered as a dynamic process, the progressing boundary can be regarded as a *wave front* propagating through the target object. This interpretation is the basis for image segmentation with the level set and fast marching methods [Sethian, 1999] (see also the fundamental paper by Osher and Sethian [1988]). The wave propagation is guided by a *speed function*. The speed function contains terms related to image features, such as image intensity and gradient (external forces), and may further consider internal forces, e.g., those that favor smooth results. Level sets are considered as an *implicit formulation* of deformable models. However, the contour γ is not manipulated directly. Instead, it is embedded as the *zero level set* in a higher dimensional function, the level set function $\psi(X,t)$, where X denotes the dependency in space and t the dependency in time. The parameters are specified in such a way that the progression becomes slow towards the target object's boundaries. More precisely, the level set function is evolved under control of the partial differential equation (PDE) in Equation 4.15. The evolving contour can be determined by extracting the zero level set.

$$\Gamma((X),t) = \psi(X,t=0) \pm d \tag{4.15}$$

d represents the distance to the surface, that is positive or negative, depending on whether the point is inside or outside. As a result of applying Equation 4.15, all points that are at height 0 of the embedding function are determined.

$$\psi_t + F|\nabla\psi| = 0 \tag{4.16}$$

The evolving function $\psi(X, t)$ is represented with a speed function F according to Equation 4.16. The speed function may consist of a number of terms. Important examples are:

- a *gradient-based term* to let the algorithm stop at regions with strong gradients, and
- a *curvature-related term*,

both suggested by Malladi *et al.* [1995].

Level set segmentation is naturally able to handle complex anatomical shapes with arbitrary topology. Note that the segmentation of such complex shapes with statistical shape models is very challenging.

Fast Marching Methods are closely related to level sets [Sethian, 1999]. Again, a PDE, namely the *Eikonal* equation (Eq. 4.17), is numerically solved.

$$|\nabla u| = C \tag{4.17}$$

where t is the time or arrival and C is a cost image, as we got to know in livewire segmentation (recall § 4.4.1). The user controls the segmentation process by placing seed points, e.g., a scribble centrally located in the target structure. These seed points $p \in P$ serve as boundary conditions $u(p) = 0$ for the solution of the PDE. The solution is searched for in a *narrow band* around the current wavefront that is initialized with the seed points. Thus, the surface (or in 3D the volume) evolves and is expanded in the direction of its local surface normal.

Design of the Cost Image The narrow band enables a fast solution. However, it also limits the flexibility. The design of the cost image C is the central problem in this segmentation technique. It should ensure that low costs arise in homogenous regions and high costs at edges. To implement this strategy, noise reduction is an essential first step [Rink and Toennies, 2008]. Vidholm *et al.* [2006] combine bilateral (edge-preserving) and Gaussian filtering to ensure very low intensity differences within a structure. A gradient image I_g that computes the gradient magnitude per voxel of the filtered input image has the desired property. The final cost image is often a linear combination between the gradient image I_g and its gradient magnitude (see Eq. 4.18 and [Vidholm *et al.*, 2006]).

$$C(x) = \alpha I_g + (1 - \alpha)|\nabla I_g(x)| \tag{4.18}$$

Finally, an *arrival time* needs to be determined to decide that the front at that time should be considered as final segmentation. The arrival time may be determined by considering the average cost (per voxel of the boundary front) of the current front. The costs typically increase from the seed points (where they are zero) and then start to decrease when the boundary is reached [Yan and Zhuang, 2003]. Level set segmentation is slower but more general than fast marching methods. In contrast to shape models, described in the next subsection, level set segmentation does not require an *explicit shape representation*, e.g., a surface mesh. There are many variants and applications of level set methods for image segmentation. The geodesic active contour is a popular edge-based variant [Caselles *et al.*, 1997].

Applications Avants and Williams [2000] and van Bemmel *et al.* [2002] segment vascular structures with level sets. The segmentation of layered anatomical structures, such as the cortex (the outermost layer of gray matter in the brain), can be performed well with level sets [Zeng *et al.*, 1999]. There are many applications with complex speed functions tailored to specific applications, such as artery-vein separation [van Bemmel *et al.*, 2003]. On the other hand, also more general speed functions were employed. Rink and Toennies [2008], for example, introduced distance-related measures in the speed function to connect portions of a contour that are close to each other and also to restrict the thickness of the target object. They applied such distance-related speed terms for the segmentation of dendrites in microscopy data and for the segmentation of the cortical surface in MRI data. Fan *et al.* [2008] refined level sets for consistent and topology-preserving segmentation of multiple objects and applied that method for the segmentation of bones and for subcortical segmentation.

4.5.3 STATISTICAL SHAPE MODELS

Statistical shape models (SSM), also known as active shape models (ASMs) are parameterizable descriptions of the shape of anatomical structures. In contrast to deformable models, SSM are based on a statistical analysis of a representative sample of training data. Due to their origin in statistical analysis, SSMs are also referred to as *statistical models*. They were introduced by Cootes *et al.* [1994]. We first describe the general principles and then discuss the requirements and limitations.

The parameterization allows to adapt the default model to different shape variants. For segmentation, parameters are searched, which optimally adapt the shape model to the target structure in a particular dataset. The model is derived from appropriate training data with a set of shapes $S_i (i = 1, \ldots, N)$, each of which is represented by the same set of M points (this set is referred to as *point distribution model*). These points should be roughly equally spaced along the surface. Note that is essential to find a corresponding point for each landmark in the other dataset.

PCA-based Shape Analysis After all anatomical landmarks for the individual shapes are determined, they are aligned with each other. In this process, the shapes are translated and rotated such that the differences between corresponding landmarks are minimal. This alignment process is actually a registration, more specifically a rigid registration where the object shape does not change (§ 4.8.1). An important tool for analyzing the variability of the landmarks' positions is the principal component analysis (PCA). This statistical method delivers a set of ordered orthogonal basis vectors that represent the directions of progressively smaller variance. The dimensionality of the correlated datasets can be reduced with the PCA results by retaining to the first principle vectors [Morrison, 2005, Jolliffe, 1986]. The use of PCA for statistical models is described in the following.

The mean shape vector $\bar{v}$ represents the average of each point M_i. The variability of the points can be expressed by means of the covariance matrix C (Eq. 4.19). The PCA of the point distribution model is a high dimensional problem (the number of dimensions corresponds to the number of landmarks and is thus often larger than 50).

$$C = \frac{1}{N-1} \sum_{1=1}^{N} (S_i - \bar{S})(S_i - \bar{S}^T) \tag{4.19}$$

With a PCA, the eigenvectors e_i and eigenvalues λ_i of C are determined, which fulfill Equation 4.20.

$$\mathrm{C} \cdot e_i = \lambda_i \cdot e_i \tag{4.20}$$

They are determined by calculating the roots of the characteristic polynomial of C of degree n. Each shape vector can be expressed as a linear model of the form:

$$S_i = \bar{S} + Cb_i = S + \sum_{k=1}^{n} E^k b_i^k \tag{4.21}$$

where $E = e^k$ is the matrix of eigenvectors of the covariance matrix.

The eigenvalues are sorted ($\lambda_i \geq \lambda_{i+1}$) and the eigenvectors are labeled such that e_i corresponds to λ_i. The order of λ_i characterizes the influence of points on the object shape. Usually, a small number of points accounts for most of the variation. This gives rise to an approximation with the largest t eigenvalues, which explain, for example, 95% of the variability of the object shape. A shape is then approximated by finding optimal weights b_s for the significant modes of variations ($e_1, e_2, \ldots, e_t$). These eigenvectors are concatenated to a matrix P_s. Equation 4.21 can now be replaced by an approximation (Eq. 4.22).

$$S_i \approx \bar{S} + P_s b_s \tag{4.22}$$

With this mechanism, a *shape space*, or an *allowable shape domain* [Cootes *et al.*, 1994] is created that is spanned by the mean shape $\bar{S}$ and the eigenvectors e_i. The space contains all linear combinations of these eigenvectors e_i. In other words, with an SSM it is feasible to segment shapes correctly, provided that each landmark does not deviate more from its mean value than all shapes in the training set. The shape parameters b represent weights that control the modes of variation and thus the variability of the shape. The variability of a particular landmark is suitably restricted. A common restriction is to permit a variance related to the statistical variance of this landmark. If the shapes are assumed to represent a Gaussian distribution, 99% of all shapes in the training data are within the bounds $\pm 3\sqrt{\lambda_i}$.

As Wimmer *et al.* [2009] point out, this shape space construction assumes that the shapes are normally distributed, which is not necessarily true. If, for example, the pelvis of men and women are analyzed and integrated in *one* model, there are distinct differences in the men and women subsects. Also a shape model for an organ derived from adult data will most likely not successfully segment the same organ in a small child, where not even the size but also the shape might differ significantly.

If too many parameters are necessary to characterize individual shapes precisely enough, very large training datasets would be required and the search process would be too laborious.

Model Fitting The fitting of the model must be properly initiated, for example, by a user-selected central point or a roughly defined shape. Starting from the mean shape, all landmarks (starting with the most significant mode of variation) are translated perpendicular to the contour and evaluated until the contour remains stable.

Requirements Although the basic idea of segmenting objects by means of SSMs is easily explained, its realization is demanding and time-consuming. The segmentation quality strongly depends on the quality of the acquired model. The model is derived from a training dataset and has to fulfill several requirements:

- The training dataset should be large enough to statistically characterize shape parameters. It is not reasonable to present a minimum number of test cases covering all applications, but as a rule of thumb, it should be more than 20 training cases.
- The training set of datasets should comprise a representative selection of the anatomical variants. If certain variants occur, they must be part of the training set. Otherwise, the model cannot be used

to fit such variants. If it turns out that an initial SSM of the target structure has many variables that characterize its shape, a larger training set is needed compared to shapes with little variability.

- The quality of the segmentations must be very high, which means that the segmentation result is either produced manually as accurate as possible or—if generated with a semi-interactive approach—carefully verified and modified, if necessary.
- A prerequisite for the comparison of training datasets is that all coordinates refer to a common reference frame. Therefore, the surfaces have to be aligned (translated, scaled, and rotated) such that the correspondence between the shapes is optimal (the distances between corresponding points is minimal).
- The model generation process relies on the definition of corresponding landmark points, which allow to compare the shapes. It is necessary that enough points are determined, which actually have a correspondence in all other segmentation results.

The list of requirements stresses that the effort to create an appropriate model is significant and only justified, if it addresses a frequent segmentation task. Landmark extraction is by far the most challenging step in case of 3D models. As a general strategy, it is useful to decompose each dataset of the training data in a certain number of patches and use this decomposition to generate topologically equivalent meshes for all datasets. The decomposition into patches enables a more robust search for point landmarks, as shown in Figure 4.24. The landmark extraction process, however, also has very specific components exploiting anatomical peculiarities. As an example, for analyzing the pelvis, the anterior pelvic plane is essential [Seim *et al.*, 2009], and thus, its extraction is a useful input for further analysis.

Applications The first application of SSM was the segmentation of the left heart ventricle in echo cardiograms and MRI data [Cootes *et al.*, 1994]. Successful applications have been realized for liver segmentation [Lamecker *et al.*, 2002] and pelvic bone segmentation (see Fig. 4.25) [Lamecker *et al.*, 2004, Seim *et al.*, 2008].

For both applications, it turned out that correspondence is difficult to realize for the whole anatomical structure. Instead, the structures are subdivided into substructures; the liver, for example, in four substructures, three of which represent liver lobes. The pelvic bone was subdivided into 11 substructures. This process has to be carried out for each dataset. Therefore, automatic support is important. Lamecker *et al.* [2002] suggest that substructures are chosen such that they can be identified automatically by locating and connecting features with high curvature.

The model generation for the pelvic bone was more challenging because of the complex topology (genus 3, which means that the pelvic bone has 3 holes). On the other hand, the shape of the pelvic bone is

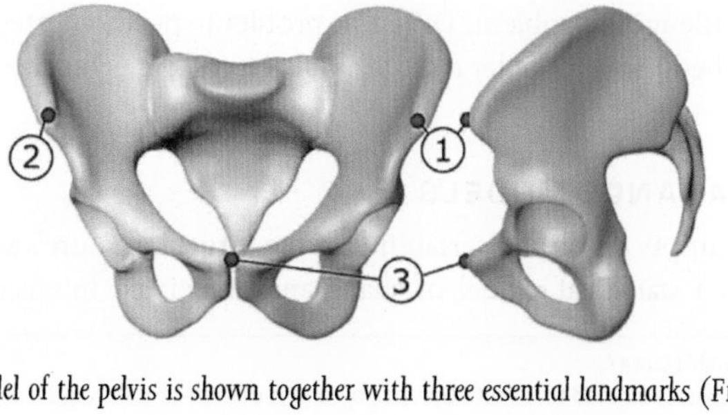

FIGURE 4.24 *The average model of the pelvis is shown together with three essential landmarks (From: [Seim et al., 2009]).*

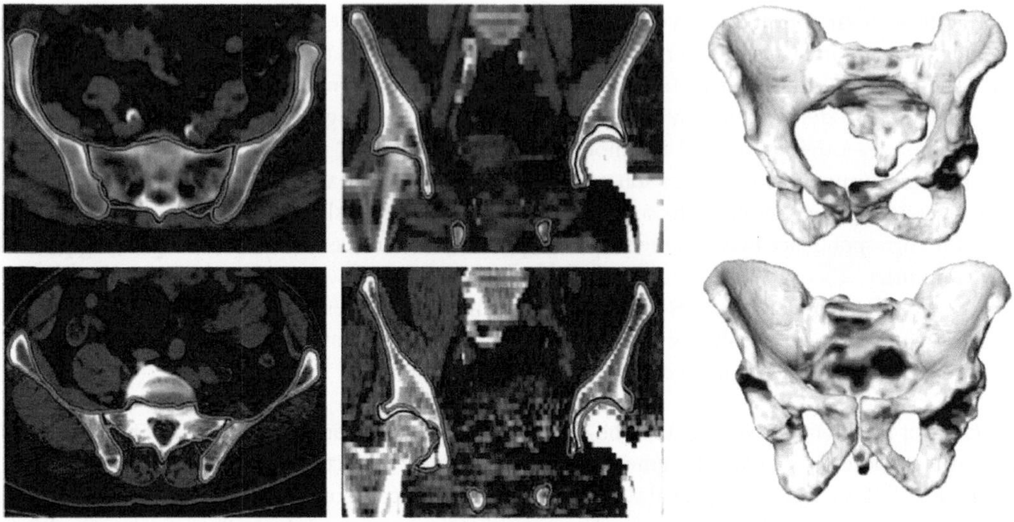

FIGURE 4.25 *The pelvic bone is segmented with a pipeline of steps with a SSM at the core. The images show transversal, coronal and 3D views. The color encodes the segmentation error that is larger in the second example where more severe pathologies occur (Courtesy of Heiko Ramm, Zuse-Institut Berlin. See also [Seim et al., 2008]).*

less variable (3 main modes of variation were considered). The liver model considers 21 modes of variation resulting from 43 datasets. Probably, a larger training set would increase the number of significant modes.

More recently, SSMs were employed to segment bones and cartilages of the knee (from MRI data) [Seim *et al.*, 2010]. This special segmentation task was the topic of a contest—the "Medical image analysis for the clinic—A grand challenge".[3] Sixty clinical datasets from patients suffering from osteoarthritis are available along with expert segmentations used as ground truth for the validation.

The solution presented by Seim *et al.* [2010], one of the award winners, is based on an initial rigid transformation using a low resolution template (some 500 vertices). This initial transformation is computed with the general Hough transform (GHT) [Ballard, 1981]. The GHT is able to detect arbitrary shapes based on an appropriate template.[4] Figure 4.26 illustrates the good correspondence between expert and fully automatic segmentation. Validation, of course, also needs to be performed in a quantitative manner that we shall discuss in § 4.7.

There are many more applications of SSMs for medical image segmentation, including tubular structures and structures with different topologies. For 3D segmentation, establishing correspondences between landmarks is the most challenging problem. Different problem-specific strategies to the correspondence problem have been described [Brechbuehler *et al.*, 1995, Brett *et al.*, 1997a, Lorenz and Krahnstöver, 1999, de Bruijne *et al.*, 2002].

4.5.4 ACTIVE APPEARANCE MODELS

Shape models capture assumptions on the variability of the target structure's shape. An active appearance model (AAM) comprises a statistical model of shape and associated intensity values. Thus, it is more

3 Contest website: http://www.ski10.org/.

4 The classical Hough transform was restricted to objects that can be analytically described, e.g., a circle or a sphere.

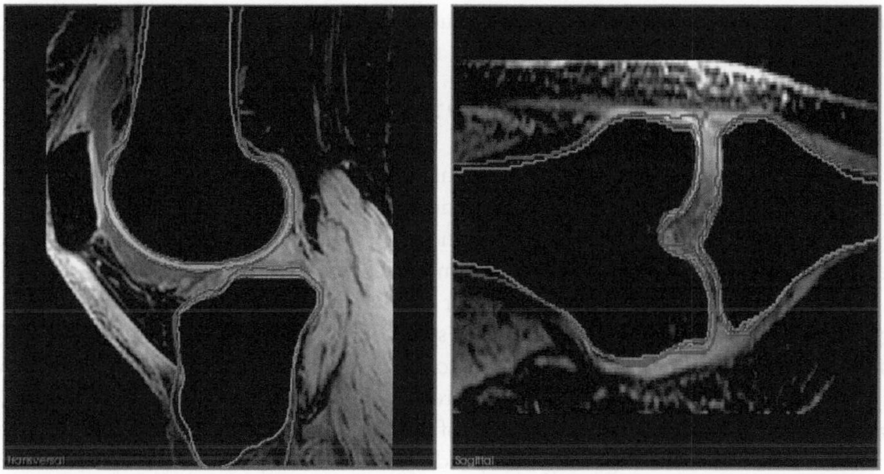

FIGURE 4.26 *Validation of an automatic knee segmentation method. The green contours were drawn by an expert, whereas the red contours were automatically generated* (Courtesy of Heiko Ramm, Zuse-Institut Berlin. *See also* [Seim *et al.*, 2010]).

specialized but cannot be applied to CT and MRI data simultaneously. The extension to AAMs has also been suggested by Cootes *et al.* [2001].

An AAM is constructed by adjusting differences between the shapes using the point distribution model and the PCA. With this strategy, each shape is transformed to the mean shape $\bar{S}$. As the shapes are sized and oriented in a different way, the transformation requires a resampling of the gray values (new pixel values in the normalized dataset are determined as weighted average of pixels in the original dataset).

In these normalized shapes, the gray value distribution is analyzed, e.g., by sampling profile vectors perpendicular to the boundary surface. The resulting intensity profiles are often analyzed with a PCA to derive a model of the intensities along the boundary—often called a *boundary model*. Again, the PCA relies on a normal distribution of the intensity profiles, which represents a simplification, since there might be characteristic categories of boundary profiles, e.g., in case of vessels or tumors close to the boundary. van Ginneken *et al.* [2002] introduced a boundary model that does not rely on a particular distribution. This boundary model was successfully applied by Wimmer *et al.* [2009] for liver segmentation in the course of a MICCAI contest.

For the segmentation with AAM, the model must be fitted to the (new) dataset. This fitting process can be guided by intensity profiles along the surface normal, which represent expectations concerning gray values and gradients. In order to enhance the correspondence between these profiles in the training data and the real data, diffusion filtering might be very useful (recall § 4.2).

Applications A comparison of AAMs and SSMs is carried out for MRI data of the knee and the brain and documents the benefit of including assumptions concerning gray level distributions [Cootes *et al.*, 1998]. Segmentation with SSMs is feasible, if the variability of the shapes of an anatomical structure is not too large. Stegmann *et al.* [2000] contributed a flexible implementation of AAMs.

For anatomical structures, which exhibit a strong individual variability or complex folding patterns, such as the brain, they are not appropriate, since they may only segment a shape that is similar to the shapes of the training set. Therefore, they are often combined, e.g., with a subsequent free form deformation to enhance their flexibility. This strategy was introduced by Weese *et al.* [2001] and later applied, e.g., by Heimann *et al.* [2006] and Kainmueller *et al.* [2007] to liver segmentation.

4.5.5 INCORPORATING MODEL ASSUMPTIONS IN REGION GROWING SEGMENTATION

In this subsection, we discuss how a general segmentation method, namely region growing, may be refined by incorporating model assumptions. In particular, *shape constraints* are often used to enhance region growing, e.g., to prevent leakage. For the segmentation of vascular structures in contrast-enhanced data, it is a reasonable assumption that the cross section of these structures is roughly elliptical. It is also justified to assume that these structures are at similar locations in adjacent slices. With these assumptions, region growing may be initiated by a seed point specified by the user. The interval for the growing process may be estimated by analyzing the 3D surrounding and evaluating how many voxels would be segmented with a particular threshold (a sudden increase in this number indicates a crossing of the border of contrast-enhanced structures). The assumption of an elliptical cross section is employed by fitting an ellipse to the detected cross section (see Fig. 4.27) and to restrict the segmentation result to this ellipse. The segmentation result in one slice is propagated to the next slice and refined with respect to the thresholds. Hennemuth *et al.* [2005] designed this approach and refined it even further with assumptions suitable to delineate coronary vessels. They have shown that even in the presence of noise and plaque reasonable segmentation results were achieved based on only one seed point specified by the user (see Fig. 4.28).

4.5.6 APPLICATION: TUMOR SEGMENTATION

This section is primarily focused on and organized according to *segmentation methods*. It does not provide an overview of specific applications, but only briefly mentions where certain methods are applicable. In this section we shall discuss one particularly important application, namely the segmentation of benign and malignant tumors. The importance of that segmentation task is due to the fact that tumor size and tumor volume directly influence tumor staging and treatment decisions. In the large portion of tumor diseases, where radiation treatment and chemotherapy is applied instead of surgical removal, tumor segmentation

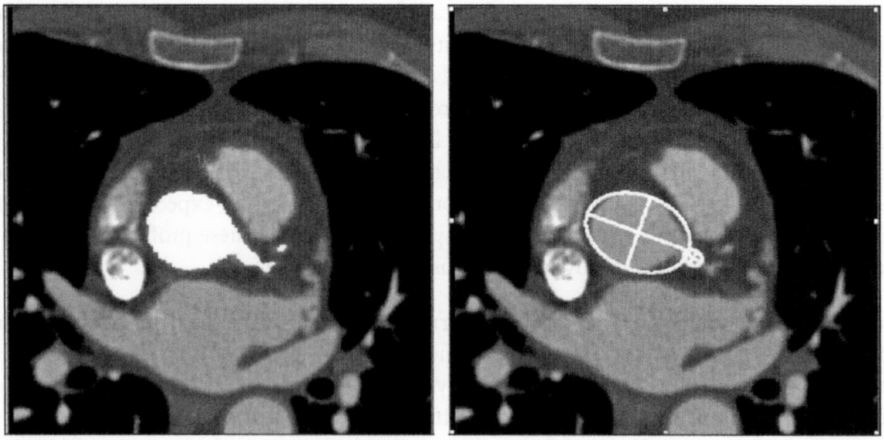

FIGURE 4.27 *An ellipse fit is applied to restrict a segmentation result, see the cross section of a coronary artery* (From: [Hennemuth et al., 2005]).

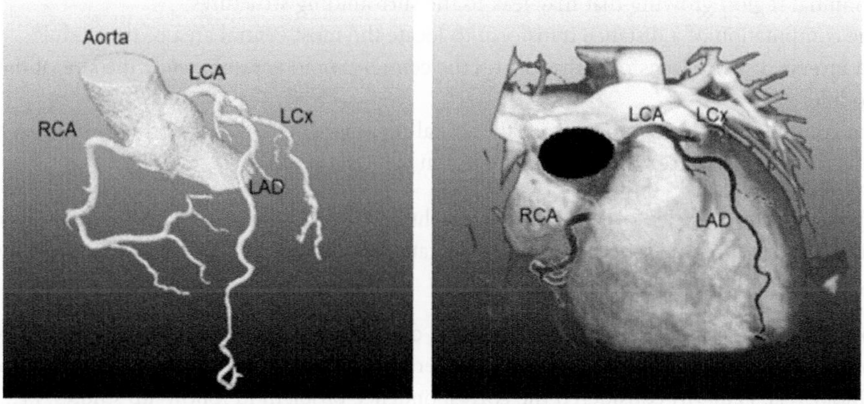

FIGURE 4.28 *Automatically segmented coronary tree with an advanced region growing. LCA and RCA denote the left and right coronary artery, LCx denotes the circumflex artery and LAD denotes the left anterior descending artery (From: [Hennemuth et al., 2005]).*

is essential to streamline follow-up investigations and to assess tumor progress reliably. Besides the pure segmentation task, detection of tumors and automatic correspondence finding between an original exam and a follow-up study as well as tumor volumetry are essential and often combined with segmentation.

Problem Statement In clinical practice, the longest axial diameter in a selected slice is determined manually (according to the RECIST criteria), or, in addition the diameter perpendicular to the longest diameter is determined to estimate the area (according to the guidelines of the World Health Organization). However, numerous studies indicate that segmentation with subsequent volumetry is significantly more reliable (see, for example, [Prasad *et al.*, 2002]). Benign and malignant tumors exhibit a large variety of biological processes and thus appear very different in medical image data (if they may be distinguished at all). They might appear *hypodense* (darker than the surrounding) or *hyperdense* (brighter than the surrounding). Also the tumor itself may be very inhomogeneous with active areas (with very strong blood supply) on the one hand and necrotic areas on the other hand. Thus, model building is particularly challenging and relies on a good selection of examples from this diversity. Probably, even with a good model, new cases will include tumor variants that are not covered by the training data.

Segmentation Techniques Several of the previously discussed methods, e.g., histogram analysis, region growing, watershed, and active contours, are relevant but often need to be combined with other methods resulting in more or less complex *segmentation workflows*. In practice, a good combination of rather simple individual techniques is often favorable compared to one very sophisticated method. Since tumor segmentation is a very active area, we can only discuss selected examples instead of giving a comprehensive overview.

Most techniques are very specific and consider only one tumor type, e.g., hepatic metastases but not hepatic carcinoma (the primary liver tumors), and only one modality, such as the technique introduced by Yim and Foran [2003]. They combined *active contours* and *watershed segmentation*. A series of simple techniques was carefully combined by Kuhnigk *et al.* [2006] to segment lung nodules, even if they are attached to other tissue or crossed by vascular structures. This method consists of the following steps:

1 an initial region growing that may leak to the surrounding structures,
2 the computation of a distance transform to locate the most central area of the nodule,
3 an inverse distance transform that dilates the central area to approximately the size of the original nodule,
4 the computation of the union from the initial region growing result and the result from step 3. This represents the area were the initial region growing leaked.

By subtracting the so-called over-segmentation, they achieve a result in which one central connected component remains and represents the final segmentation result. Figure 4.29 illustrates this principle and Figure 4.30 shows some results.

Follow-up Studies Moltz *et al.* [2009a] employ a line drawn by the user inside the tumor and determine the histogram along that line to determine parameters for further segmentation, in particular of hepatic tumors. Moltz *et al.* [2009b] considered the correspondence problem in follow-up studies, i.e., they aim at finding the same tumor in different datasets to assess growth or shrinkage. They searched for a tumor within a certain gray value interval and within roughly circular regions detected with a Hough transform.

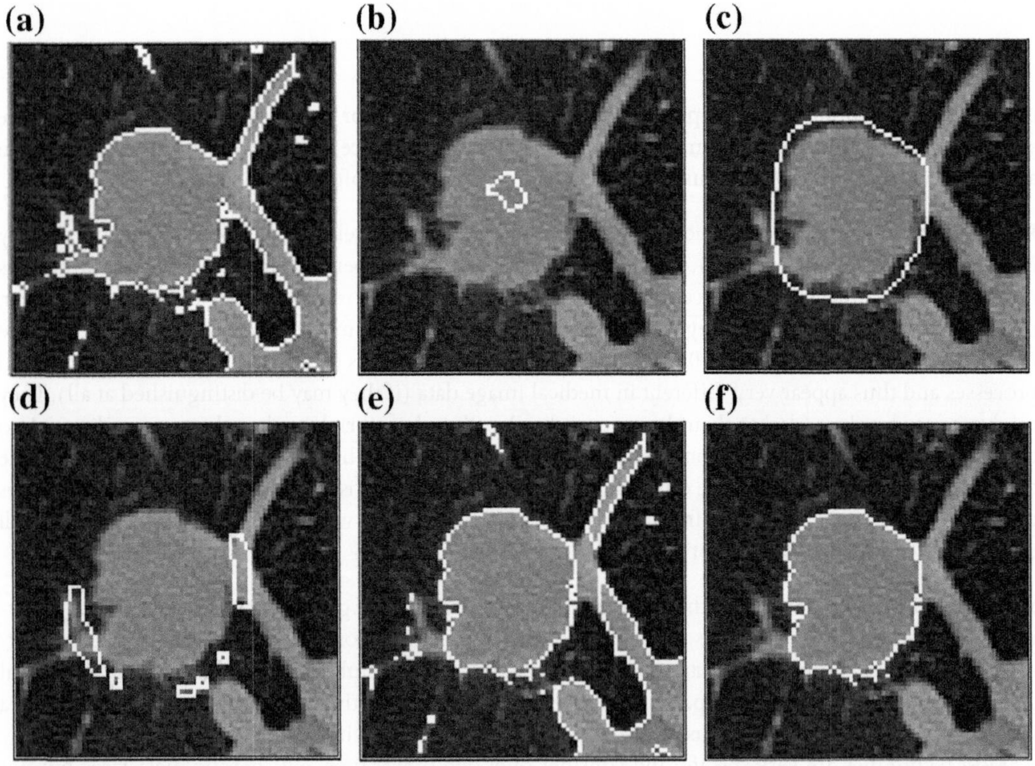

FIGURE 4.29 *Lung nodule segmentation with an initial region growing leaking into surrounding vessels (a), a subsequent distance transform (b), and an inverse distance transform (c). The union of the results from step 1 and 3 is shown in (d). (e) displays the difference set of step 1 and 3. After subtracting this set (e), one central connected component may be identified as final result (f) (Courtesy of Jan Martin Kuhnigk, Fraunhofer MEVIS Bremen).*

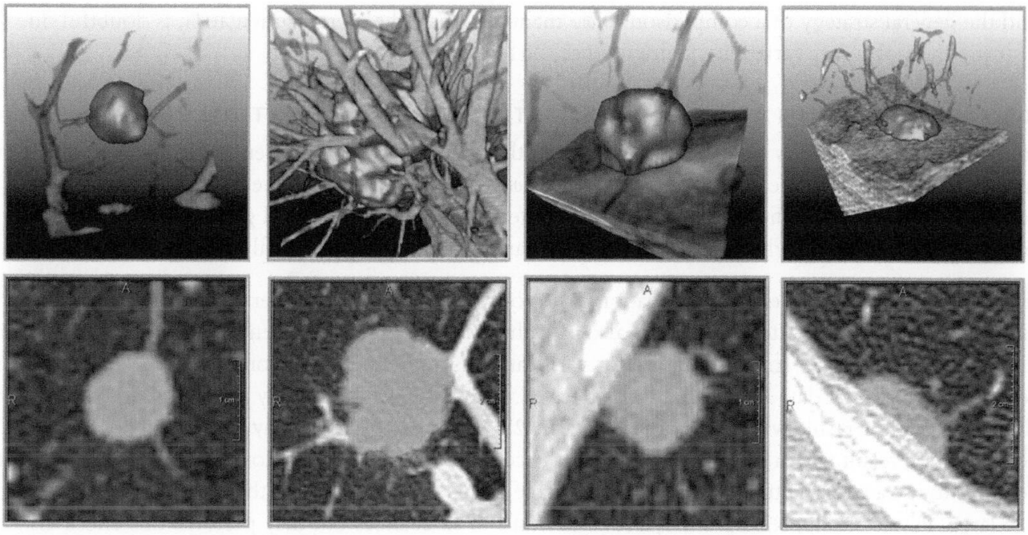

FIGURE 4.30 *Four examples of lung nodules segmented in CT thorax data and displayed in 3D (top row) and 2D (bottom row). Shape and size of the nodules are similar. However, the nodules may be attached to vessels (two cases on the left) or to the pleura (two cases on the right). Since these structures exhibit similar intensity values, simple methods are likely to fail (Courtesy of Jan Martin Kuhnigk, Fraunhofer MEVIS Bremen).*

As a next step, they employed a template matching using a similarity criterion that is frequently used in image registration (§ 4.8), namely *normalized cross-correlation*. Their method was more widely applicable, as the validation with more than 300 nodules (lung nodules, liver metastases and lymph nodes) indicates.

Segmentation Workflows Tumor segmentation is an excellent example for the importance of an appropriate segmentation workflow. The specific segmentation task benefits from a prior segmentation of surrounding and adjacent structures that are often easier to delineate. As an example, the tumor segmentation described by Seo [2005] starts with the segmentation of the liver and the hepatic vasculature to restrict the search space to liver tumors. Also Zhou *et al.* [2010] explain that the combination of organ and tumor segmentation is "a promising development." Zhou *et al.* [2010] perform such a combination with a Gaussian mixture model (recall § 4.3.3.2), searching for the parameters to characterize two tissue types, namely the liver and the liver tumors. The parameters are later used for a constrained region growing process.

Clinical Application For clinical use, it is essential that tumor segmentation methods were developed and evaluated with respect to clinically relevant conditions. As an example, tumor segmentation in CT data is, in general, easier with a large slice distance and a correspondingly high SNR [Zhou *et al.*, 2010]. Tumor segmentation methods may also be dedicated to one specific tumor type instead of a broader range of, e.g., liver and lung lesions. As a consequence, a more flexible approach is often more appropriate in practice compared to a highly automated technique that does not work beyond a very narrow application setting.

Validation Due to the importance of accurate tumor segmentation, validation is essential. The general validation principles described in § 4.7 are relevant here as well. However, often larger studies are necessary and the general strategy of a comparison to *one* manually created expert segmentation is doubtful due to a strong intra-observer variability [Schwier *et al.*, 2011].

4.5.7 VERIFICATION AND REPRESENTATION OF SEGMENTATION RESULTS

In this section we discuss two essential problems that are largely independent from the segmentation method actually used. The first problem is *verification*, i.e., the process where a user checks whether a segmentation result is sufficiently accurate for further processing. The second general problem is storage of segmentation results, where accuracy, efficiency and fast access are essential criteria.

Verification of Segmentation Results Verification is not only performed by the person actually segmenting a structure, e.g., a radiology technician, but also by a physician later using segmentation results for diagnosis and treatment planning. The core feature for verification is a possibility for comparing the segmentation result to the original data from which it is derived. This is typically done by providing an overview of the segmentation result with the original data in 2D slices. The overlay may be realized by filling the segmentation result with a color or by drawing the contour of the segmentation result. The filling variant requires to use a strongly transparent color to enable the user to see whether the segmentation is actually too large. Physicians appreciate if they are not bound to axial slices but may perform this check also in sagittal and coronal or also in oblique views (see Fig. 4.31).

Representation of Binary Segmentation Results Many segmentation approaches, e.g., region growing and watershed segmentation "decide" on the voxel level whether a voxel belongs to the target structure or not. The natural storage scheme to accurately represent such segmentation results are *binary masks* having the same size as the input image data. Other segmentation techniques, in particular some of the model-based approaches we get to know in the next section, adapt a polygonal surface mesh to the target structure. In this case, the segmentation information has an accuracy beyond the voxel level, at least for the boundary voxels. Often, even in these cases, the surface mesh is converted in a voxel representation where basically a voxel counts as foreground object if it is covered by more than 50%. This is a convenient storage scheme

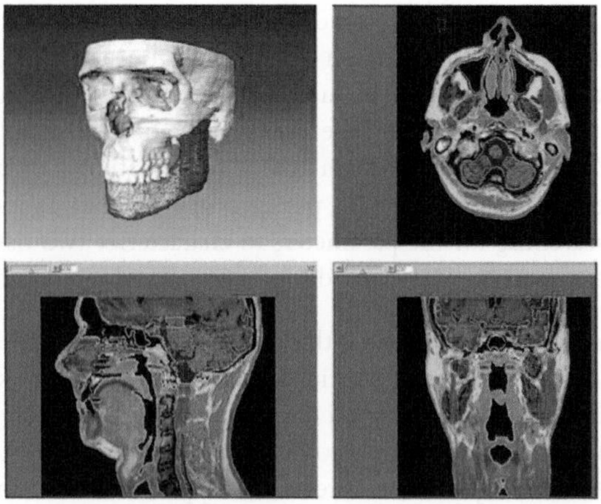

FIGURE 4.31 *Screenshot from a segmentation editor that provides the outlines of all segmentation results in three orthogonal views to enable verification by a physician. The segmentation results are employed for cranio-facial surgery planning (From: [Zachow et al., 2004b]).*

and directly supports tasks, such as the verification described above. However, this conversion ("voxelization") is a lossy process and may lead to problems, e.g., when the segmentation result should be displayed as a 3D surface visualization. A blocky staircase behavior would result. Thus, when subvoxel accuracy is available, it should be considered to represent it accurately, e.g., as a surface mesh.

Let us discuss the storage in a binary mask in more detail. Voxels labeled as "1" represent those that belong to the target structure, whereas background voxels are labeled as "0." Frequently, such a mask is called a *tagged volume* or a *label volume*. This storage scheme enables fast access in a visualization algorithm, where the original volume data and the tagged volume may be sampled simultaneously to adapt the rendering in regions belonging to the target structure.

Representing Multiple Overlapping Segmentations Binary masks may be extended to multiple segmentations, e.g., for radiation treatment or surgery planning, where potentially several dozens of structures are segmented: one label, an integer number, is assigned to each structure and the tagged volume indicates whether a voxel belongs to the background or to any of the target structures. Unfortunately, in practice, segmentation results often overlap. Therefore, situations where a voxel belongs to several segmentation masks, e.g., to a lung tumor, to the lung lobe and to the whole lung cannot be easily represented. The most general storage scheme to represent that a voxel belongs to an arbitrary subset of N segmentations is to reserve one bit for each target structure. Thus, with two bytes per voxel any combination of segmentation results for 16 target structures can be represented. In practice, more segmentation results occur frequently. As an example, the commercial service for liver surgery planning provided by MeVis Distant Services[5] regularly generates organ segmentation, segmentation of various vascular territories, segmentation of the different intrahepatic vascular structures and liver tumors. For an application like this, considerable memory consumption is required with a simple storage scheme.

Memory-efficient Storage A more efficient storage is possible, if one takes into account that only a very small subset of the theoretically possible combinations occurs. Mühler *et al.* [2010] presented a *coded segmentation scheme* that compresses the segmentation information, assigning unique labels to each combination of segmentation results that actually occurs. They give several examples from ENT and liver surgery planning and show that a one byte tagged volume is sufficient in almost all relevant situations (see Fig. 4.32). This increased efficiency is particularly important for larger studies, as they emerge in epidemiology and for training systems associated with a larger set of cases.

4.6 INTERACTION FOR SEGMENTATION

"Fully automatic, completely reliable segmentation in medical images is an unrealistic expectation" [Grady and Funka-Lea, 2006]. This statement is certainly still true, in particular for clinical data, often with less than perfect quality and often with severe pathologies that are at odds with model assumptions. The feasibility and acceptance of image analysis methods strongly depends on the required amount and style of user interaction. Some methods may produce excellent results with almost no interaction in many cases, but lack appropriate interaction facilities in other cases. Often, segmentation is an iterative process where intermediate results are fine-tuned. While some methods support a directed improvement of intermediate results, others are based on trial-and-error. Despite significant progress in recent years (see [McGuinness and O'Connor, 2010] for an overview), interaction issues in image segmentation are still

5 http://www.mevis.de/mms/en/Distant_Services.html.

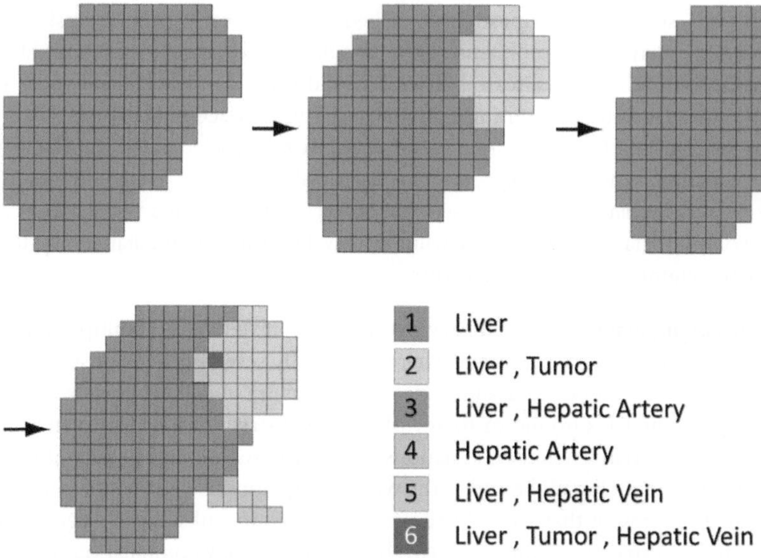

FIGURE 4.32 *Coded segmentation: To represent the overlapping segmentations of four structures, only six labels are necessary* (From: [Mühler et al., 2010]).

not widely researched. Research and development is strongly focused on algorithms and interaction is widely considered as a repair mechanism for problems where full automation is not successful.

The discussion of user interface issues for image segmentation is guided by some general considerations regarding human-computer collaboration based on [Shneiderman, 1997]. He emphasizes that computers are generally better in

- counting or measuring physical quantities,
- processing quantitative data in predefined ways, and
- maintaining performance over extended periods of time.

Humans, on the other hand, are better in

- detecting stimuli on noisy background,
- adapting decisions to specific situations, and
- selecting alternatives, if an original approach fails.

Interaction techniques for image segmentation should be designed by taking the strength and weaknesses of human beings into account. Interaction plays an essential role in three stages of the segmentation process:

1. initialization, where, e.g., markers are set or templates are roughly placed,
2. parameter specification, e.g., selection of thresholds or flooding heights, and
3. local correction of segmentation results.

We shall discuss human-computer interaction in the next chapter. In essence, general user interface principles (§ 5.5) should be considered for the tools provided for supporting the segmentation process. In particular, tools should be easy and efficient to be used and the system should provide informative feedback. User interface metaphors may be helpful to achieve these goals and we will briefly discuss some metaphors that turned out to be useful for refining object shapes.

In this section, we will not discuss the systematic evaluation of interaction techniques for segmentation and direct the reader to the evaluation framework introduced by McGuinness and O'Connor [2010].

A dedicated effort to understand interaction issues in image segmentation has been attempted by Olabarriaga and Smeulders [2001]. They emphasize that medical doctors have no difficulties to specify points inside or outside the target structure or to roughly encircle it for the initialization. However, difficulties arise, if users have to specify numerical input, such as the average gradient magnitude of the target structure. The following considerations are based on their work.

4.6.1 GENERAL TECHNIQUES FOR CORRECTING PRE-SEGMENTATIONS

Frequently, an initial segmentation result, e.g., a result of an automatic segmentation, needs to be locally corrected (stage 3). This local correction should be fast and behave in a predictable manner. Ideally, local correction is possible at the level of 2D slices as well as at the level of 3D models. The latter requirement is carefully discussed in [Kang *et al.* 2004, Grady and Funka-Lea, 2006]. Most image processing toolkits only provide 2D correction tools that are operated in 2D slices and only affect the current slice. An example is MITK (http://www.mitk.org/wiki/) that provides brushing tools to add or remove pixels. However, the 3D counterpart of such tools is significantly more effective, as Silva *et al.* [2010] demonstrated, at least for segmentations of structures covering many slices.

Compared to the large amount of segmentation techniques, there are rather few attempts to systematically explore strategies and methods for the correction of pre-segmentations. This correction may be achieved at two levels:

- modification of the surface mesh generated from the segmentation, or
- modification of the binary segmentation result (pixel or voxel level).

We discuss approaches of both categories in the following two subsections.

4.6.2 MESH-BASED CORRECTION OF SEGMENTATION RESULTS

With these techniques, meshes are deformed, e.g., by dragging vertices and displacing them and their local surrounding, by bulging surfaces with appropriate tools. These corrections do not consider image information, such as large gradient magnitude. Therefore, they are referred to as *image-independent* correction techniques [Heckel *et al.*, 2012].

Fine-grained and Coarse Modification An important issue is *scale*, that is the size of the surrounding that is influenced. Obviously, fine-grained tools support a more precise interaction but their use is time-consuming. Often, it is desirable to modify the scale flexibly depending on the nature of the segmentation problem to be solved. As an example Silva *et al.* [2010], found that in the correction of the pre-segmentation of the left ventricle a sphere with a large radius was preferred for correcting problems at the mitral valve, whereas the correction of the small outgoing tract requires a smaller radius. Immediate feedback is an essential requirement for mesh-based correction tools. This requirement is difficult to achieve if larger tools are used and a large portion of a triangle mesh needs to be recomputed. We discuss mesh processing in Chapter 6. There, we explain data structures that explicitly represent smaller or larger neighborhood information in meshes which enables a significant speed-up for operations like mesh deformations.

Correction Inspired by Polygon Modeling Besides a polygonal mesh also the mesh of a parametric surface, such as a B-spline surface, fitted to the segmentation result, may be employed for local correction. One of the first dedicated efforts to interactively correct segmentation results employed such a parametric surface [Jackowski *et al.*, 1999].

The development of *correction tools* for segmentation meshes was strongly inspired by polygon modeling in computer graphics, in particular from character generation for entertainment. Besides striking similarities, there is, of course, one essential difference, namely that correction is applied to match measured medical image data instead of just following artistic or esthetic considerations.

In polygon modeling, the Laplacian modeling framework is widely used [Lipman *et al.*, 2005]. Each vertex $\overrightarrow{v_i}$ is transformed in differential coordinates $\overrightarrow{\delta_i}$ according to Equation 4.23. In this equation, $\overrightarrow{v_i}$ is a vertex, $N(i)$ is the 1-ring neighborhood of that vertex (contains all vertices connected to $\overrightarrow{v_i}$ via an edge), and $deg(i)$ is the number of neighbors. Thus, the differential coordinate $\overrightarrow{\delta_i}$ represents the displacement vector between a vertex and the average of its 1-ring neighbors.

$$\overrightarrow{\delta_i} = \overrightarrow{v_i} - \frac{1}{deg(i)} \sum_{j \in N(i)} \overrightarrow{v_j} \tag{4.23}$$

This representation is used for object manipulation taking into account constraints, e.g., parts of the object should not be modified. One problem that may arise with all kinds of mesh-based correction tools is that the modifications may be severe and require not only to translate vertices but to *remesh* them locally. This problem arises, if the user cuts a mesh or deforms it strongly leading to degenerated triangles. We discuss remeshing briefly in the context of mesh simplification and mesh smoothing (§ 6.7.1).

At the mesh level, correction tools were developed

- to redraw contours,
- to bulge a shape,
- to pick and drag meshes, and
- to transform the centerline.

We describe examples for each of these correction tools.

Redraw The *sketch tool* makes it possible to redraw the contour locally. While such facility is widely available, an advanced realization transforms the user-drawn contour to a spline curve to ensure a smooth contour. This is particularly important if the previously applied segmentation technique generated a smooth boundary. The Laplacian modeling framework supports the interaction with the traction and sketch tool. The spline mode is also useful to yield smooth contours with the traction tool [Kang *et al.*, 2004].

Bulge Tool A bulge tool was introduced by Timinger *et al.* [2003]. They employed a circle or sphere and each vertex touched by the bulge tool was projected to the circle or sphere. The *bulge tool* developed by Proksch *et al.* [2010] (see Fig. 4.33) is similarly moved along the contour to bulge it, like elastic material can be easily deformed if touched with a certain pressure. The size of the sphere tool determines the amount of changes—a small tool better supports fine-grained manipulation.

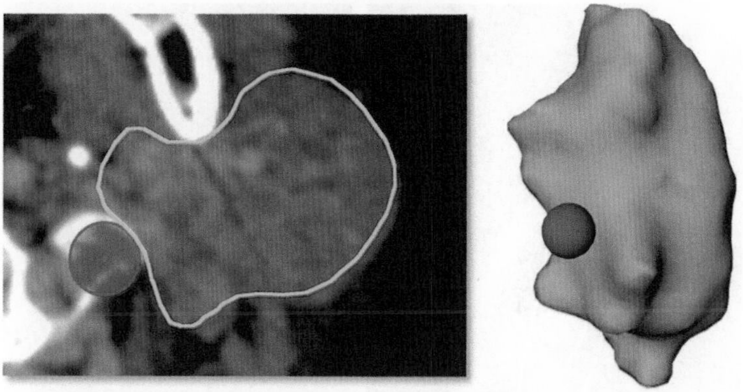

FIGURE 4.33 *A sphere-shaped bulge tool in 2D and 3D is shown to locally deform an object shape and thus to refine a segmentation result (Courtesy of Daniel Proksch. See also [Proksch et al., 2010]).*

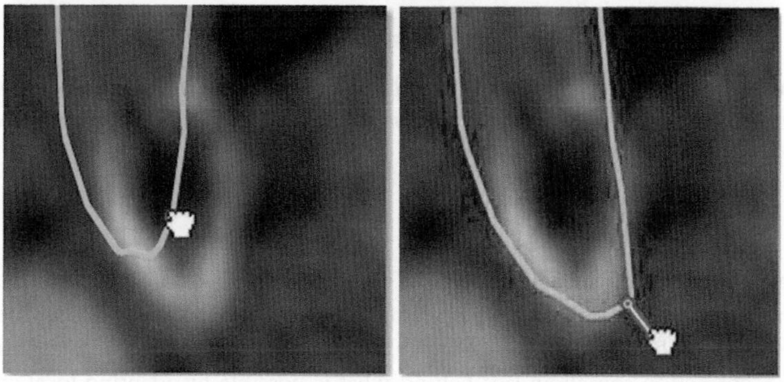

FIGURE 4.34 *A point is dragged and a certain part of the contour is adapted appropriately. A smooth transition between the modified part of the contour and the remaining one is essential (From: [Proksch et al., 2010]).*

Pick and Drag A tool to pick and drag contours enables users to move a selected point such that the contour follows [Kang et al., 2004, Schwarz et al., 2008]. The modification is restricted to a certain portion of the contour the size of which may be interactively adjusted, e.g., by rotating the mouse wheel [Proksch et al., 2010] (see Fig. 4.34).

The direction of the contour movement corresponds to the displacement vector that represents the movement of the control point. The influence of the dragging movement to the contour should naturally be reduced with increasing distance. Kang et al. [2004] discussed the use of different functions to model this reduced influence. A Gaussian is an obvious and useful choice [Schwarz et al., 2008].

Tools to Transform the Centerline The idea to correct segmentation results via transformations of the centerline is inspired by the wide use of skeleton-based modeling in graphics tools, in particular for character modeling [Kho and Garland, 2005]. Proksch et al. [2010] introduced a *bending tool* that allows to modify the local centerline. The object shape is adapted to this modification. The sketch tool for redrawing the contour and the bending tool are shown in Figure 4.35.

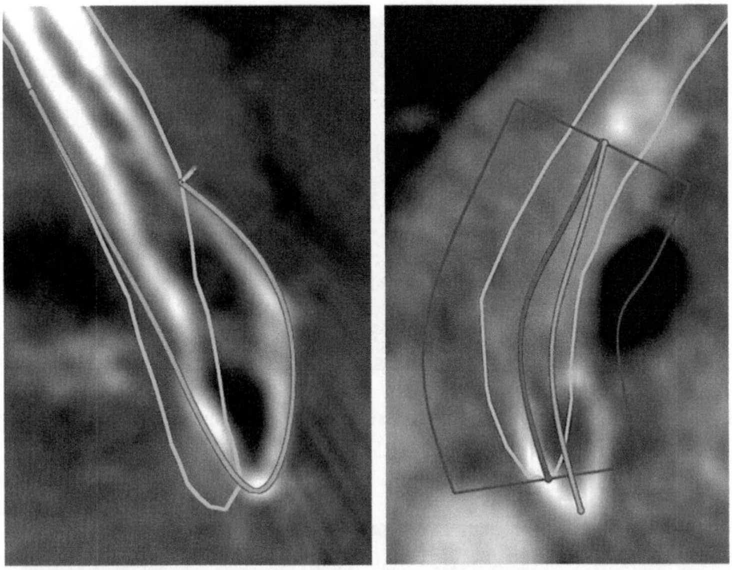

FIGURE 4.35 *The sketch tool (left) and the bending tool (right) provide further support for correcting segmentation results. The bending tool is particularly effective for elongated shapes where only a reference curve, e.g., the centerline is modified instead of the whole shape (Courtesy of Daniel Proksch. See also [Proksch et al., 2010]).*

Combining Image Features and Interactive Changes The tools described so far are rather intuitive but their effectiveness could be improved by analyzing local image features. While the original segmentation method might have used features like expected intensity values, gradient magnitude and curvature, extensively, purely interactive correction somehow lags behind what is possible by adapting local changes to image features. The first effort in this direction was performed by Timinger *et al.* [2003]. They refined a traction tool to be used in combination with an active contour model and integrated user input as additional term in the energy minimization process. An influential paper that described a general approach to such advanced correction was published in [Grady and Funka-Lea, 2006].

The editing approach also used the *affinity graph* (recall § 4.4.4 and [Grady, 2006]). Also the specific affinity computation is the same (recall Eq. 4.11). As further input, they employ the pre-segmentation, i.e., a binary mask. Finally, the editing operations are represented as seed points that either enforce the seed point to be included in the segmentation (F) or excluded (B). The affinity term, the pre-segmentation and the edit operations are integrated in an energy functional that also contains weights to control the influence of each of them. The minimization of this functional leads to a correction that considers both not only the previous segmentation and the edit operation, but also image features. This basic strategy had to be refined to also ensure that edit operations only have a local influence as we have discussed, e.g., for the traction tool. Grady and Funka-Lea [2006] suggest to weight the pre-segmentation strength with the distance to all seed points. Figure 4.36 shows an example of this approach. It can be clearly seen that the final result corresponds to the pre-segmentation in regions far away from the seed points and that the correction nicely adapts to the gradients in the data.

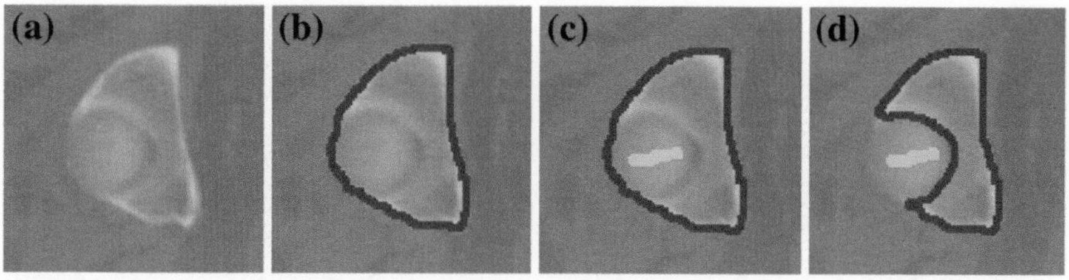

FIGURE 4.36 *This series of images shows from left to right: a slice of the original data, the pre-segmentation (blue), the correction performed by a yellow scribble to exclude that portion from the segmentation and the final result (From: [Grady and Funka-Lea, 2006]).*

4.6.3 INTERACTIVE MORPHOLOGICAL IMAGE PROCESSING

After we explained the mesh-based modification of segmentation results, we now describe the modification of the binary segmentation result as the second possible level for correction.

Threshold-based and region-oriented segmentation methods often produce such binary results. Examples for the necessity of a correction are erroneous holes within a segmentation result. If, for example, a tumor with a central necrosis occurs, region growing typically would not include the central necrosis, although it should be part of the tumor segmentation result.[6] Another frequent example are holes in the segmentation of trabecular bones [Kang *et al.*, 2004]. The use of morphological filters to enhance such segmentation problems is probably the oldest strategy for interactive correction of segmentation results [Hoehne *et al.*, 1992].

Morphological Image Processing Segmentation results can often be enhanced by morphological filters [Soille and Talbot, 2001]. Morphological filters add or remove voxels inside or from the border. Such filters operate on binary masks. Similar to noise reduction filters, morphological filters are described by a kernel matrix with a certain size. The elements, however, are restricted to be 1 or 0 to produce binary results.

Erosion and Dilation The simplest morphological filters are *erosion* and *dilation*. Erosion with a 3×3 kernel with all elements set to 1 removes all pixels, which have a neighbor pixel outside the segmentation result and hence shrink the segmentation. Typically, erosion is used to remove erroneous ("false") connections between regions. In contrast, dilation grows the segmentation along the boundary (thus closes holes and bumps in the boundary).

Opening and closing Since erosion and dilation reduce or increase the segmentation, *opening* and *closing* filters are introduced that maintain the overall size. *Opening* consists of an erosion and a subsequent dilation. Note that the image really changes with these two operations; dilation is not exactly the inverse transformation of erosion. For example, a 2×2 square would be completely removed in the erosion process and does not re-appear in the dilation. Also, small connections between parts of a segmentation result are removed. In general, opening is employed to remove small objects and to reduce convex bulges. As an example, Kuhnigk *et al.* [2006] employ opening for tumor segmentation to remove connections to adjacent vessels. This concept is very flexible: Kuhnigk *et al.* [2006] describe a *smart opening* where the size of the opening kernel is adjusted to the tumor shape and the surrounding, which is analyzed by casting rays from a central seed point and computing distances to the boundary of the initial segmentation result.

6 A necrosis describes the death of cells in an organ or tissue caused by disease or injury.

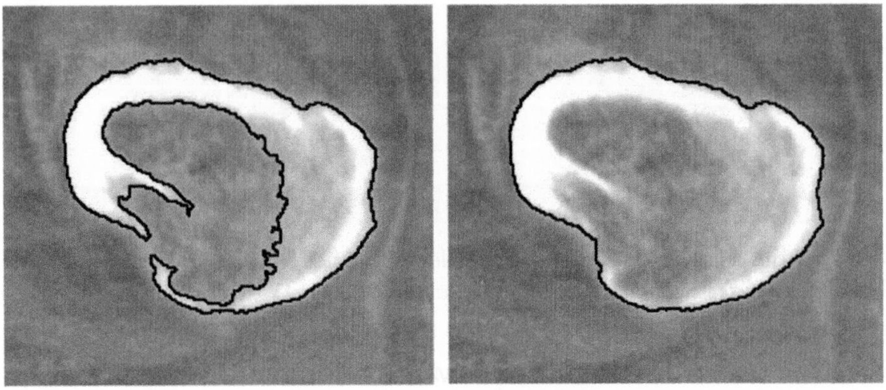

FIGURE 4.37 *A modified close filter is able to fill holes that are only partially enclosed by the segmentation (left). Threshold-based segmentation of bones in CT data frequently leads to such situations (From: [Kang et al., 2004]).*

Closing, on the other hand, dilates the segmentation result first and erodes it subsequently. Closing fills concave notches and closes (small) holes. Other parts of the segmentation result remain unchanged. This often enables to add a central necrosis to a tumor segmentation. However, closing is a difficult procedure in practice, since it only works correctly if the segmentation result contains *complete holes* without any connection to the surrounding. To cope with situations where the hole is connected to the surrounding like a cave, a number of variants of the simple closing were introduced. As an example, Kang *et al.* [2004] introduce a hole-filling tool that computes rays from the center of a hole in various directions and record how many of these rays hit the segmentation result. If this is true for most of them, e.g., for 65%, they consider this a hole to be closed (see Fig. 4.37).

Note that the morphological filter kernels ("structure elements") may not be a fully set $N \times N$ matrix to achieve specific result shapes. In these cases, we speak of *active* and *inactive* kernel entries. The application of morphologic operations may depend on certain conditions (referred to as, e.g., conditional dilation, conditional erosion). For complex segmentation tasks, such conditional morphological filters are essential. Krekel *et al.* [2006] describe a comprehensive system for the planning of shoulder implants in the shoulder, and use morphological filters in a pipeline for segmenting the relevant skeletal structures.

4.6.4 INTERACTION TECHNIQUES FOR SEMI-AUTOMATIC SEGMENTATION

In the following, we discuss selected interaction techniques and interaction problems related to widespread semi-automatic segmentation techniques that were introduced earlier in this chapter. Region-based techniques, such as region growing and watershed segmentation, require the user to set markers in the first stage (initialization). This process is usually performed in the 2D slices, often with a cross-hair cursor to support precise selection. The markers are often displayed slightly larger than a pixel to enable better recognition. If markers in different slices are selected, an overview is desirable to indicate which slices contain markers.

Interaction Techniques for Region Growing In the second stage—parameter setting—region growing benefits from dedicated support for thresholding. A diagram that indicates the size of the segmentation result for a range of thresholds (see Fig. 4.38) is useful to enable the user to predict the segmentation result [Selle *et al.*, 2002]. The creation of this *threshold-volume diagram* requires that the algorithm has been initiated for all integer values in a certain interval (recall § 4.3.4). With this feature, users can deliberately specify a

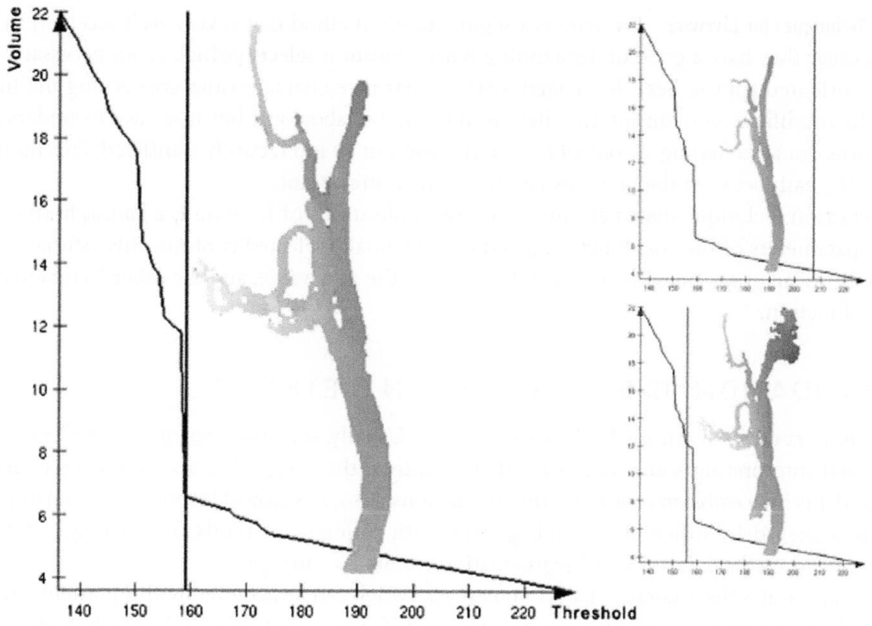

FIGURE 4.38 *For a range of intensity values the volume of the segmented structure is displayed in the threshold-volume diagram. With the vertical bar the user can specify a threshold. The visualization result is shown as a point cloud (From: [Boskamp et al., 2004]).*

threshold that prevents that the segmentation leaks into surrounding structures. Reasonable candidates can be identified as locations of large steps in the threshold curve.

Interaction Techniques for Watershed Segmentation The basic interaction of image segmentation with the watershed transform is to specify include and exclude markers. On the one hand, it is easy for users to specify which point belongs to the target structure and which does not. On the other hand, it is often difficult to estimate how many include and exclude markers have to be specified until a reasonable result is achieved. Similar to region growing, the user cannot force the boundary to be at a particular location where he or she expects the boundary to be.

Another issue of watershed segmentation is the difficulty of predicting the effects of the specification of include and exclude points. Under unfavorable conditions, the following sequence of interactions arises: the user specifies (several) markers in slice S_1 until a desired segmentation in this slice is achieved. The user moves to another slice S_2 and recognizes that the target structure is not well segmented. Again, include and exclude markers are specified until the result is satisfying in S_2. The user goes back to slice S_1 to assess the effect of the new include and exclude markers on the segmentation result there (which was satisfying before) and notices that the recently added markers resulted in a poor segmentation result of S_1. If the user—without actually understanding the underlying algorithm—has this experience, he or she might have no idea how to achieve a satisfying result in all slices. Although this frustrating scenario is not common—often a single include and a single exclude point are sufficient for segmentation—it may happen.

Interaction Techniques for Livewire Livewire is a segmentation method that is very well accepted by medical doctors because they have a good understanding what contour it selects (which is not necessarily true for the region-oriented approaches). In general, livewire has nice characteristics concerning the interactive control. The modification of an intermediate result may be laborious, but it is easy to understand. If a contour turns out to be wrong, a control (or seed) point can be interactively translated. This modification influences the path between the previous and the next control point.

An interaction technique that is essential for new applications of livewire is a *learning function* that estimates the parameters of the cost function based on a manually selected contour. This estimation process considers the mean gray value, the standard deviation of the gray value, and the other factors that are part of the cost function.

4.7 VALIDATION OF SEGMENTATION METHODS

Validation is a crucial issue in medical image analysis. Usually, scientists perform "their" validation, by analyzing and interpreting some data. For other scientists, the image data and reference is usually not available and it is impossible to reproduce the conclusions. Also, it is almost impossible to reliably compare the quality achieved by different research groups with different methods. Fortunately, databases that provide access to medical datasets and segmentation results are emerging.

Validation indicates the accuracy of a given method, which can be achieved with a particular segmentation method. The design of a study to assess accuracy is difficult, in particular, if the result strongly depends on user interactions or careful choices with respect to many parameters of an automatic algorithm. Validation is carried out primarily for automatic segmentation or for automatic support in semi-interactive segmentation methods (such as the influence of shape-based interpolation on the accuracy of livewire, recall [Schenk *et al.*, 2000].

If segmentation results primarily depend on a user-selected threshold (flooding level, intensity or gradient threshold) validation studies are carried out to evaluate the sensitivity of the parameter. If very similar results would have been obtained with slightly different parameter values, it is likely that different users would gain similar results.

4.7.1 PHANTOM STUDIES VERSUS CLINICAL DATA

For a validation, a representative sample of segmentation results is required. The size of the required sample depends on

- the variability of the target structure,
- the variability of surrounding structures that may influence the segmentation, and
- the variability of the image acquisition parameters.

Validation studies include clinical data and phantoms. In principle, a validation study with clinical data can be better transferred to the real clinical use. However, validations performed by researchers are often restricted to data with an excellent quality that are not generally available and do not include relevant pathologies. In such cases, the evaluation only indicates an upper bound for the performance of an algorithm under perfect circumstances.

Hardware and Software Phantoms Phantoms, on the other hand, are artificial data, which exhibit characteristics similar to real data. This similarity relates to size, location and overall shape of target structures. Phantoms may be physical artifacts that are imaged by CT or MRI to obtain a digital representation. An alternative is the use of *phantoms* where the *ground truth* is available. The challenge is to develop phantoms that are realistic enough to permit conclusions about segmentation accuracy for real data.

A more flexible strategy is to create *software phantoms* by means of geometric modeling software. Physical phantoms play an essential role in medical imaging where they are used to verify an imaging device and calibrate its parameters. They are also increasingly used to verify algorithms and software libraries, where they are appreciated based on the ground truth they provide.

Measurements are performed to analyze whether the known geometry, e.g., of a sphere, is correctly represented. Software phantoms may be used, e.g., to explore vascular trees with segments of varying parameters, branching angles and branching types. Phantom data may be flexibly parameterized with respect to noise levels and noise distribution, inhomogeneity artifacts and image resolution. Thus, they allow to simulate many aspects of the variability of the images. Experiments with such software phantoms are often referred to as *in silico* experiments.

Modified Clinical Data are often a viable trade-off that combines the flexibility of phantom data and the authenticity of clinical data. A modification of the noise level, for example, by adding different types and different levels of noise enables a simulation of different acquisition parameters. Such modifications are useful to draw conclusions on the noise level for which (still) acceptable results may be expected. A reasonable strategy is to use a very high-quality dataset with a high resolution and to degrade the image quality by adding noise or transforming it to lower resolution.

Validation studies target at quantitative expressions concerning the accuracy. For this purpose, *validation metrics* are required to compare the results achieved with different segmentation methods. It is desirable to use several metrics and thus to study different aspects of accuracy. Which aspect is particularly important and which level of accuracy is acceptable depends strongly on the specific application. As mentioned before, accuracy is more important, if segmentation is the basis for quantitative analysis. It is difficult to make a general statement concerning the accuracy requirements for visualization purposes. If the local neighborhood of a tumor is evaluated, the visible border surfaces should correctly reflect the spatial relations. If on the other hand, the location of a tumor inside a larger organ shall be evaluated, the requirements for the accuracy of the organ segmentation are reduced.

4.7.2 VALIDATION METRICS

Validation metrics refer to distances between segmentation results or to volume overlaps between the *gold standard* and the (new) segmentation method. The *gold standard*, typically, is a high-quality reference segmentation carried out by an expert, although it is not perfectly accurate, and reliable.

Distance and Volume-based Measures Distances between contours or boundary surfaces allow to assess worst case scenarios (maximum distance between surfaces), whereas the metrics based on the volume overlap represent average values. In the following, R denotes our reference segmentation and S denotes our segmentation with a new method. The following distance metrics are widespread:

- mean symmetric distance (avg). For the contour or surface of S the distances between each vertex and the closest vertex of R is calculated. Subsequently, for each vertex of R_i the distance to the closest vertex of S_k is computed. avg represents the mean value of these distances (Eq. 4.24).

$$d_{avg}(S, R) = \frac{\sum_{S_i} min_{R_k} d(S_i, R_k) + \sum_{R_k} min_{S_i} d(R_k, S_i)}{|S_i| + |R_k|} \tag{4.24}$$

- Hausdorff distance $d_{Hausdorff}$ (Eq. 4.25) which represents the maximum deviation between two contours or surfaces.

$$d_{Hausdorff}(S, R) = max(min\{d(S_i, R\}, min\{d(S, R_k)\}) \tag{4.25}$$

- Euclidean distance between the centers of gravity of S and R.

The above-described distance measures do not differentiate between over-segmentation, where S is constantly larger than R and under-segmentation, where S is smaller than R.

To evaluate the volume overlap, the Dice coefficient is a widespread measure. It computes the union of the volumes of R and S and relates it to the sum of the volumes of R and S (Eq. 4.26).

$$d_{Dice}(S, R) = \frac{2 * |S| \cap |R|}{|S| + |R|} \tag{4.26}$$

The $dice$ coefficient has values in the range of 0–1, with 1 representing perfect overlap.

The correlation between the results achieved with the above-mentioned metrics is rather low. In general, metrics that characterize the volume overlap lead to different assessments of the segmentation than surface distance measures. The two surface distance measures may also lead to different assessments. In general, several metrics should be employed in a validation. Zhang [1996] discusses also other validation metrics.

A promising validation strategy is to employ a collection of expert segmentations to account for the inter-observer variability. A good segmentation approach would generate results that are within the inter-observer variability. Warfield *et al.* [2002] and Maddah *et al.* [2004] described an approach where a probabilistic estimate of the "ground truth" is attempted with an expectation-maximization algorithm.

4.7.3 VALIDATION WITH PUBLIC DATABASES

Specialized databases with validated segmentation results greatly support validation and benchmarking. In recent years, considerable effort was spent on funding and developing databases with a sufficient number of datasets and all required information for validation.

An excellent example is the simulated brain database (http://www.bic.mni.mcgill.ca/brainweb/, [Collins *et al.*, 1998]). Another dedicated effort is the development of the lung image database consortium, which aims at stimulating the development of computer-aided detection algorithms for lung nodules in CT data [Armato *et al.*, 2004]. The lung image database was initiated by the National Cancer Institute in the United States (http://imaging.cancer.gov/programsandresources/InformationSystems/LIDC). According to a recent report [Armato *et al.*, 2011], data from 1018 patients containing 7371 lesions were collected from seven medical centers. Lesions were classified as nodules larger than 3 mm, nodules smaller than 3 mm and non-nodules in a standardized manner. More recently, the various MICCAI contests, e.g., on liver segmentation, knee segmentation and segmentation of coronary vasculature provide a common pool of test data with relevant pathologies and expert segmentations.

The Osteo-Arthritis Initiative (OAI), a large public-private partnership, aims at the development of quantitative image analysis of the knee joint and cartilage [Vincent *et al.*, 2010]. A large database is provided for public access: http://www.oai.ucsf.edu. It contains (August 2012) datasets of more than 4000 participants including baseline exams, several follow-up studies for a four-year period and questionnaires providing clinically relevant additional information.

4.8 REGISTRATION AND FUSION OF MEDICAL IMAGE DATA

Image registration is the process of aligning images so that corresponding features from different image data can easily be related [Hajnal *et al.*, 2001]. Image registration is an instance of an *inverse problem* where the transformation parameters are derived by the images [Fluck *et al.*, 2011]. In many clinical scenarios, it is crucial to mentally combine information related to the same patient extracted from different sources to draw conclusions. Registration is essential to compare image data and to analyze different image data in a common frame. The different image data often relate to the same patient but are acquired at different points in time, or they are acquired with different imaging modalities.

To name a few examples, where registration is required:

1. *Registration of image data acquired at different points in time.* In dynamic imaging, image data are acquired at different time points. An analysis of the dynamic processes, e.g., contrast agent uptake or metabolism, requires the correction of motion artifacts.

   Another kind of time-dependent data is generated within follow-up studies after initial treatment. It involves the acquisition of images at various stages, such as 3 months, 6 months, and 12 months after a therapy. The evaluation of these images involves a comparison, for example with respect to tumor growth. The anatomy may change during that period and the registration actually serves to analyze such a (potential) change.
2. *Multimodal registration.* A wide area of application is multimodal image registration where different acquisition techniques, such as CT and MRI, are used complementary.
3. *Registration of pre- and intraoperative data.* Therapy monitoring is based on intraoperative imaging. It is essential to relate intraoperative data to analysis results derived from preoperative data. Together with navigation systems, a correct transformation of intraoperative data to preoperative data might be used to support the localization of a pathology. To emphasize that data of the same modality are registered, this is often referred to as *intramodality registration.*
4. *Atlas-based matching.* Finally, image registration is often employed to compare the data of a particular patient with an *atlas*, which represents normal anatomical variations.

The first three categories relate to data of the same patient (intra-patient registration), whereas the last category relates to the registration of data from different patients (inter-patient registration). Despite its importance, e.g., in a cohort study, we focus on intra-patient registration. We also do not discuss 2D-3D registration as it frequently occurs in the registration of pre- and intraoperative data. While preoperatively usually a 3D dataset was acquired, intraoperatively, 2D imaging, such as fluoroscopy and ultrasound, dominate.

The commonality of these different application areas is the need to geometrically adapt several images to each other or to some kind of model. The goal of image registration is to deform or transform one dataset to optimally match another dataset that provides different information as well as similar information. The dataset to which a (new) dataset is adapted is referred to as *reference image*. According to the common terminology, the images to be registered are here referred to as *template image* (a more expressive term, less frequently used is *floating image*).

There is a huge amount of scientific literature on image registration, including whole books on sub-classes of registration problems. Usually, single components of the registration process (transformations, similarity measures, optimization, interpolation, image representation) are considered in publications. Like in segmentation, there is no standard approach due to the large variety of registration problems.

Components of Registration Algorithms The registration problem can be formulated as follows: "Transform a template image dataset geometrically such that it fits optimally to a given reference image under a given aspect". This problem statement contains several components:

- *Geometric transformation* of voxel coordinates.
- *Fitting* based on a similarity measure.
- "Optimally." The transformation should be accomplished such that the similarity measure is maximized.
- "A given aspect." The criteria for optimal matching are chosen such that particular structures are matched as good as possible. As an example, the goal might be to match vascular structures, or skeletal structures, or organs from multimodal images. It is essential to note that optimal correspondence with respect to a given aspect is often achieved at the expense of other aspects. In a follow-up study, it is essential not to match the pathologies, such as tumors, to each other. By doing so, they are enforced to be as similar as possible and the development of the tumor cannot be analyzed. Thus, a common assumption is that corresponding points and structures are used as boundary conditions for the registration.

4.8.1 TRANSFORMATION

"Global" and "local" transformations are discriminated. In both cases, after transformation an interpolation step is required to map the transformed voxels to a regular grid with integer-value coordinates.

Global Transformations Global transformations are employed to correct simple movements or as a first step before a local transformation. With increasing complexity, we can discriminate *rigid*, *affine*, and *polynomial transformations*. Rigid transformations only rotate and translate the template image. Affine transformations also include anisotropic scaling (different scaling factors in each dimension) and shearing with additional degrees of freedom. Rigid and affine transformations are realized by a matrix multiplication where the individual transformations are multiplied resulting in one 4×4 matrix that is applied to all coordinates. Polynomial transformations are often realized by means of thin plate splines. Rigid transformations are usually not sufficient to compensate complex organ motion and deformation, as they occur for example due to breathing and heart beat in abdominal regions. However, they maintain the geometry which is desirable in certain situations, e.g., in neuroanatomy where only limited movements occur.

Local Transformations These transformations are described by a *large* set of parameters that characterize locally different movements. As an example, when images are registered, that were acquired at different points in time, breathing and muscle relaxation lead to various movements that affects different tissue types in a characteristic way.

The most precise registration may be achieved by computing an optimum transformation for every voxel of the template image. Since, this often is prohibitive with respect to the computational effort, often a coarser resolution is used. This gave rise to meshes of control points that are interpreted as part of a Bezier or B-spline mesh. Thus, the transformation between the control points is assumed to change continuously and it is computed using interpolation, e.g., with a tricubic function. The density of these control points affects the number of parameters and thus the computational effort of the optimization.

Modifications of a single parameter (control point) affect only a local neighborhood. Examples for local transformations are cubic B-spline transformations [Rueckert *et al.*, 1999] and Bézier transformations [Otte, 2001]. They are appreciated because they represent smooth transformations (cubic splines are C^2

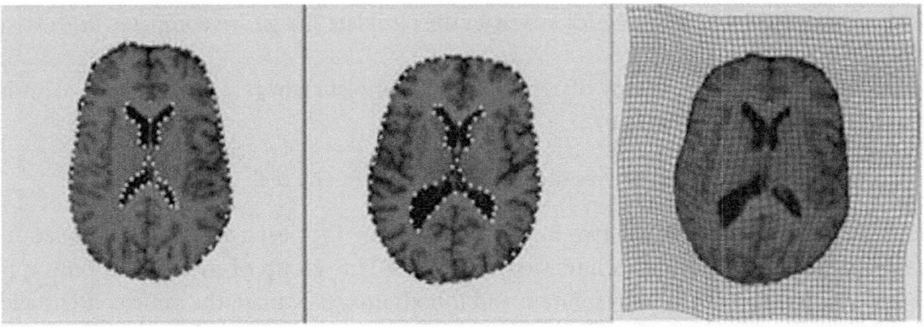

FIGURE 4.39 *A number of point landmarks characterizing the human brain and the ventricles in the reference and template image (left, middle) guides the registration. The local transformation that provides the best match between the landmarks is shown on the right by superimposing the grid of the B-spline transformation (From: [Xie and Farin, 2004]).*

continuous[7]) and exhibit a local behavior. These properties are also favorable for image registration. Figure 4.39 illustrates B-spline grid and the effects of a local transformation. The grid display may also serve for quality control, since it conveys the amount of deformation in each region of the image. These geometric transformations are widely used in computer graphics and in particular in geometric modeling. Among their applications in medicine is *computational anatomy*, a discipline that explores anatomical shapes and their variance in a systematic manner [Grenander and Miller, 1998, Miller, 2004]. The registration of anatomical structures, e.g., brain areas, from different persons to each other is at the core of computational anatomy.

Other local approaches utilize elastic models [Christensen, 1994, 1999, 2001, Rohr *et al.*, 2001] or fluid models to characterize movements [Bro-Nielsen and Gramkow, 1996, Bro-Nielsen, 1996]. The numeric solution of these models is computationally expensive, since it is based on solving partial differential equations.

Interpolation After applying a transformation to the coordinates of each voxel of the template image, usually non-integer values arise. Thus, the voxels are no longer placed at a regular grid. The distances between adjacent voxels have changed such that some of them are now close together, whereas gaps may arise in other regions of the data. Therefore, a *resampling* is necessary to map the template image to a regular grid with the same dimension as the reference image.

Resampling denotes that an interpolation at each grid point is performed. The simplest interpolation scheme is "nearest neighbor interpolation," where for each voxel of the final grid the value of the nearest neighbor (according to the Euclidean distance metric) is chosen. This simple strategy is not appropriate, since some voxels would be chosen several times, e.g., where the distance between neighbors increased and others would not be chosen at all. More advanced local interpolation schemes, such as trilinear or tricubic interpolation, take a certain number of voxels in the neighborhood into account and weight their influence depending on the distance. However, any kind of resampling induces a certain error. Depending on the chosen interpolation kernel, the image often appears smoothed after resampling.

4.8.2 FITTING

Similarity measures characterize how similar two images are. Basically, similarity measures based on intensities of voxels and based on geometric measures are distinguished:

7 A curve is C^n continuous if the nth derivative does not exhibit any discontinuity. A polynomial curve of degree n is at most $n-1$ continuous.

- *Intensity-based similarity*. Gray values of voxels in the template image are compared with voxels in the reference image.
- *Geometry-based similarity*. Positions of voxels in the template image are compared to those in the reference image [Rohr, 2001].

There are three categories of *intensity-based similarity measures* [Roche *et al.*, 1999]:

- *Voxel-based*. The intensities of the two images are compared for each voxel in a 1:1 relation, e.g., by computing the sum of squared intensity differences. This group of measures is only applicable if the two images have the same resolution and if both images contain the same content with similar intensities, e.g., time-dependent data with limited motion artifacts, such as cerebral perfusion. This assumption is not fulfilled in multimodal registration.
- *Statistic*. The normalized correlation of intensities in both images is computed. The application of this measure also requires that the same content is represented in both images. Linear transformations of intensity values can be compensated.
- *Entropy-based*. These measures are based on information theory. The mutual information [Viola, 1995, Maes *et al.*, 1997a] of the common 2D histogram of both images is computed. Normalized mutual information is a similarity metric that may be used even if the content of the images is slightly different [Studholme, 1997]. The relationship between the intensity values may be statistical. Registration based on normalized mutual information is able to match multimodal image data, such as CT and MRI.

While these similarity measures are computed automatically, the determination of anatomical landmarks in the template image as well as in the reference image, typically, requires user input. The automatic localization of corresponding landmarks is difficult. Branching points of vascular trees and sulcal landmarks in the brain are appropriate [Aylward and Bullitt, 2002, Tschirren *et al.*, 2002]. We discussed landmark extraction already with respect to the generation of point distribution models for segmentation with statistical shape models (recall § 4.5.3). Although we require less landmarks for registration, the process is similarly demanding.

Intensity-based and similarity-based registration are also combined [Johnson and Christensen, 2002]. Normalized-mutual information is the most frequently used similarity measure in particular for multimodal registration. However, the use of this measure has also considerable drawbacks [Haber and Modersitzki, 2005]. Typically, it has many local minima, which make the optimization process difficult.

Geometry-based Similarity The most frequently used similarity measure relates to corresponding *point landmarks*, either automatically determined or specified by a user. Branchings of vascular structures and other prominent anatomical features, such as tip of the nose, serve as point landmarks. The number of required pairs of landmarks depends on the transformation type. For a rigid transformation, four pairs of corresponding landmarks in the reference and the template images are necessary to determine all parameters (the landmarks may not be located at the same plane). For affine transformations, two more pairs of landmarks are necessary. If more than the required number of corresponding landmarks is available, an approximative solution is computed. Often, the Levenberg-Marquardt algorithm [Dennis and Schnabel, 1983] is employed for this purpose. It computes the transformation t with the least squared error (Eq. 4.27). P_r and P_t are the two sets of corresponding landmarks.

$$D(t) = \sum_i = 1^m \|t\left(P_r^i\right) - P_t^i\|^2 \tag{4.27}$$

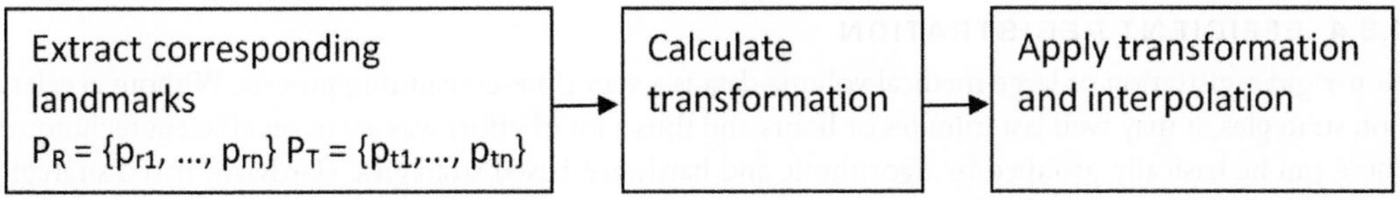

FIGURE 4.40 *Scheme of landmark-based image registration based on the sets of landmarks P_r for the reference image and P_t for the template image (Adapted From: [Hennemuth, 2012]).*

For the maximization of the selected similarity measure a numerical optimizer is used to approximate "optimal" transformation parameters. Numerical optimization is either applied to the similarity values, for example simplex, Powell or Hooke approach, or considers also derived information [Maes *et al.*, 1997b]. Figure 4.40 illustrates the steps to be accomplished during landmark-based registration.

Discussion It is difficult to judge and compare registration methods. On the one hand, they should provide an optimal match of landmarks or intensity-based features. On the other hand, they should not change the template image "too much." Thus, a human expert is needed to judge the results. As an example, a simple rigid transformation ensures that the volume of a structure does not change. However, it is often too simple to provide a sufficiently good match.

Local registration processes are often guided by some constraints. For example, the volume of certain tissue, e.g., a tumor in perfusion data, should be preserved. Without constraints, arbitrary deformations may arise that lead to misleading visualizations. For example with contrast-enhanced perfusion data, some bright spots become larger over time as a consequence of the wash-in behavior. Unconstrained registration would try to match smaller and larger spots by scaling the region correspondingly. Volume-preserving registration is often desirable [Haber and Modersitzki, 2004, Rohlfing *et al.*, 2003].

In the clinical routine, landmark-based registration is primarily used for aligning pre- and postoperative imaging. This is probably due to the fact that with this kind of registration it is relatively easy to control which regions of the target image are mapped to certain portions of the reference image.

4.8.3 MODEL-BASED REGISTRATION

When we discussed image segmentation, we got to know very flexible general techniques that are employed for a large variety of segmentation problems. On the other hand, we learnt that a high level of automation might be possible by taking *model assumptions* related to shape, location and intensity distributions into account. In a similar way, registration may benefit from specific assumptions related to movements and deformations that might be expected. Intramodality registration, for example, is used to compensate for effects due to heartbeat, breathing, muscle relaxation, tumor growth and so forth. Considerable effort was spent on modeling such movements to restrict the transformations to those that are possible and likely. As an example, Werner *et al.* [2010] modeled breathing-related movements in the thorax region to achieve a fast and reliable registration of dynamic CT thorax data. This research has a practical relevance, since it enables to adjust radiation treatment of a bronchial carcinoma to that movement instead of applying radiation to a much larger area where the tumor may occur at a certain point in the breathing cycle.

Model assumptions, thus regularize a registration problem and may lead to an appropriate behavior even in case of artifacts or severe noise. As a drawback, however, if any assumption is not fulfilled, the registration may fail.

4.8.4 EFFICIENT REGISTRATION

Non-rigid registration of large medical volume data is a very time-consuming process. Without acceleration strategies, it may well last minutes or hours and thus a lot of effort was spent on efficient techniques. These can be basically grouped in algorithmic and hardware-based strategies. Hardware-based strategies aim at parallelization and often in particular on efficiently using the GPU with its ability to perform tasks in a highly parallel manner.

Algorithmic Acceleration of Image Registration Among the software strategies to improve computation times, multi-resolution techniques and related hierarchical approaches are prominent. Multi-resolution strategies compute image pyramids related to the reference and the template image. Thus, for both images, a number of more and more coarsely related variants are computed, e.g., with a wavelet transform. The registration is first performed at the top level with coarse images and the transformation determined at one level is employed to initialize the registration at the next level, leading to faster convergence.

A related strategy is to adaptively refine the control grid of a B-spline or Bezier transform. At the highest level an initial transform for a $4 \times 4 \times 4$ control grid is determined. The control grid is adaptively refined only in those subvolumes where the registration error extends a threshold [Xie and Farin, 2004]. Thus, only for a few selected regions of the dataset where actually large deformations occur, a fine control grid is needed. Besides accelerating the registration, it avoids unnecessarily large deformations.

GPU-based Registration The operations necessary for registration may be significantly accelerated by means of graphics hardware. Even the first variants of programmable graphics hardware could be used for registration [Soza *et al.*, 2002, Hastreiter *et al.*, 2004]. Meanwhile, the increased floating point accuracy and the increased flexibility of GPUs enable even better support. As a first step, image histograms may be computed on the GPU as a basis for similarity computation, e.g., with mutual information [Fluck *et al.*, 2011].

For interactive registration, primarily global transformations are employed. Several attempts have been made to accelerate local registration by employing either graphics hardware [Soza *et al.*, 2002] or a parallel computer [Ferrant *et al.*, 2001], [Ruiz-Alzola *et al.*, 2002]. Another alternative is to employ a priori knowledge relating to the specific question. As an example, Azar *et al.* [2002] employ a model for breast deformations to accelerate local registration.

To support the transformation stage, the template image is loaded in the texture memory. Global transformations are applied to the coordinates of this texture [Fluck *et al.*, 2011]. Non-rigid transformations are more difficult to accomplish with the GPU. In their survey, Fluck *et al.* [2011] describe such approaches. The first of these techniques employed regularized gradient flow—an energy-minimizing optimization [Strzodka *et al.*, 2004, Köhn *et al.*, 2006]. Meanwhile, a number of other registration techniques are available as GPU implementations. According to Fluck *et al.* [2011], the CUDA language is primarily used for recent GPU implementations of registration techniques. In recent years, also MATLAB and JAVA users benefit from GPU support in CUDA, e.g., for segmentation and registration.

4.8.5 VISUALIZATION

Visualization is essential to verify registration results and to display the fused image data. Both visualization tasks are challenging, since the underlying data is more complex compared to image segmentation.

Verification of Registration Results While in segmentation verification may be achieved by a simple overlay of original data and segmentation results, we face more complex data in registration. In general, it is difficult to understand and verify the registration process. Checkerboard visualizations are frequently used to evaluate the registration accuracy in different portions of the data (see Stokking *et al.* [2003] for many examples). König and Peitgen [2005] discussed visualization techniques to convey the locally different amount and direction of transformation in a non-rigid local registration. This local examination is often essential because a correct transformation in certain parts of an image, e.g., where a tumor occurs, is more important than in others. Such techniques need to be refined and employed to increase the acceptance of advanced registration techniques.

Integrated Visualization of Registered Image Data Once the target image is transformed to the reference image, all image data can be explored in an integrated visualization. For the discussion of this integration we will refer to both image data as *source images*. Most integrated visualization techniques also serve for verification purposes.

Stokking *et al.* [2003] provided a comprehensive review of visualization techniques for fused image data, including a discussion of their clinical applicability and acceptance. According to them, the majority of authors introduced 2D visualization techniques. While in the conventional (single source) display of medical image data, gray scales prevail, fused visualization usually relies on the additional perceptual capacity of color vision. For color fusion, both the technically oriented RGB color space as well as the perceptually motivated HSV and HLS color spaces (recall § 3.3.2) were frequently used. With such techniques, one source image (either the template or the reference image) is mapped to one component of these spaces and one or two of the remaining components are employed for the other. As an example Stokking *et al.* [2001] mapped MRI data to the value component of the HSV space and the registered SPECT data to the hue and saturation component. The HLS space was used for the fused display ofT1-weighted and T2-weighted MRI data (for an early example, see [Weiss *et al.*, 1987]). For the same purpose, also color schemes derived from the RGB space were employed [Alfano *et al.*, 1995].

Selective and Non-selective Integration Stokking *et al.* [2003] make a useful distinction in their review. They consider a visualization technique to be *selective* when the display of (at least) one source image is restricted to regions where a certain condition is fulfilled. This condition may be an interval of intensity values or may relate to derived data, such as image gradients. In practice, however, it is more often related to a segmentation result, e.g., the brain. A selective integration may also achieved interactively, e.g., by using a lens-based exploration tool (see Fig. 4.41). On the other hand, *non-selective imaging* maps all pixels of both source images to the fused output. The potential of selective techniques is to focus the display on the diagnostically relevant information. Among the applications for fused display of medical imaging data, imaging of the brain is the prevailing example. Thus, functional imaging with fMRI, PET and SPECT is often overlaid with anatomical image data. Selective integration in these situations is often performed by thresholding the functional data to emphasize high values (activated regions in fMRI data, or increased metabolism in PET data).

Integrated 3D Visualizations The generation of integrated 3D visualizations to be used on a 2D output device is particularly challenging. The information from many slices in two source images should be displayed in one projection and yield the most important information. In most systems providing such integrated 3D visualizations, clipping planes are used to restrict which portions are visible from the source images (see Fig. 4.42). Schiers *et al.* [1989] already provided two *multimodal cutting planes* to control the display of the CT and MRI data.

Neurosurgical interventions are an example where multimodal information, in particular CT and MRI data, is frequently acquired. The registration and integrated visualization of both image data provides an overview on soft tissue structures within the context of skeletal data (see Fig. 4.43). As final example, we present two integrated visualizations of PET and CT data. Due to its increased metabolism, a tumor in the

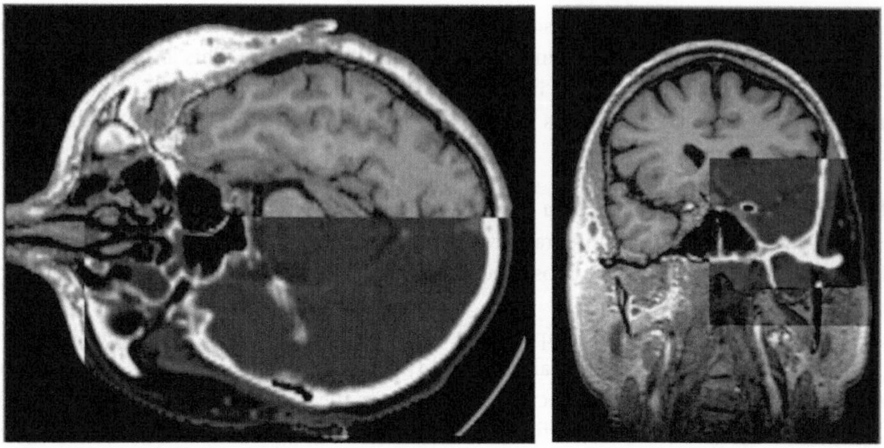

FIGURE 4.41 *Fusion of T1 weighted MRI and CT angiography data. Integrated and synchronized slice views are displayed and explored with a "fusion" lens (Courtesy of Peter Hastreiter, University of Erlangen-Nuremberg. See also [Hastreiter and Ertl, 1998]).*

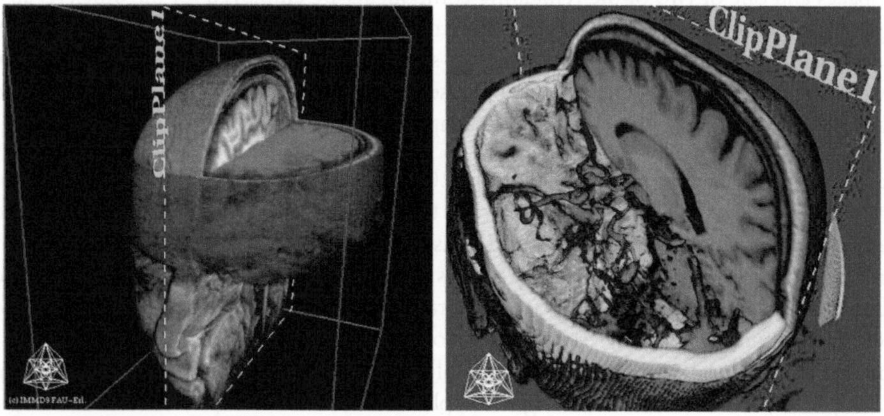

FIGURE 4.42 *Fusion of PET data showing a brain tumor, MRI data showing the brain tissue context and CT data for the exterior of the head. 3D visualizations are explored by means of clipping planes (Courtesy of Bastijn Vissers, Philips Healthcare. See also [Hastreiter and Ertl, 1998]).*

neck region is detected with PET data and integrated in a volume visualization of the skeletal structures based on CT data. The integrated visualization supports the localization of the tumor (see Fig. 4.44).

4.9 SUMMARY

In this chapter, we discussed a typical image analysis pipeline that processes medical volume data, such as CT and MRI data, and produces segmentation information for selective visualization or quantitative analysis. For clinically useful applications, it is a good strategy to attempt at automatic solutions that produce acceptable results in the majority of the cases. These solutions should be complemented by more general semi-automatic solutions for the remaining cases. Image analysis and visualization are closely connected

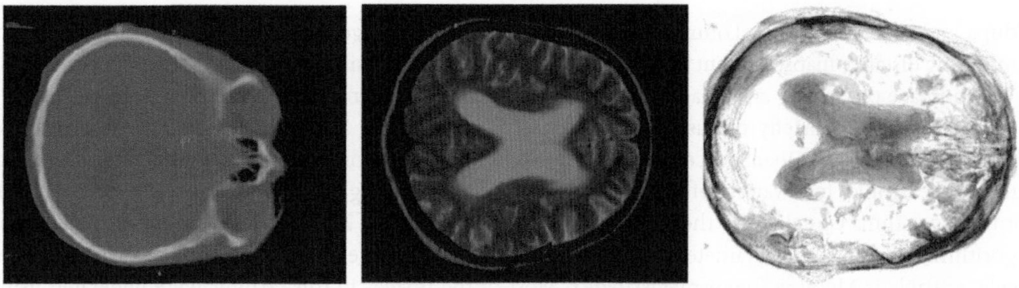

FIGURE 4.43 *The fusion of skeletal structures from CT (left) and cerebral soft tissue from MRI data (right) allows to generate integrated 3D visualizations highlighting the cerebrospinal fluid inside the skull (Courtesy of Matthias Keil, Fraunhofer Institute Darmstadt).*

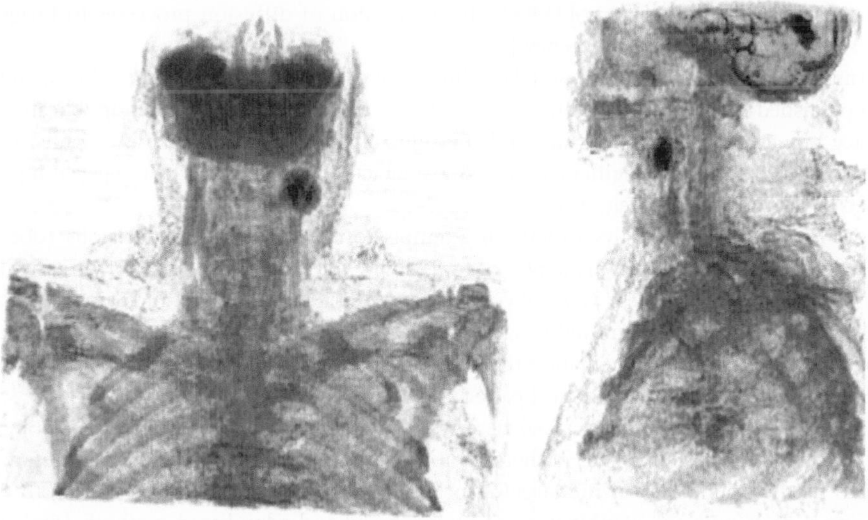

FIGURE 4.44 *Fusion of PET and CT data to convey the location of a neck tumor. The tumor is visualized based on its characteristic signal in PET data while the skeletal structures are extracted from CT data (Courtesy of Matthias Keil, Fraunhofer Institute Darmstadt).*

parts of computer support. Fast 3D visualization techniques are very useful to evaluate segmentation results. These visualizations might also be used to fine-tune the segmentation. On the other hand, segmentation is the prerequisite for high-quality visualizations of the relevant structures. While visualization techniques in general have a broad applicability, image analysis is necessarily more dependent on the specific data to which it is applied. As an example for a complex image analysis task, we discussed vessel analysis. We will revisit that topic in Chapter 11 on the visualization of vascular structures.

FURTHER READING

Many aspects of image analysis could only be touched in this chapter. Readers with interest in image analysis are referred to respective textbooks [Sonka and Fitzpatrick, 2000, Gonzales and Woods, 1998,

Udupa and Herman, 2000]. Lohmann [1998] focuses on 3D image analysis and efficient methods for computing distance maps. A recent textbook on medical image analysis is [Toennies, 2012]. We only briefly touched image processing and image analysis of ultrasound data. For a survey, see [Birkeland *et al.*, 2012].

Many algorithms briefly discussed in this chapter are available in dedicated software libraries. The platform-independent OpenSource project Insight Toolkit (ITK), for example, contains algorithms and annotated examples for a variety of segmentation tasks (www.itk.org). Yoo [2004] describes the concepts for the algorithms contained in the toolkit. Ibanez and Schroeder, [2005] explains how to assemble the algorithms and adjust the parameters appropriately. Another software library which is (in a basic version) freely available is MEVISLAB (www.mevislab.de). Most of the images in this chapter were generated using this platform.

Mathematical models of (pixel) noise in medical image data are discussed in [Hahn, 2005]. Macovski [1996] and McVeigh and Bronskill [1985] characterize noise in MRI data in dependence of acquisition parameters, such as volume size and acquisition time. The most substantial work on noise characteristics in MRI data is the PhD thesis Sijbers [1998]. The application of diffusion processes to image analysis problems is discussed by ter Haar Romeney [1994].

Concerning livewire segmentation, several modifications of the basic approach including quality studies have been published [Barrett and Mortensen, 1997, Falcao *et al.*, 1998, 1999]. These publications discuss the accuracy, efficiency, interaction issues and reproducibility of the segmentation results. Falcao and Udupa [1997] extend livewire segmentation to 3D. Interactive segmentation with special input devices is discussed in [Harders and Székely, 2003].

A whole branch of image analysis methods attempts to overcome binary decisions (does a pixels belong to an object?). They rely on principles of fuzzy logic, for example, region growing methods with a fuzzy definition of connectedness. General concepts are described in [Udupa and Samarasekera, 1996]. A specific application of fuzzy connectedness, the quantification of Multiple Sclerosis lesions, is described in [Udupa *et al.*, 1997]. Fuzzy segmentation relates to the statistical probability of connected components. This concept is a special aspect of statistical pattern recognition [Duda *et al.*, 2001].

While some of the algorithms described here were attempted at the identification of homogeneous regions (region growing, watershed), others aimed at the delineation of discontinuities, which are supposed to be the boundaries of the target structure (livewire, active contour models). A variety of research papers deals with the combination of region-based and edge-based methods [Freixenet *et al.*, 2002].

A detailed description of active contours is given in [Blake and Isard, 1998]. A collection of research papers on active contours and other variants of deformable models has been edited as a book [Singh *et al.*, 1999]. McInerney and Terzopoulos [1996] is an excellent and detailed survey on deformable models. Combinations of clustering, classification and segmentation are promising for many specialized images analysis problems, such as brain tumor segmentation from multimodal MRI data [Popuri *et al.*, 2012].

A flexible class of model-based segmentation techniques is based on *M-reps* [Joshi *et al.*, 2002, Pizer *et al.*, 2003]. M-reps are based on *medial atoms*, parts of medial axis and surfaces. They are particularly well suited to the modeling of anatomical objects, producing models that can be used to capture prior geometric information effectively in deformable models segmentation approaches.

Mass-spring models are another class of deformable models, which have been refined for image segmentation, e.g., segmentation of neck lymph nodes from CT data) [Dornheim *et al.*, 2005a,2006b]. This model-based technique will be discussed in § 20.5 where it is applied for segmentation problems in ear, nose, and throat surgery.

The segmentation of 4D (time-varying data) is currently not the focus of much research. It might be inspiring to look at a few examples, such as [Pohle *et al.*, 2004] (segmentation of the left ventricle in dSPECT data and [Qian *et al.*, 2005], segmentation of 4D cardiac MRI data). From all application areas, in medical imaging, the analysis of cardiac image data of different modalities is particularly advanced. In particular, sophisticated model-based techniques are used in this area (see [Frangi *et al.*, 2001, Lelieveldt *et al.*, 2006] for survey articles, and [Mitchell *et al.*, 2002] for the application of shape and appearance models for MRI and ultrasound data).

As a general and comprehensive overview on medical image registration, including technology, and practical implementations in a variety of medical settings, we recommend [Hajnal *et al.*, 2001]. Fast numeric solutions to registration problems are described in [Modersitzki, 2004]. Overviews on registration methods can be found in [Fitzpatrick *et al.*, 2000, Hallpike and Hawkes, 2002, Maintz and Viergever, 1998, Zitova and Flusser, 2003].

Finally, we want to direct the reader to GPU programing and its use for solving image analysis problems. Many algorithms discussed in this chapter, including noise reduction filters, segmentation techniques and registration are very time-consuming if applied to large medical volume data. They involve optimization techniques, discretization of PDE and finally the solution of large equation systems. Although GPUs were not developed for such purposes, they may be used to significantly accelerate such computations, see Owens *et al.* [2007] for a state-of-the-art report of using the GPU for such non-graphics related tasks. The PhD thesis [Schiwietz, 2008] is more specific for medical image analysis and describes GPU realizations of various algorithms, including the random walker segmentation.

Chapter 05

Human-Computer Interaction for Medical Visualization

5.1 INTRODUCTION

To efficiently support tasks in clinical practice, it is essential that not only efficient and reliable visual computing algorithms are developed, but that they are integrated in a carefully designed user interface. The goal of regular clinical use requires to put the user in focus—or as experts in Human-Computer Interaction (HCI) would call it—to adopt a *user-centered design approach*. This comprises an in-depth analysis of the tasks to be solved and the target user group. It is necessary to understand:

- which diagnostic or treatment processes are essential,
- which decisions have to be taken,
- which criteria are essential for such decisions,
- which information is needed to support such decisions, and
- how this information shall be displayed in order to be concise.

For this purpose, it is useful to analyze medical publications. Such an analysis may help to define relevant questions for the actual task analysis. Observations of users, interviews with single users or group interviews and questionnaires are among the methods used to gain this understanding. The design and development of prototypes should be carried out only based on verified assumptions about the essential usage scenarios. This process usually starts with some kind of representation of the current solution, e.g., a workflow diagram or, more informally, a set of user stories. The process continues with a representation of user needs and their priorities as well as a representation of the envisioned solution. Thus, user interface design is much more than a nice visual wrap-up for some algorithms. It is instead a complex and highly iterative process, which requires early and continuous feedback from the target user group and other relevant stakeholders. This whole process is usually termed *Usability Engineering* and a whole collection of books describes variants of this process with its stages and feedback loops. Selected examples are [Nielsen, 1993], a very practically oriented book which discusses trade-offs between the reliability of user feedback and the necessary effort, [Mayhew, 1999], a book which emphasizes different stages and the results to be achieved at each stage, and more recently [Rosson and Carroll, 2003] who describe the *scenario-based approach* to usability engineering. There are, of course, strong differences between research settings, where requirements may be vague, and more product-oriented developments, where precise functional goals and usability goals drive the whole process. We cover both situations but slightly focus on research projects.

Users of medical visualization systems are medical doctors from a specific discipline, such as radiology, surgery, nuclear medicine or radiation treatment, who use such tools for diagnosis support, treatment planning, and follow-up studies to evaluate the success of treatment. Thus, we focus on these user groups which do not include students and educational settings. With respect to research, we aim at clinically oriented research carried out by medical doctors in addition to the (time-critical) clinical routine.

Visual Computing for Medicine, Second Edition. http://dx.doi.org/10.1016/B978-0-12-415873-3.00005-5

The focus on medical doctors in clinical settings is justified, since this group is by far larger than medical students and basic researchers. Also, if these target users are provided with better-to-use tools, this has a direct impact on patient health. It is essential to be clear about the user groups: The working place of a medical doctor in a hospital, particularly in an operating room, differs so strongly from the office of a researcher or the desk of a student that it is not wise to assume that a solution developed for one of these user groups also fits the needs of the other. To discuss feasible approaches, we dive into HCI, the scientific discipline which deals with the systematic development of usable and attractive user interfaces. Since HCI is a huge topic in itself, we have to focus strongly on aspects which are particularly relevant for the clinical use of medical visualization. This chapter extends an earlier article [Preim, 2011] and is focused on the following aspects:

1. *user and task analysis* methods which carefully incorporate the context of use, usage scenarios, habits and preferences of users as well as acceptance criteria,
2. *prototyping* and evaluation techniques which support the exploration of a wide variety of techniques, options, and combinations,
3. *user interface design* principles, and guidelines,
4. a characterization of input devices and input options, such as pen, touch display, and gestural input,
5. *3D interaction techniques*,
6. user interface issues in *intraoperative situations*, and
7. strategies and recommendations which improve the *user experience*.

The first three aspects are related to the almost classical usability engineering life cycle. Aspects 4 and 5 are HCI sub-disciplines, particularly relevant for medical visualization. The 6th aspect is not directly related to any HCI discipline and contains special considerations for medicine. The last aspect covers an essential addition to the classical usability engineering. The user experience (UX) covers perceived attractiveness, joy of use and other aspects that influence how engaged users actually are. Among others, a distinct visual design, typography, the careful use of colors, shapes, and animations contribute to the user experience [Buxton, 2007]. Over and above visual design, UX encompasses the complete life-cycle of user interaction with a product, including marketing, purchasing, service, packaging, training.

In research settings, usability issues are often considered an optional or minor aspect. This attitude is not effective, since substantial feedback on your latest medical visualization or image analysis problem usually requires that users can solve real problems with it. For industrial software development, usability engineering is even mandatory and has to be conform with norms, such as IEC 62366. These norms prescribe a process which includes a precise characterization of the intended use and an evaluation based on this characterization.

Organization We start with task analysis (§ 5.2) and go on with discussing (interface) metaphors (§ 5.3), prototyping and testing (§ 5.4). To summarize essential experiences, we discuss selected user interface design principles (§ 5.5) including those related to the user experience. Among the many interaction techniques developed so far, 3D interaction is particularly relevant for medical visualization. Thus, we discuss 3D selection, 3D transformation and navigation in § 5.6. While in current practice, most medical visualization systems are operated with keyboard and mouse, more advanced input and output devices, e.g., 3D input devices, have great potential. An overview of such devices and the experiences gained in medical applications is given in § 5.7. A specially challenging situation for medical visualization is intra-operative use, where devices need to be sterile and surgeons need to focus on the patient. Interaction techniques and devices for these settings are described in § 5.8. Finally, we discuss the evaluation of interaction techniques and user interfaces (§ 5.10).

5.2 USER AND TASK ANALYSIS

Task analysis is a key element for research and development that is targeted at supporting clinical work. The failure of many attempts to create useful systems for clinicians is often largely due to an incomplete task analysis, where major requirements were not identified or their priority was underestimated. The naive approach, to simply ask users what they need, may be a reasonable start, but there are several reasons why the immediate answer to this question is not sufficient. Typical users have no idea what could be done with adequate technical support, they are accustomed to certain kind of technology and try to cope with it. Thus, user needs have to be very carefully elicited.

Besides an analysis of *tasks*, it is also essential to understand *users*, their habits and preferences, their educational background and problem-solving strategies. If you think about a present for a friend, you carefully consider which present may be attractive for your friend, taking into account many aspects of his or her life. In a similar way, the design of technology, e.g., for radiation treatment planning should carefully consider what you know about the people working in such a department. Of course, you cannot design for *one* physician, but also a special group of physicians has unique characteristics that should be uncovered.

HCI experts specialized on these activities are referred to as *user researchers*, a term that illustrates how complex, challenging and creative the analysis task actually is. Often, user researchers have a PhD in psychology and thus in-depth experience of interviewing and observation techniques. Task analysis in itself is a huge topic that can be introduced here only very briefly. For a thorough understanding, the reader is referred to [Holtzblatt, 2003, Rosson and Carroll, 2003, Benyon *et al.*, 2005].

5.2.1 TASK ANALYSIS METHODS

Modern task analysis combines a variety of methods. Here we focus on observations and interviews, which are particularly important in practice. There are different types of observation:

- *Shadowing*: Pure observation, no involvement or interruption,
- *Ethnographic studies*: Long-term immersion including the "culture" of a setting, e.g., of a surgery department, and
- *Contextual inquiry*: Short-term observation including questions, thinking aloud, etc.

We focus in the following on contextual inquiry, the probably most widespread observation technique for medical applications.

Observations are usually done first to get an initial understanding of workplaces, tasks, priorities and also constraints, e.g., with respect to acceptable input- and output devices. In particular short-term observations (less than two hours) provide quite a random view of the problems involved, since chance determines what one observes, for example certain complications, software failures and the resulting workarounds. It is essential to be aware of such problems and any potentially important non-routine aspects. Task analysis should reveal more than only the major workflows accomplished in the absence of any problems.

If users may be interrupted, questions could be asked for clarification. It is useful if users "think aloud", thus explaining what they are doing. Observations also help to get an understanding of timing. Experienced medical doctors are accustomed to think aloud, since they also train residents. How long certain procedures take in reality is an essential information, since users can usually not spend more time,

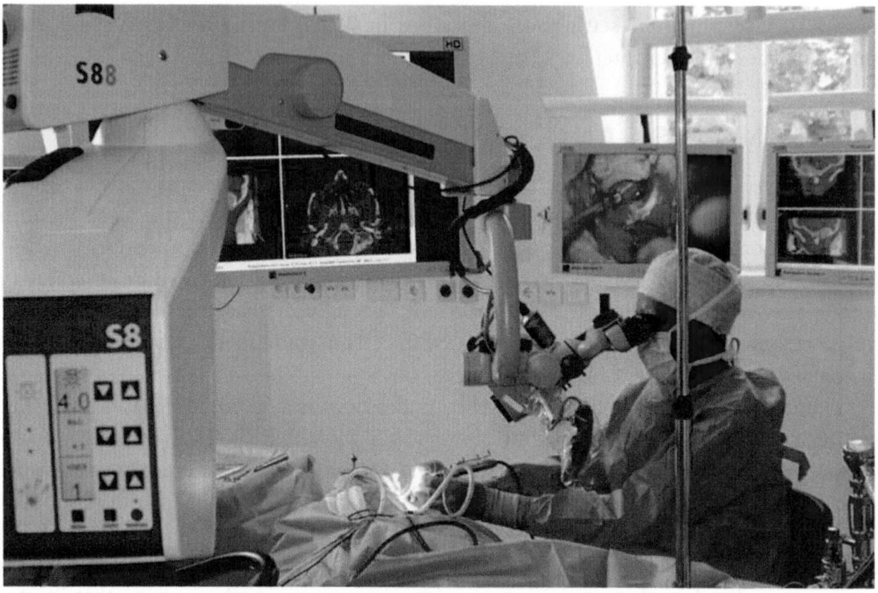

FIGURE 5.1 *A surgeon performs endoscopic surgery of the sinus region. He uses the operation microscope to see the relevant anatomy in detail. He may also use a monitor that presents the endoscopic view. The image clearly illustrates that the activity requires a great deal of precise and focused work. Computer support may provide navigational information to avoid that risk structures are hurt. However, care should be taken not to interrupt the surgeon unnecessarily or too often (Courtesy of Gero Strauss, University Hospital Leipzig).*

even if additional information may be provided by a visual computing system. For medical visualizations, observations of interventions, tumor-board discussions, and other decision-making activities as well as observations of diagnostic processes, such as the place where CT thorax data are acquired, are relevant. If possible, photos or videos should be acquired to represent the context. As an example, in Figure 5.1, the workplace of a surgeon performing an endoscopic intervention in the nasal region is shown. To interrupt them in surgery, however, is often inappropriate.

Interviews Diagnostic and treatment planning tasks are complex and demanding. It is therefore necessary to carefully prepare the analysis with suitable questions and follow-up questions in order to reveal the implicit knowledge of medical experts. Thus, a lot of background information needs to be collected and processed in advance. The website of the hospital, Wikipedia entries of the relevant diseases and medical procedures, and the pubmed database of medical research[1] are among the more useful sources.

Interviews should be prepared with a set of questions but should be designed to be flexible, allowing the asking of follow-up questions. Such interviews are referred to as *semi-structured*; they are not completely open but also not perfectly structured in the way that the exact wording of each question is prepared in advance. Follow-up questions should be used to identify and understand non-routine aspects, e.g., when the current software fails and how these problems are handled.

1 http://www.ncbi.nlm.nih.gov/pubmed.

5.2.2 WHAT HAS TO BE ANALYZED?

The details of a particular treatment are, of course, different. However, a few general questions may serve as orientation for preparing an interview or a questionnaire:

- Which pathologies should be diagnosed or treated?
- Which imaging modalities and protocols are used either in isolation or in combination for diagnosis or treatment planning?
- How is the pathology described and which alternative pathologies are considered (confirm or exclude a certain diagnosis)? As an example, how do doctors discriminate inflammation, scar and benign tumors from malignant cancer?
- How is the severity of the disease described and which criteria are employed for this description?
- What are the therapeutic consequences of the diagnosis?
- Which treatment options exist, e.g., surgery, radiation treatment, intervention? How can they be combined?
- Which criteria drive the decision for these treatment options? What are the priorities of these criteria?
- Which further details have to be determined prior to surgery or intervention, e.g., access path for a catheter or stent, extent of a surgical resection, necessity of vessel reconstructions?
- Who is involved in these decisions? Who is finally responsible?
- What kind of technical support is used during the intervention, e.g., navigation or surgical assistance systems?
- Which decisions have to be performed during an intervention?
- Which constraints, e.g., with regard to space and security, have to be considered?

It is crucial to explore these questions, to verify the answers through literature review and by discussing with several medical doctors. Finally, the results of your analysis need to be discussed with medical doctors to make sure you get it right. More often than not, it turns out that some facts have been confused or the relevance of some aspects is not correctly understood. As a consequence, the computer support should focus on generating visualizations which support *diagnostic or treatment decisions* directly. The identification of such decisions is probably the most important issue in the task analysis.

Later in a project, evaluations should focus on the influence of computer support on these questions and in particular on the decisions to be taken. Does computer support really affect surgical strategies? And if so, are the modified strategies better, e.g., with respect to avoiding complications, better assessment of risks and outcome? These questions are essential for both research-type solutions and products.

Our experience indicates that observations at clinical workplaces are a mandatory aspect of task analysis. They reveal, amongst others, how crowded with all kinds of technology modern operating rooms are and which ergonomic problems arise (see Fig. 5.2).

5.2.3 REPRESENTATIONS OF TASK ANALYSIS

Task analysis yields a wealth of data that needs to be filtered, structured, prioritized and consolidated before concise results can be extracted. Audio recordings from interviews or "think aloud" sessions, hand-written notes, and schematic drawings of workplaces or tasks are typical examples of the collected data. Filtering, of course, is a highly sensitive task. It is essential to strongly reduce the amount of data before further analysis. However, wrong decisions in the filtering process necessarily lead to incomplete task analysis results. Other problems, such as an inappropriate structure or prioritization, are likely to be detected later.

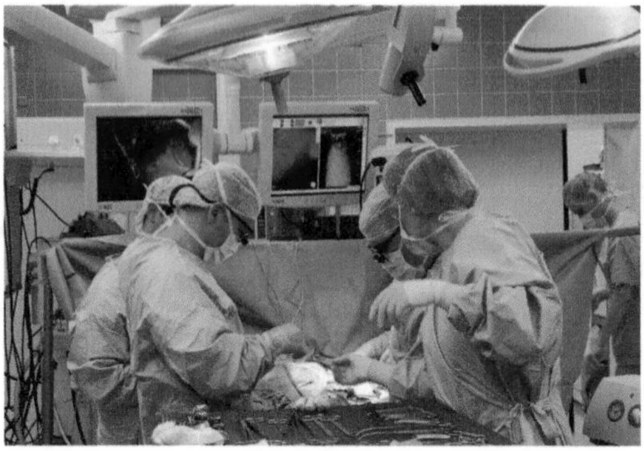

FIGURE 5.2 *The operating room (OR) setup with several monitors and a lot of complex technology. Any additional technical support has to be integrated with the existing devices—extra devices are hardly acceptable* (Courtesy of Konrad Mühler, University of Magdeburg).

There are different representations that are frequently used to convey task analysis results:

- *hierarchical task analysis* (HTA) where a task is (at multiple levels) decomposed into subtasks,
- *workflows* that capture the flow of data and information, and
- *scenarios* that are semi-informal representations providing also background information on the importance of specific parts of a solution.

In the following, we focus on workflows and scenarios, since these representations have been used and refined for medical visualization applications frequently.

5.2.3.1 Workflow Analysis

Workflow analysis and redesign is a core activity in business informatics where business processes should be designed, evaluated and optimized.

Definition 5.1. Workflows represent a process as a graph representations which contain actions or events (nodes in the graph) and their logical sequence (edges in the graph). Workflows may contain variants and may emphasize typical sequences of actions.

Workflows in Medicine The design of medical visualization may borrow from these experiences, notations and tools to identify such workflows and thus to characterize diagnosis, treatment planning, interventional procedures and outcome control. As a first step for understanding a workflow in medicine, it is highly recommended to look for official guidelines of the medical societies. Such guidelines describe in which stages of a disease a particular treatment is justified, how this treatment should be accomplished (including variants) and how (often) treatment success should be verified, e.g., with control examinations in certain intervals. In medical publications, amongst others *patient workflow*, *diagnostic workflow*, *administrative workflow*, *anesthetic workflow* and *surgical workflow* are discussed [Neumuth, 2011]. Image data and advanced visualization are relevant for only some of these workflows. In the following, we focus on *surgical workflows*, since there is a substantial and well-documented experience with the acquisition and exploitation of workflows.

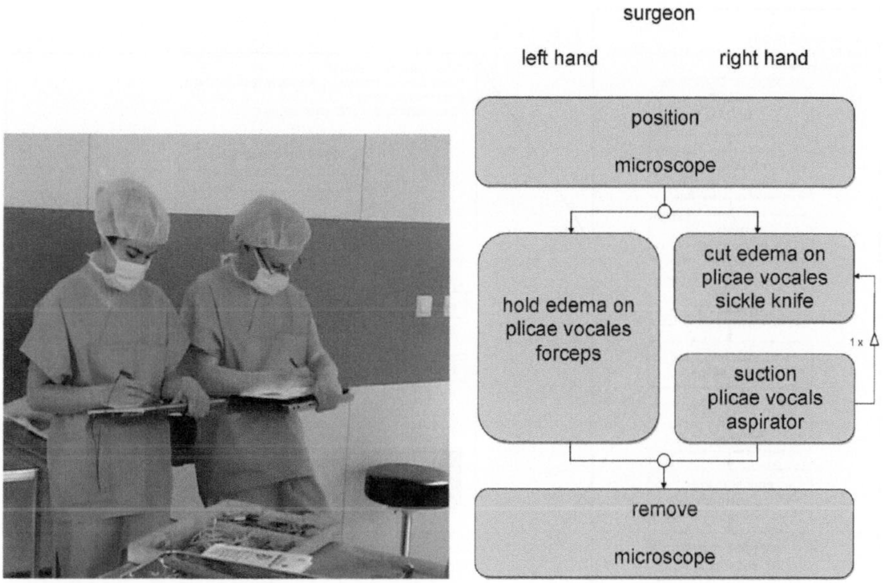

FIGURE 5.3 *A workflow for a surgical intervention in cardiology resulting from careful observations (left with a tablet PC and dedicated software) in the operating room (Based on a courtesy of Thomas Neumuth, ICCAS Leipzig).*

Surgical Workflow Analysis Due to individual patient conditions and different capabilities and preferences of surgeons the variability of workflows is considerable. Different *surgical schools* add another level of variability that is significantly higher than in standardized industrial production processes.

Not every minor variation needs to be explicitly represented – often elementary workflows may be generalized. Workflows may also encode how often certain procedures occur, and how much time they take—information that is crucial in deciding which processes may be improved by computer support [Neumuth *et al.*, 2006].

Top-Down and Bottom-Up Workflow Analysis Workflows may be derived in a top-down manner based on interviews with surgeons. These workflows have a rather low resolution but capture the experience of surgeons. On the other hand, workflows may be derived by precise measurements in the Operating Room (OR) where the use of tools, OR equipment and information is recorded (partly manually, see Fig. 5.3, partly automatically by means of various sensors). These bottom-up workflows are more detailed and contain quantitative information [Neumuth, 2011]. However, the effort to generate such workflows is considerable and includes a careful interpretation of measured and recorded events. Combinations of top-down and bottom-up approaches are possible, e.g., after a high-level workflow is determined in a top down manner, the observation of several instances of surgery serves to verify and refine that workflow. In general, workflows describe processes at various levels, thus allowing an analysis at different levels of granularity. Figure 5.4 illustrates these levels graphically for a cardio-vascular surgery. Specialized editors support the creation of workflows.

Discussion The formal character of this representation is a benefit that clearly supports the software development process. However, since this notation is not familiar to medical doctors, workflows are

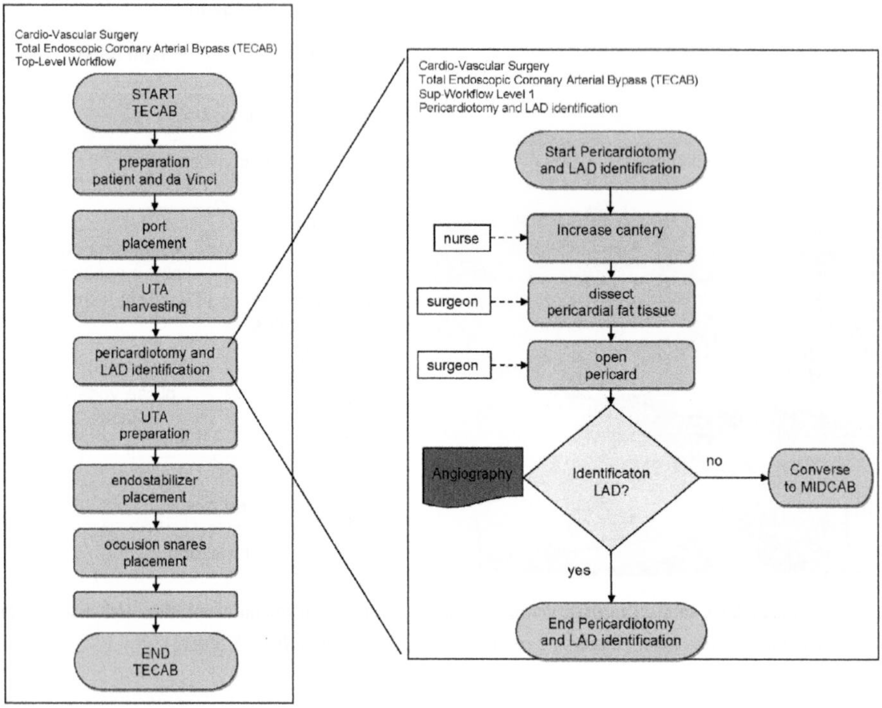

FIGURE 5.4 *A high-level workflow and a selected refinement of one step is presented. This workflow represents a coronary arterial bypass surgery—an essential intervention in cardiac surgery (Based on a courtesy of Thomas Neumuth, ICCAS Leipzig).*

not always useful for discussions with them. As a remedy, the language used in workflows to characterize different states and transitions should be carefully chosen to reflect the proper use of medical terminology. Neumuth [2011] emphasizes the need for a common language between workflow analysts and doctors.

Also, at different sites or even among different doctors at one site, there might be huge differences in their specific workflows (unlike in manufacturing and administrative procedures, medical treatment is and must be more individualized with respect to the patient and the medical doctor). Workflow diagrams can hardly represent that variability, but are often restricted to a somehow averaged instance. Finally, a workflow diagram abstracts from important aspects, such as the motivation for and relevance of some steps. Thus, the rich picture which results from task analysis must be strongly simplified to yield a workflow description.

With respect to medical visualization, the use of microscopes, navigation data, display facilities, such as ultrasound is essential to derive requirements, in particular for intraoperative visualizations.

For more information and successful examples of workflow acquisition in **surgery**, readers are referred to [Blum *et al.*, 2010, Jannin *et al.*, 2003, Neumuth *et al.*, 2009, Neumuth *et al.*, 2011, Padoy *et al.*, 2010.] Padoy *et al.* [2010] present and discuss neurosurgical workflows and carefully discuss how a standardized terminology is incorporated. Neumuth *et al.* [2011] discuss how a "mean," workflow may be derived using 102 cataract interventions from eye surgery as example. Workflow analysis with the goal to identify the current stage of surgery, to predict the next steps and to support it directly, e.g., by adjusting endoscopes's field of view or OR lightning is a promising research area to better support surgeons. At least, some surgical interventions, e.g., cataract surgery are sufficiently standardized for this kind of support.

In fact, they (and other authors) suggest to combine workflows with *ontologies* that also represent relations, such as a *lung* has *lobes*. An important recent refinement of workflow notation is to derive a few representative workflows from many observations and add percentages to the different steps and transitions between states explicitly representing how likely certain workflows are.

5.2.3.2 Scenario-Based Design

Scenarios are now widely used in HCI, in particular to characterize and envision radically new software systems [Rosson and Carroll, 2003].

Definition 5.2. **Scenarios** are natural language descriptions of a process that include statements about which technology or feature is used for which purpose. The stakeholders are explicitly mentioned. They contain different perspectives as well as motivations from users.

Scenarios are more open to interpretation, which may be considered a drawback. However, they are clearly useful as a basis to discuss with medical doctors. Although scenarios are natural-language descriptions, they follow a certain structure and contain certain elements at a minimum. Thus, they may be characterized as *semi-formal representations*.

In three projects at the University of Magdeburg, scenario descriptions have been used and discussed within the development team and with medical doctors resulting in a large corpus of descriptions, annotations and refined descriptions [Cordes *et al.*, 2009]. Figure 5.5 shows different types of scenarios and their relations as they have been used for liver surgery training, neck surgery planning and minimally-invasive spine surgery training. This scheme is a refined version of a process originally described by Benyon *et al.* [2005]. According to this scheme, initially a set of *user stories* is created to describe essential processes

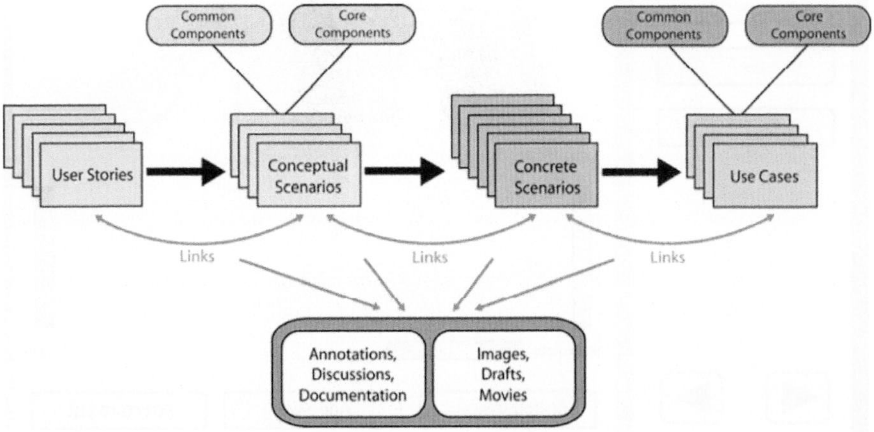

FIGURE 5.5 *To envision a system, high-level user stories are refined stepwise by providing detail on how a function should be performed and by considering constraints from the context of the intended system use. The links between the documents need to be managed (Courtesy of Jeanette Mönch, University of Magdeburg).*

from a user's perspective in natural language. User stories include explicit statements of expectations and preferences. After discussion and refinement, the user stories are refined to *conceptual scenarios* that abstract from expectations and preferences, and may summarize user stories. *Concrete scenarios* are derived to precisely describe *how* the interaction should be performed and how the system responds. Thus, a conceptual scenario might include a statement such as "vascular structures in the vicinity of the tumor are emphasized." A concrete scenario must describe the specific emphasis technique used. Finally, *use cases* are described in a more formal manner. The use cases provide dense information without background information or motivation. Use cases are a part of UML (Unified Modeling Language) and play an essential role in modern software engineering. Thus, by including use cases, a link between user interface and (classical) software engineering is provided.

The following is a short portion from a user story and the derived scenarios for a SpineSurgeryTrainer (see Fig. 5.6 and [Cordes *et al.*, 2008]):

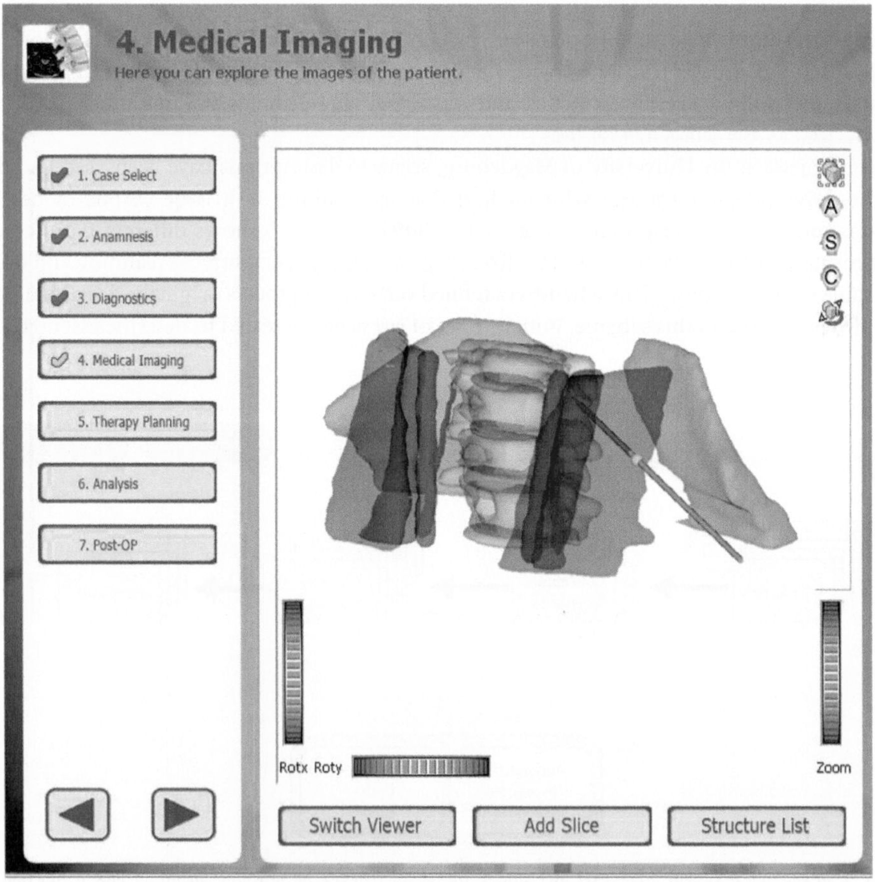

FIGURE 5.6 *A screenshot from a training system for minimally-invasive spine surgery where needle placement should be trained* (Courtesy of Jeanette Mönch, University of Magdeburg. See also Cordes et al. [2008]).

User Story: *The doctor in training has to place an injection in the area of the cervical spine for the first time. He is insecure and wants to train this procedure to test his skills and to do the real injection with self-confidence. But there is no expert and no cadaver available at the moment. Since he wants to start the training directly, he decides to train the injection virtually ...*

Conceptual Scenario: *He starts with the survey of the patient data and anamnesis. After that, he decides for an injection as therapy and starts the training of the virtual placement of the needle [Concrete Scenario 1] based on the MRI data and the 3D model of the patient's anatomy ...*

Concrete Scenario 1: *(Details of injection planning): With the mouse (left mouse click) he defines one marker for the penetration point and one for the target point of the needle in the 2D data. The needle takes up its position. In an animation the user can view the injection process of the needle to his defined position ...*

Experiences with the use of Scenarios In total, six scenarios related to cases with different levels of difficultly and different viable treatment options have been explored in this example. The discussion of such scenarios with medical doctors lead to many ideas for the exploration of the data, in particular when the decision between two alternative therapies depends on subtle details of the patient anatomy. As a consequence, it was discussed how such *transitions in surgical decisions* should be reflected in training systems. We already mentioned the importance of decisions. Here, we learned specific examples of difficult decisions and how they are taken. Slight variations in the angle between spinal disks determine whether an access from the back is possible or whether a more complex intervention from the frontal side is required to access the pathology.

In another project it turned out in the discussion of scenarios for surgical planning that the envisioned tool is also relevant for patient consulting, where surgical options are explained to the patient and to family members (see Fig. 5.7). For this purpose, a large display device is useful and the set of available features may be strongly reduced.

Combining Scenarios and Visual Components A drawback of a pure scenario-based design is that it is restricted to textual components. Scenario descriptions may be enriched with sketches, screenshots, and digital photos from important artifacts. Implants, phantom data of an anatomical region, surgical instruments or relevant objects from the desk of a medical doctor may be among these artifacts. In particular for envisioning future usage, visual components, such as sketches, screenshots, video sequences, storyboards or even cartoons are essential. To further strengthen the imagination of medical doctors and to support the reflection on the user stories, the strongly visual components of diagnostics and treatment planning systems need to be incorporated into early design stages. The set of previously described scenarios, for example, was linked with Figure 5.6.

Guidelines for Scenario Authors Another essential lesson is that scenario authors need support to create meaningful and coherent descriptions. Thus, the experiences with scenarios in a certain type of application, should be analyzed with the goal to create *guidelines for scenario authors*. These guidelines should provide guidance on the content, structure, and use of the different types of scenarios. Also hints for the use of visual components should be provided.

Combination of Scenarios and Workflows Workflows and scenarios provide useful and complementary information to guide the development process. While scenarios better support the discussion between user researchers and target users, they do not inform the actual developers in a concise manner. For the developers, a validated workflow description is a valuable support, in particular for implementing wizard-like systems which guide the user in a step-by-step manner. The systems developed at the University of Magdeburg were also based on workflow descriptions at different granularities.

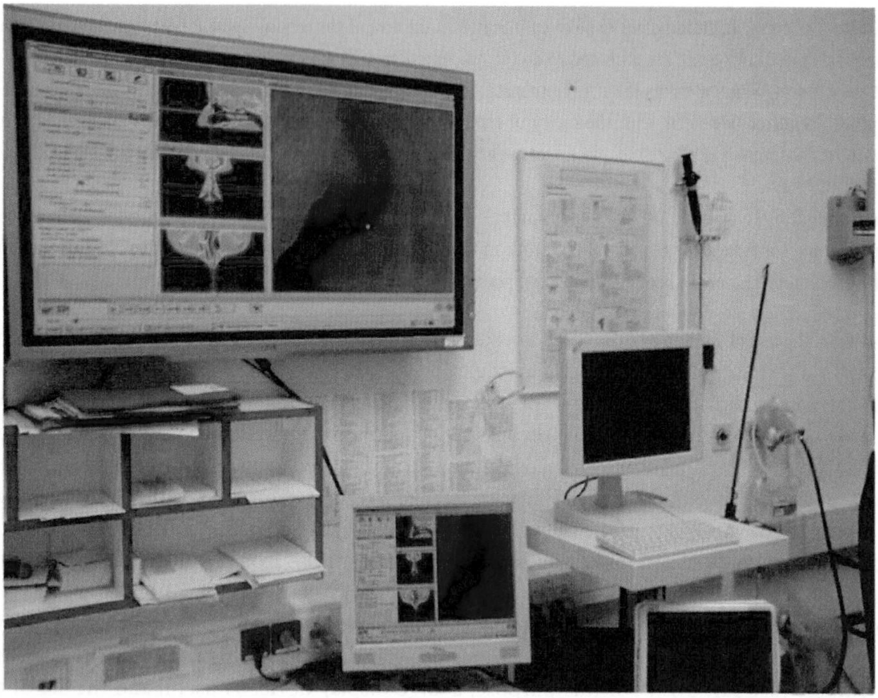

FIGURE 5.7 *The use case of patient consult was identified in a discussion of user stories for a virtual endoscopy system (planning of an endoscopic intervention in the nasal region). A large screen with 40 inch diagonal (for the patient) connected with a conventional notebook where the doctor modifies the view is an appropriate configuration (Courtesy of Gero Strauß, University Hospital Leipzig).*

Surgical planning, for example, at the highest level often follows the workflow:

- anamnesis and diagnosis,
- assessment of the general operability (Can the patient tolerate anesthesia?, Will the patient recover from a major surgery?, ...),
- resectability (Is the pathology accessible and may be removed without damage of vital structures?),
- access planning,
- in-depth planning including vascular reconstructions.

Requirements The final result of the analysis stage is usually a set of requirements, which should be

- concise,
- precise enough to verify whether they are fulfilled, and
- consistent with each other.

Requirements should be associated with a *priority* which reflects whether a certain aspect is a "must have" or a rather optional aspect, which might enlighten users but will not be sorely missed if unavailable. Obviously, requirements need to be discussed, validated and updated [Pohl and Rupp, 2009]. To make matters worse, in any non-trivial situation, requirements change over time based on first experiences with prototypes or new technologies. It is reasonable to enable a certain flexibility and thus to integrate a history mechanism in a *requirements document* which allows to keep track on any changes. For legal product development, such a mechanism is even mandatory due to legal admission procedures.

Managing Task Analysis Results Task analysis results in many different data, such as workflows, scenarios and requirements. These data should be carefully managed in a database or data warehouse to be used for longer projects and also for a set of related projects. The substantial effort of a task analysis is only justified if the results are used in an intensive manner and over a longer period of time. As a rule of thumb, task analysis is valid for a period of about 5 years.

5.2.4 UNDERSTANDING THE USER

This stage in a user interface lifecycle aims at understanding users' qualifications, preferences, needs and attitudes in order to create solutions which are acceptable and appropriate for them. User analysis usually follows task analysis and adds information. In medical visualization, users are primarily radiologists, radiology technicians, surgical nurses, medical doctors from different operative subjects, such as orthopedics, neurosurgery, or urology. The teamwork between radiologists and radiology technicians as well as between surgeons, and their surgical assistants and surgical nurses needs to be analyzed in detail to understand the roles of all parties. All decisions with respect to a computer support should consider whether and how this teamwork will likely change. Care is necessary when routine habits would need to be changed.

There are significant differences between radiologists and medical doctors from operative disciplines. While the former use the computer for a large part of their work, the latter consider their cognitive and manual skills to perform surgery as the core of their activity and use the computer only for a small portion of their work, often considering this work as less important. Consequently, radiologists are often experienced (power) users and surgeons are more likely at the level of casual users.

This difference has huge consequences for what is considered as appropriate visualization and interaction technique. While radiologists prefer a very efficient interaction even at the expense of more complexity and a longer learning period, doctors in operative subjects prefer simple easy-to-use interfaces even at the expense of longer interaction sequences and reduced flexibility. Therefore, radiologists (and medical doctors from related disciplines as nuclear medicine and radiation treatment) efficiently use systems with rather dense user interface panels, invisible interactions, such as shortcuts, popup menus and other interaction facilities that only appear in a certain context. On the other hand, doctors in operative disciplines favor simple screens with only a few large control elements. For radiologists it is essential that they can stay focused on a certain region in a 2D or 3D visualization while performing changes on the visualization parameters, such as brightness, contrast, or the currently selected slice. Thus, they prefer in-place interaction with mouse movements, such as scrolling through the slices with the mouse wheel and changing brightness/contrast with left/right up/down mouse movements. Interfaces for surgeons perform the same task with a control panel, where (large) sliders enable control of these parameters.

Of course, we simplify here and neglect the (substantial) differences between surgeons. It may turn out that the individual differences are large. To provide alternative options, sounds like the *golden rule* for coping with varying preferences. However, it must be done carefully and only if strong evidence for their necessity exists. Not only that all these different parts of the user interface need to be developed, evaluated, refined, and documented—more choices lead to additional decisions on the user's side. Usually, users are effective when they have clear workflows and do not have to decide too many things. Surgeons have to make many and severe decisions regarding treatment, thus they should not have many user interface choices.

Using Personas A particularly in-depth user analysis is based on *Persona* descriptions. This method has been introduced by Cooper [1999] and since then also has been widely used for industrial applications.

Definition 5.3. Personas characterize fictitious users comprehensively to discuss design decisions based on their suitability for one of the fictitious users. At a minimum, Personas contain information regarding the professional background, gender, age and some information related to the cultural background, professional goals and attitude of a fictitious user.

With Persona descriptions, designers and developers discuss about features and their implementation related to one or more of their Personas. Humans often and successfully speculate whether something is desirable or relevant for persons they know well. It is this specific experience that is harnessed with the use of Personas. Different Persona descriptions are needed to represent the different roles, e.g., of surgical nurses and younger and experienced surgeons.

Content of Personas Persona descriptions include leisure habits, attitudes, and other aspects that are not directly and immediately relevant for the use of the envisioned system. Pruitt and Grudin [2003] mention reading habits and learning styles as essential parts. Also the family situation, language skills, education and job responsibilities are relevant. It is also recommended to use specific citations of that fictitious Persona which makes it more personal. Furthermore, it is recommended to use photographs to provide an emotional relation to the fictitious users and to present such Personas, e.g., as posters to be clearly visible for developers.

Personas should be based on *data* derived from observations of real users, marketing research or other activities aiming at collecting data related to users. In a similar way, like activities need to be carefully studied to derive workflow diagrams and scenarios, Persona descriptions should be based on validated data of real users. Persona descriptions, similar to scenarios, are natural language descriptions. They might be somehow structured, leading to a semi-formal expression. While scenarios focus on activities, Personas focus on users.

Personas for Medical Visualization Radiology and surgery planning applications may benefit from Persona descriptions characterizing younger and more experienced medical doctors with different responsibilities and goals for their further professional development. Leading vendors, such as SIEMENS, successfully adopted this approach and use it in particular to design for the different markets. That means, they choose Personas to represent, e.g., users in the US, in Scandinavia or in Southern Europe. In such applications, the professional background (education, experience), the current role, and professional goals are the most essential ingredients.

5.2.5 CASE STUDY: TASK ANALYSIS FOR MEDICAL TEAM MEETINGS

We have discussed in § 3.9, what kinds of medical team meetings are essential with respect to diagnosis, treatment and postoperative control as well as who takes part in such meetings. Olwal *et al.* [2011] describe how they analyzed such meetings to derive requirements for computer support. They extensively employed interviews and observations over a period of 4 years. Among the meetings were 12 decision and preoperative meetings. The meetings were video-recorded for further analysis. The user researchers wanted to identify and understand patterns of interaction as well as current use of technology. Based on their analysis, they stated that additional computer support should aim at shared displays with better input options for all participating physicians. Laser pointer input was observed but considered infeasible in practice, since the pointers' footprint is small and the radiologist has to interrupt his work steering the display of medical image data.

They identified particular situations where such input is desirable, e.g., to mark regions in image data (on a large remote display) and ask (the radiologist) for details or to suggest an access or resection strategy. They also found that the radiologists' role of selecting and rotating images should be kept with computer support since (only) the radiologist is very effective in this task and also to keep his or her social role in such meetings.

5.3 METAPHORS

Metaphors are concepts from the everyday or professional life of users (the *source domain*) that are used in a new context (the *target domain*) to explain and familiarize users with new theories or new technology. Thus, metaphors play an essential role in science, for example, in biology and chemistry, where theories related to atoms ("planet model") or genes (the genetic "code") need to be conveyed. Metaphors are also essential in human-computer interaction, leading to the definition of the term *interaction metaphor*.

Definition 5.4. An **interface metaphor** is a concept from a source domain likely to be familiar to target users that is employed in the target domain of a human computer interface.

The desktop metaphor with ingredients such as "windows," "waste baskets," "post entry" is an extremely widespread interface metaphor that made graphical user interfaces popular (see Fig. 5.8 for some more examples). The identification and use of appropriate metaphors is a crucial aspect of a user-centered design process. Suitable metaphors help developers to focus on key aspects, to use appropriate terminology, but also to derive graphical representations. Beyond requirements, scenarios and workflows, the user and task analysis *may* elicit suitable metaphors. The use of metaphors may also lead to problems, e.g., when the metaphor leads to wrong conclusions on the user's side. The suitability of metaphors depends on:

- the *familiarity* of users with the metaphor,
- the *structure* and *richness* of the metaphor (What do people associate with a metaphor?), and
- the *degree of correspondence* between the source domain and the target domain, the new application where the metaphor is employed to label and visually illustrate application concepts.

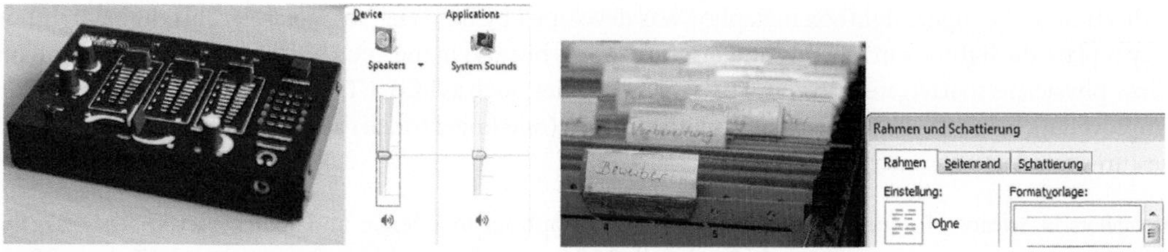

FIGURE 5.8 *Examples for real-world objects and their counterparts in graphical user interfaces. Metaphors guide icon design and behavior. However, a complete simulation of real world behavior is not attempted (Courtesy of Konrad Mühler, University of Magdeburg).*

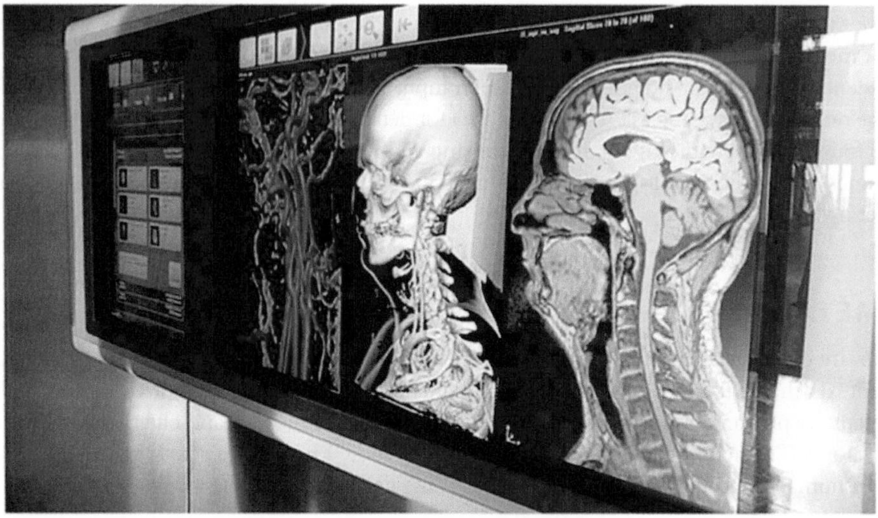

FIGURE 5.9 *The Digital Lightbox is based on a large touchscreen with similar dimensions like the real lightbox. It provides substantially more features than the original lightbox. On the left, the user may select image data, since the system is combined with a Picture Archiving System. The user operates the system via touch input. The right display enables interactions towards data enrichment, e.g., image fusion, 3D volume visualization, object and trajectory planning specification of target points, measurements, and region selection (Courtesy of Brainlab, Feldkirchen).*

Metaphors in Computerized Medicine Successful applications of metaphors in medicine are:

- virtual "endoscopy" (Chap. 13),
- digital "microscopy" (a metaphor for designing solutions for pathologists),
- the digital "lightbox" (a general metaphor for radiology workstations, particularly for X-ray based image analysis).

In § 5.8, we briefly discuss the *surgical cockpit*, a metaphor from aviation to envision integrated and centralized control in an operating room. General metaphors may incorporate more basic metaphors, e.g., the digital lightbox incorporates "magnifying glasses" and "rulers" for measurement. A sophisticated realization of the digital lightbox metaphor was developed by BRAINLAB (see Fig. 5.9). This digital lightbox may replace the lightbox in meeting and briefing rooms but also in the OR. The touch and drag movements allow physicians to navigate, zoom and fuse on modalities, such as MRI, CT, PET/SPECT. The touch gestures employed included the movement through the images (one finger touch) and the widespread two fingers gestures to select and enlarge regions.

Metaphors in Science To further study the use of metaphors in science and in interactive systems, the following sources are recommended [Blackwell, 2006, Carroll *et al.*, 1990, Fauconnier and Turner, 2008, Kuhn, 1995]. In particular, the more recent publications also discuss the limitations and the "career" of scientific metaphors. Often, metaphors were useful to foster certain discoveries and explain them to interested laypersons but hampered further progress at a certain stage when the positive aspects of the metaphor have been exhaustively used.

5.4 PROTOTYPING

Prototyping is the stage that follows after the identification of user needs and specification. Prototyping is a broad term that covers many different techniques which help to explore the design space of possible solutions. Pen-and-paper sketches, like in architecture and engineering, is a powerful prototyping technique, since ideas and concepts may be flexibly and easily expressed (see Fig. 5.10). Sketches may be performed at different levels and designers may just leave portions they have not considered so far. Sketches may serve for general layout discussions but also for more precise considerations on icon design, use of colors, etc.

In particular, if user interfaces for Tablet PCs and mobile devices should be developed it is common practice to use predefined *wireframes*. These wireframes sketch the overall appearance of the device and provide a sketching frame with an appropriate size. Since mobile devices gain importance for medical visualization these techniques are essential here. Some leading vendors, such as NOKIA, provide such wireframe templates to support design for their platform. In addition, they give many hints on how to use such wireframes for initial conceptual design as well as for detailed design using the interface elements their platform supports.

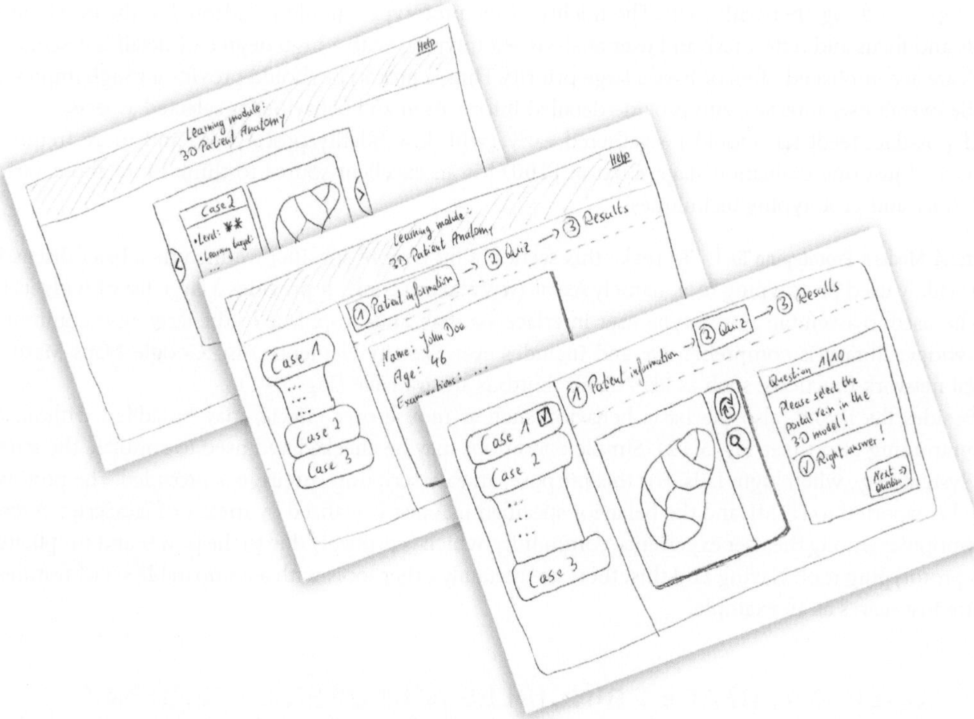

FIGURE 5.10 Sketching allows to explore design variants, such as different layout strategies for a surgical planning or training system (Courtesy of Steven Birr, University of Magdeburg).

Fidelity of Prototypes The character of a prototype should match the evaluation that it is intended for. A *high fidelity prototype* where important functions are carefully implemented enables to gather feedback on performance issues, whereas a *low fidelity prototype*, such as a set of sketches, is more suitable for discussions on the conceptual design and the overall layout.

Storyboards Individual sketches may be connected in a *storyboard* that captures the intended flow of different interaction sequences. Prototyping software which supports sketching, drawing and user interface layout may also be used to combine prototyping with the advantages of digital solutions (archiving, versioning, easy editing).

Prototyping Tools There are many tools for these purposes available. It is essential that an easy connection of different elements is possible. Diagram tools, such as MICROSOFT tool VISIO provide such facilities. MICROSOFT POWERPOINT is certainly not an ideal prototyping tool. However, due to its familiarity and widespread use for presentation purposes, it is also often used to create interactive mockups. For such purposes, not only the pure presentation facilities, but also the interactive (hypertext) elements and animations are essential.

Later, at least important parts of the software, e.g., those that implement a key scenario, may be realized in an advanced (high fidelity) prototype. If real data are not available yet, phantom data should be employed.

As in other creative engineering tasks, there is a danger to narrow the design choices too early and thus to develop towards a suboptimal solution. Different variants should be prepared and discussed among the developers and together with users. The fidelity of the prototypes should be adapted to the development goals and focus and reflect task and user analysis. Prototyping with a high degree of detail is essential for tasks are accomplished often or have a large priority. Thus, a prototype should provide a rough impression of the overall user interface and provide detailed information and behavior for selected aspects.

If possible, feedback should be gathered early (with low fidelity prototypes) and more frequently instead of just one evaluation stage. Buxton [2007] is an excellent source to think more about various sketching and prototyping techniques.

Axure: A Modern Prototyping Tool To make this section a little more specific, we include a brief discussion of a widely used prototyping tool, namely AXURE (www.axure.com). It provides a large list of widgets that can be used to assemble a prototype user interface via drag-and-drop. Due to the large user community, the widget library is comprehensive and includes even sketchy elements. Also Google-Maps-Mashups, social network functions, such as like/dislike buttons are available (Fig. 5.11).

Besides the layout, also the basic behavior, such as mouse-over effects, may be added without any programming effort (see Fig. 5.12). Simple conditions may be checked and used to simulate the state of the system, e.g., when login fails. For this purpose, an easy scripting language is provided. The prototype may be exported to HTML and the behavior specified in AXURE is realized by means of JavaScript. AXURE is very popular among the user experience community, which is probably due to the power and simplicity of this prototyping tool. Having said this, there are certainly other tools with a comparable set of features—Axure just serves as an example.

5.5 USER INTERFACE PRINCIPLES AND USER EXPERIENCE

User interface design and development involves a large amount of decisions. Principles at different levels provide a basis for discussions and decisions. At the highest level, general rules give an orientation how certain desirable properties of a user interface may be achieved. Since these high-level principles are quite

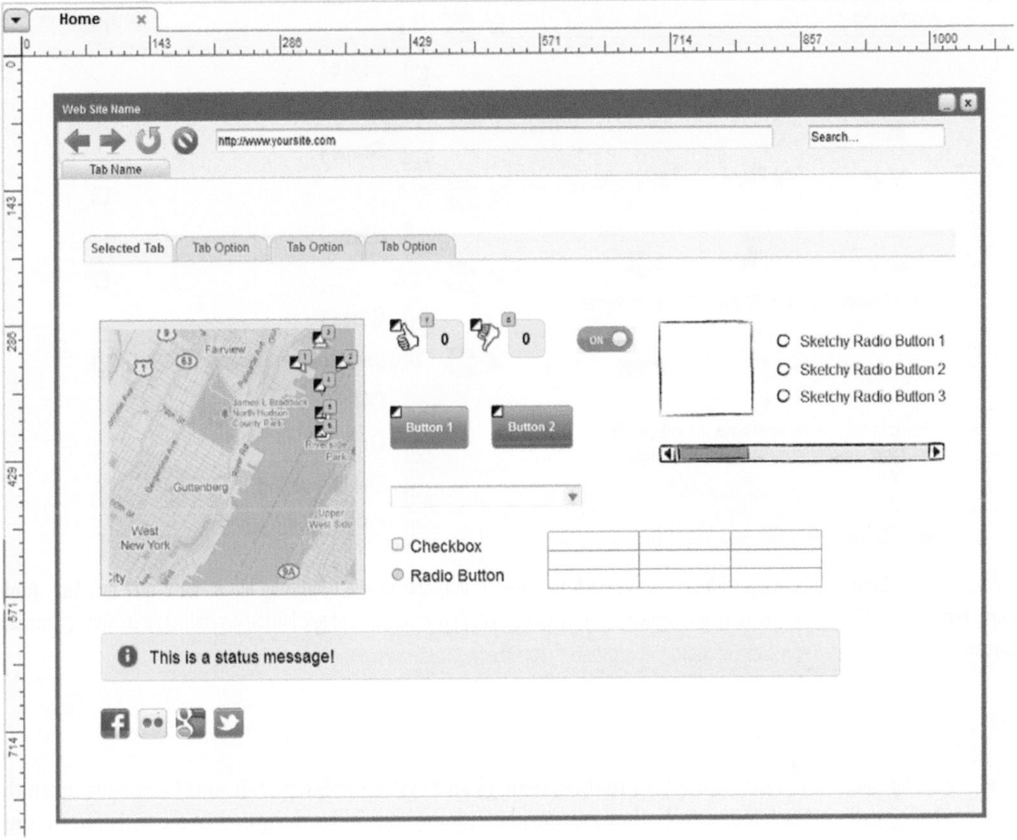

FIGURE 5.11 *A user interface is composed on top of a grid structure where various elements are arranged and aligned (screenshot of Axure).*

abstract, more detailed recommendations were derived to explain how specific user interface elements, such as scrollbars, text entry fields and menus, should be used and combined in an appropriate layout. These recommendations are integrated in so-called *styleguides* [Stewart and Trevis, 2003]. Styleguides have been developed for many specific application areas, such as mobile text entry, and for different platforms, such as Apple Human Interface Guidelines and Microsoft Windows User Experience Interaction Guidelines. Styleguides for medical applications certainly exist in the relevant companies. However, such a styleguide was not published so far.

5.5.1 GENERAL USER INTERFACE PRINCIPLES

Here, we focus on high-level principles and discuss their relevance for medical visualization. The most prominent collection of high-level principles is SHNEIDERMAN's set of eight Golden Rules [Shneiderman, 2004]. We discuss six of these rules:

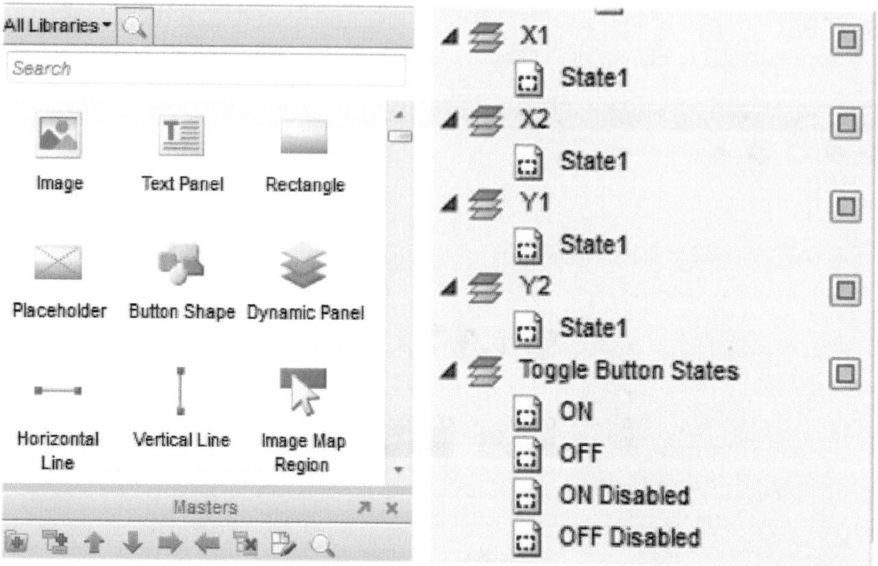

FIGURE 5.12 **Left:** *A large widget library with search functions is available to select building blocks for a user interface.* **Right:** *Simple behavior is added to the user interface elements, e.g., to change the appearance of a toggle button depending on its state (screenshot of Axure).*

- *Strive for consistency.* Terminology in menus, dialogs and system messages should be consistent in the whole system. Also, icons and other graphical elements should be designed in a consistent manner (*graphical consistency*). Interface elements should also behave consistently, providing the same actions and feedbacks. Interface elements, such as "OK" and "Cancel" buttons should be placed at similar positions in different dialogs (*layout consistency*).

  Consistency is difficult to achieve in large user interfaces, where multiple developers contribute. Consistency may be achieved by applying strict rules, using common predefined functions and interface controls and by using internal (project- or company-specific) styleguides that explain how repeated actions should be named and performed. Inconsistencies often result from changes at a certain part of an interface, e.g., when users explained that a term or label is inappropriate. To consequently change that term at *all* places in the interface, is the obvious but difficult task.
- *Aim for high performance.* In the literature on human-computer interaction, there are various experiments indicating that a response time of less than 0.1 second is perfect, since the user does not notice any delay and fluently interacts with the system. Response times between 0.1 seconds and 1 second are noticed and thus may interrupt the flow slightly. It is recommended to adapt the cursor shape, e.g., to use a wait cursor, to indicate such an action. Longer response times are indeed critical since in addition to the delay they cause, users get distracted and may lose their focus of attention. If this occurs, users need to be informed, e.g., by a progress bar. Obviously, we are highly interested in algorithms that do not require to use progress bars at least for typical input sizes. Throughout the book, we therefore discuss efficient algorithms, GPU-based realization or parallelization strategies that take advantage of modern computing hardware.

- *Provide informative feedback.* Especially beginners need feedback to understand what happens in an interactive system. The change of the cursor shape, a progress bar or messages in the status line may be used to inform the user. Loading large medical datasets over a network, registration of datasets, or advanced segmentation are among these lengthier operations.
- *Offer simple error handling.* Usability specialists try to avoid errors in using a system, e.g., by making the available commands as obvious as possible. Errors, however, may occur. Thus, it is essential that an error is clearly diagnosed with a constructive message and options to follow. In particular medical doctors working under severe time pressure expect comfortable error handling and a positive tone in any kind of system messages.
- *Permit easy reversal of actions.* Actions may have unintended consequences. One essential component to handle such situations is to provide a powerful and easy-to-use mechanism to undo such actions, including multiple actions. If actions cannot be undone, this should be clearly stated and users warned explicitly if the consequences might be severe.
- *Reduce short-term memory load.* Users should not be expected to memorize file names, data, and command names. They should be able to select items from lists and to see important state information. Recognizing names is much easier than recalling them.
- *Provide shortcuts.* Frequent and expert users aim for interaction facilities to invoke important commands quickly without the necessity to select menu or dialog items. Function keys, macros or other facilities to abbreviate interaction are essential for these users. In particular radiologists often use systems intensively and benefit from such facilities.

These general principles help to develop a *usable* interface, not necessarily an attractive user interface with compelling user experience. In addition to high-level principles, more specific guidance for menu and dialog design is essential [Galitz, 2007].

For many commercial applications, one more guideline is crucial: "Support localization for important markets early and carefully."

Developing for different markets means to develop tools to be used in different cultures. The obvious user interface-related difference between cultures, is the language. Thus, labels and other textual components have to be translated. However, this is only the tip of the iceberg. After translation, messages and labels might be much shorter or longer, resulting in layout problems. The preference and acceptability of metaphors, colors, icons, layout and font strategies are among the aspects which differ in various cultures [Hafner, 2011].

5.5.2 USER INTERFACE PRINCIPLES FOR MEDICAL APPLICATIONS

In the following, we briefly discuss some principles for radiology and surgical applications based on the experiences of the authors (thus, these principles cannot be backed with large empirical data).

- *Provide useful default values.* For most settings in a radiology or surgical application, it is reasonable to provide default values. These should be carefully chosen to minimize the necessity to change them. Viewing directions, brightness and contrast adjustment, colors and transparency values are among the many examples where carefully chosen default values are highly welcome.
- *Support clinical workflows.* In diagnosis and treatment planning, there are established workflows. Despite the individual differences among the users and the peculiarities of a particular case, these workflows should be identified and followed. As an example, in diagnosis, current image data are compared

with previous data of that patient, if available. Thus, these data may be looked up at a server and presented simultaneously.

- *Provide multiple coordinated views.* For most tasks in diagnosis, planning and intraoperative guidance, a single view is not sufficient. 2D and 3D views, 3D views in different resolutions (detail and context), map views, such as Curved Planar Reformation [Kanitsar *et al.*, 2002] or Bull's Eye Plot are needed. Developers should carefully explore which views are essential for a particular application, how they are used in an integrated manner, and how they may be synchronized. As an example, in vessel diagnosis (§ 11.7), a 3D view with a facility to select centerline voxels is essential to define a vascular region where a cross section is essential.

5.5.3 USER EXPERIENCE

User experience is a rather recent yet already widespread term which extends the older term *usability* by covering also motivational aspects. Whether or not software is considered as attractive might be seen as a vague matter of taste. However, it is well understood, which aspects indeed contribute to a good user experience. Among many others, color schemes, typography, well-balanced layouts and the use of certain shapes play an essential role [Buxton, 2007]. 3D input devices, still being rather new and unfamiliar, may contribute to a positive user experience as well (see Fig. 5.13).

In particular, the fluent interaction provided by gesture- and touch-based interfaces is considered very attractive by a large majority of users. Some commercial vendors have recognized this preference and provide viewers with multi-touch input for selecting cases and image data, for zooming in selected data and for specifying measurements, regions-of-interest etc. An innovative example is the DIGITAL LIGHTBOX (recall Fig. 5.9 on page 192). Other vendors provide similar interaction experiences, e.g., the STORZ OR 1, an integrated system for a whole operating room, is consequently focused on touch-based interaction.

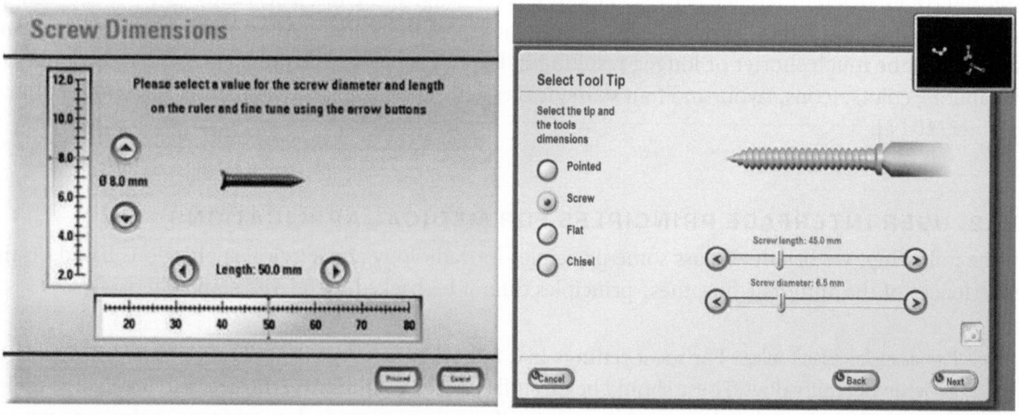

FIGURE 5.13 **Left:** *A simple elegant user interface (from 2005) with a metallic look provides an attractive tool for planning orthopedic interventions.* **Right:** *A screenshot from a more recent version of that software (from 2011). The differences between both versions are primarily at the layout level and reflect that modern trends are carefully incorporated (Screenshot of the Spine Application, Copyright Brainlab, Feldkirchen).*

5.6 3D INTERACTION TECHNIQUES

In medical visualization, 3D interaction is essential. 3D representations of the patient anatomy and of surgical instruments or implants are rotated, scaled, clipped, and individual objects may be selected in order to change their appearance. We discuss *selection* first, since it is the most fundamental 3D interaction task. We also discuss *object placement*, since it is essential, e.g., for implant placement. Interaction techniques for *rotation* and *navigation* are also explained. More specialized 3D interaction techniques, such as measurement and path planning, are discussed in specialized chapters. For all interaction tasks, we primarily consider interaction techniques that are considered as *direct manipulation*, that is they are performed by selecting and dragging 3D representations instead of using number entry or other indirect styles.

5.6.1 SELECTION TASKS

Medical visualization systems comprise a number of selection tasks:

- *Selection of points at surfaces.* This selection task is essential for landmark-based registration. Users select an anatomical landmark, such as the tip of the nose or major branchings of vessels, at a surface representation to control a matching process. Point selection is also the prerequisite for measurement tasks, such as distance and angle measurements.
- *Selection of a region of interest* (ROI). A ROI is often spherical, ellipsoidal or cubical. The interactive definition depends on the specific shape. To define a sphere or an equilateral cube, only a center point and one scalar value representing the diameter or extent, are required.
- *Selection of objects.* In treatment planning systems, users select objects representing previously segmented anatomical structures.

Picking and Snapping Selection may be performed by specifying coordinates or object names. The most intuitive interaction technique for selection tasks is *picking* where the user points at a graphical representation of the intended point, object or region. The simplest implementation of picking is *raycasting* where a ray from the 2D screen position in the direction of the camera view is computed and the first intersection of that ray with an object is the selection result. However, picking in 3D has some problems due to the limited depth cues provided by common monitor types and visualization styles. In particular, small and distant objects and objects in a cluster of other objects are hard to select. One remedy for point and object selection is *snapping* where the cursor is attracted to a surface that is close. Snapping is based on an appropriate *gravity function*. The selected surface is not necessarily the closest one. The size of the object and other measures may be considered to make it easier to select those objects that are very hard to select directly [de Haan, 2009].

Selection Feedback A user-friendly implementation requires that the user is able to predict which object will be selected if the mouse button is released. Thus, the system must convey that snapping is enabled or disabled, e.g., by changing the cursor shape, and the currently attracted object should be somehow emphasized. Multimodal feedback, e.g., auditory and visual feedback, may be a suitable option [Cockburn and Brewster, 2005]. With these ingredients, the user immediately recognizes if he or she is at the right position and saves time and effort to further increase precision. A particular selection problem that occurs quite frequently in computer-assisted treatment planning, is the selection of objects enclosed by a larger semi-transparently rendered object. The simple raycasting would not allow to select an object that is behind another one. This behavior is not intuitive, since users would assume that a clearly visible object may be selected. As a remedy, Mühler *et al.* [2010] suggest to define a *scoring metric* that considers the opacity

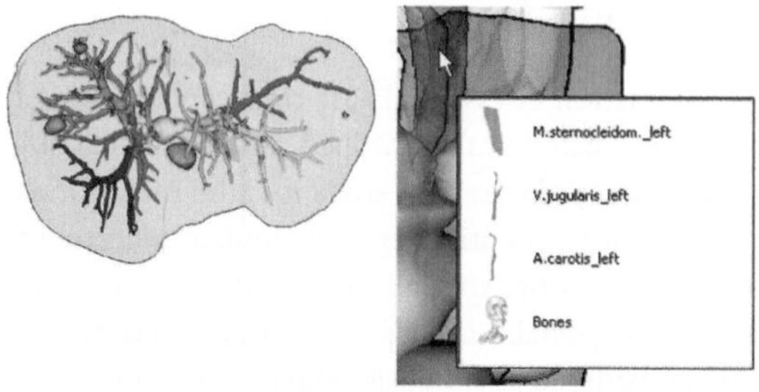

FIGURE 5.14 *In the left model, vascular structures and tumors in the semitransparent liver surface may be selected with a raycasting that prefers small opaque objects. If the user cannot select the desired object, a popup menu with object names may be used to disambiguate the selection (From: [Mühler et al., 2010]).*

and size of all objects hit by a ray. The metric is designed such that small and opaque objects, e.g., vascular structures and tumors, are preferred (see Fig. 5.14, left). The semi-transparently rendered organ surface still can be selected conveniently by pointing between the smaller objects. There are, of course, also a few situations, where a semi-transparent object has approximately the same size like an object behind. In this special case, also the advanced selection strategy cannot sufficiently disambiguate the selection. Thus, a list of possible objects (described by their name and an icon) should be presented (see Fig. 5.14, right).

5.6.2 3D ROTATION

A fundamental task in using any kind of 3D visualization is the adaptation of the viewpoint by zooming or rotation. Zooming is usually performed with a scroll widget in a viewer or the scroll wheel integrated in a mouse and poses no severe usability problems.

Rotation, however, is a tricky interaction and if you watch medical doctors carefully trying to adjust the favorite viewing direction, it turns out that this is often a tedious trial-and-error process which ends up in a sufficient but not optimal choice.

Unrestricted 3D rotation by means of a 2D display and a 2D input device is a challenging task, since only very limited depth cues are available and users often get confused when they attempt to select a specific viewing direction. Different *mappings* from a path of a 2D input device to a modification of a 3D viewing direction exist. This lack of a standard further complicates the adjustment of viewing directions.

Users expect that mouse movements are handled in a transitive manner, that is the resulting viewing direction after two mouse movements does not depend on their sequence. In particular, they expect that after several movements they may return to the original viewing direction by moving the mouse cursor back to approximately the original position. Unfortunately, with popular 3D rotation techniques, such as the virtual trackball [Chen *et al.*, 1988], the actual reaction from the system is different. Also the effect of a certain mouse movement depends on the current mouse position—the same movement has different consequences.

Virtual Trackball The *virtual trackball* (also referred to as *virtual sphere*) maps mouse movements on rotation parameters such as if a sphere would be displayed [Chen *et al.*, 1988]. The properties of the mapping change depending on whether the mouse cursor is inside the projected half sphere or not. If the current mouse position is $p_1(x_1, y_1)$ and the mouse is moved to $p_2(x_2, y_2)$ inside the half sphere, a rotation in x- and y-direction results (from P_1 to P_2). Otherwise, the same movement is mapped to a rotation in

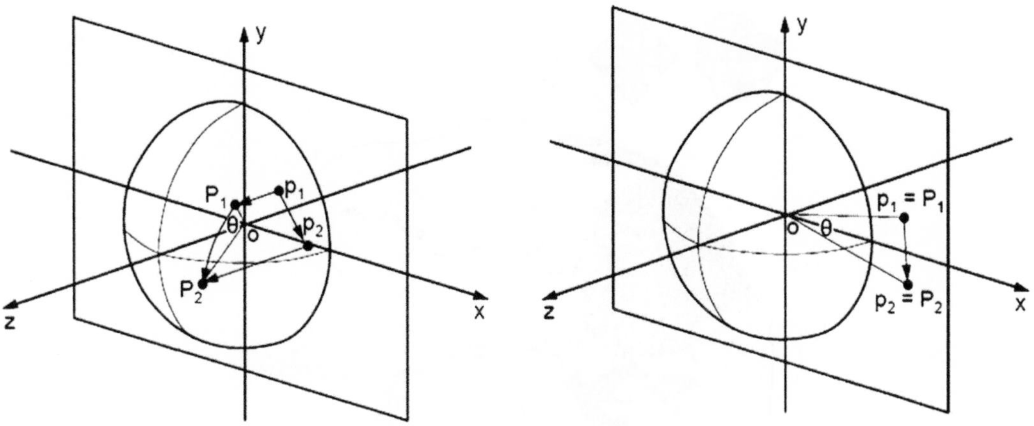

FIGURE 5.15 *Rotation by means of a virtual trackball. If the mouse cursor and the target are inside the half sphere, the camera position will be adapted according to the projection on the sphere surface—from* P_1 *to* P_2*. A mouse movement outside the half sphere (right) leads to a rotation along the z-axis (Courtesy of Ragnar Bade, University of Magdeburg).*

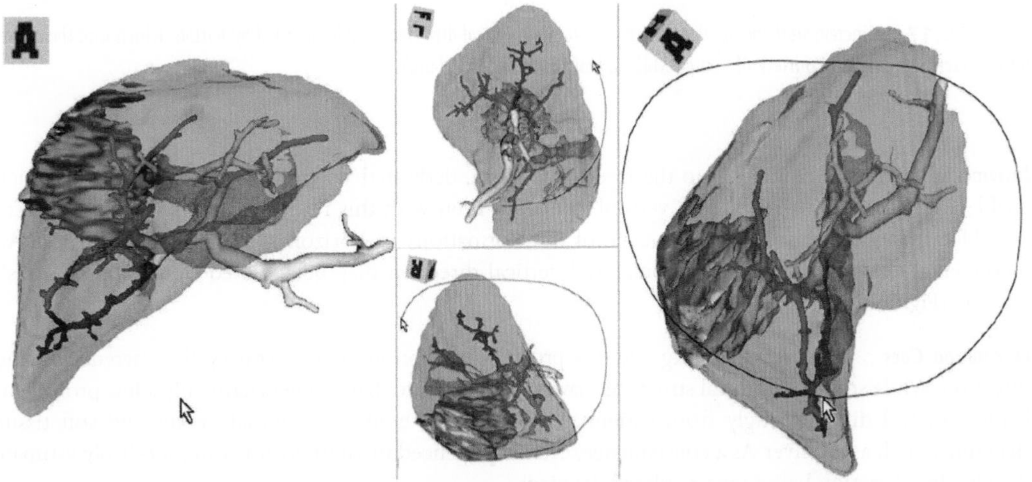

FIGURE 5.16 *An anatomical model is rotated with various movements. In the most right image, the mouse cursor returned to its initial position. However, the viewing direction differs strongly from the initial direction (Courtesy of Ragnar Bade, University of Magdeburg).*

the z-direction (Fig. 5.15). This behavior is usually not conveyed to the user. One could, for example, at least change the cursor shape when the user enters or leaves the projected half sphere. With the virtual trackball, an arbitrary 3D rotation is not possible, but instead needs to be decomposed artificially in at least two mouse movements. For user studies that compare mouse-based 3D rotation techniques with respect to efficiency and accuracy, see [Bade *et al.*, 2005] and [Hinckley *et al.*, 1997]. For a careful mathematical description of the underlying transformations, [Henriksen *et al.*, 2004] may be recommended (see Fig. 5.16).

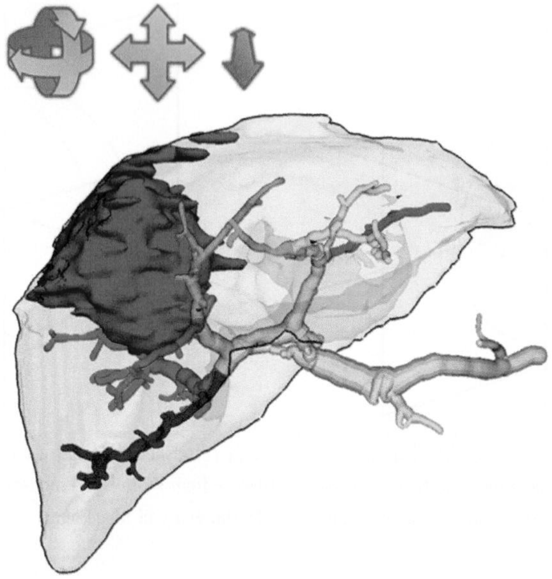

FIGURE 5.17 *An incremental change along the horizontal and vertical direction may be achieved by buttons which lend themselves for a discrete interaction (Courtesy of Konrad Mühler, University of Magdeburg).*

Incremental Rotation In addition to the free 3D rotation, dedicated widgets should be provided, which enable a rotation in horizontal and vertical direction. Even with this restriction users may adjust every possible viewing direction by a sequence of transformations in horizontal and vertical direction. An incremental change along the horizontal and vertical direction may be achieved by appropriate push buttons (Fig. 5.17).

Orientation Cues Most 3D planning systems provide orientation cues to convey the current viewing direction. While some anatomical structures have a characteristic shape, others have only a few prominent landmarks and differ strongly from patient to patient. This holds for internal organs and soft tissue structures, such as the liver. As a consequence, even experienced medical doctors cannot reliably estimate the viewing direction based on a rendered 3D view.

To provide orientation cues, 3D viewers could contain a small 3D geometry which is transformed in the same way as the 3D model of the patient anatomy. To convey the current viewing direction unambiguously, an orientation cube labeled with "H" (Head), "F" (Feet), "L" (Lateral), "A" (Anterior), ... may be employed (Fig. 5.18). Other frequently used orientation cues are a sticky figure of a man or realistic depictions of characteristic parts of the body, e.g., the skull, the skeleton or a torso. While it is obvious that orientation cues are essential, there is no verified guideline which defines where to place the orientation cue (in which of the four corners?), how to scale it, and which particular geometry to use.

5.6.3 OBJECT PLACEMENT

Object placement is the goal-directed movement of an object in a 3D model. It includes object translation and rotation. Widespread examples are planning systems for kitchen, bath and garden equipment.

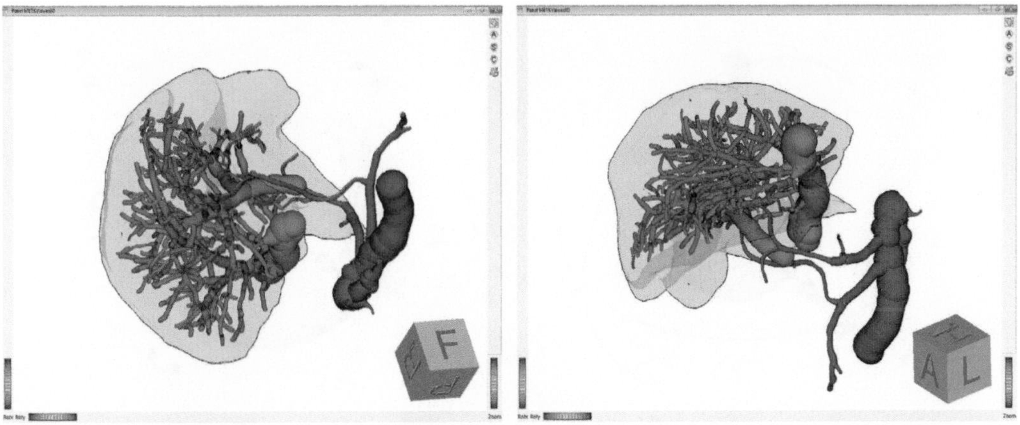

FIGURE 5.18 *A 3D model of the liver and intrahepatic vasculature was rotated. The orientation cube in the lower right corner (displayed larger than usual) indicates the viewing direction. Left the "F" is clearly visible, thus the liver is shown from the "Foot" direction. In the right image, the 3D model is shown from the "Head," "Anterior" and "Lateral" direction (Courtesy of Konrad Mühler, University of Magdeburg).*

In surgery planning, object placement is essential, e.g., in interventions where an implant needs to be selected and placed. Object placement has three subtasks [Teather and Stuerzlinger, 2007]:

- initial placement after an object type was created,
- gross placement, and
- fine placement, where objects are precisely aligned.

In the initial placement stage it is essential that the newly created object is visible. Thus, its initial position must be chosen such that the object is not hidden or too small to be recognized. A default position for all newly created objects clearly does not meet the requirements!

Gross object placement requires an appropriate 3D widget, e.g., an interaction element with a 3D geometry and handles to manipulate the individual degrees of freedom. In Fig. 5.19 such 3D widgets for 3D translation and rotation are shown. Snapping, discussed previously for selection tasks, is also essential for object placement. It may be used to attract an object to likely intended target positions [Bier, 1990]. Further constraints are often employed, e.g., the movement of an object along a certain path or inside a predefined volume is enforced. In particular, in computer-aided design, that is in engineering tasks, such constraints are carefully incorporated into widespread tools [Bukowski and Séquin, 1995]. Figure 5.20 illustrates the placement of an ear implant in an anatomical model.

5.6.4 NAVIGATION

Navigation is a widely used term with origin in steering ships. Surgical navigation or car navigation rely on technical assistance and some kind of tracking to tell the user how his position (or the position of his instrument) relates to some target region. We discuss user interface issues related to surgical navigation in Chapter 18. Here, we consider (only) the basic 3D interaction task that comprises changes of the viewpoint within a 3D model.

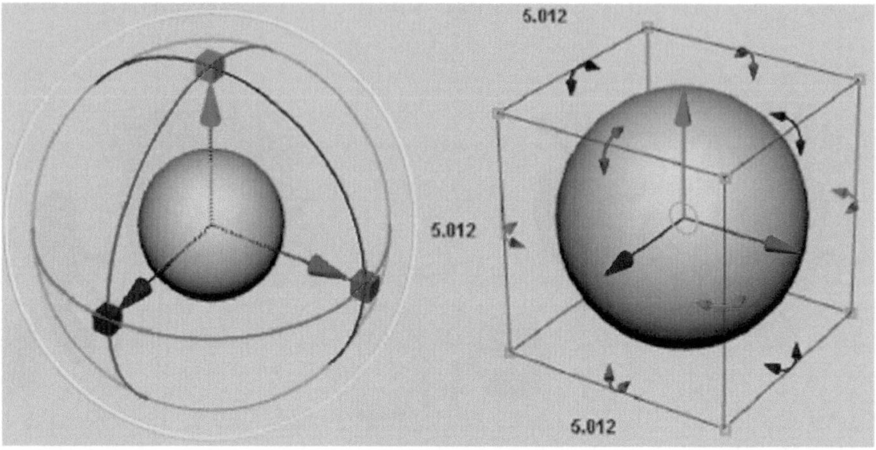

FIGURE 5.19 *3D widgets for 3D translation and rotation (screenshot from Alias Maya).*

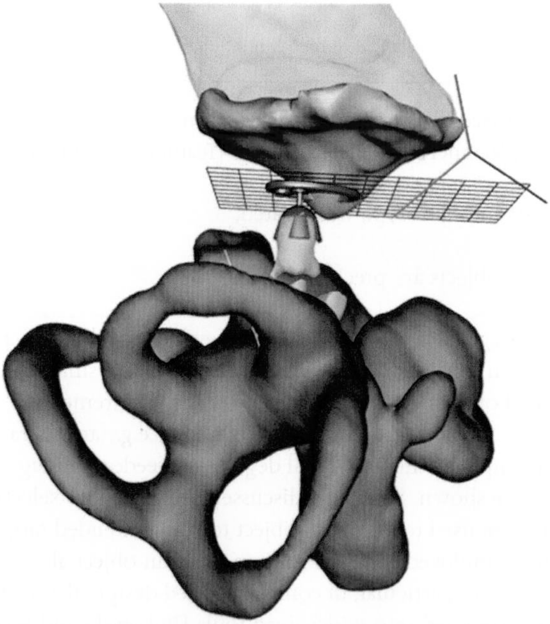

FIGURE 5.20 *As part of ear surgery planning, the precise position of an implant is shown. A coordinate plane serves as orientation for fine object placement (Courtesy of Michael Gessat, ICCAS Leipzig).*

In case of a compact 3D model it is sufficient to rotate the model and zoom. However, in case of more complex 3D models, users have to plan a path and make decisions where to go. The most essential navigation problem related to medical visualization is virtual endoscopy, where users move a camera along air-filled or fluid-filled structures. Navigation aims at either inspecting walls (colon wall, vessel wall) or at preparing an endoscopic intervention. Navigation has two components:

- *wayfinding*, the cognitive process of deciding on the path, and
- *maneuvering*, the process of moving along the selected path [Bowman *et al.*, 2004].

We discuss navigation problems in virtual endoscopy in Chapter 13. As a general remark, also navigation is usually *constrained*, such as object placement [Hanson and Wernert, 1997]. Anatomical landmarks, such as colon or vessel centerlines, are employed to guide the user, since these structures often serve as paths for diagnostic exploration. As a second general remark, both navigation components, *wayfinding* and *maneuvering*, benefit from overview maps that show the current position and orientation in a larger context instead of just presenting an internal view of a very small fraction of the anatomy. There is a wealth of literature on 3D navigation, e.g., in city models, virtual landscapes and games, e.g., Beckhaus *et al.* [2000] and Elmqvist *et al.* [2008] are inspiring. Some of these solutions might be relevant in medical visualization as well.

5.7 INPUT DEVICES

Input and output devices play an essential role for the usability of medical visualization systems. There is a large variety of input and output devices potentially relevant for medical visualization applications. The multi-touch medical visualization table described by Lundström *et al.* [2011] is an inspiring example and used for virtual autopsy and orthopedic surgery planning (see Fig. 5.21). The whole design aims at a high "similarity to a real physical situation" and a "low threshold for usage learning." This development

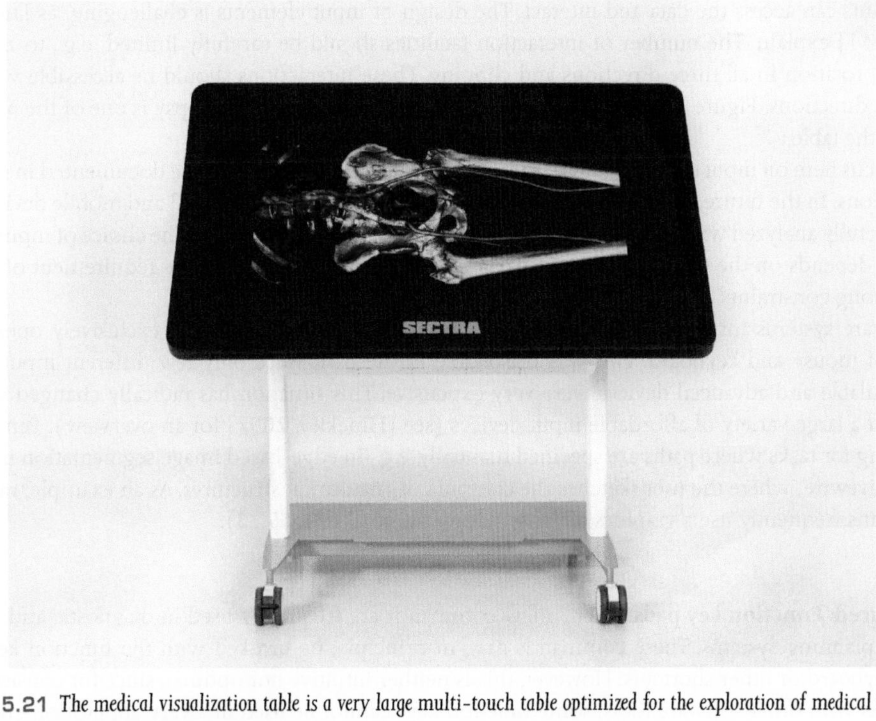

FIGURE 5.21 *The medical visualization table is a very large multi-touch table optimized for the exploration of medical image data (Courtesy of Claes Lundstroem, SECTRA).*

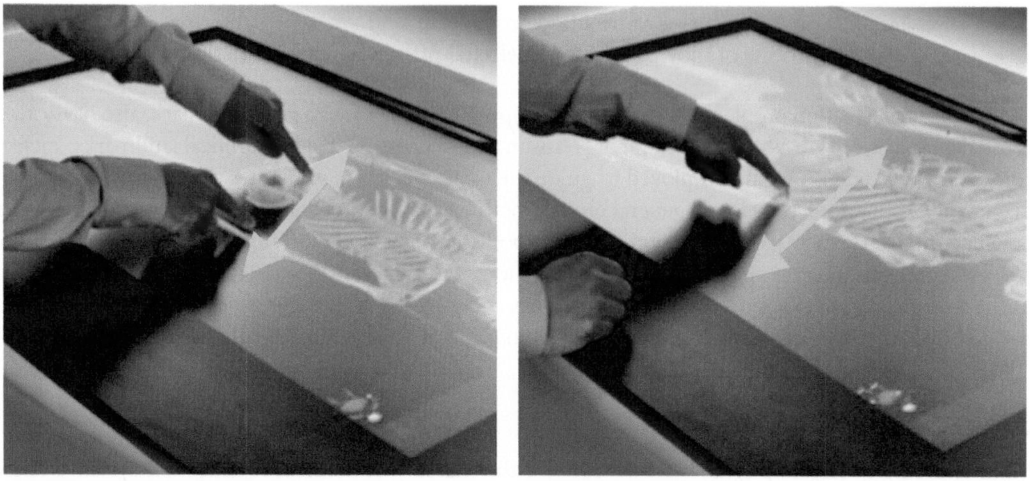

FIGURE 5.22 *Two essential gestures enable zooming (left) and rotation in the plane (right) (Courtesy of Claes Lundstroem, SECTRA).*

is guided by the metaphor that there is a *patient lying on the table*. This metaphor has various consequences. As an example, the default size, in which data is presented, corresponds to the natural size of that patient. Interaction with such tables is favorable for supporting cooperative decisions. The crucial aspect is that all participants can access the data and interact. The design of input elements is challenging, as Lundström *et al.* [2011] explain. The number of interaction facilities should be carefully limited, e.g., to zooming, panning, rotation in all three directions and clipping. These interactions should be accessible well from different directions. Figure 5.22 illustrates some of these gestures. Virtual autopsy is one of the major use cases of the table.

We focus here on input devices because there is considerable more experience documented in scientific publications. In the future, however, autostereoscopic displays [Hopf *et al.*, 2006] and mobile devices need to be carefully analyzed with respect to their potential for medical visualization. The choice of input devices strongly depends on the context of use. In particular, intraoperative use and the requirement of sterility poses strong constraints.

Software systems for medical diagnosis and treatment planning are almost exclusively operated by means of mouse and keyboard. This was reasonable in the past, since only few different input devices were available and advanced devices were very expensive. This situation has radically changed with the advent of a large variety of affordable input devices (see [Hinckley, 2007] for an overview). Pen input is promising for tasks where paths are specified manually, e.g., in edge-based image segmentation methods, such as livewire, where the user sketches the contours of anatomical structures. As an example, radiology technicians frequently use a graphics tablet with pen input (see Fig. 5.23).

Advanced: Function key pads Often, a few commands are frequently used in diagnostic and treatment planning systems. These commands may, in principle, be invoked with the function keys of the keyboard or other shortcuts. However, this is neither intuitive nor optimal, since for consistency reasons with other software tools, some function keys cannot be used in a very application-specific

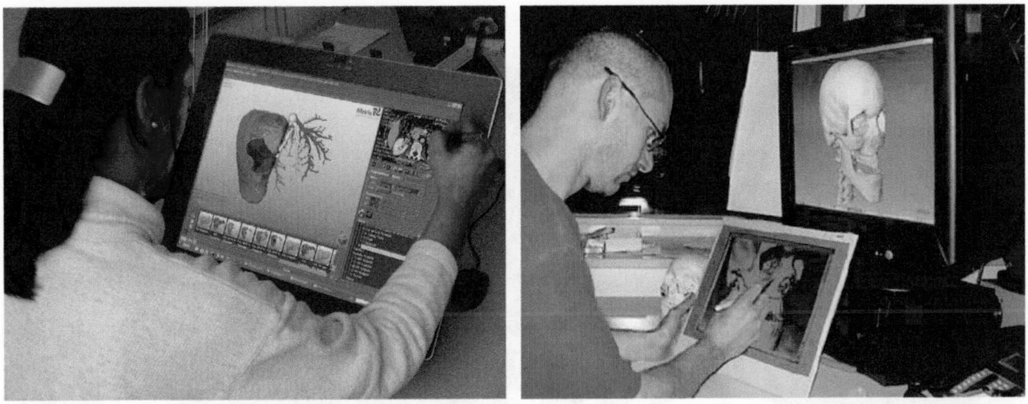

FIGURE 5.23 **Left:** *A radiology technician performs segmentation, measurement and other analysis tasks on medical imaging data. Pen-based input meets her needs for precise, fast and convenient interaction (Courtesy of MeVis Medical Solutions).* **Right:** *specification of resection lines on a 3D model of the facial bones by means of pen and graphics tablet (Courtesy of Stefan Zachow, Zuse-Institute Berlin. See also Zachow et al. [2003]).*

way. Also, to invoke the keys, the visual focus has to be put on the keyboard. As an alternative, in an airplane cockpit or a car a gear can be used without visual attention due to its specific shape, which allows to use the tactile sense to grasp it. Thus, joysticks or *function key pads* are a promising alternative. For an application in diagnosis of mammography images, a team around Anke Boedicker, MEVIS Breastcare, developed a special function pad where the size and placement of keys are carefully adapted to the frequency of use. In Figure 5.24, a general function keypad and a specific keypad for diagnosis of mammography are shown.

5.7.1 6 DOF INPUT DEVICES

3D input devices have experienced a strong development in the past 20 years. While some of them, including data gloves and AR flysticks, are primarily used in immersive virtual environments, others, such as 3D variants of the traditional mouse, are intended for desktop use. Immersive virtual environments are usually not appropriate for the tasks which discussed in this book. Thus, we focus on devices usable in a desktop environment and start with 3D mouse variants. The major motivation to develop these devices was to provide the full flexibility for 3D input, namely to enable users to translate and rotate objects in three dimensions. Since this results in an overall of six degrees of freedom, they are referred to as 6 DOF devices.

6 DOF devices differ in their shape and controls (the form factor) and consequently in the convenience of use for a longer time. Some devices are moved freely in the air and their position and orientation is tracked. Examples are the FlyMouse and the RingMouse attached to a user's finger [LaViola *et al.*, 2009]. This interaction style may be learned easily. However, it is not comfortable for long term use, since the supporting surface, which makes traditional mouse usage convenient, is missing. Also, it is difficult to use such devices to issue commands or change modes, such as it could be done with mouse buttons. Therefore, such devices did not gain widespread use, neither in medicine nor in other professional domains. The Cubic

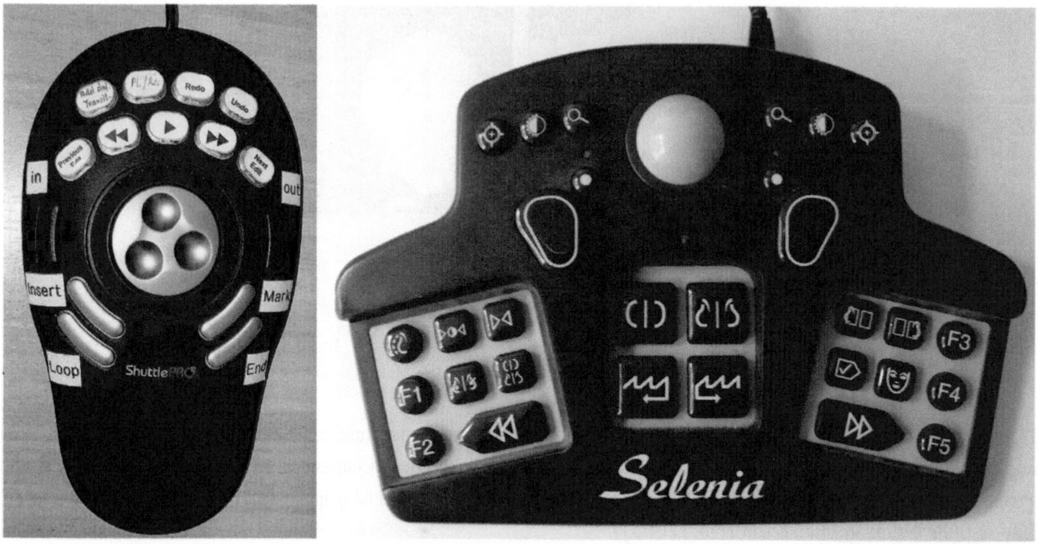

FIGURE 5.24 **Left:** *A general function pad may be used to provide fast access for the most important interactions.* **Right:** *A dedicated function pad has been developed and refined in various iterations to provide fast access to frequent commands in a diagnostic system for mammography data. Magnifying glasses, contrast adjustments, simultaneous display of both mammography images of a woman are among the functions that can be invoked via the function pad (Right image: Courtesy of MeVisBreastCare).*

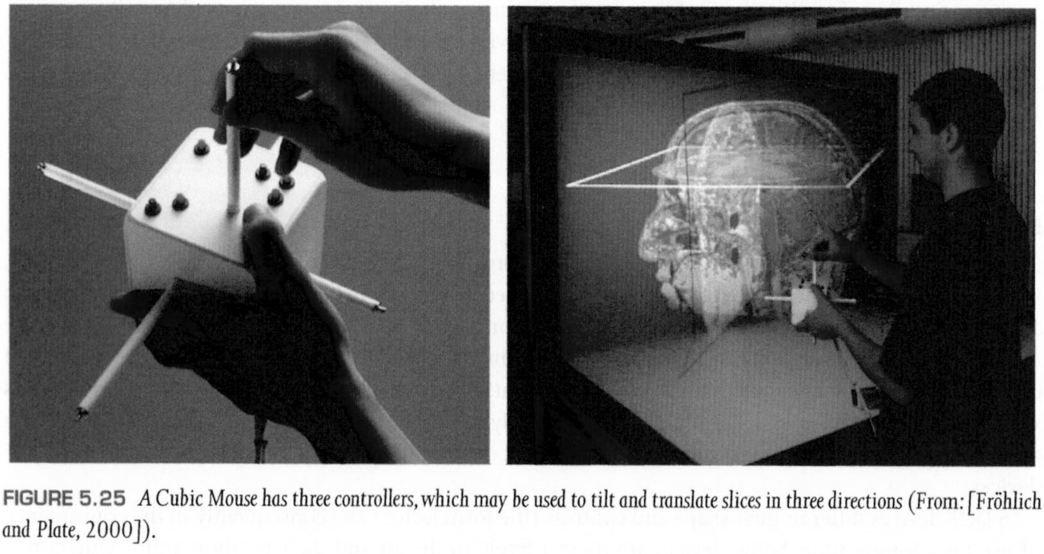

FIGURE 5.25 *A Cubic Mouse has three controllers, which may be used to tilt and translate slices in three directions (From: [Fröhlich and Plate, 2000]).*

MOUSE [Fröhlich and Plate, 2000] is an interesting device for direct interaction with medical volume data (see Fig. 5.25). The three handles enable a natural selection of slices in x-, y- and z-direction. Also, oblique slices may be naturally defined. Despite these promising properties, however, also the concept of the CUBIC MOUSE did not gain widespread acceptance.

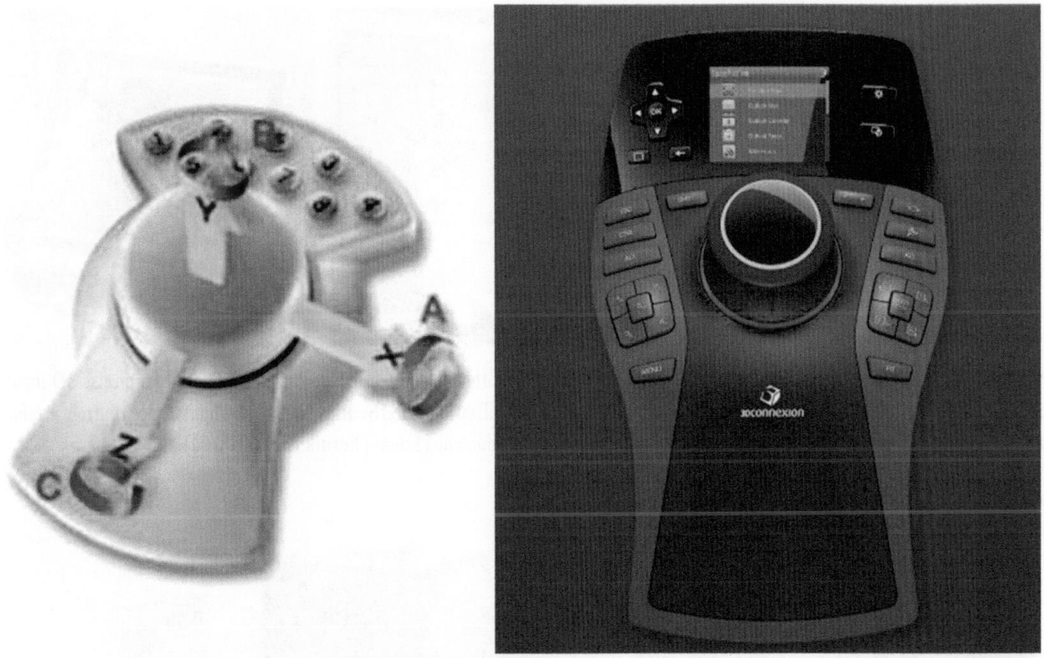

FIGURE 5.26 *The SpaceMouse (left) and the SpacePilot (right) are widespread examples for 6 DOF input devices. The controller is dragged to control the z-direction of the movement. Both devices are associated with several buttons that can be used as function keys. The keys can be operated without leaving the 6 DOF input device.*

More promising are 6 DOF devices, which are as conveniently used as the traditional mouse and which are equipped with a variety of buttons to enable flexible command input without the need to change the input device. Examples of such systems are the SpaceMouse and the more recently developed SpacePilot (see Fig. 5.26). Instead of decomposing a 3D translation somehow artificially in orthogonal movements, 6 DOF devices enable a natural translation thus reducing the mental effort.

Applications The SpaceMouse and the SpacePilot devices gained widespread use in combination with computer-aided design tools used in engineering. They serve for the variety of interaction tasks to be performed when designing complex geometric models for building new machines and devices. 6 DOF input devices may be used simultaneously to another input device, leading to bi-manual interaction. While there are many studies related to comparisons of 3D input devices, very few consider realistic medical tasks.

In medicine, 3D input devices may be used for interactive 3D segmentation and for steering tasks. Bornik *et al.* [2006] introduced a 3D input device attached with buttons and scroll wheel that could be tracked and used for precise 3D interaction (see Fig. 5.27).

Krüger *et al.* [2008] have exploited the SpaceMouse to steer the virtual camera in an endoscopic application, specifically the planning of endoscopic sinus surgery (see Fig. 5.28). It turned out that users, despite of being unfamiliar with this device, could follow an ideal path more precisely and faster compared to a 2D mouse.

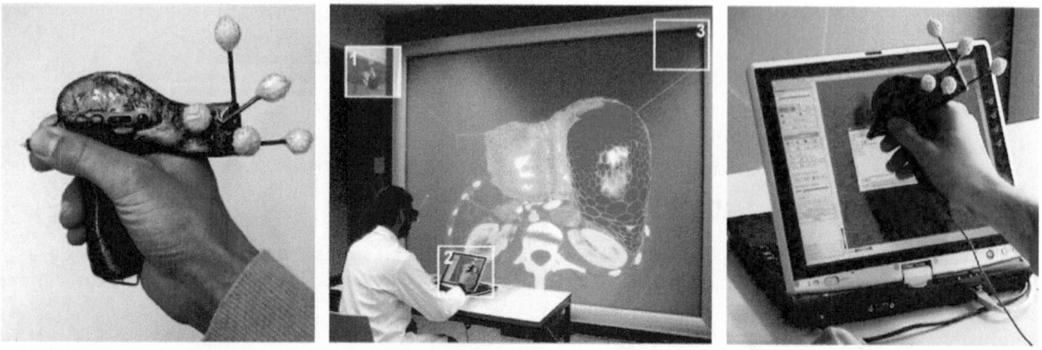

FIGURE 5.27 **Left:** *A special 3D input device with reference spheres that enable a spatial localization is useful for precise 3D input.* **Middle:** *The 3D input device may be used to control a large 3D visualization directly.* **Right:** *The 3D input device controls a tablet PC where an application is started to be used in semi-immersive environment (From: [Bornik et al., 2006]).*

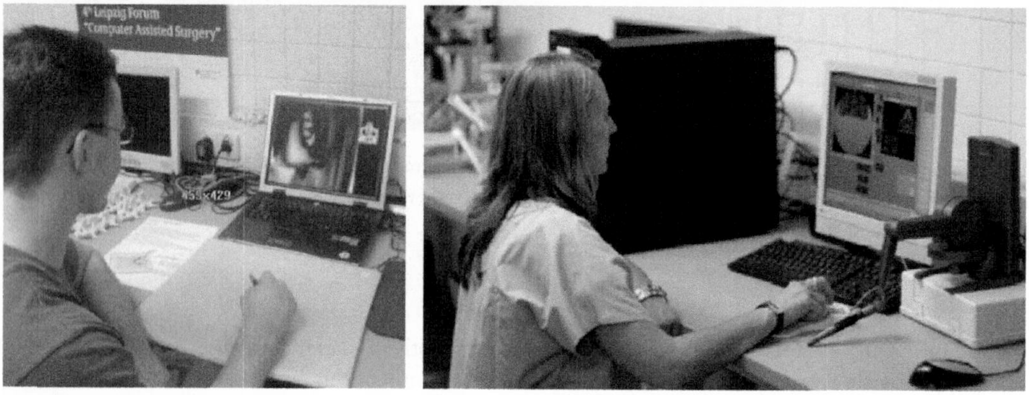

FIGURE 5.28 *Different input devices, such as the graphics tablet with a stylus (left) and the Phantom which provides haptic feedback (right), are used for controlling virtual endoscopic views. The graphics tablet with a pen and 3D mouse have been explored for controlling virtual endoscopy in the sinus.*

Ritter *et al.* [2000] have presented a 3D anatomy teaching system, where the SpaceMouse served to explore 3D anatomical structures. They have not deeply studied the performance, but users obviously liked this method of exploration. In particular for educational purposes, where the user's motivation plays an essential role, the acceptance is a crucial factor. Implant and needle placement are among the tasks to be supported by providing 6 DOF devices.

5.7.2 TACTILE INPUT DEVICES

Touch input is essential for surgeons who benefit substantially from their ability to infer information from touching different tissue and applying just the right amount of force to insert instruments or to cut tissue. The exploration of a complex 3D environment and the placement of objects in that environment benefit from integrating further cues besides visual depth cues. Tactile (or haptic) input devices are usually

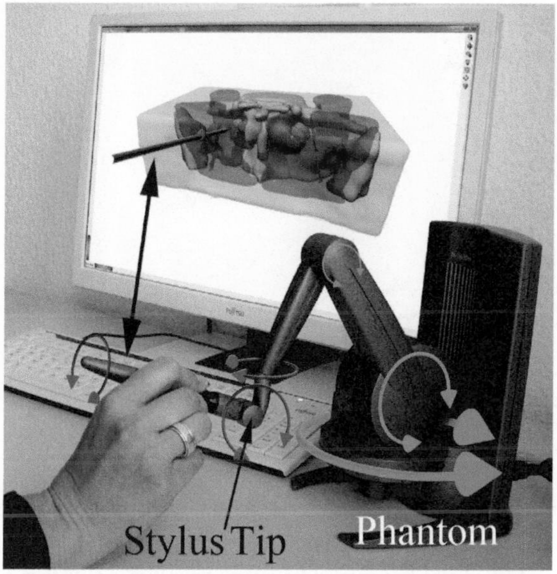

FIGURE 5.29 *A haptic device is operated with a stylus. The arrows illustrate the different degrees of freedom. The device is used to train needle insertion in the spine. The different elasticity of soft-tissue structures and bones are modeled to provide realistic feedback (Courtesy of Kerstin Kellermann, University of Magdeburg).*

electromechanical desktop devices where the user inserts a finger into thimble of holds a stylus. The stylus is supported by a mechanical arm (see Fig. 5.29).

Haptic devices enable users to feel whether they reach a surface by providing tactile feedback. The amount of feedback may be adjusted to the different tissue types and the angle between cursor movement and surface normal. Tactile feedback must be provided very fast, since the tactile sense has a high temporal resolution. While an update of the geometric model with a frequency of 50 Hz is sufficient for purely visual feedback, a much higher frequency of 1000 Hz is required to faithfully represent touch sensations. Tactile input devices differ in the forces, which may be generated as feedback. Since tactile input devices were quite expensive, they were not widely used, except in research settings. This has changed meanwhile. The PHANTOM Desktop system delivers higher fidelity, that is a more realistic haptic sensation and supports stronger forces, whereas the PHANTOM Omni aims at a wider market with lower prices. The customization of end effectors is possible, e.g., to integrate effectors that resemble surgical instruments (see Fig. 5.30).

From an HCI perspective, current haptic devices are not optimal, since their use is fatiguing over time. Research attempts try to develop a device that may be released and remain at their previous position, similar like the mouse at the desktop [Formaglio *et al.*, 2008].

Data Gloves Another type of haptic input employs *data gloves*, a kind of wearable user interface. While a physician in the daily routine would rarely use such a device with cables a specialized medical technician frequently performing tasks, such as segmenting relevant objects in medical image data, might benefit from such a device if it provides useful feedback. A study of glove input in comparison to conventional 2D input devices was performed by Zudilova-Seinstra *et al.* [2010]. 30 participants performed selection and positioning tasks related to medical image data (selection of a region of interest in visualizations of

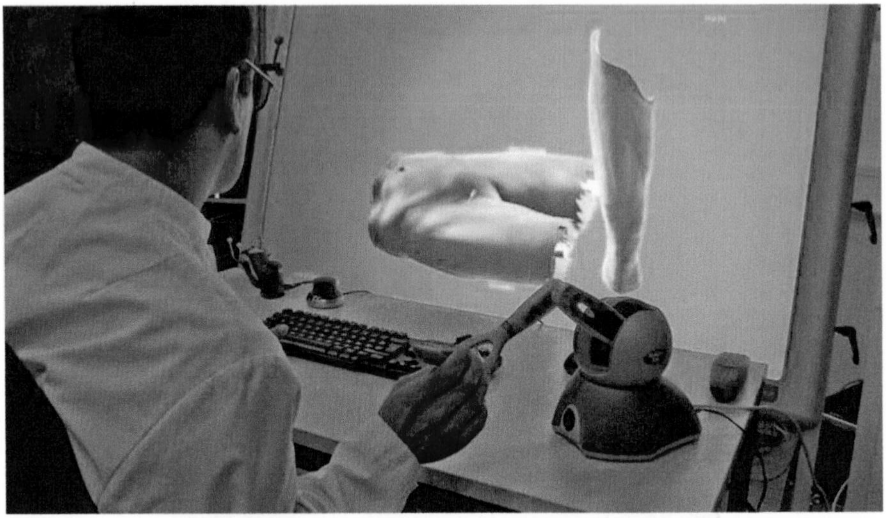

FIGURE 5.30 *The Phantom Omni device from Sensable provides haptic feedback. It can be used to provide touch sensations and thus further depth cues. Moreover, haptic feedback is essential for surgery simulation, e.g., to train regional anesthesia. The device is integrated in a* workbench, *a semi-immersive VR environment* (From: [Ullrich et al., 2010]).

vascular structures and repositioning vessel centerlines). The 6 DOF input possible with the data glove turned out to be more useful for the selection task. Due to the strong experience of users with the 2D mouse and the unfamiliarity with the data glove the performance with the 2D mouse was better. However, longitudinal studies where users get familiar with a data glove and develop more routine in using it, may lead to more favorable results.

In medicine, the most relevant use of haptic input so far is in surgery simulation systems where they are used for handling elastic deformable surfaces. In particular, needle insertion is often trained with haptic feedback [Gerovichev *et al.*, 2002, Ullrich *et al.*, 2010, Coles *et al.*, 2011]. Tactile feedback is also useful if users draw on virtual objects or to support camera control. Since these kinds of functions are essential in virtual endoscopy, it is reasonable to equip such systems with tactile feedback. Haptic input has also been explored for image segmentation (§ 4.3) where it provides additional feedback and potentially eases the task of seed point selection (in 3D data). Promising results were reported by [Harders and Székely, 2003, Malmberg *et al.*, 2006, Vidholm *et al.*, 2006]. However, none of these methods has gained widespread acceptance so far.

5.8 HCI IN THE OPERATING ROOM

Time-consuming planning of surgical interventions is primarily accomplished in case of complex and severe interventions, e.g., when rare anatomical variants occur or surgery close to vital risk structures is necessary. In these situations, it is often necessary to compare the intraoperative situation with the preoperative plan to rehearse preoperative planning or to adapt the plan due to new findings, such as an additional metastasis. Meeting these requirements is challenging. Accurate navigation systems are needed, intraoperative data has to be precisely registered to the preoperatively acquired patient data, registration has to be updated fast and reliably when the anatomical situation changes, e.g., due to brain shift or soft tissue deformation. Computer-assisted surgery research is focused on these algorithmic challenges [Peters and Cleary, 2008]. Computer support during surgery, however, is also an area where ergonomic considerations are of paramount importance due to the complex technical environment and the space restrictions of an operating room. Moreover, it has to be considered that surgeons have highly specialized capabilities which they have learnt over a long time. They have to rely on these capabilities and likely resist major changes, unless they really provide an enormous benefit. Careful and reliable workflow analysis (recall § 5.2.3.1) is an important source of information for designing user interfaces for the operating room.

Current and Future Operating Rooms Operating rooms currently integrate a large variety of different devices and technology. These devices may be mounted on ceilings or walls, but an awful lot of them is mounted on mobile cars. This is flexible and allows to adapt the OR to different surgical or interventional procedures. At the same time, surgeons suffer from this flexibility, since they cannot rely on having certain devices at fixed positions.

When surgeons think about the operating rooms (OR) of the future [Satava, 2003, Feussner, 2003] they demand a more *integrated* environment where isolated technology is melted. This integration is essential to improve usability (learning effort) and safety, since less devices occupy the rather limited space. Operation rooms should be integrated with the information flow in the hospital, including access to diagnostic information and surgical planning. This need is urgent, particularly for minimally-invasive surgery, where a detailed understanding of the regional anatomy is essential. Intraoperative imaging as well as teleconsultation facilities will be more and more integrated in advanced ORs and lead to further needs for integration. As Feussner [2003] points out, the design of future ORs must no longer rely exclusively on the surgeon's memory. Moreover, surgeons generate new information, such as intraoperative findings, that need to be documented as fast and as comfortable as possible.

Satava [2003] made an important point related to one of the typical task analysis questions, that we raised in § 5.2, namely who is actually responsible in the emerging ORs of the future: this is likely to be the surgeon. Thus, despite all assistance staff and all the industrial needs and preferences, the final responsibility stays with the surgeon and consequently his or her needs have extraordinary priority.

Surgical Cockpits The shared vision of leading companies and researchers is the *surgical cockpit*, a metaphor derived by aviation that clearly conveys the integration of all control facilities at a single place. Since 2009 first realizations of the cockpit metaphor are available and generally appreciated by surgeons. However, they have one serious drawback: the devices used in the OR are integrated in a proprietary user interface from *one* vendor. This vendor develops either every component himself or acquires some solutions and integrates them into to the company-specific solution. The future software interfaces need to be *open* and *standardized* , similar as DICOM is the standardized format for exchange and presentation of imaging data. Open interfaces allow to more flexibly construct operating room technology, combining the strength of different vendors. These developments will take considerable time, not only since standardization in itself is a lengthy process but also, since challenging regulatory questions and questions of accountability arise.

Intraoperative Displays Without any doubt the use of image data and related planning information in the OR will be further increasing. Meanwhile, the first prototypes of radiology workstations adapted for use in the OR were evaluated. With respect to the user interface, an important question is the selection and placement of a proper display in an OR that is already overloaded with various equipment, e.g., from anesthesia. Challenging ergonomic issues arise, e.g., when endoscopic surgery is performed and the monitor has to be placed in a way that it is not too distracting to look at it during surgery

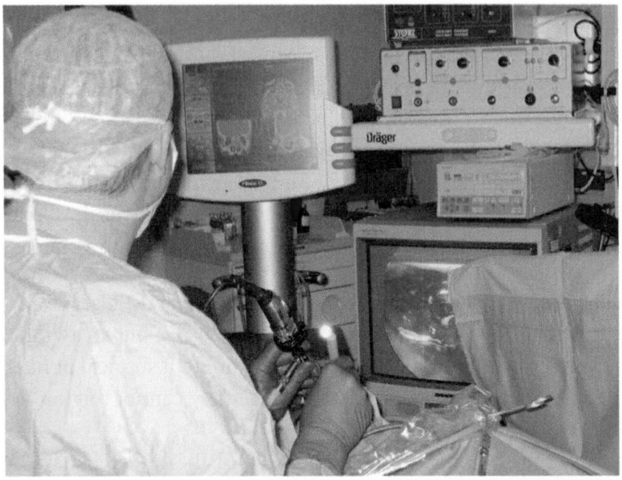

FIGURE 5.31 *During a navigated intervention of the paranasal sinus the surgeon has to shift his attention from the patient to the endoscopic monitor which presents the images from inside the patient. When he operates close to critical structures he has to focus on the monitor of the navigation system which indicates the instrument position in relation to preoperatively acquired CT data.*

[Hanna *et al.*, 1998]. Even more challenging is the choice of a display position when a navigation system is used, since an additional monitor has to be placed (see Fig. 5.31). Since the user primarily employs the endoscopic monitor, the monitor of the navigation system should be close.

Visualizations used in these settings have to be carefully adapted to this situation, e.g., by avoiding a too dense display of information. The user has to operate software intraoperatively meeting the requirements of sterility. Voice control has been extensively studied but seems not promising, amongst others, because the environment is generally noisy. More promising is gesture input, which is a research focus in various groups. Ritter *et al.* [2009] use the Wii interface to operate 3D visualizations (see Fig. 5.32), whereas Chojecki and Leiner [2009] and Kollorz *et al.* [2008] employed gestures to operate a touchscreen.

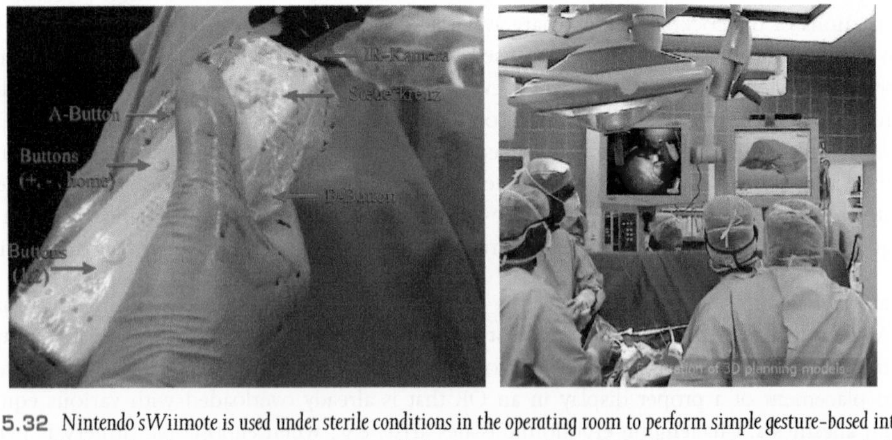

FIGURE 5.32 Nintendo's*Wiimote* is used under sterile conditions in the operating room to perform simple gesture-based interactions with the 3D model derived in the planning stage (Courtesy of Felix Ritter, Fraunhofer MEVIS Bremen. See also Ritter et al. [2009]).

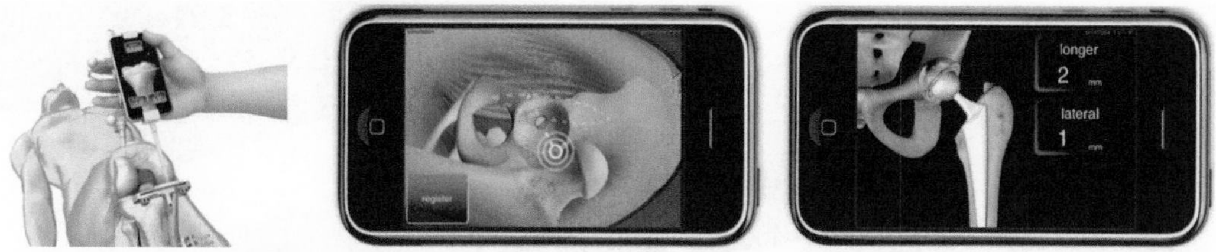

FIGURE 5.33 *A mobile device is associated with sensors and surgical instruments to provide up-to-date information (left). The device is used to perform landmark-based registration and measurements of femur length in hip surgery navigation (middle and right) (Courtesy of Brainlab, Feldkirchen).*

Touchscreens are now widely used as OR interfaces. All of these solutions are based on intensive clinical cooperations with extensive observations in operating rooms and are now in a state where first trials in realistic settings showed the feasibility.

A promising solution has been developed by BRAINLAB in the framework of the project DASH. In this project displays were integrated with surgical instruments providing relevant information and interaction facilities in the typical surgeon's view (see Fig. 5.33).

Advanced: Foot interaction. In interventional radiology and in surgery a variety of pedal-like devices are operated with a foot, like the foot pedals to steer a car. For example, the height of the OP table or position of light sources may be adjusted by pressing and releasing a foot pedal. Foot interaction raises no problems with sterility and can be performed when both hands are busy. Actually the motivation for a hands-free interaction is crucial for foot interaction. Of course, foot interaction has limited precision, compared to interaction based on the fingers. Thus, it cannot be used for, e.g., defining target points for distance measurements. Foot interaction is not a mainstream research topic in human-computer interaction but there are experiences and initial guidelines that may be used for developing OR user interfaces.

Input devices for foot interaction were developed since the 1980s [Pearson and Weiser, 1986]. Meanwhile mature and cost effective solutions are available, partially based on the large demand in gaming and entertainment industry, such as the development of the WII BALANCE BOARD. For an introduction in the concepts and major applications of foot interaction, see [Pakkanen and Raisamo, 2004] and [Schöning *et al.*, 2009]. For use in the OR, of course, safety considerations are much more important than in entertainment applications. The design of such interfaces must ensure that no confusion among different pedals occur, in particular if the invoked functions are potentially dangerous. Surgeons sometimes complain that different foot-operated devices are part of an OR. Since their position is not fixed like the foot pedals in a car, confusion is a frequent problem.

Advanced: Remote control for Angiography. Modern angiography devices enable to perform interventions, such as catheter-based stenting under real-time imaging control. Thus, the position of an instrument is immediately visible. The imaging modality is a kind of X-ray with a flexible C-arc (actually an adapted version of an industrial robot). Angiography devices can produce various

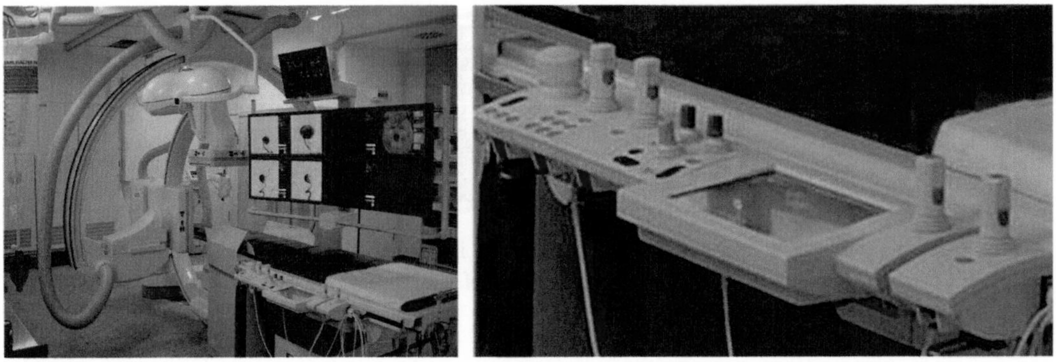

FIGURE 5.34 *Challenging user interface questions arise at the C-arm that is used for interventional radiology, in particular for angiography. The C-arm is a flexible robot arm that may be adapted to optimally image the patient. The resulting images are shown at the set of screens. The user may control the visualizations remotely by a set of joysticks attached beside the patient table, see the enlarged inset of the user interface (right image) (Photo provided by Martin Skalej, University Hospital Magdeburg).*

visualizations. Contrast, brightness and zoom level may be adapted, but also rotations and threshold-based isosurface renderings may be enabled. To control the visualization is essential in order to understand whether a complication occurred, whether treatment is successful or whether the instruments need to be relocated. The user interface for these adjustments is currently a *remote control* with a few joysticks and other knobs that can be operated by touch, that is without looking at these interaction elements (see Fig. 5.34). Researchers and developers currently explore alternative interaction styles, such as gesture input.

5.9 MOBILE COMPUTING

The widespread use of mobile devices is an essential trend also for medicine where it allows to access information immediately at the point of care, e.g., in patient-consulting discussion. Already Flanders *et al.* [2003] stated that improvement in handwriting recognition, display characteristics and wireless networking make PDAs (Personal Digital Assistants) valuable tools for review of patient data, decision support by providing educational material and for remote access to radiology information systems (RIS). In particular, mobile devices have a great potential to provide a convenient access to electronic medical records (EMR)—electronic patient data that was considered almost invaluable before the advent of mobile computing due to difficult access. Amongst others, access to current laboratory data, correct drug dosage, interactions of drugs and alternatives, order entry for examinations are essential features mobile devices provide. For a radiologist, mobile access to a worklist and the PACS system, is a highly welcome feature [Raman *et al.*, 2004].

With respect to displaying image data, even the generation of PDAs with low resolution displays were accepted. As Flanders *et al.* [2003] pointed out: "a clinician is likely to be more than willing to accept some compromises in image quality to attain portable access to medical images." For a radiologist, however, compressed scaled down versions of medical image data cannot be employed for diagnosis. The latest generation of mobile devices provides enough spatial resolution and computing power even for the demands of radiologists.

In addition to clinical practice, mobile computing plays a growing role in medical education where a large number of Apps meanwhile supports a large variety of learning goals. Thus, some faculties of medicine in the US equip their new students with the most recent iPad to prepare them to use the iPad consequently along to perform self-study.

Medicine is often blamed to be conservative, adopting new technology slowly. This attitude is probably because of the strong safety requirements which imply that users need to rely on instruments and methods they have substantial experience with. Considering this conservative attitude, it is remarkable how quickly users as well as industrial suppliers embrace recently introduced mobile devices, in particular the APPLE IPHONE and the IPAD and comparable devices. While the obvious use case for mobile devices is to support physicians with relevant patient information at the bedside, also patients or their loved-ones may benefit. Hospital patients are often anxious and severely under-informed about the diagnosis and treatment. In a substantial study of emergency case patients, Vardoulakis *et al.* [2012] found that they highly welcome dedicate information presented to them at a mobile phone.

Special Usability Concerns with Mobile Devices While the interaction concepts, metaphors and development strategies described in this chapter are valid for mobile computing as well, a number of peculiar aspects have to be considered [Chittaro, 2011]. Mobile devices have a huge potential with many built-in sensors that enable a context-sensitive and personalized interaction. However, the reduced screen size, limited resolution, and processing speed require special developments and not just the transfer from desktop applications. The most essential difference is display size that increased strongly for desktop applications but continues to be small for mobile devices. For visualization applications, that are most essential in the scope of this book, the strong increase in graphics capabilities in recent mobile devices is essential and enables powerful applications in principle provided that the device- and context-related constraints are carefully considered.

Mobile devices together with wireless connectivity meet an urgent need, namely to have the relevant information immediately available at different places, e.g., at the bedside of the patient. These systems already enable the selection of cases and image data, zooming in selected data and specifying measurements. In particular, the ability to access medical image and other patient data at the bed of the patient and to enter additional information is highly welcome by medical doctors. Moreover, mobile devices may be used to enter information in a digital manner, instead of taking handwritten notes, which later have to be entered into a hospital information system. The following set of images illustrates a mobile solution, an "App," developed by SIEMENS primarily to support the patient visit (Fig. 5.35).

Scenarios for Mobile Computing in Medical Team Meetings Besides the individual use of mobile devices, e.g., during patient visits, mobile devices have a great potential to support team meetings, such as tumor board meetings and preoperative planning. In such meetings, one doctor, usually a radiologist operates a computer and thus controls what is displayed (recall § 3.9). Technology might be used to enhance collaboration. A notorious problem with currently dominant technology is that physicians want to locate certain regions in image data and describe it verbally due to the lack of an appropriate pointing device. While some experienced surgeons are extremely capable in such verbal descriptions, younger doctors have more difficulties and thus the communication with the radiologist becomes ineffective. Various mobile devices might be used by the participants to localize regions they want to bring to the attention of all group members. Olwal *et al.* [2011] investigated devices with smaller and larger displays (IPAD, IPOD) and devices without display, such as a graphics tablet that are just used for positioning. Such technology support is

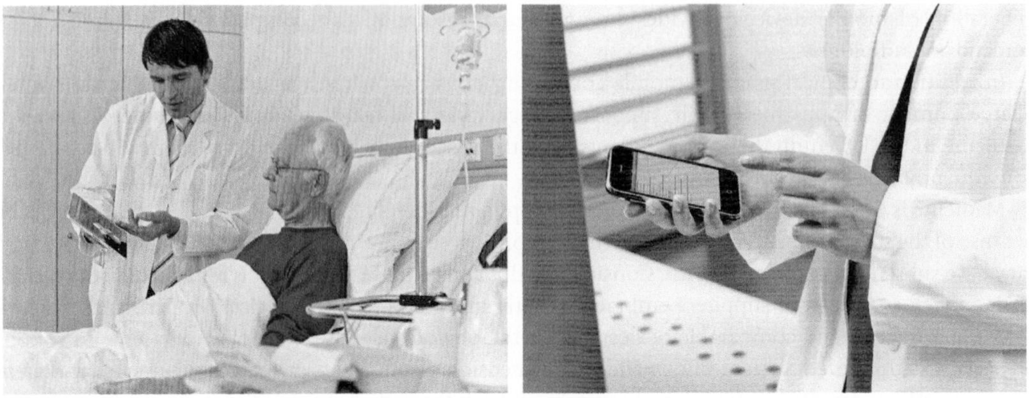

FIGURE 5.35 *Tablet PCs are increasingly used in hospitals, since they provide the necessary information where needed* (From: [Knapheide, 2011]) (Copyright: SIEMENS Healthcare).

not without risk with respect to the social consequences. Radiologists are afraid to lose the attention of the participants, if each of them has a mobile device to interact with. Also, it must be ensured that people interact in a coordinated manner with a large display. While in conventional meetings, participants are often very experienced and know well when it is acceptable to interrupt the speaker, social roles have to be adapted to situations with heavy technology support. The discussion of these issues in [Olwal *et al.*, 2011] is enlightening.

User Interface Design Design choices for small mobile devices have to consider the very limited screen space. The permanent display of a status value, such as the current transfer function, is not feasible. Instead, such values are only temporarily shown, e.g., when the user invokes a command or when the mouse cursor reaches a certain region on the screen. When short textual commands are possible, menu selection might be better than too many buttons [Raman *et al.*, 2004].

For developers it is essential to consider styleguides (recall § 5.5) for mobile platforms. Styleguides for the Apple products and for the Android platform are particularly important. They encompass, e.g., guidelines for the different kinds of icons, launcher icons for programs and menu icons for options. Also the use of tabs, the design of a home screen and the use of gestures benefits from such styleguides.

Gesture-Based Interaction Different interaction paradigms may be used to operate mobile devices. Pen-based interaction enables a rather precise interaction. However, a dedicated interaction device is required. The most frequently used interaction technique with mobile devices is *single-touch* and *multi-touch interaction*. Frequently used single-touch gestures include:

- *tap* and *double tap* which correspond to a single or double click,
- *press* where a finger touches a position for a longer time,
- *drag* where an object is moved with a continuous finger movement, and
- *flick* where move a finger very fast, e.g., to enable scrolling or to switch between windows.

Multi-touch gestures are often composed of single-touch gestures, e.g., *press and tap* or *press and drag*. Frequent multi-touch gestures are *rotate* where two fingers are placed and perform a 2D rotation, *pinch* where two fingers are moved to each other and, the opposite, the *spread* gesture where two fingers touching the screen close together before being moved away from each other. All these gestures were employed by Olwal *et al.* [2011] to support medical team meetings including zooming, panning and scrolling through image stacks. This implies to design all custom controls to be large enough for convenient selection with touch. Interactive rendering is crucial, since users expect a high update rate such that the 3D data closely follow the movement of the finger's.

The design of an appropriate gesture set is a challenging task. Certain gestures, e.g., for zooming images, are already established and should be used in a similar way like in other systems. A gesture set should be carefully limited and the individual gestures should be unique to avoid that they are easily misinterpreted as other similar gestures. It is also discussed to enable users to perform gestures and assign functions to their specific gestures. Thus, the system "learns" gestures similar like speech recognition systems learn the voice of the user by recording how they pronounce words in a predefined text. Gestures, however, should not be considered as a single interaction style, but instead be combined with other (traditional) widgets.

Visualization for Mobile Computing Tablet PCs and even smart phones may also be employed for visualization of medical volume data. Interactive volume rendering may be achieved by means of the Open GL ES (Embedded Systems) standard that supports a variety of platforms with very different configurations with respect to memory size and CPU clock rate. Open GL ES is based on a subset of the Open GL standard developed for desktop computers earlier. Among the supported platforms are not only the Apple products (iPad, iPhone, iPod Touch) but also Android, Nokia and Samsung phones.[2] Thus, developers do not need to adapt their systems manually to the details of different platforms. The Open GL ES 2.x versions (available since 2008) offer a programmable 3D pipeline which provides a great potential for advanced medical visualization.

To perform volume rendering, as a memory and compute-intensive application, is challenging. Initially, client-server-based solutions were developed [Stegmaier *et al.*, 2002]. In these settings, the computations are performed on a powerful server and the solutions include image compression, streaming and decompression for presenting data on a mobile device (the thin client). These network-based solutions suffered from latency, bandwidth and availability problems. Moser and Weiskopf [2008] and Butson *et al.* [2013] discussed the use of texture-based volume rendering on mobile devices using Open GL ES. Moser and Weiskopf [2008] presented the first system where mobile rendering was not performed in a client-server fashion. The key feature of mobile volume rendering is the initial use of low resolution buffers and sampling leading to coarse images that are further refined if the user stops the interaction and a static image is rendered in high quality (see Fig. 5.36).

Medical Applications There is a growing number of research prototypes but also commercial mobile systems. The CGM Mobile App and Bedside from IMS Maxims present patient lists and patient data after selection in the list on the Apple products iPhone and iPad. They are intended for home visits of medical doctors and for the visit in the hospital.

In contrast to the previously mentioned systems, Mobile Osirix also provides access to medical imaging data. Brightness and contrast are adjusted with simple touch gestures. Also 3D renderings may be zoomed and rotated. Mobile Osirix is dedicated to the Apple platforms. Finally, in telemedicine, there is a growing number of mobile applications operated with touch input. Volonte *et al.* [2011] employed the iPad for planning and intraoperative use of thoracic surgery. They used the results (screenshots and videos) of preoperative planning in the OR with an iPad inserted in a sterile plastic bag. Butson *et al.* [2013] presented

2 See http://en.wikipedia.org/wiki/OpenGL_ES, for a complete list and more information on Open GL ES.

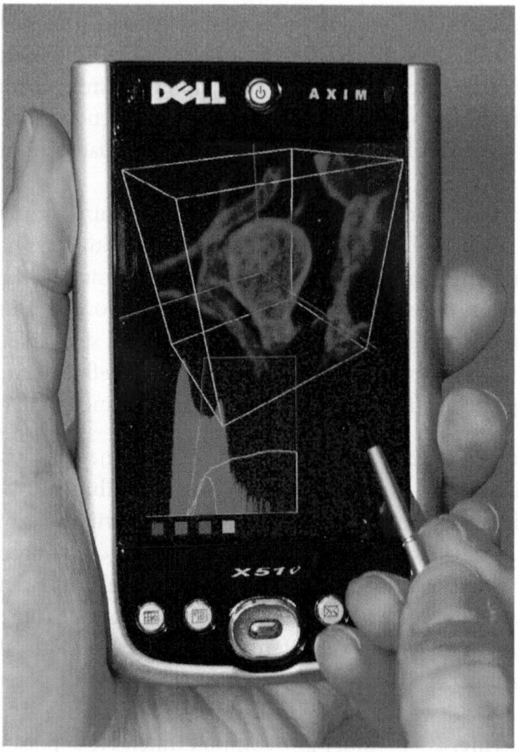

FIGURE 5.36 *The user adjusts the transfer function for volume rendering on a smartphone. Pen-based interaction is used to manipulate transfer function parameters (From: [Moser and Weiskopf, 2008]).*

a system where deep brain stimulation, e.g., for patients suffering from Parkinson's disease, was planned with a Smart Phone. The whole planning process could be strongly accelerated based on the immediate visual feedback.

Discussion This section primarily emphasized the great potential of mobile devices for using medical images. However, risks and problems also need to be considered. Among them are theft and loss of mobile devices, unauthorized access to data, synchronization with databases and usability problems due to the small display size.

5.10 EVALUATION

Evaluation is the process where prototypes or completed systems are carefully checked and evaluated either by users or usability experts. The "think aloud" technique, like in early task analysis, is helpful. Logging protocols, which represent the actions taken by the user, are often an invaluable help. Eye-tracking may be a useful ingredient, e.g., to compare visualization techniques with respect to their effect on viewing patterns. However, for most solutions it is not necessary and the interpretation of eye-tracking results is quite challenging. Besides subjective assessments of users, physiological measures, such as pulse rates, indicating workload, in particular mental workload are increasingly used to understand how much attention different variants of user interfaces require [Saleem and Russ, 2009].

Evaluations require *tasks*, which users or usability experts should perform in order to structure the evaluation of a system. Depending on the purpose of the evaluation and the stage of the system development, the tasks may be or less precise. In any case, the tasks should be *relevant* for the users, that is they should occur frequently in practice or are for another reason, e.g., patient safety, important. Evaluation also needs measures which might be qualitative and subjective, e.g., perceived ease of use or preference or quantitative such as *task completion time* or *accuracy*.

In the following, we briefly explain different kinds of evaluation. This discussion comprises evaluations carried out at different stages in the development process and evaluations, performed either by asking user interface experts or by testing with potential users.

5.10.1 FORMATIVE AND SUMMATIVE EVALUATIONS

HCI researchers make a basic distinction between *formative* and *summative* evaluations. Formative evaluations are carried out *during* the development and serve to receive feedback for guiding the further development. Summative evaluations characterize the final system with respect to:

- ease of use,
- ease of learning,
- error rates, and
- task completion time.

Moreover, other usability factors, e.g., related to user satisfaction, are essential. At most minor problems may be addressed in this late stage. The user experience-related factors are integrated in evaluations, e.g., it is relevant to understand very good or very bad experiences users had with a system.

For medical visualizations, both kinds of evaluations are essential. Formative evaluations are accomplished with a few users in an informal way. Preparation includes the selection of tasks to be performed and the selection of questions to be answered. The questions should include open questions that stimulate discussions. Task selection is one of the most challenging aspects in the preparation of an evaluation. A well-defined task analysis is essential, since workflows and scenarios determined in this stage provide a useful guidance for an evaluation. The selection of test persons is another serious aspect. In particular, the availability of medical doctors for such purposes is usually bad. It has to be carefully thought how many test persons are actually needed (often a small number is sufficient to identify most of the problems), whether medical doctors are needed for all aspects of an evaluation, and what particular experience the users need to have. While some aspects, such as general medical visualization techniques, might be assessed even by students in a reliable way, specialized techniques, such as those for bloodflow visualization, require highly specialized medical doctors.

Formative Evaluations In early stages, sketches and mockups may be used. Ongoing formative evaluation is essential for research projects where a large design space is explored [Buxton, 2007]. One general recommendation is to let users compare alternatives. Users are more critical and discuss more intensively if they may select between a few alternatives instead of having to comment on the only one solution presented to them. Evaluations might be applied in more artificial settings, e.g., in the office of a developer or even a user interface lab with dedicated facilities to record user actions. Alternatively, user interfaces may be evaluated at the user's place, e.g., in the noisy environment where CT data are analyzed or even in an operating room. Both strategies have advantages and disadvantages. For most scenarios discussed in this book, evaluations at the user's place lead to more insights, since the constraints of the real world become obvious.

Summative Evaluation often aims at a statistic analysis with a larger number of participants. Many aspects of such an evaluation need to be carefully considered, such as the selection of test persons, the specific questionnaire design and the statistical methods used for evaluation. Such summative evaluations have rarely been accomplished in medical visualization. The few such evaluations were web-based questionnaires and—as a trade-off between the number of test persons and their suitability—often not only medical doctors were included.

As a consequence, more insights usually result from formative or informal summative evaluations where a few users are carefully observed and interrogated. In medical visualization, typical tasks include the description of the morphology and spatial surrounding of a pathology, its classification and the assessment of its operability. How long medical doctors need for their decision, how secure they are and whether their assessment is actually correct, are among the aspects which might be explored.

5.10.2 INSPECTION-BASED AND EMPIRICAL EVALUATIONS

Another basic distinction is between *inspection-based* and *empirical* evaluation. The above discussion is focused on empirical evaluation, that is on an evaluation with (potential) users. Inspection-based evaluations are performed by usability experts, that is by persons with substantial experience in the design, development and evaluation of user interfaces [Nielsen and Mack, 1994]. Usability inspection is inspired by the much older *code inspection*, where experienced software developers inspect the code of another developer in order to identify problems. In a similar way, a user interface is analyzed in usability inspection with respect to conformance to styleguides and potential usability problems. The most in-depth inspection method is the *cognitive walkthrough*, where the whole user interface is analyzed [Polson *et al.*, 1992, Blackmon *et al.*, 2003]. *Heuristic evaluation* is a less demanding approach.

Usability experts may not only notice problems, but also prioritize them or make recommendations how to solve them. Medical applications have a lot of peculiarities. Thus, usability experts without any experience in medical applications can only detect a subset of the real usability problems, based on their general know-how of menus, dialog and form design or web usability. A usability expert with background in medicine instead may also suggest alternative solutions for special tasks based on his knowledge of competing products or related projects. Heuristic evaluations may not replace tests with real users. Instead, both may be used complementarily, e.g., a heuristic evaluation prior to an empirical evaluation in order to remove obvious flaws.

5.10.3 EVALUATION OF INTERACTIVE SEGMENTATION TECHNIQUES

In Chapter 4, we got to know a large variety of segmentation techniques, most of them are semi-automatic and depend on interactive initialization, steering of parameters and correction of initial results. In addition to the different algorithmic aspects and interaction techniques, also different input devices, such as haptic input, pen input and 3D input devices were introduced to enhance segmentation. Thus, it is crucial to evaluate these interactive components of image segmentation, to compare them and to identify which interaction techniques and input devices are particularly useful for certain segmentation tasks. Such a comparison, of course, includes validation (recall § 4.7) where the accuracy of the results related to some ground truth is determined with various distance and volume overlap metrics. However, from a user-centered perspective more criteria need to be considered. In particular:

- the *perceived ease of use*,
- the *perceived accuracy*,
- the appropriateness of feedback, and as a more quantitative measure,
- the *task completion time*

are essential [McGuinness and O'Connor, 2010].

To perform an evaluation of segmentation techniques, a careful selection of datasets, including those with clinically relevant pathologies and frequent artifacts is necessary. If new technologies or input devices should be compared against those that are familiar to users, a careful preparation is necessary to compensate for the missing experience with new technology. Users should not only answer multiple choice questions or assign values at a Likert scale but should be encouraged to make free comments. Here are a few examples collected by McGuinness and O'Connor [2010] in their comparison of four segmentation techniques. A user uttered the system "reacted well to local changes without causing too much global deformation" and another one likes that "small localized scribbles only have a local effect." For other techniques they explained that "adding one scribble may completely change the segmentation." Thus, in particular issues of feeling in control and algorithm responsiveness may be analyzed by means of such verbal comments.

5.10.4 POST MARKET CLINICAL FOLLOW UP

Long-term research projects and industrial projects also consider evaluation after the first version of the system is installed and used in clinical practice. This "post market clinical follow up" is essential to collect feedback and prioritize ideas for future product versions or future research projects. For industrial projects, it is mandatory to collect and analyze this kind of feedback.

5.11 CONCLUSION

The development of visualization systems for clinical medicine requires in-depth analysis of interventions, equipment, usage scenarios and user characteristics. In particular, it is essential which decisions need to be taken, which information is employed for these decisions and how this decision making process may be improved.

The design of new solutions should comprise a substantial prototyping stage where variants of visualizations, view arrangements and interactions are discussed early and refined correspondingly. The scope of input devices should be carefully considered. This includes a combination of devices which may be used bimanually. Graphical user interface design is an important issue even in research settings. Medical doctors expect easy-to-use and attractive user interfaces, which are perceived as engaging and motivating. Visualization researchers usually do not have an appropriate qualification for all tasks mentioned above. Therefore, cooperations with HCI researchers and practitioners are highly recommended. People with a background in psychology, visual design and user interface programming may be part of interdisciplinary teams to progress medical visualization in a user-centered way.

There are more HCI-relevant topics to be included in future medical visualization systems. An important aspect is whether medical doctors trust the visualizations and analysis results presented to them. In other security-relevant areas, such as aviation, a "level of trust" is determined in order to evaluate this aspect. Research on uncertainty visualization may be a good source to fine-tune visualization parameters in order to arrive at an appropriate level of trust.

Outlook With respect to foreseeable future developments it is likely that mobile devices with wireless connection and multi-touch input will play an essential role. Leading manufacturers, such as BRAINLAB,

MEDTRONIC, and SIEMENS, already provide systems adapted to the use of multi-touch tablet computers. While this first generation of multi-touch software is often a direct "translation" to the software environment of tablet-PCs, future systems will likely take more advantage of the bi-manual operation mode. As an example Wagner *et al.* [2012] investigated how tablet-PCs are hold, which areas are easy to be reached and how interaction may be adapted to these findings.

Also, sensors, cameras and user interfaces originally developed for gaming have a high potential for controlling intraoperative applications. As an example, the MICROSOFT KINECT[3] enables to control devices by body movements based on a 3D camera. For the operating room, these and related developments are interesting. While most of the interaction techniques and devices discussed in this chapter focused on single-user interaction, collaborative activities such as tumor board meetings and other decision meetings also benefit from specific computer support. The necessary technical developments have been performed, thus, such applications are likely to arise in the future. We will discuss selected HCI issues in later chapters where advanced interaction techniques are essential, e.g., for measurement, labeling, access planning, and virtual resection.

Summary for Industrial Developers In this chapter, we put emphasis on research settings. For practitioners, regulatory issues with respect to usability are essential. In particular, the European norm EN 60601-1-6, its (identical) international norm IEC 60601-1-6 and its successor IEC 62366 are relevant here. It might be interesting that this norm for medical devices discusses requirements for both usability and safety, stressing that both strongly depend on each other. These norms prescribe a *process* involving a careful task analysis, as explained in § 5.2, and a careful evaluation in particular with respect to safety-relevant aspects. Also, the role of styleguides for development and evaluation is emphasized. Thus, to be legally admitted, medical devices including software need to be based on verifiable usability criteria and a carefully documented process aiming towards these criteria. From the viewpoint of legal admission user experience issues are not crucial. If a fancy multi-touch input, for example, is at odds with safety requirements, for any industrial purpose, safety, of course, has priority. Most ingredients to successfully follow this process have been described in this chapter. Regulatory requirements stress risk analysis and management more than has been done in this chapter. Workflow analysis and scenario descriptions are a useful basis to identify risks and discuss solutions how the risks can be managed. Also post-market surveillance is considered a mandatory part of the usability engineering process.

FURTHER READING

For those who are broadly interested in HCI, it is recommended to select at least two books to get different perspectives. Shneiderman and Plaisant [2009] is a popular and comprehensive general textbook on user interface design. Some other general HCI textbooks have been mentioned in this chapter, i.e., Benyon *et al.* [2005], Rosson and Carroll [2003]. Galitz [2007] is a comprehensive textbook on GUI design (selection of typefaces, point size, layout strategies as well as label and caption styles). In this book, many examples are given where initial designs are iteratively improved based on evaluations and guidelines.

3D interaction is an HCI subdiscipline that is particularly relevant for medical visualization. While a lot of research in this area aims at immersive virtual reality, there is also substantial research for more widespread input and output facilities, as they are relevant for medical visualization. Bowman *et al.* [2004] is a comprehensive introduction. The same authors gave many tutorials on 3D user interaction at leading

3 http://de.wikipedia.org/wiki/Kinect.

conferences—most of the tutorial notes were kindly made available online. The yearly IEEE symposium on 3D user interfaces is also a valuable source of information.

Mobile interaction is also a whole branch of HCI with dedicated conferences. Most essential for medical visualization is the development of visualization techniques suitable for mobile devices and their smart screens. Olwal *et al.* [2011] discuss requirements and prototypes for medical team meetings. Birr *et al.* [2011a] discuss scenarios for using mobile devices in collaborative and educational settings, such as surgery planning and training. The use of mobile devices in radiology and their potential use to speed up workflows is explained in Flanders *et al.* [2003], Ratib *et al.* [2003], and Raman *et al.* [2004]. Papers dealing with exploring other kinds of image data, such as geographic data are also inspiring [Chittaro, 2006, Paelke *et al.*, 2003]. Paek *et al.* [2004] describe how large, shared displays may be combined with mobile devices to offer multiple users to the large display.

Remote control of OR devices, such as lightning facilities, was investigated in recent years, using touch input, voice control [Finke *et al.*, 2010] and more recently gestures with the Microsoft KINECT Sensor that do not require any cables [Hartmann and Schläfer, 2012]. The motion sensing abilities of the KINECT have also been used for controlling medical images in the OR under sterile conditions [Klumb *et al.*, 2012].

We focused on visual interaction and feedback with a few remarks on tactile input. In particular for intraoperative use, auditory feedback is essential as well, e.g., to warn the surgeon when approaching structures at risk. The synthesis of appropriate sounds, a strategy when to initiate sounds and how to parameterize them are crucial for effective use. Warnings of different urgency are not the only situation where sound is essential. Wegner [2010] presented early ideas, concepts and prototypes on using audio feedback during surgery. A general discussion of audio in medical applications can be found in Jovanov *et al.* [1999]. However, these prototypes were only informally evaluated. More recently, refined prototypes were developed for anesthesia monitoring, e.g., [Mondor and Finley, 2003], and for surgical navigation [Black *et al.*, 2010]. Advanced surgeon-computer interfaces for intraoperative use were introduced by Kassil and Stewart [2009] and Onceanu and Stewart [2011]. Kassil and Stewart [2009] attached a small LCD display and video camera to a surgical drill and used the LCD to display the tool position with respect to a planned trajectory. Onceanu and Stewart [2011] introduced a sterile surgical joystick that makes use of an existing surgical tool and should replace verbal delegation. Saleem and Russ [2009] discuss how HCI theories, concepts and guidelines may be used for information systems to be used in clinical settings. The focus in on task and activity analysis and evaluation techniques, including aspects such as situation awareness and mental workload. This comprehensive paper is an excellent pointer to further relevant publications.

Readers interested in the evaluation of medical visualization systems should consider the general thoughts on user studies in visualization by Kosara *et al.* [2003] as well as the insight-based evaluation by Saraiya *et al.* [2005]. Ideally, medical visualization systems are evaluated with medical doctors not only as passive sources of information but instead as those who guide the evaluation towards relevant medical problems. Among the few examples of such evaluations are Lamadé *et al.* [2000] who investigated advanced 3D liver surgery planning and Fischer *et al.* [2009a], who evaluated virtual endoscopy for surgery planning. There is little work on exploring input devices for planning and diagnosis. Sherbondy *et al.* [2005b] and Krüger *et al.* [2008] explored the efficiency and accuracy of users with different input devices. Both studies comprised pen input and 3D input devices for navigating in angiography data and in the sinus region.

Part II

Visualization and Exploration of Medical Volume Data

Part II is devoted to the visualization of medical volume data and to basic interactions with them. Visualization algorithms should be fast, and should provide accurate and smooth renditions of the underlying medical image data. We discuss software aspects and GPU programming to realize good trade-offs between these conflicting goals. Image analysis, and in particular, image segmentation results are taken into account, e.g., by selectively visualizing segmented anatomical structures.

Volume data can be visualized by directly projecting the data to the screen (direct volume rendering, DVR) or by generating an intermediate representation, which is subsequently rendered (indirect volume rendering). Chapter 6 is devoted to surface-based visualization. Isosurfaces are based on an isovalue selected by the user and display the surface that connects all elements of a volume dataset where this isovalue occurs. Another flavor is surface visualization related to (binary) segmentation results. We also discuss postprocessing of such surfaces, in particular mesh smoothing and mesh reduction.

Chapter 7 provides an introduction to direct volume rendering including different rendering pipelines and compositing techniques. Chapter 8 describes advanced volume rendering techniques, in particular volume illumination and other techniques that enable an improved shape and depth perception. Efficient GPU-based techniques are a focus of this chapter, provided by the contributing author Timo Ropinski, Linköping University.

After the introduction of volume visualization techniques, we discuss *volume interaction* (Chap. 9). This includes advanced transfer function design for volume rendering. Without dedicated support, users have to experiment with many possible transfer function settings before an appropriate specification is found. Since the first edition, many new and promising concepts were introduced, such as size-based and shape-based transfer functions, that are carefully explained. We also discuss clipping and virtual resection. Clipping, virtual resection, and transfer function design are often combined to specify which parts of the data should be displayed.

Labeling and measurement techniques are also examples for the interactive use of medical volume data (Chap. 10). Labels and measurements are special kinds of annotations that enhance medical visualizations for diagnosis and particularly for documentation. The integration of these components raises issues of visual design, e.g., appropriate use of layout strategies, color, fonts, and line styles to provide a clear representation of medical image data and related annotations. The qualitative analysis of spatial relations is added through measurements that may directly support treatment decisions. The size and extent of a tumor strongly influences applicable therapies. The angle between bony structures may influence whether the anatomy is regarded as normal or whether treatment is necessary. We discuss algorithms that compute such measures effectively and precisely. Interactive measurements and automatic measurements which employ segmentation information are covered.

Visual Computing for Medicine, Second Edition. http://dx.doi.org/10.1016/B978-0-12-415873-3.00031-6

Chapter 06

Surface Rendering

6.1 INTRODUCTION

Surface rendering is one of the two major rendering modes for medical volume data. Instead of classifying volume data and mapping it directly to the viewport, surface rendering is based on an indirect surface mesh representation. This mesh is either generated by *extracting an isosurface* from the original volume data or by *transforming a segmentation result*. As we have discussed in § 4.6.2, surface renderings may not only visualize the final segmentation result, but also intermediate results that are interactively corrected, e.g., by dragging or bulging. In particular, in this use case, a fast update of the surface mesh is crucial.

Surface rendering of volume data was primarily motivated by two issues: it was much faster than volume rendering, since a mesh has a significantly lower memory footprint than a volume dataset and it provides clearly recognizable images with depth cues such as illumination. These original advantages have somehow lost their relevance when GPU rendering became more and more powerful and could be used to support all stages of direct volume rendering. Thus, even advanced volume rendering of typical medical datasets can be performed in real-time. However, surface rendering is available in any radiologic workstation and in most therapy planning systems, since users are familiar with this display mode. In the last years, three developments occurred that raised the importance of surface extraction and surface rendering:

- With the increased use of biophysical simulation, there is a need for surface meshes as a basis for volume grids that are used for simulations.
- Interactive 3D visualizations are used in web browsers and mobile settings. Although direct volume rendering is also feasible in such settings, surface renderings are prevailing due to the lower memory requirements.
- Surface mesh construction becomes increasingly important for 3D printing. For challenging treatment planning questions, relevant portions of the human anatomy are modeled and printed in 3D to enable an in-depth collaborative discussion of treatment options.

In this chapter, we focus on general requirements and solutions for surface rendering. We include the use of surface rendering in web browsers and in mobile settings. Mesh simplification is more essential in mobile use to cope with bandwidth problems. We postpone the additional requirements related to surface meshes used as input for volume grid generation and simulation to Chapter 19.

Organization We start this chapter with a brief discussion of the surface extraction process. In particular, we explain typical problems when contours in volume data are transformed into surfaces (§ 6.2). In this section, we also explain widespread data structures to represent surfaces. We go on and explain Marching Cubes—the most essential algorithm to carry out this transformation (§ 6.3). This section includes improvements with respect to quality and performance. In § 6.4, we describe how the methods described before can actually be used for generating high-quality surface renderings in unsegmented data. This includes preprocessing to reduce noise, adequate support in the selection of isovalues and the simultaneous visualization of several isosurfaces.

Visual Computing for Medicine, Second Edition. http://dx.doi.org/10.1016/B978-0-12-415873-3.00006-7

In advanced therapy planning, such as radiation treatment planning, the target objects are segmented. A relevant problem is thus the transformation of segmentation results into surface meshes (§ 6.5). In particular, binary segmentation results cause severe aliasing artifacts when they are visualized in a straightforward manner. Since the human visual system gets strongly distracted by aliasing artifacts, we have to discuss mesh smoothing and explain a number of methods that differ in computational effort, accuracy, and visual quality. We extend this discussion by introducing advanced mesh smoothing methods (§ 6.6). They are tailored to specific artifacts and consider various constraints to provide better trade-offs between accuracy and smoothness. Finally, we discuss surface rendering for mobile and web-based therapy planning and training (§ 6.7).

6.2 RECONSTRUCTION OF SURFACES FROM CONTOURS

In this section, we discuss the topology of surfaces, neighborhood relations as a special aspect of topology, and finally data structures that represent surface meshes.

6.2.1 TOPOLOGICAL PROBLEMS

The topology of surfaces is characterized by the number of connected components and by the so-called *genus*. The genus of a surface is the maximum number of non-intersecting cuts that leave the surface connected [Wood *et al.*, 2004]. A torus, for example, has genus 1, whereas a sphere has genus 0. Most anatomical surfaces, e.g., the brain, have a genus of 0. Thus, the computation of the genus in an extracted surface may reveal *topological noise*—excessive topology that needs to be detected and removed.

Segmentation often results in contours in the individual slices. The determination of surfaces from such contours is challenging, since three problems have to be solved [Meyers *et al.*, 1992]:

- the *correspondence problem*. Which of a potential number of contours in slice n corresponds to a contour in slice $n+1$?
- the *tiling problem*. How should the vertices of contour C_n in slice n be connected to contour C_{n+1} in slice $n+1$?
- the *branching problem*. If a contour C_n in slice n corresponds to C_{n+1_a} and C_{n+1_b} in slice $n+1$, the question arises, where the contour actually splits.

Figure 6.1 shows several possible solutions of the correspondence problem in case that the number of contours in adjacent slices is different (contours may split or merge). While the correspondence problem is related to the branching problem, it may also occur in isolation, in particular if the contour curves change strongly between adjacent slices.

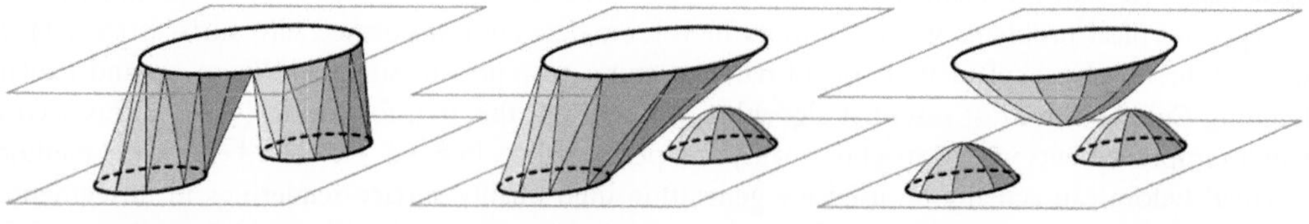

FIGURE 6.1 *Three possible solutions to the correspondence problem in case of a topology change (a bifurcation) (Courtesy of Ragnar Bade, University of Magdeburg).*

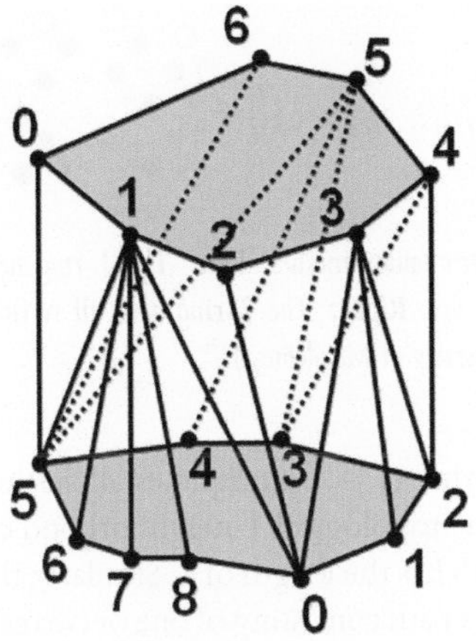

FIGURE 6.2 *The contour in slice n has seven vertices, whereas the contour in slice n + 1 has nine vertices. There are many possible triangulations. Favorable triangulations lead to compact objects with a low surface area and a high volume* (Courtesy of Ragnar Bade, University of Magdeburg).

The tiling problem is illustrated in Figure 6.2. Several authors discussed optimal triangulations between contours in adjacent slices. These include:

- maximization of the volume,
- minimization of the surface,
- preference for a connection that moves the barycenter in slice n close to the barycenter of slice $n + 1$.

Efficient solutions for this problem are based on search processes in graphs [Keppel, 1975, Fuchs *et al.*, 1977]. Thus, a *cost function*, a weighted combination of the three criteria mentioned above, is used to search for a path through all vertices of the two contours with minimum costs. We already discussed such minimum path search in image segmentation (recall § 4.4.1).

The topology of a surface may be well represented by the *reeb graph* [Carr *et al.*, 2000]. To construct this graph, an axis-aligned sweep through the volume is performed to determine the contours in each slice. Each contour in one slice represents a node in the reeb graph and edges represent the connection between contours in subsequent slices. Nodes with more than two neighbors reflect a branching. Cycles in the reeb graph indicate a structure with holes. Algorithms to clean the topology of surfaces frequently employ that graph. In a valid triangle mesh, no triangles overlap. Also there are no T-junctions or holes in a regular mesh.

6.2.2 NEIGHBORHOOD RELATIONS IN SURFACE MESHES

Most algorithms that process surface meshes operate on a local neighborhood of each vertex, e.g., to smooth or simplify the mesh. This local behavior enables efficient solutions. In the following, we employ V as a set of vertices of a surface mesh. There are primarily two different terms of neighborhood, e.g.:

- *topological neighborhood*, and
- *Euclidean neighborhood*.

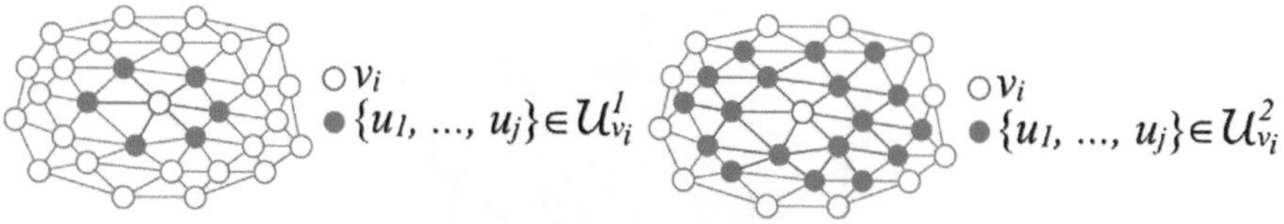

FIGURE 6.3 Topological neighborhood in triangular meshes. **Left:** The 1-ring neighborhood (contains all vertices u_j directly connected with an edge to the current vertex v_i). **Right:** The 2-ring adds all vertices that are directly connected to the vertices of the 1-ring (Courtesy of Ragnar Bade, University of Magdeburg).

The topological neighborhood of vertex $v_i \in V$ comprises all vertices $u_j \in V$ that are connected to v_i through a path of a certain length. The topological 1-neighborhood comprises exactly all u_i that share an edge with v_i, thus the connecting path has the length of 1. Similarly, the topological 2-neighborhood contains all vertices connected to v_i with a path consisting of one or two edges (Fig. 6.3). These neighborhoods are often shortly referred to as the 1-ring or 2-ring. The topological 2-neighborhood has significantly more vertices. Thus, even in a data structure that enables an efficient access to all adjacent vertices, any computation that involves this neighborhood is more compute-intense.

The *Euclidean neighborhood* of vertex v_i comprises all vertices $u_j \in V$ that have an (Euclidean) distance $\leq d$ to v_i, where d is a distance threshold. While the topological neighborhood may contain vertices that are rather distant, the Euclidean neighborhood has a circular (in 2D) or spherical (in 3D) shape, effectively limiting the distance. In practice, the 1-ring has a couple of advantages for many applications. The neighboring vertices u_j may be determined faster (without distance computations) and it always contains a certain number of elements that are usually needed, e.g., for robust mesh smoothing. However, Euclidean distances are also employed for some surface rendering problems in medicine, e.g., in vessel visualization with implicit surfaces (§ 11.6.2).

6.2.3 REPRESENTATION OF SURFACE MESHES

There are various data structures that represent surface meshes. We briefly describe a lean and compact data structure that is often used for rendering surface meshes. Moreover, we describe data structures that provide more information related to the topology of a triangle mesh and thus more direct access to information needed to simplify, smooth, or otherwise process a triangle mesh.

Shared Vertex Representations If surface meshes should only be rendered and not processed in any further way, a lean data structure with low memory consumption is often preferred. Shared vertex representations are optimal for this purpose.[1] It consists of a *vertex list* that comprises the coordinates of all vertices and of an *indexed face list*. The face list contains pointers to the vertex list, e.g., an entry (5, 6, 8) specifies that a polygon has the vertices with the indices 5, 6, and 8 in the vertex list. This indirection has several advantages over a direct list with all vertices of all polygons. In a regular triangle mesh, each vertex belongs to six triangles. Thus, the coordinates (3 float values with 4 bytes each) need to be redundantly stored six times, instead of one integer representing the index. Moreover, the indirect storage scheme explicitly represents that a certain vertex belongs to six triangles. If, for example, this vertex is modified, only one 3D vector, representing the coordinates, needs to be updated. If the mesh only consists of triangles, each triple of indices represents a triangle. In the more general form, an indexed face set may contain mixed polygons, e.g., triangles and quadrilaterals. In this case, a special entry, often -1, is used to indicate the

1 These data structures are also known as *IndexedFaceSet*, a name that corresponds to an OPEN INVENTOR class.

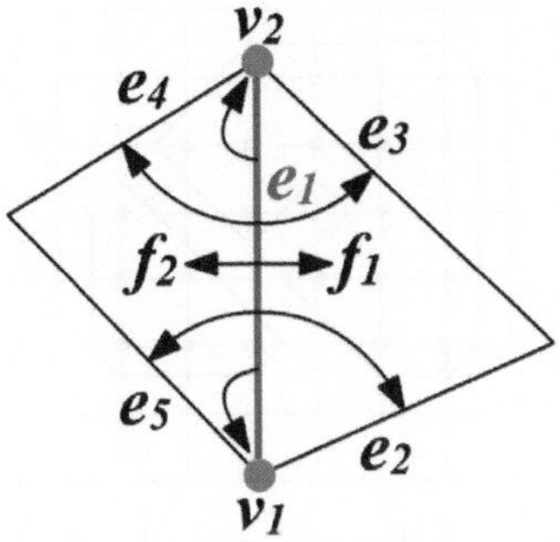

FIGURE 6.4 *Winged-edge data structure: an edge e_1 has pointers to its two vertices (v_1, v_2), to edges that share these vertices (e_2, e_3, e_4, e_5), and to the two faces that contain e_1 (Courtesy of Ragnar Bade, University of Magdeburg).*

separation between different polygon descriptions. Widespread toolkits for medical visualization, such as OPENINVENTOR, provide classes for storing meshes in indexed face lists.

For many operations performed on polygonal meshes, an indexed face set does not provide direct support. As an example, it is often necessary to determine the two faces that share an edge in a mesh. In an indexed face set, this requires a search through the whole data structure. It would be more convenient, if such neighborhood relations are directly stored. Ideally, any adjacency relations between faces, edges, and vertices are explicitly represented. Since this would require compute-intense preprocessing and result in a large data structure, different subsets of these relations are represented in data structures, such as the winged-edge data structure [Baumgart, 1975] and the half-edge structure [Botsch *et al.*, 2002].

Winged-edge Data Structure The winged-edge data structure is centered on *edges*. In this data structure, each edge has a pointer to the two vertices and to the two adjacent faces. Moreover, an edge as part of an edge list has a pointer to its successor and its predecessor (see Fig. 6.4). For algorithms that iterate over vertices of a mesh and modify them according to their neighborhood (recall § 6.2.2), this data structure is not ideal, since neighbors of vertices cannot be directly accessed.

Half-edge Data Structure The half-edge structure splits each edge into two edges with the same coordinates but opposite direction. Each half-edge points to its opposite half-edge, one vertex (the so-called target vertex), the opposite and the previous half-edge, and the incident polygon. Half-edge-based structures are provided by CGAL[2] and OPENMESH.[3] For algorithms that require the insertion or deletion of elements, double-linked lists are provided, whereas array representations are favorable for algorithms that only modify existing mesh elements, since the access to array elements is faster. Thus, the algorithms that should be applied determine an appropriate data structure. Botsch *et al.* [2010] provide a good overview on mesh processing and related data structures.

6.3 MARCHING CUBES

Among the many available algorithms for the extraction of isosurfaces from volumetric image data [Hansen and Johnson, 2004] there is one classical algorithm: the Marching Cubes [Lorensen and Cline, 1987]. Essentially, the Marching Cubes algorithm examines each individual volume cell and generates a triangulation in case the isosurface intersects the cell. Thus, the process of extracting an isosurface from a

2 http://www.cgal.org.
3 http://www.openmesh.org.

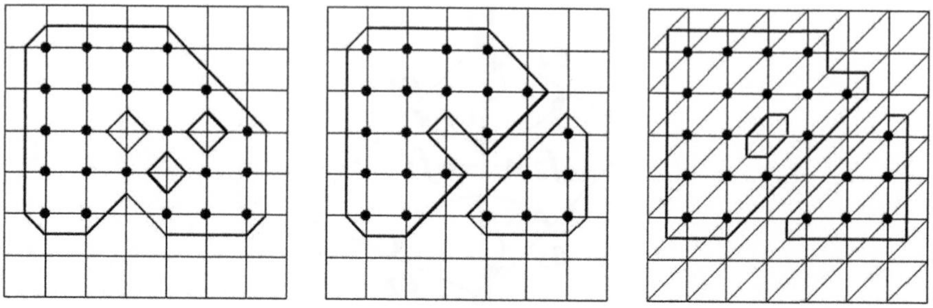

FIGURE 6.5 *Possible contours of a set of pixels with three ambiguous cells. From left to right: Marching Square contouring with case 4; contouring with the complementary case 4a; contouring after triangulation (Marching Triangles). All results are valid but they are topologically different, i.e., the number of holes and components is different (Courtesy of Dirk Bartz).*

volume is decomposed in individual cells and treated locally. A cell consists of four sample points in one plane and four in an adjacent plane. In a dataset with $N \times M \times O$ elements, there are $N-1 \times M-1 \times O-1$ cells to consider. The final surface is composed of the local contributions. The major innovation of Marching Cubes was the use of a lookup table—the case table—for every possible triangulation. This enabled a significantly faster triangulation of the specified isosurface. In the following, we will call the grid connections between pixels (and voxels in 3D) *cell edges*. Marching Cubes assumes that a contour is passing through a cell edge between two neighboring voxels with different states exactly once. Based on that assumption, it generates a contour crossing through the respective cell edges.

Since Marching Cubes operates locally, inconsistencies of the triangulation resulting in holes may arise. In the following, we will first discuss the 2D version of Marching Cubes, the *Marching Squares* algorithm. Afterwards, we continue with Marching Cubes itself.

6.3.1 MARCHING SQUARES

The Marching Squares algorithm computes isolines from 2D images [Schroeder *et al.*, 2001]. In essence, Marching Squares examines all image cells of four pixels. For each cell, the pixels (or corners) are examined if they are greater or equal the isovalue or threshold. If that is the case, the respective pixel states are set or reset otherwise. In total, this generates $2^4(=16)$ possible combinations of set or reset pixels.

If we interpret the pixel states as digits of a number, this number may serve as index to a table that enumerates all 16 cases for the respective contour lines. Most of these cases are very similar. With rotations and inversion of the set/reset pixel states we can reduce the number of cases to five possible configurations.

Unfortunately, two cases have an ambiguous solution that cannot be decided without further information. In these cases, two pixel states are set and two are reset, and the two set pixels are diagonally located. Both set pixels can either be connected, or separated. Figure 6.5 (left, middle) shows the impact of the chosen case on the resulting contour. One remedy to avoid the ambiguity is to use a different cell type, e.g., a triangulation, which would generate a unique contour (Fig. 6.5, right). However, the transformation of quadrilateral cells to triangles is not unique. Thus, the ambiguity is just translated.

6.3.2 BASIC ALGORITHM

We will now look into the Marching Cubes algorithm [Lorensen and Cline, 1987]. The Marching Cubes algorithm solves five tasks to extract a surface from volume data:

1 determination of the case index of each cell,
2 determination of the intersected edges,

3 computation of intersections by means of linear interpolation,
4 triangulation of the intersections, and
5 computation of outward-pointing surface normals for illumination.

Marching Cubes processes each volume cell independently.

Determination of the Case Index and Intersected Edges The eight voxels of the volume cell have an assigned state, indicating whether their respective voxel value is greater, equal, or smaller than the specified isovalue τ. The state of each voxel is interpreted as a binary digit (1 for inside, and 0 for outside) and composed into an eight-bit number $index$. Figure 6.6 (left) shows which voxel state goes to which position.

After the case index for the cell is determined, the cell edges that are intersected by the isosurface can be looked up in the case table. In Figure 6.6 (right), six cell edges are intersected by the isosurface.

As an example, in case 9 ($9 = 1 * 2^0 + 1 * 2^3$), the states of voxel V_0 and voxel V_3 are set. We now have 256 possible configurations of voxel states, and hence we have 256 possible triangulations of a volume cell. However, not all of these configurations generate different triangulations. Most cases can be sorted into 15 equivalence classes,[4] taking into account rotation or mirroring (on a plane). Figure 6.7 illustrates all 15 classes, as listed by Lorensen and Cline [1987]. This reduction was more essential when Marching Cubes was invented than it is today: It enables to store the state of two cells in the eight bits of a byte, effectively reducing the storage consumption of the case table. Figure 6.7 also reveals that at most four triangles are generated as local contribution of a cell.

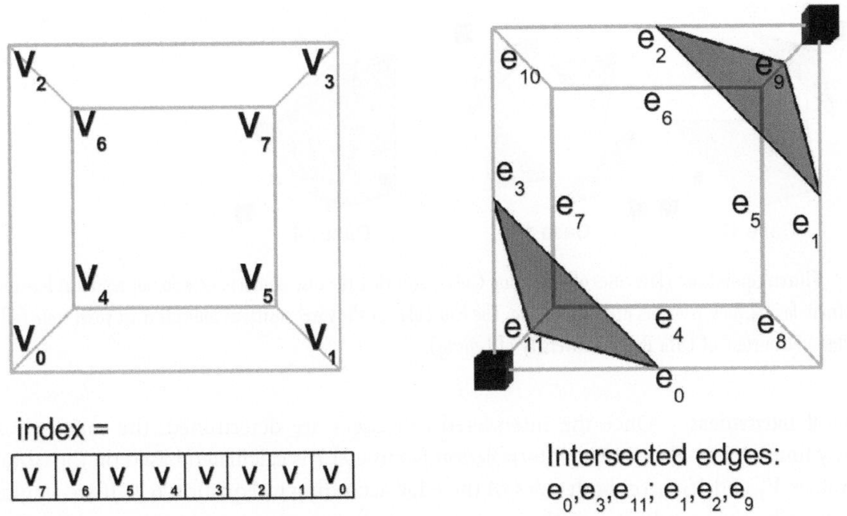

FIGURE 6.6 Voxel and edge indexing of the Marching Cubes algorithm. **Left:** To compute the case table index, the voxel indices compose an eight-bit index, depending on if they are set or reset. **Right:** The case table contains a list of the intersected edges. In this example, edges e_0, e_3, e_{11} and edges e_1, e_2, e_9 are intersected. The blue cubes at the voxel positions indicate a set voxel state (Courtesy of Dirk Bartz).

4 Some papers or lecture notes mention only 14 equivalence classes, but there are really 15 classes. Since only 14 classes actually contain a part of the isosurface, this might be the cause of confusion.

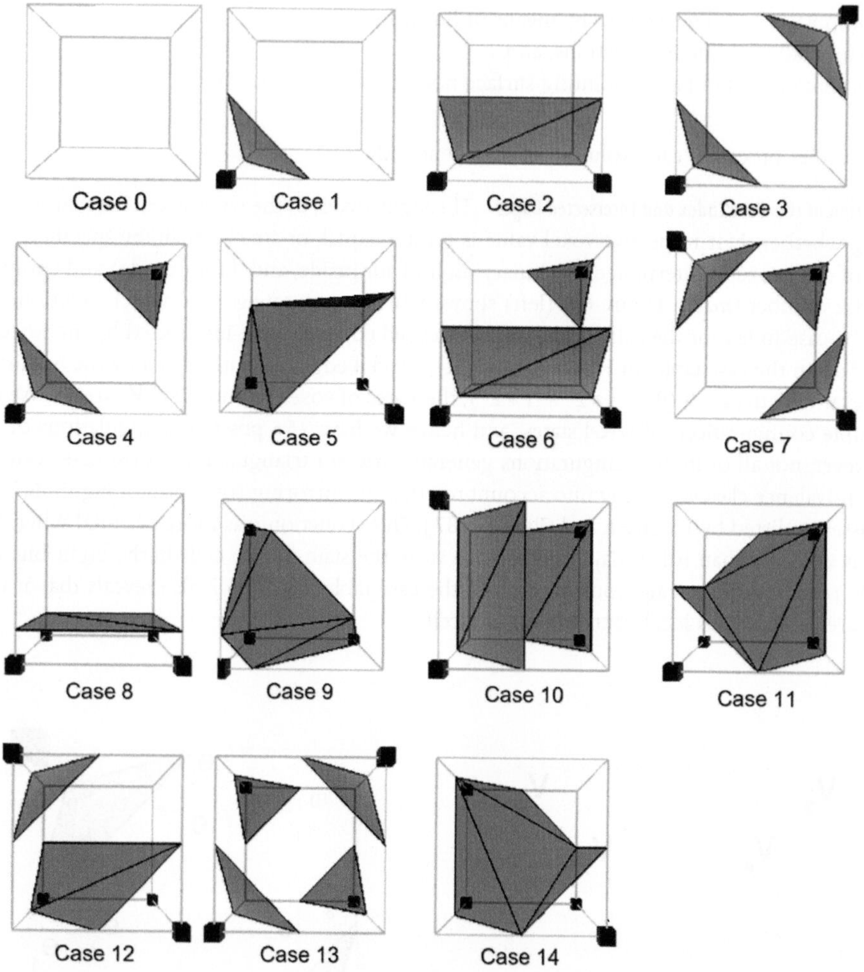

FIGURE 6.7 *Fifteen equivalence class cases of Marching Cubes. Not that the case numbers here do not represent bit states. Magenta triangles are front-facing, gray triangles are back-facing. The blue cubes at the voxel positions indicate a set voxel state (all other voxels have a reset state) (Courtesy of Dirk Bartz, University of Leipzig).*

Computation of Intersections Once the intersected cell edges are determined, the intersection itself is calculated by linear interpolation. The interpolation parameter t is calculated based on the isovalue τ and the voxel values V_j and V_{j+1} on both sides of the edge according to Equation 6.1. If we assume that X_j and X_{j+1} describe the coordinates of the respective voxels, we can compute the respective intersection X_e with the linear interpolation according to Equation 6.2.

$$t = \frac{\tau - V_j}{V_{j+1} - V_j} \tag{6.1}$$

$$X_e = X_j + t \cdot (X_{j+1} - X_j) \tag{6.2}$$

If the isovalue τ is closer to the voxel value V_{j+1}, the respective edge vertex moves closer to that voxel. Respectively, the edge vertex moves closer to the left voxel, if τ is closer to the voxel value V_j. If t is exactly zero or one, the surface would pass through a vertex of the cell. This causes problems in the subsequent triangulation, where a degenerated triangle would arise. Thus, t is often slightly modified to yield a valid triangulation.

Triangulation of the Intersections If we combine the interpolated intersections with the information how the edge intersections are composed into triangles—which is also stored in the case table—we can now determine the triangles.

Computation of Outward-pointing Surface Normals Finally, the surface normals need to be computed to enable a shaded visualization that clearly depicts the corresponding shape. Usually, surface normals are determined based on the orientation of the triangle. However, in the context of surface extraction, we might approximate the gradients of the scalar field by computing intensity differences. The use of the original data of the scalar field leads to a more precise definition of surface normals. This computation is performed for the three vertices of a triangle and as a simple solution it is averaged. The resulting gradient needs to be normalized for the use in an illumination model. The very same strategy is used for the integration of illumination in direct volume rendering.

6.3.3 DISCUSSION

In the following, we discuss some limitations of Marching Cubes and potential improvements. Marching Cubes, like any surface extraction method, is based on the *binary* decision whether portions of a cell belong to the surface or not. Thus, isosurfaces are appropriate for distinct surfaces, such as teeth, skin, and bones extracted from CT data (see Fig. 6.8). However, they are misleading if generated from noisy and inhomogeneous data or when the underlying phenomena are amorph with more fuzzy boundaries.

Topology Problems First, we discuss Marching Cubes in relation to the three problems explained in the transformation from contours to slices (recall § 6.2). Marching Cubes does not solve the *correspondence*

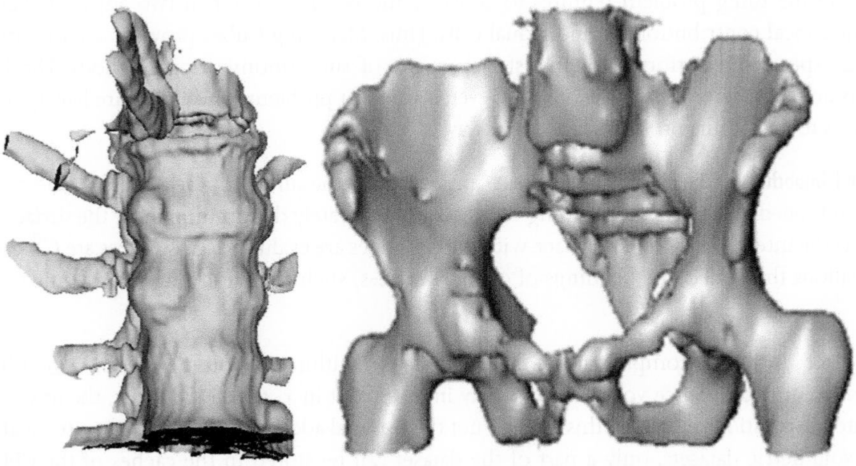

FIGURE 6.8 Isosurfaces extracted from CT data with Marching Cubes. **Left:** A portion of the spine in the breast region. **Right:** Pelvis extracted from CT data (Courtesy of Wolf Spindler, Fraunhofer MEVIS, and Ragnar Bade, University of Magdeburg).

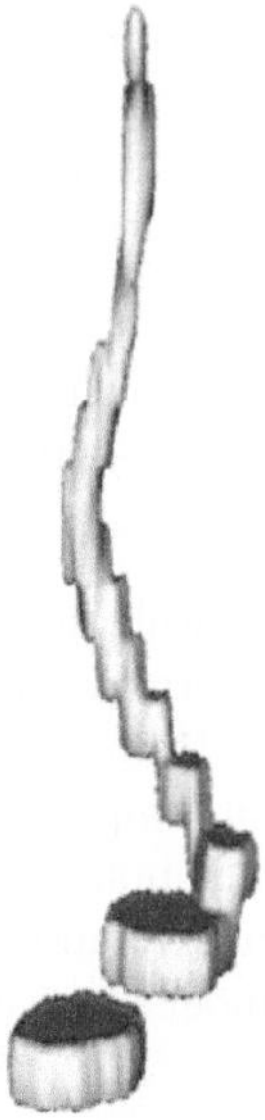

FIGURE 6.9 *A Marching Cubes result of the segmentation of an elongated, partially strongly curved blood vessel (V. Jugularis). The contours in adjacent slices do not always overlap. Thus, Marching Cubes cannot generate a connected surface. The dataset has a rather low resolution between the slices (3 mm), compared to an in-plane resolution of 0.5 mm.*

problem. The contributions from adjacent slices to a surface are only connected if they overlap in these slices. This is very likely, in particular for compact large objects and for data with a low distance between the slices. However, if both requirements are not fulfilled, disconnected surface components arise, as Figure 6.9 illustrates.

The solution of the *tiling problem* is acceptable but not optimal. Any optimal solution to the correspondence problem and the tiling problem requires to consider the whole contour in two adjacent slices instead of only their local contributions in individual cells. Thus, Marching Cubes provides a trade-off between quality and speed and performs much faster than any of such optimization methods. The branching problem is not considered explicitly. This, however, is the least problem, since there are hardly any general assumptions to tackle this problem in a better way.

Accuracy and Smoothness The Marching Cubes computation of the surface is a reasonable trade-off between accuracy and speed. Instead of subdividing each cell and accurately determining how the surface proceeds inside, only the intersections of the surface with the cell edges are evaluated. Isosurfaces are C^0-continuous approximations that reflect the bendings of curved surfaces, such as anatomical shapes, only to a limited extent.

Cache Coherence After the computation of the triangulation within one volume cell, the algorithm *marches* to the next volume cell. Since voxels are typically indexed first in x, then in y and z, the next cell has an incremented x-position. However, this is often not the optimal addressing scheme. As in most algorithms for large volumetric datasets, only a part of the dataset can be stored in the caches of the CPU. Hence, an implementation of the Marching Cubes algorithm will benefit enormously if it adopts a *cache-sensitive* processing that takes into account how the voxels are organized in memory.

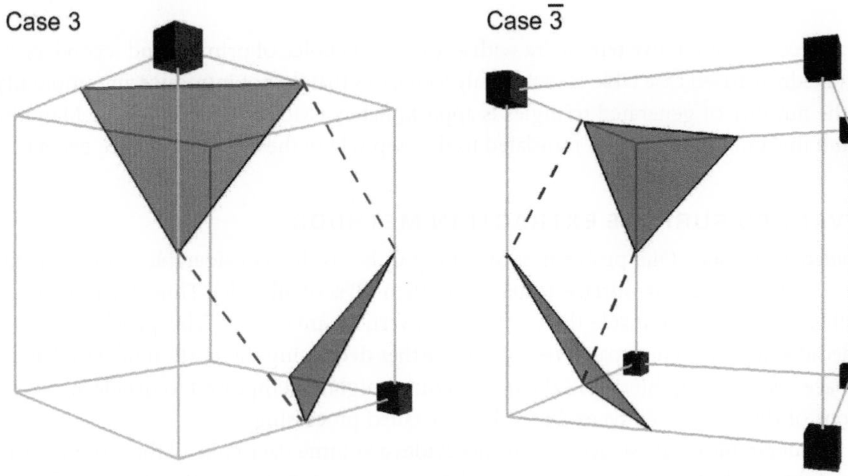

FIGURE 6.10 *Possible Marching Cubes triangulations for two neighboring volume cells. The left cell is triangulated to separate set voxels (case 3), the right neighboring cell is triangulated to connect set voxels (case $\overline{3}$). Both are valid triangulations, but they generate an inconsistent triangle interface with holes. The dashed lines indicate the triangle edges of the respective other cell (Courtesy of Dirk Bartz, University of Leipzig).*

Ambiguities in 3D Similar to the 2D case, Marching Cubes suffers from ambiguities. Depending on how intersections are triangulated, connected, or separated surfaces arise. The ambiguities may also cause inconsistencies, such as holes (see Fig. 6.10). Here, the very assumption that the isosurface extraction can be performed locally breaks down and the solution is not only ambiguous, as in the 2D case, but wrong (true isosurfaces are connected as long as they do not cross the border of the dataset). This problem (and others) of the Marching Cubes algorithm has been detected quite rapidly [Dürst, 1988] and a number of remedies have been suggested. An interesting idea from Wu and Sullivan [2003] is based on user input: the user specifies *connectivity priorities* and thus indicates whether the foreground structure or the background structure should be connected, if possible.

Asymptotic Decider Nielson and Hamann [1991] suggested to interpolate a point on the face that is shared by both cells to provide information if the set voxels should be connected or separated. They exploit the fact that the contours on that face are hyperbolic and reconstruct the face interpolation point (or bilinear saddle point) with the asymptotes of the hyperbolas.

Case Table Refinement An alternative solution to the computation of additional interpolation points is the refinement of the original Marching Cubes case table. Chernyaev [1995] modified the case table to 33 cases to address the above-mentioned face and cell ambiguities. A similar approach was proposed by Cignoni *et al.* [2000], where the triangulation is progressively refined to address ambiguities. The probably most widely used solution is implemented in VTK [Schroeder *et al.*, 2001], where the full 255-case table[5] is used to avoid inconsistencies.

Marching Tetrahedra Similar to marching triangles in 2D, Shirley and Tuchman [1990] proposed the use of tetrahedra as cell type. In order to generate the respective tessellation of the Cartesian grid dataset, every

5 Only case 0 (no set voxel) and case 255 (eight set voxels) are combined into one case that does not contain an isosurface.

cuboid cell is decomposed in five tetrahedra with a consistent choice of primary and secondary diagonals. The new tetrahedron-based case table contains only four cases that do not introduce any ambiguity. On the downside, the number of generated triangles is approximately twice as large as for the Marching Cubes algorithm and the ambiguity is again translated to the step where the tetrahedrons are generated.

6.3.4 ADVANCED SURFACE EXTRACTION METHODS

Efficient Isosurface Extraction One problem of Marching Cubes is that considerable effort is spent on cells that do not contribute to the isosurface (often more than 90% of all cells). Thus, for more than 90% of the cells, either all vertices are inside the surface or all vertices are outside. This problem was aggravated in the last decades with a higher spatial resolution, further decreasing the portion of cells that contribute to an isosurface. As a remedy, hierarchical data structures might be employed to decide at a coarser level, which regions of the dataset can be excluded from detailed processing.

An *octree* is a hierarchical data structure that subdivides a volume dataset in all three dimensions in half, resulting in eight child blocks, the *octants*. The subdivision is continued until one octant represents one volume cell of eight voxels. If the volume dataset has a resolution of a power of two in each dimension, e.g., $512 \times 512 \times 256$, this process can be applied in a straightforward manner. Otherwise, a special treatment is needed.

A *kd-tree* is a slightly different data structure. Instead of subdividing the volume dataset in all three dimensions at the same time, only one dimension is chosen, generating a binary partition at every subdivision step. Note that the orientation of subdivision plane can be changed step by step. A similar data structure is the *BSP tree* (Binary Space Partitioning Tree), which uses arbitrary oblique subdivision planes.

Octrees, kd-trees, and BSP trees are hierarchical and recursive tree structures, where the root node represents the whole dataset. The depth of the tree is determined by the maximum subdivision level, which is usually the cell level where a block (or node) is represented by a volume cell of eight voxels.

All these data structures may be employed for accelerating isosurface extraction. Per node the minimum and maximum intensity value that occurs within the cells is represented. Therefore, such trees are called *MinMax trees*. For a particular isovalue i, the tree is traversed in a top-down manner and only nodes where i is between min and max need to be further considered. The traversal is performed until the level of the elementary cells that are treated like in the Marching Cubes algorithm. This very idea was introduced by Wilhelms and van Gelder [1992] using octrees. This algorithm was widely used, e.g., for multiresolution representation of isosurfaces and refined, e.g., in [Livnat *et al.*, 1996], where kd-trees have been employed.

> **Advanced topic: Precise marching cubes.** The Marching Cubes algorithm does not deliver the isosurface with maximum accuracy. Trilinear interpolation with sampling points inside each cell delivers better results. However, the computational effort is prohibitive if this interpolation scheme would be applied to the whole dataset with a fine subdivision of each cell. Allamandri *et al.* [1998] and Cignoni *et al.* [2000] developed an algorithm that adaptively refines the surface representation in cases where the contours in adjacent slices change strongly. The resulting surfaces are at the same time more accurate and smoother. However, the computational effort, even with the adaptive scheme is large. For each refined cell, it is two orders of magnitude slower compared to Marching Cubes. The higher accuracy is also related to a larger number of triangles per surface mesh. Thus, not only surface extraction but also rendering is slower.

Advanced topic: Fuzzy isosurfaces. It may be desirable to create isosurfaces for structures with fuzzy surfaces. Instead of a precise threshold, an interval $[i_1; i_2]$ is defined to control the surface extraction. The surface corresponding to $(i_1+i_2)/2$ will be rendered opaque. Surfaces corresponding to values i in $[i_1, i_2]$ are rendered semitransparently, where the transparency increases according to $(i_1+i_2)/2-i$. This method was introduced by VOXAR in the 1990s.[6] It may also be used in combination with segmented medical image data, in particular if fuzzy segmentation or classification are used.

6.3.5 HARDWARE-ACCELERATED ISOSURFACE EXTRACTION

It would be highly desirable to perform surface extraction fast, even for larger datasets, so that the user can interactively modify an isovalue and can immediately see the resulting surface as feedback. Even with hierarchical data structures, this is difficult to achieve, since these data structures have to be rebuild at least partially when the isovalue is changed. There have been various attempts to perform Marching Cubes on the GPU, e.g., Pascucci [2004], Kipfer and Westermann [2005]. Unfortunately, these attempts suffered from the limited flexibility of the GPU at that time. There was no possibility to create geometry simply with fragment and vertex shaders. Thus, the number of triangles needs to be predetermined and a lot of unnecessary degenerated triangles were generated and had to be removed later. With the advent of shader model 3 and the geometry shader, more efficient isosurface extraction on the hardware was feasible.

As an example, we briefly describe the method by Dyken *et al.* [2008]. The cells of the 3D space are processed independently and in parallel to yield the output stream. It is based on a hierarchical data structure, referred to as *histogram pyramid*. The histogram pyramid is a stack of hierarchical 2D textures where the *base texture* has the full resolution and each element in the upper levels integrates 2×2 texels by summing up their values (in contrast to a mipmap where upper levels contain the average). The entries in the histogram pyramid represent the number of output elements to be generated, that is the number of triangles (a cell in 2D space contains up to two triangles). Thus, exactly the required geometry is created. For the sake of brevity, we refer the reader to [Dyken *et al.*, 2008] and restrict to a brief discussion of the results. The authors carried out a performance analysis, among others with medical data, e.g., a CT head dataset, and two MR brain datasets where the brain and the cerebral vasculature were extracted. The datasets had a resolution of $256 \times 256 \times 256$ each and the test was performed with various graphics cards. With the best GPU, frame rates of 53, 37, and 55 were observed. The differences result from the number of relevant cells contributing to the isosurfaces. A CUDA implementation was also provided and was only slightly slower (43, 34, 31 frames per second). Thus, even with a higher number of slices, as they occur, e.g., in the thorax region, isosurface extraction may be performed in less than a second.

6.4 SURFACE RENDERING OF UNSEGMENTED VOLUME DATA

In this section, we discuss practical problems and solutions related to surface renderings. First, we emphasize that prior smoothing of the image data favors the extraction of smooth isosurfaces. We also discuss the selection of isovalues. Medical doctors should be supported in this process to avoid a lengthy interaction and sub-optimal results. In particular for treatment planning, often several isosurfaces need to be extracted and displayed simultaneously. We discuss both, the efficient extraction of such isosurfaces and their visualization.

6 Voxar is now a part of Toshiba Medical Visualization Systems, http://www.tmvse.com/.

6.4.1 PREPROCESSING VOLUME DATA FOR VISUALIZATION

At the image data level, there are primarily two kinds of techniques that potentially favor subsequent surface extraction. If data are strongly anisotropic, severe aliasing artifacts may occur in extracted surfaces. The interpolation of intermediate slices reduces these problems at the expense of an extended memory consumption. Noisy data, e.g., CT data with a rather low radiation and a high spatial resolution, benefits from smoothing of the volume data. In principle, both techniques may be combined. However, since they both affect accuracy, this has to be performed with care, e.g., by analyzing the resulting errors. In the following, we discuss these methods.

Resampling Volume Data Interpolation of intermediate slices aims at a reduction of anisotropy, or, even better, at the generation of an isotropic volume with equal resolution in all spatial directions. It may be performed with different methods, resulting in different quality but also computational effort. Linear interpolation is the simplest method, whereas cubic B-spline interpolations, Hermite and Lanczos interpolations are more advanced. To yield isotropic data, it is usually not sufficient to interpolate in between existing slices, but to resample the data completely. Such resampling has a certain smoothing effect and thus might slightly degrade accuracy. Figure 6.11 compares surfaces extracted from anisotropic and from resampled isotropic data, where cubic B-splines were employed as resampling filter.

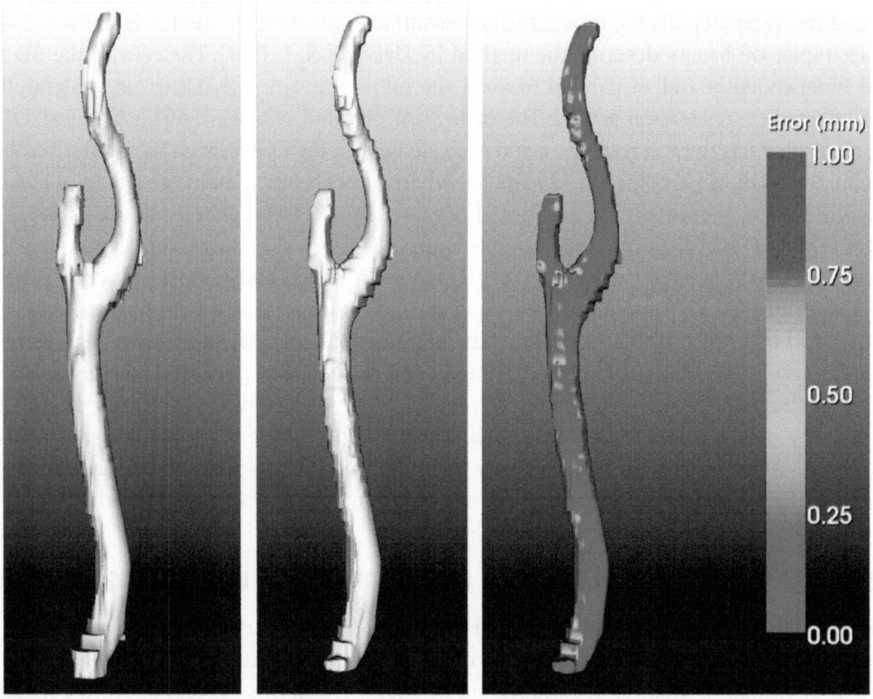

FIGURE 6.11 Effect of the interpolation of intermediate slices on isosurface extraction. **Left:** The surface of the *A. carotis* is extracted from CT data with a typical resolution of $0.453 \times 0.453 \times 3$ mm. **Middle:** The data were resampled in the z-direction to an isotropic grid with cubic B-splines before surface extraction. Aliasing effects are slightly reduced but could not be removed. **Right:** The difference between both surfaces is analyzed and color-coded (Courtesy of Tobias Mönch, University of Magdeburg).

Volume Smoothing We discussed volume smoothing in § 4.2.4 and learnt that there are simple methods that are independent from the actual data and replace intensity values based on a weighted average of surrounding values, such as the Gaussian filter. Advanced but also more compute-intensive algorithms work in an adaptive manner. They may preserve edges or adapt their behavior to other local properties of the data. We discussed some prominent examples, such as bilateral filtering and anisotropic diffusion. Figure 6.12 compares isosurface generation without smoothing, after smoothing with a small Gaussian filter kernel, and after smoothing with the non-linear anisotropic diffusion method. In Figure 6.13, the

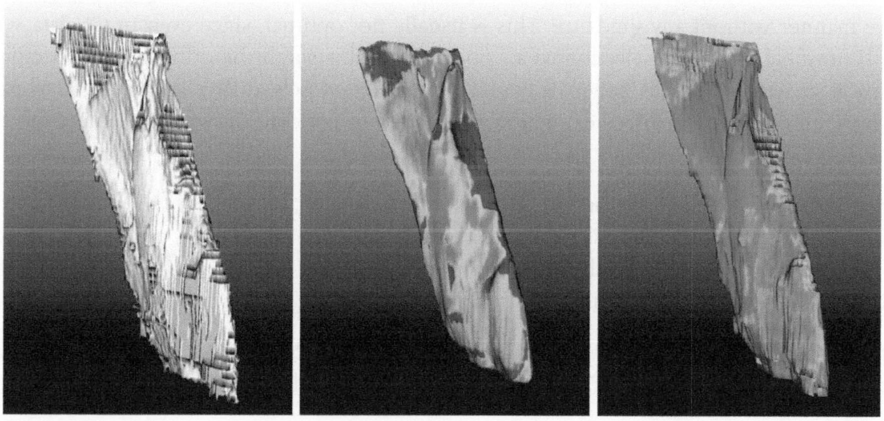

FIGURE 6.12 *Effect of volume smoothing on isosurface extraction. Color encodes error.* **Left:** *A noisy surface of a neck muscle extracted from the original data.* **Middle:** *Gaussian smoothing in a $3 \times 3 \times 3$ neighborhood prior to surface extraction leads to a surface with lower curvature.* **Right:** *Anisotropic diffusion reduces noise more effectively and thus leads to a further reduction in the curvature (Courtesy of Tobias Mönch, University of Magdeburg).*

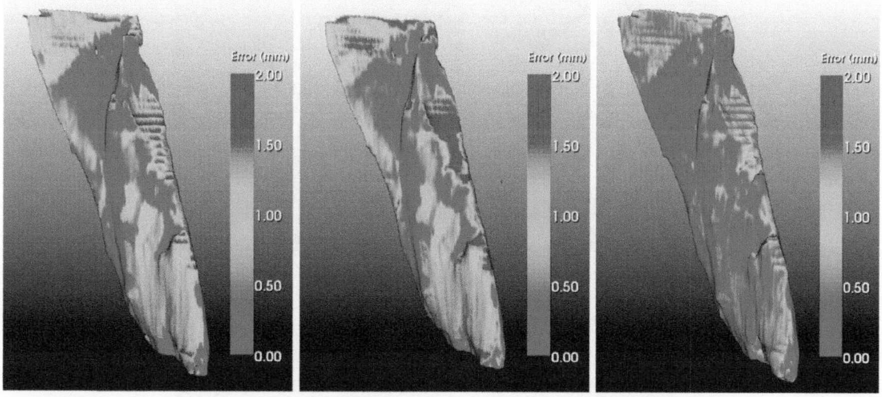

FIGURE 6.13 *Volume smoothing with larger filter kernels. The anisotropy in the data is considered by using anisotropic kernels.* **Left:** *Gaussian smoothing in a $9 \times 9 \times 3$ neighborhood and the error induced by smoothing.* **Middle:** *Gaussian smoothing in a $9 \times 9 \times 5$ neighborhood.* **Right:** *Anisotropic diffusion in a $9 \times 9 \times 5$ neighborhood with $\sigma = 450$ (Courtesy of Tobias Mönch, University of Magdeburg).*

same methods are employed but the kernels have a larger size. It becomes obvious that the diffusion filter preserves the original shape much better. In case of strongly anisotropic data with large distances between the slices, filter kernels should reflect that anisotropy, e.g., a $9 \times 9 \times 3$ kernel size is more appropriate than a $9 \times 9 \times 9$ kernel. As a consequence, moderate smoothing of CT and MRI data may be recommended as a preprocessing step prior to surface extraction. The specific choice of filters and parameters should consider the resolution of the data and the signal-to-noise ratio.

6.4.2 SELECTION OF ISOVALUES

Isosurface visualization requires the proper choice of an isovalue. The isovalue may be chosen in a purely interactive manner without any guidance. This is usually not optimal, since even in CT data with standardized Hounsfield units, the selection of an optimal isovalue might be difficult. The specific density of anatomical structures, such as bones or contrast-enhanced vessels, differs from patient to patient. At the very least, an effective isosurface extraction is required to perform the selection effectively (recall § 6.3.5).

Histogram as Support for Isovalue Selection As a first level of support, the histogram of the dataset may be displayed and labeled to enable the user to select a certain value. In many cases, users are interested in an isovalue that represents a peak, a local maximum in the histogram or a value slightly below that peak to ensure that a certain structure is included in the isosurface (see Fig. 6.14).

Previews for Isovalue Selection A further support may be provided by rendering a few thumbnail images and enable the user to select from them. This *gallery concept* is widespread in radiology workstations. It may be

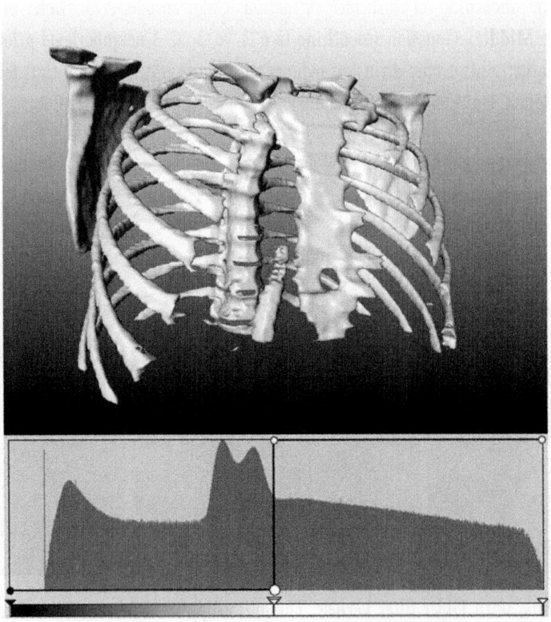

FIGURE 6.14 *A histogram of a CT thorax dataset is used to select isovalues for surface rendering. Here, a high isovalue (see the vertical line) is chosen to display skeletal structures. The first peak represents air, which fills the lungs. The other peaks represent lung tissue and other soft tissue structures (Courtesy of Tobias Mönch, University of Magdeburg).*

combined with some kind of intelligence. In a particular dataset, such as CT thorax data, there is a limited number of typical diagnostic goals for isosurface rendering, e.g., the bones only, or bones and soft tissue should be displayed. Thus, the thumbnails may employ a few isovalues and their presentation might be labeled with meaningful names.

6.4.3 MULTIPLE AND NESTED ISOSURFACES

Isosurface extraction approaches are often used to extract *one* surface. In particular for the visualization of multiple segmented anatomical structures, different objects need to be distinguished and rendered accordingly.

Extraction of Multiple Isosurfaces The brute force approach to extracting two (or more) isosurfaces is to apply Marching Cubes several times in sequence. There are, however, more efficient methods that visit each cell only once to decide whether they intersect one of the isosurfaces and to determine the related triangles in the same pass. As an Gerstner and Rumpf [1999] used a tetrahedral decomposition of hexahedral cells and built a hierarchical data structure to efficiently skip regions that do not contribute to any isosurface.

Visualization of Multiple Isosurfaces A basic distinction can be achieved by using different material parameters, e.g., different colors, for different objects (see Fig. 6.15). Unfortunately, some objects contain other objects and will hence occlude them. The optimal visualization of nested surfaces is a challenging issue. Obviously, a fully opaque rendering of the outer surface completely hides the internal surface. With an appropriate amount of transparency both are visible to a certain extent. Such a combined visualization enables an overview and thus an understanding of the location of inner surfaces within outer surfaces. Note that for the correct rendering all geometry primitives must be depth-sorted from back to front to allow the correct alpha blending in OpenGL or other graphics APIs (Application Programming Interfaces).

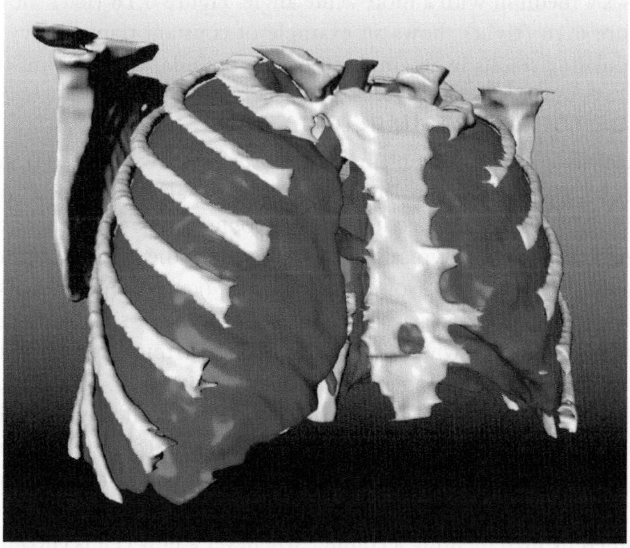

FIGURE 6.15 Lung and ribs are displayed by means of two isovalues. Since the ribs do not occlude the lung strongly, both may be rendered opaque (Courtesy of Tobias Mönch, University of Magdeburg).

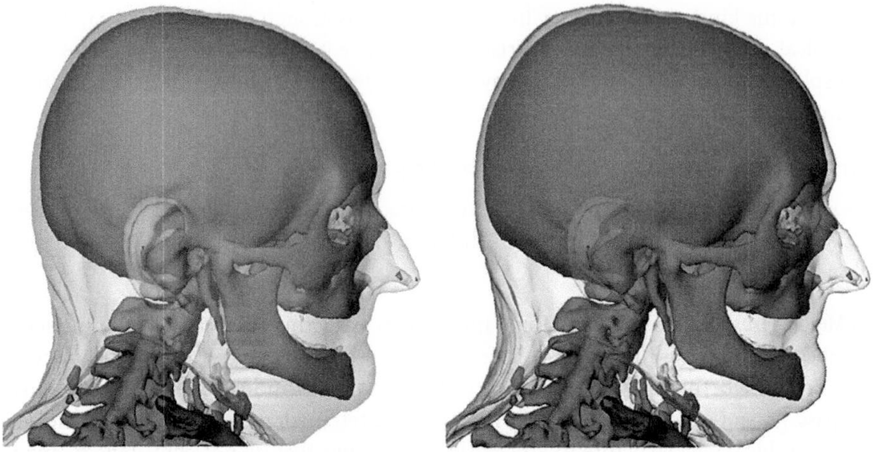

FIGURE 6.16 *Transparency-modulated Marching Cubes models [Stalling et al., 1999].* **Left:** *Constant transparency modulating increases the opacity for faces orthogonal to the viewing direction.* **Right:** *Oriented transparency modulating (Courtesy of Detlev Stalling, Zuse Institute Berlin).*

While this approach allows to see virtually all objects, it does not enable a good perception of the location of the internal object in relation to the outer object. In order to address this, the transparency can be adapted for each triangle. Stalling *et al.* [1999] presented such an approach where the transparency of a triangle is adapted based on its orientation toward the viewer. If it is parallel to the user, a small α-value is chosen, and a large α-value if the triangles are oriented more orthogonal to the user. This is a variation of a much older concept by Kay and Greenberg [1979], which assumes that a light ray will be more attenuated if it traverses a medium with a more acute angle. Figure 6.16 (left) shows an example of this technique, while Figure 6.16 (right) shows an example of constant transparency modulation. Overall, this transparency modulating results in an emphasis on the boundary of the semi-transparent objects.

6.4.4 ISOSURFACE TOPOLOGY SIMPLIFICATION

Connected Component Analysis A typical problem when isosurfaces are extracted from noisy image data, is that many small disconnected regions arise. Due to noise, the isovalue might be erroneously exceeded for just a few pixels. Often, the user is interested in one large connected component or at most a few components. Many disconnected components typically represent noise in the data. Thus, prior volume smoothing would lead to a strongly reduced number of components. To better support the user, surface extraction might be combined with a *connected component analysis* (CCA). This rather simple algorithm visits all cells of a dataset and starts a new component when a cell occurs that contributes to the isosurface. Other cells are labeled as background component. Once a new component is initialized, the CCA iteratively visits neighboring cells and labels these cells as parts of the initialized components if they also belong to the isosurface. That is basically the functionality of a region growing algorithm (recall § 4.3.4). In contrast to region growing, it does not stop after the first component is completed but searches for cells that are not labeled to find further components. The CCA stops when no more cells are unlabeled. In the CCA, the size of a component may easily be determined by incrementing a counter whenever a new cell is encountered that belongs to the component. Thus, the components may be sorted according to their size and, for example, to display only the largest component. Figure 6.17 illustrates how the CCA may be used to clean a visualization.

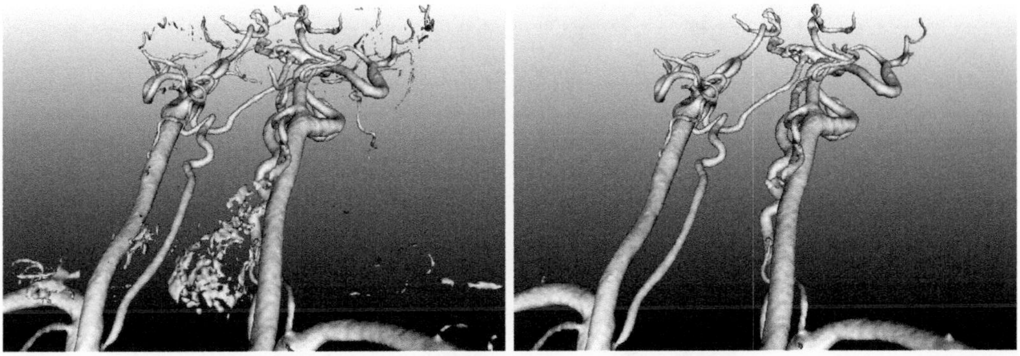

FIGURE 6.17 *An isosurface was created to display the neck and cerebral vasculature. As result of the noisy image data, many isolated components arise. With a reduction to the largest connected component, the relevant anatomy can be clearly displayed (Courtesy of Tobias Mönch, University of Magdeburg).*

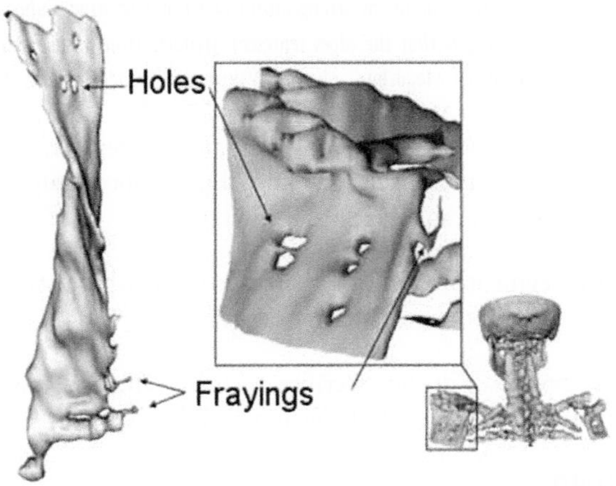

FIGURE 6.18 *Holes in a skeletal surface as a consequence of noisy data (Courtesy of Ragnar Bade, University of Magdeburg).*

Removing Excessive Topology Isosurface extraction frequently leads to holes. This might also happen in manually segmented data due to the lack of coherence in the slices. A number of methods have been developed that analyze the topology and simplify it if it is excessively complex. Figure 6.18 shows a medical surface model with erroneous holes in a muscle.

6.5 SURFACE RENDERING OF SEGMENTED VOLUME DATA

In the following, we consider the use of 3D binary segmentation results for isosurface visualization. The segmentation result is characterized by a *segmentation* or *label volume*. One value represents voxels belonging to the segmentation mask and a second value represents background voxels. Tomographic medical image data exhibit anisotropic voxels (slice distance is considerably larger than the in-plane resolution). A straightforward visualization of (binary) segmentation information represented in strongly anisotropic data leads to typical staircase artifacts and noisy surfaces (see Fig. 6.19, middle). For a correct and convenient perception

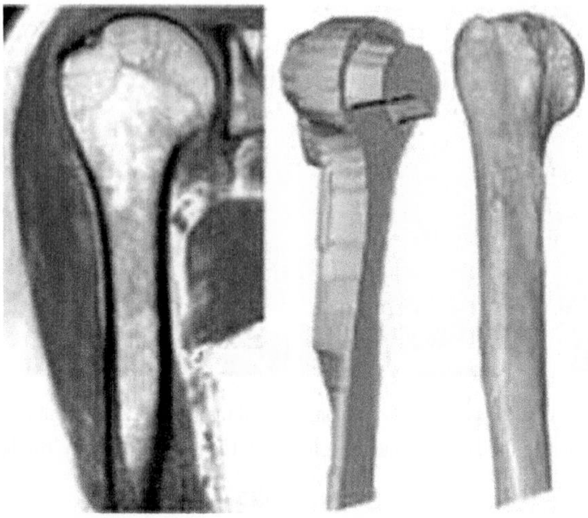

FIGURE 6.19 **Left:** *MR slice view.* **Middle:** *Due to the strong anisotropy, the Marching Cubes extraction yields a surface with strong edges.* **Right:** *A photo of that bone reveals that the edges represent artifacts from image acquisition and not features of the anatomy (Courtesy of Ragnar Bade, University of Magdeburg, photo: [Wikimedia Foundation Inc. 2005]).*

of shapes and spatial relations, the models should look naturally to resemble, e.g., the intraoperative experience of surgeons. The natural appearance refers to smoothness, since anatomical structures usually do not exhibit sharp edges. The problem can be tackled in two stages:

- at the image level, the segmentation information may be post-processed and smoothed, and
- the polygonal mesh may be processed and smoothed.

It is essential that these processes do not sacrifice accuracy. Thus, we consequently consider both improvements in smoothness and the side effects on accuracy.

6.5.1 PREPROCESSING

Also the surface visualization of segmented data benefits from preprocessing, similar to the preprocessing strategies discussed for the original data (recall § 6.4.1). The segmentation information may be used to enhance both resampling and volume smoothing.

Resampling Volume Data With segmented data, resampling may be strongly restricted to a ROI that just comprises the segmentation result. Thus, the resampling effort and the memory consumption may be strongly reduced. In addition, a more advanced interpolation technique may be applied. Instead of grey value interpolation, the shape of the contours representing the segmentation result in different slices should be interpolated. Thus, *shape-based interpolation* is frequently used [Raya and Udupa, 1990]. Shape-based interpolation takes two contours, represented as binary volumes, as input and generates a desired number of intermediate contours. Figure 6.20 compares surfaces extracted from segmentation in the original anisotropic data with surfaces extracted after shape-based interpolation. Please note that the aliasing effects are strongly reduced and the effect is stronger than by resampling that does not consider the shapes.

Smoothing Segmentation Results for Visualization Isosurfaces from segmentation results are created by using an intermediate value (between the value for the segmentation mask and background) as isovalue. As an

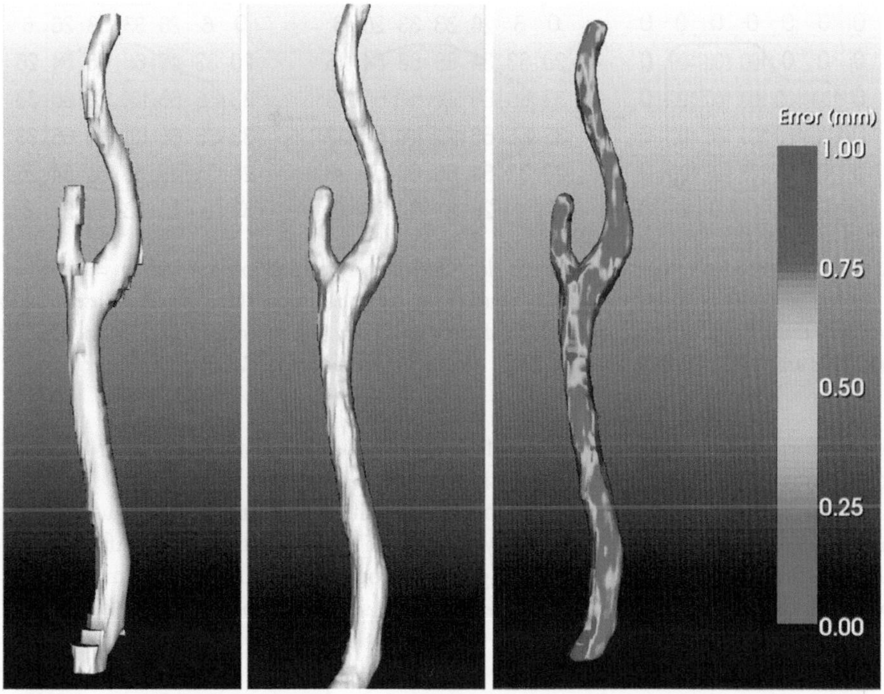

FIGURE 6.20 *Effect of shape-based interpolation on isosurface extraction.* **Left:** *The surface of the segmented A. carotis is extracted from CT data with a resolution of 0.453 × 0.453 × 3 mm.* **Middle:** *Shape-based interpolation between the contours of the segmented A. carotis was applied prior to surface extraction. The data were resampled to an isotropic grid and cubic B-splines were applied for the interpolation.* **Right:** *The difference between both surfaces is analyzed and color-coded (Courtesy of Tobias Mönch, University of Magdeburg).*

example, 100 may denote voxels belonging to the segmentation mask, 0 represents background voxels, and 50 is used as isovalue. The simple isosurface generation suffers from strong aliasing artifacts, which become obvious as discontinuities in the surface normals. Therefore, it is useful to "smooth" the boundary in the segmentation result at the voxel level. Otherwise, intersections of an isosurface and a cell are always located at the center of an edge; never at any intermediate position. This explains why aliasing artifacts are significantly particularly severe when surfaces are extracted from *binary* volumes.

Fuzzy Boundaries Morphological operations may be employed to improve the appearance of visualizations that are based on binary segmentation results. In essence, they provide *fuzzy boundaries*. This is achieved by transforming the narrow region around the segmentation boundary such that the intensity values vary rather smoothly from background to foreground. This very idea was introduced by Lakare and Kaufman [2003]. They suggested to use the corresponding voxels in the original data to provide a visualization that considers both the segmentation and the acquired medical image data.

Smoothing Segmentation Results with Morphologic Operations In the following, we describe an efficient approach to smooth the segmentation result with morphological image processing [Neubauer *et al.*, 2004a].

We denote with v_1 the value of the segmentation result and with v_2 the value of the background voxels. τ represents the isovalue which is computed as $(v_1 + v_2)/2$. The method is based on morphologic

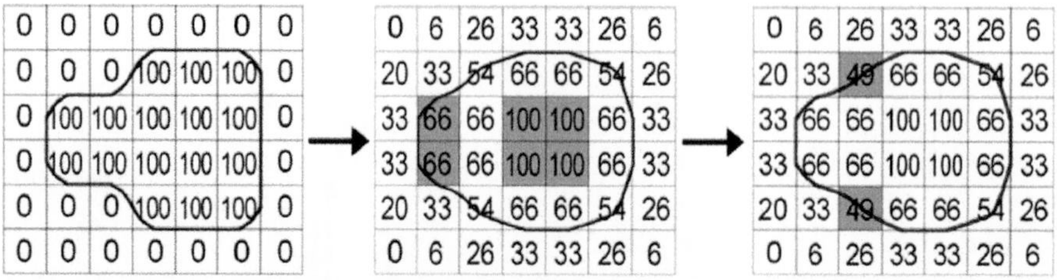

FIGURE 6.21 *Smoothing binary segmentation results (left) through morphological operators with $v_1 = 0, v_2 = 100$, and $\tau = 50$. The dark gray voxels in the left part (middle) would be removed by an erosion. This is avoided to preserve the object shape. In a last step, voxels that belong to the segmentation result and have a value below 50 are corrected (right). Instead of a binary volume, nine different values arise and lead to reduced discontinuities (Courtesy of André Neubauer, VRVis Wien).*

operations performed in a defined distance of the original object boundary and it is constrained to maintain the foreground-background classification.

Each voxel near the object boundary is assigned a new value v, with $v_1 \leq v \leq v_2$ using the following algorithm: A reference mask V_{ref} is created by eroding the segmentation result. After the erosion, all voxels of V_{ref} are assigned the value v according to Equation 6.3, which in essence moves the isosurface closer to the background value, thus farther away from the segmented object.

$$v = v_2 - (v_2 - v_1) * \frac{1}{3} \tag{6.3}$$

During erosion, the algorithm checks whether the shape has significantly changed such that small features on the boundary of the segmented object would be lost [Neubauer *et al.*, 2004b]. Significant changes are defined as removed voxels which are not adjacent to the original segmentation. These voxels are not removed (see Fig. 6.21).

After the modified erosion, two dilation operations are performed. The boundary voxels of the reference mask are tracked as reference voxels with the dilation front. Each voxel V that is added through dilation is therefore associated with a reference voxel V_{ref} and acquires the value

$$v = v_{ref} - (v_2 - v_1) * \frac{d}{3} \tag{6.4}$$

with d being the Euclidean distance from V to V_{ref} and v_{ref} being the value of V_{ref}. The method can be generalized to a wider filter region (with more erosion and dilatation steps). To preserve the segmentation result, it is desirable that all voxels which belong to the segmentation result yield a value above τ. This is achieved by a correction with a small positive δ in a final step. The resulting isosurface is at most one voxel away from the surface that would result from the original data.

This algorithm yields a near-linear value degradation from the reference mask outwards. It can be applied to smooth larger regions by eroding and dilating several times, see Figure 6.22. The algorithm retains the basic object shape and volume.

6.5.2 BASIC MESH SMOOTHING

In the following, we describe rather simple and general mesh smoothing techniques. In general, mesh smoothing does not change the number of vertices and the topology of a surface mesh. Instead, only the coordinates of vertices are changed. Thus, almost all mesh smoothing techniques are *topology preserving*. Before

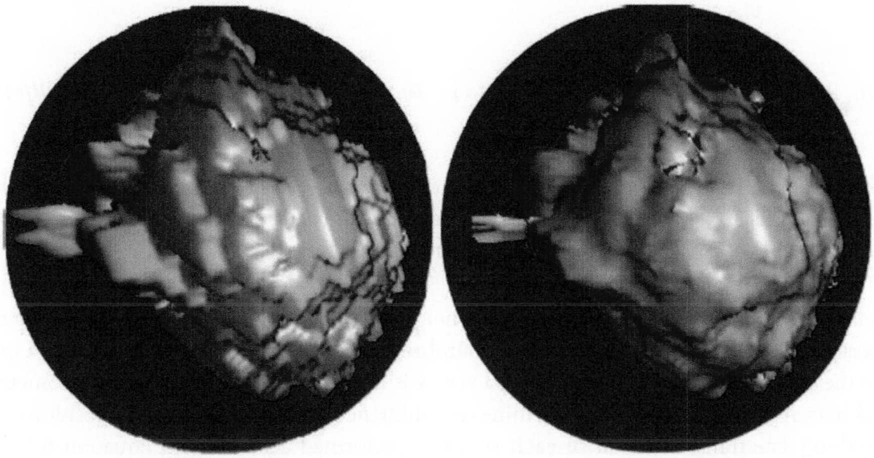

FIGURE 6.22 **Left:** 3D visualization based on the raw segmentation result. **Right:** The distracting interpolation artifacts are effectively reduced with smoothing based on a larger filter kernel. The circular images are from virtual endoscopy and resemble real endoscopic views (Courtesy of André Neubauer, VRVis Wien).

we describe these techniques, we introduce the differential properties of curvature that are fundamental to mesh smoothing.

Curvature Efficient smoothing of a surface model reduces bumps and bulges. This leads to lower *curvature values*. Curvature characterizes how strongly the surface deviates from a plane. Curvature along a surface that lives in 3D space is measured along two directions: along the principal curvature direction and along an orthogonal direction. Based on these two measures κ_1 and κ_2, various curvature measures are defined, e.g.,

- mean curvature ($H = 1/2(\kappa_1 + \kappa_2)$), and
- Gaussian curvature ($K = \kappa_1 \cdot \kappa_2$).

Curvature measures are derived from 2nd order partial derivatives and thus can only be defined for smooth continuous surfaces with at least C^1 continuity. A polygonal mesh does not fulfill this requirement, actually it is locally flat and exhibits no curvature. For approximating curvature values, higher order polynomial surfaces, e.g., quadric or cubic surfaces, are optimally fitted to a polygon mesh. There are various approaches, differing in accuracy and computational effort, see e.g., [Razdan and Bae, 2005, Taubin, 1995b]. For our purposes, it is sufficient to state that curvature can be effectively approximated and used to evaluate smoothing algorithms. The chosen curvature value can be color-coded on the surface, and additionally histograms of curvature values may be displayed and analyzed. We discuss curvature estimation both related to curvature values and curvature directions in more detail in § 12.3, since it plays an essential role in illustrative visualization.

Laplacian Smoothing The Laplacian filter or operator is the simplest smoothing method, and it is widely available in visualization and geometric modeling toolkits (see Fig. 6.23). It is sometimes called *relaxation filter*. The term *relaxation* is related to the effect on the surface where the bending energy is reduced—the surface is relaxed. The filter is applied iteratively to a polygonal mesh and produces smooth surfaces after an appropriate number of iterations. In most implementations, it is applied to the 1-ring neighborhood,

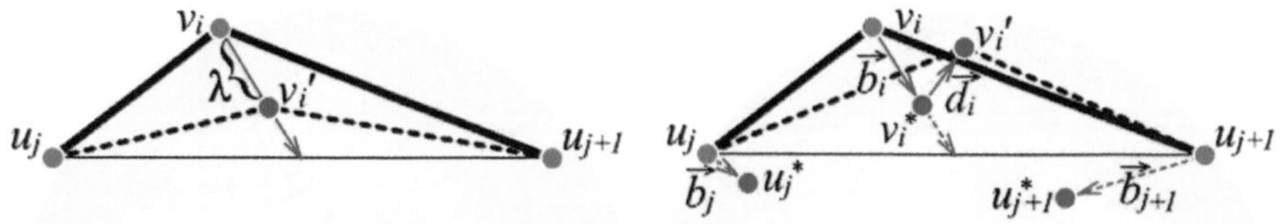

FIGURE 6.23 **Left:** *The Laplacian filter applied to a polygonal curve moves vertex* v_i *in the direction of its neighbors according to the weighting factor* λ. **Right:** *A correction after the Laplacian reduces the effect of the first smoothing step. The correction moves in a direction derived by the local normal vectors (Courtesy of Ragnar Bade, University of Magdeburg).*

since this is faster compared to the more extended neighborhoods. Because of this, it is also referred to as *umbrella operator*. This term relates to the fact that an umbrella has a central vertex, connected to a number of vertices in the surroundings. In each iteration, a vertex is moved in the direction of the geometric center of its neighbors. A weighting factor λ determines the influence of the original vertex position to its value after smoothing. The transformation of each vertex is performed according to Equation 6.5, where v_i is the previous position of a vertex, and v_i' is its new position and u_j are vertices of the neighborhood from v_i. Thus, the Laplacian operator is a discretized version of the Laplacian for continuous analytical functions, applicable to polygonal meshes. The number of iterations and the weighting factor λ are the two parameters that determine the amount of smoothing.

$$v_i' = v_i + \frac{\lambda}{m}\sum_{j=1}^{m}(u_j - v_i)v_i, \; u_j \in V, \; v_i \neq u_j, \; \forall u_j \in U_{vi} m = \|U_{vi}\| \tag{6.5}$$

Since all neighbors are treated equally in the smoothing process, the method leads to deformations of the surface when regions with significantly smaller edges are close to regions with large edges. In surface models, directly extracted from regular volume grids, this problem is not severe. If meshes are simplified and compressed, however, subsequent smoothing should properly weight the vertex contribution according to the distance from the current vertex.

An essential drawback of Laplacian smoothing is that smoothness is achieved at the expense of accuracy. Small details may be lost, since the method is not adaptive, similar to the Gaussian filter in image smoothing. Volumes typically shrink considerably. These problems are particularly relevant in medical applications where 3D visualization should provide faithful renditions suitable for treatment decisions. These drawbacks gave rise to a number of refinements that are discussed in the following.

Laplacian with Correction The Laplacian with an additional correction was introduced by Vollmer *et al.* [1999] to reduce volume shrinkage. In this approach, vertices are translated in roughly the original direction by a certain amount after Laplacian smoothing. The specific direction and the amount are derived from the previous position of that vertex and the averaged translation of its direct neighbors. This algorithm is rather time-consuming, since each step is more compute-intensive and more steps are required compared to the original Laplacian. However, more accurate results are achieved. A drawback is that the Laplacian with correction has four parameters (two in addition to the two of the Laplacian). Thus, users need guidance to adjust these parameters. Figure 6.24 illustrates the working principle of the Laplacian and the Laplacian with correction on a 2D polygonal curve.

The λ/μ Filter The λ/μ filter (also referred to as low-pass filter) combines a positively and a negatively weighted Laplacian filter that are applied alternately [Taubin, 1995a]. The result is similar to the Laplacian with correction and leads to more accurate results than the original Laplacian. In particular, volume

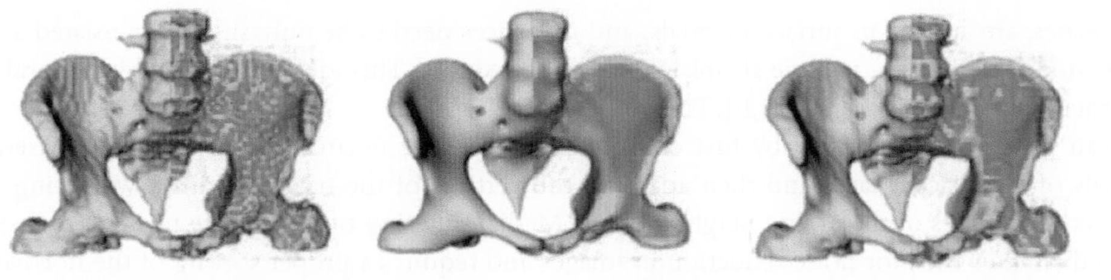

FIGURE 6.24 *Mesh smoothing and resulting maximum curvature in the right part (green represents zero and red represents maximum values).* **Left:** *Original surface of a pelvis extracted from binary thresholded CT data.* **Middle:** *After Laplacian smoothing with 20 iterations and $\lambda = 0.7$.* **Right:** *Laplacian smoothing with correction but identical number of iterations and weighting factor λ. The surface is not that smooth but represents the anatomy more faithfully (Courtesy of Ragnar Bade, University of Magdeburg).*

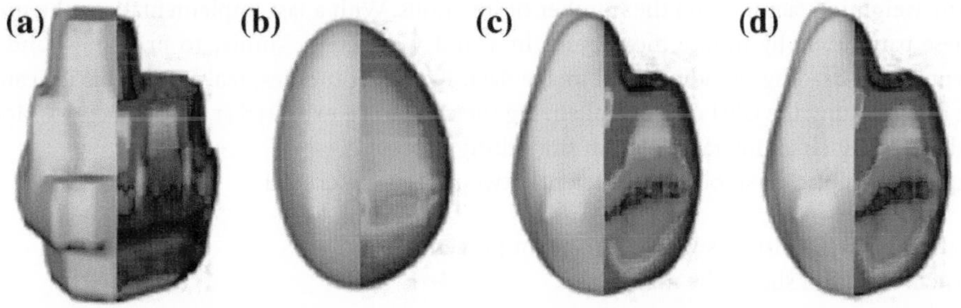

FIGURE 6.25 *Due to their small size lymph nodes are eligible for substantial volume shrinkage. Mesh smoothing and resulting maximum curvature (green represents zero, red represents maximum positive values, blue represents maximum negative curvature). (a) original surface, (b) after Laplacian smoothing with 50 iterations and $\lambda = 0.9$, (c) after Laplacian smoothing with correction, and (d) after applying the low-pass filter (Courtesy of Ragnar Bade, University of Magdeburg).*

shrinkage is strongly reduced. The λ/μ filter is particularly often employed to yield smooth and accurate surface meshes for grid generation in finite element simulation (§ 19.3.3). In Figure 6.25, the effect of the λ/μ filter is compared to other smoothing filters for a surface model of a lymph node.

The three filters described so far, benefit from a data structure that enables a fast traversal of vertices with immediate access to their 1-ring neighbors.

Mean Curvature Flow Smoothing with the *mean curvature flow* was introduced by Desbrun *et al.* [1999] to perform smoothing independently from the triangulation. With this approach, smoothing is applied in the direction of the local surface normal and the amount of smoothing is determined by the *mean curvature*. With the mean curvature flow the new position of v_i' is computed according to Equation 6.6.

$$v_i' = v_i + \frac{\lambda}{G}\sum_{j=1}^{m}(\cot\alpha_{ij}\cot\beta_{ij})(u_j - v_i)v_i \in V,\ u_j \neq u_j,\ \forall u_j \in U_{v_i} m = \|U_{v_i}\| \qquad (6.6)$$

Smoothing with the mean curvature flow preserves the shapes better compared to standard Laplacian smoothing, but it does not preserve the volume well.

Mean and Median Smoothing of the Surface Normals Discontinuities of surface normals are pronounced by lighting models and thus clearly visible. If similar methods, that were discussed so far for vertex coordinates, are applied to surface normals, and if vertices need to be only slightly translated according to the modified normals, volume shrinkage might be reduced. This idea was realized by several groups, in particular by Yagou *et al.* [2002a,b], Tasdizen *et al.* [2002].

Mean filtering is performed by first computing the average normal $\vec{m}$ for a triangle based on the normals of all adjacent faces and then adapting the vertices of the triangle with a weighting factor λ considering vertices of the 1-ring neighborhood. Median filtering of the surface normals is inspired by the median filter used for noise reduction in images and requires a proper sorting of the normals in the neighborhood. The normal $\vec{m}$ is then replaced by the median in this sorted sequence of normals.

6.5.3 INTERACTIVE REAL-TIME MESH SMOOTHING

Mesh smoothing, like mesh extraction, is an operation that should be performed fast enough to enable real-time adjustment of parameters. As an example, Laplacian smoothing is controlled by two parameters, namely the weighting factor λ and the number of iterations. With a fast implementation, the user might adjust these parameters by mouse movements in x and y direction, similar to brightness and contrast adjustments in the reading of radiological image data. For larger meshes, real-time behavior can only be achieved by exploiting the GPU or by parallelizing the code to be executed at multiple cores. Mönch *et al.* [2012] described such an interactive mesh smoothing process.

To implement Laplacian smoothing efficiently, two aspects are crucial:

- Data structures must be suitable for stream processing.
- Synchronization should be minimized.

In the following, we describe such an interactive mesh smoothing approach introduced by Mönch *et al.* [2012]. Proper data management is crucial to achieve high performance on throughput processors. While generic mesh data structures (recall § 6.2.3) are often optimized for editing of the topology, the performance suffers from too many memory indirections. The data structure described in the following ensures that the processors' cache line mechanism is utilized well, as required data is contiguously stored in memory. The processing benefits from prefetching the coordinates of the next vertices. To cope with the memory latency, modern CPUs can analyze the instructions and execute them out-of-order to lower the impact of memory fetches. SIMD (single instruction multiple destinations) allows wider memory fetches and operations per clock. NVIDIA's SIMT (single instruction multiple threads) model, established with CUDA, widened the data processing further running thousands of threads in parallel.

ALGORITHM 1 Pseudocode of Laplacian smoothing

for i $= 0 \rightarrow$ *iterations* **do**
  for all v $\in$ *Vertices* **do**
    v_s.*Initialize*()
    for all $v_n \in$ v.*GetNeighbors*() **do**
      $v_s \leftarrow v_s + v_n$
    end for
    $v_s \leftarrow v_s /$ v.*NumNeighbors*()
    $v_s \leftarrow v + \alpha \cdot (v_s - v)$
  end for
end for

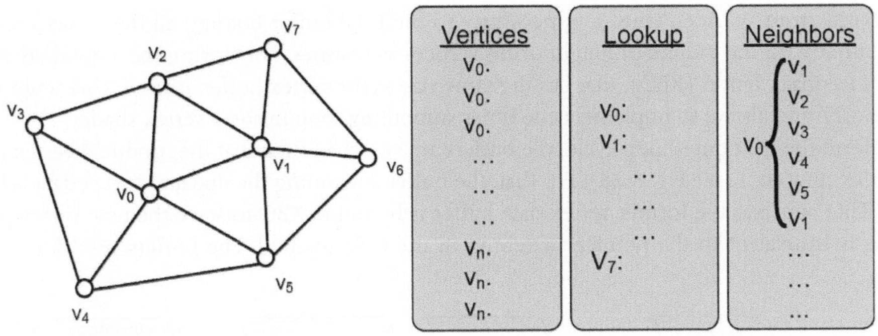

FIGURE 6.26 *The data for hardware-accelerated mesh smoothing is organized in three arrays: vertex coordinates, a lookup table holding information on the number of neighboring vertices, and their location in the list of neighboring vertices (From: [Mönch et al., 2012]).*

We consider the pseudocode of Laplacian smoothing (Alg. 1), since a number of other smoothing techniques have the same algorithmic structure. The algorithm (see Alg. 1) consists of an outer loop (line 1), which cannot be parallelized, since it requires the results of a former cycle (line 7). The second loop (line 2) can be executed free of synchronizations within one iteration. For the Laplace+HC- and the low-pass filter, an additional correction step has to be considered.

The data structure for fast CPU and GPU-based mesh smoothing is depicted in Figure 6.26. In this data structure, each vertex holds information on its neighboring vertices. Thus, an array for the vertex coordinates and a second array for the indices of neighboring vertices is created. For each vertex, the list of neighboring vertices is finalized by adding the first neighbor to the list again. This duplicate neighbor index simplifies the code for average vertex normal generation from the adjacent triangles. Through counterclockwise sorting of the list the 1-ring neighborhood may be created quickly. Furthermore, a lookup table contains neighborhood information, such as the number of neighboring vertices and the location (offset) of the indices of neighboring vertices in the neighbor index list.

CPU Implementation with OpenMP CPU-based smoothing filters can easily be extended by OpenMP which is supported by a variety of compilers, e.g., Microsoft Visual C/C++ 2008 [Mönch *et al.*, 2012]. Especially the iteration over the vertices within one smoothing cycle can be parallelized. After computing the new vertex positions, the pointers to the input and output arrays need to be switched, such that the subsequent smoothing iteration continues with the updated vertex positions as new input. The required normal update is carried out likewise.

OpenGL Implementation Smoothing through OpenGL involves the usage of shaders. Vertex shaders are primarily designed to output positions and they execute code for *one* vertex without natively providing further geometry information, such as the location of neighboring vertices. To provide access to the previously described data structure (see Fig. 6.26), vertex buffer objects (VBOs) and texture buffer objects (TBOs) are used. OpenGL provides a buffer-centric data model, in which the programmer can manage memory on the device and bind it to different functionalities of the rendering pipeline. VBOs allow to upload vertices and related vertex attributes to the graphics card. Up to 16 attributes (4D vectors) may be attached to a vertex. This is sufficient to store the 1-ring neighborhood. For mesh smoothing, this includes the vertex's own position and the neighborhood lookup data. Within the vertex shader, only the attributes of the current vertex can be accessed. Since mesh smoothing requires information on the location of neighboring vertices, TBOs are employed which allow arbitrary access to any location within bound buffer objects from a shader. Thus, it is necessary to bind the buffer holding all the vertex coordinates, and the buffer with the indices of neighboring vertices as textures. For storing the smoothed vertices, a transform feedback buffer (XBO), that has the same size as the vertex buffer, is used. This setup is shown in Figure 6.27 and allows to implement the inner smoothing loop inside a vertex shader.

To perform the next outer loop cycle, the buffers are switched such that the modified vertex positions become the input data (see Fig. 6.28). For that, the buffer containing the updated vertex data is bound as VBO and TBO, whereas the former vertex data buffer is bound as XBO to store the new vertex positions. Thus, this is equivalent to the pointer switching in the CPU method. The buffers used for smoothing

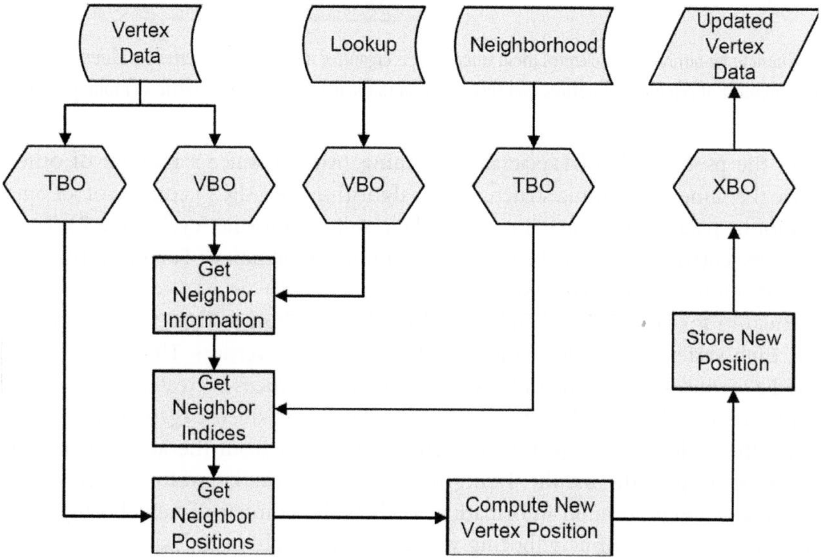

FIGURE 6.27 The interaction between the different buffer objects required for accessing neighborhood information and output of the results (From: [Mönch et al., 2012]).

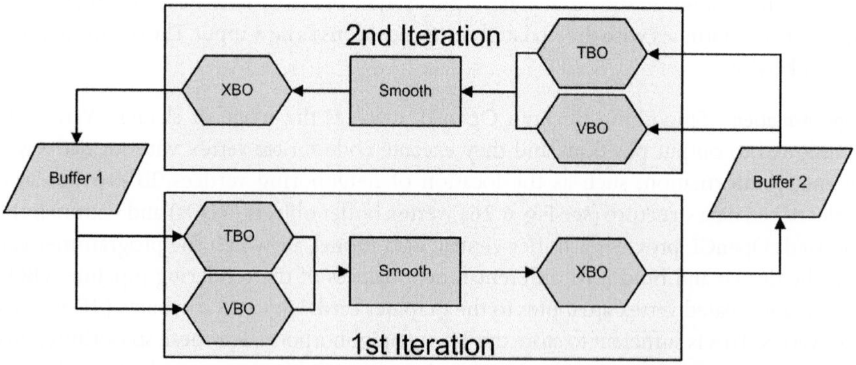

FIGURE 6.28 The input and output buffers are switched after each smoothing cycle by binding them as VBO/TBO and XBO (From: [Mönch et al., 2012]).

computations can subsequently be used for rendering. The VBOs for vertex data and lookup, as well as the neighborhood TBO can again be employed to gain all neighborhood information and finally compute the updated vertex normals. Since the data is already located in graphics card memory, it can directly be used for visualization. As a result, the OpenGL approach is advantageous for smoothing with an immediate visual feedback. The execution of GLSL code depends on the employed OpenGL extensions. For the described setup, at least OpenGL 3 is required.

6.5.4 EVALUATION OF SMOOTHING APPROACHES

Before we discuss the appropriateness of the basic smoothing methods for medical surface models, it is necessary to elaborate on evaluation criteria that go beyond a subjective visual evaluation.

A first objective criterion is the *distance* between a surface considered to be correct and a smoothed surface. Often, it is reasonable to consider the Marching Cubes result as correct, although the simple linear interpolation introduces a slight error. We can thus compare a smoothed surface with the original surface by computing the Hausdorff distance between them. We got to know this measure in the validation of image segmentation. The Hausdorff distance is a kind of worst-case approximation of the distance between the surfaces; the average distance is usually significantly lower. A second widely used measure is *volume preservation*, that measures how strongly the volume after smoothing differs from the original volume.

Comparison of Basic Mesh Smoothing Filters Bade *et al.* [2006] compared the effects of basic mesh smoothing filters to the visualization of medical surface models. A set of six surface models was selected, including elongated and branching anatomical structures, large compact structures, such as organs, and small compact structures, such as lymph nodes. Different types of anatomical structures were considered, since optimal approaches or optimal parameters might differ depending on the geometry and size of the considered objects. For all smoothing filters, different parameters were selected to understand at which levels optimal trade-offs between accuracy and smoothness are achieved. The 1-ring and 2-ring neighborhood were employed (see Fig. 6.29).

The comparison focused on the measurements described above. The whole analysis was quite complex, since six shapes, two neighborhoods, three smoothing methods, four different iteration numbers, and six smoothing factors were considered, resulting in 864 measurements. For smoothing compact objects (e.g., organs, lymph nodes), the low-pass filter and the Laplace+HC with a weighting factor λ between 0.5 and

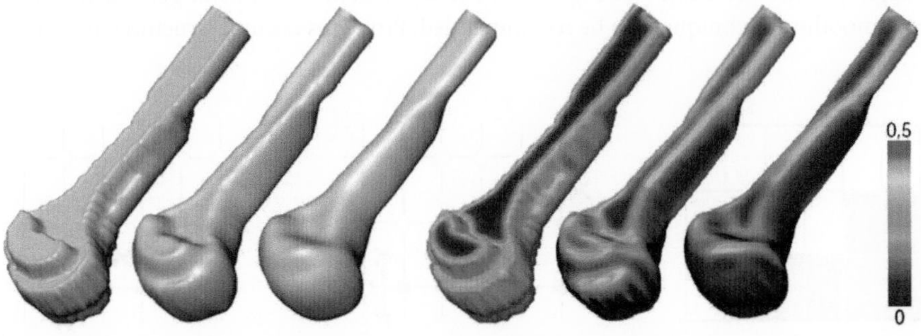

FIGURE 6.29 *Curvature is used to assess the effect of smoothing. From left to right: the Marching Cubes surface generated from the binary segmentation of a bone, Laplacian smoothing with 1-ring neighborhood, Laplacian smoothing with 2-ring neighborhood. The same three models are shown with color-coded curvature. The strong reduction of high-frequency noise leads to significantly reduced curvature (Courtesy of Ragnar Bade, University of Magdeburg).*

0.9 and with 20 to 50 iterations turned out to be equally appropriate. For flat objects, smoothing with the low-pass and Laplace+HC filter yielded the best results. However, the low-pass filter slightly better preserves the volume and shape. A weighting factor between 0.5 and 0.7 and 20 iterations turned out to be appropriate. For elongated and branching vascular structures, partially represented with a few voxels in their cross sections, all methods performed badly. This gives rise to specific surface extraction methods for vascular and other branching structures (see § 11.5).

6.6 ADVANCED MESH SMOOTHING

While the methods described above treat the whole mesh equally, advanced methods are adaptive and modify the smoothing process depending on a local analysis. This enables them to better preserve features or to provide error bounds. Such adaptive methods, similar to the global methods, are inspired by image processing techniques, such as anisotropic diffusion. These methods are referred to as *feature-sensitive* and are widespread in processing engineering data, such as CAD models[7] [Kobbelt *et al.*, 2001]. However, if these methods are applied to surface models derived from medical image data, they identify staircase artifacts as features to preserve. Only recently, adaptive methods specific for medical image data have been developed.

6.6.1 CONSTRAINED MESH SMOOTHING

Dedicated attempts have been made to wrap binary volume data with smooth surfaces. This principle is closely related to the segmentation with snakes (recall § 4.5.1), where energy minimizing surfaces are fitted to the image data and attracted to features, such as edges. Gibson [1998] applied the principles of energy-minimization, to generate smooth surfaces from binary medical volume data. Initially, the centers of each boundary cell of a binary volume are extracted and connected. In an iterative energy minimization process, each vertex is modified but never leaves a cube region with a size that corresponds to the resolution of the data (Fig. 6.30). In particular, the "terraces" in binary segmented data can be handled appropriately by their method of fitting a surface around the binary segmentation result. The iterative relaxation process is constrained by a voxel environment—created by the volume cells that contain at least one boundary voxel of the binary segmentation and at least one background voxel. This concept is referred to as *Constrained elastic surface nets* (CESN). Such constraint may even be used to give a guarantee on the preciseness of the surface.

Later, Bade *et al.* [2007] used a diamond-shaped region to restrict the movement of each vertex and enables a slightly better precision (see Fig. 6.31). For segmentation results of general anatomical shapes constrained smoothing techniques can be recommended. Problems occur if structures are at least partially

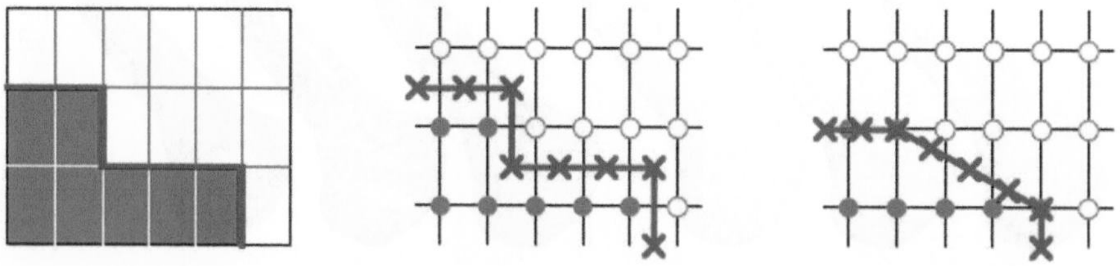

FIGURE 6.30 *Constrained elastic surface nets: The vertices of the red surface are iteratively modified and reduce even staircasing artifacts without leaving a voxel-sized cubical region (Courtesy of Ragnar Bade, University of Magdeburg).*

7 CAD here denotes computer-aided design, whereas it denotes more frequently in the book computer-aided detection.

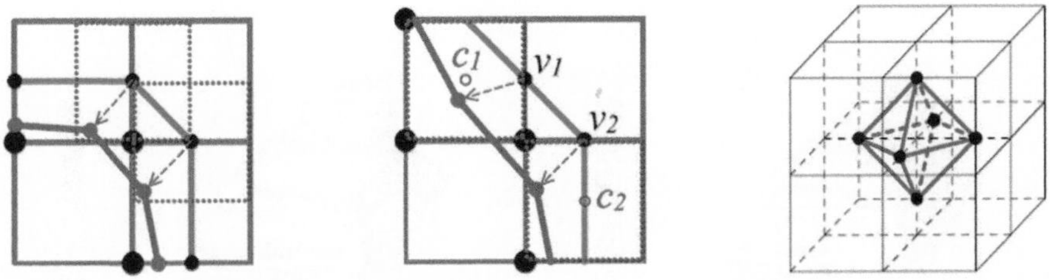

FIGURE 6.31 *Diamond-constraint smoothing: The movement of vertices is restricted to a 3D diamond-shaped region centered around their initial coordinate (Courtesy of Ragnar Bade, University of Magdeburg).*

very thin, since they may degenerate to a line. With CESN and related techniques there is no guarantee that the topology of the surface can be preserved.

6.6.2 CONTEXT-AWARE SMOOTHING

In a series of publications, MÖNCH and colleagues identified features to preserve in medical image data and designed methods to modify existing smoothing techniques that restrict smoothing to certain regions or reduce the amount of smoothing to preserve features. These methods are summarized as *context-aware* smoothing [Mönch *et al.*, 2011a].

Distance-aware smoothing. Since surface visualizations are frequently in therapy planning, an essential aspect is to preserve such distances. That means that interactive or automatic measures[8] after smoothing should yield reliable results. Thus, smoothing needs to be adapted in regions of a surface where another surface is located close. Mönch *et al.* [2010a] introduced this concept and referred to it as *distance-aware smoothing*. Otherwise, more aggressive smoothing is appropriate. Figure 6.32 illustrates distance-aware smoothing. This strategy leads to visualizations where the amount of detail varies according to the amount of smoothing. From a perceptual point of view, the viewer is directed towards the important regions with more detail.

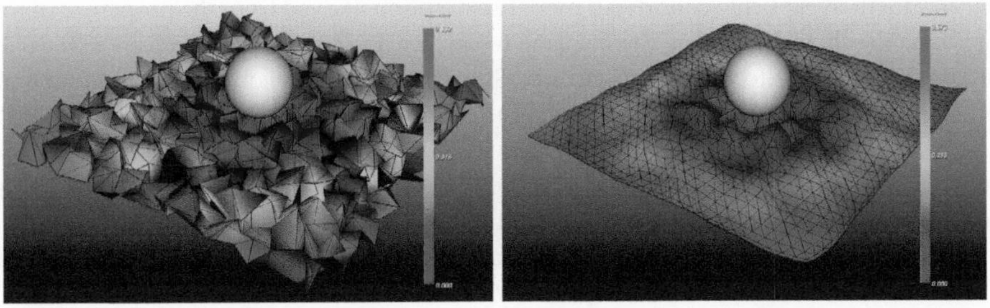

FIGURE 6.32 *Principle of distance-aware smoothing. The noisy plane (left) is strongly smoothed in regions that are far from the sphere (right). In regions close to the sphere, however, smoothing is strongly reduced. The plane geometry is color-coded according to the distance, with red representing low distances (Courtesy of Tobias Mönch, University of Magdeburg).*

8 Measurement techniques are discussed in Chapter 10.

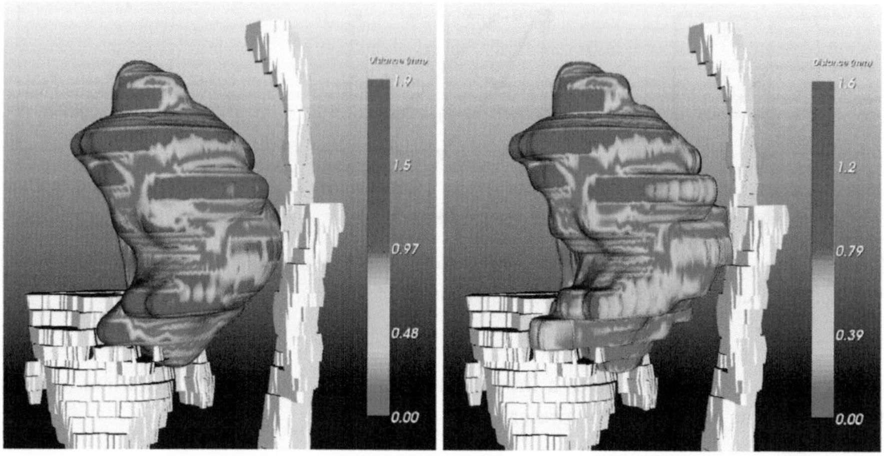

FIGURE 6.33 *Distance-aware smoothing preserves the distance between a tumor and an adjacent vascular structure.* **Left:** *Uniform Laplacian smoothing.* **Right:** *Distance-aware smoothing. The damping factor included in the smoothing process is linearly adapted to the distance to adjacent structures (Courtesy of Tobias Mönch, University of Magdeburg).*

To implement this strategy, the minimum distance $dist_{min}$ between each pair of objects is incorporated a smoothing damping factor $damp$ that may be combined with any existing smoothing technique. When the distance is below a threshold, distance-aware smoothing is enabled. The damping factor $damp$ is 1 (maximum damping) in regions with a distance of $dist_{min}$ and decreased in other regions. $damp$ may be decreased either linearly or exponentially until 0. Figure 6.33 presents an example with linear scaling.

Advanced topic: Staircase-aware smoothing. To provide smooth visualizations without strong side-effects, Mönch *et al.* [2010b] described a method that detects staircases from anisotropic tomographical data. This method explicitly considers a model assumption derived from the properties of medical imaging data. The slicing direction, the in-plane resolution and the slice distance are extracted from the DICOM data and used to search for staircases. Smoothing is modified with weights that represent the detected staircases. As Figure 6.34 indicates, the same amount of smoothness is achieved with better accuracy. This *staircase-aware* smoothing takes longer, since a preprocess is necessary to identify the staircases and the smoothing process is slightly more complex. The modifications due to distance computations and due to staircases may be combined.

Staircase-aware smoothing is related to an approach presented by Xu *et al.* [2006]. They analyzed a mesh to classify vertices in *noise vertices* (probably due to noise or reconstruction errors) and *feature vertices*, focusing smoothing on the noise vertices. Since this approach was also inspired by and tested with contours from tomographical data, the methods are closely related. However, Xu *et al.* [2006] also refine meshes adaptively, whereas Mönch *et al.* [2010b] leave the mesh complexity constant. The method from Xu *et al.* [2006] is less specialized, not explicitly searching for staircases.

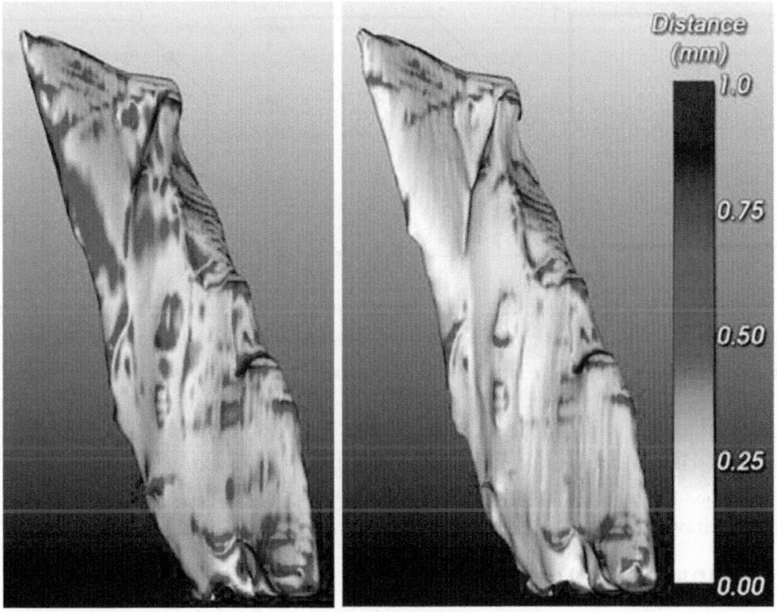

FIGURE 6.34 *A muscle model, where staircases were detected to scale the smoothing factor appropriately.* ***Left:*** *Uniform smoothing leads to larger displacements along the surface.* ***Right:*** *The distance to the original surface before smoothing is color-coded. Only close to the staircases, notable differences exist (From: [Mönch et al., 2011a]).*

6.6.3 EXTRACTING SURFACES FROM LABEL VOLUMES

Label volumes contain multiple segmentation results. If a label volume should be used, e.g., to generate surfaces from all inner organs, there are cells (consisting of the eight adjacent vertices considered in Marching Cubes) that represent more than two different values. Thus, surface extraction is more complex than the definition of just one material transition. Moreover, any post-processing, such as smoothing operations, must consider the special problems of multiple materials to avoid that the surfaces intersect later. Hege *et al.* [1997] introduced "a generalized Marching Cubes"—an approach to extract smooth surfaces from non-binary *label volumes*. They extended the original Marching Cubes and considered the different topological states if three, four, or even more materials exist in one cell. They could show that in a cell with three materials 44 additional cases occur. In cells with four different materials, another 66 topological different states are possible. Together with the 15 cases from a binary situation, 59 and 125 cases respectively have to be considered. For three materials, the configurations are carefully illustrated. However, it is not sufficient to consider just more cases. The boundaries between different materials in the inner of the cell needs to be taken into consideration, leading to vertices not only along at edges, but also at faces and in the internal part of a cell. Thus, as a consequence of this complex setup, a lookup-table with a manageable size (below 1 MByte) is only feasible for up to three materials. According to Hege *et al.* [1997] penetrating surfaces have to be avoided.

Later, Wu and Sullivan [2003] described the multimaterial Marching Cubes algorithm that provides an alternative to the "Generalized Marching Cubes." They renounce on the idea of using a case table to prepare a triangulation for every possible case. Similar to Hege *et al.* [1997], in case that the four vertices that constitute a face of the cells share more than two materials, additional face center points are introduced. Figure 6.35 illustrates some possible configurations and the surfaces defined in this case.

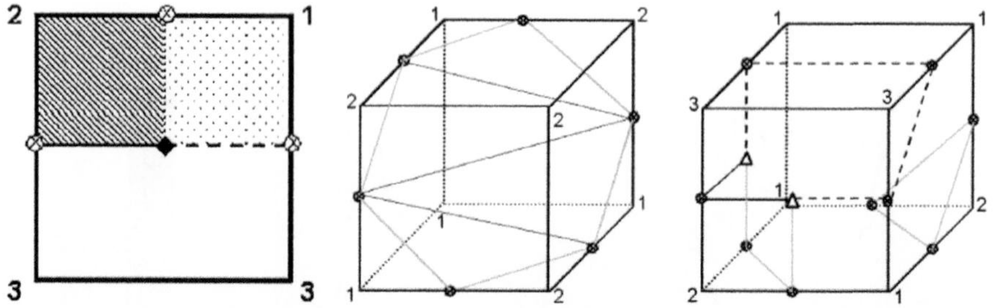

FIGURE 6.35 *Multimaterial Marching Cubes.* **Left:** *A 2D example with three materials where a central point is inserted to generate consistent isolines.* **Middle:** *A 3D example with three materials where no face centers need to be inserted.* **Right:** *A 3D configuration with three materials where two face centers were introduced for surface extraction (Inspired by [Wu and Sullivan, 2003]).*

Surface extraction is quite complex in cells where more than two materials exist. In the large majority, where only two materials are present, the standard Marching Cubes extraction may be performed. With this strategy, all surfaces can be generated in one pass and with a similar performance like the classical Marching Cubes. A drawback is that the number of generated triangles is large.

6.6.4 EVALUATION OF ADVANCED MESH SMOOTHING

In this subsection, we build on the evaluation criteria discussed in § 6.5.4. These criteria are, of course, also essential for the advanced smoothing approaches. However, they need to be adapted to the context-specific character of advanced methods. As an example, for the evaluation of distance-aware smoothing, the distance evaluation needs to be performed at a finer level. It is essential that distances to critical structures are preserved accurately, whereas global distance measures or volumetric overlap are less relevant. Consequently, distance-aware smoothing was primarily evaluated with respect to its effect on minimal distance computations. Similarly, staircase-aware smoothing should be evaluated with respect to its local effect close to the identified artifacts. Advanced smoothing techniques combine a feature detection step and a sophisticated smoothing approach considering these features. Obviously, the computational demands are increased compared to basic methods. Thus, a substantial performance analysis should also be part of the evaluation.

6.7 MESH SIMPLIFICATION AND WEB-BASED SURFACE RENDERING

A promising usage context of 3D medical visualization is its use directly in the web browser. While web-based interactive 3D renderings are feasible in principle since the 1990s, only recently convenient use is possible. On the one hand, with new standards such as HMTL 5, 3D renderings may be used without the need to install any plugin—an improvement that is crucial in hospitals, where it is often not allowed to install additional software. On the other hand, the bandwidth of current internet connections enables interactive 3D visualizations of at least moderately sized surface meshes. Surface renderings are based on polygonal meshes that have a much lower storage footprint than medical volume data. Thus, in the foreseeable future, mesh-based surface rendering is the better option for web-based medical visualization. In medicine, two application types are prevailing:

- interactive surgical planning, and
- interactive medical education

In the following, we discuss web-based surface rendering for these applications.

6.7.1 MESH SIMPLIFICATION

For web-based surface rendering, the size of surface models is crucial. Several strategies are used to cope with the related bandwidth problems. The most general strategy is to transform a surface mesh M in a low resolution mesh M' that is as close as possible to the original mesh but encompasses a significantly lower number of vertices and polygons. A good trade-off between accuracy and size of the mesh can only be achieved with adaptive methods that remove only geometrical details not contributing significantly to the shape. Flat regions with no or only low curvature may be strongly reduced, whereas regions with high curvature can only be reduced mildly.

The selection of a difference metric is crucial. In theory, it should reflect how much a model is visually changing. In practice, however, this is difficult to measure. Hence, a number of specific difference metrics are used, such as the geometric distance in object space (e.g., the Hausdorff distance), the pixel distance in screen space, or the differences in the attribute space (e.g., normals, colors, or textures).

Mesh simplification may take as input

- a certain target number of polygons,
- a certain percentage of reduction in size, or
- an error that should not be exceeded.

Vertices and/or edges are classified with respect to their relevance by assessing the error that would be introduced by removing them. Based on this assessment, geometrical details are removed until the target size or percentage is reached. It is essential that, after removing a vertex, a local *remeshing* provides a local triangulation in that area. Edge collapse is a simplification operation and means that one vertex v_s is moved to an adjacent vertex v_t and then deleted. Remeshing means that after removal of a vertex and the associated edges the affected part of the mesh is transformed in a triangle net (see Fig. 6.36). This is always possible. Among the possible triangulations, one is searched for where the triangles are as equi-lateral as possible.

Thus, in contrast to mesh smoothing, mesh simplification often alters the topology of a surface mesh. Garland and Heckbert [1997], Hoppe *et al.* [1993], and Lindstrom and Turk [1998] described powerful mesh simplification algorithms.

Progressive Meshes Instead of just producing *one* strongly reduced mesh, it might be reasonable to generate a sequence of reduced meshes. If the user opens a corresponding website, a strongly reduced base mesh is shown first. This base mesh M_0 may not be reduced further without changing the topology. If the user does not manipulate the visualization, refined versions are loaded. Instead of providing a number of complete meshes, it is reasonable to store a base mesh and the local differences to more refined meshes

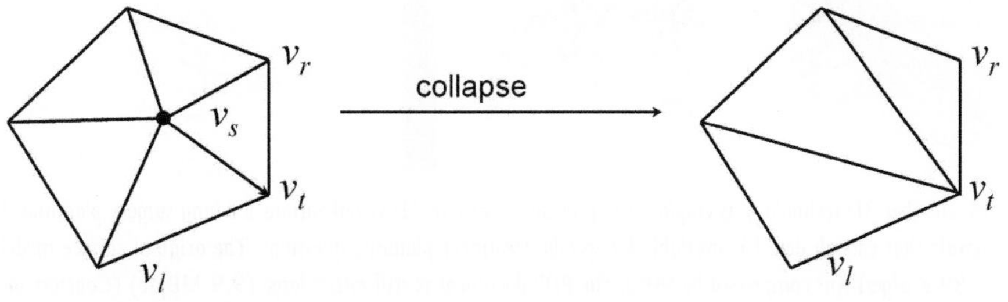

FIGURE 6.36 *After an edge collapse, the resulting loop of edges is triangulated such that no degenerated triangles arise.*

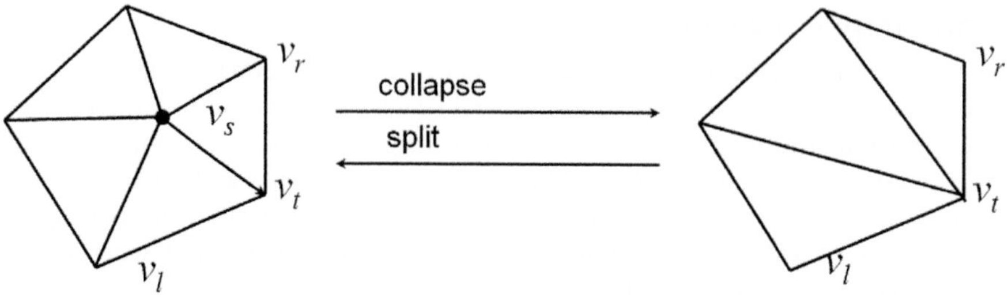

FIGURE 6.37 *Representation of a collapse/split. For the collapse of an edge, its left and right neighbor as well as the remaining vertex are stored. The coordinates of the removed vertex are also stored to be able to restore the edge in a split operation.*

$(M_1, M_2, \ldots, M_n)$. This is feasible if there are invertible transformations to reduce the mesh. This idea is known as *Progressive meshes* [Hoppe, 1996]. Figure 6.37 illustrates the invertible edge collapse operation employed for generating reduced meshes from the original mesh M_n.

The chosen simplification approach depends largely on the required accuracy for the simplified model. In particular the requirements for the boundary between the different objects are important. If adjacent objects are simplified separately, cracks between the polygonal surfaces may appear and need to be re-triangulated.

There are a number of surveys on the variety of mesh simplification algorithms, error metrics, and applications [Garland, 1999, Luebcke *et al.*, 2004].

6.7.2 WEB-BASED SURGICAL PLANNING

For regular clinical use, the development of Acrobat 3D PDF is promising. PDF documents are widely used for the exchange of documents among physicians. If the familiar experience of using PDF documents can be combined with the functionality to interactively explore a 3D model of the relevant patient anatomy,

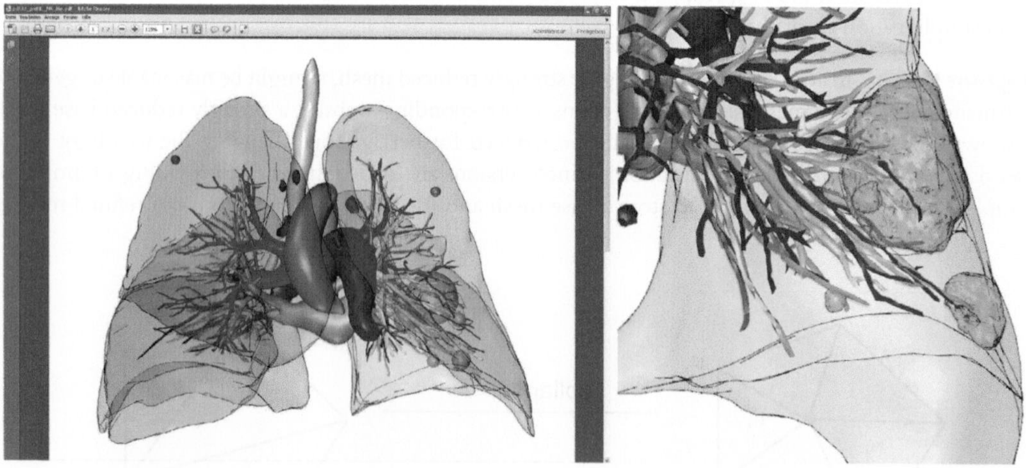

FIGURE 6.38 *Acrobat 3D technology is employed to provide interactive 3D visualizations for lung surgery planning. The close-up view (right) reveals that enough detail is available for specific treatment planning questions. The original surface model (1.463 K vertices and 2.289 K edges) was compressed by 90%. The PDF document is still rather large (9.9 MByte) (Courtesy of Steven Birr, University of Magdeburg).*

it is more likely that these functions are actually used. Figure 6.38 shows an example of a documentation and planning system for thorax surgery, presented by Birr *et al.* [2011b].

The use of Acrobat 3D PDF for surgery planning was pioneered by MeVis Distant Services in 2009 and is regularly performed for liver surgery planning in case of liver tumors and for planning transplantation surgery. They also take care of reducing the geometric models and provide sets of carefully defined 3D models that depict the vascular anatomy, the risk associated with surgery and a number of resection proposals. In Figure 6.39, the hepatic veins are shown and color-coded with respect to their distance to the tumor—the analysis of affected vascular structures is one essential step in surgery planning.

6.7.3 WEB-BASED MEDICAL EDUCATION

In § 5.9 we discussed the mobile use of medical (image) data. Surface renderings prevail in mobile settings, because they can be easily used in any web-browser. Computer-based training applications increasingly support web and mobile usage, and as a consequence, such support is expected by medical users. Figure 6.40 presents an example where 3D rendering in the web browser is employed for medical education.

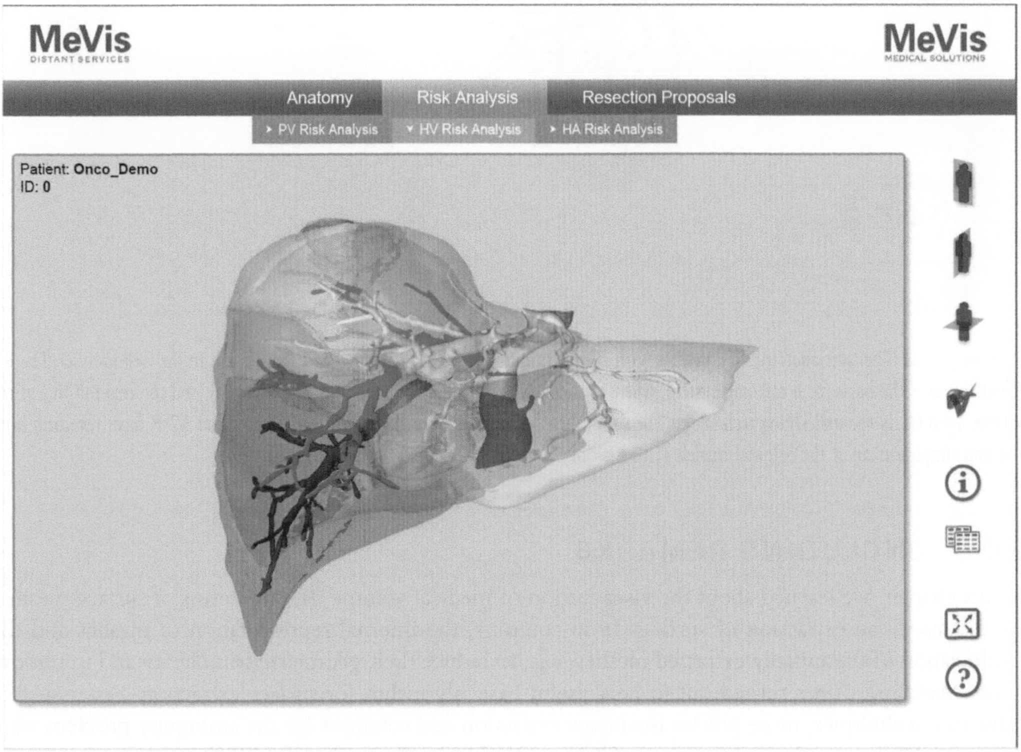

FIGURE 6.39 *Acrobat 3D technology is used for liver surgery planning. The liver and the hepatic vein (one of three vascular systems in the liver). The color of the vascular branches indicates their distance to a tumor (red represents regions in the 2 mm margin around the tumor). A set of 10 3D models, sharing large parts of the geometry are provided to support the complete surgical planning process with appropriate 3D models (10.6 MByte) (Courtesy of MeVis Distant Services).*

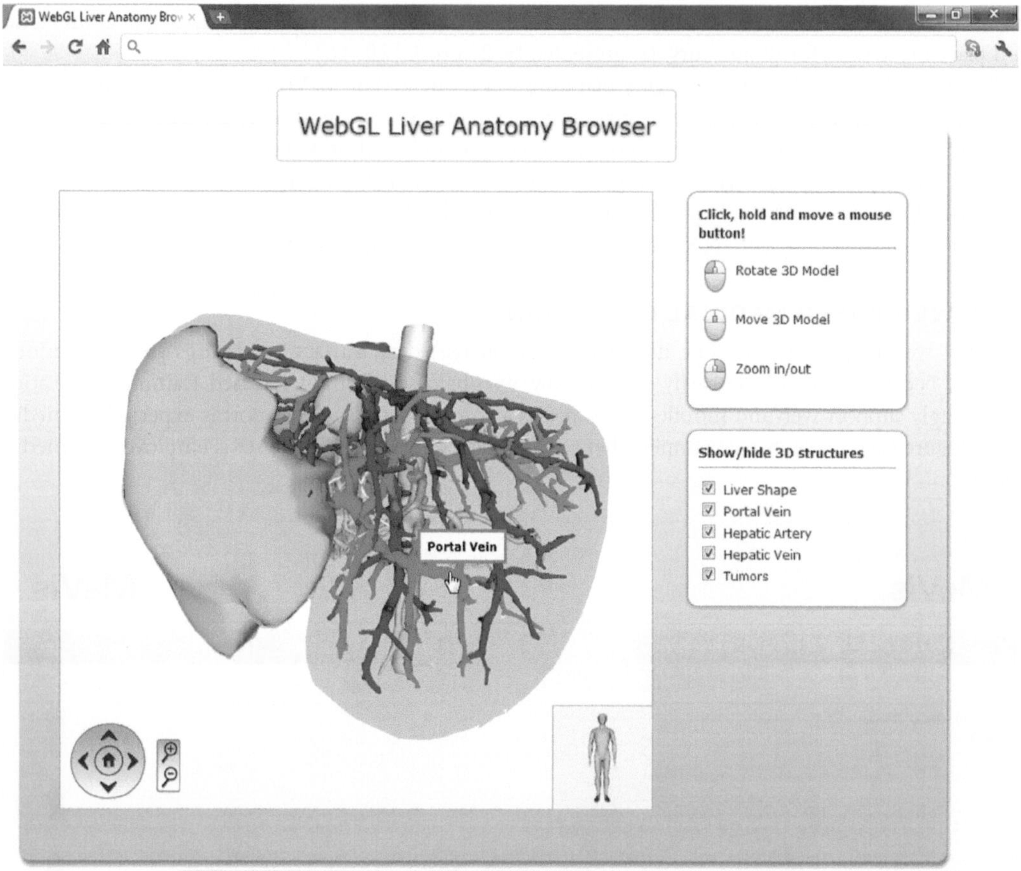

FIGURE 6.40 *The liver anatomy of a patient with a large tumor (yellow) is presented as surface mesh in the web browser. The 3D visualization is the basis for a training system, where medical doctors should assess the vascular anatomy and the resectability of the patient. Web GL is the underlying technology. The surface meshes have an overall size of 26 K vertices and 52 K faces resulting from a strong simplification of the original models (Courtesy of Steven Birr, University of Magdeburg).*

6.8 CONCLUDING REMARKS

In this chapter, we learned about the visualization of medical volume data by means of surface meshes. We discussed the extraction of surfaces from contours, the internal representation of meshes and the modification of the initially extracted meshes, e.g., to reduce their geometric complexity and to remove noise. Marching Cubes turned out to be a useful basic algorithm for surface extraction. Faster surface extraction techniques, more precise isosurface extraction and solutions for the ambiguity problem were discussed. Mesh smoothing was discussed in considerable detail to reflect on different usage scenarios. In particular, the surface extraction from binary and strongly anisotropic volume data causes severe aliasing artifacts which give rise to smoothing techniques. Curvature measures enable an objective discussion of the achieved effects on smoothness. Accuracy was evaluated, e.g., with respect to volume shrinkage and surface distances to original unaltered surfaces. The relation between noise reduction at the image data level and the resulting surfaces was described. We discussed methods also with respect to performance issues that are particularly important when surface meshes are used in web-based environments. While our focus in this chapter was on the visual exploration on surface meshes for standard visualization, surface extraction is also the basis for illustrative rendering (Chap. 12) and for biophysical simulations (Chap. 19).

Surface Meshes for 3D Printing We have not discussed the emerging use case of generating medical surface models for 3D printing. Physical models of anatomical structures have a great potential for surgical planning and medical education. 3D printers have strongly increased in their capabilities, e.g., to employ different materials and colors, and even transparency and their price has been reduced considerably making the technology much more available. Schmauss *et al.* [2012], e.g., describe, how physical 3D models are used for planning heart valve replacement and Mönch *et al.* [2011b] describe the generation of physical vascular surface models with complex pathologies. Also for planning stent implantation [Armillotta *et al.*, 2007] and for educational purposes physical models are essential [Knox *et al.*, 2005]. In all these cases, the geometry is represented with surface meshes that should be smooth and accurate.

In addition, some specific requirements have to be considered, e.g., adjacent parts of a complex geometry should not be too close to each other to avoid that they merge in the model generation process. Also, depending on the quality of the 3D printer, very thin branches are not stable enough to be constructed. These specific requirements often need special editing with mesh processing software.

FURTHER READING

We discussed data structures for meshes only briefly. For an in-depth discussion, we refer to [Botsch *et al.*, 2002, Sieger and Botsch, 2011] and to a recent book on mesh processing [Botsch *et al.*, 2010]. Mesh simplification was also only briefly discussed. Cignoni *et al.* [1998] provides an overview.

Mesh smoothing may also be performed based on subdivision. These approaches add vertices and edges to rough portions of a mesh to represent it at a finer scale and thus provide a smooth appearance in regions where the original resolution was insufficient to capture curved regions appropriately [Xu *et al.*, 2006]. Theisel [2002] showed how exact contours of 3D regular volumes may be determined by triangular rational cubic Bezier patches. Curvature estimation is an essential aspect of mesh processing. Discrete differential geometry operators, in most cases tailored to triangular nets, are used for this purpose [Meyer *et al.*, 2002, Desbrun *et al.*, 2006].

Chapter 07

Direct Volume Visualization

In the previous chapter, we discussed surface rendering as an important method for the visualization of medical volumetric data. Surface rendering is also called indirect volume visualization, as it relies on the generation of an intermediate representation of the dataset, the surface, that can then be rendered. Because this intermediate representation is not the original dataset itself, this is called indirect.

In direct volume visualization, the volumetric dataset is directly represented visually without generating an intermediate representation. This is generally done by somehow projecting the volumetric information onto the viewing plane. This chapter will discuss the major strategies and variations that can be employed for this projection. Direct volume visualization is often called direct volume rendering, or in short, volume rendering.

Furthermore, the complexity of direct volume visualization algorithms is driven by the number of voxels of the dataset and by the number of pixels of the viewing plane. In contrast, the complexity of a polygonal representation of an isosurface is driven by the number of polygons, and not by the viewing plane resolution. Consequently, many polygons will have only a small contribution, in particular if they have a projected size of one pixel or less.

Organization In this chapter, we will focus on the theoretical aspects of direct volume visualization, in particular the employed physical model (§ 7.1) and the mathematical foundation of the resulting *volume rendering equation*. Section 7.2 addresses the processing order of the volume rendering pipeline that evaluated the volume rendering equation and its components such as sampling and compositing (§ 7.3). We then discuss the volume raycasting algorithm, after which we compactly treat the implementation of direct volume raycasting on the GPU.

In the next chapter, we will discuss advanced direct volume visualization techniques such as volumetric illumination and artificial depth enhancements. Since this book's focus is on visualization in medicine in general, our discussion of direct volume rendering is by definition focused in these two chapters. A more in depth discussion can be found in the recent book by Engel *et al.* [2006].

7.1 THEORETICAL MODELS

Rendering in general is the interaction of light, objects, and the medium in between, which in practice breaks down into the interaction of particles and media. It is typically described with absorption, emission, and scattering and has its physical foundation in the *transport theory of light*. This theory is modeled in its steady state (or stationary) version by the linear Boltzmann equation that describes the increase or decrease of the intensity of particles in space [Krüger, 1990b].

In direct volume rendering, this complex model is usually simplified. The influence of a changing medium is ignored, different wavelengths, diffraction, and scattering are not modeled. These simplifications lead to the rendering equation as introduced by Kajiya [1986].[1] If we further remove refraction and

1 Note that scattering found its way into the global illumination research area with the introduction of Bidirectional Reflectance Distribution Functions (BRDFs) and Subsurface Scattering (SSS).

Visual Computing for Medicine, Second Edition. http://dx.doi.org/10.1016/B978-0-12-415873-3.00007-9

reflection[2] from the model—which is called a *Low Albedo* scenario [Blinn, 1982a]—,we have reached the standard physical model of volume rendering, the *density emitter model* introduced by Sabella [1988]. This model only considers *emission* and *absorption* and essentially models every contributing particle in a volume dataset as a tiny light source, the light of which is attenuated by the material it encounters while traveling through the volume dataset.

7.1.1 EMISSION

The general assumption behind the emission part of the physical model is that each contributing particle in a volume dataset is a tiny light source which emits its light through-out the volume. In the emission-only physical model this light is not attenuated and not scattered, hence it is without any interaction with the volume [Hege *et al.*, 1993, Max, 1995]. An example of this situation is a glowing, but mostly transparent (no absorption and no scattering) gas. This light source is modeled by the *source term* $Q_\lambda(s)$, where λ specifies the wavelength of the emitted light, and s specifies the direction of the light. Later, we will model s as a ray that travels from the viewpoint through the volume and that accumulates the light (see Fig. 7.1).[3]

From now on, we will further simplify the source term by computing it for one fixed wavelength, thus using only $Q(s)$ as source term. Differential equation 7.1 models the intensity $I(s)$ at position s along a ray S, based on the source term $Q(s)$:

$$\frac{dI}{ds} = Q(s) \tag{7.1}$$

The solution is found by computing the integral:

$$I(s) = I_{s_0} + \int_{s_0}^{s} Q(t)dt \tag{7.2}$$

where s_0 is the entry point into the volume. Here, I_{s_0} is the initial value of light intensity when the ray enters the volume. It can be considered as some kind of ambient background light. The source term $Q(s)$ represents the actual contribution of the volume dataset to the final image.

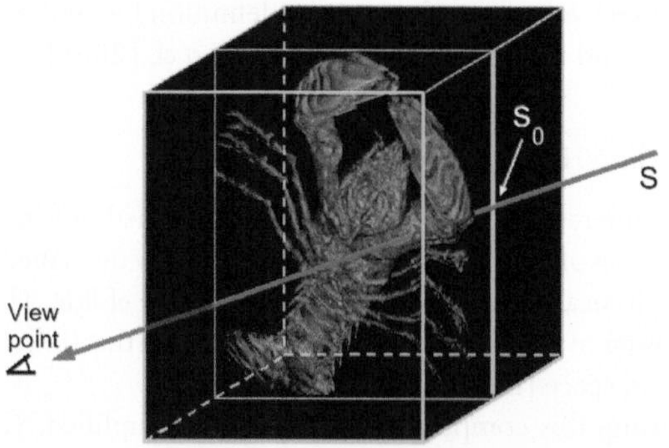

FIGURE 7.1 *A ray S traverses a volume dataset and accumulates contributions starting from the entry point s_0 toward the viewpoint.*

---

2 There is still a diffuse specular lighting component as part of the Phong lighting model.

3 Different publications present these models with varying conventions. Either the ray moves toward the viewpoint (eye), or away from the viewpoint. Our convention is the same as that of Hege *et al.* [1993] and Max [1995], while Sabella [1988] cast the ray away from the viewpoint.

In practice, $Q(s)$ is derived from $v(s)$, the sample value in the volume dataset at position s, by applying a *transfer function* $T_F(.)$. The transfer function maps data samples to optical characteristics, generally color and opacity. In one of its simplest forms, the transfer function is a 1D function of the volume scalar values, yielding for each possible volume scalar value an opacity. When the transfer function yields opacity, it is called the *opacity transfer function* or OTF. Similarly, transfer functions can be specified for color, for example mapping from the volume sample scalar value to a hue, saturation and value (HSV) or red, green and blue (RGB) tuple. When a transfer function yields color, it is called the *color transfer function* or CTF.

Transfer functions are often implemented as lookup tables. In Chapter 9, more advanced transfer function approaches, for instance also making use of volume gradients, are discussed.

The source term at position s is usually also illuminated, typically by the Phong lighting model [Phong, 1975], which we briefly discuss in § 7.2. This, however, extends the basic density-emitter model of Sabella [1988], which assumes just a (homogenous) participating media cloud. Instead, the Phong illumination model interprets each sample as an object which is illuminated by external light sources.

7.1.2 ABSORPTION

Since our physical model interprets the volume dataset as a cloud of a homogenous medium, we also need to specify how this medium attenuates light. Our absorption-only physical model assumes any light intensity will be absorbed by all the particles [Max, 1995]. Equation 7.3 defines this absorption at position s along ray S within the volume with the following differential equation:

$$\frac{dI}{ds} = -\tau(s) \cdot I(s) \tag{7.3}$$

Max [1995] calls $\tau(s)$ the extinction coefficient. It represents the differential density of the material that the light ray passes through, and hence attenuates the intensity of the ray as it passes through the volume. It also corresponds to the opacity of the sampled value at s specified by the opacity transfer function. Transparency and opacity are complementary values. If we assume a transparency range of $t \in [0 \ldots 1]$, we can compute the opacity by $\alpha(s) = 1 - t(s)$.

Integrating the differential equation 7.3 yields

$$I(s) = I_{s_0} \cdot e^{\left(-\int_{s_0}^{s} \tau(t)dt\right)} \tag{7.4}$$

where $T_{s_0}(s) = e^{\left(-\int_{s_0}^{s} \tau(t)dt\right)}$, the *accumulated transparency*, can be used to calculate how much of the initial intensity I_{s_0} at position s_0 is let through to position s. The higher the constituent $\tau(t)$ attenuation values, the lower the accumulated transparency will be, resulting in much less of the initial intensity passing through.

7.1.3 VOLUME RENDERING EQUATION

The standard physical model for direct volume rendering employs emission and absorption [Max, 1995]. Hence, we combine both terms to

$$dI/ds = Q(s) - \tau(s) \cdot I(s) \tag{7.5}$$

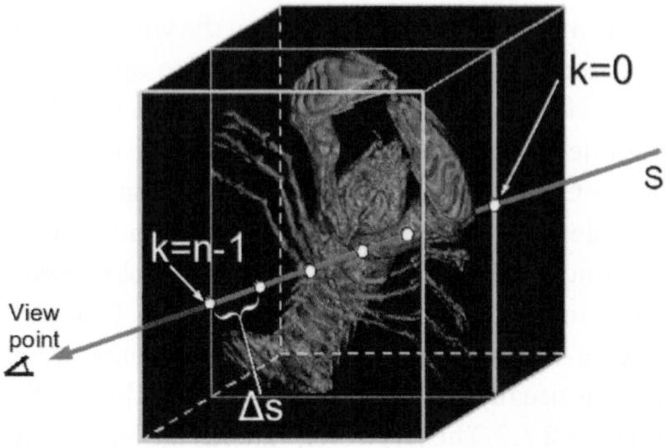

FIGURE 7.2 *A discretized ray S traverses a volume dataset and accumulates contributions at sampling points s_k starting from the entry point k = 0 through k = n − 1. Note that appropriate sampling would require many more samples than illustrated in this figure (Courtesy of Dirk Bartz, University of Leipzig).*

and find as solution for that differential equation the *Volume Rendering Equation* 7.6:

$$\begin{aligned} I(s) &= I_{s_0} \cdot e^{\left(-\int_{s_0}^{s} \tau(t)dt\right)} + \int_{s_0}^{s} Q(p) \cdot e^{\left(-\int_{p}^{s} \tau(t)dt\right)} dp \\ &= I_{s_0} \cdot T_{s_0}(s) + \int_{s_0}^{s} Q(p) \cdot T_p(p)dp \end{aligned} \tag{7.6}$$

with $T_x(.)$ the attenuation function.[4]

This equation cannot be solved analytically in a practical fashion for most volume rendering applications, so we solve it numerically. This is typically done with a Riemann sum and a fixed step size Δs that scales the current sampling position k along ray S with $k \cdot \Delta s$ (see Fig. 7.2). Before we discretize the volume rendering equation, we first discretize and simplify the attenuation term T_{s_0} into T_0, where we assume that the entry point of the ray S into the volume is now at location 0 instead of s_0:

$$\begin{aligned} T_0(s) &= e^{\left(-\int_0^s \tau(t)dt\right)} = e^{\left(-\sum_{k=0}^{n-1} \tau(k\cdot\Delta t)\Delta t\right)} \\ &= \prod_{k=0}^{n-1} e^{-\tau(k\Delta t)\cdot\Delta t} = \prod_{k=0}^{n-1} t_k \end{aligned} \tag{7.7}$$

with $n-1$ as the final position $(n-1)\cdot\Delta s$ along the ray S and with t_k as the transparency at the discrete sample point k. If we now discretize the volume rendering equation (Eq. 7.6) with $s_k = k \cdot \Delta s$ representing the position s along the ray, $Q_k = Q(s_k)$ representing the source term $Q(s)$, and the discretization of the attenuation term in equation 7.7, we get

$$I(s) = I_0 \prod_{k=0}^{n-1} t_k + \sum_{k=0}^{n-1} Q(k \cdot \Delta s) \cdot \Delta s \prod_{j=k+1}^{n-1} t_j \tag{7.8}$$

4 Note that the previously mentioned different conventions of the direction of the ray use different integration ranges of the attenuation function, reflecting the accumulation ranges. With our convention, the attenuation accumulates from the current sampling point p (Eq. 7.6) to the volume exit point s toward the viewpoint. The other convention would use switched integration bounds.

This equation describes how a ray S with the initial value of the first summand in Equation 7.8 traverses the volume dataset and accumulates at discrete locations k contributions. These contributions are based on the local source term Q_k that is attenuated by the transparency (or opacity) that has been accumulated from t_j at the sample locations j along that ray. While this equation provides the theoretical basis for direct volume rendering, it also governs how the voxels of the volume datasets contribute to the final rendered image. The specifics of how the volume rendering equation is evaluated, are determined by the volume rendering pipeline.

7.2 THE VOLUME RENDERING PIPELINE

The volume rendering pipeline specifies the order of the individual operations that are used to evaluate the discrete volume rendering equation (Eq. 7.8). An overview of these operations is given in Figure 7.3. Differences between direct volume rendering algorithms generally come down to variations of the order of operations, or of the individual operations, such as the interpolation approach that is employed in the sampling step.

Sampling The volume rendering equation describes a ray that traverses a volume dataset. Volume contributions are accumulated at discrete locations along this ray. The process of selecting these locations, and then calculating the corresponding volume contributions, is called *sampling*.

There are at least two important issues to take into account when implementing sampling. First, a suitable sampling distance Δs has to be chosen. The smaller this distance, the more accurate the numerical approximation of the volume rendering integral will be, and the higher quality the resultant renderings will have. However, the shorter the sampling distance, the more samples have to be evaluated, resulting in a significantly longer rendering time. As is often the case, a trade-off between speed and quality has to be made.

Second, a suitable interpolation method should be selected. As we discussed in Section 2.2, the actual dataset values are only defined on the grid locations and the values between these grid values must be interpolated. The choice of an interpolation method also influences sampling, since the order of the interpolation methods specifies the support on which that interpolation is defined. A first-order trilinear interpolation function, for example, takes into account the immediate voxel neighborhood of the sample value. In contrast, a third-order tricubic interpolation function considers a significantly larger voxel neighborhood and hence provides a low-pass filtering of that sampled region. This becomes even more clear, if we consider that interpolation functions are volumetric data filters with the respective filter kernel.

Classification and Illumination Once the location and the value of the sampling point s has been determined, its contribution $Q(s)$ must be computed. The sample value is first classified using the transfer functions introduced in § 7.1.1. The result of this classification is a color value $O_d(s)$ that is then used as part of a lighting simulation to compute its illuminated contribution $Q(s)$, a process also known as *shading*. Typically, the *Phong reflection model* [Phong, 1975] is used for this purpose. The Phong reflection model, also known as Phong illumination or Phong lighthing, simulates the interaction of an ambient and one or more directional light sources with an object, in this case the volume sample at location s. The shaded

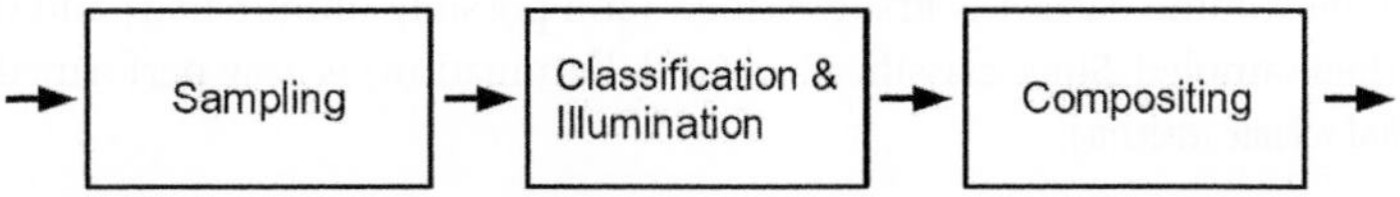

FIGURE 7.3 *Post-classified volume rendering pipeline.*

color $Q(s)$ is calculated for each color component and for a single directional light source as follows:

$$Q(s) = I_a k_a O_d(s) + I_d k_d O_d(s) \left(\mathbf{N(s)} \cdot \mathbf{L}\right) + I_s k_s \left(\mathbf{V} \cdot \mathbf{R}\right)^n \tag{7.9}$$

with the following operands:

I_a	ambient light intensity
k_a	ambient reflection coefficient
$O_d(s)$	object diffuse color at s
I_d	light source diffuse component
I_s	light source specular component
k_d	diffuse reflection coefficient
$\mathbf{N(s)}$	surface normal/volume gradient at s
$\mathbf{L}$	direction of light source
k_s	specular reflection coefficient
$\mathbf{R}$	direction of specular reflection; $\mathbf{L}$ reflected about $\mathbf{N(s)}$
$\mathbf{V}$	direction of viewer
n	specular reflection exponent

The first, or ambient, term of the equation models non-directional scattered light being reflected equally well in all directions. The second, or diffuse, term models the reflection of directional light. The more the incoming directional light is aligned with the object surface normal, the more it will be reflected. In volume rendering, the local volume gradient is used as the surface normal in the lighting equations. The last, or specular, term models specular highlights on the object surface. The more the view direction as aligned with the reflection of the incoming light, the more intense the specular highlight will be. The exponent n is high (200 or more) for shiny surfaces, in which case the specular highlights are small and bright, or small for dull surfaces.

The attenuation factor $\tau(s)$ or its discretized representation complement transparency t_j is determined using the *opacity transfer function* (OTF). The higher the opacity, the more the current volume sample will attenuate any light propagating through it and the less transparent it will be. When opacity is set to zero for a particular volume sample, that sample disappears completely from the final rendition, that is, it has maximal transparency. In effect, the OTF determines, which part of the volume contribute to the final image and which parts do not.

Compositing Once the sample values have been computed, classified, and illuminated, they must be accumulated along the ray according to the physical model. This accumulation is called compositing, and it is the numerical approximation of the volume rendering. Compositing will be discussed in more detail in § 7.3.

7.2.1 PRECLASSIFIED VOLUME RENDERING PIPELINE

The previous paragraphs and Figure 7.3 described the postclassified[5] volume rendering pipeline, where sampling is performed before classification and illumination. Figure 7.4 describes a different order of operations, where the volume dataset is first classified (and possibly illuminated) and the resulting color volume dataset is then sampled. Since classification (and illumination) is now performed before sampling, it is called *preclassified volume rendering*.

5 Also known as post-shaded or post-illuminated.

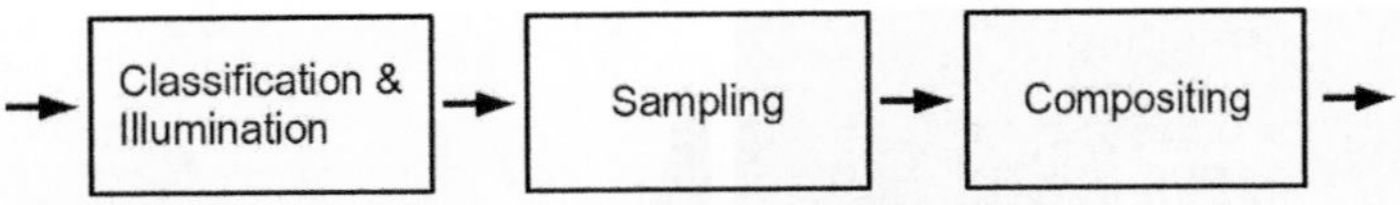

FIGURE 7.4 *The preclassified volume rendering pipeline changes the order of classification and sampling.*

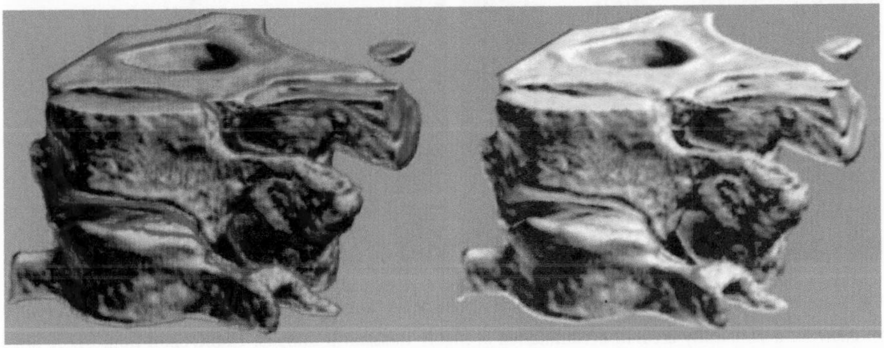

FIGURE 7.5 *Color bleeding artifact on a reconstructed vertebra dataset. From [Wittenbrink et al., 1998] (Courtesy of Craig Wittenbrink, NVIDIA Corporation and Tom Malzbender, Hewlett-Packard Corporation).*

The big advantage of preclassified volume rendering is that classification and illumination are computed for every voxel, hence we can tell in advance, which voxel will contribute and which voxel will not based on the classification. Furthermore, we can perform most of the expensive illumination calculations, like the approximation of the normal, in a preprocessing stage, albeit increasing the memory footprint by the need to store the normals for every voxel. Finally, the preclassified color volume can be used in cases where no on-the-fly illumination can be performed, as was the case for the original volume rendering approaches based on 3D-texture mapping [Cullip and Neumann, 1993, van Gelder and Kim, 1996].

There are also a number of disadvantages associated with preclassified volume rendering. First, the changes of the sampling value domain—from data values to color values—introduces several problems. Interpolation in color space is not as straightforward as in the original data space. Depending on the color model, a sampling value between two different colors, e.g., on the boundary of an object, can result in a third color, as it can be seen in Figure 7.5. This artifact is known as *color bleeding*, due to the red color shift, and it is similar to the interpolation artifacts known as staircasing. Wittenbrink *et al.* [1998] analyzed this issue and provided a solution to it, called *opacity-weighted interpolation*. This variation of the interpolation rescales the color value of the voxels by dividing them by their respective transparency values before interpolating the contribution of the sample point. Second, high-frequency details in the transfer functions cannot be presented properly by preclassification [Mueller *et al.*, 1999].

7.3 COMPOSITING

As we already briefly discussed in the previous section, *compositing* describes how the individual contributions from the sample points are accumulated. *Compositing* is the discrete, numerical approximation of the volume rendering equation as shown in Equation 7.8. Since the contribution per sampling point may be small and is further attenuated by the accumulated attenuation factors, we require data types for compositing that provide a high accuracy and fidelity. These requirements are further increased by

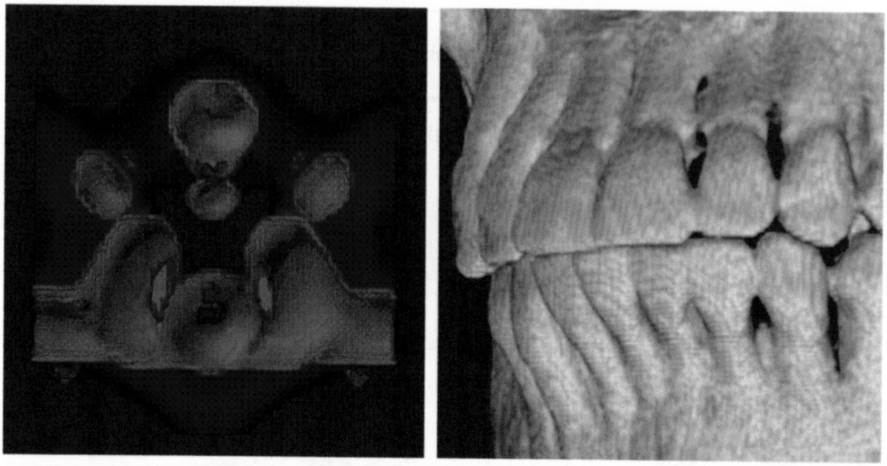

FIGURE 7.6 *Compositing accuracy issues.* **Left:** *Probability cloud of electrons in a protein molecule. The fidelity of compositing data type does not allow for a sufficiently accurate accumulation of highly transparent samples.* **Right:** *Skull from 3D X-ray. Insufficient compositing fidelity is causing color staircasing [Meißner et al., 2000] (Courtesy of Michael Meißner, Universität Tübingen).*

opacity-weighted interpolation, since that requires an additional division for every computed color at the samples. These requirements, however, are not always met. Several direct volume rendering systems provide here only a limited accuracy that in turn leads to color staircasing, a variation of the color bleeding and interpolation artifacts. An example of this is shown in Figure 7.6.

The basic compositing operator is the *over-operator* that was introduced by Porter and Duff [1984] for the compositing of images. Equation 7.10 shows how the overoperators works for a ray with three sampling points ($n = 3$) and $C_k = Q(k \cdot \Delta s)$:

$$\begin{aligned} I(s) &= I_0 \prod_{k=0}^{2} t_k + \sum_{k=0}^{2} C_k \prod_{j=k+1}^{2} t_j \\ &= I_0(t_0 \cdot t_1 \cdot t_2) + (C_0 \cdot t_1 \cdot t_2 + C_1 \cdot t_2 + C_2) \\ &= C_2 + t_2(C_1 + t_1(C_0 + t_0 \cdot I_0)) \\ &= C_2 \text{ over } (C_1 \text{ over } (C_0 \text{ over } I_0)) \end{aligned} \quad (7.10)$$

The overoperator is associative, but not commutative. This means that the order of composited samples cannot be changed, but the order of evaluation can. This gives rise to two directions of composition, *back-to-front* and *front-to-back*. The former composes sample on the ray from the back end of the volume dataset to the front (toward the viewpoint) [Levoy, 1988]. Back-to-front compositing is described by Equation 7.11, where the contribution at sample position k is computed by the previous contribution weighted by the transparency t_k at the current sample, plus the color C_k at the current sample. The initial value I_0 is given by boundary condition, or the ambient background light. The final result is given by I_{n-1}, the accumulated intensity at the final sample position.

$$I_k = I_{k-1} \cdot t_k + C_k, \forall k = 1, \ldots, n-1 \quad (7.11)$$

In *front-to-back* compositing, samples are composited from the front (entry point into the volume from the viewpoint) of the volume dataset along the ray to the back end of the dataset [Drebin *et al.*, 1988,

Upson and Keeler, 1988] (see Fig. 7.2). This is described by Equation 7.12, where we start at the volume exit point $n-1$ of the ray and accumulate color I_{k-1} at the next sampling position, based on the accumulated color I_k at the current sampling position, plus the color at the current sample position C_k weighted by the accumulated transparency $\hat{t}_k$. In contrast to back-to-front compositing, we now must also explicitly compute the accumulated transparency $\hat{t}_{k-1}$ at the next sampling position, based on the transparency t_k at the current sampling point, and the already accumulated transparency $\hat{t}_k$. In contrast to back-to-front compositing in Equation 7.11, the final result is stored in I_0 and $\hat{t}_0$.

$$
\begin{aligned}
I_{n-1} &= C_{n-1} \\
\hat{t}_{n-1} &= t_{n-1} \\
I_{k-1} &= I_k + C_k \cdot \hat{t}_k, \forall k = n-2, \ldots, 0 \\
\hat{t}_{k-1} &= t_k \cdot \hat{t}_k, \forall k = n-2, \ldots, 0
\end{aligned}
\tag{7.12}
$$

7.3.1 COMPOSITING VARIATIONS: PSEUDO X-RAY, MIP, CVP, AND MIDA

Now that we have specified the basic compositing operator, we can employ it in different compositing variations (see Figs. 7.7 and 7.8). If we sample the casted rays until we find two sample points above and below a certain intensity threshold, we reconstruct the isosurface of that threshold. This compositing mode is called *First Hit*, since it terminates once the sample points hit the isosurface with the specified threshold. This compositing mode is similar to polygonal isosurface extraction. However, the isosurface is sampled instead of approximated with polygons. If our sampling rate is too low, we experience aliasing and visual artifacts. Furthermore, first hit compositing usually does not compute the exact intersection of the ray with the isosurface; it only computes the nearest sample points. Hence, small details of the isosurface may be missed if they are too small for our sampling rate. Some compositing algorithms therefore explicitly calculate the intersection point and its contribution to the compositing.

Pseudo X-ray or *averaging* accumulates sample values along the rays throughout the whole volume (see Fig. 7.7, left). Voxel values are simply averaged along the rays, whereas color and lighting information are typically not considered. Overall, this leads to a representation that appears similar to X-ray images (Röntgen images), hence its name. Such renderings can also be used in educational systems for radiologists to simulate X-ray images. Unfortunately, this method also takes into account dark background voxels, which may darken the composed image. This can be prevented by considering only sample values above a certain intensity threshold. This variation is called *threshold-sensitive compositing* and is demonstrated in Figure 7.7 on the right.

A popular compositing mode is *Maximum Intensity Projection* (MIP), which searches for the sample point with the highest intensity value. MIP therefore uses an MAX-operator along the compositing ray (see Fig. 7.8 left). With MIP compositing, the anatomical structures with the highest intensities can be visualized efficiently. This is particularly useful for bone structures (CT) and contrast-enhanced vascular structures, where the measured intensity is significantly above the regular tissue signal (recall Chap. 2). Since MIP is searching for the maximum sample value along the ray, it must traverse the whole volume dataset to locate it, which can involve significant time consumption.

Another drawback of MIP is that it does not provide information on how deep the shown structure is located in the volume, since no attenuation information is used. This leads to the peculiar effect that two MIP projections from opposite directions (e.g., front and back of the volume) will be identical for the same orientation. Furthermore, small and usually darker vessels are outshone by the larger and brighter vessels. For such cases Siebert *et al.* [1991] proposed the *Closest Vessel Projection* (CVP), which takes the first sample

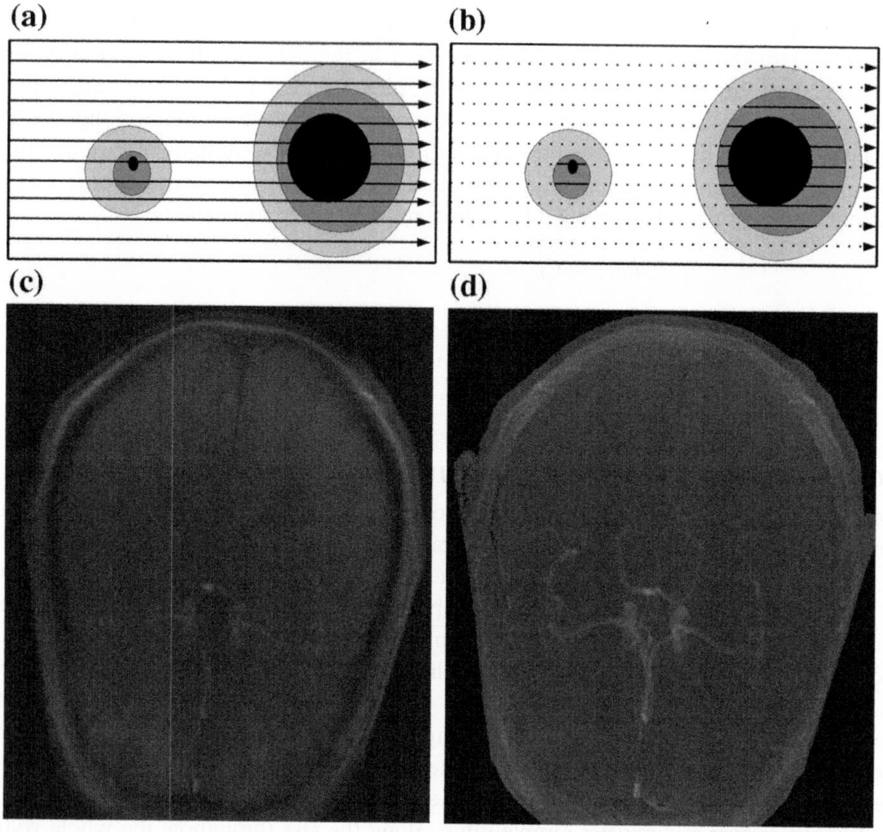

FIGURE 7.7 *Pseudo X-ray and threshold-sensitive compositing. The illustrations at the top show how the rays traverse the volume, sampling the objects therein. Solid lines indicate which parts of the ray actually contribute to the final value. The bottom row shows example renderings of an MR Angiography dataset. On the left, (a) and (c) show pseudo X-ray compositing, where all samples along the ray are composited. On the right, (b) and (d) show threshold-sensitive compositing, where only samples above a certain threshold, in this case 10% of the maximum value, are composited. The vessels are much more clearly visible in the rendering on the right.*

with a local maximum that surpasses a specified threshold (see Fig. 7.8, right). As we have discussed earlier, scanned datasets always experience some sort of noise, which will create very small local maxima along the ray. Therefore, the sensitivity of detecting the local maximum must be carefully tuned. In some cases, it might be necessary to traverse the ray a few samples further to ensure that we found a true local maximum. CVP is closely related to first hit raycasting, but differs in the choice of the sample point. The difference can be seen in Figure 7.8 (right), where the sixth ray from the top find the local maximum of the black ellipsoid. First hit raycasting stops already at the larger middle gray ellipsoid (similar to the seventh ray), which already satisfies the threshold.

The lack of depth and shape cues in MIP was addressed by Bruckner and Gröller [2009] with a technique called *Maximum Intensity Difference Accumulation* or MIDA. MIDA combines the advantages of standard DVR and MIP, and enables a smooth transition between the two, depending on the type of data that is being visualized. Instead of only rendering the maximum value along the ray, MIDA keeps track of each sample along the ray where a new maximum is found. Compositing is performed at each of these points, with

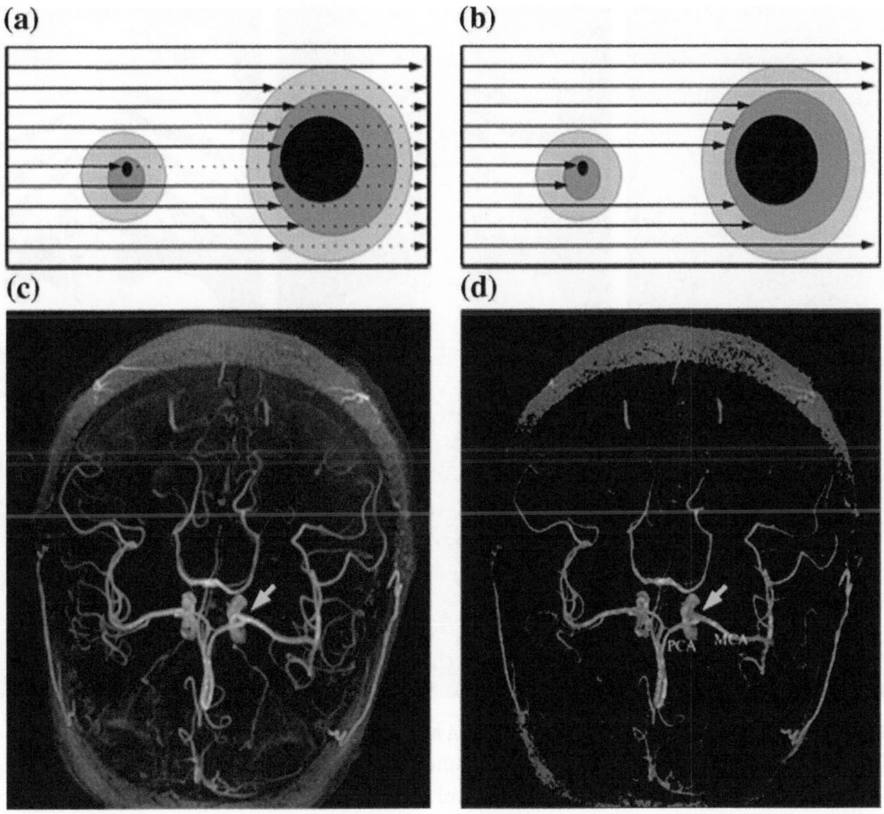

FIGURE 7.8 Maximum Intensity Projection (MIP) and Closest Vessel Projection (CVP) compositing. The illustrations at the top show how the rays traverse the volume, sampling the objects therein. In this case, the solid parts of the arrows point to the volume samples that are selected for the final image. The bottom row shows example renderings of an MR Angiography dataset. On the left, (a) and (c) show MIP compositing, where only the highest value along the ray is selected. On the right, (b) and (d) show CVP compositing, where the first sample above a certain threshold, in this case 10% of the maximum value, is selected. The difference in depth perception is visible at the left carotid siphon (yellow arrow) of the left internal carotid artery (ICA), where the MIP suggests that the left middle cerebral artery (MCA) and left posterior communicating artery are located in front of the siphon.

the magnitude of the difference with the new maximum is used to emphasize the contribution of the corresponding sample. Surface-based shading is also employed at these inflection points to further improve shape perception. Figure 7.9 shows a comparison between DVR, MIDA, and MIP.

7.3.2 THIN SLAB VOLUME RENDERING

All of the compositing variations discussed above consider the full volume. While this is a useful setting for many applications, it is difficult to use if only the local neighborhood of a specific location is examined. Napel *et al.* [1993] proposed the use of *thin slabs* in the context of a MIP, in order to focus only on pulmonary (see Fig. 7.10) and cerebral blood vessels (see Fig. 7.11). Thin slab volume rendering considers only a small number of slices from the full volume dataset, specified by two synchronized clipping planes. It thus enables inspection of the local image data. This allows for a better representation of the spatial coherence

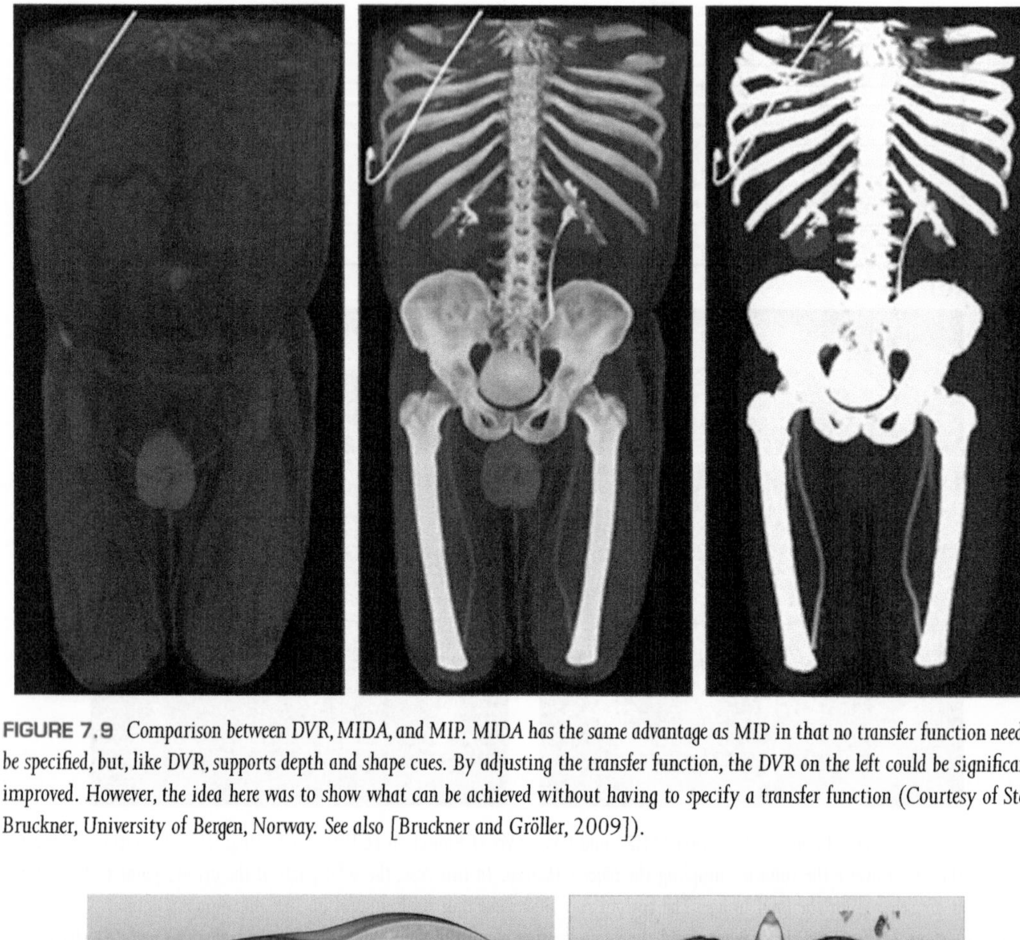

FIGURE 7.9 Comparison between DVR, MIDA, and MIP. MIDA has the same advantage as MIP in that no transfer function needs to be specified, but, like DVR, supports depth and shape cues. By adjusting the transfer function, the DVR on the left could be significantly improved. However, the idea here was to show what can be achieved without having to specify a transfer function (Courtesy of Stefan Bruckner, University of Bergen, Norway. See also [Bruckner and Gröller, 2009]).

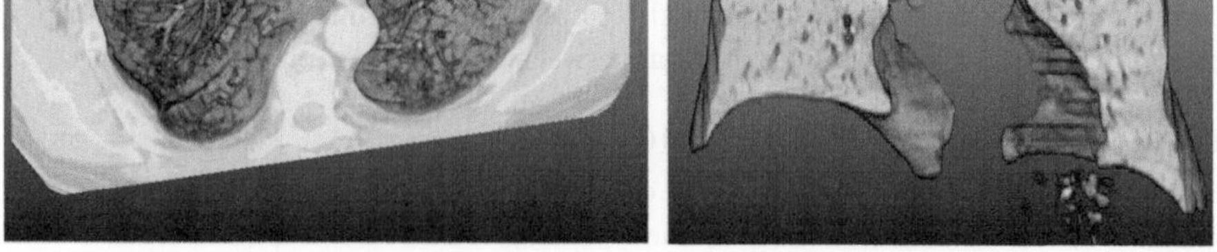

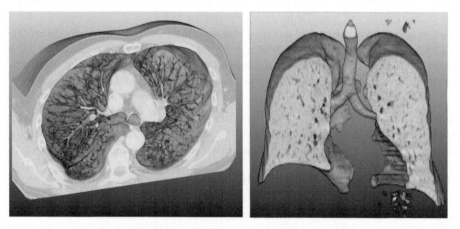

FIGURE 7.10 Slab volume rendering of about 10 cm of CT thorax data. The left image shows the arterial and venous part of the blood vessel tree of the lungs. Right below the heart, we can also see the beginning of the left and right bronchi (empty tube-like structure with staircases). In the right image, another transfer function was specified to analyze the lung. **Left:** a sagittal view, **right:** an axial view (Courtesy of Volker Dicken, Fraunhofer MEVIS Bremen).

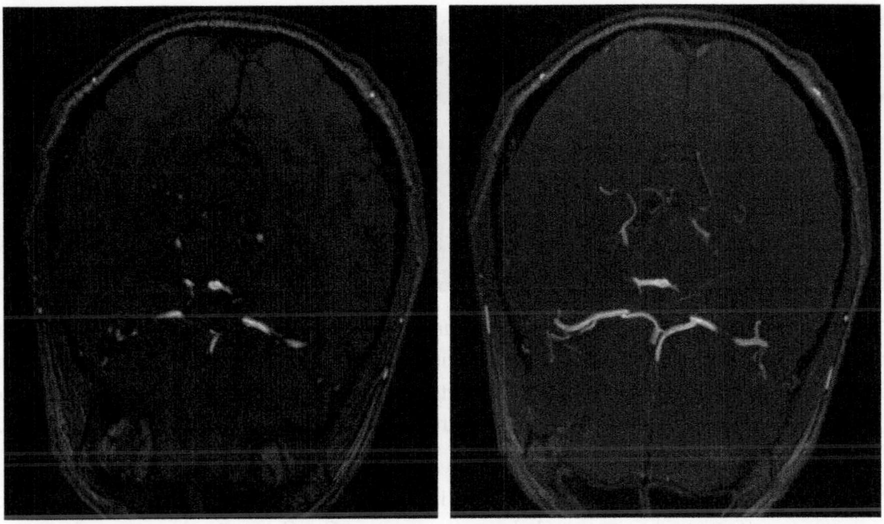

FIGURE 7.11 *Representations of an MR Angiography dataset.* ***Left:*** *single slice representation,* ***Right:*** *thin slab maximum intensity projection.*

between individual slices (see Fig. 7.11 left). One of the major motivations for Thin Slab MIP was better depth perception of local blood vessels. While this goal is better achieved with CVP, thin slab rendering became a popular technique in a more general setting. In that context it is also known as *thick slice volume rendering* or simply as *slab volume rendering*.

Slab rendering is an accepted variant for certain diagnostic tasks, in particular if a large number of slices is involved such as in CT thorax examinations [Napel *et al.*, 1993]. In particular Maximum-Intensity Projections (MIPs) are frequently slab volume rendered (see Fig. 7.11 right). The user may change the displayed portion of the data by moving the mouse over an image (typically using the mouse wheel) thus sliding through the data. The acronym STS for *sliding thin slab* is often used for this type of exploration (recall [Napel *et al.*, 1993]). Slab rendering and other visualization techniques to explore CT thorax data are discussed by Dicken *et al.* [2003].

7.3.3 PRE-INTEGRATED VOLUME RENDERING

As we have mentioned earlier, the frequency range of a volume dataset can be increased depending on the transfer function used. In particular, a binary transfer function that specifies a threshold for an isosurface will increase the frequency spectrum tremendously. This effect can be demonstrated if we consider that a sampling ray has a sample point before and after the isosurface. Therefore, the actual intensity transition will be missed. The obvious solution for this situation is to increase the sampling rate of the ray. This, however, will also increase the computational costs of sampling significantly. An alternative was proposed in the form of *preintegrated volume rendering* by Engel *et al.* [2001]. Instead of composing the contributions at sample points, they propose to compose ray segments between the sample points. This assumes that there is only a linear variation of the intensity between the sample points. While this is not totally true for all scanned datasets,[6] it is a reasonable approximation of the situation (see Fig. 7.12).

6 Voxels in measured volume datasets are computed by a complex set of filter operations based on the measured raw data. Most of these filter operations are not linear.

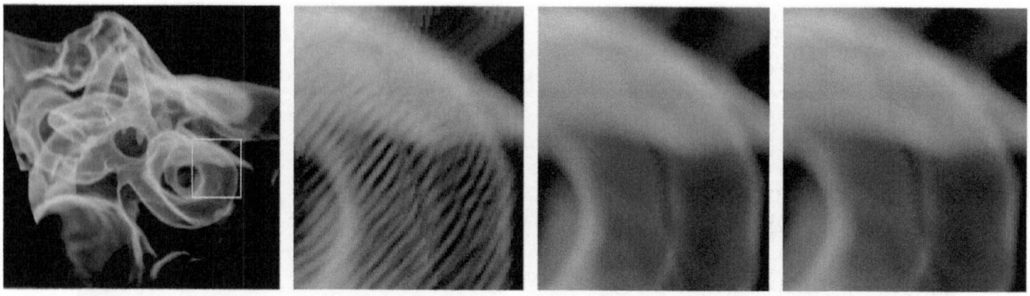

FIGURE 7.12 *Volume rendering of a CT dataset of the inner ear with Vestibule and Cochlea (left most image) with close-up of a part of the Vestibule. Middle left: Postclassified volume rendering with 128 slices; the interpolation artifacts are clearly visible. Middle right: Preintegrated volume rendering with 128 slices; no artifacts are visible. Right: Postclassified sampled volume rendering with 284 slices with the same quality as the middle right image (Courtesy of Klaus Engel, Siemens AG. See also [Engel et al., 2001]).*

The ray segments represent pre-integrated contributions along the rays. Their values depend on the local attenuation coefficients τ_k, τ_{k+1} and the source terms C_k, C_{k+1}. Furthermore, the contribution depends on the distance Δs_k between the two sampling points. If we consider our current discrete volume rendering model, we use a constant sampling distance Δs. Hence, the ray segment contributions depend only on the sampling values at position k and $k+1$. If we precompute all possible combinations of current (k) and next ($k+1$) sampling values, we get a 2D lookup table of values, where each dimension has as many entries as we have possible voxel values. For an 8bit voxel depths, the 2D table has 256×256 entries. Since we precompute the transparencies and the source terms, we need two such lookup tables. Note that we need to recompute the lookup tables for every change in the transfer functions.

7.4 VOLUME RAYCASTING

Direct volume rendering is most often implemented as *volume raycasting*. This algorithm is a more or less direct mapping of the volume rendering equation and the volume rendering pipeline.

For each pixel in the resultant image, one or more rays are cast through the volume. The rays can traverse the volume in parallel to each other, in which case an *orthographic projection* of the volume is performed. More commonly, the rays fan out from the virtual camera according to the *view frustum*, resulting in a *perspective projection* of the volume. Due to this ray configuration, objects further away from the camera appear smaller in the projection, emulating how we perceive real world scenes. Besides these two main projection types, a multitude of effects can be achieved by modifying the ray configuration. For example, by curving the rays, space can be effectively warped, enabling interactive volume deformation [Correa et al., 2006b].

At regular intervals Δs along each ray, the volume is sampled. Generally a trilinear interpolation is used, but higher quality reconstruction kernels can also be used at the cost of rendering speed. The interpolated voxel sample, and any number of related values such as the first and second derivatives, are transformed into color and opacity by the transfer function (§ 7.1.1). The looked up color and opacity are then illuminated, often using the Phong lighting model (§ 7.1.1). Other more advanced lighting models can be used. In most cases, the local volume gradient is required as an approximation of the local surface normal, in order to simulate interaction with directional light sources. The volume gradient is most often calculated using central differences, recall § 2.3.3. Convolving with the Gaussian derivative kernel yields higher quality gradients, but is computationally more expensive. The illuminated color and opacity are then composited with previous samples along the ray using the Equation 7.8, the discretized volume rendering equation. When the ray exits the volume, it is terminated and the accumulated color and opacity are assigned to the pixel from which the ray originated.

Volume raycasting is an *image-order* algorithm, as it iterates over the resulting image. *Object-order* algorithms iterate over the volume data, for example calculating for each voxel its complete contribution to the final image. An example of this will be mentioned in § 7.6.

7.5 EFFICIENT VOLUME RENDERING

Straightforward raycasting is a computationally challenging algorithm. For each pixel in the rendering, one or more rays have to be cast through the volume, along which a large number of samples have to be interpolated, looked up, illuminated and composited. By a conservative estimate, for a single 512 × 512 image, more than 250 million samples have to be evaluated with the steps just listed. For interactive use, this whole process has to be done at more than 15 images per second.

It was initially not possible to achieve interactive performance of the raycasting of reasonably large datasets on normal single CPU computers. Understandably, since the first direct volume rendering developments, acceleration techniques were already a high priority.

There are currently various strategies for the acceleration of volume rendering, thus enabling real-time rendering even with illumination and other special effects that we introduce in Chapter 8. Most notable is the use of the GPU. GPU support may be combined with acceleration strategies at the software level. Here, we discuss two basic algorithmic techniques for speeding up volume raycasting. In the next section (§ 7.6), we discuss GPU-based strategies.

Early Ray Termination This technique leverages the fact that there are generally a number of structures in any volume rendering that are occluded by other structures, and tries to terminate ray integration when a ray has entered such an opaque occluding structure, instead of letting it reach the other side of the volume [Levoy, 1990]. In other words, when a given front-to-back ray has accumulated close to full opacity, none of the samples further along that ray can contribute to the final image, as they are in fact fully occluded. At this point, ray computation can be safely terminated, saving time. Typically, the used opacity threshold is set to 95%.

Empty Space Skipping This technique leverages the observation that most volume datasets are quite sparsely populated. This means that along any given ray, probably only a fraction of its samples contribute to the final image. However, in a straightforward implementation, each of the samples has to be evaluated to determine whether it contributes or not, taking up valuable computation time.

Empty space skipping techniques employ extra data structures with which it can be quickly determined whether a given segment of a ray should be evaluated or can be safely skipped. For example, the volume can be partitioned into subvolumes, where for each subvolume a flag is stored indicating whether it contains only transparent voxels, i.e., it is empty, or not. Alternatively, the minimum and maximum scalar values are stored for each subvolume. In this case, certain assumptions have to be made about the transfer function to determine whether a subvolume is empty or not.

For each ray, the subvolumes it intersects with are determined. The entry and exit points for each subvolume determine a ray segment. Casting a ray can now be formulated as visiting each of its segments in order. Segments with empty subvolumes are skipped, whereas other segments are evaluated from subvolume entry to exit point.

Hierarchical Data Structures These subvolumes can be more efficiently queried by making use of hierarchical data structures such as *octrees* [LaMar *et al.*, 1999] (see Fig. 7.13). Each octree node represents a subvolume.

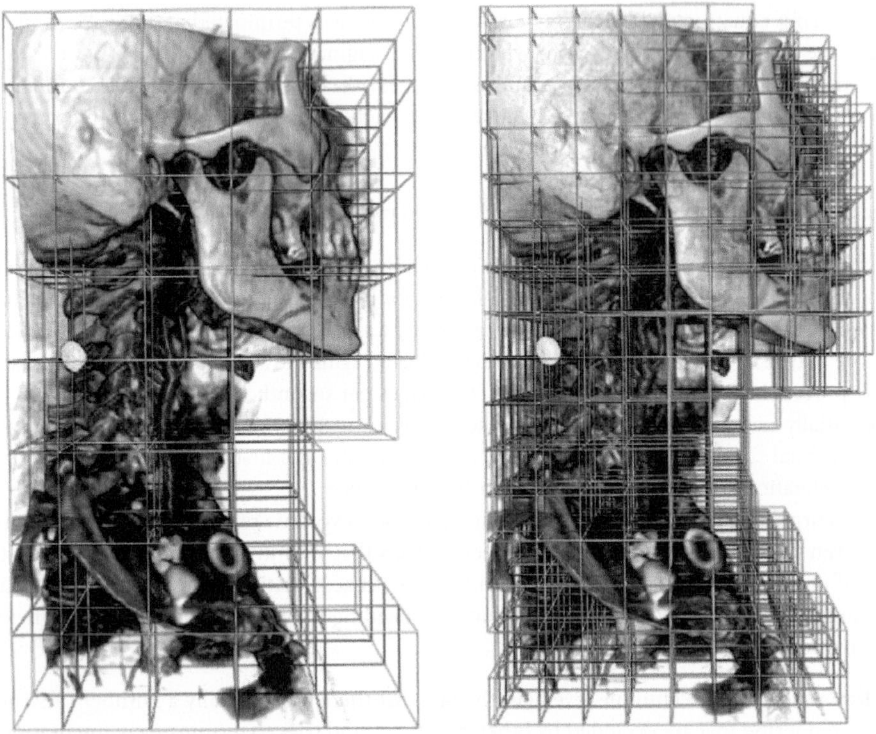

FIGURE 7.13 *Efficient volume rendering with octrees. In the left image, the octree node size equals 64 × 64 × 64 voxels and in the right image 32 × 32 × 32 voxels (Courtesy of Florian Link, MeVis Medical Solutions).*

Due to its hierarchical nature, the octree can be used to determine efficiently which subvolumes, and even which aggregated subvolumes (higher up in the octree), are intersected by the current ray, and whether these spaces can be skipped or not.

The octree nodes slightly overlap to enable correct interpolation. The overhead and additional storage depends on the octree level. The best octree resolution may be adaptively selected based on the camera frustum and the available memory [Link *et al.*, 2006].

7.6 DIRECT VOLUME RENDERING ON THE GPU

As discussed in the previous section, early ray termination and empty space skipping are two basic but effective techniques for speeding up volume raycasting. Over the years, there have been many more contributions toward speeding up direct volume rendering. This section focuses on the use of commodity graphics hardware for interactive volume rendering. However, we start with a short summary of other notable optimization efforts.

Westover [1989] proposed an elaborate reformulation of direct volume rendering, called *splatting*, where the contribution of each voxel to the final image was calculated (the so-called splat) and aggregated. As this *object-order* algorithm ideally visited each voxel only once, in contrast to standard raycasting, an *image-order* algorithm, that samples each voxel potentially a number of times per rendered frame, it was a promising performance optimization. However, the handling of each voxel as an atomic contribution to the final image led to reconstruction artifacts, especially in the case of interleaved voxels. A number of remedies to this problem were proposed [Mueller et al., 1999], but none yielded results as high quality as a good raycasting implementation.

Shear-warp volume rendering was another significant reformulation that traversed the volume in an efficient manner, and then warped the resultant image to compensate for the deformation caused by the efficient traversal [Lacroute and Levoy, 1994]. One of the first dedicated direct volume rendering hardware platforms, the VolumePro, was based on this approach [Pfister *et al.*, 1999].

Algorithmic optimizations and advances in PC hardware would eventually result in software raycasting implementations that run interactively on current off-the-shelf multi-core CPUs. However, the incredible development highly parallel graphics processing units (GPUs) have undergone over the past years, primarily driven by the gaming industry, have turned them into an almost ideal platform for direct volume rendering. With this in mind, we continue our discussion of GPU-based direct volume rendering.

GPU Raycasting Cullip and Neumann [1993] first described the general idea of storing volume data as a 3D texture on the graphics hardware, and then specifying a sampling surface, or *proxy geometry*, onto which the texture was sampled and interpolated by the graphics hardware. Proxy geometry could consist of planes that are aligned with the volume, of planes aligned with the image plane, or even of spherical shells around the viewing point. After interpolation, the graphics hardware would take care of compositing the textured proxy geometry to form the final volume rendering.

A decade after the introduction of 3D textures for GPU-based volume rendering, Krüger and Westermann [2003] proposed addressing a major drawback of texture-based volume rendering approaches: Regardless of the varying characteristics of the volume data being rendered, and hence the differing degrees of contribution to the final image, each and every part of the volume intersected sampled by proxy geometry would be fully interpolated, sampled, composited, and so forth. In the light of the fact that most volume datasets are quite sparsely populated with visible features, this represents a great deal of unnecessary calculations. Their solution was to implement volume raycasting directly on the GPU, using the new shader extensions (GPU instructions) that were gradually coming available. Doing this would on its part make possible the implementation of existing raycasting improvements such as early ray termination and empty space skipping.

Their algorithm was based on two preparatory passes, followed by a number of interleaved main and intermediate passes. At the highest level, rays traversed the volume from the viewpoint, sampling and compositing the volume in parallel.

- In the first preparatory pass, the front faces of the volume bounding box were rendered to a 2D RGB texture, resulting in a texture with color components containing the first intersection points between the rays and the volume.
- In the second preparatory pass, the bounding volume back faces were rendered, making use of the 2D front faces texture, resulting in a new texture with RGB components representing the normalized ray directions.
- In each of N main passes, making use of the entry point and direction textures, M steps along the rays would be sampled, composited and then blended with the result of the previous main pass. If a ray had exited the volume, its opacity would be set to maximum.
- In each of the intermediate passes, interleaved with the main passes, rays were terminated if their accumulated opacity was above a certain threshold.

Two additional textures were used to encode empty blocks in the volume. These textures were accessed and acted upon during the intermediate passes to jump over empty blocks in the volume. Using these relatively straightforward techniques, frame rates ranging from 13.6 to 23.4 were obtained using a 2003 consumer graphics card on the well-known benchmark volume datasets *head*, *aneurysm*, *foot*, and *engine*.

Notable extensions to GPU raycasting include the single pass formulation that was made possible by the then-introduced support of branching and looping in fragment shaders [Stegmaier *et al.*, 2005], as well as various data structures that enable the rendering of large volumes that do not fit into texture memory [Engel *et al.*, 2006].

Because raycasting is an *embarrassingly parallel problem*, the performance of GPU raycasting has improved significantly since its introduction, and is still improving, along with the increased parallelism and texture memory in each new generation of GPU technology. Based on the quality, performance and straightforward implementation that can be achieved with GPU raycasting, we believe that this will remain the *de facto* standard for direct volume rendering in the years to come.

7.7 SUMMARY

In this chapter, we provided a brief presentation of the theoretical foundations of direct volume rendering. Specifically, we described a physical model that consists of emission and absorption in a low albedo situation with the volume rendering equation. This model was named by Sabella [1988] as the *density emitter model* and it omits the influence of scattering, diffraction, refraction, reflection, participating (inhomogeneous) media, and wavelength. Also, relativistic effects are completely ignored.

Direct volume rendering is organized by the volume rendering pipeline, which allows for pre and postclassified volume rendering with different consequences for the quality and the accuracy of the direct volume rendering algorithms. The final step of compositing the various contributing samples enables different modes, which in turn generate different visual representations of the data.

We then described volume raycasting, an important algorithm for direct volume rendering, concluding with a discussion of acceleration strategies, both in software and on the GPU. In the next chapter, we will discuss a number of advanced direct volume rendering techniques.

FURTHER READING AND EXPERIMENTATION

Experimenting with state of the art direct volume rendering implementations can help in understanding the practical implications of the material we have discussed in this chapter. Fortunately, a number of high-quality direct volume rendering systems are freely available, often as open source. ImageVis3D[7] is an open-source implementation of 2D texture-based volume rendering and GPU raycasting. The free version of MeVisLab[8] contains the Giga Voxel Renderer (GVR), a high-quality GPU-based volume renderer for large and time-varying volumetric datasets. VTK-based tools such as ParaView[9], DeVIDE[10] and OsiriX[11] provide user-friendly access to the various volume rendering implementations in VTK, including software-based multi-core, 2D texture, 3Dtexture, and GPU raycasting implementations. Voreen[12] is a visual programming

7 http://www.imagevis3d.com/.
8 http://www.mevislab.de/.
9 http://www.paraview.org/.
10 http://graphics.tudelft.nl/Projects/DeVIDE.
11 http://www.osirix-viewer.com/.
12 http://www.voreen.org/.

environment that focuses on volume rendering. There are more tools available, but we mention only the ones we have experience with.

There are many articles that describe the foundations of direct volume rendering. A comprehensive presentation of the physical models typically used for volume rendering was prepared by Max [1995]. Hege *et al.* [1993] provide also an excellent overview of the theoretical foundations.

The basics of the physical model is the transport theory of light and was described by Krüger [1990a,b]. It is the more general version of the Rendering Equation presented by Kajiya [1986], which omits the participating media and assumes a vacuum and that light is emitted, scattered, and absorbed on surfaces only. The Rendering Equation also ignores any kind of wavelength dependencies. Blinn [1982a] described the physical model of single scattering events or low albedo situations with an example of the dust particle rings of Saturn. In that paper, he first introduced the notion of a density cloud with certain optical properties. Kajiya and Herzen [1984] extended the model to multiple scattering events, or high albedo situations.

Four important articles on direct volume rendering were published in 1988. Sabella [1988] specified the optical basis of direct volume rendering with the density emitter model. The use of the Phong lighting model was proposed by Drebin *et al.* [1988], Upson and Keeler [1988], Levoy [1988], and the specification of opacity transfer functions was proposed in all four papers. Although the opacity transfer function already implied the classification of different materials, this was only discussed by Drebin *et al.* [1988]. Furthermore, they introduced color transfer functions in addition to the opacity transfer function. Levoy, however, also proposed the use of gradient magnitudes to emphasize boundaries [Levoy, 1988].

While most direct volume rendering applications work sufficiently well with the discussed models, Rau *et al.* [1998], Weiskopf *et al.* [1999] modeled also relativistic effects for ray tracing, where in particular the geometric distortion [Rau *et al.*, 1998] and the Doppler and searchlight effects [Weiskopf *et al.*, 1999] were examined.

Gobbetti *et al.* [2008] describe how multi-gigabyte volumes, that do not fit in texture memory, can be interactively rendered with a single-pass GPU raycasting approach that utilizes an out-of-core octree and adaptive loading of the data onto the GPU. Crassin *et al.* [2009] developed a similar approach to this problem in parallel to Gobetti and colleagues. Through the use of a *virtual octree*, i.e., an octree of which the contents are calculated only when necessary, Beyer *et al.* [2011] managed to render interactively terabyte-sized volumes.

An important issue is also the validation of volume rendering algorithms, e.g., the assessment of interpolation schemes, gradient estimation, and other parameters with respect to the perceived accuracy. Pommert and Höhne [2002] and Pommert [2004] carefully investigated these issues using various phantoms with known geometry, such as spheres.

Chapter 08

Advanced Direct Volume Visualization

8.1 INTRODUCTION

In the previous chapters we have described the volume visualization pipeline and discussed several volume rendering algorithms. With the advent of modern GPUs, an increasing number of existing algorithms have been adapted, or new algorithms have been specifically developed to enable advanced GPU-based volume rendering. As a consequence, it became possible to reach interactive frame rates even for large datasets and when using high sampling rates. With the further development of modern GPUs and the resulting performance increases, more computation time was available during rendering and thus the usage of more advanced algorithms became feasible. Since these approaches should be considered as extensions to the existing volume rendering paradigms rather than new algorithms, we describe them separately within this chapter. We have grouped the covered advanced direct volume rendering algorithms into two classes, based on the main challenges which have been addressed over the last years in this area. Advanced volume rendering techniques are motivated to a large extent by perceptual issues. Thus, color, contrast, and gray value perception are essential (recall § 3.3). In addition, we discuss *depth perception* in this chapter in order to discuss how advanced rendering supports the interpretation of spatial relations.

Volumetric Illumination and Depth Enhancement While the standard volume rendering integral, based on emission and absorption, allows to convey the basic structures inherent to a volumetric dataset, it does not take the perceptual capabilities of the human visual system into account. However, several studies have been conducted, which indicate that incorporating these capabilities results in an improved perception, which could either allow a more accurate or a more rapid spatial comprehension. The *dark-means-deep* paradigm is a relatively old model for understanding and describing depth relationships [Nicolaides, 1941]. It is often motivated by the color diminishing due to environmental fog. In a more recent work, Langer and Bülthoff [2000] were able to show that the underlying illumination model has a direct impact on the spatial comprehension of a scene. These are just two examples of a vast amount of work indicating perceptual benefits when incorporating the human visual capabilities during image generation. Accordingly, a lot of research has been dedicated toward this aspect. Two trends can be observed to reach this goal. First, focusing on *mimicking the illumination capabilities* present in the real world, and second, using *more abstract depth enhancement* techniques, for which no counterpart can be found in real-world illumination. Within this chapter we will address both of these areas.

Organization We will start with the volumetric illumination techniques by discussing the supported illumination types, the underlying illumination model, and different GPU-based algorithms that support these illumination types. § 8.2 discusses volumetric illumination techniques, which have been developed with the goal to mimic real-world lighting properties. § 8.3 covers non-illumination-based depth enhancement techniques used in medical visualization. While these techniques have been developed with a similar goal as the illumination techniques described in § 8.2, i.e., an improved communication of the front-to-back arrangements in a scene, the techniques do not obey to physical laws observed in the real world.

Visual Computing for Medicine, Second Edition. http://dx.doi.org/10.1016/B978-0-12-415873-3.00008-0

8.2 VOLUMETRIC ILLUMINATION

Shading has the potential to improve the quality of volume rendered images, as used in medical visualization. While the previously discussed approaches (recall § 7.2) are similar to surface-based shading techniques, in recent years illumination models have been developed, which take into account the volumetric nature of the data to be visualized [Rezk Salama *et al.*, 2009]. This development is motivated by perceptual benefits of advanced illumination effects [Wanger, 1992]. More recently, the benefits of advanced illumination techniques could also be demonstrated in various user studies [Šoltészová *et al.*, 2011, Lindemann and Ropinski, 2011]. This is especially important for medical visualization, as these perceptual benefits allow a better communication of the relative positioning of anatomical structures of interest. Thus, a lot of research has been dedicated toward replacing the standard emission absorption model. As the emission absorption model conveys the basic structures represented in a volumetric dataset (see Fig. 8.1, left), it is only capable of simulating local lighting effects, where light is emitted and absorbed locally at each sample point processed during rendering. Hence, though all structures are clearly visible in these images, the arrangement and size of structures is sometimes hard to convey. As can be seen in Figure 8.1 (right), advanced illumination models not only increase the degree of realism, but also enable improved comprehension. While Figure 8.1 (left) shows the overall structure of the rendered CT dataset of a human heart, the shadows added in Figure 8.1 (right) provide additional depth information.

In this section, we focus on advanced volumetric illumination models, which are applicable in medical diagnosis or surgical planning, as they allow interactive data exploration, i.e., rendering parameters can be changed interactively. This data exploration often occurs in the medical workflow, for instance when estimating the distance of structures at risk to an intervention path. When developing these techniques, several challenges need to be addressed:

- A volumetric optical model must be applied, which usually results in more complex computations due to the global nature of the illumination.
- Interactive transfer function updates must be supported. This requires that the resulting changes to the 3D structure of the data, which for instance arises when changing the set of visible anatomical structures, must be incorporated during illumination.
- Graphics processing unit (GPU) algorithms need to be developed to allow interactivity.

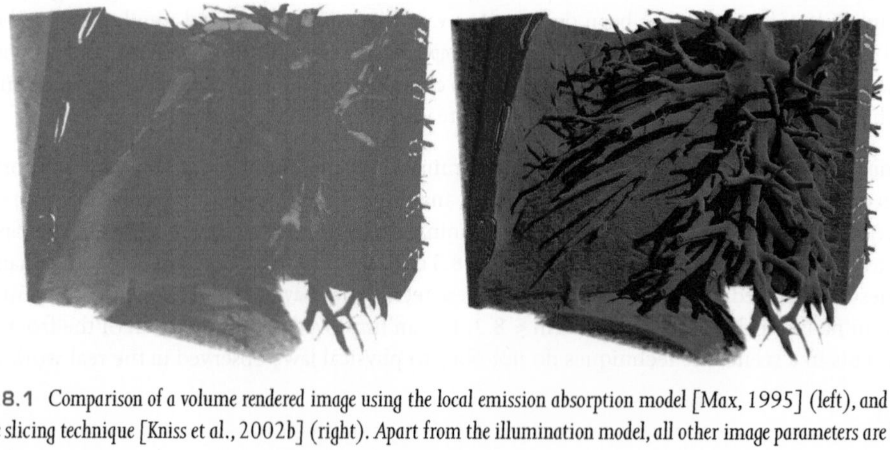

FIGURE 8.1 *Comparison of a volume rendered image using the local emission absorption model [Max, 1995] (left), and the global half angle slicing technique [Kniss et al., 2002b] (right). Apart from the illumination model, all other image parameters are the same.*

Illumination Effects The approaches for volumetric illumination deal mainly with three effects, which are intended to mimic physical light volume interaction:

- Ambient occlusion—By incorporating the degree of occlusion in the neighborhood of a voxel, the usually local shading term is modified.
- Shadowing—As in conventional computer graphics algorithms, the directional shadowing contribution is considered during the rendering process.
- Scattering—Due to the translucent properties of a volume, scattering effects need to be taken into account to achieve a high degree of realism.

To present a structured overview, we classify the discussed techniques based on their technical realization, their performance behavior, and their perceptual capabilities, and we will further comment on their applicability within medical visualization. To start, we will discuss the emission absorption model, which we successively enrich to later support global volumetric illumination effects. We then present the classification of existing volumetric illumination techniques and discuss the covered techniques in more detail. Since one of the main motivations for developing volumetric illumination models is improved visual perception, we will also discuss recent findings in this area with respect to medical visualization. Finally, we will provide the developer of medical visualization systems with a comparative overview of the discussed techniques, which is aimed at supporting the selection of an appropriate illumination algorithm from a technical point of view.

8.2.1 VOLUMETRIC ILLUMINATION MODEL

In this section we derive the volume illumination model frequently exploited by the advanced volume illumination approaches. The model is based on the optical model derived by Max [1995] as well as on the extensions more recently described by Max and Chen [2010]. For clarity, we have included the definitions used within the model as a reference below.

Mathematical notation

$L_s(\mathbf{x}, \boldsymbol{\omega}_o)$	Radiance scattered from $\mathbf{x}$ into direction $\boldsymbol{\omega}_o$.
$L_i(\mathbf{x}, \boldsymbol{\omega}_i)$	Radiance reaching $\mathbf{x}$ from direction $\boldsymbol{\omega}_i$.
$L_e(\mathbf{x})$	Radiance isotropically emitted from $\mathbf{x}$.
$s(\mathbf{x}, \boldsymbol{\omega}_i, \boldsymbol{\omega}_o)$	Shading function used at position $\mathbf{x}$. It is dependent on the incoming light direction $\boldsymbol{\omega}_i$ and the outgoing light direction $\boldsymbol{\omega}_o$.
$p(\mathbf{x}, \boldsymbol{\omega}_i, \boldsymbol{\omega}_o)$	Phase function used at position $\mathbf{x}$. As the shading function s, it is dependent on the incoming light direction $\boldsymbol{\omega}_i$ and the outgoing light direction $\boldsymbol{\omega}_o$.
$\tau(\mathbf{x})$	Extinction occurring at $\mathbf{x}$.
$T(\mathbf{x}_l, \mathbf{x})$	Transparency between the light source position $\mathbf{x}_l$ and the current position.
L_l	Initial radiance as emitted by the light source.
$L_0(\mathbf{x}_0, \boldsymbol{\omega}_o)$	Background intensity.

Similar to surface-based models, in volume rendering lighting is computed per point, which is in our case a sample $\mathbf{x}$ along a viewing ray. The radiance $L_s(\mathbf{x}, \boldsymbol{\omega}_o)$ which is scattered from $\mathbf{x}$ inside the volume into direction $\boldsymbol{\omega}_o$, can be defined as:

$$L_s(\mathbf{x}, \boldsymbol{\omega}_o) = s(\mathbf{x}, \boldsymbol{\omega}_i, \boldsymbol{\omega}_o) \cdot L_i(\mathbf{x}, \boldsymbol{\omega}_i) + L_e(\mathbf{x}) \tag{8.1}$$

where $L_i(\mathbf{x}, \boldsymbol{\omega}_\mathbf{i})$ is the incident radiance reaching $\mathbf{x}$ from direction $\boldsymbol{\omega}_\mathbf{i}$, $L_e(\mathbf{x})$ is the emissive radiance and $s(\mathbf{x}, \boldsymbol{\omega}_\mathbf{i}, \boldsymbol{\omega}_\mathbf{o})$ describes the actual shading, which is dependent on both the incident light direction $\boldsymbol{\omega}_\mathbf{i}$ as well as the outgoing light direction $\boldsymbol{\omega}_\mathbf{o}$. Furthermore, $s(\mathbf{x}, \boldsymbol{\omega}_\mathbf{i}, \boldsymbol{\omega}_\mathbf{o})$ is dependent on parameters which may vary based on $\mathbf{x}$, as for instance the optical properties assigned through the transfer function. In the context of volume rendering $s(\mathbf{x}, \boldsymbol{\omega}_\mathbf{i}, \boldsymbol{\omega}_\mathbf{o})$ is often written as:

$$s(\mathbf{x}, \boldsymbol{\omega}_\mathbf{i}, \boldsymbol{\omega}_\mathbf{o}) = \tau(\mathbf{x}) \cdot p(\mathbf{x}, \boldsymbol{\omega}_\mathbf{i}, \boldsymbol{\omega}_\mathbf{o}) \tag{8.2}$$

where $\tau(\mathbf{x})$ represents the extinction coefficient at position $\mathbf{x}$ and $p(\mathbf{x}, \boldsymbol{\omega}_\mathbf{i}, \boldsymbol{\omega}_\mathbf{o})$ is the phase function describing the scattering characteristics of the participating medium at position $\mathbf{x}$.

Scattering is the physical process which forces light to deviate from its straight trajectory. The reflection of light at a surface point is thus a *scattering event*. Depending on the material properties of the surface, incident photons are scattered in different directions. When using the raycasting analogy, scattering can be considered as a redirection of a ray penetrating an object. Since scattering can also change a photon's frequency and thus its wavelength, a change in color becomes possible. Max [1995] presents accurate solutions for simulating light scattering in participating media, i.e., how the light trajectory is changed when penetrating translucent materials.

In polygonal rendering, single scattering accounts for light emitted from a light source directly onto a surface and reflected unimpededly into the observer's eye. Multiple scattering describes the same concept, but incoming photons are scattered multiple times. To generate realistic images, both *indirect light* and *multiple scattering events* have to be taken into account. Both concepts are closely related; they only differ in their scale. Indirect illumination means that light is reflected multiple times by different objects in the scene. Multiple scattering refers to the probabilistic characteristics of a scattering event caused by a photon being reflected multiple times within an object. While light reflection on a surface is often modeled using bidirectional reflectance distribution functions (BRDFs), in volume rendering *phase functions* are used to model the scattering behavior. A phase function can be thought of as being the spherical extension of a hemispherical BRDF. It defines the probability of a photon changing its direction of motion by an angle of θ. In interactive volume rendering, the Henyey-Greenstein model $G(\theta, g) = \frac{1-g^2}{(1+g^2-2g\cos\theta)^{\frac{3}{2}}}$ is often used to incorporate phase functions. The parameter $g \in [-1, 1]$ describes the anisotropy of the scattering event. A value $g = 0$ denotes that light is scattered equally in all directions. A positive value of g increases the probability of forward scattering. Accordingly, with a negative value backward scattering will become more likely. If $g = 1$, a photon will always pass through the point unaffectedly. If $g = -1$ it will deterministically be reflected into the direction it came from.

Shadowing, where the attenuation of external light traveling through the volume is incorporated, can be considered in this model by defining the incident radiance $L_i(\mathbf{x}, \boldsymbol{\omega}_\mathbf{i})$ as:

$$L_i(\mathbf{x}, \boldsymbol{\omega}_\mathbf{i}) = L_l \cdot T(\mathbf{x}_\mathbf{l}, \mathbf{x}) \tag{8.3}$$

This definition is based on the standard volume rendering integral, where the light source is located at $\mathbf{x}_\mathbf{l}$ and has the radiance L_l and $T(\mathbf{x}_\mathbf{l}, \mathbf{x})$ is dependent on the transparency between $\mathbf{x}_\mathbf{l}$ and $\mathbf{x}$. It describes the compositing of the optical properties assigned to all samples $\mathbf{x}'$ along a ray and it incorporates emission and absorption, such that it can be written as:

$$L(\mathbf{x}, \boldsymbol{\omega}_\mathbf{o}) = L_0(\mathbf{x}_\mathbf{0}, \boldsymbol{\omega}_\mathbf{o}) \cdot T(\mathbf{x}_\mathbf{0}, \mathbf{x}) + \int_{\mathbf{x}_\mathbf{0}}^{\mathbf{x}} o(\mathbf{x}') \cdot T(\mathbf{x}', \mathbf{x}) d\mathbf{x}' \tag{8.4}$$

While $L_0(\mathbf{x_0}, \boldsymbol{\omega_o})$ depicts the background energy entering the volume, $o(\mathbf{x}')$ defines the optical properties at $\mathbf{x}'$, and $T(\mathbf{x_i}, \mathbf{x_j})$ is dependent on the optical depth and describes how light is attenuated when traveling through the volume:

$$T(\mathbf{x_i}, \mathbf{x_j}) = e^{-\int_{\mathbf{x_i}}^{\mathbf{x_j}} \tau(\mathbf{x}')d\mathbf{x}'} \quad (8.5)$$

Since volumetric data is discrete, the volume rendering integral is in practice approximated numerically, usually by exploiting a Riemann sum.

According to MAX, the standard volume rendering integral simulating absorption and emission can be extended with these definitions to support single scattering and shadowing:

$$\begin{aligned} L(\mathbf{x}, \boldsymbol{\omega_o}) = {} & L_0(\mathbf{x_0}, \boldsymbol{\omega_o}) \cdot T(\mathbf{x_0}, \mathbf{x}) \\ & + \int_{\mathbf{x_0}}^{\mathbf{x}} (L_e(\mathbf{x}) + (s(\mathbf{x}', \boldsymbol{\omega_i}, \boldsymbol{\omega_o}) \cdot L_i(\mathbf{x}', \boldsymbol{\omega_i}))) \cdot T(\mathbf{x}', \mathbf{x}) d\mathbf{x}' \end{aligned} \quad (8.6)$$

with $\boldsymbol{\omega_i} = \mathbf{x_l} - \mathbf{x}'$, $L_0(\mathbf{x_0}, \boldsymbol{\omega_o})$ being the ackground intensity and $\mathbf{x_0}$ being a point behind the volume. When extending this equation to support multiple scattering, it is necessary to integrate the scattering of light coming from all possible directions $\boldsymbol{\omega_i}$ on the unit sphere.

8.2.2 ALGORITHM CLASSIFICATION

To give a comprehensive overview, we will introduce the following classification within this section, which allows us to compare advanced volumetric illumination techniques. The classification has been developed to provide decision support, when choosing advanced volumetric illumination techniques. This is especially important, as the integration of advanced illumination models into legacy medical visualization systems requires matching them with the existing technology. Thus, we will first cover the most relevant algorithm properties that need to be considered when making such a decision.

Rendering Paradigms The most limiting property of advanced volumetric illumination algorithms is the dependence on an underlying rendering paradigm. In the past, different paradigms allowing interactive volume rendering have been proposed. These paradigms range from a shear-warp transformation [Lacroute and Levoy, 1994], oversplatting [Mueller *et al.*, 1999], and slice-based rendering [Cabral *et al.*, 1994] to volume raycasting [Krüger and Westermann, 2003]. Besides their different technical realizations, the visual quality of the rendered image also varies with respect to the used rendering paradigm [Smelyanskiy *et al.*, 2009]. Many illumination approaches have been developed, which allow a performance gain by being closely bound to a specific rendering paradigm (e.g., [Kniss *et al.*, 2002b, Schott *et al.*, 2009]). Nowadays, the two rendering paradigms most commonly used when visualizing medical volume data, are slice-based rendering and raycasting. Figure 8.2 shows a schematic representation of these two approaches. When performing raycasting (see Fig. 8.2, left), viewing rays are sampled independently. As this is done on a pixel basis, raycasting is considered as image-based technique. Figure 8.2 (left) depicts the samples, which are in this case uniformly distributed, for the current ray which is emphasized.

Shadowing Effects To integrate shadowing effects, the light source visibility must be determined for each sample along each ray. The most straightforward way of doing this is to send shadow rays or shadow feelers from each sample toward the light source, as shown for the current sample. Slice-based volume rendering (see Fig. 8.2, right) is an object-based rendering paradigm, as slices intersecting the volume are rendered sequentially, either from back to front or vice versa. While the most obvious approach for shadow generation is also the evaluation of shadow rays, another more efficient approach is often exploited. When

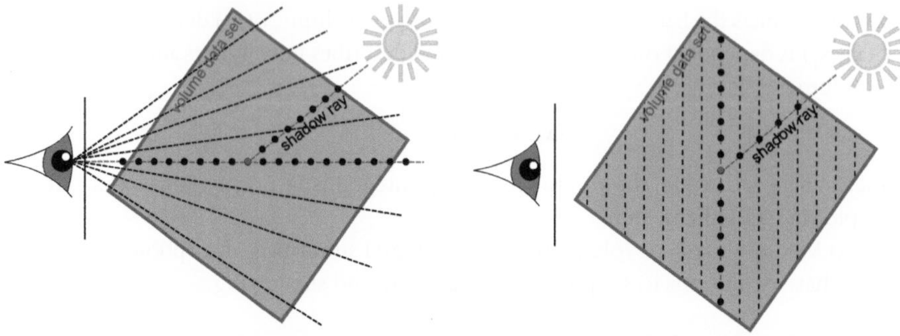

FIGURE 8.2 *Schematic representation of raycasting (left) and slice-based volume rendering (right). Samples are depicted as black disks, while the current sample, for which light source visibility is evaluated, is shown in red.*

using a shadow ray sample distribution, which is inline with the distances between the rendered slices, the sequential nature of the slicing rendering can be exploited to compute the light source visibility more efficiently. In Figure 8.2 (right), where the light source is located behind the volume, a back-to-front slice processing would allow to compute the visibility iteratively for each slice, and forward it to the next slice to be rendered. Especially when integrating volumetric illumination into existing visualization systems, the underlying rendering paradigm might be limiting when choosing an appropriate algorithm. Therefore, the considerations made in Figure 8.2 have to be taken into account, and we will further discuss this dependency.

Illumination Effects Another crucial property is, which illumination effects are supported by a certain algorithm. This is on the one hand specified based on the supported lighting, and on the other hand on the light interaction and propagation inside the volume. The supported illumination can vary with respect to the number and types of the light sources. Supported light source include:

- point light sources,
- directional light sources,
- area light sources, and
- textured light sources.

Since several algorithms focus on ambient visibility computation, we also consider an *ambient light source*, which is omni-directional and homogeneous. As some algorithms are bound to certain rendering paradigms, they may also be subject to constraints regarding the light source position. Finally, the number of supported light sources varies, where either one or many light sources are supported. With respect to the light interaction and propagation inside the volume, the discussed algorithms also vary. While all algorithms support either local or global shadowing, though at different frequencies reaching from soft to hard shadows, scattering is not supported by all approaches. Algorithms which support scattering may either support the simulation of single or multiple scattering events. We will discuss these capabilities for each covered technique and relate the supported illumination effects to those described by Max [1995].

Technical Resources Applying advanced illumination techniques in volume rendering involves a trade-off between rendering performance and memory consumption. The two most extreme cases on this scale are entire precomputation of the illumination information, and recomputation on the fly for each frame.

We will compare the techniques with respect to this trade-off by describing the performance impact of these techniques as well as the required memory consumption. We will review their performance capabilities with respect to rendering and illumination update. Some techniques trade illumination update times for frame rendering times and thus allow higher frame rates, as long as no illumination-critical parameter has been changed. We discuss rendering times as well as illumination update times, whereby we differentiate whether they are triggered by lighting or transfer function updates. Recomputations performed when the camera changes are considered as rendering time. The memory footprint of the covered techniques is also important, since it is often limited by the available graphics memory. Some techniques precompute an illumination volume, e.g., [Schlegel *et al.*, 2011], while others store much less or even no illumination data, e.g., Kniss *et al.* [2002b].

Clipping and Geometry Finally, it is important whether a volumetric illumination approach can be combined with clipping planes and allows to combine geometry and volumetric data. While clipping is used in many medical visualization scenarios, the integration of polygonal geometry data is for instance important when volume data along with surgical instruments, catheters or implants.

Classification Categories To enable easier comparison of the existing techniques, we classified them into five groups, based on the algorithmic concepts exploited to achieve the resulting illumination effects. The thus obtained groups are:

- *Local region-based* techniques, which consider only the local neighborhood around a voxel.
- *Slice-based* techniques, which propagate illumination by iteratively slicing through the volume.
- *Light space-based* techniques, which project illumination as seen from the light source.
- *Lattice-based* techniques, which compute the illumination directly on the volumetric data grid without applying sampling.
- *Basis function-based* techniques, which use a basis function representation of the illumination information.

While this classification is solely performed based on the concepts used to compute the illumination itself, and not for the image generation, it might go hand in hand, e.g., when considering the *slice-based* techniques, which are bound to the slice-based rendering paradigm. A comparison of the visual output of one representative technique of each of the five groups is shown in Figure 8.3. As it can be seen, when changing the illumination model, the visual results might change drastically, even though most of the presented techniques are based on the formulation by Max [1995] of a volumetric illumination model. The most prominent visual differences are the intensities of shadows as well as their frequency, which is visible based on the blurriness of the shadow borders. Besides the five main groups supporting fully interactive volume rendering, we will also briefly cover *raytracing-based* techniques, and those only limited to *isosurface illumination*. While the introduced groups allow a sufficient classification for most techniques, some approaches could be classified into more than one group. For instance, the shadow volume propagation approach [Ropinski *et al.*, 2010a], which we have classified as lattice-based, could also be classified as light space-based, since the illumination propagation is performed based on the current light source position.

In the following sections, we will describe all techniques in a formalized way. For each group, we will provide details regarding the algorithms themselves with respect to their technical capabilities as well as the supported illumination effects. We will start with a brief explanation of each algorithm where we relate the exploited illumination computations to Max's model (see § 8.2.1) and provide a conceptual overview of the implementation. Then, we will discuss the illumination capabilities with respect to supported

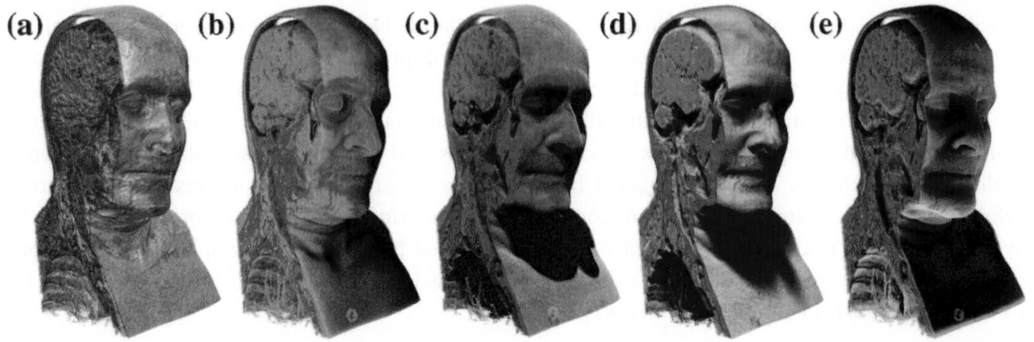

FIGURE 8.3 *Visual comparison when applying different volumetric illumination models to a computed CT scan of a human head with clipping applied. (a) Gradient-based shading [Levoy, 1988], (b) directional occlusion shading [Schott et al., 2009], (c) image plane sweep volume illumination [Sundén et al., 2011], (d) shadow volume propagation [Ropinski et al., 2010a], and (e) spherical harmonic lighting [Kronander et al., 2012]. Apart from the used illumination model, all other rendering parameters are constant.*

light sources and light interactions inside the volume, before addressing performance impact, memory consumption, and applicability in medical visualization.

8.2.3 LOCAL REGION-BASED TECHNIQUES

As the name implies, the techniques described in this subsection perform the illumination computation based on a local region. Thus, when relating volumetric illumination techniques to polygonal computer graphics, these techniques could be best compared to local shading models. While the still most frequently used gradient-based shading is exploiting the concepts underlying the Blinn-Phong illumination model [Levoy, 1988], other techniques are more focused on the volumetric nature of the data to be rendered. Also with respect to the locality, the described techniques vary. Gradient-based shading relies on a gradient and thus takes only adjacent voxels into account. Other techniques, as for instance *dynamic ambient occlusion*, take into account bigger, though still local, regions [Ropinski *et al.*, 2008b]. Thus, by using local region-based techniques, only direct illumination is computed, i.e., local illumination not influenced by other parts of the scene. Hence, not every other part of the scene has to be considered when computing the illumination for the current object, and the rendering complexity is reduced from $O(n^2)$ to $O(n)$, with n being the number of voxels. This difference is of importance when considering the applicability in the medical domain, as only when taking into account all parts of the volume during illumination computation, distances between anatomical structures can be estimated globally.

Gradient-based volumetric shading [Levoy, 1988] is today still the most widely used shading technique in the context of interactive volume rendering. It exploits voxel gradients as surface normals to calculate local lighting effects. The actual illumination computation is performed in a similar way as when using the Blinn-Phong illumination model [Blinn, 1977] in polygonal-based graphics, whereas the surface normal is substituted by the gradient derived from the volumetric data. The local illumination at a point $\mathbf{x}$ is computed as the sum of the three supported reflection contributions: diffuse reflection, specular reflection and ambient lighting. Diffuse and specular reflections both depend on the normalized gradient $| \bigtriangledown \tau(f(\mathbf{x}))|$, where $f(\mathbf{x})$ is the intensity value given at position $\mathbf{x}$. Thus, we can define the diffuse reflection as:

$$L_{diff}(\mathbf{x}, \omega_i) = L_l \cdot k_d \cdot max(| \bigtriangledown \tau(f(\mathbf{x}))| \cdot \omega_i, 0) \quad (8.7)$$

Thus, we can modulate the initial diffuse lighting L_l based on its incident angle and the current voxel's diffuse color k_d. In contrast to diffuse reflections, specular reflections also depend on the viewing angle, and thus the outgoing light direction $\boldsymbol{\omega}_\mathbf{o}$. Therefore, $\boldsymbol{\omega}_\mathbf{o}$ is also used to modulate the initial light intensity L_l and the voxel's specular color k_s:

$$L_{spec}(\mathbf{x}, \boldsymbol{\omega}_\mathbf{i}, \boldsymbol{\omega}_\mathbf{o}) = L_l \cdot k_s \cdot max\left(|\nabla \tau(f(\mathbf{x}))| \cdot \frac{\boldsymbol{\omega}_\mathbf{i} + \boldsymbol{\omega}_\mathbf{o}}{2}, 0\right)^{\alpha} \quad (8.8)$$

α is used to influence the shape of the highlight seen on surface-like structures. A rather large α results in a small sharp highlight, while a smaller α results in a bigger smoother highlight. To approximate indirect illumination effects, usually an ambient term is added. This ensures, that voxels with gradients pointing away from the light source do not appear pitch black. Since this ambient term does not incorporate any spatial information, it is the easiest to compute as:

$$L_{amb}(\mathbf{x}) = L_l \cdot k_a \quad (8.9)$$

Local Ambient Occlusion is a local approximation of ambient occlusion, which considers the voxels in a neighborhood around each voxel [Hernell *et al.*, 2007]. Ambient occlusion goes back to the obscurance rendering model, which relates the luminance of a scene element to the degree of occlusion in its surroundings [Zhukov *et al.*, 1998]. To incorporate this information into the volume rendering equation, Hernell *et al.* [2007] obtain the neighborhood information of each sample with rays (see Fig. 8.4, left), and replace the standard ambient term $L_{amb}(\mathbf{x})$ by:

$$L_{amb}(\mathbf{x}) = \int_{\Omega} \int_{\delta(\mathbf{x},\omega_i,R_\Omega)}^{\delta(\mathbf{x},\omega_i,a)} g_A(\mathbf{x}') \cdot T(\mathbf{x}', \delta(\mathbf{x}, \omega_i, a)) d\mathbf{x}' d\omega_i \quad (8.10)$$

where $\delta(\mathbf{x}, \omega_i, a)$ offsets the position by a along the direction ω_i, to avoid self occlusion. R_Ω specifies the radius of the local neighborhood for which the occlusion is computed, and $g_a(\mathbf{x})$ denotes the light contribution at each position $\mathbf{x}$ along a ray. Since the occlusion should be computed in an ambient manner, it needs to be integrated over all rays in the neighborhood Ω around the position $\mathbf{x}$.

Different light contribution functions $g_A(\mathbf{x})$ are presented. To achieve sharp shadow borders, the usage of a Dirac delta is proposed, which ensures that light contributes only at the boundary of Ω.

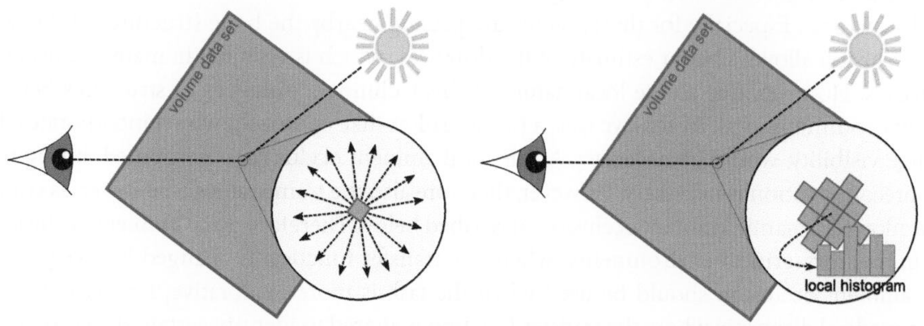

FIGURE 8.4 *When computing local ambient occlusion, rays with a certain length are cast into the volume starting from each voxel (left). Dynamic ambient occlusion instead, neglects spatial information and represents the neighborhood environment through local histograms (right).*

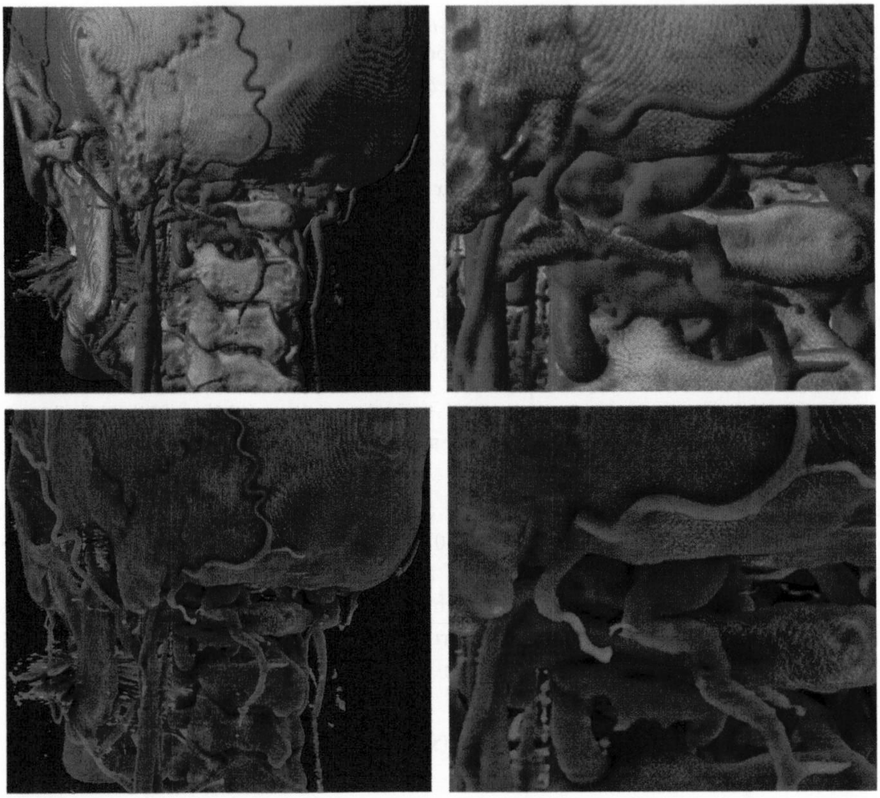

FIGURE 8.5 *Application of local ambient occlusion to a contrast-enhanced CT scan of a human head. In comparison to gradient-based shading (top), local ambient occlusion allows a better comprehension of the vessel structures as well as the distance to the bone structures (bottom) (From: [Hernell et al., 2007]).*

Figure 8.5 shows the application of local ambient occlusion to a contrast-enhanced CT scan of a human head. Compared to gradient-based shading, local ambient occlusion allows a better communication of the vessel structures. Especially for those, which are passing nearby the bone structures of the skull, local ambient occlusion allows a better estimate of the distances, which is essential in many medical visualization scenarios. However, due to the local nature of this technique, distances of structures being further apart are not communicated. To achieve this, a more shadow-like approach, which incorporates the entire light source visibility, would be necessary. As the local ambient occlusion is computed during rendering time, no precomputation is necessary. However, therefore also the frame rate is a bit lower, as compared to the application of dynamic ambient occlusion, described below. Therefore, local ambient occlusion should be used in memory-critical environments, where the transfer function is changed less frequently, while dynamic ambient occlusion should be used when the task is more explorative, for instance when performing a medical diagnosis where the transfer function is altered to identify certain structures of interest.

When using local ambient occlusion, smoother results can be achieved when the ambient light source is considered volumetrically. This results in adding a fractional light emission at each sample point, whereby varying emissive properties for different tissue types can be included. Another example is shown in

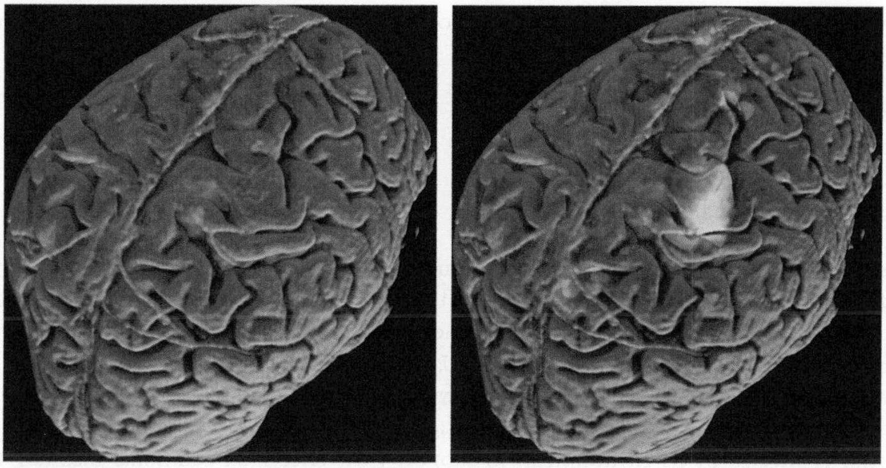

FIGURE 8.6 *An application of local ambient occlusion in a medical context. Usage of the occlusion term allows to convey the 3D structure, while multimodal emissive lighting allows to integrate fMRI activity as additional modality. (Brain activity is shown respectively during a language task and a math task (Courtesy of Khoa Tan Nguyen, Linköping University. See also [Nguyen et al., 2010]).*

Figure 8.6, where brain activity, derived from functional MRI (fMRI), is represented by the additional emissive term, together with the occlusive term representing the underlying 3D structure [Nguyen *et al.*, 2010].

Applicability Local ambient occlusion is not bound to a specific rendering paradigm. When combined with gradient-based lighting, it supports point and directional light sources, while the actual occlusion simulates an exclusive ambient light only. This allows interactive rendering, while the exploited multiresolution data structure needs to be updated whenever the transfer function has been changed. The memory size of this multiresolution data structure depends on the size and homogeneity of the dataset. In a follow-up work, the usage of clipping planes during the local ambient occlusion computation is discussed [Hernell *et al.*, 2009]. As shown in Figure 8.6, local ambient occlusion is beneficial for medical visualization, when combining it with multiple modalities. However, due to its local nature it cannot be used to communicate distances between anatomical structures on a global scale.

Dynamic Ambient Occlusion is a histogram-based approach, which allows integration of ambient occlusion, color bleeding, and basic scattering effects, as well as a simple glow effect that can be used to highlight regions within the volume [Ropinski *et al.*, 2008b]. While the techniques presented by Hernell *et al.* [2009] exploit a ray-based approach to determine the degree of occlusion in the neighborhood of $\mathbf{x}$, dynamic ambient occlusion uses a precomputation of intensity distributions for each voxel's neighborhood. The main idea of this approach is to modulate these intensity distributions with the transfer function during rendering, such that an integration over the modulated result allows to obtain the occlusion. The intensity distributions are stored as normalized local histograms (see Fig. 8.4 (right)), whereby the number of bins can be user-defined. When storing one normalized local histogram for each voxel, this would result in a large amount of data which needs to be stored and accessed during rendering. Therefore, a similarity-based clustering is performed on the histograms, whereby a vector quantization approach is exploited. After clustering, the local histograms representing a cluster are available as a 2D texture table, which is accessed during rendering. Additionally, a scalar volume dataset is generated, which contains a cluster ID for each voxel, which associates the voxel with the corresponding row storing the local histogram in the 2D texture.

During rendering, the precomputed information is used to support four different illumination effects:

- ambient occlusion,
- color bleeding,
- scattering, and
- a simple glow effect.

Therefore, the representative histogram is looked up for the current voxel and then modulated with the transfer function color to produce the final color. To integrate ambient occlusion into an isosurface-based volume renderer, the ambient intensity $L_{amb}(\mathbf{x})$ is derived from the precomputed data. This operation is performed through texture blending on the GPU, and thus allows to update the occlusion information in real-time. To apply this approach to direct volume rendering, the environmental color E_{env} is derived in a similar way as the occlusion factor O_{env}. Color bleeding can be simulated, as the current voxel's color is affected by its environment. To support glow effects, an additional mapping function can be exploited, which is also used to modulate the local histograms stored in the precomputed 2D texture.

Applicability Dynamic ambient occlusion is not bound to a specific rendering paradigm, though in the original paper it has been introduced in the context of volume raycasting [Ropinski *et al.*, 2008b]. Since it facilitates a gradient-based Blinn-Phong illumination model, which is enriched by ambient occlusion and color bleeding, it supports point, distant and ambient light sources. While an ambient light source is always exclusive, the technique can be used with several point and distant light sources, which are used to compute L_{diff} and L_{spec}. Since the precomputed histograms are constrained to local regions, only local shadows are supported, which have a soft appearance. Therefore, distances between anatomical structures of different regions cannot be communicated. For the precomputation stage, Ropinski *et al.* [2008b] report expensive processing times, which are required to compute the local histograms and to perform the clustering. In a more recent approach, Mess and Ropinski [2010] propose a CUDA-based algorithm that reduces the precomputation times by a factor of up to ten. Since the histogram computation takes a lot of processing time, interactive clipping is not supported, as it would affect the intensity distribution in the voxel neighborhoods.

8.2.4 SLICE-BASED TECHNIQUES

The techniques covered in this section are all bound to the slice-based rendering paradigm introduced by Cabral *et al.* [1994]. This volume rendering paradigm exploits a stack consisting of a high number of rectangular polygons, which are used as a proxy geometry to represent a volumetric dataset. Different varieties of this paradigm exist. Today, 3D-texture mapping is most frequently used to store the volume data and map it to image plane-aligned polygons.

Half Angle Slicing was introduced by Kniss *et al.* [2002b]. It is the first of the slice-based approaches, which synchronizes the slicing used for rendering with the illumination computation, and the first integration of volumetric illumination models including indirect lighting and scattering within interactive applications. It orients the slicing direction according to the half angle between the view and the light direction in order to propagate illumination as coming from the light source (see Fig. 8.7, left). The indirect lighting is modeled as:

$$L_i(\mathbf{x}, \boldsymbol{\omega}_i) = L_l \cdot T(\mathbf{x}_l, \mathbf{x}) \tag{8.11}$$

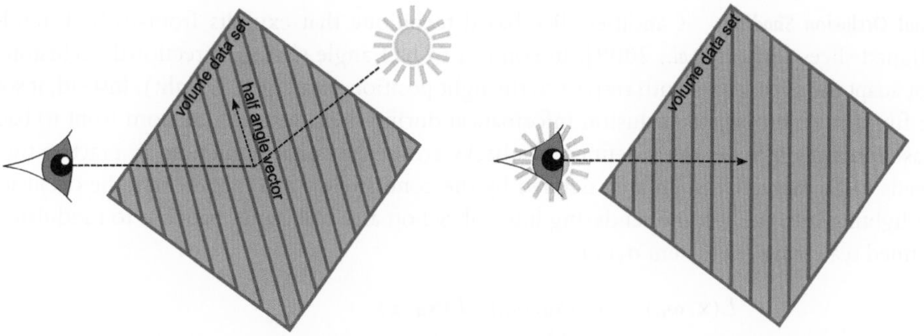

FIGURE 8.7 *Half angle slicing orients the slicing direction according to the half angle between the view and the light direction (left). Directional occlusion shading allows only light sources coinciding with the virtual camera, as occlusion information is propagated through the image plane-aligned slices from front to back (right).*

To include multiple scattering, a directed diffusion process is modeled through an angle-dependent *blur function*. Thus, the indirect lighting is rewritten as:

$$L_i(\mathbf{x}, \omega_\mathrm{i}) = L_l \cdot T(\mathbf{x}_\mathrm{l}, \mathbf{x}) + L_l \cdot T(\mathbf{x}_\mathrm{l}, \mathbf{x}) Blur(\theta) \tag{8.12}$$

where θ is a user-defined cone angle. In addition to this modified indirect lighting, which simulates multiple scattering, half angle slicing also exploits a surface shading factor $S(\mathbf{x})$. $S(\mathbf{x})$ can either be user-defined through a mapping function or derived from the gradient magnitude at $\mathbf{x}$. It is used to weight the degree of emission and surface shading, such that the illumination $C(\mathbf{x}, \omega_\mathrm{i}, \omega_\mathrm{o})$ at $\mathbf{x}$ is computed as:

$$C(\mathbf{x}, \omega_\mathrm{i}, \omega_\mathrm{o}) = L_e(\mathbf{x}) \cdot (1 - S(\mathbf{x})) + s(\mathbf{x}, \omega_\mathrm{i}, \omega_\mathrm{o}) \cdot S(\mathbf{x}) \tag{8.13}$$

$C(\mathbf{x}, \omega_\mathrm{i}, \omega_\mathrm{o})$ is then used in the volume rendering integral as follows:

$$\begin{aligned} L(\mathbf{x}, \omega_\mathrm{o}) = {} & L_0(\mathbf{x_0}, \omega_\mathrm{o}) \cdot T(\mathbf{x_0}, \mathbf{x}) \\ & + \int_{\mathbf{x_0}}^{\mathbf{x}} C(\mathbf{x}', \omega_\mathrm{i}, \omega_\mathrm{o}) \cdot L_i(\mathbf{x}', \omega_\mathrm{i}) \cdot T(\mathbf{x}', \mathbf{x}) d\mathbf{x}' \end{aligned} \tag{8.14}$$

In a follow up work, Kniss *et al.* [2003a] have proposed enhancements of their optical model by using phase functions.

Applicability Due to the described synchronization, half angle slicing is bound to slicing rendering. It supports one directional or point light source located outside the volume, and allows to produce shadows having hard, well-defined borders (see Fig. 8.1 (right)). By integrating a directed diffusion process in the indirect lighting computation, multiple scattering can be simulated, which allows a realistic representation of translucent materials. Half angle slicing performs two rendering passes for each slice, one from the point of view of the observer and one from that of the light source, and thus allows to achieve interactive frame rates. Since rendering and illumination computation are performed in a lockstep manner, besides the three buffers used for compositing, no intermediate storage is required. Clipping planes can be applied interactively, which makes it a good candidate to be used in medical visualization. Also, the ability to generate hard shadows communicating spatial structures clearly (see Fig. 8.1, right) is beneficial for medical visualization.

Directional Occlusion Shading is another slice-based technique that exploits front-to-back rendering of view-aligned slices [Schott *et al.*, 2009]. In contrast to half angle slicing, directional occlusion shading does not adapt the slicing axis with respect to the light position (see Fig. 8.7, right). Instead, it solely uses a phase function to propagate occlusion information during the slice traversal from front to back. Since this phase function $p(\mathbf{x}, \boldsymbol{\omega}_\mathbf{i}, \boldsymbol{\omega})$ is defined as a backward-peaked phase function, in practice the integral only needs to be evaluated in an area defined by the cone angle θ. To incorporate the occlusion-based indirect lighting into the volume rendering integral, Schott and colleagues propose to modulate it with a user-defined scattering coefficient $\sigma_s(\mathbf{x})$:

$$L(\mathbf{x}, \boldsymbol{\omega}_\mathbf{o}) = L_0(\mathbf{x_0}, \boldsymbol{\omega}_\mathbf{o}) \cdot T(\mathbf{x_0}, \mathbf{x}) + \int_{\mathbf{x_0}}^{\mathbf{x}} \sigma_s(\mathbf{x}') \cdot L_i(\mathbf{x}', \boldsymbol{\omega}_\mathbf{i}, \boldsymbol{\omega}) \cdot T(\mathbf{x}', \mathbf{x}) d\mathbf{x}'. \tag{8.15}$$

The implementation of occlusion-based shading is similar to front-to-back slice rendering. However, similar as in half angle slicing [Kniss *et al.*, 2002b], two additional occlusion buffers are used for compositing the lighting contribution.

Phase function. The phase function $p(\mathbf{x}, \boldsymbol{\omega}_\mathbf{i}, \boldsymbol{\omega})$ used within directional occlusion shading is defined as:

$$p(\mathbf{x}, \boldsymbol{\omega}_\mathbf{i}, \boldsymbol{\omega}) = \left\{ \begin{array}{ll} 0 & \text{if } \boldsymbol{\omega}_\mathbf{i} \cdot \boldsymbol{\omega} < \theta(\mathbf{x}) \\ \frac{1}{2\pi \cdot (1 - \cos(\theta))} & \text{otherwise.} \end{array} \right\} \tag{8.16}$$

where $\boldsymbol{\omega}$ is the viewing direction and the $\boldsymbol{\omega}_\mathbf{i}$'s are lying in the cone, which points with the tip along $\boldsymbol{\omega}$. Similar to the approach by Kniss *et al.* [2003a] this is a peaked phase function where the scattering direction is defined through the cone angle θ. This (backward-) peaked behavior is important in order to support synchronized occlusion computation and rendering. Thus, $p(\mathbf{x}, \boldsymbol{\omega}_\mathbf{i}, \boldsymbol{\omega})$ can be used during the computation of the indirect lighting as follows:

$$L_i(\mathbf{x}, \boldsymbol{\omega}) = L_0(\mathbf{x_0}, \boldsymbol{\omega}) \cdot \int_{\Omega} p(\mathbf{x}, \boldsymbol{\omega}_\mathbf{i}, \boldsymbol{\omega}) \cdot T(\mathbf{x}_\mathbf{i}', \mathbf{x}) d\omega_i \tag{8.17}$$

where the background intensity is modulated by $p(\mathbf{x}, \boldsymbol{\omega}_\mathbf{i}, \boldsymbol{\omega})$, which is evaluated over the contributions coming from all directions $\boldsymbol{\omega}_i$ over the sphere.

Applicability Due to the fixed compositing order, directional occlusion shading is bound to the slice-based rendering paradigm and supports only a single light source, which is located at the camera position. The iterative convolution allows to generate soft shadowing effects, and incorporating the phase function accounts for first order scattering effects (see Fig. 8.8 (left) and (middle)). The performance is interactive and comparable to half angle slicing. Since no precomputation is used, no illumination updates need to be performed. Accordingly, also the memory footprint is low, as only the additional occlusion buffers need to be allocated. Finally, clipping planes can be used interactively. A recent extension by Schott *et al.* [2012] allows to integrate geometry and support light interactions between the geometry and the volumetric media.

Multidirectional Occlusion Shading introduced by Šoltészová *et al.* [2010] extends the directional occlusion technique to allow for a more flexible placement of the light source. Therefore, the convolution kernel is

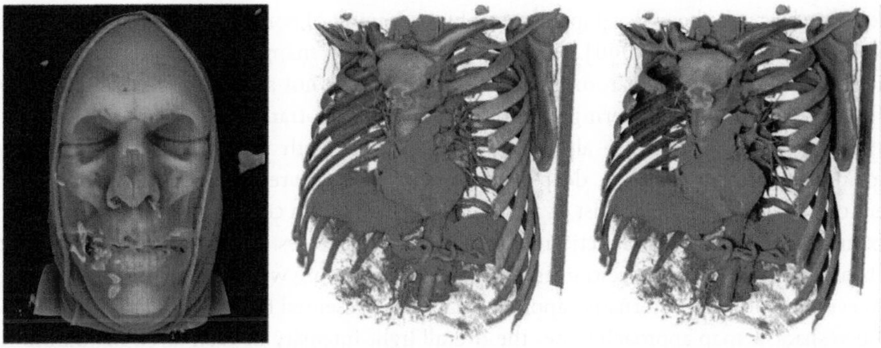

FIGURE 8.8 *Directional occlusion shading [Schott et al., 2009] integrates soft shadowing effects (left). Multidirectional occlusion shading [Šoltészová et al., 2010] additionally supports different lighting positions, (middle and right) ([Schott et al., 2009] and [Šoltészová et al., 2010], Left image courtesy of Mathias Schott, middle and right image courtesy of Veronika Šoltészová).*

exchanged, which is used for the iterative convolution performed during the slicing. Directional occlusion shading yields the assumption that the light source direction is aligned with the viewing direction, and therefore does not allow for changing the light source position. Multidirectional occlusion shading avoids this assumption by introducing more complex convolution kernels. Instead of performing the convolution of the opacity buffer with a symmetrical disk-shaped kernel, Šoltészová *et al.* [2010] propose the usage of an *elliptical kernel* derived from a tilted cone c. They derived the convolution kernel from the light source position and the aperture θ defining c. Due to the directional component introduced by the front-to-back slicing, the tilt angle of the cone is limited to lie in $\left[0, \frac{\pi}{2} - \theta\right]$, which restricts the shape of the filter kernel from generating into hyperbolas or parabolas. The underlying illumination model is the same as with directional occlusion shading, whereas the indirect lighting contribution is modified by exploiting ellipse-shaped filter kernels.

Applicability As standard directional occlusion shading, multidirectional occlusion shading uses front-to-back slice rendering, which tightly binds it to this rendering paradigm. Since the introduced filter kernels allow for modeling light sources at different positions, multiple light sources are supported. However, due to the directional nature, light sources must be positioned in the viewer's hemisphere. Shadowing and scattering capabilities are the same as with directional occlusion shading, i.e., soft shadows and first order scattering is supported. However, since different light positions are supported, shadows can be made more prominent in the final image when the light direction differs from the view direction. This effect is shown in Figure 8.8, where Figure 8.8 (middle) shows a rendering where the light source is located in the camera position, while the light source has been moved to the left in Figure 8.8 (right). Due to the more complex filter kernel, the rendering time of this model is slightly higher than when using directional occlusion shading. The memory consumption is equally low.

8.2.5 LIGHT SPACE-BASED TECHNIQUES

As light space-based techniques we consider all techniques where illumination information is directionally propagated with respect to the current light position. Unlike the slice-based techniques, these techniques are independent of the underlying rendering paradigm. However, since illumination information is propagated along a specific direction, these techniques usually support only a single light source.

Deep Shadow Mapping has been developed to enable shadowing of complex, potentially semi-transparent structures [Lokovic and Veach, 2000]. While standard shadow mapping supports basic shadowing by projecting a shadow map as seen from the light source, it does not support semi-transparent occluders which often occur in volume rendering. In order to address semi-transparent structures, opacity shadow maps serve as a stack, which store alpha values instead of depth values in each shadow map [Kim and Neumann, 2001]. Nevertheless, deep shadow maps are a more compact representation for semi-transparent occluders. They also consist of a stack of textures, but in contrast to the opacity shadow maps an approximation to the shadow function is stored in these textures. Thus, it is possible to approximate shadows by using fewer hardware resources. Deep shadow mapping was first applied to volume rendering by Hadwiger *et al.* [2006]. An alternative approach has been presented by Ropinski *et al.* [2008a]. While the original deep shadow map approach stores the overall light intensity in each layer, in volume rendering it is advantageous to store the absorption given by the accumulated alpha value in analogy to the volume rendering integral. Thus, for each shadow ray, the alpha function is analyzed, i.e., the function describing the absorption, and approximated by using linear functions.

To have a termination criterion for the approximation of the shadowing function, the depth interval covered by each layer can be restricted. However, when the currently analyzed voxels cannot be approximated sufficiently by a linear function, smaller depth intervals are considered. Thus, the approximation works as follows. Initially, the first hit point for each shadow ray is computed, similar as for standard shadow mapping. Next, the distance to the light source of the first hit point and the alpha value for this position are stored within the first layer of the deep shadow map. At the first hit position, the alpha value usually equals zero. Starting from this first hit point, each shadow ray is traversed and checked iteratively whether the samples encountered so far can be approximated by a linear function. When processing a sample where this approximation would not be sufficient, i.e., a user-defined error threshold is exceeded, the distance of the previous sample to the light source as well as the accumulated alpha value at the previous sample are stored in the next layer of the deep shadow map. This is repeated until all layers of the deep shadow map have been created.

Advanced topic: Shadowing function error. When generating the deep shadow map data structure, an error threshold is introduced to determine whether the currently analyzed samples can be approximated by a linear function. In analogy to the original deep shadow mapping technique [Lokovic and Veach, 2000], this error value constrains the variance of the approximation. This can be done by adding (resp. subtracting) the error value at each sample's position. When the alpha function does not lie anymore within the range given by the error threshold, a new segment to be approximated by a linear function is started. A too small error threshold results in a too close approximation, and more layers are needed to represent the shadow function.

The shadowing information represented in the deep shadow map data structure can be used in different ways. A common approach is to use the shadowing information to diminish the diffuse reflectance L_{diff} when using gradient-based shading. Figure 8.9 shows examples for applying deep shadow mapping to a CT scan of a human hand, where different light source positions are used. As can be seen, the shadowing effects allow a good estimate of the spatial arrangements of the vessels. This is even more prominent when changing the light source position, which is not possible when using ambient light sources, as they are used by the ambient occlusion techniques described above. Furthermore, the global nature of the shadows makes communication of the arrangements lying further apart more easy, which also cannot be

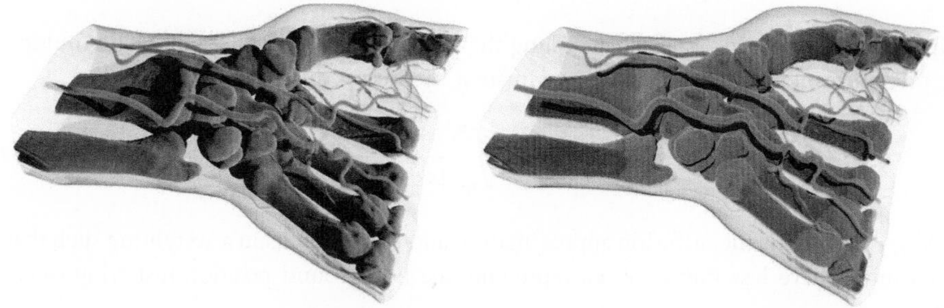

FIGURE 8.9 *CT scan of a human hand with deep shadow mapping in combination with direct volume rendering (Courtesy of Markus Hadwiger, King Abdullah University of Science and Technology (KAUST), as inspired by [Hadwiger et al., 2006]).*

done with the local ambient occlusion approaches. Therefore, when investigating structural arrangements, as for instance in preoperative planning, deep shadow mapping should be used. However, when a better communication of local structures is required, for instance when diagnosing bone fractures, the ambient nature of the local approaches would be beneficial. Instead of modifying the diffuse reflectance, deep shadow mapping can also be used to directly modulate the emissive contribution L_e at $\mathbf{x}$.

Applicability The deep shadow mapping technique is not bound to a specific rendering paradigm. It supports directional and point light sources, which should lie outside the volume, since the shadow propagation is unidirectional. Therefore, only a single light source is supported. Both rendering time and update of the deep shadow data structure, which needs to be done when lighting or transfer function changes, are interactive. The memory footprint of deep shadow mapping is directly proportional to the number of used layers.

Image Plane Sweep Volume Illumination allows the integration of advanced illumination effects into a GPU-based volume raycaster by exploiting the plane sweep paradigm [Sundén et al., 2011]. By using sweeping, it becomes possible to reduce the illumination computation complexity and achieve interactive frame rates while supporting scattering as well as shadowing. The approach is based on a reformulation of the optical model that either considers only single scattering with a single light direction, or multiple scattering resulting from a rather high albedo [Max and Chen, 2010]. To have shadowing effects of higher frequency and more diffuse scattering effects at the same time, these two formulations are combined. This is achieved by adding the local emission at $\mathbf{x}$ with the following scattering term:

$$g(\mathbf{x}, \omega_o) = (1 - a(\mathbf{x})) \cdot p(\mathbf{x}, \omega_l, \omega_o) \cdot I_{ss}(\mathbf{x}, \omega_l) + a(\mathbf{x}) \cdot \int_\Omega p(\mathbf{x}, \omega_i, \omega_o) \cdot I_{ms}(\mathbf{x}, \omega_i) d\omega_i \tag{8.18}$$

Here, ω_l is the principal light direction and ω_i are all directions from which light may enter. $a(\mathbf{x})$ is the albedo, which is the probability that light is rather scattered than absorbed. Thus, $I_{ss}(\mathbf{x}, \omega_l)$ describes the single scattering contribution, and $I_{ms}(\mathbf{x}, \omega_i)$ describes the multiple scattering contribution. Similar to the formulation presented by Max and Chen [2010], the single scattering contribution is written as:

$$I_{ss}(\mathbf{x}, \omega_l) = T(\mathbf{x}_l, \mathbf{x}) \cdot L_0 + \int_{\mathbf{x}_l}^{\mathbf{x}} T(\mathbf{x}', \mathbf{x}) \cdot \tau(\mathbf{x}') \cdot L_e(\mathbf{x}') d\mathbf{x}' \tag{8.19}$$

Multiple scattering is simulated by assuming the presence of a high albedo making multiple scattering predominant and allowing to approximate it by using a diffusion approach:

$$I_{ms}(\mathbf{x}, \omega_i) = \nabla_{diff} \int_{\mathbf{x}_b}^{\mathbf{x}} \frac{1}{|\mathbf{x}' - \mathbf{x}|} \cdot L_e(\mathbf{x}')d\mathbf{x}' \tag{8.20}$$

Here, ∇_{diff} represents the diffusion approximation and $\frac{1}{|\mathbf{x}'-\mathbf{x}|}$ results in a weighting such that more distant samples have less influence. $\mathbf{x}_b$ represents the background position just lying outside the volume.

The computation of the scattering contributions can be simplified when assuming the presence of a forward-peaked phase function such that all relevant samples lie in direction of the light source. Thus, the computation can be performed in a synchronized manner by splitting the integrals and solving them piecewise. Image plane sweep volume illumination facilitates this splitting based on the current state of the sweep line, and performs a synchronized ray marching. During this process, the view rays are processed in an order such that those being closer to the light source in image space are processed earlier. This is ensured by exploiting a modified plane sweeping approach, which iteratively computes the influence of structures when moving further away from the light source. To store the illumination information accumulated along all light rays between the samples of a specific sweep plane, a 2D illumination cache in form of a texture is used.

Applicability Image plane sweep volume illumination has been developed as a ray-based technique and thus can only be used with this rendering paradigm. It supports one point or directional light source, and simulates global shadowing and multiple scattering effects. Since all illumination computations are performed directly within a single rendering pass, it does not require any preprocessing and does not need to store intermediate results within an illumination volume, which results in a low memory footprint. The interactive application of clipping planes is inherently supported. Together with the high rendering quality achieved by adopting the raycasting paradigm and the low memory footprint, this makes image plane sweep volume illumination an excellent candidate for state-of-the-art volume rendering within medical visualization. Figure 8.10 shows the applicability of image plane sweep volume illumination to MRI data being subject to an inherently low signal-to-noise ratio. Even for these modalities, the structures contained in the medical volume dataset, are communicated clearly.

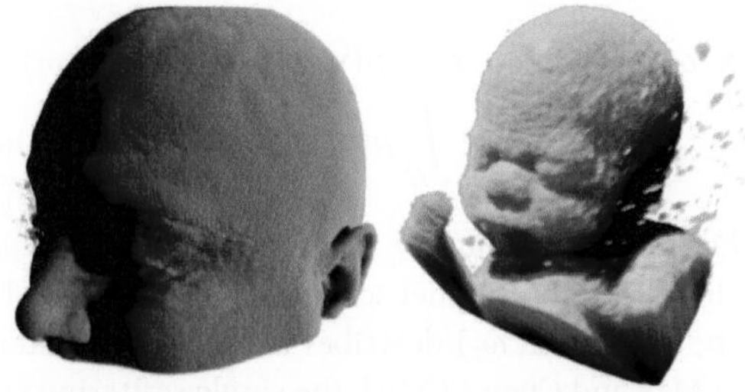

FIGURE 8.10 *Application of image plane sweep volume illumination to MRI (left) and 3D ultrasound data (right). Also with these modalities, which suffer from a low signal-to-noise ratio, image plane sweep volume illumination allows to communicate structures clearly.*

Shadow Splatting has been first proposed by Nulkar and Mueller [2001]. As the name implies, it is bound to the splatting paradigm, which is exploited to attenuate the lighting information, as it travels through the volume. Therefore, a shadow volume is introduced, which is updated in a first splatting pass, during which light information is attenuated as it travels through the volume. In the second splatting pass, which is used for rendering, the shadow volume is fetched to acquire the incident illumination. The indirect light computation in the first pass can be described as:

$$L_i(\mathbf{x}, \boldsymbol{\omega}_\mathrm{i}) = L_l \cdot T(\mathbf{x}_\mathrm{l}, \mathbf{x}) \tag{8.21}$$

Phong shading is employed, whereas the diffuse and the specular lighting intensity is replaced by the indirect light $L_i(\mathbf{x}, \boldsymbol{\omega}_\mathrm{i})$.

Zhang and Crawfis [2003] present an algorithm, which does not require to store a shadow volume. Their algorithm exploits two additional image buffers for handling illumination information. These buffers are used to attenuate the light during rendering, and to add its contribution to the final image. Whenever a contribution is added to the final image buffer seen from the camera, this contribution is also added to the shadow buffer as seen from the light source.

Shadow splatting can be used for multiple point light and distant light sources as well as textured area lights. While the initial algorithm [Zhang and Crawfis, 2002] only supports hard shadows, a more recent extension integrates soft shadows [Zhang and Crawfis, 2003]. When computing shadows, the rendering time is approximately doubled with respect to regular splatting. The algorithm by Zhang and Crawfis [2003] updates the 2D image buffers during rendering and thus requires no considerable update times, while the algorithm of [Nulkar and Mueller, 2001] needs to update the shadow volume, which requires extra memory and update times. With an extension, the integration of geometry also becomes possible [Zhang *et al.*, 2005].

8.2.6 LATTICE-BASED TECHNIQUES

As lattice-based techniques, we classify all approaches that compute the illumination directly based on the underlying grid. While many of the previous approaches are computing the illumination per sample during rendering, the lattice-based techniques perform the computations per voxel, usually by exploiting the nature of the lattice. In this section, we also focus on techniques, which allow interactive data exploration, though it should be mentioned that other techniques working on non-regular grids exist [Qiu *et al.*, 2007].

Shadow Volume Propagation is a lattice-based approach where illumination information is propagated in a preprocessing through the regular grid defining the volumetric dataset. The first algorithm realizing this principle has been proposed by Behrens and Ratering [1998] in the context of slice-based volume rendering. Their technique simulates shadows caused by attenuation of one distant light source. These shadows, which are stored within a shadow volume, are computed by attenuating illumination slice by slice through the volume. More recently, the lattice-based propagation concept has been exploited by Ropinski *et al.* [2010a] to allow high frequency shadows and low frequency scattering simultaneously. Their raycasting-based technique approximates the light propagation direction in order to allow efficient rendering. It facilitates a four channel illumination volume to store luminance and scattering information obtained from the volumetric dataset with respect to the currently set transfer function. Therefore, similar to Kniss *et al.* [2003a], indirect lighting is incorporated by blurring the incoming light within a given cone centered about the incoming light direction. However, shadow volume propagation uses blurring only for the chromaticity and not for the intensity of the light (luminance). Although this procedure is not physically correct, it generates harder shadow borders, which improve the perception of spatial structures [Wanger, 1992]. Thus, the underlying illumination model can be specified as follows:

$$L(\mathbf{x}, \omega_o) = L_0(\mathbf{x_0}, \omega_o) \cdot T(\mathbf{x_0}, \mathbf{x}) + \int_{\mathbf{x_0}}^{\mathbf{x}} (L_e(\mathbf{x}) + s(\mathbf{x}, \omega_i, \omega_o)) \cdot T(\mathbf{x}', \mathbf{x}) d\mathbf{x}' \tag{8.22}$$

where $s(\mathbf{x}, \omega_i, \omega_o)$ is calculated as the transport color $t(\mathbf{x})$, as assigned through the transfer function, multiplied by the chromaticity $c(\mathbf{x}, \omega_o)$ of the in-scattered light and modulated by the attenuated luminance $l_i(\mathbf{x}, \omega_i)$:

$$s(\mathbf{x}, \omega_i, \omega_o) = t(\mathbf{x}) \cdot c(\mathbf{x}, \omega_o) \cdot l_i(\mathbf{x}, \omega_i) \tag{8.23}$$

Color modulation. The transport color $t(\mathbf{x})$ as well as the chromaticity $c(\mathbf{x}, \omega_o)$ are wavelength-dependent, while the scalar $l_i(\mathbf{x}, \omega_i)$ describes the incident (achromatic) luminance. Multiplying all together results in the incident radiance. Chromaticity $c(\mathbf{x}, \omega_o)$ is computed from the in-scattered light

$$c(\mathbf{x}, \omega_o) = \int_{\Omega} \tau(\mathbf{x}) \cdot p(\mathbf{x}, \omega_i', \omega_o) \cdot c(\mathbf{x}, \omega_i') d\omega_i' \tag{8.24}$$

where Ω is the unit sphere centered around $\mathbf{x}$. To allow the unidirectional illumination propagation, $p(\mathbf{x}, \omega_i', \omega_o)$ has been chosen to be a strongly forward-peaked phase function:

$$p(\mathbf{x}, \omega_i', \omega_o) = \begin{cases} (\omega_i' \cdot \omega_o)^{\beta} & \text{if } \omega_i' \cdot \omega_o < \theta(\mathbf{x}) \\ 0 & \text{otherwise} \end{cases} \tag{8.25}$$

The cone angle θ is used to control the amount of scattering and depends on the intensity at position $\mathbf{x}$, and the phase function is a Phong lobe whose extent is controlled by the exponent β, restricted to the cone angle θ.

During rendering, the illumination volume is accessed to look up the luminance value and scattering color of the current voxel. The chromaticity $c(\mathbf{x}, \omega_o)$ and the luminance $l_i(\mathbf{x}, \omega_i)$ are fetched from the illumination volume and used within $s(\mathbf{x}, \omega_i, \omega_o)$. In cases where a high gradient magnitude is present, specular reflections and thus surface-based illumination is also integrated into $s(\mathbf{x}, \omega_i, \omega_o)$.

Applicability Shadow volume propagation can be combined with various rendering paradigms and does not require a noticeable amount of preprocessing, since the light propagation is carried out on the GPU. It supports point and directional light sources, whereby a more recent extension also supports area light sources [Ropinski *et al.*, 2010b]. While the position of the light source is unconstrained, the number of light sources is limited to one, since only one illumination propagation direction is supported. By simulating the diffusion process, shadow volume propagation supports multiple scattering. Rendering times are quite low, since only one additional 3D texture fetch is required to obtain the illumination values. However, when the transfer function is changed, the illumination information needs to be updated and thus the propagation step needs to be recomputed. Nevertheless, this still supports interactive frame rates. Since the illumination volume is stored and processed on the GPU, a sufficient amount of graphics memory is required.

Piecewise Integration computes global light transport by dividing rays into k segments and evaluating the incoming radiance [Hernell *et al.*, 2008] using:

$$L_i(\mathbf{x}, \omega_\mathbf{i}) = L_0 \cdot \prod_{n=0}^{k} T(\mathbf{x}_n, \mathbf{x}_{n+1}) \tag{8.26}$$

Short rays are first cast toward the light source for each voxel and the piecewise segments are stored in an intermediate 3D texture using a multiresolution data structure [Ljung *et al.*, 2006]. Then, again for each voxel, global rays are sent toward the light source sampling from the piecewise segment 3D texture. In addition to direct illumination, first order in-scattering is approximated by treating scattering in the vicinity as emission. To preserve interactivity, the final radiance is progressively refined by sending one ray at a time and blending the result into a final 3D texture.

Applicability The piecewise integration technique can be combined with other rendering paradigms, even though it has been developed for volume raycasting. It also supports a single directional or point light source, which can be dynamically moved, and it includes an approximation of first order in-scattering. Rendering times are low, since only a single extra lookup is required to compute the incoming radiance at the sample position. As soon at the light source or transfer function changes, the radiance must be recomputed, which can be performed interactively and progressively. Three additional 3D textures are required for the computations. However, a multiresolution structure and lower resolution grid are used to alleviate some of the additional memory requirements.

Summed Area Table techniques were first exploited by Díaz *et al.* [2008] for computation of various illumination effects in interactive direct volume rendering. The 2D summed area table (SAT) is a data structure where each cell (x, y) stores the sum of every cell located between the initial position $(0, 0)$ and (x, y) such that the 2D SAT for each pixel p can be computed as:

$$SAT_{image}(x, y) = \sum_{i=0, j=0}^{x,y} p_{i,j} \tag{8.27}$$

A 2D SAT can be computed incrementally during a single pass and the computation cost increase's linearly with the number of cells. Once a 2D SAT has been constructed, an efficient evaluation of a region can be performed with only four texture accesses to the corners of the regions to be evaluated. Díaz *et al.* [2008] proposed *Vicinity Occlusion Mapping* (VOM), which effectively utilizes two SATs computed from the depth map, one which stores the accumulated depth for each pixel and one which stores the number of contributed values of the neighborhood of each pixel. The vicinity occlusion map is then used to incorporate view-dependent ambient occlusion and halo effects in the volume rendered image. The condition for which a pixel should be occluded is determined by evaluating the average depth around that pixel. If this depth is larger than the depth of the pixel, the neighboring structures are further away, which means that this structure is not occluded. If the structure in the current pixel is occluded, the amount of occlusion, i.e., how much the pixel should be darkened, is determined by the amount of differences of depths around the corresponding pixel. A halo effect can be achieved by also considering the average depth from the neighborhood. If the structure in the pixel lies outside the object, a halo color is rendered which decays with respect to the distance to the object.

Applicability Density Summed Area Table [Díaz *et al.*, 2010] utilizes a 3D SAT for ambient occlusion, calculated from the density values stored in the volume. This procedure is view-independent and supports incorporation of semi-transparent structures, while it is more accurate than the 2D image space approach [Díaz *et al.*, 2008]. However, while only eight texture accesses are needed to estimate a region in a 3D SAT, the preprocessing is more computationally expensive and it results in a larger memory footprint. However, the 3D SAT does not need to be recomputed if the view changes. Desgranges and Engel also describe a SAT-based inexpensive approximation of ambient light [Desgranges and Engel, 2007]. They combine ambient occlusion volumes from different filtered volumes into a composite occlusion volume.

Extinction-based Shading and Illumination is a recent technique by Schlegel *et al.* [2011], where a 3D SAT is used to model ambient occlusion, color bleeding, directional soft shadows, and scattering effects by using the summation of the exponential extinction coefficient. As the summation of the exponential extinction coefficient in their model is order-independent, the use of a 3D SAT and efficient aggregate summation decreases the computational cost significantly. The directional soft shadows, and scattering effects are incorporated by estimating a cone defined by the light source. The approximation of that cone is performed with a series of cuboids. Texture accesses in the SAT structure can only be performed axis-aligned, thus the cuboids are placed along the two axis-aligned planes with the largest projection size of the cone toward the light. Schlegel and colleagues do this by defining the primary cone axis to be the axis with the smallest angle to the vector toward the light source and then defining two secondary axes (of four possibilities) which are afterward used to form two axis-aligned planes.

Applicability Extinction-based shading and illumination is not limited to any specific rendering paradigm. The technique can handle point, directional and area light sources. For each additional light source, the extinction must be estimated, which means that rendering time increases with the number of light sources. In terms of memory consumption, an extra 3D texture is required for the SAT, which can be of lower resolution than the volume data while still producing convincing results.

8.2.7 BASIS FUNCTION-BASED TECHNIQUES

Basis function-based techniques cover approaches where the light source radiance L_l and transparency (visibility) $T(\mathbf{x}_l, \mathbf{x})$ from the position $\mathbf{x}$ toward the light source position $\mathbf{x}_l$ are represented using a *basis function* to compute the incident radiance in Equation 8.3. Since radiance and visibility are computed independently, light sources may be dynamically changed without an expensive visibility update. Furthermore, the light source composition may be complex, as they are projected to another basis which is independent of the number of light sources. This can be especially beneficial in medical visualization, as complex lighting setups are known to better communicate spatial arrangements, which can be given by anatomical structures. Up to now, the only basis functions used in volume rendering are *spherical harmonics*. However, to incorporate future techniques into our classification, we have decided to keep this group more general. There are two key properties of spherical harmonics which are worth special mentioning. The first is that efficient integral evaluation can be performed, which supports real-time computation of the incoming radiance over the sphere. The second property is that it can be rotated on the fly, and thus supports dynamic light sources. Since it is beyond the scope of this chapter to provide a detailed introduction to spherical harmonics-based lighting, we focus on the volume rendering-specific properties, and refer to Sloan *et al.* [2002] for further details.

Spherical Harmonics While spherical harmonics were first used in volume rendering by Beason *et al.* [2006] to enhance isosurface shading, in this section, we cover algorithms applying spherical harmonics in direct volume rendering. Later, Ritschel [2007] has applied spherical basis functions to simulate low-frequency shadowing effects. To enable interactive rendering, a GPU-based approach is exploited for the computation of the required spherical harmonic coefficients. Therefore, a multiresolution data structure similar to a volumetric mipmap is computed and stored on the GPU. Whenever the spherical harmonic coefficients need to be recomputed, this data structure is accessed and the ray traversal is performed with increasing step size. The increasing step size is realized by sampling the multiresolution data structure in different levels, whereby the level of detail decreases as the sampling proceeds further away from the voxel for which the coefficients need to be computed.

More recently, spherical harmonics were used to support advanced material properties [Lindemann and Ropinski, 2010]. The authors exploit the approach proposed by Ritschel [2007] to compute spherical harmonic coefficients. During raycasting, the spherical integral over the product of an area light source and voxel occlusion is efficiently computed using the precomputed occlusion information. Furthermore, realistic light material interaction effects are integrated while still achieving interactive volume frame rates. By using a modified spherical harmonic projection approach, tailored specifically to volume rendering, it becomes possible to realize non-cone-shaped phase functions. Thus, more realistic material representations become possible.

One problem with using a basis function, such as spherical harmonics, is the increased storage requirement. Higher frequencies can be represented when using more coefficients, thus obtaining better results. However, each coefficient needs to be stored to be used during rendering. Kronander *et al.* [2012] address this storage requirement issue and decrease the time to update the visibility. In their method, both volume data and spherical harmonic coefficients exploit the multiresolution technique of Ljung *et al.* [2006]. The sparse representation of volume data and visibility allows substantial reductions with respect to memory requirements. To also decrease the visibility update time, a two-pass approach is used. First, local visibility is computed over a small neighborhood by sending rays uniformly distributed on the sphere. Then, piecewise integration of the local visibility is performed in order to compute global visibility [Hernell *et al.*, 2008]. Since both local and global visibility have been computed, the user can switch between them during rendering and thus reveal structures hidden by global features while still keeping spatial comprehension.

Applicability The spherical harmonics-based methods are not bound to any specific rendering paradigm, although only volume raycasting has been used by the techniques presented here. An arbitrary number of dynamic directional light sources are supported, i.e., environment maps. Area and point light sources are also supported, each adding an overhead, since the direction toward the sample along the ray changes and the spherical harmonics representation of the light source must be rotated. Very naturally looking images can be generated with complex light setups and material representation (see Fig. 8.11), in contrast to the hard shadows of techniques like half angle slicing. However, storage and computation time limits the accuracy of the spherical harmonics representation, thus restricting the illumination to low frequency effects. In general, light sources are constrained to be outside of the volume. However, when using local visibility, e.g., by Kronander *et al.* [2012], they may be positioned arbitrarily. The rendering time is interactive, only requiring some (typically one to four) extra texture lookups and scalar products. The light source representation must be recomputed or rotated when the illumination changes, but this can be performed in real-time. However, the visibility must be recomputed when the transfer function or clip plane changes, which is expensive but can be performed interactively [Kronander *et al.*, 2012]. We refer to Kronander *et al.* [2012] for an in-depth analysis of how to trade-off memory size and image quality.

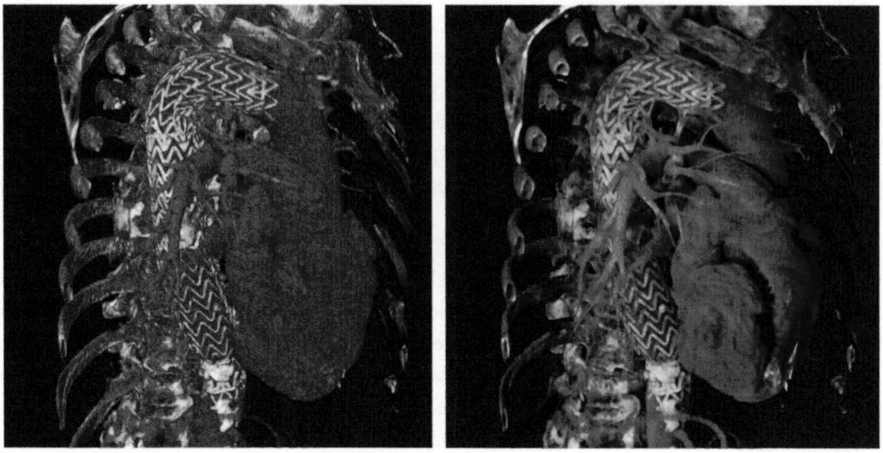

FIGURE 8.11 *A CT scan of a human torso rendered with diffuse gradient-based shading (left) and spherical harmonic lighting (right). When using spherical harmonic lighting, the cylindrical structure of the stent embracing the aorta is more prominent (From: [Kronander et al., 2012]).*

8.2.8 RAYTRACING-BASED TECHNIQUES

The work discussed above focuses on increasing the lighting realism in interactive volume rendering applications. This is often achieved by making assumptions regarding the lighting setup or the illumination propagation, e.g., assuming that only directional scattering occurs. As raytracing has been widely used in polygonal rendering to generate realistic images, a few authors have investigated raytracing for volume rendering. Gradients, as used for the gradient-based shading approaches, can also be exploited to realize a volumetric raytracer supporting more physically correct illumination. One such approach, considering only first order rays to be traversed, has been proposed by Stegmaier *et al.* [2005]. They are able to simulate mirror-like reflections and refraction by casting a ray and computing its deflection. To simulate mirror-like reflections, they perform an environment texture lookup. More sophisticated refraction approaches have been presented by [Li and Mueller, 2005, Rodgman and Chen, 2006].

To produce images of high realism, stochastic Monte Carlo raytracing methods have also been used for interactive volume rendering. The benefit of these approaches is that they are directly coupled with physically based light transport. The first Monte Carlo-based approach has been presented by Rezk-Salama [2007]. It supports shadowing and scattering, whereby interactivity is achieved by constraining the expensive scattering computations to selected surfaces only. With respect to the gradient magnitude it is decided if a boundary surface, potentially initiating a scattering event, is present. The approach supports interactive frame rates and a high degree of lighting realism.

More recently, Kroes *et al.* [2011] have presented an interactive Monte Carlo raytracer, which does not limit the scattering to selected boundary surfaces. Their approach simulates several real-world factors influencing volumetric illumination, such as multiple arbitrarily shaped and textured area light sources, a real-world camera with lens and aperture, as well as complex material properties. This combination allows to generate images showing a high degree of realism (see Fig. 8.12). To adequately represent both volumetric and surface-like materials, their approach blends between BRDF-based and a phase function-based material representation.

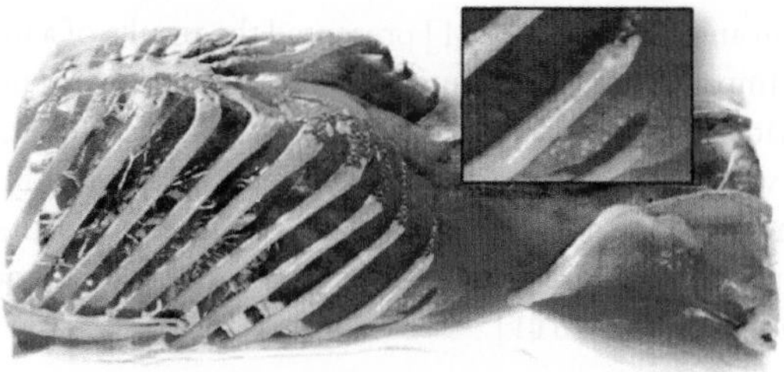

FIGURE 8.12 *Monte Carlo raytracing allows to incorporate gradient-based material properties and the modeling of camera apertures to generate highly realistic images (From: [Kroes et al., 2011], courtesy of Thomas Kroes).*

Advanced topic: Isosurface-based techniques. Besides the algorithms discussed above, which can be combined with direct volume rendering and are therefore the focus of this chapter, several approaches allow advanced illumination when visualizing isosurfaces. While when dealing with direct volume rendering a transfer function may extract several structures having different intensities and thus optical properties, when dealing with the simplest form of isosurface rendering, only a single isosurface with homogeneous optical properties is visible. This reduces the combinations of materials, which interact with each other, and produces complex lighting effects drastically. Several approaches have been proposed, which exploit this reduced complexity and thus enable advanced illumination with higher rendering speeds and sometimes lower memory footprints. Vicinity Shading, which simulates illumination of isosurfaces by taking into account neighboring voxels, was the first approach addressing advanced illumination for isosurfaces extracted from volume data [Stewart, 2003]. In a precomputation the vicinity of each voxel is analyzed and the resulting value, which represents the occlusion of the voxel, is stored in a shading texture which can be accessed during rendering. Wyman *et al.* [2006] and Beason *et al.* [2006] focus on a spherical harmonics-based precomputation, supporting the display of isosurfaces under static illumination conditions. Penner and Mitchell [2008] exploit an ambient occlusion approach to render smoothly shaded isosurfaces.

8.2.9 PERCEPTUAL IMPACT

Besides the technical insights and the achievable illumination effects, the perceptual impact of the current techniques is also of relevance. Although the perceptual qualities of advanced illumination techniques are frequently pointed out, remarkably little research has been done in order to investigate them in a systematic fashion. One study, showing the perceptual benefits of advanced volumetric illumination models, was conducted to analyze the impact of the shadow volume propagation technique [Ropinski *et al.*, 2010a]. The users, participating in this study, had to perform several tasks depending on the depth perception of static images, where one set was generated using gradient-based shading and the other one using shadow volume propagation. The results of the study indicate that depth perception is more accurate and performed faster when using shadow volume propagation.

Šoltészová *et al.* [2011] evaluated the perceptual impact of chromatic soft shadows. Inspired by illustrators, they replace the luminance decrease usually present in shadowed areas by a chromaticity blending. They could show the perceptual benefit of these chromatic shadows with respect to depth and surface perception. However, their results also indicate that brighter shadows might have a negative impact on the perceptual qualities of an image.

More recently, Lindemann and Ropinski [2011] presented the results of a user study, in which they have investigated the perceptual impact of seven volumetric illumination techniques. Within their study, depth and volume-related tasks had to be performed. They could show that advanced volumetric illumination models make a difference when it is necessary to assess depth or size in images. However, they could not find a relation between the time used to perform a certain task and the used illumination model. The results of this study indicate that the directional occlusion shading model has the best perceptual capabilities [Lindemann and Ropinski, 2011].

8.2.10 TECHNICAL CONSIDERATIONS

When integrating advanced illumination algorithms into a medical visualization system, it is important to know about the capabilities of the techniques to be realized, as for instance light sources and supported illumination effects have a strong impact on this choice. Therefore, we provide a comparison taking into account the most important properties of the handled algorithms. Table 8.1 relates the algorithms to each other, by considering light source properties, illumination effects, performance behavior, memory consumption, and the effect when applying to a low signal-to-noise ratio (SNR). The possible supported light types are, directional lights (D), point lights (P, area lights (A), textured lights (T), and omni-directional ambient light sources (*AMB*). The constraints, regarding the number of light sources, are also compared, where "-" means that this measure is not applicable and "N" means, that there are no conceptual limits with respect to the number of light sources. As the incorporation of scattering directly influences the visual outcome, whereby for instance skin or certain organs can be represented at a higher degree of realism when using scattering, we compare the support of scattering effects as there can be no (✖) scattering, single scattering (S) or multiple scattering (M). Memory usage and rendering times are classified as lying between very low (○○○) and very high (●●●). Especially when considering the explorative nature of image-based medical diagnosis, where the radiologist must be able to adapt the windowing to investigate the features contained in the data, interactive editing of the transfer function is essential. Therefore, we also denote when a transfer function triggers a frame update (▲▲). As in some application scenarios light source changes may be of interest, we have also indicated updates required on light source changes (☀). For a radiology workstation with transfer function presets, an algorithm without transfer function update triggers or a fast update should be chosen. However, when using transfer function presets only, the transfer function update triggers are less important. Finally, the medical system integrator should be aware of the capabilities of the used imaging modalities. As the signal-to-noise ratio varies drastically in the medical domain, where CT for instance has a high SNR and MRI has a lower SNR, it is of importance how the SNR effects the outcome of the chosen illumination algorithm. Therefore, we distinguish between insensitivity with respect to SNR (✔) and sensitivity with respect to SNR (✔).

8.3 ARTIFICIAL DEPTH ENHANCEMENTS

In many areas of medical imaging, 2D visualizations of the—in most cases inherently 3D—datasets are sufficient to communicate the desired information. 3D is exploited only in application areas where the depth information is essential to provide physicians with insights. While 3D imaging does not pose a problem nowadays, the communication of complex 3D and 4D structures through medical visualization is impaired by mainly three reasons: First, the structures and shapes of organs and the accompanying abnormalities may vary. Thus, the viewer cannot resort to experiences and expectations in the perception process, which happens when perceiving things in everyday life where we have an unconscious understanding of the depth structure. Therefore, it is especially hard for novices to spatially comprehend imaging modalities, such as 3D ultrasound.

Method	Light Source			Scattering	Refresh Time		Memory	SNR
	Type(s)	Location Constraint	#		Render	Update		
Gradient-based [Levoy, 1988]	D, P	None	N	✖	● ○ ○	○ ○ ○	○ ○ ○	✖
Local Ambient Occlusion [Hernell *et al.*, 2009]	D, P, AMB	–	–	✖	● ○ ○	● ● ●	● ● ○	✔
Dynamic Ambient Occlusion [Ropinski *et al.*, 2008b]	D, P, AMB	–	–	S	● ○ ○	● ○ ○	● ● ●	✔
Half Angle Slicing [Kniss *et al.*, 2003a]	D, P	Outside	1	S,M	● ● ○	○ ○ ○	● ○ ○	✔
Directional Occlusion [Schott *et al.*, 2009]	P	Head	1	S	● ● ○	○ ○ ○	● ○ ○	✔
Multidirectional Occlusion [Šoltészovà *et al.*, 2010]	P	View Hemisphere	N	S,M	● ● ●	○ ○ ○	● ○ ○	✔
Deep Shadow Mapping [Hadwiger *et al.*, 2006]	D, P	Outside	1	S,M	● ○ ○	● ● ○	● ● ○	✖
Image Plane Sweep [Sundén *et al.*, 2011]	D, P	None	1	S,M	● ● ○	○ ○ ○	● ○ ○	✔
Shadow Splatting [Zhang *et al.*, 2005]	D, P, A	Outside	1	S,M	● ○ ○		● ○ ○	✔
Piecewise Integration [Hernell *et al.*, 2008]	D, P	None	1	S	● ○ ○	● ● ○	● ● ●	✔
Shadow Volume Propagation [Ropinski *et al.*, 2010b]	D, P, A	None	1	S,M	● ○ ○	● ● ○	● ● ●	✔
Extinction-based Shading [Schlegel *et al.*, 2011]	D, P, A, AMB	None	N	S	● ○ ○	● ● ○	● ● ○	✔
Spherical Harmonics [Kronander *et al.*, 2012]	D, P, A, T, AMB	Outside	N	S,M	● ○ ○	● ● ●	● ● ●	✔
Monte Carlo Raytracing [Kroes *et al.*, 2011]	D, P, A, T, AMB	None	N	S,M	● ● ●	● ● ●	● ○ ○	✔

TABLE 8.1 Comparison between the different illumination methods.

Unavailability of Binocular Disparity The second reason, making depth perception of medical 3D data difficult, is the unavailability of binocular disparity. In nature, we perceive the depth information of close objects by exploiting the viewing parallax given by the distance between our eyes. Although in visualization this can be simulated by using stereoscopic techniques, either instrumenting the user with special glasses or using autostereoscopic displays is necessary. Both techniques are currently not sufficient for everyday use as well as for multiple observers. Thus, binocular disparity is in most cases not present when analyzing 3D medical data. In medical diagnosis, physicians often view 3D datasets under motion by rotating them interactively in order to improve depth perception. Because of the rigidity of the structures, the rotation of, for instance, a vessel complex, may give clues about its geometry. The thus exploited depth cues are motion parallax, and the dynamic change of occlusion arising when performing a rotation. It is obvious that motion cannot be used to enhance spatial comprehension of static images as they may appear in reports or print publications. Furthermore, when a group of people watches a dataset, it is not easy to talk about certain medical aspects while the object of interest is in motion. Due to these problems, besides the illumination approaches discussed before, several other depth enhancement techniques have been developed in the past. Most of these techniques are inspired by drawing styles used in medical illustrations, such as for instance line drawings used to emphasize/deemphasizes structures. We refer to these techniques as *artificial depth enhancement techniques*, as they try not to accomplish spatial comprehension by applying a physical real-world model, as it is for instance done when performing volumetric illumination, but as they try to impose depth through other approaches. A detailed review on the influence of depth cues on depth perception can be found in Wanger [1992]. The unphysical nature of these effects can also be seen as a benefit, since it gives the user more control over changing the rendering parameters.

For estimating the interplay of depth cues, different models have been proposed. They all take into account the combination of different depth cues and postulate a way in which these depth cues contribute to the overall depth perception. The models incorporate for instance the weighted linear sum [Bruno and Cutting, 1988], a geometric sum [Dosher *et al.*, 1986], or the reliability of depth cues in the context of other cues and additional information [Young *et al.*, 1993].

8.3.1 COLOR-CODING

Colors are often used to encode depth information in an image. The most widely used technique, which is also applied in medical visualization, is a color-coding which associates dark colors with areas further behind. Despite its simplicity, this technique improves the communication of spatial information drastically. When using dark-bright color combinations for this effect, it is also referred to as the *dark-means-deep principle* [Nicolaides, 1941]. Since this principle is inspired by environmental fog, which results in a darker appearance of structures located further away from the viewer, it is sometimes also referred to as *aerial perspective*.

The *chromadepth technique* is another color-based depth enhancement approach [Steenblik, 1987]. It communicates depth based on the fact that the lens of the eye refracts colored light with different wavelengths at different angles. Although this effect can be supported by diffraction grating glasses, watching appropriate images without instrumentation can also improve the depth perception. The color-coding itself is applied in the same way as the dark-means-deep metaphor, whereby the distance to the viewer is responsible for the applied coloring. Nevertheless, instead of varying the luminance of the original color value, chromadepth varies the hue instead. The advantage of this technology is that one can perceive depth in chromadepth pictures also without wearing eyeglasses. However, the selection of colors is limited, since the colors code the depth information of the picture. When the color of an object is changed, its observed distance would also be changed.

Depth Perception in Angiography Ropinski *et al.* [2006] have developed 3D medical visualization techniques to support depth perception in angiography datasets through the application of chromadepth. To reduce the visual complexity introduced through the rainbow color mapping, which is frequently used when applying chromadepth, they apply a simplified color map. They have chosen to use a gradient running from red to blue, instead of the rainbow color map. This has several benefits. First, the high wavelength difference of red light (780 nm) and blue light (450 nm) results in a different focus point within the human eye. The shorter wavelength of the blue light results in a higher refraction, and therefore the point of focus lies closer to the lens, which results in blue objects being perceived to be farther away. This is also the effect exploited in chromadepth images, whereas only two colors are used, namely those with the highest contrast in terms of depth perception. Another aspect important for choosing blue and red for color-coding depth information is that the human eye has a higher color resolution for the colors red and green than for blue. Furthermore, the time to respond to a signal varies according to the color used; dark colors lead to a relative high response time, whereas light colors ensure quick response times. Accordingly, by mapping front structures to red and back structures to blue, similar effects can be achieved as when applying the standard chromadepth approach. This is also indicated by a user study conducted by Ropinski *et al.* [2006]. Their results indicate that the pseudochromadepth color modification could make the comprehension of medical vessel datasets more efficient (see Fig. 8.13).

GPU-based Depth Enhancement Svakhine *et al.* [2009] present a collection of fast GPU-based algorithms to enhance depth perception in volumetric medical visualization. Besides the large- and small-scale feature emphasis discussed further below, they also employ color-based techniques which improve depth perception by mimicking the effects of aerial perspective. In order to give the user more control on how to emphasize features based on their depth value, they introduce a *depth filtering function*. By using this function, the depth enhancement can be constrained to a subset of the overall depth extend only. Thus, it can be avoided to apply depth enhancements also to features close to the user, which is—according to the authors—not desirable in many cases. Nevertheless, to be able to exploit this approach, meaningful depth values need to be available, which usually are not generated when using a slice-based volume renderer, as done by the authors. Therefore, they introduce a *feature transfer function*, which they set to 1 for the samples belonging to the feature of interest, and 0 otherwise. Based on the thus modified depth values, the authors present how to use depth color blending and depth cueing.

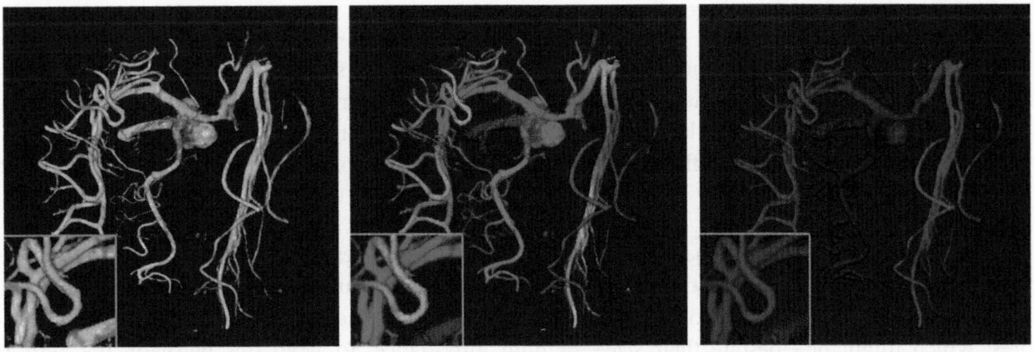

FIGURE 8.13 Depth cues through color coding as applied to an angiography dataset. The depth is not encoded in the color (left), chromadepth (middle) pseudo chromadepth reduced to red and blue (right) (From: [Ropinski et al., 2006]).

Advanced topic: Depth color blending. EBERT and RHEINGANS have introduced depth color blending [Ebert and Rheingans, 2000], which introduces a depth color $Color_{depth}$, which represents the color blend at the maximum depth, i.e., the largest value in the depth buffer. Thus, the new sample color can be computed as $Color_{new} = (1.0 - \delta) \cdot Color_{old} + \delta \cdot Color_{depth}$, where δ is the depth value of the current sample and $Color_{old}$ is its original color. The presented depth cueing technique exploits a similar approach, whereas colors are blended with gray based on their depth value $\delta : Color_{new} = (1.0 - \delta) \cdot Color_{old} + \delta \cdot Color_{gray}$.

8.3.2 HALOS

Halos usually result from effects related to illumination. However, we cover them within this section, as they are often obtained without considering the rules of light transport. Some of the discussed illumination approaches can also be used to allow the integration of halos, for instance dynamic ambient occlusion [Ropinski *et al.*, 2008b] or vicinity shading technique [Stewart, 2003].

Bruckner and Gröller [2007b] propose an approach to enhance depth-perception of volume rendered images with *halos*. In contrast to the application of volumetric illumination models their halo approach allows flexible parameter changes and thus supports manual emphasis of structures of interest. To do so, they employ a slice-based rendering algorithm, which composites view-aligned slices from front to back. During slicing, they apply a three step process, which generates and propagates the halos. Thus, no additional data needs to be stored, which avoids preprocessing, and thus allows to change all relevant visualization parameters interactively. The three consecutive steps applied during rendering are:

- halo seeding,
- halo generation, and
- halo mapping and compositing.

Within the halo seeding stage it is determined where halos appear later on. While there are several possibilities for seeding halos, BRUCKNER and GRÖLLER propose to place the halos around contours of objects by taking the angle between the view vector and the local gradient into account. If these vectors are nearly orthogonal, the according sample point is considered as a contour point and a halo is seeded.

To control the localization of the introduced halos, they introduce a halo mapping function. This mapping function is based on three components:

- First, the value influence function which allows to restrict halo seeding to specific intensity ranges.
- Second, the directional influence function which allows to restrict halo rendering to certain directions, as given by the angle between the view vector and the gradient.
- And finally, the positional influence function which allows to control the occurrence of halos based on a user-defined position.

Based on the thus generated halo seeds, the actual halos are created in the halo generation stage. While low-pass filtering would be the straightforward approach to transform the halo seeds into halos, it has several drawbacks. Most importantly, it might extinguish the seeds of small high-frequency features, which might be—despite their size—of high importance. To avoid this behavior, the authors present a spreading approach which preserves halos of small features while still producing a smooth halo field.

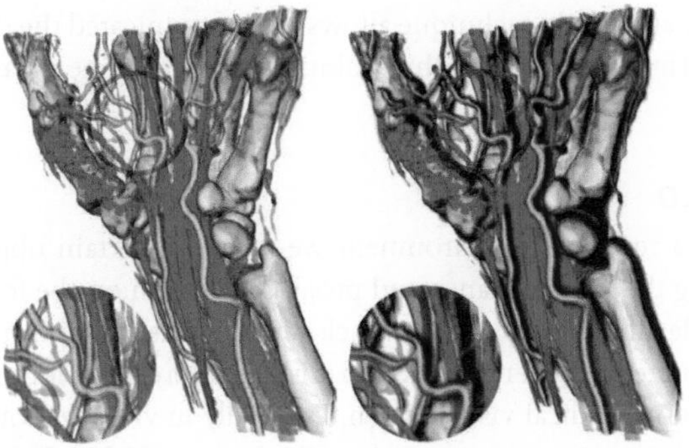

FIGURE 8.14 *Volumetric halos allow for increasing depth perception. A standard volume rendering (left), as compared to the application of halos as described by Bruckner and Gröller (right) (From: [Bruckner and Gröller, 2007b]).*

In the halo mapping and compositing stage, the generated halos are mapped to colors and opacities before they are blended with the original volume data. In this stage, two types of halos are distinguished: emissive halos and occlusive halos. Emissive halos can be compared to the scattering resulting from glowing objects which are placed in gloomy environments. In contrast, the generation of occlusive halos can be compared to the application of a view plane-aligned shadow map. To transform halos into these representations, the halo mapping function is used. By using this technique, flexible volumetric halos can be generated at interactive frame rates. Figure 8.14 shows an example which has been generated with the described approach. While Figure 8.14 (left) shows the original rendering, Figure 8.14 (right) demonstrates the enhanced depth perception when applying the described halo approach.

Halo-based Feature Emphasis The techniques presented by Svakhine *et al.* [2009] enables an approach inspired by medical illustrations. It exploits lines as halos to emphasize the features of interest. While previous line-based techniques allow for emphasizing the contours of objects, SVAKHINE and colleagues also focus on structural changes along the surfaces in a volume dataset. Thus, it becomes possible to emphasize large- and small-scale features at the same time. The authors exploit the unsharp masking principle, which is widely used in image processing to sharpen pictures. Very briefly described, unsharp masking allows to generate a sharped version of the original picture I_o, by subtracting I_o from a Gauss filtered version I_G of itself. The result of this operation is referred to as the unsharp mask $\Delta I = I_G - I_o$. The *halo-based feature emphasis* is inspired by a modified *unsharp masking* technique, which performs the operation on the signal stored in the depth buffer instead of the color buffer [Luft *et al.*, 2006]. The depth buffer necessary to perform this operation is generated as follows. Based on the *feature transfer function* and the *main opacity function*, the depth value of a slice is only written to the depth buffer if both are unequal to 0. To also emphasize small-scale features, for which the depth contrast would not be high enough, a modified unsharp masking is performed on the gradient field derived from the volume. To compute the differences between gradients adjacent in screen space, the dot product is used and thus the modified unsharp masking on the gradient field becomes possible. Thus, more small-scale features can be highlighted as compared to the standard unsharp masking approach. The authors also describe how to extend the approach to handle multiple features.

Everts *et al.* [2009] have proposed to use depth-dependent halos in order to illustrate dense line data, as they arise when visualizing DTI datasets. To support a halo effect, which is depth-dependent, they introduce geometric profiles which are sweeped along the fibers extracted from the DTI data. The V shape of these geometry profiles, which are positioned with the lower angular point at each fiber pointing away from the camera, ensures that the halo technique allows to communicated the distance between two fibers based on the halo width. Thus, by applying this technique to dense line datasets, a coherent illustrative style can be achieved.

8.3.3 DEPTH OF FIELD

When we look around in a real world environment we focus on certain objects located at a particular distance. All objects, having the same distance and projection region on the fovea as the objects in focus, are perceived sharply, while all other objects being closer or farther away from the viewer are perceived blurry. This gradual effect increases is denoted as *depth of field* or *depth of focus*. It can be simulated in computer graphics and thus exploited in medical visualization. Especially in visualization, depth of field effects can be combined with semantics to support user steering [Kosara *et al.*, 2001]. This avoids the unknown focus problem, which usually occurs when no head tracking device is used.

In recent years, a few approaches supporting depth of field rendering for volumetric data have been proposed. Ropinski *et al.* [2006] have integrated a modified depth of field effect into angiogram visualization. Thus, they were able to represent some parts of the imaged vessels more blurry. The approach works by taking into account the depth value which is associated with each sample. Based on this depth, the σ value of a Gaussian filter kernel is adapted in such a way that structures further away are more affected than structures nearby. This is similar to the kernel size-based approach employed for depth-dependent blurring proposed by Svakhine *et al.* [2009]. To overcome the problem of unknown focus, Ropinski *et al.* [2006] apply the following heuristic approach to determine the structures in focus. When viewing angiogram images, the view is usually changed by rotating the object. Through this rotation some of the vessel structures lying in the back get occluded by the parts lying in front. Thus, more distant objects are harder to perceive, and therefore the authors assume that the viewer is focusing on the vessels being closer to the camera. For this reason, the depth of field effect is only applied to those parts of a vessels whose distance from the viewer exceeds a certain threshold. This threshold is given as percentage of the depth

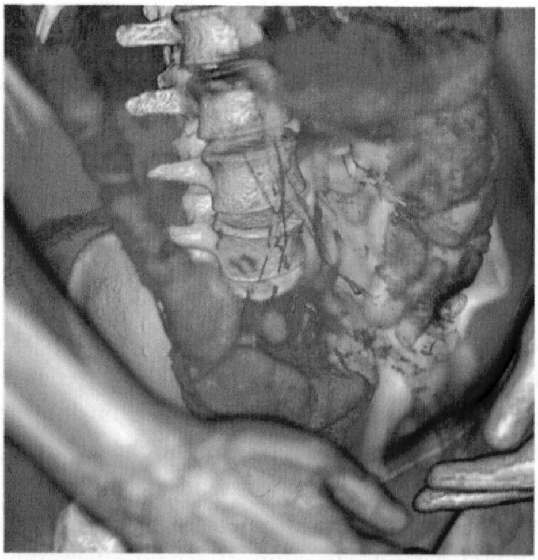

FIGURE 8.15 *Application of an interactive depth of field effect, obtained by a slice-based volume rendering approach (Courtesy of Mathias Schott, University of Utah. See also [Schott et al., 2011]).*

interval of the vessel dataset. This threshold distance is related to the depth mapping function proposed by Svakhine *et al.* [2009] to limit their depth enhancements to certain depth ranges.

Recently, a more sophisticated depth of field effect for interactive slice-based volume rendering has been presented by Schott *et al.* [2011]. The technique exploits iterative blurring of view-aligned slices used during the volume rendering process. Based on the presented camera model, the authors derived an iterative convolution filter, which allows to simulate the depth-based blurring for different camera parameters. The actual convolution is then performed in a lockstep manner along with the actual slicing during rendering. Therefore, the authors propose to generate two view-aligned slicing stacks: one for those slices located behind the focal plane, and one for those slices located in front of the focal plane. While the first stack is traversed in front-to-back manner, the second stack needs to be traversed in back-to-front manner in order to perform the iterative convolution. Figure 8.15 shows a depth of field enhanced volume rendering which has been generated with the described approach.

8.4 CONCLUDING REMARKS

We have discussed advanced volume rendering techniques and their application in the medical domain. The common purpose of the handled techniques was to increase image comprehension, as the understanding of spatial arrangements is essential for several tasks within medical visualization. We have handled mainly two types of approaches, illumination-based techniques and artificial depth enhancements. The illumination-based techniques borrow from reality, as they model and simplify real-world lighting interactions to better communicate structures and their spatial arrangements. We have seen how these techniques vary with respect to their illumination capabilities, and how these influence their applicability in the medical domain. While current techniques allow to generate realistically looking images at interactive frame rates, only very little is known about the actual benefits when applying the approaches in medical diagnosis. Latest studies rather investigate the perceptual impact of these techniques in a general sense. Obtaining more information about their behavior within the medical area is especially interesting, with respect to medical certification to which radiological workstations are subject to. While the illumination-based techniques mainly facilitate shadowing and scattering to communicate spatial structures, the artificial depth enhancements which are often motivated by medical illustrations exploit color-coding, haloes, and depth of field effects. Despite the many differences, there are also overlaps between illumination-based approaches and artificial depth enhancements. When for instance considering depth-based color blending, it is based on atmospheric illumination effects. Furthermore, the halo-based approaches can be related to illumination techniques, where the light source position coincides with the camera, as the halos can also be thought of as shadows. Again, only little is known about the impact of these techniques in a medical domain, though as they are widely applied in medical illustrations, medical doctors should be accustomed to many of these. Since interactivity is essential in medical visualization, the techniques covered within this chapter have been selected with respect to their performance. Thus, most techniques can be realized on modern GPUs.

Interactivity is important in many fields of medical visualization. When for instance a radiologist performs a medical diagnosis or a surgeon plans an intervention, interactive exploration of volumetric data is essential. When dealing with structural modalities, the medical expert is interested in relative positioning and size of organs and other anatomical features. In many of these cases, 3D representations are essential, since the features of interest might not be located in adjacent slices. Within this chapter we have discussed interactive 3D visualization techniques, which support the data exploration process, as performed in these medical disciplines. Having the these tasks in mind, we have focused on volumetric illumination models and depth enhancement strategies. These techniques allow to better communicate spatial arrangements and reveal an occlusion-free view to anatomical features, which are otherwise hidden deep inside the body. While volumetric illumination models and depth enhancement techniques support an improved depth perception of volume rendered images, smart visibility techniques allow for revealing potentially occluded objects of interest. We have learned how scattering and shadowing effects can be achieved by extending the standard volume rendering integral. Furthermore, how these effects can be achieved interactively by using GPU-based techniques, which might associate them with certain rendering paradigms. Recent findings indicate that the perceptual benefits of the presented techniques vary, and directional occlusion shading is beneficial in many scenarios. The benefit of the artificial depth enhancement techniques is the individual parameter control. Though, for clinical applicability it is important that meaningful presets are available. We have further learned about color-based effects, halos, and depth of field effects.

FURTHER READING

Due to the diversity of the covered approaches, this chapter cannot be complete. Therefore, several sources are recommended for further reading. The theory behind the volumetric illumination models is extensively discussed by MAX's article [Max, 1995]. The course notes by Rezk Salama *et al.* [2009] present a comprehensive overview of different volumetric illumination techniques.

Future Work Though the techniques presented in this chapter allow to generate realistic volume rendered images at interactive frame rates, still several challenges exist to be addressed in future work. When reviewing existing techniques, it can be noticed that although the underlying optical models already contain simplifications, there is sometimes a gap between the model and the actual implementation. In the future it is necessary to narrow this gap by providing physically more accurate illumination models. The work done by KROES and colleagues [Kroes *et al.*, 2011] can be considered as a first valuable step into this direction. One important ingredient necessary to provide further realism is the support of advanced material properties. Current techniques only support simplified phase function models and sometimes BRDFs, while more realistic volumetric material functions are not yet integrated.

Another challenging area, which needs to be addressed in the future, is the integration of several data sources. Although, Nguyen and colleagues [Nguyen *et al.*, 2010] have presented an approach for integrating MRI and fMRI data, more general approaches potentially supporting multiple modalities are missing. Along this lines, also the integration of volumetric and geometric information needs more consideration. While the approach by Schott *et al.* [2012] allows an integration in the context of slice-based rendering, other volume rendering paradigms are not yet supported.

Chapter 09

Volume Interaction

9.1 INTRODUCTION

In this chapter, we discuss techniques for the exploration of medical volume data. Exploration in this context refers to the specification of which portions of the data should be visible and how they should be displayed. The techniques we describe are used to modify the brightness, contrast and opacity of voxels, and thus the contrast between different materials. A crucial problem is to provide user interfaces and interaction techniques that enable physicians to specify their intent as directly as possible. The intent of physicians is to emphasize certain tissues, material boundaries, or spatial relations between adjacent structures, e.g., around a pathology. Simple user interfaces, however, just provide a transfer function editor, where the user has to spend much effort in order to come up with a visualization that is at least close to the above-mentioned visualization goals. Moreover, physicians think in terms of diagnostic and treatment decisions, e.g., with respect to infiltration and resectability. The raw parameters of a transfer function are too low level to enable convenient assistance for such questions.

This chapter builds on the introduction in human-computer interaction (Chap. 5). Thus, the techniques presented throughout the chapter aim at simple and efficient interaction and often use results from data analysis to provide high-level support. Care, however, is necessary to hide the details of data analysis from physicians. They should not be asked to specify a number of parameters that control a clustering approach for instance, since the choice of such values is not related to their *domain knowledge* which is *tissue-centric* [Lundstrom *et al.*, 2006].

Another strategy to provide guidance for achieving a particular visualization goal is to assume that users are familiar with the data and understand the significance of the represented structures. Thus, high-level support with *immediate visual feedback* is desirable to enable medical doctors to employ their domain-specific knowledge appropriately. In particular if segmentation information is available, volume interaction may be significantly improved.

Volume interaction also comprises techniques to *geometrically* specify which portions of the data are visible, e.g., with clipping planes or cutting geometries that are moved inside the data. In this way, virtual resections can be performed in order to define which portions of an organ remain after a pathology is removed from a certain area with a certain safety margin. Figure 9.1 shows clinically relevant examples of volume-rendered images prepared with a combination of volume interaction techniques.

In contrast to geometric modifications that are inherently local, transfer functions are global transformations that map data with certain properties (wherever they occur in the data) to opacity and colors. While simple transfer functions only employ the intensity value range (1D transfer functions), more advanced strategies incorporate a second dimension, e.g., the gradient magnitude that indicates the local inhomogeneity of the data. In general, 1D TFs allow to separate *materials*, whereas 2D TFs, in particular with gradient magnitude as the second dimension, also allow to emphasize *material interfaces* or *material boundaries*. Similar to our strategy in other chapters, we present both widely available solutions used in clinical practice as well as research prototypes that may inspire the development of next generation systems for radiology and related disciplines.

Visual Computing for Medicine, Second Edition. http://dx.doi.org/10.1016/B978-0-12-415873-3.00009-2

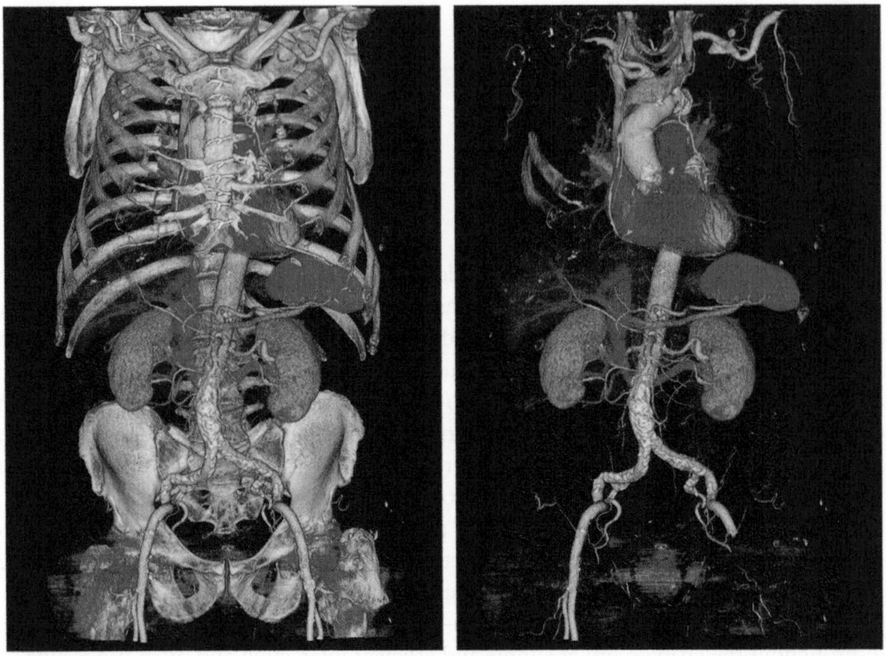

FIGURE 9.1 *Two volume renderings of the same CT dataset. The left image provides a better sense of depth. However, calcifications are partly obscured. In the right image, bony structures were automatically removed prior to volume rendering (Courtesy of Hoen-Oh Shin, MH Hannover).*

Organization We start with a discussion of strategies for the specification of 1D TFs and discuss two approaches to support the user in the TF specification (§ 9.2). Interaction techniques for the specification of multidimensional TFs are described in § 9.3. As selected examples for multidimensional transfer functions, we introduce gradient- and LH space-based transfer functions in § 9.4. In § 9.5, we discuss the use of local TFs that assign different optical properties to different regions of the data. Picking in semitransparent renderings of volume data is a basis for further interactions, such as highlighting and labeling. The mapping of a screen point position to a voxel in world coordinates representing the intended 3D point in space, however, is difficult. In § 9.6, we describe selected volume picking techniques.

In § 9.7, we describe clipping and some of its variants, such as selective clipping and box clipping that determine visibility with rather simple planar widgets. More complex geometries are involved in virtual resection (§ 9.8) and cutting (§ 9.9). Virtual resection is motivated by the desire to preoperatively specify the shape and extent of a resection, whereas cutting primarily serves educational purposes.

9.2 ONE-DIMENSIONAL TRANSFER FUNCTIONS

Let us begin the discussion of transfer functions with a few more motivational thoughts. REZK-SALAMA stated that the technical problems of efficiently rendering medical volume data are solved, but "In practice, in particular in medical practice, the existing solutions are still not used as frequently as one would expect... Physicians often experience difficulties in managing the complexity of visual parameters" [Rezk-Salama *et al.*, 2006]. These authors quote their cooperating physicians with statements such as "Try to make the vessels sharper." and "Improve the contrast between skin and bone a little bit." when transfer functions should be adjusted. The following discussion is focused on data analysis and user interface strategies that reduce the gap between such high-level specifications and the low-level parameters of a transfer function.

Classification and Assignment of Optical Properties Transfer function specification is a two-step process.

- In the first stage, materials are *classified*, e.g., with respect to representing bones, skin, or vessels.
- In the second stage, visual properties are assigned to the classified materials.

The first stage may be performed interactively, e.g., by adapting a trapezoidal function to the histogram, as it was suggested in the pioneering work by Drebin *et al.* [1988]. The slope of the trapezoid indicates *uncertainty* in the border areas, a kind of fuzzy membership. Other shapes, such as tents or Gaussian curves, are also possible to reflect this increasing uncertainty in the border regions. The second stage may be performed by an editor that assigns colors and opacities to the trapezoid.

Focus on Semi-automatic Techniques At first glance, one should aim at a fully automatic solution for the classification process. However, as we have discussed with respect to image segmentation, fully automatic solutions are rarely able to cope with the large anatomical variety and variety in imaging parameters. Also, tissue types can simply not be discriminated reliably in histograms. Thus, the focus lies on the more promising *semi-automatic techniques* that support the users substantially but enable adaptation and flexible combination from some basic types.

The intensity values of a dataset represent the *domain* of a transfer function, whereas color and opacity represent the *range*. In principle, the range may comprise any visual property, such as shininess or refraction index. In medical visualization practice, opacity, gray values, and colors are of primary concern. However, the question what kind of representation is chosen—color or gray levels—depends largely on the target audience. While radiologists often prefer gray level renderings, surgeons benefit from colored visualizations with a natural appearance.

Opacity Transfer Functions TFs determine which structures are visible and how they are displayed. Among the different functions, the *opacity transfer function* is the most important, since it determines which portions of the data are visible. Usually, high opacities are assigned to important features of the data to ensure that they are not obscured by uninteresting regions. TFs are designed to isolate relevant structures and to suppress other structures. Without dedicated support, TF specification is tedious because the parameter space is huge and the relation between the modification of a parameter of the TF and the resulting change in the visualization is indirect and hard to predict.

Histogram Display Since TF design is largely based on the histogram (see Fig. 9.2), it also makes sense to refine the visual representation of the histogram. Zooming and logarithmic axis scaling can be used to improve the usability of the histogram display. Furthermore, more meaningful information can be employed by adding basic statistical values, such as the standard deviation, average, minimum, and maximum values. In particular the latter two are frequently used to indicate peaks.

Transfer Function Specification Approaches In the following, we discuss different approaches to the design of 1D transfer functions. According to Pfister *et al.* [2001], we distinguish

- *interactive approaches* (or unassisted approaches) that do not provide any kind of data analysis to guide the user,

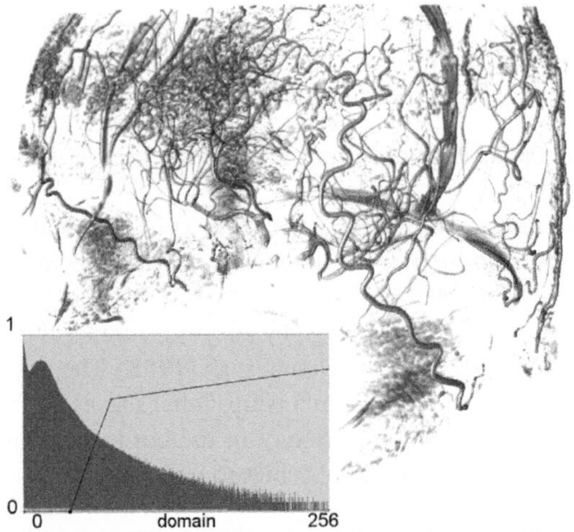

FIGURE 9.2 *An MR-TOF dataset of the brain, acquired with a 7 Tesla device, is displayed with the opacity transfer function shown in the lower left corner (overlaid to the image histogram). Most of the data are completely transparent (see the values around the peak of the histogram where opacity is mapped to zero). Thus, primarily vascular structures are visible. However, a reliable classification based on a global 1D TF is not possible for such data (Courtesy of Rocco Gasteiger, University of Magdeburg).*

- *data-driven approaches* that are based on an analysis of the data, e.g., with respect to local clusters or visibility, and
- *image-driven approaches* that provide support by analyzing rendered images or portions thereof.

The classification above is not perfectly orthogonal since *interactive approaches* obviously exploit features of the images as well as *image-driven approaches*. Thus, in contrast to the original classification, we employ the term *unassisted* instead.[1]

9.2.1 UNASSISTED TECHNIQUES

The major concept of unassisted techniques is a transfer function editor that enables the placement and adjustment of control points that define transfer functions for opacity and color. While transfer function editors are part of every medical visualization library, such as Voreen or MEVISLAB, they are rarely used in clinical practice. Instead, a simplified interaction technique is employed to specify relatively simple transfer functions, in particular to enable *windowing*.

In this technique, opacity TFs are adjusted with mouse movements, e.g., when the right mouse key is pressed. Horizontal and vertical movements are mapped to modifications of the center and width of an opacity ramp, very similar to windowing in 2D slice data, where brightness and contrast (the parameters of a ramp function for gray values) are affected. This parameterization has to be learned, but once the user is familiar with this concept, a fluid interaction is possible, where the user can focus on portions of the image data instead of shifting the attention between user interface components and data display.

In medical research, more fine-grained control is desirable. A transfer function editor must at least provide mechanisms to add, delete, and move control points. Direct manipulation combined with a display of numerical values is the default interaction style.

1 Based on a discussion with Claes Lundstroem.

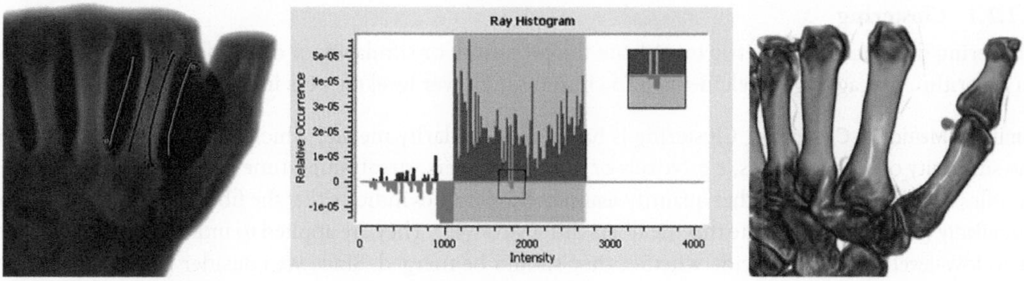

FIGURE 9.3 **Left:** *The user creates two pairs of strokes (green and blue) in a volume rendering of a CT hand dataset.* **Middle:** *Histograms in the corresponding colors are shown and used to define transfer functions.* **Right:** *The resulting volume rendering clearly reveals the skeletal structures (From: [Ropinski et al., 2008c]).*

Predefined Transfer Functions In clinical practice, often predefined transfer functions are employed. Thus, for a certain examination, such as CT head, or CT neck, or CT thorax, there are a couple of predefined TFs each of which emphasizes one tissue type.

Stroke-based Transfer Functions There are a number of concepts for TF specification that replace the editing of TF parameters by some kind of drawing operations in slice data [Tzeng *et al.*, 2003] or rendered images. This general concept is convincing, since users now *directly* interact with image data instead of indirectly manipulating functions related to the histogram space. Note that thus the frequent focus switch between the displayed data and the histogram view, which characterizes a trial-and-error specification, may be avoided.

These direct manipulations are particularly useful to emphasize small structures that are clearly visible and recognizable in slice data for an experienced user but not discernible in histogram space where their footprint is too low. As an example, Ropinski *et al.* [2008c] provide a *stroke-based* interaction, where users roughly delineate the target structure and assign a stroke width to define a region in the data that should be emphasized. The histogram of the voxels belonging to that stroke is analyzed in order to define the transfer function (see Fig. 9.3).

This particular concept is not purely interactive but combined with image-driven interaction concepts described later. For effective use, it should be avoided that the user has to delineate a target structure, e.g., a vessel precisely. As an example, user input may snap to nearby boundaries with a livewire-like interaction (recall § 4.4.1). Despite strategies to avoid overly precise drawings, zooming is provided to specify such strokes, in particular for smaller structures.

9.2.2 DATA-DRIVEN TRANSFER FUNCTIONS

In this subsection, we extend the idea of employing the intensity histogram for TF specification and discuss how the histogram of derived quantities may be used to support TF design and thus make it more reproducible. In recent years, primarily new data-driven transfer function specification techniques were introduced to provide a semi-automatic TF specification.

TF specification is a more general problem than isovalue or threshold specification for surface rendering. Methods which derive salient and potentially appropriate isovalues (recall for example [Bajaj *et al.*, 1997]) are relevant for TF specification where higher opacity is assigned to an interval around critical isovalues. We start this subsection with some general remarks on *clustering*—the grouping of data elements according to similarity. Clustering is essential for data-driven transfer functions but also for other tasks in medical visualization, e.g., to simplify visualizations of blood flow or fiber tracts.

9.2.2.1 Clustering

Clustering data includes a metric to evaluate the proximity or similarity of data. The core of clustering is an algorithm that aggregates elements into clusters and lower level clusters into higher level clusters.

Similarity Metrics for Clustering Clustering is based on a similarity metric, which enables the assessment of the similarity of data elements, e.g., voxels or in later chapters, streamlines, time-intensity curves, or fiber bundles. Similarity metrics either quantify *similarity* (high values indicate that the fibers are almost equal) or *dissimilarity* (high values indicate that the fibers differ strongly). They are applied to individual data elements or to low-level clusters to decide whether they should be merged. Since we consider here the similarity of voxels, we refer to data elements as v_i. Note that data elements may also be higher dimensional, e.g., a feature vector. In the case of volume data classification, the intensity, gradient magnitude, and Gaussian curvature along the principal curvature direction may together form a feature vector. For volume classification, the location of a voxel, and not only its attributes, is essential for the derivation of locally coherent clusters.

Most similarity metrics are symmetric, yielding the same value for the pairs of data elements (v_i, v_j) and (v_j, v_i). With distance-based metrics, v_i and v_j are regarded as belonging to the same cluster if a distance $d(v_i, v_j)$ is below a threshold d. There are many metrics to characterize the distance between two data elements, e.g., the mean of closest point distances and the Hausdorff distance.

Clustering Algorithms Clustering imposes a classification on the data. Based on similarity metrics, data elements are grouped in clusters. The evaluation of the metric leads to a *proximity matrix*, where for each pair of elements the proximity is recorded. Simple clustering algorithms rely on a predefined number of clusters. Examples for this type of algorithms are k-means [Hartigan and Wong, 1979], or fuzzy c-means [Kannan *et al.*, 2013], where a data element has a probability of belonging to a cluster. These methods are iteratively applied starting from initial (randomly selected) cluster centers, subsequently assigning elements to these clusters. According to quality criteria, such as *compactness* of clusters, the centers are displaced. The process is repeated until the cluster centers no longer move significantly and the process has thus converged. Figure 9.4 shows an intermediate and the final stage of k-means clustering. k-means clustering is a *local optimization* that is not reproducible, since the result depends on the initially selected centers.

An improved version of k-means, called *k-means++* [Arthur and Vassilvitskii, 2007] is less sensitive to the initial cluster centers. Fuzzy clustering methods are relevant for transfer function design in volume data, since they may represent border areas between tissue types and the probability may be used as input for opacity or color mapping.

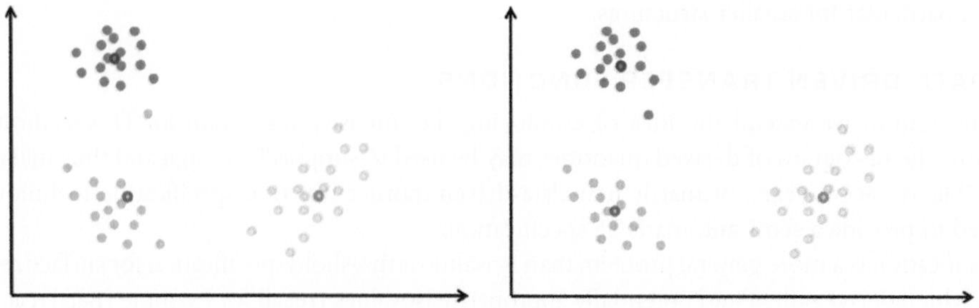

FIGURE 9.4 *Clustering in 2D space with k-means. The data should be decomposed in three clusters.* **Left:** *An intermediate result where one element—close to the green elements—is assigned to another cluster based on the distance to the cluster center.* **Right:** *After a final iteration the point moved to the green cluster. Thus, finally, the clusters are compact. Note that the shape is convex, that is the clusters may be achieved with linear separation (Courtesy of Sylvia Glaßer, University of Magdeburg).*

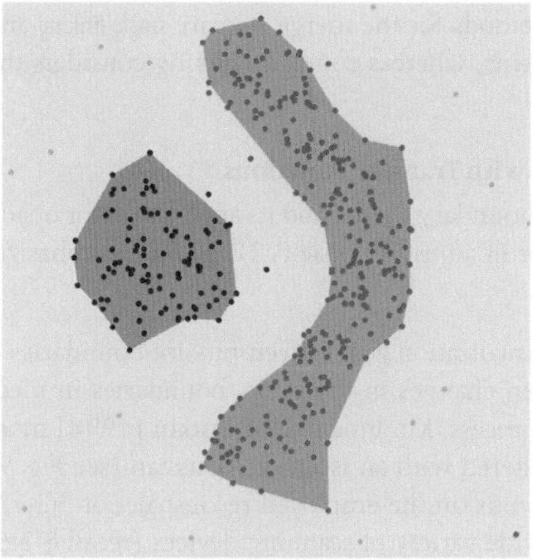

FIGURE 9.5 *Clustering in 2D space with DBSCAN. Outliers are not assigned to any cluster and the cluster shapes may be concave. The number of clusters was determined by the algorithm and not provided as input parameter (Courtesy of Wikimedia).*

While some clustering approaches, such as k-means, are restricted to produce convex shapes, others are able to produce any kind of clustering shape. Density-based clustering, such as DBSCAN [Ester *et al.*, 1996] and OPTICS (Ordering Points To Identify the Clustering Structure) [Ankerst *et al.*, 1999], may produce concave shapes, see Figure 9.5 for an example. These density-based clustering approaches rely on two parameters: the minimum number of points that a cluster should have (*minPoints*) and the maximum distance to consider for a cluster ε.

Clustering algorithms differ with respect to their result. *Hierarchical clustering* algorithms generate a nested hierarchy of partitions. At different levels of the hierarchy a different number of clusters arises. *Partitioning algorithms*, on the other hand, produce a single partitioning of the data. Clustering algorithms may assign each element to exactly one cluster (hard clustering) or compute a membership probability. The latter class of algorithms is referred to as *fuzzy clustering*.

Hierarchical Clustering The basic strategy for hierarchical clustering is as follows:

1 Each item is regarded as an individual cluster.
2 The two most similar clusters (with respect to the similarity metrics) are merged.
3 The second step is repeated until only one cluster remains.

Figure 9.6 illustrates hierarchical clustering.

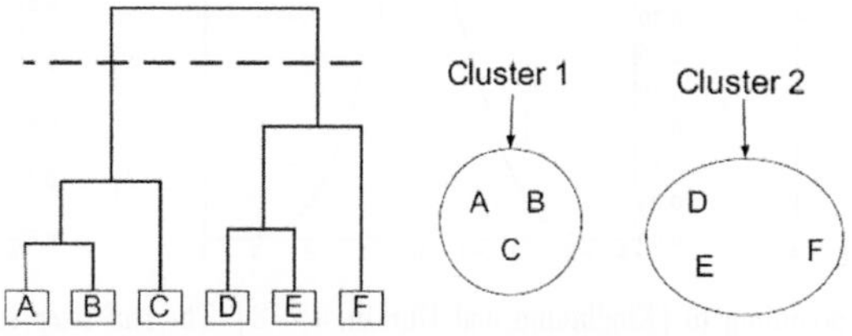

FIGURE 9.6 *A graph represents the results of hierarchical clustering (left image). With a cut (see the dotted line) a particular classification with two cluster results (right) ([Moberts, 2005]).*

Two simple and popular methods for the merge step are *single linking* and *complete linking*. Single linking considers the closest pair of items, whereas complete linking considers the maximum distance between a pair of items.

9.2.2.2 Boundary Emphasis with Transfer Functions

In the following, we discuss a boundary model and its application for opacity TF specification. This model is designed to support the user in adjusting opacity TFs, which emphasize boundaries at the expense of homogeneous regions.

Boundary Model An essential visualization goal is to emphasize boundaries in the data. While ideal boundaries are represented by sudden changes in the value, boundaries in medical image data are smoothed due to the image acquisition process. Kindlmann and Durkin [1998] model boundaries in medical volume data by a step function filtered with an isotropic Gaussian (see Fig. 9.7). Thus, the extent to which boundaries are smoothed depends on the employed reconstruction filter, but the general appearance of boundaries is the same for a wide variety of scanning devices (recall § 2.5).

A boundary can be identified by looking for voxels with a local maximum slope (local maximum in the first order derivative) and zero-crossing in the second order derivative. Actually, this assumption has been used in computer vision for a long time to develop edge detection filters in image analysis.

Kindlmann and Durkin [1998] used these assumptions and created a *histogram volume* H where each entry represents $f(x)$, $f'(x)$, and $f''(x)$ for a particular value x. They defined a position function p [Kindlmann and Durkin, 1998] (Eq. 9.1):

$$p(v) = \frac{-h(v)}{g(v)} \tag{9.1}$$

where v is an intensity value, $g(v)$ represents the average gradient magnitude for all voxels with value v, and $h(v)$ is the average second order derivative in gradient direction. $p(v)$ describes the average distance of a data point with value v from a boundary.

Generating Opacity TFs The analysis of the histogram volume allows to detect a boundary and to estimate its width. According to the boundary model, a Gaussian is fitted to the data surrounding a boundary. The σ-parameter of the Gaussian characterizes the steepness of the function. Based on this information, the user can select a *boundary emphasis function*, which finally determines *how* the respective boundary is visualized. The predefined functions have different width, height, and shape, e.g., tent functions or box shapes.

The opacity TF results by multiplying p with a boundary emphasis function. Defining opacity as a function of distance to a boundary is more intuitive than defining opacity as a function of data value.

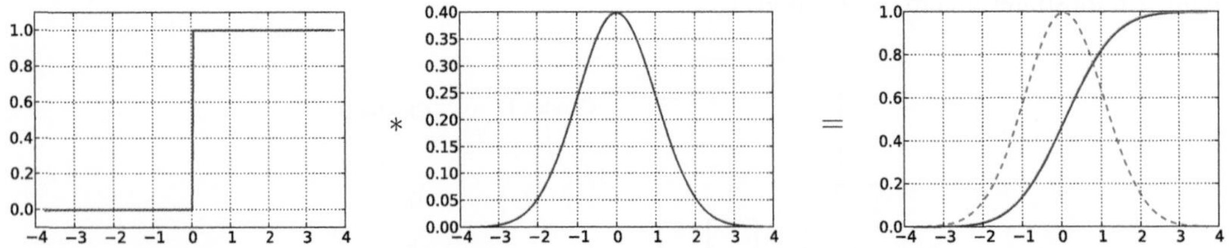

FIGURE 9.7 Boundary model according to [Kindlmann and Durkin, 1998]. The real steep edge is blurred with a (Gaussian) low-pass filter resulting in a gradual change in image intensity. The largest gradient in the resulting image (see the red dashed line) occurs at the position of the original edge. The width of the Gaussian depends on the particular acquisition device.

Although the method proposed by Kindlmann and Durkin [1998] is based on strong assumptions with respect to the appearance of boundaries, it is a crucial contribution to TF specification. In cases where the assumptions are not valid, such as inhomogeneous MRI data, preprocessing might transform the data such that the boundary model becomes applicable.

9.2.2.3 Reference Transfer Functions

Static presets with a fixed lookup table may efficiently support direct volume rendering. They are, however, limited in their applicability to structures with standardized data values, e.g., Hounsfield values in CT data. This requirement is not fulfilled for example for MRI data, but also does not account for contrast agent inhomogeneity in contrast-enhanced CT data.

Therefore, there is a need for data-driven support, which adapts a preset carefully specified for one dataset to other datasets that are similar with respect to the pathology, modality, and imaging parameters. According to Rezk-Salama *et al.* [2000a], we refer to this flexible preset as a reference transfer function (TF_{ref}). If we have defined this function for a dataset D_{ref} and now analyze a similar dataset D_{new}, we are looking for a transformation $t(TF_{ref})$ adapted to the characteristics of D_{new}.

TF Transform According to the Histogram The first strategy discussed by Rezk-Salama *et al.* [2000a] to adapt TF_{ref} is to analyze the histogram H_{ref} and to define how the histogram of a new dataset (H_{new}) has to be transformed to match the histogram of D_{ref} in an optimal way. This can be formalized as follows:

$$H_{new}(v) \approx H_{ref}(t(v)) \tag{9.2}$$

where H_{ref} is the histogram of the reference dataset. The matching process is guided by a similarity metric D_t, which evaluates the differences between the frequencies of all values v in D_{ref} and D_{new}.

This matching process has to consider that not only the position and shape of the peaks along the domain are modified but also the frequency values might differ strongly. Therefore, the histograms are normalized first.

$$D_t(H_{ref}, H_{new}) = \sum |H_{ref}(v) - H_{new}(v)| \tag{9.3}$$

Figure 9.8 illustrates the non-linear transformation of the histogram and its effect on the transformation. A further improvement may be achieved by using the **position function** p (recall Eq. 9.1 and [Kindlmann and Durkin, 1998]) instead of transforming the histogram.

9.2.2.4 Visibility-Driven Transfer Functions

With conventional TF design, the visibility of certain anatomical structures is a *consequence* of adjusting transfer function parameters. Correa and Ma [2009] suggest to control visibility directly by computing **visibility histograms** as a basis for visibility-driven transfer functions. Visibility-based transfer functions are actually an instance of a data-driven TF specification.

A visibility histogram "represents the visibility of sample values from a given viewpoint" [Correa and Ma, 2009]. The visibility of a sample is determined by the selected opacity transfer function (OTF) and the visibility of the samples in front of it along the viewing ray. Thus, an entry in the visibility histogram VH is incrementally computed according to Equation 9.4 and the visibility $\alpha(s)$.

$$VH[x] = VH[x] + (1 - \alpha(s)O(x) \tag{9.4}$$

$O(x)$ represents the result of applying the OTF to the sample point x and $\alpha(s)$ represents the current visibility along the ray. This value has to be updated for the next sampling point along that ray according

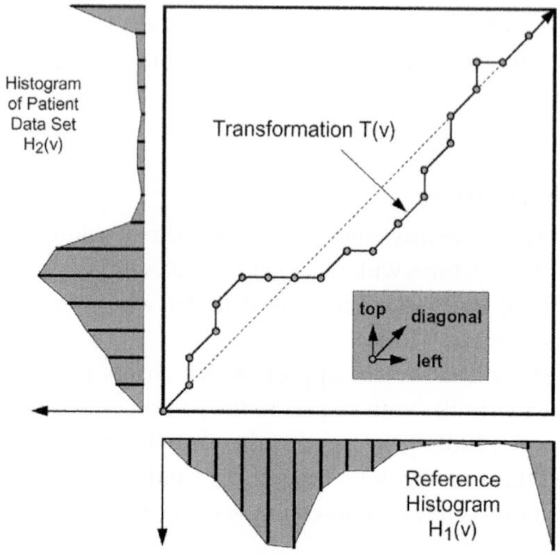

FIGURE 9.8 *A non-linear one-dimensional transformation of the data value range is carried out in order to adapt a new dataset to the histogram of a reference dataset (From: [Rezk-Salama et al., 2000a]).*

to Equation 9.5.

$$\alpha(s + \Delta s) = (1 - \alpha(s))O(x) + \alpha(s) \tag{9.5}$$

Similar to conventional histograms, visibility histograms indicate patterns, in this case occluding patterns. Figure 9.9 indicates how strongly skin and flesh occlude skeletal structures although only moderate opacity values are assigned to them.

There are many details to consider for which we refer the reader to Correa and Ma [2009] and its more recent extension Correa and Ma [2011]. We want to mention some important issues: the binsize of the visibility histogram and the sampling resolution for computing visibility need to be carefully chosen. An efficient histogram computation, using GPU techniques, is required to achieve sufficient update rates. Instead of "only" guiding the users, visibility computations may also be used along with user-specified constraints to optimize opacity transfer functions.

Limitations and Extensions The original concept was only applied to 1D TFs and thus exhibits the natural limitations, e.g., with respect to the discrimination of tissues with overlapping intensity intervals. Also, the computation was performed for *one viewpoint*, meaning that after a rotation the resulting visualization could be very inexpressive.

Correa and Ma [2011] applied the concept of visibility-driven TFs also to multidimensional TFs, primarily to intensity-gradient magnitude-based 2D histograms. Furthermore, they computed *omni-directional visibility histograms*. Thus, an opacity TF is selected guided by these histograms that leads to expressive visualization for *all* viewpoints. Of course, such an OTF cannot be optimal for a single viewpoint but it is advantageous for an exploration process.

9.2.2.5 Shape-Based Transfer Functions

Praßni *et al.* [2010] combine shape classification with transfer function design. They start with a simple pre-segmentation based on windowing and compute the skeletons of the resulting voxels with at least a certain visibility. Based on these skeletons they classify objects with respect to *tubiness*, *blobbiness*, or *surfaceness*.

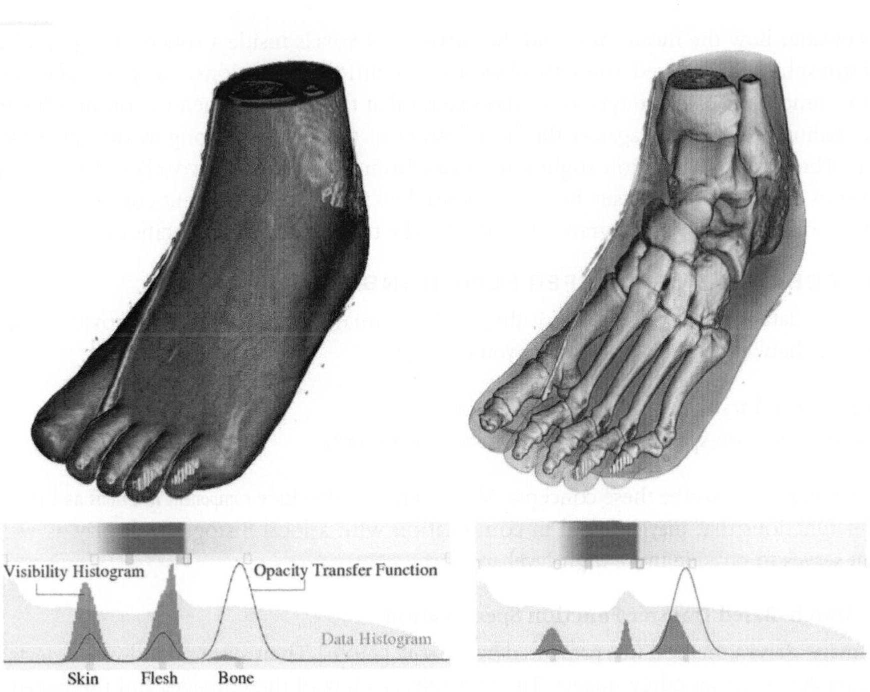

FIGURE 9.9 *CT data are roughly classified according to their intensity values in skin, flesh, and bone. The visibility histogram on the left (see the purple plot) indicates that bone is largely occluded by skin and bone, although the opacity transfer function (red line) assigns high values to bone. The image on the right is based on an opacity transfer function where skin and flesh are assigned very low levels making the bones visible. The peaks in the visibility histogram are thus lower for skin and flesh and higher for bones. The background histogram (light gray) is the overall intensity histogram (From: [Correa and Ma, 2009]).*

High tubiness characterizes tube-like structures with a high extent in one direction and low extents in the two orthogonal directions. High surfaceness is found in objects that have a large extent in two directions and small extent in the orthogonal direction, e.g., the skull-cap and high blobbiness relates to compact structures, like most organs, e.g., liver, and kidney.

This classification is a fuzzy process that assigns a *degree of membership* to each of the three classes. The transfer function specification is based on the membership values. As an example, a transfer function that emphasizes tubular structures (well approximated by a generalized cylinder) highlights vascular structures, nerves, and some skeletal structures. In contrast to previous volume classification schemes, not only local neighborhoods around a voxel are considered, as it is done, e.g., within the vesselness computation described by Frangi *et al.* [1998] and Joshi *et al.* [2008]. As a limitation, the process strongly depends on the pre-segmentation, which may cause instabilities in the resulting skeletons.

9.2.2.6 Statistics-Based Transfer Functions

A number of approaches to transfer function specification are based on statistics in local neighborhoods. Some of these methods consider fixed neighborhoods starting from user-defined seed points, whereas other consider dynamic neighborhoods, the size of which is determined by a local analysis. Most notable is the method entitled "moment curves" by Patel *et al.* [2009].

They consider how the mean value and the variance of voxels inside a spherical region change if the radius of that sphere is increased. There are obviously two different situations: the spherical region may stay inside one homogeneous tissue type or it may extend that tissue type. When the mean value is recorded along the radius, it converges against the "true" value of that tissue, as long as the sphere stays inside that tissue. The standard deviation slightly increases from zero (the seed voxel) until convergence and then increases again when the tissue boundary is reached. Thus, these moment curves provide additional information, over and above histograms, that guides the transfer function specification.

9.2.3 IMAGE-DRIVEN TRANSFER FUNCTIONS

In contrast to data-driven methods, here the rendered images are analyzed to provide support for TF specification. There are two basic image-driven concepts:

- search-based transfer function specification,
- transfer function specification based on local histograms.

In the following, we describe these concepts. Moreover, we introduce *component functions* as building blocks of transfer functions that may be used in combination with a local histogram display as well as a *layer concept* that serves to provide more high-level support.

9.2.3.1 Search-Based Transfer Function Specification

The first image-driven method was presented by He *et al.* [1996]. Their system randomly selects TF parameters and renders corresponding images. The user selects a few of these images and the system generates new images with TF parameters between the selected images. Thus, instead of manipulating TF parameters directly, the user chooses among images, which ideally represent a wide scope of possible TFs. Compared to the trial-and-error specification, image-driven specification is more goal-oriented and requires less knowledge of the user. A technical challenge is to render a sufficient number of preview images fast enough.

A *genetic algorithm* is employed to "breed" a TF from the initial population which is optimal for the user's needs. This concept is convincing, since the TF space is huge and only partially understood for a specific dataset, which is exactly the kind of problem where genetic algorithms are designed for. However, genetic algorithms strongly depend on the underlying fitness function. Since users cannot be assumed to be familiar with fitness functions and their effect on transfer functions and volume renderings, in practice they rely on the built-in fitness function. In more recent times, the use of *genetic algorithms* for optimizing transfer function design gained some attention, most notably by Wu and Qu [2007]. However, it is still restricted to research settings.

Gallery Concept The ideas of He and colleagues were generalized and enhanced by Marks *et al.* [1997]. Their "Design galleries" represent a general approach for selecting parameters in a multidimensional space. Marks *et al.* [1997] mention camera and light specification as possible applications of their approach. TF specification with this approach is accomplished by selecting previews to guide the search process. The parameter space is more regularly sampled. In contrast to He *et al.* [1996] very large sets of preview images are generated and arranged in a "Design Gallery" from which the most appealing image might be selected. The gallery concept is now widely used in radiology workstations (recall § 9.2.1), where a small set of preview images, named with the anatomical structures they emphasize, are provided.

9.2.3.2 Specification with Component Functions

Component functions fit well to the mental model of physicians considering transfer function design as a tissue-centric process where they emphasize certain structures and hide others. Thus, transfer functions

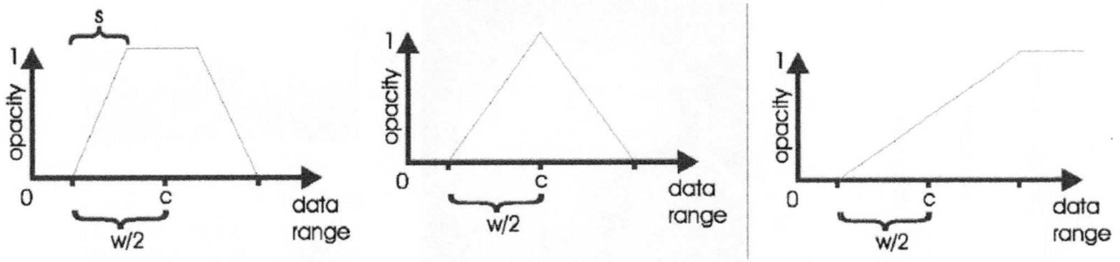

FIGURE 9.10 *Component functions for 1D TF design. All components are characterized by width w and center c. The trapezoid (left) has an additional parameter that refers to slope s. From left to right: trapezoid, tent, and ramp (Adapted from: [Castro et al., 1998]).*

may be defined based on *component functions* (hereafter CF), which are simple basis functions such as ramps, boxes, and tents (see Fig. 9.10) [Castro *et al.*, 1998]. To specify a CF, the user has to set a small number of parameters. Often the setting of a center, a width, and a maximum opacity is sufficient. The required flexibility to specify 1D TFs is achieved by combining CFs. Thus, this concept is widely used, e.g., by Ropinski *et al.* [2008c] combined with a *layer concept*.

Component functions are not restricted to be piecewise linear. Also sine functions (first half with positive values) or Gaussian bell-shaped functions have been used. They are motivated by the better fit to typical peaks in histograms. Again, a careful user interface design is essential. It should enable an intuitive selection of the active component function, a movement of that CF in the horizontal direction, a stretch in the vertical direction and an adaptation of width parameters.

9.2.3.3 Transfer Function Specification Based on Local Histograms

The computation of the histogram in a specific region of interest within the dataset, or along a line defined in the dataset may be helpful to emphasize small-scale features. The last-mentioned line histograms are called intensity profiles and may exhibit intensity transitions between different materials. The general concept underlying these facilities is called *probing*, where the user "queries" data values which guide the TF specification. The simplest probing functionality, however, is to select a particular position and "read" the value at this position.

Component Functions and Local Histograms Since relevant structures are often too small to generate a discernible footprint in the global histogram, local histograms can be useful to adjust the components. Also in local regions, the target structure may be separated from structures with similar intensity. In Figure 9.11, we show how a component function is parameterized by means of histograms, which refer to a selected quadrilateral region and a line in a slice. The additional effort to specify the local regions is clearly justified.

It is possible to combine CFs such that their intervals overlap. In this case, some rule is necessary to combine several non-zero values from different CFs in the overlapping regions. A simple and generally applicable strategy would be to assign the maximum value to the corresponding visualization parameter. König and Gröller [2001] suggest to combine fast previews of selected thumbnails with a facility to compose transfer functions by means of component functions.

9.2.3.4 Layer Concepts for Transfer Function Design

The layer concept for TF design is another useful concept to hide the details of TF specification and to adjust the parameters at a higher level. This high-level specification is achieved by providing *layers* that roughly correspond to tissue types and thus also adheres to the tissue-centric mental model of physicians. The layer

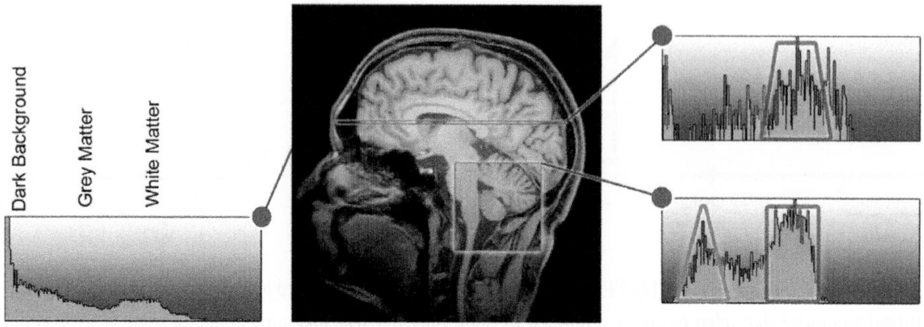

FIGURE 9.11 *Slice from an MRI dataset with labeled global histogram (left) and local histograms of a thin line and a rectangular region (right). In these local histograms, the white matter appears much more pronounced and can be used to place component functions (Courtesy of Mathias Neugebauer, University of Magdeburg).*

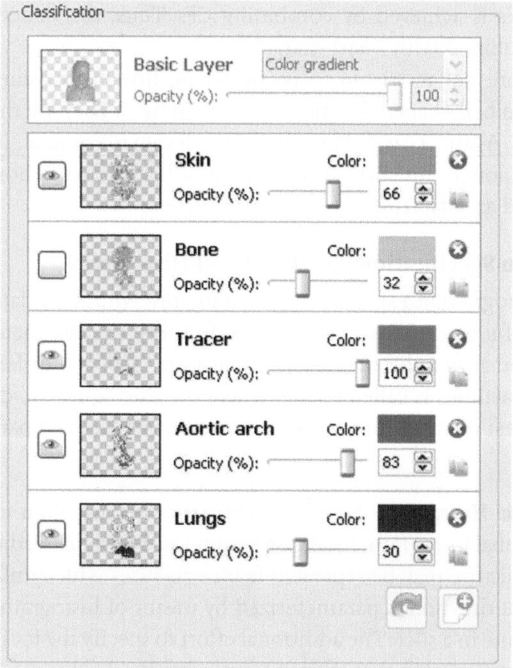

FIGURE 9.12 *A layer concept for TF design. A labeled preview image for each layer is provided. A color chooser and a slider for opacity adjustments are available to adjust the appearance of the respective layer. These specifications are mapped to tent-shaped component functions and merged to an overall transfer function (From: [Ropinski et al., 2008c]).*

concept is known from image processing software where the different layers are designed independently and then overlaid. Different authors have explored a layer concept for TF design, e.g., Rezk-Salama et al. [2006], Rautek et al. [2007], Ropinski et al. [2008c]. Figure 9.12 shows the user interface provided by Ropinski et al. [2008c]. Despite its appealing character, layer concepts are not able to fully solve the task of TF design in many cases, since the relevant components often cannot be discriminated in 1D histograms.

9.3 MULTIDIMENSIONAL TRANSFER FUNCTIONS

With 1D TFs, the ability to emphasize structures is limited to those which can be distinguished based on their data values. In Chapter 2, we discussed CT data and presented Hounsfield units for some structures, such as pancreas (10...40), heart (20...50), liver (50...60), and kidney (50...70). Obviously, transfer functions based on Hounsfield values only are not able to visually discriminate structures, such as liver and kidney. In order to better discriminate features, multidimensional TFs have been developed, which use additionally derived data, such as gradient magnitude or curvature metrics. However, the increased flexibility of multidimensional TFs is achieved at the expense of an enlarged parameter space. Therefore, we have to consider facilities to guide the parameter specification process.

In this section, we introduce general concepts of using multidimensional transfer functions, such as 2D histograms, 2D component functions, and user interfaces to specify them. As a specific example, we discuss *size-based transfer functions*, a concept, where feature size is used as the second dimension in the transfer function range.

Multidimensional TF is a term that summarizes all TFs with a higher-dimensional domain. In addition to data values, gradient magnitude, approximated second order derivatives, curvature-related measures, and distance to reference objects have been employed successfully. In principal, multidimensional TFs allow the user to produce excellent visualizations in particular of CT data. However, much effort is required to specify TFs, and different users (medical doctors) would probably get quite different results. Despite the potential of three- or even higher-dimensional ranges, we therefore restrict the discussion to 2D transfer functions. The very idea of using and interacting with a histogram display would be challenging when three or more dimensions are involved.

Similar to 1D TF specification, sufficient flexibility on the one hand and reduced interaction effort on the other hand are desired in 2D TF design. The design of appropriate user interfaces is more difficult, since more data dimensions are involved. We elaborate the idea of extending component-based 1D TF specification (recall § 9.2.3) to 2D TFs. The composition of a TF based on predefined but adjustable component functions is promising for the larger parameter space of 2D TFs. If the components are restricted to linear shapes, the necessary transformation to a lookup table can be easily accomplished by bilinear interpolation. To support interactive exploration, lookup tables must be computed fast enough.

In the following, we discuss some general concepts of 2D TF specification before we discuss the special cases of gradient-based and distance-based TFs. The dimensions of the TF domain are denoted by V_0 and V_1.

9.3.1 HISTOGRAMS FOR 2D TRANSFER FUNCTIONS

As we have discussed for 1D TF design, the histogram presentation aids the TF specification. Each item in the histogram represents a small range of values in both dimensions. Therefore, we have to consider the 2D histogram, which raises the question how frequency along the two dimensions may be displayed effectively.

Visualization of 2D Histograms The frequency of each item may be encoded in different ways, for example as height in the 3rd dimension. Due to occlusions, however, this is not effective. A more effective technique is to map frequency to gray values. Often, a frequency of 0 is mapped to white and the maximum frequency is mapped to black (see, e.g., Fig. 9.13).

For 2D transfer functions, all considerations related to 1D TFs are also valid: the histogram should be scaled appropriately taking into account, which data actually occur. Logarithmic scales might be a useful option, and histogram analysis may facilitate TF specification. Probing is even more valuable for designing 2D TFs. Users select individual voxels or small regions (in 2D slice visualizations) and query their values in both dimensions indicated in the 2D histogram. This feature is essential because users are not aware of such values. A cluster analysis may be combined with a gallery concept such that one TF is generated per cluster and the resulting images are shown as selection.

User Interfaces for 2D TF Design The basic interaction technique for 2D TFs is to employ *widgets* that enable selections of regions in 2D histogram space or to *probe* data and to highlight corresponding regions in histogram space. Selections require the adjustment of control points or edges. Still the most advanced system for interactive TF specification was presented by Kniss *et al.* [2002a]. Their system also incorporates 3D widgets to explore histogram volumes.

Histogram Analysis More powerful guidance is possible when TFs are not only shown but also analyzed with respect to connected regions, clusters, or peaks. Kotava *et al.* [2012] describe techniques for precise peak localization in higher-dimensional histograms. Although useful in some cases, peaks often represent overlaps of tissue types and are not particularly interesting [Maciejewski *et al.*, 2009]. Maciejewski *et al.* [2009] employed clustering techniques, e.g., to analyze the gradient vs. intensity histogram space. They employed non-parametric clustering, that is the number of clusters is not predefined by the user. The highly non-linear shapes of these clusters could hardly have been interactively selected by 2D widgets.

Conversion of 2D Transfer Functions to Lookup Tables The issue of transforming the 2D TF to lookup tables is essential, since lookup table sizes should consider the available hardware support (in order to facilitate interactive exploration). This may reduce the accuracy of TF specification in both dimensions (for example to 256 data values instead of 4096). The presentation of the histogram should reflect the sizes of the lookup tables to which the transfer functions are transformed. Therefore, frequencies reflect a small interval along the V_0 and the V_1 direction, called a *bin*. A typical number of bins is 256×256, which also represents a typical size of hardware-supported lookup tables in modern graphics processing units [Vega *et al.*, 2004]. It is not necessary that the number of bins is equal in both dimensions. As an example, more bins may be used to sample the intensity dimension compared to a second dimension, such as distance or gradient magnitude.

Within the 2D histogram, the user might select regions by means of graphics primitives. Rectangles, trapezoids as well as triangles are typical shapes of such primitives. Primitives are modified with respect to position and size, either by means of direct manipulation or by means of numeric input (see Fig. 9.13). The selection of regions is the first step to derive a subset of the TF domain. In a second step, the behavior of the TF within that subset has to be specified.

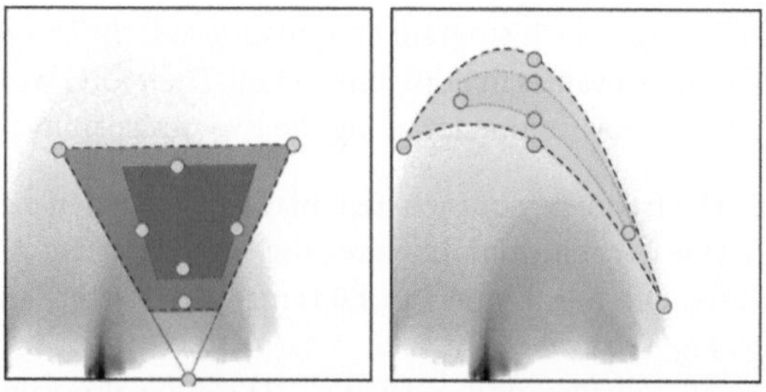

FIGURE 9.13 *2D histograms (gradient magnitude and intensity) with graphics primitives to select subdomains as basis for 2D TF specification. The inner primitives represent the area that is fully opaque and the areas between the inner and outer primitives represent the data values that are mapped to semitransparent values. The areas outside the primitives are rendered fully transparent (From: [Rezk-Salama et al., 2006]).*

9.3.2 2D COMPONENT FUNCTIONS

In this subsection, we assume a rectangular region in the 2DTF domain and discuss TF specification based on templates (component functions) for these 2D domains. The following sequence of interactions is carried out to set the parameter of a 2D CF:

- selection of *intervals* in both dimensions V_0 and V_1,
- selection of a *template*, which describes the adjustment of color and opacity values inside the selected ranges, and
- selection of an *opacity* and a *color value*.

Interval Selection The intervals in the V_0 and V_1 dimension define which tissues are visualized. To specify the intervals, four values have to be defined which represent the borders of ranges (F_{1min}, F_{1max}, F_{2min}, F_{2max}).

A valuable support is to convey to the user the relation of the current settings to slice-based visualizations. For this purpose, 2D views may be combined with colored overlays indicating which pixels are affected by the current interval specification.

Templates The template of a CF is adaptable by the selected intervals of $[F_{1min}, F_{1max}] \times [F_{2min}, F_{2max}]$. For the description of these templates we need two additional variables: We denote: $F_{1center} = F_{1min} + (F_{1max} - F_{1min})/2. F_{2center} = F_{2min} + (F_{2max} - F_{2min})/2$.

The following list contains a selection of useful 2D templates described in [Tappenbeck *et al.*, 2006].

1. *Constant values in the selected intervals (2D extension of a 1D box).* The template is assigned a constant level in $[V_{0min}, V_{0max}] \times [V_{1min}, V_{1max}]$. Outside the selected intervals, the template decreases to 0 with high slope or suddenly without a smooth transition.
2. *Constant values in the selected intervals (2D extension of a trapezoid).* The template is assigned a constant level in $[V_{0min}, V_{0max}] \times [V_{1min}, V_{1max}]$. Outside these intervals, the template decreases slowly toward zero. Zero is reached at the borders of a larger interval $[V_{2min}, V_{2max}]$, $[V_{3min}, V_{3max}]$.
3. *Increasing/decreasing values in the V_0 and in the V_1 dimension.* The template linearly increases from 0 to a maximum between V_{0min} and $V_{0center}$ and linearly decreases above. The CF exhibits the same behavior in the V_0 direction, which leads to a pyramidal shape of CF where the maximum is reached at $(V_{0center}, V_{1center})$—the center of the rectangular subdomain selected by the user.
4. *Increasing values in the V_0 dimension and constant values in the V_1 dimension.* The template is similar to the third. However, the maximum occurs not only at a point but along the line between $(V_{0center}; V_{1min})$ and $(V_{0center}; V_{0max})$.

These transfer function types are illustrated in Figure 9.14.

9.3.3 REPRESENTATION OF 2D TRANSFER FUNCTIONS

The internal representation of 2D transfer functions is essential for their efficient application. 1D transfer functions are usually represented as a linear list of control points with an associated height. The transfer function is an interpolation along the 1D TF domain. Transfer functions for a two-dimensional domain require a 2D grid to represent control points and values, unless they are evaluated on the fly, which is currently possible with programmable graphics hardware. Rectilinear grids are often useful to represent 2D TFs and perform the bilinear interpolation. In contrast to regular grids, rectilinear grids enable to represent some regions in the 2D domain with higher resolution. On the other hand, these grids still have a clear row-column structure of the control points that makes processing easy and efficient.

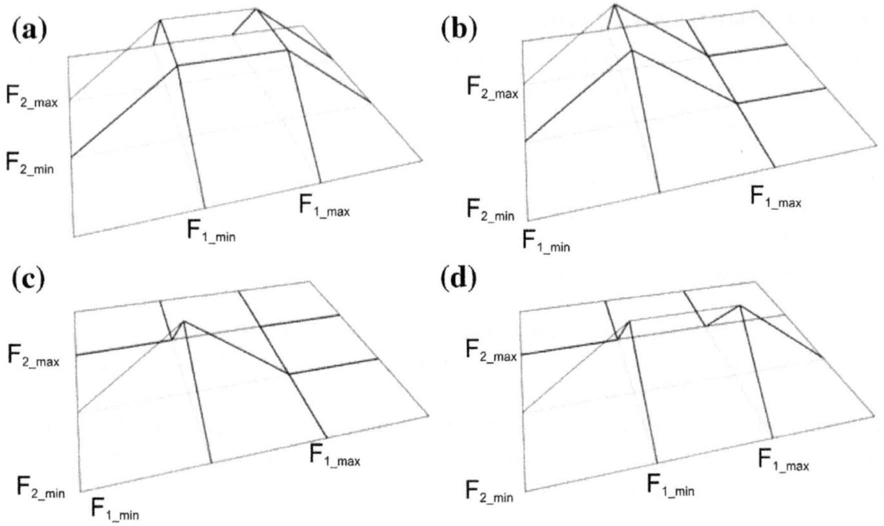

FIGURE 9.14 *Two-dimensional component functions that may be placed, scaled, and combined to define a transfer function over any kind of two-dimensional domain (From: [Tappenbeck et al., 2006]).*

9.3.4 SIZE-BASED TRANSFER FUNCTIONS

A promising idea discussed and realized by C. Correa is to employ *scale* as an additional dimension in transfer function design. Thus, users would be able to combine intensity values and scale to assign colors and other optical properties. This concept enables a clear display of rather small features that may be obscured otherwise. It also enables to adjust colors such that suspicious regions are emphasized, e.g., dilatations of a vascular system [Correa and Ma, 2008].

This concept is not easy to realize and we only sketch the basic approach here. Size-based transfer functions are inspired by scale-space theory and its successful application in computer vision, where for example, multiscale approaches are employed to detect edges or other features at different scales. Multiscale approaches may be realized with discrete levels, e.g., image pyramids, where pixels at one level are summarized to elements at a higher level. This summarization is usually carried out by Gaussian fitering. Such discrete levels, as Correa and Ma [2008] explain, are not an optimal basis for size-based transfer functions, since features are not located precisely. Even with a higher order interpolation between different scales the localization of features is worse compared to those based on *continuous* scale-space representations, e.g., based on wavelets. The specific continuous scale-space representation used by Correa and Ma [2008] is based on a modified linear diffusion process. This may be controlled by one parameter that is a trade-off between robustness against noise and the accuracy of feature detection.

With the scale space constructed, the user now has a typical 2D transfer function domain with intensity and scale and benefits from a 2D histogram representing the distributions of these values. Figures 9.15 and 9.16 explain how this technique is used. The situation displayed in Figure 9.16 is an example where the use of gradient magnitude would not significantly improve the discrimination between vascular structures and bones, since the bones are rather small and their gradient magnitude values are similar to that of vascular structures.

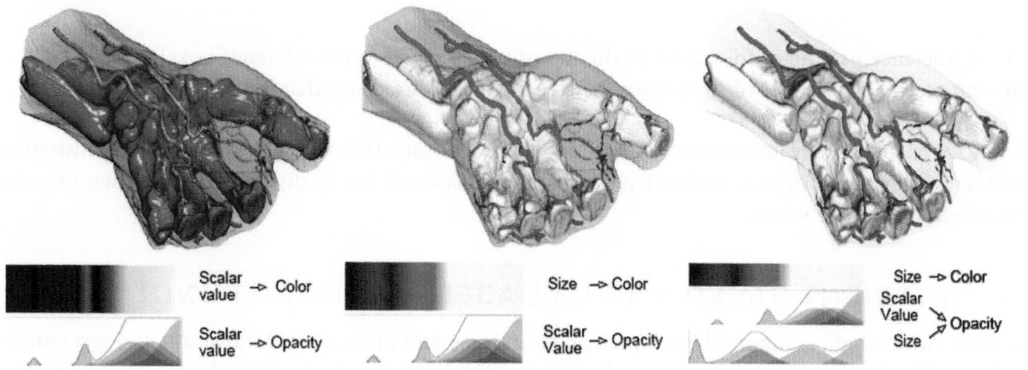

FIGURE 9.15 **Left:** *With a 1D TF vascular structures and bones cannot be discriminated.* **Middle and right:** *Size-based transfer functions, enable a discrimination based on color and an emphasis of small structures, such as veins with an appropriate opacity transfer function (From: [Correa and Ma, 2008]).*

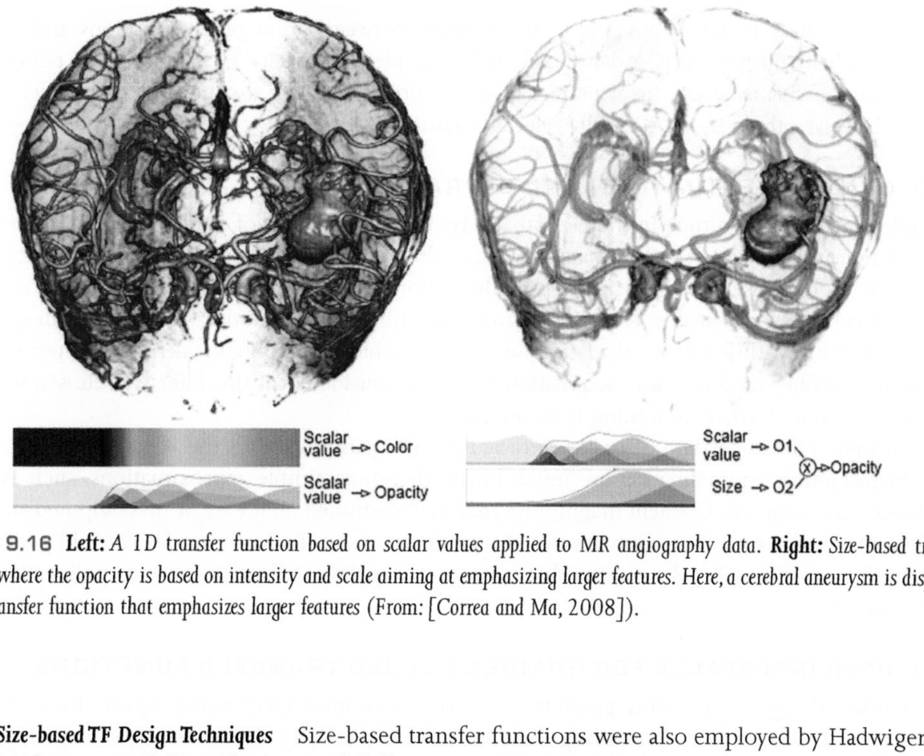

FIGURE 9.16 **Left:** *A 1D transfer function based on scalar values applied to MR angiography data.* **Right:** *Size-based transfer function where the opacity is based on intensity and scale aiming at emphasizing larger features. Here, a cerebral aneurysm is displayed with a transfer function that emphasizes larger features (From: [Correa and Ma, 2008]).*

Further Size-based TF Design Techniques Size-based transfer functions were also employed by Hadwiger *et al.* [2008] and Wesarg *et al.* [2010]. They used different procedures to generate the structure size information and finally the size-intensity histograms. Hadwiger *et al.* [2008] employed a region growing process at automatically defined seeds. Similarly, Wesarg *et al.* [2010] start such growing processes searching for adjacent structures with similar intensities at multiple scales (actually, they suggest to use six scales). The growing process is controlled by

1 a tolerance parameter (deviation of the intensity compared to the reference voxel) and
2 an acceptable number of invalid voxels in the neighborhood size that is analyzed.

Among the examples they investigated more closely, is an abdominal CT, where the size-intensity histogram enables to discriminate organs, such as liver and kidney, that could not be discriminated by their intensity or gradient magnitude values.

9.4 GRADIENT-BASED AND LH-BASED TRANSFER FUNCTIONS

There are two strategies employed to emphasize boundaries and thus material transition in direct volume rendering. The first strategy was to use gradient magnitude as a second parameter for the TF specification [Levoy, 1988]. A second much more recent strategy employs the so-called LH space where the lowest (L) and highest (H) values of path-crossing boundaries are analyzed, presented in histograms and employed for transfer function specification [Serlie *et al.*, 2003, Sereda *et al.*, 2006a]. In this section we describe and illustrate both approaches.

9.4.1 GRADIENT-BASED TRANSFER FUNCTIONS

Gradient magnitude makes it possible to differentiate between homogeneous regions and transition regions. Gradient magnitude is usually exploited to guide the opacity TF. This is often referred to as *opacity-weighted gradient magnitude*. In principle, gradient direction could also be used as transfer function domain. However, there are no clinically relevant examples so far.

9.4.2 GRADIENT ESTIMATION AND STORAGE

To employ gradient magnitude in the TF domain, requires an estimate of gradients. Gradients represent first order derivatives which are estimated in discretely-sampled data based on some differences (recall § 2.3.3). It might be useful to apply a low-pass filter before the gradient calculation is actually carried out, since gradients are very sensitive to noise. Convolving with the Gaussian derivative kernel integrates this low-pass filtering with gradient calculation, and is preferable if computational resources permit it. The reconstruction filter used in image acquisition has to be considered. If this filter was chosen to acquire smooth images, no further smoothing is recommended.

Compared to the calculation of *gradient directions* for high-quality shading, the accuracy demands for the gradient magnitude approximation are much lower. Therefore, simple approximations, such as central differences, are common. Gradient magnitudes may be determined on the fly or precomputed and stored in a separate *gradient volume*. The computation of a gradient can be efficiently accomplished by means of a gradient filter, usually a $3 \times 3 \times 3$ filter that is iteratively applied to the volume and applies the selected differentiation scheme.

9.4.3 USER INTERFACES FOR GRADIENT-BASED TRANSFER FUNCTIONS

User interface design for adjusting gradient-based visualizations is challenging. Again, this process may be supported substantially by presenting a 2D histogram (recall Fig. 9.13). Gradient magnitude is less standardized than intensity values. The values depend on the reconstruction filter as well as on the voxel spacing. Therefore, fixed presets with respect to the gradient magnitude direction are only applicable if exactly the same image acquisition parameters are used.

In the 2D histogram, gradient magnitude strongly differs with some very high values and a lot of smaller values. A linear scale would not allow to detect weaker boundaries in the histogram. Therefore, it

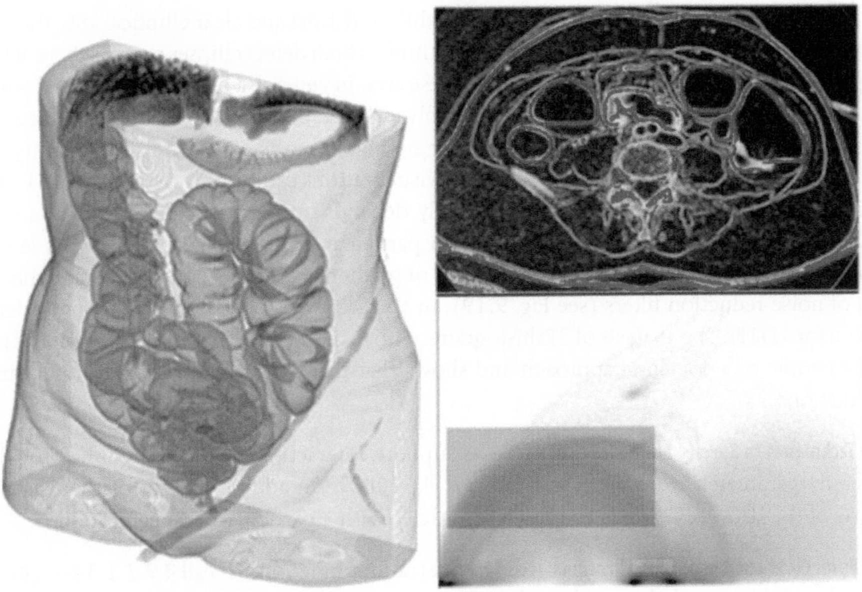

FIGURE 9.17 *The volume rendering (on the left) emphasizes the boundary of the colon as well as the air skin boundary. The opacity TF is combined with two rectangular regions in the 2D histogram (lower right)—each corresponding to one transition. The rectangles impose a condition to the gradient magnitude as well as to data values. All voxels, which fulfill these conditions (included within the rectangles) are highlighted in the 2D slice visualization (upper right) (From: [Shin et al., 2003]).*

is recommended to employ a logarithmic gray level scale for gradient magnitude. The TF specification may be accomplished by means of the interaction facilities discussed in § 9.3. Together with the 2D histogram presentation and slice-based visualizations of the affected regions, TF specification may be carried out effectively. In Figure 9.17, we present an example where a volume-rendered image is shown along with its TF specification carried out by means of 2D histograms.

9.4.3.1 Arcs in Gradient Magnitude/Intensity Histograms

In order to provide dedicated support for gradient-based TF specification, it is necessary to investigate the characteristics of the gradient magnitude/intensity histogram. The 2D histograms of gradient magnitude and data values are characterized by *arcs*, which represent the transition between two tissue types (see Fig. 9.13). These arcs can be well explained by means of the boundary model illustrated in Figure 9.7. Due to the smoothed appearance of a boundary, there is not a single peak in gradient magnitude for a particular value. Some user interfaces for gradient-based TF should employ the typical arcs. In principle, the user can be supported in two different ways.

- Arcs may be automatically detected and parameterized to derive transfer functions, which are subsequently fine-tuned by the user.
- The user may be provided with graphics primitives, which are appropriate to select arcs.

Automatic Determination of Arcs If the 2D histogram exhibits distinct and clear elliptical arcs, the determination of these arcs is feasible by means of special algorithms, which detect ellipses or parts thereof [Xie and Ji, 2002, e.g.,]. Parabolas and ellipses may be fitted to these arcs. In general, a better fit is obtained with ellipses.

However, if data from the clinical routine are involved, these 2D histograms often exhibit a noise level too high for automatic detection of arcs. Currently no algorithm is able to reliably identify such arcs. With the interactive specification of arcs, expressive visualizations can be achieved. It should be noted that the gradient magnitude/intensity histogram strongly depends on the particular acquisition parameters, such as the reconstruction filter in CT scanning. In particular, hard reconstruction filters lead to noisy histograms (see Fig. 9.18). The renderings by means of gradient-based TFs may be considerably improved by means of noise reduction filters (see Fig. 9.19). In § 9.2.2, we introduced *data-driven* transfer function specification for 1D TFs. The analysis of 2D histograms with respect to arcs representing material transitions is also an example of a *data-driven* approach and shows that this basic idea extends to multidimensional transfer functions.

Interaction Techniques to Specify Half-elliptical Arcs As support, interaction facilities might be provided which allow to easily parameterize elliptical arcs [Vega *et al.*, 2003]. An additional aid for the user is to show which parts of the data are mapped to non-zero opacity with a particular TF specification.

Reference TFs for Gradient-based Visualizations Reference transfer functions (recall § 9.2.2.3 and [Rezk-Salama *et al.*, 2000a]) may be extended to gradient-based TFs. Vega *et al.* [2003] realized this extension and applied it to effectively generate high-quality renderings of cerebral MRI data and thus to support the diagnosis of cerebral aneurysms. For highly standardized image acquisition, the automatic adjustment turned out to be feasible and reliable.

9.4.3.2 High-Level User Interfaces for Gradient-Based Visualizations

Rezk-Salama *et al.* [2006] extended on their previous work by a more general interaction concept. It is inspired by character animation tools that incorporate a number of mechanisms for specifying the desired effects, e.g., that a character smiles, at a rather high level. Similar to their previous work they employ training data, e.g., 20 MRI datasets and the transfer functions specified and optimized for them, e.g., with appropriate widgets and 2D histogram visualizations. Transfer functions are optimized for all major tissue types, e.g., bone, skin, and vessels.

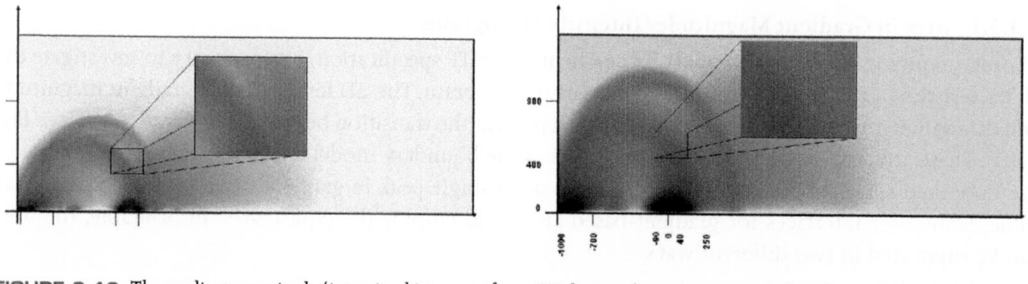

FIGURE 9.18 *The gradient magnitude/intensity histogram for a CT dataset (intensity is mapped to the x-axis). The left dataset was acquired with a soft reconstruction filter whereas the right image was acquired with a hard reconstruction filter. The adjustment of gradient magnitude-based TFs is easier to accomplish with soft reconstruction filters resulting in a less blurred histogram (Courtesy of Diana Stölzel, University of Magdeburg).*

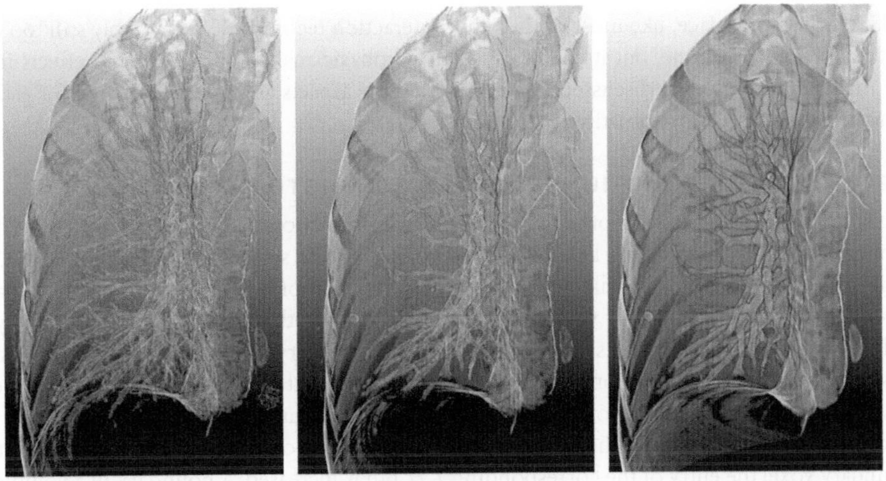

FIGURE 9.19 *Gradient magnitude-based visualization of lung vasculature.* **Left:** *Application to CT data with a hard reconstruction filter.* **Middle:** *The CT data were exposed to median filtering.* **Right:** *With median and Gaussian filtering the data were preprocessed to provide improved conditions for gradient magnitude-based transfer functions (Courtesy of Diana Stölzel, University of Magdeburg).*

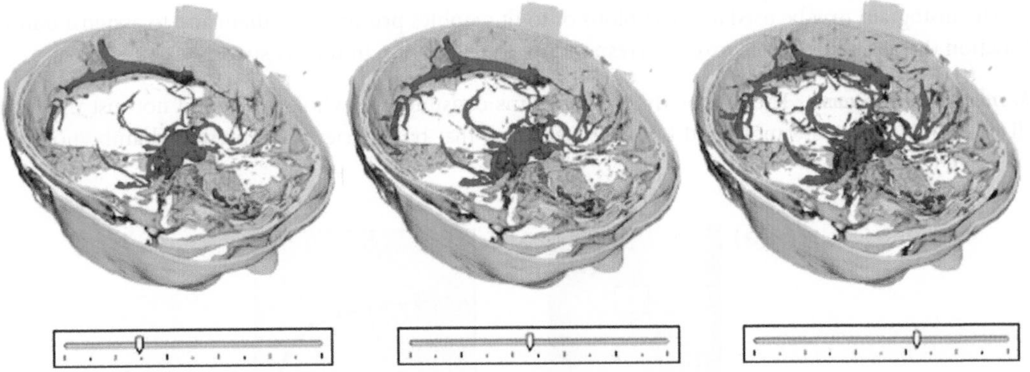

FIGURE 9.20 *Based on the analysis of 20 training datasets, templates for transfer functions were developed and analyzed with the PCA. A slider is moved to adapt the "vessels" template (From: [Rezk-Salama et al., 2006]).*

Their goal is to provide flexible specifications based on these optimized transfer functions. They achieve this by considering transfer functions as arrays of floating point numbers. These points in a high-dimensional space are analyzed with a Principal Component Analysis (PCA) assuming that the data represent a normal distribution. As the most essential result, they consider the first eigenvector (corresponding to the largest eigenvalue) enabling to adjust a single parameter. In contrast to navigating in a high-dimensional space, the user moves a slider corresponding to the first eigenvector direction to select a transfer function (see Fig. 9.20). Such a slider labeled "Adapt template" is available for each tissue type. As a second facility, users may adjust the visibility of the tissue types again with a slider.

This kind of user interface, like most of the other interaction techniques, is probably still too complex for most physicians in routine, but it enables specialized physicians to achieve desired effects in a goal-directed manner. Although we discussed *high-level user interface* aspects as a special strategy for *gradient-based transfer functions* it is in fact more broadly applicable.

9.4.4 2D TRANSFER FUNCTIONS BASED ON LH HISTOGRAMS

The LH histogram is an alternative representation of useful information for boundary emphasis. Compared to the intensity-gradient magnitude histogram, boundaries can be selected with less ambiguity. The LH histogram is based on intensity profiles across boundaries instead of computing the gradient magnitude just for single voxels. For a boundary voxel an intensity profile in both directions is determined by tracing the gradient direction. The process is stopped if either the boundary region obviously ends or a certain length is achieved. A boundary region most often ends when the intensity reaches a plateau representing the transition to a homogeneous region inside a certain material. Figure 9.21 illustrates this tracing process.

L and H denote the lowest and the highest intensity values that occur along these paths, and thus, for each boundary voxel the entry of the corresponding LH bin is increased. A boundary in a volume dataset typically results in a clearly visible blob structure in the LH histogram, at least if that boundary exceeds a minimum length. The very idea of LH histograms was introduced by Serlie *et al.* [2003] in the special context of electronic cleansing of virtual colonoscopy datasets, where it was used to determine the mixture of materials present in a boundary voxel. As a broad concept for TF design it was presented in Sereda *et al.* [2006a]. In Figure 9.22 we show a cerebral MRI dataset, its LH histogram and a volume-rendered image based on selection in LH space.

The histogram may be used to select blobs or to fit graphics primitives to them and to assign a transfer function that is applied to all voxels corresponding to that region in the LH space.

Mirrored LH Histograms The mirrored LH histograms consume the whole space and not just the upper diagonal parts. They are motivated by the observation that boundaries are represented ambiguously in

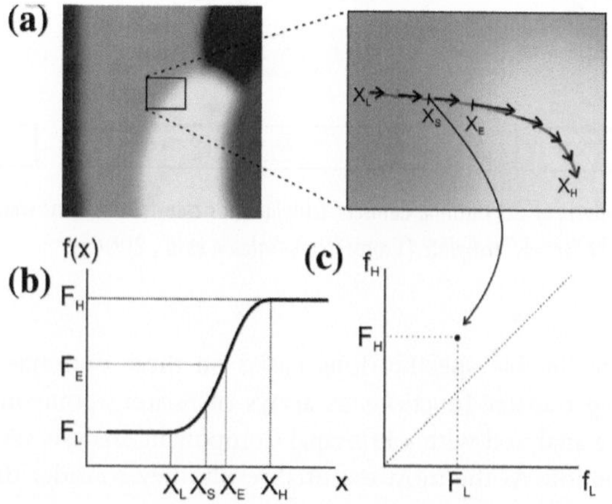

FIGURE 9.21 *The top left image includes a border region (enlarged on the top right). Starting at the boundary voxel X_S the gradient field is integrated leading to an intensity profile (b). The values F_L and F_H denote the lowest and highest values and determine the point in the LH histogram (c) that represents that border voxel (From: [Sereda et al., 2006b]).*

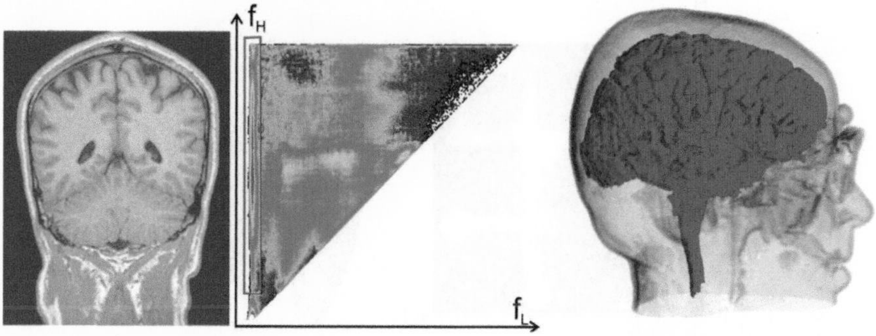

FIGURE 9.22 *The LH histogram (middle) of a cerebral MRI dataset (left) serves as a basis to select subspaces and assign a transfer function. In the right image, the corresponding rendered image is shown (Courtesy of Petr Sereda, Technical University of Eindhoven).*

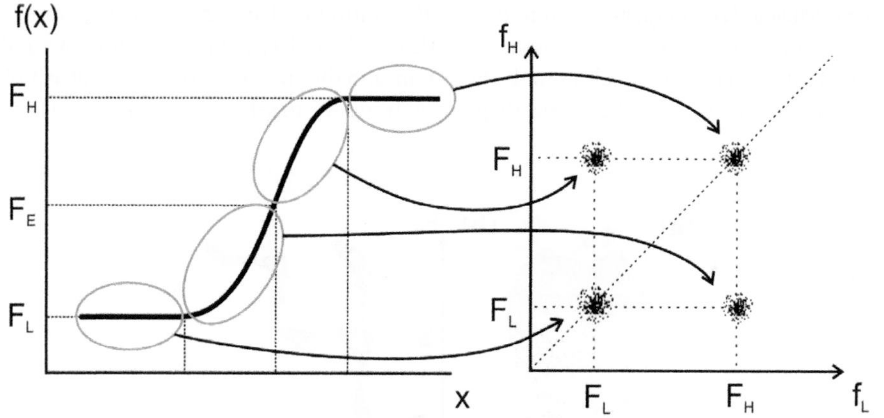

FIGURE 9.23 *The mirrored LH histogram contains entries in the upper section when the voxel's intensity is above the edge intensity F_E. Otherwise, they project to the lower half (From: [Sereda et al., 2006b]).*

the original LH space. The mirrored LH histograms require an estimation where the boundary actually occurs and which intensity value F_E represents this edge. Thus, along the path some voxels exhibit intensity values above F_E and others below F_E. This enables a discrimination of the part of the border to which they belong. The mirrored LH histograms were introduced by Sereda *et al.* [2006b] (see Fig. 9.23). The authors also applied a hierarchical clustering to the data in LH space grouping regions with similar boundary characteristics together. Hierarchical clusterings may be adjusted to create more or less fine-grained groupings. These may be used to assign transfer functions to the computed clusters (see Fig. 9.24). The advantage of the computation and exploration of the LH space is a better identification and delineation of boundary regions. However, this is achieved at the expense of an expensive tracking process along each boundary voxel. Thus, the LH computation needs to be performed in a preprocess to enable interactive classification [Praßni *et al.*, 2009].

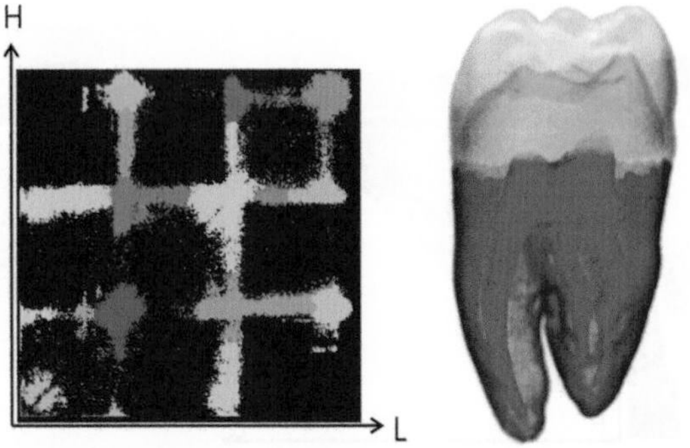

FIGURE 9.24 The mirrored LH histogram of the tooth dataset with the result of a hierarchical clustering (left) is used for volume rendering. The boundaries are more pronounced than would be possible with the original LH histogram (Courtesy of Petr Sereda, Technical University of Eindhoven).

Efficient Computation of LH Histograms Praßni et al. [2009] introduced an efficient algorithm to compute the boundary paths for LH histogram construction. Also the boundary paths are continuous and slightly improve the clarity of the resulting blobs in the histogram and thus the selection and emphasis of features (see Fig. 9.25). It is essential that free-form shapes may be drawn to select regions in the LH histogram.

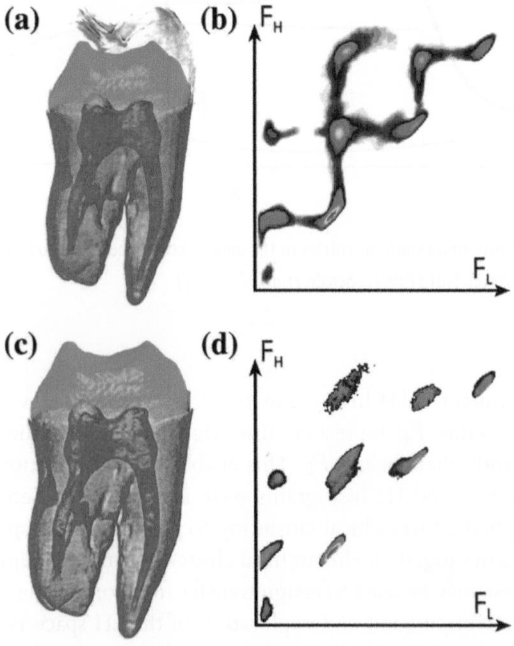

FIGURE 9.25 Original LH histogram (a) and a derived visualization of the tooth dataset (b). The improved method with clear easy-to-select blobs leads to an improved volume rendering (c) LH histogramme related to c (d) (From: [Praßni et al., 2009]).

9.5 LOCAL AND DISTANCE-BASED TRANSFER FUNCTIONS

All types of transfer functions discussed so far relate to features which are independent of the position of data values. The expressiveness of volume-rendered images is limited by the difficulty to locally control the mapping process. Visual parameters are usually defined globally for the whole dataset. In medical applications, however, selected anatomical structures are relevant, whereas surrounding tissues serve as anatomical context only. In such situations, local TFs [Tiede *et al.*, 1998] are appropriate, since they permit to apply different visual parameters to different subvolumes and thus to locally discriminate tissues. Relevant structures may be enhanced by rendering them with higher opacity.

Local TFs are defined for different regions in the dataset. With local TFs, another feature is introduced that increases flexibility and potentially the expressiveness of volume renderings at the expense of an enlarged parameter space. If we want to assign n TFs, we have to define n regions and one TF for each. The use of local TFs is viable if regions are already defined, either as regions-of-interest or as segmentation results.

Local TFs for Detail-and-context Views The presentation of an overview combined with the presentation of details on demand is one of the general principles for effective interactive visualization [Shneiderman and Bederson, 2003]. This principle also applies to the exploration of medical volume data. A powerful exploration facility is to let the user navigate through the volume to define a region to be displayed enlarged in a separate detail view. Such views can be enhanced by local TFs, which are fine-tuned to the anatomical structures which are investigated in them. Rezk-Salama *et al.* [2000b] defined reference function TFs for both an overview as well as a detail view (see Fig. 9.26, where an overview of vascular structures and a

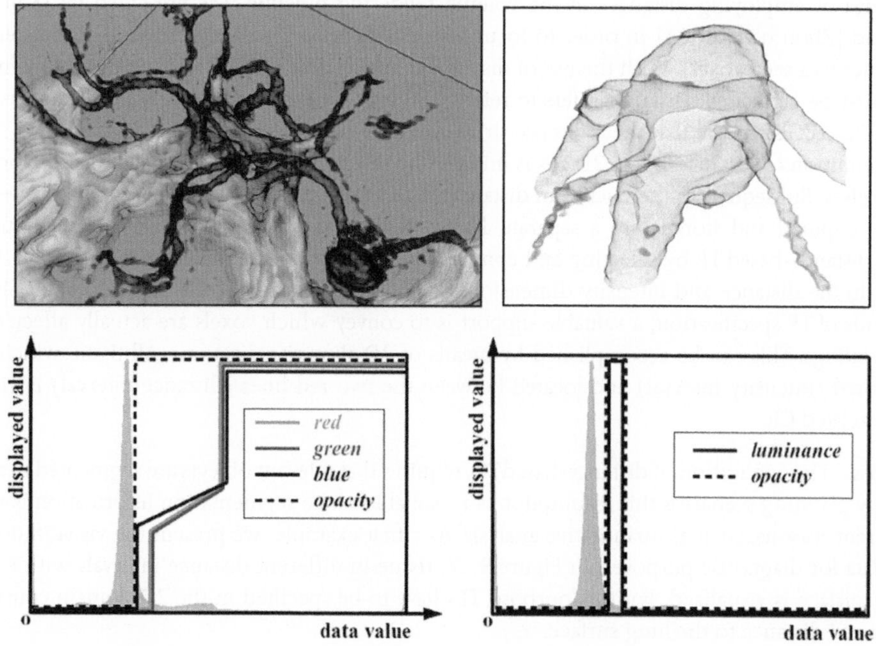

FIGURE 9.26 *Different templates of TFs are used for an overview (left) and detailed analysis (right) of vascular structures. Top row: visualizations of cerebral vessels, bottom row: related transfer functions (From: [Rezk-Salama et al., 2000b]).*

detailed analysis of potential cerebral aneurysms is facilitated). The adjustment of reference TFs (recall § 9.2.2.3) is efficient for this kind of exploration.

Compared to a surface visualization, direct volume rendering restricted to a lung lobe contains more information, in particular with respect to smaller vessels which are usually segmented incompletely.

Realization of Local Transfer Functions Efficient direct volume rendering by means of local TFs is demanding. High performance requires to use hardware-supported lookup tables which either restricts the number of local TFs or the size of an individual local TF.

With local TFs also the rendering process has to be modified. A conceptually simple, yet not efficient variant is to apply a multi-pass rendering, where one region is rendered by means of different lookup table in each rendering pass. As long as two TFs are used, for example a focal region and a peripheral region, the stencil buffer of the graphics hardware may be employed.

9.5.1 DISTANCE-BASED TRANSFER FUNCTIONS

In this subsection, we discuss a special class of multidimensional TFs, where *distance* is employed as a second dimension (in addition to the image intensity). Distance-based transfer functions are another concept to provide *local* control. Distance-based TFs are motivated by the fact that the interest of the user is often determined by the distance to reference surfaces, such as margins around a tumor or regions close to an organ's boundary. With distance-based TFs, it is possible to deliberately show voxels within a certain margin to the (curved) organ surface. If this distance is continuously changed, the user may inspect an organ by slicing orthogonal to the organ surface, which may be effective, for example, in the search for lung nodules in CT thorax data.

The idea of employing distances in the volume rendering pipeline was presented by [Kanda *et al.*, 2002] and [Zhou *et al.*, 2004] in order to focus visualizations on a particular region (characterized by the distance to a seed voxel). With the use of distance in the TF domain, the local control of the mapping process may be facilitated. Distance refers to reference surfaces of anatomical structures, such as organs. Distance-based TFs require that the reference structures have been segmented in advance.

The definition of distance-based 2D TFs is initiated by selecting an object to which the distance specification refers. Subsequently, the Euclidean distance of all voxels to the boundaries of the selected object will be computed and stored into a separate *distance volume.*[2] Based on this information, the user may define a distance-based TF by selecting and composing 2D component functions (recall Fig. 9.14). The intervals in the distance and intensity dimension are chosen by means of the 2D histogram. Similar to other kinds of TF specification, a valuable support is to convey which voxels are actually affected by the current settings. This can be accomplished by means of 2D slice visualizations. All tissue which is light blue colored (intensity interval) and located between the two red lines (distance interval) is visualized with the related CF.

Applications The application of distance-based TFs requires that relevant objects are segmented in advance. In therapy planning scenarios this assumption is reasonable, since segmentation information is required for different reasons, such as quantitative analysis. As a first example, we present the visualization of CT thorax data for diagnostic purposes. In Figure 9.27, tissue in different distance intervals with respect to the lung surface is visualized. For this purpose, TFs have to be specified in the 2D domain consisting of intensity and distance to the lung surface.

---

2 Efficient approximate approaches for the distance computation are described in [Lohmann 1998].

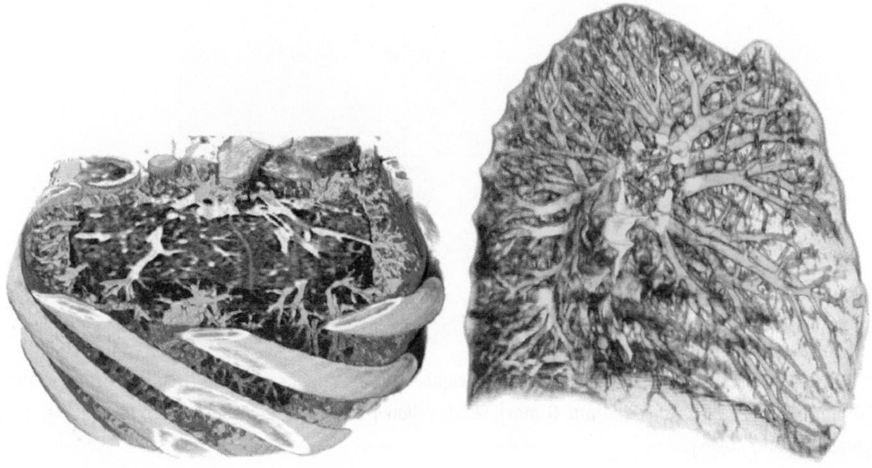

FIGURE 9.27 **Left:** *Overview visualization of CT thorax data with four distance intervals to show bones, lung surface, lung vessels, and lung opaque.* **Right:** *3D visualization of a lung lobe and the vessels inside the lung. The distance-based TF was adjusted such that the surface of the lung lobe and the vascular structures inside are visualized (From: [Tappenbeck et al., 2006]).*

There are four distance-intensity intervals defined to assign color and opacity values unequally. To visualize bones, a distance interval of [–40 mm, 0 mm] and an intensity interval of [100 HU, 1450 HU] is employed. In these intervals, a linear interpolation between black and white in the intensity dimension and a linearly increasing opacity from 0 to 1 in the distance dimension are applied (distance values outside of target structures are negative). For the visualization of lung surface, lung vessels, and opaque lung tissue, three distance-intensity intervals are defined.

Thus, it is possible to visualize opaque tissue in one distance interval, and lung surface, lung vessels, or transparent lung tissue in another. In this example, component functions are used, which have a constant behavior in the distance dimension. It is also possible to define distance-dependent color and opacity mappings.

In Figure 9.27 (right), we show one lobe of the lung and the internal vessels are visualized. The TF for the lung lobe is specified such that two distance intervals are rendered: the surface [0 mm, 2 mm] and the inner vessels [2 mm, 160 mm]. For both intervals, different opacity and color properties are used. Thus, a special tissue can be visualized in a different manner by exploiting distance.

Tumor Surgery Planning In surgery planning, the distance from (malignant) tumors to vascular structures is crucial. A valuable support can be provided with distance-based TFs with the tumor as segmentation target structure and with colors employed to convey the distance of vascular branches. Such visualizations provide an overview to vascular branches in certain safety margins around a tumor (see Fig. 9.28). It is also possible to completely suppress structures beyond a certain distance of a tumor. These visualizations convey more information than a single distance measure.

Discussion Distance-based volume rendering is closely related to focus-and-context rendering [Bruckner et al., 2005]. Indeed, distance-based TF specification provides additional facilities for focus-and-context rendering. The major difference is that the visualization properties are adapted to specific distances. This

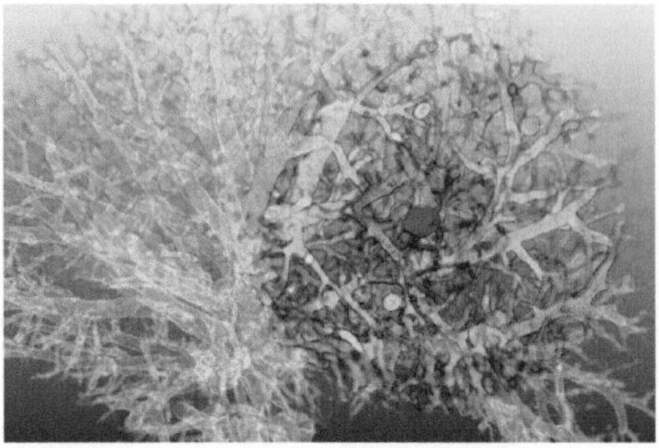

FIGURE 9.28 *Distance-dependent coloring of vessels in the neighborhood of a tumor inside the liver. Four distance intervals are used: tumor red* [0 mm, 3 mm], *vessels red* [−15 mm, 0 mm], *vessels yellow* [−30 mm, −15 mm], *vessels green* [−45 mm, −30 mm] (From: [*Tappenbeck et al.*, 2006]).

is crucial for clinically relevant tasks, such as tumor surgery and radiation treatment planning, where acceptable safety margins are based on established guidelines. The idea of *distance weighting* may be extended in several ways. Kerwin *et al.* [2010] generate additional effects, e.g., lighting effects based on distance, leading to a spot light effect for the target structure. Moreover, they introduce *weighted distances*, that is distance values incorporating relations between distances and intensity values. Weighted distances as such were used, e.g., for graph-based segmentation, where the weightings represent specific costs associated with the path from one voxel to another (recall § 4.4). This concept leads to substantial degrees of freedom also for transfer function design. However, this flexibility comes at the price of increased effort to adjust such distance metrics.

9.5.2 LOCAL TRANSFER FUNCTIONS

In the following, we describe a data-driven approach, e.g., a strategy to assist the design of local transfer functions by means of a local histogram analysis. These local data-driven strategy is motivated minor features, which might be essential, are not visible in the global histogram.

The local TF scheme introduced by Lundstrom *et al.* [2006] is motivated by the observation that boundary emphasis is not sufficient for a number of important medical diagnosis tasks. As an example, volume rendering of vascular structures should reliably display the morphology and enable precise measures of the local diameter. Lundstrom *et al.* [2006] suggest to incorporate probabilistic tissue classification with a Gaussian mixture model (recall § 4.3.3.2) and locally analyze histograms in small neighborhoods. These neighborhoods are designed to be non-overlapping and volume filling. As an example, cuboid neighborhoods may be employed. Each block should be small enough so that an interesting feature likely dominates the local histogram. Lundstrom *et al.* [2006] suggest $8 \times 8 \times 8$-sized voxels. The histogram analysis is focused on a certain range of intensity values, i.e., only blocks are considered where at least a certain percentage of the individual voxels exhibit values in that range. Therefore, this process is called *partial range histogram* analysis.

The local transfer function assignment can be performed in a fully automatic manner without the user having to specify such interval ranges. For this purpose the following procedure is employed [Lundstrom *et al.*, 2006]:

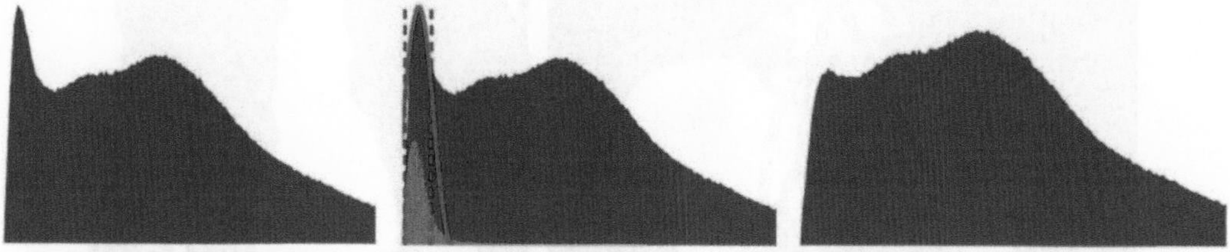

FIGURE 9.29 *The highest peak in the global histogram (left image) is detected. A partial range histogram is computed for all blocks that are dominated by intensity values close to that peak (middle) image. These voxels are removed from the histogram and the next highest peak is determined (From: [Lundstrom et al., 2006]).*

1 The highest peak in the global histogram is selected.
2 A partial range histogram for the middle part of that peak is computed and then removed from the main histogram.
3 The first two steps are repeated until the whole histogram is analyzed.
4 As a final step, similar partial range histograms are merged.

The process is illustrated in Figure 9.29. With these partial range histograms, it is also possible to selectively emphasize structures of a certain size—thus similar effects like those with size-based transfer functions, (recall § 9.3.4) may be achieved.

Each partial range histogram is modeled by a Gaussian. The partial range represents the interval $[\mu - \alpha, \mu + \alpha]$. Merging is applied to histograms having peaks very close to each other and similar width. The process runs smoothly for tissues where the intensity is the same across the whole volume dataset. However, for MRI data or CT data with inhomogeneous contrast agent distribution, this is not the case. In such situations, these inhomogeneities should be corrected (recall § 4.2.5). The partial range histograms are employed as a basis for tissue classification. With this method, promising results were achieved. As a validation, the classification was compared with manual segmentation and although the volume overlap was very low, the peak intensity of tissue types was close to the chosen gold standard. Thus, this technique was one of only a few successful attempts to efficiently assign transfer functions to MRI data. In Figure 9.30 a few application examples are presented. A clinical evaluation of this work describing the value in diagnosis was performed by Persson *et al.* [2006].

9.6 ADVANCED PICKING

Picking refers to direct-manipulative selection by pointing (recall § 5.6.1). Picking in volume data is essential, e.g., to highlight the selected structure, or to adjust an associated slice view, or to place a label for documentation related to the selected point [Kohlmann *et al.*, 2009]. Kohlmann *et al.* [2008], for example, illustrate the usefulness of adapting 2D slice views to the position selected in 3D space.

In 3D data visualizations, picking with a 2D pointing device is ambiguous since many voxels are projected to the selected position in screen space. In volume-rendered images, typically many voxels are assigned to semitransparent appearance based on the transfer function. Thus, the basic strategy to assign a selected point to the first opaque voxel is not appropriate in most cases. A simple alternative is to employ a *opacity threshold*, that is the first voxel along the ray that exceeds this threshold is selected. Obviously, it is not straight-forward to devise an appropriate threshold, neither for an algorithm, nor for the user.

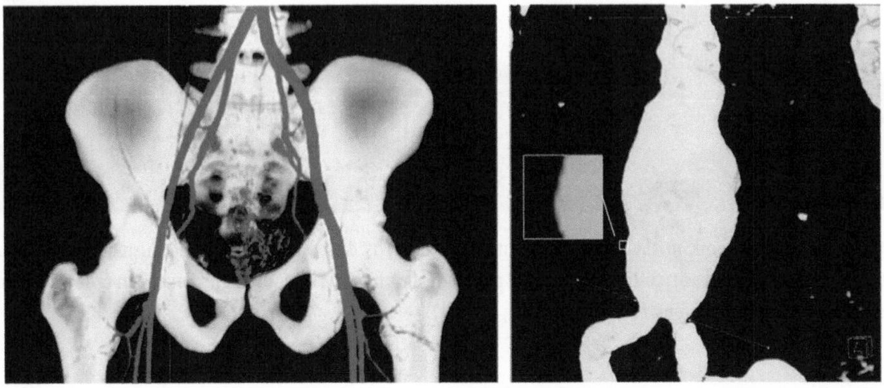

FIGURE 9.30 **Left:** *A clear separation from vessels and spongy bones from CT data was achieved with automatically determined local transfer functions.* **Right:** *An abdominal aortic aneurysm could be displayed with an automatically generated transfer function such that the diameter measurement (compared with manual segmentation) is very accurate (From: [Lundstrom et al., 2006]).*

As Wiebel *et al.* [2012] recently demonstrated the whole concept of an opacity threshold for picking is questionable. The user probably wants to select the most visible structure at a particular screen space position. This structure may be visible, not because of a single voxel with high opacity, but instead of a sequence of voxels with a certain accumulated opacity. In the following, we describe two advanced picking techniques:

- contextual picking, where metadata is employed to select the intended world-space position, and
- visibility-oriented picking.

9.6.1 CONTEXTUAL PICKING

The basic idea of Kohlmann *et al.* [2009] is to employ the meta data associated with medical image data to narrow down the choice of a selected point to enhance picking. DICOM data (recall § 3.4) indicate the type of examination (*study description*) and the related anatomical region (*body part examined*). As an example, in an angiography, the user is likely interested in reins or arteries, where as some diagnostic decisions in orthopedic require to closely examine skeletal structures.

To employ this information for picking is not entirely straightforward. Kohlmann *et al.* [2009] create a knowledge base of ray profiles for the different tissue types. Thus, they aim to exploit patterns that occur in the intensity profiles of rays that select, e.g., vascular structures and bones. Obviously, such viewing rays differ significantly even for the same type of structure, but indeed some patterns are rather stable. In CT data, the Hounsfield values may be exploited and the thickness of some anatomical structures is rather similar. Based on these observations, they analyzed many viewing rays for each of the typical structures and compute for each of them a *mean ray profile*. The major attributes of these profiles are intensity values and gradient magnitude. With this information, they enhance picking by computing the similarity of the particular selection ray profile to these predefined profiles, taking into account also the purpose of this examination to finally disambiguate picking (see Fig. 9.31). Figure 9.32 presents and example for ray profiles and the derived mean ray profile. Obviously, this techniques is somehow limited to the predefined profiles, although an interface is described to extend the knowledge base.

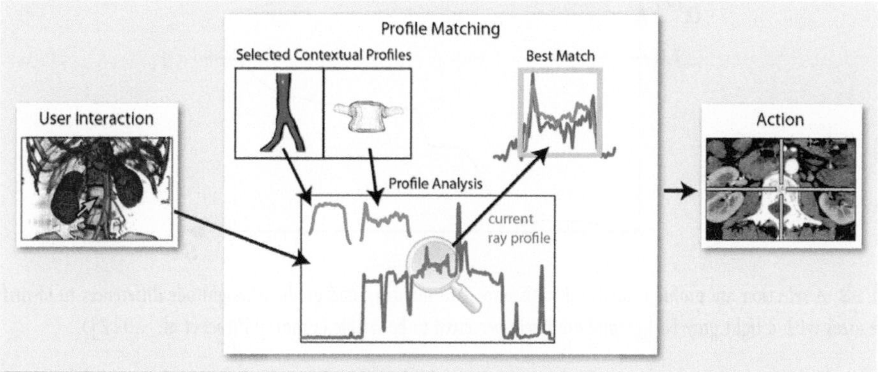

FIGURE 9.31 *The contextual picking approach integrates the current user input (selection in volume-rendered data in screen space) and a knowledge base with predefined ray profiles. The current selection ray profile is analyzed stepwise to determine an optimal fit. As a consequence, the selected point in 3D space is derived and used to trigger a subsequent action. In this case, the crosshair cursor in a 2D slice view indicates the corresponding position in 2D. Note that this also involves to select the "right" slice (From: [Kohlmann et al., 2009]).*

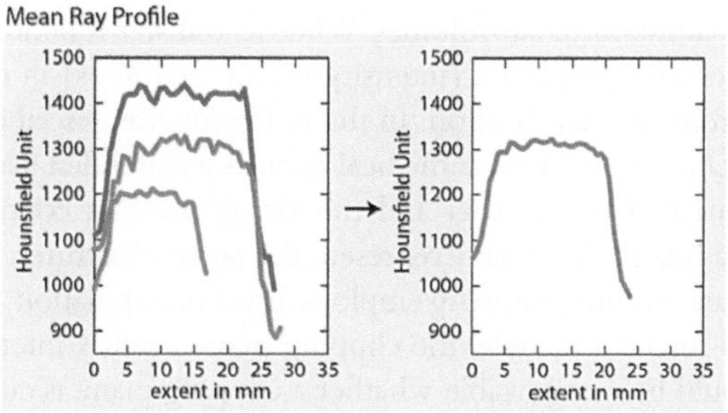

FIGURE 9.32 *The left view contains three selection ray profiles for an Aorta. The right view shows the derived mean ray profile that is used for matching new picking actions (From: [Kohlmann et al., 2009]).*

9.6.2 VISIBILITY-BASED PICKING

The recently introduced visibility-based picking technique is more broadly applicable and does not require any meta knowledge, e.g., from DICOM data [Wiebel et al., 2012]. Instead, it is based on perceptual observations and aimed at selecting just the structure that the user would probably consider as the visible structure at that position in screen space. The selection ray is analyzed with respect to the intensity profile, the profile of gradient magnitude and the second derivative in the gradient direction. With this analysis, visible borders are derived (see Fig. 9.33) and the most likely point in world space is determined. The authors refer to their method as "WYSIWYP: What You See Is What You Pick". The feasibility of the approach was verified in a substantial user study with a 20 test persons and 36 test images. The users had the task to move a cross-sectional plane in the 3D rendering to indicate the z-coordinate of the position, they perceive as target of their selections. The major test of accuracy was a comparison between the points, the users wanted to select and the actually selected points. For this comparison, the mean and standard deviation of the 20 test persons was computed for all the 36 test images. In 32 out of 36 images, the

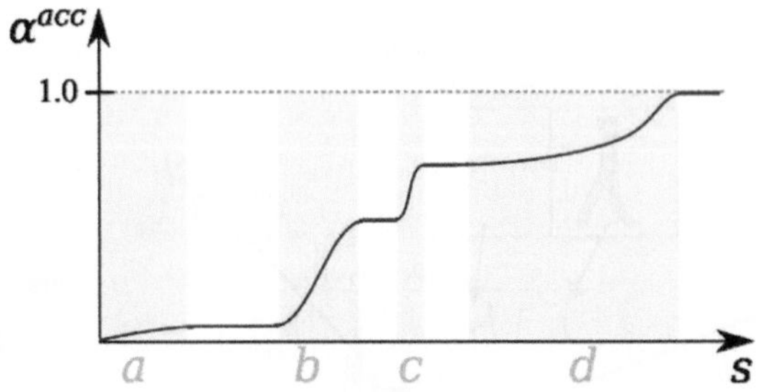

FIGURE 9.33 *A selection ray profile is analyzed with respect to intensity and gradient magnitude differences to identify visibility borders. The areas with a light gray background are likely perceived to be visible (From: [Wiebel et al., 2012]).*

difference between the computed and intended position was smaller than the standard deviation between different test persons indicating a very good accuracy in the large majority of the cases.

9.7 CLIPPING

Clipping is a fundamental interaction technique to explore medical volume data [Hoehne *et al.*, 1987]. It is used to restrict the visualization to subvolumes. Whereas transfer functions restrict the visualization to those parts which have certain properties (intensity values, gradients) in common, clipping exclude certain geometric shapes from the visualization. In the following we describe interaction techniques to specify and to modify the clip geometry with medical doctors as intended users.

Clipping planes are translated by the user and the visualization is continuously updated. Usually, clipping planes may also be tilted to optimally represent the target structures. Rapid feedback is essential for the exploration of the data. Intuitive clipping employs direct manipulation, for translating and rotating a clipping plane. With this interaction style, the clipping plane itself is interactive—representing a 3D widget. For the user, it should be recognizable whether a clipping plane is currently selected and active. Handles (small iconic arrows) might be displayed to control the translation.

Integration of Clipping Planes with Direct Volume Rendering and Surface Rendering In combination with volume rendering, clipping is conceptually easy to accomplish. In the final stage of volume rendering a voxel is tested as to its spatial relation to the clipping planes. Voxels affected by the clipping plane are discarded completely. Unless the resolution of the underlying volume data is coarse, there is no need to calculate subvoxel representations of the clipping plane. Subvoxel accuracy, however, is desirable in case of illuminated volume rendering to faithfully represent the gradient information. If the clipping plane is moved along the viewing direction the 3D visualization is similar to conventional slice-based 2D viewing (the difference is that volume rendering is usually semitransparent).

For surface representations each triangle is tested whether it should be drawn or not. If triangles are larger (covering several pixels in the rendered image) they must be cut, resulting in new vertices. As surface visualizations result in sharp boundaries, the effect of not calculating precise boundaries with cut triangles is more obvious than in volume rendering.

If other than planar clipping is desired, the complexity increases considerably [Lorenson, 1993]. A variety of methods for non-linear clip geometries employs the z-buffer of the graphics hardware. As an example, Lucas *et al.* [1992] enable arbitrary convex clip geometries by means of rendering into two z-buffers, where the additional z-buffer contains the boundaries of the clip volume.

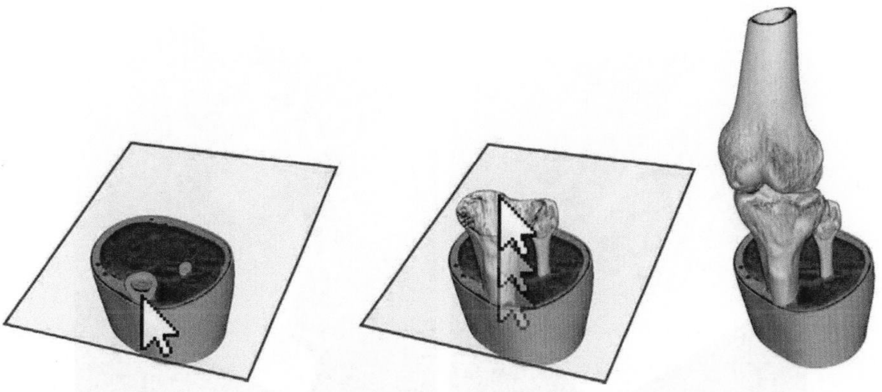

FIGURE 9.34 *Selective clipping. After placing a clipping plane, the user specified which structures should be extruded instead of being clipped (Courtesy of Jose Díaz, Polytechnic university of Catalonia. See also [Díaz et al., 2012]).*

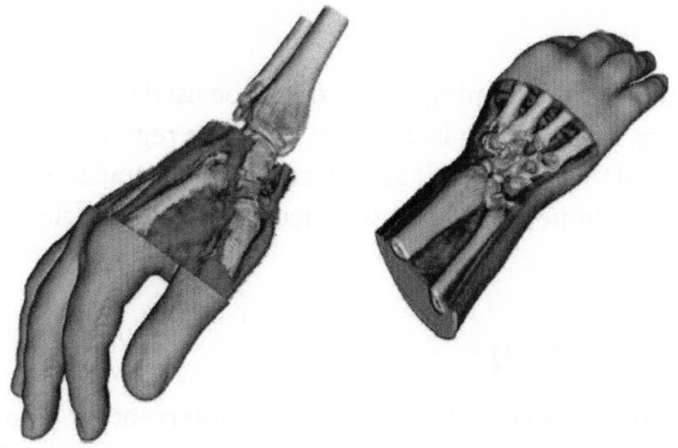

FIGURE 9.35 *Examples for selective clipping using a hand dataset.* **Left:** *One selective clipping plane is placed in the dataset.* **Right:** *With a second clipping plane, the position of the bones can be shown more clearly (Courtesy of Jose Díaz, Polytechnic university of Catalonia. See also [Díaz et al., 2012]).*

Selective Clipping A variant of clipping, primarily used if segmented structures are available, is selective clipping, where clipping is only performed when certain conditions are fulfilled. Selective clipping was introduced almost simultaneously in [Lorenson, 1993] and in [Tiede et al., 1993] and is widely used to emphasize structures (those which are not affected by clipping) while presenting contextual information (structures which are partially visible due to clipping). The interaction to create such visualizations is illustrated in Figure 9.34. In Figure 9.35, two examples are shown.

Selective clipping is also useful for surgery planning. For visualizations of the head region the symmetry might be employed by placing a selective clipping plane as (vertical) symmetry axis. Selective clipping may also be applied in combination with arbitrary clip geometries (see § 9.8).

Selective clipping is also feasible without segmentation information. Here, different transfer functions might be applied for regions affected by the clipping plane and the remaining volume. Another common application of selective clipping is *thin slab volume rendering*, where two synchronized parallel clipping planes specify a set of volume slices which are rendered.

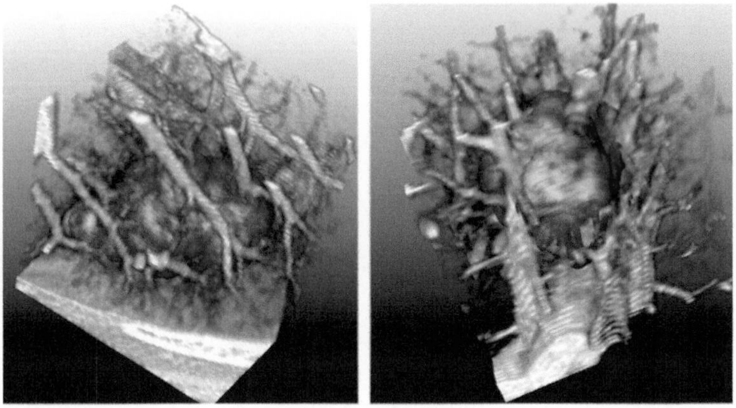

FIGURE 9.36 *Local volume rendering for the evaluation of the surrounding of a lung tumor in CT thorax data. The tumor is visualized as isosurface, whereas the vascular structures around are rendered as direct volume rendering (Courtesy of Volker Dicken, Fraunhofer MEVIS).*

Box Clipping The combination of six clipping planes might be used to define a subvolume. This variant is often referred to as *box clipping*. Box clipping is useful to explore a region in detail, for example, the region around a tumor (Fig. 9.36). 3D widgets, such as a HandleBox Manipulator, might be used to define and modify the clip box. The subvolume might be presented as a single isolated view or combined with an overview.

9.8 VIRTUAL RESECTION

Resection refers to the removal of tissue during a surgical intervention. The planning process of such an intervention using medical volume data is referred to as *virtual resection*. Virtual resection is a core function of many intervention planning systems. In difficult cases, the exploration of resection strategies directly supports the questions whether or not the resection is feasible at all and how it can be optimally performed. A virtual resection can be used for a quantitative analysis with respect to the volume of the intended resection or the percentage of an organ which that has to be removed.

Technically, a user must be able to specify an arbitrarily-shaped 3D clip geometry as resection volume and the clip geometry should be rendered quickly and accurately. Modern APIs, such as OpenGL, however, only support clip geometries composed of clipping planes.

Virtual resection functions have to fulfill several requirements:

1. The user must be able to specify a virtual resection intuitively and precisely.
2. Modification must be supported in order to change virtual resections either to correct them or to explore other variations.
3. Virtual resections should be visualized immediately with high quality.

According to the first requirement medical doctors should be able to decide in detail which anatomical structures will be removed. For example, the question whether or not a certain vascular structure will be cut is often essential, because a complex vascular reconstruction may be required. The modification of a virtual resection is crucial in order to support a flexible exploration of the resection strategies. It is essential that virtual resections might be modified on different scales. The last requirement refers to the update and rendering mechanism which is used to show the effect of a virtual resection. This aspect has to be considered since medical volume data is typically large and the update should take place with interactive frame rates.

There are several possibilities how a virtual resection might be specified. Some methods are restricted in the shape of resections which can be produced. For example, the extrusion of shapes, such as prisms, along a path cannot serve as general approach to define arbitrarily shaped resection volumes. On radiological workstations, such techniques are primarily provided to explore data and to ensure an unoccluded view to relevant anatomical structures.

In the following, we focus on real-time interaction techniques which can produce any desired shape of the clip geometry. We briefly describe two straightforward approaches to virtual resection in the following subsections. In § 9.8.2, we introduce an approach inspired by surgical procedures.

9.8.1 VIRTUAL RESECTIONS BY DRAWING ON SLICES

Another approach to virtual resection is inspired by the communication between surgeons and radiologists discussing a resection; some slices of the CT or MRI data are copied to paper and the resection is marked by drawing on the slices with a pen or mouse. By drawing on slices, a resection can be specified as precisely as desired. However, this process is time-consuming, if the entire resection volume should be specified, since often some 50 to 100 slices are involved. This kind of virtual resection is similar to segmentation with edge-based methods and can also be enhanced with interpolation methods. Instead of drawing on *all* slices, the user might skip many slices on which the contour is computed by shape-based interpolation. While the interaction with this approach is restricted to 2D, the 3D visualization is used to evaluate the result and to discuss the shape of resections (see Fig. 9.37).

9.8.2 VIRTUAL RESECTION WITH A DEFORMABLE CUTTING PLANE

In the following, we describe a more sophisticated approach to virtual resection to support the clinical resection planning. It is based on a surface representation of an organ, usually achieved with explicit segmentation of that organ. The user draws lines on the (3D) surface of an organ to initialize the virtual

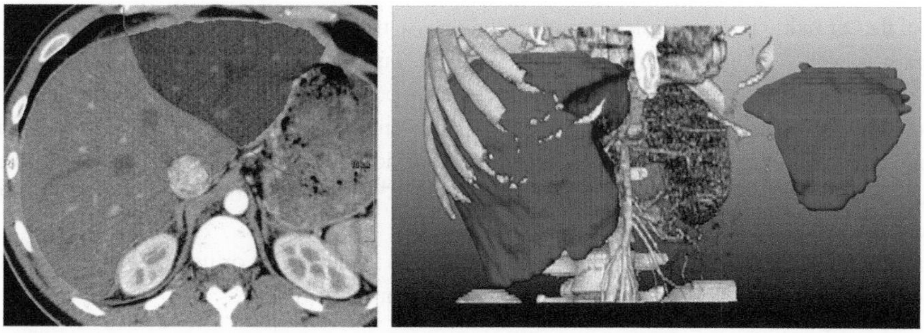

FIGURE 9.37 *Virtual liver resection by drawing on the slices. Using the liver segmentation mask, only one line per slice has to be drawn cross over the organ. In the 2D view (left image) the contour has been specified on selected slices. After the interpolation, the result is displayed in the 3D view. The virtually resected and the remaining portion of the liver are separated to support the evaluation of the shape of virtual resections (Courtesy of Andrea Schenk, Fraunhofer MEVIS Bremen).*

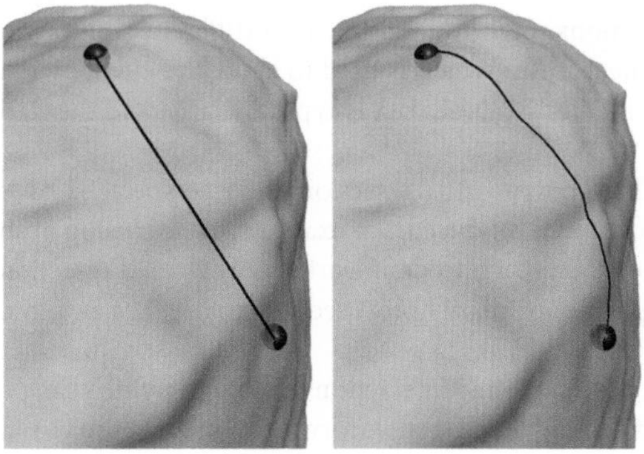

FIGURE 9.38 Euclidean (left) versus geodesic distance (right) between surface points.

resection. From these lines, which characterize the boundary of the cutting plane, a mesh is generated that represents the initial cutting plane. The plane is deformed locally to fit the lines drawn by the user.[3] This cutting plane can be interactively modified to refine the virtual resection. The method described in the following is based on [Konrad-Verse *et al.*, 2004].

9.8.2.1 Defining Cutting Plane Boundaries

The idea to specify a cutting plane based on drawing actions dates back to [Yasuda *et al.*, 1990] and was refined by Delingette *et al.* [1994]. With this approach, the user employs a 2D pointing device and controls the movement of a cursor on a 3D surface. This control is accomplished by casting a ray from the viewpoint through the 2D point (marked by a pointing device) to the 3D position on the surface. The mapping considers the current projection parameters and the z-buffer in order to select the first visible surface along the projection ray [Zachow *et al.*, 2003]. The mouse motion is sampled and represented as a sequence of 3D coordinates. Note that the coordinates are not restricted to coincide with the vertices of the mesh.

Definition of the Cut Path If the sampled points of the mouse movement are sufficiently close to each other, the cut path is well defined and the individual connections between points do not matter. Otherwise, different strategies of connecting points on the surface are possible. The Euclidean distance represents the shortest distance between successive points. However, the straight line between these points may intersect the organ's surface. A better choice is to employ the geodesic shortest path which connects points on the 3D surface with a path on that surface (see Fig. 9.38 left).[4] These and other issues of mesh cutting are discussed by Bruyns *et al.* [2002].

The drawing process can be carried out using a mouse as input device or using a pen which is directly pointed on the screen or a digitizing tablet. The latter is more intuitive.

---

3 In contrast to clipping planes which are actually flat, cutting planes after deformation are two-manifolds but not planar.

4 A geodesic is a generalization of the notion of a "straight line" to "curved spaces." The definition of geodesic depends on the type of "curved space." If the space carries a natural metric, then geodesics are defined to be (locally) the shortest path between points on the space. The term "geodesic" comes from geodesy, the science of measuring the size and shape of the earth. In the original sense, a geodesic was the shortest route between two points on the surface of the earth. (Source: Wikipedia)

9.8.2.2 Generation of the Initial Cutting Plane

The following algorithm describes how lines drawn by the user on a surface are converted into an initial cutting plane. The lines are transformed into a pointset (representing each pixel of the digitized mouse movement).

1 *Determine the oriented bounding box of the lines drawn by the user.* The oriented bounding box is computed by a principal component analysis (PCA) of the pointset P forming the lines. The center of gravity is subtracted from all points p_i resulting in a new pointset P^{norm}. Based on this pointset, the covariance matrix A is determined. The eigenvectors of A define a local right-angled coordinate system of the pointset. The normalized eigenvectors are composed to a transformation matrix M_{rot} that describes the mapping from P into a local coordinate system with respect to the cutting plane.

2 *Determine the orientation and extent of the cutting plane.* The vectors (e_1, e_2) corresponding to the two largest eigenvalues (λ_1, λ_2) resulting from the PCA of A define the cutting plane's orientation. The plane is determined by the following equation, where x represents any vector which satisfies Equation 9.6.

$$E : (x - v) \cdot e_0 = 0 \tag{9.6}$$

where $\cdot$ denotes the dot product (see Fig. 9.39 for a sketch). This strategy is useful for organs where the extent is strongly different in the three directions. In case of an almost spherical object the eigenvalues are very similar and the orientation of the initial plane might be unexpected.

3 The center of the cutting plane (E) is chosen to be v, the center of gravity of P. This plane is then divided into a regular grid with quadrilateral cells. The resolution of the mesh is chosen such that the requirements of surgeons to specify typical resection shapes can be satisfied. The default size of

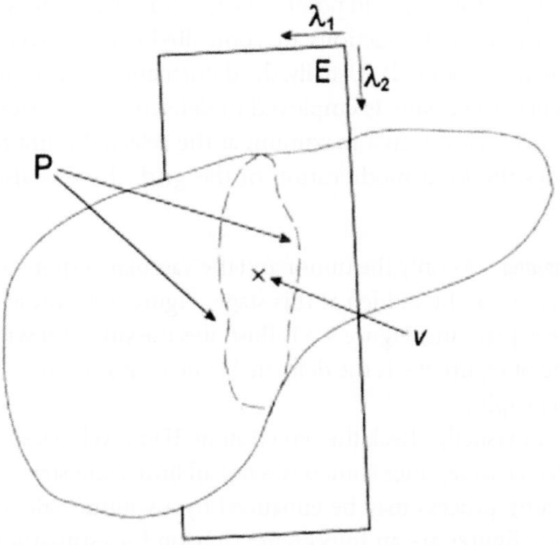

FIGURE 9.39 Definition of the plane E based on the (dashed) lines P drawn by the user. v represents the center of gravity of P and λ_1 and λ_2 point in the directions of the two largest eigenvectors of E (Courtesy of Arne Littmann and Olaf Konrad Verse, Fraunhofer MEVIS).

the mesh is determined by (λ_1, λ_2); the extent of the mesh is twice as long in the direction of the corresponding eigenvectors.

4 *Project Y into E.*

$$y_i^P = \begin{pmatrix} 1 & 1 & 0 \end{pmatrix} \cdot y_i \tag{9.7}$$

5 *Calculate displacements.* The mesh is displaced in the e_0 direction to fit the original pointset. This is accomplished by scanning all grid cells $y_{m,n}$ and testing whether any point of the transformed points y_i is projected in this cell. The displacement $d_{m,n}$ is computed as the maximum z-component of all y_i which are projected into $y_{m,n}$.

$$d_{m,n} = \|z_i\|_{\max} * \operatorname{sgn}(z_i) \tag{9.8}$$

where z_i represents the z-component related to y_i and "sgn" represents the signum function.

$$z^0_{m,n} = y_{m,n} + d_{m,n} \cdot e_0 \tag{9.9}$$

As an alternative, $d_{m,n}$ could be set to the average distance of the relevant points. The maximum, however, seems better suited because strong bulges specified by the user are better represented.

6 *Smoothing.* After these distances have been calculated for the whole mesh they are processed by Laplacian smoothing (recall § 6.5.2).

The resulting mesh is rendered and appears smooth due to the applied Gouraud shading. The user can switch between two 3D visualization modes; one showing the complete scene, while the other one is focused on the structures of interest, namely the tumor, the vessels, and the deformable cutting plane.

9.8.2.3 Modification of Virtual Resections

The resection can be refined by translating grid points. The user can define the sphere of influence as well as the amplitude of the deformation. Both functions are controlled with a direct-manipulative style (mouse movements at the point which is modified). Usually, the deformation direction is orthogonal to the plane. Within the sphere of influence, the cosine is employed to determine the extent of the displacement (the extent of the displacement decreases from a maximum at the selected point to zero at the border of the sphere of influence). Besides the local modification of the grid, there is also a facility to translate the whole mesh.

Application in Liver Surgery Planning As only the tumor and the vascular systems are essential for the decision where to cut, the organ surface can be hidden at this stage. Figure 9.40 presents an example of an initial plane defined for liver surgery planning. Figure 9.41 illustrates the situation when the user starts to modify the plane. In the right image of Figure 9.41, the deformable plane is modified (the modification is slightly exaggerated to show the principle).

Of course, the surgeon can visually check the resection in 2D as well. Despite the intuitive clearness of 3D visualization, this is indispensable, since sometimes not all important structures can be segmented with reasonable effort. The planning process may be enhanced by a volume calculation of both the resection and the remaining part. Such figures are an important criterion for estimating the operation risk.

Transformation of the Resection Boundary to a Resection Plane There are viable alternatives to the transformation described above, where a planar projection of the boundary is deformed to represent the points specified by a user. *Minimal surfaces* are another well-defined representation of a surface specified by a given boundary.

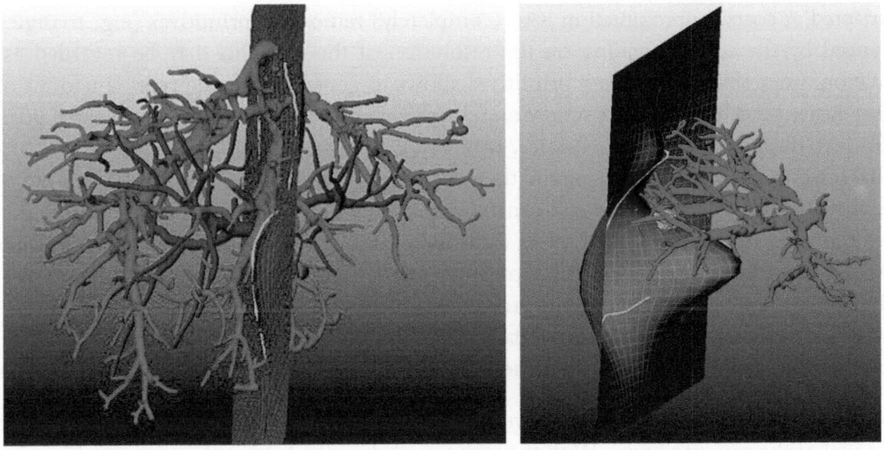

FIGURE 9.40 *Based on the two lines drawn on the object surface, an initial resection has been specified which might be refined by the user (Courtesy of Arne Littmann, Fraunhofer MEVIS).*

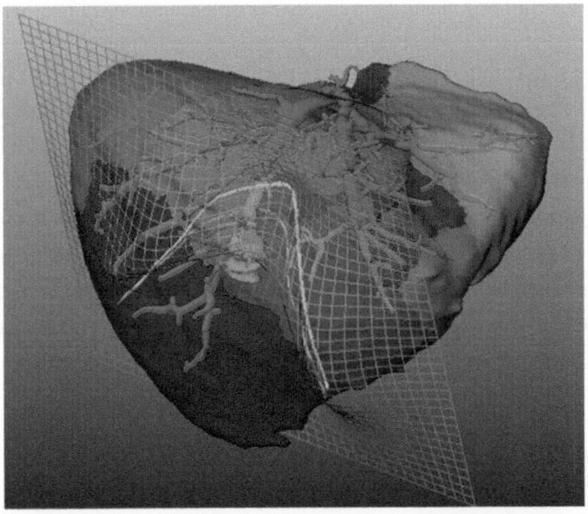

FIGURE 9.41 *Left: As soon as the cutting plane is initialized, the surrounding organ is removed in order to support fine-tuning of the plane with respect to blood vessels. Right: The initial cutting plane is translated with an adjustable sphere of influence (Courtesy of Milo Hindennach, Fraunhofer MEVIS).*

Minimal surfaces are constructed such that they exactly match the given boundary. The vertices of the inner parts of the surface are determined in an optimization process which generates a surface with the minimum surface area. Minimal surfaces are also characterized by a low mean curvature, which is a nice property since surgeons also prefer (near) planar surfaces. Computational methods to generate minimal surfaces are given in [Pinkall and Polthier, 1993].

Visualization Once the resection plane is specified, the organ should be visualized with the defined cutting region removed. There are many variants how this can be accomplished. At the surface level, the mesh may be adapted. A coarse approximation is to (completely) remove all primitives (e.g., triangles) which are influenced by the cut. Depending on the resolution of the grid this may be regarded as a crude approximation. Remeshing intersected primitives allows to generate accurate representations of the cut surface (see Bruyns *et al.* [2002] for a survey on remeshing after mesh cutting). An essential goal of these algorithms is to limit the introduction of new primitives. To generate a closed surface model of an organ after virtual resection, the resection plane and the remaining surface model of an organ must be combined.

If the virtual resection is complete, it can be displayed in different ways. The realistic approach—to remove the resection volume entirely—is *one* possibility. The resection volume can be regarded as a new visualization object that can be flexibly parameterized, e.g., rendered semitransparently. It might be specified whether objects are clipped against resection volumes or not (recall *selective clipping* in § 9.7). It is often useful to display also tumors and vascular structures in resection volumes. Again, such adjustments can be specified as default values to enhance the reproducibility and effectiveness of intervention planning.

Application Areas In craniofacial surgery, conventional planning is based on drawing lines on a stereolithographic model of the patient's bones. With the techniques described above the same kind of specification may be applied to plan surgical interventions with 3D models (see Fig. 9.42). Compared to the conventional planning, considerably more flexibility exists and it is possible to evaluate the effects of different strategies [Zachow *et al.*, 2003].

9.8.2.4 Evaluation

To understand how surgeons use deformable cutting planes, an informal evaluation was carried out by Konrad-Verse *et al.* [2004]. The use of the deformable cutting plane was regarded as promising, which is probably due to the fact that an aspect of real surgical procedures (marking resection lines on organ surfaces) is simulated with this approach.

Some comments of surgeons reveal desirable refinements. For example, the distance from the resection plane to a tumor should be continuously displayed to indicate the safety margin associated with the virtual resection. In this vein, a useful option would be to prevent that the plane is moved too close to the tumor (a "no go" zone around the tumor). Another desirable function is to render the deformable cutting plane semitransparently.

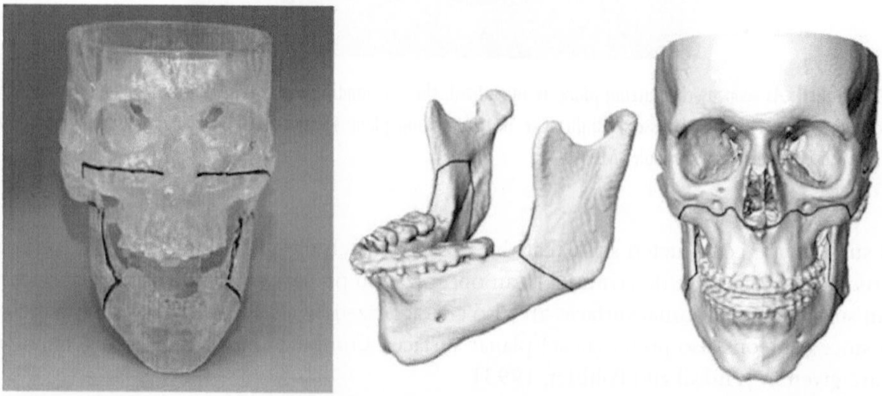

FIGURE 9.42 *Conventional osteotomy planning based on a stereolithographic model (left). Virtual resection based on a 3D model of the patient's bones (middle, right) (Courtesy of Stefan Zachow, Zuse Institute Berlin).*

Usually, the initial viewing direction when the user starts drawing on the organ's surface is not appropriate to draw the line on the entire organ. Currently, this process must be interrupted to rotate the virtual camera. This process (sequences of drawing, rotating, drawing, ...) can be improved using two-handed input, where one hand (using one input device) is used to control the virtual camera, and the other is used for the specification of the virtual resection. People are very effective in coordinated movements with both hands (see [Hinckley *et al.*, 1998] for the use of two-handed input in neurosurgery planning).

9.9 CUTTING MEDICAL VOLUME DATA

Cutting facilities are important for surgery simulation. With such functions users move a cutting device—often a *virtual scalpel*—through medical volume data and simulate cutting procedures. Collision detection (determine which parts of the geometric model are touched by the cutting device) and tactile feedback are essential for educational purposes where prospective surgeons are trained. The development of surgery simulators is driven by similar reasons than flight simulators used to train pilots. A visually realistic environment and handling should be used to avoid the risks of real-world training with living patients and to reduce the cost involved with training by an expert. In contrast to flight simulators, where the user moves primarily in a static scenery, surgery simulators have to consider many interactions between cutting devices and human tissue, such as elastic deformations and bleedings. We restrict the discussion here to the cutting procedures in surgical simulators where the geometry affected by the cutting is regarded as static (and not as deformable soft tissue). Cutting is related to cutaway views and ghostviews—illustrative rendering techniques that modify visibility. Such techniques are summarized as *smart visibility techniques* and are described in § 12.10.

Mensmann *et al.* [2008] introduced *cutting templates* that may be placed and dragged in a geometric model to remove the geometry cut by them. These templates also support irregular geometries as they are typically used in medical illustration. An essential aspect is that the widgets remain at the surface when they are dragged. Figure 9.43 shows examples of this system.

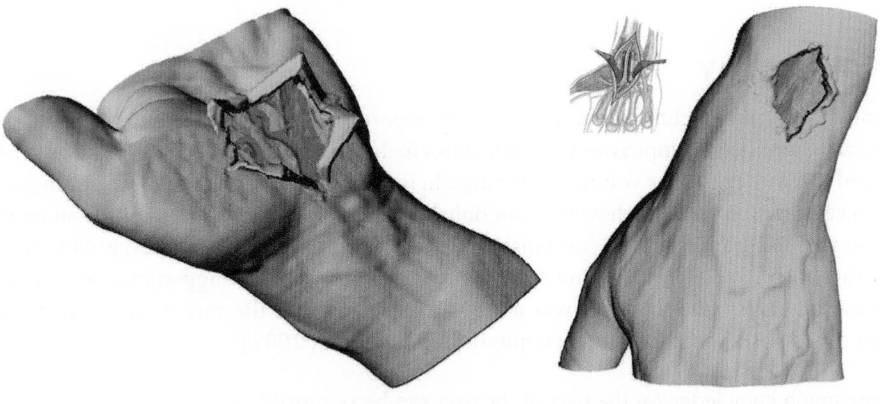

FIGURE 9.43 *Cutting templates are used to create visualizations with a similar expressiveness like surgical illustrations* (From: [Mensmann et al., 2008]).

9.9.1 HIGH-QUALITY REPRESENTATION OF CUT SURFACES

As a first step, surgical tools, such as scalpels, scissors and drilling devices are to be included in the 3D scenario. Also a behavior is associated with the models and facilities to parameterize the geometry. As the tools are moved and operated in the virtual environment, collision detection algorithms are employed to determine whether a cut is performed and which part of the overall model is affected. Surgical cutting is a challenging application for collision detection because the requirements for accuracy and speed are high, and arbitrary (not necessarily convex) shapes are involved.

If virtual resection is accomplished by means of a volume representation, the resolution of the cut surface is limited to the resolution of the underlying data. For the visualization of irregular cut surfaces, which arise after cutting or drilling, this is not appropriate because sharp edges lead to severe "staircase" artifacts. Pflesser *et al.* [2002)] developed a visualization technique which considers the cut surface at subvoxel resolution and estimates surface normals based on gradients. With their method, tools, such as a drilling device, can be moved arbitrarily in 3D space. Once shape, position, and orientation are specified, the cutting is voxelized with a weighted filtering technique. Pflesser *et al.* [2002] emphasize that existing cut surfaces should be preserved (the term *progressive cutting* is used for this feature). Therefore, the portion of an existing cut region that is unaffected by the new cut is determined, resampled, and combined at subvoxel resolution with the new cut.

The method has been applied in a simulator for petrous bone surgery (surgery in the ear region). A virtual scalpel and adjustable drilling devices might be employed to practice surgery. The precise simulation of drilling procedures is motivated by the delicate structures in this area (e.g., the facial nerve).

A 6 DOF-haptic input device, a Phantom® from SensAble Technologies, is used to provide the tactile feedback necessary for surgery training. Appropriate tactile or haptic feedback is difficult to achieve because a high framerate is required (1000 updates per second are required [Avila and Sobierajski, 1996]).

9.9.2 VIRTUAL RESECTION AND SURGERY SIMULATION

There are some differences and some similarities between surgery simulation and virtual resection. Virtual resection techniques are intended for experienced surgeons who actually plan a surgical procedure. Specialized hardware, such as those for tactile feedback, should not be assumed for virtual resection. In general, virtual resection is not focused on the realistic simulation of a procedure but on decision support based on the interaction with the data of a particular patient.

9.10 SUMMARY

We presented interaction techniques and high-level support for TF design, clipping and cutting. Transfer functions can be adjusted to emphasize various features in the data. In particular, multidimensional TFs may be employed to create expressive volume renderings. In routine diagnosis and therapy planning, the potential of such visualization facilities, however, can only be realized if the interaction effort can be restricted.

The most promising approach is a combination of predefined functions, suggestions which are adapted to the histogram of the TF domain and facilities to refine presets and suggestions. Except for special applications, fully automatic solutions will not be able to cope with the variety of medical image data. The design of TFs poses some fundamental questions [Gerig *et al.*, 2002]:

- How much knowledge on the part of the user can be assumed?
- Is it more appropriate to provide guidance in the exploration process without limiting flexibility or is it more appropriate to restrict parameter settings to some predefined subsets?

- Which context information should be presented to support parameter settings?
- Is it more appropriate to rely on subjective evaluations (selection of thumbnail images) or to guide the process by objective measures, such as those resulting from histogram analysis?

There is a considerable similarity between segmentation and TF design. With segmentation, a binary decision is made as to whether a voxel or a part of it belongs to a certain structure. TF specification is used to visualize and highlight structures. However, visibility is not a binary, but a fuzzy decision based on assigning different opacity values. It is therefore justified to call opacity TF specification as a kind of *fuzzy segmentation* [Udupa, 2000]. There is a close relation between segmentation and TF specification with respect to local TFs based on segmentation results.

We extend the discussion of transfer function specification in § 11.7 where we explain how specific tasks in the diagnosis of vascular structures may be solved by combining vessel segmentation, histogram analysis, and transfer function generation. Diagnostic tasks include the emphasis of plaques in coronary arteries and the understanding of spatial relations around vascular pathologies such as aneurysms and arterio-venous malformation.

We also discussed interaction techniques for clipping, cutting, and virtual resection as further facilities to adjust visualizations and restrict the visibility of structures and regions. Clipping and cutting may be combined with transfer function design to explore volume data and generate visualizations that support specific clinical tasks.

Future Work We have not considered new input and output devices, since not much work was carried out in this area. In the future, gesture input, multi-touch devices, such as the medical visualization table [Lundström *et al.*, 2011], and stereo output likely play a crucial role in volume interaction. An interesting area for future work is the integrated visualization of several volume datasets after image registration, for example CT and PET data. Transfer function specification for fused volume data is of course even more challenging than the problems discussed in this chapter. Promising results are presented in [Kniss *et al.*, 2003b]. Schulze and Rice [2004] demonstrated volume rendering with four channel datasets. Recently, Kotava *et al.* [2012] introduced accurate algorithms for multidimensional peak finding to support TF specification on multiple fields. Despite the recent progress, we consider multifield transfer functions more as an area of future work than an area with established methods. Other future areas, relate to time-dependent and vector-valued volume data, e.g., perfusion data or measured blood flow. The basic concepts of computing histograms, analyzing them, and providing semi-automatic support are certainly relevant for these more complex data as well. However, the specific realization will be challenging.

FURTHER READING

Pfister *et al.* [2001] give an enlightening overview of purely interactive, data-driven, and image-driven transfer function specification approaches applied to carefully selected CT and MRI datasets. Tzeng *et al.* [2003] combine machine learning techniques, such as support vector machines, with a painting metaphor to allow more sophisticated classification. Similar to the reference TF, the TF derived for one dataset can be adapted to another (similar) dataset. For colored volume renderings, color maps have to be defined. This process may also be guided by high-level support regarding human color perception [Bergmann *et al.*, 1995].

The concept of distance-based transfer functions has been combined with non-linear magnification in the focal region [Wang *et al.*, 2005a]. Thus, smooth transitions between enlarged and "normally" scaled regions of the volume are possible.

An inspiring idea is to change transfer functions over time along a path [Correa and Silver, 2005]. An application in medical visualization is to use the centerline of a vascular structure as a path and to parameterize the temporal changes such that the bloodflow can be visually represented.

3D ultrasound data is an attractive imaging technique due to the low costs associated with it. A dedicate effort to model tissue boundaries in ultrasound data is described in [Hönigmann *et al.*, 2003]. Based on these considerations, boundaries are detected and opacity TF design is directed at illustrating boundaries.

We have not discussed curvature-based TFs in detail, although they enrich the effects achievable by means of volume visualization considerably. The idea of using *curvature* in the TF domain was introduced in [Hladuvka *et al.*, 2000] and enhanced in [Kindlmann *et al.*, 2003]. In particular, the principal curvatures κ_1 and κ_2 were employed to emphasize ridges and valleys in volume data and to achieve some effects from Non-Photorealistic rendering.

The focus in the discussion of TF design was on adjusting gray values, color and opacity. The concepts presented for this task are also applicable for more advanced visualization parameters, such as lightning specifications [Lum and Ma, 2004] and illustrative rendering parameters [Bruckner and Gröller, 2007a, Rautek *et al.*, 2007].

Spatialized transfer function were introduced by [Röttger *et al.*, 2005]. This special variant of local transfer functions, maps positional information to color. Caban and Rheingans [2008] employ texture features derived from volume regions as a basis for transfer functions. Somewhat related to size-based transfer functions, is the effect of frequency-based transfer functions [Vuçini *et al.*, 2011]. Here volume data is Fourier-transformed and scatterplots of amplitudes vs. frequencies are generated (instead of histograms) to guide transfer function specification and thus to deliberately emphasize either low or high frequency features.

Schulze-Döbold *et al.* [2001] and later Shen *et al.* [2008] describe volume rendering in virtual environments, primarily for educational purposes. Volume interaction and in particular transfer function specification with 3D widgets is a focus of these descriptions. Forsberg *et al.* [2011] introduced *model-based transfer functions* that consider the large dynamic range of medical image data. Instead of simple histogram-based operations to restrict this range, they employ a model of tissue types and their intensity values to which a new dataset is registered to support a model-based assignment of gray values and opacity. Lindholm *et al.* [2010] provided strategies for locally adapting transfer functions. With their system, *semantic rules*, such as "render iodine uptake close to the liver" could be realized. Even earlier, Rautek *et al.* [2007] aimed at integrating semantics in volume rendering to bridge the gap between high-level intents of users and the low-level transfer function parameters.

An interesting line of research is also to compute further statistical properties, e.g., mean values and standard deviations [Haidacher *et al.*, 2010] or skewness and standard deviations of local distributions [Maciejewski *et al.*, 2013] to create attribute spaces that better represent features in the data compared to simple histograms. *Peeling* of volume data, where the exploration is guided by layers meaningful for the user, is a promising volume exploration technique [Malik *et al.*, 2007].

Chapter 10

Labeling and Measurements in Medical Visualization

10.1 INTRODUCTION

Tumor staging, the assessment of the severity of a vascular disease, the resectability of a patient, and many other essential tasks depend on a quantitative assessment of pathological structures and the spatial relations between them and adjacent anatomical structures (see Fig. 10.1). The diameter and length of a stenosis and the angle between bones after fracture are just a few examples of measures directly relevant to treatment decisions. In treatment monitoring, the essential goal is to assess whether a pathology shrinked down, stayed constant or grew despite treatment. Distance, angle, cross-sectional area and volume measurements are performed to support such tasks. Measurements always require a discussion of their accuracy, since unreliable measurements may mislead users. In general, more reliable measurements are possible with the recent advances in image acquisition—medical image data with a high signal-to-noise ratio and a high spatial resolution is a prerequisite for precise measurements. In this chapter, we deal with the integration of measures in 2D and 3D visualizations assuming segmentations of the target objects to be sufficiently precise for computing measures.

Annotations of relevant structures and regions play a role in various settings, e.g., in diagnostics and individual treatment planning, but also in medical team meetings. They serve to focus discussions and to represent major results of the collaborative decision making process.

Measurements are either based on interactively selected points or automatic procedures that take segmentation results as input. Combinations are also possible, e.g., when the user moves interactively along the surface of one object and yields the automatically computed minimum distance from the selected point of another object. Due to their crucial role, measurements need to be integrated in visualizations to convey clearly to which structures they belong. The integration may also increase trust in the measure. However, it is not easy to achieve a convenient integration. Problems, such as the potential occlusion of measurement numbers and lines and the selection of colors and fonts to ensure sufficient contrast and legibility have to be tackled. These problems are similar to labeling where names of anatomical structures or other short information are integrated in visualizations. This chapter is dedicated to these two related tasks: the integration of measurements, and textual labels primarily in 3D visualizations.

Organization First, we discuss general concepts for integrating labels and measurements in 3D visualizations (§ 10.2). We go on and discuss interactive distance measurements (§ 10.3). While distance measurements need to be precise, it is sometimes desirable to manually estimate measures roughly, e.g., with an interactive ruler. Such tools are also introduced in that section. Automatic measurements of distances and largest diameters are described in more detail in § 10.4. Interactive angular measurements and automatic measurements of angles are discussed in § 10.5. A short discussion of measurements in virtual environments follows in § 10.6. Finally, we discuss labeling of 3D surface models and 2D slice views in § 10.7.

Visual Computing for Medicine, Second Edition. http://dx.doi.org/10.1016/B978-0-12-415873-3.00010-9

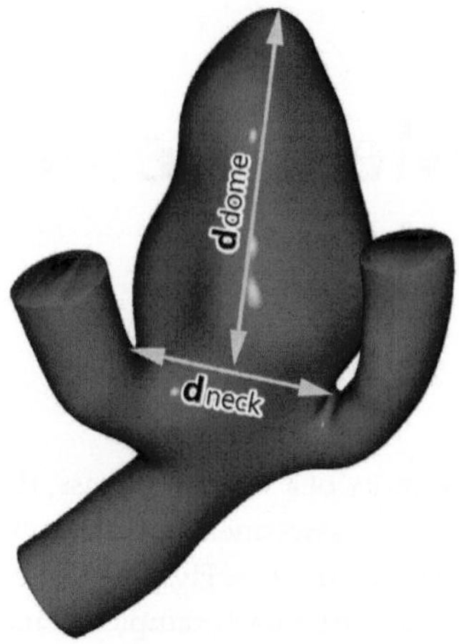

FIGURE 10.1 *The neck diameter of a cerebral aneurysm d_{neck} and the height of the aneurysm dome d_{neck} are essential measures in the diagnosis and treatment planning of this vascular disease* (Courtesy of Mathias Neugebauer, University of Magdeburg).

10.2 GENERAL DESIGN ISSUES

Labeling and measurements are *annotations* that relate to one or more anatomical or pathological structures. They play an essential role in diagnosis and documentation, in particular to represent *why* certain diagnostic and treatment decisions were taken. Although labeling is of essential importance for educational purposes, it is also relevant for clinical medicine.

The most widespread form of labeling is the assignment of a name to *one* structure, but whole groups of anatomical structures may also be related to one label. Measurements, such as the largest diameter of a pathology or the volume of an organ, may also be related to one structure. Distance and angular measurements, in contrast, usually relate to two structures. In all these labeling and measurement tasks, it is crucial that

- annotations are *visible* and *legible*,
- the relationship between anatomical and pathological structures to their annotation is clearly *recognizable*, and
- the overall design and layout of an annotated 3D model is *aesthetically pleasing*.

Visibility and Legibility The first requirement means that the annotations should be large enough, should appear with a sufficient contrast to the 3D model and should be rendered undistorted (or with low perspective distortion). Sans serif fonts, such as Helvetica or Arial, should be employed to improve legibility. To control the size of an annotation, that is integrated with a 3D model requires to consider the current viewing projection and the resulting size in 2D image space. The choice of an appropriate color is also difficult, in particular if the measure or label is drawn on top of the anatomical model. The use of a semi-transparent rectangle is a viable solution to prevent strong changes in the background color.

Recognizable Relation between Annotations and Reference Objects The second requirement is usually fulfilled by using lines that connect objects, or points that define a measure to the annotation. The specific layout of these *reference lines* strongly depends on the kind of measure or label. However, as a general rule, it must be ensured that such lines are *visible* and *recognizable*. Visibility requires that no other structures occlude such a line. Recognizability primarily means that the whole line is drawn in a color that exhibits a sufficient contrast to the anatomical structures. Either the color for such lines differs strongly (ideally in hue and saturation) from *all* other colors, or the annotation line is drawn with two colors. As an example, a white line embedded in two parallel black lines always yields a good contrast.

Aesthetics The third requirement sounds a bit vague and just like a matter of taste but should not be considered as optional. The use of fonts, lines with various attributes, and colors for anatomical structures, labels, and measurements might easily lead to confusing and overwhelming visualizations. Optimal choices of all these parameters require an understanding of color and font design. At the very least, visual clutter, resulting from too many information and too many (highly saturated) colors should be avoided. In particular labels may be arranged in a pleasing way in either columns or around a 3D model without many crossing lines.

Another dimension of aesthetics relates to dynamic changes caused by interactive exploration. When the user zooms or rotates a 3D model, annotations, in particular the spatial layout, need to be adapted. Coherent placements of annotations and reference lines or smooth transitions should be preferred to reduce mental load. Trade-offs between good static layout and convenient interactive behavior are necessary. Frankly, it is easier to criticize annotated visualizations from an aesthetics point of view than it is to automatically compute a layout that is aesthetically pleasing.

The reader is encouraged to carefully look at the images in the whole chapter and consider to what extent the general design recommendations with respect to visibility, recognizability, and layout are considered.

10.3 INTERACTIVE MEASUREMENT OF DISTANCES AND VOLUMES

In this section, we discuss interactive measurements of distances, based on a pair of points selected by the user in 2D or 3D visualizations (§ 10.3.1) and rough estimates of sizes based on 3D visualizations (§ 10.3.2).

10.3.1 INTERACTIVE DISTANCE MEASUREMENT

Distance measures are still carried out primarily in 2D slice views where users can exactly locate points. If both reference points are located in the same slice, this is convenient and fast. If the points are located in different slices, users have to scroll in the slices and to remember the slice in which they selected the first point. This is more cumbersome and it is also difficult to provide good feedback. 3D distance measures may be performed more intuitively in 3D visualizations of relevant objects. The selection of the two points, usually at surfaces, is a typical *selection task* (recall § 5.6.1).

3D Geometry A *distance line widget* can be realized as a 3D geometry (a cylinder with two cones as arrowheads) or as a (flat) line with arrows. While the flat line may be hardly visible if its orientation remains fix, it may also be adapted to the current orientation of the camera. Figure 10.2 compares these variants. In all subfigures, a weakly saturated color with a good contrast to object colors and background color is chosen. In an informal evaluation a continuous adaptation of the distance line widget (Fig. 10.2c) was judged as poor and even the selection of an orthogonal projection (Fig. 10.2d) was rated lower compared to the 3D widget (Fig. 10.2a) [Rössling *et al.*, 2009].

Interactive Use To be used interactively, the distance line needs *sensitive regions* where it can be selected to control the movement of either the whole distance line or one of the endpoints. These sensitive regions

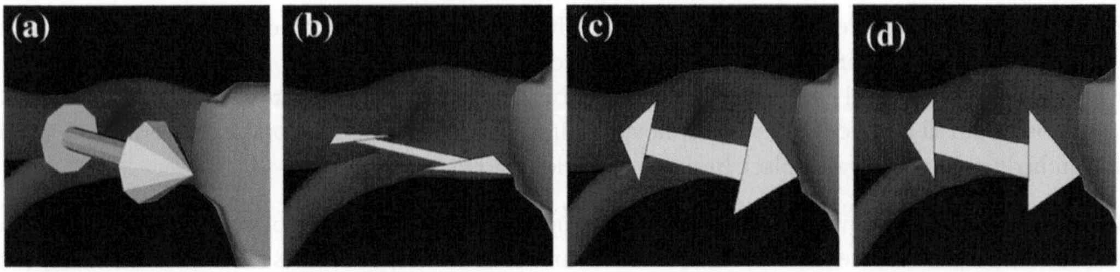

FIGURE 10.2 *A distance line widget may be realized with a full 3D geometry (a) or as static double-sided arrow. Without adaptation to the viewing direction the arrow may be hardly seen (b). If the arrow is projected in the view plane (c) it is optimally recognizable but changes its orientation as the scene rotates. As a trade-off, one of the three orthogonal projections may be chosen such that only major rotations "flip" the arrow (Courtesy of Ivo Rössling, University of Magdeburg).*

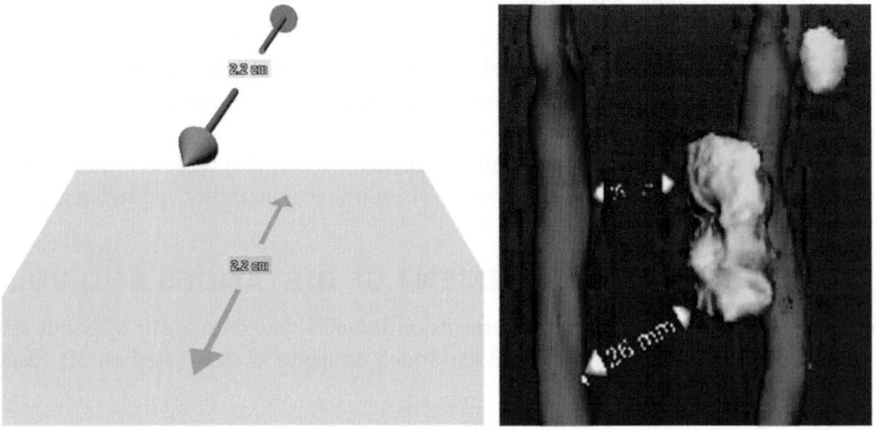

FIGURE 10.3 *A 3D widget for interactive distance measurement.* ***Left:*** *The measurement number is embedded in the cylindrical distance line. A small rectangle is used as uniformly colored background for the measure (From: [Preim et al., 2002]).* ***Right:*** *An ENT surgeon determines the distance between a tumor and the Aorta carotis interna at two different locations to assess the risk of surgical intervention (From: [Rössling et al., 2011]).*

should be large enough to be conveniently selected, e.g., the complete arrows in Figure 10.2. The use of colors in case of several distance lines and the placement of the label in 3D are discussed in [Preim *et al.*, 2002]. Figure 10.3 (right) illustrates the use of the distance line widget.

A distance line widget should be placed by *rubberbanding*, a direct-manipulative techniques that is widely used in 2D and 3D graphics programs to create and place 3D geometries, such as rectangles, ellipsoids, and lines. The distance line is controlled by the mouse cursor with a pressed mouse button and it appears always as it would look when the button would be released. In particular, the measurement number has to be updated fast. If distances in 3D surface models are measured (see Fig. 10.3, right), *snapping* is useful to support the selection of points residing at the surface (recall the discussion of selection techniques in § 5.6.1). In volume rendered images, the distance line widget may be attracted by voxels that are visible and exhibit strong gradients [Reitinger *et al.*, 2006a,b].

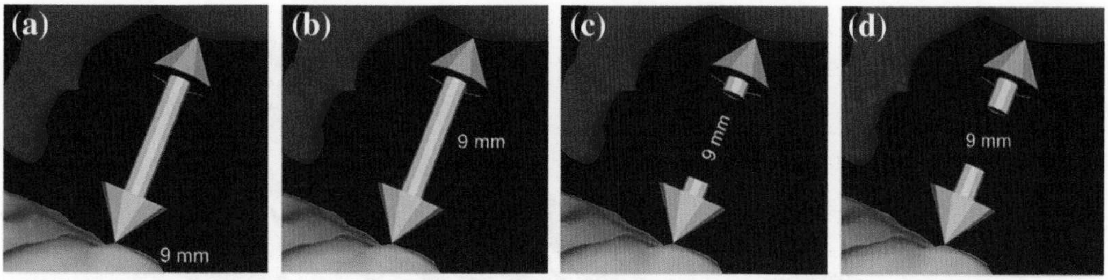

FIGURE 10.4 *There are different variants for the placement of measures besides the distance line. Close to one reference point (a), besides the center of the distance line (b) or integrated in the distance line (c) and (d). The image in (c) exhibits the most obvious relation between the number and the distance line, (d) shows the measure in the most legible manner from left to right (Courtesy of Ivo Rössling, University of Magdeburg).*

Discussion In Figure 10.3, a 3D widget for distance line measurement is presented that fulfills the general design considerations for measurement widgets (recall § 10.2). The two images differ in the placement of the measurement number. The placement in the middle is optimal, since the relation between the arrow glyph and the number is clearly visible, even in case of other distance lines. However, depending on the specific distance and camera view, the arrow glyph might be too small to embed the measurement number. In this case, one of the two endpoints should be selected to place the number, or the number is only displayed when the measure is large enough to accommodate it. These and other variants are compared in Figure 10.4. In all subfigures, a sans serif font is employed. In a small and informal evaluation with medical doctors and computer scientists, the integration of the measurement line to accommodate the label (Fig. 10.4c and d) was preferred by all test persons. The three medical doctors preferred the perspective display (Fig. 10.4c), whereas the computer scientists preferred the flat arrow (Fig. 10.4d) [Rössling *et al.*, 2009].

Accuracy As feedback, the measure should always be presented. This raises the question, how accurate the displayed measure should be. The accuracy of the measure reflects the spatial resolution of the data. Thus, if the diagonal size of a voxel is in the order of 2–3 mm, an accuracy of 1 mm is appropriate (see Fig. 10.4). For CT or MRI datasets with a very high spatial resolution 0.1 mm is recommended, but any further increase in accuracy does not reflect the characteristics or CT or MRI data and should therefore be avoided. Some authors presented the uncertainty resulting from the spatial resolution, i.e., 9.0 ± 0.8 mm. With this strategy, they consequently convey an internal information related to the maximum accuracy that can be achieved with distance measures. However, discussions with medical doctors reveal that this is not preferred. On the one hand, the measure is presented in a more complex way, on the other hand, medical doctors are aware of the spatial resolution and the limited accuracy of measures. Moreover, they are aware that there are more severe sources of inaccuracy, e.g., whether the full extent of a tumor is visible in CT data. Thus, an uncertainty specification in distance or other measures is even considered as misleading by some doctors, since they pretend an unrealistic level of accuracy.

10.3.2 ESTIMATION OF QUANTITATIVE VALUES

Besides precise measures, that involve a certain effort to select points or other features accurately, a rough approximation of quantitative values is often useful. The viewers used in radiology workstations provide a scale which indicates the real size of certain features visible in the radiologic images. This scale is used,

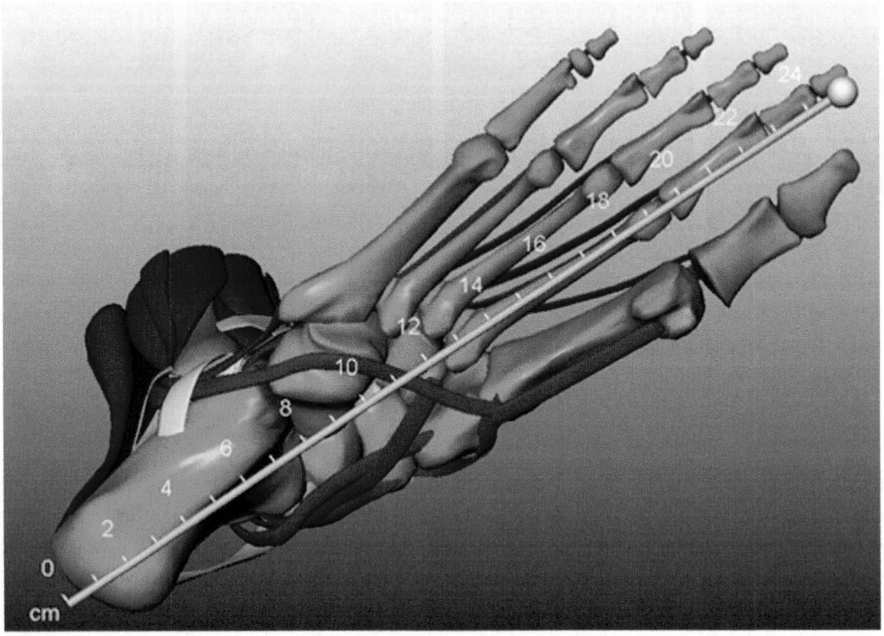

FIGURE 10.5 *A 3D ruler widget may be flexibly placed in space to estimate sizes. The measurement ticks are realized as small circles. Thus, they are visible from each direction (From: [Preim et al., 2002]).*

e.g., to estimate the extent of anatomical structures in slice-based 2D visualizations. A similar feature is desirable for a 3D visualization. However, the relation between the size of a feature in image space to its real size is not linear in case of perspective projections.

In real life, *rulers* are employed to estimate distances. A ruler, like the scale in the legend of a slice view, contains many labeled values at equal spacings. Unlike the scale it can be integrated in a 3D visualization and freely placed there. The general design issues related to colors and visibility are essential for the use of 3D rulers as well. Preim *et al.* [2002] and Reitinger *et al.* [2006a] discuss the design of ruler widgets that are inspired by rulers in real life but adapted in their appearance and behavior to the exploration of 3D visualizations. The ruler widget, introduced in [Preim *et al.*, 2002], is intended for desktop use (see Fig. 10.5). The design of Reitinger *et al.* [2006a] aims at use in a virtual reality environment (see § 10.6). To assess the size of an object, 3D widgets for scaling may be extended with additional features to calculate and present their current size (see Fig. 10.6).

Implementation of Interactive Annotations It might be interesting that most developments presented in this chapter were realized in the Open Inventor framework, which provides a set of 3D widgets and a powerful mechanism for subclassing and specialization. This object-oriented, cross-platform graphics toolkit was developed by Silicon Graphics and is now available as a product from the Visualization Sciences Group.[1] Rössling *et al.* [2009] employed the visualization toolkit (vtk)[2] for their interactive measurement.

1 http://vsg3d.com/open-inventor/sdk.
2 http://www.vtk.org/.

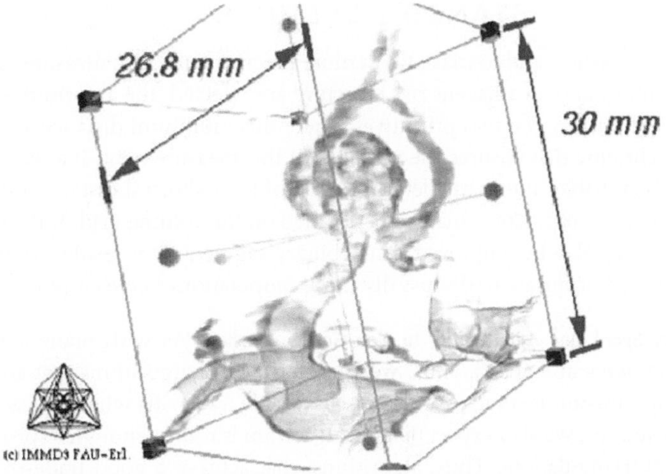

FIGURE 10.6 *A 3D widget for scaling objects was extended by measurement labels that are automatically updated whenever the widget changes. The measurement labels are arranged to be always readable from left to right. Here the widget is used to assess a cerebral aneurysm. The height of the aneurysm dome and the neck size (recall Fig. 10.1) are thus assessed (Courtesy of Peter Hastreiter, Friedrich-Alexander-Universität Erlangen-Nürnberg. See also [Hastreiter et al., 1998]).*

Approximation of Volumes For some diagnostic and treatment planning tasks it is essential to roughly estimate the volume of pathological structures. Some ideas for this task were introduced in [Preim *et al.*, 2002] and discussed in the first edition of this book. In particular, a bounding volume is interactively placed and combined with a selection of voxels based on intensity values. A more recent idea from Reitinger *et al.* [2006a] is the use of a *measurement jug* with an appropriate scale. The user may drag objects in that jug. Thus, volumes, e.g., from several metastases, may be added and the user gets an idea of the overall volume (Fig. 10.7). With segmented structures, of course, a more precise volume estimation is possible. But the idea of the measurement jug remains appealing due to the intuitive interaction.

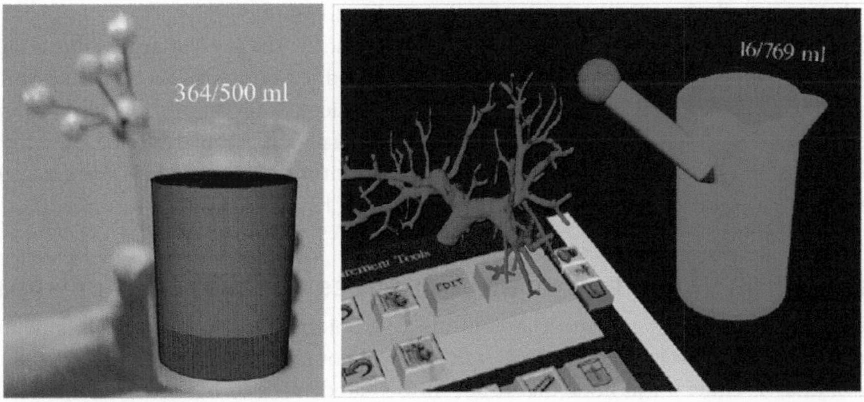

FIGURE 10.7 *A measurement jug with a known volume is employed for volume estimations. Each object that is dragged in the jug is represented there by a cylinder scaled in height to yield the equivalent volume. In the right image, it is shown how a tumor model is moved in the jug (From: [Reitinger et al., 2006a]).*

10.4 AUTOMATIC DISTANCE MEASURES

To accelerate distance measures and to make them more precise, automatic measures are highly desirable. As an example, if a tumor and an adjacent risk structure are selected, the algorithm should compute the minimum distance and display the two primitives where this minimum distance actually occurs, ideally with an emphasis technique that ensures the visibility of this measurement. If a reliable segmentation of the target structure is available, automatic determination of their shortest distance is feasible. In case of a binary segmentation, the computation may be performed on the volume grid. If the segmentation yields a triangle mesh, this may also be employed. Since binary segmentation results are usually converted to polygonal meshes, it is appropriate to discuss distance computations between polygonal meshes.

Requirements: *Accuracy, Speed, and Applicability* to Non-Convex Meshes As with many algorithms, there is a trade-off between accuracy and speed. Thus, we are interested in algorithms that are as fast as possible, ideally without compromising accuracy. We also discuss viable trade-offs where still acceptable accuracy is achieved with fast solutions. We also expect that the algorithm is robust enough to provide a reliable result for all kinds of valid triangulations. Thus, algorithms, that achieve a good trade-off between accuracy and speed based on restrictions, e.g., to convex surfaces, are not appropriate. This aspect is essential, since a variety of algorithms indeed assume convex geometries as input [Bobrow, 1989, Lin and Canny, 1991]. These algorithms were designed for robotic applications where machine parts and other regular, often convex objects occur. While these algorithms are not directly applicable in medical visualization and surgical planning, they may serve as inspiration. In particular, the idea of hierarchically decomposing the geometric space, where the two objects live, and computing *candidate pairs* between the nodes of that hierarchy is essential to efficiently determine minimal distances.

Hierarchic Decomposition The algorithm from [Quinlan, 1994], where hierarchies of bounding spheres were employed for a fast computation, may be adapted. Most algorithms employ some parameters, e.g., the maximum depth of trees or the maximum size of nodes at each level. The careful choice of such parameters leads to roughly balanced trees where the overhead to construct the data structure is appropriate. For medical visualization, however, such parameters need to be hidden from users, since medical doctors obviously lack the knowledge in making wise decisions on such parameters. As an example, Preim *et al.* [2002] discussed how the two essential parameters of QUINLAN's algorithm may be determined automatically for a large variety of surfaces with different complexities.

A highly accurate algorithm would determine a pair of points on the two surfaces where their distance is minimal. These points may live at edges or even correspond to vertices of the mesh, but more likely they live at the face; some distance away from edges and vertices. Some minimal distance computation approaches restrict their result to a pair of vertices. This is, usually, an acceptable trade-off, provided that the polygonal mesh has a uniformly high resolution. The algorithm presented in [Preim *et al.*, 2002], and more carefully explained in [Preim and Bartz, 2007], Chapter 13 is based on this simplification.

10.4.1 BOUNDING VOLUMES AND SPATIAL TREES FOR DISTANCE COMPUTATION

A hierarchic decomposition of the space around the two objects leads to two tree representations of the related anatomical surfaces. At the top of each tree is a bounding volume that covers the complete surface. Each node is either a leaf node that is not further subdivided or has **children** that cover a smaller subspace. Please note that the top level bounding boxes of the two objects and subboxes of the two anatomical surfaces may overlap. Such a hierarchic decomposition may be employed to determine at each level which pairs of nodes $(n_{1a}; n_{2b})$[3] are candidates to contain the points with minimum distance or, in other words, to exclude a pair of nodes where the minimum *cannot* occur. For this purpose, the distances between bounding volumes are determined to define both a lower and an upper bound for the distances between all primitives represented by these bounding volumes.

The basic strategy has two components:

- *Bounding volumes* with simple and regular shapes should be defined for the nodes of the spatial tree structure. The bounding volume should be simple such that distance computation between them is extremely fast.
- The space should be decomposed hierarchically in a balanced way resulting in a *spatial search tree*.

Thus, instead of searching for minima at all faces of a complex surfaces the search can be restricted to regions where the bounding volumes are close to each other.

Choice of a Bounding Volume If we consider two pairs of nodes n_{1a}, n_{2b} and n_{1c}, n_{2d} and find, by comparing their corresponding bounding volumes, that the maximum distance d_{max} between n_{1a}, n_{2b} is smaller than the minimum distance d_{min} between n_{1c}, n_{2d}, we can reliably state that the minimum distance between the two surfaces does not occur at any part of the surfaces represented by n_{1c} and n_{2d}. Thus, we can spare the effort of determining distances between vertices, edges, and faces of the potentially complex subsurfaces represented by the bounding volumes n_{1c} and n_{2d}.

On the other hand, it should be possible to compute the bounding volumes for a subset of the surface representation very fast as well. Finally, the bounding volumes should cover the related geometry completely, but tightly. The tighter the bounding volumes represent the geometry, the more accurate the distance estimations are and, as a consequence, the more pairs of nodes can be excluded early. Figure 10.8 compares three potentially useful bounding volumes, namely spheres, axis-aligned bounding boxes (AABB), and oriented bounding boxes (OBB). From the image, it is immediately clear that the OBB is the tightest bounding volume approximation. The sphere is the widest bounding volume, thus, many sphere-sphere comparisons at different levels are needed to restrict the search for the minimum. The AABB does not reflect the orientation of the object and thus is significantly larger than the OBB of that object. However, it has two clear advantages over the OBB: minimum and maximum distances between a

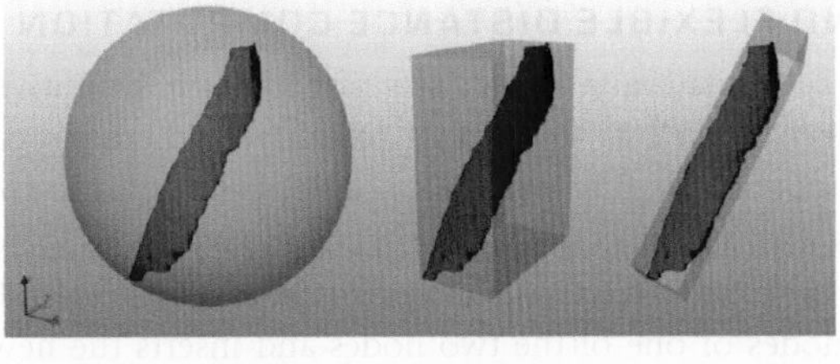

FIGURE 10.8 *A comparison of bounding volumes.* **Left:** *The bounding sphere does not fit an elongated structure (M. sternocleidomastoideus) well.* **Middle:** *The axis-aligned bounding box (AABB), provides a better fit and is easy to compute.* **Right:** *The best fit is achieved with the oriented bounding box (OBB). However, the computation of the OBB is significantly more complex (From: [Rössling et al., 2010]).*

3 We refer to the nodes of the first object tree as n_{1i}, and to those of the second object tree as n_{2j}.

pair of AABBs can be computed faster, and even more important: The AABB of an object can be computed more efficiently. In essence, the AABB exhibits the advantages of the sphere (easy construction and fast determination of distances between them), but provides a tighter bounding volume. Thus, the currently best minimum distance computation algorithm relies on trees of AABB representations [Rössling *et al.*, 2010] ("best" refers to speed and accuracy; faster algorithms, e.g., in collision detection do generate only approximate results). For more discussion on bounding volume, see the survey of Gottschalk *et al.* [1996].

Generation of a Spatial Search Tree As preprocessing for the actual minimum distance computation, *spatial search trees* for the related surface meshes need to be constructed. This construction process can be performed top-down (starting with a node representing the complete surface) or bottom-up (starting with vertices, edges and faces of the mesh and summarizing them according to their distance). Usually, the leave nodes of the tree contain a predefined maximum number of geometric primitives—a parameter that the developers should define, not the users, as discussed above. To design a flexible and general solution, it is wise to consider multiple types of primitives (e.g., vertices, edges, faces, etc.). Thus, the algorithm may also be used to compute the minimum distance between a skeleton, e.g., a vessel centerline, and a surface [Rössling *et al.*, 2010].

The two most widespread spatial tree structures are octrees and kd-trees [Langetepe and Zachmann, 2006]. Rössling *et al.* [2010] employed a tree structure that is similar to the octree but more balanced and thus leads to a higher performance. The original octree starts with an axis-aligned box and subdivides it at each level exactly at the middle point of that box. Instead, Rössling *et al.* [2010] compute the *barycenter* or *center of gravity* and use this point as pivotal point to decompose the tree. This *Split* procedure stops when the nodes contain less than a predefined maximum number of primitives.

The better balance of this tree has the consequence that, on average, the trees have a lower number of levels; they are not that deep. This is achieved at the expense of a higher construction effort, since the barycenters at all levels need to be computed. If this computation is integrated in the construction of the tree, where all vertices are traversed anyway, the additional effort is rather small. While usually the minimum distance between two surfaces is determined, Rössling *et al.* [2010] introduced a modification to be able to process also line segments or points. For this purpose, barycenters are weighted with $w = 1, 2, 3$ for points, line segments, and triangles, respectively. The search tree may be completely determined in a preprocessing step or it may be selectively refined on demand during computations on the fly. Figure 10.9 illustrates the decomposition based on the barycenters.

10.4.2 EFFICIENT AND FLEXIBLE DISTANCE COMPUTATION

An algorithm for distance computation takes two sets of geometric primitives as input and returns the minimum Euclidean distance as well as the pair of primitives where it occurs. In the following, we describe the approach introduced by Rössling *et al.* [2010] based on the spatial search tree described above. The algorithm starts with a *priority queue* (a concept that is widely used in computational geometry) that contains the two root nodes. It extracts the first pair (the root nodes) and refines the distance query with respect to the child nodes of one of the two nodes and inserts the new pairs resulting from that refinement in the queue. In each step, the bounding boxes of the two currently considered nodes provide a lower bound of the minimum distance for all primitives contained in the two boxes. This lower bound is employed as *priority value* that determines the order of the queue's elements. If this node is chosen for (further) refinement, the larger of the two bounding boxes is refined.

While in the initial steps only distances between boxes or between a box and a primitive are determined, at some point the first primitive-primitive test takes place and computes a "real" distance. This distance may

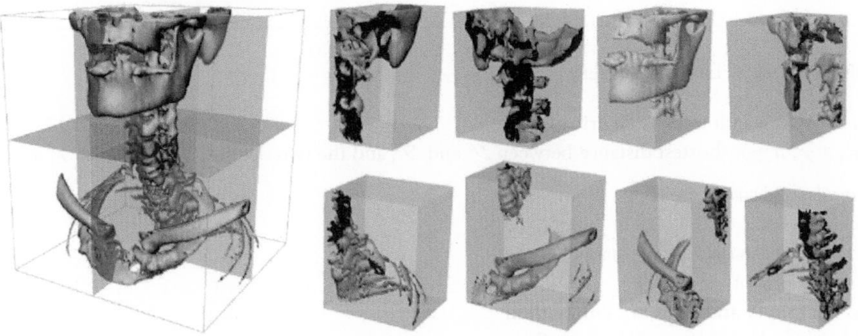

FIGURE 10.9 *For a skeletal model (left), a spatial tree is constructed. The top-down decomposition of the first level is illustrated. The barycenter of the whole model is employed as pivotal point to decompose the space. The AABB of the relevant geometry is determined to compute bounds for the distances between primitives contained in that node (From: [Rössling et al., 2010]).*

still be slightly larger than the bound computed for the two bounding boxes and likely even larger than the bound for some other pairs of boxes. Thus, further elements of the queue may need to be examined, leading to new distance values and to reinsertions in the priority queue. The search terminates when the head of the queue has a priority that is at least the minimum distance determined so far. Algorithm 2 formally describes the minimum distance computation according to Rössling *et al.* [2010].

Advanced topic: Performance of minimal distance computation. We briefly discuss performance issues, since response times have a strong influence on user satisfaction and efficiency (recall § 5.5.1). The specific numbers are not crucial. Instead, the following discussion should provide guidance how performance should be discussed.

Rössling *et al.* [2010] made a couple of experiments on an Intel Pentium 4 processor at 3.2 GHz with 1 GB RAM averaging values over five experiments to get reliable results. For small to moderate object sizes, such as those consisting of some 3.000 vertices each, the minimum distance could be computed in some 40 ms (milliseconds) in the highest accuracy (considering the actual faces). The process could be accelerated to 10–15 ms by taking into account only the vertices (slight reduction in accuracy). These timings relate to an *On-Demand* split of the spatial search tree. In all experiments, the *On-Demand* split yielded better results than the *Full Split*, that is, the additional construction time of the full split does not pay off in the actual distance query although the query time was almost negligible. This, of course, only holds if the preprocessing is used only once. When the user moves over a surface and is interested in the minimum distance to a second surface starting from the current cursor position, the same preprocessing results are employed frequently. While for moderate input sizes the delay is not noticeable, for larger input sizes efficiency becomes crucial to avoid disturbing waiting times.

Compared to the algorithm introduced in [Preim *et al.*, 2002], ROESSLING's algorithm is faster for all kinds of object sizes (the comparison relates to vertex-vertex distances). While the difference is rather small for small to medium object sizes (factor 2–3), it becomes two orders of magnitude for the largest example shapes. Thus, for larger objects ROESSLING's algorithm is even more precise and faster. The largest pair of objects, that was considered, consisted of 129 K vertices and 110 K vertices representing a large skeletal structure and skin. In this example, the overall response time

ALGORITHM 2 Shortest Distance Query

Input: $\mathscr{S}, \mathscr{T}$: two search trees as described above
Output: $(d, \pi_{\mathscr{S}}, \pi_{\mathscr{T}})$: shortest distance between $\mathscr{S}$ and $\mathscr{T}$, and the two defining primitives $\pi_{\mathscr{S}}, \pi_{\mathscr{T}}$

Initialize return values and priority queue:

initialize $d \leftarrow \infty$
initialize $\pi_{\mathscr{S}} \leftarrow$ invalid, $\pi_{\mathscr{T}} \leftarrow$ invalid
create empty priority queue Q
if $\mathscr{S}$ is not empty **and** $\mathscr{T}$ is not empty **then**
    add $(\mathscr{S}, \mathscr{T}, \text{dist}(\mathscr{S}.\text{bbox}, \mathscr{T}.\text{bbox}))$ to Q
end if

Keep refining head of Q until shortest distance is found:

while Q not empty **do**
    assign $(\mathscr{A}, \mathscr{B}, \alpha) \leftarrow \text{Head}(Q)$
    if $d \leq \alpha$ **then**
        return $(d, \pi_{\mathscr{S}}, \pi_{\mathscr{T}})$
    end if
    if $\mathscr{A}$ contains only one primitive $\pi_{\mathscr{A}}$ **and** $\mathscr{B}$ contains only one primitive $\pi_{\mathscr{B}}$ **then**
        update $d \leftarrow \alpha$
        update $\pi_{\mathscr{S}} \leftarrow \pi_{\mathscr{A}}, \pi_{\mathscr{T}} \leftarrow \pi_{\mathscr{B}}$
    else
        RefineHead(Q)
    end if
end while
return $(d, \pi_{\mathscr{S}}, \pi_{\mathscr{T}})$

Function RefineHead(Priority Queue Q)
Selectively refine the query towards one of the two tree nodes stored at the head of Q:

assign $(\mathscr{A}, \mathscr{B}, \alpha) \leftarrow \text{Head}(Q)$
RemoveHead(Q)
if B contains exactly one primitive **or** $\text{Vol}(\mathscr{B}.\text{bbox}) < \text{Vol}(\mathscr{A}.\text{bbox})$ **then**
    for all $\mathscr{A}_i \in \mathscr{A}.\text{children}$ **do**
        let $\alpha_i \leftarrow \text{dist}(\mathscr{A}_i.\text{bbox}, \mathscr{B}.\text{bbox})$
        add $(\mathscr{A}_i, \mathscr{B}, \alpha_i)$ to Q
    end for
else
    for all $\mathscr{B}_i \in \mathscr{B}.\text{children}$ **do**
        let $\alpha_i \leftarrow \text{dist}(\mathscr{A}.\text{bbox}, \mathscr{B}_i.\text{bbox})$
        add $(\mathscr{A}, \mathscr{B}_i, \alpha_i)$ to Q
    end for
end if

was 3 seconds (including only 0.14 seconds for the actual computation provided that the *Full Split* preprocessing was carried out).

This discussion can only provide a rough insight into performance issues. Performance depends not only on object sizes but also on the ability of the algorithm to quickly rule out large portions of the geometry. As an example, if two roughly parallel elongated structures, such as blood vessels in the neck region, are selected as input, many primitive pairs have to be considered. But as a general statement, due to the complex nature of anatomical shapes run-time behavior in practice is much better than any purely theoretical analysis would yield. With current multicore technology, better results are, of course, feasible. However, due to the increased spatial resolution of the source data, input sizes are growing as well.

10.4.3 CLINICAL EXAMPLES

The determination of minimal distances between two anatomical surfaces may be an essential help in surgical planning. If the minimum distance between a vital structure, such as the A. carotis and a metastasis, is below a threshold, a *safety margin violation* occurs and the metastasis may only be removed with a higher risk for tumor residuals. If the minimum distance is very low, this may indicate an *infiltration*. If not only the primitives with the absolute minimum distance are returned, but instead all pairs of primitives with very low values, the outline of a contact area may be determined (due to the inaccuracy of image acquisition, processing and segmentation a contact or infiltration is likely or at least possible if the measured distance is very low).

The flexible algorithm developed by Rössling *et al.* [2010] also supports other measurement tasks. If one object represents the surface of an object and the second object represents the centerline of the same object, the algorithm returns the minimum diameter. For a potentially pathological vascular structure this may represent the most critical point of a stenosis and the measure is relevant, e.g., to assess whether a catheter with a certain diameter may be inserted into that segment of the vessel. Another example, discussed in Rössling *et al.* [2010], is the assessment of constrictions of the respiratory tract (*tracheal stenosis*) where again the outer surface and the centerline are the input for the minimum distance computation.

The two objects might also represent an outer and an inner boundary, e.g., the outer and inner boundary of the myocard. In this case, regions with minimum (or maximum) wall thickness are computed. Finally, maximum distances can be computed as well. As Rössling *et al.* [2010] point out, the maximum distance between an object's triangle mesh and itself returns the maximum diameter of that object—a value that is essential for tumor staging.

10.4.4 MEASURING THE EXTENTS OF OBJECTS

The extent of an object o can be roughly characterized by its axis-aligned bounding box (AABB). This, however, is not a precise measure, since the size of the AABB depends on the orientation of an object. After rotation, a different measure is obtained, although the object itself has still the same size. The oriented bounding box (OBB) avoids this and provides a box with an orientation adapted to the shape of the object. The longest side of the OBB is a better approximation of the longest diameter of an object. Guidelines for tumor diagnostics and staging require that the longest diameter is determined. The conventional manual approach is tedious: The slice, where the tumor appears to be largest, is selected and the extent is determined by manual placement of two points. Since the maximum diameter does not necessarily show up in any axial slice, this approach is unreliable.

Once the maximum diameter is computed, it needs to be presented clearly. Since the line that connects the two primitives, where the maximum diameter occurs, is usually hidden, semi-transparent rendering of the related anatomical structure is a feasible variant (Fig. 10.10b). In an informal study, the semi-transparent rendering was clearly preferred and the other three variants were considered as confusing by several test persons [Rössling *et al.*, 2009]. Figure 10.11 illustrates a clinical example and the value of an automated approach to maximum diameter computation. The manual approach (Fig. 10.11, left) corresponds to the RECIST criteria and thus represent the current clinical standard.

The OBB determination, which can be carried out automatically after image segmentation, produces a reliable result. It is based on the principal component analysis (PCA) [Sonka *et al.*, 1999]. We briefly sketch this approach. First, the center of gravity (COG) of object o is calculated. The covariance matrix A (a symmetric 3×3 matrix) is computed taking into account all vertices of o. The normalized eigenvectors $\overrightarrow{e_i}$ of A form a local right-angled coordinate system with origin at the COG of o. The eigenvectors $\overrightarrow{e_i}$ specify a rotation matrix C from the regular Cartesian space into the object coordinate system. In order to get the exact extent in each of the three directions, o is transformed to o' by rotating o according to

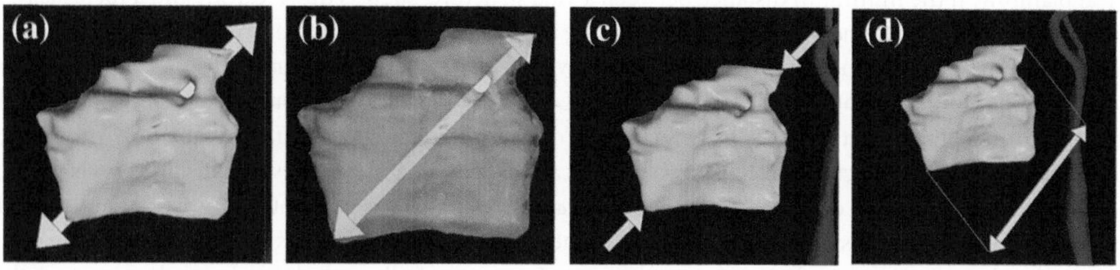

FIGURE 10.10 *The largest diameter is represented by a line that is barely visible (a). Semi-transparent rendering better conveys the largest diameter (b). Alternatives, inspired by conventions from engineering drawings, are to point to the reference points from outside (c) or to use auxiliary lines (d) (Courtesy of Ivo Rössling, Dornheim Medical Images. See also [Rössling et al., 2010]).*

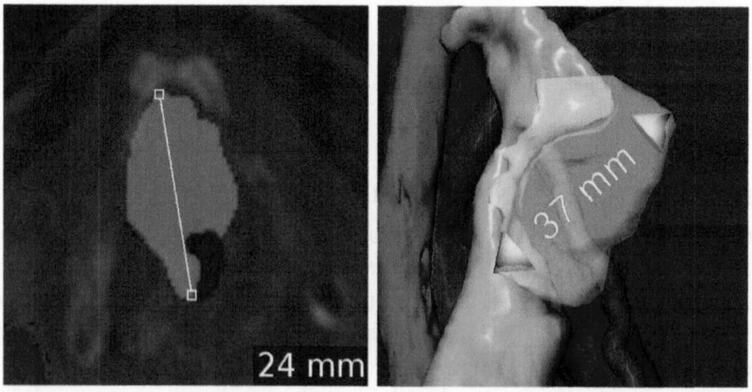

FIGURE 10.11 **Left:** *An experienced ENT surgeon estimated the largest diameter of the yellow tumor based on an interactive measure in a 2D slice view to be 24 mm.* **Right:** *Automatic analysis reveals that it is in fact 37 mm and thus clearly above 3 cm—an essential threshold for tumor staging (From: [Rössling et al., 2010]).*

the rotation C. As object o' is axis-aligned, the axis-aligned bounding box (AABB) of o' can be easily determined. The length of the axes of the AABB represents the length of the main axis (see Fig. 10.12).

It might be useful to display not only the longest diameter of an object but the complete oriented bounding box. This may be done by either displaying the (enclosing) box or by displaying three orthogonal distance lines that intersect at the barycenter (thus, inside the reference object). The latter requires to render the related object semi-transparently. The box display and the distance lines may also be presented along with each other. ROESSLING also considered the display of three distance lines that intersect at one vertex of the OBB (the lower, left, frontal vertex), again with or without a display of the complete box (Fig. 10.13).

The extent is visualized by either the longest distance line or by three orthogonal distance lines intersecting at the COG (Figs. 10.12 and 10.13, left). Numbers are placed at the endpoints to reduce the problem of overlapping information. As the distance lines proceed inside, the object, for which these

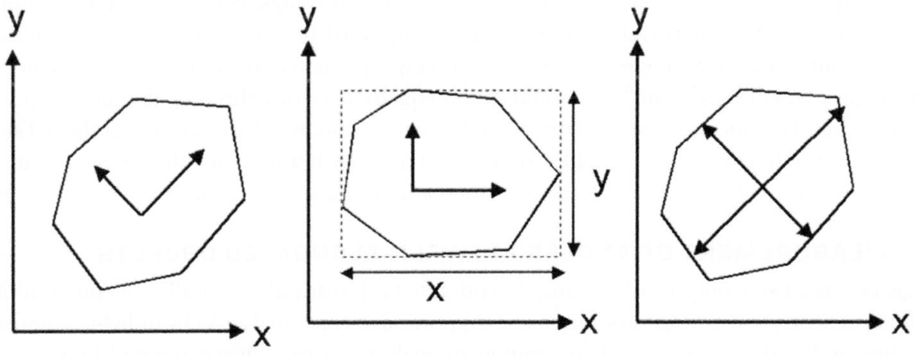

FIGURE 10.12 *Eigenvectors of an object are defined using the covariance matrix (left). Object o is rotated according to the Jacobian matrix to define the oriented bounding box (middle). o is rotated back and the main axis is visualized with distance lines (right).*

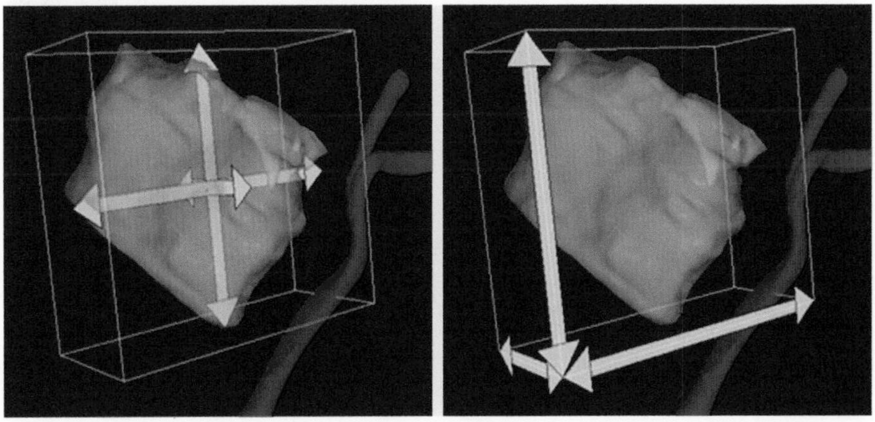

FIGURE 10.13 *The OBB of an object is displayed with three orthogonal distance lines intersecting at the barycenter (left) or at one vertex of the OBB. To better convey the extent, the full box may be displayed (with thin lines and desaturated colors to avoid visual clutter) (Courtesy of Ivo Rössling, University of Magdeburg).*

measurements have been carried out, is rendered semi-transparently. Please note that the lines representing the maximum diameter, e.g., in Figure 10.13 (left), do not end at the object's surface, which might be considered confusing.

10.5 ANGULAR MEASUREMENTS

In diagnosis and treatment planning, angular measurements are often used to evaluate the orientation of elongated structures with regard to some vector or midline. Angles that describe different orientations of objects are often important for the assessment of the severity of complex bone fractures (e.g., whether a surgical intervention after fractures of the arm is required, depends on the angle between the bones).

Angular measurements are more complex than distance measurements. Users have to select three points. A 3D widget must provide three separate handles for this purpose. Similar to interactive distance measures, the measure needs to be carefully placed to be legible. In Figure 10.14 (left), the measurement number is embedded in a transparent rectangle at the apex of the angle. Since it is difficult to place an angle in a 3D model precisely, *orientation aids* are useful. In Figure 10.14 semi-transparent planes orthogonal to the legs are integrated. If an angle would be only visually represented by two lines, an ambiguity would arise: an angle x and the angle $360° - x$ would appear equally. To resolve this disambiguity, the inner part of the angle must be indicated. A semi-transparent display is recommended to avoid that the 3D anatomy is not occluded too heavily (see Fig. 10.14). An informal usability test indicated that the semi-transparent circular segment is preferred over alternatives, such as a semi-transparent triangle [Preim *et al.*, 2002].

10.5.1 MEASUREMENT OF ANGLES BETWEEN ELONGATED OBJECTS

The angle between two elongated objects may be computed automatically. Clinically relevant examples can be found in dentistry and orthopedics. Automatic support can be provided again by utilizing segmentation information and performing a principal component analysis for two objects selected by the user. For automatic angular measurements, it is sufficient to know the eigenvector corresponding to the largest

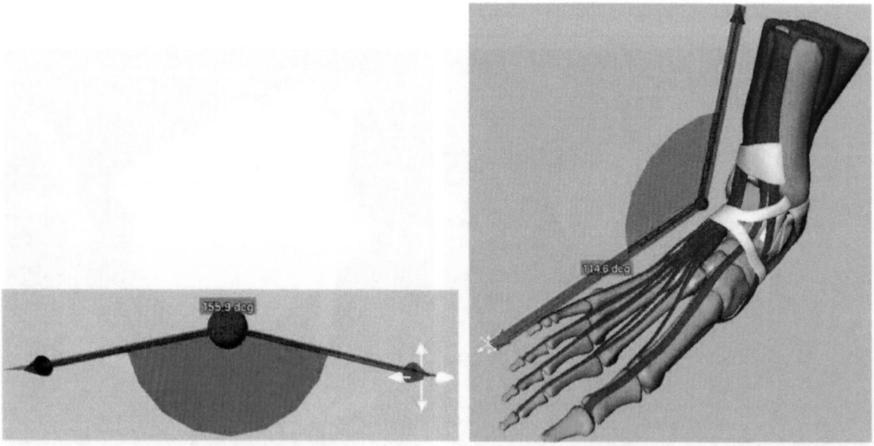

FIGURE 10.14 *With an appropriate 3D widget, angles can be determined interactively. The 3D widget exhibits a clear spatial shape. The inner part (between the legs) is indicated as a semi-transparent circular segment.* ***Right:*** *application of angular measurements in the surface model of a foot) (From: [Preim et al., 2002]).*

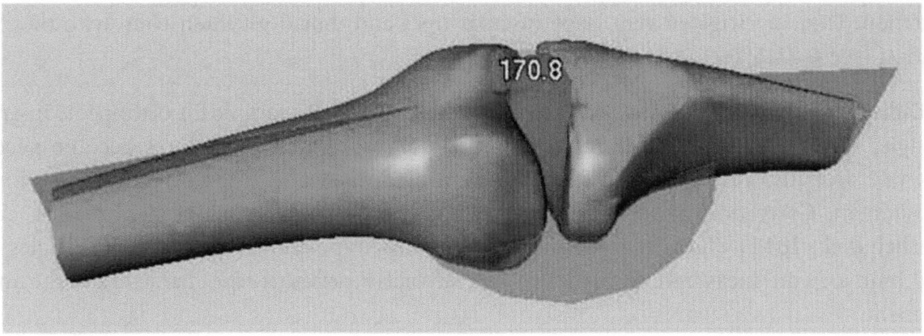

FIGURE 10.15 *Automatic measurement of angles based on a principal component analysis of the two elongated bones* (From: [Preim et al., 2002]).

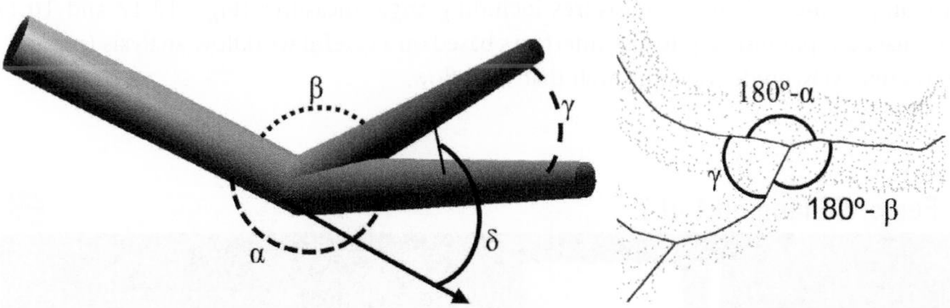

FIGURE 10.16 **Left:** *The angles characterizing a bifurcation: the main angle α between the parent and larger daughter vessel, the secondary angle (β) between the parent and smaller daughter vessels, the in-plane angle (γ) between the daughter vessels, and the out-of-plane angle (δ) between the plane defined by the daughter and parent vessels.* **Right:** *example for a bifurcation angle α is not indicated, since it is barely visible due to the projection* (Courtesy of Thomas Wischgoll, Wright State University. See also [Wischgoll et al., 2009a]).

eigenvalue for both objects.[4] The angle between these directions is automatically calculated and an angle measurement tool may be placed which conveys this angle. The legs of the angle are parallel to the direction of the computed eigenvectors and the apex of the angle is placed at their cross section (see Fig. 10.15).

10.5.2 MEDICAL APPLICATIONS

Branching Angles in the Vascular System Angular measurements are essential in selected medical research problems. As an example, several research groups aim at a better understanding of the development of vascular trees. They are interested in the formation of vascular structures and the relation between geometric measures (*morphometry*) and physical attributes such as blood pressure and flow velocity. Wischgoll *et al.* [2009a] analyzed such morphometric measures for the cardiovascular system. Branching angles play an essential role in this analysis (see Fig. 10.16). Not only individual angles, but also their frequency distribution is relevant. The research project described in Wischgoll *et al.* [2009a] aims at a comprehensive analysis of morphometric features, such as diameter, length, and branching angles in relation to the function of coronary arteries. Branching angles were determined automatically based on a centerline

4 This measure is only reliable for elongated objects where one eigenvalue is significantly larger than the other two.

representation. They investigated very large vascular trees and thus dealt intensively with their efficient visualization (see § 11.5.1.2).

Planning Orthopedic Interventions Osteotomies around the knee are an example for orthopedic interventions where angles between skeletal structures are essential. These surgical procedures become necessary in case of severe arthritis, a frequent and strongly age-related disease, and to correct other serious forms of misalignment. Correction is necessary to enable a good alignment between hip, knee, and ankle joint [Perlich *et al.*, 2011]. In order to define the osteotomy type and correction angle, angles between bone and limb axes are measured. In particular, the *femorotibial mechanical angle* characterizes the amount of misalignment.

Osteotomy planning is supported by 2D and 3D tools, whereas 2D tools are based on radiography data and 3D tools employ CT data. Automatic support for the definition of these angles is desirable, in particular for 3D osteotomy planning. Triangle meshes of the femur and the tibia are thus required. A leading vendor for surgical planning and guidance in orthopedics is BRAINLAB. The following screenshots indicate the importance of various measures including angle measures (Figs. 10.17 and 10.18). These applications have simple and easy-to-use interfaces based on a careful workflow analysis (recall § 5.2.3.1). The systems effectively guide users through that workflow.

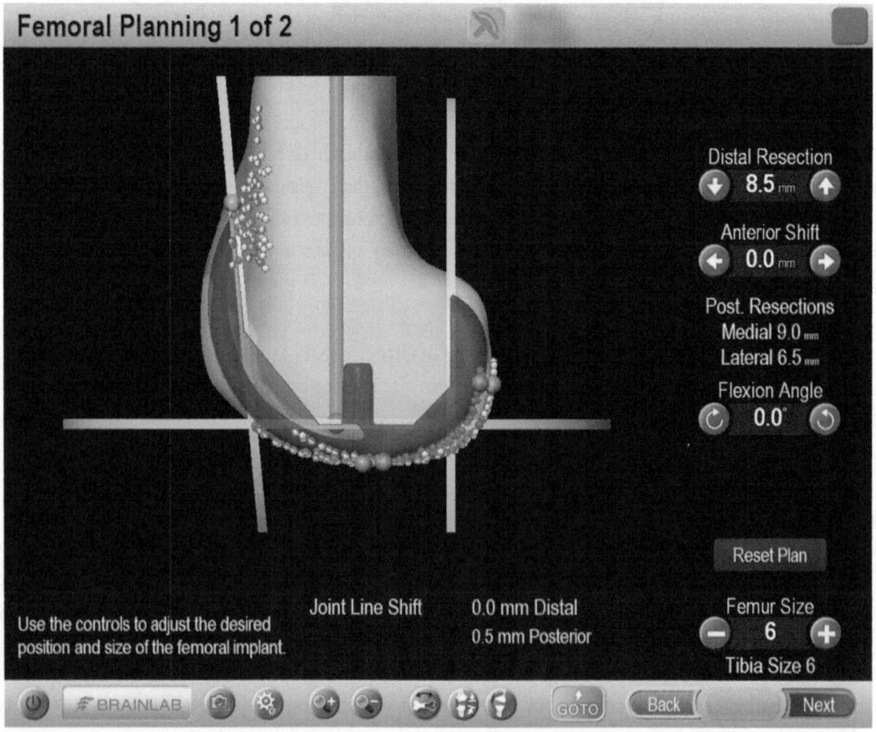

FIGURE 10.17 *Total Knee Replacement: planning of Tibia implant, adjustment of implant sizes, angles, resection levels. These measures have an influence on the resulting leg length, leg alignment, range of motion, and finally the durability of the implant (Courtesy of Brainlab, Feldkirchen).*

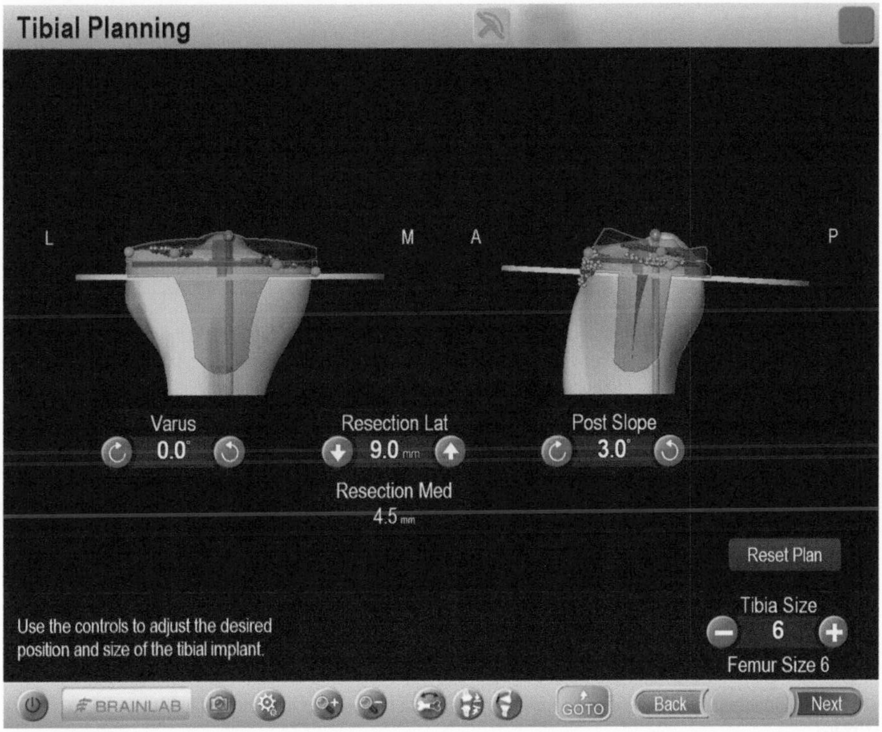

FIGURE 10.18 *Total Knee Replacement: planning of Femur implant. Implant size and angles as well as resection levels are measured in two projection directions (L(ateral)-M(edial) and A(nterior)- P(osterior)) (Courtesy of Brainlab, Feldkirchen).*

10.6 MEASUREMENTS IN VIRTUAL REALITY

So far, we have not discussed input and output devices and basically assumed that a notebook or desktop PC with mouse and keyboard is employed. Clearly, measurements in a complex 3D model benefit from 3D input and output devices that provide better cues for shape perception and more intuitive handling of a 3D model. In particular, 3D input devices, such as the SpacePilot or the Phantom, may enable a more intuitive selection in 3D (recall § 5.7). Measurement tasks may be supported in a natural way by providing bimanual interaction [de Haan, 2009]. Thus, the two endpoints of a distance line may be selected in parallel (Fig. 10.19).

A long-term research project on surgery planning performed at the TU Graz also yielded inspiring solutions for measurement tasks [Reitinger *et al.*, 2006a]. In Figure 10.20, examples for distance and angular measures are presented. The ruler is a physical artifact that is tracked by a camera and controls a ruler widget in the VR environment.

10.7 LABELING 2D AND 3D MEDICAL VISUALIZATIONS

Labeling, like measuring, may be performed *automatically* or *interactively*. Interactive labeling may be realized by temporarily displaying a name when the mouse is over an object or by selecting objects and drawing

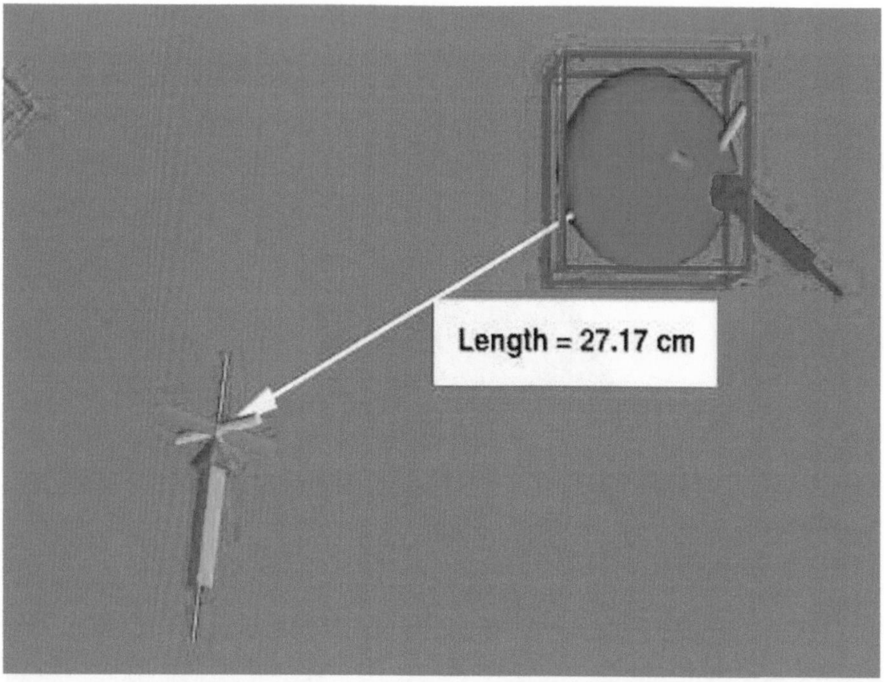

FIGURE 10.19 *Bimanual interaction for distance measurement. Each hand defines one vertex of a distance line (Courtesy of Gerwin de Haan, TU Delft).*

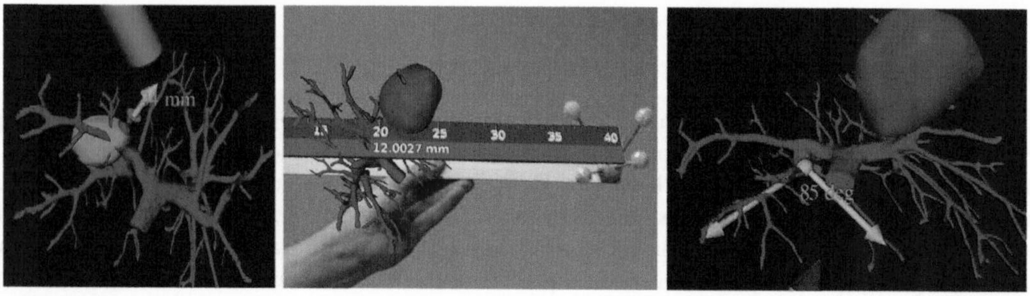

FIGURE 10.20 *Interactive measurement of distances (left), approximation of sizes with a ruler (middle) and angular measurement (right) in a Virtual Reality environment. Distance measurement is supported by snapping which is enabled with a button on the input device (pen) (Courtesy of Bernhard Reitinger, Graz University of Technology. See also [Reitinger et al., 2006a]).*

a reference line to guide the label placement. While these features are useful, automatic labeling where the system arranges textual labels, is an essential ingredient for such systems in order to use the potential of multiple labels. We discuss labeling of static 3D models but also consider *dynamic labeling* where users zoom and rotate and labels need to be adapted.

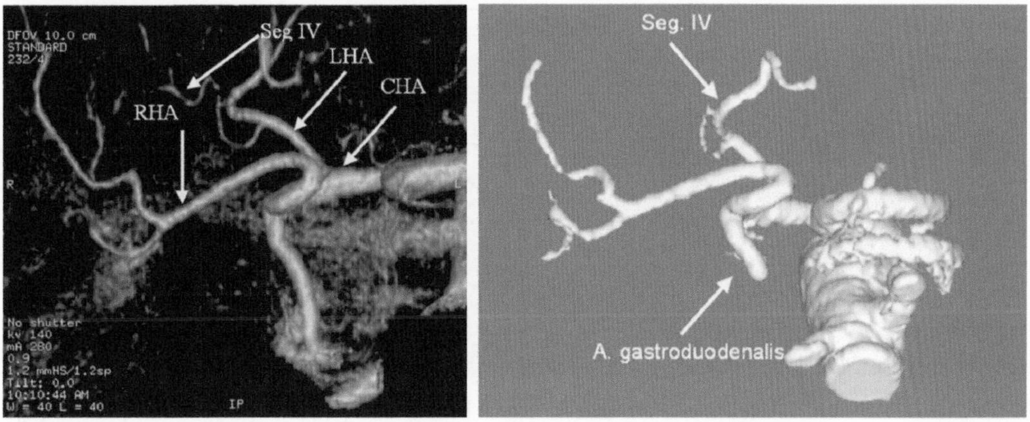

FIGURE 10.21 *With a modern radiology workstation, 3D renderings (left a volume rendering, right isosurface rendering) may be interactively annotated. Here, the arterial blood supply of the liver is shown to discuss whether the patient is eligible for live donor liver transplantation. (LHA—left hepatic artery, RHA—right hepatic artery, CHA—common hepatic artery, SEG IV—artery that supplies liver segment IV) (Courtesy of Christoph Wald, MGH Boston).*

Labeling of medical visualizations benefits from an analysis of labeled images in textbooks. Many decisions with respect to the label layout, described in this section, are inspired by textbooks, in particular from anatomy where often a multitude of labels is carefully arranged around an image. While for interactive use the number of simultaneously visible labels is usually small, for documentation purposes, sometimes more labels are stored.

Labeling is essential in anatomy and other medical training systems (see Chap. 21) to familiarize learners with anatomical structures but also for routine treatment planning. Thus, any modern radiological workstation provides facilities to manually annotate structures, e.g., with lines, arrowheads, and textual labels. As a first example, see the 3D manually annotated renderings of hepatic vasculature, serving for treatment planning in Figure 10.21.

Similarly, Figure 10.22 shows labeled 3D visualizations which are regularly generated by MeVis Medical Solutions[5] to provide the essential information for liver surgery planning. In particular, branches of the vascular system are labeled, since many further analysis steps, such as the computation of vascular territories, depend on the correct identification of these branches and their assignment to liver segments. There are two labeling strategies:

- *internal labeling* where the object name is embedded in the shape of the related object, and
- *external labeling* where the object is connected via a reference line with a textual label.

Both strategies are also employed in maps and technical drawings. Algorithms for internal labeling are often rather complex, e.g., when labels should be accommodated in elongated curved structures, such as rivers in geographic maps or vascular structures in medicine. In the following, we describe the labeling strategies first for 3D models and later for slice-based visualizations.

5 http://www.mevis.de/mms/Distant_Services.html.

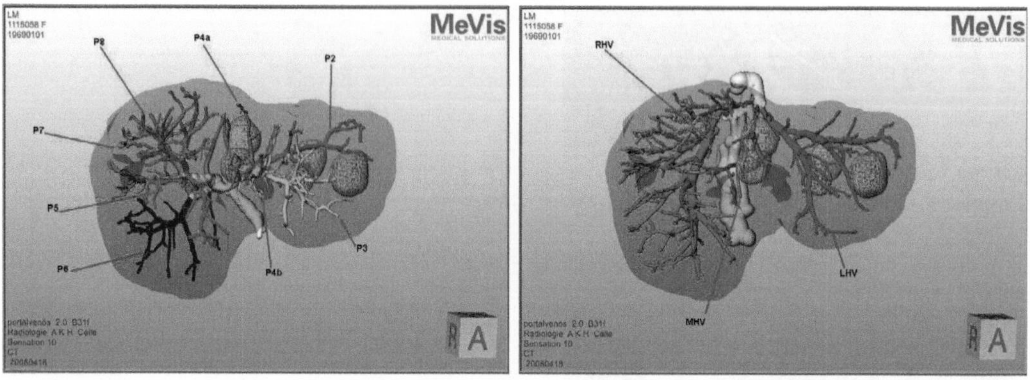

FIGURE 10.22 *A 3D model of the liver anatomy where the vascular branches of the portal vein (left) and the hepatic vein (right) are labeled to support surgical planning and documentation of preoperative decisions. The left image conveys how the portal vein branches are assigned to the eight portal vein segments, whereas the right image indicates the assignment of venous branches to the left, right, and middle hepatic vein (LV, RV, MV) (Courtesy of Fraunhofer MEVIS).*

10.7.1 INTERNAL LABELING OF 3D MEDICAL SURFACE MODELS

Internal labels should be [Cipriano and Gleicher, 2008]:

- visible,
- legible, and
- shape-conveying.

A label is shape-conveying if it is placed such that the recognition of the labeled shape is supported well. Cartographers discriminate two processes in placing labels that are meanwhile also used for the annotation of medical shapes:

- *labeling* is the process of defining a path where the label should be placed.
- The second process, called *lettering*, defines the spacing and precise display of the letters along that path.

Labeling Internal labels are placed on top of the graphical representation of an object and should fit the 2D shape of that object. Thus, the use of internal labels is only feasible for objects that are large enough to accommodate a label and that are not partially obscured by other objects. With respect to legibility, it is preferred to present labels horizontally. If this is not possible, Götzelmann *et al.* [2005] suggest to place a label along the centerline. This strategy is also used by other authors, such as Cipriano and Gleicher [2008)]. If the centerline branches, a path needs to be selected that is long enough. The skeleton or medial axis path may be smoothed to reduce curvature and to gently accommodate a label. However, in general, labels along curved paths are hard to read.

Lettering The readability of internal labels may be improved by computing individual spacings between any two letters (instead of monospacing) and by incorporating thresholds on the allowable curvature of the path [Götzelmann *et al.*, 2005, Cipriano and Gleicher, 2008].

Internal labels related to 3D models are projected on the object surface. However, care has to be taken to ensure legibility. In particular noisy surfaces cannot be directly used to project a label on top. A promising

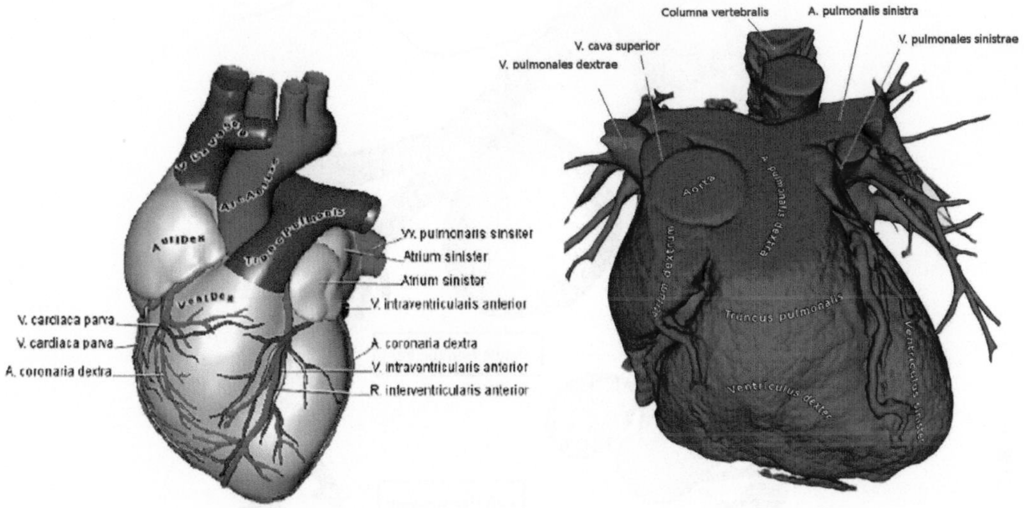

FIGURE 10.23 *Internal and external labels were placed automatically. The placement of internal labels is guided by the skeleton (From: [Götzelmann et al., 2005] and from: [Ropinski et al., 2007]).*

approach is to fit a (smooth) Bezier patch to a 3D surface that should be labeled [Ropinski *et al.*, 2007]. Similarly, Cipriano and Gleicher [2008] describe a process where a *scaffold surface* is created from the surface to label, including morphological oprations, such as hole filling. However, the legibility of internal labels may suffer from different background colors and low contrast. Figure 10.23 illustrates *hybrid labeling* where internal and external labeling is combined.

10.7.2 EXTERNAL LABELING

External labeling aims to fulfill a couple of requirements. Labels should

- not overlap with other labels or objects,
- identify an object unambiguously, and
- be placed such that they are close to related objects (proximity).

The use of external labels requires *anchor points* and *reference line* as additional graphical elements. The selection of anchor points is crucial to establish a clear correlation between a label and its reference object. Despite the problems of providing a correlation between a textual label and related visual objects, we regard *external labels* as the more promising approach for CBT (Computer-based training) systems. The most obvious advantage of external labels is better legibility, since external labels are placed on top of a background in uniform color.

A somewhat mixed situation occurs when a large object, e.g., an organ, is used as background to place labels on top, in particular if a close-up is shown (Fig. 10.24). Again, anchor points and reference lines are employed but due to shading, a uniform background color may not be guaranteed. Moreover, external labels do not restrict the perception of the shape of visual objects, which is essential in medicine where object shapes are irregular and complex. Figure 10.25 provides an example where the labels are arranged around the object guided by its silhouette. Algorithms for automatically placing labels around medical surface models are described in [Preim *et al.*, 1997, Hartmann *et al.*, 2004, Bruckner *et al.*, 2005].

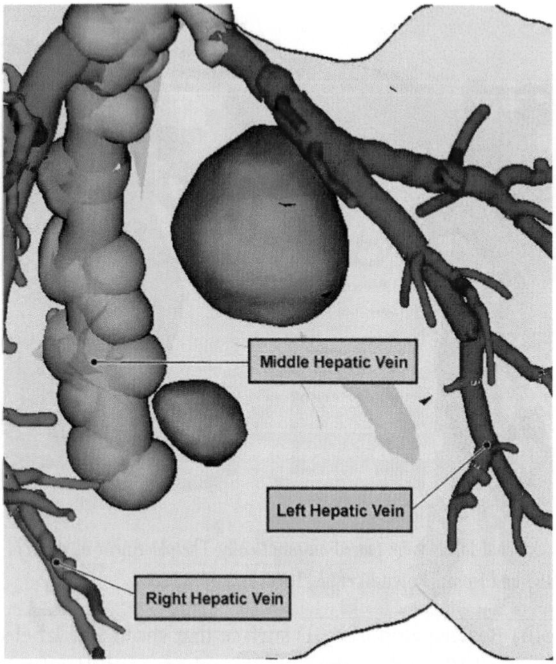

FIGURE 10.24 *If no free space is available, annotations are placed above large structures, such as organs, that serve as background (From: [Mühler and Preim, 2009a]).*

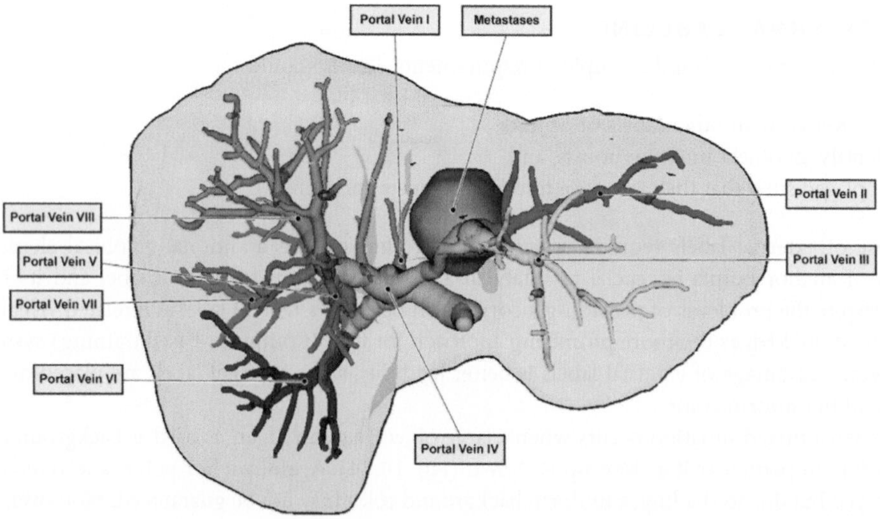

FIGURE 10.25 *External labeling with labels automatically arranged around the silhouette of the overall model. Sections of the hepatic vasculature and a tumor are labeled. Labels are embedded in rectangles with a light background (From: [Mühler and Preim, 2009a]).*

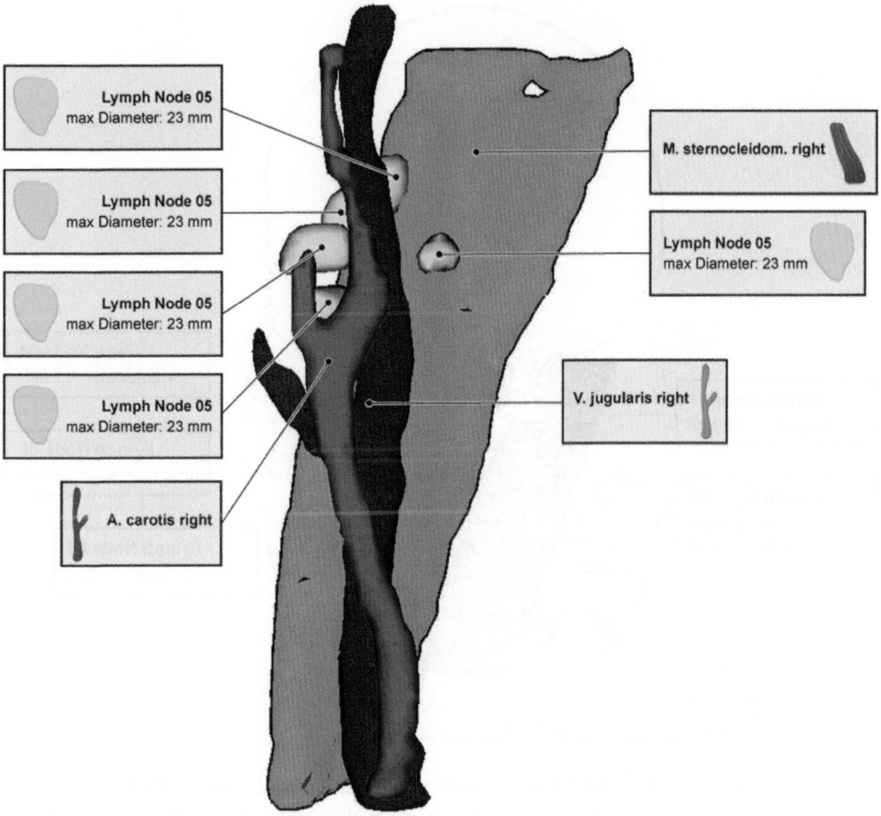

FIGURE 10.26 *The relation between anatomical structures and their textual labels may be improved by adding icons that represent the type of anatomical structure, e.g., muscle, lymph node, or vascular structure* (From: [Mühler and Preim, 2009a]).

It is often difficult to recognize the relation between labels and reference objects in complex scenes with several labels. A surgeon, Prof. Oldhafer, from Asklepios hospital Hamburg uttered the idea of adding icons to textual labels to represent the object type. Mühler and Preim [2009a] realized this idea that turned out to be an advantage in a user study (Fig. 10.26). In specific applications it may be useful to define a particular *labeling style* similar to defining other layout attributes for specific applications.

Dynamic Adaptation When 3D models are interactively explored, the whole geometry consisting of objects and labels changes and thus a dynamic adaptation is required. Götzelmann *et al.* [2005] explain that the use of internal and external labels should change as a consequence of zooming. When the user gets closer to an object, at a certain distance an external label should be replaced by an internal label. The size of the label, however, should not change. When 3D models are rotated, other adaptations of labels and reference lines need to be considered, e.g., the horizontal and vertical placement of labels may be adjusted to avoid that long lines arise and too many lines cross each other [Preim *et al.*, 1997]. Mühler and Preim [2009a] investigated adaptations of labels to reflect the changing visibility of the reference objects. In Figure 10.27 labels relating to objects invisible after rotation are combined with *curved arrows* instead of reference lines.

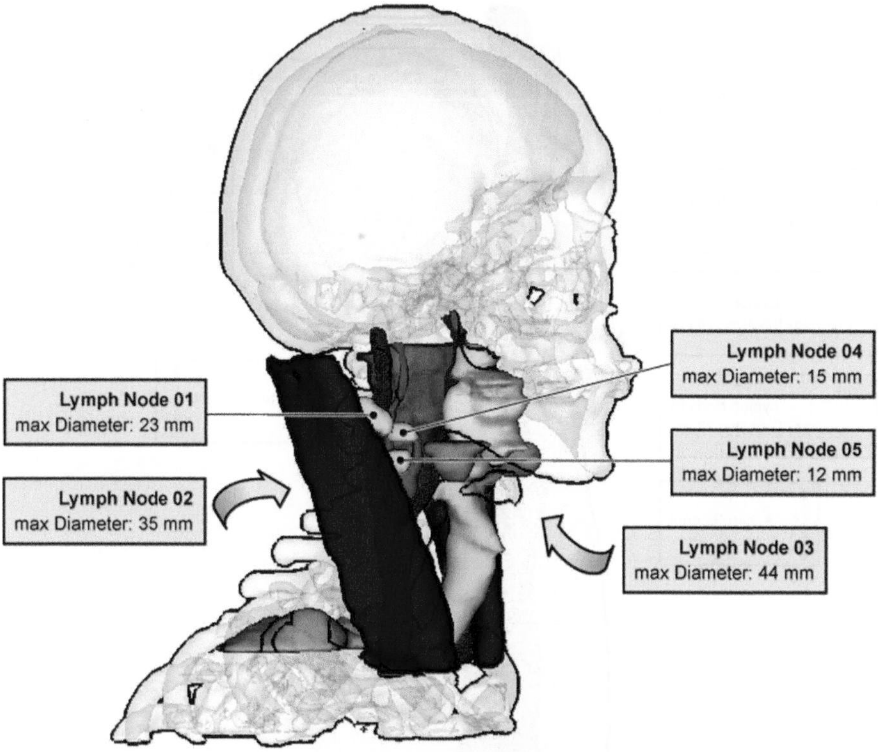

FIGURE 10.27 *A 3D model was rotated after labels for lymph nodes have been enabled. Lymph nodes that are no longer visible are indicated with a curved arrow. The direction of the arrow roughly points in the direction of that object as a navigation aid. Pressing such an arrow rotates the model to make the related object visible (From: [Mühler and Preim, 2009a]).*

This adaptation indicates that there are labeled objects, but to make them visible the scene needs to be rotated. The curved arrows are designed as interactive widgets: when they are selected, a small animation is initiated which rotates the scene and makes the related object visible.

Since textual labels occupy a large amount of space, it might be a good option to display them only temporarily. Sonnet *et al.* [2004] described a system for the exploration of complex geometric models, e.g., models of an engine. An object is rendered transparently when the mouse pointer is on top of it. As a consequence, internal structures and the center of gravity become visible. If this center is selected, the related label and a short explanation are displayed as long as no other object is selected.

10.7.3 LABELING SLICE-BASED VISUALIZATIONS

Labeling and measurements in 2D slice views are also highly relevant for diagnosis and documentation. As an example, in oncology, follow-up examinations to monitor chemotherapy and radiation treatment planning are frequent. Metastasis need to be identified, quantified (diameter, volume, mean gray value), and labeled with these values. Again, crossing lines should be avoided, labels and associated structures should not overlap with each other and labels should be placed close to the associated structure. Moreover, the dense content of a slice of CT or MRI data should not be hidden strongly.

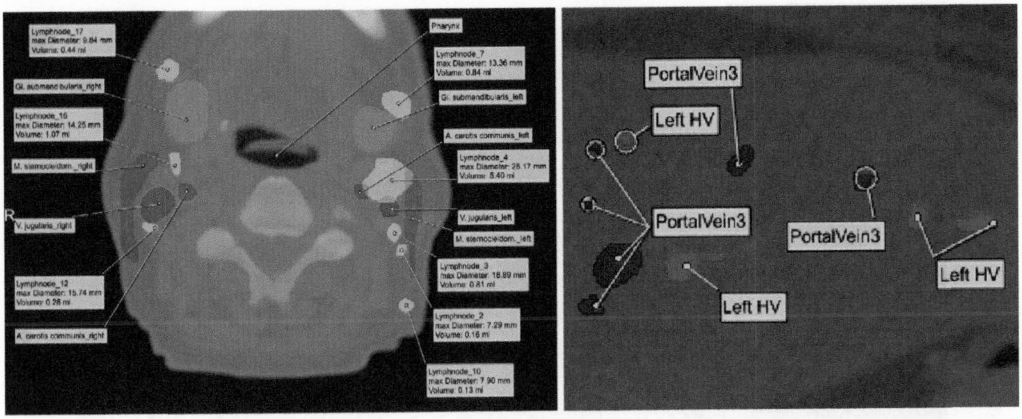

FIGURE 10.28 *Labeling segmented anatomical structures in 2D slice views. External labels in the background (left) or internal labels in the immediate vicinity of anatomical structures are viable (Courtesy of Konrad Mühler, University of Magdeburg).*

With respect to fonts and colors, similar considerations like in 3D visualizations are required. In general, labeling and measurement in 2D are simpler than in 3D where occlusion has to be considered. Despite this, appropriate labeling of 2D slice visualizations should be supported by an automatic layout. Like in 3D, external labels in the background portions of slices and internal labels close to the anatomical structures are possible (see Fig. 10.28).

The labels in Figure 10.28 are created with an algorithm introduced in Mühler and Preim [2009b]. The following steps are performed to generate labels for segmented structures:

1 **Connected components** are identified to represent which regions need to be labeled and which space is available for placing labels.
2 For each component, **anchor points** are determined based on an Euclidean distance transform. The point with the largest distance to the component's boundary is used as anchor point.
3 For each component, **candidate positions** for labeling are determined taking the individual label size into account.
4 Initially, labels are placed at the closest candidate position.
5 Labels are iteratively rearranged to **avoid crossing lines**. The final step benefits from the candidate positions determined in step 3.

There are a couple of special situations that need to be considered.

Grouping Disconnected Components Branching and elongated anatomical structures with a small diameter appear as disconnected components in slice views. As long as these small regions are close to each other, they may be summarized by *one* label (Fig. 10.28, right). Often, in particular cross sections of vessels and nerves are very small. Thus, it is better to encircle them than to select an anchor point (see again Fig. 10.28, right).

Internal Labels If large portions of a slice view are occupied by one large anatomical structure, such as the lung, the algorithm described above would yield label positions which are far away from the related anatomical structures. Therefore, such a large structure may be considered as background where internal labels are allowed to hide it partially. This process may be automated as well, taking into account the

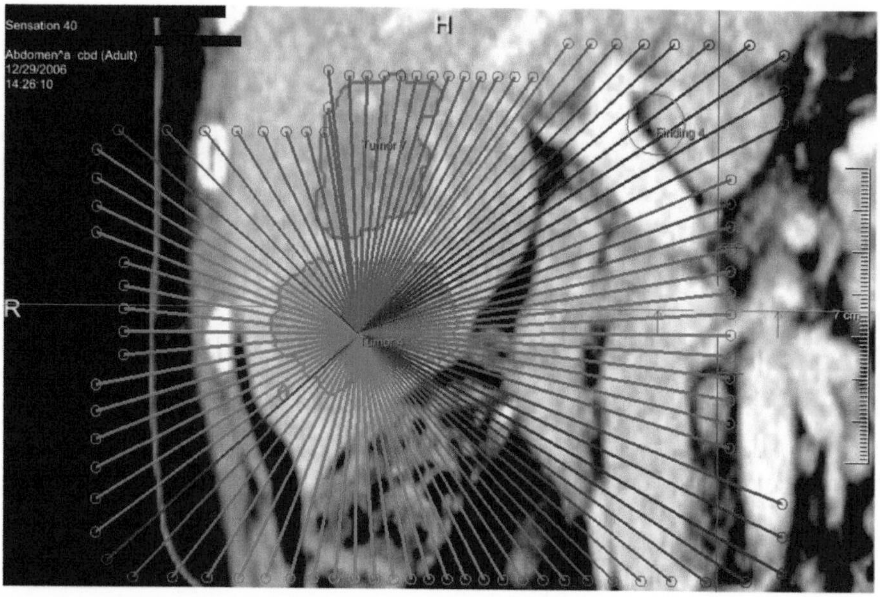

FIGURE 10.29 *Appropriate labeling positions for a tumor are searched in discrete (180) directions. The green rays represent suitable directions, where no other findings would be obscured (From: [Mogalle et al., 2012]).*

category of anatomical structures. Thus, vascular structures and tumors probably should be occluded by labels, whereas for organs this is often acceptable.

Coherency between Slices The major use case of slice-based visualizations is to browse through the slices. If this is not adequately considered, the labeling algorithm produces new labeling positions for one object in any slice. Thus, labels "jump" around when the slices are browsed through. Since this is obviously disturbing, the labeling position and extent is left constant whenever possible—new components might be labeled with somewhat longer reference lines.

Constrained Labeling If multiple labels, possibly multiline labels should be placed, a rigorous optimization strategy is necessary to determine a good layout that does not violate any requirements. Global optimization algorithms are notoriously slow. Thus, a local optimization, e.g., following the gradient-descent strategy, is more promising to achieve a good trade-off between quality and speed. Recently, Mogalle *et al.* [2012] presented an algorithm that sampled directions for label placement starting from the center of the reference object. Starting from an initial label configuration that possibly violates several requirements, labels are shifted as often as necessary to achieve a satisfying layout. Figure 10.29 illustrates the search process, and Figure 10.30 shows a result of that process. Of course, there are even situations, where no instance of a layout is satisfying. In the oncology applications that motivated this work, they are, however, rare, since not more than ten metastasis are considered according to the guidelines for evaluating treatment response. Despite this work was based on an in-depth task analysis related to follow-up investigations in case of cancer treatment, further evaluation is necessary to fully understand the benefit of the labeling approach and the need for further refinement.

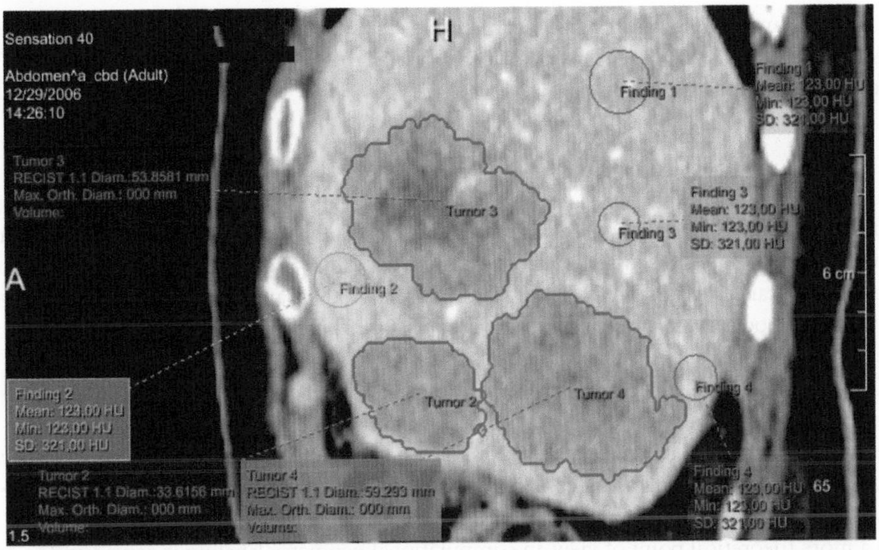

FIGURE 10.30 *In total, seven findings are automatically labeled primarily at the border of the images (From: [Mogalle et al., 2012]).*

10.8 SUMMARY

Measurement facilities are part of general and specialized diagnostic workstations and surgical planning systems, such as the 3D SLICER [Gering *et al.*, 1999b] and the TUMORTHERAPYMANAGER [Rössling *et al.*, 2011]. In particular angular measures and distance measures between surface meshes are essential for many specific tasks. Automatic measures are significantly more reliable than interactive measures, e.g., of longest diameters. Medical doctors are sometimes not aware of the large amount of uncertainty involved in manual, purely interactive measures. Thus, the ability to reliably measure is an important motivation for segmentation. Even interactive measures may be supported by snapping (to surfaces) and appropriate views, e.g., combinations of 2D and 3D views.

With respect to measurement lines and labeling we also discussed aesthetic issues, such as layout and colors. These aspects influence perception, e.g., whether measurements and labels are correctly and efficiently associated with anatomical structures. We discussed a few results from informal studies, but these are too limited to make final conclusions. Therefore, we presented several variants in this chapter and would recommend that treatment planning systems offer a few choices to enable users to adjust labeling and measurement styles to their preferences. Larger studies with more complex and realistic tasks as well as precise measures of task completion time and error rate are necessary.

Open Questions Despite the progress in the last years and the recognized importance of labeling and measurement, these fields have not matured in a way that is similar to map labeling. Often, individual measures and (internal) labels are placed and the interaction between these individual decisions is not carefully considered. The techniques described in this chapter are *general techniques* applicable for a wide range of medical applications. To gain acceptance in clinical practice, such techniques need to be fine-tuned for specific treatment planning and documentation settings. This would include the definition of labeling and measurement templates with default values for specific anatomic structures. As a very step in that direction, Mori *et al.* [2011] recently described a system that is dedicated to the annotation of vascular structures in the abdominal region.

FURTHER READING

The accuracy of diameter and volume measurements as well as the clinical impact of such measurements for treatment monitoring is discussed in [Bornemann *et al.*, 2007]. The focus of the authors is follow-up studies after lung cancer treatment. The same authors refined their analysis in a large study where more than 200 lymph nodes were investigated [Fabel *et al.*, 2008]. Manual, semi-automatic and automatic measures of hypo and hyper dense hepatic metastasis were investigated by Keil *et al.* [2008].

Labeling is widely studied in cartography. The most essential reference is still the classic text from Eduard Imhof that discriminated different types of labeling tasks, criteria for labeling and viable labeling strategies including trade-offs between the various criteria [Imhof, 2008]. More recently, also in cartography interactive and animated maps are considered and the classic principles were adapted to these settings [Harrower, 2003, Harrower and Sheesley, 2007].

From a more theoretical point of view, in computational geometry labeling is considered as optimization problem under constraints (desirable properties) [Christensen *et al.*, 1995, Doddi *et al.*, 1997, Wagner and Wolff, 1995, Petzold and Gröger, 2003]. The specific problem of labeling line features was investigated by Wolff *et al.* [2000] and may serve as orientation for labeling vascular structures. Map labeling is still an active field of research. As an example Bekos *et al.*, [2010] study how boundary labels (at the boundary of a map) may be generated efficiently without leading to intersection lines.

It might be inspiring to analyze such labeling techniques and to investigate whether some principles may be transferred to medical visualization. Fekete and Plaisant [1999] introduced labeling techniques for information visualization, classified many existing techniques, and discussed the combination of lens-based interaction with labeling. Cmolík and Bittner [2010)] described the generation of label layouts consisting of external labels using various measures.

With respect to medical visualization, labeling techniques discussed in [Götzelmann *et al.*, 2005, 2006, Ali *et al.*, 2005] are relevant. These and other more recent publications investigate *dynamic labeling*, that is, adaptations of labels when 3D scenes are interactively explored or panning and zooming occurs during exploration of digital maps [Been *et al.*, 2006, Stein and Décoret, 2008].

Similar to labeling, distance computation is an active research topic in computational geometry (and applications in robotics) [Bobrow, 1989, Lin and Canny, 1991, Gottschalk *et al.*, 1996]. In particular distance computations are performed in the context of collision detection—thus, they need to be very fast as well.

Part III

Advanced Medical Visualization Techniques

Part III "Advanced visualization techniques" starts with the visualization of anatomical tree structures, such as vascular and bronchial trees (Chap. 11). We describe different methods that produce comprehensible visualizations at different levels of detail and accuracy. Surface- and volume rendering techniques were developed and fine-tuned for the peculiarities of anatomical tree structures. Among the surface methods, a number of implicit surface representations have been introduced recently that enable a smooth and accurate visualization. While this chapter was restricted to surface-based visualizations in the first edition, we provide more detail on volume rendering techniques, tailored, e.g., for the diagnosis of vascular diseases. Focus-and-context rendering, transfer functions for emphasizing elongated structures as well as plaques and stents inside vessels are introduced.

Chapter 13 is devoted to virtual endoscopy. Virtual endoscopy has a great potential for surgery training and treatment planning, as well as for diagnosis and intraoperative navigation, because it has less restrictions than real endoscopy (the virtual camera can go everywhere) and is more comfortable for the patient. Visualization and navigation techniques in the virtual human are the issues which are discussed in this chapter. We cover image processing, surface and volume rendering, and user guidance. Highly realistic and efficient rendering is a focus. We also consider different application areas, primarily virtual colonoscopy, bronchoscopy, and angioscopy, focusing on clinical applicability and studies investigating the effect of virtual endoscopy in practice.

In Chapter 12, illustrative rendering and emphasis techniques are described. These techniques are essential for medical education and for therapy planning. In recent years, many new techniques were introduced that represent features of complex (anatomical) surfaces, e.g., various feature lines. Also new hatching and stippling methods are discussed. Finally, smart visibility techniques, such as cutaway views and ghosted views are discussed.

In the last chapter of Part III, we discuss "Projection-based Medical Visualization Techniques" (Chap. 14). This completely new chapter is motivated by a variety of successful applications that incorporate map-like projections. Vessel flattening, brain and colon flattening, tumor maps, Bull's Eye plots in cardiology are just some of the examples, where 3D geometries are transformed to map projections to give an overview. Such projections from a higher to a lower dimensional space are related with distortions and a loss of information. We carefully discuss different strategies and their limitations.

Visual Computing for Medicine, Second Edition. http://dx.doi.org/10.1016/B978-0-12-415873-3.00032-8

Chapter 11

Visualization of Vascular Structures

11.1 INTRODUCTION

For diagnosis as well as for many therapy planning tasks it is crucial to understand the branching pattern and morphology of tree-like anatomical structures, such as nerves, vascular, and bronchial trees. A slight difference in vascular topology may lead to a strong difference in the treatment strategy. For therapy planning, it is of paramount importance to recognize shape features and morphology of vascular structures as well as spatial relations between vascular and other relevant structures. Such an analysis allows to recognize vascular abnormalities, to judge possible complications during surgery and thus directly supports the decision making process.

For a convenient interpretation, the curvature, the depth relations, and the diminution of the diameter toward the periphery should be depicted correctly. For diagnosis it is essential to reliably recognize and assess vessel wall abnormalities, such as narrowings (stenosis) or dilated parts (aneurysms) as well as plaque and thrombus formation. Primarily CT and MR angiography are employed. Digital subtraction angiography (DSA), a variant of X-ray, is also available as a 3D imaging technique. It is referred to as *rotation angiography* and provides data with a very high spatial resolution. However, it is a rather invasive procedure [Giachetti and Zanetti, 2004. Thus, we focus on processing and visualizing information derived from CT and MR angiography data. In particular for diagnosis, 2D views of the original data, derived information, such as oblique reformations and changes of the vessel diameter, need to be integrated carefully with 3D views.

We restrict here to the analysis of *static* data where the blood vessels are assumed as rigid structures. This is, of course, a simplification, since blood vessels are elastic structures that change slightly during the blood cycle depending on the alternating pressure and flow. Blood flow data provides valuable information and plays an increasing role in understanding vascular diseases. We discuss the acquisition, analysis and interpretation of flow data in Chapter 19.

Organization We describe how vascular structures may be enhanced and visually separated from skeletal structures (§ 11.2). With such enhancements, direct volume rendering provides appropriate visualizations. To further support diagnostic tasks, *projection techniques* have been developed primarily to be used in combination with direct volume rendering (§ 11.3).

We briefly explain image analysis (segmentation and centerline extraction) techniques, which are a prerequisite for high-quality vessel visualization (§ 11.4). We continue with surface visualization techniques using the vessel segmentation result. *Model-based* and *illustrative* surface visualizations of vascular trees serve primarily for treatment planning. They are based on model assumptions, such as a circular cross section. These methods either fit graphics primitives, such as cylinders or truncated cones, along the skeleton, or generate parametric or implicit surfaces to represent the circular cross section (§ 11.5). In contrast, *model-free approaches* do not enforce any assumptions but display vascular structures, as they have been segmented. To achieve a high visual quality and ease interpretation, smoothness is aimed at. Again, implicit surface visualization techniques are a viable solution (§ 11.6).

Visual Computing for Medicine, Second Edition. http://dx.doi.org/10.1016/B978-0-12-415873-3.00011-0

Adapted volume rendering also has a great potential for visualizing vascular structures in particular for diagnostic purposes (§ 11.7). We present strategies for transfer function specification and local volume rendering techniques, using the segmentation result to emphasize certain regions. Specific applications comprise the diagnosis of cerebral and abdominal aneurysms as well as the diagnosis of the coronary heart disease. In this section we also discuss how multiple views may be employed for the diagnosis of vascular diseases. In particular, we discuss the coordination between such views.

11.2 ENHANCING VASCULAR STRUCTURES

Ideally, the contrast agent is equally distributed in all vascular structures that are relevant for diagnosis. However, the contrast agent spreads with a certain speed and thus cannot reach a complete vascular tree at a particular point in time. Moreover, the contrast agent diffuses in the surrounding and leads to irregularly increased image intensity values. This non-uniform spatial distribution is referred to as *contrast agent inhomogeneity*. A simple technique to compensate for this artifact is a so-called *background compensation* [Selle *et al.*, 2000]. With this technique, the different background values in regions of the data are estimated and adaptively corrected. This process is based on the assumption that the intensity difference between contrast-enhanced and surrounding structures is similar throughout the data.

Another general problem is the small scale of vascular structures. A large portion of the voxels belonging to a blood vessel are boundary voxels. These voxels comprise vessel portions and other tissues leading to an averaging of the image intensities (*partial volume effect*). As a consequence, small side-branches of vascular structures may be hidden and larger branches may appear smaller than they actually are.

Finally, the image intensity of contrast-enhanced vascular structures in CT data is in the same range as bony structures. In some regions of the body, these bony structures may be far away from the vascular structures and can be efficiently removed by applying clipping planes. However, in other regions, such as the skull, this is often not feasible, since they are too close to each other.

11.2.1 EMPHASIS OF ELONGATED STRUCTURES

As preprocessing for vascular analysis, a special "vesselness" filter has been proposed by Lorenz *et al.* [1997] and refined by Frangi *et al.* [1998]. It is based on the symmetric Hessian matrix, which summarizes the second order derivatives of the intensity variations ($I_{xx}, I_{xy}, I_{xz}, I_{yy}, I_{yz}, I_{zz}$). The remaining three entries are obtained by symmetry ($I_{yx} = I_{xy}, \ldots$). These derivatives cannot be computed analytically but are estimated by applying an appropriate filter.

The Hessian has three real-valued eigenvalues λ_i that can be used to determine the likelihood of a voxel to belong to a line-shaped structure. The eigenvalues are sorted such that ($|\lambda_1| \geq |\lambda_2| \geq |\lambda_3|$). For an ideal line-shaped structure, the following relation holds: $\lambda_1 \gg \lambda_2 \approx \lambda_3$. With appropriate weight parameters this analysis may be used to enhance vascular structures. This analysis should be carried out at different scales to cope with vessels of a different diameter. Frangi *et al.* [1998] applied the filter in a multiscale approach, performing the eigenanalysis at different scales and chosing that scale where the maximum vesselness was computed. A vesselness filter in CTA data always gives a signal, even in case that there is not tubular structure. To get expressive results, only regions with a *significant signal* of the filter should be emphasized. The refined "vesselness" filter is widely used and yielded an improved visualization (MIP, Direct Volume Rendering, Fig. 11.1) as well as a better segmentation. This preprocessing step, however, is computationally expensive and often applied as an offline process.

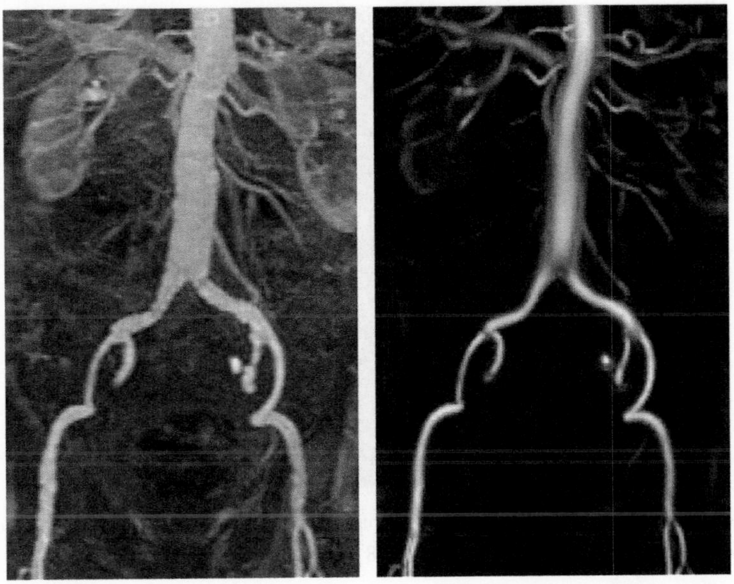

FIGURE 11.1 *A MIP image of an MRA dataset is generated (left). The "vesselness" filter is applied to suppressing other structures (From: [Frangi et al., 1998]).*

Entropy-based Vesselness Filtering Since only tubular structures are determined by the "vesselness" filter, the detection of vessels in branching areas leaves room for improvement. The multiscale approach is also limited in dealing with varying vessel diameters, due to its limitation to fixed diameters. These issues were dealt with by Joshi *et al.* [2008], who used a mix of Hessian- and entropy-based filtering. Their entropy factor was generated from analyzing the polar profiles of each voxel. For each direction, the variance in intensities and average intensity are computed within the neighborhood (these neighborhood voxels along one direction are referred to as *profile*). The likelihood of clusters within such profiles is used to calculate the vesselness. Compared to the Hessian-based technique, the profiles do not require multiple runs for different vessel diameters, and especially the quality around branching points has been improved (see Fig. 11.2). Figure 11.3 illustrates that even better results are achieved if both methods are combined. The specific solution from Joshi *et al.* [2008] is too slow for clinical use, but there is substantial room for performance optimizations.

Limitations The geometric assumptions underlying the vesselness computation are not very specific. Basically, any cylinder-shaped structure, including tendons and bones, are thus emphasized. Physicians can discriminate these structures and vascular structures very well. However, an annoying situation arises, if "real" vessels are nearby and get obscured from these erroneously emphasized structures. This gives rise to the following discussion, to automatically discriminate bones from contrast-enhanced vessels.

11.2.2 BONE REMOVAL

In most regions of the human body, (contrast-enhanced) vascular structures and skeletal structures cannot be reliably discriminated [Zheng *et al.*, 2008]. Bone removal is part of modern radiology workstations. Simultaneously, calcified plaque is removed, which enables the evaluation of a (possible) stenosis. In most

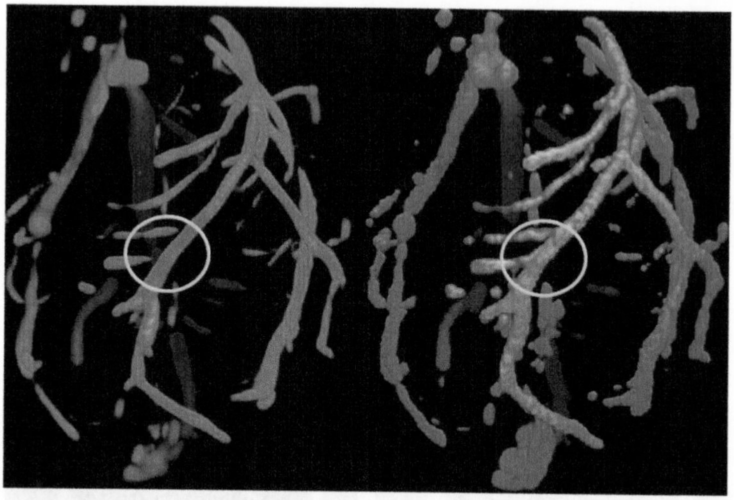

FIGURE 11.2 Comparison of the Hessian-based (left) and entropy-based (right) emphasis. The encircled branching clearly reveals the differences between both approaches (From: [Joshi et al., 2008]).

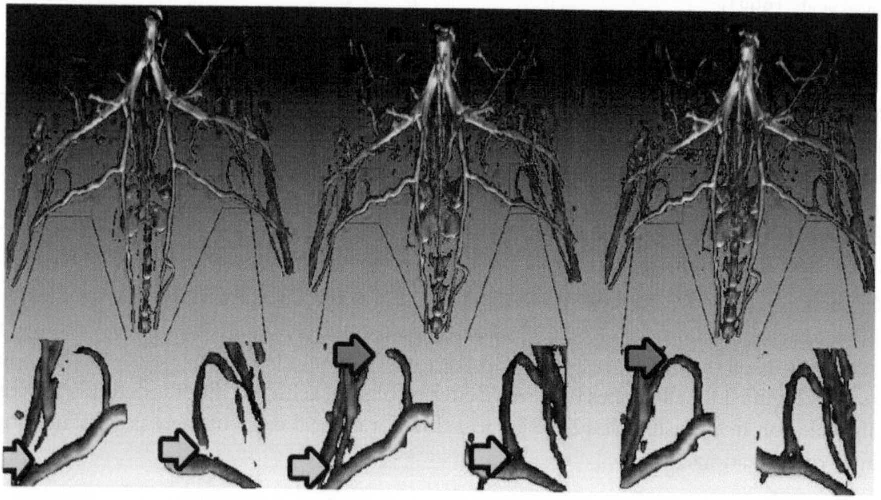

FIGURE 11.3 Comparison of the Hessian-based (left) and entropy-based (middle), polar profile, vessel filters. The green arrows mark benefits of the earlier method, and the yellow arrows show improvements of the latter. The final (right) image shows a combination of both techniques (From: [Joshi et al., 2008]).

cases, it is sufficient if the user marks a connected skeletal component with one click of a pointing device to initiate a (more or less advanced) region growing method to roughly segment this structure (see Fig. 11.4). Specific solutions have been developed for using the full information from Dual Energy CT (recall [Zheng et al., 2008]).

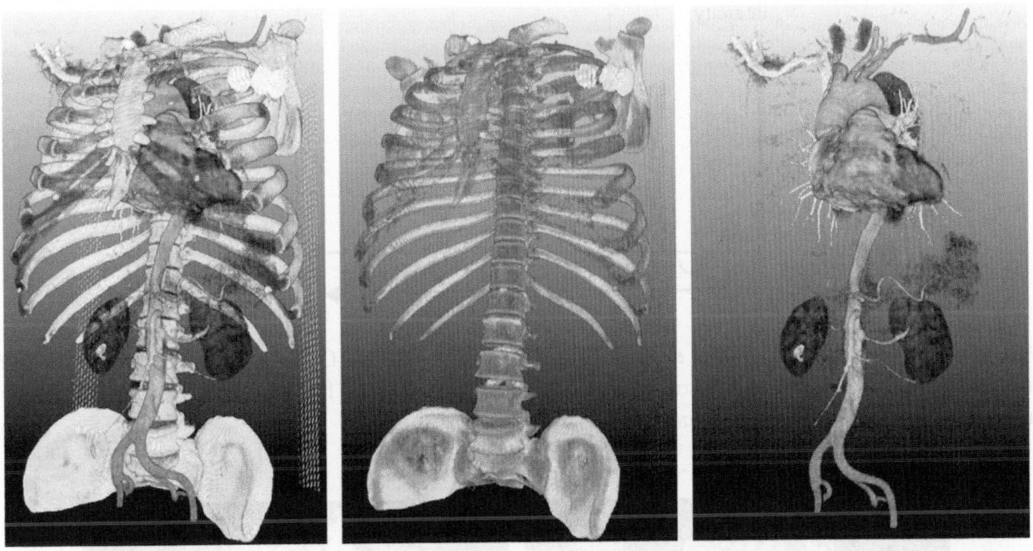

FIGURE 11.4 *DVR of vascular structures. Original scene (left), bones to be removed (middle), and resulting visualization restricted to the heart, the kidney, and vascular structures (right). Bone removal significantly improves the display of vascular structures (Courtesy of Johann Drexl, Florian Link and Horst Hahn, Fraunhofer MEVIS).*

11.3 PROJECTION-BASED VISUALIZATION

A number of projection techniques have been developed to convey the complex information of vascular structures. While many tasks in radiology are still performed with conventional 2D slice views, the longitudinal and branching structures of vasculature can be better perceived with techniques providing a better overview. With this goal in mind, a number of projection-based techniques have been developed and are described in the following.

11.3.1 MAXIMUM INTENSITY AND CLOSEST VESSEL PROJECTION

For the visualization of vascular structures, Maximum Intensity Projections (MIP) are frequently used. In cardiovascular diagnosis, MIP indicates calcified plaques. A related projection technique is minimum intensity projection (MINIP) that depicts the minimum value along the ray and may reveals soft plaques [Mistelbauer *et al.*, 2013].

However, MIP and MINIP do not correctly reflect depth relations because voxels might be displayed, although other voxels with high opacity are closer to the camera. Moreover, small vessels tend to disappear completely. Therefore, it is essential to rotate such visualizations or to use precomputed videos of such rotations in order to benefit from depth cues resulting from the motion parallax. The image intensity of the selected voxels is usually linearly mapped to the brightness of a gray value. Thus, it is not necessary to adjust a transfer function. For clinical users, the simplicity of MIP images is a great advantage—MIP rendering is just enabled or disabled.

As a modification of the MIP, closest vessel projections (CVP), also called *Local MIP*, have been introduced [Zuiderveld, 1995]. The CVP scheme is as follows: for each ray, the first *local maximum* with an intensity above a user-defined threshold t is projected to the image instead of the global maximum. Thus, small

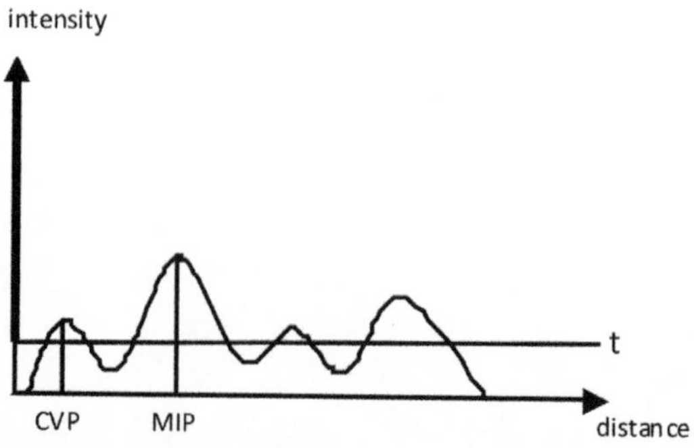

FIGURE 11.5 *The profile along a ray is evaluated differently within the MIP and CVP scheme. In a MIP image, the global maximum, independent of its position is chosen, whereas in CVP the ray is traced starting from the viewing position and the first local maximum beyond a threshold t (see the horizontal line) is selected.*

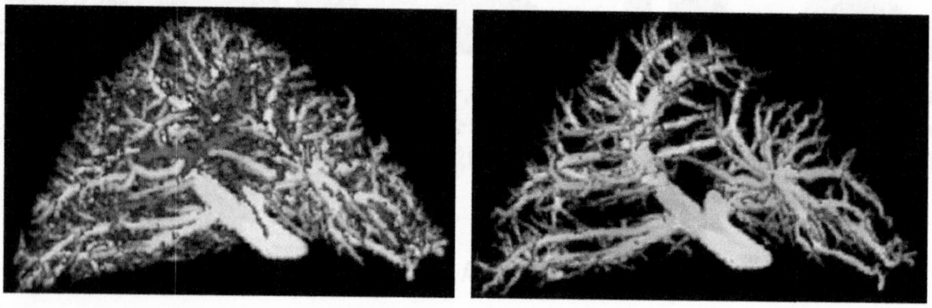

FIGURE 11.6 *Closest vessel projection of a corrosion cast of the human liver.* **Left:** *A low threshold,* **right:** *a higher threshold.*

vessels in front of large vessels (with higher intensities) are visible. However, the user has to specify t appropriately (Fig. 11.5). As a rule of thumb, a certain percentage of the global maximum intensity of the whole dataset is usually appropriate and "suggested" as default value. With the methods described so far, the interaction to explore vascular structures is restricted (Fig. 11.6). For example, it is not possible to selectively hide or emphasize vessels.

Advanced topic: Real-time MIP. MIP and CVP are usually realized as raycasting. CVP benefits from early ray termination, which naturally is applied to stop the calculation after the local maximum is determined. MIP, on the other hand, requires always to compute the intensity values along the whole ray. Thus, it is slower than conventional Direct Volume Rendering. There have been several suggestions to accelerate MIP computation, e.g., by adaptive resampling [Fang *et al.*, 2002], by using templates in parallel projection [Mroz *et al.*, 1999] and by optimizing storage schemes where data are stored according to their sorted value [Mroz *et al.*, 2000]. Today, GPU-based strategies are more promising. As an example, Kye and Jeong [2008] employ occlusion culling applied to blocks of the data, scaled such that cache-efficient GPU rendering is enabled. Thus, they can exploit the GPU-supported *occlusion queries*.

11.3.2 MAXIMUM INTENSITY DIFFERENCE ACCUMULATION

Bruckner and Gröller [2009] introduced the **maximum intensity difference accumulation** (MIDA) to highlight possibly occluded structures. They altered the blending to favor classified samples that have a higher opacity than previous samples. Thus, similar to MIP, high opacity structures are not covered by the accumulation of many low opacity structures. The MIDA construction scheme is compared with MIP and DVR generation in Figure 11.7.

Their control value allows a seamless transition from regular DVR to MIDA to MIP (see Fig. 11.8). Although this is a rather general volume rendering technique, it is especially useful for rendering vascular structures. The segmentation of vascular structures allows to adjust a TF to the image intensities, in

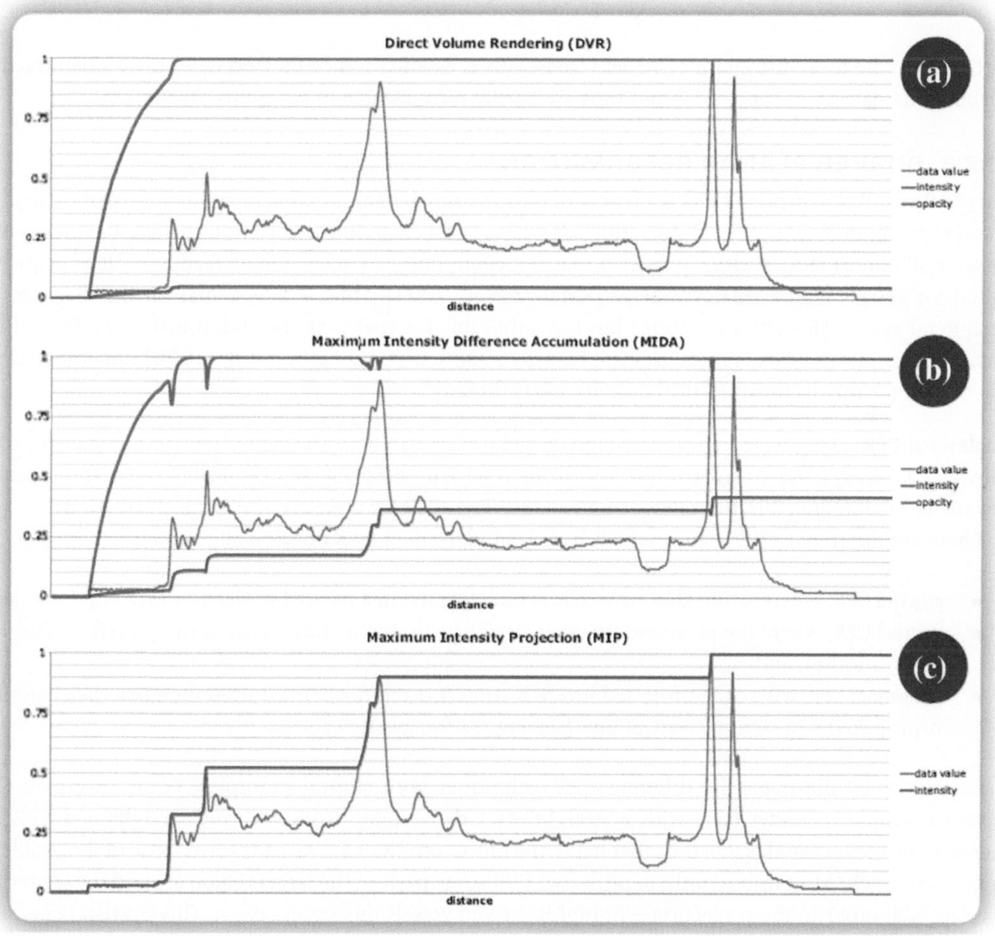

FIGURE 11.7 *The same ray profile is evaluated differently in (a) DVR, (b) MIDA, and (c) MIP. In DVR, opacity soon reaches its maximum and more distant voxels do not contribute. In MIDA, intensity differences are highlighted by applying high opacity. MIP just looks for the global maximum and assigns this to intensity (brightness) (From: [Bruckner and Gröller, 2009]).*

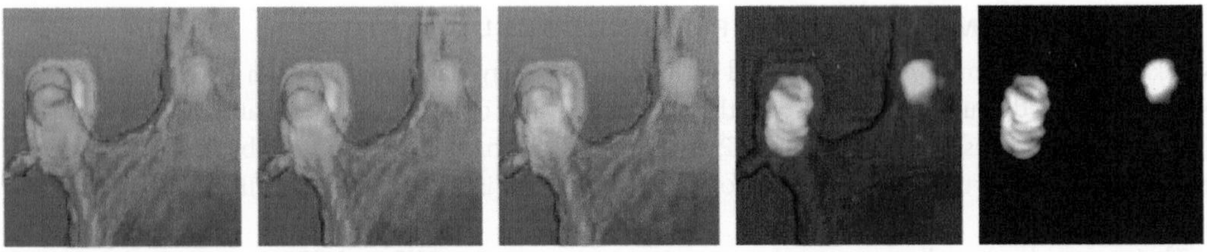

FIGURE 11.8 *Maximum intensity difference accumulation applied to coronary vessels in CT data. From left to right the MIDA control value γ is changed from -1 (a) to 0 (c) to 1 (e). This is equivalent to blending from DVR to MIDA to MIP. Compared to the original MIDA implementation, the opacity values for MIDA blending were different than for DVR to achieve a higher contrast* (From: [Kubisch *et al.*, 2012]).

particular to the local histogram of vessel voxels. This is essential, since they occupy only a small fraction of the entire dataset (some 2–5%) and thus are hardly recognizable in the global histogram.

11.3.3 CURVED PLANAR REFORMATION

Curved Planar Reformation (CPR) is a family of reformatting techniques that integrate information along a vessel segment in the absence of bifurcations. It is based on a centerline description and allows to recognize vessel wall abnormalities easily, provided that the centerline was accurately determined. It is primarily suited for vessels with a small diameter [Kanitsar *et al.*, 2005]. Thus, it is essential for the diagnosis of peripheral vessels [Koechl *et al.*, 2003] but less applicable for analyzing the abdominal aorta. One of the earliest descriptions of its clinical use date back to 1998 where Achenbach *et al.* [1998] documented the use of CPR for the diagnosis of the coronary heart disease.

***Single Vessel* CPR** The more traditional single vessel CPR is based on the centerline (to be determined at subvoxel accuracy) and a vector v_i (vector of interest). Lines starting at a centerline point and oriented toward v_i are integrated in the CPR generation (see Fig. 11.9 for a sketch of the transformation).

There are different CPR variants, which have been described by Kanitsar *et al.* [2005]:

- *projected* CPR, where a thin slice of voxels is transformed in a parallel projection (see Fig. 11.9, left),
- *stretched* CPR, where the projected image is stretched along the dimension of the centerline (see Fig. 11.9, middle), and
- *straightened* CPR, where the projected image is stretched and further distorted such that the centerline is projected to a straight vertical line (see Fig. 11.9, right).

Figure 11.10 illustrates the different CPR techniques with clinical examples. While projected CPR is rather simple to understand with a straightforward mapping, stretched, and straightened CPR are increasingly more complex. On the other hand, the more complex CPR variants solve some of the problems of projected CPR. Most importantly, in projected CPR some parts of the target region around the centerline overlap each other in the projection—in highly curved vessels this occurs often. This overlap is handled with a compositing scheme, such as MIP. However, the very problem of overlapping projections conflicts with the goal of providing an overview of the entire vessel lumen.

Bone removal (recall § 11.2.2) may be necessary for projected CPR in case that bony structures are close to vascular structures, e.g., at the carotid artery [Kanitsar *et al.*, 2005]. Stretched CPRs avoid any

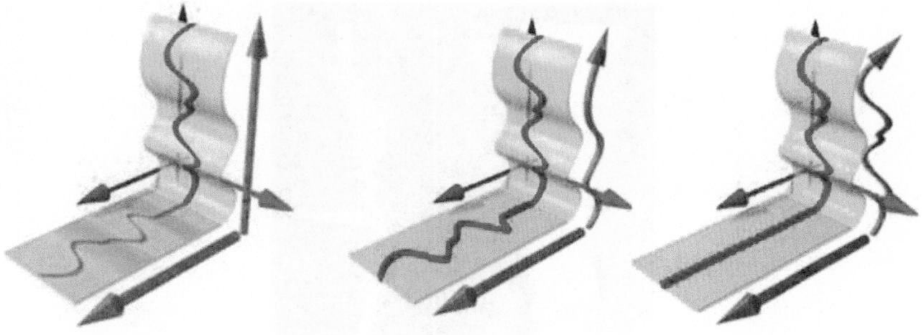

(a) Projected (b) stretched (c) straightened

FIGURE 11.9 CPR generation schemes: (a) projected where information perpendicular to the centerline is just projected (b) stretched where the projection is enlarged such that no overlapping projections occur (c) straightened where the centerline is mapped to a straight line so that the original curvature is no longer recognizable (From: [Kanitsar et al., 2005]).

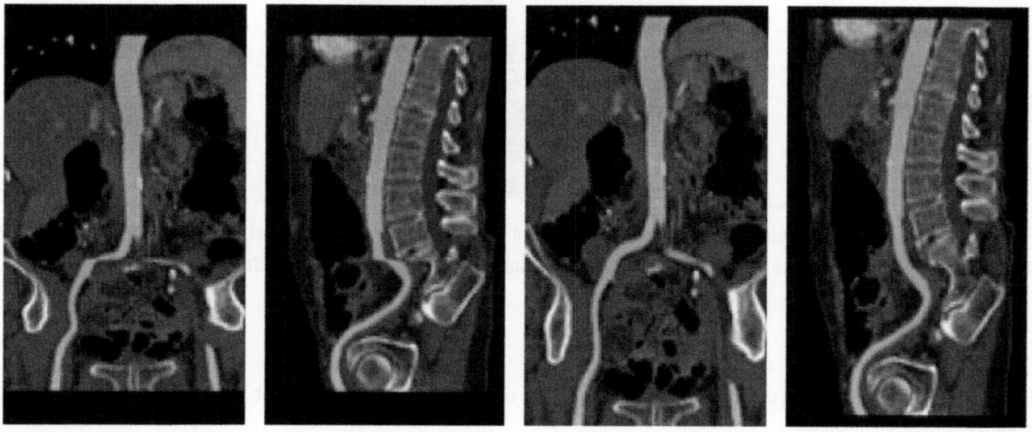

(a) (b) (c) (d)

FIGURE 11.10 Comparison of CPR methods: a coronal and sagittal display of a projected CPR (a,b), stretched CPR (c,d) (From: [Kanitsar et al., 2005]).

overlap, but in contrast to straightened CPRs, the curvature of the centerline (and thus the whole vascular structure) is preserved. Moreover, the stretched CPR is an isometric mapping procedure. As Kanitsar et al. [2005] point out, this property is essential for planning vascular surgery, such as endovascular stenting of aneurysms, where accurate length measurements are essential. Thus, stretched CPR provides the best trade-off for many applications.

For the evaluation of plaques and stenotic changes, a straightened CPR may be combined with a quantitative analysis of the change of the (minimal or average) diameter in all slices (Fig. 11.11).

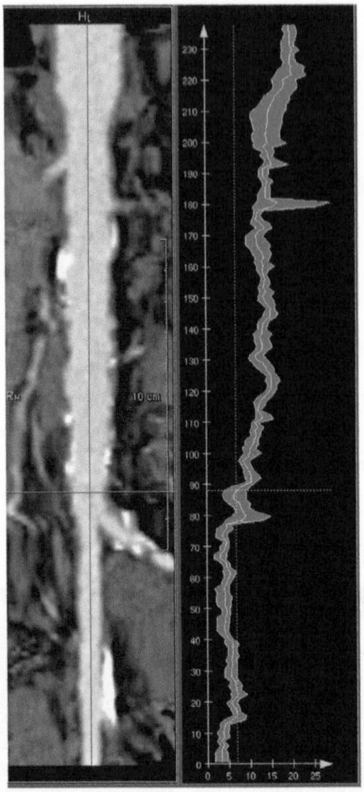

FIGURE 11.11 *For a quantitative analysis of vascular diseases, a straightened CPR view (left) and the corresponding cross-sectional measurement diagram (right) are useful (Courtesy of Tobias Boskamp, MEVIS Medical Solutions Bremen).*

User Interaction Several interaction techniques have to be provided to use CPR views. The user should be able to

- define a vessel segment, for which a CPR is generated,
- move along the centerlines, and
- rotate around the centerline.

For the first task, it is sufficient to select two points with a pointing device (pen or mouse). The movement can be naturally accomplished with the scroll wheel of a mouse, provided that the CPR is generated vertically. Rotation around the centerline should be constrained to a particular direction. In case of a vertically aligned centerline, the horizontal component of a mouse movement is naturally mapped to a rotation around the centerline. Interaction techniques for these tasks are discussed in more detail in [van Schooten *et al.*, 2010].

As an example, the visual analysis of coronary vessels is shown in Figure 11.12. The user marked two points (see the yellow spheres) to define the vessel segment. Please note that the CPR view is horizontally aligned here which is a less frequently used but also viable option. Figures 11.11 and 11.12 are screenshots

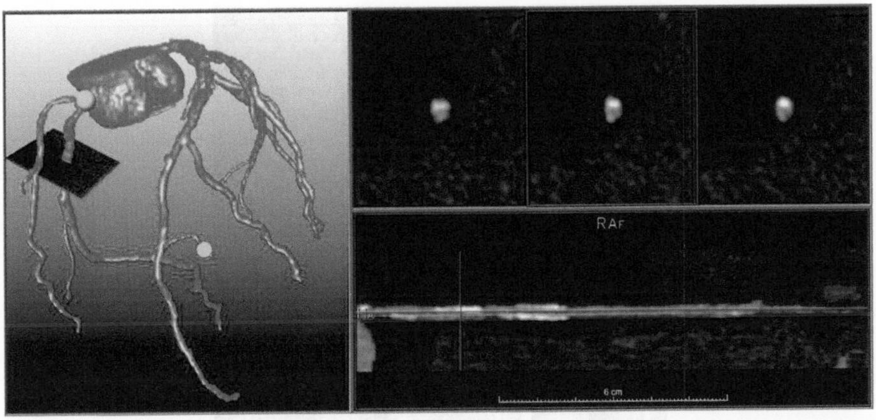

FIGURE 11.12 *Integrated visualization for the diagnosis of coronary vessels. In the 3D overview (left), the user marked two points in the tree to which the detailed analysis relates. The straightened CPR view (bottom part) contains calcifications (appearing bright). The upper right views show cross-sectional slice views in the neighborhood to the current position of the cross-sectional view in the left view (Courtesy of Anja Hennemuth, Fraunhofer MEVIS Bremen).*

of the VascuVision system developed at Fraunhofer MEVIS Bremen (see [Gerhards *et al.*, 2004] for a clinical evaluation).

Multipath CPR The exploration of a single segment of a vascular tree is of limited value, since for most tasks vascular trees have to be explored in their entirety. CPR may be extended thus that a non-overlapping projection of all branches is generated. The resampling process is rather complex, since bounding hull primitives for each segment have to be computed and carefully arranged to provide an easy-to-understand projection [Kanitsar *et al.*, 2003, 2005].

In Figure 11.13, a comparison of a stretched CPR and a dedicated multipath CPR of peripheral vessels is shown. The multipath method, introduced by Kanitsar *et al.* [2005], carefully prevents that vascular segments obscure each other introducing slight modifications. A clinical evaluation of multipath CPR is presented in [Roos *et al.*, 2007], where this method has been compared with MIP for the diagnosis of the peripheral arterial occlusive disease within 10 patients.

Curvicircular Feature Aggregation A recent extension of CPR was presented by Mistelbauer *et al.* [2013]. While CPR views require that the user rotates the views around the centerline to get a comprehensive view of plaques and other vessel wall abnormalities, they integrate the information in *one* static image. One image, of course, cannot convey the full information necessary for diagnosis, but it may give a good overview and enable goal-directed interaction to explore a suspicious region in more detail.

The basic idea of the *curvicircular feature aggregation* is to sample the region around the vessel centerline in concentric circular paths and integrate the information, e.g., with maximum or minimum intensity projection. The result critically depends on the sampling strategy. The sampling density is controlled by a specific arc or by an arclength. The latter generates more sampling points for outer regions. This advanced visualization concept is not familiar to users and thus requires effort to understand the image generation and to interpret the results. Despite the low familiarity, radiologists appreciated the technique in comparison to CPR views [Mistelbauer *et al.*, 2013].

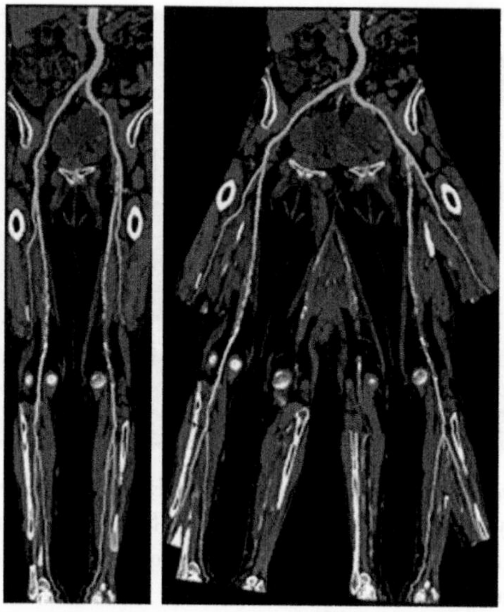

FIGURE 11.13 *A CTA dataset of the peripheral vessels in coronal view.* **Left:** *A straight CPR applied to the whole tree,* **right:** *a dedicated projection which avoids that vessel segments obscure each other. However, the right visualization is not familiar (From: [Kanitsar et al., 2005]).*

11.4 VESSEL ANALYSIS

For the reconstruction and high-quality visualization of anatomical tree structures several image processing and analysis steps have to be carried out. In particular, the centerline of these structures and the local diameter are needed in order to visualize tree structures with circular cross sections. With this information, visualizations may be restricted to branches where the diameter is above a threshold. Such restricted visualizations may support surgeons who try to avoid damage of vascular structures above a certain diameter or—if this turns out to be impossible—consider vascular reconstruction. The exploration of vascular trees is supported with the pipeline of analysis steps illustrated in Figure 11.14.

Basically, there are approaches where vessels are first segmented and then skeletonized and approaches which start by searching the centerline in each slice and continue by searching the cross section of a vessel for each detected centerline voxel. If it is important to detect small vessels in the periphery, multiscale approaches are often successful in combining segmentation results derived in different resolutions. As with other areas of image analysis, there is a trade-off between general methods with a wide scope and highly specialized algorithms, which incorporate model assumptions about parts of the human body or particular image acquisition protocols.

11.4.1 VESSEL SEGMENTATION

After appropriate preprocessing, e.g., with anisotropic diffusion filtering [Krissian, 2002, Metz *et al.* 2007] or Hessian-based filtering, vessel segmentation is an important element of the vessel analysis pipeline (Fig. 11.14).

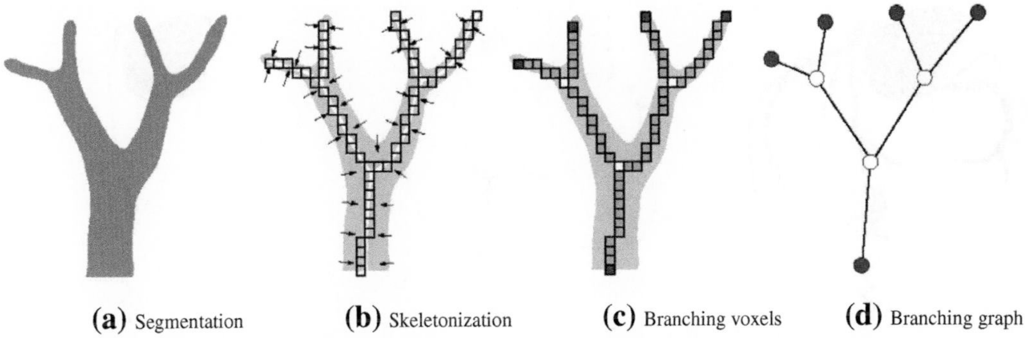

FIGURE 11.14 *Vessel segmentation, skeletonization (construction of a one voxel-width representation in the centerline of the branches) and reconstruction of a branching graph illustrated in the 2D-case. Points in the skeleton with more than two neighbors are considered as branching points and form the nodes in the branching graph (From: [Selle et al., 2000]).*

Basic Region Growing For vessel segmentation region growing algorithms (recall § 4.3.4) are often used. The growing process is initiated with a user-defined seed point and adjacent voxels are accumulated when they satisfy a homogeneity criterion. A simple criterion is a threshold that is adjusted such that contrast-enhanced voxels of vascular structures are separated from surrounding tissue. Simple intensity-based methods usually do not deliver accurate results, since smaller vessels exhibit a lower value due to the smearing effect of the point-spread function. Thus, region growing terminates prematurely if at one voxel no neighboring voxel is found which satisfies the growing criterion.

Advanced Region Growing To trace vascular structures as long as possible into the periphery, an initial region growing segmentation result may be frozen and incrementally expanded guided by seed points specified by the user. Based on an analysis of the neighborhood of these additional seed points, local thresholds are estimated. With this strategy, the periphery of vascular structures is segmented with other (lower) thresholds than the central parts. Another strategy to vessel segmentation is to look for voxels not only in the immediate neighborhood (either with a sophisticated region growing variant or with a completely different segmentation approach).

For vascular structures, region growing may be refined by employing the assumption of elliptical cross sections (recall [Hennemuth *et al.*, 2005]). This approach for coronary artery segmentation was later refined by controlling the growth fronts separately and thus to better avoid leakage [Bock *et al.*, 2008].

Level Sets and Fast Marching The progressing boundary of the segmentation process can also be interpreted as wave front that propagates through the segmented object. This interpretation forms the basis of the level set and fast marching methods that have been used for vessel segmentation [Wu *et al.*, 2011b]. Local image features, such as intensities, gradients, and textures, control this propagation adaptively. Therefore, the front is rapidly moved toward those regions, which are likely part of the vascular system, and is hindered from others [Kubisch *et al.*, 2012]. Level set methods were also successfully used to segment pathological vascular segments, such as coronary arteries and plaques [Müller and Mäder, 2008].

Vessel Tracking A variation of segmentation is *vessel tracking*, in which a path along the vessel is extracted from a given starting point. While some methods extract single paths (with given start and endpoint), others can locate the entire vessel tree and correctly handle vessel branching. Image intensities, path length,

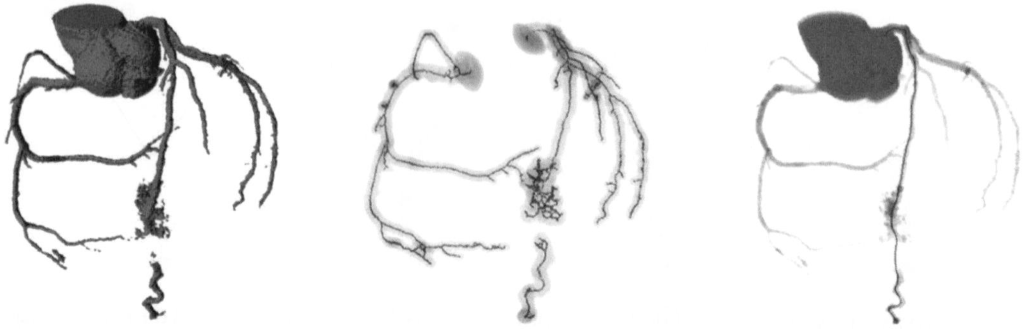

FIGURE 11.15 *Segmentation and centerline detection in coronary arteries. Since one major artery was not segmented completely a search in the neighborhood was initiated to come up with a connected vessel centerline (From: [Hennemuth, 2012]).*

curvature, and vesselness, are among the features to be used for path extraction [Hennemuth, 2012]. In the ROTTERDAM CORONARY ARTERY ALGORITHM EVALUATION FRAMEWORK [Schaap *et al.*, 2009] many methods have been compared with respect to accuracy, speed, and user interaction. More recently the "Coronary Artery Tracking Challenge" stimulated substantial research in robust tracking even of branches in the periphery. The approach described in Friman *et al.* [2010] was considered the best approach in that challenge. It is based on 3D templates and multiple hypothesis tracking. Figure 11.15 gives an example of a result of that algorithm.

Besides a powerful segmentation algorithm, a fast and goal-directed interaction is essential to fine-tune the result (e.g., adjustments of thresholds and definition of additional seed points). Comprehensive overviews on vessel segmentation are given in [Kirbas and Quek, 2004, Boskamp *et al.*, 2006, Lesage *et al.*, 2009. An example for a recent and highly specialized vessel segmentation method is given in [Schaap *et al.*, 2011] for coronary vessels. In general, there is a tendency toward integrating more anatomical knowledge and thus to provide more specialized solutions.

Specialized Segmentation Tasks While for some applications, e.g., surgery planning where vascular structures are at risk (but not pathological), the segmentation of the vessel lumen is sufficient, diagnostic tasks often involve specialized segmentation problems. As an important example, the diagnosis of the coronary heart disease benefits from a selective analysis of plaques and thrombus. Giachetti and Zanetti [2004] discuss the segmentation of calcified plaque and thrombus in abdominal CT data, comparing *thresholding* and *deformable models* in a validation with 40 patient datasets. Similarly de Bruijne *et al.* [2004] developed a specific solution for the segmentation of aortic aneurysms.

11.4.2 SKELETONIZATION AND GRAPH ANALYSIS

For visualizing vascular tree structures the vessel skeleton and the local vessel diameter are often required. The skeleton[1] of an elongated tubular structure is usually a polyline. However, for a whole vascular tree with a number of branchings, a more complex skeleton arises that consists of a corresponding number of branches. According to Wan *et al.* [2002] we define a continuous skeleton and its approximation in a discrete 3D space as follows.

1 Note that, *skeleton* and *centerline* are used as synonyms.

Definition 11.1. In a continuous space, the **continuous skeleton** of an object is a set of (infinitely thin) space curves. The skeleton is the locus of all centers of the maximum enclosing circles (in 2D space) or the maximum enclosing spheres (in 3D space).

Definition 11.2. In a discrete 3D space, the **discrete skeleton** is a one-voxel wide line representation which proceeds in the center of a volumetric object.

The differences between the definition for continuous objects and skeletons of discrete representations is shown in Figure 11.16.

Based on the definitions above, we discuss general requirements for skeletonization algorithms for tubular 3D objects according to [Wan *et al.*, 2002, Negahdar *et al.*, 2006]. Discrete skeletons should exhibit the following properties:

- *Centeredness.* The skeleton should be as exactly as possible in the middle of the tubular structure, staying away as much as possible from the walls.
- *Connectivity.* The skeleton should be connected such that it consists of directly connected voxels.
- *Robustness.* Slight changes to the shape of an object should change the shape of an object only slightly.
- *Invariance against affine transformations.* If an affine transformation t, e.g., a rotation, is applied to the skeleton of an object $s(o)$, the same skeleton should result as if t would be applied to o before skeletonization. Thus, it is required that $t(s(o)) = s(t(o))$.
- *Singularity.* The skeleton should not exhibit manifolds or self-intersections.
- *Efficiency.* The skeleton should be computed fast to enable real-time use.

Skeletonization by Thinning Algorithms, which compute skeletons, may successively erode the segmentation result, until a one-voxel wide line remains. This process is modified to ensure topological correctness. Thus, only *simple* points are actually removed. Simple points are no terminal points (having only one

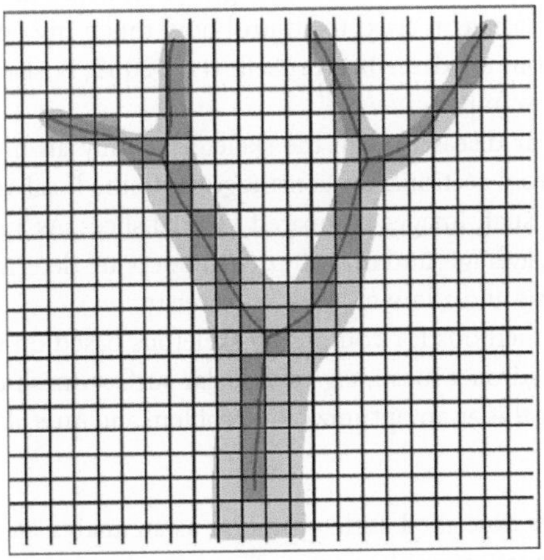

FIGURE 11.16 *The dark line represents the skeleton of the gray shape. The dark gray pixels represent the discrete skeleton. The deviation between the continuous skeleton and an ideal discrete skeleton is less than one voxel* (Courtesy of Dirk Selle. See also [Selle *et al.*, 2002]).

neighbor skeleton voxel) and do not represent branchings (having more than two neighboring voxels). Skeletonization based on erosion is called *thinning*. This iterative peeling process is time-consuming for larger objects. Since in each step the connectivity of the resulting skeleton has to be ensured [Wan *et al.*, 2002]. Accelerated thinning-based techniques were introduced by Ge *et al.*, [1996] and later by Paik *et al.*, [1998].

Actually, skeletonization of discrete 3D objects with *anisotropic voxels* is more difficult. The anisotropic character must be explicitly considered to compensate for the fact that an erosion in the z-direction may be considerably larger than for the x- and y-directions. Thinning-based skeletonization algorithms, in general are accurate (fulfill the centeredness-requirement).

Skeletonization by Distance Transformation Distance transforms of an object o assign a signed distance to each voxel that represents the distance to o. The result of a distance transform is referred to as a *distance map*. For skeletonization, distance transform is applied to an object that consists of the boundary voxels of a segmented anatomical structure, e.g., a vascular tree. In a second step, the distance map is employed to determine the skeleton that basically connects voxels with the highest values. Distance transforms may be computed precisely, taking longer, or be approximated in a fast mode. The precise computation of the Euclidean distance metric involves the square root and thus is time-consuming. With this metric, the distance between face-connected neighbor voxels equals 1, edge-connected voxels have a distance of $\sqrt{2}$ and vertex-connected voxels a distance of $\sqrt{3}$. Approximations, that consider only integer values, are much faster. Different approximations are used, e.g., 1, 2, and 3 [Zhou, and Toga 1999] or 3, 4, and 5 [Ge *et al.*, 1996], or even more precise 10, 14, and 17 [Wan *et al.*, 2002]. As Wan *et al.*, [2002] point out, distance transforms lead to fast skeleton computation and ensures that the skeleton remains inside the target object. However, they tend to "hug the corners," that means they are not perfectly *centralized*.

Removal of Irrelevant Side-branches Very small side-branches often arise due to noise or partial volume effects (see Fig. 11.17). Small side-branches may correctly reflect the anatomical situation, but may also be the consequence of the discrete representation. A filter, which controls these side-branches, may consider the length of a terminal side branch in relation to the length of an adjacent branch as well as the gradient along the branch. A *sensitivity parameter* is used to control how much information is filtered out (*pruning*). Examples for such filter functions are described in [Selle *et al.*, 2002, Boskamp *et al.*, 2004, Negahdar *et al.*, 2006]. Figure 11.17 gives an example.

For the diagnosis of vascular diseases, even the skeleton is only an intermediate result. It might be used for the visualization of cross-sectional areas orthogonal to the local vessel centerline. A stenosis can be detected much better with such images compared to axial slices. As an example for further analysis, cross-sectional areas, minimal, average, and maximum diameters are determined. These measures support the diagnosis of a vessel stenosis and allow to assess its severity.

While we consider mainly methods for computing skeletons based on segmentation results, it is also possible to compute them based on a mesh, e.g., a vascular surface mesh created with Marching Cubes. Wang and Lee [2008] consider this as an optimization problem and Au *et al.* [2008] compute the skeleton based on mesh contraction.

Direct Skeletonization So far, we described skeletonization as an analysis step, which is carried out after segmentation using the segmentation result as input. There are also algorithms which compute the vessel skeleton immediately (without prior segmentation). Similar to the livewire segmentation they are based on a minimal path computation which considers gray values, local contrasts as well as the length and

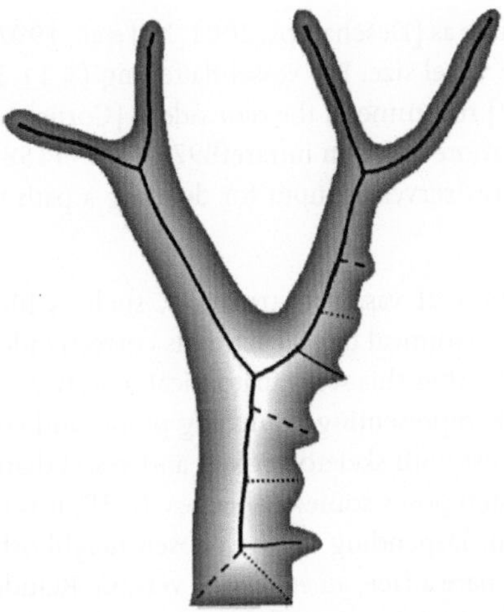

FIGURE 11.17 *Irrelevant side branches are suppressed by a threshold applied to distance transform gradient. All lines represent the skeleton with a threshold of 0.8 (only a few branches are filtered out). With the threshold reduced to 0.6 the dotted branches are removed. Further reduction to 0.4 removes the dashed branches also. The solid lines which probably represent the interesting shape information here are obtained with a threshold of 0.0 (Courtesy of Dirk Selle. See also [Selle et al., 2002]).*

curvature of the resulting path. Usually, the user has to specify an initial point (on the centerline) and an initial direction and the algorithms extrapolates in the given direction with a small increment and searches for a new centerline point [Wink *et al.*, 2000]. The result of direct skeletonization often is a set of path's, that is not all portions are connected. As Wu *et al.*, [2011b] discuss, a postprocessing step, that tries to connect vessel segments with similar directions, located close to each other, improves the result. Manual intervention may be necessary, in particular when artifacts occur.

Direct skeletonization is fast, however, the resulting paths may strongly deviate from the true centerlines, in particular at branchings. Direct skeletonization methods are discussed in [Frangi *et al.*, 1999, Hernandez-Hoyos *et al.*, 2002, Wu *et al.*, 2011b].

Comparison Between Direct and Indirect Skeletonization The direct skeletonization approach is usually faster, since the segmentation step which is tedious and error-prone is completely avoided. However, direct skeletonization is often less accurate in particular in strongly bended parts of a vessel and near branchings. If noticeable deviations occur, the user has to fine-tune the parameters of the underlying optimal path calculation, which is probably difficult and it is not clear that this process converges against the true centerline. Accuracy is critical for centerline determination both for visualization as well as for the diagnosis of vascular diseases. With respect to the requirements discussed in § 4.3.1, in particular *robustness* and *reliability*, there is an advantage for indirect methods. The segmentation result is a verifiable intermediate result which may be fine-tuned by specifying seed points for example. Consequently, indirect skeletonization currently dominates in clinical applications.

The results of the widely available skeletonization algorithms differ in particular with respect to their accuracy (deviation to the centerline). Kruszynski *et al.* [2006] discuss these differences in a quantitative way which is essential for a morphometric analysis. For generating model-based surface visualizations, the accuracy of known algorithms, such as [Deschamps, 2001, Näf *et al.*, 1997] is sufficient, since the deviation is usually small compared to the voxel size. For vessel flattening (§ 11.3.3), a particularly high accuracy is required. Ropinski *et al.* [2009] recommend the *curve skeleton* [Cornea *et al.*, 2007] for this purpose.

We discuss skeletonization in more detail in intrarefB978-0-12-415873-3.00013-4§ 13.3.2.3, where the centerline of tubular structures serves as input for defining a path that guides the virtual camera in virtual colonoscopy.

Graph Analysis For the exploration of vascular structures, such as hiding a subtree, it is essential to represent them as a graph. If an anatomical tree structure is correctly identified it should not contain any cycle (cycles should be removed). After this step, anatomical trees may be represented as directed acyclic graph $G = (V, E)$ with nodes V representing branching points and edges E representing connections between them. For each edge, a list with skeleton voxels and vessel diameters along this edge should be represented. The graph analysis step poses some challenges. In 3D, it is often ambiguous which skeleton voxel actually forms the junction. Depending on the chosen neighborhood definition (6-, 12-, or 26-neighborhood for voxels which share a face, an edge, or a vertex). Reinders *et al.* [2000] discuss this issue and suggest to consider the voxel which has three face-connected neighbors as the junction node. If none such node exists, a voxel which shares edges or faces with three voxels is chosen. This way, the analysis becomes usually unambiguous.

A branching graph (see Fig. 11.14) may be used for filtering vascular trees based on a bifurcation hierarchy. The branching graph may be further analyzed to tackle another special problem of vessel analysis, namely the separation between several connected vascular trees, which arise, e.g., in the liver where the portal vein, the arteries, and the hepatic vein are close to each other. This problem is analyzed in [Selle *et al.*, 2002] and as a consequence various geometric descriptors are used to detect wrong connections. Such processes do not work in a fully automatic manner. Thus, manual correction facilities where users may add or remove edges in the branching graph, are mandatory.

11.4.3 DIAMETER ESTIMATION

As a side effect of skeletonization the local vessel diameter may be derived, e.g., in a thinning-based skeletonization it is registered how many voxels in a certain direction had to be removed to yield the centerline. This information, together with the known dimensions of a voxel, lead to a radius information. Thus, as a result of skeletonization, a list of skeleton voxels with the associated diameter is registered. The diameter is essential for model-based surface visualization techniques, but also enables interaction techniques, such as pruning the vascular tree according to a diameter criterion [Selle *et al.*, 2002]. Since vascular structures are not perfectly circular, different diameters may result for one voxel. Thus, it is useful to store, minimum, average, median, and maximum diameter per voxel. Consequently, the decision, which diameter-related value should be used for visualization and exploration may be postponed.

More advanced methods for diameter estimation start a growing process at each skeleton voxel to determine either a circle or an ellipse that optimally matches the cross section taking also local gradient information into account [Wu *et al.*, 2011b]. The advanced methods for circle fitting and ellipse fitting were introduced in [Luboz *et al.*, 2005] and [Krissian *et al.*, 2006] respectively.

Enhancement of Skeletons and Diameter Information Due to the discrete nature of radiological data, distracting aliasing effects occur if the skeleton is immediately used for visualization or camera movement inside vascular structures. Jagged lines appear instead of straight lines and curved line segments are also not faithfully represented. To eliminate these effects, skeletons are smoothed, e.g., with a low-pass filter. A Gaussian that is discretely approximated by the binomial filter (the elements of the filter are the binomial coefficients)

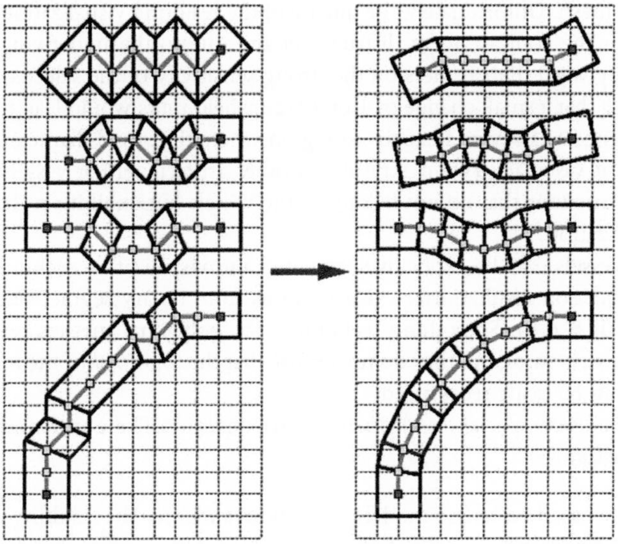

FIGURE 11.18 *Smoothing with a binomial filter of size 3 ([121]-kernel). The jaggy skeleton with all elements located at grid positions (left) is smoothed whereas skeleton elements are no longer forced to be located at grid positions. Small quadrilaterals represent the center of voxels. Note that start and endpoints of the skeleton are not affected (Courtesy of Horst Karl Hahn, Fraunhofer MEVIS. See also [Hahn et al., 2001]).*

is appropriate to smooth the edges of the skeleton (see Fig. 11.18). For all voxels of the skeleton with two neighbors, e.g., in the absence of branchings, the resulting skeleton is strongly improved. However, at bifurcations the simple smoothing causes undesirable effects. Specialized solutions for this problem using weights for the individual contributions are described in [Hahn *et al.*, 2001]. As an alternative, Negahdar *et al.*, [2006] introduce additional subvoxels in regions where the skeleton exhibits strong discontinuities. Another viable strategy that generates continuous curved centerlines is the application of a subdivision scheme and the use of a spline interpolation, e.g., Catmull-Rom splines.

The local vessel diameter exhibits discontinuities as well. These might be due to a disease affecting the vessel wall, but it is more likely an artifact of the image acquisition and analysis. Since model-based approaches are not used for detailed diagnosis, it is reasonable to assume that the diameter should be smooth as well. In the *truncated cone-visualization* described in [Hahn *et al.*, 2001], the same filtering strategy applied to the skeleton is also applied to the diameter information.

Wu *et al.* [2011b] postprocess the cross-sectional areas instead of the skeleton. In particular, they identify regions of the skeleton where strong discontinuities occur. This is achieved by comparing a cross section in each (oblique) slice with the cross section in adjacent slices. If the difference to both of them is too strong, an artifact is assumed and the probably erroneous cross section is replaced by the average of its neighbors.

11.5 MODEL-BASED SURFACE VISUALIZATION

The most common surface reconstruction technique is Marching Cubes with an appropriate threshold (isosurface rendering) applied to the original intensity data. Marching Cubes generates a watertight twomanifold triangle mesh. Unfortunately, the quality of the resulting visualizations is relatively low due to inhomogeneities in the contrast agent distribution and due to the underlying linear interpolation. Textbooks on radiology warn their readers on the strong sensitivity of the selected isovalue on the visualization by illustrating that a small change of 1 or 2 Hounsfield units would lead to a different diagnosis (e.g., presence or absence of a severe stenosis—a region where the vessel diameter is strongly reduced). Isosurface rendering of vascular structures results in other artifacts: either vessels appear disconnected in the periphery, or structures that do not belong to the vessels but exhibit similar intensity values, are included in the visualization.

As an alternative, vessels may be explicitly segmented and visualization techniques be applied to the (often binary) segmentation result. Surface visualizations from binary segmentation exhibit distracting aliasing artifacts (recall § 6.6). Smoothing techniques for polygonal meshes may improve isosurface renderings of vascular structures, but they do not ensure that the topology of the resulting tree structures remains correct and can be easily recognized.

These problems gave rise to special vessel visualization techniques. There are two classes of surface-based vessel visualization methods:

- methods that are based on certain model assumptions and force the resulting visualization to adhere to these assumptions, and
- methods that adhere strictly to the underlying data (*model-free* methods).

In this section, we describe methods of the first class and refer to them as *model-based*. With these methods, vascular trees are reconstructed such that the branching pattern and geometrical properties (vessel diameter, curvature) are easy to interpret. The benefit of the *reconstruction* of vascular structures for a visualization which emphasizes the connectivity and shape features was recognized early [Gerig *et al.*, 1993]. Meanwhile, special visualization techniques for anatomical tree structures, in general, and vascular trees in particular were developed. In the following two sections, we consider two approaches to vessel visualization:

- *explicit surface reconstruction.* This category of methods explicitly generates a polygonal mesh of a vascular system based on the detected centerline and the associated diameter information.
- *implicit surface reconstruction.* These methods generate a scalar field based on implicit equations. A polygonal mesh arises by thresholding the scalar field.

Most of the explicit reconstruction techniques employ a *generalized cylinder* with the skeleton as 3D curve representing the centerline and a closed circular cross section perpendicular to it. From the cross section, the local diameter of the generalized cylinders may be derived. Since the cross section in general is not circular, it must be decided whether the minimum, the maximum, or the mean diameter is chosen. Tubes, truncated cones as well as parametric surfaces, such as B-Splines, are specific examples of graphics primitives used for explicit surface reconstruction techniques. The resulting surfaces are often triangle meshes [Hahn *et al.*, 2001, Oeltze and Preim 2004, Schumann *et al.*, 2007] but also quadrilateral primitives are employed [Felkl *et al.*, 2004, Wu *et al.*, 2011b]. Both types of graphics representations benefit from hardware support for efficient rendering.

11.5.1 RECONSTRUCTION WITH CYLINDERS AND TRUNCATED CONES

The reconstruction and visualization are based on the *model assumption* that the cross section of non-pathological vessels has a circular shape [Masutani *et al.*, 1996]. This assumption turned out to be appropriate for therapy planning procedures where vascular structures are not pathological themselves but represent important anatomical context. A second model assumption, more or less integrated in the explicit and implicit reconstruction techniques, is that vessels are smooth structures where the diameter and the orientation of the centerline do not change abruptly. Again, this assumption may be violated in case of pathologies. Skeletons and derived diameters are often postprocessed with a low-pass filter to consider this model assumption.

Masutani *et al.* [1996] fitted cylinders along the skeleton to visualize vascular structures. However, severe discontinuities occur at branchings where cylinders with different diameters coincide. To overcome this problem, Hahn *et al.* [2001] employed truncated cones (TC), which are able to represent the constriction of the vessel diameter appropriately. The method is therefore referred to as *TC visualization*.

For the visualization, a vascular tree must be mapped to a set of lists L_i which comprise sequential edges of a vascular tree. The edges of each list represent a path at which the TCs are extruded. Along one path, surface normals and colors are interpolated such that a smooth appearance results. At the touching points between two paths, visible discontinuities arise. To minimize these distracting artifacts, as many edges as possible are assigned to one list.

The quality of the visualization depends on two parameters:

- the accuracy of the polygonal approximation of truncated cones (the number of vertices per TC), and
- the sampling rate along the path (the number of generated cones).

11.5.1.1 Quality Aspects of Vascular Reconstructions

Minimum accuracy for the first parameter means that the circular cross section of cones is represented via a triangle. With the minimum sampling rate, one TC is generated to represent the complete path between two bifurcations. With the maximum sampling rate, one truncated cone is generated between two voxels along the path. A reasonable trade-off between quality and speed is to employ 8–12 vertices to approximate the circular cross section of each TC and to use the maximum sampling rate (one TC represents the vascular tree between two subsequent voxels).

One problem with a straightforward TC visualization is the appearance at endpoints. Without special care, vessels seem to end abruptly instead of showing a natural smooth end. To improve this, the end of each path may be capped by a half-sphere. With these ingredients, images like in Figure 11.19 may be generated.

The TC visualization technique has been extensively used for preoperative planning in liver, kidney, and pancreas surgery. As an example, the improved vessel visualization is used for oncologic liver surgery where it is essential to recognize the spatial relations around a malignant tumor and to estimate how the destruction or removal of this tumor affects the blood supply. The TC visualization is part of the software assistant called MeVis Liver Explorer which is used at various hospitals in an image analysis distant service (MeVis Distant Services) where more than 7000 interventions in various countries have been planned until 2011.

11.5.1.2 Efficient Realization of Vascular Reconstructions

When vascular trees are derived from very high resolution data and thus get really large, the geometric models needed to represent such trees with cylinders or truncated cones in high quality become very large. Even larger vascular trees arise, when vascular models are composed from different datasets or

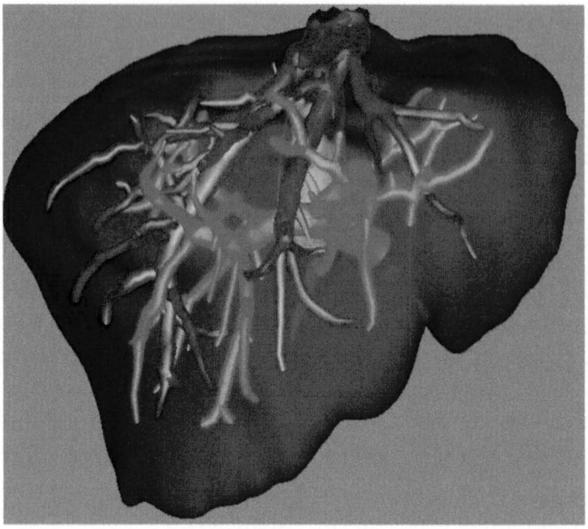

FIGURE 11.19 *Visualization of the intrahepatic vascular anatomy (hepatic vein and portal vein) inside the semi-transparent liver (Courtesy of Wolf Spindler, Fraunhofer MEVIS. See also [Selle et al., 2000]).*

from simulation models where assumptions of vessel growth are employed. As an example for such large models, Wischgoll *et al.* [2007] reconstructed coronary vessel trees down to the capillary level (see Fig. 11.20 for an example). The consequent use of large triangle strips as a general strategy is recommended. In the following, additional techniques are briefly discussed as to their ability to accelerate rendering.

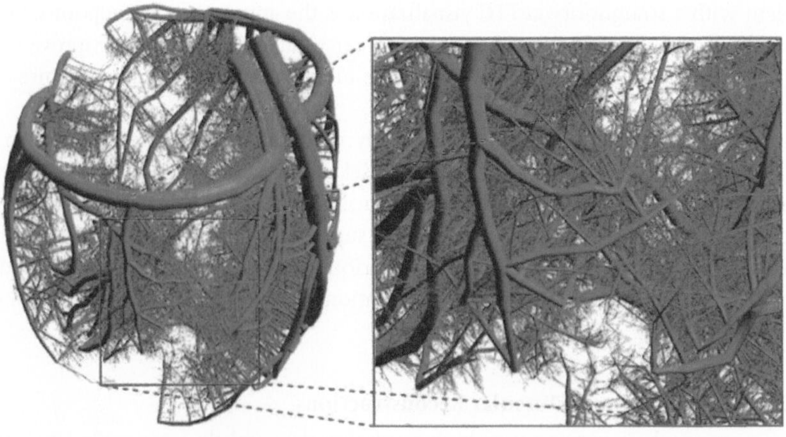

FIGURE 11.20 *Complete representation and close-up view of the vasculature of a pig heart rendered with truncated cones (From: [Wischgoll et al., 2007]).*

Advanced topic: Level-of-detail rendering. A general computer graphics strategy to cope with large geometric models and provide reasonable performance is to use the level-of-detail (LOD) concept. With this concept, there are different geometric representations for the same object, and the rendering system selects one of them depending on its distance to the viewer. Thus, cylindrical or conical vessel segments are provided at a high level of detail, e.g., with 16 vertices representing one circular cross section and with two lower levels of detail with 8 and 4 vertices only. There is, of course, an overhead, since the additional representations have to be stored and the rendering system must perform some computations to select the corresponding representation. This technique improves the performance of an explicitly reconstructed vascular tree despite this overhead [Wischgoll *et al.*, 2007]. However, the distance computation needs to be efficiently realized based on a spatial subdivision (octree). With a naive distance computation, no performance gain is achieved.

Occlusion and backface culling. In general, *occlusion culling* is a reasonable performance gaining strategy. Hidden geometry is identified and excluded from further rendering steps (projection, lightning, rasterization). However, it is not of much value for the visualization of vascular trees, since only few vessel segments are completely hidden (and can be excluded) [Wischgoll *et al.*, 2007]. Instead, since vessel segments are rather thin, most segments are partially visible and the additional effort to identify hidden segments does not pay off.

Backface culling, the removal of triangles which point away from the viewer, has a better cost-efficiency if it is efficiently implemented. Since the vessel segments have arbitrary orientations, backfaces have to be identified individually for each segment. Thus, a considerable amount of computation is involved even with an efficient realization. On average half of the triangles can be excluded from further rendering.

Rendering with imposters. The rendering process may be significantly accelerated if an imposter, placed parallel to the viewing plane is employed instead of a full 3D geometry. This very idea has been developed in the visualization of flow data [Stoll *et al.*, 2005] but was adapted to vascular trees [Wischgoll *et al.*, 2005] and DTI fiber tracking [Merhof *et al.*, 2006a]. A vessel segment is thus replaced with either a flat triangle strip with a few vertices or, even more efficient, with one quadrilateral (the projection of a truncated cone has a quadrilateral shape). Special care is taken for vessel segments which are looked at such that their circular cross section becomes visible.

Without further considerations, however, the vascular tree would appear completely flat. The essential depth cues come from shading and lead to an intensity gradient from the truncated cone's border toward the center. This effect can be efficiently mimicked with a small shader program that combines two 1D textures for specular and diffuse reflection in a 2D texture (see Fig. 11.21).

It must be noted that these acceleration strategies are only applicable for vessel visualizations based on graphics primitives.

Discussion All surface reconstruction methods that fit graphics primitive *explicitly* to the skeleton tend to get problems in highly curved areas, where the cross sections may intersect. These problems lead to the generation of primitives that are partially inside and thus not appropriate for virtual endoscopy. Moreover, noticeable discontinuities and the outer surface result. To avoid these problems, the skeleton may be sampled with a lower density in such regions. However, this is at odds with the accuracy requirement. Highly curved areas need a particularly high sampling to represent the geometry well.

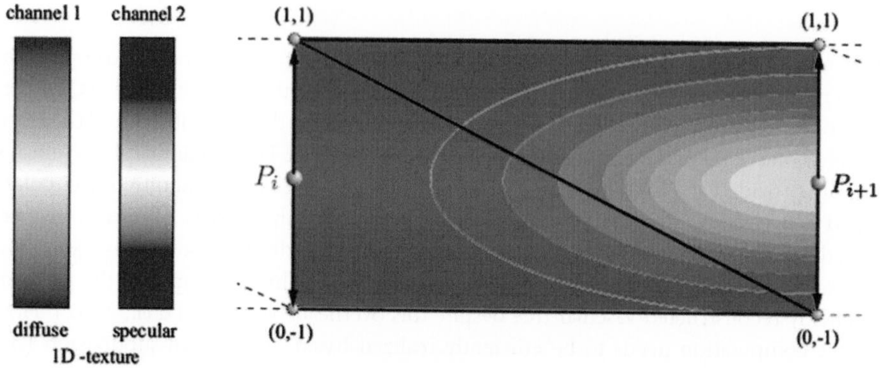

FIGURE 11.21 *Two 1D textures represent the shading effect along a cylinder. They are combined in a 2D texture and may be used for displaying vascular trees with 2D imposters (From: [Merhof et al., 2006a]).*

11.5.2 VISUALIZATION WITH PARAMETRIC AND SUBDIVISION SURFACES

The most advanced explicit reconstruction technique is based on *subdivision surfaces* and has been developed at the VRVis research center in Vienna [Felkl *et al.*, 2002, 2004]. This method is also an instance of the generalized cylinder approach. An initial *base mesh* is constructed along the vessel centerline. This base mesh consists of quadrilateral patches and can be subdivided and refined according to the Catmull-Clark subdivision technique described in [DeRose *et al.*, 1998]. The smoothness of the final model depends on the iteration depth of the refinement step.

The algorithm can handle different branching types in a uniform and efficient manner. The algorithm requires non-overlapping cross sections along vessel segments but also at joints (the latter is a more severe restriction). The application of this technique to "real" clinical data is illustrated in Figure 11.22. As an alternative, subdivision surfaces may also be composed of triangles. For this purpose, the Catmull-Clark subdivision scheme must be replaced with the Loop scheme [Wu *et al.*, 2010].

Input Trees Versus Input Loops While the method developed at the VRVis expects an *input tree*, actually some vascular structures in the arterial system are loops. The most important example is the Circle of Wilis in the cerebral vascular system. Therefore, Wu *et al.* [2011b] developed an algorithm that also processes loops of vessel segments in a correct manner.

Visualization of Partially Segmented Vessels Model-based visualization techniques are also applicable if only incomplete segmentation is available. Pommert *et al.* [2001] built a geometric model for anatomy education based on the Visible Human Dataset. Small vessels and nerves which could only be detected in part (or not at all) have been modeled by placing ball-shaped markers which are connected with cubic B-splines resulting in smooth visualizations (see Fig. 11.23) even at branchings. With splines the shape of the modeled tree structures may be locally changed by translating the position of the markers.

The obvious alternative is the use of cylinders fitted to the manually placed points leading to piecewise a linear appearance. Cubic B-splines are superior for educational purposes not only because of the smoother result, but also because the smooth connection is anatomically more plausible. In clinical applications (treatment planning), a disadvantage of the perfectly looking B-splines is that a higher accuracy is pretended than actually available with an incomplete segmentation.

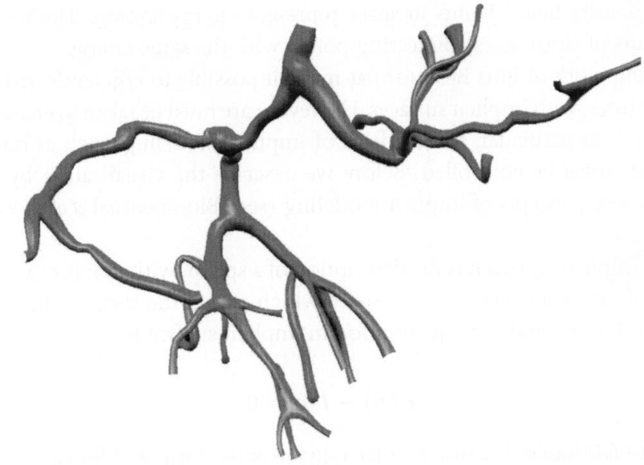

FIGURE 11.22 Subdivision surfaces applied to a vessel tree derived from clinical data (Courtesy of Petr Felkel).

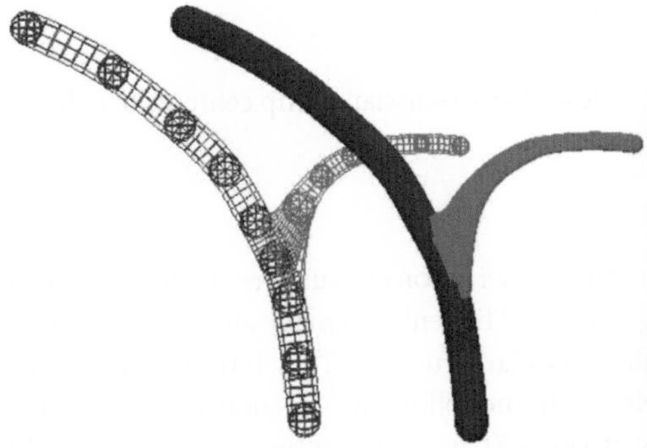

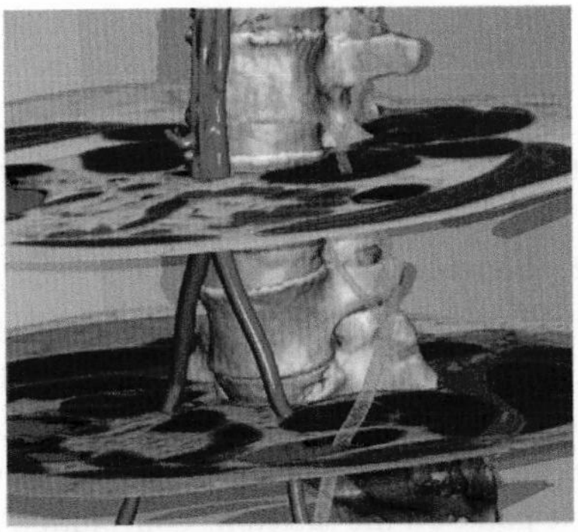

FIGURE 11.23 Small anatomical tree structures are modeled by placing ball-shaped markers and represented as a special variant of splines (From: [Pommert et al., 2001]).

11.5.3 IMPLICIT RECONSTRUCTION OF VASCULAR TREES

As an alternative, we describe a radically different approach based on implicit surfaces introduced in [Bloomenthal and Shoemake, 1991]. Instead of explicitly describing the geometry, anatomical structures are described by implicit equations and visualized by polygonizing the resulting scalar field. Implicit modeling is known for the generation of smooth surfaces. The smoothness, however, is often achieved at the expense of accuracy. We study the so-called unwanted effects and describe how they are avoided.

11.5.3.1 Introduction

Implicit surfaces describe the surface by an equation, which is often more compact than its parametric counterpart. Especially in modeling smooth, deformable objects, implicit surfaces unfold their full strength. Blinn [1982b] introduced implicit surfaces in computer graphics. He developed *Blobby Molecules* to visualize electron density fields. Points in space represent energy sources. The resulting energy fields are visualized by means of isosurfaces connecting points with the same energy.

Later, the pioneering work of JULES BLOOMENTHAL made it possible to efficiently visualize skeletal structures, such as vascular trees, with implicit surfaces. However, care must be taken to ensure that the structures are faithfully visualized. In particular, some effects of implicit modeling, such as bulging and blending between skeleton parts must be controlled. Before we describe the visualization by means of *convolution surfaces* we introduce some concepts of implicit modeling (see [Bloomenthal *et al.*, 1997] for an in-depth discussion).

An example for an implicit equation is the description of a sphere with radius r: $x^2 + y^2 + z^2 - r^2 = 0$. This formula represents all points $\mathbf{p}(x, y, z)$ in space which are on the surface of a sphere with radius r centered at the origin. The generalized equation for an implicit surface is:

$$F(p) - Iso = 0 \tag{11.1}$$

$F(p)$ is called the *scalar field function* because a scalar value may be computed for each point p. Iso denotes an *isovalue* used for generating an *isosurface*, which represents all points where the implicit equation is zero.

The function employed by Blinn [1982b] is given in Equation 11.2:

$$F(p) = be^{-\sigma \|c-p\|^2} \tag{11.2}$$

where c is the center of an electron. Equation 11.2 describes a Gaussian bump centered at c, having height b, and standard deviation σ.

11.5.3.2 Convolution Surfaces

Bloomenthal and Shoemake [1991] extended implicit descriptions to surfaces defined by skeletal primitives, e.g., line segments or polygons (see Fig. 11.24). This enhancement allows to generate smooth generalized cylinders which is essential to visualize vascular structures. They introduced *Convolution Surfaces* to model the surface of an object around its skeleton. In the following, S denotes a skeleton and s refers to a single point on the skeleton. Convolution Surfaces (CS) avoid bulges and creases for non-branching

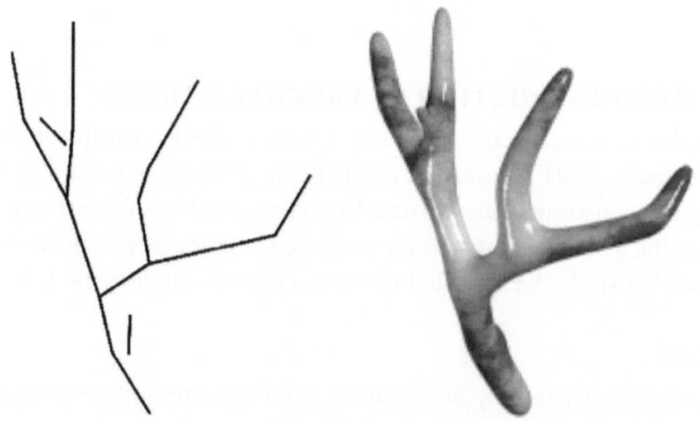

FIGURE 11.24 Example of a simple skeleton and the resulting convolution surface (From: [Jin et al., 2001a]).

skeletal structures. The scalar value is calculated according to Equation 11.3:

$$F(p) = f(S, p) = \int_S e^{\left(\frac{-\|s-p\|^2}{2}\right)} ds \tag{11.3}$$

where $f(S, p)$ is the convolution of a skeleton S with a three-dimensional Gaussian filter. In contrast to other implicit surfaces, the value is computed considering *all* points of the skeleton by integration.

Convolution surfaces utilize a concept, which is well known from signal processing, namely the modification of a signal by a filter (recall § 4.2.4 where noise reduction with convolution filters was discussed). For a Gaussian filter, Equation 11.3 may be rewritten as:

$$F(p) = f(S, p) = (h \otimes S)(p) \tag{11.4}$$

where S is the signal, h is the filter function and $\otimes$ denotes the convolution operator. For the visualization of vasculature, the skeleton corresponds to the signal. The selected filter function should smooth this signal and thereby suppress high frequencies. A low-pass filter is most suitable for that purpose. The resulting field around the skeleton corresponds to the scalar field mentioned above. By constructing an isosurface through this field the CS is formed.

The superposition property of convolution (Eq. 11.5) guarantees that two abutting segments produce the same convolution as does their union. The superposition property also permits the convolution of a complex object primitive by primitive in an arbitrary order instead of considering the skeleton as a whole.

$$h \otimes (S_1 + S_2) = (h \otimes S_1) + (h \otimes S_2) \tag{11.5}$$

Filter Selection For vessel visualization, the underlying filter function should be continuous, monotonic, and it should have finite support (or be negligible beyond a certain distance). Only a few filter functions fulfill these criteria and allow to create a CS which faithfully represents a given local radius information. In [Bloomenthal, 1995], a Gaussian function (Eq. 11.6) is utilized for convolution.

$$h(p) = e^{-d(p,S)^2\omega}, \quad \omega = \ln 2, \quad d(p, S) > 0 \tag{11.6}$$

ω is referred to as the *width coefficient* and equals $1/(2\sigma^2)$ where σ is the standard deviation. The distance between point p and the line segment skeleton S is denoted by $d(p, S)$.

The choice of a filter function must also consider computational speed. By definition of a CS (Eq. 11.3), the entire skeleton needs to be considered when calculating the scalar value at a point p. To improve the performance, the computation of the scalar field might be restricted to bounding volumes along line segments (parts of the vessel skeleton between two branchings). The tightness of a suitable bounding volume depends on the filter function (in particular on the distance from the center to points where the function value is negligible) [Oeltze and Preim, 2005]. The Gaussian allows to employ tight bounding volumes because it drops much faster toward zero than many other kernels, such as those described in [Hornus *et al.*, 2003].

Correct Representation of the Radius Information To let the CS converge against a given radius, appropriate isovalues and width coefficients ω must be selected. BLOOMENTHAL employed an isovalue of 1/2 so as to let the CS pass through the segment endpoints. Now, let us consider the CS of a sufficiently long cylinder and a point p which is located exactly on the surface and in the middle of it. Here, the integration filter equals 1, since the kernel is fully subtended by the segment. With the constraint that $d(p, H) = r(H)$ for point p on the CS it follows from Equation 11.1:

$$F(p) = e^{-(r(H)/r(H))^2\omega} - 1/2 = e^{-\omega} - 1/2 = 0 \tag{11.7}$$

Thus, $\omega = \ln 2 \approx 0.6931$. ω might be used as parameter to control the amount of blending.

11.5.3.3 Blending and Bulging

The ability to create smooth transitions between simple objects intending to form a complex organic shape is a strength of implicit surfaces. For a CS, blending corresponds to an integration of the filter along the entire skeleton. At the skeleton joints, the scalar fields of adjacent primitives overlap. The CS constructed through the resulting field forms a smooth envelope of the underlying joint. Blending may have negative effects on the visualization of vascular structures.

Blending Strength at Branchings With the initial filter design [Bloomenthal and Shoemake, 1991], the transitions at branchings were very smooth but deviated strongly from the skeleton. This is undesirable and in some cases the radiologist's interpretation of the topology is even hampered. Therefore, a narrower filter kernel should be used to produce a surface which tracks the skeleton more faithfully.

Unwanted Blending For precise modeling of complex shapes it is essential to control the blending between different parts. Concerning anatomical tree structures, segments whose skeleton is not connected should not blend with each other. Opalach and Maddock [1993] use a *restricted blending graph* to solve this problem. Based on the topology of the given skeleton, primitives are classified into *blendable* and *unblendable* primitives.

Bulging As shown in [Bloomenthal, 1995], convolution surfaces exhibit bulges at branchings. This effect is disturbing for the visualization of vascular structures since a bulge might be easily mistaken for a pathological variation, e.g., an aneurysm.

Consequences The Gaussian is the only filter function which allows the correct visualization of the radius information and provides a parameter, the width coefficient ω, which can be used to control the amount of blending. However, a modification of the original kernel is essential to reduce the blending strength at branchings and other unwanted effects (unwanted blending and bulging). Furthermore, the polygonization of scalar fields might be accelerated by using tighter bounding volumes [Oeltze and Preim, 2004].

11.5.3.4 Filter Modification

An evaluation of different ω values yielded that a value of $5\ln(2) \sim 3.5$ is suitable to prevent the undesired effects on the one hand by still maintaining the desired effects (smooth blending). With considerably larger width coefficients, blending would be avoided and the CS visualization leads to almost exactly the same result than the TC visualization, except for the construction of polygons inside the vascular surface at branchings. Note that ω has been increased with the effect that the filter function is narrower (Fig. 11.25). In order to correctly represent the radius information along a line segment, a recalculation of the isovalue (Iso) is required (Eq. 11.8)

$$F(p) = e^{-(r(H)/r(H))^2 5\ln 2} - Iso = e^{-5\ln 2} - Iso = 0. \tag{11.8}$$

Hence, $Iso = 1/32 = 0.03125$.

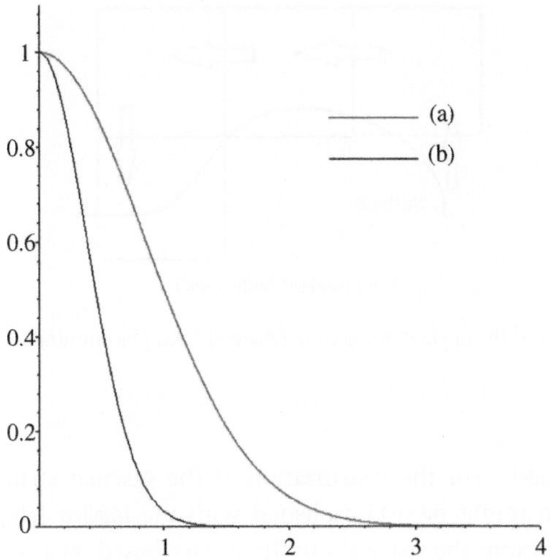

FIGURE 11.25 *Gaussian function from* BLOOMENTHAL *(a) compared to the modified version with increased width coefficient and narrower shape (b) (From: [Oeltze and Preim, 2004]).*

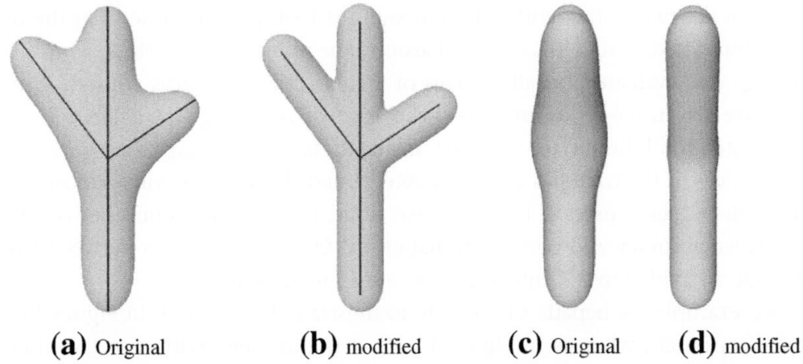

FIGURE 11.26 *Transitions at branching, (a): convolved with original filter function ($\omega = \ln(2)$), (b): convolved with modified filter ($\omega = 5\ln(2)$). The semi-transparent visualization reveals the underlying skeleton. (c): side view of the same skeleton convolved with original Gaussian filter. (d) side view of the skeleton convolved with modified filter that avoids bulging (From: [Oeltze and Preim, 2005]).*

To illustrate the effect of this filter function, a simple skeleton with a trifurcation (four coinciding branches) might be employed. Figure 11.26 (a) and (b) show how the blending strength is reduced for the simple skeleton. Also, bulging is avoided with the modified filter function (see Fig. 11.26, c, d). Oeltze and Preim [2004] discuss the influence of ω on smoothness, accuracy, and speed in more detail.

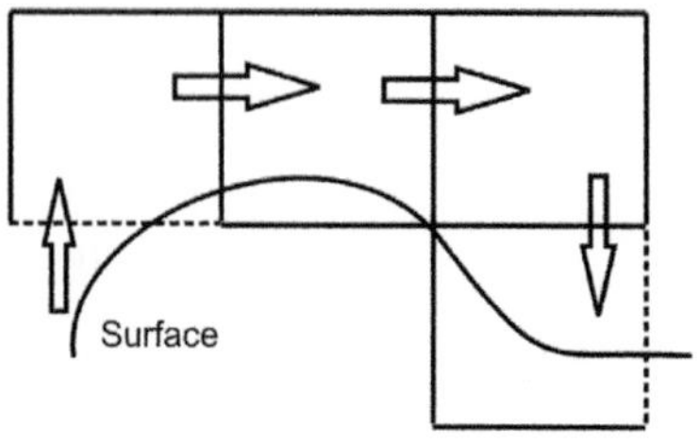

FIGURE 11.27 *Working principle of the implicit polygonizer (Adapted from [Bloomenthal, 1994]).*

Construction of a Geometric Model For the visualization of the vascular structures the CS is transformed into a triangle mesh, which might be accomplished with the *Implicit Polygonizer* [Bloomenthal, 1994]. The implicit polygonizer partitions the space about the surface based on a continuation scheme presented by Wyvill *et al.* [1986]. An initial cube is centered at an arbitrary point on the convolution surface (see Fig. 11.27). The root of an anatomical tree may serve as seed point for computing the position of the initial cube. The size of the cube should be derived from the voxel size of the underlying data to reflect the resolution of the data and to prevent that small details of the vessel tree are ignored.

The implicit function f is evaluated in the neighborhood of the seed point, and a point with opposite polarity of f in the neighborhood of the root is determined. The zero crossing of f—determined by binary subdivision between the two points with different signs of f—represents a point at the desired surface. The initial cube is translated so that it is centered around the point on the surface.

In the next stage, f is evaluated for all vertices of a cube and those faces consisting of vertices with opposite polarity are determined. Continuation proceeds by generating new cubes across any such face. This process is repeated until the surface is closed. Inside these cubes, triangles are generated to represent the surface. The vertices of the triangles are again determined along edges with opposite polarity. Binary subdivision along the edges is used to locate intersections. The maximum number of subdivision steps is a trade-off between accuracy and computational effort. Often, it is chosen between five and ten (ten means that the edge is divided in 2^{10} intervals to locate an intersection).

We present two examples of hepatic vasculature to illustrate this method. In Figure 11.28, the vasculature is rendered separately, whereas in Figure 11.29, it is combined with direct volume rendering of surrounding structures. The latter example is more realistic.

Validation and Evaluation Complex visualization techniques need to be verified with respect to their accuracy (*validation*) and evaluated with respect to their usefulness. For both tasks, a careful selection of datasets representing the spectrum of clinically relevant cases needs to be determined. In the validation it is essential to determine how strongly the generated surfaces deviate from standard methods, such as Marching Cubes. The validation benefits from a combination of clinical data and artificial data (software phantoms) to study the behavior at certain branching types in detail. The essential question in the evaluation is whether or not the more advanced visualization techniques indeed improve the interpretation of either radiologists or surgeons. This improvement might be characterized by better diagnostic or treatment planning decisions, or by an improved perceived appearance, particularly for the surgeon or by time saving. These issues are discussed in [Oeltze and Preim, 2005].

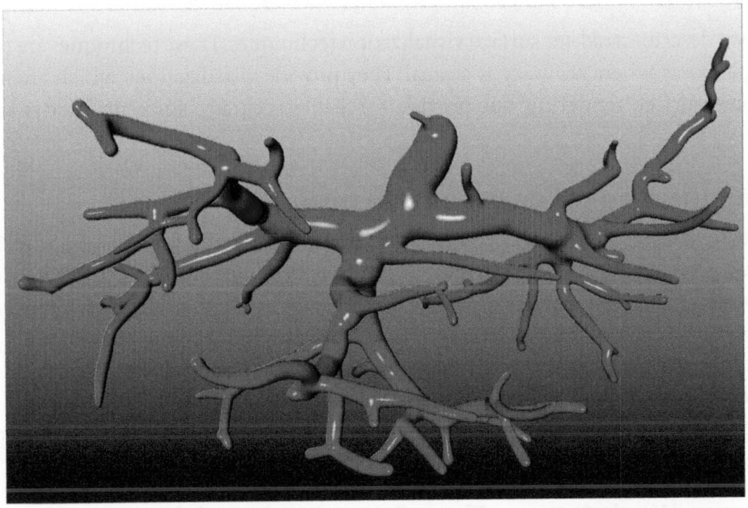

FIGURE 11.28 Visualization of the portal vein derived from a clinical CT dataset with 136 edges by means of convolution surfaces. Computation time was 54 seconds, including all precomputations. Once the model is generated, it can be transformed in real time (Courtesy of Steffen Oeltze, University of Magdeburg).

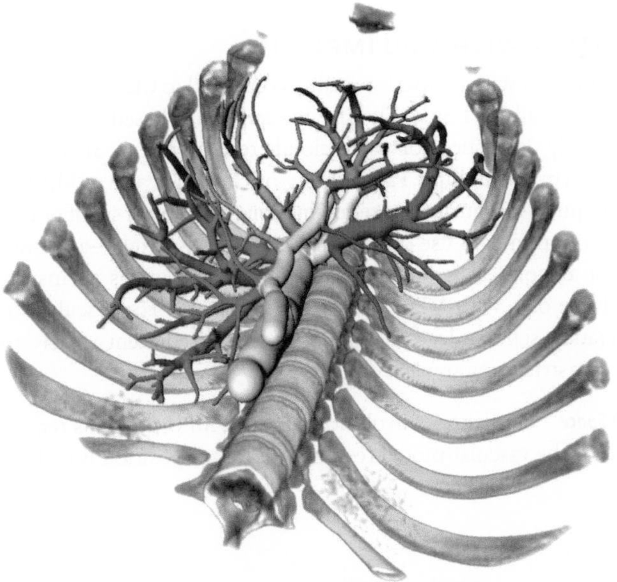

FIGURE 11.29 Combined visualization of bony structures (rendered using volume rendering) and of vessels (rendered with convolution surfaces). The color indicates vascular territories, so-called segments, supplied by the vessels (Courtesy of Christian Rieder, Fraunhofer MEVIS Bremen).

11.6 MODEL-FREE SURFACE VISUALIZATION

In this section, we describe *model-free* surface visualization techniques. These techniques are primarily useful for diagnostic purposes where accuracy is crucial. They provide visualizations which are much smoother than conventional surface rendering but provide a reliable accuracy, since no model assumptions are enforced.

11.6.1 SMOOTHING SURFACE VISUALIZATIONS

Aliasing artifacts in surfaces may be reduced in a smoothing step (recall § 6.5.2). Appropriate smoothing of vascular structures, however, is challenging and often does not lead to the desired results. Simple smoothing procedures, such as Laplacian smoothing, should not be used at all because they may easily change the topology of vascular trees, i.e., a vascular tree may be decomposed at a thin portion where the few connecting parts are removed as a consequence of smoothing. Better results are achieved with error-controlled smoothing approaches, such as low-pass filtering [Taubin, 1995a] and the improved Laplacian smoothing introduced in [Vollmer *et al.*, 1999]. However, even these advanced approaches may lead to severe errors, such as topological inconsistency [Cebral and Lohner, 2001].

Visualization of Segmented Vascular Structures The quality may be enhanced if the relevant vessels are explicitly segmented prior to surface reconstruction. Strong terracing artifacts are typical for surfaces generated from binary segmentation results (recall § 6.5). The best general method to smooth visualizations of binary segmentation results is Constrained Elastic Surface Nets (CESN) [Gibson, 1998] (recall § 6.6.1). However, for small vascular structures, the constraint to a particular cell is not sufficient, since these are often only one voxel wide. Such structures degenerate after smoothing to a line.

11.6.2 VISUALIZATION WITH MPU IMPLICITS

A vascular surface visualization with a superior quality compared to CESN can be developed using implicit visualization techniques (recall § 11.5.3). The specific method is based on MPU implicits [Ohtake *et al.*, 2003], a method originally developed for point clouds resulting from 3D laser scanning with implicit surfaces. MPU is an acronym for Multiple Partinioning of Unity. The use of MPU implicits for visualizing anatomical structures requires to transform a segmentation result into a set of points. A simple and general solution for this transformation is to use centers of all boundary voxels—a method used by Braude *et al.* [2007] for a variety of anatomical structures. This general solution is an instance of the pipeline for rendering medical volume data with MPU implicits (Fig. 11.30). For vascular structures, however, this simple point set generation scheme leads to problems, e.g., if adjacent vessels are very close or in the periphery where vascular structures are very thin.

Decomposition of the 3D Space Similar to convolution surfaces, MPU implicits require a 3D decomposition of the whole space where the vascular model resides. This decomposition is realized as an adaptive octree

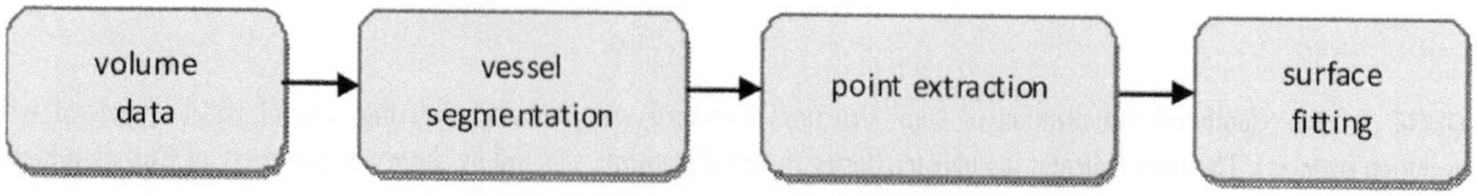

FIGURE 11.30 Pipeline for vessel visualization with MPU implicits.

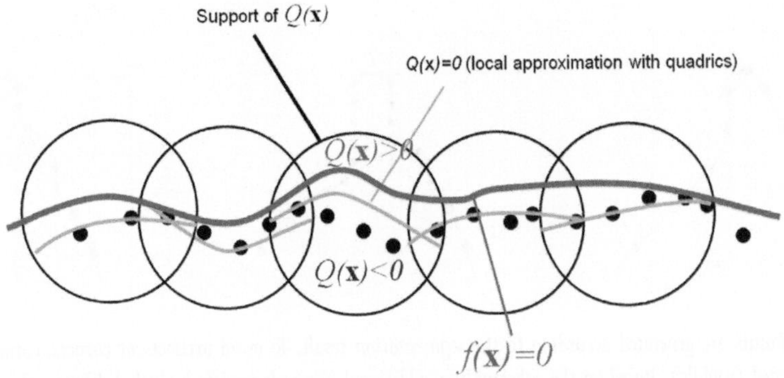

FIGURE 11.31 Principle of MPU surface generation. Instead of the 3D spheres, circles illustrate how smooth quadratic functions are fitted locally to all sampling points (small black circles) and finally superimposed in a global function (Courtesy of Christian Schumann, Fraunhofer MEVIS Bremen).

which represents where the points are located in space. The tree has a deeper level in regions where many points reside and a low level in empty regions. For each octree node, a sphere is generated, which serves as neighborhood where a quadric surface is approximated to the points inside of that sphere (see Fig. 11.31). An important decision relates to the size of the spheres: They should be large enough to cover a reasonable number of sampling points but not that large that too many points have to be considered. Since a general quadratic function from x, y, z has ten coefficients, at least ten points are required to determine a unique set of coefficients. The points may be scattered arbitrarily in space. Thus, within a certain fixed radius of the sphere, too many or too few sampling points may be contained. Ohtake *et al.* [2003] suggest to start with a low radius and use it if sufficient points are contained.[2] Otherwise, the radius is iteratively enlarged by a certain percentage until enough points are contained. Each sampling point p has a certain *support*, a region around p where the quadratic function is above zero representing a non-zero influence of p. The influence drops from a maximum of 1 at p to 0 according to a Gaussian function (recall Fig. 11.25 and the discussion of convolution surfaces). The local approximations within several spheres overlap (see Fig. 11.31). Thus, the local approximation results are blended in the border regions to yield one global result. Mathematically, this is achieved as a weighted average of the local approximations according to Equation 11.9

$$f(x) = \frac{\sum_i w_i(x) Q_i(x)}{w_i(x)} \tag{11.9}$$

Advanced Point Generation The simple use of the segmentation results' boundary voxels' center as points is not optimal [Wu *et al.*, 2010]. To prevent that small vascular structures collapse, Schumann *et al.* [2007] suggested to include additional subvoxels at thin and elongated structures (Fig. 11.32). They also describe some neighborhood-dependent rules for point placement to generate smooth MPU visualizations (Fig. 11.33). As further steps, the surface has to be constructed by means of polygonization and surface normals have to be estimated. Depending on the point constellation Schumann *et al.* [2007] employed either a gradient-based method for normal generation or simply used the normal vector of the outer face of the

2 A variant of the MPU implicit construction was employed by the same authors for reliably defining ridge and valley lines (§ 12.5.3) on surfaces [Ohtake *et al.*, 2004]).

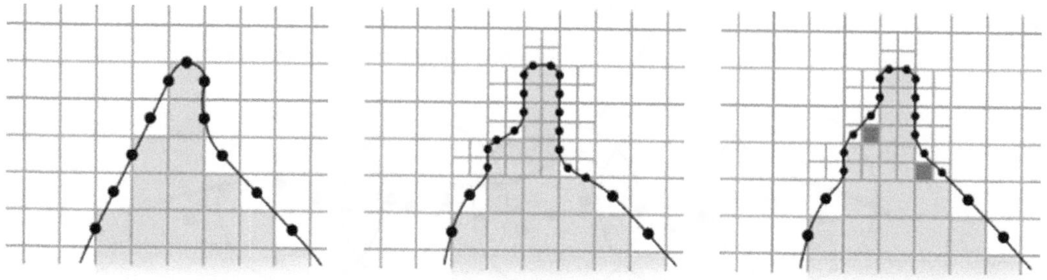

FIGURE 11.32 *Points are generated according to the segmentation result. To avoid artifacts at corners, corner regions, and thin features are subsampled (middle). Based on the subsampling, additional subvoxels need to be included before the generation of points (right) (From: [Schumann et al., 2007]).*

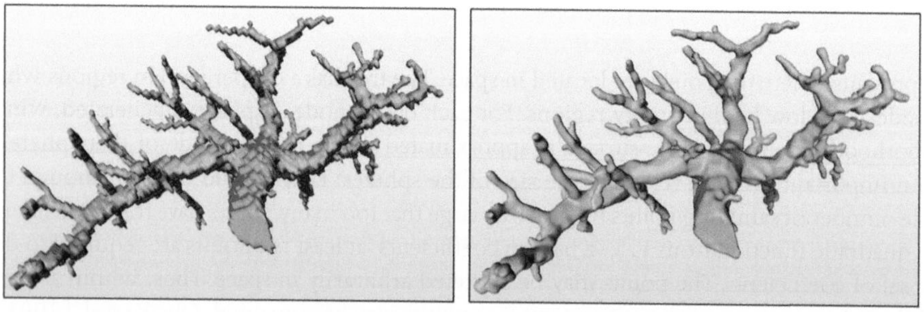

FIGURE 11.33 *A segmented liver tree is visualized with Marching Cubes (left) and with MPU implicits (right). The appearance is strongly improved and the accuracy of the visualization is maintained. Without any optimization, however, the MPU implicits' generation takes considerably longer (13 seconds vs. 2 seconds) (Courtesy of Christian Schumann, Fraunhofer MEVIS. See also [Schumann et al., 2007]).*

boundary voxel. For the generation of the triangle mesh they used the implicit polygonizer [Bloomenthal, 1994].

For clinical applicability it is essential that all parameters to control this process, e.g., the sphere radius, are determined from the input data. The parameters are chosen such that unwanted blending or other undesirable effects are avoided. Thus, a medical doctor does not need to adjust parameters, nor has to understand the underlying algorithm. Hence, Schumann *et al.* [2007] also describe an automatic estimation of appropriate default values for all relevant parameters of their implicit mesh generation pipeline.

Validation and Discussion The desired smoothing effect was verified by computing and analyzing maximum curvature values (see § 12.3 for a discussion of curvature estimation at polygonal meshes). A smoothed visualization of a certain geometric model is characterized by significantly reduced curvature values (Fig. 11.34).

Compared to a visualization of the same data with convolution surfaces, the MPU implicit visualization is significantly more precise, but at the expense of a little lower smoothness. The surface generation process based on the segmentation result and a few introduced points in the center of adjacent subvoxels even

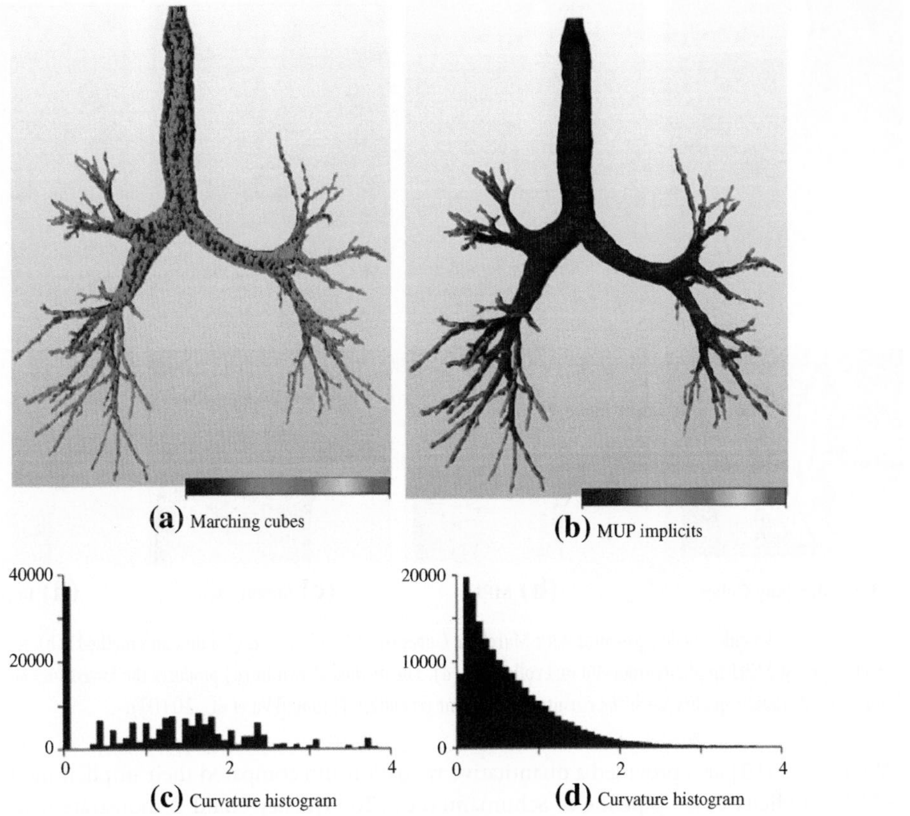

FIGURE 11.34 *A segmented bronchial tree rendered with Marching Cubes (a) and MPU implicits (b). Both surface models are color-coded according to maximum curvature. In the bottom part, the corresponding histograms of Gaussian curvature values are shown. Maximum curvature values are lower in the MPU implicits visualization and the histogram has a shape where the frequency decreases monotonically for larger vascular trees (From: [Schumann et al., 2007]).*

allows to compute a boundary for the maximum deviation to a perfectly accurate visualization of the segmentation result.

While Schumann *et al.* [2007] could show the applicability of MPU implicits for the smooth and accurate visualization of vascular surfaces, several steps of their approach have been improved by Wu *et al.* [2010]. They used the point generation strategy from Schumann *et al.* [2007] but came up with another implicit surface representation, namely "Poisson Surfaces." This includes a more advanced surface normal estimation scheme using covariance analysis of points in a certain neighborhood. This enables a smoother impression if lightning is enabled.

They also significantly improved the generation of the triangle mesh by making it adaptive to the estimated local curvature. This allows to reduce the overall number of triangles without degrading quality. Moreover, triangles with a better quality (almost equilateral) are thus generated (see Fig. 11.35). This is a crucial advantage for the generation of simulation models (see § 19.3). Schumann *et al.* [2008] also provided a modification of their original method to enable simulations. However, they need an additional remeshing step.

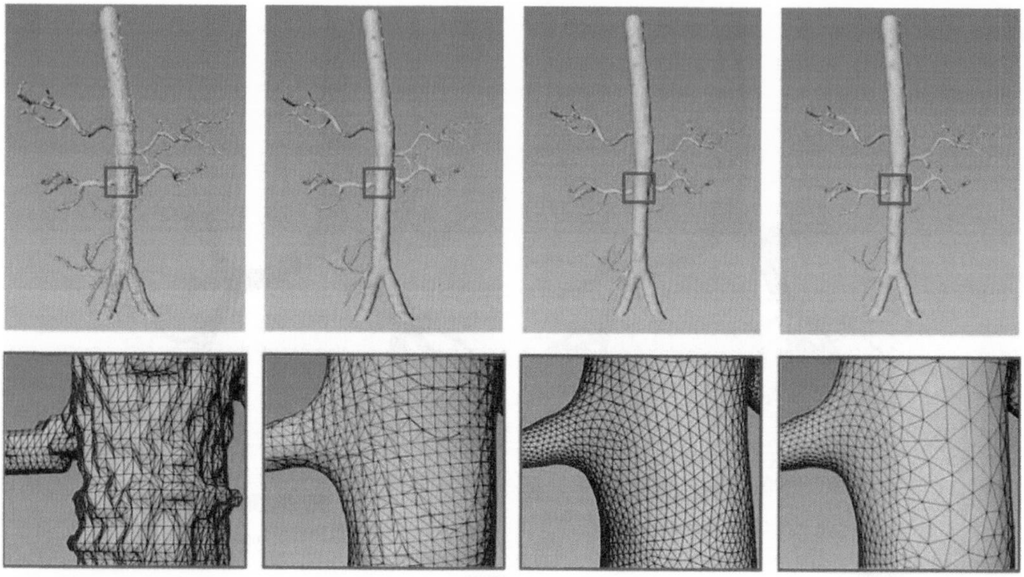

(a) Marching Cubes **(b)** MPUI **(c)** Subdivision **(d)** Improved MPUI

FIGURE 11.35 *Vascular models generated with Marching Cubes (a), MPU implicits (Schumann's method) (b), subdivision surfaces (c), and improved MPU implicits from Wu and colleagues (d). The method shown in (d) produces the lowest number of triangles and achieves a good triangle quality with the curvature-dependent generation (From: [Wu et al., 2010]).*

Wu *et al.* [2010] also provided a quantitative validation and compared their implicit method as well as the MPU implicits-based pipeline of Schumann *et al.* [2008]. They could demonstrate that both variants of the MPU implicits exhibit a very low error (the maximum error was always below two voxel diagonal sizes), whereas subdivision surfaces lead to an error three to four times larger.

11.6.3 IMPLICIT RECONSTRUCTION WITH SWEEPING

Recently, Hong *et al.* [2012] introduced an implicit surface reconstruction method that is model-free, like [Schumann *et al.*, 2007], but provides smooth results based on a *sweeping approach*. Sweep objects arise when a shape is moved along a path, e.g., by translation and rotation.

It achieves a better quality by using the vessel centerline and decomposing the surface reconstruction in the following steps:

- Capture each cross section with the vessel centerline and represent it as a point set.
- Provide a smooth and accurate representation of intersections perpendicular to the centerline.
- Integrate these profiles with a *sweeping* technique by weighting the individual contributions.

This implicit sweeping method does not suffer from any restrictions to the shape. Even highly curved regions that cause problems when reconstructed explicitly, are represented without artifacts. The cross sections are represented with a special kind of 2D splines, called *2D piecewise algebraic splines* [Li and Tian, 2009]. Figure 11.36 illustrates how the pointset of a cross section is transformed in a 2D curve with the 2D spline technique. While the very idea of implicit sweep objects is not new [Crespin, *et al.* 1996], Hong *et al.* [2012] make it usable for the first time for the complex topology of vascular (and bronchial)

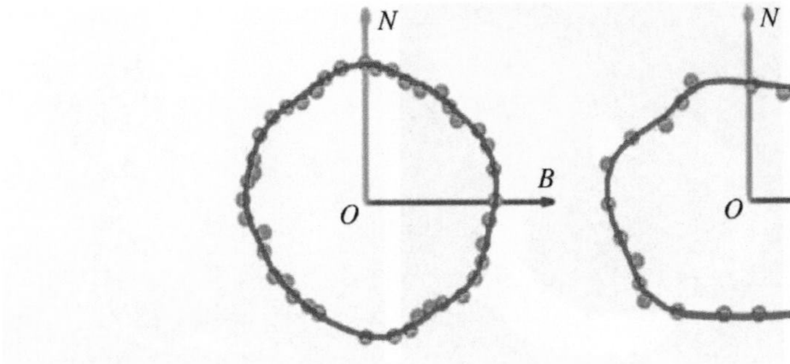

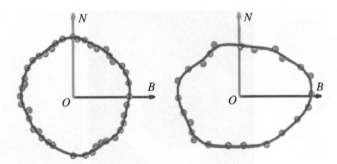

FIGURE 11.36 The cross section of a vascular structure given by a pointset is represented by implicit splines resulting in a smooth transition (From: [Hong et al., 2012]).

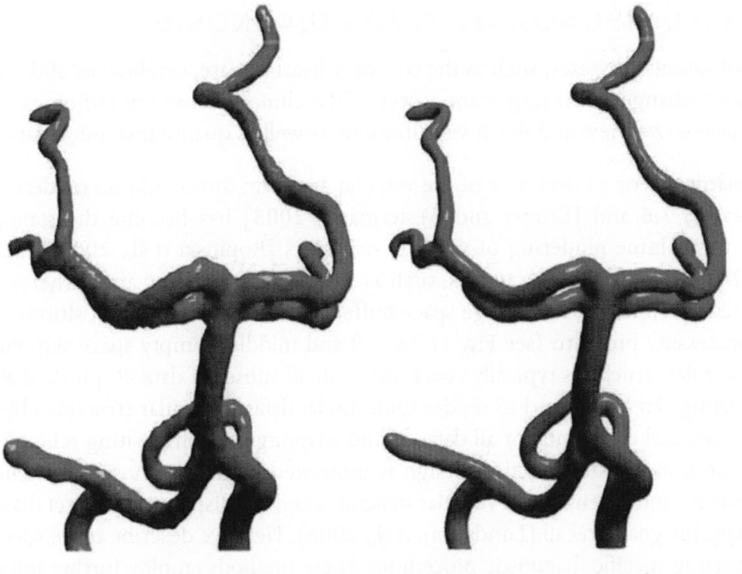

FIGURE 11.37 Cerebral vasculature reconstructed from MRA data with implicit methods. **Left:** Reconstruction with MPU implicits, **right:** clearly improved reconstruction with implicit sweeping (From: [Hong et al., 2012]).

trees. In case of branchings, several branches contribute to the implicit surface. The individual components are weighted accordingly and smoothly blended. The notorious over-blending property of implicit surfaces (bulging, ...) could be avoided. With going into details we want to mention at least one major ingredient of that method: the points along the centerline $S(s)$ are transformed in the Frenet frame. This frame is a 3D coordinate system, where the T component represents the tangent of the curve, the N component the normal and, the B component the binormal. A vascular tree computed with this method is shown in Figure 11.37 (right). It is compared with the MPU implicit reconstruction (Fig. 11.37, left). The only disadvantage is the high computational effort—the method takes 1–2 minutes as an efficient GPU-based implementation for average-size datasets.

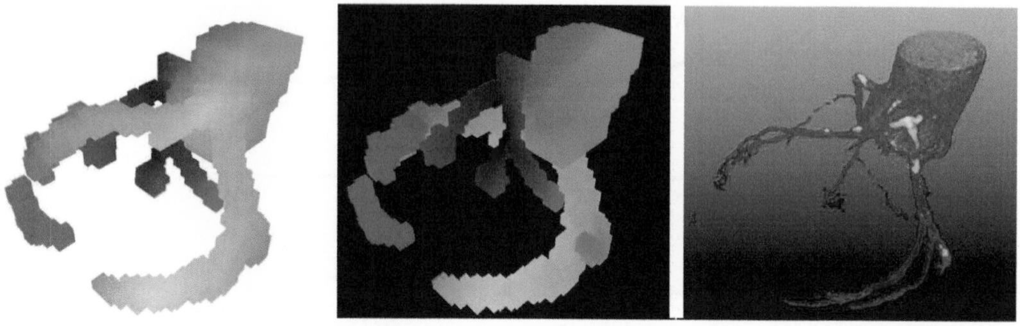

FIGURE 11.38 *GPU raycasting with position buffers applied to coronary vessels in CT data. An approximated mesh hull of the volume is rasterized into ray-start- (left) and ray-end-position (middle) buffer. Both are used for the final volume rendering (right) through a viewport-spanning quad mesh (From: [Kubisch et al., 2012]).*

11.7 VESSEL VISUALIZATION FOR DIAGNOSIS

The diagnosis of vascular diseases, such as the coronary heart disease, cerebral, or abdominal aneurysms, as well as stenotic changes is an important aspect of the clinical routine in radiology departments. For diagnostic purposes, overview and detail visualizations as well as quantitative information are essential.

Direct Volume Rendering For an overview of the vascular anatomy, direct volume rendering is useful. GPU raycasting (recall § 7.6 and [Krüger and Westermann, 2003] has become the state-of-the art technique also for the volume rendering of vascular structures [Ropinski *et al.*, 2009, Glaßer *et al.*, 2010a, Kubisch *et al.*, 2012]. Acceleration strategies, such as empty space skipping and early ray termination, are essential in efficient rendering. Two image space buffers for ray start and end positions are used as input for the pixel processing program (see Fig. 11.38, left and middle). Empty space skipping is particularly useful, as the vascular structures typically cover only a small subset of data. Ropinski *et al.*[2009] explain how GPU raycasting can be adapted to render multimodal data of vascular structures by computing and integrating ray start and endpoints for all datasets and adapting the compositing scheme.

A lot of research in transfer function design is motivated by the diagnosis of vascular diseases. The separation between contrast-enhanced vascular structures and the display of a correct diameter of vascular structures are specific goals (recall [Lundstrom *et al.*, 2006]. Here we describe more specialized methods aiming at supporting specific diagnostic procedures. These methods employ further information, in particular segmentation information and are fine-tuned to highlight structures, such as atherosclerotic plaque in coronary arteries.

Multiplanar Reformatting An important ingredient for such a system is a multiplanar reformatting (MPR) view which presents the original data orthogonal to the local vessel centerline. This cross-sectional view, however, has to be mentally integrated in an overview of the vascular tree (Fig. 11.39). The 3D visualization, in this context, serves to verify the image analysis results and to locate detailed information in the overall structure [Boskamp *et al.*, 2004].

Transfer Functions for Diagnosis of Vascular Diseases A number of advanced transfer function design concepts, such as gradient-based transfer functions (§ 9.4.1) and size-based transfer functions (§ 9.3.4) are largely motivated by diagnosing vascular diseases. Despite some promising results, none of these approaches considers two frequent problems in visualizing CT angiography data:

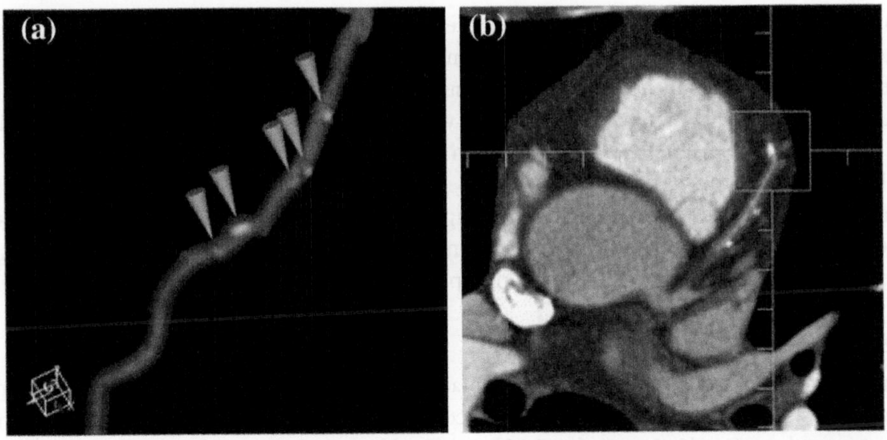

FIGURE 11.41 *A segmented branch of the coronary arteries is displayed via volume rendering. Arrows point at suspicious regions where possibly calcified plaque occurs (left). For each suspicious region, the corresponding part in the 2D slice view is emphasized (From: [Wesarg et al., 2006]).*

- MR time-of-flight (TOF),
- *MR angiography* is increasingly used, and
- *rotation angiography* as high-end imaging modality is available at some university hospitals.

In the following, we focus on CT and MRI data due to their widespread use.

Cerebral aneurysms develop from a congenital or acquired weakness of stabilizing parts of the cerebral arterial vessel wall. They bear a high risk of rupture with often fatal consequences for the patient. On the other hand, treatment options, such as neurosurgical interventions and endovascular coiling (a set of small wires is inserted in the aneurysm to slow down and stop further blood flow), exhibit a substantial risk. Neurosurgery is necessary if the location of the aneurysm is unfortunate for access with a catheter and for giant aneurysms (>2.5 cm).

To gain insight into the cause and evolution of cerebral aneurysms and to support treatment decisions, a detailed characterization of morphology (size, shape), morphodynamics (pulsatile change of morphology), and hemodynamics (blood flow pattern) is important. We will discuss the hemodynamics in aneurysms in Chapter 19. Here, we restrict to the static visualization of vascular structures.

Arterio-venous Malformations (AVMs) are direct connections between arteries and veins. This short circuit is characterized by coils of vessel branches and needs treatment by either endovascular interventions or surgery. The prevalence of this disease is not quite clear, e.g., Weiler *et al.* [2012] state that 0.01–0.5% of the population are affected. With respect to the visualization challenges, AVMs in the brain are similar to cerebral aneurysms. Martin *et al.* [2000] discuss the treatment options and the related experiences in detail.

There have been several attempts to support the diagnosis of cerebral aneurysms. Puig *et al.* [1997] modeled typical bifurcations and pathologies in cerebral vasculature to identify and emphasize aneurysms and stenosis in patient-specific data. Five different graphics primitives are used to reconstruct the vascular tree. The focus of their work is on the geometric continuity and on realistic shading. Boskamp *et al.* [2006]

report on another system that is able to detect and emphasize potential aneurysms. This was achieved by a complex vessel analysis pipeline, including a quantitative analysis of vessel diameters.

Correa and Ma [2008] introduced *size-based transfer functions* (recall § 9.3.4). One of their showcase examples was to highlight aneurysms as parts of a vascular system that typically is large. Thus, using the size of a feature as a dimension for transfer function specification, it may be discriminated and presented, e.g., with a different color.

Recently, Chen *et al.* [2012], used level set propagation for the segmentation of the related vessels and displayed the wavefront propagation front as a hint for the blood flow. They further used augmented reality techniques to support the decision making process (where to clip).

11.7.1.2 Focus-and-Context Rendering

One general strategy to employ the vessel segmentation is to design transfer functions which emphasize the segmented vasculature and provide additional context information. This general strategy is known as *focus-and-context rendering* (see [Krüger *et al.*, 2006] and [Bruckner *et al.*, 2010] for surveys).

The case study of Neugebauer *et al.* [2009b] is based on MR TOF data which yield a high signal from blood moving into the direction of the slice plane normal. The focus-and-context rendering scheme described in the following is a special example derived from general principles of focus-and-context rendering (§ 12.10).

They suggest an adaptation of the transfer function to the segmented aneurysm region to highlight the aneurysm and its immediate inflow and outflow region. This can either be achieved with tagged volume rendering where the segmented target structure is rendered with a transfer function that ensures its visibility or with a hybrid rendering where the target region is rendered as isosurface and the contextual vasculature is displayed via volume rendering.

The data have to be filtered to reliably exclude skin and non-vascular tissue. By exploring ten datasets with varying intensity values and from different scanner devices, the following pipeline with four steps was derived:

1. **Binary threshold.** Due to the high intensity values of vessels in MR TOF data, thresholding removes most of the disturbing data. Because of individual varyings between datasets, the threshold selection is based on the equalized histogram, which compensates for image intensities and overall contrast between vessels and tissue. The mean value position p in the equalized image histogram is used to define the refined threshold as $T = p * 0.5$, which was found to be roughly $I_{max} * 0.25$. After thresholding, the image contains all relevant arteries, but also parts of high intensity brain tissue, skin, as well as noisy parts of other tissue (see Fig. 11.42, (b)).
2. **Connected Component Analysis.** Voxels belonging to arteries form large components, whereas skin and tissue-related voxels split up into several small components (see Fig. 11.42, (b)). Therefore, a connected component analysis (CCA) may distinguish between relevant (arteries) and irrelevant structures. The noise is removed by discarding all components smaller than 0.01% (empiric threshold) of the overall dataset volume. Removal of the skin components is achieved by taking into account that the arteries are located along the center medial axis of the head (Fig. 11.42, (c)). The bounding boxes of all components are projected into the transverse plane. Since the arteries are close to the center of the whole dataset and run mostly vertically, their bounding box centers are clustered in this plane. In contrast, the skin components exhibit a lower clustering rate. This observation may be used to robustly exclude the skin components (see [Kubisch *et al.*, 2012] for details of this separation).

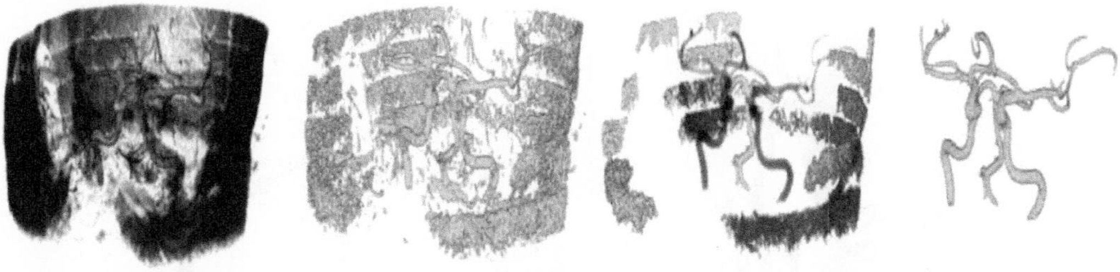

(a) original data (b) after thresholding (c) after CCA (d) removal of skin

FIGURE 11.42 *Different stages of the filtering processes: original data (a), threshold applied (b), connected component analysis discarding small structures (c), removal of outer skin structures (d) (From: [Kubisch et al., 2012]).*

3 **Preservation of relevant details.** The CCA reliably identifies the large arteries. Small vessels that potentially emanate from the aneurysm body, cannot be identified this way. They have a small diameter (2–3 voxels), are often fragmented because of the low spatial resolution of the MR scan and exhibit low contrast differences with respect to the surrounding tissue. Thus, those vessels exhibit characteristics similar to noise and other artifacts—structures which are removed in the CCA-based processing. Since these small vessels may be diagnostically relevant, they should be included in the context visualization.

For this purpose, a distance field from the main vessels is generated. Finally, it is weighted by the original intensity values of the volume data (D) and used in the 3D view (E). An experienced radiologist is able to visually distinguish between noise and small vessels, if the view at the region containing the small vessels is not occluded. Hence, the region near the aneurysm is included in the context visualization without any filtering. Again, there are a couple of algorithmic details and parameters to control this process precisely [Kubisch *et al.*, 2012].

4 **Final mask creation.** The result of the CCA-based processing is a binary volume. This volume is processed with a dilation filter with a $3 \times 3 \times 3$. Thus, it is ensured that the vessel surface is represented completely when masking the original data. This mask is combined with a mask resulting from the previous step by applying the arithmetic image operation *max*. As a result, a mask that will preserve the main arteries and low contrast information near to the aneurysm surface arises.

With the use of 1D TFs, the final visualization is presented in Figure 11.43. To avoid artifacts around the mesh, its voxelized version was subtracted from the original volume data. Otherwise, the double representation of the same structure would lead to problems.

Treatment Planning for *AVMs* Arterio-venous malformations (AVM)s are also treated by embolization with coils or surgically. Treatment planning for AVMs is based on similar data, e.g., MR-TOF or MRA and T1-weighted MRI and involves similar visualization tasks. Again, the vascular pathology needs to be located and the surrounding vascular structures, in particular the inflow vessels (*feeders*) and the draining veins needs to be understood. Moreover, there are frequently "en-passage" arteries passing the AVM that should not be ligated. The complete understanding of that complex vascular anatomy is further hampered by the fact that not a single image modality is able to capture all relevant information.

Bullitt *et al.* [2001] thus suggested to segment the feeding arteries and outgoing veins to selectively visualize essential components of the vascular architecture. Focus-and-context visualizations where color

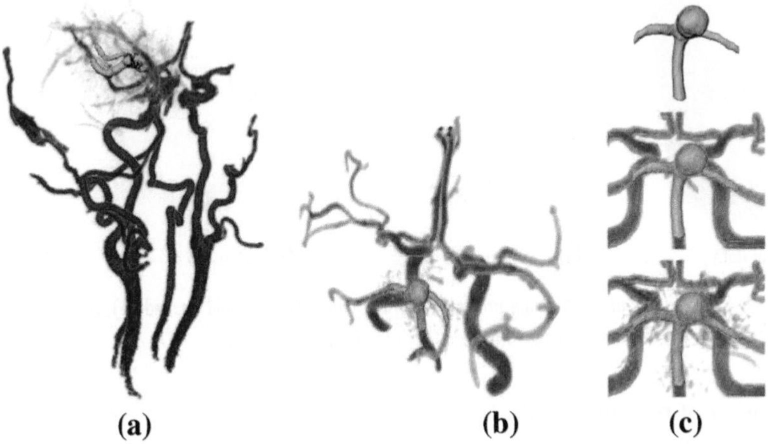

FIGURE 11.43 *The focus-and-context visualization as a hybrid combination of isosurface rendering (aneurysm region) and volume rendering of the surrounding vessels. (a) and (b) Show different 1D transfer functions. (c) Illustrates the benefits of context information by showing vessels of a growing distance field. Small vessels originating from the aneurysm become visible (From: [Kubisch et al., 2012]).*

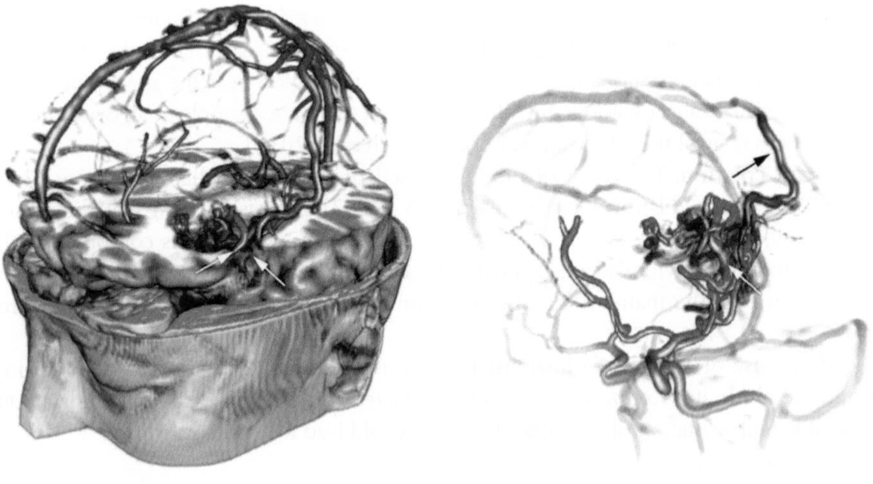

FIGURE 11.44 *Visualization of the neurovascular anatomy for diagnosis and treatment of AVMs.* **Left:** *The complete context is displayed.* **Right:** *a focused visualization where the AVM core is emphasized and shown along with the supplying vessels (the feeders). The right image provides the essential information for treatment planning (Courtesy of Florian Weiler, Fraunhofer MEVIS Bremen).*

and transparency are adjusted to emphasize the AVM and to display the essential context as well are useful (see Fig. 11.44). Such visualizations, of course, require careful preprocessing. Weiler *et al.* [2011] employ for example the "vesselness" filter to enhance vascular structures. In an extension of that work, Weiler *et al.* [2012] presented a multimodal framework, that is able to process and fuse DSA, CTA, and MRI data. The exploration of the multimodal data employs the strategies, presented in § 4.8.5, e.g., to employ different clipping planes for each modality.

11.7.2 DIAGNOSIS OF THE CORONARY HEART DISEASE

11.7.2.1 Medical Background

Coronary heart disease (CHD) is the leading cause of death in western nations. Atherosclerotic CHD is the result of inflammatory modifications leading to accumulations in the coronary artery wall, so-called plaques. Plaque deposits contain different accumulations and can be classified into soft, fibrous and hard plaques. The lipid-rich soft plaques are prone to rupture and thus very dangerous. For individual soft plaque characterization, imaging modalities such as intravascular ultrasound and Optical Coherent Tomography with a very high spatial resolution can be employed. However, this modality is still rare. Fibrous plaques and hard plaques consist of more dense accumulations and are more stable.

Hard plaque deposits contain calcium accumulations and are thus also referred to as *calcified plaques*. The overall coronary calcium acts as an indicator for the patient's whole plaque burden. The early stages of atherosclerotic CHD do not necessarily lead to *significant stenoses*, since they can be compensated by a positive remodeling of the vessel wall, see Figure 11.45. Therefore, the evaluation of the coronary artery lumen is insufficient for the assessment of the patient's plaque burden, and the pathological change of the vessel wall has to be taken into account. Evaluation of the lumen and the vessel wall is carried out in 2D MPR and CPR views (recall Fig. 11.12).

Thus, the major goals in the diagnostic process are:

- assessment of the vessel morphology,
- assessment of the regional distribution of plaques, and
- assessment and quantification of the plaque decomposition.

CT *Angiography Data* While the discrimination between different plaque types was limited with 16-slice and 64-slice CT technology, the most recent generation of CT scanners with 256 slices enable a discrimination of plaque types [Yang *et al.*, 2010]. With the recent improvements of multislice spiral CT data, where 64, 256, and even 320 slices are acquired simultaneously, CT data play an essential role in the diagnosis. With the short acquisition times it is now possible to depict the coronary arteries in a sufficient quality, even for patients with accelerated heart beat or other abnormalities. With non-invasive contrast-enhanced CT coronary angiography (CTA), the coronary heart disease may be reliably excluded.

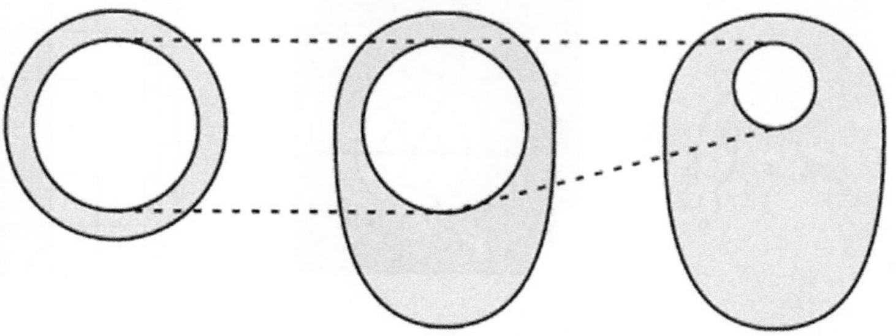

FIGURE 11.45 *Illustration of remodeling in cross-sectional views. Left, a normal vessel wall (gray) is depicted. Early stages of CHD are compensated by positive remodeling—an increasing wall thickness (center). Negative remodeling, caused by progressive CHD, yields a stenosis (right) (Courtesy: Sylvia Glaßer, University of Magdeburg).*

Especially for asymptomatic patients with a high risk (due to increased blood pressure, age and body mass index), CTA is employed for non-invasive identification, characterization, and quantification of atherosclerotic CHD. For a thorough description of CHD, treatment options, imaging modalities, and an integrated computer support, see [Hennemuth, 2012].

Quantification is carried out by applying *calcium scores* to the data, e.g., the AGATSTON SCORE which defines a threshold for hard plaques as the sum of the mean plus twice the standard deviation of the non-enhanced blood intensity [Agatson *et al.*, 1990].

CT data is also used for monitoring of coronary stents (artificial support devices, e.g., stainless steel mesh tubes that are placed in a coronary artery to keep the vessel open).

11.7.2.2 Designing Local Transfer Functions

In the following, we focus on the visual analysis of CT data. This problem has been analyzed in [Glaßer *et al.*, 2010a], where a prototypic solution is presented. The automatically generated transfer functions can be interactively changed by modifying two offsets. The first offset O_1 defines the relative position of the hard plaque separation, that is S_6. The second offset, O_2, determines the average vessel wall intensity and thus the control point S_3.

The specific visualization goal was to emphasize the vessel wall with its deposits. The 3D visualization employs an analysis of the vessel voxels' histogram and the vessel wall voxel's histogram (the segmentation of the coronary arteries can be accomplished semi-automatically, e.g., [Friman *et al.*, 2010] detects also small vascular structures in the periphery).

A Gaussian distribution of the intensity values in CT data is assumed. Its parameters μ and σ are determined by an optimal (least square) fit to the intensity distribution of the vessel voxels (actually the segmentation result needs to be postprocessed to account for boundary voxels partially belonging to other tissue). It turned out that $\mu_{blood}, \sigma_{blood}$ differ strongly, i.e., by more than 100 HU values, from dataset to dataset. These two dataset-specific parameters are employed to determine the threshold for calcified plaques.

To selectively emphasize the vessel wall, a local histogram analysis [Lindstroem *et al.*, 2005] for each coronary artery branch is performed (see Fig. 11.46). To identify these branches, the centerline of the segmented coronary artery tree is generated. The centerlines are transferred into a tree representation where each branch consists of a list with the corresponding centerline voxels and is linked to adjacent

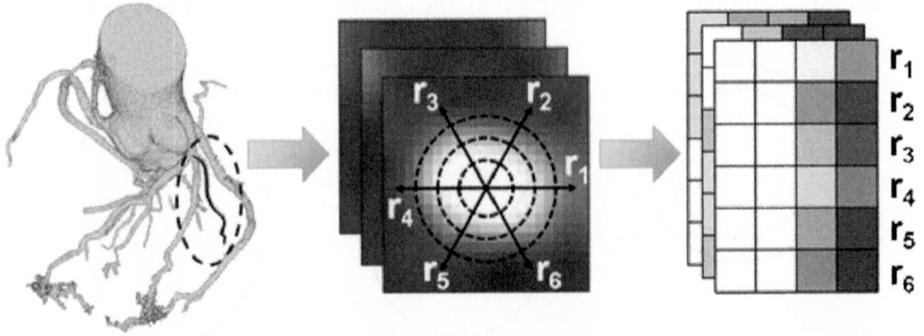

FIGURE 11.46 *Extraction of the IPV. For each voxel of the local centerline of a coronary branch (left), a certain number (e.g., 6) of rays perpendicular to the centerline is casted (middle). Along the rays, intensities are sampled and stored in a slice of the IPV (right). Repeating this procedure for each centerline voxel of the branch yields the complete IPV (From: [Glaßer et al., 2010a]).*

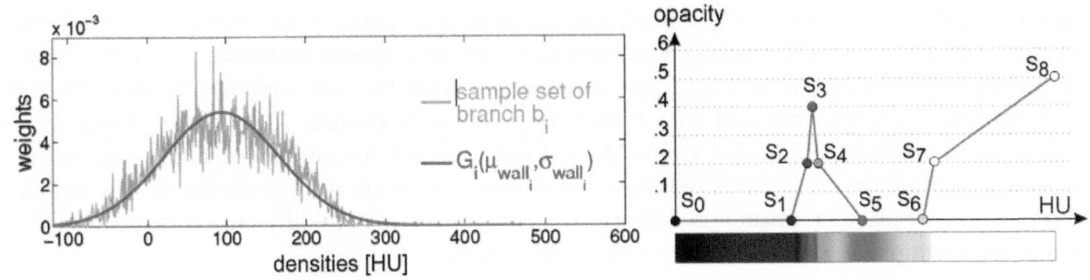

FIGURE 11.47 The transfer function specification is carried out by calculation of $\mu_{\text{blood}}, \sigma_{\text{blood}}$ and $\mu_{\text{wall}}, \sigma_{\text{wall}}$. Supporting points S_0 to S_8 are derived. Opacity values are linearly interpolated between the points. Since the HU values differ from dataset to dataset, the x-axis is not labeled (From: [Glaßer et al., 2010a]).

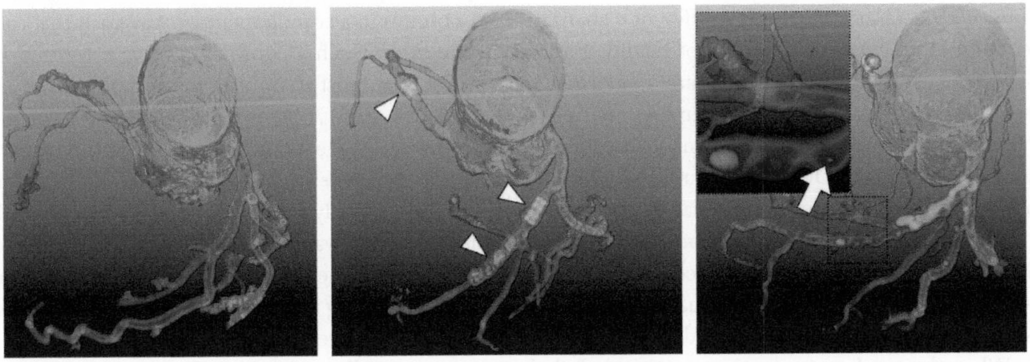

FIGURE 11.48 Direct volume rendering of three CTA datasets. The transfer function specification is based on an analysis of the segmented coronary arteries. On the left, the DVR view indicates a very low overall plaque burden. The dataset in the middle exhibits three stents (arrowheads), whereas the visualization on the right shows many hard plaques. Even small hard plaques are recognizable (arrow) (From: [Glaßer et al., 2010a]).

branches. The local histograms for the vessel intensity approximation are generated by the intensity profile volume (IPV) extraction for each branch of the centerline.

The TF specification is carried out by determining supporting points, which depend on the mean intensity and standard deviation of the bloodpool ($\mu_{blood}, \sigma_{blood}$) and the vessel wall ($\mu_{wall}, \sigma_{wall}$). Figure 11.47 illustrates how the Gaussian parameters are estimated and used for generating control points for the opacity transfer function. Figure 11.48 presents some examples of the renderings achieved with these transfer functions. In a similar way, parameters for a 2D transfer function (colors, brightness) are derived to emphasize wall abnormalities also in 2D.

11.7.2.3 Multimodal Vessel Visualization for Disease Understanding

Visualization techniques may also support medical research aiming at better disease understanding. With respect to the CHD, this relates to an understanding of the cellular and molecular processes in the vessel wall leading to plaque formation [Ropinski et al., 2009]. As an important contribution to this goal an interdisciplinary team at the University of Münster acquired a series of PET and CT data of small animals (mice) in high resolution. PET data indicates inflammatory plaque activity. Visualization served the purpose of presenting the multimodal data in a fused manner. After appropriate (semi-interactive) registration, they employed an efficient GPU raycaster. Moreover, they aimed at *comparative visualization* of different datasets and described a normalization process to cope with the substantial biologic variability. Besides DVR, they also generated CPR views enhanced with branching points as landmarks. Their system clearly shows the benefits of multiple coordinated views. Medical research and disease understanding requires also a reliable quantification, e.g., of wall thickness and degree of stenosis. As a result, the system supports the comparison of plaque formation in different animals which represent different genotypes as well as different interventions, e.g., they were fed with different diets.

11.7.3 MULTIPLE COORDINATED VIEWS

The diagnosis of vascular diseases and treatment planning require a precise understanding of vascular structures and their surroundings. We have discussed the potential and limitations of a number of vessel visualization techniques. However, none of these techniques can present the entire relevant information. Thus, it is necessary to combine different visualization techniques in a complementary way such that one technique presents information not readily available in the other. Such a combination is performed in different views, e.g., views for volume rendering, MIP, or CPR. The most straightforward implementation is to design these views as independent facilities to explore the data. A better alternative is to provide synchronization facilities, which enable a coupling of different views, e.g., the adaptation of the camera position in MIP and DVR. Such coupled views are referred to as *multiple coordinated views*. The combination of a global 3D overview of a vascular tree and a close-up of the currently selected region is often helpful.

A particular useful combination integrates DVR and CPR views. van Schooten *et al.* [2010] could demonstrate that users enjoyed such synchronization mechanisms. They compared different navigation strategies using a task where users had to find segmentation errors using DVR and straightened CPR views. Navigation along the centerline and rotation around the vector of interest were supported.

When the synchronization was not enabled, the test persons usually enabled it. When synchronization was enabled, users were 40% faster and made 20% less errors. The interaction patterns were quite different among the users. This relates to the use of both views for selection and navigation. In summary, at 66% of the overall time users interacted with the DVR view.

11.8 SUMMARY

The visualization of vascular structures is challenging due to their small size and complex topology. For advanced diagnostic or therapeutic problems dedicated visualization techniques are required. The accuracy of the visualization as well as the removal of annoying discretization artifacts are the two major and conflicting goals. For diagnostic processes, accuracy is more important, as it gives rise to techniques without model assumptions. For therapy planning, minor deviations are usually acceptable and therefore model-based techniques are appropriate. Among the model-based techniques, noticeable differences in the visual quality exist. Methods based on subdivision surfaces and convolution surfaces produce better results at the expense of increased computational effort. Advanced model-based techniques avoid any discontinuities at branchings as well as inner polygons.

Various direct volume rendering techniques have been successfully employed for diagnosis. The quality of vessel visualization benefits from preprocessing and filtering, which highlight elongated circular structures (*vesselness*). A histogram-based TF specification is particularly useful when applied to segmented vessels. For a vessel diagnosis system (e.g., [Boskamp *et al.*, 2004]), the combination of 2D and 3D views is essential, as only their combination can reveal the adequate detail and overview information. Automatically generated visualizations and an analysis of changes in the local vessel diameter might be used to emphasize potentially relevant or suspicious portions. Compared to surface-based techniques, DVR may also display important changes of the vessel wall and not only its general shape. For clinical routine, fast, reliable, and easy to setup techniques are favorable.

The analysis of vascular structures shall be important in four other chapters: In Chapter 10, we discussed measurements related to vascular structures, in Chapter 12, we discuss how illustrative techniques may enhance depth perception of vessel visualizations, in Chapter 13, vascular models are employed for generating fly-through animations, and in Chapter 19, geometric models of vascular structures serve as a basis for blood flow simulations.

FURTHER READING

For more details on skeletonization, see [Telea and van Wijk, 2002] and [Strzodka and Telea, 2004]. The latter provides a solution that is directly supported by the graphics hardware. Luboz *et al.* [2005] present a pipeline for vessel reconstruction from CT angiography datasets with semi-automatic tools using clinical and phantom data. It is aimed at neuroradiological interventions to treat cerebral ischemic strokes. There is recent work on flattening vascular structures for providing an overview on their topology [Saroul *et al.*, 2003, 2006, Won *et al.*, 2006]. A dedicated effort from Won *et al.* [2013] aims at displaying heavily branching vascular structures uncluttered using the abdominal aorta to showcase the potential. Kretschmar *et al.* [2012] introduced a model-based technique that generates intersection-free surfaces from centerlines with complex outlines. Vascular segments are described by local signed distance functions and combined using Boolean operations. An octree-based surface generation strategy computes watertight, scale-adaptive meshes with a controllable quality. Recently, Sibbing *et al.* [2012] presented a method that generates high-quality vascular surface models, consisting of quadrilaterals. They decompose a vascular tree into junctions and tube components and improve an initial surface model by remeshing to obtain smooth surfaces and high quality meshes appropriate for simulations.

Dedicated research has been conducted to fine-tune volume rendering, reformatting, and MIP to the diagnosis of vascular diseases such as diseases of the lower extremities [Roos *et al.*, 2009], renal artery stenosis [Rubin *et al.*, 1994, Rubin and Napel, 1997], analysis of vascular calcifications [Raman *et al.*, 2008b], cervicocranial arteries [Sparacia *et al.*, 2007], Aortoiliac and Peripheral Arterial Walls [Raman *et al.*, 2011]. A clinical evaluation of bone removal is presented in [Raman *et al.*, 2008a].

Chapter 12

Illustrative Medical Visualization

12.1 INTRODUCTION

A large portion of the previous chapters was dedicated to explain how medical volume data may be rendered precisely, efficiently and in high quality, including illumination effects and depth enhancement to provide a realistic expression of the underlying 3D geometry. In this chapter, we build on these rendering approaches and refine them by discussing *illustrative techniques*.

These illustrative techniques were developed to create renditions that consider *perceptual capabilities* of humans. As an example, humans infer information about shape not only from realistic shading but also from hatching and from outlines that support the mental separation of nearby objects rendered in similar colors. We have discussed perceptual issues relevant for interpreting medical image data in § 3.3, where we focused on contrast and color perception as well as in § 8.2.9, where we discussed illumination techniques and their impact on depth and shape perception. Illustrative techniques are also motivated by human cognitive processes, such as attention and situation awareness. Thus, the additional degrees of freedom of illustrative visualization should be used to emphasize what the author the visualization considers important.

Illustrative visualization techniques are inspired by the work of professional scientific and medical illustrators, who developed an impressive set of techniques that depict objects and relations in an abstract manner, leaving out details, or simplifying them [Briscoe, 1996]. These illustrations are based on many experiences and are guided toward specific goals, special aspects that should be emphasized, e.g., the spatial order of objects, their particular shape, or some details of the overall shape. Illustrative techniques provide more freedom to guide the viewer's attention, compared to conventional visualization techniques. In particular, *abstraction* plays an essential role in high-level illustrative visualization techniques. With abstraction, we refer to any attempt to adjust the level of detail, to simplify parts of a medical visualization or even omit them. In this chapter, we will discuss how such goals may be realized with computer-generated visualizations.

However, we shall not explain how visualizations are created that are as close as possible to manually created medical illustrations. Instead, we explain techniques that use the specific capabilities of interactive 3D rendering and consider the exploration of the data as an essential aspect. Thus, similar to the discussion in previous chapters, we focus on efficient (real-time) rendering and easy parameterization.

Low- and High-level Illustrative Techniques Illustrative visualization is a broad and somehow vague term. It covers pen-and-ink illustration techniques, such as silhouette, crease line and hatching generation (*low-level illustration technique*). Also illustrative illumination models and color selection influence *how* a given geometry is visualized (see Fig. 12.1).

High-level illustration techniques consider *what portion of the geometry* is displayed. As an example, objects may be removed, clipped or rendered transparently to reveal other objects behind. This particular category of illustration techniques is usually called *smart visibility* techniques and includes cutaways, ghosted and section views. Obviously, low-level and high-level techniques may be combined. In particular, the sparse

Visual Computing for Medicine, Second Edition. http://dx.doi.org/10.1016/B978-0-12-415873-3.00012-2

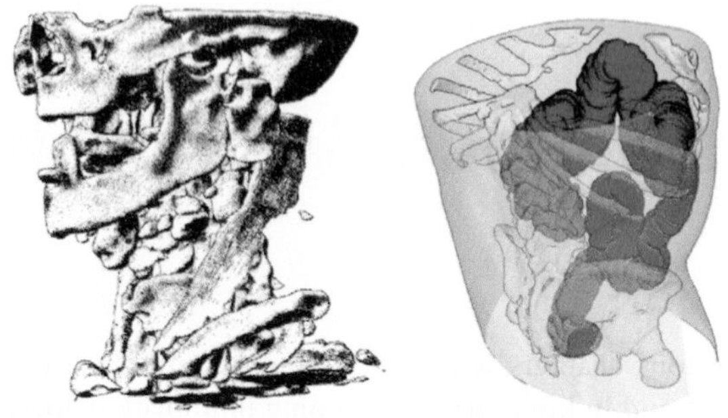

FIGURE 12.1 *Illustrative visualizations of medical image data.* **Left:** *The neck anatomy is depicted with a combination of illustrative shading and hatching.* **Right:** *The colon and other anatomical structures of the stomach region are depicted with silhouettes and toon shading. The focus is on the colon that is depicted in a saturated color (Courtesy of Roland Pfisterer and Zein Salah, University of Magdeburg).*

nature of most pen-and-ink techniques allows to render less important features in a more abstract manner, whereas shading may be employed for focus objects.

Similar to manually created illustrations, application-specific knowledge is employed in the generation of illustrative medical visualization, e.g., someone has to decide which objects should be emphasized. In this chapter, we discuss illustrative techniques guided by a user's perspective. Thus, time-consuming error prone parameterization is not feasible. Instead, the relevant knowledge must be either derived from the dataset or be derived from a description, which characterizes a set of similar cases. Similar to predefined transfer functions, *predefined illustration styles* for certain objects are essential.

Illustrative Visualization and NPR Illustrative visualization is related to the computer graphics term *Non-Photorealistic Rendering*, or short NPR. The term NPR is used since around 1990 when the seminal paper of Saito and Takahashi [1990] clearly illustrated that complex 3D shapes can be rendered more "comprehensible" by using certain *feature lines*. Later, two books summarized the NPR developments of the first decade [Gooch and Gooch, 2001, Strothotte and Schlechtweg, 2002]. NPR covers all rendering techniques that do not aim at photorealistic rendering and is thus an umbrella also for illustrative visualization. However, many NPR techniques indeed simulate the techniques of painters e.g., oil paintings or water color paintings as a kind of digital art with esthetics as major motivation. Often, NPR techniques are employed for entertainment; not to convey a particular kind of information as clearly as possible. In medical visualization, a clear depiction of medical volume data is essential and limits the degrees of freedom. Thus, illustrative visualization is the more focused term that covers rendering techniques serving clear visualization goals, namely to convey shape information efficiently. For a more detailed discussion of NPR and illustrative visualization Rautek *et al.* [2008] is recommended. They point out that strictly speaking "illustrative visualization" is a tautology, since "both illustration and visualization amplify cognition using visual representations." In medical visualization, either surfaces or volume data are rendered in illustrative styles. For illustrative volume rendering, the term *volume illustration* was introduced by Ebert and Rheingans [2000].

Organization We start with a general overview of potential medical application areas in § 12.2. In § 12.3, we describe curvature-related measures and discuss how they are approximated in case of polygonal surface meshes. We explain specific low-level illustrative rendering techniques starting with an introduction to feature line rendering (§ 12.4) and go on with an in-depth discussion of geometry-dependent feature lines, such as silhouettes, and lighting-dependent feature lines (§ 12.5 and 12.6).

Stippling (§ 12.7) and hatching (§ 12.8) are discussed as surface illustration techniques. Illustrative shading (§ 12.9) may be combined with stippling and hatching but also used in combination with conventional surface rendering. Finally, smart visibility techniques are discussed in § 12.10. These techniques support focus+context visualization within medical visualization in order to allow for emphasizing features of interest while at the same time deemphasizing other features.

12.2 MEDICAL APPLICATIONS

In the scope of this book, we consider visualization techniques primarily aiming at medical diagnosis, treatment planning, outcome control, intraoperative support, medical research, or medical education. With only few exceptions, a common pre-requisite for illustrative medical visualization is the segmentation (recall § 4.5) of all relevant structures from volumetric medical image data, limiting applications to those where the segmentation effort is justified. The few exceptions are related to anatomical structures that can be easily delineated, such as skeletal or air-filled structures in CT data where an appropriate transfer function may be sufficient to extract relevant anatomical structures. In the scientific literature in computer graphics and visualization, these examples of very low clinical relevance are frequently used which might be misleading. More recent examples of illustrative visualizations not based on segmentations employ MR-DTI data to visualize fiber tracts. This very special application is postponed to Chapter 15.

Medical Education Illustrative rendering requires high quality data where noise is effectively removed. Thus, the overall effort to *prepare* data is substantially higher compared to traditional surface and volume rendering. Illustrative medical visualization usually is discussed as valuable for *medical education*, that is with specific learning objectives in mind, e.g., in anatomy to convey complex spatial relations and their variance among individuals. This also corresponds to the observations from Rautek *et al.* [2008] who found that illustrative techniques are primarily used for knowledge communication, e.g., in presenting research results and in educational settings.

Although there are only few educational systems that rely on illustrative visualization, education is a likely useful application area. In medical textbooks illustrations still play an essential role because they obviously enable an effective understanding of complex anatomical or surgical situations. If illustrations of a similar quality may be provided and flexible exploration is supported, such as rotation and clipping, this *active exploration* certainly supports a deep understanding. In educational systems, the segmentation effort and other tasks to *author* an illustration are justified, since the same illustrated model may be reused frequently.

Clinical Applications Diagnosis, on the other hand, is probably not an essential application area for illustrative visualization, since the relation between original data and visualizations is very complex involving complex postprocessing. However, for treatment planning and for intraoperative support, carefully adapted illustration techniques have a role. For treatment planning, often internal objects and embedding structures need to be seen simultaneously—a situation where smart visibility techniques are useful. As an example, in Figure 12.2 ghosted views are generated to show enlarged (potentially malignant) lymph nodes. The circular cross section of the affected region is also highlighted in the 2D view.

More and more, data from different sources need to be integrated in treatment planning and illustrative techniques may be designed such that they allow to cope with that complexity. The first important example was radiation treatment planning where anatomical information, derived from CT data was

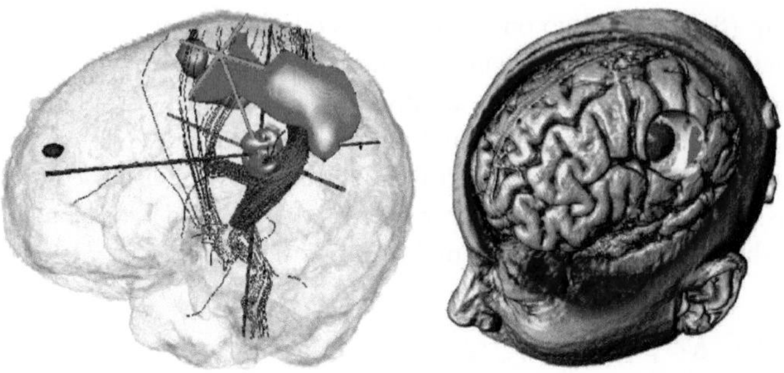

FIGURE 12.2 **Left:** *An illustrative technique, namely ghosted views, carefully adapted to surgical needs in neurosurgery planning. Ghosted views are employed to reveal the path to a deep seated tumor.* **Right:** *Silhouettes, a low-level illustrative rendering technique is employed to incorporate fiber bundles as context information (Courtesy of Christian Rieder, Fraunhofer MEVIS Bremen. See also [Rieder et al., 2008]).*

visually combined with isodose simulations to predict the chances and risks of a particular configuration of radiation sources [Interrante *et al.*, 1995]. We will discuss intraoperative illustrative visualization in § 18.7.4. Here it might be sufficient to stress that the overlay of intraoperatively acquired data with preoperative data is the major problem where low and high-level illustration techniques may support an enhanced depth perception of these inherently complex data.

12.3 CURVATURE APPROXIMATION

In this chapter, we discuss a large variety of line-based illustrative techniques, such as feature lines and hatching. Most of them employ *curvature-related measures* to control the placement of lines. We introduced curvature briefly in § 6.5.2. Here we extend that discussion with more details and illustrations.

Curvature-related measures may be directly derived from a mathematical description of a smooth (curved) surface, such as a sphere. However, surface models reconstructed from medical image data or from derived segmentation results are planar polygonal surfaces, e.g., triangle meshes or quadrilaterals. Thus, the boundary surfaces of the anatomical structures are flat and consequently the curvature is zero. To approximate curvature-related measures, two basic strategies exist:

- the curvature is approximated only locally, e.g., by analyzing the surface normals within a certain neighborhood, or
- a smooth (at least C^1 continuity) surface is fitted to the surface model.

The first approach is usually implemented by reconstructing a local polynomial representation that optimally fits to a point and its local surrounding. The latter approach may also be locally applied to a subset of a polygonal mesh. To limit the computational effort, polynomial surfaces of a low degree (two or three) are fitted to the polygonal surface. Frequently, a quadratic surface is employed for this purpose:

$$z(x, y) = ax^2 + bxy + cy^2 + dx + ey + f \tag{12.1}$$

To compute the six coefficients of Equation 12.1 at least six points are required. These six points might represent the 1-ring-neighborhood around a vertex.

12.3.1 CURVATURE-RELATED MEASURES

Many authors state that regions with "high curvature" are emphasized. This raises the question what exactly is measured to assess curvature. Actually, there are number of curvature-related measures and the exact output of an algorithm, of course, depends on the specific curvature measure. Curvature computation at a point p is based on an approximation of the unit surface normal N_p. As an example, if p corresponds to the vertex of a mesh N_p may be estimated as the average of the surface normals of all faces that share this vertex. The curvature estimation is related to a local coordinate system centered at p where the tangential directions x_1 and x_2 as well as the surface normal N_p form the basis. Such a local parameterization of a continuous surface enables the computation of two principal curvature directions that are orthogonal to each other as well as the associated principal curvature values κ_1 and κ_2. By convention $\kappa_1 \geq \kappa_2$ and κ_1 is the maximum curvature and κ_2 the minimum curvature.

If both κ_1 and κ_2 are positive at a point p the surface is elliptical in the surrounding. If either κ_1 and κ_2 are close to zero, the surface has a parabolic shape and if κ_1 and κ_2 have opposite signs, the surface is hyperbolic (see Fig. 12.3).

Various curvature measures are derived from κ_1 and κ_2:

- the *Gaussian curvature* K is computed as $\kappa_1 \cdot \kappa_2$. It is often used to highlight regions where one principal curvature value is negative, i.e., in hyperbolic regions.
- the *mean curvature* H is computed as $(\kappa_1 + \kappa_2)/2$. With this measure, the flatness of a region is assessed.
- the *absolute curvature* is computed as $|\kappa_1| + |\kappa_2|$

Figure 12.4 shows how curvature along a curve and along a smooth surface is defined. If a general quadratic surface (recall Eq. 12.1) is employed for curvature estimation, κ_1 and κ_2 may be directly computed as follows:

$$\kappa_1 = a + c + \sqrt{(a-c)^2 + b^2} \tag{12.2}$$

$$\kappa_2 = a + c - \sqrt{(a-c)^2 + b^2} \tag{12.3}$$

A very simple approach to decide whether the curvature along adjacent faces is high is to consider the dihedral angle between them. It is computed according to Equation 12.4.

$$\phi = \pi - arccos\frac{< \vec{n_1} \cdot \vec{n_2} >}{\|\vec{n_1}\| \cdot \|\vec{n_2}\|} \tag{12.4}$$

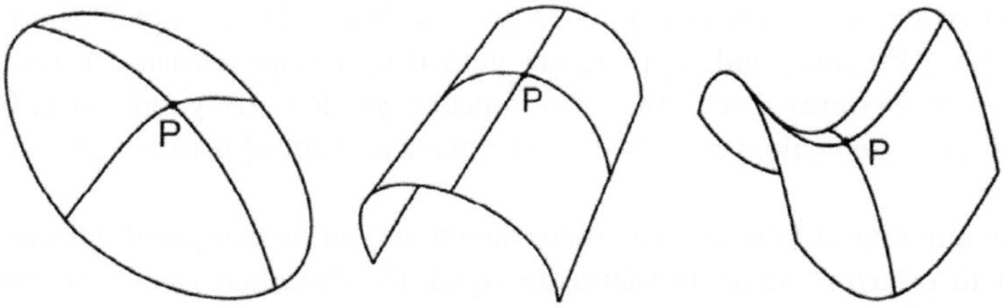

FIGURE 12.3 *Curvature analysis enables to discriminate between elliptical points (left), a parabola (middle), and hyperbolic points (right).*

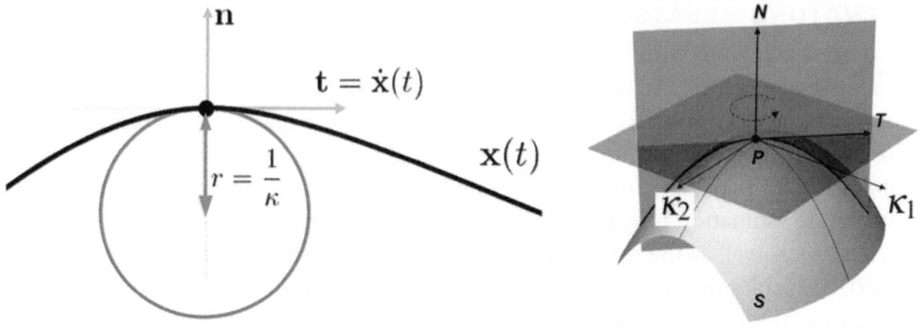

FIGURE 12.4 **Left:** The curvature k along a curve x(t) is determined. It is indirectly proportional to the radius r of circle fitted to the curve. The curvature is positive in convex regions of the curve. **Right:** The curvature along a surface is determined in a 3D coordinate system centered at P. κ_1 and κ_2 denote the minimum and maximum curvature.

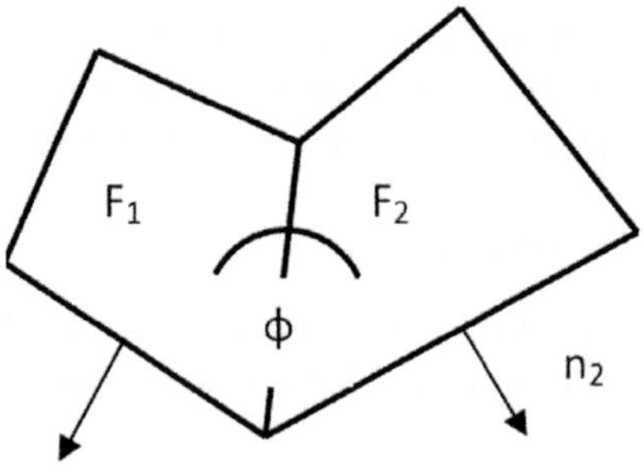

FIGURE 12.5 Three faces f_1, f_2, and f_3 and their surface normals $\vec{n_1}$, $\vec{n_2}$, and $\vec{n_3}$ are shown as part of a surface model. f_1 and f_2 share e_1. Thus, the dihedral angle at that edge characterizes the angular difference between $\vec{n_1}$, $\vec{n_2}$. Similarly, the angular difference between $\vec{n_2}$, $\vec{n_3}$ represents the dihedral angle at e_2. Crease lines are defined as edges, where the dihedral angle is below a threshold.

Thus, for parallel faces ϕ equals 180°, whereas for convex portions of the surface, $\phi < 180°$ (see Fig. 12.5). Figure 12.6 shows how curvature values are distributed along a surface model. As expected, vessel segments with a low diameter exhibit a high mean curvature.

12.3.2 CURVATURE ESTIMATION FOR ILLUSTRATIVE VISUALIZATION

While some illustrative visualization techniques, e.g., some feature lines, employ *curvature values* to decide where to draw lines, hatching, and stippling are guided by *principle curvature directions* (see Fig. 12.7). The curvature direction estimated with the cubic function yielded very good results [Goldfeather and Interrante, 2004]. Also the method described by Rusinkiewicz [2004] is frequently used for illustrative visualization.

This raises the question of how accurate these directions can be computed. Obviously, at umbilical points, where both principal curvature values are equal, the directions cannot be reliably computed. However, even at other portions of a polygonal mesh, slight surface approximation errors may lead to strong changes of the principal curvature directions, leading to noisy curvature direction vector fields. Although the noise may be reduced with appropriate filters, this introduces further errors. For a detailed

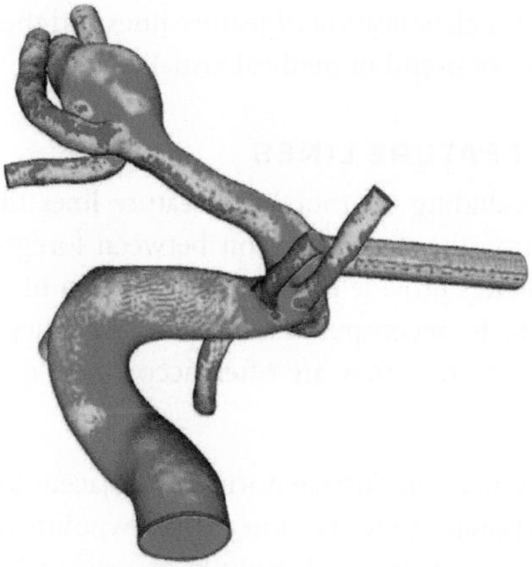

FIGURE 12.6 *A cerebral vascular structure is shown and the mean curvature is color-coded. Low curvature regions are depicted as green, moderate values as yellow, and high curvature as red (Courtesy of Kai Lawonn, University of Magdeburg).*

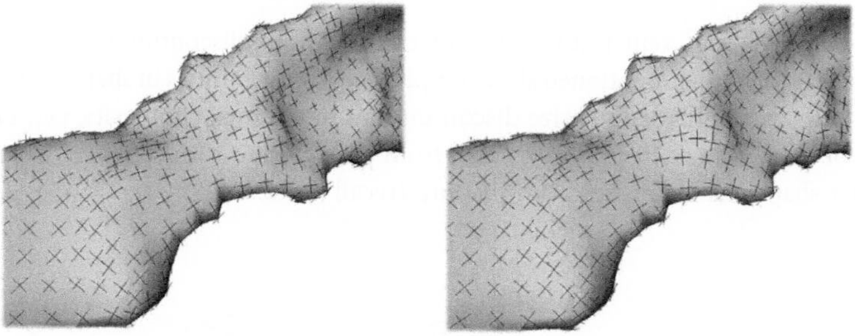

FIGURE 12.7 *The approximated principal curvature directions along a neck muscle segmented from CT data. In the left image, a quadratic function is fitted to the local neighborhood, whereas in the right image additional data are used to fit a cubic function (Courtesy of Rocco Gasteiger, University of Magdeburg).*

discussion of curvature estimation techniques with respect to accuracy and performance, see [Goldfeather and Interrante, 2004]. They describe and compare methods developed earlier, e.g., [Taubin, 1995b] and [Meyer *et al.*, 2003] and introduce new method. Curvature estimation is also a useful ingredient for mesh processing techniques, such as mesh smoothing (recall § 6.5.2) and mesh simplification.

12.4 AN INTRODUCTION TO FEATURE LINES

The use of feature lines in visualization is motivated by perceptual theories and experiments. The influential theory of vision [Marr, 1976] states that the first stage of visual perception involves the extraction of features, such as contours. According to this theory, the extracted features support the assessment of shape and relative depth. Feature lines cover a wide range of lines or *strokes* that depict discontinuities in surface shape, visibility of specific regions, and illumination. Silhouettes, ridge and valley lines, and highlight lines are examples of feature lines that will be discussed in this section. We describe these different feature lines first at a high level leading to a classification of feature lines and then explain in more detail how the lines are derived and where they are useful in medical visualization.

12.4.1 AN OVERVIEW OF FEATURE LINES

Silhouettes (sometimes called occluding contours) are feature lines that depict the visible boundaries of an object, effectively supporting the discrimination between foreground object and background or between different objects. Silhouettes provide essential information in basically all applications. They are view-dependent and thus have to be recomputed after rotations. They do not provide any cues of the shape of surfaces facing the viewer. Thus, they are often accompanied by one or more of the following line representations:

- *sharp creases* connect edges where the surface normal of adjacent faces changes strongly,
- *suggestive contours*, that incorporate contours of nearby viewpoints [DeCarlo *et al.*, 2003],
- *ridge and valley lines*, that represent the local minima of principal curvature magnitude [Interrante et al., 1995], and
- *apparent ridges* that depict points where the curvature along the view-dependent curvature directions is maximal [Judd *et al.*, 2007]. Thus, ridge and valley lines are view-independent, whereas apparent ridges emphasize shape details that appear strongly bent from the current viewpoint.

Figure 12.8 compares different feature lines that characterize discontinuities in surface shape and visibility. While the feature lines mentioned above emphasize discontinuities in shape and visibility, recently feature lines were discussed that emphasize discontinuities in the image intensity, i.e., in the brightness. The integration of these feature lines is motivated from perception research where clear evidence exists that humans infer shape characteristics from shading (recall § 8.2.1):

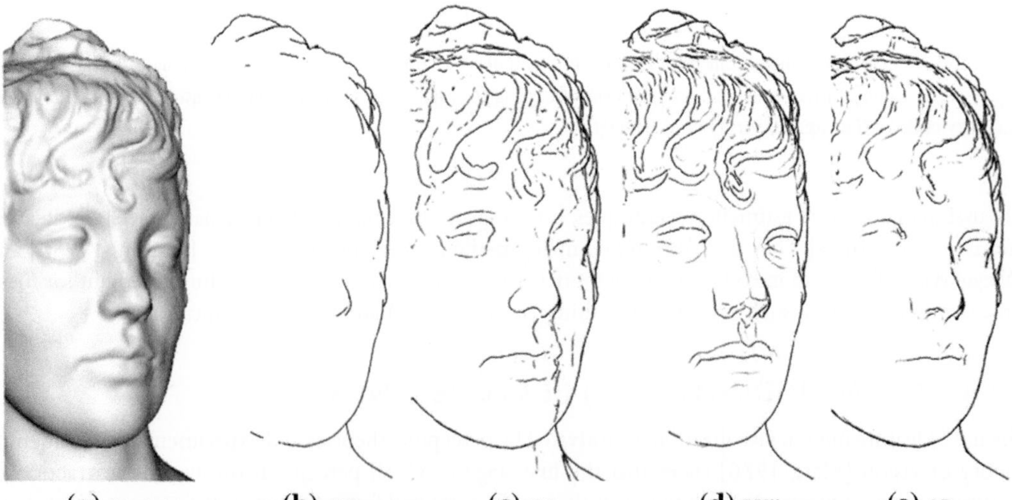

(a) Shaded **(b)** Silhouettes **(c)** SC **(d)** RVlines **(e)** AR

FIGURE 12.8 *A shade view is compared with various feature lines: From left to right: Silhouettes, suggestive contours, ridge and valley lines, and apparent ridges (From: [Judd et al., 2007]).*

Feature Line	Order of Feature	View-Dependent
Silhouettes	first-order	yes
Crease lines	first-order	no
Suggestive contours	second-order	yes
Ridge and valley lines	third-order	no
Apparent ridges	third-order	yes

TABLE 12.1 *Frequently used feature lines that depend on surface shape and visibility only.*

Feature Line	Order of Feature	View-Dependent
Isophote lines	first-order	no
Laplacian lines	third-order	yes
PELs	third-order	yes
Highlight lines	second-order	yes

TABLE 12.2 *Frequently used light-dependent feature lines.*

- *isophotes*, connect regions that exhibit the same image intensity (brightness),
- *PELs (Photic extremum lines)*, that illustrate discontinuities in the illumination depending on light source placement [Xie *et al.*, 2007],
- *Laplacian lines* [Zhang *et al.*, 2009], and
- *highlight lines*, assume a light source at the camera position and indicate regions that exhibit a local maximum in image intensity [DeCarlo and Rusinkiewicz, 2007].

For a classification of feature lines it is useful to characterize which information is used. We refer to techniques that use the first derivative of the original data as *first-order* techniques, information that employs the second or third (partial) derivatives as *second- and third- order techniques*. Moreover, feature lines differ in their dependence on the current view and on light source specification. This information is summarized in the Tables 12.1 and 12.2. For all techniques we add whether it is view-dependent or not. View-dependent feature lines have the inherent drawback that they need to be recomputed whenever the view direction changes. On the other hand, they are more natural, since in reality recognizable features strongly depend on the viewing direction. Thus, some authors recommend to use view-dependent feature lines.

12.4.2 GENERAL ASPECTS OF FEATURE LINE RENDERING

Before we explain the determination and use of the individual feature lines, we briefly discuss a few general aspects:

- smoothing the underlying data,
- efficient data structures for surface meshes,
- stylization, i.e., the assignment of graphical attributes to feature lines,
- frame coherence, and
- relevance filtering, i.e., the control of the amount and distribution of depicted feature lines.

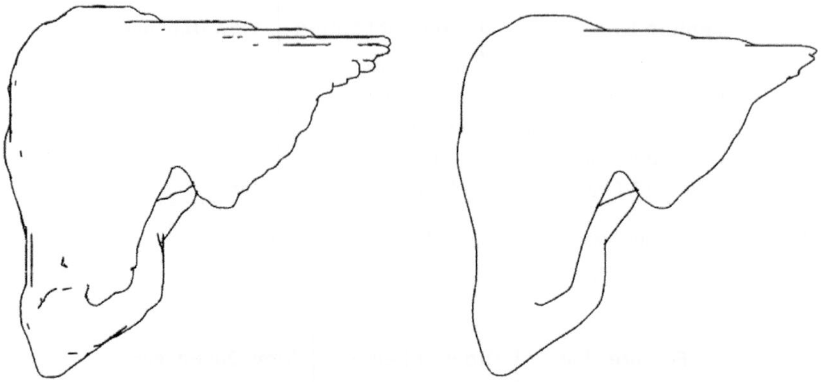

FIGURE 12.9 *Silhouette generation of the liver.* **Left:** *The isosurface representing the original segmentation result is employed. The resulting staircase artifacts are distracting and confusing, since they have no anatomical basis.* **Right:** *The triangle mesh of the isosurface was smoothed with a relaxation filter* (Courtesy of Christian Tietjen, University of Magdeburg).

Smoothing In general, feature line detection algorithms assume that the underlying data (volume data or polygonal meshes) are sufficiently smooth. Feature lines represent discontinuities at surfaces. If discontinuities represent high frequency noise related to image acquisition, distracting, and erroneous lines are generated [Hertzmann and Zorin, 2000]. While many computer graphics publications employ geometric models that are manually created with advanced polygon modeling tools, medical visualization is based on noisy routine data. In particular if the volume dataset is highly anisotropic or if the isosurfaces are based on a segmentation (recall § 6.3) severe problems may occur.

These problems can be avoided by interpolating additional slices with a higher order interpolation scheme, such as cubic B-splines, or by smoothing the polygonal meshes (recall § 6.5.2) or volume data. In Figure 12.9, the effect of smoothing a surface on the resulting silhouettes and feature lines is shown.

While it is in most cases essential to smooth models, in case of coarse models, it is reasonable to apply *mesh sharpening* where modifications of the surface normals are applied to enhance the geometric features of objects [Hao *et al.*, 2010]. That is particularly useful for flat regions, that rarely occur in anatomy, but may occur in surgical instruments or other devices to be included in medical visualization.

Efficient Data Structures for Surface Meshes While feature lines may be extracted from a flat "polygon soup," it is often advantageous to use a data structure that provides *local connectivity information*. In particular, this enables to "stylize" feature lines, e.g., to adapt line styles to distance or visibility. Connectivity information enables to access adjacent polygons directly (polygons which have a common edge or a common vertex). This information is represented, for example, in a winged-edge data structure [Baumgart, 1975] (recall § 6.2.3). All feature line algorithms may also be used with a simpler data structure where just a list of vertices and faces is available (a *shared vertex representation*, recall § 6.2.3). However, without explicit connectivity information, much time is spent on searching the whole mesh for adjacent elements.

Stylization The assignment of line styles, color, transparency, or other visual attributes to feature lines is referred to as *stylization*. In NPR, sophisticated stylization techniques were developed that resemble artistic styles often involving some randomness in the placement and parameterization of graphics primitives. Thus, strokes or brush types are simulated. In illustrative visualization, neither artistic appearance nor

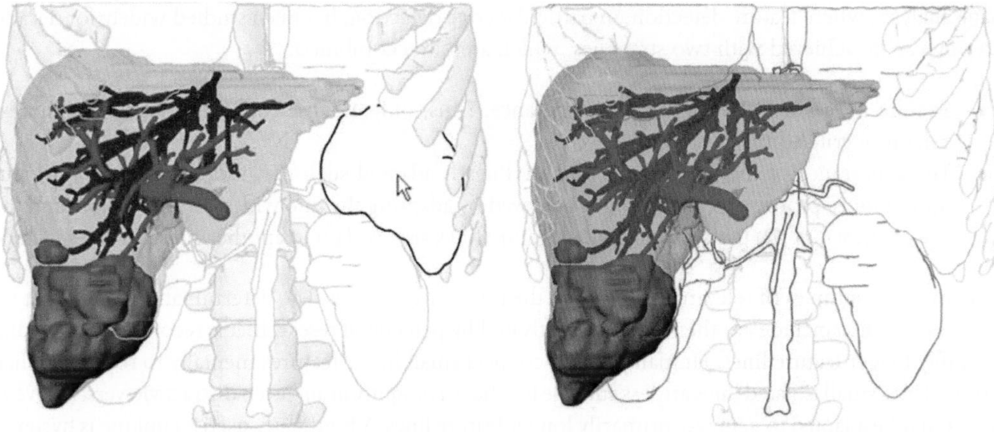

FIGURE 12.10 Silhouettes and crease lines have been determined and are stylized in a different manner. In the left image, line thickness is adapted to emphasize the silhouette of the selected object, while in the right image colors are employed to distinguish different anatomical structures (From: [Tietjen et al., 2005]).

randomness are desirable, since this is at odds with the generation of frame-coherent interactive exploration. In illustrative medical visualization, the primary goal is to render images comprehensibly, e.g., by providing additional depth or shape cues. As an example, line width in technical and medical illustration is often adapted to the distance—a depth cue that is also used in computer-generated illustrations [Raskar and Cohen, 1999].

To emphasize feature lines, it is useful to draw them with a specific width. This may be achieved by extruding the feature lines in the direction of the surface normal [Hao *et al.*, 2010]. The width modification can be used to emphasize silhouettes as outer contours, as it is frequently done in scientific illustration. Figure 12.10 illustrates different stylizations. The image also shows how surface and feature line rendering may be combined effectively. Often, some silhouette edges appear thin and weak. This may be effectively avoided by adapting the surface normal (see [Hao *et al.*, 2010] for a couple of examples).

Frame Coherence For the application of feature lines but also for stippling and hatching techniques in medical visualization systems, *frame coherence* is crucial. Frame coherence refers to a consistent display of surfaces, lines, and points in consecutive frames of an animation or interactive movement. Frame-coherent visualizations avoid that small features suddenly pop out or disappear from frame to frame and ensure that features are drawn at constant positions in 3D space. If frame coherence cannot be ensured, the user's attention—strongly and unconsciously attracted by movements—is guided by such artifacts instead of toward relevant features. Thus, similar to the smoothing issue, it is not primarily a matter of esthetics but an urgent goal for efficient communication. In general, object-space approaches, where lines are drawn at surfaces provide frame coherency, whereas image-space approaches require substantial effort to ensure frame-coherent behavior.

Relevance Filtering Most of the feature lines described in the following occur at many places in complex wrinkled anatomical models (even after smoothing). To avoid visual clutter, it is essential to control the amount of generated feature lines and their appearance. Solutions for this problem may be derived from image analysis, where feature detection, in particular edge detection, has been studied widely for decades. Filtering can be achieved with two strategies, which are often combined:

- Feature lines are filtered as to their relevance. Thus, only a subset of feature lines that fulfills a relevance criterion is drawn.
- The appearance of the (remaining) feature lines is adapted such that more relevant feature lines appear more prominently. This can be achieved by adapting the line width, the line color (and thus the contrast), or the transparency when feature lines are overlaid to another surface representation.

We discuss examples of relevance filtering in the following sections. The determination of relevant feature lines may also include another criterion motivated by perceptual research: it is recommended to draw preferably longer feature lines. Humans tend to connect small linear features mentally to recognize shape features. Thus, small isolated lines are less suitable for shape recognition and even distract viewers. Relevance criteria may be adapted to generate primarily longer feature lines. A frequently used technique is hysteresis thresholding, where two thresholds t_1 and t_2 are used and as soon as a line segments' relevance exceeds the higher threshold, a feature line is tracked as long as the segments exceed at least the lower threshold t_2. Thus, it may be effectively avoided that a longer feature line is interrupted because some segments slightly fail the relevance threshold. To completely avoid small feature lines by incorporating a minimum length threshold, is a less elegant but also viable option. This whole discussion indicates that illustrative techniques involve a couple of parameters that need to be carefully adjusted. As we have discussed in Chapter 5, flexibility is a double-edged sword. To avoid unnecessary complex interactions, meaningful default values should be derived.

12.5 GEOMETRY-DEPENDENT FEATURE LINES

In this section, we describe the feature lines introduced in Table 12.1. We discuss geometric definitions of these feature lines, their detection in polygonal meshes and their use. The examples are not restricted to medicine, but focused on smoothly varying complex wrinkled surfaces, as they dominate in medicine. We discuss all general issues introduced in § 12.4, in particular issues of smoothing and relevance filtering and performance issues.

12.5.1 SILHOUETTE GENERATION

The term "silhouette" can be traced back to Étienne de Silhouette, who was French secretary of finance in the 18th century. He was cutting silhouette portraits of his friends, which outline only the outer shape of the subject that differentiates it from the background. Hence, the silhouette looks pretty much like the shadow of that person.

12.5.1.1 Silhouette Definition

Definition 12.1. For continuously differentiable surfaces, such as B-spline surfaces, the **silhouette** S is defined as the set of points p_i on the object's surface where the surface normal $\overrightarrow{n_i}$ is perpendicular to the vector from the viewpoint $\overrightarrow{v} = (p_i - c)$, Thus, the dot product between $\overrightarrow{n_i}$ and $\overrightarrow{v}$ is zero, with c being the camera position for perspective projections (Eq. 12.5):

$$S = P : | < \overrightarrow{n_i}; \quad p_i - c >= 0 \tag{12.5}$$

This widely used definition of a silhouette in computer graphics is similar to the daily life definition of a *contour*. But since the term contour is used in computer graphics to specify an isosurface (or iso-contour), we refrain from using it in this context. Silhouettes are *first-order feature lines*, thus, they are defined for surfaces with C^1 continuity (quadratic surfaces or surfaces of higher polynomial order).
For polygonal models, the definition above cannot be applied directly, because normals are only defined for faces and vertices but not for arbitrary points. However, silhouettes can be found along edges, which separate front- and back-facing polygons. A simple approach for the determination of silhouettes will be to search for edges that share a front- and a back-facing polygon and to compose them. However, this simple approach generates many artifacts. We will discuss at page 576 how silhouettes may be determined in a way that avoids discontinuities and artifacts.

12.5.1.2 Silhouette Extraction in Volume Data

When silhouettes are computed based on discrete voxel data, the gradient $\vec{g_i}$ of the voxels need to be approximated with a gradient estimation scheme. A threshold for the gradient magnitude has to be supplied to restrict the extraction of silhouettes to regions with strong transitions that may represent edges. The scalar product of normal $\vec{g_i}$ and viewing direction $\vec{v_i}$ is rarely exactly zero. Therefore, Equation 12.5 is usually replaced with Equation 12.6 with an appropriate threshold ε:

$$S = \{P|(\langle\vec{g_i}\,;\,\vec{v}\rangle) < \varepsilon\} \tag{12.6}$$

Unfortunately, the choice of ε is difficult and the resulting set of voxels considered to be silhouette voxels will be of varying thickness, depending on the local surface curvature. Therefore, Equation 12.6 is usually refined with a constant k used as exponent, leading to Equation 12.7 [Csébfalvi *et al.*, 2001]. The varying thickness is thus reduced but not avoided completely. Nagy and Klein [2004] later described a hardware-assisted silhouette extraction technique, which produced for the first time silhouettes of constant thickness (see Fig. 12.11). The description of this algorithm is too complex to be briefly included here (see [Nagy and Klein, 2004]).

$$S = \{P|1 - (\langle\vec{g_i}\,;\,\vec{v}\rangle)^k| < \varepsilon\} \tag{12.7}$$

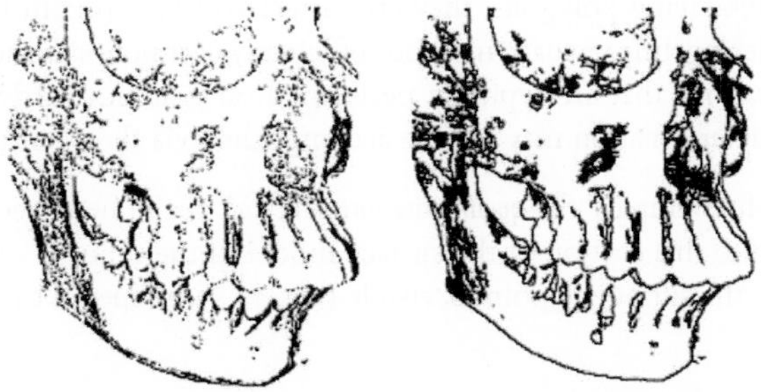

FIGURE 12.11 *Silhouettes with constant width may be derived. The left image is based on the definition in Equation 12.7. The right image was created with the algorithm described in [Nagy and Klein, 2004] (From: [Nagy and Klein, 2004]).*

12.5.1.3 Silhouette Generation

The following discussion of techniques is structured according to the two tasks that have to be performed: The determination of

- a set of silhouette edges s_i and
- the visible subset $\tilde{s}_i \subset s_i$.

In general, *image*- and *object-space* methods are available for these tasks. While object-space methods evaluate vertices, edges (or other graphics primitive) of the model, image-space methods operate on different buffers, which contain per pixel information. While simple object-space algorithms operate on *all* graphics primitives, more advanced algorithms reduce the computational effort, e.g., using hierarchical data structures. Obviously, image-space methods depend on the current resolution used for image generation. Image-space methods often solve both tasks, whereas object-space methods usually only determine silhouette edges and rely on a subsequent visibility algorithm to determine $\tilde{s}_i$. Visibility algorithms, again, may operate on image- or object-space. Thus, *hybrid* algorithms combine an object-space detection of silhouette edges with an image-space visibility algorithm.

As always, the result of an image-space method depends on the resolution where the object-space approach may deliver precise results in any given resolution. The increased precision and flexibility of object-space methods comes at the price of a more complex implementation and, even more important longer runtimes.

Image-space Techniques In particular, the z-buffer (depth buffer) and the normal-buffer (representing the z-coordinate and the normal of the polygon rendered at each pixel) are useful to determine silhouette edges. Strong discontinuities in these buffers indicate the boundaries between objects and, thus, silhouettes. Edge detection methods from conventional image processing are employed for this purpose (recall [Hertzmann and Zorin, 2000]). An alternative approach exploits the depth-buffer of OpenGL that contains the depth value of the graphics primitive that is closest to the virtual camera [Lander, 2000]. In conventional rendering the depth buffer is initialized with a very high value ($maxdepth$). Subsequently, each primitive is rasterized and each pixel of that primitive is drawn when it passes the depth test (when its depth value is lower (LESS) than the current value of the depth buffer at that position. For silhouette rendering this behavior is adapted in the following way.

After rendering the front-facing polygons (flat white for silhouette rendering only), the depth buffer function is changed from LESS to LEQUAL (less equal) and the back-facing polygons of the same object are rendered in a wire-frame mode. Since the rasterized pixels of the silhouette have the same depth value for the front- and the back-facing polygons, they are rasterized twice (depth function is LEQUAL) and hence appear on the rendering. Image-space methods efficiently compute silhouettes, since they are based on fast framebuffer operations that are typically performed on graphics hardware [Raskar and Cohen, 1999]. The visible edge determination may also be accomplished via the z-buffer in image space.

Object-space Techniques often employ the *quantitative invisibility* of a silhouette section by intersecting rays from the camera position to that section of the surface model. If the number of intersections, the quantitative invisibility, is odd, the silhouette point is visible (except some special cases that need to be treated differently).

Subpolygon Silhouettes from Surface Meshes Simple object-space silhouette algorithms only evaluate the normals of the vertices. A silhouette may occur in a polygon with vertices that exhibit a sign change of the scalar product between surface normal and viewing direction. Depending on the local curvature of these

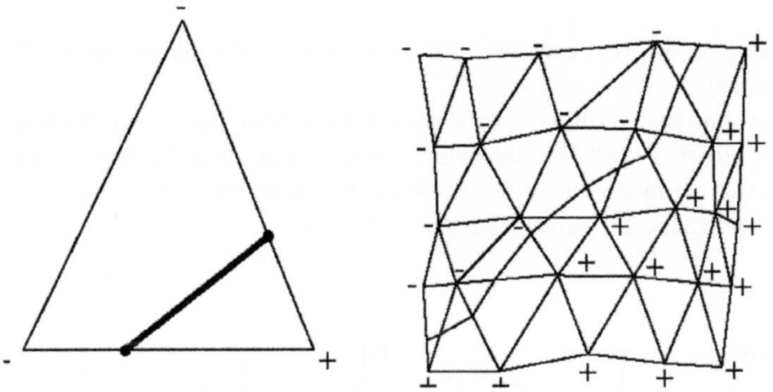

FIGURE 12.12 *Computation of a subpolygon silhouette for an isolated triangle (left) and a polygonal mesh (right) (Courtesy of Aaron Hertzmann).*

polygons, the scalar product at the vertices have a varying magnitude. If we consider varying polygon sizes, the polygon edges might be poor silhouette approximations and exhibit interpolation or staircasing artifacts. Instead, we can compute a refined silhouette by computing a piecewise linear approximation of the silhouette within the respective polygons (see Fig. 12.12) [Hertzmann and Zorin, 2000].

Advanced topic: Efficient silhouette detection. Simple object-space algorithms exhaustively consider all edges of a mesh whether they belong to the silhouette or not. Since this is time-consuming for large models, a couple of acceleration strategies were developed. For the sake of brevity, we only describe their main idea. Since silhouettes (and other view-dependent feature lines) need to be computed in every frame, performance is indeed an essential issue.

Gooch *et al.* [1999] presented hardware-accelerated and software-only accelerations of silhouette detection. The hardware acceleration heavily uses the stencil buffer and is less flexible, while the software acceleration is based on *hierarchic Gaussian Maps* (the Gauss map of an edge is a great arc on the sphere of orientations, see illustrations and details in [Gooch *et al.*, 1999]). The edge-buffer is a data structure, introduced in [Buchanan and Sousa, 2000] to accelerate silhouette detection. Instead of iterating over all edges of a polygonal model it allows to iterate over the faces (the number of faces is lower). Also randomized algorithms have been suggested by Markosian *et al.* [1997]. These algorithms are based on the observation that edges with lower dihedral angles[1] have a higher probability of being silhouette edges and hence edges are sorted by their dihedral angle and silhouettes are looked for in the neighborhood of such high probability edges. An acceleration by a factor of five was achieved, however a small number of silhouette edges may be missed. This is not an essential problem, in particular, if the algorithm operates in a progressive manner, looking for further silhouette lines, when the user is not rotating the model. Isenberg *et al.* [2003] gives a good survey on these (somewhat older) silhouette generation techniques from surfaces.

We also briefly discuss efficient extraction of silhouettes directly from volume data. This is essential when data without segmentation information need to be processed. Also, if per-voxel segmentation results are available, it might be useful to extract silhouettes directly from the voxel representation. Naive algorithms for silhouette detection from volume data employ the silhouette definition from Equation 12.6 directly. This is unfortunate, since it cannot ensure that the silhouettes have a constant width (depending on the local curvature and the chosen ε value silhouettes are thicker in regions with low curvature).

A basic algorithm to determine feature lines from volume data is the *Marching Lines* algorithm [Thirion and Gourdon, 1996]. This algorithm is a modification of the Marching Cubes algorithm (recall Chap. 6) that computes lines instead of surfaces. Among other, it may be used to extract crease lines and ridge and valley lines from regular volume data.

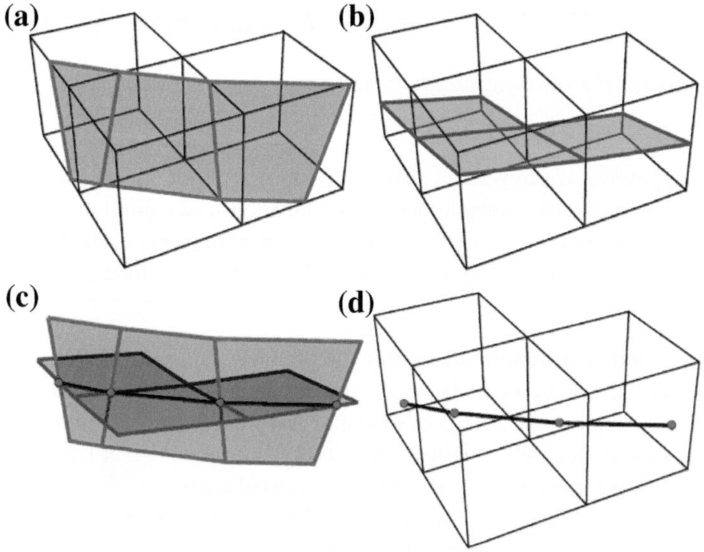

FIGURE 12.13 *Efficient extraction of silhouettes from volume data: (a) The isosurface F for a particular threshold is computed and intersected with the contour surface (shown in blue in (b). The resulting line (c) is tracked with a Marching Lines algorithm (From: [Burns et al., 2005]).*

Burns *et al.* [2005] presented an algorithm based on the observation that silhouettes likely occur at edges with a low dihedral angle. They operate, however, on the voxel level, determining first relevant voxels and than using a variant of the *Marching Lines* algorithm to find precise interactions of silhouettes with edges of the voxel grid. The basic strategy is illustrated in Figure 12.13: an isosurface F is located with a surface reconstruction technique, a contour surface (where the view vector is perpendicular to the voxels' gradient) is located and the silhouette is determined as the intersection of the isosurface and the contour. For the approximation of the voxel gradient, a gradient estimation scheme, e.g., central differences (recall § 2.3.3) is employed. Figure 12.14 presents a result of the algorithm.

A strategy applicable in both, mesh-based and voxel-based silhouette extraction, is to exploit *temporal coherence*. Thus, silhouettes in one frame are likely close to silhouettes computed for the previous frame. Burns *et al.* [2005] discussed various seeding strategies where they start searching silhouette portions and compared their performance. Finally, it should be mentioned that silhouette extraction from volume data

1 see Fig. 12.5 for a sketch of the definition of the dihedral angle.

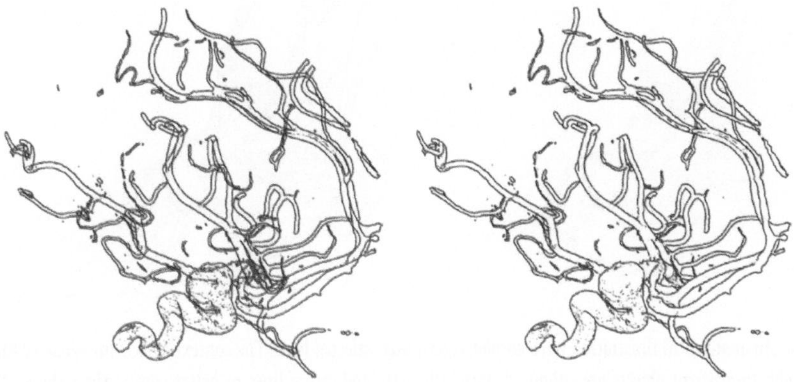

FIGURE 12.14 *Vascular structures and a cerebral aneurysm are shown via their silhouettes. In the left image, visibility of the silhouette lines is neglected leading to clutter in some areas, whereas in the right image only visible silhouette portions are shown (From: [Burns et al., 2005]).*

could also be accomplished by a GPU-implementation that may achieve a better performance [Nagy and Klein, 2004].

Stylization of Crease Lines and Silhouettes When both silhouettes as well as crease lines are integrated in one image, it is often recommended to render them in a different manner. Raskar and Cohen [1999] discusses examples from technical illustration where silhouettes are drawn thicker than crease lines (this may be achieved with extrusion along the surface normal (recall [Hao *et al.*, 2010]). Also, the color may be used to distinguish the different line features. Whereas silhouettes are usually dark, crease lines as inner edges are sometimes depicted with white lines. In general, object-space feature line extraction enables considerably more freedom to stylize the lines based on analytic description.

12.5.2 CREASE LINES

Definition 12.2. **Crease lines** are composed of edges in a polygonal model where the orientation of the adjacent faces changes strongly. As a measure for the difference in surface orientation, the dihedral angle along an edge between the coinciding (outward pointing) face normals is computed (see Fig. 12.5). The edge belongs to a crease lines if the dihedral angle (Eq. 12.4) exceeds a threshold t.

Similar to silhouettes, crease lines are *first-order feature lines*. When drawing crease lines, discontinuities in the surface shape are emphasized. Crease lines are by their definition *independent of the viewing direction* and thus need to be computed only once. The parameter t allows to adjust how many crease lines will be drawn. Obviously, with small t values, many edges fulfill the condition of belonging to a crease line. A good choice of t strongly depends on the specific geometric model: when applied to a noisy model with many discontinuities, higher t values are appropriate compared to a perfectly smooth model. Figure 12.15 illustrates the use of images-space silhouettes and crease lines to convey the shape of context objects. However, the underlying model has a very high quality and is not directly derived from routine medical image data.

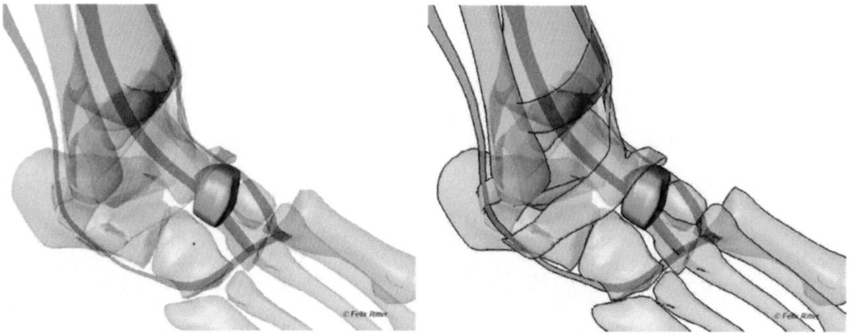

FIGURE 12.15 *An anatomical illustration with emphasis on a user-selected bone. The context objects are rendered highly transparent (left). On the right, transparent objects are enhanced with silhouette and crease lines to better convey their shape. Note that only a few crease lines at some bones are included based on a high threshold (Courtesy of Felix Ritter, Fraunhofer MEVIS Bremen).*

The threshold t is obviously the essential *relevance parameter* as we discussed at page 572. Hysteresis thresholding for generating longer crease lines and adjustment of graphics attributes to fade only slightly relevant feature lines are useful refinements of the general crease line drawing process.

While crease lines are usually determined to be drawn as lines, they may also be used in combination with other illustrative rendering techniques. This combination exploits that crease lines and their immediate neighborhood represent *salient surface features*. Thus, they may be used to guide the placement of stippling points (see § 12.7) and of hatching strokes.

Similar to silhouettes, crease lines may be directly derived from volume data, replacing the surface normals with the approximated gradients. However, similar to silhouettes, it is difficult to generate crease lines with constant and predefined width.

12.5.3 RIDGE AND VALLEY LINES

Ridge and valley lines, as the name implies, have their origin in topography and geomorphology where digital terrain and elevation models are analyzed and refined by tracking *ridges* and *valleys*. Interrante *et al.* [1995] argue that in particular the explicit display of valley lines is perceptually motivated, since valley regions usually appear dark and with little contrast. While we discuss these lines here only as illustrative visualization technique, there are numerous other applications of ridge and valley lines. They are used to characterize shapes, to decompose them in subsurfaces and in image registration where these lines serve as features to be derived from target and reference dataset to align them in an optimal way.

Mathematically, ridge and valley lines may be precisely defined for smooth oriented surfaces based on computing derivatives of principal curvatures (see [Koenderink, 1990, Interrante *et al.*, 1995, Ohtake *et al.*, 2004]) for detailed explanations).

Definition 12.3. A **valley line** is the set of all points of a continuous surface (with at least C^3 continuity) where the curvature k_{min} in the principal direction t_{min} exhibits a local minimum associated with the largest negative curvature.

A local minimum is attained when the derivative of the curvature in the direction of k_{min} is zero.

Definition 12.4. A **ridge line** is the set of all points of a continuous surface where the curvature k_{max} in the principal direction t_{max} exhibits a local maximum associated with the largest positive curvature.

Ridge and valley lines are view-independent third-order feature lines. The local maxima of the curvature represents the zero crossing of the derivative in the t_{max}-direction.

Computation of Ridge and Valley Lines at Polygonal Meshes To employ this definition for polygonal surface meshes, as they result from surface reconstruction, the curvature must be estimated (recall § 12.3). Curvature estimation is essential for all second- or third-order feature lines, e.g., for most light-dependant feature lines.

The expressiveness of ridge and valley lines depends strongly on the curvature estimation method actually used. Interrante *et al.* [1995] smoothed surface normals as a basis for curvature estimation. The curvature itself was approximated with finite differences. Fitting implicit or other polynomial surfaces—the second group of curvature estimation techniques—is a viable option [Ohtake *et al.*, 2004], since it leads to smooth representations. However, the computation of a globally smooth surface approximation is very time-consuming. Note that in general curvature is a second-order feature, thus at least C^2 continuous polynomials (cubic functions or higher order polynomials) are required. The specific solution introduced by Ohtake *et al.* [2004] employs local compactly supported basis functions fitted to the data. This solution is highly attractive, since high performance and robust line detection are achieved.

Smoothness of surfaces is particularly important for determining these third-order feature lines, since the noise level increases with additional derivatives. Ridge and valley lines may coincide with crease lines depending on the crease line threshold and the steepness of ridges as well as the narrowness of valleys. Figure 12.16 illustrates the use of ridge and valley lines overlaid to a surface visualization of the Michelangelo statue. As a second example, ridge and valley lines are shown that depict the Max Planck bust. Ridge and valley lines convey most of the salient features of a human face (Fig. 12.17). However, the generated ridge and valley lines are often isolated where a human artist would draw connected lines.

Filtering and Stylization In a typical surface model derived from measured data, a large number of ridge and valley lines occurs. Thus, they need to be filtered in a similar way like crease lines. The major criterion for filtering is a threshold for the curvature in the relevant regions, i.e., a criterion that evaluates how significant the computed minima and maxima actually are. Ohtake *et al.* [2004] compute the integral over ridge and valley lines with respect to the maximum curvature along the lines. This integral value is used as *relevance parameter*. This strategy is established and used similarly for filtering other feature lines. Figure 12.18 indicates the consequences of different thresholds for the filtering of ridge and valley lines.

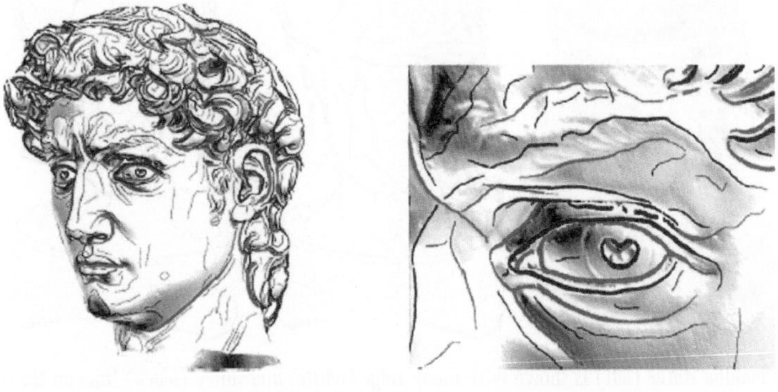

FIGURE 12.16 *A test model rendered as surface overlaid with ridge and valley lines. Ridge lines are drawn in blue, valley lines in red (Courtesy of Kai Lawonn, University of Magdeburg, inspired by [Ohtake et al., 2004]).*

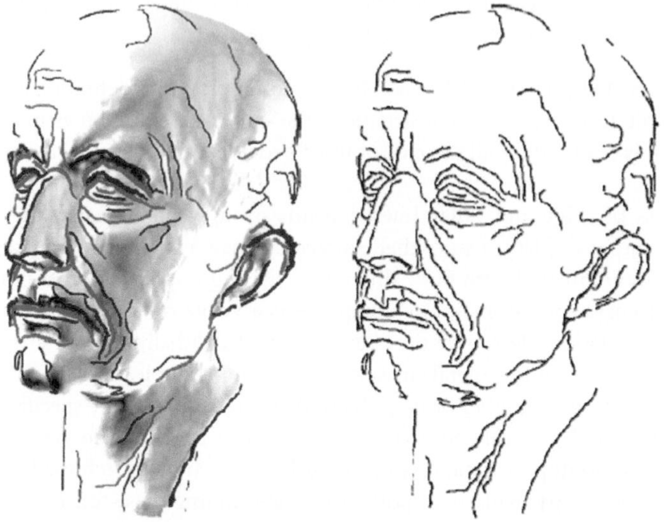

FIGURE 12.17 The Max Planck bust as surface model overlaid with ridge and valley lines (left) and as line drawing only (Courtesy of Kai Lawonn, University of Magdeburg, inspired by [Ohtake et al., 2004]).

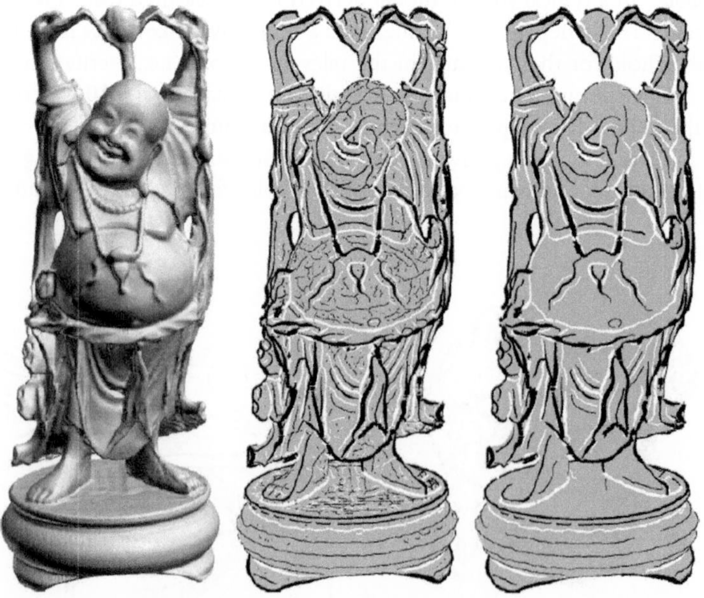

FIGURE 12.18 The buddha statue (left) is shown with many ridge (white) and valley (black) lines on the right. (Courtesy of Kai Lawonn, University of Magdeburg, inspired by [Ohtake et al., 2004]).

If both, ridge and valley lines are included in a visualization, they should be distinguished by their color. Often, e.g., in Figure 12.18, valley lines are depicted with dark color and ridges with bright colors. In the examples above (Figs. 12.16 and 12.17), red and blue colors have been used instead.

Interrante *et al.* [1995] have explored various stylization techniques for a specific medical example, namely radiation treatment planning where the isodose distribution is shown. They strongly filtered the lines, mapped the relevance of the remaining lines to opacity (emphasizing the most relevant feature lines) and avoided short ridge and valley lines.

12.5.4 SUGGESTIVE CONTOURS

An interesting extension of the more traditional silhouettes are *suggestive contours* introduced by DeCarlo *et al.* [2003]. They include contours derived from closely related viewpoints to generate expressive renderings, which convey complex shapes with concavities convincingly. Suggestive contours are widely used and represent an essential state-of-the-art line drawing technique.

Definition 12.5. **Suggestive contours** of a continuous surface (at least C^2 continuity is required) represent the set of points where the dot product between the surface normal $\vec{n}$ and the view vector $\vec{v}$ has a local minimum. At these points, radial curvature is zero and the curvature in the projected view direction is positive.

Suggestive contours naturally extend silhouettes. Suggestive contours are second-order features. Radial curvature is measured in the radial plane that is orthogonal to the tangent plane at each point. The surface normal and the view vector projection in the tangent pane form the two coordinates of the radial plane (see Fig. 12.19).

The above definition of suggestive contours turned out to be incomplete. Thus, DeCarlo *et al.* [2003] extended it and required points that are contours in "nearby" viewpoints, but do not have "corresponding" contours in any closer views. With this extended definition, q' in Figure 12.20 is no suggestive contour point, whereas r belongs to the suggestive contour. Finally, DeCarlo *et al.* [2003] suggested to define an angular range of $90°[-45°; \cdots + 45°]$ from the current viewpoint as the "nearby" region.

Suggestive contours may represent lines that were not part of the silhouette (anticipating their appearance) or they elongate a line that is part of the silhouette. In the latter situation, a seamless transition between the lines belonging together is essential. An essential advantage of suggestive contours is their

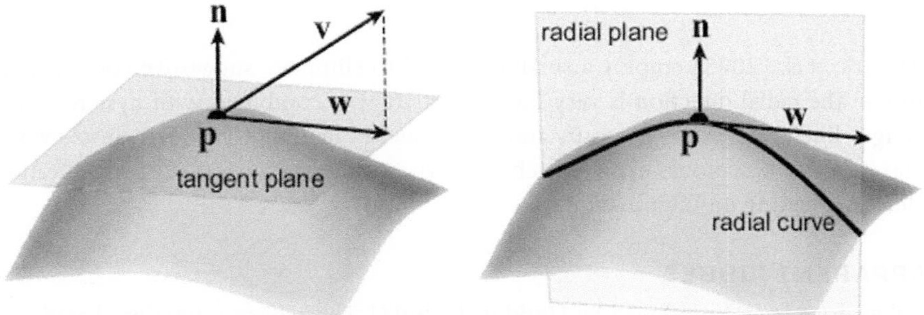

FIGURE 12.19 *The view vector v is projected in the tangent plane at p (left) leading to the vector w. The radial plane is defined by the normal vector n and w (Courtesy of Kai Lawonn, University of Magdeburg, inspired by [DeCarlo et al., 2003]).*

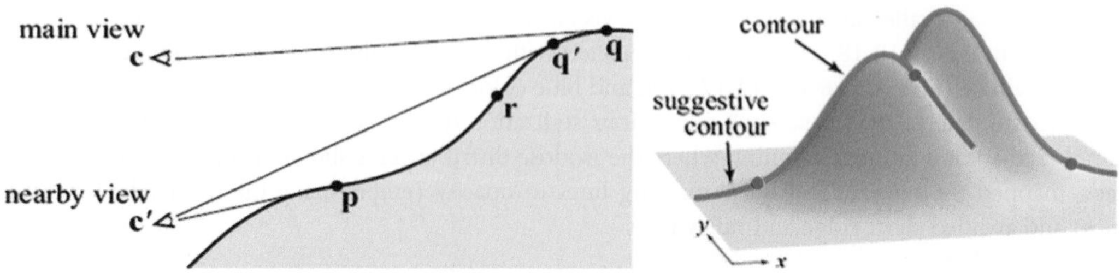

FIGURE 12.20 **Left:** *A surface is shown in the radial plane. While q is a silhouette point, q_i is a suggestive contour point that is derived from point p with 0 curvature.* **Right:** *The image emphasizes silhouette regions (green) and suggestive contours (blue) (Courtesy of Kai Lawonn, University of Magdeburg, inspried by [DeCarlo et al., 2003]).*

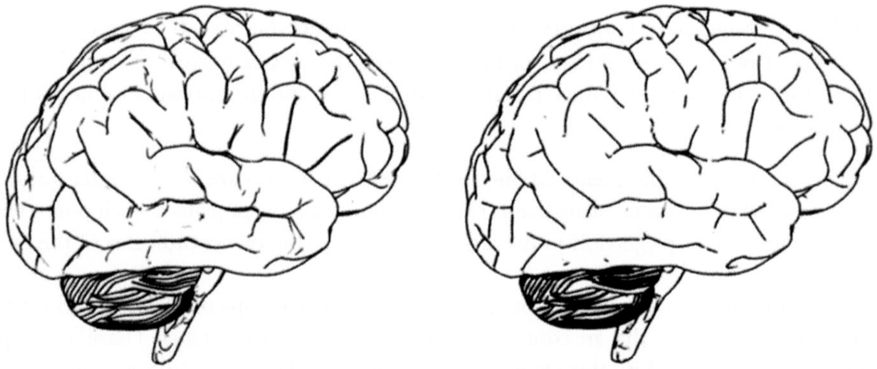

FIGURE 12.21 *Depiction of a brain model.* **Left:** *Suggestive contours.* **Right:** *Apparent ridges (From: [Judd et al., 2007]).*

temporal coherence. While conventional silhouettes may strongly change after small rotations, suggestive contours are more constant [DeCarlo *et al.*, 2004]. Temporal coherence is an advantage for animations as well as for interactive 3D renderings. However, suggestive contours fall into the class of view-dependent features. Figure 12.21 compares suggestive contours with apparent ridges, which are described in the next section.

Filtering DeCarlo *et al.* [2003] employ a small threshold to eliminate suggestive contour points where the curvature in the radial direction is very low. This strategy is combined with hysteresis thresholding to prefer longer lines. Suggestive contours add to silhouettes naturally. However, in convex regions of a surface, no suggestive contours arise, which gives rise to the discussion of further feature lines, in particular lines depending on illumination.

12.5.5 APPARENT RIDGES

Apparent ridges have been introduced by [Judd *et al.*, 2007]. These feature lines are based on curvature estimation, resembling ridge and valley lines, but compute curvature in a view-dependent manner. Thus, it is evaluated how strongly certain regions appear to be bent from a given camera position. Curvature of

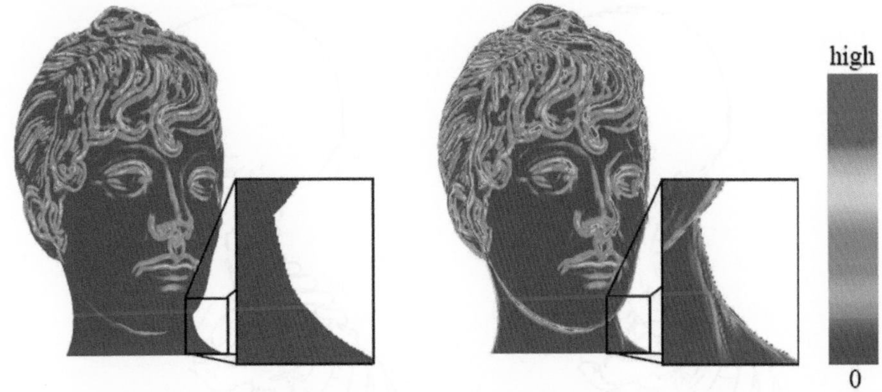

FIGURE 12.22 *Ridge and valley lines are guided by the maximum curvature (left) whereas apparent ridges utilize view-dependent curvature that is significantly different at the side faces (From: [Judd et al., 2007]).*

the object and perspective foreshortening contribute to the perception of curvature. This leads to a formal definition [Judd *et al.*, 2007]:

Definition 12.6. An **apparent ridge** of a continuous surface is the set of all points where the maximum view-dependent curvature reaches a local maximum in the view-dependent curvature direction.

At front faces where the surface normal and the view direction are almost parallel, the maximum curvature in normal direction is very similar to the maximum curvature in view direction (Fig. 12.22). Thus, apparent ridges and ridge and valley lines occur almost at the same positions. However, in surface regions facing away from the viewer, there are noticeable differences, leading to different lines to be detected. In Figure 12.21 suggestive contours and apparent ridges are compared. It is striking that the brain's sulci are better depicted with single valley lines, whereas suggestive contours appear as double lines close to the actual valley. The specific algorithm for finding apparent ridges on polygonal meshes is sophisticated, but similar to the location and tracking of ridge and valley lines, i.e., zero crossings of curvature are determined again with the method of Ohtake *et al.* [2004].

Like ridge and valley lines, apparent ridges evaluate third-order features of surfaces and are thus very noise-sensitive. To generate Figure 12.23 from clinical data, the underlying curvature field was heavily smoothed.

Similar to previously discussed feature lines, the direct application of the definition of apparent ridges leads to the determination of (too) many lines. Essential features are those where not only a local maximum in view-dependent curvature occurs but where this maximum achieves high values. Thus, thresholding based on this maximum is essential. Judd *et al.* [2007] suggest to derive the threshold from the average edge length of the mesh, leading to a threshold that is independent from scale. Moreover, it is reasonable to filter apparent ridges with respect to their length to avoid too many distracting small lines. Figure 12.23 illustrates this influence.

Performance Since apparent ridges are view-dependent and involve heavy computation, performance is a serious issue. Without careful optimization, apparent ridges can only for small models be generated in real time. As the comparison of Zhang *et al.* [2009] reveals the computation of apparent ridges is

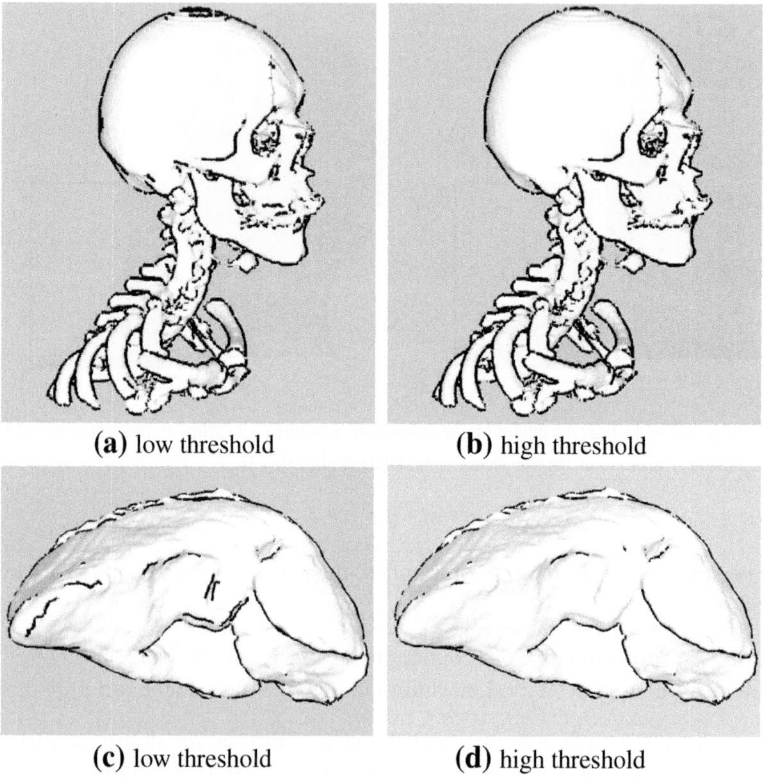

FIGURE 12.23 *Influence of the length threshold for apparent ridge generation. In (a) and (c), a low threshold (0.4) is chosen, whereas (b) and (d) exhibit less lines due to a higher threshold of 0.8. Both surface models are derived from clinical CT data (Courtesy of Tobias Hann and Werner Schöne, University of Magdeburg).*

approximately five times slower than the computation of suggestive contours and ten times slower than silhouette generation (for a wide variety of meshes of different sizes).

12.5.6 STREAMLINE-BASED ILLUSTRATIVE RENDERING

Complex anatomy cannot be faithfully represented by feature lines only. Hatching, on the other hand, is often overwhelming with too many lines. Recently, Lawonn *et al.* [2013b] presented a method that is based on *streamlines*, a vector field visualization technique. To apply this technique, they computed four vector fields for a triangle mesh, namely those that correspond to the first and second principal curvature direction and their inverse. Curvature directions are defined as discussed in § 12.3 [Rusinkiewicz, 2004]. The streamlines are computed by integrating the vector field in the forward and backward direction.

Streamline seeding is restricted to areas of the mesh close to the contour. For this purpose, a *contour margin* is defined as the subset of all triangles where the angle to a nearby contour is below a threshold, e.g., 20°. After preprocessing (subdivision and smoothing) this technique yields good results as a user study indicated (see Fig. 12.24). In Figure 12.25, the streamline-based rendering is compared with apparent ridges and suggestive contours. Among the examples, used by the authors to study their techniques, is also a surface mesh of the trachea for endoscopic viewing.

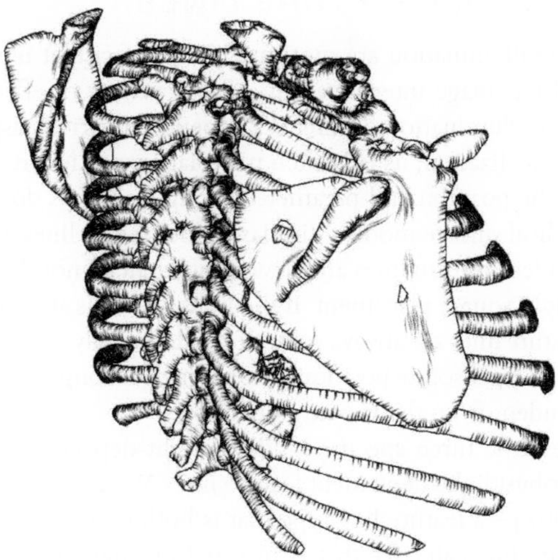

FIGURE 12.24 The skeletal structures extracted from CT thorax data are displayed with streamlines seeded in the contour margin (Courtesy of Kai Lawonn, University of Magdeburg).

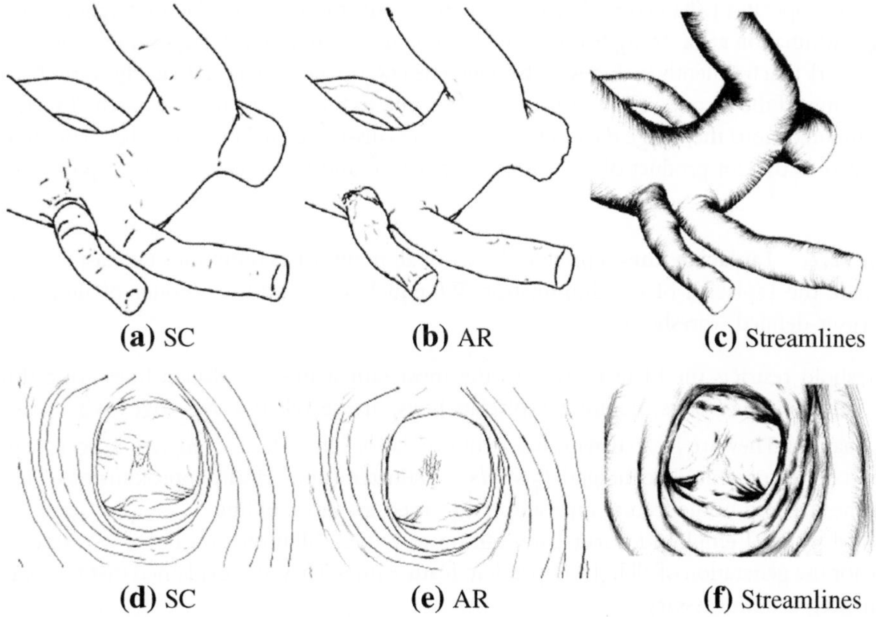

FIGURE 12.25 Suggestive contours, apparent ridges, and streamline-based illustrative rendering (from left to right) are compared. The geometric model in the top row represents a vascular surface and the model in the bottom row a trachea shown from an endoscopic perspective (Courtesy of Kai Lawonn, University of Magdeburg).

12.6 LIGHT-DEPENDENT FEATURE LINES

Feature lines that incorporate illumination are motivated by the fact that illumination differences guide the viewer and are essential for image interpretation. A large variety of effects may be shown by light-dependent feature lines, since illumination differences depend on various aspects, such as refractiveness and specularity. In medical visualization, usually such material properties are not available and not particularly important. However, the position and parameters of light sources do affect shape perception also when applied to typical medical surface models. Similar to the feature lines described above, we will also discuss whether light-dependent feature lines are view-dependent or not. This discussion is complicated by the dependency on the light source placement. If the light source is at a fixed position, as it is in many settings, light-dependent feature lines are always view-dependent. Only when the light sources are relative to the polygonal model, e.g., their absolute position is transformed along with the model, light-dependent feature lines may be independent from the viewing direction.

In the following, we describe three specific kinds of light-dependent feature lines. We start with *Laplacian lines* that are rather robust light-dependent feature lines. We also discuss *Photic Extremum Lines* (PELs) introduced by [Xie *et al.*, 2007]—a feature line type that is both light- and view- dependent. Finally, we discuss *Highlight lines*, a feature line category that is inspired by suggestive contours. We do not discuss *isophotes* in detail. This rather simple first-order feature line connects regions with the same illumination. Isophotes are briefly discussed in § 12.9 on illustrative shading.

12.6.1 LAPLACIAN LINES

Laplacian lines are inspired by an established edge detection technique from image processing—the *Laplacian of Gaussian* (LoG) operator [Zhang *et al.*, 2009]. It is perceptually motivated by the observation that intensity changes in illumination are a strong feature used by humans to infer object shape and further inspired by illustrator's work that frequently includes such edges.The LoG operator exploits that edges are characterized as zero crossings of the second-order derivatives. However, to account for noisy data, the Laplacian is not directly computed from the image data but instead of a Gaussian kernel of image data. The illumination I is computed as the dot product of the surface normal $\vec{n}$ and the direction from a point to the light source $\vec{l}$.

Definition 12.7. Laplacian lines represent the set of all points of a continuous (at least C^3 continuity) surface where the Laplacian of the illumination ∇I equals zero and the amount of illumination ΔI exceeds a (user-defined) threshold t.

The threshold restricts the identification to the most salient lines. Laplacian lines are a third-order feature of surfaces. The points, defining Laplacian lines, are searched along edges where the sign of $\langle \vec{n} \cdot \vec{l} \rangle$ changes. They are located with linear interpolation. In order to generate longer, perceptually more important feature lines, the integral $\int_S \nabla I ds$ is evaluated (numerically approximated). This integral represents the strength of the feature lines and is also used for thresholding.

Zhang *et al.* [2009] employed normal smoothing to reduce "illumination noise"—a strategy that is reasonable for the generation of all light-dependent feature lines. They also explained that for clean regular meshes this step is not necessary.

Discussion In contrast to apparent ridges the major component, the ∇I computation, may be precomputed. Thus, the performance is similar to silhouettes and suggestive contours where even models of approximately 1 million. Vertices may be rendered in real time. Zhang *et al.* [2009] compare Laplacian lines with other feature lines by means of a variety of examples and show the effects of different parameter choices. Laplacian lines are generated in convex and concave regions, an advantage over suggestive contours. However, they fail to represent sharp corners correctly, similar to the LoG operator from which it inherits strength and limitations.

12.6.2 PHOTIC EXTREMUM LINES

Similar to Laplacian lines, Photic extremum lines are inspired by a certain class of edge detectors in image processing. These edge detectors locate edges at regions in images where the gradient magnitude reaches a local minimum. In contrast to image processing, in the visualization of surface meshes PELs are detected in object space and all information related to the illumination are available as input. PELs depict regions on a surface where significant changes in illumination occur.

Definition 12.8. **Photic extremum lines** represent the set of all points of a continuous (at least C^3 continuity) surface where the variation of illumination in the direction of its gradient reaches a local maximum (according to Eqs. 12.8 and 12.9) [Xie *et al.*, 2007].

$$D_w = \|\nabla f\| = 0 \tag{12.8}$$

$$D_w \cdot D_w \|\nabla I\| < 0 \tag{12.9}$$

where ∇ represents the surface gradient and the direction d equals $\nabla f / \|\nabla f\|$ and $f = n \times v$.

According to Xie *et al.* [2007] light models should emphasize shape variations by means of illumination variation to support shape perception. The widespread Phong model computes illumination as the weighted sum of *ambient*, *diffuse*, and *specular reflection*.

The ambient reflection compensates for the lack of higher order lighting effects, such as multiple reflections and refractions, by adding a constant term. Thus, ambient reflection is independent from shape variations and therefore not relevant for feature line determination.

Specular reflection strongly depends on the viewing specification and illumination (specular highlights arise when the reflected light vector and the view vector are very close to each other). Thus, specular reflection also does not reflect surface shape.

As a consequence, the diffuse reflection, as the only term that reflects surface shape should receive the maximum weight and the other two terms may be neglected for feature line definition (for conventional shading, the other terms, of course, are essential).

Major and Auxiliary Light Sources Xie *et al.* [2007] show that expressive feature lines may be generated with a major directional light source with lighting rays parallel to the view vector. However, not all potentially relevant details appear with one major light source. Thus, additional auxiliary light sources may be integrated to better reveal interesting portions. Light source placement is obviously a demanding task. Thus, a system that requires the user to manually place light source in a trial-and-error manner is not suitable for medical doctors. However, Xie *et al.* [2007] explained that automatic suggestions based on a geometric analysis are feasible and yield good results.

Smoothing and Filtering Similar to the generation of Laplacian lines, "illumination noise" is suppressed by smoothing of normals and the removal of irrelevant (small) PELs is performed in a similar way by thresholding the integral of illumination changes along a line. Relevant medical examples are shown in Figures 12.26 and 12.27 where two embedded surfaces are displayed with silhouettes and PELs. Figure 12.27 indicates that toon shading for both objects might be combined with the feature lines without overwhelming visual complexity.

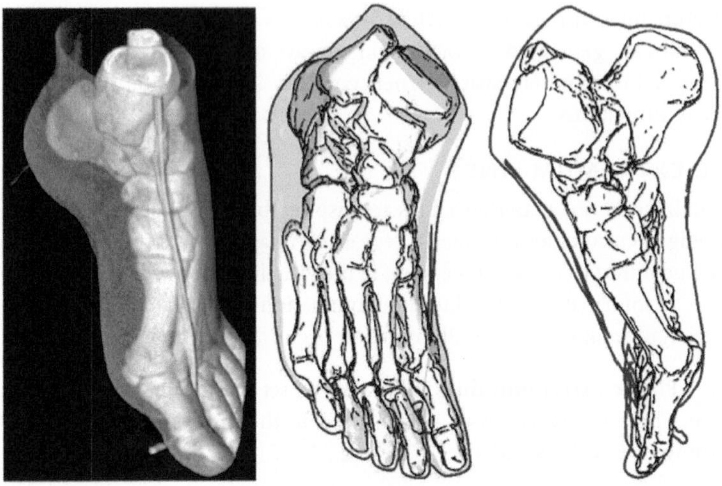

FIGURE 12.26 *Two different tissue types, here skeletal structures and skin, may be shown simultaneously by rendering the outer surface transparent (left image). An alternative is to employ PELs (for the inner object) and silhouettes (for the outer object) which might be enhanced by toon shading (middle). The feature lines of both objects are discriminated by their color (From: [Xie et al., 2007]).*

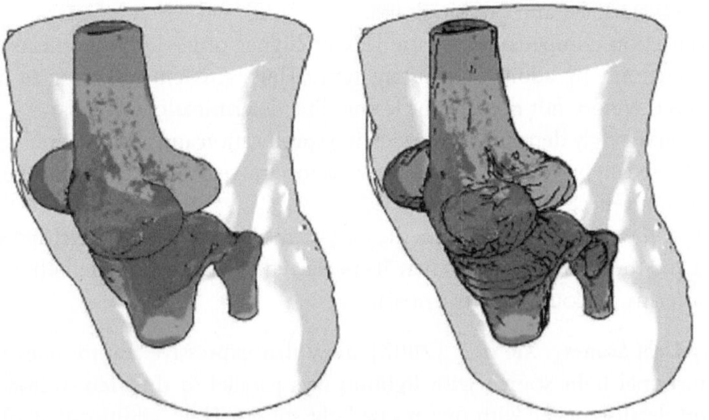

FIGURE 12.27 *Silhouettes and PELs are combined for a nested surface visualization. The rich details of the wrinkled bony structures are depicted clearly. Optionally, toon shading may provide additional shape cues (From: [Xie et al., 2007]).*

Efficient Realization Since the software-based computation of PELs is time-consuming, a real-time alternative was developed that employs the GPU [Zhang *et al.*, 2010a]. This approach exploits a texture where each pixel represents the gradient of the illumination ∇I computed for one vertex of the surface. A further texture represents the direction $\nabla I / \|\nabla I\|$ per vertex. The gradient computation is realized very precisely using a tangent plane, locally adapted to the one-ring neighborhood of a vertex. The computation may be parallelized well so that the whole approach may be performed in a single rendering pass. Over a range of surface models, the GPU implementation accelerates the PEL computation by an order of magnitude (a factor between 12 and 16) [Zhang *et al.*, 2010a]. The efficient PEL generation is faster than the generation of other advanced feature lines, such as apparent ridges and Laplacian lines.

It turns out that without modification not enough lines are generated to depict the details of the object shape. When combined with *exaggerated shading* [Rusinkiewicz *et al.*, 2006], expressive visualizations of medical surface models may be generated (Fig. 12.28). Exaggerated shading represents a non-photorealistic shading model inspired by terrain rendering. The local illumination is modified with a factor derived from the local curvature along the two major principal directions. Thus, surface details are emphasized based on the local curvature. This modification has the same goal as the placement of auxiliary light sources in the original PEL approach. The automatic emphasis, of course, is much more useful in practice. However, the emphasis is controlled by two parameters that need to be carefully defined.

Filtering Also for PELs, filtering is essential to control the number of generated lines. The relevance filtering process for the original (software-computed) PELs [Xie *et al.*, 2007] works at a global level using a threshold t for the illumination gradient in a very similar way as for Laplacian lines. Thus, the illumination gradient is integrated over a whole PEL $\int_S \nabla I ds$ and compared to t to decide whether it is relevant or not. With a

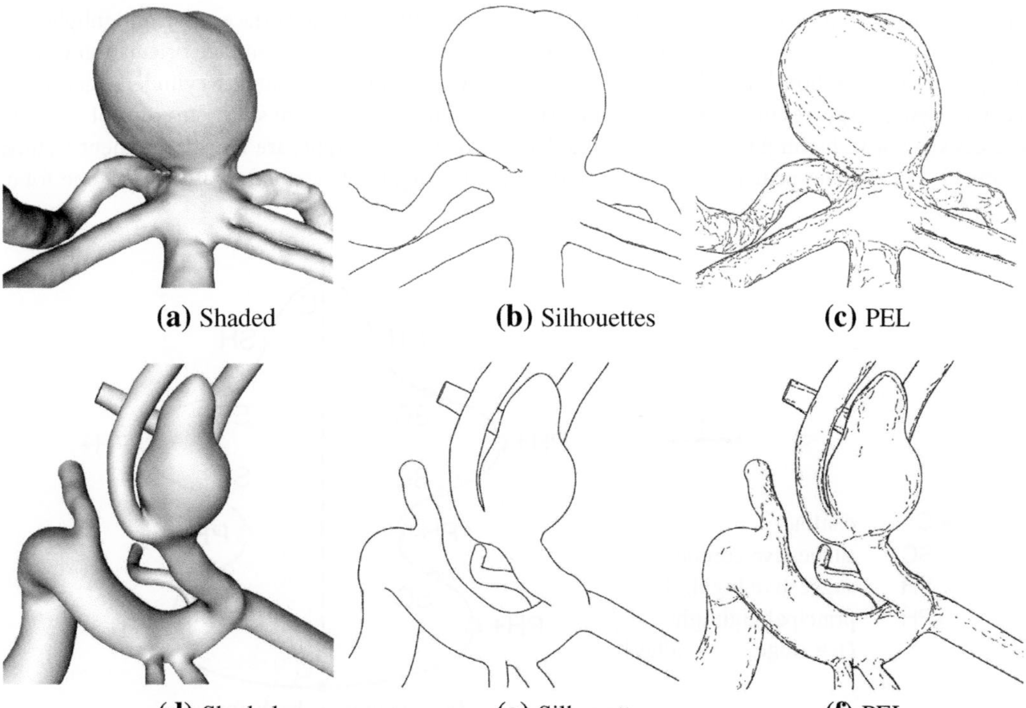

FIGURE 12.28 *Photic extremum lines (PEL) applied to surface models of cerebral aneurysms, parts of the cerebral vasculature that exhibit a pathology. The images on the left show the surface models with conventional shading. The images in the middle depict the silhouettes of the corresponding surface meshes. The images on the right employ exaggerated shading and computes the PELs with a moderate threshold of two (Courtesy of Jonas Singe, University of Magdeburg).*

GPU-based implementation, small fragments of PELs are generated and the relevance filtering needs to be adapted. Singe [2012] suggest to compute the average illumination gradient in a surface mesh to derive a threshold t in relation to that average. As an example, to use the double average turns out to be a suitable choice (see Fig. 12.28).

12.6.3 HIGHLIGHT LINES

Highlight lines were introduced by DeCarlo and Rusinkiewicz [2007] to convey discontinuities in image intensity due to illumination. They are strongly related to *suggestive contours* that connect the darkest regions in an image when illuminated by a light source at the camera position. Highlight lines instead connect the brightest regions (and are usually drawn in white). DeCarlo and Rusinkiewicz [2007] distinguishes highlight lines in

- *suggestive highlights* that appear "at view-dependent inflections," and
- *principal highlights* that appear at points where the viewing direction coincides with a principal curvature direction (see Fig. 12.29 for a sketch).

While suggestive contours represent local minima of $\langle \vec{n} \cdot \vec{v} \rangle$ ($\vec{n}$ representing the surface normal and $\vec{v}$ the view vector), highlight lines represent local maxima of $\langle \vec{n} \cdot \vec{v} \rangle$. Thus, while suggestive contours roughly represent intensity valleys (not necessary valleys of the surface mesh), highlight lines roughly represent intensity ridges. These ridges occur in regions where the surface orientation changes strongly in one direction but only slightly in the orthogonal direction. Thus, at cylinders such ridges occur, however, at spheres they are not present. Principal highlights represent strong maxima of $\langle \vec{n} \cdot \vec{v} \rangle$, whereas suggestive highlights are just maxima. Thus, principal highlights are more prominent features. Figure 12.30 illustrates principal highlights and suggestive highlights applied to a golf ball. The robust

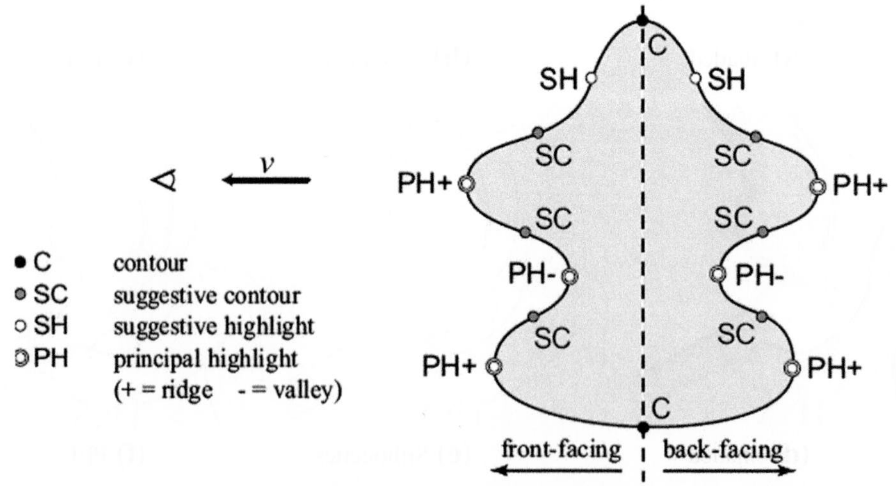

FIGURE 12.29 *A side view of a shape with points emphasized that belong to various feature lines if the shape is looked at from the given camera position. The emphasized points at the backside become important if a transparent rendering style is chosen (Courtesy of Kai Lawonn, University of Magdeburg, inspried by [DeCarlo and Rusinkiewicz, 2007]).*

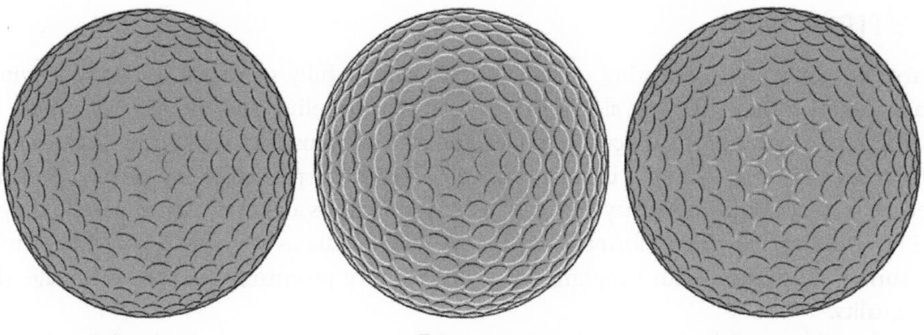

FIGURE 12.30 *A golf ball with its bumps is displayed with various feature lines. (a), silhouettes (S) and suggestive contours (S + SC) are shown. (b) adds suggestive highlights (SH), whereas (c) adds principal highlights (PH) both shown in white. Note that there are many more suggestive highlight lines compared to only a few principal highlights (Courtesy of Kai Lawonn, University of Magdeburg, inspired by DeCarlo and Rusinkiewicz (2007)).*

computation of highlight lines is not-trivial, see [DeCarlo and Rusinkiewicz, 2007]. With respect to rendering, a viable strategy is to render contours and suggestive contours in black and both kinds of highlight lines in white on a dark background. Semitransparent rendering with faded (hidden) highlight lines is also feasible [DeCarlo and Rusinkiewicz, 2007].

12.6.4 DISCUSSION

We have discussed various feature lines that may be derived automatically from surfaces based on differential geometry. These feature lines support different aspects of shape perception, but they are not completely orthogonal. The more recently introduced apparent ridges and suggestive contours more naturally represent relevant surface features than crease lines and ridge and valley lines.

While all these feature lines are used in traditional illustration, where static images are created, they are not equally important when 3D models are animated or interactively explored. Interrante *et al.* [1995] argued that *view-dependent* silhouettes are less effective during exploration. On the other hand, many essential properties of shape are view-dependent and even in traditional animations silhouettes are often employed. Thus, it is reasonable to consider view-dependent feature lines also for interactive exploration. *View-independent* feature lines, such as crease lines and ridge and valley lines, remain at constant positions at the surface, which is an advantage for exploration.

Certainly, view-dependent techniques should be incorporated when the user stops the exploration temporarily or when a screenshot for *documentation* is taken. Support for documentation is often insufficient in treatment planning. Thus, this application is useful in surgery and radiation treatment planning.

Feature lines might be used in combination with more compact line representation described in the following sections but also in combination with surface rendering, where they act as a (semi-transparent) overlay. A particularly important application is the use of feature lines for the display of nested surfaces where feature lines indicate the outer surface as a kind of opacity texture map. Since the application of ridge and valley lines to radiation treatment planning (display of isodose intensity surfaces and anatomy), this strategy has been used successfully [Interrante *et al.*, 1995].

12.7 STIPPLING

Since sparse line drawings, consisting of feature lines cannot fully convey a smoothly varying shape, such as anatomical surfaces [Cole *et al.*, 2009], we consider stippling and hatching as a more compact line drawing representation of surfaces. Again we focus this discussion on the peculiarities of medical visualization instead of providing a comprehensive overview. In particular, we do not explain how a computer-generated stipple image may be generated that resembles a photo or a manual stippling [Martín *et al.*, 2011]. Stippling may be performed directly on volume data as well as on polygonal surfaces. We focus on surface illustration with stippling, since this is more promising for medical image data with moderate quality.

These surface illustration techniques place graphics primitives not only guided by feature lines. Instead, larger portions of surfaces are covered to provide additional shape cues. Compared to hatching, stippling better depicts objects which do not exhibit ridges, valleys, or other regions of high curvature. Stippling is a surface illustration technique where *points* or *dots* are used as graphics primitives. It is an old technique to convey brightness by adapting the placement and density of points—traditionally a tedious manual process. Hodges [1989] contains numerous excellent examples of traditional stippling images used for scientific, technical, and medical illustration.

12.7.1 ESSENTIAL PARAMETERS OF STIPPLING

According to Deussen *et al.* [2000], there are three essential parameters of stippling that effect the perceived darkness and different materials:

- *dot spacing*. This is most important parameter. Dots should be placed such that no clear holes or clusters arise.
- *dot size*. Dot size may be varied according to brightness, but the largest dots are no larger than twice the smallest ones.
- *dot shape*. The individual dots shape may vary simulating the effect of a pen that is pushed on paper with a varying angle. If it is pushed perpendicularly to paper, a perfect circular shape arises. The more tilted the pen is, the more the elongated the ellipsoidal shape becomes.

Usually the size and shape of stippling dots remains constant with computer-generated stippling. Thus, shape characteristics are illustrated only by means of the distribution of dots, particularly by adapting their density [Lu *et al.*, 2002]. The constant shape and size of computer-generated stippling dots is a striking difference to manual stippling where both shape and size but also the tonal value differs from stipple dot to stipple dot, e.g., due to changes in the pressure of a pencil.

Dot Spacing may be adjusted such that some areas are emphasized, e.g., based on appropriate user input. Often dot spacing should convey target tones that may result from conventional shading (dark areas should be displayed with many dots). For a particular tone, the dots should be roughly equally distributed. A first idea would be to distribute a certain target number of dots just randomly. This, however, is neither expressive nor esthetically pleasing. A regular distribution, such as a grid, however, is also not appropriate. Thus, a more complex strategy combining some regularity with randomness is required.

A Voronoi diagram is a useful data structure to achieve a roughly equal distribution. It assigns a region, a *cell* C_p to each point p such that each part of C_p is closer to p than to any other point. Therefore, the points are also called *generating points*. While a Voronoi diagram can be computed for each set of point, obviously not each set of points is well-spaced. As Meruvia-Pastor and Strothotte [2002] explain, this is due to the fact that the generating points (often strongly) deviate from the center of mass of the Voronoi cells. A special instance of Voronoi diagrams, *centroidal Voronoi diagrams* have their generating points coincident with the centers of mass. For dot spacing, an algorithm that iteratively translates an initial point set to a point set that generates a centroidal Voronoi diagram is very helpful. Meruvia-Pastor and Strothotte [2002] describe such an algorithm and combine it with nine stippling levels to be used for different brightness levels.

Also Secord [2002] defined a Voronoi decomposition of the surfaces to guide the dot placement. With this approach, expressive visualizations may be generated, but the technique does not support interactive exploration. While Voronoi-based techniques for stippling dominated for some time, Martín *et al.* [2011] more recently explained that stippling dots should also be placed at essential feature lines. However, in the absence of such characteristic features, notable chains of stippling dots should be avoided.

To avoid distracting patterns in the stippling texture, deliberately some kind of randomness is introduced. Secord [2002] describes this manual process and comments that stippling is particularly suited to convey smooth objects without sharp edges, as they occur in archaelogical and medical illustrations.

12.7.2 FRAME-COHERENT STIPPLING

Computer-generated stippling first aimed at reproducing the results of the manual process in static images [Deussen *et al.*, 2000]. Often, a photograph or a photo-realistically rendered images was taken as input and the distribution of stipple dots should mimick the brightness distribution of the input image. An editor with special tools may be used to fine-tune the distribution of dots. This is related to half-toning, a technique also exploited in computer graphics and aiming at avoiding regular patterns due to the arising aliasing effects. It is widely recognized that a particular distribution used for half toning is optimal for stippling—the so-called *blue noise distribution*. It is a random distribution with the constraint that no two dots are closer to each other than a minimum distance. Cook [1986] investigated this distribution and characterized it in the frequency domain where it has a clear spike at one frequency and a low level of noise at other frequencies. With this distribution, neither holes, nor clusters, nor regular patterns are perceived. In computer graphics, this distribution was realized as a Monte-Carlo technique, a stochastic approach, aiming at alias reduction in photo-realistic rendering, such as ray tracing [Cook, 1986]. While in these applications, stochastic sampling was used to generate sampling positions along rays, they are relevant for stippling directly to place stippling dots. Efficient dot generation is a challenge for large detailed geometric models where many dots need to be distributed (see Ascencio-Lopez *et al.* [2010], Balzer *et al.* [2009] for possible solutions).

In medical visualization, stochastic sampling might be useful when a medical illustrator carefully generates a textbook image or an image for a poster. However, for the much more frequent use cases of interactive explorations or animations, one special requirement has to be considered: stippling dots should be frame-coherent. To achieve frame coherence, the positions of stippling dots need to be defined either in object space, i.e., on a 3D surface, or in a texture-space, where a unique mapping of that texture to a 3D surface model needs to be defined.

Object-space Stippling Meruvia-Pastor and Strothotte [2002] described one of the first frame-coherent stippling techniques. It considered rotation and zooming of objects. Zooming poses a special requirement, since the density of dots must be adapted to the size of an object in viewport coordinates. Thus, stippling dots need to be inserted when zooming in and removed when zooming out. This lead them to create a hierarchy corresponding to the underlying surface mesh. The hierarchy is constructed by subdividing the original mesh, leading to more polygons and, thus, more points and by simplifying it, leading to more abstract representations of the model. While it is straightforward to define discrete abstraction levels with discrete sets of stippling dots coherence requires smooth transitions when zooming in and out.

Texture-based Stippling The major motivation for a texture-based approach is performance. Object-space approaches are rather slow and, thus, not appropriate for interactively handling large models. There a number of problems to solve. A texture needs to be designed that

- enables smooth and natural transitions when objects are magnified, and
- integrates different levels of tone.

When objects are magnified the stippling dots should maintain their size and the shading tones should be constant over the enlarged area (see Fig. 12.31, right). Thus, the stippling dots cannot be scaled in the same manner as the 3D object.

Scale-independent Textures A constant behavior during zooming requires that stippling dots appear while magnifying and disappear while minifying the related object. The solution for this general problem in texture mapping is *mip-mapping*, where different levels of a texture are precomputed and the appropriate level is selected. To achieve seamless transitions between these levels, self-similar textures are required. Solutions for this problem are described in [Lu *et al.*, 2003] and [Baer *et al.*, 2007].

The different brightness levels are achieved by precomputing textures for discrete brightness intervals. The shading tones are designed such that darker tones comprise all stippling dots of lighter tones (see Fig. 12.31, left).

Distortion-free Stippling Textures Baer *et al.* [2007] introduced a texture-based stippling approach that employs the texture mapping hardware for efficient image generation. The challenge is to determine a surface for texture mapping that avoids strong projective distortions of stipple dots. Cube mapping, where a complex geometry is represented by a surrounding cube, is not optimal, since it is a too coarse representation. The *polycube mapping*, introduced by Tarini *et al.* [2004], enables a more detailed representation that leads to only slight distortions. Inspired by this work, Baer *et al.* [2007] developed a stippling approach based on another multicube decomposition (they used regularly sized subcubes instead of an adaptation

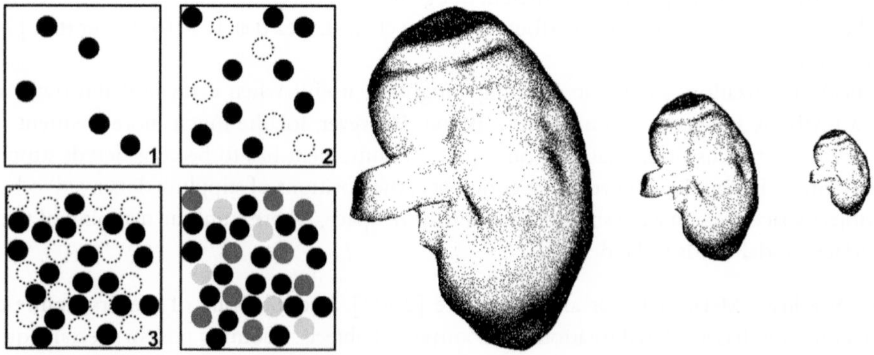

FIGURE 12.31 Using texture mapping for stippling. **Left:** Different texture layers representing different levels of brightness. **Right:** Stippling dots are added when the user zooms in and removed when the user zooms out to maintain the distribution of dots (Courtesy of Alexandra Baer, University of Magdeburg).

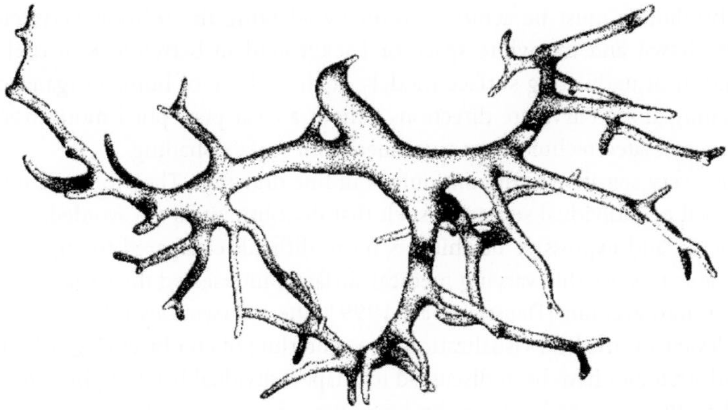

FIGURE 12.32 *With an efficient stippling approach it is possible to apply stippling textures with minimal distortions to surface models of vascular trees. Stipple dots are uniform in size and shape. With their distribution, boundaries are emphasized. The vascular surface model was generated with Convolution surfaces (Courtesy of Alexandra Baer, University of Magdeburg).*

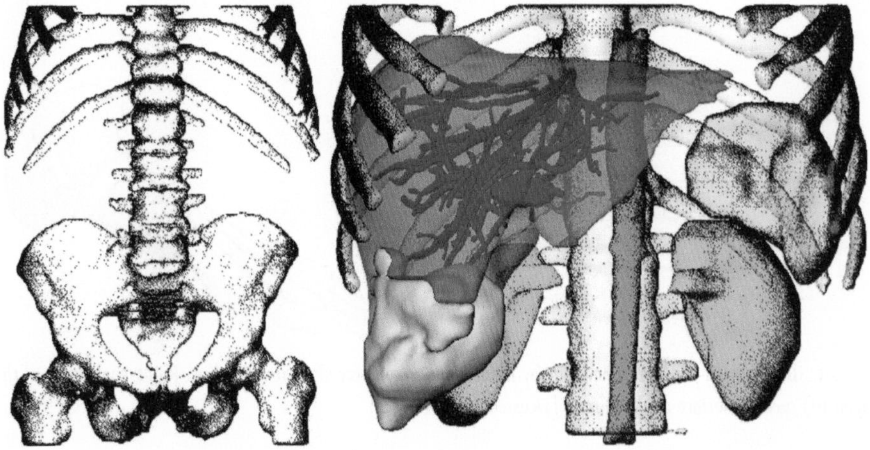

FIGURE 12.33 **Left:** *Stippling the pelvis and other skeletal structures.* **Right:** *Stippling combined with colored surface shading (From: [Baer et al., 2007]).*

of cube-size to surface features). This method was used, e.g., to efficiently stipple vascular structures and (Fig. 12.32). The use of colors can be restricted to a few regions, which are particularly relevant, such as the branches of a vascular tree close to a tumor. In Figure 12.33 more examples of stippling.

12.8 HATCHING

Hatching is traditionally used for shading in anatomical illustrations. The basic rendering primitive for hatching is a line. However, the desired effects usually require that attributes, such as line width, are carefully adapted to convey brightness. Similar to stippling, hatching lines usually have a constant color.

Thus, the target brightness must be achieved again by adapting the relation between the area where hatching lines are drawn and the white space or background in between. Kim *et al.* [2003] showed that depth perception of undulating surface models, such as those of human organs, can be effectively enhanced by hatching along curvature directions. This is a clear perceptual motivation for considering hatching either as an isolated technique or combined with surface shading.

Humans are also very sensitive to discontinuities in line drawings. Therefore, complex hatching lines have to be composed of individual segments such that discontinuities are avoided. In general, the generation of convincing and expressive hatching is more difficult compared to stippling. Early hatching techniques, applicable to smoothly varying medical surfaces, intersected the surfaces at regular distances taking illumination into account [Deussen *et al.*, 1999]. The intersections follow either a user-specified curve or, more relevant for medical visualization, the centerline of an object (Fig. 12.34).

Many ideas and strategies have been discussed to adapt individual hatching lines to the desired target brightness. To adapt the distance between the lines, turned out to be disappointing, since the arising patterns are disturbing. More in alignment to traditional illustration, line segments are placed regularly but their length and width is adapted. Figure 12.35 illustrates a robust method developed by Rössl *et al.* [2000].

Hatching is particularly useful, when embedded surfaces need to be displayed and the outer surface is hatched instead of being rendered semi-transparently. For clinical applications, it is essential that

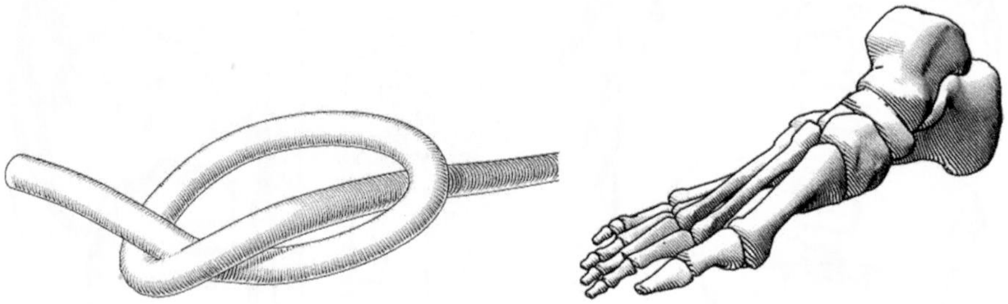

FIGURE 12.34 *Illumination-modulated hatching by intersecting a geometry along its centerline. Right: application of this principle to a (high quality) medical surface model (From: [Deussen et al., 1999]).*

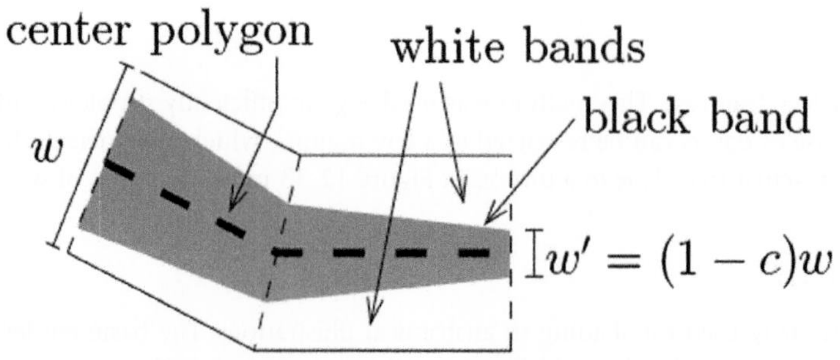

FIGURE 12.35 *Only a portion of the stroke is drawn to reflect the desired density (Inspired by [Rössl et al., 2000]).*

- the user interaction to generate hatching is minimized,
- hatching lines are generated in real-time, and
- frame-coherent exploration is enabled where hatching lines move consistently instead of suddenly appearing and disappearing.

Our discussion of hatching techniques is based on these requirements. We first describe hatching techniques that employ curvature information to emphasize surface shape (§ 12.8.1). We continue with discussing how domain-specific knowledge, e.g., preferential directions may be combined with curvature-based hatching and then describe how these refined techniques were applied for hatching (§ 12.8.2). Special hatching techniques are needed for particular structures, such as muscles, which are hatched by medical illustrators according to their fiber orientation [Dong *et al.*, 2001]. This a priori knowledge may be combined with a geometric analysis that involves principal curvature directions (§ 12.8.3). Finally, we discuss hatching based on volume data (§ 12.8.4).

12.8.1 CURVATURE-GUIDED HATCHING

Advanced hatching techniques are based on differential properties of the underlying surface shape—similar to the feature line generation. In particular, curvature along the principal directions plays an essential role to guide hatching line placement and enable a better shape perception than conventional shading [Kim *et al.*, 2003]. Thus, curvature is approximated to project hatching lines in the curvature direction on the surfaces.

Among the early attempts to employ curvature for hatching is the work of [Rössl *et al.*, 2000] that employed triangular surface meshes. An essential problem is that the meshes need to be subdivided in regions with roughly homogenous curvature to avoid discontinuities at transitions. Rössl *et al.* [2000] performed this task with both interactive and geometry-derived techniques. When combined with silhouettes, expressive rendering could be achieved (see Fig. 12.36). A second direction for hatching was computed to support cross-hatching, that is particularly useful to represent darker regions of the output image and thus to increase the perceived contrast (see Fig. 12.36). These renderings could be precisely adjusted to give the impression of a certain *tone*.

The relation between smoothed geometric models and illustrative renderings is also emphasized by [Rössl *et al.*, 2000]. They suggest to incorporate mesh smoothing techniques in illustrative rendering

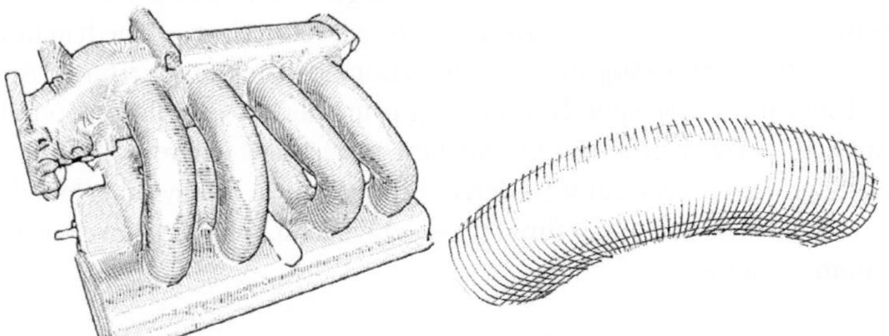

FIGURE 12.36 Curvature-guided hatching modulated by lighting applied to an engine block. The right image illustrates cross-hatching in dark regions (Courtesy of Christian Rössl, University of Magdeburg).

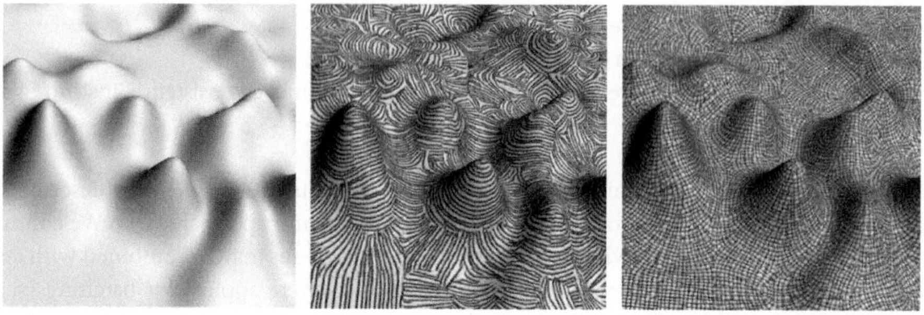

FIGURE 12.37 *Three examples from a study testing shape perception.* **Left:** *Phong shading.* **Middle:** *Lines representing one principal direction.* **Right:** *Lines in two principal directions* (From: [Kim *et al.*, 2003).

systems. This enables to flexibly adjust the level of detail in illustrated visualizations—by subdividing the mesh, more details arise and by smoothing details may be omitted.

Evaluation of Hatching In the study of Kim *et al.* [2003], users had to estimate surface normals. The results showed that the 3D shape was better perceived with hatching lines in the direction of maximum curvature. Slightly better results were achieved with hatching lines in direction of the two principal curvatures (Fig. 12.37, right).

Due to the characteristics of anatomical models and the quality of datasets, common hatching approaches, which are only based on curvature information, are not appropriate and sometimes fail due to singularities[2] in the curvature vector field. Instead, a priori knowledge needs to be incorporated to achieve robust hatching and to generate hatchings that correspond to the expectations of viewers mainly raised by the familiar look of textbook illustrations. Muscles in traditional illustrations, for example, exhibit a typical hatching that reflects the underlying fiber structure. Thus, we focus on object-space approaches where the hatching lines are aligned with the surface meshes. Again, image-space techniques do not provide frame coherence and are resolution-dependent. A special instance of object-space hatching is the texture-based approach where hatching is realized by the efficient texture-mapping hardware.

12.8.2 MODEL-BASED HATCHING OF MUSCLES AND VASCULAR STRUCTURES

In the following, we describe the automatic generation of a curvature and model-based vector field for vessel structures and elongated muscles (based on [Gasteiger *et al.*, 2008]. Observations from anatomy textbooks indicate that vessels and muscles have a specific *preferential direction*. The hatching lines are placed *radially* around vessel surfaces and *along* the fiber direction for muscle structures. Although the radial alignment for vessel structures corresponds to the first principle curvature direction, this does not hold for rough vessel surfaces derived from routine medical image data where noise prevents a strict radial orientation. Muscle fiber directions cannot be derived by curvature or any other purely geometry-based approach (see Fig. 12.38a). The following three steps generate an appropriate vector field depending on the underlying anatomical surface:

1 adaptive curvature estimation,
2 definition of a model-based preferential direction, and

2 A singularity is a point in the vector field where the local vector is zero. In a curvature field, thus, no directional information is available.

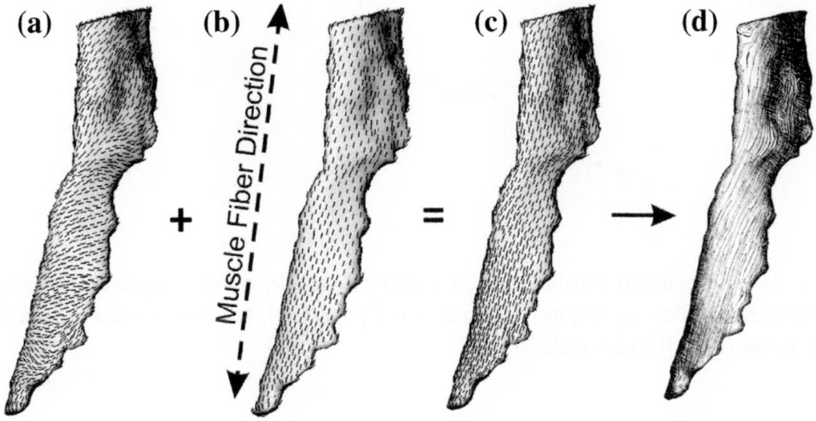

FIGURE 12.38 *Curvature- and model-based hatching: (a) curvature estimation, (b) approximation of preferential direction (depicted as arrow), and (c) combination of (a) and (b) to the final model-based vector field, (d) employing TAM textures aligned to the vector field (From: [Gasteiger et al., 2008]).*

3 combination of 1 and 2 to the final vector field. The last step resolves singularities for vessels and muscles because of their inherent preferential direction. The structure type (vessel, muscle) is stored during the prior segmentation process. Finally, hatch textures, e. g., Tonal Art Maps are mapped onto the surface with lapped patches.

The three steps and their results are illustrated in the subfigures of Figure 12.38.

While Gasteiger *et al.* [2008] employed the Laplacian filter to smooth the anatomical surfaces, Xie *et al.* [2007] employed the bilateral filter to smooth surface normals. The smooth model is used to estimate the curvature direction of each original vertex p. Due to the simple surface topology (number of convex and concave vertices) of muscle structures, a quadratic surface fitting method with topology-independent parameterization is appropriate. Vessel structures exhibit a more complex surface where a topology-independent parameterization does not always preserve the ordering of neighbors around p. Hence, a topology-dependent parameterization by approximating geodesic polar coordinates is better suited. Gasteiger *et al.* [2008] used the parameterization introduced by Rössl *et al.* [2000].

In order to obtain model-based preferential directions, the skeleton of elongated structures is useful (skeletonization was discussed in § 11.4.2). The result of the skeletonization is a graph G, which contains the edges e_i as connections between different branchings. Each edge consists of the skeleton voxels s_j .

The local radial alignment for vessel structures corresponds to the direction which is perpendicular to the local direction of the skeleton. To compute this vector, we need the nearest local skeleton direction for each vertex. Figure 12.39 (left) illustrates a vessel section with its corresponding edge e_i and some skeleton voxels as black squares. Through each s_j a plane $E(s_j)$ is placed that is defined by s_j and its direction vector (black arrow). The direction vector is calculated by central differences of its two adjacent skeleton voxels s_{j+1} and s_{j-1}. Additionally, the nearest plane $E(s_j)$ to p is defined. The "up" vector (blue arrow) that is perpendicular to the direction vector, lies within $E(s_j)$ and describes the local radial direction of p. The projected vector of this direction to the tangent plane of p is the local (normalized) preferential vector r_p is determined. For complex vessels the corresponding skeleton edge e_i for each vertex p before the nearest plane is selected (see Fig. 12.39, right, where a vascular tree of the liver

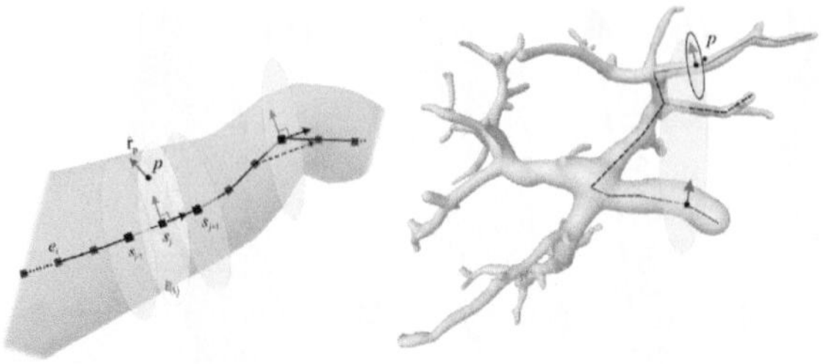

FIGURE 12.39 *Definition of the preferential direction r_p at a vertex p of a vascular structure. Projection of the "up" vector (blue) of the corresponding intersection plane $E(s_j)$ (b) into the tangent plane of p as r_p (red).* **Left:** *A small portion of a vascular tree.* **Right:** *A complete vascular tree (From: [Gasteiger et al., 2008]).*

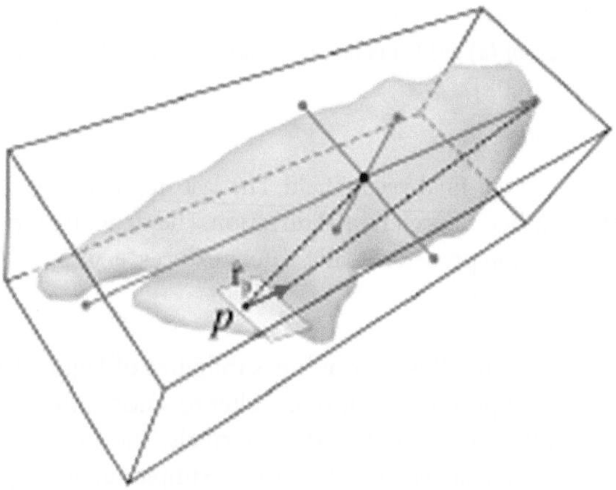

FIGURE 12.40 *Approximation of the skeleton by the OBB and choosing the longest axis (blue) as r_p (From: [Gasteiger et al., 2008]).*

is shown). There are two planes nearby at p, but only the green line with the bordered plane, is the corresponding edge to p to get the right local "up" vector.

Preferential Directions for Muscle Structures For elongated muscle structures the fiber direction, which indicates the course between origin and onset of the muscle, is essential. This orientation may be roughly approximated by the longest principle axis of the object-oriented bounding box (OBB). Figure 12.40 shows a muscle structure surrounded by its OBB as well as the corresponding principle axes. Among all three directions the vector u is the longest and r_p is defined as the projection of u to the tangent plane of each p.

12.8.3 COMBINATION OF CURVATURE AND PREFERENTIAL DIRECTION

With the approach described above, we obtain two kinds of direction information for vessel and muscle structures: curvature information in terms of both principle directions, and preferential directions

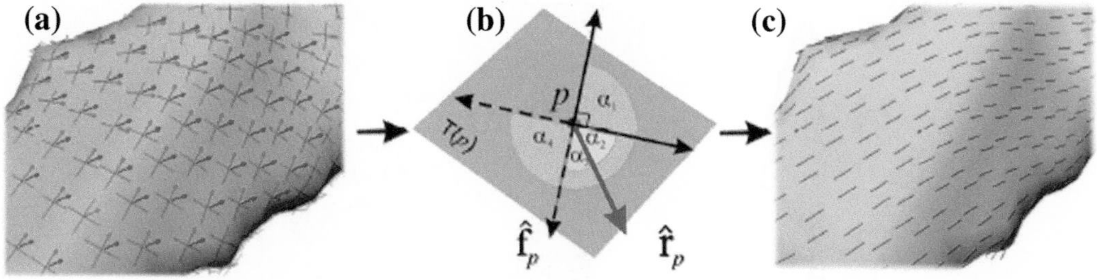

FIGURE 12.41 *(a) Curvature information (crosses) and preferential direction (red arrow = r_p) at each vertex p, (b) selection of the principle direction, which has the smallest angle to r_p denoted as f_p, (c) resulting optimized model-based vector field (From: [Gasteiger et al., 2008]).*

depending on the underlying anatomical structure. This information needs to be combined to yield a stable vector (see Fig. 12.41).

In Figure 12.41(a), for each vertex its two principle directions are shown as black crosses and one preferential direction is shown as red arrow. Figure 12.41(b) illustrates all directions for the vertex p in its tangent plane $T(p)$. Additionally, the enclosed angles between r_p and the principle directions (two principal directions in forward and backward manner) are included. For the initial vector field, the principle direction, which has the smallest angle to r_p, is selected and denoted as f_p (indicated by a blue arrow in Figure 12.41a). The resulting vector field may still exhibit some discontinuities (see Fig. 12.41a) where each selected principle direction is highlighted (blue). The alignment of each f_p to the preferential direction r_p and to its neighborhood may be improved by following a global geodesic course of the vector field. The solution of Gasteiger *et al.* [2008] is based on an *energy minimization* formulation. Finally, a direction vector for every face is computed by averaging the directions of the face vertices. Figure 12.41c gives an example for the results after the optimization.

In summary, a geodesic vector field without singularities is computed. It is aligned to the preferential direction, and guided by the local curvature information. Figure 12.42 shows the resulting hatching for an isolated object and as part of an anatomical illustration inspired by the needs for neck surgery planning. The relative position between lymph nodes (yellow) and muscles (brown) should be depicted clearly. Hence, lymph nodes are opaque, bones (gray) and muscles are semi-transparent. Additionally, all structures are highlighted with their silhouettes. Since the whole approach operates in object space, frame-coherent zooming and scaling is possible. The computation of the vector field requires considerable effort. Gasteiger *et al.* [2008] reported on preprocessing times of about 30 seconds for anatomical structures of moderate resolution. However, this effort is only needed once.

12.8.4 HATCHING VOLUME MODELS

One of the first volume illustration approaches addressed hatching. [Treavett and Chen, 2000]. A slightly different approach was proposed by Dong *et al.* [2003] who used segmentation information to reliably calculate silhouettes and principal curvature directions. With volume hatching, strokes are generated, which take the intensity values of the volume data into account. Also, in contrast to surface hatching, interior voxels close to the surface make a contribution to the hatching. Based on gradient estimation schemes, the local orientation of a surface in the volume data is approximated to calculate lighting information. Thus, the depth cues provided by shadings are also provided.

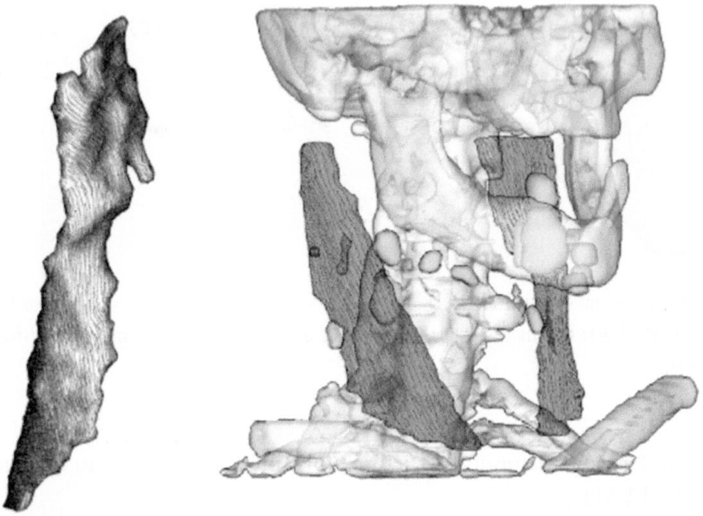

FIGURE 12.42 **Left:** *Hatching the M. sternoclaidomastoideus with a combination of curvature and model-based information. In regions with low illumination, the dark tones hide surface characteristics (see the boundaries of the muscle).* **Right:** *The same neck muscle is hatched and integrated in the visualization of the neck anatomy (From: [Gasteiger et al., 2008]).*

Hatchings based on volume information allow to produce smoother hatching lines compared to purely surface-based methods. Dong *et al.* [2003] describe a method where smooth patches are fitted to the intensity values of eight adjacent voxels. In contrast to a polygonal isosurface with its discontinuities in the surface normal, these patches provide smooth transitions of the orientation.

Dong *et al.* [2001] describe methods for approximating the muscle fiber orientation to guide hatching lines (see Fig. 12.43). The general principle here is to derive material properties to guide hatching directions. Frame coherence is achieved by an object-space approach (using illuminated 3D strokes as rendering primitives). The stroke generation is currently rather slow and the techniques are not widely evaluated, but they indicate the great potential of hatching techniques for medical visualization applications.

12.9 ILLUSTRATIVE SHADING

Shading provides essential cues for depth and shape perception. Therefore, we discussed the integration of shading in volume rendering (recall § 8.2) and the generation of feature lines that represent illumination discontinuities. In the following, we analyze lighting situations in (medical) illustrations (§ 12.9.1) and discuss how these may be adopted to 3D surface illustration. *Shading* in the following refers to the use of brightness for displaying object features. This is a broader definition compared to the general computer graphics definition where shading relates to brightness caused by illumination (only). Shading in this broader sense is based on different parameters. These parameters are mapped into a *Shading Map* where different weights may be used to control the influence of these parameters. The resulting Shading Map is used as a lookup for the final intensity at a certain area [Tietjen *et al.*, 2008]. Thus, a shading map may be used to control hatching and stippling but also material properties, such as transparency. Since additional parameterization options lead to more complex user interfaces, we discuss a simplification

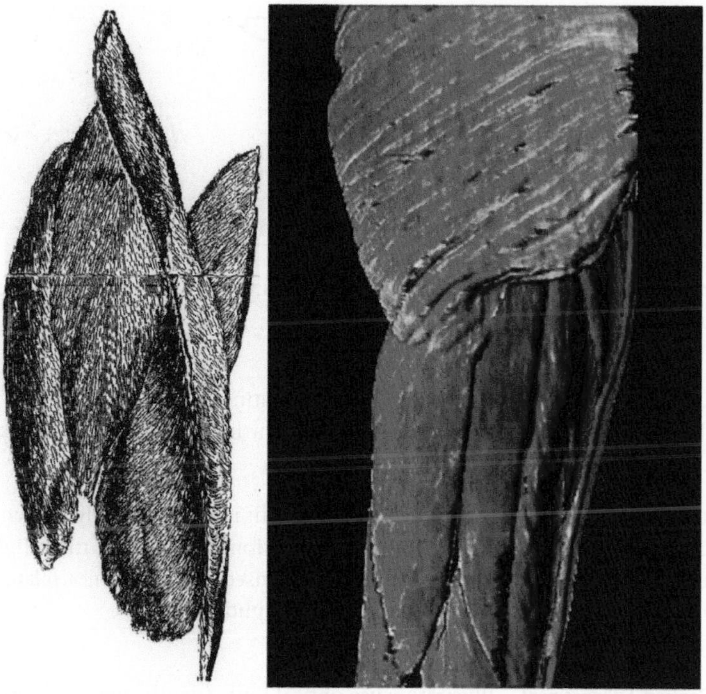

FIGURE 12.43 *Volumetric hatching of different human muscles. The image quality is impressive. However, it is based on the Visible Human dataset—a dataset with a quality that is still not available in clinical routine data (From: [Dong and Clapworthy, 2005]).*

based on *templates* and *high-level shading parameters* summarizing a couple of more elementary parameters. This discussion is based on [Tietjen *et al.*, 2008] and [Pfisterer, 2008] where 20 elementary shading parameters were identified and summarized to four high-level parameters. Templates and high-level parameters enable a guided interaction, which provides a reasonable trade-off between flexibility and ease of use.

12.9.1 SHADING IN MEDICAL TEXTBOOKS

The illustrator has the possibility to arrange the lighting proportions to achieve an optimal perceptibility of the structure's shape and surface. For a detailed analysis of these methods, see [Hodges, 1989, Hamel, 2000] and the excellent master thesis by Pfisterer [2008] on which this section is primarily based.

Conventional and Reflected Lighting A light source from the top left is often used and corresponds to the natural perception of the daylight. In reality, reflected light ensures that shadowed areas appear not completely black. The reflected light is used as scatter lighting to make structures apparent that are not directly illuminated.

Plateau Lighting is suitable to emphasize the silhouette and for figure-ground-separation. This results in an enhanced perception of the overall shape. For roundish structures, the center appears brighter and border areas are darker.

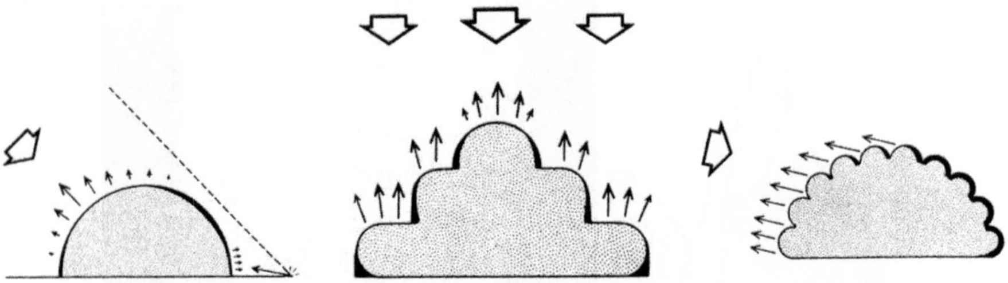

FIGURE 12.44 *Frequently used lightning configurations in scientific illustrations. From left to right: conventional main light, plateau lighting, and raking light (Adapted from: [Hodges, 1989]).*

Backlighting In contrast to the plateau lighting the backlighting separates an object from a dark background. The backlighting has a lower effect than the plateau lighting and is often used in addition to plateau illumination.

Raking Light Details are optimally recognizable when the light is approximately tangential to the surface, although the raking light does not affect the overall impression of a realistic main light source. For the illustration of the object's surface, additional techniques are used, which are not related to the incidence of light. Ridges and valleys may be highlighted to improve lighting.

Figure 12.44 illustrates these lighting configurations.

Depth Cueing and Contrast Enhancement Illustrators use optical hints (depth cues) to support the perception of depth in 2D drawings clearly. In nature, the scattering of light and fog cause that distant objects appear brighter and with low contrast. The atmospheric perspective gives also a clue of depth. Furthermore, the distance between overlapping objects is frequently emphasized by projecting a shadow onto the rear object. This shadow seems to be caused by a light source from the direction of the observer. The shadow is independent of the main light source and is only applied locally. Thus, it differs from a shadow in reality. Additionally, the front object is brightened at the boundaries to aid the contrast to the rear object, similar to the backlighting. In addition, a high contrast range makes illustrations appear more dynamic and increases the amount of perceived information at the same time. Histogram-based transformations facilitate such high contrast range images.

Stippling and hatching are based on the placement of (usually) black stipples or strokes to create an impression of gray values. Thus, for every pixel a target gray value must be determined based on a (local) lighting model. In the following, a system for a flexible computation of an illustrative shading is described. To adopt the computer-generated shading to geometric models, it is necessary that the shading arrangements are provided as parameters in an appropriate user interface.

12.9.2 REALIZATION OF THE EXTENDED SHADING

The overall pipeline employs the geometry, that is the vertex position and vertex normal, as input. In a preprocessing step, individual contributions to the shading map are computed and weighted according to user input. The resulting shading map is used as input for an illustrative rendering system. The whole pipeline (Fig. 12.45) may be realized on the GPU. The OpenGL Framebuffer Objects (FBO) extension is used. Every parameter is mapped to one FBO. To process additional static values to the GPU, e.g., curvature, user vertex attributes provided by OpenGL are used. Lighting is computed per fragment and therefore for every point of the surface. However, histogram operations have to be performed for the whole image.

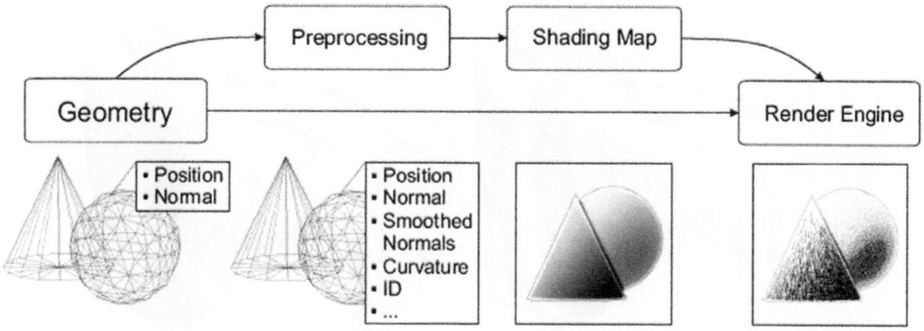

FIGURE 12.45 *The render engine, e.g., a hatching renderer, takes the geometry and the shading map as input. The whole computation is view-independent (From: [Tietjen et al., 2008]).*

Hence, the local brightness of a surface depends on surrounding objects. It is not possible to render the brightness in a normal fragment shader. Therefore, the brightness distribution should be computed in a separate process and used in the final rendering process [Tietjen *et al.*, 2008].

While lighting and curvature are computed more efficiently in object space, others, e.g., histogram operations are performed in image space. Object-space computations are performed only once and all results are transformed in image space to be combined flexibly. The combination of all parameters yields the so-called *extended shading map*—a map associated with the current camera position and screen resolution, representing the brightness for every pixel. Figure 12.46 illustrates the resulting effect. Mesh or normal smoothing is essential to avoid artifacts (Fig. 12.47).

Feature lines might be integrated but should not appear too prominently (Fig. 12.48). Tietjen *et al.* [2008] discuss reasonable choices for all parameters (default values) as well as their summary to high-level parameters. The most essential high-level parameters are (modified from [Tietjen *et al.*, 2008]):

- *Boundary enhancement*. Besides the feature line thickness, the ratio between main and plateau light affects the intensity of the object's boundary. The ratio may be combined with feature line thickness to one high-level attribute (Fig. 12.48).

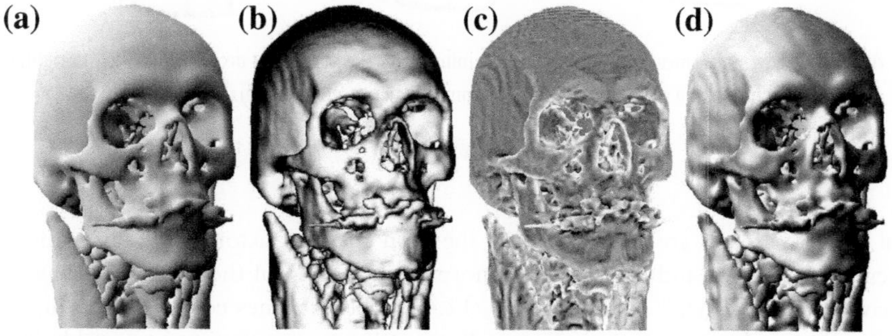

FIGURE 12.46 *Combination of the surface representation parameter: (d) is the weighted sum of the main light map (a), the plateau light map (b) and a curvature map (c), and an additional histogram equalization (From: [Tietjen et al., 2008]).*

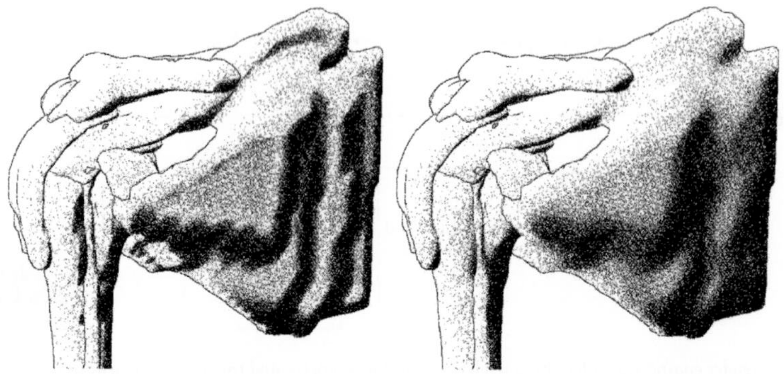

FIGURE 12.47 *A shoulder model with strong artifacts arising from binary segmentation (left). With strong normal smoothing, pleasant illustrative shading may be obtained (From: [Tietjen et al., 2008]).*

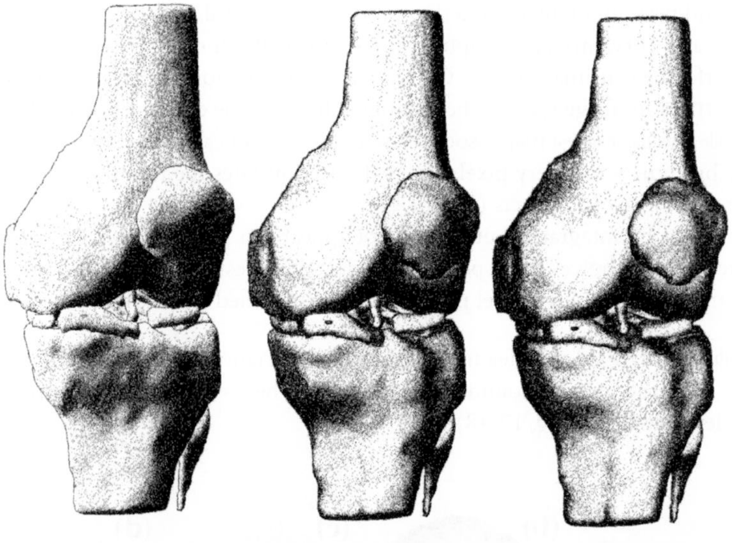

FIGURE 12.48 *Boundary enhancement of a knee model: the influence of the main light decreases from left to right, whereas feature line thickness and plateau light have an increasing influence (From: [Tietjen et al., 2008]).*

- *Detail amplitude.* Details are emphasized by the toon shading factor of the raking light as well as the curvature weight and extenuated by normal smoothing of the main light. These parameters are combined to a detail amplitude (Fig. 12.49). The extremes correspond to high details and additional smoothing respectively. The medium setting is according to a normal lighting.
- *Surface enhancement.* Back light, depth shadow, and atmospheric perspective contribute to the surface enhancement.

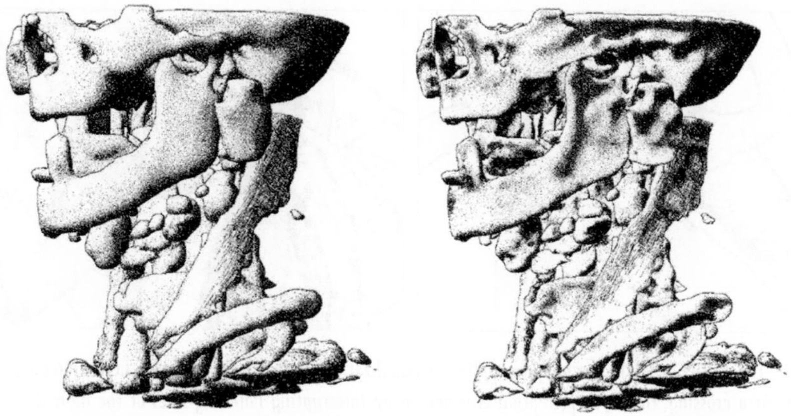

FIGURE 12.49 *Detail amplitude applied to a model of the neck anatomy: on the left, only main light and smoothed normals are used. On the right, smoothing decreases, toon shading and curvature weight increases. The muscles are rendered with the hatching technique described in § 12.8 (From: [Tietjen et al., 2008]).*

The shading framework was implemented on an NVidia GeForce 7900GS graphics card. The weights of the parameters do not influence the frame rates. The frame rates for the shading map generation varied between 7.5 and 20 fps for geometric models with 25–225 K polygons and a viewport size of 512 × 512. As an example, for the neck anatomy (94 K polygons, Fig. 12.49) the shading map was generated with a frame rate of 14 fps.

12.9.3 ILLUSTRATIVE VISUALIZATION OF VASCULAR TREES

Illustrative techniques, such as hatching and silhouette generation, serve two purposes in the context of vessel visualization:

- they enhance the shape perception, and
- they may encode additional information on the vessel's surface.

In this section, we describe the use of illustrative techniques for vascular structures, geometrically represented with model-based techniques, such as truncated cones or implicit surfaces (recall § 11.5).

Enhancing Shape Perception Hatching lines require an appropriate parameterization of the vessel surface. Usually, hatching lines are guided by principal curvature directions. So far, such a parameterization has only been performed for vessels represented by concatenated truncated cones. Ritter *et al.* [2006] presented a texture-based and hardware-supported approach to hatching vessels composed of truncated cones (recall Hahn *et al.* [2001]). Figure 12.50 presents two examples of their work. Hatching was selectively employed to indicate distances between two branches at bifurcations. In a rather large user study, Ritter *et al.* [2006] could demonstrate that the desired effect on shape perception was actually achieved.

The illustrative shading strategy described in § 12.9 is also useful for illustrative rendering of vascular structures. In Figure 12.51, the use of shading maps reflecting the distance to the viewer (atmospheric perspective) is shown. However, since vascular surface models tend to be large (225 K polygons in this example), it is difficult to enable real-time transformations.

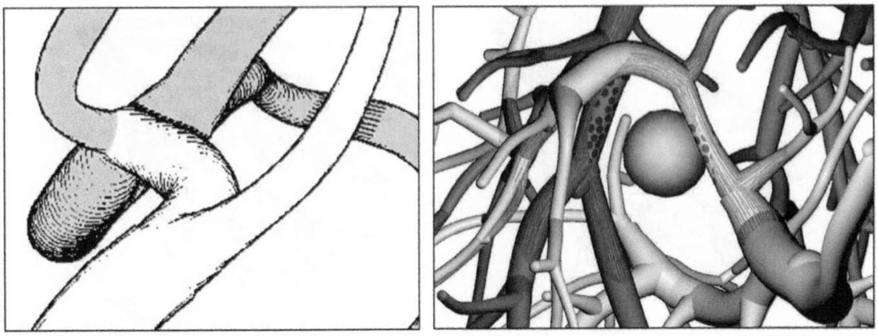

FIGURE 12.50 *Illustrative rendering techniques applied to visualizations with truncated cones.* **Left:** *Hatching lines support the shape perception. At a crossing, the depth perception is enhanced by interrupting hatching lines at the more distant vessel branch.* **Right:** *Two colors serve to distinguish two vascular trees. Different textures are mapped onto the surface to indicate distance intervals to a simulated tumor (yellow sphere) (Courtesy Christian Hansen, Fraunhofer MEVIS Bremen).*

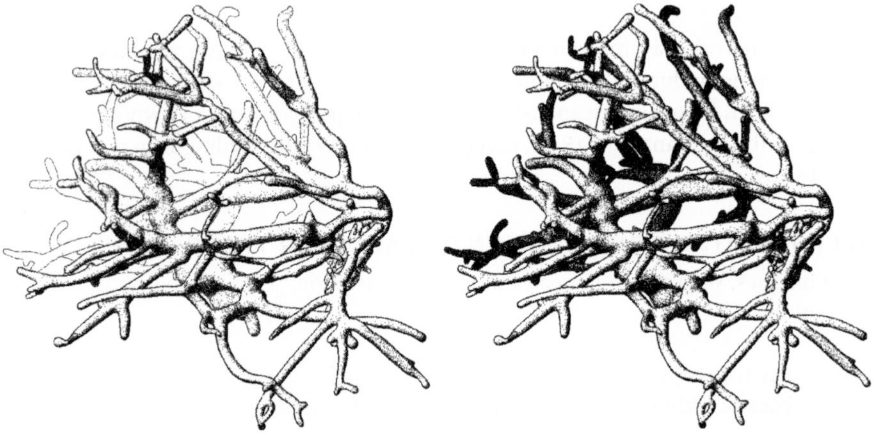

FIGURE 12.51 *A surface of the hepatic vasculature was generated with convolution surfaces and rendered with a shading map with atmospheric perspective enabled for better depth perception. The background intensity differs in both images (From: [Tietjen et al., 2008]).*

Enhancing Depth Perception with Color A further support for depth perception of vascular structures may be achieved if the colors of silhouette and hatching strokes are adapted. Chu *et al.* [2008] realized such an illustrative vessel rendering system exploiting the perceptual effect of *chromostereopsis*. This term relates to the fact that humans tend to perceive certain colors as advancing colors and others as receding, assuming that objects appearing in this color are further away. In general, what artists refer to as *warm colors*, e.g., red, orange, and yellow, are advancing colors, supporting the perception that crossing branches in these colors are in the front, whereas *cold* colors, such as cyan and blue, depict more distant objects. The chromostereopsis effect is discussed in [Thompson *et al.*, 1993].

Encoding Information on Vessel Surfaces Illustrative techniques bear a great potential to encode additional information on vessel surfaces. The density and orientation of hatching lines, for example, are attributes which can be distinguished efficiently. Thus, hatching can be used to encode two or even three nominal values (see Fig. 12.52). Another illustrative rendering technique, inspired from technical drawings, is to adapt the line style (solid, dashed, dotted) to the spatial relations. Thus, relations, such as "in front of," "within," and "behind," can be clearly communicated [Hansen *et al.*, 2010b] (see Fig. 12.53). The authors refer to this technique as *distance-encoding silhouettes*.

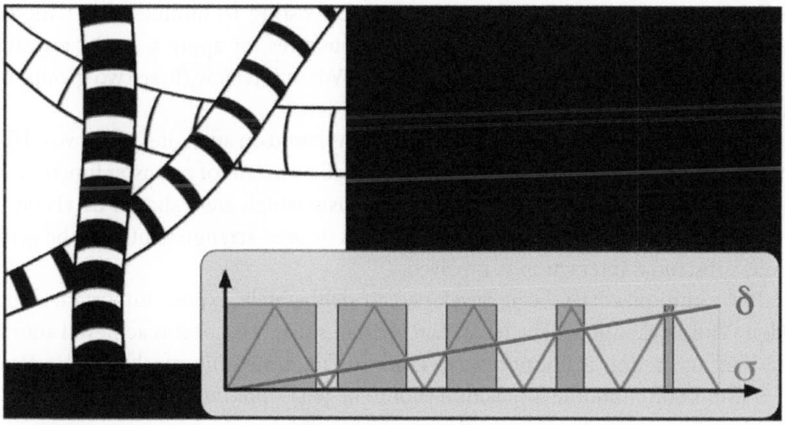

FIGURE 12.52 *The distance to the viewer (δ) is encoded by the thickness of strokes. A sawtooth function (σ) is compared with the distance. If δ is greater than the value of σ, a black fragment is generated, otherwise a white fragment (Courtesy of Christian Hansen, Fraunhofer MEVIS Bremen).*

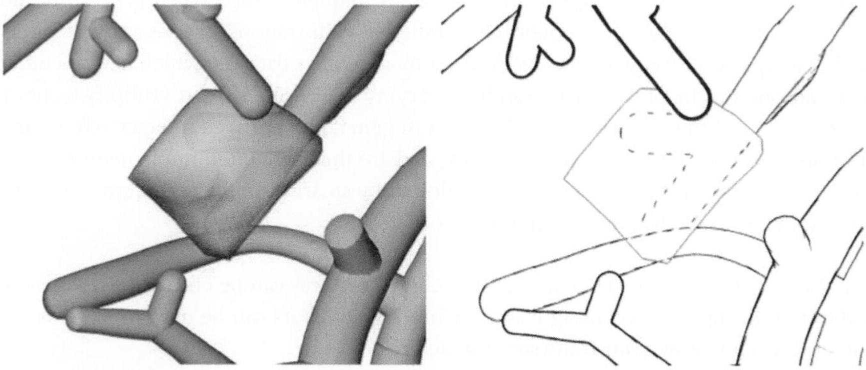

FIGURE 12.53 *A close-up view of a tumor (yellow) and adjacent vascular structures with classical semi-transparent surface rendering (left). The depth information can be conveyed more clearly with depth-enhanced silhouettes (right) (Courtesy of Christian Hansen, Fraunhofer MEVIS Bremen).*

We will later extend this discussion and show how illustrative visualization techniques may be used in intraoperative visualization where vascular trees derived from preoperative data are shown on top of video or live images of real surgery (Chap. 18).

12.10 SMART VISIBILITY

Smart visibility techniques enable an unobstructed view on features of interest. Thus, it becomes possible to steer the user's focus and emphasize information of high relevance. Especially when dealing with medical volume data, it is difficult to ensure an unoccluded view if this information is located deep inside the body. While transparency serves as a basic approach, which is inherently given through the emission absorption model, more elaborate techniques have been developed. Existing techniques either modify the visual attributes associated with the represented anatomical structures, or apply a spatial transformation that changes the relative positioning of anatomical structures. We will review these two groups of approaches and provide background information as well as technical details.

In traditional volume rendering, visibility of structures is based on attributes of the voxel data (intensity, gradient magnitude, curvature measures) and can be adjusted by means of a transfer function. Furthermore, clipping planes may be used to specify on a geometric basis which areas should be visible. In principle, with advanced cutting and virtual resection techniques, all desired arrangements may be generated (recall § 9.8). However, substantial interaction is involved.

Smart visibility techniques have been developed to deliberately expose important structures which would be hidden [Viola *et al.*, 2005]. The term *smart* indicates that this effect is achieved automatically. This does not mean that interaction is not necessary at all. In fact, a steering mechanism is essential, e.g., to specify "What is important?" But the interaction should be performed at this high level of communicative intents instead of the low level of precisely adapting visual styles.

Techniques, such as ghosted views, section views, and cutaways—known from technical illustrations—have a great potential for treatment planning [Krüger *et al.*, 2006, Kubisch *et al.*, 2010]. They have been applied to explore neck lymph nodes, to reveal tumors and vascular structures in abdominal organs, and to convey the location of other internal structures (see Fig. 12.54). Among the medical applications are also augmented reality solutions for intraoperative support—(see § 18.7.4).

Smart visibility techniques are inspired by approaches frequently used when generating illustrations [Viola *et al.*, 2005]. Medical atlases with their hand crafted 3D illustrations serve as a source of inspiration. Such occluded setups occur frequently, as medical scanners acquire datasets, which have no inherent view dependency and can thus be projected as seen from varying views. Since smart visibility techniques must achieve their goals for different views, and views can in general be changed interactively, smart visibility techniques must also support rapid visual feedback, and are therefore often implemented on the GPU.

There are three main approaches, which are exploited by smart visibility techniques in order to grant an unobstructed view to the features of interest:

- First, the visual attributes of occluding or occluded features can be changed. Transparency can be used to see through an occluding feature, while signal colors can be used to emphasize a feature of interest occluded by semi-transparent structures.
- The second concept, often applied when realizing smart visibility, is based on deformation of the occluding features, such that an unoccluded view is obtained. While changing the visual attributes does not alter the topology of the dataset to be visualized, deformation results in topology changes, though in a continuous manner.

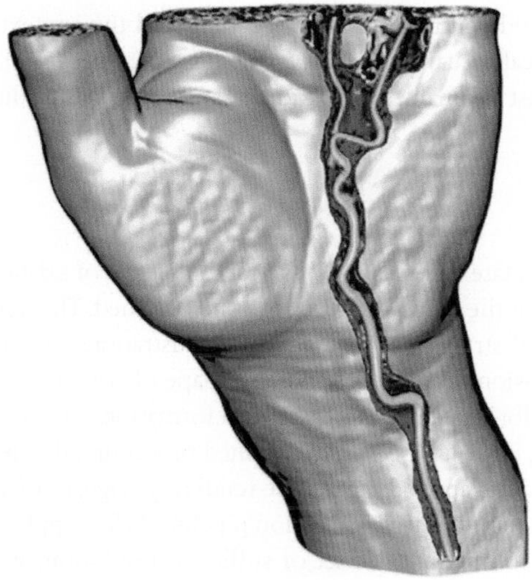

FIGURE 12.54 *Cutaways enable an occlusion-free view of otherwise occluded structures* (Courtesy of *Ivan Viola, Vienna University of Technology, described in [Viola et al., 2006]*).

- The third approach are *exploded views* where no deformations are applied, but occluding parts are transformed such that they do not block the view to the features of interest anymore.

While deformation allows to intuitively understand the original topology, since continuity is obeyed, exploded views represent a disassembly based on the parts of the object.

Smart visibility techniques, in contrary, have been developed by intentionally neglecting the laws of light propagation. Thus, modifying the way light reaches the viewer makes it possible to achieve the desired occlusion-free view. Because of this non-physical behavior and because many smart visibility techniques have been inspired by actual illustrations, they are also considered as illustrative visualization techniques. While neglecting the physical realism is acceptable and necessary, the designer of a smart visibility technique must still assure that visual coherence of the visualization is remained. Only by generating a visually coherent representation the interrelation between features of interest and the rest of the dataset can be perceived intuitively.

In the following sections, we will review selected smart visibility techniques, which have been proposed in the context of medical visualization. We will present the reviewed techniques in two sections. In the first, we cover cutaways and ghosted views, while we cover deformations in the second section. As smart visibility techniques are closely related to focus+context techniques, we will also refer to the feature of interest as *focus*, while we will denote the rest of the data as *context*.

12.10.1 CUTAWAYS

Clipping is frequently used in different medical diagnosis tasks. While both axis-aligned clipping and clipping along arbitrary planes can be achieved easily in combination with standard volume rendering techniques, more advanced cutaway techniques require more effort. Diepstraten *et al.* [2003] describe different approaches in the context of technical illustrations. All presented techniques simplify a structure for illustration by discarding irrelevant or obscuring parts of a dataset. The authors note that illustrators often prefer cutaways, as they allow no ambiguous interpretations of the depth ordering. Furthermore, cutaways provide a good contrast between the focus and the context structures. They can also be applied in the area of medical visualization. Nevertheless, the removal of medical structures, such as organs or their subparts, must be enabled to avoid the ambiguities introduced through smart visibility techniques.

12.10.1.1 Deformations

Many cutaway techniques facilitate deformations, as occluding parts of a dataset are cut and deformed such that an occlusion-free view on the focus structures can be obtained. This results in a shape deformation, rather then a relocalization of structures. In anatomical illustrations, deformations are widely used, as they allow spatial comprehension despite the modified shape of structures. Several such techniques have been proposed, which allow for generating interactive deformations of volumetric datasets acquired with medical scanners [Chen *et al.*, 2007]. Based on the applied procedure, the deformation process can either be interpreted as a transformation applied during the rendering stage, or of a data transformation, applied within the data enhancement stage in the visualization pipeline. When applying it in the data enhancement stage, revoxelization is used to obtain a dataset of sufficient resolution, which can be visualized using standard volume rendering algorithms. This approach is also referred to as *forward mapping*. The problem with approaches falling in this category is that the revoxelization performance is often slow. Therefore, simplified deformation data structures have been proposed, which allow an efficient deformation by exploiting GPU technology.

Revoxalization Correa *et al.* [2006a] present metaphors for illustrative volume deformations, which can be applied to support revealing internal structures interactively. They propose different operators, which allow the user to deform the data before the rendering stage. By focusing on the interactivity, these techniques can be used to generate impressive illustrations. Schulze *et al.* [2007] have presented an alternative approach based on the ChainMail algorithm. Their technique is focused on small subparts of large datasets only. While several other techniques exist for deforming volume data prior to rendering, usually high computational costs for resampling and additional memory is needed for the deformed volume. Furthermore, resampling artifacts are an arising problem when using these approaches.

Rendering Transformation Applying deformations directly during rendering in the last stage of the visualization pipeline has the benefit that no intermediate data representation needs to be stored, and thus the sampling of the original volume dataset is used. Kurzion and Yagel [1997] present ray deflectors as an efficient way to transform the viewing rays during rendering, rather than the dataset itself. As all similar algorithms, this way of deformation is less intuitive to understand by the user and thus needs to be accompanied with powerful interaction techniques. Rezk-Salama *et al.* [2001] present an approach, where iterative subdivision of the dataset is performed, and the actual deformation is applied by transforming the texture coordinates which define which parts of the volume are accessed during rendering. The approach presented by Mensmann *et al.* [2008] is tailored toward GPU-based volume ray casting. Similar to the approach by Schulze *et al.* [2007], the ChainMail algorithm is employed. However, in contrast, the deformation is closely linked with the rendering. In fact, the proxy geometry used for rendering is transformed, such that a modified GPU-based volume ray caster can be used to render the results of the deformation. The cutting operations preceding the deformation stage, are performed with high-level cutting templates which can be altered by using a point-and-drag interface. While deformation is as a technique often applied in medical visualization, several alternative approaches have been proposed to obtain an occlusion-free view on focus objects.

12.10.1.2 Volumetric Lenses

Cutaway and other smart visibility techniques are related to *lenses*. Similar to lens-based interaction, visualizations are *locally* changed. Whereas traditional lenses provide a magnified view, *magic lenses* allow for changing the used visualization style in the focus region. Magic lenses can be continuously moved over an image, or automatically moved to investigate all instances of focus objects, e.g., all segmented tumors. The magic lens metaphor has been originally proposed for use in 2D applications. Later on, 3D extensions, and more recently volumetric versions, which can be applied in medical visualizations, have been proposed. Two different kinds of shapes are commonly used to reveal the focus structures [Kubisch *et al.*, 2010]:

- *Primitive-based* lenses are specified by an enclosing primitive, such as a bounding cylinder or bounding box, which is used to make the target structure, and a narrow margin, visible.
- *Anatomy-based* lenses are derived directly from the anatomical focus structure (usually by a dilatation with an appropriate margin), and

Primitive-based LaMar *et al.* [2001] were the first to apply 3D magic lenses to volumetric datasets. Their approach allows to magnify the focus region by allowing a continuous transition into the context regions. Wang *et al.* [2005a] explore this direction by comparing various magnification lenses, which enlarge the focus area while preserving structures in the context area. Ropinski *et al.* [2005] propose a general approach for magic lenses, which separates the focus and the context region by applying different rendering styles. They use the depth buffer and an additional depth test in order to perform this separation during rendering. For convex lens shapes, this leads to a three pass rendering algorithm, where the focus rendering style is applied in the second pass, while the context rendering style is applied in the first and the third rendering pass. They employed this approach for multimodal visualization [Ropinski *et al.*, 2005].

Anatomy-based The anatomy-based approach (see Fig. 12.55, right) has the benefit of accentuating the shape of the anatomical target structure. It also reduces the amount of the geometry to be removed. However, a complex shape with many details, such as bumps, might also add too much noise to the

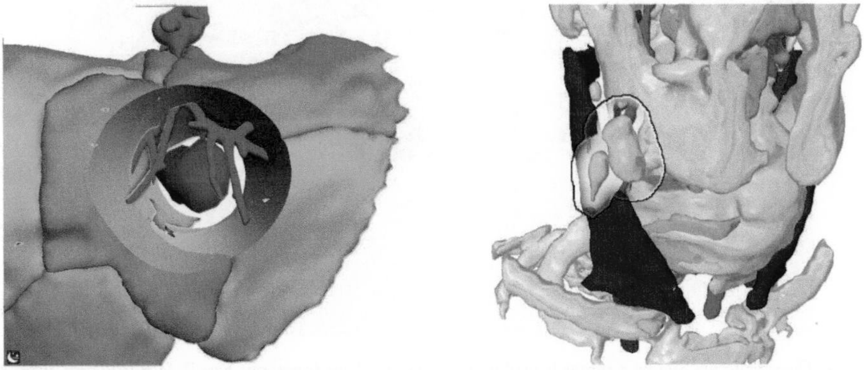

FIGURE 12.55 **Left:** *A primitive shape was applied to a liver dataset to reveal an (artificial) tumor and the vascular structures.* **Right:** *an anatomy-based cut shape is defined to emphasize two nearby lymph nodes in the neck area. While the left image shows a cutaway view, the right image shows a ghosted view where the obscuring anatomy (a large muscle) is partially visible (From: [Kubisch et al., 2010]).*

scenery. As a remedy, the anatomical region may be strongly smoothed to provide a simplified cut shape. Whereas smoothing in medical visualizations is usually performed with care not to compromise accuracy, for this illustration purpose the cut region may be smoothed more aggressively (see Fig. 12.56). As maximum flexibility is desired, cut shapes can often be defined interactively.

Burns *et al.* [2007] combined *contextual cutaways* with feature enhancement techniques. A contextual cutaway is defined by the screen space shape of an object and the current camera position. Based on this object's image footprint a frustum is generated, in which a cutaway is applied. To allow a smoother integration of this cutaway into the scene, several frustums with different opening angles are defined, and a slightly different cutting approach can be applied within them. Thus, the border of the cutaway region can be designed as a transition between the original rendering style and the faded out representation used within the core of the cutaway region. An example of this approach is shown in Figure 12.57, where it is applied to show internal structures within a CT scan of a human torso.

Kubisch *et al.* [2010] present a similar approach to reduce occlusion of structures of interest. They focus on the following scenario: Primary tumors and metastasis should be treated with local therapies, such as surgery, radiation treatment or interventions. The location of tumors, especially the proximity to surrounding risk structures, such as major blood vessels, should be displayed for supporting treatment decisions, such as resectability or extent of a surgical procedure as well as access planning. Therefore, the technique, which they call *breakaway view*, cuts out the surrounding of an object of interest by using depth-based clipping. Their approach focuses on surface-based representations. Due to the polygonal nature of the data, the clipping against arbitrary shapes results in open areas, which are closed by using a GPU-based capping approach. While the actual clipping is performed through fragment tests performed

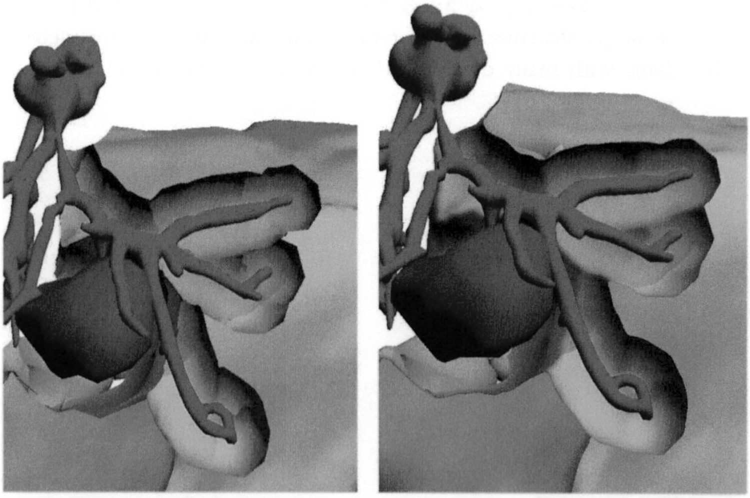

FIGURE 12.56 *The vasculature around a tumor is used to guide the cut shape (anatomy-based). While the cut shape in the right image is derived by precisely dilating the vasculature, it has been strongly smoothed for the generation of the right image. The smoothed variant avoids sharp edges that strongly direct the user's attention (From: [Kubisch et al., 2010]).*

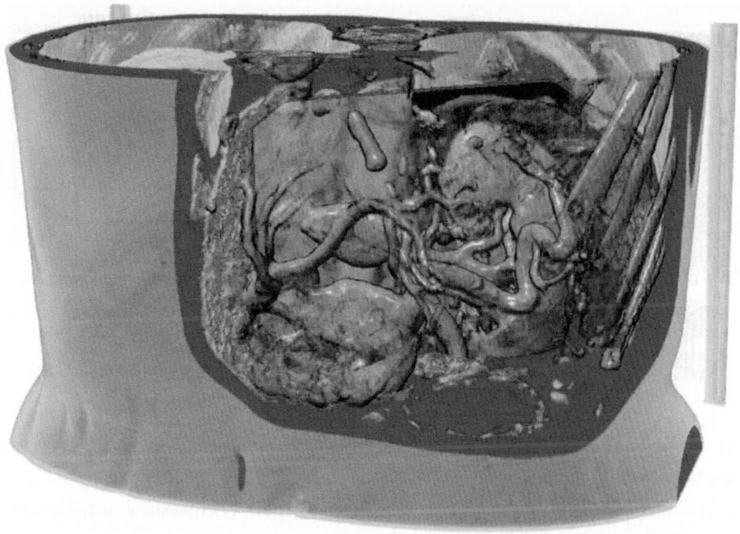

FIGURE 12.57 *Contextual cutaway applied to a CT scan of a human torso, whereby the cutaway shape is defined by the integrated ultrasound slice. While an occlusion-free view to the internal structures is granted, the contextual structure of the torso is still conserved (Courtesy of Martin Haidacher, Miracor Medical Systems. See also [Burns et al., 2007]).*

against the clipping geometry, the capping is performed by exploiting the stencil buffer. To further enhance the resulting representations, the authors describe how to add fake shadows through unsharp masking [Luft *et al.*, 2006], which support a better integration of the structures of interest into the clipping region.

12.10.2 GHOSTED VIEWS

The use of standard primitive shapes, such as cones, boxes, and cylinders draws attention due to their regularity that contrasts to the irregular organic shapes. Since tumors typically exhibit blob-like shapes, cylinders and cones are appropriate containers for them. However, for other anatomical target structures, such as vasculature, a regular bounding volume is extremely large and thus inappropriate. Even for tumors, lymph nodes, and other compact focal structures, the anatomy-based approach has some advantages, since it indicates the anatomy and a safety margin around the tumor—a region that is essential for any kind of local tumor therapy planning. For this purpose, the cut geometry should be rendered semi-transparently instead of being completely removed (see Fig. 12.55, right). This *ghosting* called approach is frequently used in illustrations of surgical interventions [Hodges, 2003]. Although the transparency introduced with ghosting techniques allows ambiguous depth interpretation, several ghosting approaches have been described for medical visualization.

Viola *et al.* [2004] present a ghosting technique, which is based on an *importance function*. With the thus assigned importance values, they alter the visibility of occluding structures (see Fig. 12.58). To support a

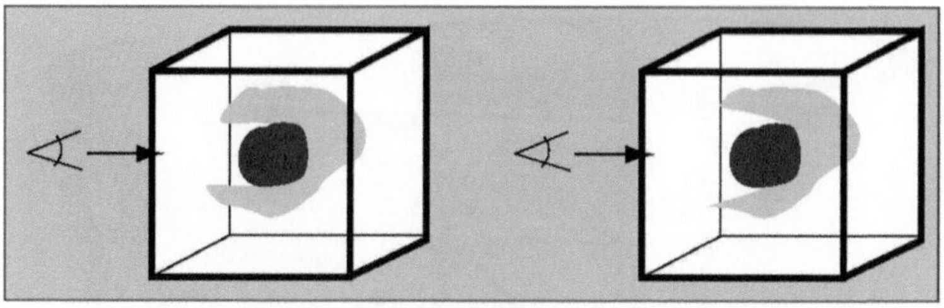

FIGURE 12.58 *Viola and Gröller enable ghosting by exploiting an importance function that maps intensity values to importance values. The importance values can be used to alter the visibility of occluding structures* (From: [Viola et al., 2005]).

better integration of focus and context regions, they present different approaches for partially blending out the context parts covering the focus region.

Bruckner and Gröller [2005] present ghosting as part of their VolumeShop, which supports interactive volume illustration. While the standard emission absorption model incorporates transparency to simulate non-opaque structures available in the real world, their approach allows for assigning a high degree of transparency to occluding structures. By interactively painting on the screen, the degree of transparency can be increased for selected structures without breaking the continuity of the visualized parts.

Bruckner *et al.* [2006] employ an interactive ghosting approach. Through a flash light metaphor the user can interactively specify the region of interest. The transparency of occluding structures is then increased based on the gradient as well as the specular reflections. Thus, a sufficient amount of contextual information is available, such that focus and context can be integrated intuitively.

Krüger *et al.* [2006] present another more surface-oriented approach, called ClearView. By allowing the interactive application of continuous blending between different transparent surface representations in a volume, they achieve an intuitive highlighting with good depth cues. The technique is based on observations made in modern illustrations, and performs visibility adaption based on:

- regions of high curvature,
- distance to the viewer, and
- distances between surfaces in the direction of the normal of a focus surface.

In many cases when a focus region is present, some of the contextual information in front of the focus region is obtained in order to provide a clear depth relation. These context clues are mainly given by features having a high curvature, such as ridges on surfaces. Based on this observation, the presented approach exploits one or more *opaque focus layers* and one or more *semitransparent context layers*, inspired by the ClearView principle. To estimate those features being visible on the context layers, although they cover the focus area, the authors use a curvature estimation scheme which can be evaluated on the fly during rendering. During compositing, the resulting feature intensity and two other surface-based methods can be used. The viewing distance metric relates the degree of blending based on the distance of two surfaces based on their distance along the viewing ray. In contrast, the normal distance metric relates the degree of blending to the distance along the normal of the current surface sample. Furthermore, the compositing can be confined to specific regions of interest. Figure 12.59 shows the application of the ClearView technique when using the normal distance weighting (left) and the curvature-based compositing (right).

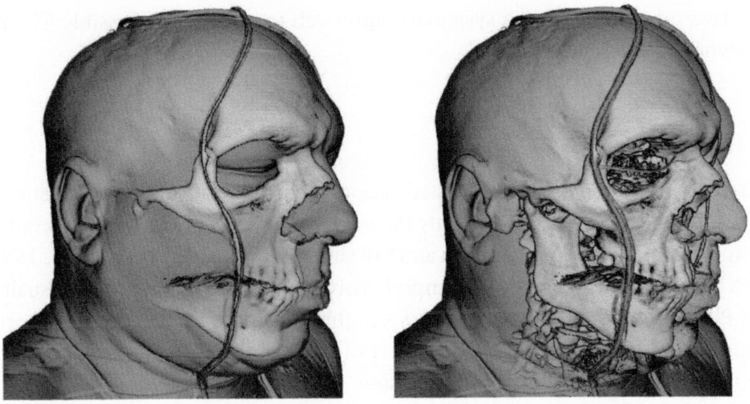

FIGURE 12.59 *Application of the ClearView ghosting technique when using the normal distance weighting (left) and the curvature-based compositing (right) (From: [Krüger et al., 2006]).*

12.11 CONCLUSION

In this chapter we got to know various illustrative visualization techniques that are promising to support medical applications, such as surgery planning and training. These techniques are motivated by research on visual perception that clearly indicates that perception of complex shapes and spatial relations benefits from an emphasis of boundaries and other relevant details. It is inspired by solutions from art and scientific illustration. The development and use of illustrative visualization techniques was a very creative endeavor not only mimicking traditional techniques but providing solutions for interactive exploration and animation. Among the special aspects to consider is the frame-coherent placement of graphics primitives and the development of fast techniques using GPU facilities.

We started this chapter with an overview of *feature lines* that illustrate discontinuities in shape, visibility, or illumination. Thus, an advanced geometric analysis of shape and their relation to light sources and cameras is essential. To employ these techniques for enhancing medical visualization, however, is not straightforward. Medical surface models are noisy. without care artifacts and noise are recognized as features to be emphasized. Thus, there is a close link between surface extraction and, in particular mesh smoothing, for illustrative visualization of patient data. Feature line visualizations require smooth and regularly tesselated surface models that are usually not the immediate result of surface extraction from CT or MRI data but require preprocessing, such as subdivision and smoothing.

In addition to line features, we discussed surface illustration with stippling and hatching. These techniques have many parameters and as a consequence impose many degrees of freedom. For medical illustrators this flexibility is an advantage. For routine use of such techniques, however, appropriate default values for these parameters need to be determined to enable an efficient use.

Finally, we have addressed smart visibility techniques, from which some can already be found in modern surgical planning tools. As occlusion is a driving problem, the acceptance of these approaches is more likely in the medical domain.

While we explained illustration techniques on a technical level with some hints to perception and cognition, we have omitted a discussion of esthetic aspects. Obviously, the assembly of illustrative and other techniques influences the perceived attractiveness of the resulting visualizations and the applications in which they are embedded. While esthetics may be considered a matter of taste and thus a very subjective issue, there is increasing evidence that a systematic approach to esthetics is possible. The rather new field of *computational esthetics* explores such issues.

FURTHER READING

For readers with more interest in illustrative visualization, early publications from SALISBURY and WINKENBACH are highly interesting, since they discuss not only the technical problems and solutions but also their motivation and the background in art [Winkenbach and Salesin, 1994, Salisbury *et al.*, 1994, 1996, Winkenbach and Salesin, 1996]. There is one general and comprehensive textbook on "illustrative visualization" [Gooch *et al.*, 2002]. The Phd thesis from STEFAN BRUCKNER is a highly recommended source of information [Bruckner, 2008]. Lawonn *et al.* [2013a] compared a number of advanced feature line renderings based on typical medical surface models and feedback from physicians.

Treavett and Chen [2000] and Sousa *et al.* [2005] applied illustrative techniques to scientific and medical datasets to provide more comprehensible renditions for medical education and in particular surgery training. Jainek *et al.* [2008] applied illustrative rendering to represent the location of brain activation areas (derived from MRI and fMRI). Their system was extended by Born *et al.* [2009] to include DTI data as well.

Gorla *et al.* [2003] described a surface texturing algorithm that enables the automatic synthesis of a desired texture over the surface of an arbitrary object such that both discontinuity and distortion are minimized. This technique enables hatching of complex anatomical surfaces and perceptual studies that evaluate the subtle effects of texture orientation on shape perception.

Hiller *et al.* [2003] extended stippling to other object types than disks. Schlechtweg *et al.* [2005] introduced RENDERBOTS, a general technique to support the flexible generation of various illustrative styles, such as stippling and hatching, that can also be flexibly combined. Kopf *et al.* [2006] came up with an advanced method for computing blue noise point distributions rapidly. The paper, an expressive video and even the source code is available online. More recently, van Pelt *et al.* [2008] described an inspiring GPU-based stippling Busking *et al.* [2008] investigated particle systems for generating illustrative visualizations. They employed user-selectable rules to create a variety of illustrative styles in a unified manner.

The method described by Potter *et al.* [2009] is dedicated to architectural walk troughs and improves the depth perception compared to simple texture-mapped renditions. Schlömer *et al.* [2011] recently described a flexible and simple optimization strategy for distributing point sets—an essential prerequisite for stippling.

Smart visibility techniques are discussed in a review [Viola and Gröller, 2005], while deformation techniques for sampled data are extensively described in the state-of-the-art report by Chen *et al.* [2007].

Chapter 13

Virtual Endoscopy

13.1 INTRODUCTION

Endoscopy is a diagnostic procedure that is used by pulmonologists to diagnose bronchial diseases, such as lung cancer, by gastroenterologists to detect changes of the colon wall, and by a number of other medical disciplines. The cameras attached to the tip of an endoscope provide full color images of internal structures at high resolution and with very good quality. However, it is an invasive diagnostic procedure where sedation of the patient is necessary and complications, not only associated with anesthesia, may occur. Thus, it is an essential goal to reduce the necessity of such procedures.

Inspired by "real" fiber endoscopy, the walls of vascular and air-filled structures, such as the colon, can be explored by means of internal rendering of CT or MRI data. Such virtual endoscopy should resemble fiber endoscopy, e.g., similar wide-angle optics should be simulated to enable efficient diagnosis and treatment planning. Virtual endoscopy can partially, but not completely, replace fiber endoscopy as a diagnostic procedure. Moreover, it may be used in a complementary manner. While real vessel walls are opaque, in virtual endoscopy some areas may be rendered semi-transparently to reveal important structures behind the cavity that is explored (the "look behind the wall"). While in patients, the passage of an area in the bronchial or a vascular tree may be blocked by a severe stenosis, the virtual camera in a 3D model may pass that region. Thus, *endoscopy* is a metaphor, highly useful for developers and users of virtual endoscopy applications.

In principle, virtual endoscopy may provide the same information as the underlying CT or MRI data. However, the internal rendering may significantly improve the detection and characterization of pathologies along walls. In particular, the assessment of anatomical structures with a complex morphology, e.g., the bronchial tree and the colon, benefits from internal views and guidance through that anatomy. However, internal renderings alone do not provide sufficient context and orientation. At least one additional view is required to indicate the position and orientation of the endoscope.

In the related medical disciplines, there is a general agreement that in a number of applications the effort of preparing medical image data for virtual fly-throughs is justified. As an example, whenever possible the invasiveness of fiber endoscopy and the required general anesthesia should be avoided in case of children. As a consequence, major vendors provide and continuously refine virtual endoscopy packages. Despite the general acceptance of virtual endoscopy there are ongoing debates on specific diagnostic and treatment planning questions where exactly virtual endoscopy should be used and how it should be integrated in clinical workflows.

Virtual endoscopy is a classic area in medical visualization. After the first conference publications appeared in late 1994 [Vining *et al.*, 1994a,b], the first full papers appeared almost simultaneously [Lorensen, 1995, Hong, *et al.*, 1995, Geiger and Kikinis, 1995] and since then the field has evolved rapidly. Virtual endoscopy was first performed in a non-interactive manner using precomputed movies that display the cavity of interest from inside [Lorensen, 1995]. Since this is not sufficient to achieve a high diagnostic accuracy, methods for real-time exploration were developed. With more computing power available, interactive virtual endoscopy was first provided based on surface representations. Interactive control of volume rendered endoscopy was first restricted to high-end graphics workstations [Gobbetti *et al.*, 1998] and only

Visual Computing for Medicine, Second Edition. http://dx.doi.org/10.1016/B978-0-12-415873-3.00013-4

recently became widespread. Diagnostic applications started with virtual colonoscopy [Hong *et al.*, 1995, 1997], virtual bronchoscopy [Vining *et al.*, 1994a], and virtual angioscopy [Gobbetti *et al.*, 1998].

Endoscopic surgery is a special kind of minimally-invasive surgery, where natural holes, e.g., in the paranasal sinus are employed to access and remove pathologies. Virtual endoscopy may provide a planning and training environment for such endoscopic surgical interventions [Auer *et al.*, 1997, Yagel *et al.*, 1996].

Organization In this chapter, we first discuss the medical and technical background, i.e., optic endoscopy and its limitations as well as the potential of virtual endoscopy in (§ 13.2). Then, we explain which kinds of image data are acquired and how they are processed to enable virtual endoscopy (§ 13.3). We also discuss how a path may be generated that is suitable to explore the target region. With respect to rendering, we discuss the peculiarities of rendering rather narrow internal structures, since these peculiarities enable a particularly efficient rendering (§ 13.4). The performance gain may be used to integrate effects that increase the visual realism—an aspect that is relevant for surgical planning and training. Our discussion of rendering aspects includes surface rendering and volume rendering.

Virtual endoscopy involves a number of user interface issues, e.g., how users control the virtual camera, how they can deviate from the pre-planned path and how additional views may support the interpretation of the current internal 3D rendering (§ 13.5). Finally, we give a survey on the most essential clinical applications, namely virtual colonoscopy, virtual bronchoscopy, and virtual angioscopy focusing on specific clinical questions and the evaluation (§ 13.6). Thus, the sensitivity and specificity of diagnosing and grading certain diseases are considered. In addition to these *diagnostic* applications, we also consider a surgical intervention, the transphenoidal surgery of the pituitary gland. This endoscope-assisted neurosurgical intervention benefits from endoscopic viewing in treatment planning and during surgery.

13.2 MEDICAL AND TECHNICAL BACKGROUND

While there are a number of specific aspects of using (virtual) endoscopes for exploring different cavities in the human body, in this section we emphasize general aspects and discuss the specific aspects later. Endoscopes consist of an optical fiber that is moved to the target area. The camera at the tip of the endoscope delivers full color information of the walls of the inspected cavities. This image is displayed on an appropriate monitor. High resolution monitors with a resolution of 1920×1280 are common. Sufficient light must be provided to enable images with high contrast. The optical fiber itself can be flexible or stiff. The choice of the optic fiber depends on the location, shape, and size of the target region. As an example, a typical endoscope for neurosurgery has a small diameter in order to minimize the impacted brain tissue. The small diameter reduces the ability to transport sufficient light through the fiber to the endoscope head. Building a stiff fiber to allow a maximum of light [Duffner *et al.*, 1994] compensates for this effect. Besides the light source, an endoscope consists of the optic fiber for a camera to transport the acquired image to a monitor, and has one or more "working tubes" that are used to move tools, such as pliers, to the target area. Lenses at the tip of the endoscopes usually have a large opening angle in order to provide a sufficient overview. Unfortunately, this also aggravates optical effects such as the fish eye view [Freudenstein *et al.*, 2001]. An essential aspect of endoscopy is digital signal processing: the video stream is "stabilized" to provide a consistent view of internal structures not hampered by small movements of the camera.

Limitations of Endoscopy Several drawbacks are associated with endoscopy. It is unpleasant for patients and involves a risk due to sedation or general anesthesia or due to the mechanical interaction between the endoscope and the wall of an anatomical structure, e.g., in case of a colonoscopy. In diagnostic colonoscopy, the risk of bleeding due to colon perforation amounts to 0.1% and the mortality to 0.02%. Although these numbers are low, they are serious in particular for screening a healthy population. Schauer *et al.* [1997] discusses such risks in detail.

Endoscopy results as well as the risks of complications highly depend on the experience of the operator. Furthermore, some areas of interest cannot be reached by the endoscope due to folds and plaits or obstructive diseases. Handling and control of endoscopes is often difficult, mainly due to limited flexibility, the limited field of view, and a very limited depth perception. Endoscopic surgery lacks the fast access for open surgery in case of serious complications, such as strong bleeding. Therefore, careful planning and realization of these procedures is essential in order to avoid such complications.

Video Capsule Endoscopy This rather new endoscopy variant employs an orally administered capsule endoscope and uses the peristaltic movement to travel through the gastro-intenstinal (GI) tract. Major indications are gastrointestinal bleeding and suspected Crohn disease. First, it was used for small bowel diseases only, but meanwhile it is also used in pilot studies for the whole GI tract [Filip *et al.*, 2011]. The first capsule was admitted by the FDA in late 2003 for children.

The images delivered by the camera inside the capsule have a very good quality. However, the movement of the capsules is rather slow (24–48 hours for the whole GI tract). The image data are transmitted using radiofrequency signals and are recorded at the patients' waist. After completion, they are downloaded by a physician [Li *et al.*, 2007]. The comprehensive overview given by Li *et al.* [2007] includes the two products PillCam ESO and PillCam SB for the evaluation of the esophagus and the small bowel.

The larger the lumen of the explored cavity the more the capsule tumbles and thus the images are hard to interpret. Therefore, image processing attempts to stabilize the images and enable a robust interpretation. Recently, video was evaluated with respect to its ability for supporting colon cancer screening [Mussetto *et al.*, 2012]. Gossum and Ibrahim [2010] report on new ways to steer capsules, e.g., by magnetic manipulation and new diagnostic uses.

Virtual Endoscopy primarily mimics fiber endoscopy, but since there are no mechanical restrictions, it has a wider applicability. While real angioscopy is restricted to the arteries with a large diameter, virtual angioscopy is also employed in smaller vessels [Gobbetti *et al.*, 1998]. Moreover, additional and useful information may be displayed that is not visible in fiber endoscopy. Additional information may include hidden objects but also waypoints or other signs added in a planning step to support surgery [Scharsach *et al.*, 2006]. The display of this additional information may be accomplished in a flexible manner. Thus, instead of simulating the natural appearance, colors, and shading may be adapted to ensure a good contrast and emphasis of essential structures, such as nerves, nearby vessels, or tumors. Table 13.1 summarizes the differences between virtual and fiber endoscopy.

	Fiber Endoscopy	**Virtual Endoscopy**
Information	full color information, tactile impression of walls	intensity values (CT, MRI), look behind the wall, measures of local diameters
Limitations	size of the cavity, directly visible structures	no treatment possible
Risks	general anesthesia, perforation of cavity	non-invasive, radiation (in case of CT data)

TABLE 13.1 *Comparison: Virtual and fiber endoscopy.*

Diagnosis and Screening The most interesting goal is the replacement of the optical endoscopic procedure by the virtual endoscopic analogon. As diagnostic alternative, virtual endoscopy has the potential of reducing the costs significantly. In colonoscopy, for example, the interior colon wall is inspected for pathologies such as polyps. In case no suspicious areas are found, assuming a sufficient sensitivity, no further intervention is necessary. In the opposite case, however, an intervention may be necessary to acquire additional information through an endoscopic biopsy or to remove an identified pathology. Virtual endoscopy is also discussed in the context of screening examinations, where a whole age or risk group is examined, which is too costly to perform with optical endoscopy. We discuss such applications in § 13.6.

Potential of Endoscopic Views An interesting question is *why* virtual endoscopy enables a better diagnosis compared to viewing axial (or reformatted slices) or external 3D rendering? This question arises, since the same data is just displayed in a different manner. On the one hand, virtual endoscopy is an excellent example where the visualization is restricted to the relevant portion. Radiologists explore exactly the cavity they are interested in and are not distracted by other information. On the other hand, in virtual endoscopy even small details of the size of a few voxels are visible for several seconds: the user slowly moves along the, cavity and has more time to detect and interpret features. However, these details are the results of post-processing, e.g., thresholding, smoothing, or transfer function specification. Thus, the details visible in virtual endoscopy need to be interpreted carefully.

Limitations of Virtual Endoscopy for Diagnosis Certain diseases, such as mucosal abnormalities, can only be displayed with fiber endoscopy. Moreover, the assessment of suspicious regions in fiber endoscopy can be enhanced with irrigation and suction, where, e.g., secretions may be just removed. Finally, the ability to touch structures provides additional potentially diagnostically relevant information.

Training and Teaching Virtual endoscopy combined with a tissue simulation model allows the training of physicians without the necessity to employ animals or patients. Unfortunately, no available tissue model allows accurate simulations at sufficient simulation speed of a complex organ system. This is still an active research topic. With respect to teaching, virtual endoscopy can be used to instruct students on the anatomy of patients from interior viewpoints. Note that virtual endoscopy applications are based on volumetric patient datasets. No texture and color information of the organ is acquired, hence it cannot be properly represented. This can be a substantial flaw for a training application.

Intervention and Therapy Planning The currently most frequently employed scenario is intervention and therapy planning, where virtual endoscopy is used to explore access ways, potential complications, or the specific patient anatomy. A clear advantage of virtual endoscopy-based planning is the possibility to visualize anatomical structures that are not visible through optical endoscopy. This includes risk structures such as blood vessels, but also areas that are not accessible to optical endoscopy. In this chapter, § 13.6.1–13.6.3 describe such applications.

Intraoperative Navigation Finally, virtual endoscopy can be applied in connection with image-guided surgery (see Chap. 18) to provide an additional intraoperative navigation aid for a minimally-invasive intervention. The basic idea to this scenario arises from the fact that optical endoscopy is often limited to inside views of the visited cavity. All anatomical structures beyond the cavity wall are usually not visible. With virtual endoscopy, this can be different when additional information is provided. Consequently, a combination of optical and virtual endoscopy can provide valuable information to significantly reduce the complication rate of minimally-invasive surgery.

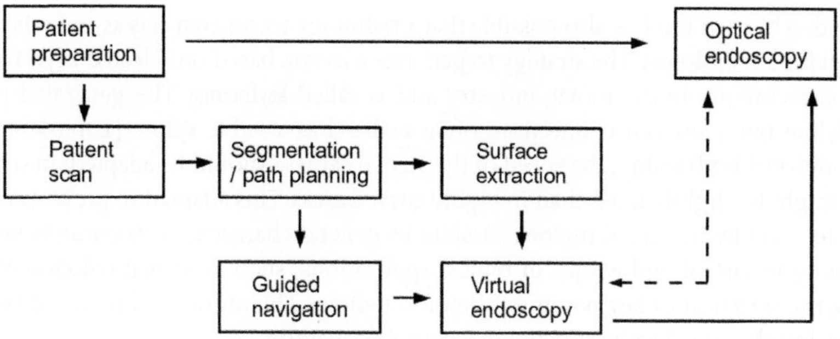

FIGURE 13.1 *Workflow of a virtual endoscopy system in contrast to optical endoscopy. The dotted line indicates that sometimes both are necessary, e.g., virtual endoscopy after optical endoscopy to reach further in a narrow or obstructed cavity. "Surface extraction" may be performed with isosurfacing or a special volume rendering technique, called first hit raycasting* (Courtesy of Dirk Bartz, University of Leipzig).

13.3 PREPROCESSING

Virtual endoscopy requires image data in a high spatial resolution and quality. In particular, motion artifacts, for instance due to breathing, may hamper the use of image data. Thus, the advances in imaging, e.g., multislice CT data and prospective motion correction are essential for endoscopic applications, such as angioscopy, colonoscopy, and bronchoscopy.

13.3.1 PREPROCESSING WORKFLOW

The overall workflow is depicted in Figure 13.1. The most essential goal of preprocessing is to provide a path to guide the user through the relevant cavity. The other steps are needed to prepare the generation of a path.

The first step to prepare endoscopic viewing is the *segmentation* of the target cavity (see Fig. 13.1). The choice of an appropriate segmentation technique and the specific parameters, of course, depend on the specific structure. As a general remark the related segmentation tasks are rather easy. In particular, air-filled structures in CT data, such as the colon and bronchial tree, exhibit a strong contrast to the surroundings that enables threshold-based segmentation. The segmentation of contrast-enhanced vascular structures is also a rather simple task. However, in case of small vascular structures, partial volume effects and an inhomogeneous contrast agent distribution may lead to problems that require a more elaborate segmentation. In some regions of the body, pathologies can make the segmentation task challenging. While the segmentation of the paranasal sinus in healthy patients is quite easy (except the partial volume effect relevant for the bony details), it becomes difficult in case of severe mucosal swellings.

13.3.2 PATH PLANNING

A path through the cavity of interest is required for generating a movie, but also essential for interactive exploration where the user may be guided to a complex anatomy with highly curved or branching portions.

13.3.2.1 Keyframing

A rather simple and general strategy for path planning is to let the *author* of a visualization specify a set of keypoints that are automatically connected to form a path and to generate a "fly-through." The author may later use this video himself but it is also possible that a radiology technician acts as an author and prepares the fly-through for a radiologist. The strategy to generate a movie based on selected keyframes is a widely used animation technique in the movie industry and is called *keyframing*. The generated path is usually not just a polyline but a smooth connection, often realized as a cubic spline [Lorensen, 1995].[1] Also, inspired by traditional keyframing, the speed of the virtual camera should be adapted: in straight portions of the path, it might be slightly faster than in highly curved areas. This adaptation prevents that the field of view changes too rapidly in curved regions. Despite its general character, keyframing is not widely used for path planning in virtual endoscopy. In typical applications, such as virtual colonoscopy and virtual bronchoscopy, the selection of key points is often too tedious. The number of required keypoints is not overwhelming, but they need to be selected in a complex anatomy.

13.3.2.2 Robot Motion Planning

Lorensen [1995] already presented an alternative approach that computes a path automatically based on the result of a previous segmentation. He adapted a solution strategy developed in *robot motion planning*. Robot motion planning serves to find a suitable, or rather an optimal, path from a start position to a target in a 2D floor where a number of constraints have to be considered. These constraints are primarily obstacles that prevent the robot to move from start to end on a straight line.

Translated to virtual endoscopy, a path is searched for which moves the virtual camera from a start point, e.g., the root of the bronchial tree to a target deep in the periphery where the walls of the cavity represent the constraints. Besides hard constraints, other criteria may be integrated, e.g., strong and sudden changes of the orientation should be avoided (for perceptual reasons) and the visibility of a large portion of the wall of the cavity should be ensured.

Problems of this category may be considered as the search for a path with minimum costs where the cost of a path is determined by its length and weighting factors that are chosen such that the constraints are considered. We discussed such problems and solutions, e.g., in image segmentation, where the livewire algorithm employs this strategy (recall § 4.4.1).

13.3.2.3 Skeletonization for Path Planning

The most frequently used strategy to compute a path for virtual endoscopy is to employ the result of a skeletonization algorithm. To support the navigation in virtual endoscopic exploration, the path should be smooth and centralized.

The user often has to specify two points of the skeleton to define the path as the portion of the skeleton that connects these points (in some colonoscopy systems). The skeletonization does not provide a perfect basis, since the orientation may change strongly. Similar to keyframing, a smooth path may be generated, e.g., by fitting a cubic spline to the skeleton to provide a more suitable representation. The path generation should also consider that the virtual camera is always oriented in a *stable viewing direction* to avoid sudden twists and turns [Paik *et al.*, 1998].

Once a path is defined with one of the methods described above, a movie may be generated that enables the exploration of the cavity with VCR[2]-based interaction (play forward and backward, stop,...). An efficient solution for creating such movies is to render panoramic images, a technology that was introduced by Apple with their Quick-Time format [Tiede *et al.*, 2002]. If virtual endoscopy is available as a movie, this has the essential advantage that the examination is *documented*.

---

1 A cubic spline is C^2 continuous and thus the curvature-related properties change continuously.

2 Video Cassette Recording.

Path Planning for Virtual Colonoscopy Skeletons to be used as a path for virtual colonoscopy should fulfill the general requirements for skeletonization discussed in § 11.4.2. In addition, the skeletonization approach should be robust against some typical problems of the appearance of the colon. Even after perfect preparation some folds of the colon may collapse leading to multiple segments or loops in skeletons if not carefully prevented [Ge *et al.*, 1996]. Early approaches required the user to select a start and endpoint to yield *one continuous* curve and further user input to avoid self-intersections. Later, Wan *et al.* [2002] achieved a high level of automation. With their method, also appropriate start and endpoints were computed. To achieve a smooth curve suitable for camera movements, Ge *et al.* [1996] used Catmull-Rom splines and applied them to a downsampled skeleton (every fifth skeleton voxel was employed).

Path Planning for Virtual Bronchoscopy Path planning for virtual bronchoscopy is guided by specific requirements. The bronchial tree does not exhibit folds or other properties that might lead to self-intersecting skeletons. However, the bronchial tree branches and the related skeleton are more complex. The efficient method from Zhou and Toga [1999] computes such skeletons. However, the position of branching points is not precise. The algorithm introduced by Paik *et al.* [1998] (and discussed earlier) was also applied to compute multiple paths in a bronchial tree. Negahdar *et al.* [2006] introduced an efficient approach that is based on a start point in the root of the bronchial tree. The start point is automatically located in the central axis of the trachea. Also, all endpoints are computed automatically and a sophisticated distance metric is used that computes distance transform quickly and precisely. The rough discrete skeleton is enhanced and smoothed as also discussed for vessel visualization in § 11.4.2.

13.4 RENDERING FOR VIRTUAL ENDOSCOPY

Virtual endoscopy mimics the visual representation of an optical endoscope. Hence, the optical properties of the endoscopes need to be mapped to the parameters of the virtual camera. Next to the camera distortion (fish eye and barrel distortion), this requires the *perspective rendering* of the dataset, which is not possible for all rendering algorithms and acceleration strategies. The two basic alternatives are indirect (surface) and direct volume rendering, which are discussed next. A good overview of the different rendering options was given by Neubauer *et al.* [2005] (see Fig. 13.2). Russ *et al.* [2010] and Krüger *et al.* [2008] described more recent rendering techniques.

13.4.1 INDIRECT VOLUME RENDERING

Indirect volume rendering is based on a polygonal surface representation of the respective body cavities (recall Chap. 6). This approach has several advantages and disadvantages that need to be considered. First, a polygonal representation offers good control over the visual result of the rendering. Transparencies can be easily specified and enable a concise visualization of the participating anatomical structures. Furthermore, many methods are available to improve the appearance and quality of the polygonal meshes that represent the body organs. Finally, graphics hardware allows fast and flexible rendering of polygonal objects, in particular perspective transformations come at no extra costs.

Processing Polygonal Models for High-quality Rendering On the downside, the visual quality of most indirect volume rendering methods is not as good as for many direct volume rendering approaches. In particular the standard Marching Cubes approach (see § 6.3) does not provide trilinear interpolation of the triangle vertices, which results in severe aliasing artifacts (see Fig. 13.3, (a) and (d)) for zoomed views close to the voxel resolution. Typically, the camera is very close to surfaces in endoscopic viewing. Therefore, aliasing problems are more severe than in external rendering.

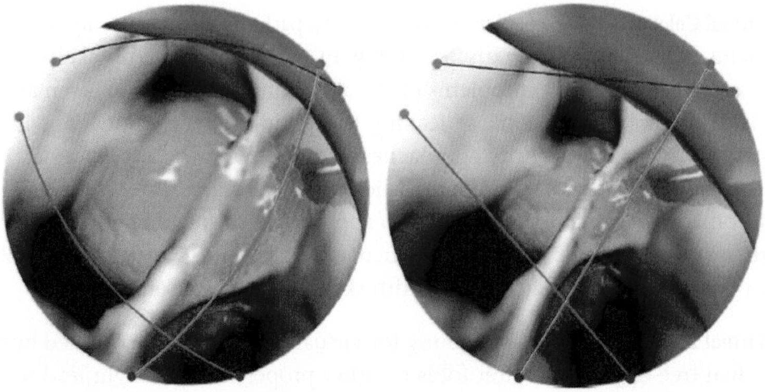

FIGURE 13.2 *Barrel distortion of a simulated endoscopic camera.* ***Left:*** *distorted camera image;* ***right:*** *undistorted camera image (Courtesy of André Neubauer. See also [Neubauer et al., 2005]).*

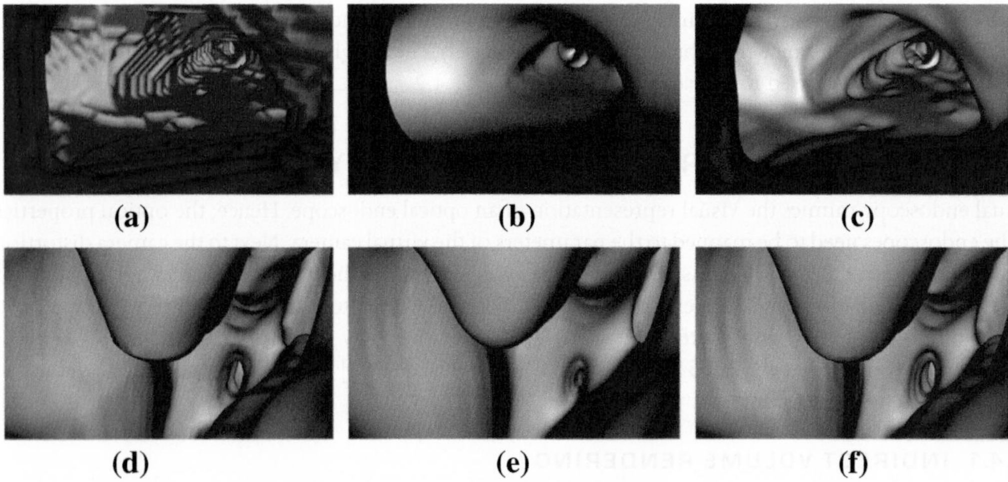

FIGURE 13.3 *Artifacts in isosurface generation and noise reduction with Laplacian smoothing; (a): the binary segmentation mask of a bronchial tree is directly transformed to a (jaggy) surface; (b): with strong Laplacian smoothing artifacts but also relevant information are removed; (c): the low-pass filter leads to a good trade-off between accuracy and smoothness. (d): endoscopic view of a surface of the nasal bony anatomy derived from the original data; (e): Laplacian smoothing of the nasal bony anatomy; (f): Again, the low-pass filter better preserves anatomical details (Courtesy of Tobias Mönch, University of Magdeburg).*

These artifacts can be avoided by heavy smoothing with a simple filter, such as the Laplacian (see Fig. 13.3, (b) and (e)). Heavy smoothing, however, may easily remove subtle landmarks for orientation or even diagnostically relevant information. Thus, a smoothing technique with error corrections, such as the low-pass filter is more appropriate (see Fig. 13.3, (c) and (f)).

Furthermore, the two stage process of surface extraction and subsequent rendering allows no flexible refinement of the isovalue that describes the surface, except if an advanced GPU-based real-time surface extraction technique is used (recall § 6.3.5). However, this sounds worse than it actually is, since most virtual endoscopy applications use an already carefully determined surface classification.

13.4.2 DIRECT VOLUME RENDERING

Direct volume rendering (see Chap. 7) computes the visual contribution of the target anatomy without generating a polygonal representation. This enables more flexibility for the exploration of the appropriate classification.

The first virtual endoscopy systems using volume rendering employed texture-based volume rendering to cope with the real-time requirements [Gobbetti *et al.*, 1998]. Meanwhile, most virtual endoscopy systems that use direct volume rendering employ a special version of ray casting—called *first hit ray casting*. In this method the view space is searched for the first sample that indicates the isosurface of a respective organ representation [Neubauer *et al.*, 2005, Krüger *et al.*, 2008].[3] In general, ray-casting approaches have the advantage that endoscopic views have viewpoints close or at least not far away from the surface, and hence the first hit sample is usually found rapidly. To further accelerate this sampling process, *space leaping* or empty space traversal methods are applied to skip large parts of the cavity itself. Note, however, that even in these relatively small spaces, *perspective ray divergence* must be addressed to provide sufficient sampling.

When anatomical objects behind the surface of the currently visited cavity should be displayed as well, first hit ray casting must be adapted to include those objects. Neubauer et al. [2005] split the respective rendering elements into foreground and background objects and renders them into a foreground and background image. Based on the depth information that has been computed during ray casting, the background image is blended with the foreground image. Figure 13.4 demonstrates the fusion of fore- and background in the context of pituitary gland surgery (see § 13.6.4). While the left image shows the blending of fore- and background with a fixed blending parameter, the right image considers the depth distance between fore- and background for the pixelwise blending. Note that if background objects are rendered semi-transparently, regular ray casting (no first hit) must be used.

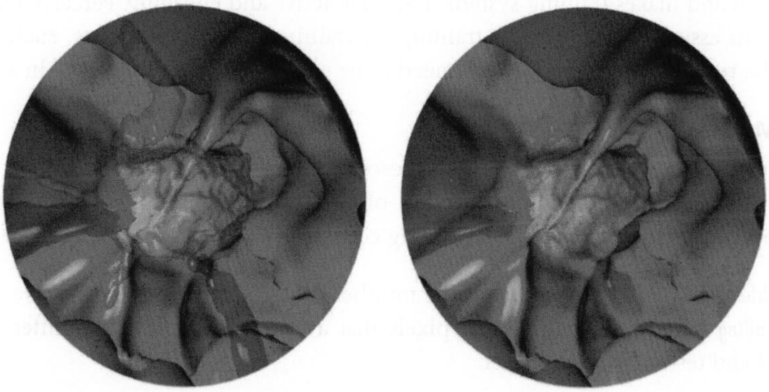

FIGURE 13.4 *Blended fore- and background images for first hit ray casting.* ***Left:*** *The images are blended with a constant blending parameter.* ***Right:*** *The images are blended considering the distance between fore- and background (Courtesy of André Neubauer. See also [Neubauer et al., 2005]).*

3 Neubauer's approach is actually an object-space order, cell-based ray-casting method that composes ray segments from different voxel bricks ("macro cells").

13.4.3 HYBRID RENDERING

The hybrid combination of isosurface and direct volume rendering enables the simultaneous display of endoscopic tools and pointers along with the target anatomy [Scharsach *et al.*, 2006]. While endoscopic tools are naturally represented as polygonal meshes, a flexible visualization of the target anatomy benefits from direct volume rendering, in particular to adjust the display of hidden structures. With modern graphics hardware, hybrid endoscopy rendering may be efficiently supported. Scharsach *et al.* [2006] describe a ray-casting fragment shader that performs surface and volume rendering in one rendering pass. The shader comprises two ray-casting loops that perform first hit ray casting and a subsequent direct volume rendering. For large clinical datasets and a 512×512 viewport they achieved interactive performance (at least 28 fps), even if the target cavity was highly transparent. Meanwhile, recent hardware enables an even better performance even for rendering larger models reflecting recent progress in CT and MRI acquisition.

13.4.4 ADVANCED RENDERING

Depending on the specific application, more advanced rendering techniques (recall Chap. 8) are used for virtual endoscopy. Illumination effects help to convey the complex spatial relations more clearly. The shadowing effects simulated by ambient occlusion provide a more realistic representation of the 3D geometry compared to standard Phong lightning. Depth-dependent light attenuation further improves depth perception (see Fig. 13.5). These advanced techniques may not compromise interactive rendering speed—a fluent interaction is indispensable for endoscopic viewing. With recent advances in GPU hardware, efficient implementations enable advanced rendering with sufficient performance.

For diagnostic applications, it is desirable that residual flood is clearly separated, which may be achieved with appropriate transfer functions [Russ *et al.*, 2010]. As a further technique to generate high-quality visualizations of endoscopic views, texture mapping may be employed to stimulate the appearance of "real" vessels, bronchial segments or colon walls (see Fig. 13.6).

This kind of enhancing endoscopic views is a double-edged sword: It adds information that is not derived from the underlying image data and thus pretends a level of realism that may be misleading. Therefore, this feature is usually not employed for diagnostic purposes. However, it leads to a higher level of immersion and makes training systems more attractive and engaging. Perceived similarity to real interventions is an essential criterion for training. In training, often also effects, such as bleeding are simulated and the resulting visualizations just need to be plausible and not "correct" in a narrower sense.

13.4.5 GEOMETRY CULLING

When isosurfaces are extracted from large (high resolution) medical image datasets with the Marching Cubes algorithm, the resulting polygonal models often consist of several million triangles. There are basically two approaches to deal with the rendering complexity of large polygonal models:

- *Mesh simplification* (recall § 6.7) reduces the number of polygons that represent the isosurface, and
- *geometry culling* reduces the number of pixels that are drawn in the framebuffer before they are rasterized and tested by the z-buffer.

Geometry culling removes groups of polygons (objects) from the rendering pipeline that are invisible. In order to maintain efficiency, several heuristics are employed. Hence, not all invisible polygons are culled, but only those that are detected by the heuristics. At the same time, a culling approach must be conservative in order to ensure that only invisible polygons are culled. For virtual endoscopy, more than 90% of the geometry can usually be culled by a combination of view frustum and occlusion culling [Bartz and Skalej, 1999] (see Fig. 13.7).

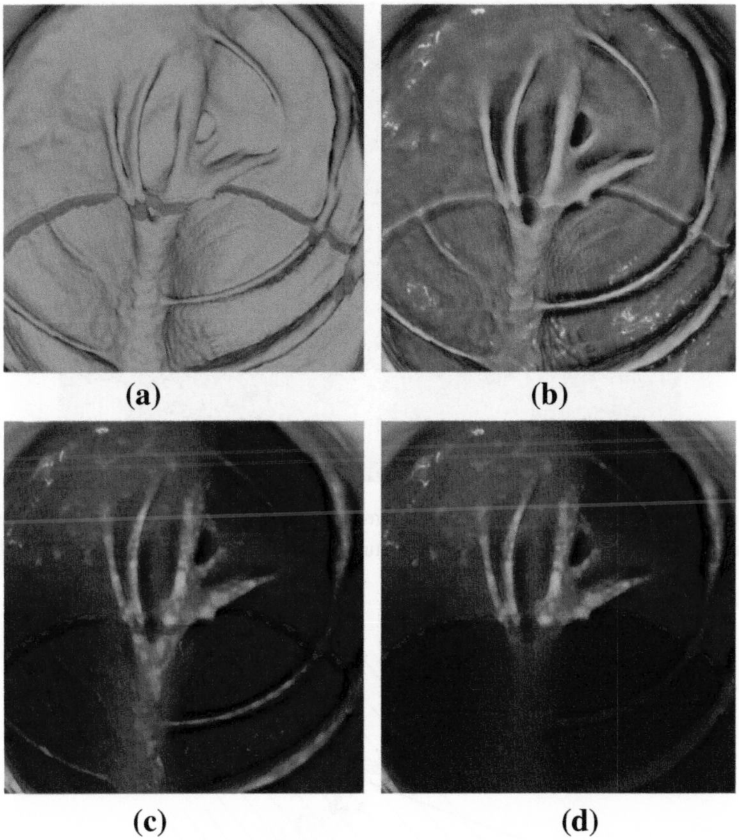

FIGURE 13.5 *Advanced rendering options for virtual endoscopy. Top left: Screen-space ambient occlusion. Top right: Simple diffuse shading of detail textured isosurfaces. Lower left: Fluid visualized transparently. Lower right: Combining these effects with light attenuation and shadows further enhance depth perception.* (Courtesy of Christoph Russ, ETH Zurich. *See also* [Russ et al., 2010]).

Advanced topic: geometry culling. Three classes of culling can be employed:

- backface culling,
- view frustum culling, and
- occlusion culling.

Backface culling removes all triangles that face away from the viewpoint. Since the back- and frontfaces of a triangle are decided through the direction of its normal, this test essentially checks if the normals are pointing away from the viewpoint. Since backface culling requires a consistent orientation of the tested triangles, the vertices of all triangles are enumerated in either anti-clockwise or clockwise fashion.

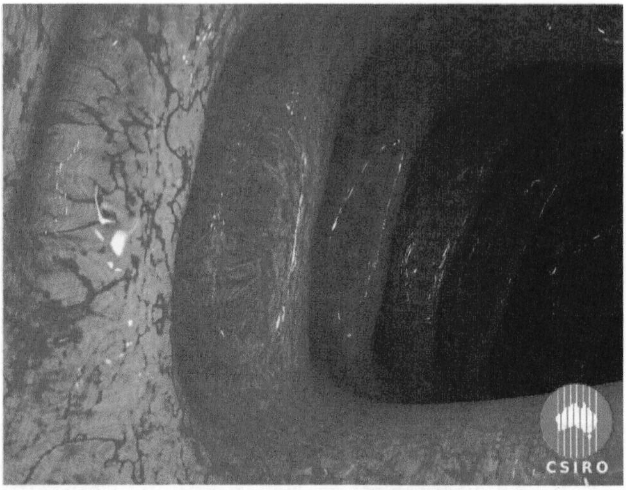

FIGURE 13.6 *A glossy texture is applied to the colon wall to create a realistic impression. While training systems benefit from the added realism, diagnostic applications should not employ such textures (Courtesy of Christoph Russ, CSIRO, Brisbane, Australia).*

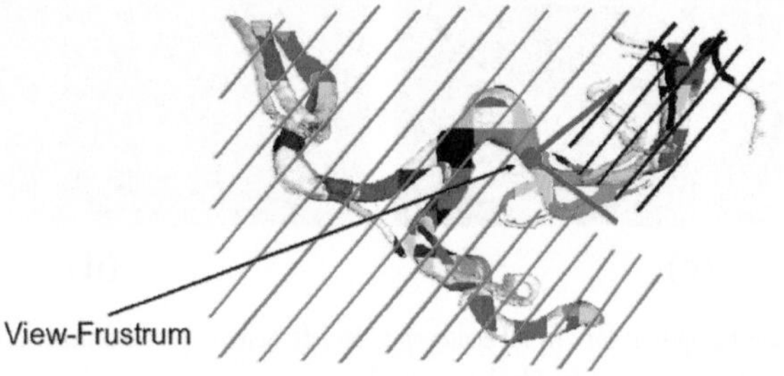

FIGURE 13.7 *An arterial cerebral blood vessel tree is culled. The different colored blocks are an octree decomposition of the geometry of the model. The red lines show the view frustum, whereas the red circle indicates the view-position. The green hatched area shows the geometry culled by view frustum culling, the blue hatched area shows the geometry culled by occlusion culling (Courtesy of Dirk Bartz, University of Leipzig).*

View frustum culling tests if the object is at least partially located within the view frustum. If not, the whole object cannot be visible from the current viewpoint. Usually, view frustum culling will not check the whole object, but only the vertices of its bounding volume (BV). These vertices represented by that BV are transformed according to the viewing transformation and then tested if they are within the view frustum. This approach has one major drawback: If the BV contains the whole view frustum—a rare but possible configuration—none of the BV vertices will be within the view frustum. Hence, the test will incorrectly return that the object is not visible Bartz *et al.* [1999a].

While the previous culling techniques are fairly standard, the actually used *occlusion culling* approach can be very diverse. Cohen-Or *et al.* [2003] presented a survey of a variety of culling and visibility approaches. A standard approach utilizes *occlusion queries* that are supported by the hardware of modern graphics subsystems. The functionality of this *occlusion culling flag* was first used by Bartz and Skalej [1999]. After view frustum culling, the remaining objects intersecting with the view frustum are processed from front to back (view frustum culling implicitly depth sorts the objects).[4] First, the BV of the front-most object is tested for occlusion using the occlusion culling flag. If the BV of this object is not occluded (which does not mean that it is visible, since we are conservative), it is rendered. Otherwise, it is culled and the algorithm tests the next object. There are numerous improvements of the basic algorithm, such as using a test hierarchy [Staneker *et al.*, 2004], using an occupancy map to avoid redundant occlusion queries [Staneker *et al.*, 2003], and to group individual queries [Staneker *et al.*, 2006] to reduce the query overhead. Scharsach *et al.* [2006] described a culling strategy for hybrid rendering (recall § 13.4.3). They created a brick structure, consisting of $8 \times 8 \times 8$ voxel-sized bricks. Based on this data structure, they employed an objects-space empty space skipping.

Note that transparency modulation and occlusion culling do not fit well together. A translucent representation allows to see behind translucent object—a concept that violates the very idea of occlusion. Moreover, occlusion culling queries are best processed in a front to back manner, while transparency requires a back to front sorting for correct blending. However, if the respective scene elements are carefully sorted and tested, they can be still used together [Bartz *et al.*, 2003].

Stereo Rendering For the perception of spatial relations, stereo rendering may provide additional and useful depth cues. Although conventional endoscopes generate monoscopic images so far, there were early efforts to provide stereo rendering in virtual endoscopy [Lorensen, 1995, Gobbetti *et al.*, 1998]. Stereo rendering requires more computational power and either users have to wear glasses or autostereoscopic monitors need to be employed. So far, there were no large studies that investigate whether the additional effort is justified by a significantly improved accuracy in diagnosis or treatment planning.

13.5 USER INTERFACES FOR VIRTUAL ENDOSCOPY

The efficient use of virtual endoscopy requires that a number of tasks are efficiently and intuitively supported by appropriate user interfaces and interaction facilities. This relates to

- the interactive exploration of the endoscopic view,
- the integration of the endoscopic view with other views on the data as well as,
- a number of settings that adjust display options in the view components.

Thus, both 3D interaction and GUI design are essential. Within the endoscopic view, camera control is important and thus discussed in detail. GUI design may be inspired by the interaction facilities provided to control fiber endoscopes. Often, these provide a number of sliders to adjust, e.g., the brightness and controls to adapt the angle of the optical system. A less obvious interaction is point picking [Gobbetti *et al.*, 1998] which is essential to interactively annotate features or measure distances. Annotation of findings and measurement of distances are crucial for a diagnostic report and for treatment decisions.

4 The actual occlusion status of the tested objects depends on the traversal order. Since front-most objects typically occlude objects in the back, they should also be tested and rendered first.

13.5.1 CAMERA CONTROL AND NAVIGATION

If a predefined path exists, video recorder functionality such as forward, backward, and speed control are provided to explore the prerendered endoscopic views. This, however, is not appropriate if a movement is only possible in the forward direction of that path, since users miss a substantial fraction of pathologies. In fiber endoscopy the endoscope tip may be flexibly rotated at least in the horizontal direction to create more views from the current position. In principle, moving the endoscope forward and backward and rotating it enables to see the whole cavity except for large complex-shaped folds. Thus, rotation should be provided in an intuitive way (users should be able to rotate the endoscope without looking at some distant interface controls). We discussed such controls also for conventional viewing of (axial) slices where brightness, contrast, and the selected slice should be modified with cursor keys instead of sliders that require to shift the focus of visual attention (recall § 3.6.6).

Orientation Cues in Virtual Endoscopy To understand the current viewing direction, the use of small 3D geometries, like orientation cubes or simplified skeletons for *external* views, was discussed in § 5.6.2. In virtual endoscopy, the orientation cues should be integrated in the endoscopic view, of course, without heavily obstructing it. Dirk Bartz employed a double pyramid to indicate the camera position and orientation [Bartz *et al.*, 1999b, 2001, 2003]. This structure is shown outlined to reduce occlusion and labeled with the anatomical directions, such as "ventral," and "dorsal." The SinusEndoscopy system [Krüger *et al.*, 2008] employs three orthogonal lines, representing a coordinate system in the endoscopic view and a straight line in the associated 2D view. In the 2D views, the orientation of the lines represents the orientation of the camera and the start point of the lines indicates the camera position for the endoscopic view (Fig. 13.13, page 536).

Forward and Backward Navigation In addition, investigation in virtual colonoscopy clearly reveals that users detect more pathologies if also a rear view is provided and used (95% instead of 70% [Dachille *et al.*, 2001]).[5] Thus, either the whole exploration along the path should be performed twice in forward and backward direction or at least at any point the user should be able to generate a rear view [Vilanova *et al.*, 1999]. The investigation in both directions is also referred to as "tandem colonoscopy," a term that is used in the review article from [van Rijn *et al.*, 2006].

Reliable Navigation A specific variation of the planned navigation approach is *reliable navigation* [He and Hong, 1999], where viewing of all interior surface parts is guaranteed. This, however, can also result in an over-coverage of parts of the cavity, and thus in a lower examination efficiency. Note that planned navigation does not require an interactive volume rendering, since no user interaction is involved.

Navigation Strategies To support the navigation paradigm, three different options are available [Hong *et al.*, 1997]:

- automatic navigation,
- manual or free navigation, and
- guided navigation.

Automatic or planned navigation relies on a predefined camera path through the representation of the respective body cavity. This camera path must specify positions and view directions (orientations) of the virtual

5 Hikers often notice that when they return a path they recognize many features that they did not notice when they moved along the path in the opposite direction.

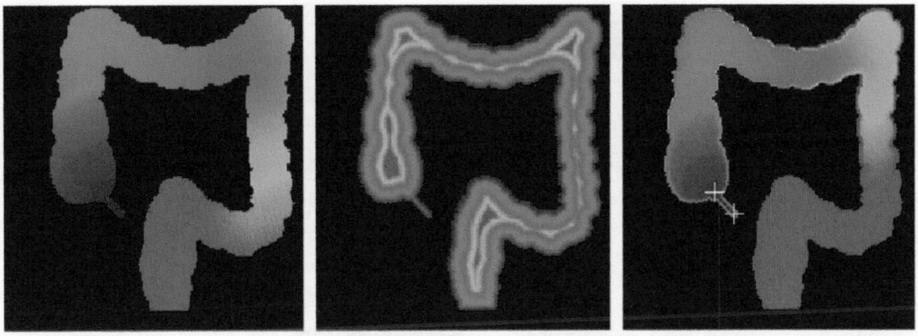

FIGURE 13.8 *Distance maps for guided navigation.* **Left:** *distance to target (blue).* **Middle:** *Distance to surface.* **Right:** *Combined distance map. The distance-to-surface influence is only visible at the surface boundary [Hong et al., 1997] (Courtesy of Shigeru Muraki, AIST Japan).*

camera. Afterwards, a fly-through is computed based on that path. While this option offers a good overview of the target area, it requires the refinement of the camera path—and the subsequent regeneration of the fly-through—to capture details that were previously not sufficiently visible.

In *manual or free navigation* the camera is transformed freely. For virtual endoscopy applications, free navigation poses severe difficulties due to the high complexity of many body cavities. Furthermore, the lack of collision avoidance mechanisms, and the difficulties adding those to a free navigation system, worsen this issue. Since free navigation relies on the direct interaction of the user with the system, it also requires interactive rendering speed. Lags between interaction and the resulting rendering accumulate and cannot be tolerated.

The best option for virtual endoscopy combines navigation flexibility with guidance and is hence called *guided navigation*. It combines a set of constraints which guide the user to a predefined target area. This strategy is often referred to as *auto-piloting* [Ge *et al.*, 1996]. It typically indicates the distal end of a body cavity. Hong *et al.* [1997] implemented a guided navigation system by employing a set of distance maps that are interpreted as potential fields. One type of distance maps (see Fig. 13.8, left) implements a current toward the target area (blue), and another type (middle) implements a collision avoidance system (see [Hong *et al.*, 1997] for details). The potential field approach is motivated by the *submarine metaphor*. Thus, according to the potential field, the submarine glides toward a goal.

If these fields are combined (Fig. 13.8, right) and explored with a physically-based camera model, this system realizes an intuitive navigation system. They compare a combined navigation model with a microfied submarine traveling through a blood stream inside the body, a scenario of the academy award movie "Fantastic Voyage" (20th Century Fox, 1966).

13.5.2 VIEWS FOR INTERACTIVE VIRTUAL ENDOSCOPY

An essential user interface aspect for any interactive virtual endoscopy solution is the selection of views, their initial layout and the interaction facilities offered to change that layout. The internal 3D view is not sufficient to provide enough orientation cues and to precisely locate pathologies or other relevant features, e.g., for surgical planning. The following views are often provided along with the virtual endoscopic view:

- an external 3D rendering,
- a plane that displays the cross section corresponding to the camera position and orientation,

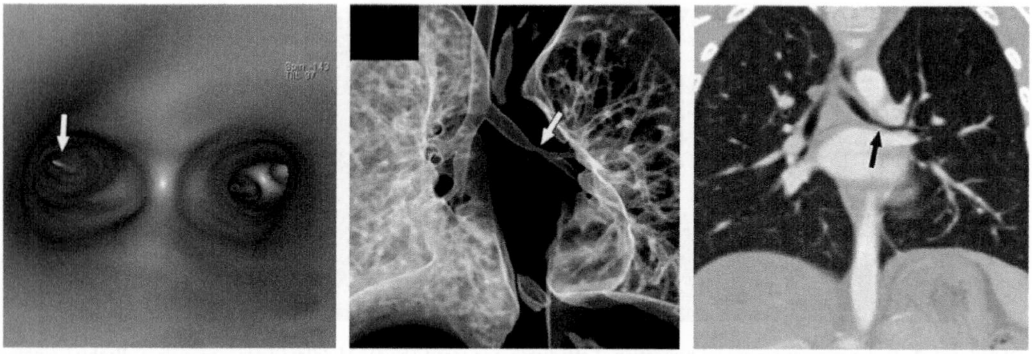

FIGURE 13.9 *Multiple-coordinated views assist the assessment of polyps during virtual colonoscopy.* ***Left:*** *The 3D unfolded cube display (ViewForum, Philips Healthcare; [serlie et al., 2001a]) is used for fly-throughs.* ***Middle:*** *The reformatted slice view shows a detail view of the polyp, in this case submerged under contrast-enhanced residual stool.* ***Right:*** *The external 3D volume rendering shows the global approximate location of the polyp (Courtesy o Iwo Serlie, Philips Healthcare. See also [Horton et al., 2007]).*

- an axial slice view, and
- further reformatted slice views (sagittal and coronal views).

They are combined such that interactions, e.g., selections, are synchronized between the different multiple coordinated views: Figure 13.9 gives an example for combined views in a virtual colonoscopy system.

An external 3D rendering should be employed to provide an overview on the target cavity. It might also be used to show the (precomputed) path. This external rendering is sometimes referred to as "bird's eye view," indicating the overview character [Lorensen, 1995].

These additional views need to be synchronized with the virtual endoscopic view to provide an effective exploration. Thus, the user should easily recognize how the endoscopic view relates to the other views and where certain findings are. The additional views literally provide a different perspective on the data and enable to double check whether a suspicious area is indeed (with high likelihood) a pathology. In particular virtual endoscopy based on surface rendering critically depends on the selected threshold. Suspicious areas may turn out as artifacts when looking in cross-sectional or other slice views. These additional views occupy screen space and may strongly reduce the space for the main endoscopic view. Thus, it should be possible to enlarge the endoscopic view or switch to a full screen mode where the whole display space is available for the endoscopic view. Virtual endoscopy benefits from a multimonitor solution or a large display device (recall § 3.6.6.2).

13.5.3 GRAPHICAL USER INTERFACE

Research systems and systems for clinical practice vary in their functionality and user interface. While research systems are typically proof-of-concepts, they are often a starting point for a commercial system. The critical difference between the available commercial systems, however, is often not the available rendering speed or quality, but lies in the careful arrangement of their functionality. In particular, the adaptation of the system to the clinical routine of a hospital or any other doctor's practice is important [Pickhardt, 2003].

13.5.4 INPUT DEVICES

While most professional workspaces in medicine are still equipped with mouse and keyboard, these input devices are not optimal for camera control and other tasks. Camera control, for example, in some computer games is often performed with a joystick that enables intuitive control of speed and direction. Similarly, Wolfsberger *et al.* [2004] were the first to employ a joystick combined with collision detection and haptic feedback to enable steering of the virtual endoscope.

Gobbetti *et al.* [1998] already investigated the use of a 3D Space Ball and a viscous friction force field for camera control (recall the discussion of input devices in § 5.7). Heng *et al.* [1999] suggested a pen as input device to modify the path and to control the virtual camera in virtual bronchoscopy. Later, Krüger *et al.* [2008] compared the effectiveness of a 3D Space Ball, the Phantom and a pen attached to a graphics tablet and could show that users could follow a predefined path through the nasal cavities faster and more accurate than with the 2D mouse. This result indicates the potential of these input devices, since the users (ENT surgeons) were very familiar with the mouse and had no experience with the other input devices. However, despite these research efforts, examples of the use of such advanced input devices are almost impossible to find.

13.6 APPLICATIONS

Virtual endoscopy plays an essential role for a large number of diagnostic and treatment planning tasks. In the following, we describe three selected diagnostic applications:

- virtual colonoscopy,
- virtual bronchoscopy, and
- virtual angioscopy.

These applications were selected, since they are widespread and computer support in these areas is mature. The specific names relate to the specific cavity that is explored from inside. In case of colonoscopy, this is the colon where polyps are searched. Virtual bronchoscopy aims at an exploration of the bronchial tree, in particular to search direct or indirect signs of lung cancer, and angioscopy is a term that summarizes all endoscopy-like renderings in vascular structures, such as the coronary or cerebral arteries.

As an example for a treatment planning application, we discuss transphenosoidal surgery of the pituitary gland in § 13.6.4.

13.6.1 VIRTUAL COLONOSCOPY

Medical Background The colon is a part of the human alimentary system that temporarily stores waste material and absorbs vitamins and water [Zhao, 2011]. Colon cancer is a frequent type of cancer and the third leading cause of cancer death in the Western world. However, if detected early, the five-year survival rate exceeds 90% [McFarland *et al.*, 2008]. Thus, prevention and early detection of colon cancer have an essential importance.

Colon cancer occurs at the colon wall as a consequence of mutations in the cell division process. Colonoscopy aims at exploring the colon wall to detect inflamed tissue, ulcers, and polyps. Such polyps are caps on the colon wall that have a certain risk to transform into malignant cancer. This risk strongly depends on the size of the polyp and since the polyps usually grow slowly before they eventually transform into cancer, larger polyps are clinically more relevant. There is an ongoing debate on the threshold for clinical relevance and the necessity of treatment; 6, 8, or even 10 mm are often considered as the threshold. Thus, the sensitivity and specificity of polyp detection is the major criterion for colonoscopy and virtual colonoscopy as well. In the revised guidelines for colon cancer prevention and diagnosis McFarland *et al.* [2008] summarize the results of more than 6,000 patients where virtual colonoscopy was applied, and based on a sensitivity of 90% for detecting polyps sized 10 mm or larger they recommend virtual colonoscopy as comparable to optical colonoscopy.

There are also a number of studies, which report considerably lower sensitivity and specificity. However, in these studies, either suboptimal image data were used or physicians had low experience. Thus, virtual colonoscopy requires experienced readers and all aspects, including preparation, need to be performed in a standardized high quality. At the same time, the radiation exposure should be reduced, in particular, if virtual colonoscopy is used as a screening method.

Currently, optical colonoscopy and barium enema are the major procedures available for examining the entire colon to detect clinically relevant polyps. Since colon cancer, similar to other types of cancer, primarily affects older people, colonoscopy was established as a screening procedure for people over 50 years of age (one examination every 10 years is recommended). In optical colonoscopy, a fiber-optic probe, called a *colonoscope*, is introduced into the colon through the rectum. By manipulating the tiny camera attached to the tip of the probe, the physician examines the inner surface of the colon to identify abnormalities. Due to the complex geometry of the colon wall with many folds and deep valleys it is difficult to reach all areas. This invasive procedure takes about half an hour and requires intravenous sedation (taking some extra time), resulting in high costs. Barium enema in contrast requires a great deal of physical cooperation from the patient when the X-ray radiographs of the colon are taken at different views. Additionally, its sensitivity can be as low as 78% in detecting polyps in the range of 5–20 mm [Morosi *et al.*, 1991].

Rendering for Virtual Colonoscopy Optical colonoscopy and barium enema are expensive or circumstantial making them less ideal for screening examinations. Also patient acceptance is low. Consequently, virtual colonoscopy was proposed to limit optical colonoscopy to cases in which either a suspicious polyp was found (which induced a biopsy or removal of the polyp) or which were inconclusive in virtual colonoscopy [Vining *et al.*, 1994a]. The latter happens if (shape) defects of the graphical representation of the inner colon surface cannot be identified as polyps or residual stool.

After cleansing and inflating of the colon (both actions are also required for optical colonoscopy), a CT or MRI scan is performed. The resulting image stack is pre-processed and examined using a virtual endoscopy system. Usually, a path is generated that starts at the proximal end of the colon and ends at the rectum (Fig. 13.10). Hong *et al.* [1997] compare the results of optical and virtual endoscopy based on polyps found in both procedures. In particular, they compare snapshots of two polyps (see Fig. 13.11). The first polyp (see Fig. 13.11, left) is located in the descending colon, close to the sigmoid colon (lower arrow). It is of a size of 8 mm and hence of high clinical relevance. Figure 13.11 (top row) images show the information represented by optical colonoscopy, while bottom row images show the information provided by virtual colonoscopy. The shape information of the polyp is well represented by the virtual technique. However, texture information is not available, while it is very helpful in optical colonoscopy (although not obvious in Fig. 13.11, top row) to identify false positive polyps, which are often remaining stool and residual fluids.

The second polyp is of a size of 4 mm and it is located in the transverse colon, not too far away from the hepatic (right) flexure (upper left arrow). Similar to the previous polyp, the actual location is quite different from the rough estimation in the overview image of optical colonoscopy, which locates the polyp in the ascending colon (see Fig. 13.11, middle).

A study of the advantages of virtual colonoscopy compared to optical or conventional colonoscopy was presented by Fenlon *et al.* [1999]. The authors found that the performance of virtual colonoscopy is comparable to optical, as long as the data resolution is sufficient to detect polyps of the respective size. Problems arose due to residual stool, which often was the cause of a false positive finding.

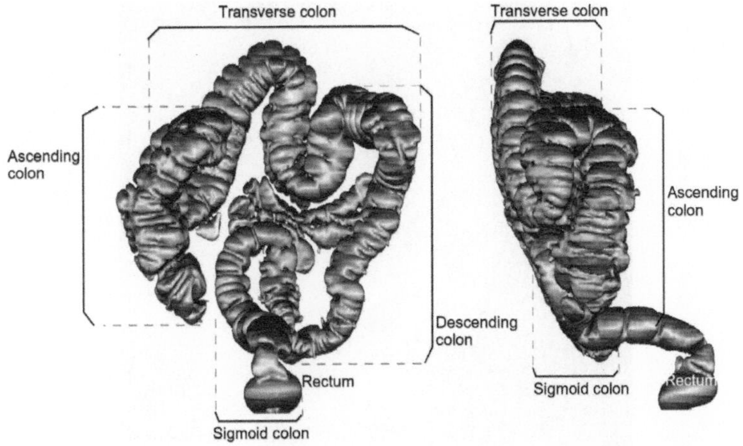

FIGURE 13.10 *Colon dataset. The colon is composed of ascending colon, transverse colon, and descending colon. After the sigmoid colon it exits through the rectum. The left image shows a coronal view, the right image shows a sagittal view (Courtesy of Dirk Bartz, University of Leipzig).*

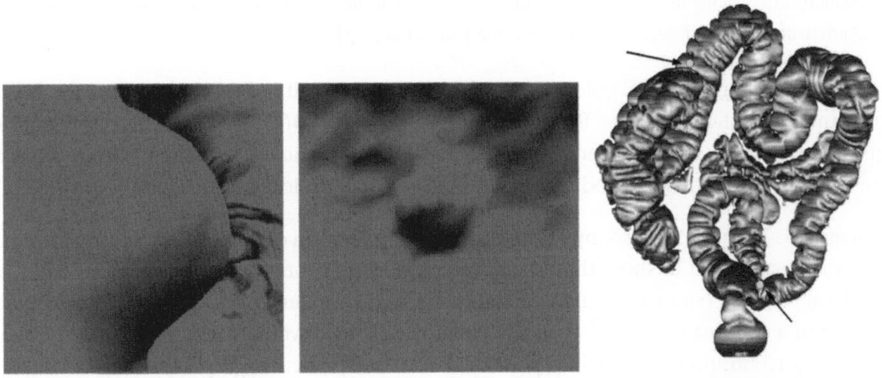

FIGURE 13.11 *Polyps in virtual colonoscopy. Polyps in virtual colonoscopy.* **Left:** *An 8 mm polyp;* **middle:** *A 4 mm polyp;* **right:** *colon overview. The top arrow (yellow marker) indicates the 4 mm polyp, the bottom arrow (yellow marker) indicates the 8 mm polyp (From [Hong et al., 1997]).*

Pickhardt et al. [2003] presented an even larger study[6] that essentially confirmed the findings by Fenlon et al. [1999]. Interestingly, they found several positively identified polyps in virtual colonoscopy which had not been found in the initial optical colonoscopy. Only after a re-examination taking into account the virtual colonoscopy information, these polyps were identified by optical colonoscopy.

Pickhardt et al. [2003] also pointed out that the result of virtual colonoscopy depends significantly on the dataset preparation and the way how virtual colonoscopy is applied. Digital cleansing of the data (tagging of identified stool and residual fluids) enabled a better surface representation of the colon. Furthermore, they showed that a full 3D representation enables a better polyp identification instead of the examination of

6 A large subset of datasets used for that study can be found at http://nova.nlm.nih.gov/WRAMC. Every approach on identifying polyps should be benchmarked with these datasets to get comparable results.

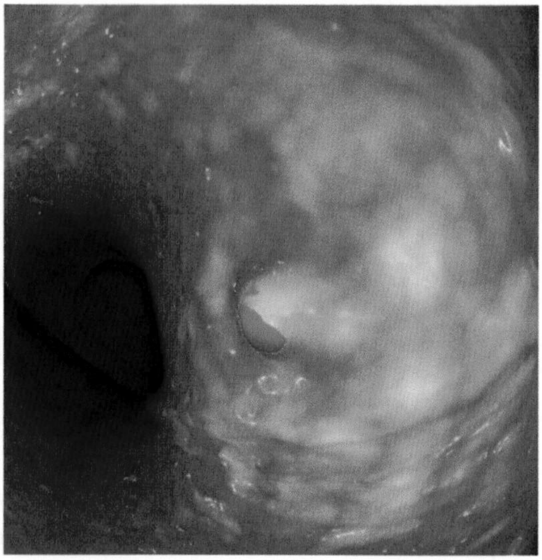

FIGURE 13.12 *A polyp is detected based on curvature analysis and emphasized with a uniform color. The colon wall is rendered using a non-photorealistic shading model in order to minimize distractions for the viewer, thus enabling them to focus on curvature highlights (Courtesy of Christoph Russ, ETH Zurich. See also [Russ et al., 2010]).*

the axial slices only. Overall, virtual colonoscopy achieved a sensitivity of more than 88% for polyps larger than 6 mm, and a specificity close to 80% (see McFarland *et al.* [2008] for a summary of other studies). Radiologists experienced in virtual endoscopy achieve this diagnostic accuracy within approximately 15 minutes, which makes this method significantly faster than optical colonoscopy [Zhao, 2011].

Electronic Cleansing Virtual colonoscopy requires careful preparation of patients, including cathartic bowel preparation and insufflation to show the tissue boundary more pronounced. For correct diagnosis of the colon wall, fecal residues (stool and fluid) need to be tagged completely. This is usually performed by oral administration of a contrast material,[7] typically barium. This inconvenient procedure may be replaced by image processing techniques in principle [Lakare *et al.*, 2000]. The image processing variant is referred to as *electronic cleansing*. More advanced methods were later introduced by Wang *et al.* [2005b] and Näppi and Yoshida [2008]. However, due to partial volume effects and artifacts, this procedure may also remove diagnostically relevant information. An overview of electronic cleansing is given by Cai and Yoshida [2011].

Combining CAD and Virtual Colonoscopy In § 3.6.4.2 we briefly discussed computer-aided detection methods that support the diagnosis of polyps along the colon wall. Most of these schemes analyze surface curvature to find suspicious regions and emphasize the polyp cap. Such CAD schemes may be combined with virtual colonoscopy to intuitively reveal where the lesions occur [Zhao *et al.*, 2006]. The workflow (recall Fig. 13.1) is enhanced by including CAD after surface reconstruction. Thus, instead of realistically displaying only the colon wall, relevant features, such as principal curvature directions, are overlaid in the endoscopic view (see Fig. 13.12).

Projection Techniques Finally, it should be mentioned that projection techniques (recall Chap. 14) are also relevant for virtual colonoscopy. In particular, colon unfolding was developed in order to show all relevant

7 Please note that this contrast material is strongly different from contrast agents used in CT angiography.

aspects of the colon wall at a glance without occlusion, see § 14.3.3. Of course, this overview is achieved at the expense of distortions. Thus, in unfortunate situations, diagnostically relevant polyps are distorted too heavily to be correctly assessed. In summary, the projection view should not be the only display of the colon wall that is actually looked at.

13.6.2 VIRTUAL BRONCHOSCOPY

Virtual bronchoscopy summarizes internal renderings of the bronchial tree based on CT and MRI data (with CT being the dominant modality) [Ferguson and McLennan, 2005]. Data with high spatial and temporal resolution is acquired during breath hold. Virtual bronchoscopy is promising, e.g., for planning and guiding biopsies [Negahdar *et al.*, 2006]. The first clinical report of diagnosing 20 patients with virtual bronchoscopy is from Vining *et al.* [1996]. The survey article from Ferguson and McLennan [2005] lists a number of crucial requirements for computer support:

- accurate visualization of airway structures,
- accurate visualization of the relation to adjacent structures, e.g., vascular structures, and
- the ability to correctly measure pathological variations, e.g., size and width of a stenosis.

In the following, we briefly explain the medical background and later discuss rendering for virtual bronchoscopy.

Medical Background The exchange of the air takes place in the lungs within the blood and airway vessels. Both systems consist of pipe-like structures, which split successively into smaller ones creating the blood vessel and tracheo-bronchial tree. The trachea connects the bronchial tree with the upper airways. At the main bifurcation, the main bronchi branch supplies the left and right lung. Inhaled air is distributed in the bronchial tree down to the alveoli where the oxygen/carbon dioxide exchange takes place. The exhausted air is transported back to the trachea during exhale. The lung function may be hampered by a number of pathologies, such as tumors (lung cancer), pulmonary embolism, emphysema, fibrosis, tubercolosis, and asthma. Fiber bronchoscopy plays an essential role in the diagnosis of such diseases, in the precise localization as well as in planning further interventions such as biopsy or lung surgery. Since fiber bronchoscopy is an invasive procedure that requires anesthesia and carries a risk for complications, e.g., by hurting segments of the bronchial tree, virtual bronchoscopy was developed and refined to restrict the use of fiber bronchoscopy.

Pulmonary Diseases and CT Data For the diagnosis of pulmonary diseases, CT is still the dominant modality due to the good contrast between air-filled and surrounding structures. The advances in CT scanner technology enabling data acquisition with higher spatial and temporal resolution, were crucial for virtual bronchoscopy, since the thorax region is particularly susceptible for motion artifacts. With 64-multislice technology, the image acquisition is fast enough to scan the whole thorax during breath hold even in case of severely ill patients or children. The spatial resolution enables to trace the bronchial tree to the fifth or sixth branching order. According to more recent publications, even the 7th and 8th branching order may be extracted [Ferguson and McLennan, 2005]. A number of clinical investigations indicate that tracheal and bronchial abnormalities, such as stenosis and obstructions are identified with high sensitivity. Hoppe *et al.* [2004] determined a sensitivity of 98% in detecting tracheobronchial stenosis (compared to 96% with pure slice-based viewing). However, in particular at the segmental level of bronchii the specificity is rather low (below 50% in [Hoppe *et al.*, 2004]). As Boiselle *et al.* [2002] point out, secretions may easily be confused with polypoid lesions, leading to false positives.

Use Cases for Virtual Bronchoscopy Virtual bronchoscopy is also employed to precisely measure length and width of obstructing lesions. This is an essential advantage compared to fiber bronchoscopy where the obstruction often blocks the passage and thus prevents to fully assess and quantify a lesion. The only major limitation is that mucosal abnormalities, such as mucosal infiltration, are not visible in CT data and in derived endoscopic views [Wever *et al.*, 2004].

While the diagnosis of airway lesions is an established application, more complex applications are currently evaluated. Among them is the guidance for biopsies and other interventions, where spatial relations, e.g., between lymph nodes and the bronchial tree need to be correctly depicted [Ferguson and McLennan, 2005]. A review article from Jones *et al.* [2005] summarizes 27 studies that compare virtual and conventional fiber bronchoscopy. The majority of the patients considered in all these studies was diagnosed with lung cancer (63%), rendering this suspicion as the most important diagnosis. The second most essential patient group had a lung transplantation and bronchoscopy was performed to evaluate potential anastomotic abnormalities.

Rendering for Virtual Bronchoscopy Surface rendering is the most dominant rendering technique in virtual bronchoscopy, as a large number of clinical reports indicate. It requires a careful adjustment of thresholds. One global threshold does not enable the visualization of the whole bronchial tree [Wever *et al.*, 2004]. Instead, results acquired with different thresholds need to be combined. This is due to the partial volume effect that leads to different intensity values for voxels belonging to thinner or thicker portions of the bronchial wall. Wever *et al.* [2004] employed a threshold of −520 HU for the central bronchial tree and decreased that value to −720 HU for the most distal (small) portions of the bronchial tree. Similarly, Hoppe *et al.* [2004] recommended to adjust the threshold for the central airway between −400 and −550 HU and to reduce this value down to −800 HU for distal branches. This combination of thresholds is similar to an explicit segmentation of the bronchial tree that was described by Bartz *et al.* [2003]. They refined a region growing approach with different thresholds to cope with the varying intensities. Figure 13.13 illustrates their virtual bronchoscopy system. Hoppe *et al.* [2004] argue that not only the threshold

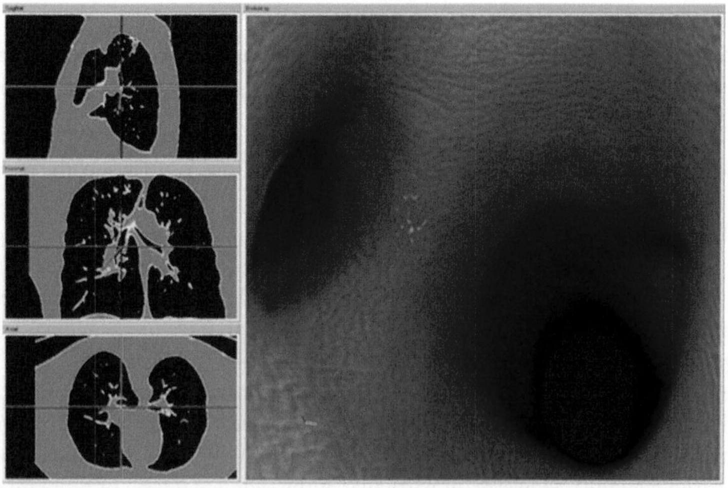

FIGURE 13.13 *A virtual bronchoscopy view and the associated orthogonal slice views (Courtesy of Christoph Kubisch, University of Magdeburg).*

but also the cone angle of the endoscope should be adapted to the caliber of the bronchial segments (they recommend to adjust the angle between 50° and 80°.

Surprisingly few papers discuss path planning for virtual bronchoscopy. Among them is the work of Heng *et al.* [1999], who argue for a restricted movement along the centerlines that are determined semi-automatically based on paths with a minimum cost.

13.6.3 VIRTUAL ANGIOSCOPY

For diagnostic tasks as well as for planning vascular interventions, virtual fly-throughs in vascular structures are a useful option [Gobbetti *et al.*, 1998]. In particular the search for arterial wall changes, such as plaques, stenoses, and thrombus formation in case of atherosclerosis, e.g., in the coronary arteries benefits from the guided exploration of the internal vessel lumen [van Ooijen *et al.*, 2007, 2000]. Also the planning of endovascular stent grafts or the later control of implanted stents benefits from endoscopic renderings [Sun *et al.*, 2010]. This is a special instance of virtual endoscopy, called ***virtual angioscopy***. The feasibility of virtual angioscopy in particular for the assessment of the coronary arteries was strongly improved by recent developments of CT technology that enable a higher spatial and temporal resolution. Also dual source CTs with their better ability to discriminate different tissue types enabled more expressive virtual angioscopy, in particular of coronary arteries [van Ooijen *et al.*, 2007]. Figure 13.14 integrates a slice view, an overview rendering and an endoscopic view. In Figure 13.15 the endoluminal visualization of a stent in the carotid arteries is visible.

Some of the described vessel visualization methods, e.g., model-based approaches using cylinders or truncated cones (recall Chap. 11) are not appropriate for virtual angioscopy at all due to the construction of polygons inside the vessel lumen. Other model-based approaches facilitate a fly-through. However, their accuracy is not sufficient for planning vascular surgery. Instead, model-free approaches are more suitable. It is essential to combine detailed views of the inner structures with an overview of the anatomical structures (see Fig. 13.16). A specific transfer function design that emphasizes the vessel wall as well as calcified plaques and stents was introduced in § 11.7.2 [Kubisch *et al.*, 2012].

Implicit Surfaces Vascular surfaces computed with implicit surface representations (recall [Hong *et al.*, 2012, Wu *et al.*, 2010]) have the advantage that collision detection of the virtual camera with the vessel

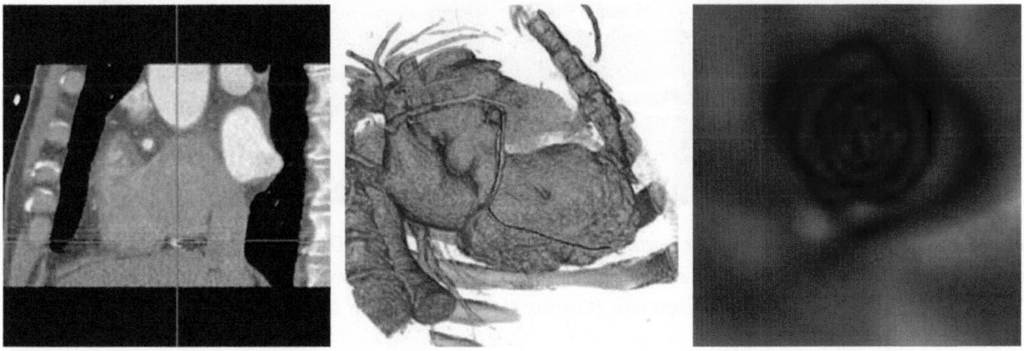

FIGURE 13.14 *Three views are combined to explore the carotid arteries. The left view shows a reformatted slice of the CT data with the camera position emphasized. The volume rendering in the middle presents an overview and shows the trajectory of the whole path that the virtual camera takes. Again, the current position is emphasized. With this information, the endoscopic view on the right may be better explored (From: [van Ooijen et al., 2007]).*

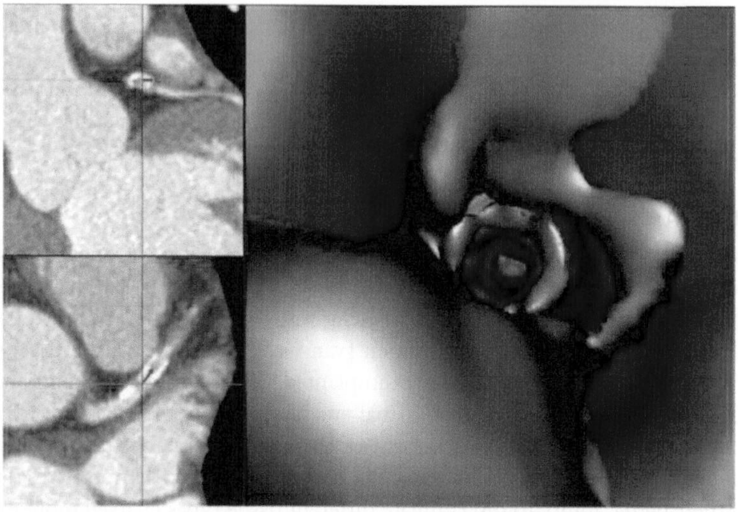

FIGURE 13.15 *In the main view on the right, a stent in the carotid arteries is explored to assess whether it remains in a correct position. The two slice views on the left indicate the position and orientation of the virtual camera (From: [van Ooijen et al., 2007]).*

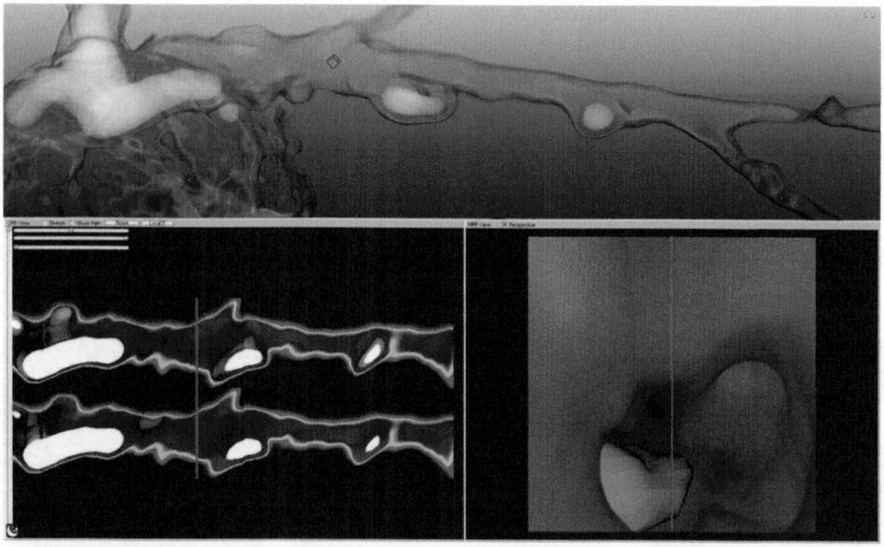

FIGURE 13.16 *Virtual angioscopy for the diagnosis of a coronary heart disease. A 3D overview shows a large coronary vessel and the plaque inside. A small sign indicates the camera position for the endoscopic view (lower right). The vertical line in the lower left 2D view corresponds to the line in the endoscopic view (Courtesy of Christoph Kubisch, NVIDIA).*

walls may be easily performed. The underlying implicit function evaluates to zero, if a point $p(x, y, z)$ is on the wall and the sign of the result indicates whether p is inside or outside. This kind of signed distance function replaces the computation of a potential field that is used in other endoscopy methods. However, the potential field could also be used for guidance within a vascular surface. The implicit surface reconstruction requires other mechanisms to steer the virtual camera, once the centerline was left. Moreover, the smoothness of these shapes is beneficial. Hong *et al.* [2011] introduced a virtual angioscopy system that employs indeed the implicit spline surface representation discussed in Hong *et al.* [2012].

Applications A dedicated application of virtual angioscopy, namely the diagnosis of neurovascular diseases, was described in [Bartz *et al.*, 1999b]. The navigation inside vascular structures is usually accomplished with guided navigation concepts, used in other areas of virtual endoscopy, e.g., virtual colonoscopy. Virtual angioscopy was also an important aspect of the Virtual Vasculature project [Abdoulaev *et al.*, 1998, Pili *et al.*, 1997] that is dedicated to the exploration of cerebral vessels. In this project, virtual angioscopy is combined with vascular fluid dynamic simulations.

Although the exploration of the coronary arteries is by far the most essential application of virtual endoscopy, the technique is not restricted to this region. Virtual angioscopy may also be applied to cerebral vasculature [Bartz *et al.*, 1999b]. In particular, the assessment of cerebral aneurysms [Colpan *et al.*, 2007] and the control of implanted stents [Orbach *et al.*, 2006] benefits from virtual angioscopy.

Virtual angioscopy of the pulmonary arteries supports the detection of pulmonary embolisms [Sun *et al.*, 2010].

13.6.4 VIRTUAL ENDOSCOPY FOR MINIMALLY-INVASIVE NEUROSURGERY

After discussing three essential diagnostic applications, we shall discuss an intervention in the brain as an example for surgical applications of virtual endoscopy. For surgeons, it is essential to become familiar with the relevant patient anatomy and its peculiarities, in particular with risky constellations (see Chap. 17). Endoscopic viewing enhanced with tools to clip obstructing geometry and to measure distances supports this process. The particular intervention is minimally-invasive surgery of the pituitary gland. Computer-assisted planning tools were developed in a long-term research project between the VRVis research center and the General hospital (both in Vienna, Austria, key researchers: Katja Bühler, PhD and Stefan Wolfsberger, MD). The following subsection briefly describes both the technical design and implementation of endoscopic planning tools as well as their clinical use.

The pituitary gland is an important part of the endocrine system of the body. It regulates the production and distribution of many hormones for many different tasks such as growth, milk production (of females), stimulation of the adrenal and thyroid glands, of ovaries and testes, and skin pigmentation. It is located in a small bone cavity, the *sella turcica* (near the base of the skull, and next to the brain and important blood vessels). The target anatomy is depicted in Figure 13.17.

Endoscopic Treatment of Pituitary Tumors An endoscopic intervention of the pituitary gland is usually performed in cases of a (typically benign) pituitary tumor. This tumor can cause headaches, impaired vision due to the compression of the optical nerve by the tumor, and most importantly an excess production of hormones, which in turn causes a severe imbalance of the endocrine system [Neubauer *et al.*, 2005]. This kind of surgery is very demanding, since the target anatomy is complex and difficult to fully understand with the limited field of view in endoscopy.

A standard interventional approach is endonasal transsphenoidal pituitary surgery, which uses a rigid rod-lens-based endoscope that accesses the target area through the nose (endonasal), the *sphenoid ostium* to the *sphenoid sinus* (transsphenoidal, see Fig. 13.18). Since the sphenoid ostium is usually too small to accommodate the endoscope, it must be enlarged by a bone puncher, a process that is called a *sphenoidotomy*. The same applies to septa located in the sphenoid sinus. This step is also used to assess size and location of the pituitary gland and other important anatomical structures behind the floor of the *sella turcica* [Neubauer *et al.*, 2005]. The pituitary gland, and hence the tumor, is located behind this, which must be opened using

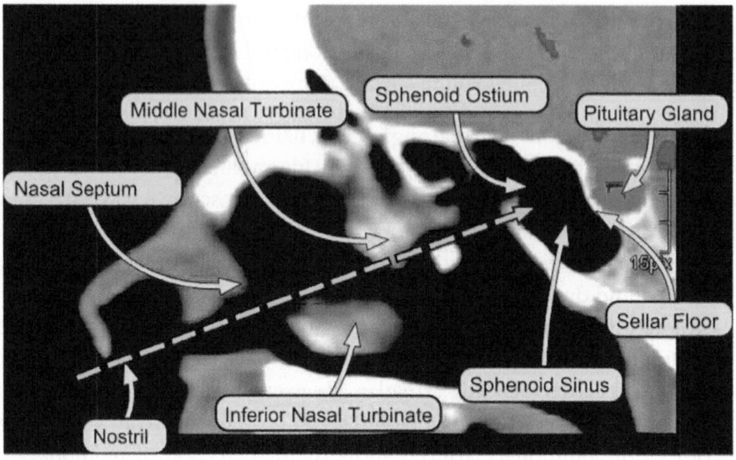

FIGURE 13.17 *The endonasal transphenoidal approach and the relevant anatomical structures (From: [Schulze et al., 2010]).*

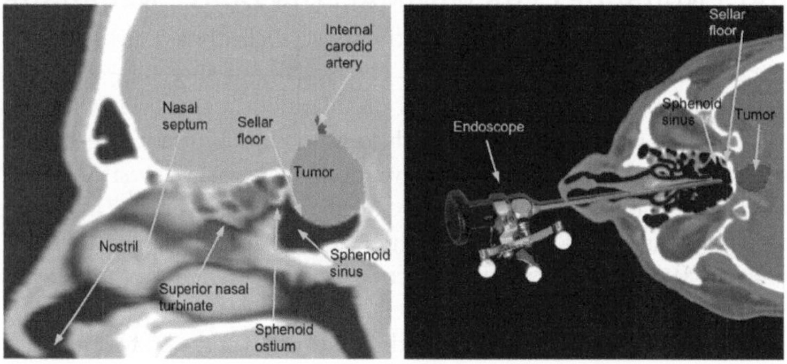

FIGURE 13.18 *Location of and approach to pituitary tumors. The endoscope approaches the pituitary gland through the nose and the sphenoid sinus. Sagittal (left) and axial (right) slice with segmented tumor (green) [Neubauer et al., 2005] (Courtesy of André Neubauer, VRVis Wien).*

a drill or a chisel. The bone puncher is again used to enlarge the opening for a full access of the tumor. Subsequently, the tumor can be removed. In case that the tumor is located within the pituitary gland, the gland must be dissected to provide access to the tumor. After the removal of the tumor, the new cavity must be filled with body tissue of the patient, such as fat and muscular tissue from the abdomen. The sella floor is reconstructed using available parts of the bone and fibrinous glue.

Due to the complex anatomy of the paranasal sinus, nearby arterial blood vessels, the pituitary gland and the brain tissue, a careful planning of the intervention is needed. Neubauer *et al.* [2005] presented a system—STEPS—for the planning of this intervention.

Virtual Endoscopy of the Pituitary Gland requires the identification of important anatomical structures for a proper visualization. Since this planning requires the representation of structures of the skull and a good soft-tissue contrast, CT and MRI scans of the patients are performed. Tumors of the pituitary gland can be quite small and may be difficult to segment [Neubauer *et al.*, 2005].

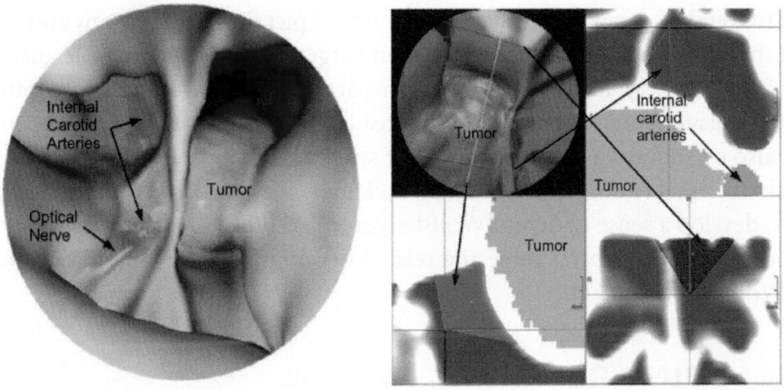

FIGURE 13.19 **Left:** *View from the sphenoid sinus to the pituitary gland (green) behind the sella floor. The segmented optical nerve (blue) and the internal carotid arteries (red) are also shown [Neubauer et al., 2005].* **Right:** *Endoscopic view of the tumor (bright green) of the pituitary gland with multiplanar reconstruction of the standard slices that contain the current viewpoint. The slices represent also their view contribution to the endoscopic view by representing the respective intersection of the slices with the endoscopic view in all four representations: sagittal (green), axial (red), coronal (blue) [Neubauer et al., 2004b].*

Direct volume rendering is performed as described in § 13.4.2. The surface of the endonasal structures and of the sphenoid structures is handled as *foreground object*, while tumor, pituitary gland, blood vessels, and optical nerve are treated as *background objects*. Figure 13.19 shows two examples of the virtual endoscopy of the pituitary gland. The left image shows a fused visualization of the sphenoid sinus, where the sella floor and the surrounding bone structure are rendered semi-transparent, thus exposing the tumor (bright green), the internal carotid arteries (red), and the optical nerve (blue). The pituitary gland is completely occluded by the tumor. The right image shows a similar situation, where only the tumor is visible in front of the pituitary gland. Next to the endoscopic view, three multiplanar slice projections (red, green, blue) are visible. These slice projections show the intersection of the slices with the segmented dataset from the current endoscopic viewpoint. Next to the endoscopic visualization of the virtual procedure, STEPS enable to simulate steps of the minimally-invasive procedure. In particular, it simulates several cutting tools that remove tissue during the procedure, such as the bone puncher. These tools actually change the data volumes of the respective tissue behind the impact region. This impact region is defined by a circular projection onto the surface of the tissue and the depth of the tissue before it enters the underlying tissue. Note, however, that a real tool defines the impact depth by the applied force and the material properties, not just by geometric means.

Clinical Evaluation Wolfsberger *et al.* [2006] report on the clinical use of the planning tools. Planning and surgery were performed in 32 patients with pituitary adenoma. CT imaging was used, since it provides a very good delineation of bony structures in the nasal cavity that serve as landmarks for orientation. Preoperative planning, including segmentation, image registration and exploration of the anatomy lasts 13 minutes on average [Schulze *et al.*, 2010]. A later more comprehensive report by Wolfsberger and Neubauer [2011] is based on more than 100 surgeries.

Deviations of the septum represent an essential anatomical variant that may be expressively visualized with the STEPS system. In some patients, a wide opening of the sella floor is required. This situation is risky, since surgery is close to the internal carotid artery that may not be damaged at all circumstances. Virtual endoscopy helped to evaluate the patient-specific risk. Also the clear display of the wideness of the nasal corridor, of bony landmarks and the location of the sphenoid ostium were useful.

In essence, virtual endoscopy was considered helpful to depict the nasal anatomy and the sphenoid sinus and it improved the intraoperative orientation later in surgery, since unpredictable anatomical variations are visualized prior to surgery. In particular, the transparent 3D visualization of the pituitary gland, the tumor and the adjacent anatomical landmarks was considered as helpful. Although the tool aims at surgical planning, it was also considered as a valuable tool for surgical training. Surgeons, however, also remarked a major drawback of virtual endoscopy, namely the lack of haptic feedback from immediate tissue contact that is essential to develop a sense of depth [Wolfsberger *et al.*, 2004]. A recent survey on the use of virtual endoscopy in neurosurgery compares these and related developments focusing on planning and training [Neubauer and Wolfsberger, 2013].

13.7 CONCLUDING REMARKS

Virtual endoscopy in the colon as well as in the bronchial and arterial trees is an essential diagnostic procedure, which provides complementary information compared to CT or MRI data and may replace fiber endoscopy for certain diagnostic questions. With dedicated support (adapted segmentation and path planning), the effort to prepare virtual endoscopy could be significantly reduced and a number of studies indicate that the remaining additional effort is justified to improve diagnostic accuracy and obtain additional relevant information. Navigation inside the cavities of the human body remains challenging. Collision detection and a simulation of haptic feedback in case that the walls of the cavity are touched may further improve the steering of the virtual camera. Virtual endoscopy cannot fully replace fiber endoscopy, which provides additional information that is essential to assess, e.g., mucosal abnormalities in the bronchial tree or in the paranasal airways.

Besides screening and diagnosis, virtual endoscopy is useful for planning interventions and may provide a *roadmap* for biopsies and related procedures. Ongoing research and development aims at combining preoperative virtual endoscopy with intraoperative navigation. A number of projects show that virtual endoscopy is also useful as a training tool and for patient consult. As a case study, we later discuss virtual endoscopy in the paranasal sinuses as part of the chapter on computer support in ENT surgery (Chap. 20).

Outlook Medical research papers on virtual endoscopy often contain labeled images. Instead of full anatomical names that could not be accommodated, numbers are used and explained in a legend. As an example from otoscopy, Rodt *et al.* [2002] contains six screenshots with five to ten labels each. Such labeled screenshots are highly useful for documentation. An interesting task for future research is to adapt labeling algorithms (recall Chap. 10) to the peculiarities of endoscopic views. Another task for documenting results is to contribute to a standardization of viewpoints for such screenshots. Ideally, camera position and orientation is chosen to show the same anatomical landmarks for different patients. Again, this is performed manually so far, see for example [Rodt *et al.*, 2002], but could be automatized as well.

FURTHER READING

It is interesting to read some clinical papers describing and illustrating specific diagnostic processes where virtual endoscopy plays an essential role. The pubmed database contains a large number of such papers. Wever *et al.* [2004] and Boiselle *et al.* [2002] contain many cases where virtual bronchoscopy is employed. There are more clinically relevant applications than could be described in this chapter. As an example, Shen et al. [2011] described virtual endoscopy for analyzing the gastric wall with the goal to detect cancer in an early stage.

Chapter e14

Projections and Reformations

14.1 INTRODUCTION

In 2002, the American Heart Association proposed a standardized segmentation and accompanying 2D Bull's Eye Plot of the myocardium, or heart muscle, of the left heart ventricle [Cerqueira *et al.*, 2002a]. Figure e14.1 shows how the Bull's Eye Plot (BEP) is constructed by projecting segments of the myocardium onto the horizontal plane, almost as if folding open the heart. Based on this standardized segmentation, information from 3D scans, such as for example the presence of scar tissue, can also be projected onto the Bull's Eye Plot and presented in a clear and unambiguous fashion. The cardiac BEP is a simple but excellent example of *reducing* complex 3D data to a standardized 2D representation that greatly facilitates the interpretation and communication of that data.

In medical visualization, there are a number of similar techniques that are employed to reduce 3D data, either by projection or reformation, to effective 2D visual representations. Straightforward projection, as employed in the standard 3D graphics pipeline, also serves to reduce 3D data to a 2D representation. However, in this chapter we discuss examples that go a step further in terms of complexity and effectiveness.

We have classified these reductive techniques broadly into two groups: *projections* and *reformations*. In projections, 3D information is accumulated, or flattened, along one or more directions to obtain a 2D image. In reformations, 3D information is sampled along some geometry that can later be flattened, and the sampled information along with it. There are examples that have characteristics of more than one class. The Bull's Eye Plot mentioned above is an example of a projection (data is aggregated through the heart wall) with elements of reformation (reformatting to the plane is performed along the geometry of the heart wall), whereas multiplanar reformatting (MPR), or slicing through volumetric data, is clearly a straightforward example of reformation.

14.2 OVERVIEW

We have further grouped the techniques into different types based on their core principles. In this section, we briefly define the different types. In the subsequent sections, we discuss each of the examples in more depth. The types are defined as follows:

- *Anatomical unfolding* techniques rely on a surface describing some anatomical, usually wrinkled, shape in detail, and then unfold that surface, along with the information it holds, onto the view plane. examples motivated by the great deal of self-occlusion that occurs when viewing these complex surfaces.The geometry is fully determined by the anatomy, in contrast to anatomical planar reformation, where the geometry is only partly determined by the anatomy, usually by some sort of center line.
- With *Anatomical planar reformation/projection* techniques, an *anatomically-guided* planar geometry is derived along which samples from the original data can be interpolated and/or aggregated. The planar geometry is then flattened, taking the sampled data along with it.

Visual Computing for Medicine, Second Edition. http://dx.doi.org/10.1016/B978-0-12-415873-3.00014-6

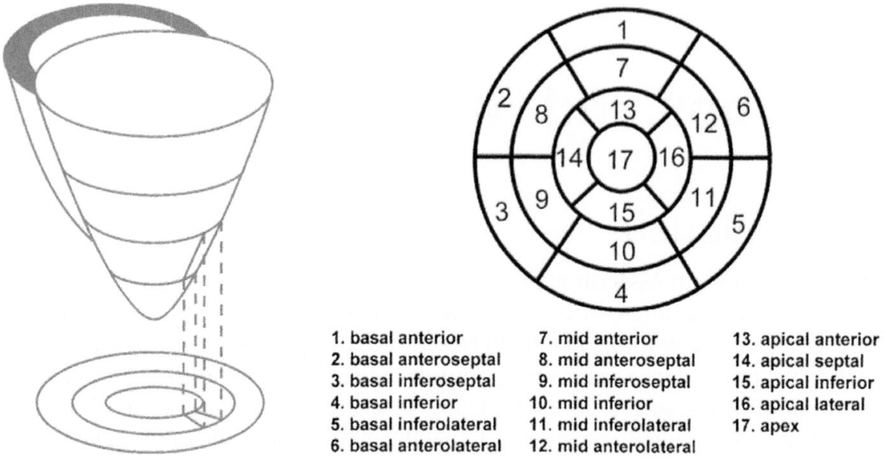

FIGURE e14.1 The cardiac Bull's Eye Plot. **Left:** Principle of construction (courtesy of Steffen Oeltze, University of Magdeburg). **Right:** The resulting myocardial (heart muscle) segments (Courtesy of Konrad Mühler, inspired by Cerqueira et al. [2002a]).

Name	Reference	Type
Cardiac/Volumetric Bull's Eye Plot	Cerqueira *et al.* [2002a], Termeer *et al.* [2007]	AU
Colon Unfolding	Vilanova *et al.* [2001]	AU
Brain Flattening	Fischl *et al.* [1999]	AU
Curved Planar Reformation	Kanitsar *et al.* [2002]	APR/P
Articulated Planar Reformation	Kok *et al.* [2010]	APR/P
Tubular Straightening	Angelelli and Hauser [2011]	APR/P
Tumor Maps	Rieder *et al.* [2010]	MP
Liver Resection Surface Maps	Lamata *et al.* [2008], Hansen *et al.* [2010c]	MP
Colonoscopy Maps	Vos *et al.* [2003], Paik *et al.* [2000]	MP
Aneurysm Maps	Neugebauer *et al.* [2009a]	MP

TABLE e14.1 Projection and reformation techniques discussed in this chapter. AU = Anatomical Unfolding, APR/P = Anatomical Planar Reformation and/or Projection, MP = Map Projection. We list a subset of the references.

- *Map projection* techniques are named after the methods used in cartography to represent the surface of a sphere, typically the earth, on a plane in order to create a map. We explicitly include techniques that map non-spherical objects to a plane.

Table e14.1 shows the list of techniques that we have selected, along with their types and an example reference.

14.3 ANATOMICAL UNFOLDING

In this section, we discuss four essential examples of anatomical unfolding. We start with the Bull's eye plot, a kind of anatomical unfolding that is frequently used in clinical practice and go on with brain cortex and colon unfolding. Brain cortex unfolding is widely used in neurosciences, whereas colon unfolding is motivated by the efficient search for polyps and early stages of colon cancer along the complex colon anatomy. Multiply branched vessel unfolding is used to investigate branching blood vessel structures for stenoses and other pathologies.

14.3.1 CARDIAC BULL'S EYE PLOTS

In the introduction, we have already discussed the cardiac *Bull's Eye Plot* [Cerqueira *et al.*, 2002a], where parts of the muscle wall (myocardium) of the left ventricle of the heart are projected onto 17 standardized segments, arranged into concentric circles. This can also be seen as an unfolding of the conical heart wall geometry onto the plane, with the apex of the cone being the innermost of the concentric circles. The great strength of this layout is that it is instantly recognized and understood by cardiologists and other cardiac imaging professionals worldwide. Complex 3D information can be mapped onto the 17 segments, and users are instantly able to reconstruct mentally the 3D origin of the projected information without the need for any interaction.

Termeer *et al.* [2007] identified three issues with the standard BEP, namely that the segments had the risk of giving a quantized view of the data, that they were not able to show both the amount of scar *and* the distribution of scar at the same time and that the traditional BEP did not provide any anatomical information. In order to address these limitations, they introduced the *volumetric BEP, or VBEP*.

Figure e14.2 shows the principle behind the construction of the VBEP. It is similar to the BEP in that the conical shape of the ventricle is unfolded onto the plane. However, where the BEP accumulated data through a particular segment of the heart wall and projected the accumulation onto the relevant segment of the plot, TERMEER proposed volume rendering the full thickness of the heart wall. This resulted in a continuous, instead of segmented, representation of the data. Furthermore, the VBEP was enhanced with anatomical context in the form of the projected coronary arteries as well as two dots representing the locations where the right ventricle meets the left ventricle. Figure e14.3 shows a BEP and VBEP side-by-side.

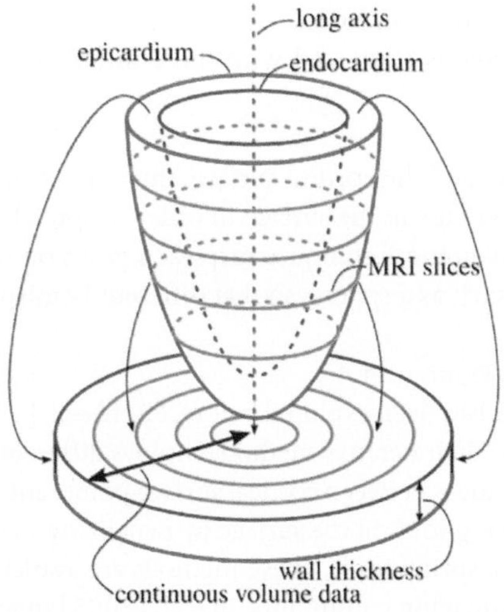

FIGURE e14.2 The principle behind the construction of the Volumetric Bull's Eye Plot (VBEP). The heart wall is unfolded in the same way as for the BEP, but the thickness of the wall is maintained through volume rendering. Furthermore, this results in a continuous, unsegmented visualization of information mapped throughout the thickness of the myocardium (From: [Termeer et al., 2007]).

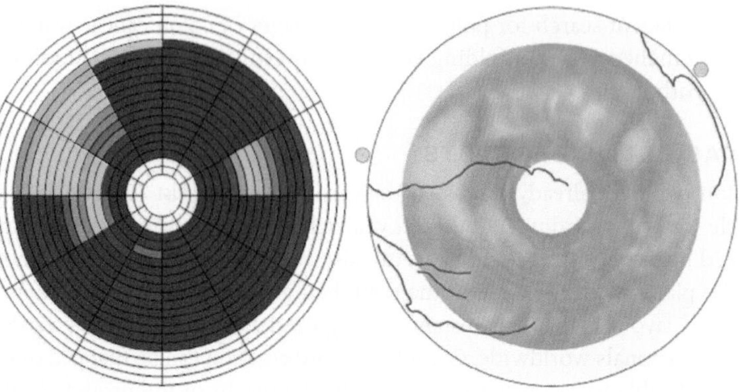

FIGURE e14.3 *A BEP and VBEP side-by-side. The BEP aggregates and represents a single attribute value per segment, while the VBEP renders the underlying data continuously. The coronary arteries are projected as red lines, while the two dots outside the outermost circle show the locations where the right ventricle joins the left ventricle (From: [Termeer et al., 2007]).*

14.3.2 BRAIN CORTEX FLATTENING

The outside layer of the brain is called the cerebral cortex. This layer consists of gray matter which is formed mostly by neurons. In humans, as well as in other large mammals, the cortex consists of many folds. It is estimated that between 60% and 70% of the cortex is buried in the grooves formed by the cortical folds, also known as the sulci [Zilles *et al.*, 1988]. When analyzing or visualizing for example functional brain imaging data as acquired by fMRI, the folded nature of the cortex poses a challenge. How can neural activity, which takes place mostly in the folded cortex, be effectively visualized if such a large percentage of the cortex itself is hidden in folds?

In neuroimaging, this challenge is addressed with three different anatomical unfolding techniques [Fischl *et al.*, 1999]:

- Inflation techniques "blow up" the cortical surface, thus smoothing out all folds.
- Flattening techniques make cuts in the surface in order to spread it out on a planar surface.
- Parameterizable surface mapping techniques map each point on the cortical surface to a different parameterizable surface, such as a sphere, so that different hemispheres can be easily compared.

Three examples are shown in Figure e14.4.

Although these three solutions had been explored before, Fischl *et al.* [1999] presented a unified method that minimizes metric distortion. Their iterative method employs different *cost functions* incorporating terms for maintaining the geodesic distances between cortical surface points and their neighbors (this minimizes the metric distortion), for removing folds in the surface by penalizing negative oriented face area, and for smoothing out the surface with a spring force. These methods are available in the FreeSurfer software,[1] a system widely used in the neuroimaging community. Ju *et al.* [2005] quantitatively evaluate and compare Fischl's methods with five alternative approaches for cortical surface flattening.

1 http://surfer.nmr.mgh.harvard.edu/.

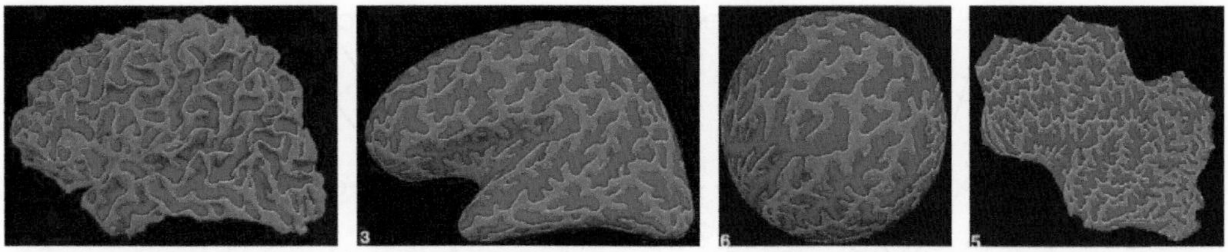

(a) Folded **(b)** Inflated **(c)** Sphere **(d)** Flattened

FIGURE e14.4 *Three different ways of anatomically unfolding the brain cortex: inflation, mapping to a sphere and flattening (From: [Fischl et al., 1999]). Sulci are red and gyri green in all cases.*

14.3.3 COLON UNFOLDING

In virtual colonoscopy (§ 13.6.1), graphics techniques are used to render the inside of the colon based on CT data, so that polyps, fleshy outgrowths on the inside wall of the colon that are precursors of colon cancer, can be visually detected. The colon also contains many folds, resulting in a significantly larger inner surface for the absorption of nutrients from food. However, inspecting the inside wall of the colon is complicated, as large parts of the surface, including potentially polyps, are hidden inside colonic folds. Colon unfolding techniques address this problem by attempting to flatten all folds, then to open up the tubular colon and finally to project the flattened and opened-up colon to a plane for inspection.

Early techniques to unfold the colon were straightforward [Wang and Vannier, 1995]. First, the centerline of the colonic cavity was computed. Then, a number of cross sections, orthogonal to the centerline and sampled over its length, were determined. The centerline was then straightened and the cross sections stacked upon each other accordingly. The straightened colon contained by the stacked cross sections was then unfolded and viewed using standard volume rendering techniques.

However, sharp curves in the centerline would cause cross section undersampling on their outsides and intersecting cross sections on their insides. This could lead to respectively missing polyps or rendering geometry multiple times. Therefore, several improvements have been proposed. In a follow-up publication addressing the intersection problem, Wang *et al.* [1998] suggested to use curved cross sections determined by simulated electrical field lines exiting from electrical charges distributed over the length of the colon centerline. When this is done with charges distributed over the full length, curved cross sections would not intersect, but the method could still cause substantial distortion due to oversampling and undersampling. This problem was alleviated by considering only a 2.5 cm window along the colon centerline around the currently extracted cross section. The technique was qualitatively evaluated by a radiologist, experienced in virtual colonoscopy, on two patient datasets.

Unfolding by Non-Linear Ray Sampling By casting rays initially radially outwards from the colon centerline for each successive cross section, but then following the gradient direction of the centerline distance map, Vilanova *et al.* [2001] efficiently solved the problem of intersecting cross sections. Figure e14.5 shows the difference between standard orthogonal cross sections and non-linear rays. The volume data was sampled along each curved ray and volume rendering was performed, stopping when the ray hit the colon wall. This resulted in a 2D parameterization of the inside colon wall, with the distance along the centerline being the one parameter and the radial index of the ray within its cross section being the other. The sampling of the colon wall by this parameterization was of course not uniform, so a direct mapping to 2D would result in severe distortions. The sampling was therefore nonlinearly scaled, using an iterative algorithm, to compensate for these distortions and maintain area preservation. Finally, undersampling in

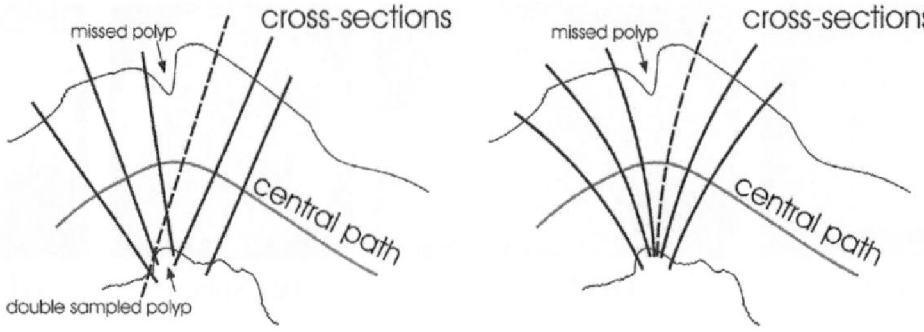

FIGURE e14.5 *On the left, a 2D view of cross sections orthogonal to the colon centerline with a missed and doubly sampled polyp shown. On the right, non-linear ray sampling solves the multiply sampled geometry problem, but without undersampling correction could still miss polyps (From: [Vilanova et al., 2001]).*

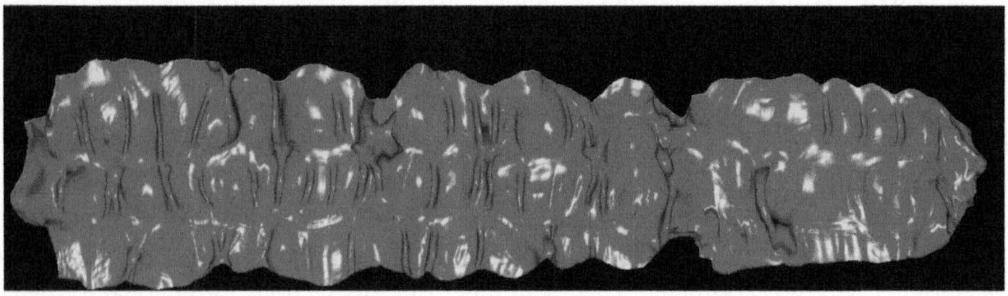

FIGURE e14.6 *Unfolded colon after non-linear sampling (From: [Vilanova et al., 2001]).*

the resultant scaled grid was detected and remedied by interpolating extra intermediate samples from the inside colon surface. This approach efficiently yields overviews of the complete inner surface of the colon, while minimizing distortion, duplication and undersampling. It was tested on three datasets, and in one case also compared with a physical dissection, but not yet clinically evaluated. Figure e14.6 shows an example of a colon that has been unfolded using this technique.

Unfolding by Conformal Mapping Haker *et al.* [2000] took a different approach to colon unfolding in basing their technique on an explicit triangulated surface representation of the colon, which could then be conformally mapped onto a flat surface. A *conformal mapping* preserves angles, and hence the local geometry of the folded colon surface. The method made use of a finite element procedure to approximate numerically the function mapping from the folded colon surface to the plane. It resulted in a completely flattened geometry which had to be visually enhanced either with a surface coloring representing mean curvature or a shading map (that is the mapped normals from the original unflattened surface) to facilitate surface feature recognition in the flattened view. This method was not evaluated for clinical use.

Hong *et al.* [2006] presented a related approach, in that they also started from a triangulated mesh which was then conformally mapped to the plane using the finite element method. However, their approach introduced two interesting variations. First, they employed an explicit step for the removal of small topological handles from the mesh, thus filtering out this type of topological noise.

Second, they used direct volume rendering (DVR) techniques (see § 7) to render the flattened colon image, in order to add shading and hence to improve shape perception of the embedded polyps in the flattened representation. For each pixel in the flattened image, the corresponding 3D position and camera

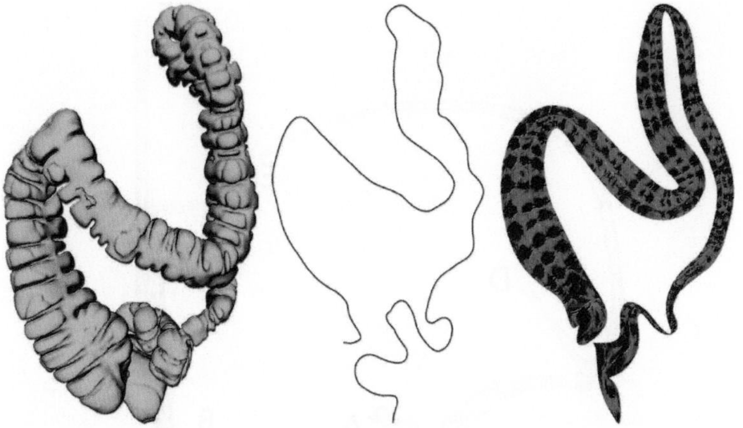

FIGURE e14.7 *Context-preserving maps of tubular structures. On the left the original colon surface is shown. In the middle the 3D centerline has been mapped to 2D, and on the right the colon has been conformally mapped to the plane and deformed according to the 2D centerline (From: [Marino et al., 2011]).*

would be used by a GPU fragment shader to calculate the correct shading. The work does not mention any clinical evaluation.

Up to now, all colon unfolding techniques also straightened the colon, yielding a single rectangular image. This facilitates finding polyps in a single view. However, the 3D trajectory of the colon is completely discarded in the process, leaving only the length along its centerline to help the user with localization. To address this problem, Marino *et al.* [2011] proposed deriving context-preserving maps of tubular structures, in which they unfolded the colon using the same harmonic mapping approach as Hong *et al.* [2006], but managed to project its 3D trajectory onto the plane while still retaining a large part of its 3D trajectory (see Fig. e14.7).

After deriving the centerline (or 3D skeleton) of the colon, it was projected either onto its best anatomical view plane, or, if that is not known, a plane that minimizes structural overlap and centerline intersections. After this initial projection step, the projected centerline segment length was corrected for projection distortion, after which intersections were removed and finally close segments were spaced apart.

The colon surface was then conformally mapped to the plane, after which that plane was deformed according to the projected centerline of the colon. This would yield a flattened map that still managed to retain a great deal of the context contained in the 3D trajectory of the colon. This context-preserving flattened map could then be rendered using volume rendering techniques, as explained previously.

Map projections have also been employed in the context of virtual colonoscopy. This is discussed in § 14.5.3.

14.3.4 MULTIPLY BRANCHED VESSEL UNFOLDING

In contrast to the colon, which has no branches, blood vessels often branch, forming trees with multiple branch points. The unfolding of these multiply branched structures is also possible, as was shown by Zhu *et al.* [2005]. They first showed how a Y-shaped vessel bifurcation could be conformally mapped to the plane. This was done by constructing three smooth curves, running from the base of the Y to the point at which it splits into two branches, and then up the two respective branches. These curves define a cut

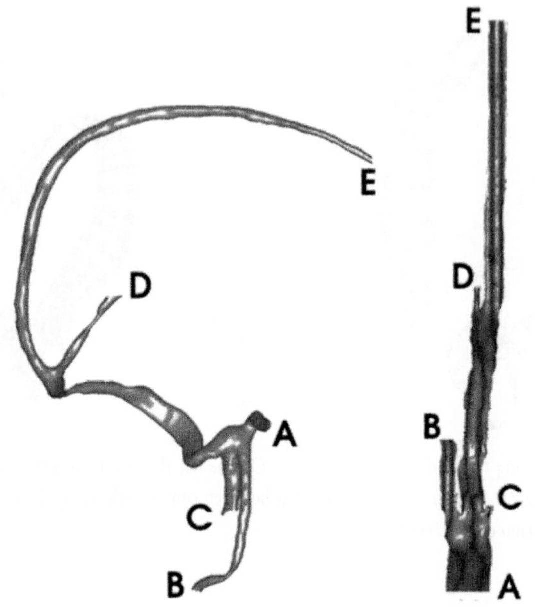

FIGURE e14.8 *Conformal mapping of multiply branched vessels from brain MRA. On the left is the original surface, on the right the conformally mapped, non angle-preserving, map view. Vertices have been shaded with their original normal vectors* (From: [Zhu *et al.*, 2005]).

on the Y-shaped surface that could be used with the finite element method to determine a conformal mapping to the plane.

For conformally mapping a more complex multiply branched vessel tree, they would first determine the *harmonic skeleton* of the vessel tree. The *harmonic skeleton* is similar to the central line or straightforward skeleton, but was called so due to its particular implementation. A surface-based region growing was started at the root of the tree. Whenever a branch point was reached, the triangle-based distance from the root would be associated with it. By determining the centroids of clustered distance values, the central line could be determined. In subsequent steps, the skeleton was refined.

With this skeleton, the vessel tree could be decomposed into multiple Y-shaped segments, each of which could be conformally mapped to the plane. This would finally yield a single view of the whole tree on the plane, that could optionally be further processed to yield also an area-preserving mapping. Figure e14.8 shows an example of applying this approach to a brain MRA dataset. Curved planar reformation, see § 11.3.3, offers a different method, one that does not employ explicit unfolding or conformal mapping, for the visualization of curved and branching structures on the plane.

14.4 ANATOMICAL PLANAR REFORMATION/PROJECTION

As mentioned above, anatomical planar reformation and projection techniques derive a planar geometry based on the most relevant anatomical structures for a given problem domain, then reformat or project the original data along or onto that geometry, finally flattening the planar geometry along with the data. One of the most well-known examples of anatomical planar reformation techniques is CPR

[Kanitsar *et al.*, 2002, Vrtovec *et al.*, 2005], where the planar geometry is formulated along vascular structures that are to be visualized, which finally results in a 2D flattened visualization of the vascular structures and their surroundings. CPR is discussed in some detail in § 11.3.3 where also branching multivessels are considered. In this section, we will examine two additional examples, one based on projection and the other on reformation. In both cases, elongated tubular structures are involved. The techniques are motivated by the diagnostic goal of detecting any suspicious change along the tubular anatomy.

14.4.1 TUBULAR STRAIGHTENING

Angelelli and Hauser [2011] presented an anatomical planar projection approach for visualizing flows through tubular structures, applied to the specific problem of visualizing blood flow through the human aorta as measured with Phase-Contrast MRI (PC-MRI). Their technique is based on determining the centerline of the aorta and then either reformatting the original space and data, or reformatting flow visualization primitives, along the straightened centerline. In the former case, the straightened data domain can be visualized with traditional flow visualization techniques.

Tubular straightening offers similar advantages to other planar reformation techniques: The focus structure, for example the aorta, along with the information in and around it, has been straightened so that it can be more easily viewed in its flattened configuration. Also due to the same structure being flattened in the same way, side-by-side comparisons become more useful. Figure e14.9 shows the general procedure behind tubular straightening and side-by-side comparison.

Rib Straightening Kiraly *et al.* [2006] presented a similar technique for the visualization of ribs from CT data. Such rib visualizations are primarily motivated by the search for bone metastasis in the case of cancer patients. In conventional slice-based or 3D visualizations, the mandatory search for such metastasis

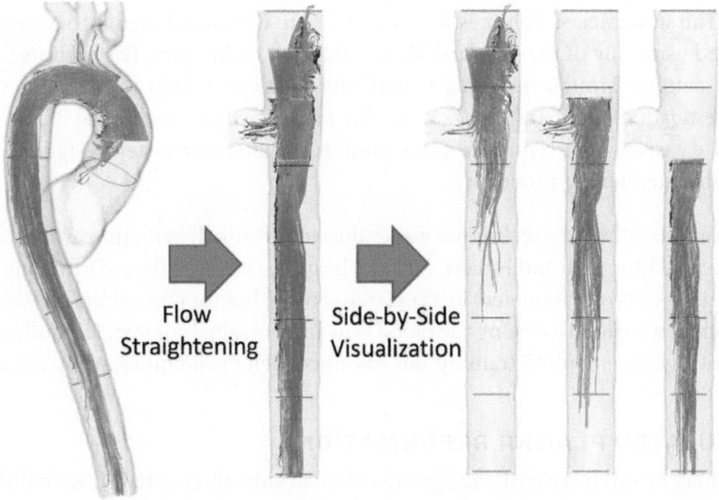

FIGURE e14.9 *Straightened aorta with streamlines visualizing the blood flow for a single timestep. Due to the straightening, different timesteps or, in this case, different streamline seeding configurations can be shown side-by-side (From: [Angelelli and Hauser, 2011]).*

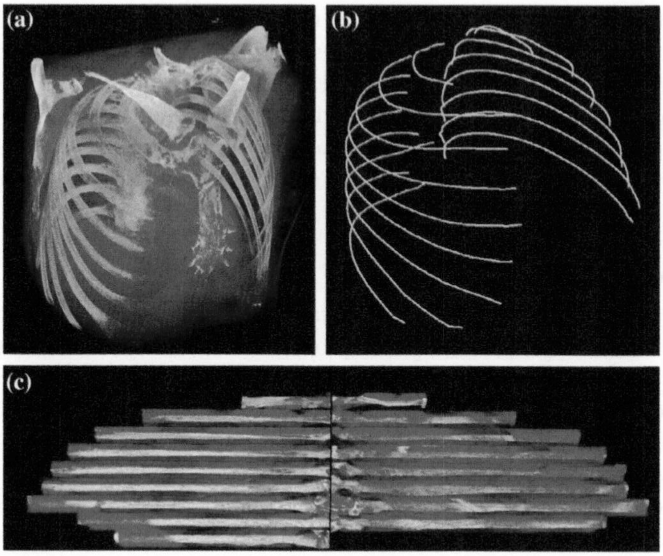

FIGURE e14.10 *Example of the rib straightening technique. At the top left, a volume rendering of the original CT data. At the top right, the extracted and smoothed centerlines. At the bottom, a single slice through the straightened data* (From: [Kiraly et al., 2006]).

is tedious. After segmenting the ribs and determining their smooth centerlines, the data around each rib was reformatted by resampling from planes positioned orthogonally to its centerline, at regular intervals along its length. The straightened volumes for each rib were then combined into a single dataset which could be visualized using any of the standard 3D visualization techniques. The authors found that simply viewing the slice cutting through the centers of all ribs yielded the best results. This view enabled the simultaneous investigation of all ribs, for example for tumors, where traditional 3D visualization of the non-straightened dataset would require a great number of interaction steps. Figure e14.10 shows an example of the rib straightening procedure.

Evaluation The aorta straightening technique was evaluated informally with the cardiovascular MRI group at an academic hospital [Angelelli and Hauser, 2011]. The group believed the reformatting to be potentially useful for comparison of flow parameters in a research setting, but for clinical staff it would require some training, as physicians were used to seeing the blood flow in its original context. The authors make the good point that CPR initially also required training but has since then been embraced by clinical practitioners.

14.4.2 ARTICULATED PLANAR REFORMATION

In molecular imaging research experiments, groups of small animals are imaged with different modalities at different time points. In general, animal movement can't be constrained, so postures are potentially different for each animal, at each timepoint and for each modality. This greatly complicates high-level and fine-grained comparison between different animals and between timesteps, a central activity in molecular imaging research.

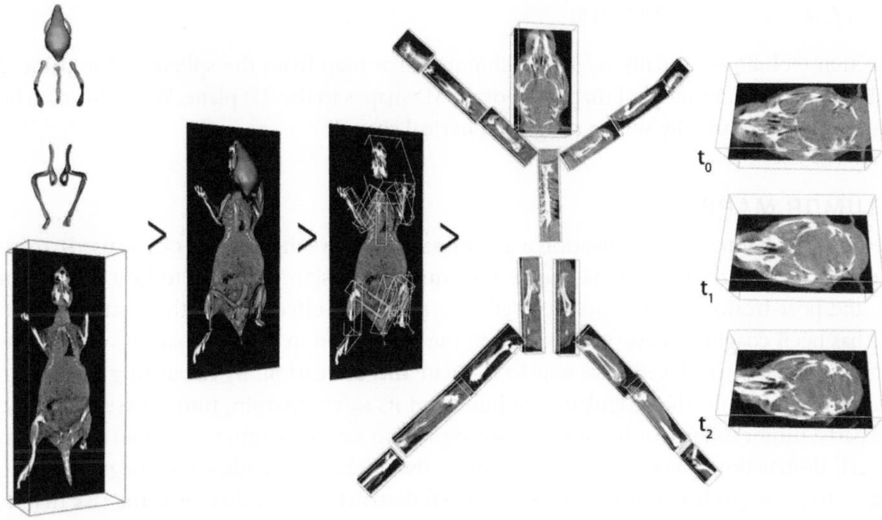

FIGURE e14.11 *The complete articulated planar reformation (APR) processing pipeline [Kok et al., 2010]. First, a labeled skeletal atlas is mapped to the new data using articulated registration. Using the known location of all atlas bones in the new data, sub-volumes surrounding these bones are calculated using PCA. These sub-volumes are transformed back to a standardized flattened skeleton space where different datasets can be easily compared (Courtesy of Peter Kok, Delft University of Technology).*

Kok *et al.* [2010] addressed this problem by reformatting the data based on a standardized planar (flattened) arrangement of a mouse atlas skeleton, and then visualizing the original data reformatted along this flattened skeleton. Figure e14.11 shows all steps of the presented procedure.

All small animal datasets were mapped to the same mouse atlas skeleton via articulated registration [Baiker *et al.*, 2010]. In articulated registration, the mouse atlas skeleton is registered fully automatically to any CT dataset by taking into account the different range of motion constraints of each skeletal joint. Using the iterative closest point transform, the different bones are registered in a hierarchical fashion to the CT data: First the spine, then the head taking into account the neck range of motion, then the upper arms taking into account the range of motion of the shoulders, and so forth.

As a result of this registration, each of the bones in the mouse atlas skeleton could be positioned in the target CT dataset. Using principal component analysis, object-aligned bounding boxes surrounding each of the bones in the CT dataset could be determined. These bounding boxes, along with the CT data that they contained, were then mapped back to the planar layout of the mouse atlas skeleton.

This process was repeated for all mice and all timepoints, after which global and local comparisons could be more easily performed. For global comparison, difference metrics could be mapped onto the mouse atlas skeleton, while for local comparison the user could zoom in on any of the now planar bones and perform side-by-side comparisons of the raw CT data.

Evaluation The technique was evaluated separately with the scientific leaders of two large small animal and molecular imaging research groups, who found the standardized planar layout to be a valuable tool for comparison of study data. The possibility of performing group studies, that is being able to reformat the data of a large cohort of small animals, could be of significant added value.

14.5 MAP PROJECTIONS

Map projection techniques usually refer to techniques that map from the sphere to the plane. Here we additionally discuss techniques that map from other 3D shapes to the 2D plane. We begin with *tumor maps*, an anatomical structure usually with a roughly spherical shape.

14.5.1 TUMOR MAPS

Percutaneous radio-frequency (RF) ablation is a minimally-invasive therapy that can be used to treat tumors in the liver. Electrodes are inserted via needle-puncture of the skin and used to heat up and kill tumor cells. Pre- and post-treatment CT scans are used to evaluate the effectivity of the treatment by checking that tissue has been coagulated everywhere within the tumor and in a safety margin surrounding it.

Rieder *et al.* [2010] introduced *tumor maps* to facilitate this evaluation. By calculating the intersection of the segmented tumor with the coagulation volume and its safety margin, tumor tissue can be classified into three parts: tumor tissue that lies inside the coagulation safety margin is assumed to have undergone complete cell destruction (shown in green), tumor tissue that lies within the coagulation region but outside the safety margin has probably undergone cell destruction, but there is some risk that this is not the case (shown in yellow) and tumor tissue that falls completely outside of the coagulation region has not been successfully ablated (shown in red).

As shown in Figure e14.12, the color-coded tumor surface is shown in its 3D context, and visualized with a tumor map which shows the complete color-mapped outer surface of the tumor map projected onto the 2D plane, in this case using the area-preserving Mollweide map projection. By default, the authors employ a longitude-latitude mapping, a cylindrical mapping that simply maps longitude and latitude to a rectangular coordinate system. Due to the distortion at the poles, they then optionally apply either the area-preserving sinusoidal projection or the area-preserving Mollweide projection. The tumor map is further enhanced with directional cues, being primarily the A, P, L, R, H, and F (anterior, posterior, left, right, head, foot) labels, well-known from medical imaging workstation consoles.

Using the tumor map, the full outside surface of the tumor, color-coded with the three different coagulation zones, can be viewed in a single 2D image. However, the anatomical context is missing. To address this issue, the authors designed synchronized interaction between the tumor map and the

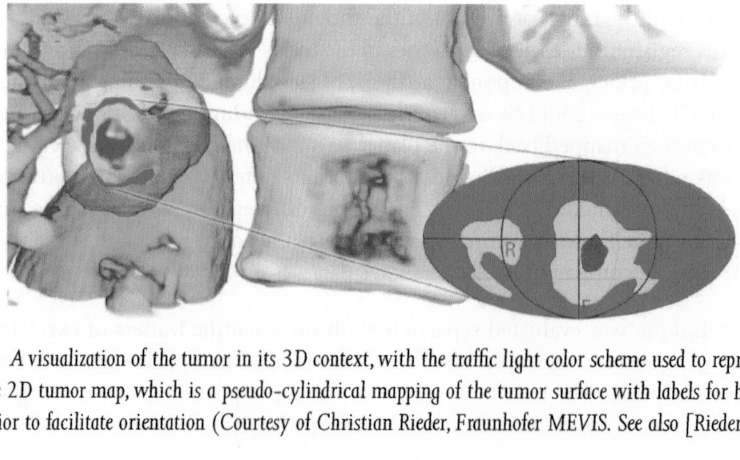

FIGURE e14.12 *A visualization of the tumor in its 3D context, with the traffic light color scheme used to represent ablation state. The inset shows the 2D tumor map, which is a pseudo-cylindrical mapping of the tumor surface with labels for head, foot, left, right, anterior and posterior to facilitate orientation (Courtesy of Christian Rieder, Fraunhofer MEVIS. See also [Rieder et al., 2010]).*

accompanying 3D visualization. Clicking on the tumor map highlights the corresponding point in 3D, while dragging on the tumor map rotates the 3D view accordingly.

Evaluation The authors made the case that the advantage of being able to view the entire outside surface of the tumor was obvious enough not to require an evaluation. Instead, they evaluated in a user study with fifteen users whether scene rotation to pre-specified zones of interest via the tumor map was faster than traditional methods, and found that navigation with the straightforward longitude-latitude map was the fastest, followed by the Mollweide, and that both were significantly faster than normal trackball rotation. An informal evaluation was also conducted with five experienced physicians, who found the tumor map useful for the initial observation of ablation zones, and for the initial marking of suspicious areas.

14.5.2 LIVER RESECTION SURFACE MAPS

Liver tumors are surgically removed in a process called hepatectomy, or liver resection. During this procedure the part of the liver containing the tumor is surgically removed, avoiding as far as possible critical structures such as the portal and hepatic veins. During the surgical planning stage, a straight or curved resection plane, along which the liver will be resected, is specified. This is explained in more detail in Section 17.5.4 of Chapter 17.

Lamata *et al.* [2008] first proposed using a simplified representation of the planned Resection Map and critical structures for intraoperative visualization, and called their representation the *Resection Map*. The Resection Map consisted of two views. The surgical view showed the resection plane orthogonal to the view plane, along with risk structures within a user-configurable distance to that plane and within the *progress window*. The progress window was defined on the second view, called the progress view, showing the resection plane parallel to the view plane. In this view, all critical structures could also be seen, with color-coding to represent their closeness to the resection plane. Figure e14.13 shows an example of the Resection Map display.

Hansen *et al.* [2010c] extended this idea by projecting critical structures (tumor, hepatic and portal veins) onto the resection surface. The distance of the critical structures to the resection surface was also represented by a segmented color-coding as can be seen in Figure e14.14.

Evaluation Based on a preliminary and informal evaluation by surgeons, Risk Maps "may prevent a possible damage to risk structures and thus enhance patient safety during liver surgery" [Hansen *et al.*, 2010c]. In follow-up work, Risk Maps were further evaluated in two studies measuring whether and how Risk Maps facilitate the process of surgical risk assessment [Hansen, 2012]. In the first study, resection planes were presented to three experienced surgeons, randomly with or without Risk Maps, after which they had to mark areas at which they expected risk or difficulty during the resection. Surgeons were faster with Risk Maps, but not significantly so. Through the accompanying questionnaire they did indicate that Risk Maps were helpful in assessing risk. In the second experiment, a mix of scientists and radiological technicians had to identify risk structures close to a virtual instrument tip, with and without using Risk Maps. Identification of risk structures was significantly faster with Risk Maps than without.

Resection Maps were first evaluated with guided interviews with five surgeons from two European hospitals [Lamata *et al.*, 2008]. During these interviews, surgeons indicated that the risk maps could potentially lead to an increase in confidence and that they could serve as a sufficient guidance tool. Resection Maps would have the most utility supporting irregular resection planes. Surgeons would have preferred the progress window to update automatically. In a follow-up study, the technique was further evaluated with three surgeons from three hospitals using Resection Maps in the execution of seven hepatectomies [Lamata *et al.*, 2010]. Based on the Likert scale questionnaire, Resection Maps were positively received.

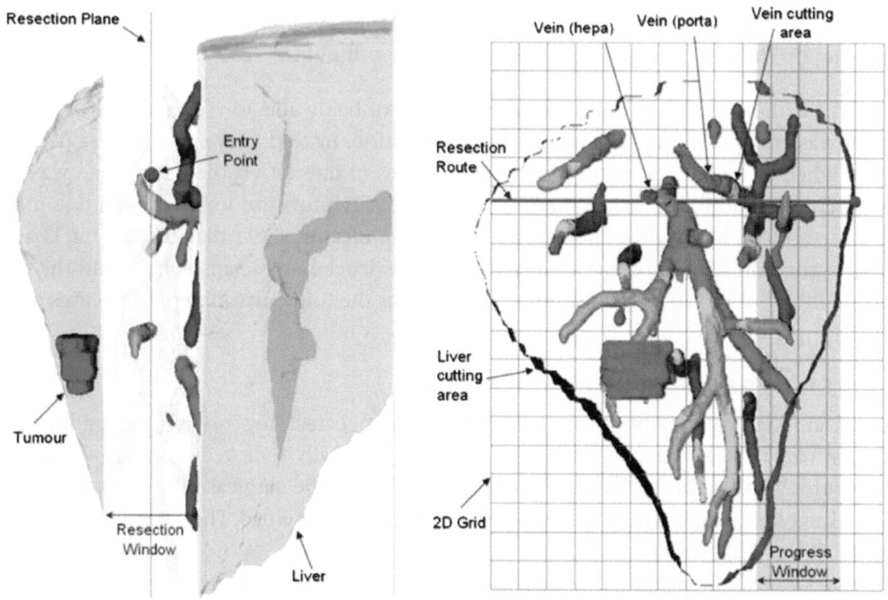

FIGURE e14.13 *The Resection Map as proposed by Lamata et al. [2008]. On the left the surgical view is shown, and on the right the progress view.*

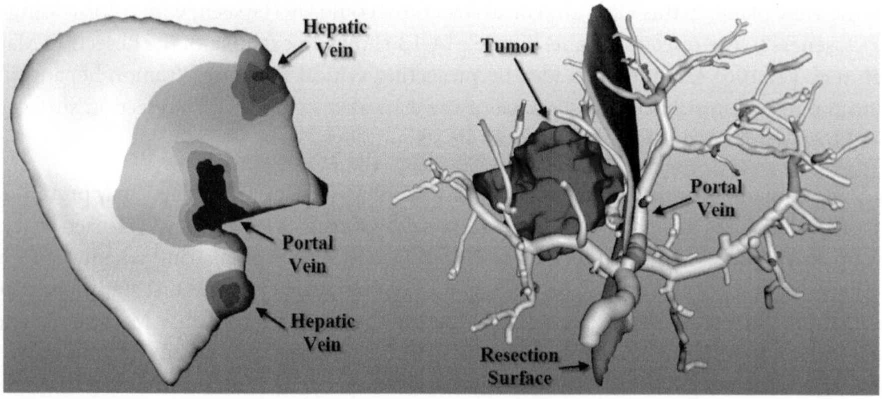

FIGURE e14.14 *On the left, an example of the liver risk map, showing the proximity of the tumor in red, and the hepatic and portal veins in green and blue, respectively. The distance of the hepatic and portal veins is encoded in lighter color segments. On the right, the curved resection plane is shown in its anatomical context (From: [Hansen et al., 2010c]).*

14.5.3 COLONOSCOPY MAPS

In Section 14.3.3, anatomical unfolding was employed to flatten the folds and virtually dissect the colon, resulting in a flattened surface that can in principal be inspected more easily for polyps.

Paik *et al.* [2000] investigated Mercator and stereographic map projections as an alternative solution to the problem of ensuring visibility of a large percentage of the folded colon wall. Instead of unfolding and dissecting the colon, flythroughs are generated along the colon centerline. At regular points along the centerline, a map projection of the full surroundings was generated, instead of just the forward and backward facing views, as was commonly done. The map projection results in a flattened view of the full surrounding colonic landscape. This is the same as a map projection of the earth, except that the observer finds itself within the colon looking outward.

This theme was further explored in Serlie *et al.* [2001], where the authors proposed rendering six projections at 90% viewing angles at regular points along the centerline, and then displaying flythroughs as a sequence of unfolded cubes.

Evaluation On nine random patient datasets, it was found that the Mercator map projection guaranteed 98.8% surface visibility. Forward and backward facing views could only compete with this at a high view frustum angle, which resulted in quite some visual distortion and hence lower sensitivity. With two experienced radiologists and synthetic polyps in a real dataset, more polyps were detected with Mercator and stereographic map projects than with normal endoscopic rendering or even viewing raw axial slices.

The unfolded cube technique was compared with forward and backward facing views [Vos *et al.*, 2003]. Two experienced radiologists used both display methods to study the data of thirty patients. It was found that the unfolded cube was significantly faster and ensured more visibility of the inner colon surface, although sensitivity and specificity were not significantly different between the two methods.

14.5.4 ANEURYSM MAPS

Blood flow simulations result in flow data and scalar flow features, such as pressure, velocity, and wall shear stress (WSS). In particular, WSS plays an essential role in the understanding of initiation and progression of vascular diseases. A simple solution to display scalar flow features is to show the surface of the relevant vascular region with the scalar flow feature color-mapped onto it.

The disadvantage of this simple solution is that only a small portion of the surface is visible at the same time. By using a map projection that shows the five sides not currently facing forward, in a flattened arrangement, all scalar information can be shown simultaneously. However, a map exhibits distortions. Furthermore, a simple map can be hard to relate to the complex 3D anatomy of pathological vessels. A combination of a faithful 3D anatomy representation and a map view, where interaction in both views are synchronized, could help to address this problem.

Neugebauer *et al.* [2009a] introduced a map display for scalar flow features where the 3D anatomy model is presented in a central part and flow features of the left, right, bottom, up, and back side are presented as flat regions of a map surrounding the anatomical view. When the user selects a point in one of the map views and drags it toward the center, the 3D anatomy model is rotated such that this point becomes visible (see Fig. e14.15). Also, a rotation of the 3D view of the anatomical model is possible and results in an update of the map views. This enables a systematic exploration of all regions. Neuroradiologists emphasized that this technique enables a better exploration of scalar flow features at opposite sites. There are many details to consider, such as map layout, interaction techniques, color selection and display of additional hints that are discussed in Neugebauer *et al.* [2009a].

Despite encouraging feedback so far, more evaluation and corresponding refinements are necessary to make this strategy broadly applicable. While it is applicable to non-stationary flows in principle, it is likely that modifications are necessary if the scalar flow features change over time and lead to frequent changes of the map view and the 3D model view.

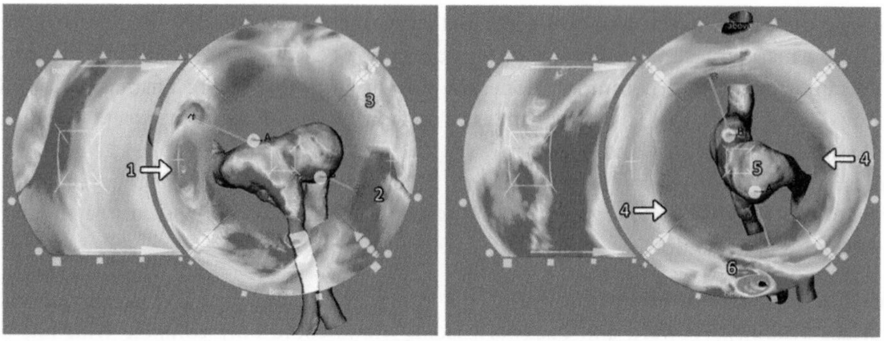

FIGURE e14.15 *A 3D model of the relevant vascular anatomy is surrounded by map views that display scalar flow features of five sides (features at the left, right, bottom, and up side are shown at the corresponding ring portions). Scalar features of the backside are shown at the most right display. The lines pointing from the map portions to the 3D view indicate correspondences, where scalar features are shown in both views. If the user drags a point, representing an interesting feature from a map view to the center, the anatomical model is rotated to make that region visible. All map views change accordingly (From: [Neugebauer et al., 2009a]).*

14.6 CONCLUSION

In this chapter we have discussed a number of medical visualization techniques that deal with the problem of intelligently transforming 3D data into 2D. The techniques are based either on reformation or projection. Reformation-based techniques sample data along a certain geometry embedded within the source 3D dataset, and then flatten that embedded geometry, taking the sampled data with it. Projection-based techniques aggregate data over any number of arbitrarily defined projection frustums.

We further grouped the techniques into three types. Anatomical unfolding techniques make use of an anatomically defined, usually folded, surface in the data, which is then unfolded and flattened, along with the data defined on or close to it. Anatomical planar reformation and projection techniques define a planar geometry, guided by tubular or skeletal structures in the data, and then flatten the planar geometry, along with the data defined on or close to it. Map projection techniques, originating from cartography, employ various approaches to project 360° views to 2D. The choice of technique type is guided by domain expertise and tasks on the one hand, and by what can be extracted from the data on the other. For example in the case of CPR, the domain task is to inspect visually the condition of a geometrically complex blood vessel, focusing on abnormalities such as stenoses, occlusions, aneurysms, and vessel wall calcifications. Furthermore, the blood vessel can be extracted from the data. Because the blood vessel geometry is available, and a plane intersecting the vessel is appropriate for detecting the mentioned abnormalities, a planar reformation is the most suitable technique type.

Ware [2001] argued that, based on the characteristics of human spatial perception, we should definitely favor 2D layout over 3D when designing graphics. Furthermore, he recommended that 3D objects should be used to represent data entities, in the context of a 2D layout, as such objects are easier to identify and remember. The techniques discussed in this chapter satisfy these, and to a certain extent all the other, guidelines that form part of Ware's *2½-D attitude* to the design of visual displays. Through intelligent projection or reformation, three-dimensional medical data is transformed to a two-dimensional layout, while maintaining the three-dimensional characteristics of embedded objects. These representations offer advantages in terms of minimizing occlusion and in terms of enabling effective interaction, for example the fast rotation-to-target demonstrated by Rieder *et al.* [2010].

Based on the perceptual and interaction advantages, together with the observation that medical datasets are steadily growing in size and complexity, we think that projections and reformations that are able to simplify 3D to 2D in an elegant and effective fashion will become increasingly important and widespread in medical visualization.

Part IV

Visualization of High-Dimensional Medical Image Data

Part IV discusses the visualization of high-dimensional medical image data. Thus, in this part we consider time-dependent data, as well as 3D vector and tensor data.

A special variation of MRI is Diffusion Tensor Imaging (DTI). With this modality, the inhomogeneity of the direction of (water) diffusion can be non-invasively determined. Strongly directed diffusion occurs for example in the whiter matter of the human brain, and thus indicates the direction and location of fiber tracks. This information is highly relevant, in particular in neuroradiology and neurosurgery. The analysis and visualization of DTI data poses many challenges, which are discussed in Chapter 15. In contrast to the first edition, we extend the scope here and consider DTI just one method to explore brain connectivity.

Chapter 16 describes techniques to explore and analyze perfusion data, a special instance of time-dependent volume data. These data have a great potential for medical diagnosis, e.g., for the assessment of tumors, where malignant tumors exhibit a stronger vascularization than benign tumors. This effect cannot be observed in static images. Techniques for the efficient visualization and analysis of such data are important, because the huge amount of dynamic volume data cannot be evaluated without dedicated software support.

Visual Computing for Medicine, Second Edition. http://dx.doi.org/10.1016/B978-0-12-415873-3.00033-X

Chapter 15

Visualization of Brain Connectivity

15.1 INTRODUCTION

The human brain consists of approximately 10^{11} (one hundred thousand million, or one hundred US billion) brain cells, or neurons [Murre and Sturdy, 1995]. Each neuron consists of a cell body, or *soma*. The shorter fibers extending from the cell body are called dendrites, and act as the inputs to the neuron. The axon is a usually much longer fiber, up to one meter in length, also extending from the cell body. It is protected by the myelin sheath. The axon functions as the output of the neuron.

Each axon ends in a number of fine branches called *presynaptic terminals*. Axons can also have branching terminals along their length. Terminals generally come into close proximity of the dendrites of other neurons. The region between the presynaptic terminal of one neuron and the dendrite of the next is called the *synaptic gap*, while the connection itself is called the *synapse*.

Signals are passed from one neuron to the next via the synapses. A signal can be electrical, in which case an electrical current passes from axon to dendrite, or chemical, in which case neurotransmitters cross the gap and bind to receptors in the receiving dendritic site. A *neuron* weights and adds up the inputs it receives via its dendrites. If the weighted sum of the inputs reaches a certain threshold, the neuron will fire an action potential, that is, it will send an electrical signal out via its axon. There are approximately 10^{15} (one thousand million million, or one thousand US quadrillion) such connections between all neurons in the human brain [Murre and Sturdy, 1995]. There is a strong hypothesis that the structure of this large and complex network plays an important role in human cognition [Sporns *et al.*, 2004, 2005]. In other words, the way in which the network is connected "places specific constraints on brain dynamics, and thus shapes the operations and processes of human cognition" [Sporns *et al.*, 2005].

Furthermore, when the network is modified, either by a connectivity-related pathology or other brain disorder, or by surgical intervention, brain function can be drastically affected. Pathologies that affect brain connectivity include Alzheimer's, schizophrenia and epilepsy [Guye *et al.*, 2010]. Stroke, tumors, and multiple-sclerosis are associated with brain lesions which can also affect brain networks. Understanding of the brain networks involved helps to predict the behavioral consequences of the various pathologies, and is an increasingly important component in the planning of neurosurgical intervention.

The brain is our most important organ. It cannot be replaced, and its function cannot be artificially taken over. When it is damaged or shuts down, the whole organism is at risk. *The brain defines who we are.* In this light, it is of great importance to understand the working of the brain, and the effect of pathologies and of treatment on it. In this context, studying brain connectivity is clearly crucial.

This chapter discusses mainly techniques for the *in vivo* acquisition and visualization of macroscopic brain connectivity. We are interested in the large scale connective network of the whole human brain, hence *macroscale connectivity*. *Mesoscale connectivity* refers to connectivity at the scale of a few micrometers, at which local neuronal circuits, such as a single functional column of the cortex, can be studied. *Microscale connectivity* refers to the study of connectivity between single neurons. We distinguish between three different types of brain connectivity.

Visual Computing for Medicine, Second Edition. http://dx.doi.org/10.1016/B978-0-12-415873-3.00015-8

- *Structural connectivity* refers to the network of anatomical links, such as bundles of neuronal axons, between different regions of the brain. Often, this type of data describes the geometry of the axon bundles connecting the different parts.
- *Functional connectivity* refers to the network formed by the correlation of time-dependent brain activity between different regions of the brain.
- *Effective connectivity* refers to the influence that different brain regions exert on each other. This is usually based on statistical correlation as well, but integrates some assumed model of connectivity between the involved brain regions.

Unlike structural and functional connectivity, effective connections are directed. Because both functional and effective connectivity rely on the functional coherence between different parts of the brain, they represent the point-to-point connectivity, and do not describe the actual structure of the connections. Functional and effective connectivity information can be represented as a matrix, with the participating brain regions enumerating the rows and the columns, and each position holding the connectivity between its row and column regions.

Many forms of diffusion MRI can be used to derive structural connectivity, while EEG, MEG, and fMRI yield functional connectivity, and indirectly effective connectivity. Importantly, structural connectivity data can be transformed to point-to-point connectivity, by for example counting the number of connections, the total size of a connective bundle, or aggregating the amount of diffusion over a given connection. § 15.4.1 contains a number of such examples. Information on the anatomical trajectory of the connection is discarded, and replaced with the derived connectivity measures, yielding, as is the case with functional connectivity, a matrix of connectivity measures between various pairs of brain regions.

In the rest of this chapter, we structure this discussion of *macroscopic brain connectivity* visualization techniques according to the different types of data and the classes of techniques shown in Figure 15.1. Due to the possibility of transforming structural connectivity to a connectivity matrix, which is identical to the type of data used for functional and effective connectivity, we distinguish between visualization techniques for structural connectivity on the one hand, and visualization techniques for connectivity matrices on the other.

Organization We start with an overview of the various acquisition techniques that can be used to measure, in-vivo, macroscopic connectivity in the human brain. We then discuss in detail first the techniques that apply to the visualization of structural connectivity. We have further subdivided these techniques into three types: Scalar reduction, glyphs, and global multiscale. Following the structural techniques, we treat techniques that focus on the visualization of point-to-point brain connectivity, of which functional

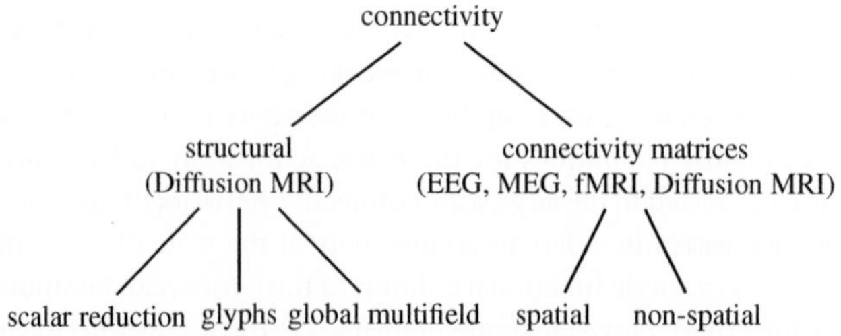

FIGURE 15.1 *Techniques for the visualization of macroscopic connectivity. The two main groups of techniques deal respectively with structural connectivity and with connectivity matrices. Imaging techniques are added in parentheses.*

connectivity is one example. These techniques are either spatial, or non-spatial, depending on whether connectivity is visualized in its anatomical context.

15.2 ACQUISITION OF CONNECTIVITY DATA

In this section, we give compact explanations of a number of modalities for the acquisition of macroscopic brain connectivity information. In the subsequent section we give an overview of the analysis and visualization techniques that can be applied to such information.

15.2.1 EEG AND MEG

Electroencephalography, or EEG, is defined as the time-dependent difference in voltage measured at two different locations, at least one of which is on the scalp [Fisch and Spehlmann, 1999]. The voltage signal that is measured on the scalp is caused by voltage sources in the cortex that cause a flow of current through the intermediate tissue up to the surface of the scalp. This flow of current is called *volume conduction* and has a significant effect on the voltage that is finally measured. The voltage sources are in fact each thousands of synchronized *postsynaptic potentials*. Postsynaptic potential refers to the voltage signal on the cell membrane of a signal-receiving neuron, in other words the signal on the receiving side of the synapse.

The *International 10–20 system* is a convention for placing EEG electrodes. Under this convention, 19 electrodes, each labeled with a letter-digit code, are placed at standard locations, as well as ground and reference electrodes. However, in *multi-channel* or *high-density* EEG, up to 512 electrodes can be used.

In *magnetoencephalography*, or MEG, sensors called magnetometers are used to measure the localized magnetic field on the scalp. An example of a MEG scanner can be seen in Figure 15.2. This magnetic field measured on the scalp is caused by electrical currents within large groups of synchronized neurons. The currents are also associated with postsynaptic potentials, so a MEG signal is ultimately caused by the same neurophysiological process as an EEG signal. The magnetometers need to be highly sensitive, as the magnetic field is very weak. Currently, SQUIDs, or superconducting quantum interference devices, are most commonly used for this purpose. Similar to EEG, up to a few hundred sensors, arranged over the scalp, can be used.

Unlike EEG, MEG does not require a reference measurement. Although the magnetic field is attenuated more severely by the distance between source and sensor, it does not get distorted as severely as EEG by the tissue between source and sensor. In practice, this means that MEG yields better spatial resolution, but is limited to measuring superficial cortical activity. Furthermore, MEG equipment is significantly more expensive and harder to transport.

Both MEG and EEG systems have better than millisecond temporal resolution. By calculating the correlation between the time-dependent signals acquired by all sensors, a network of functional connections can be derived. However, this sensor-level connectivity can give an inaccurate representation of the underlying source connectivity, as the activity of each source is picked up by multiple sensors. This phenomenon is called *field spread*. Methods also exist for the calculation of source-level connectivity [Schoffelen and Gross, 2009]. Usually these start by reconstructing the sources responsible for the sensor measurements using inverse methods [Baillet *et al.*, 2001] and then derive the functional connectivity between prespecified regions of interest. Full connectivity matrices for the whole brain can also be calculated, but extracting meaningful information from such matrices has proven challenging [Schoffelen and Gross, 2009].

15.2.2 MAGNETIC RESONANCE IMAGING

The principles of MRI, or magnetic resonance imaging, are explained in § 2.6. We recapitulate them here in order to explain diffusion MRI and later functional MRI. In MRI a strong magnetic field is applied over

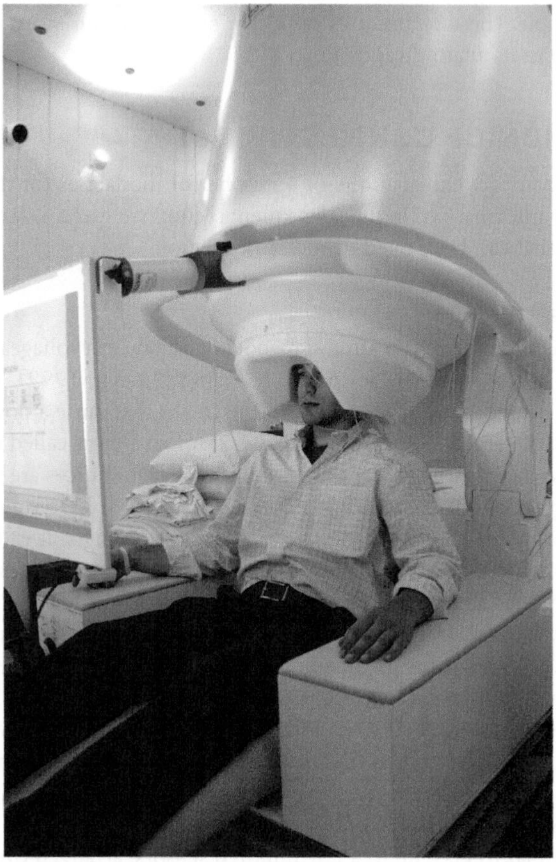

FIGURE 15.2 *MEG scanner with patient (Courtesy of the National Institute of Mental Health, National Institutes of Health, Department of Health, and Human Services).*

the subject that is to be scanned. Unpaired protons, mostly those in the nuclei of the hydrogen atoms that form part of water molecules, precess about the magnetic field direction at the Larmor frequency ω, an angular frequency that is related to the strength of the magnetic field B at that point by the gyromagnetic ratio γ. This precession is analogous to that of a spinning top in the gravity field.

When a radio frequency pulse is applied with a certain frequency, all protons precessing at exactly that frequency will resonate and precess in the plane orthogonal to the magnetic field. When the radio frequency pulse is switched off, these protons return to their lower energy state precessing around the magnetic field. In doing this, they release the energy difference as photons which are detected by the scanner as an electromagnetic signal. The speed at which protons regain their lower energy state, or the relaxation time, is related to the type of material they find themselves in.

The magnetic field is deliberately varied in strength across three-dimensional space, so that protons at different positions precess at different frequencies and will resonate at different frequencies, which in turn enables MRI to generate volume data describing the subject being scanned. These variations in field strength are referred to as magnetic field gradients. For a more detailed discussion of MRI acquisition, we refer the reader to the overview by Hendee and Morgan [1984].

An MRI scanner applies a strong magnetic field over the subject that is to be scanned. Unpaired protons, mostly those in the nuclei of the hydrogen atoms that form part of water molecules, precess about the main direction of the magnetic field B at the Larmor frequency ω, an angular frequency that is related to the strength of the magnetic field at that point by the gyromagnetic ratio γ. This precession is analogous to that of a spinning top in the gravity field.

When a radio-frequency pulse with that specific frequency is applied, all protons precessing at exactly that frequency will resonate and precess in the plane orthogonal to the magnetic field. When the radio-frequency pulse is switched off, these protons return to their lower energy state precessing around the magnetic field. In doing this, they release the energy difference as photons which are detected by the scanner as an electromagnetic signal. The speed at which protons regain their lower energy state, or the relaxation time, is related to the type of material they find themselves in.

The magnetic field is deliberately varied in strength through three-dimensional space, so that protons at different positions precess at different frequencies and will resonate at different frequencies, which in turn enables MRI to generate volume data describing the subject being scanned. These variations in field strength are referred to as *magnetic field gradients*.

15.2.3 DIFFUSION MRI

Water molecules at any temperature above absolute zero undergo Brownian motion or molecular diffusion [Einstein and Fürth, 1905]. In free water, this motion is completely random, and water molecules move with equal probability in all directions (*isotropic diffusion*). In the presence of constraining structures, such as the axons connecting neurons together, water molecules move more often in the same direction than they do across these structures (*anisotropic diffusion*).

When such a molecule moves, the two precessing protons of its hydrogen nucleus move as well. When this motion occurs in the same direction as the diffusion gradient q (an extra magnetic field gradient that is applied during scanning) of a diffusion-weighted MRI scan, the detected signal from that position is weakened, or attenuated.

This MRI signal attenuation and the diffusion that causes it can be modeled by the following equation [Le Bihan *et al.*, 2001]:

$$\frac{S}{S_0} = e^{-b \cdot \mathrm{ADC}} \tag{15.1}$$

Where S_0 is the signal without diffusion weighting, also known as the baseline image, S is the signal with diffusion weighting, b is the "b value" and ADC is the apparent diffusion coefficient, representing the amount of diffusion in $\frac{\mathrm{mm}^2}{s}$. The b value, with unit $\frac{s}{\mathrm{mm}^2}$, consists of factors describing the strength and duration of the gradient pulse, and the time between pulses. The diffusion is qualified as "apparent," as it bundles the effects of different types of properties, and is also dependent on the used b value. This equation holds for diffusion in a single direction.

By applying diffusion gradients in a number of different directions, anisotropic water diffusion can also be measured.

Diffusion Tensor Imaging When at least six directions are acquired, the b value becomes the **b** matrix and the ADC becomes a 3×3 symmetric diffusion tensor **D**, defined as:

$$\mathbf{D} = \begin{matrix} D_{xx} & D_{xy} & D_{xz} \\ D_{yx} & D_{yy} & D_{yz} \\ D_{zx} & D_{zy} & D_{zz} \end{matrix} \tag{15.2}$$

This diffusion tensor describes molecular mobility along perpendicular directions of the MRI reference frame (D_{xx}, D_{yy}, D_{zz}), as well as the coupling between these directions. This type of MRI acquisition is called diffusion tensor imaging, or DTI. As mentioned above, the shape of the diffusion (and hence the elements of the diffusion tensor) at a certain point is affected by the structures running through it.

High Angular Resolution Diffusion Imaging DTI is not able to capture more than one principal direction per sample point. If two or more neural fibers were to cross, normal single tensor DTI would show either planar or more spherical diffusion at that point. The full diffusion probability density function, or PDF, is a function $f(\mathbf{p}, \mathbf{r})$ describing the probability of water diffusion from each voxel position $\mathbf{p}$ to all possible three dimensional displacements $\mathbf{r}$ in the volume. This is a six-dimensional function, as for each 3D voxel position, a complete 3D volume of probabilities has to be stored.

In order to reconstruct the PDF, about 500 or more diffusion-weighted MRI volumes have to be acquired successively. This is called *diffusion spectrum imaging* or DSI [Hagmann *et al.*, 2006] and is the canonical way of acquiring the complete 3D water diffusion behavior. However, the time and processing required to perform full DSI complicate its use in research and practice.

Alternatively, the 3D diffusion profile around every point can be sampled with 40 or more directions [Tuch *et al.*, 1999, 2002]. Based on such data, multiple diffusion tensors can be fit to the data [Tuch *et al.*, 2002] and higher order diffusion tensors can be used [Özarslan and Mareci, 2003], spherical harmonics can be used to approximate the apparent diffusion coefficient on the sphere [Frank, 2002], or a model-free method such as Q-Ball imaging [Tuch, 2004] can be applied. Q-Ball yields as output an orientation distribution function, or ODF. The ODF is related to the diffusion PDF in that it describes for each direction the sum of the PDF values in that direction. It can be visualized as a deformed sphere of which the radius in any direction represents the amount of diffusion in that direction. Figure 15.3 shows examples of a PDF and an ODF around a single point in a diffusion dataset.

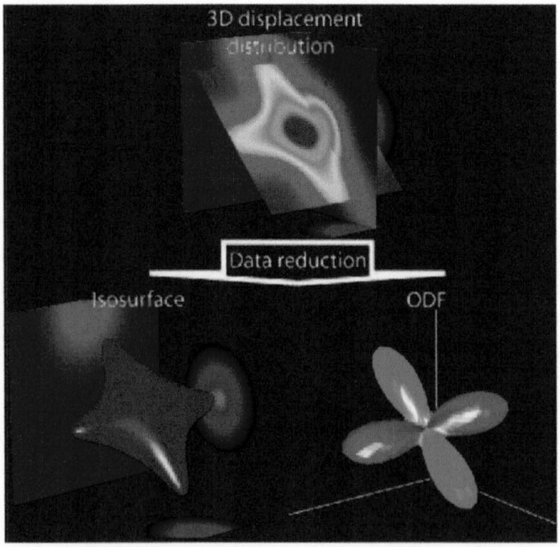

FIGURE 15.3 *Illustration of the 3D diffusion probability function (PDF) at the top, an isosurface of equal probability at the bottom left, and the orientation distribution function (ODF) at the bottom right (From [Hagmann et al., 2006]).*

Following Descoteaux *et al.* [2009], we group these techniques involving a higher number of diffusion directions, including DSI, under High Angular Resolution Diffusion Imaging, or HARDI.

15.2.4 FUNCTIONAL MRI

Blood-oxygen-level dependence, or BOLD, is a special type of MRI that is able to measure increased levels of blood oxygenation [Ogawa *et al.*, 1990]. Because they require more glucose from the bloodstream, active neurons cause higher blood oxygenation in nearby veins. Based on this principle, functional MRI, or fMRI, uses BOLD to image time-dependent 3D neural activity in the brain [Ogawa *et al.*, 1992].

fMRI can also be used to derive functional or *effective connectivity* in the brain. Functional connectivity is determined by calculating the temporal correlations between the fMRI signals originating from different parts of the brain [Friston, 1994]. This is done either while the subject performs a specific task, for example, tapping with a finger, in order to assess how the brain network is applied during that task, or during *resting state*. In this latter case, functional MRI is acquired with the subject in a relaxed mental state, in other words, not performing some task or another. This type of data, called *resting-state fMRI*, can be used to study the functional organization of the brain.

Connectivity data can be determined between a specific seed region or voxel and one or more other regions or voxels, or exhaustively between all regions or voxels in the brain.

The spatial resolution of the resultant dataset ranges from 1 mm spacing in the case of region-based studies to 4 mm spacing in the case of whole brain studies. The temporal resolution can be as high as 1 second.

Effective connectivity, defined as the causal influence one neuronal system exerts over another, is dependent on a model of the connectivity between the participating regions. For example, the signal at one position could be expressed as the weighted sum of the signals elsewhere [Friston, 1994]. If the model is invalid, the effective connectivity derived from fMRI is also invalid.

15.3 VISUALIZATION OF STRUCTURAL CONNECTIVITY

Vilanova *et al.* [2006] proposed a classification of that DTI visualization methods could be classified based both on the dimensionality to which the tensor is reduced and on the ability of the methods to show local or global information. Their classification includes the following types:

1. *Scalar indices* reduce the multivalued tensor data to one or more scalar values.
2. *Volume rendering* techniques map from the derived scalar indices to 3D projections of the data that give indirect information about the shape of the tensor.
3. *Tensor glyphs* are able to represent visually and directly the tensors without having to reduce their dimensionality.
4. *Vector field visualization* reduces the tensors to vectors, for example by selecting the principal eigenvectors of the tensors, and then visualizes those vectors with, for example, streamlines.
5. *Beyond vector field visualization* groups all techniques that make use of more of the tensor information and are able to show global information, for example, stream surfaces.

Here we propose a simplification of this classification to group all structural connectivity visualization techniques. We divide all methods into three classes:

1. *Scalar Reduction* approaches reduce the multifield data that describes structural connectivity to one or more scalars, and then apply any of the known scalar visualization techniques to the reduced data.

2 *Glyphs* visually represent point samples of the multifield data as completely as reasonable. These could be diffusion tensors, or even HARDI orientation distribution functions (ODFs).
3 *Global Multifield* techniques aim to retain more of the multifield information, and aim to represent more global features of the data, often linking together samples based on the connective structures that they sample.

One could argue that scalar reduction and glyph techniques do not directly represent the structural connectivity, but instead the point-wise diffusion information. However, the visualizations generated by these techniques are most often used to study the connectivity, albeit implicitly. For this reason, we have classified them as structural connectivity visualization techniques.

15.3.1 SCALAR REDUCTION

Using scalar metrics, such as the *fractional anisotropy* (FA), multifield DWI data can be reduced to one or more scalar values and then displayed using traditional scalar visualization techniques, for example, multiplanar reformation or volume rendering.

Diffusivity and Anisotropy Metrics for DTI Most DTI metrics either measure the amount or the shape of the diffusion. These are called respectively *diffusivity* and *anisotropy metrics*. Both types of metrics are often based on the eigenanalysis of the diffusion tensor matrix **D**. Since **D** is a symmetric real valued matrix, it has three real and non-negative eigenvalues, denoted λ_i, and three orthogonal eigenvectors, denoted e_i.

Diffusivity metrics are essential to assess the direction-independent component of diffusion. Such metrics may be used as a filter to select which voxels should be actually visualized. Often, the mean diffusivity λ_{mean} is used for this purpose. λ_{mean} is simply the average of the three eigenvalues λ_i. Alternatively, the maximum of the λ_i values may be used as a measure for the diffusivity at a particular location.

The variance of the eigenvalues is a natural anisotropy metric (Eq. 15.3). It does not depend on the order of the eigenvalues and is a relatively stable metric.

$$c_{\text{var}} = (\lambda_1 - \lambda_{mean})^2 + (\lambda_2 - \lambda_{mean})^2 + (\lambda_3 - \lambda_{mean})^2 \tag{15.3}$$

The trace of the diffusion tensor $\text{Tr}(\mathbf{D}) = D_{xx} + D_{yy} + D_{zz}$ has also been proposed as a more robust measure of the mean diffusivity that can also be used in cases when the whole diffusion tensor cannot be acquired [Le Bihan *et al.*, 2001].

The anisotropy can be more specifically described by making use of a characterization of anisotropy that is based on the sorted eigenvalues with $\lambda_1 \geq \lambda_2 \geq \lambda_3$. This leads to the barycentric space depicted in Figure 15.4. A barycentric space is a coordinate system defined on a triangle. All points in this space have coordinates, here c_p, c_l, and c_s, with values between 0 and 1. At the vertices of the triangular space, one coordinate equals 1 and the other two coordinates equal 0. At the edges of the triangle, one coordinate equals 0, and the sum of the two other coordinate equals 1. c_p, c_l, and c_s are defined as follows [Westin *et al.*, 1999]:

$$c_l = \frac{\lambda_1 - \lambda_2}{\lambda_1 + \lambda_2 + \lambda_3} \tag{15.4}$$

$$c_p = \frac{2 * (\lambda_2 - \lambda_3)}{\lambda_1 + \lambda_2 + \lambda_3} \tag{15.5}$$

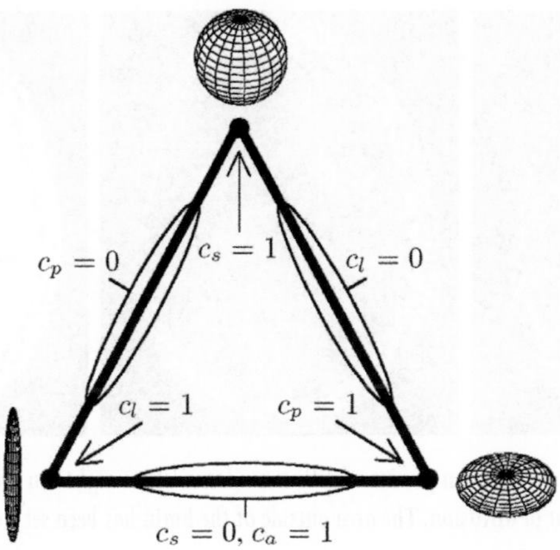

FIGURE 15.4 *Barycentric space of anisotropies with linear and planar anisotropy as well as spherical isotropy at the corners (From: Kindlmann et al. [2000]).*

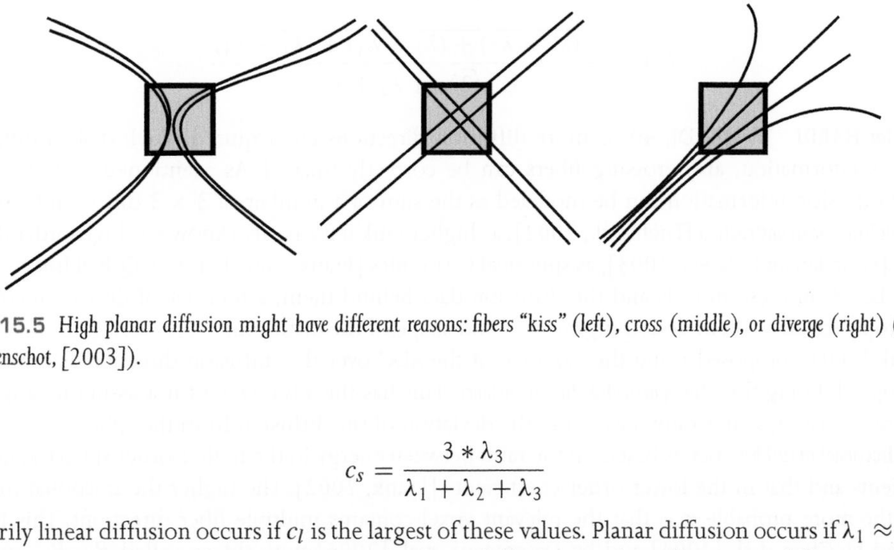

FIGURE 15.5 *High planar diffusion might have different reasons: fibers "kiss" (left), cross (middle), or diverge (right) (Redrawn from: Berenschot, [2003]).*

$$c_s = \frac{3 * \lambda_3}{\lambda_1 + \lambda_2 + \lambda_3} \tag{15.6}$$

A primarily linear diffusion occurs if c_l is the largest of these values. Planar diffusion occurs if $\lambda_1 \approx \lambda_2$ and $\lambda_2 \gg \lambda_3$ which leads to a large c_p value. High planar diffusion might indicate very different situations which cannot be discriminated due to the small size of fibers compared to the resolution of DTI data. Fibers may "kiss," cross, or diverge (see Fig. 15.5) [Moberts et al., 2005]. Moreover, bending fibers lead to high planar diffusion too.

If all eigenvalues are similar, the c_s value is largest. This corresponds to isotropic diffusion. The factors 2 and 3 in Equations 15.5 and 15.6 have been inserted to ensure that c_p and c_s are in the range from zero to one and that all measures sum up to 1. Figure 15.6, c_l, c_p, and c_s, for a coronal brain section are compared.

Based on these properties, an anisotropy measure, the *anisotropy index* (Eq. 15.7) can be derived:

$$c_a = 1 - c_s \frac{\lambda_1 + \lambda_2 - 2 * \lambda_3}{\lambda_1 + \lambda_2 + \lambda_3} \tag{15.7}$$

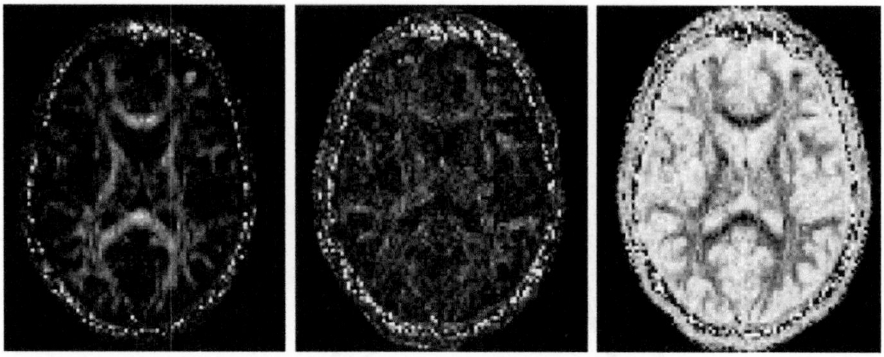

FIGURE 15.6 *Linear, planar, and spherical component of diffusion (from left to right) in a coronal brain section. White indicates a high level of the respective component of diffusion. The area outside of the brain has been set to black (From: Benger et al. [2006]).*

Fractional anisotropy, or FA, is also a single anisotropy measure that is based on the eigenvalues of the diffusion tensor. We document it here as it is very frequently used in DTI-based research. FA, defined in Equation 15.8, also characterizes the amount of anisotropy but does not give information about its shape.

$$FA = \frac{\sqrt{(\lambda_1 - \lambda_2) + (\lambda_2 - \lambda_3) + (\lambda_1 - \lambda_3)}}{\sqrt{2}\lambda_1 + \lambda_2 + \lambda_3} \tag{15.8}$$

Metrics for HARDI In HARDI, 40 or more diffusion directions are acquired [Tuch *et al.*, 1999, 2002]. With this information, also crossing fibers can be correctly imaged. As mentioned in § 15.2.3, this kind of diffusion information can be modeled as the sum of a number of 3×3 diffusion tensors, also called *multitensor reconstruction* [Tuch *et al.*, 2002], as higher rank tensors, also known as high-order diffusion tensors [Özarslan and Mareci, 2003], as spherical harmonics [Frank, 2002] or with Q-Ball Imaging [Tuch, 2004]. Based on these models and the diffusion data behind them, a number of derived metrics have been proposed, all of them describing the size and shape of the diffusion.

Frank [2001] proposed using the variance of the ADC over the diffusion direction as a measure of anisotropy, dubbing this the *spherical diffusion variance*. This has the advantage of not assuming any specific model of diffusion, as it is only measuring the deviation of the diffusion from the sphere.

The *fractional multifiber index*, is based on the ratio between energy in the higher-order spherical harmonic coefficients and that in the lower order coefficients [Frank, 2002]. The higher the fractional multifiber index, the more probable it is that the relevant voxel contains multiple fiber directions. This idea was extended by Chen *et al.* [2004] and by Descoteaux *et al.* [2006] with the so-called R_0, R_2, and R_{multi} ratios, also based on the spherical harmonic coefficients. These measures can be used to distinguish between isotropic, one-fiber, and multifiber voxels. In the generalization proposed by Descoteaux *et al.* [2006], large R_0 and/or small ADC variance is isotropic. If not, then large R_{multi} is multifiber. Everything else is one-fiber. Chen *et al.* [2004] made use only of R_0 and R_2 to distinguish, in a similar way, isotropic, double fiber and single fiber voxels.

Based on *generalized DTI*, their higher rank tensor approach, Özarslan *et al.* [2005] proposed generalized measures of diffusivity and anisotropy that can be used on HARDI data. It is shown how the mean diffusivity can be calculated, analogous to the case of the rank-2 DTI tensor, as a linear combination of an increasing number of higher rank tensor elements. The *generalized anisotropy*, or GA, is based on the variance of the normalized diffusion coefficients, which themselves are also derived from the higher rank diffusion tensor.

Finally, the standard deviation of the orientation distribution function (ODF) yielded by Q-Ball Imaging can be used to calculate the *generalized fractional anisotropy*.

As can been seen from these examples, diffusion measures either rely on the shape of the diffusion as described by the tensor modeling it, or by the variation of the diffusion, defined as a function on the sphere. Diffusion spectrum imaging (DSI) yields the full diffusion probability density function, or PDF, which can be transformed to the ODF [Hagmann *et al.*, 2006, Wedeen *et al.*, 2008], which in turn can be used to calculate diffusivity metrics.

Slice-Based Visualization Once the diffusion-weighted data has been reduced by applying one or more of the scalar metrics, existing scalar data and volume visualization techniques can be applied.

As we have discussed in § 1.3, radiologists are accustomed to exploring volume data with slice-based 2D visualizations. The main advantage of 2D visualization is that every voxel contributes to the visualization and can be selected to inspect quantitative values. A slice-based visualization with the usual interaction functionality, such as browsing through the slices (cine-mode) and interactive modification of the presentation lookup-table (mapping of anisotropic measures to gray values or colors), is an appropriate starting point for our discussion of visualization techniques.

Color-Coding Diffusivity and Anisotropy Color maps for the diffusivity and anisotropy metrics discussed above should be carefully chosen. To get rid of background voxels, an appropriate mean diffusivity λ_{mean} threshold should be selected. Instead of absolute values, thresholds have to be adapted to the image histogram. The design of color-mapping schemes which convey the quantitative nature of tensor data unambiguously is a complex task.

Color-Coding Directional Information The directional information encoded in the diffusion tensor may be color-coded in various ways. In order to avoid confusion, directional information should not be combined with other parameters, such as diffusivity. An important aspect of encoding the principal diffusion direction is that the orientation of diffusion is meaningless: parallel and antiparallel vectors (e_1 and $-e_1$) convey the same information with respect to the diffusion direction. In order to compare and evaluate color schemes, some requirements are discussed. According to [Pajevic and Pierpaoli, 1999], color schemes should:

- be *perceptually linearized*,
- be *independent of the reference frame* in which the data are acquired, and
- use *principal colors* (red, green, blue, cyan, magenta, and yellow) for principal directions (along the x-, y- and z-direction as well as along directions bisecting the xy-, the xz-, and the yz-plane).

In addition, an anisotropy metric should be used as a filter to avoid that directional information in isotropic regions is visualized where it is meaningless and confusing. The second requirement is crucial in order to compare DTI data from different patients or scanners. To fulfill this condition, an anatomical coordinate system is required which is based on landmarks that can be reliably identified in each dataset. If DTI data are analyzed, the landmarks have to be selected and the data are aligned with the coordinate system. Pajevic and Pierpaoli [1999] suggest a coordinate system with the yz-plane corresponding to the sagittal plane aligned with the interhemispheric fissure and the y-axis corresponding to the anterior-posterior intercommissural line.

Based on an appropriate coordinate system, colors may be assigned by considering the polar coordinates of the principal diffusion direction. A normalized vector is uniquely characterized by a polar θ and an azimuthal angle ϕ. Pajevic and Pierpaoli [1999] suggest to encode the polar angle with the hue component

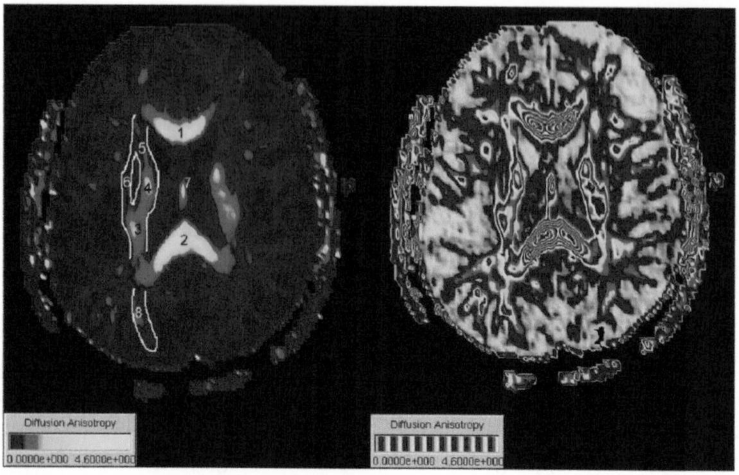

FIGURE 15.7 **Left:** *an exponential color map is used for anisotropy.* **Right:** *A cylindrical color map indicates mean diffusivity. Such a color map is not unique (different values are mapped to the same color), but the frequency of changes may be observed well* (From: [*Wünsche*, 2004]).

and the azimuthal angle with the saturation component of the HSV color space. This is a viable strategy. However, the hue component of the HSV space is not (nearly) perceptually linear. Brightness may be used to encode anisotropy. In order to avoid that too much information is encoded, a few discrete brightness values may be employed [Schlüter *et al.*, 2005].

A wide-spread color scheme is to map the x-, y-, and z-component of the normalized e_1 vector to the red-, green-, and blue-component of a color. Wünsche (2004) found that linear mappings of diffusion metrics to colors are not optimal for the interpretation of fiber tracts. Instead, he used exponential color maps for visualizing anisotropy and a cylindrical color map for mean diffusivity where subtle differences are recognizable and high contrasts arise (see Fig. 15.7).

Combining Color and Transparency to Convey Directional Information A common extension of color-coding is to employ transparency. Since DTI data are primarily analyzed with respect to the direction of principal diffusion, it is reasonable to use opacity (the inverse of transparency) to represent anisotropy. For example, the more isotropic diffusion becomes, the more transparent the representation. With this strategy, directional information is only pronounced if it is reliable. The use of transparency requires some background information, either a constant background color or anatomical information, such as a T2-weighted image (see Fig. 15.8).

Direct Volume Rendering By the straightforward mapping of an opacity and color gradation to the barycentric c_p, c_l, and c_s anisotropy index spaces discussed in § 15.3.1, a transfer function can be specified. Kindlmann *et al.* [2000] dubbed this process *barycentric mapping*. With this transfer function, a direct volume rendering can be made that visually represents these scalar metrics.

In Figure 15.9, parts of the volume with a high c_s index, that is regions with isotropic diffusion, are rendered transparently. A color gradation from longitudinal to planar diffusion helps to distinguish between these two types of diffusion.

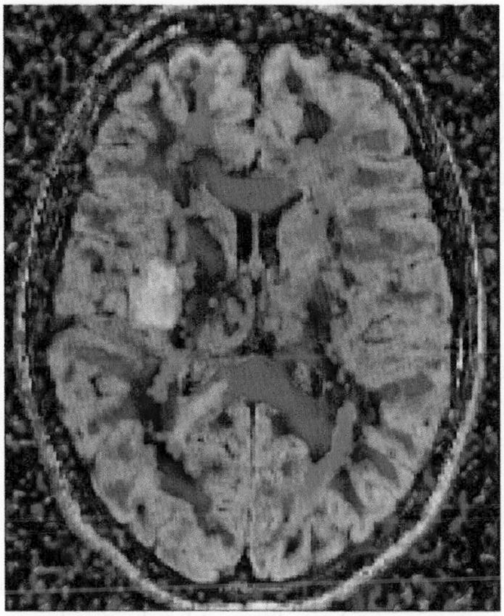

FIGURE 15.8 *The components of the principal eigenvector are mapped to the red-, green- and blue-component of color. Transparency indicates linear anisotropy. In regions with low linear anisotropy, the T2-weighted image is displayed. A malignant tumor in the left half becomes obvious as bright region with very low linear anisotropy (From: Benger et al. [2006]).*

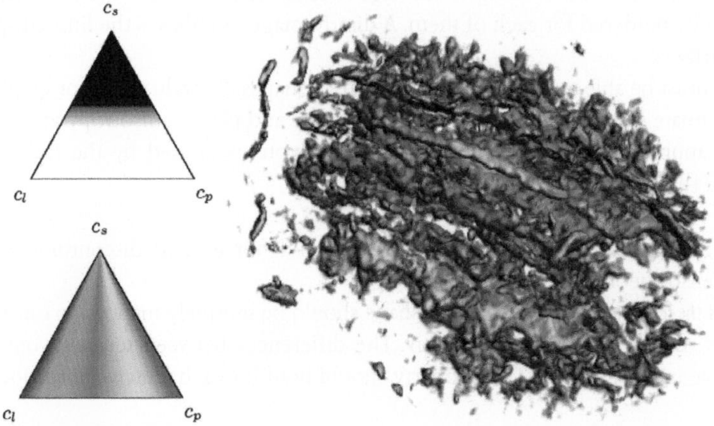

FIGURE 15.9 *Direct volume rendering of DTI data. Opacity and color transfer functions have been specified on the barycentric* c_l, c_s, *and* c_p *space, as shown on the left. On the right the resultant volume rendering is shown (From: [Kindlmann et al., 2000]).*

The lit-*tensors* technique can be used to enhance the shading of these volume renderings [Kindlmann et al., 2000]. In areas of linear anisotropy, the same lighting model as for illuminated streamlines is used. In areas of planar anisotropy, surface shading is used. In all other areas, smooth interpolation is performed between the two different lighting models. The lit-tensors lighting approach was combined with standard Phong shading based on the gradient of the opacity.

15.3.2 Glyphs

Glyphs can be used to represent samples from structural connectivity datasets, with no or significantly less reduction than is the case for the scalar reduction approaches. For example, the eigensystem of a diffusion tensor can be mapped directly to an ellipsoid, or the HARDI-derived orientation distribution function (see § 15.2.3) can be displayed as a field of deformed spheres. In the following, we make a distinction between glyph techniques for DTI data, that can be represented as traditional rank-2 diffusion tensors, and those for HARDI data.

15.3.2.1 DTI Glyphs

Glyphs convey second-order tensor data by mapping their eigenvalues and eigenvectors to the orientation and shape of a geometric primitive, such as a cylinder or a cuboid. Glyph-based visualizations transform a glyph geometry G into a tensor glyph G_T through Equation 15.9:

$$G_T = R^{-1}ERG \tag{15.9}$$

E is a diagonal matrix which consists of the eigenvalues λ_i and R is a rotation matrix which transforms the coordinate system of the dataset to the basis formed by the (orthogonal) eigenvectors [Kindlmann, 2004b].

Since the diffusion tensor has three non-negative real-valued eigenvalues, glyph geometries such as cubes, generalized cylinders (with ellipsoidal cross sections) and ellipsoids are typical choices. For such glyph geometries, the principal, medium, and minor axes correspond to the eigenvectors e_i and the glyphs are scaled in each dimension according to the eigenvalues λ_i. Cubes have the advantage that only few polygons need to be rendered for each of them. A disadvantage of cubes is the limited spatial perception due to the flat surfaces.

Tensor glyphs must be able to depict all possible tensor shapes. To evaluate tensor glyphs, the triangular barycentric coordinate system (recall § 15.3.1) with linear and planar anisotropy and spherical isotropy at its vertices is appropriate. The evaluation of tensor glyphs is guided by the following criteria (cf. [Kindlmann, 2004b]):

1. *Continuity*. Small changes in the tensor shape should not lead to discontinuous changes in the resulting tensor geometry.
2. *Uniqueness of the tensor geometry*. Each tensor shape should be uniquely mapped to one tensor geometry.
3. *Unambiguous visualization of the tensor geometry*. The differences between tensor geometries should be recognizable in image space. This property should hold for each viewing direction.

Kindlmann (2004b) demonstrate that cylinders fail with respect to the first requirement: small changes of the tensor shape may lead to a switch of the orientation of the cylinder in the case that planar and linear anisotropy have similar values. Cuboids do not exhibit such a discontinuous behavior. However, they are not uniquely defined in case of zero planar anisotropy. Ellipsoids fulfill the first and second requirement. As we will discuss later, they fail with respect to the third requirement which gives rise to more advanced tensor glyphs based on the concept of superquadrics.

Ellipsoid Tensor Glyphs The orientation and size of an ellipsoid conveys the space in which water molecules, originating at the ellipsoid's center, diffuse. The ellipsoid has the advantage that it depicts all information of the diffusion tensor in a simple shape.

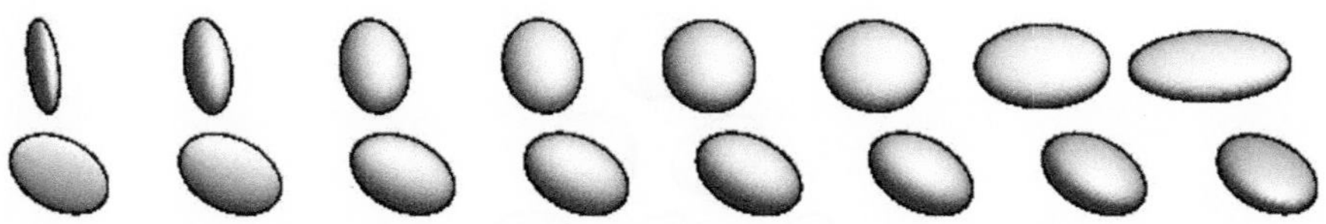

FIGURE 15.10 *Ellipsoids in the upper image are perceived as similar although they are actually quite different. The same ellipsoids are depicted in the lower image. Due to a different viewing direction the ellipsoids can be better discriminated (From: [Kindlmann, 2004a]).*

Limitations The major problem of ellipsoidal tensor glyphs is their ambiguity in image space: Under certain viewing directions, different tensor shapes are difficult to discriminate. Depending on the projection direction, the extent of the ellipsoid in the z-direction is difficult to assess (see Fig. 15.10). Only shading provides cues to differentiate a sphere and an ellipsoid with small extent in the viewing direction. In principle, some information loss in the projection from 3D to 2D cannot be avoided. However, as Westin *et al.* [2002] showed, the information loss may be reduced with more advanced geometric shapes.

Superquadric Tensor Glyphs With superquadric surfaces as tensor glyphs, all requirements discussed at the beginning of this section are met. Superquadric surfaces are widely used in visualization and graphics since their introduction by Barr (1981). The use of superquadrics for visualizing DTI data was suggested by Kindlmann (2004a). Superquadrics may be represented implicitly by Equation 15.10.

$$q(x, y, z) = (x^{\frac{2}{\alpha}} + y^{\frac{2}{\alpha}})^{\frac{\alpha}{\beta}} + z^{\frac{2}{\beta}} - 1 = 0 \tag{15.10}$$

The angles α and β control the shape of superquadrics. Ellipsoids are special variants of superquadrics. If α equals β, Equation 15.10 can be simplified and results in the implicit representation of a sphere. For their use as tensor glyphs, the space of superquadrics is restricted to a subset defined by $\beta \leq \alpha \leq 1$. Superquadric tensor glyphs can now be defined with respect to the anisotropy measures c_l and c_p and a user-controlled sharpness parameter γ [Kindlmann, 2004a] according to Equation 15.11.

$$\alpha = (1 - c_p)^\gamma \tag{15.11}$$

$$\beta = (1 - c_l)^\gamma \tag{15.12}$$

The edge sharpness parameter γ controls how pronounced edges occur with growing values of c_p and c_l (see Fig. 15.11). The edge sharpness parameter is user-defined, however some heuristics may be employed to come to a reasonable adjustment. Lower values for γ are appropriate in noisier regions of the data.

15.3.2.2 HARDI Glyphs

HARDI data is most commonly visualized using deformed spheres as glyphs. At each point, a sphere is deformed according to the orientation distribution function, or ODF. Recall from § 15.2.3 that the ODF is a function that sums, for each direction on the sphere, the diffusion probabilities for that direction. In other words, it reflects the amount of diffusion for each direction on the sphere. Schultz and Kindlmann [2010] suggests calling such deformed spheres *spherical polar plots*.

Q-Ball imaging [Tuch, 2004] yields the ODF representation directly. The ODF, as a function on the sphere, can also be represented by spherical harmonics. Furthermore, higher-order diffusion tensors [Özarslan and Mareci, 2003] can be converted to their spherical harmonic representations [Hlawitschka and Scheuermann, 2005]. The diffusion ODF can be directly represented by deforming the vertices of a

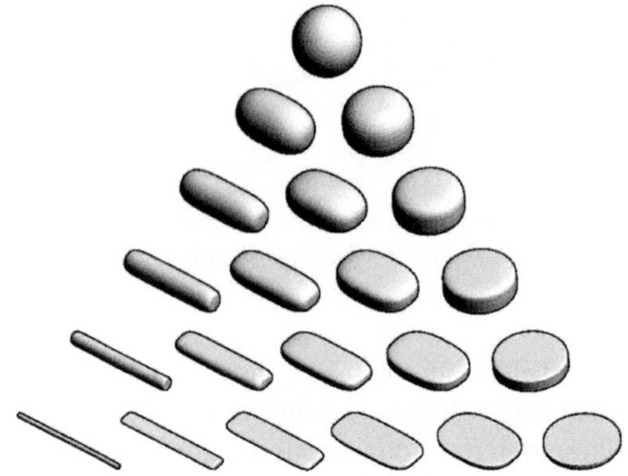

FIGURE 15.11 *Superquadric tensor glyphs in the barycentric space with sharpness factor 1.5 (From: [Kindlmann, 2004b]).*

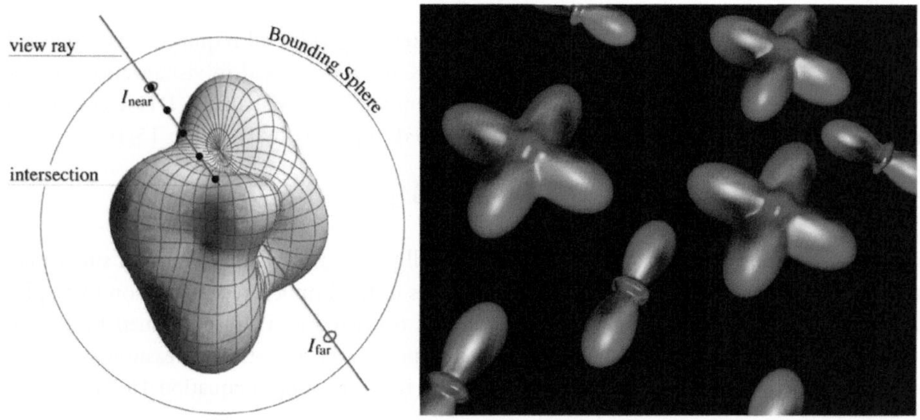

FIGURE 15.12 *Raycasting ODFs based on their spherical harmonic representation. On the left the raycasting setup is shown, on the right glyphs showing a synthetic field of crossing fibers (From: Peeters et al. [2009]).*

tessellated icosahedron, or by raycasting the spherical harmonics describing the ODF [Peeters *et al.*, 2009]. The raycasting approach offered performance advantages over rendering, for each glyph, an icosahedral mesh with more than 2000 vertices. Figure 15.12 shows the raycasting configurating as well as an example of the raycasted HARDI glyphs.

Schultz and Kindlmann [2010] introduced the 3D *Higher Order Maximum Enhancing* (HOME) glyphs, a generalization of second-order tensor ellipsoids, to visualize higher order tensors. For symmetric tensors of even order l, the vectors on the unit sphere are transformed by $l-1$ applications of the tensor-vector inner product between $\mathscr{T}$ and $\mathbf{v}$:

$$\mathbf{h}(\mathbf{v}) = \mathscr{T} \cdot^{l-1} \mathbf{v} \qquad (15.13)$$

This equation can be applied to the vertices of a finally sampled icosahedron, and will yield glyphs that significantly sharper maxima than the simple ODF-deformed spheres [Schultz *et al.*, 2009, Schultz and Kindlmann 2010], a property which is especially useful when investigating crossing fibers. The diffusion maxima and their variable-sized regions of influence are explicitly partitioned and colored using the

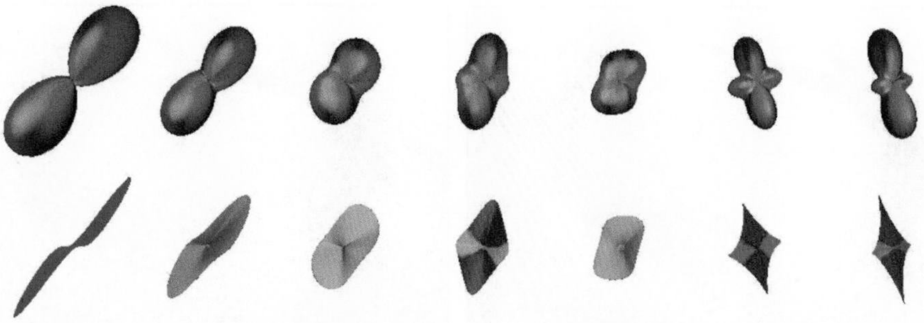

FIGURE 15.13 *Higher Order Maximum Enhancing (HOME) glyphs in the bottom row, with the corresponding traditional polar plot in the top row. HOME glyphs have sharper maxima. Maxima have been color-coded according to direction, and color-saturated according to sharpness (Courtesy of Thomas Schultz, University of Bonn. See also Schultz and Kindlmann [2010]).*

widely accepted XYZ-RGB approach, while the peak sharpness is used to modulate color saturation, giving further visual feedback on the exact shape of the diffusion. Figure 15.13 shows example HOME glyphs, with corresponding traditional ODF glyphs.

This results in a field of complex glyphs representing at each point the diffusion profile at that position. In contrast to DTI glyph techniques, regions of crossing fibers can in general be identified.

15.3.2.3 Visualization of Glyphs

For the visualization of tensor information in a selected slice, a 2D array of tensor glyphs is created.

Controlling Density An important aspect of the visualization of tensor glyphs is their placement and scaling. Without special care, elongated glyphs in areas of high diffusion may overlap, resulting in visual clutter. On the other hand, if the glyphs are too sparsely spaced in order to ensure that no overlap occurs, the connection between them is difficult to recognize. Laidlaw *et al.* [1998] suggest to normalize the glyphs such that their largest extent is equal. This normalization gives a better overview of the anatomy and pathology. However, with this normalization, the magnitude of the diffusion tensor is no longer visually represented.

Jittered Placement If tensor glyphs are rendered at node positions of the regular grid of the underlying DTI data, the structure of the grid becomes obvious and compromises image interpretation. Image interpretation may be considerably improved by slightly (randomly) disturbing tensor glyphs positions. This technique is called *jittering* and is used for example in vector visualization with arrow-shaped glyphs. Figure 15.14 illustrates the effect of jittering for an easier interpretation of DTI data with ellipsoids.

3D Visualization Glyphs are well suited for 2D visualization. However, for the investigation of the whole 3D data, additional or completely different visualization techniques are desirable. Glyphs fail to convey complex 3D data, since they occlude each other, and their connectivity is not visually represented. Taking into account the metrics defined in § 15.3.1, the display of tensor glyphs may be restricted, for example to those regions with high mean diffusivity and strong anisotropy. Figure 15.15 illustrates the use of superquadrics for depicting a slice of DTI data of the human brain.

Color Schemes for Diffusion Glyphs Tensor glyphs are usually color-coded. Color may represent the orientation of the principal eigenvector as described in § 15.3.1. It is desirable that the perceived difference of colors

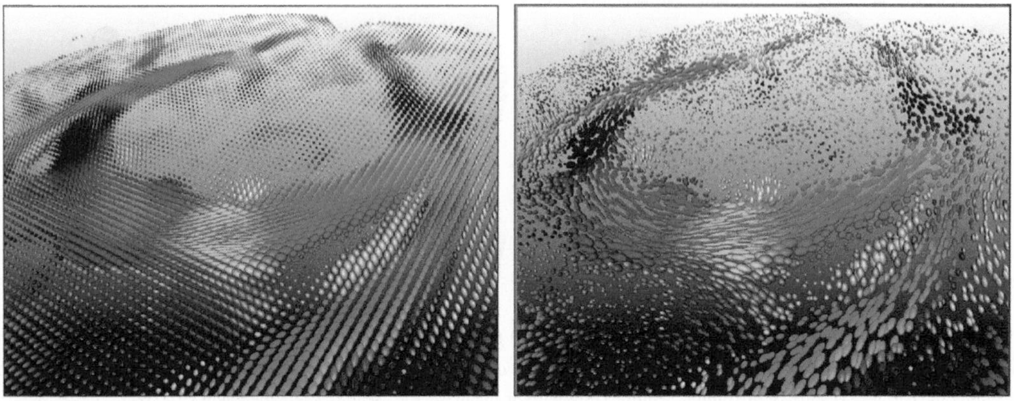

FIGURE 15.14 *In the left image, ellipsoids are centered at the original grid positions thus highlighting the regular grid. By slight random translations (jittering), the distracting effect of the grid is removed. Glyphs are colored according to the principal eigenvector (Courtesy of Mathias Schlüter and Olaf Konrad, Fraunhofer MEVIS Bremen).*

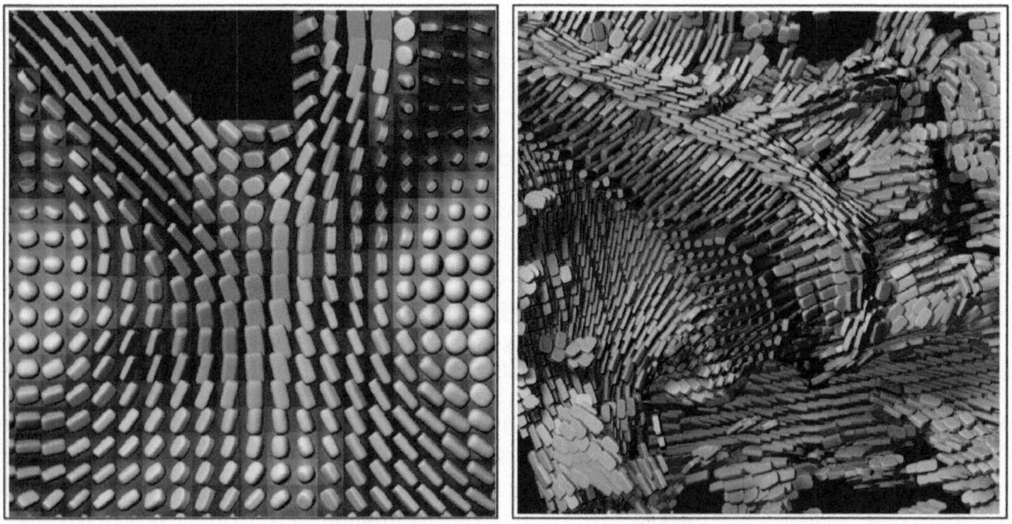

FIGURE 15.15 *Superquadric tensor glyphs applied to a slice of DTI data (left) and to a 3D view (right) (From: [Kindlmann, 2004b]).*

for adjacent glyphs are small if the major orientation differs only slightly. As discussed earlier, the HSV color space is appropriate for this purpose.

Schlüter *et al.* [2004] derived a color scheme which is very effective for the analysis of slices. This color scheme enables the encoding of anisotropy, for example, the anisotropy index (Eq. 15.7) as well as the projection of the largest eigenvector e_1 onto the current slice. The orientation of e_1 is mapped to the hue component, whereas the length of the projection is mapped to the saturation. Finally, the brightness

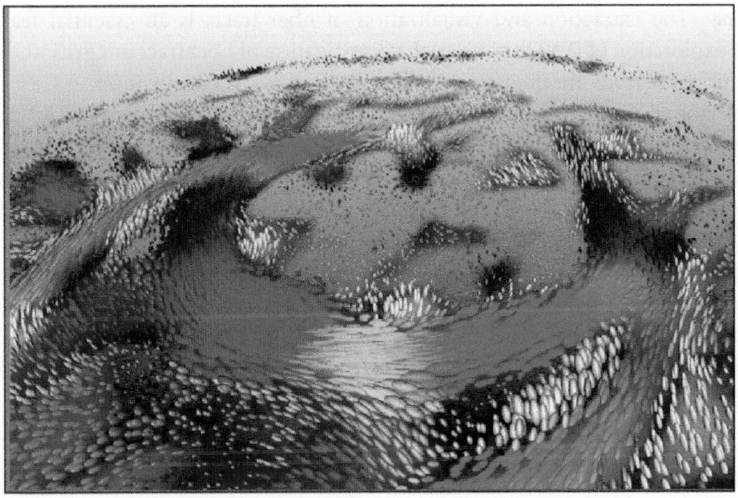

FIGURE 15.16 *Ellipsoids represent diffusion tensors in a selected oblique plane. The HSV color model is employed to color-code the major orientation of the data, its projection to the selected plane and fractional anisotropy (Courtesy of Mathias Schlüter, Fraunhofer MEVIS Bremen).*

further conveys the anisotropy. Figure 15.16 presents ellipsoidal tensor glyphs colored according to the described color scheme. In particular for distant or partially occluded ellipsoids, color is useful as an additional visualization parameter, although it does not present more information than the ellipsoid.

Combining DTI and HARDI Glyphs The necessity of acquiring HARDI data in regions of the brain containing crossing fiber bundles has been shown. However, many regions are known to contain more straightforward, non-crossing, fiber bundles. In these regions, the additional effort of processing and visualizing HARDI data is not justified. In order to address this problem, Prčkovska *et al.* [2011] proposed a data-driven classification of the acquired data, determining on a per-position basis whether HARDI data is required, or normal DTI data would suffice. Based on this classification, either straightforward DTI or more complex HARDI glyphs are used. Their visualizations were further enhanced with DTI fiber tracts.

15.3.3 GLOBAL MULTIFIELD

Global Multifield techniques visualize global information of the inherently multiply valued field. In structural connectivity, these are for the largest part *fiber tracking* [Mori and Barker, 1999], also known as *tractography* [Basser and Jones, 2002] techniques that attempt to derive the anatomical trajectories of neural fibers from diffusion-weighted imaging (DWI) data.

In the following, we use DWI as a blanket term to refer to DTI and HARDI data. DTI is only able to capture a single fiber direction per point, whereas HARDI is able to capture multiple fiber directions per point. As is the case for both the scalar reduction and glyph-based techniques, global multifield visualization techniques are in essence the same for both types of data, but have to take into account this crucial difference. We will discuss first the general visualization approach, and then focus on the differences between the two types of data.

Fiber Tract Modeling The extraction and visualization of fiber tracts is an essential feature of software assistance for the exploration of DWI data, since the investigation of fiber tract integrity and the connectivity of different functional regions are the principal motivation for DWI acquisition.

Before we describe approaches toward this goal, we need to stress that fiber tract modeling is based on coarsely and discretely sampled data, which exhibits considerable noise and is exposed to various artifacts. Fiber tract modeling requires continuous data fields resulting from interpolation and approximation. The derived directional information for DTI, for example, is only reliable in a rather small portion of the data [Benger *et al.*, 2006].

Fiber tract extraction may lead to incoherent pathways, may show connectivity between brain regions that are in reality not connected or, more seriously, fail to extract fibers where connectivity is present. Therefore, any clinical application of these methods is only justifiable if users with long-term experience carefully interpret these "connectivity" data and correlate them to their knowledge of the white matter anatomy, as well as to the original data and other less abstract visualization techniques.

There are two major approaches to fiber tracking, or tractography: *deterministic* and *probabilistic*.

Deterministic Approaches attempt to extract a number of discrete trajectories, representing actual fiber bundles, from DWI data. The shape of the diffusion descriptor at each voxel, for example a diffusion tensor, higher order tensor or ODF, is employed to compute the contiguous pathways of nerve fiber tracts. Fiber tracking usually starts by selecting a region of interest from which seed points are selected by the user or determined automatically. Starting from these seed voxels, adjacent voxels allowing for a similar diffusion direction or directions are sought. Fiber tracts are reconstructed by interpolating directions between voxels in the neighborhood of the current tracking position. Finally, fiber tracts are visualized by either lines or some form of line-shaped polygons.

Probabilistic Approaches calculate the probabilities that a single source region is connected to a number of destination regions. This can be done for a whole volume of DWI data, yielding a probability volume, describing for each voxel the probability of that voxel being connected to the selected source voxel [Koch *et al.*, 2002]. Given such a probability volume, it is straightforward to derive a number of high-probability fiber tracts emanating from the source voxel. In clinical practice and research, the deterministic approaches are by far the most used and researched.

These visualization techniques summarize information and provide a more abstract view compared to glyph-based visualizations of DWI data, which depict for each voxel its individual diffusion descriptor.

15.3.3.1 Streamlines as Neural Pathways: Computation and Visualization

By definition, a streamline is tangent everywhere to the vector field V it is defined on. Streamlines (further discussed in § 19.2.4) can also be thought of as the trace of massless particles that are advected through the vector field. Streamlines have their origin in vector field analysis and visualization. They are a natural metaphor for DWI visualization, where the data can be reduced to a vector field describing the locally dominant direction of diffusion. These types of streamlines do not completely represent tensor information.

For DTI visualization, streamline computation is usually applied to the principal eigenvector e_1. For HARDI visualization, either the direction of maximum diffusion is selected in each voxel, or multiple streamlines are computed for a number of diffusion maxima in each voxel. This is described in more detail later in this section. Mathematically, streamlines are computed by integrating the vector field along a path s (see Figure 15.17):

$$s = \int \vec{V}\, ds \tag{15.14}$$

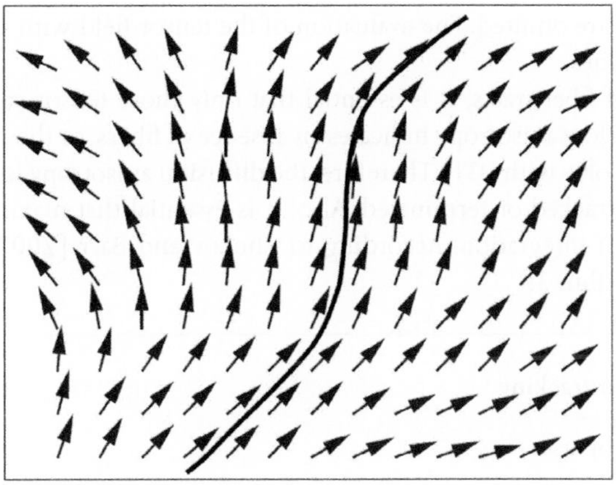

FIGURE 15.17 *Sketch of a vector field and a particular streamline computed by numerical integration (Courtesy of Noeska Smit, Delft University of Technology, inspired by [Hege and Stalling, 1997]).*

Integration is carried out along a path in forward and backward direction starting from an initial seed point (Eq. 15.14). At each grid location, the streamline corresponds to the local vector $\vec{V}$. In the case of a single diffusion maximum per voxel, there is only one streamline at each position in V except at singularities, so-called critical points where the magnitude of the vector is zero. Such singularities represent e.g., sources, sinks or center points of the vector fields enclosed by streamlines. In the case of multiple diffusion maxima per voxel, multiple streamlines do cross. Mathematically, these crossing streamlines exist in different but overlapping vector fields, corresponding to the multiple diffusion maxima per voxel.

Due to the discrete nature of the data, the integral (Eq. 15.14) is numerically approximated, for example, by Runge-Kutta or Euler schemes. Numerical approximations are based on a certain step size, where higher accuracy is achieved with smaller step sizes. As usual, increased accuracy is achieved at the expense of higher computational effort. An appropriate step size depends on the expected frequency of sudden changes.

The visualization of streamlines does not indicate the magnitude of a vector which is often an essential feature. A common technique is to color-code streamlines, for example with low magnitudes corresponding to green and high magnitude to red. In the case of DWI data, color-coding could be applied to reveal the amount of diffusion along the direction of maximum diffusion. As a variant of this strategy, the brightness can be employed to convey diffusion anisotropy. Schluter *et al.* [2005] used this variant to explore fiber tracts, near malignant brain tumors. With this strategy, dark fiber tracts indicate fiber destruction.

For visualization with streamlines, different integration limits are used which affect the length of the resulting streamlines. In general, longer streamlines are preferred, since a few longer streamlines are easier to interpret compared to many small streamlines. On the other hand, longer streamlines exhibit larger errors due to the accumulation of errors along the path. Streamlines are terminated either when the integration limits are reached, or a critical point with a very low magnitude of the local vector is encountered, or the local anisotropy becomes too low, or if the curvature of the streamline exceeds a defined threshold.

Adaptation of Streamlines for Tensor Data DTI data have a low resolution. Therefore, numerical integration is accomplished with small step sizes, such as a quarter of a voxel cell size, to prevent that important features, e.g., sharp turns, are omitted. The evaluation of the tensor field with subvoxel accuracy requires proper interpolation schemes.

For the visualization of fiber tracts, it is essential that only those tensor values are combined which exhibit strong anisotropy (low anisotropy indicates an absence of fibers, or the presence of fiber structures that are too complex to resolve with DTI). Therefore, the diffusion anisotropy is a useful criterion whether a fiber should be further tracked or terminated. Also, it is essential that maximum diffusivity exceeds a certain limit at any step of integration. According to Zhukov and Barr [2002], we can integrate these considerations with Algorithm 3:

ALGORITHM 3 Control fiber tracking

```
 1: Region R ⇐ selected by user
 2: for all P in R do
 3:    Tp ⇐ filter(T, P, ellipsoid)
 4:    cl ⇐ anisotropy(Tp)
 5:    if cl > eps then
 6:       e1 ⇐ direction(Tp)
 7:       trace1 ⇐ fibertrace(P, e1)
 8:       trace2 ⇐ fibertrace(P, −e1)
 9:       trace ⇐ trace1 + trace2
10:    end if
11: end for
```

In line 3, the diffusion tensor at point P is determined by interpolating the tensor field T with a filter kernel which corresponds to the diffusion ellipsoid. In line 4, a linear anisotropy measure is derived and compared with some threshold *epsilon* (line 5) in order to assess whether a significant linear diffusion occurs. If this is the case, the principal eigenvector e_1 of the tensor T_p at P is determined. Tracking is performed in forward and backward direction (opposing direction of e_1). The two traces are connected with each other.

In Algorithm 4, the *fibertrace* procedure is outlined. Filtering again considers the ellipsoid of the tensor P. As additional parameter, the current direction e_1 is considered. If the anisotropy at the new point P_n is above the threshold it is added to the trace and fibertracking continues. The termination criterion of fiber tracking may be a sophisticated combination of several measurements. At least, a linear anisotropy measure should be taken into account.

Usually, fiber tracking is modified to avoid very short fibers, since they are less reliable and distracting in the visualization. These modifications are performed as a correction step after an initial determination of fibers. Also, some constraints with respect to the curvature are often included in order to avoid sudden changes of the fiber direction. These constraints are reasonable, since sudden changes often represent a wrong path.

In regions of complex diffusion, selection of the direction of maximum diffusion can lead to arbitrary and incorrect new trajectories. Alternatively, anisotropy thresholds could terminate streamlines too soon. In order to address these problems, Weinstein *et al.* [1999] presented the *tensorlines* tractography algorithm. The vector for the current streamline propagation step v_p is calculated as follows:

$$\mathbf{v}_p = c_l \mathbf{v}_1 + (1 - c_l)((1 - w_{\text{punct}})\mathbf{v}_{\text{in}} + w_{\text{punct}} \mathbf{v}_{\text{out}})$$

ALGORITHM 4 Fibertrace (P, e_1)

```
trace ⇒ add(P)
repeat
    P_n ⇐ integrate_forward(P, e_1, step_size)
    T_p ⇐ filter(T, P_n, ellipsoid, e_1)
    c_l ⇐ anisotropy(T_p)
    if c_l > eps then
        trace ⇒ add(P_n)
        P ⇐ P_n
        e_1 ⇐ direction(P)
    end if
until c_l < eps
```

Where c_l is the linear anisotropy metric, $\mathbf{v}_1$ is the principal eigenvector, $\mathbf{v}_{\text{in}}$ is the vector at the previous propagation step and $\mathbf{v}_{\text{out}}$ is that vector transformed by the diffusion tensor at the current position. w_{punct} is a user-configurable parameter specifying to what extent the streamline should puncture through planar tensors oriented orthogonally to its path. In areas of low linear diffusion, i.e., when c_l is small, tensorlines make use a combination of the previous propagation direction and the shape of the local tensor to stabilize their trajectories.

Adaptation of Streamlines for HARDI Since HARDI voxels can represent multiple crossing fibers, tractography methods have to be adapted. Wedeen *et al.* [2008] proposed an elegant extension of DTI fiber tracking algorithms that works on full DSI data. Their method started by transforming the full diffusion PDF to the diffusion ODF. This was done by evaluating, for a fixed number of radial directions, defined by the vertices of a tessellated sphere (in this case the 362 vertex 6-fold geodesated icosahedron), the integral of the PDF over each direction. In other words, the ODF w over direction u was defined as follows:

$$w(u) = \int p(\rho u)\, \rho^2 d\rho \tag{15.15}$$

With $p(\rho u)$ being the PDF value at position ρu and $\rho^2 d\rho$ the corresponding discrete volume element. Calculating this integral for each of the 362 vertices yielded a deformed sphere representing the ODF.

In each voxel, the directions of maximum diffusion were then found by extracting the local maxima of the ODF. For all directions of maximum diffusion in all voxels, bi-directional path propagation was started. As a path would enter a new voxel, a single direction of maximum diffusion would be chosen that resulted in the least curvature for the incoming path, and the process would be continued. If none of the new directions of maximum diffusion would result in a low enough path curvature, or the path would end up outside of the brain, it would be terminated.

Descoteaux *et al.* [2009] suggested an approach differing in two ways. First, by deconvolving the diffusion ODF, in their case from Q-Ball Imaging, with the estimated fiber ODF kernel, the sharper fiber ODF is derived. Whereas the diffusion ODF describes the directions of diffusion, the fiber ODF describes the directions of the fiber bundles going through a point. Second, instead of performing multiple bidirectional path propagation for each ODF maximum, their tracking algorithm would split or fan out into as many paths as there were fiber diffusion maxima at any new sample point (see Fig. 15.18).

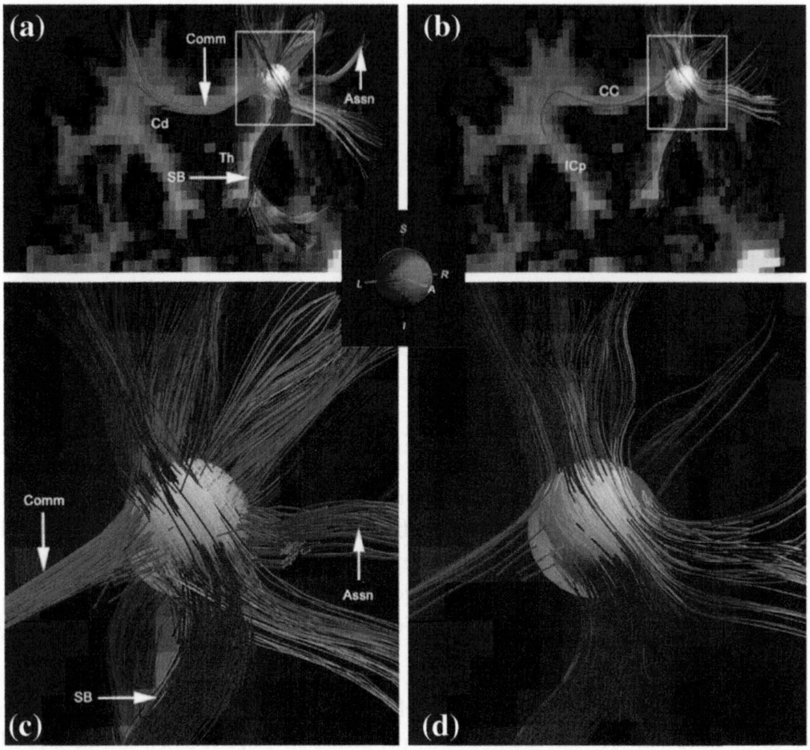

FIGURE 15.18 *Comparison of DSI tractography on the left with DTI tractography on the right, within the human centrum semiovale. With DSI the various crossing fiber bundles are well-represented and identifiable, with DTI far less so (From: [Wedeen et al., 2008]).*

Seeding Strategies A crucial issue for visualizing DWI data with fiber tracking is selecting an appropriate seeding strategy. Fiber tracking easily results in visual clutter if the number and density of pathways is not controlled appropriately. Three simple strategies are:

- regular seeding, where tracing is started at regularly spaced locations;
- random seeding, where a predefined number of pathways are traced at randomly selected positions;
- jittered regular seeding, a trade-off between the previous two techniques where the positions of regularly sampled seed voxels are slightly (randomly) perturbed. (In § 15.3.2.3 DTI glyph positions were jittered to suppress the distracting effect of their regular placement.)

None of these simple techniques guarantees that the selected seeding points are in some way particularly relevant.

Another strategy is manual seeding, where the user decides where tracking starts. With this method, the user has fine-grained control. However, in case of patients with strongly abnormal anatomy (often due to pathological changes) it might be very difficult to select appropriate seed regions.

Manual seeding addresses the problem of visual clutter, but it is challenging picking the desired regions of interest without actually having seen the full tractography. Aspects of interactive region of interest specification and full-brain fiber tracking can be combined in order to address this problem. It is possible to perform full-brain fiber tracking, followed by the interactive selection of fiber bundles of interest within the full-brain fiber tracking [Sherbondy *et al.*, 2005a, Blaas *et al.*, 2005].

With respect to assessing fiber directions and fiber connectivity, a strategy is desirable which is based on anisotropy metrics. Shen and Pang [2004] introduced this strategy and employed anisotropy measures, such as c_l, and a certain threshold value. The threshold is used to compute an isosurface representing portions of the DTI data with the corresponding anisotropy level. Seed points are selected on these surfaces with some additional rules, for example, to ensure that the lines are not traced too close to each other.

Streamlines with Controlled Density An essential aspect of streamline-based visualization is the density of the resulting streamlines. Since some fiber tracts can diverge, very sparse as well as cluttered regions arise when the density is not controlled. In sparse regions, essential features might be omitted whereas in cluttered regions relevant features are hard to recognize.

In flow visualization, streamline density is controlled in the following way: An initial streamline is tracked and new seedpoints are chosen in a certain distance d_{seed}. Starting from these new seedpoints streamlines are tracked forward and backward until the distance to an existing streamline falls below the desired minimum distance d_{sep} [Jobard and Lefer, 1997]. While d_{sep} is provided by the user, d_{seed} is automatically determined and must be higher than d_{sep}.

These techniques have been adapted for fiber tracking [Vilanova *et al.*, 2004]. An efficient 3D implementation of evenly spaced streamlines was presented in [Merhof *et al.*, 2005b] (see Fig. 15.19). Instead of a global distance, the streamline density might be automatically adapted to an anisotropy metric with higher density in regions with major white matter tracts (Fig. 15.20).

Evaluating Fiber Segments Instead of Individual Voxels Due to the noisy character of DTI data, fiber tracking can unreliably terminate because at a single voxel the computed linear diffusion is very low. This low diffusion may be due to the averaging property of the partial volume effects and does not reliably represent an area with low diffusion. As an example, if diverging fibers meet in the volume represented by a voxel, the average diffusion may be low although there is actually strong diffusion. The tensorlines [Weinstein *et al.*, 1999] mentioned earlier are one way of addressing this problem. Alternatively, instead of single voxels, moving averages for anisotropy and curvature could be evaluated in a small **fiber window** (a portion of the fiber centered at the current position). In Algorithm 4, the anisotropy test of the current voxel should be

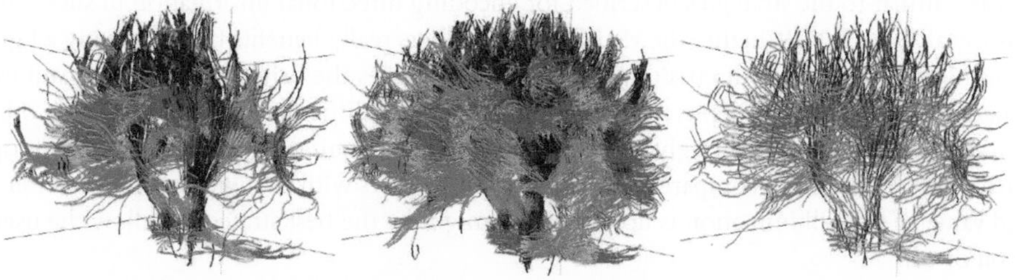

FIGURE 15.19 *Comparison of standard fiber tracking (left) with even streamline placement. In the middle d_{sep} equals 1.5 mm and in the right image d_{sep} equals 5 mm (From: Merhof et al. [2005b]).*

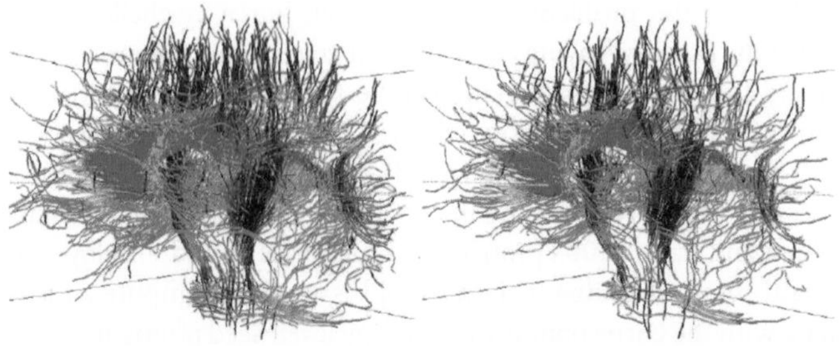

FIGURE 15.20 *Adaptive streamline placement with higher density in regions with higher fractional anisotropy. In the left image, the distance varies from 0.5 to 3 mm; in the right image from 0.5 to 5 mm (From: Merhof et al. [2005b]).*

replaced by considering a fiber window. Schluter *et al.* [2005] demonstrates that this leads to more robust tracking especially in the vicinity of white matter lesions.

Uncertainty in Fiber Tracking Besides the significant effect of image noise, fiber tracking algorithms are also dependent on a number of configurable parameters. Different permutations of these parameters can have drastic effects on the resultant tractography. Brecheisen *et al.* [2009] presented a visual exploration tool for studying the sensitivity of fiber tracking algorithms to parameter changes. They focused on the specific case of different stopping criteria, and showed how small changes could lead to incorrect termination and even erroneous pathways. Importantly, their approach enabled visualizing also the sensitivity of tract-based features to parameter changes.

In further work, Brecheisen *et al.* [2013] presented approaches for the explicit visualization of confidence, or uncertainty due to image and model noise, in probabilistic fiber tracking results. After generating a group of fibers through each of a number of seed points using probabilistic fiber tracking techniques (related to those discussed in § 15.3.3.4), they were able to assign a confidence value to each fiber by calculating its distance from the mean fiber of that given group. Confidence intervals could be graphically configured, after which the different intervals, each representing a group of fibers, was visualized as an outlined silhouette. An example of this is shown in Figure 15.21.

Algorithm parameters, image noise and model noise can all have significant effects on fiber tracking, and the user should be made explicitly aware of these. With these and other examples, Brecheisen [2012] made the case that fiber tractography visualizations should explicitly represent uncertainty. We believe that this is an important issue for medical visualization in general.

Illumination of Streamlines Streamlines, representing fiber tracts, are usually color-coded. The color-coding strategies are similar to the strategies described for encoding directional information in slice-based visualizations (recall § 15.3.1). Whether the visualization of fibers really benefits from applying a light model to the streamlines is a point of discussion. A light model changes the brightness of colors and makes the relation between colors and the depicted anisotropy values more difficult to recognize. On the other hand, shading information is usually thought of improving shape recognition. An example of both options is shown in Figure 15.22, which compares the visualization of fibers with and without illumination. Because the added value of such illumination is not certain, it might be the best strategy to allow the user to turn lighting on or off.

Streamlines Versus Streamtubes The visualization of fibers with streamlines has the advantage that is a fast method due to its low geometric complexity. However, lines with more than one pixel in width often

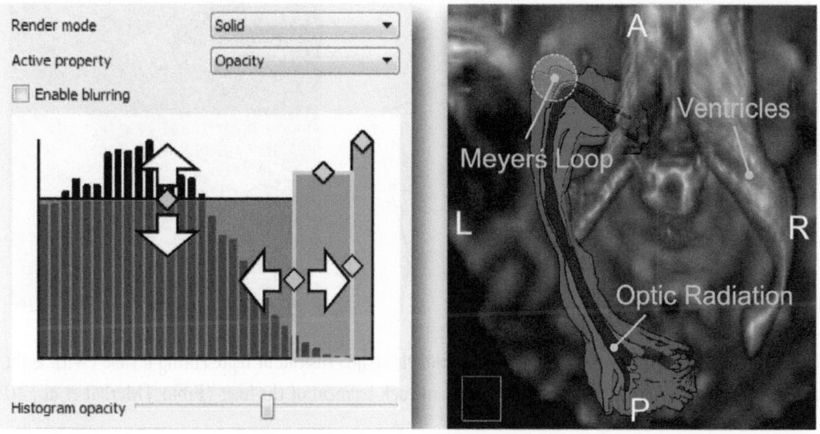

FIGURE 15.21 *Visualization of fiber confidence intervals on the right using illustrative silhouettes and outlines (from lowest confidence to highest confidence: red, green and blue). Confidence intervals and visual parameters have been configured with the histogram widget on the left (From: [Brecheisen et al., 2013]).*

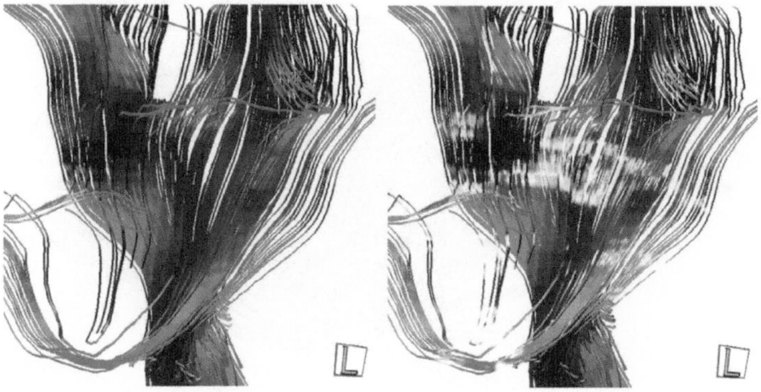

FIGURE 15.22 Comparison of fiber visualization without (left) and with illumination (right) (From: [Merhof et al., 2005a]).

show gaps in highly curved areas. Depth perception is not supported when lines with a constant density are employed [Merhof *et al.*, 2006b]. Streamtubes on the other hand provide a better visual quality with the depth cues of a shaded surface visualization at the expense of higher rendering load. Merhof *et al.* [2006b] presented a new technique that combines the quality of streamtubes with the performance of streamlines. They employ triangle strips with only two triangles per segment to represent the fiber (Fig. 15.23, left). The triangles are textured such that they appear as shaded surfaces (Fig. 15.23, right).

Illustrative Rendering of Lines The idea of efficiently enhancing depth perception by making use of shaded triangle strips was further explored by Everts *et al.* [2009] using an illustrative visualization (recall Chapter 12) approach. Instead of texturing triangle strips to look like streamlines, they added so-called *depth-dependent halos*. Each fiber is rendered as a view-aligned triangle strip. The center of the strip is black, to represent the fiber, while the outsides are white, to represent the halo. The outsides of each strip are bent

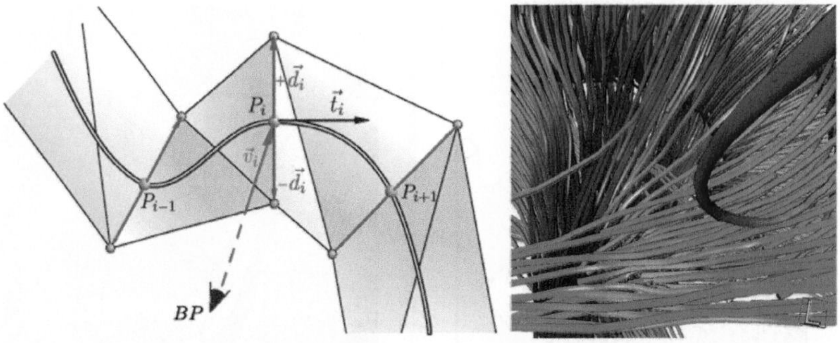

FIGURE 15.23 *Efficient visualization of DTI fibers with triangle strips. Instead of representing a tube (with eight triangles), two textured triangles oriented toward the viewer are used to represent each segment of the fiber (From: [Merhof et al., 2006a]).*

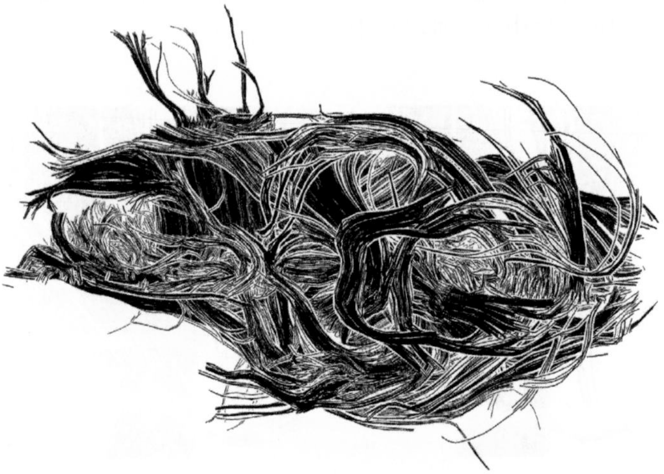

FIGURE 15.24 *Visualization from below of DTI tractography using depth-dependent halos. Due to the depth-dependent halos, fibers that run close together are visually clustered, whereas individual fibers that fan-out are emphasized (From: Everts et al. [2009] supplemental material).*

away from the viewer, resulting in a surface that looks like it was created by extruding a baseless triangle along the fiber trajectory. This geometry results in a maximal occluding halo when fibers at different depths cross each other, but a minimal halo when they run together at the same depth. When applied to a DTI tractography, this technique results in visualizations such as the one in Figure 15.24.

Multimodal Visualization Often DTI data are explored together with other anatomical data. The visualization of information derived from several datasets requires to restrict the visualization to relevant portions or properties. With respect to DTI data, an abstract or aggregated visualization, such as fiber tracking results, is a viable option.

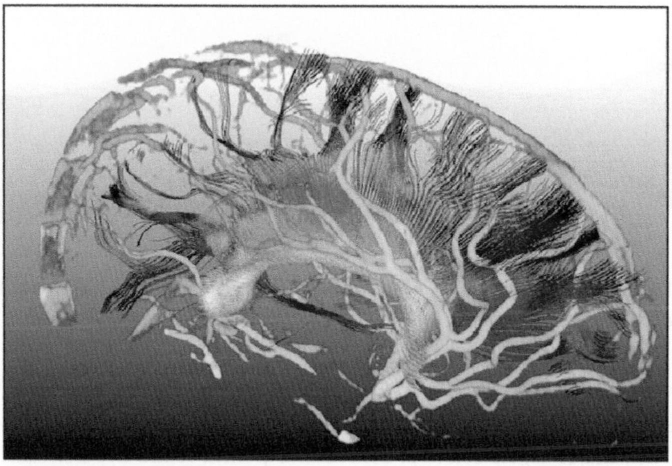

FIGURE 15.25 *DTI fiber tracking combined with vascular structures extracted from MRI data (Courtesy of Mathias Schlüter and Horst K. Hahn, Fraunhofer MEVIS Bremen).*

Anatomical image data are also used for the diagnosis, since they provide a higher spatial resolution. The integration of fused multimodal visualizations requires a priori registration. Instead of discussing all options to integrate DTI-based visualizations with other data, we present two examples to illustrate the expressiveness of such visualizations. Figure 15.25 integrates MR angiography data with the results of fiber tracking from DTI data.

Integration of Anatomical Landmarks 3D visualizations of diffusion tensor data can benefit from the integration of landmarks that serve as anatomical context. The eyes as well as the ventricles are appropriate landmarks for brain images. Wünsche [2004] showed that eyes and ventricles could be identified and delineated robustly by means of their diffusion characteristics.

15.3.3.2 Hyperstreamlines and Stream Surfaces

Hyperstreamlines were developed in order to convey more information on tensor data than streamlines, which actually restrict the information presented to the direction of the principal eigenvector. Features, such as torsion or minor eigenvalues, are not conveyed with streamlines.

Hyperstreamlines owe their name to the analogy of streamlines and were designed as a special visualization technique for second order tensor fields [Delmarcelle and Hesselink, 1992, 1993]. Similar to streamlines, hyperstreamlines follow diffusion from a number of seed points. Instead of connecting the points determined by integration with a line, a polygon is swept along the detected path. The polygon is stretched in a transverse plane in order to reflect the magnitude of the other eigenvalues. Different graphics primitive may be used to encode the magnitude of the minor eigenvalues (λ_2 and λ_3) in the cross section. Delmarcelle and Hesselink [1992] consider stretching a circle at every point to form an ellipse and rendering a cross with the length of the two lines conveying the related magnitudes. The first variant leads to tube-shaped hyperstreamlines, whereas the latter leads to a helix. An appropriate trade-off between quality and speed has to be made when the graphics primitive is mapped to a polygon. Reina *et al.* [2006] suggest to use 16 vertices to represent the cross section at each sampling point. It might be necessary to subdivide the hyperstreamline (computation of additional profiles along the path) in case of

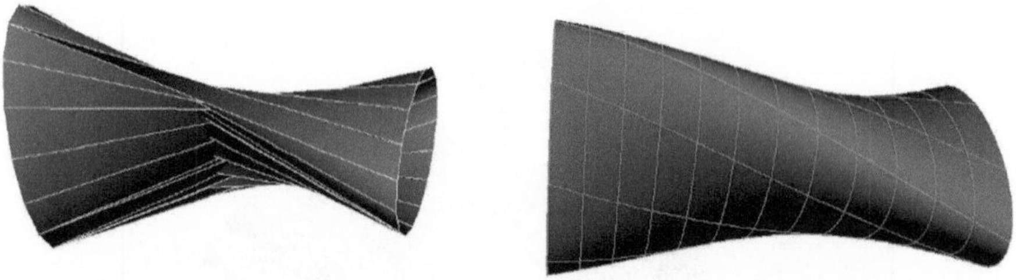

FIGURE 15.26 *Without subdividing the path, linear interpolation between cross-sectional profiles may lead to self-intersections (left). With appropriate subdivision this can be effectively avoided (right) (From: Reina et al. [2006]).*

strong torsion (see Fig. 15.26). The number of the required additional profiles can be derived from the angle between the two major eigenvectors at consecutive points. If the hyperstreamline diameters vary strongly, they may overlap each other. It is therefore reasonable to normalize the diameters or to scale the diameters such that a certain limit is not exceeded. The streamtubes proposed by Zhang *et al.* [2003] are an extension of hyperstreamlines that address the varying diameter problem, as well as solutions for creating visualizations containing dense sets of hyperstreamlines, and representing planar diffusion.

Streamsurfaces are primarily used to depict tensor information in case the diffusion is predominantly planar. In such regions, λ_1 and λ_2 define a plane. Streamlines and streamsurfaces can be combined in a natural way to indicate linear as well as planar diffusion (see Fig. 15.27). In a seed region, streamlines are tracked. If the streamlines reach voxels with primarily planar diffusion streamline tracking is not terminated. Instead a stream surface is generated. Streamline tracking is continued behind the region with primarily planar diffusion.

15.3.3.3 Exploration of Fiber Tracts through Clustering

So far, we have discussed how individual streamlines or tensorlines can be derived and visualized as a representation of neural pathways. We refer to these streamlines or tensorlines as fibers, although each fiber usually already represents a bundle of axons, due to the limited resolution of the acquiring scanner. Fiber tracking techniques aggregate more data relative to visualizations of individual measurements, for example tensor glyphs. However, from a surgical point of view, single fibers are still of minor interest. Instead, whole clusters of fibers are essential for surgical planning [Nimsky *et al.*, 2005].

The computation of clusters of fibers yields an even more abstract visualization. With clustering information, DWI data can be explored at different levels of detail, where a global view includes the clusters and local views show the fibers of selected clusters [Moberts *et al.*, 2005]. With respect to the problems in tracking fibers in noisy low resolution data, the major problem of any clustering technique is its dependency on the fiber tracking results.

Clustering, or **bundling**, is motivated by knowledge of neuroanatomy and driven by clinical applications. Reliable assessments of white matter connectivity and fiber disruption is very difficult to achieve by exploring individual fibers alone [Gerig *et al.*, 2004]. Fiber bundles that correspond to known structures, such as the corpus callosum or the pyramidal tract, are the basis for further analysis, such as the exploration of anisotropy measures along a fiber bundle.

Clustering fiber tracts is a special example of the general clustering task (recall § 9.2.2.1), where n-dimensional data are grouped to support further analysis.

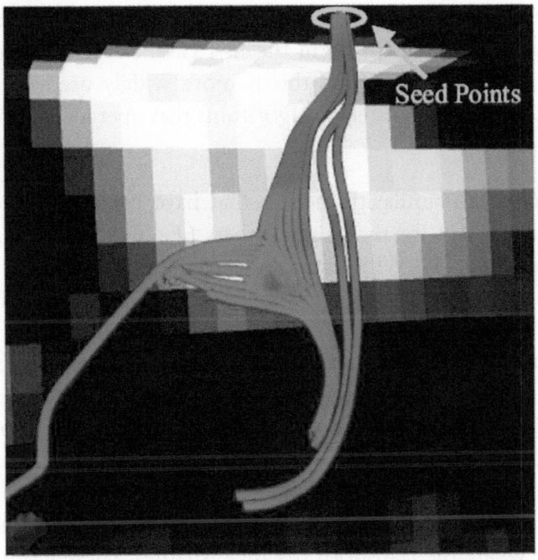

FIGURE 15.27 *Combining streamlines and streamsurfaces to visualize primarily linear and planar diffusion* (From: [Vilanova et al., 2004]).

There are many similarities between the clustering of fiber tracts on the one hand and the clustering of streamlines in flow visualization [McLoughlin *et al.*, 2013, Yu *et al.* 2012] on the other. Elements of the clustering approaches documented here can be found in both sets of literature.

The characteristic features of the clustering problem considered here guide the selection of similarity metrics and clustering algorithms. Fiber bundles occur in various shapes and sizes. Some fiber bundles are composed of a few long fibers forming a tube structure, whereas other fiber bundles contain more smaller bundles that diverge.

Figure 15.28 indicates that a pair of fibers from the same bundle which are *not* direct neighbors can have very different shapes. Since clinical DTI data are noisy, missing parts of bundles may occur and detected pathways may be erroneous.

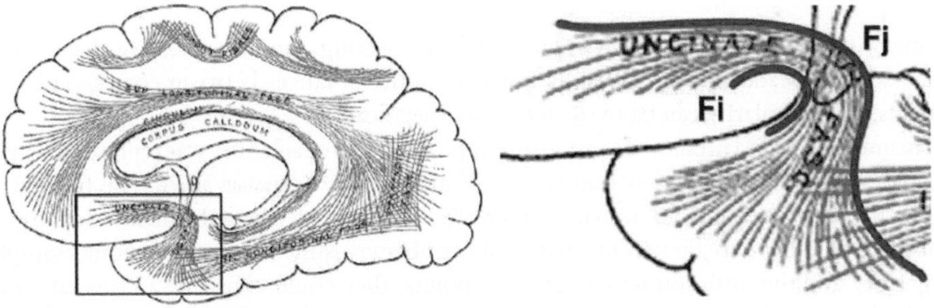

FIGURE 15.28 *White matter bundles of the brain. The right view presents a closeup of the left view. Fibers of one anatomical structure might differ considerably in shape and size* (From: [Brun et al., 2003]).

The first step in fiber clustering is either to represent each fiber as a feature vector, or to determine the pairwise similarity for all involved fibers. In the first case, standard clustering techniques such as k-means can be used. In the second case, and this is more widely used for fiber tract clustering, the pairwise similarity is used as input to clustering algorithms that operate on pairwise similarities, such as hierarchical or spectral clustering.

Similarity Metrics for Clustering All similarity metrics that have been evaluated for fiber clustering are symmetric, yielding the same value for the pairs of fibers (F_i, F_j) and (F_j, F_i). Each fiber F_i is a 3D curve represented by a set of points p_k. With distance-based metrics, F_i and F_j are regarded as belonging to the same bundle if a distance $d(F_i, F_j)$ is below a threshold θ. There are many metrics to characterize the distance between two 3D curves.

The closest distance between bundles F_i, F_j is defined on the pair of points $(p_{ik} \in F_i, p_{jl} \in F_j)$ where the distance is minimal. In general, this metric is not appropriate as similarity metric for fiber clustering, since the closest distance between two bundles is zero if they converge, diverge, or cross. Figure 15.28 contains several distinct bundles, where individual fibers overlap. These fibers would act as a "bridge" and the bundles would be erroneously merged. Other global distance measures are the mean of closest point distances and the Hausdorff distance. The Hausdorff metric is relevant here, because it allows to remove outliers (where the Hausdorff distance is large). These global distance measures result in large distances for fibers of different length and for diverging fibers. The Hausdorff distance between fibers of different length or between fibers, which are very close but diverge at some point, is large. Thus, these fibers will not be assigned to the same cluster, although they may anatomically belong to the same structure. The average closest distance has the advantage that information concerning the whole fibers F_i and F_j is considered.

Advanced Similarity Metrics Due to the problems of simple similarity metrics, more advanced metrics have been explored [Gerig *et al.*, 2004]. Ding *et al.* [2003] suggest a metric based on a subdivision of fibers into segments. These segments of the fibers F_i and F_j are then analyzed to find corresponding segments and distance metrics are applied to pairs of corresponding segments. Since no similarity metric is appropriate in all cases, a tool to assist in the exploration of DWI data should enable to adjust also the weights of all criteria.

In addition to applying distance measurements between points on the curve, similarity can also be derived from the parameters characterizing the fibers as entire curves. Examples are

- the distance between the centers of gravity,
- curvature information, e.g., average mean curvature along a path

Fiber geometry can be more completely represented by selecting a more expressive shape model, such as quintic B-splines [Maddah *et al.*, 2008]. By calculating the distances between corresponding B-spline control points, fiber similarity can be measured more specifically.

Wassermann *et al.* [2010] presented a promising approach where each fiber was represented by a blurred *indicator function*, and the indicator function was itself modeled as a *Gaussian process*. The blurred indicator function, or characteristic function, shown in Figure 15.29, returns 1 where the fiber is definitely present, and gradually goes to 0 where there is no chance of the fiber crossing. Based on the points sampled along a fiber trajectory and the diffusion tensors at those points, they could construct a Gaussian process that integrated both a smoothness constraint as well a as the shape of the diffusion along the fiber. In other words, this Gaussian process would evaluate to the indicator function, blurred according to both a fiber smoothness constraint and the direction of diffusion.

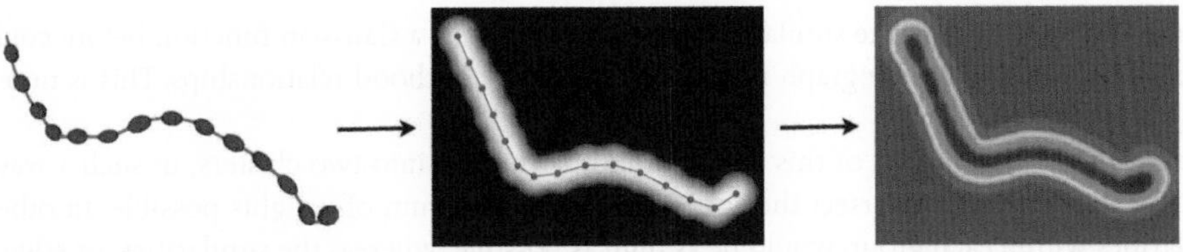

FIGURE 15.29 *Fibers and fiber bundles can be represented by blurred indicator functions, which yields 1 where the fiber is definitely present and gradually go to 0 where it is definitely not. A number of important clustering operations, such as similarity and merging, are greatly simplified using this representation (From: [Wassermann et al., 2010]).*

The indicator functions generated in this way can be merged by simple averaging, yielding a new indicator function representing the merged bundle. Furthermore, fiber or bundle similarity is represented elegantly by the normalized inner product between indicator functions.

Clustering Algorithms For the clustering of fiber tracts based on pairwise similarity, hierarchical clustering, and spectral clustering have both been investigated in multiple efforts. In the following, we also touch upon the shared nearest neighbor clustering approach proposed by Moberts *et al.* [2005] for fiber tracts.

Hierarchical Clustering Hierarchical clustering can be *divisive*, in which all fibers are initially combined into one super-cluster which is then iteratively split until each cluster is a single fiber, or *agglomerative*, in which all fibers are initially clusters which are then iteratively combined until there is only a single cluster. Both algorithms result in a clustering tree, with the super-cluster at the root, and the fibers at the nodes. The tree can be cut at any level to obtain the desired number of clusters. Agglomerative hierarchical clustering, or AHC, is more commonly used for fiber clustering.

An important component of hierarchical clustering is the method of calculating the similarity or distance between two clusters. In *single linkage*, the shortest distance between the two clusters is used, i.e., the distance between the two closest fibers from both clusters. In *complete linkage*, the maximum distance is used, and in *average linkage*, the mean of the two distances. There are more variations of this theme, each with different implications for clustering performance.

Corouge *et al.* [2004b] presented an algorithm that propagates cluster labels to closest neighbors. The algorithm assigns each unlabeled fiber to the cluster of its closest neighbor if the similarity metric is above a certain threshold. Although it shares similar aspects, this is strictly speaking not hierarchical clustering, as they did not explicitly construct a cluster tree, instead choosing to make use of a similarity threshold that controlled the final number of clusters. Zhang and Laidlaw [2004] presented one of the first examples of whole brain DTI fiber clustering using real agglomerative hierarchical clustering with single linkage. Jianu *et al.* [2009] integrated the agglomerative hierarchical cluster tree as an interactive dendogram in a coupled-view 3D DTI data visualization system.

Spectral Clustering In *spectral clustering*, the pairwise fiber similarity is used to represent each complete fiber trajectory as a single point in a high-dimensional spectral embedding space. This is a powerful concept, as it is not necessary to try and represent each fiber as a high-dimensional feature vector directly, instead focusing only on the design of a suitable similarity metric.

Based on the excellent tutorial by von Luxburg [2007], we present here a brief summary of the general procedure. One of the fundamental ideas behind spectral clustering, is that the objects that are to be clustered, together with their pairwise similarity, can be represented as an undirected similarity graph. The objects that are to be clustered are the nodes and the weighted edges between them represent the pairwise similarities. Usually, the similarities are transformed by a Gaussian function before constructing the similarity graph, so that the graph represents local neighborhood relationships. This is necessary for the subsequent analysis.

Determining the *minimum cut* of this graph would partition it into two clusters, in such a way that the partition, or the *cut*, would intersect the edges with the lowest sum of weights possible. In other words, the similarities within each group would be as high as possible, whereas the similarities, or edge weights, between them would be as low as possible. This sounds like an ideal approach to clustering.

However, the *minimum cut* often separates a single node from the rest, instead of partitioning the nodes into two reasonably sized clusters. This problem can be addressed by instead applying the *normalized cut* [Shi and Malik, 2000], which determines a partition that minimizes inter-cluster similarity while at the same time yielding clusters that are balanced in terms of the weights of their edges. Unfortunately, where the minimum cut is straightforward to solve, the *normalized cut* is NP hard.

Spectral clustering is a way to solve a relaxed version of this balanced minimum cut problem, based on the *graph Laplacian matrix* of the similarity graph. The graph Laplacian matrix L can be easily derived from the pairwise similarity matrix, which is itself just a representation of the similarity graph. The field dedicated to the study of the graph Laplacian is called *spectral graph theory*. There are multiple formulations of the graph Laplacian in literature, we show here the unnormalized graph Laplacian L:

$$L = D - W \tag{15.16}$$

W is the similarity matrix and D is the degree matrix, a diagonal matrix with the vertex degrees d_i on the diagonal. Vertex degree d_i is the sum of all similarities between vertex i and its connected neighbors.

The eigenvalues and eigenvectors of the graph Laplacian, also called its spectrum, are related to the structure of the graph. For example, the number of 0 eigenvalues is equal to the number of connected components in the graph.

After having computed L, spectral clustering can the be performed as follows:

1. Compute the eigenvectors of the $n \times n$ graph Laplacian L corresponding to the k *smallest* eigenvalues, with k being the desired number of clusters and n the number of objects, for example fiber tracts.
2. Construct a new $n \times k$ matrix U with as its columns the k eigenvectors of L.
3. Apply k-means clustering to the n k-dimensional points represented by the n rows of U, yielding k clusters.
4. The U row indices of the points belonging to a cluster correspond to the row indices of the original W and L matrices, and hence to nodes in the similarity graph.

Spectral clustering approaches generally follow this same straightforward procedure, but vary slightly for example when different graph Laplacian formulations are used. The variation we have summarized here is *unnormalized spectral clustering*, based on the *unnormalized graph Laplacian* in Equation 15.16.

In summary, objects are transformed to a high-dimensional spectral embedding space, where, due to the properties of the graph Laplacian, straightforward clustering can easily group similar elements. Importantly, only a suitable similarity function is required. Objects, or fibers, do not have to be explicitly represented as high-dimensional feature vectors.

The application of this technique to fiber tract clustering has been extensively studied [Brun it et al., 2004, Klein *et al.*, 2007, O'Donnell and Westin, 2007]. Interestingly, many applications recursively apply spectral clustering with $k = 2$ until the desired number of clusters is attained (a form of divisive hierarchical clustering), instead of computing the desired number of clusters at once. Although there are indications that the second approach might generate better results [Klein *et al.*, 2007], the first approach is useful when the final number of clusters is not known *a priori*, or when a cluster-tree is desired.

Shared Nearest Neighbor Clustering Moberts *et al.* [2005] evaluated the *shared nearest neighbor clustering* [Ertöz *et al.*, 2003] for clustering fiber data. This algorithm is based on the assumption that two fibers that share a high number of neighbors probably belong to the same cluster. It is particularly useful for clustering items of different size and shape even in noisy data. It works as follows [Moberts *et al.*, 2005]:

1 A k nearest neighbor graph (kNNG) is constructed from the proximity matrix. In this graph, nodes represent items (individual fibers) and edges connect nodes with their k nearest neighbors.
2 A shared nearest neighbor graph (SNNG) is a weighted graph constructed from NNG. Edges in SNNG exist only between items that belong to each others shared neighbors. More precisely, if p belongs to the k closest neighbors of q and q belongs to the k closest neighbors of p, they are connected through an edge. Depending on the position of p in q's nearest neighbor list and q in p's nearest neighbor list, a weight factor is computed to differentiate between near and far nearest neighbors.
3 Clusters are obtained by removing edges from SNNG if their weight is below a threshold. This threshold determines the number of resulting clusters.

Visualization and Quantification of Fiber Bundles Clustering may be used for a variety of purposes. A quantitative analysis of fiber bundles is often more interesting than the quantification of individual fibers. Diffusion parameters, such as mean diffusivity along and perpendicular to the major fiber direction, as well as geometric properties, such as mean curvature, are relevant for neuroanatomical studies [Corouge *et al.*, 2004a]. Fiber bundles may also be analyzed with respect to their anisotropy properties. Gerig *et al.* [2004] found that anisotropy significantly changes along bundles, but also across them.

With respect to visualization, it might be useful to restrict the visible fibers to those which belong to a bundle with a certain minimum number of fibers. This restriction is motivated by the fact that fibers without adjacent similar fibers have a high probability of being erroneously detected. Figure 15.30 compares fibers and the visualization of the largest clusters.

There are different strategies for the visualization of fiber bundles. The general strategy is to generate some kind of hull to "wrap" a bundle. The hull representing a bundle may be derived by computing a centerline and cross sections at different locations on the centerline. In principle, different geometries may be employed to visualize the hull. Graphics primitives, such as cylinders or ellipsoids may be fitted along the centerline—similar to model-based visualizations of vascular structures (recall § 11.5). The resulting visualizations, however, may strongly differ from the detected fibers.

Another more accurate visualization was introduced by Enders *et al.* [2005]. Instead of graphics primitives, boundary polygons are defined in planes orthogonal to the skeleton. Boundary polygons are defined by connecting the intersections of fibers with the cross sectional area perpendicular to the centerline at a particular sampling point. These boundary polygons may be immediately visualized as lines or connected with adjacent polygons to form surfaces. In Figure 15.31, the visualization of the optical and nerve tract are shown. As Enders *et al.* [2005] point out, these boundary polygons should not be directly used for the visualization. Instead, the convex hull, as a simpler representation should be employed. For each tract, two visualizations have been generated which comprise different portions of the fibers.

Representative Fibers Alternatively, a single fiber representing the whole cluster, called the *representative* or *prototype* fiber [O'Donnell *et al.*, 2009], can be visualized instead of the whole bundle. Such a representative fiber can be selected by the user, or be determined by automatic means. For example, the longest fiber in

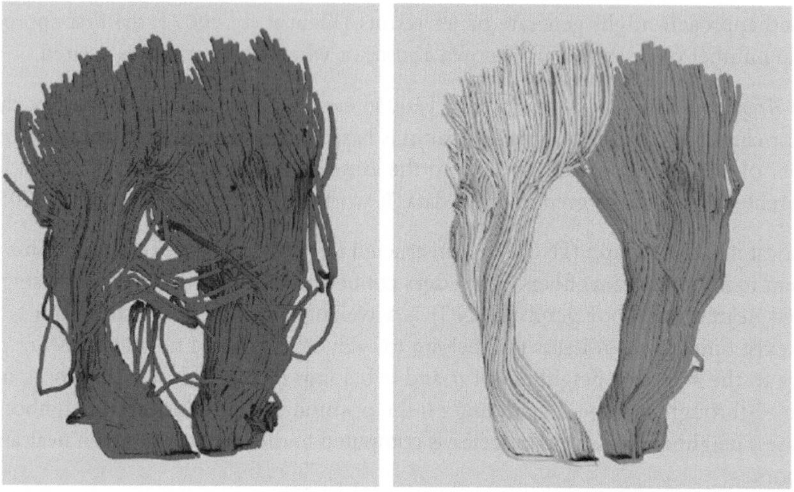

FIGURE 15.30 *Clustering of sets of tensorlines (left) to fiber bundles (right) in the area of the corticospinal tract. It was specified that two clusters (left and right corticospinal tract) should be looked for. Tensor lines which were not considered as members of the two largest clusters where removed. The curve distance metric introduced by Ding et al. [2003] has been modified in this particular cluster algorithm (From: [Gerig et al., 2004]).*

the bundle could be chosen [Maddah *et al.*, 2006], or the fiber that is closest to the mean of the fibers in bundle could be selected. The mean fiber can be determined based on a parametric representation of the fiber shapes [Maddah *et al.*, 2008]. O'Donnell *et al.* [2009] proposed selecting the fiber passing through the positions intersected by the most other fibers in the bundle.

Showing only the representative of fiber clusters results in a visualization that shows the global trajectories of all found clusters, but with far less occlusion. While this might be a desirable property in some cases, the spatial extent of the bundle is not shown at all. This can be remedied by for example adding again a semi-transparent hull showing the whole cluster.

Uncertainty in Fiber Bundle Visualization Ideally, the visualization of a fiber bundle should also reflect the uncertainty involved in fiber tract determination. This can be achieved by visualizing results generated with slightly different anisotropy thresholds in fiber tracking or slightly modified parameters of the clustering algorithm. A transparent overlay of two or three of such surfaces is an expressive visualization of such an analysis. In addition, a combination of individual fibers and a transparent hull is expressive, since it conveys how individual lines have been summarized to clusters (Fig. 15.33). In § 15.3.3.1, overlapping clusters of fibers with varying confidence intervals were visualized using illustrative silhouette and outline rendering techniques.

Focus-and-context Rendering Röttger *et al.* [2012] applied different focus-and-context techniques to various combinations of fibers and fiber hulls. With this approach, they managed to show the important fiber bundle hulls, but also illustrate the trajectories of the fibers contained within, see Figure 15.32. Furthermore, by showing two crossing bundles alternatively as hull and as fibers, and explicitly visualizing the intersecting areas in both representations, clear visualizations of the crossings could be made.

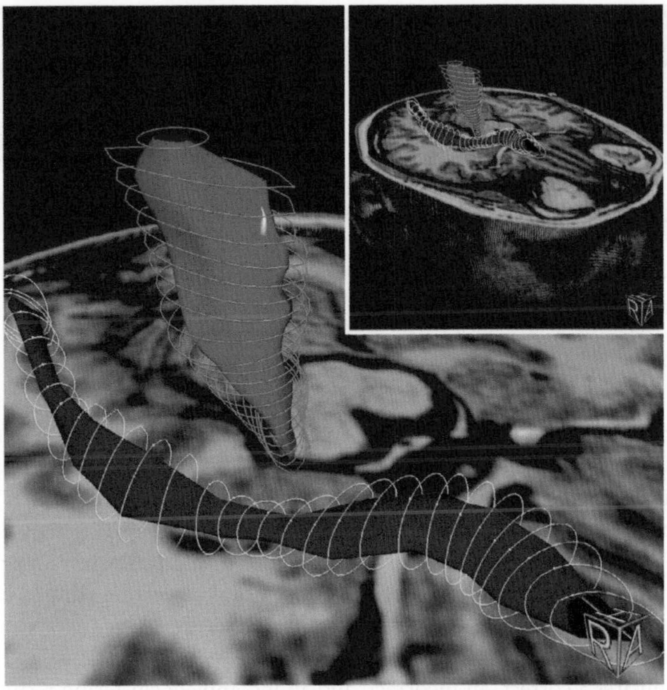

FIGURE 15.31 Combination of direct volume rendering of high resolution MRI T1 data with pyramidal (red) and optic tract (blue). The rings around the surface represent more defensive approximations. For surgical planning, more safety is achieved if the region inside the rings is preserved (From: [Enders et al., 2005]).

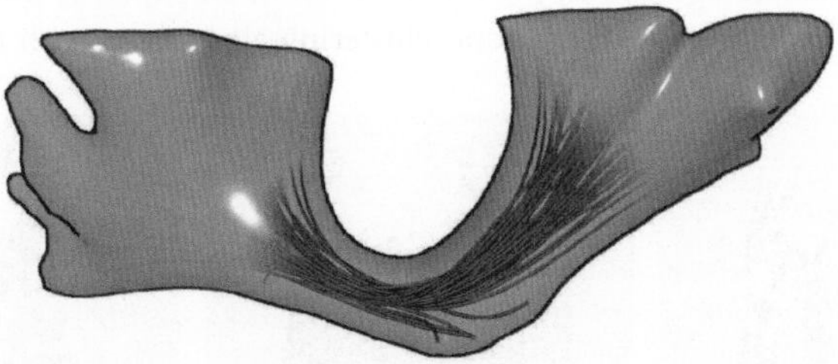

FIGURE 15.32 Focus-and-context visualization techniques, in this case a view-dependent cutaway, supports the understanding the relation between a fiber hull and the tracked fibers that it contains (Courtesy of Diana Röttger, University of Koblenz-Landau. See also [Röttger et al., 2012]).

While these visualization options are certainly valuable, validation studies and more experience are needed to provide a technical and clinical definition of safety margins [Nimsky et al., 2006a].

Validation of Fiber Clustering Validation is a crucial issue, in particular if fiber clustering is to be used for neurosurgery planning and monitoring. As a first step toward validation, two terms are essential to characterize the quality of a clustering technique [Moberts et al., 2005]:

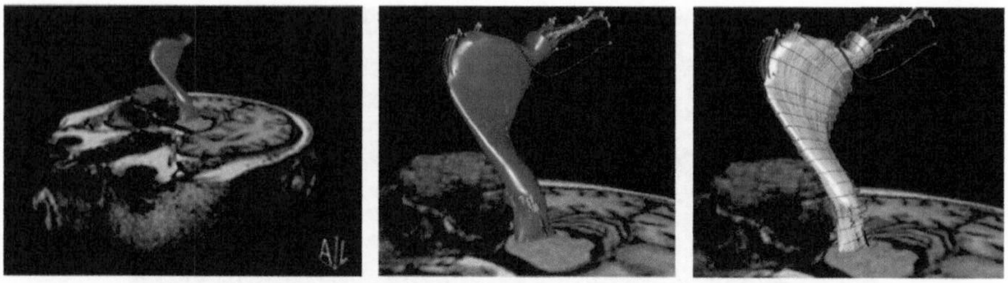

FIGURE 15.33 *A fiber bundle is shown as opaque surface (left), as opaque surface combined with individual fibers (middle), as combination of a transparent surface and rings with individual fibers* (From: [Enders et al., 2005]).

- *completeness* and
- *correctness*

Maximum completeness is achieved if all fibers, which belong to a particular nerve tract, are assigned to this nerve tract. Correctness characterizes whether all fibers that are assigned to a particular nerve tract really belong to this nerve tract. Incorrect fibers might be composed of parts which belong to different anatomical structures. The relation between correctness and completeness is exactly the same as the relation between sensitivity and specificity that characterize diagnostic processes. Maximum completeness could be easily achieved by considering all fibers as one cluster; correctness in this case is very low. The other extreme would be to assign each fiber to a different cluster—resulting in maximum correctness but very low completeness.

Figure 15.34 compares a correct, an incorrect, and an incomplete clustering result. Incorrectness and incompleteness should not be weighted equally. Incomplete but correct results can be easily corrected by marking clusters that belong together. Incorrect results, on the other hand, are difficult to improve, since many individual fibers have to be selected and assigned to another cluster [Moberts, 2005].

Validation of clustering algorithms requires a gold standard. Similar to the gold standard used for the validation of segmentation algorithms, the classification of an expert is used. The goal of validation processes is to characterize similarity metrics and clustering algorithms with respect to their influence

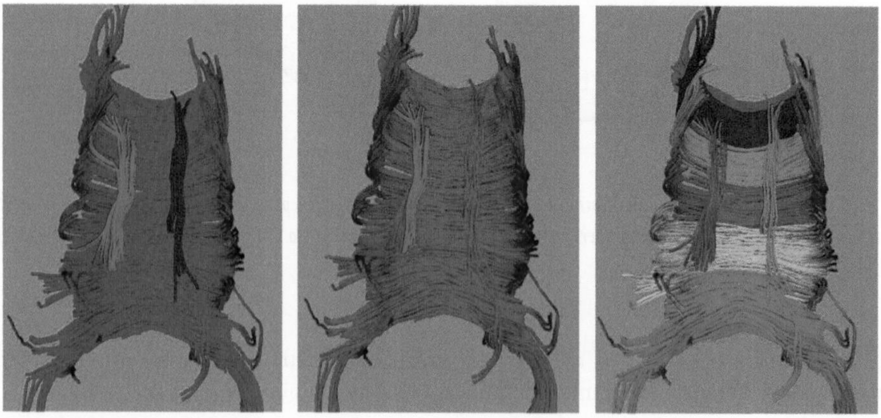

FIGURE 15.34 *The correct clustering result provided by a physician (left) compared with an incorrect (middle) and an incomplete (right) clustering. While the incomplete result could be easily modified into the correct result, the correction of the incorrect result requires considerably more interaction* (From: [Moberts et al., 2005]).

on completeness and correctness. Most of these algorithms have parameters which allow to adjust the trade-off between completeness and correctness. If one parameter, such as the number of desired clusters, is considered, a curve arises that depicts the influence of this parameter on completeness and correctness. Such curves enable the comparison of different algorithms and metrics.

Moberts *et al.* [2005] presented a framework for validating clustering algorithms and compared basic similarity metrics and clustering algorithms by means of this framework. Besides correctness and completeness, they discussed a variety of other metrics to evaluate clustering approaches. The shared nearest neighbor clustering turned out to be the best algorithm. Their results should be regarded as preliminary, since they are based on a few neuroanatomical structures only. Nevertheless, their framework is sound and substantial.

15.3.3.4 Probabilistic Tractography

In traditional deterministic tractography, the probable trajectories of bundles of neural fibers are extracted. However, such a trajectory is a binary representation: Either the fiber bundle is present or not.

In probabilistic, or stochastic, tractography, diffusion data is used to determine the per-voxel probability that given voxel is structurally connected to a selected source voxel [Koch *et al.*, 2002]. For a selected source voxel, such probabilities can be determined for a whole slice or volume of data. Given such a volume, one can then trace a trajectory of maximum probability from the selected source voxel to a specific target voxel. One could also extract an isosurface, which would by definition enclose a region of high probability (higher than the iso-value) connectivity between the selected source voxel and the rest of the probability volume.

Koch *et al.* [2002] presented a technique for probabilistic tractography where a number of particles, starting at the selected source voxel, performed a random walk through the diffusion data. At each new voxel, the probability of walking to a neighboring voxel was based on the measured diffusion along that direction, both in the current and potential new voxel. Too sharp turns were assigned zero probability. A random direction, following the calculated probability distribution, was then chosen. This process was continued for a specific particle until its path reached a maximum length, or when it reached a low anisotropy region. The whole process was terminated when a certain number of paths had been terminated, at which point the number of visits to each voxel was counted. This number represented the probability that a particle would defuse to that voxel from the selected source voxel, and hence the probability that a structural connection was present between the two voxels.

Figure 15.35 shows an example of their algorithm's output. Bright yellow signifies high probability and darker orange lower probability. The start voxel is indicated with a large arrow at the top left. In this case the simulation was performed on a single slice, but the algorithm generalizes to 3D.

Such Monte Carlo algorithms can be computationally intensive. However, due to the independence of each random walking particle, it is straightforward to implement on the GPU. However, the required amount of texture memory can be a limited factor. By making use of a simplified model of diffusion, McGraw and Nadar [2007] were able to implement their probabilistic fiber tracking technique, similar to that of Koch *et al.* [2002], to the GPU, leading to interactive stochastic fiber tracking on real-world 3D DTI datasets.

15.4 VISUALIZATION OF CONNECTIVITY MATRICES

Where structural connectivity data almost always describes the anatomical trajectory between two points in the brain, *functional connectivity* data usually only describes the degree of connectivity between two regions, mostly based on some kind of neural activity correlation between those two regions. This means that in

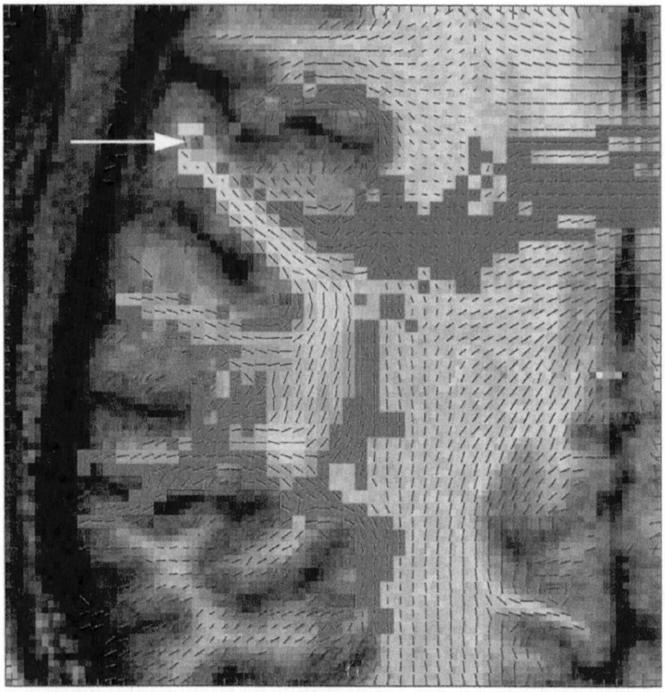

FIGURE 15.35 *Example of Monte Carlo probabilistic tractography algorithm. Bright yellow indicates that a large number of random walk particles, starting at the arrow at the top left, diffused through that voxel. Orange indicates a smaller number, and no color indicates that a voxel was never reached (From: [Koch et al., 2002]).*

almost all cases, data can be reduced to a graph, with each region being a vertex, and each connection being an edge. The edge only signifies a connection and may represent its strength, usually no information about the anatomical trajectory of the implied connection is involved. Alternatively, functional connectivity data for N regions can also be represented as an $N \times N$ connectivity matrix, with each position, defined by its row i and its column j, holding the degree of connectivity between regions i and j.

As explained in the introduction, structural connectivity data can also be easily transformed to this type of point-to-point connectivity. Once we have connectivity matrices, it does not matter whether they have been derived from structural connectivity data, or come directly from functional connectivity data, we can apply the same visualization techniques.

Visualization techniques for connectivity matrices can be classified into two main groups. *Spatial methods* take into account the anatomical embedding of the connection endpoints that are involved. In other words, the real spatial locations of the connected regions are taken into account. *Non-spatial methods* do not rely on the anatomical embedding of the data, and make use of many abstract representation techniques from information visualization.

15.4.1 NON-SPATIAL METHODS

Connectivity Distance Scatter Plots In probably the most abstract example of brain connectivity visualization, Salvador *et al.* [2005] explored the relationship between resting-state fMRI correlation (see § 15.2.4) and

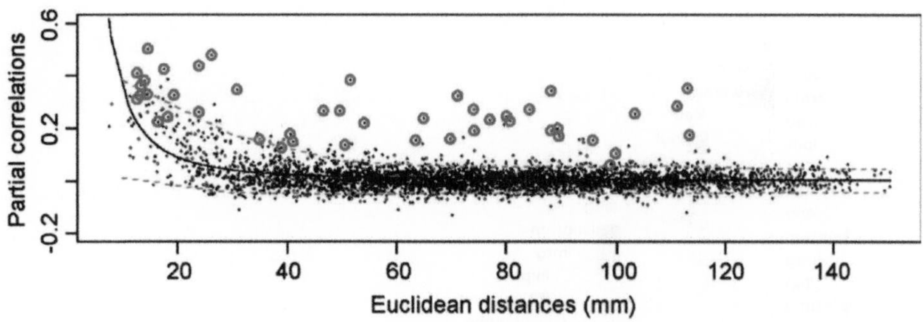

FIGURE 15.36 *Scatter plot of resting-state fMRI correlation over anatomical distance. An inverse square law, shown by the solid curve, is to be expected. A number of outliers have been selected, and are shown in the linked anatomical views (From: Salvador et al. [2005]).*

anatomical distance by using, among other representations, the scatter plot (see Fig. 15.36 for a related example). They discovered an inverse square law relation between connectivity and anatomical distance.

Connectivity Matrix Bitmaps When functional connectivity is represented as a $N \times N$ matrix, correlation is often used as connectivity metric (like in other symmetric correlation matrices). Depending on the metric, it can also be likened to the *distance matrix* from graph theory, or the *(dis)similarity matrix* from statistics.

These matrices are often visualized by color-coding each location according to the value it holds. Figure 15.37 shows an example from the NIPY project, where the resting-state fMRI-derived correlation between a relatively small number of regions is shown. In the case of a large matrix, for example with resting-state fMRI connectivity between thousands of voxels, this yields a large bitmap. In this case, smooth interaction, including panning, zooming, and linked selection, is a crucial component of an effective visualization [Van Dixhoorn *et al.*, 2012]. Another important element is using an anatomical ordering of the regions or voxels in the matrix visualization, so that regions or voxels that are anatomically close are also grouped on the horizontal or vertical axes of the matrix.

The connectivity matrix representation is effective as an overview visualization, and enables the visual detection of peaks in the connectivity between groups of voxels.

Non-spatial Node-link Diagrams are a natural metaphor for the visualization of network or graph data. They have the advantage over matrix-based visualization that the location of the nodes can be used as an extra visual channel. However, the connections are usually encoded as links, contributing a great deal of extra visual complexity.

Generally when node-link diagrams are used to visualize connectivity, node position is influenced by the anatomical location of the brain region it represents. However, here we treat the non-spatial case, the primary instance of which is when node location is used to encode grouping or hierarchy. Figure 15.38 shows a circular example, where the participating brain regions are shown on the outermost ring, grouped together according to the brain lobe or greater region containing them.

In this case, DTI data, which is inherently structural, has been transformed to point-to-point connectivity data, again yielding an $N \times N$ connectivity matrix. The number of fibers yielded by DTI tractography between two regions, reflecting the thickness of the tracked bundle, is used as a measure of connectivity. The average FA over each such bundle is used as a additional connectivity metric. The colored curves in the visualization represent connections between regions. The blue, red and green colors represent bundles with FA in respectively the lower, middle and upper third of the FA distribution. In other words, green

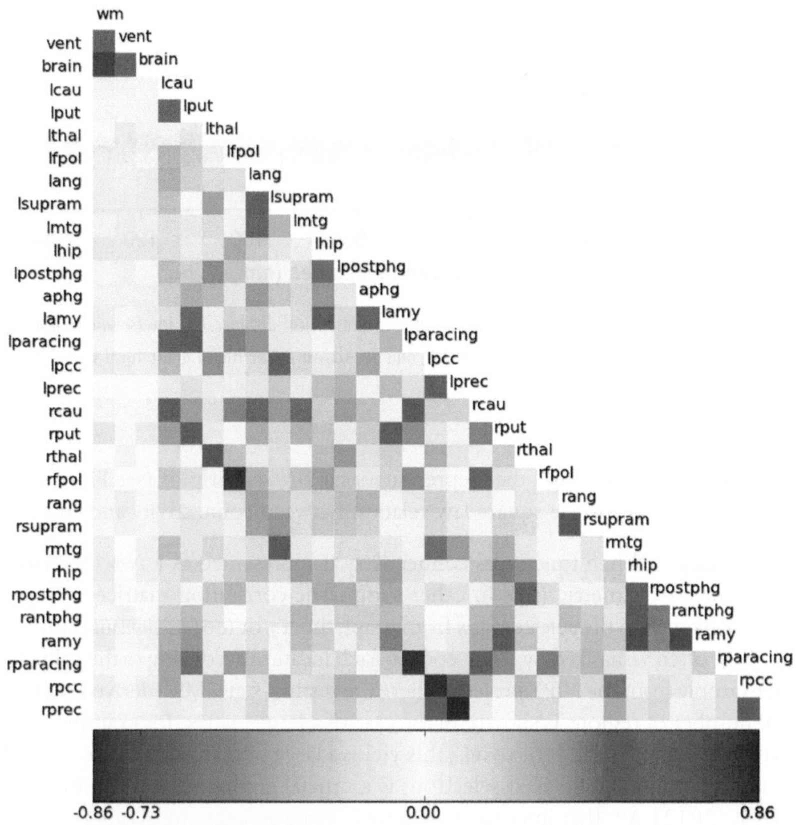

FIGURE 15.37 *Connectivity matrix showing the resting-state fMRI correlation between different regions of interest in the brain, color-coded from negative correlation to positive correlation (From: Neuroimaging in Python, or NIPY— http://nipy.sourceforge.net).*

fibers represent connections with a high average anisotropy. The opacity of the curves reflect the number of tracked fibers per connection.

Hierarchical Edge Bundles (HEB), introduced by Holten (2006), can also be classified as a circular node-link diagram, but have the unique characteristic that hierarchical connectivity can be represented by bundling together connections that terminate in the same parent nodes. By changing the bundling strength, HEB can be configured to show the low-level node-to-node connections, the more high-level node-group-to-node-group connections, or anything in between.

Van Dixhoorn *et al.* [2010] applied hierarchical edge bundles to resting-state fMRI connectivity data, having grouped the regions first by lobe and then by brain hemisphere. Modha and Singh [2010] applied the technique to connectivity data from the macaque brain collected by the CoCoMac project.[1] The CoCoMac data is based on anatomical tracer studies, but was also reduced to functional-like $N \times N$ connectivity data and used to produced visualizations such as the one in Figure 15.39. Again the regions have been grouped by lobe. Due to the bundling characteristic, the high level connectivity between the different lobes and groups of brain regions can also be appreciated. Note in this case that each curve

1 http://cocomac.org/.

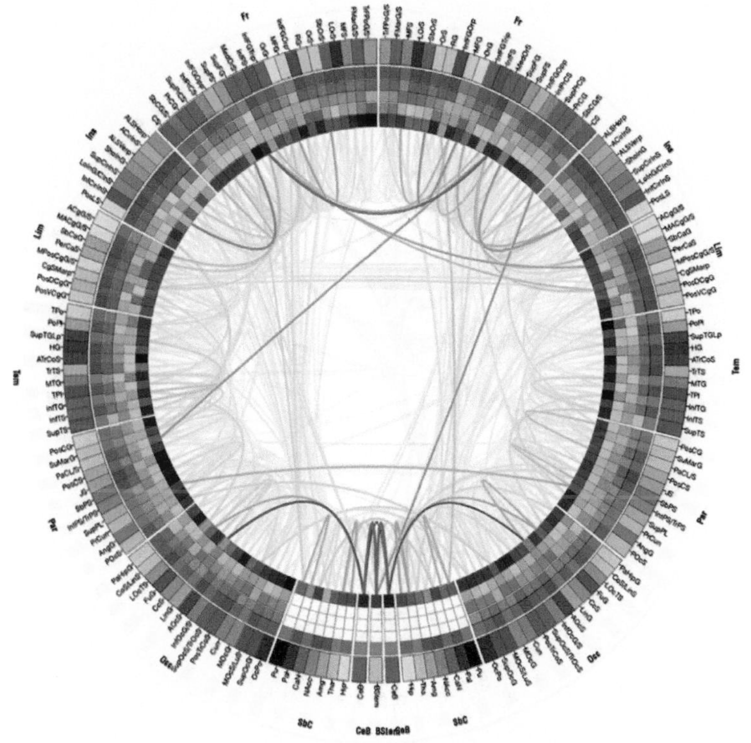

FIGURE 15.38 *Circos visualization of the structural connectivity, processed to look like functional connectivity data. The brain regions are shown on the outside ring, grouped by lobe or greater containing region: namely the frontal, insular, limbic, temporal, parietal and occipital lobes, and the brain stem, the cerebellum, and the non-cortical regions. The five rings inside that show various measures measures, such as degree of connectivity or cortical thickness (the cortex is the outer layer of the brain, see § 14.3.2). The curved edges represent the connectivity between regions (From: Irimia et al. [2012]).*

represents the existence of a connection in the CoCoMac data, but not the strength of that connection. Had such information been available, the opacity could have been used to represent it.

15.4.2 SPATIAL METHODS

In the previous section, we discussed methods that deal with connectivity matrices in a non-spatial way, for the largest part in order to emphasize the connectivity and its inherent hierarchy. However, in many cases it makes sense to show the data in its anatomical context. These *spatial methods* can be further described as being either *explicit* or *implicit*. In the explicit case, the connections themselves are visually represented, while in the implicit case, the regions that are involved in a connective network are the focus of the visualization.

Spatial Node-link Diagrams Similar to the non-spatial case, node-link diagrams can again be used to represent, explicitly, brain connectivity matrices. However, in the spatial case the anatomical location of the various participating brain regions can be integrated in the visualization. In other words, the nodes of the node-link diagram are positioned according to their real anatomical locations, or at the very least inspired by their real locations.

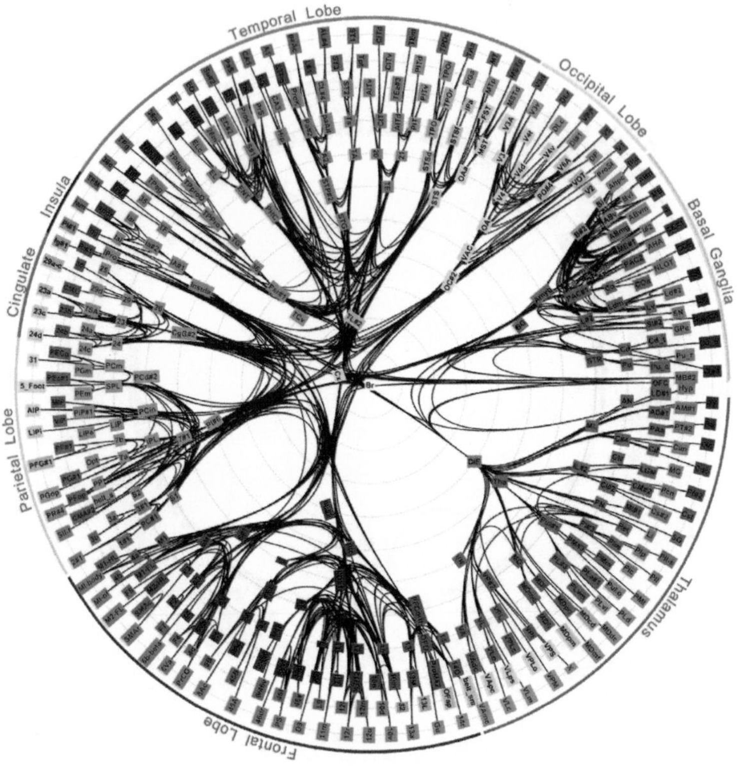

FIGURE 15.39 *Connectivity in the macaque brain, visualized using hierarchical edge bundles. Brain regions have been grouped according to their containing lobe (From: [Modha and Singh, 2010]).*

Figure 15.40 shows an example where a 258-node 3D anatomical node-link network has been used to visualize a brain connectivity matrix, in this case derived from structural Diffusion Spectrum Imaging (DSI) MRI data. Such visualizations have also been used for resting-state fMRI connectivity [Worsley *et al.*, 2005]. As can be seen from the example, such visualizations can become overly complex. Interaction facilities, such as filtering and selection, based on for example a connectivity threshold, or regions of interest, are required for the effective interpretation of such depictions. Alternatively, simplification techniques, such as hierarchical edge bundling, can also be applied in a spatial context [Böttger *et al.*, 2012].

In order to visualize functional connectivity, or the frequency-dependent coherence, from high-density EEG (recall § 15.2.1), Ten Caat *et al.* [2007] presented Functional Unit Maps, or FU maps. An example of a FU Map is shown in Figure 15.41. First the positions of the EEG electrodes on the scalp are mapped to a two-dimensional image. Here, sets of spatially adjacent electrodes that show high coherence are grouped together. Spatial adjacency is determined through the Voronoi tessellation of the electrodes. Each such group is called a Functional Unit, or FU. All the Voronoi tiles representing the electrodes belonging to a group are assigned one color. When the average coherence between two complete FUs exceeds a certain threshold, it is shown with a color-coded edge. With this technique, the complexity inherent in the full high-density coherence network is elegantly taken care of.

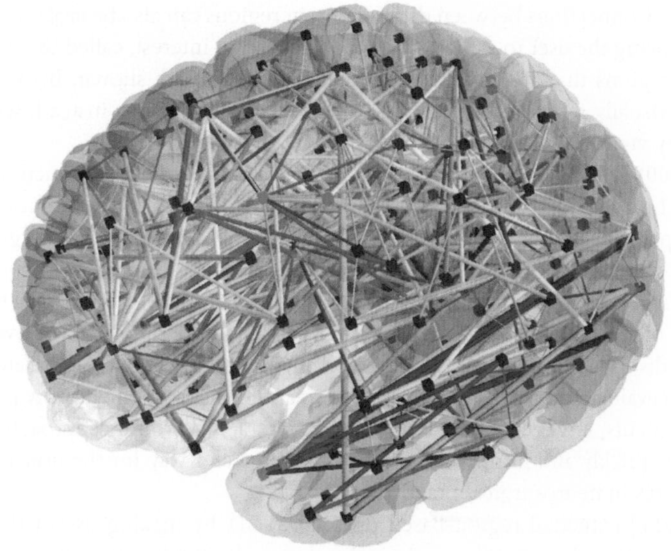

FIGURE 15.40 Image rendered with the ConnectomeViewer application, depicting the DSI-derived connectivity matrix between 258 regions with a 3D anatomical node-link diagram (Image courtesy of the Connectome Mapping Toolkit (CMTK) developers, see http://connectomeviewer.org/).

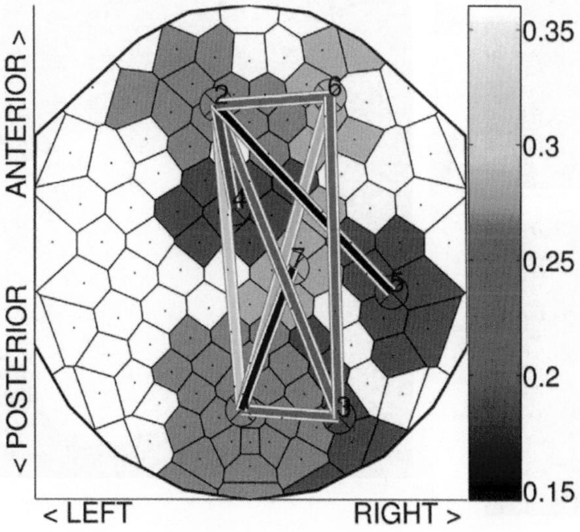

FIGURE 15.41 Functional Unit (FU) Maps for the visualization of high-density EEG connectivity. Each EEG sensor is surrounded by its Voronoi region. Sensors that show high coherence are grouped into functional units, and are displayed with the same color. Significant coherence between functional units is represented as edges between their centroids (Courtesy of Michael ten Caat, Itémedical, The Netherlands. See also Ten Caat et al. [2007]).

Region-based Probing Connections between different brain regions can also be *implicitly* represented. This is usually done by allowing the user to indicate a region or voxel of interest, called the seed region or voxel, at which point all regions that are connected to that seed region are shown. Because the connections themselves are not visually represented, but only the participating regions instead, we classify this as an implicit connectivity visualization technique.

Shimony *et al.* [2009] did some of the first work on using resting-state fMRI functional connectivity for surgical planning. They demonstrated that critical functional networks could be found based on resting state fMRI, and proposed that knowledge of these networks could help guide the surgical approach. Their demonstration was based on selecting seed regions in the brain, and examining the networks connected to those regions. Böttger *et al.* [2011] extended their work by creating a software tool that allowed for the interactive probing of seed regions. With their system, the seed region could be moved around, and the connected regions, displayed on the standard three orthogonal slices, would be updated at 10 frames per second. Based on an evaluation with four neurosurgeons and the data of one healthy participant as well as eight brain lesion patients, it was concluded that such an interactive probing approach helped to pinpoint functional networks quickly and intuitively, and had potential as a way for the non-invasive exploration of functional networks in neurosurgical practice.

Eklund *et al.* [2011] extended region-based probing to 3D, by making use of the GPU to calculate interactively the correlations between the seed voxel and up to 20,000 brain voxels. Each correlation is also calculated at 1,000 different time lags, in order to compensate for transmission delay in the communication between different brain regions. Their application, a screenshot of which is shown in Figure 15.42, uses

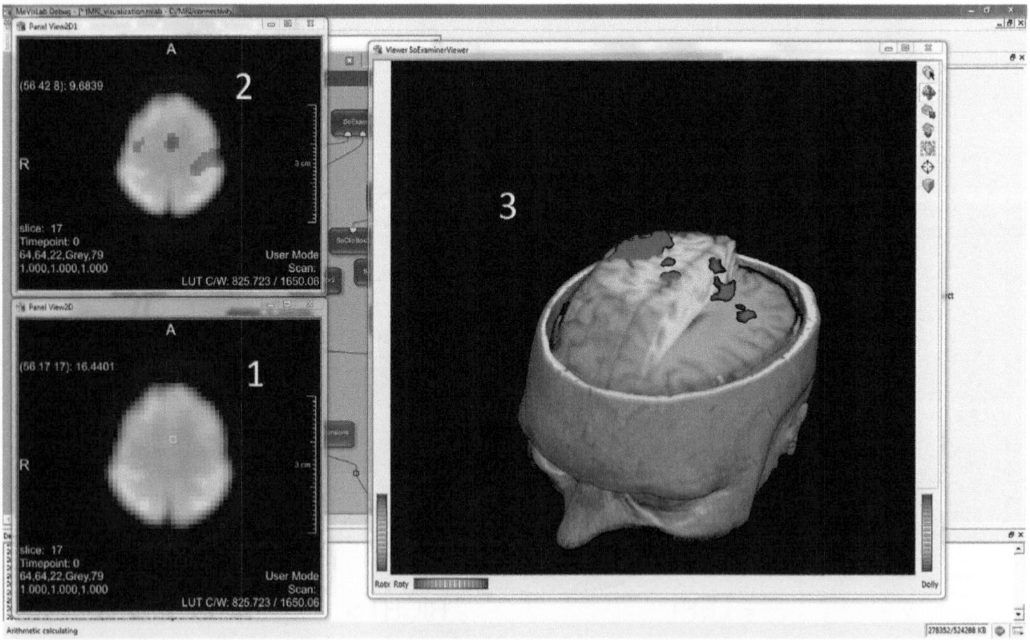

FIGURE 15.42 *GPU-based interactive calculation and visualization of 3D resting-state fMRI connectivity. A seed voxel has been selected on the slice at the bottom left. The 3D rendering at the right and the slice at the top left show other parts of the brain that have a significant correlation with the seed voxel (From: Eklund et al. [2011]).*

interactive volume rendering to visualize, in 3D, all brain regions that have a correlation higher than a certain threshold with the currently selected voxel. The work of Van Dixhoorn *et al.* [2012] enabled direct 3D probing on the cortical surface, in addition to probing on the slice views. Furthermore, it was possible to perform side-by-side comparisons of different resting-state fMRI connectivity datasets. With the freely available InstaCorr AFNI module, 3D region-based probing can also be performed [Cox, 2011].

Showing the participating regions but not the connections themselves helps to design a less cluttered visualization of complex brain connectivity matrix data. This is especially important in the case of voxel-based resting-state fMRI connectivity, where the connectivity graph contains 20,000 nodes. Furthermore, pointing at a region and then seeing which other regions it is connected with is a natural metaphor for querying the connectivity information.

15.5 SUMMARY

This chapter dealt with the visualization of macroscopic connectivity in the human brain. Understanding this macroscopic connectivity plays an important role in our fundamental understanding of how the mind works. In addition, being able to study brain networks *in vivo* facilitates our understanding of the many serious diseases that affect brain connectivity, and will play an increasingly important role in neurosurgical planning. The visualization techniques detailed in this chapter all play a role in this study.

After first giving an overview of the different acquisition techniques that are able to generate data on in-vivo brain connectivity, we discussed various visualization approaches. During this discussion, we distinguished between two main types of macroscopic connectivity. Structural connectivity describes the geometry of a neural connection or bundle of connections between different brain regions, while connectivity matrices usually only store measures of the connectivity between all pairs of regions. Visualization techniques for the first are predominantly spatial, showing connectivity in its spatial context, whereas the second group of visualization techniques can be both non-spatial and spatial, depending on whether the focus is on the hierarchy inherent in the brain's architecture, or the anatomical locations of the connected regions.

The study of brain connectivity has become increasingly important over the past years. This importance will only continue to grow; Understanding brain connectivity is considered to be a key step toward understanding how the human mind works. Initiatives such as the Human Connectome Project and the Blue Brain Project only serve to underline the value of this research. Due to the complexity and the variability of the networks involved, visualization plays a crucial role in these developments.

FURTHER READING

Pfister *et al.* [2012] presented a compact summary of visualization techniques for connectivity at all three scales: Macro-, meso-, and micro-scale connectivity. Dercksen *et al.* [2012] make the case for interactive visualization specifically in meso-scale connectivity, where the neural network in a single cortical column of the rat brain is analyzed, based on sectioned data imaged with a transmitted light brightfield microscope.

Jones [2010] presents a critical overview of the use of diffusion MRI for the reliable quantification of *in vivo* connectivity, voicing strong doubts as to the accuracy of both voxel-based connectivity measures, e.g., FA, and tractographic connectivity measures. He concludes by making suggestions toward the improvement of this type of connectivity quantification, for the largest part based on integrating information from other sources such as measures of axon density, axon caliber, and myelination. It is indeed very important to understand and communicate the limitations of the techniques used.

Global tractography or fiber reconstruction techniques attempt to generate a tractography that globally fits the acquired data as well as possible, hence yielding a consistent view of the structural connectivity architecture in the whole white matter volume. With such techniques, fiber crossings can be successfully detected even in normal diffusion tensor data [Fillard *et al.*, 2009], as the neighboring tensors contribute information maximally to the crossing point. More recently, advances have resulted in global fiber reconstruction techniques that operate quickly enough for practical application, even on HARDI data [Reisert *et al.*, 2011].

Chapter e16

Visual Exploration and Analysis of Perfusion Data

16.1 INTRODUCTION

Compared to static image data where the morphology of anatomical and pathological structures is represented with high spatial resolution, dynamic image data characterizes functional processes, such as metabolism and blood flow. These functional processes are often essential to detect diseases at an early stage or to discriminate pathologies with very similar morphology. Important examples of dynamic medical image data are functional MRI, where the activation of brain regions is imaged, dynamic PET and SPECT, where the temporal distribution of a radioactive tracer is measured to assess metabolic processes, and perfusion imaging, where the perfusion of tissue with blood is measured. We focus on perfusion data, which are acquired to support essential diagnostic tasks, e.g., stroke diagnosis, the assessment of different types of tumors and the diagnosis of the coronary heart disease.

In perfusion imaging, the distribution of contrast agents (CA) is registered to assess the microcirculation of blood and tissue kinetics. *Microcirculation* relates to the flow through the capillaries. These vascular structures are far too small to be seen directly in medical imaging data. However, perfusion imaging reflects the overall blood supply accumulated by many small capillary structures. Signal intensities after the administration of a CA are recorded. Whether or not a CA reaches a particular region and subsequently accumulates there, how long it takes until the maximum amount of CA is achieved as well as other parameters are determined for medical diagnosis. These parameters are substitutes for physiological parameters such as tumor perfusion and vessel permeability, which e.g., characterize the malignancy of a tumor [Choyke *et al.*, 2003].

Visual exploration of perfusion data is primarily based on the derived perfusion parameters, which represent features of time-intensity curves (TICs). These parameters are derived for each voxel of the perfusion data and represent a high-dimensional space, usually of five to eight parameters. The analysis of data in this space aims at understanding the correlation between these parameters as well as the local distribution of single perfusion parameters. Since the time dependency is not represented in the perfusion parameters, often parameter maps along with TICs have to be analyzed. The comprehensible and simultaneous display of these curves and parameter maps poses considerable challenges for the layout. The basic principles of deriving, filtering, and analyzing time-intensity curves were developed for the analysis of scintigrams in the 1970s and refined for the analysis of X-ray image sequences [Hoehne *et al.*, 1981].

The visual exploration is challenging due to the character and the quality of the data: They exhibit various artifacts and thus the visualization also serves the assessment of the reliability of the original data and the assessment of preprocessed data, where artifacts are reduced. In contrast to static CT data, no absolute scale for the intensity values exists. Therefore, simple visualization techniques with predefined (absolute) settings are not applicable. As a consequence of these difficulties, image processing and visualization have to be tightly integrated and a variety of visualization techniques is needed to detect and characterize important features.

Visual Computing for Medicine, Second Edition. http://dx.doi.org/10.1016/B978-0-12-415873-3.00016-X

Perfusion data are rarely used as the only imaging modality for diagnosis. MR perfusion data, e.g., are usually interpreted along with other MRI data. For the sake of brevity, we cannot explain such comprehensive diagnostic procedures in detail, but we will mention which additional modalities are used.

Organization This chapter is organized as follows: In § 16.2, we give a brief overview on the medical background in selected application areas. In § 16.3, we briefly describe image data processing, which enhances the expressiveness of basic and advanced visualization techniques (§ 16.4).

Research in the last years revealed that a combination of data analysis techniques, such as dimension reduction and clustering, with visual exploration is essential to advance perfusion imaging. In § 16.5 we introduce such visual analysis techniques and their application to perfusion data.

The application of advanced exploration and analysis techniques in the most essential areas is described in case studies on cerebral perfusion (§ 16.6), tumor perfusion (§ 16.7) and cardiac perfusion (§ 16.8). There are a couple of more application areas, where perfusion imaging gained considerable importance. Selected examples, including prostate and renal perfusion, are discussed in § 16.9.

16.2 MEDICAL IMAGING

In perfusion imaging, a certain amount of a CA is injected intravenously and its distribution is measured by a repeated acquisition of subsequent images covering the volume of interest [Axel, 1980]. The CA causes signal changes and works as a tracer of the blood. Perfusion imaging, however, differs strongly from static imaging, since greater care must be exercised in injection rate and dose, image timing and image analysis. While Choyke *et al.* [2003] assessed that "currently, such imaging techniques are mainly performed in a research context", they are now widely used.

Spatial and Temporal Resolution Perfusion imaging is possible with a high spatial and temporal resolution. However, spatial and temporal resolution cannot be increased at the same time due to the time required for image acquisition. As an example, cerebral MRI perfusion data have a low spatial resolution (2 mm pixel spacing), but high temporal resolution (2 seconds), whereas dynamic MR mammography has a high spatial resolution (0.7 mm pixel spacing) at the expense of a lower temporal resolution (1 minute). Spatial and temporal resolution also have an influence on the signal-to-noise ratio (SNR): higher resolution is usually achieved at the expense of a lower SNR. As an example, Ingrisch *et al.* [2010] investigated the influence of temporal resolution (between 1 and 5 seconds) and the SNR on quantitative lung perfusion parameters and found that the accuracy breaks down beyond a temporal resolution of 3 seconds.

DSC and DCE MRI Basically, variants of two imaging sequences are used for MR perfusion imaging:

- *Dynamic Susceptibility Contrast* (DSC) imaging, a T2*-weighted sequence that exploits the susceptibility effect. The magnetic susceptibility of different anatomical structures gives rise to local inhomogeneities in the magnetic field that is measured with T2* gradient echo sequences and a paramagnetic contrast agent.
- *Dynamic Contrast-Enhanced* (DCE) imaging, where T1-weighted MRI data are acquired. DCE imaging displays the long-term (>1 min) diffusion process of tracer particles through the membranes of the microvessels.

DCE-MRI is typically used for breast cancer diagnosis, whereas DSC-MRI and CT are employed for the diagnosis of ischemic stroke.[1] In DCE imaging, a signal enhancement is achieved in areas of CA accumulation. In contrast, DSC-MRI leads to a decrease of signal intensity where the CA accumulates.

1 A strongly restricted or blocked blood supply of tissue based on pathologies in surrounding vasculature is referred to as *ischemia*.

Particularly CT, PET, SPECT, and MRI data are employed for perfusion imaging. In the following, we focus on MRI perfusion, since this is the most widespread modality in tumor diagnosis. Moreover, MRI outperforms CT in stroke diagnosis, since the entire brain can be scanned (instead of a limited volume with CT) and it has shown to have at least a similar sensitivity and specificity in comparison to PET and SPECT in the diagnosis of the coronary heart disease. However, in comparison to CT, the feasibility of MRI is restricted due to the low availability, superior costs, and patient-specific difficulties with obtaining MRI, e.g., claustrophobia [Wintermark *et al.*, 2005].

An essential problem in perfusion imaging is the lack of standards and normalization: the signal change over time strongly depends on the scanner, on parameters of contrast agent administration, on the specific timing, and even on the menstruation cycle of woman. One essential use case, that we therefore consider throughout this chapter, is *medical research*, aiming at the improvement of perfusion imaging.

Perfusion Parameters For the diagnosis, regions of interest (ROIs) in healthy and suspicious regions are defined, and time-intensity curves (TIC)—averaged over all voxels in the selected region—are analyzed. Typical TICs from cerebral and breast tumor perfusion are presented in Figure e16.1. The curves observed in myocardial perfusion diagnosis are similar to those of cerebral perfusion. In both application areas, regions exhibiting no significant or a delayed and diminished enhancement (red and green curves in Fig. e16.1, left) are of interest. However, in breast tumor perfusion, regions showing a high early enhancement followed by rapid wash-out, i.e., a decrease of signal intensity afterwards, are especially suspicious (red curve in Fig. e16.1, right).

To achieve a more quantitative description of the curve shape, perfusion parameters are derived from the TICs. Depending on the application area, different perfusion parameters are relevant. However, some parameters are of general interest for almost all application areas (see Fig. e16.2). Before we describe these parameters, we introduce two parameters necessary for a reliable evaluation. The *CA arrival* represents the point in time when the signal enhancement actually starts, whereas Time_{End} refers to the end of the first CA passage. The *Baseline* represents the average intensity before CA arrival (see Fig. e16.2). These parameters are determined to focus the evaluation of the time-intensity curve on the relevant portion.

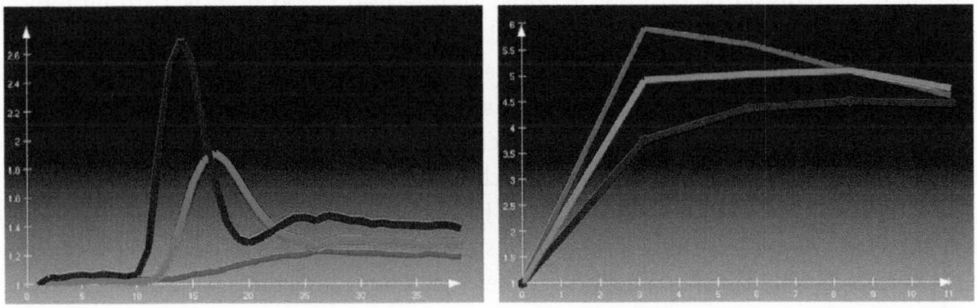

FIGURE e16.1 *Average time-intensity curves in different regions selected in perfusion data.* **Left:** *Cerebral perfusion—TICs for regions of gray matter in the brain (40 measurements). The blue curve shows normal brain perfusion. The red curve indicates no significant perfusion in the infarction core. The green curve shows decreased and delayed perfusion around the core.* **Right:** *Breast tumor perfusion—TICs of different regions in breast tissue (5 measurements). The enhancement relative to the signal intensity at the first points in time is shown to assess a suspicious tumor being benign or malignant. The red curve is especially suspicious because of its strong wash-out, which is typical for malignant tumors.*

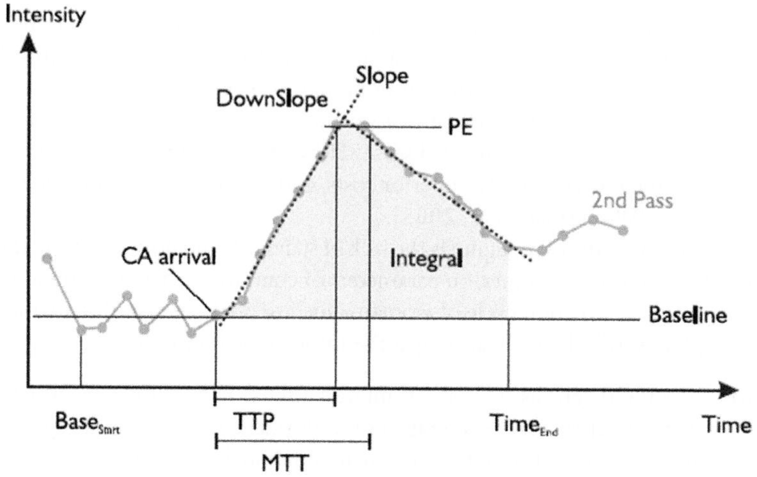

FIGURE e16.2 *A typical time-intensity curve in cardiac perfusion with a significant first pass and an alleviated second pass of contrast agent traversal annotated with the essential parameters to evaluate the first pass. Similar curves are observed in cerebral perfusion diagnosis.*

Assessing perfusion considering the actual *CA arrival* (time), Time_{End}, and the *Baseline* are essential to compare perfusion analysis results from different scanning devices and patients. Major diagnostically relevant perfusion parameters are:

- *Peak Enhancement* (PE). The maximum value normalized by subtracting the baseline.
- *Time To Peak* (TTP). The point in time where PE occurs, normalized by subtracting the CA arrival time. This parameter allows to assess whether blood supply is delayed in a particular region. If the peak is not a significant maximum or the temporal resolution is low, the TTP value is not expressive. The signal change in the interval between CA arrival and TTP is referred to as *wash-in*, whereas the signal change in the time between TTP and Time_{End} is referred to as *wash-out*.
- *Integral*. For a certain time interval (often representing the first cycle or pass of blood flow) the area between the curve and the baseline, the approximated integral, is computed. Together, PE and *Integral* indicate reduced blood flow. Reduced and delayed blood flow is a strong indicator for a damaged region, for example in cerebral stroke or cardiac diagnosis.
- *Mean Transit Time* (MTT). In the time interval used for the integral calculation, MTT specifies the first momentum of the curve. It is normalized by subtracting the CA arrival time.
- The *Slope* characterizes the steepness of the curve during wash-in. Depending on the temporal resolution, different regression methods, such as the gamma-variate and a linear fit are used to characterize the curve progression. The term *Up-Slope* in cardiac diagnosis relates to the maximum slope between two or three subsequent time steps between CA arrival and TTP.
- The *Down-Slope* characterizes the steepness of the descending curve during wash-out and is computed similar to the *Slope*.

Additional parameters are employed for specific applications (see § 16.6–16.8). All these parameters characterize the shape of the time-intensity curves; they are referred to as *descriptive* or *phenomenological* perfusion parameters [Franiel *et al.*, 2011]. In contrast, we later introduce a smaller set of perfusion parameters that result from adapting a pharmacokinetic model to the measured data. The perfusion parameters are sometimes difficult to compute, e.g., the definition of the contrast arrival time in noisy data is challenging (see Cheong *et al.* [2003] for a theoretical investigation). Also the precise determination of the MTT parameter in DSC data is challenging and may be performed with an adaptive fitting method [Li *et al.*, 2003].

Storage of Parameter Volumes Several tools for the visual exploration of perfusion data compute the essential perfusion parameters for all voxels of the dataset and store them in *parameter volumes*. With this strategy, *parameter maps* (color-coded slices of the parameter volume) or 3D visualizations of one or more parameters may be generated rapidly. If perfusion parameters are only needed for selected subsets, e.g., a ROI around a tumor, they may be computed on-the-fly.

16.2.1 CEREBRAL PERFUSION

In contrast to leaky vessels in malignant tumors, microvessels in normal brain tissue do not leak as a result of the blood brain barrier. Consequently, there is no enhancement in the extracellular volume. Instead, we observe the "first pass" of the CA through the vessel components. About 10 seconds after the first pass of blood circulation, a broadened second pass can be seen. The volume of blood in each voxel is diagnostically relevant. It is measured by the integral parameter.

CT and MRI are used to assess cerebral perfusion. MRI studies suffer from a lower spatial resolution compared to CT, but allow scanning of the entire brain, and are thus better suited to detect an infarction, if its location is not a priori known. In CT perfusion, generally a restricted volume is acquired. To reduce image noise, a large slice thickness (10 mm) is employed [König *et al.*, 2001].

CT images are used to discriminate cerebral hemorrhage and ischemic stroke. In case of an ischemic stroke, cerebral perfusion images are used to assess the existence and the extent of "tissue at risk" surrounding the core of the stroke. "Tissue at risk" is characterized by reduced and delayed perfusion. Surgical and chemical interventions aiming at revascularization may salvage at least parts of the "tissue at risk" [den Boer and Folkers, 1997].

16.2.2 TUMOR PERFUSION

The process of CA enhancement in a tumor can be described by the diffusion of tracer particles from the inside of blood vessels into the extravascular space and vice versa before it becomes excreted in the kidneys [Furman-Haran *et al.*, 1997]. The *permeability* of the vessel walls and the *extracellular volume fraction* determine the amplitude and the shape of the TIC. Time-intensity curves—which show a high early enhancement followed by a rapid wash-out, i.e., a significant decrease of signal intensity afterwards—are especially suspicious (see Fig. e16.1, right), because they indicate *strong perfusion* and *high permeability* of vessels. Strong perfusion often results from tumor-induced vessel growth (*neoangiogenesis*) and sprouting of existing capillar vessels. The newly formed vessels are leaky and therefore highly permeable, leading to a rapid wash-out [Knopp *et al.*, 1999]. Less suspicious are curves showing a plateau later on (green curve), or regions that continue to enhance (blue curve). This is typically observed in benign tumors. To compensate for different imaging parameters, TICs are normalized with respect to first point in time leading to *relative enhancement curves* (RE curves). Thus, RE curves always start at zero at the first point in time. Figure e16.3 illustrates the correspondence between ROIs selected in slice views and the related RE curves.

In DCE-MRI mammography, longer acquisition times are employed (compared to cerebral perfusion with DSC-MRI) to enable a high spatial resolution.

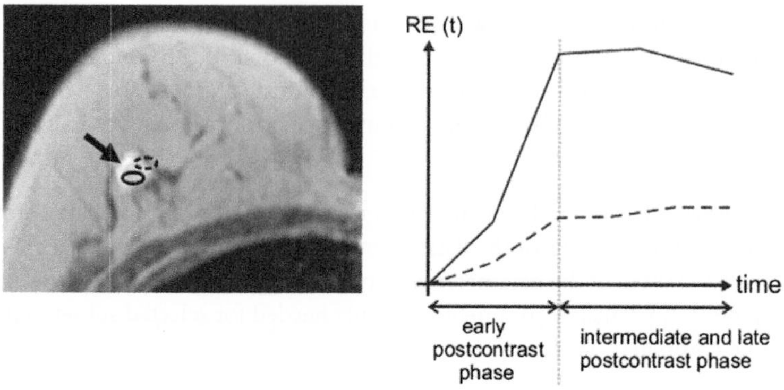

FIGURE e16.3 *Evaluation of the relative enhancement of a suspicious breast tumor. Two elliptical ROIs have been defined in the slice view (left). For both ROIs, the related time-intensity curves are shown. The dotted ellipse comprises a benign portion of a tumor. Its kinetics is reflected in the dotted curve. The fully drawn ellipse represents malignant tissue where the contrast enhancement is strong and wash-out characteristics are observed (From: [Glaßer et al., 2010b]).*

16.2.3 CARDIAC PERFUSION

Perfusion data is also crucial in the diagnosis of the coronary heart disease (CHD). At an early stage, the CHD is characterized by a perfusion defect caused by a stenosis (an abnormal vessel narrowing). The localization of the perfusion defect with respect to the myocardium combined with anatomical knowledge about the supplying coronary arteries is essential in detecting stenosis as well as in early CHD diagnosis [Oeltze *et al.*, 2006].

Data acquisition is typically accomplished according to the standards of the American Heart Association (AHA) [Cerqueira *et al.*, 2002b] (Fig. e16.4, left). The slices are acquired during breathhold and they are electrocardiogram (ECG)-triggered over a period of at least 40 consecutive heart beats. Typical parameters for cardiac perfusion data are: matrix: 128×128, slice thickness 8 mm. In contrast to cerebral and tumor

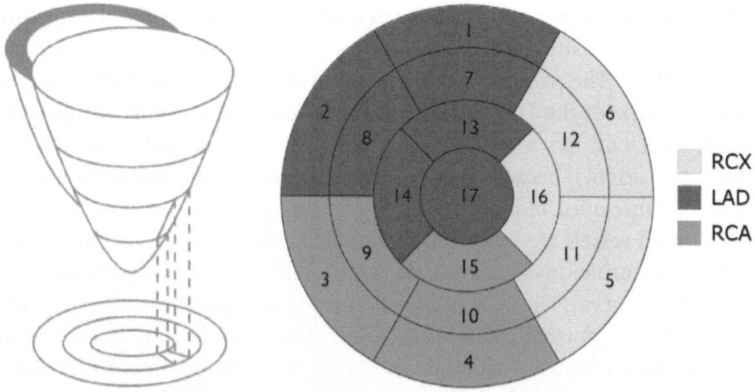

FIGURE e16.4 **Left:** *AHA-based acquisition of myocardial perfusion data in short-axis views. Schematic representation of the left ventricle that is imaged with three to four slices dissecting the left ventricle basally, centrically, apically, and at the apex.* **Right:** *Bull's-eye plot and AHA-based nomenclature. The plot is generated by projecting the myocardial segments onto a plane. The segments are colored according to the supplying coronary branch (Courtesy of Steffen Oeltze, University of Magdeburg).*

perfusion data, which continuously cover the volume of interest, cardiac perfusion data exhibit large gaps (slice thickness: 8 mm and 10 mm gaps) and only three to four slices are acquired.

Rest and Stress Perfusion The acquisition of perfusion data is often carried out at rest and under drug-induced stress. The stress test may even reveal marginal stenosis and is usually performed prior to the test at rest using identical imaging parameters. The major application of stress perfusion is the analysis of a known stenosis with respect to their hemodynamic relevance.

According to the AHA standard, the myocardium is divided into 17 segments based on a correspondence between those regions and the supplying coronary branch: ramus circumflex (RCX), left anterior descending (LAD), and right coronary artery (RCA). The perfusion parameters characterizing the CA distribution for each segment are computed (per voxel), averaged (for all voxels of the respective segment) and visualized separately by means of polar coordinates in a color-coded *Bull's-eye plot* (Fig. e16.4, right).

The detection and localization of a perfusion deficit as well as the assessment of the severity are directly relevant for treatment decisions. Major diagnostic tasks to be performed are:

- to evaluate whether the patient suffers from CHD,
- to evaluate the severity of the disease, and
- to assess the vascular supply of less perfused tissue. For an overview of MR-based diagnosis of the CHD, see Edelman [2004].

16.3 DATA PROCESSING AND DATA ANALYSIS

In the following we describe preprocessing and analysis techniques that enable an expressive visualization of perfusion data. While motion correction (§ 16.3.1) and the calibration of signal intensities (§ 16.3.2) are widely used, we also discuss segmentation and pharmacokinetic modeling that enable advanced visual analysis and exploration techniques.

16.3.1 MOTION CORRECTION

Motion correction is essential when breathing, heartbeat, patient movement, or muscle relaxation occur (Fig. e16.5). Without motion correction, subtraction images are filled with bright artifacts and TICs are misleading. Motion artifacts might hide relevant signal changes, but can also be mistaken for signal changes that are actually not present. Successful motion correction ensures that a voxel with coordinates (x, y, z) at time t_1 corresponds to a voxel with the same coordinates at time t_2. A significant amount of research was directed at *prospective motion correction* in the image acquisition stage. Thus, data acquisition may be gated according to the cardiac cycle or (partially) repeated automatically if motion is detected. However, even with state-of-the-art imaging, motion cannot be completely avoided.

Motion Correction is an instance of *registration*, a frequent task in medical image analysis (recall § 4.8). Registration is often tackled as an optimization problem where data of one image are transformed to optimally match features of a *reference image*. A *similarity metric* is employed to determine the objective function for the optimization.

Choice of a Reference Image The choice of the reference image affects the quality of registration. In perfusion imaging, the reference image is usually the image related to the first point in time. If, however, perfusion occurs in large portions of the volume, another point in time should be considered with an average amount of perfusion. Often, a post-contrast image has the highest similarity to all other images. Since

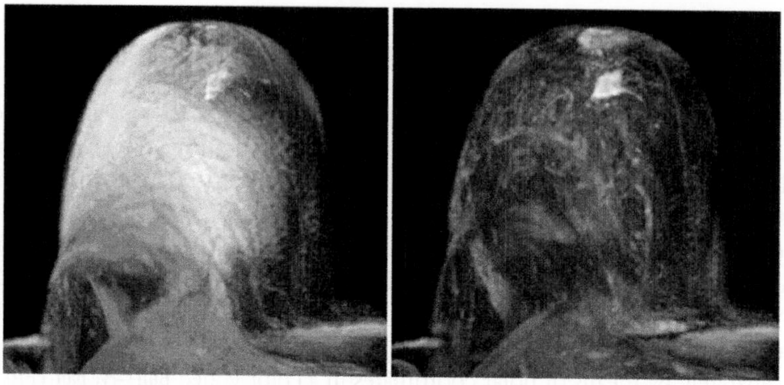

FIGURE e16.5 *Subtraction volumes of DCE-MRI mammography data rendered as MIP (Maximum Intensity Projection). Due to respiration, the data (left) exhibit bright artifacts in regions that are not aligned. After aligning the data (right), the volume becomes more transparent and reveals an enhancing tumor (Courtesy of Sven Kohle, Fraunhofer MEVIS Bremen).*

many images are involved (and not only two like in many other registration tasks), registration should be performed fully automatically and not rely on landmarks specified by a user.

For DCE-MRI mammography data, rigid registration approaches, which (only) transform the whole static dataset are not sufficient. Breathing and muscle relaxation result in considerable soft tissue deformations. Elastic (non-rigid) registration approaches, that consider local transformations, perform better in terms of registration quality. The registration algorithm described by Rueckert *et al.* [1999] is a good basis, which employs *normalized mutual information* [Wells-III *et al.*, 1996] as similarity measure. Originally developed for in DCE-MRI mammography, it is now also used for motion correction in other application areas. However, it is a global one-step registration that might not optimally match all local details. Thus, in § 16.7 we briefly discuss more advanced techniques. In cerebral perfusion, rigid registration is usually sufficient, since breathing and heartbeat have no noticeable effect.

16.3.2 CALIBRATION OF SIGNAL INTENSITIES

While CT imaging provides calibrated signal intensities in "Hounsfield" units, MRI signals are dependent on the scanning sequence used. Therefore, the raw signals are frequently converted into relative concentration of the CA, referred to as *concentration time curves* (CTC). The conversion depends on the imaging sequence used. For T1-weighted MR images, the transformation is based on the assumption of a linear correspondence between CA concentration and signal intensity, which holds quite well for gradient-echo MR sequences [Choyke *et al.*, 2003]. In DSC-MRI data the standard conversion formula is Equation e16.1 (see [Rosen *et al.*, 1990]):

$$C(t) = \frac{-\ln(S(t)/S_0)}{k_2 TE} \tag{e16.1}$$

where $C(t)$ is the CA concentration at time t, S_0 is the baseline averaged signal intensity before CA arrival, $S(t)$ is the signal intensity at time t, TE is the echo time, and k_2 is a constant that depends on imaging and tissue parameters. For all sequences used, the *arterial input function* (AIF) plays an essential role.

Definition 16.1. The *arterial input function* AIF is a time-intensity curve averaged for a small region of a large artery after a bolus of contrast agent was applied. The selected region must belong completely to the artery. The AIF serves to normalize TICs and derived perfusion parameters and thus to standardize the evaluation of perfusion data.

Determination of the Arterial Input Function The AIF exhibits an earlier peak, a higher peak intensity, and a narrower shape compared to the curves derived in the tissue supplied by that artery. Since the manual determination of the AIF is an error-prone process, automatic approaches have been developed. Mouridsen *et al.* [2006], for example, employed k-means clustering and Kohlmann *et al.* [2011] provided a sophisticated image analysis pipeline to determine the branching of the pulmonary trunk to determine the AIF for lung perfusion studies.

To achieve a valid transformation, the AIF should be determined for the individual patient and not assumed to correspond to a standard value from the literature. The individual AIF is influenced by many factors including hematocrit value, cardiac function, and renal output [Franiel *et al.*, 2011] that differ strongly among patients. As a further step, the normalized TICs are deconvolved with the AIF—a transformation that yields the cerebral blood flow in cerebral perfusion data. Still, these values are semi-quantitative and further transformation would be necessary to yield quantitative parameters [Oeltze *et al.*, 2009]. In practice, these additional transformations are rarely performed, since they require patient-specific data, such as hematocrit values, that might be unavailable.

Transformation to Relative Enhancement Curves In contrast to the rather complex transformation in DSC data, DCE-MRI data are easier to process. The original TICs are transformed in *relative enhancement curves*. Thus, they are normalized with respect to first point in time and represent the percentage increase compared to the time before contrast arrival. Neither an arterial input function, nor a deconvolution is required.

The conversion of raw data to semi-quantitative parameters is accomplished by modern commercial software tools for perfusion data analysis, such as nordic ICE.[2]

16.3.3 SEGMENTATION

As in many other fields of medical visualization, segmentation may provide valuable information for both further analysis and expressive visualization. To further analyze the enhancement kinetics of a tumor, it is essential to segment it [Glaßer *et al.*, 2010a]. Thus, the further analysis may be restricted to decomposing the suspicious tumor, e.g., with clustering or other region decomposition techniques. Diagnostic reports and preoperative planning requires reliable information on the location of pathologies. Thus, advanced systems employ segmentation information, e.g., breast tumor, skin, chest wall, nipple, and other landmarks to automatically calculate spatial distances and create a report according to the BIRADS (Breast Imaging Reporting and Data System) recommendations.

Segmentation of time-dependent data is challenging. Model-based segmentation techniques, such as Statistical Shape Models or Active Contours (recall § 4.5), are frequently used. In most cases segmentation is performed after motion correction and the segmentation result from one-time step is propagated to other time steps. The correctness of the segmentation result can be observed by slicing through the images and a good correspondence between the derived contours and the image features indicates that motion correction was successful. An alternative is to employ temporal information instead of spatial information [Boykov *et al.*, 2001]. Thus, voxels are summarized in the segmentation process based on the similarity of their TIC. Segmentation and registration mutually influence each other. If segmentation is performed first, the segmentation result may be used to constrain the motion correction process. As Song *et al.* [2006] show, both processes can be intertwined such that a rough initial motion correction is used before segmentation

2 www.nordicneurolab.com.

and later fine-tuning of the registration. They could improve the overall efficiency of both tasks. Although their work was specific for kidney segmentation in renal perfusion, the concept is more broadly applicable.

Tumor Segmentation in perfusion data may be performed with a fuzzy c-means clustering [Chen *et al.*, 2006] and neural networks [Lucht *et al.*, 2002]. Behrens *et al.* [2007] give an overview on segmentation tasks and solutions for breast tumor perfusion.

Figure e16.6 shows volume rendering of perfusion data with a segmented breast lesion integrated as colored surface. Segmentation information may also be used to steer a ghost view technique that emphasizes a tumor, showing its location, and thus providing an overview (see Fig. e16.7).

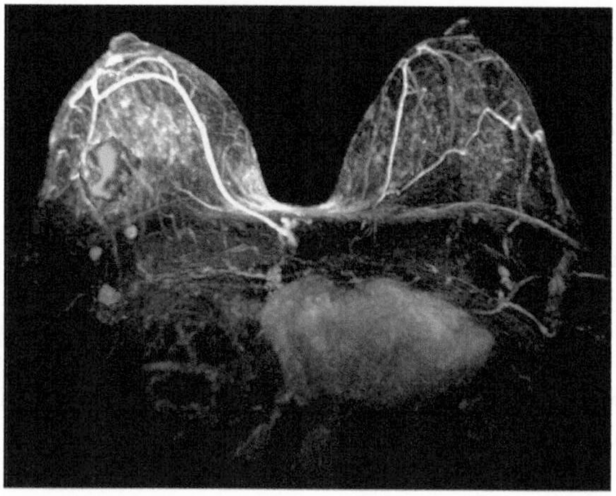

FIGURE e16.6 *Segmentation information is used to emphasize a breast lesion in its surrounding (Courtesy of Sarah Behrens, Fraunhofer MEVIS Bremen).*

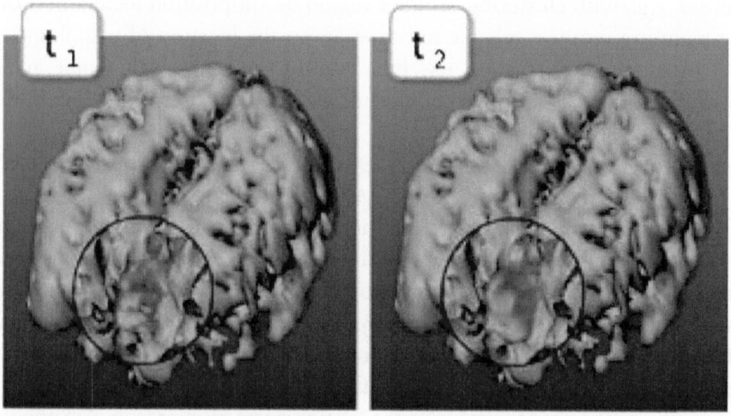

FIGURE e16.7 *In a longitudinal study with cerebral perfusion data, the development of brain tumors is analyzed. As an initial step to reveal gross changes, ghosted views are generated showing the segmented tumor in its surrounding (Courtesy of Sylvia Glaßer, University of Magdeburg).*

Discussion In order to remove occluding structures, it is necessary to segment them. For some applications, such as stroke or infarct diagnosis, it is useful to restrict the visualization to relevant structures (ventricles of the heart or brain tissue). Segmentation methods must be carefully adapted to the peculiarities of dynamic 3D image data. Usually, both assumptions related to the *morphologic image information* and to the *enhancement characteristics* are employed to identify and delineate anatomical and pathological structures in perfusion data.

16.3.4 NOISE REDUCTION

Noise reduction in perfusion data is performed similarly to noise reduction in static image data. Thus, Gaussian filters (discretized as binomial filters) are used as simple techniques. To better preserve features, 3D anisotropic diffusion filters are chosen (at the expense of computation time). Their use should be restricted to regions in the dataset where the signal intensity does not change strongly between subsequent time steps to preserve contrast agent accumulation [Song *et al.*, 2006]. Since time-intensity curves exhibit high-frequency noise, smoothing in the temporal dimension is essential for a reliable analysis. Lysaker *et al.* [2003] introduced an appropriate filter based on partial differential equations, which simulate a diffusion process, and applied it to DCE-MRI mammography data. Oeltze [2010] combined smoothing in the spatial domain with a 3×3 Gaussian filter with smoothing in the temporal domain with a 1×3 Gaussian filter.

For the generation of parameter maps, such as MTT and Integral, the "right" points in time must be chosen (recall § 16.2). Smoothed visualization may support this selection. Nevertheless, smoothing may also introduce errors and should be applied carefully. In combination with motion correction, which also has a smoothing effect, details may no longer be recognizable. Another noise reduction strategy is to fit a *gamma variate*, a non-symmetric Gaussian function. Gamma functions are used, e.g., for evaluating cerebral and cardiac perfusion data that exhibit a high temporal resolution. Furthermore, gamma functions restrict the evaluation of TICs to the contrast agent's first pass. Also wavelet transforms and Wiener-like filtering have been successfully used for smoothing perfusion data [Wirestam and Stahlberg, 2005]. There is a lack of guidelines or even consensus how data should be smoothed. In the publications mentioned above, the authors primarily (often shortly) explained their choice but did not compare various methods.

16.3.5 PHARMACOKINETIC MODELING

Descriptive parameters are derived without any assumptions, which makes it easy to use them. Although they can be employed for standardized evaluation of relative enhancement curve evaluation in DCE-MRI, they are not directly related to physiologic parameters and bound to specific scanners and protocols. Thus, they are not appropriate as a basis for a multicentric study. A more advanced method for the analysis of perfusion data is to employ a *pharmacokinetic model*. These models relate to physiological parameters, such as permeability of vasculature and the extracellular space. Moreover, pharmacokinetic models are employed to assess the effect of treatment, in particular antiangiogenetic treatment [Zwick *et al.*, 2010].

To employ a pharmacokinetic model, the model parameters are fitted to CTCs resulting from the transformation of the TICs. These models may lead to a more standardized image interpretation—the model parameters are less dependent from the imaging sequences and protocols than the general perfusion parameters.

Tofts Model The first influential and still widely used pharmacokinetic model is the two-compartment model developed by Tofts and Kermode [1991] that has been primarily used for assessing tumor perfusion. The *Tofts model* considers the vascular space and the extravascular extracellular space (EES) [Choyke *et al.*, 2003]. The CA enters the tumor through the vascular space and diffuses into the EES. The rates of diffusion

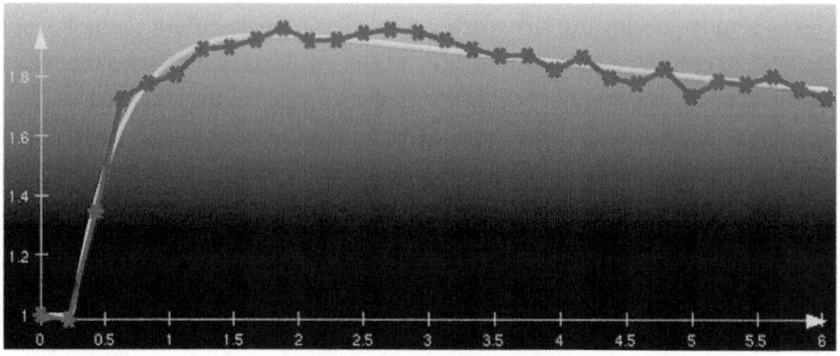

FIGURE e16.8 *The Tofts model parameters for the fit to a time-intensity curve are* $K = 0.5$ *and* $v = 50\%$ *which suggests a malignant disease.*

depend on the interface between capillaries and the EES, as well as on the concentration of the CA in the EES and in the vascular space. As a practical limitation, a high temporal resolution of at least 2 seconds is required [Franiel *et al.*, 2011]. Since this high resolution is not achieved in clinical routine imaging, except that only one slice is acquired, the value of this kind of modeling is reduced. However, even with a lower temporal resolution, pharmacokinetic modeling may be useful, as many studies indicate. As a rule of thumb, at least ten points in time should be employed for curve fitting.

The basic parameters of the Tofts model are the vascular permeability $K[1/\text{min}]$ and the extracellular volume fraction v. K affects the amplitude of the TIC, and the quotient of K/v affects the shape of the curve. A least squares fit to the TICs allows to estimate the parameters of the Tofts model (Fig. e16.8) [Furman-Haran *et al.*, 1997]. The estimated model parameters are also used for deriving parameter maps (recall Fig. e16.10). Englmeier *et al.* (2004) describe pharmacokinetic modeling of breast tumor perfusion data based on data acquired at 32 points in time.

Discussion In general, pharmacokinetic modeling is focused on cancer diagnosis, treatment monitoring, and disease understanding. In addition to confirming cancer diagnosis, such models may be used for *tumor grading*, an assessment of tumor biology that is essential for prognosis and treatment decisions, such as chemotherapy. As an example, Radjenovic *et al.* [2008] could show that mamma carcinoma with grade 2 differed significantly from those with grade 3 with respect to the two parameters of the Tofts model (possible grades are 1, 2, and 3 with three being the most aggressive tumor type). Such a sensitivity analysis is typically based on a correlation with histopathological reports where tumor grading can be determined reliably (and is considered as ground truth).

Zwick *et al.* [2010] and Franiel *et al.* [2011] give overviews on pharmacokinetic modeling and its limitations. They consider a couple of more recent and complex models and explain their assumptions, parameters, and application. According to these surveys, still primarily the two simpler and oldest models ([Tofts and Kermode, 1991] and [Brix *et al.*, 1991]) are used in clinical routine. These models are also realized in widely available commercial software.

16.3.6 CLASSIFICATION OF PERFUSION DATA AND COMPUTER-AIDED DETECTION

Another venue of analyzing perfusion data relates to a statistical analysis as well as to mining and knowledge discovery techniques. In particular, the classification of DCE-MRI mammography data by means of *artificial neural networks* and clustering techniques is an active research area [Chen *et al.*, 2006, Lucht *et al.*, 2001,

Meyer-Bäse *et al.*, 2007, Twellmann *et al.*, 2005]. As an example, Twellmann *et al.* [2005] applied an artificial neural network architecture that combines unsupervised and supervised techniques for voxel-by-voxel classification of temporal kinetic signals derived from DCE-MRI mammography data. Chen *et al.* [2006] developed a *fuzzy c-means clustering*-based technique to automatically identify characteristic kinetic curves from segmented breast lesions in DCE-MRI mammography data. Nattkemper and Wismuller [2005] described the application of *self-organized maps* to time curve features of DCE-MRI mammography data and discuss how the results may be visually represented as color-coded cross sections. The region decomposition method by Glaßer *et al.* [2010a] employs a four-dimensional feature vector derived from the TIC and aims at supporting ROI selection. The classification of small enhancing lesions is challenging and has been tackled in [Schlossbauer *et al.*, 2008].

Data classification is also aimed at in other application areas of perfusion data, such as classification of brain tissue by means of self-organizing maps and fuzzy c-means clusterings [Wismüller *et al.*, 2006], and semi-automatic region selection by means of an *independent component analysis* (ICA) [Kao *et al.*, 2008].

Computer-*Aided* Detection For tumor perfusion, in particular thresholds for the early enhancement are employed to detect suspicious lesions ([Dorrius *et al.*, 2011]). According to this review, radiologists with less experience attain a higher sensitivity with CAD systems. In the context of this chapter, CAD is interesting, since it leads to new results that must be adequately presented (along with other relevant data).

Since the most important application of perfusion data analysis is diagnosis, there have been various attempts to automatically detect and emphasize pathological structures. Such computer-aided detection (CAD) solutions have been developed, e.g., for tumor perfusion in order to improve the accuracy and shorten the time for diagnosis. Automatic classification may be useful in a screening setting in order to replace the opinion of a second radiologist or to direct a radiologist to suspicious regions. Widespread practical use is probably hampered by the low standardization of image acquisition. Thus, an automatic classifier that was explored with one scanner and protocol may need extensive training and adaptation when used for data from another hospital.

16.4 VISUAL EXPLORATION OF PERFUSION DATA

In this section, we describe general techniques that are widely used (§ 16.4.1) and later more advanced exploration techniques, such as the multiparameter visualization (§ 16.4.2). Even if advanced exploration and analysis techniques are available, basic techniques are often used first to get an overview and an initial understanding of a dataset that may guide the further analysis.

Based on the discussion of perfusion parameters, we formulate the following major questions for perfusion data analysis (see also [Oeltze, 2010]):

- Which parameters are most essential to characterize perfusion?
- How are perfusion parameters related to each other?
- How do imaging parameters affect perfusion parameters?

We discuss these issues in all case studies.

16.4.1 BASIC VISUALIZATION TECHNIQUES

Basic techniques to visualize and analyze perfusion data include:

- *cine-movies*, which step through all points in time for a selected slice,

- *subtraction images*, which depict the intensity difference between two selected points in time, and
- color-coded *parameter maps* for a selected slice. A parameter map depicts the value of a perfusion parameter in a pixelwise manner (see Fig. e16.10).

Cine-movies The cinematic depiction of gray scale images in a movie loop is helpful to assess image noise and artifacts [Choyke *et al.*, 2003], but especially for the assessment of enhancement patterns.

Subtraction Images Provided that motion is compensated, the resulting differences in subtraction images reflect contrast agent accumulation or wash-out. Subtraction images may also be used for quality control; the injection of a CA leads to an increase of signal intensity (in T1-weighted images). If the subtraction for two points in time, t_2 and t_1 after CA arrival with $t_2 > t_1$, leads to a negative value, it is likely that the pixels do not correspond to each other due to motion artifacts. If this occurs, motion correction is indispensable for a meaningful analysis.[3]

In Figure e16.9, two subtraction images are shown, which are used for the diagnosis of an ischemic stroke. Both reveal a dark area in the right hemisphere (left part of the images). This is suspicious, since it does not occur in the corresponding region of the left hemisphere. The region that is dark in both images, depicts the core of an ischemic stroke. Around this region, a larger area appears dark in the early subtraction image (left), but bright in the subtraction image, which refers to a later time (right). This region shows the "tissue at risk" around a stroke core.

Subtraction images provide valuable information for the diagnosis. However, there is no assistance in choosing the "right" points in time for subtraction images. Moreover, the 2D data are only used to visually detect abnormalities. Subtraction images do not provide quantitative information, which could make the diagnostic results more reproducible. Cine movies and subtraction images may be combined with interaction facilities that enable to select regions and further analyze such regions.

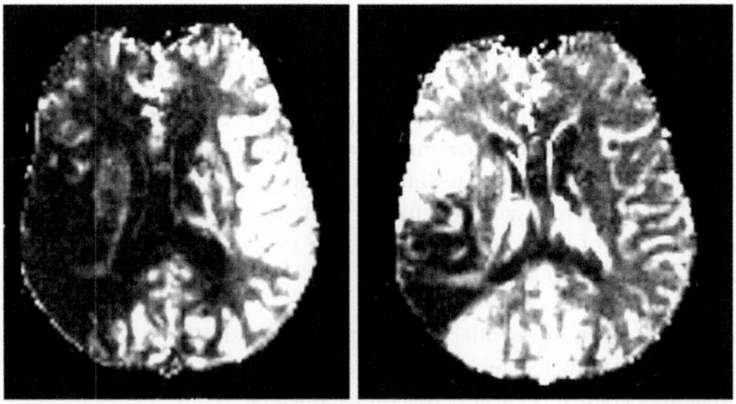

FIGURE e16.9 *Subtraction images to analyze cerebral perfusion. The T2 images have been inverted.* **Left:** *difference between* t_6 *and* t_2; **right:** t_{17} *and* t_2. *The low perfusion in a larger portion of the right hemisphere (left part in the image!) characterizes the infarct zone. In the right image, the late enhancement in a part of the right hemisphere represents the "tissue at risk". It is characterized by a high signal intensity. A brain segmentation algorithm has been applied to restrict the visualization to brain tissue (Courtesy of Jonathan Wiener, Boca Raton Community Hospital).*

3 In T2-weighted imaging, the intensity decreases after CA arrival. In these cases, the quality control must be adapted.

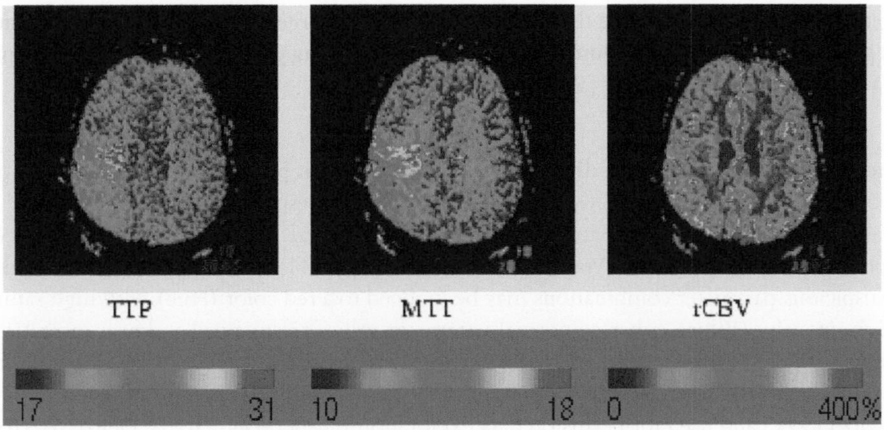

FIGURE e16.10 *Parameter maps for TTP, MTT, and the regional cerebral blood volume (roughly corresponding to the general perfusion parameter Integral) of a cerebral MRI perfusion dataset are depicted. The delayed blood flow in the right hemisphere (left part of the images) becomes obvious (Courtesy of Jonathan Wiener, Boca Raton Community Hospital).*

Parameter Maps are displayed as color-coded images (see Fig. e16.10). Parameter maps were introduced by Hoehne *et al.* [1981]. Besides parameter images, it is common to compute time-intensity curves for user-selected ROIs. Often, a parameter map is used first to detect interesting or suspicious regions, whereas time-intensity curves in selected regions are analyzed later. Parameter maps represent are part of commercial tools, such as SIEMENS syngo Volume perfusion.

Summary Basic visualization techniques for exploring perfusion data include subtraction images, parameter maps and the display of TICs [Behrens *et al.*, 1996, König *et al.*, 1998, Meyer *et al.*, 1999]. In clinical routine, diagnosis is often restricted to these basic techniques. In particular, in urgent cases like ischemic stroke diagnosis, more advanced methods are not used due to the additional time required. The diagnostic quality often depends on appropriate data acquisition and processing techniques, in particular techniques that limit motion in the acquisition stage or correct it later (motion correction).

In the following, we describe advanced visualization and analysis techniques for exploring perfusion data. These advanced techniques are motivated by three essential drawbacks of basic visualization techniques. They do not support:

- the integration of several parameter maps in one image,
- the integration of information derived from perfusion data with morphologic information from another dataset, e.g., with higher spatial resolution that is essential for the precise localization of pathologies, and
- the integration of detection and visualization of extracted features.

The following subsections show how these problems may be tackled.

16.4.2 VISUALIZATION OF MULTIPLE PERFUSION PARAMETERS

The integrated analysis of several perfusion parameters in a suspicious region is essential for various diagnostic tasks [Sorensen *et al.*, 1999]. To support the analysis, we discuss the appropriateness of integrated *multiparameter visualizations*. Multiparameter visualization is an established research area. Here we borrow from this long experience in that area (see the survey of [Wong and Bergeron, 1997]. These visualizations are based on precomputed parameter volumes where the corresponding perfusion parameters are represented for each voxel of the original dataset [Preim *et al.*, 2009].

Advanced topic: Two- and three-dimensional color scales. In principle, color may be employed for two or three perfusion parameters as well. Among the widespread color spaces, the HSV space (describing a color by its Hue, Saturation, and Value component) is the best choice, since it is perceptually roughly linearized [Ware, 2000]. To be compatible with expectations of users, the most suspicious parameter combinations may be mapped to a red color (Hue) with high saturation and high intensity (Value), whereas normal parameter values are mapped to lower saturation and intensity values and a bluish hue component. With this approach, the viewer's attention is directed to suspicious regions. To overcome the limitations of color, color icons have been introduced by Levkowitz [1991] and used for perfusion data exploration [Glaßer *et al.*, 2010a, Oeltze, 2010].

Color-coded volume rendering of perfusion data and derived pharmacokinetic modeling parameters were suggested by Englmeier *et al.* [2004]. A discrete two-dimensional color scale was used where four different hues and five different brightness/saturation values were employed to reflect the two parameters of a two-compartment model (recall § 16.3.5). A better discernibility of the contrast enhancement compared to gray value rendering was observed.

However, the simultaneous visualization of three quantitative values relating to data with high spatial frequency is in general very hard to interpret. The correct interpretation of two or even three perfusion parameters by means of one color cannot be achieved by preattentive vision. Oeltze *et al.* [2006] investigated methods where color (for one perfusion parameter) is combined with another visualization technique for visualizing a second parameter.

Isolines, height fields, or orientations of textures might be employed to combine several parameters within a single image [Tyler, 2002]. In particular, the combination of isolines and colors can be easily interpreted.

Combining isolines and color-coding. Isolines connect regions where the investigated perfusion parameter has a certain value. Isolines are easily computed by the Marching squares algorithm [Schroeder *et al.*, 2001]. Noise reduction is particularly important in order to prevent that many irrelevant small and distracting isolines or relevant but jaggy lines result (see Fig. e16.11). In contrast to color-coding, which supports a fast qualitative interpretation, isolines are not interpreted at a glance but allow a more quantitative interpretation.

Exploration of Multiple Parameter Images with Lenses Lenses are frequently used to explore conventional medical images such as X-ray. Digital lenses—working as pixel magnifiers—are also used in digital image exploration to analyze small scale phenomena within enlarged visualizations. The interaction with movable viewing lenses (*magic lenses*) is useful for exploring multidimensional data where lenses do not magnify information but show different information in the lens region [Bier *et al.*, 1993]. For parameter maps, lenses may show information relating to one parameter in the context of a map of another parameter. With this interaction style, the user starts by selecting a foreground and a background parameter (for example TTP and MTT) and then moves a lens (a rectangle or an ellipse) to select either of the parameter set. Instead of completely replacing the foreground display in the lens region, it might be shown as a semi-transparent combination of information of the foreground and background parameter (see Figs. e16.12 and e16.20).

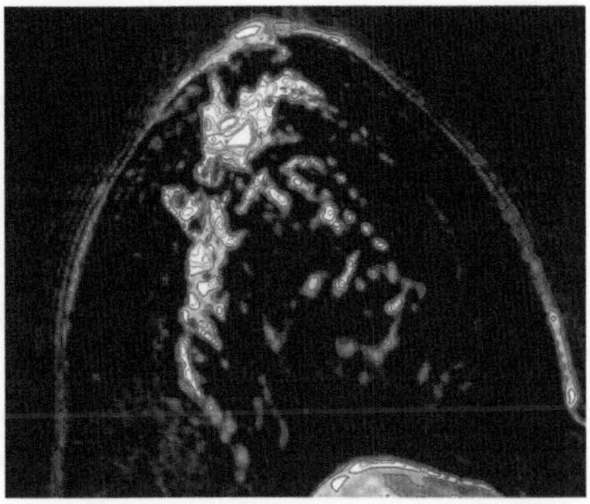

FIGURE e16.11 *Ten isolines, evenly distributed over the whole range of data, depict a perfusion parameter derived from DCE-MRI mammography. The data and the resulting isolines are smoothed (Courtesy of Olaf Konrad, Fraunhofer MEVIS Bremen).*

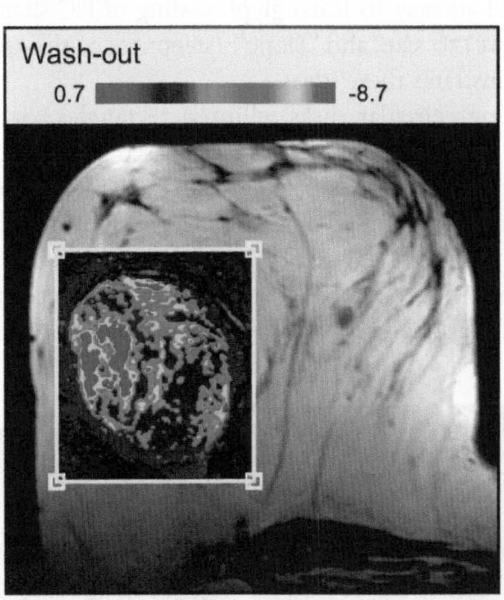

FIGURE e16.12 *Exploration of DCE-MRI mammography data with a lens. Parameter wash-out is projected through the lens. A blue color indicates a continuous enhancement for a later period in time, a green color indicates a plateau in the time-intensity curve. A yellow and in particular a red color indicate a strong "wash-out" behavior (From: [Oeltze, 2010]).*

Glyph-based Visualization of Multiple Parameters Glyphs represent a standard technique in the visualization of multifield data.

Definition 16.2. A **glyph** is a simple geometric primitive, such as ellipsoid or superquadric, which is positioned with respect to the original data points in space and whose attributes, e.g., color, extension, size, and orientation, are modified according to the values they represent.

Glyph-based visualizations of multiple perfusion parameters were introduced by Oeltze *et al.* [2008] with a focus on an intuitive mapping of perfusion parameter values to glyph shape. Intuitive mapping

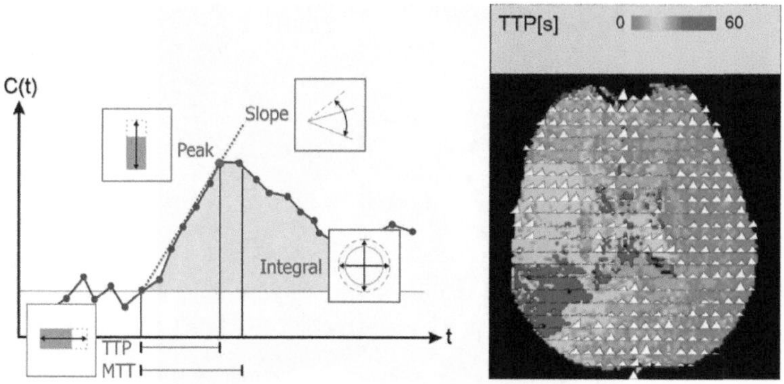

FIGURE e16.13 **Left:** *glyph shapes are designed to correspond to the basic shape of a TIC.* **Right:** *application of these intuitive glyphs to cerebral perfusion data (From: [Oeltze, 2010]).*

here refers to the generation of an easy-to-learn glyph coding of TIC shape, e.g., by mapping parameter "Integral" (area below the curve) to size, and "Slope" (steepness of the ascending curve) to orientation. The sketch in Figure e16.13 illustrates these ideas.

Several 2D glyph shapes, e.g., circular disks, ellipses, rectangles, or toroids, with different visual attributes besides color have been implemented in slice-based visualizations. Initial tests showed that the placement of one glyph per data point results in too small glyphs due to the limited screen space (see Fig. e16.14, left). Hence, a multiresolution glyph display has been proposed in [Oeltze, 2010] to improve the readability of the glyph attributes (see Fig. e16.14, right). The display incorporates different resolution layers, which can be interactively explored by the user. It is essential to include a *glyph legend* in such visualizations to convey how color, shape, size, and orientation of a glyph are related to the underlying data.

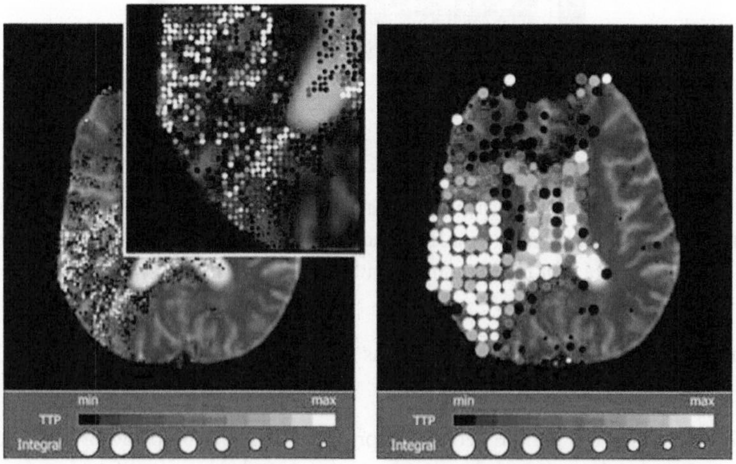

FIGURE e16.14 *Glyph-based visual exploration of cerebral perfusion parameters. The glyph display in all images has been restricted to suspicious regions by means of smooth brushing.* **Left:** *One circular disk is placed per data point. Changes in glyph size are hard to interpret. A magnification (inlet) improves the readability but involves a loss of context information and spatial orientation.* **Right:** *The application of a lower resolution layer solves the problem (Courtesy of Arvid Malcyczyk, University of Magdeburg).*

16.4.3 INTEGRATING DYNAMIC INFORMATION AND MORPHOLOGY

Relevant perfusion parameters can often only be extracted for a restricted region, e.g., where perfusion takes place. However, the display of other constituents, such as the bony structures, might provide substantial anatomical context. Also other surrounding tissues that are not enhancing, can be of indispensable diagnostic value. Therefore, it is useful to add spatial reference information in the regions not containing dynamic information. A reasonable strategy to realize this principle is to color-code dynamic information and to display the reference data in the background using a gray scale. Depending on the resolution of the image data, the integration of dynamic and morphologic information should be carried out in 2D slice visualizations or 3D renderings. For DCE-MRI mammography data with more than 50 slices, 3D renderings are appropriate, whereas cerebral and cardiac perfusion data provide a too small number of slices.

16.4.4 PROBING AND ANNOTATING OF PERFUSION DATA

Another way to depict temporal curves specified at every position of the data is to render them outside of their spatial location. The most common way is to show a set of time-dependent graphs for a set of pre-selected spatial locations, respectively. With this approach, however, one might lose the correspondence between the spatial position of the measured data and the curve data itself.

MLEJNEK and colleagues proposed the *Profile Flag*, an intuitive tool for browsing and annotating temporal data [Mlejnek *et al.*, 2005, 2006]. It enables the visualization of spatial or temporal curves closely connected to the rendering of the anatomical structure of the data without removing any parts thereof. The Profile Flag looks like a board-pin-like glyph that consists of a banner, a marker, a range selector, and a set of needles (see Fig. e16.15, left). The Profile Flag can be positioned on and dragged along the surface or inside of the inspected anatomical object. For *probing* of the underlying data, the set of needles is positioned beneath the surface of the probed structure at locations of interest. Each needle defines the position of one probed location or curve. The flag pole is a cylinder, which connects the banner with the range selector. The range selector defines the size of the ROI, i.e., it encloses the set of needles. For perfusion data, the probed information is taken along the time axis at a specific 3D location. Probing positions may be performed, e.g., with a spherical range selector or a more complex geometry (see [Mlejnek *et al.*, 2006] for details).

The probed curve data is visualized on the banner. Several types of banners can be defined, e.g., a single-profile banner only shows the probed values at the position of a single needle. Profile Flags can be

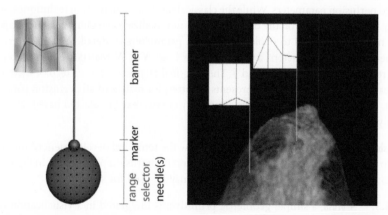

FIGURE e16.15 *Sketch of a Profile Flag (left) and DCE-MRI mammography data with two regions annotated by Profile Flags (right): a healthy region (left part of the right image) and a malignant region (right part) (Courtesy of Matej Mlejnek, TU Vienna).*

moved along the object's surface, while showing the underlying probed time-intensity curves. Multiple Profile Flags can be placed to emphasize differences between areas from different spatial locations, e.g., healthy vs. suspicious regions (see Fig. e16.15, right). For the visualization of dynamic data, the horizontal axis usually corresponds to the time axis. Therefore, for time-varying data, the banner visualizes the time steps along the horizontal axis, while the vertical axis shows the values for each measured time step. Additionally, for sparse temporal data (i.e., just a few time steps), vertical lines are included in order to facilitate reading off the values at particular timesteps. In order to avoid visual clutter, a banner is shown that represents the average of all probed curves.

Summary Advanced visual exploration techniques still play no major role in routine diagnosis. As Oeltze [2010] points out, they are rarely part of commercial tools and are considered as "bonus features." NeuroSuite [Nowinski *et al.*, 2008] and DynaCad , a product from Invivo [Wiener *et al.*, 2005] are among the tools integrating 3D visualizations. The low influence of advanced techniques after being around for a couple of years indicates a need for serious studies to assess whether advanced techniques indeed lead to a better diagnosis with respect to sensitivity, specificity, localization of features, and other relevant clinical aspects. We have described advanced techniques here to give an overview of techniques that have been carefully developed and to stimulate further research and development.

16.5 VISUAL ANALYSIS OF PERFUSION DATA

This section briefly introduces the concept of visual analytics and then describes its use for perfusion data.

16.5.1 VISUAL ANALYTICS

Visual analytics relates to the combination of data analysis, information visualization, and interactive exploration [Thomas and Cook, 2005, Keim *et al.*, 2010]. Data analysis comprises dimension reduction, such as Principal Component Analysis (PCA), cluster analysis (recall § 9.2.2.1) with a known or unknown number of clusters as well as pattern analysis. Data analysis aims at the automatic detection of correlations and trends. In visual analytics, such data analysis techniques are steered by means of appropriate visualizations and the data analysis results are integrated in visualizations.

This combination has a great potential to understand perfusion data along with the multidimensional space of derived perfusion parameters. While the classical medical visualization techniques, such as volume rendering, may give an overview on the data, information visualization techniques, such as *parallel coordinates* and *scatterplots*, may be employed to explore perfusion parameters in detail. While scatterplots represent the relations between two parameters, a *scatterplot matrix* is an $N \times N$ matrix where each element S_{ij} is a scatterplot correlating the parameters i and j. The diagonal elements of a scatterplot matrix S_{ii} show the histogram of parameter i. Figure e16.16 presents a scatterplot matrix of all perfusion parameters derived for one dataset. With such visualizations, time-intensity curves may be selected based on their properties, instead of (only) based on a selected spatial region.

Linking and Brushing Parallel coordinates naturally show the temporal development of the signal intensity, but may be also used to indicate the distribution of different perfusion parameters. In Figure e16.17 seven perfusion parameters for all voxels are displayed and may be used for selection.

Definition 16.3. A *brush*, a simple geometric primitive, is integrated in a visualization of *attributes* and selects all points in the spatial domain that exhibit the features specified with the brush in the attribute view.

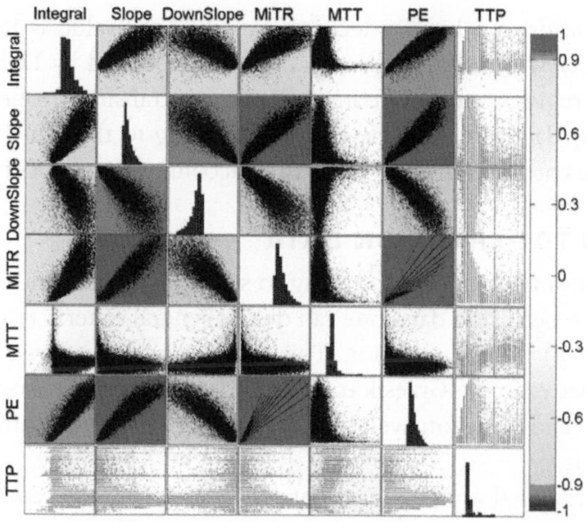

FIGURE e16.16 *A scatterplot matrix summarizes the correlation between each pair of perfusion parameters. The background color of each scatterplot represents the amount of positive or negative correlation. A high positive or negative correlation is emphasized with highly saturated colors. The analysis was performed for a DCE-MRI mammography dataset (From: [Oeltze et al., 2007]).*

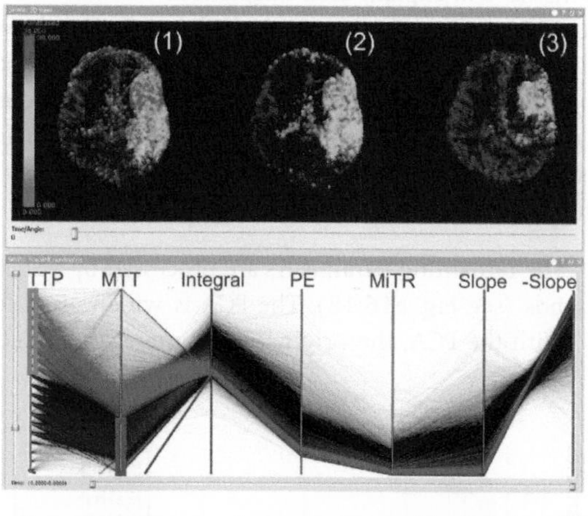

FIGURE e16.17 *A parallel coordinate view with one axis representing one (descriptive) perfusion parameter. A brush along the MTT axis selects a certain range. All voxels where the MTT value is inside that the brushed range are emphasized in the parallel coordinates to show how the MTT value relates to other perfusion parameters. The corresponding voxels are also highlighted in three spatial views (top row) (From: [Oeltze et al., 2009]).*

The most frequently used brush type is an axis-aligned rectangle—a primitive that allows to select ranges in two dimensions. The attributes in our specific example are perfusion parameters and attribute views are primarily scatterplots and parallel coordinates. The combination of selection (with a brush) and highlighting in spatial views is called *Link and Brush*. The concept is often applied to select attribute ranges in scatterplots. Thus, in Figure e16.17, a brush selects voxels based on their MTT value and highlights the corresponding voxels in three slice-based visualizations.

While a brush usually leads to a binary decision (an attribute value is inside a brush or not), the decision may be more fuzzy with *smooth brushes*, a concept introduced by Doleisch and Hauser [2002]. Smooth brushes have two regions: an inner core and an outer transition zone. A smooth brush may for example be used to display data semi-transparently that belong to the transition zone and render data opaquely that belong to the core region. Smooth brushes account for the uncertainty in the data selection.

16.5.2 APPLICATION TO PERFUSION DATA

In medicine, visual analytics in general is promising to study high-dimensional data, medical multifield data, and cohort studies. For perfusion data, one can define general criteria (e.g., maximal deviation from a predefined reference curve) for the selection. This strategy was employed along with the *Profile Flags* (recall § 16.4.4). As another example Grzesik *et al.* [2000] employed higher-dimensional histograms to explore MRI perfusion data and diffusion-weighted MRI data. Their system aimed at discriminating tissue in ischemic stroke diagnosis.

Oeltze *et al.* [2007] introduced a pipeline of data analysis techniques and information visualization techniques to efficiently explore the space of perfusion parameters. They came up with a layout of different views combining information visualization techniques and original data that is related to other medical multifield techniques [Blaas *et al.*, 2007b, Blaas, 2010]. This general strategy was recently refined for specific applications [Oeltze *et al.*, 2009, Glaßer *et al.*, 2010a]. Here, we present the general strategy and later in the case study sections we will explain their adaptation.

A *correlation analysis* is carried out to investigate which perfusion parameters strongly correlate (Fig. e16.16). The amount of correlation is quantified by a *correlation coefficient* that is 0 for uncorrelated attributes, 1 for a perfect positive correlation and -1 for a perfect negative correlation. Here, we employ the *Pearson correlation* that characterizes *linear* dependency of attribute pairs. Visually, a strong correlation is obvious if all attribute pairs are located on one straight line. In case of strongly correlated parameters, one of them is removed from further analysis.

Principal Component Analysis The remaining parameters are processed by a *Principal Component Analysis* (PCA) in order to detect major trends (see Fig. e16.18). The PCA is widely used for dimension reduction in multidimensional statistics. With the PCA, the original attributes are replaced by principal components

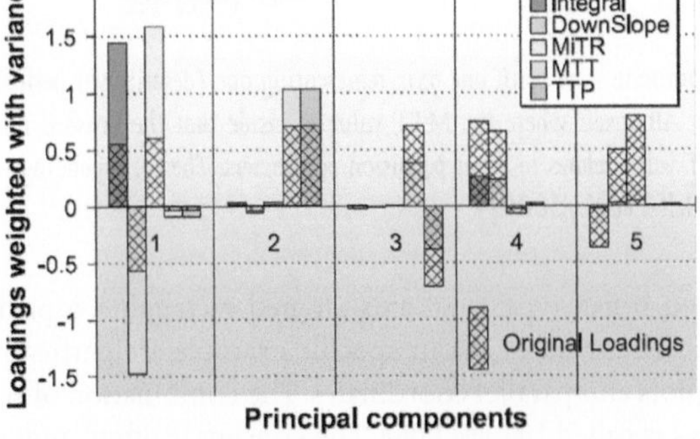

FIGURE e16.18 *After excluding four highly correlated parameters, a PCA was performed. While the first principal component (with integral, MiTR and negative Down-Slope as major contributions) indicates the amount of perfusion, the second principal component (with MTT and TTP as major contributions) represents the speed of enhancement (From: [Oeltze et al., 2007]).*

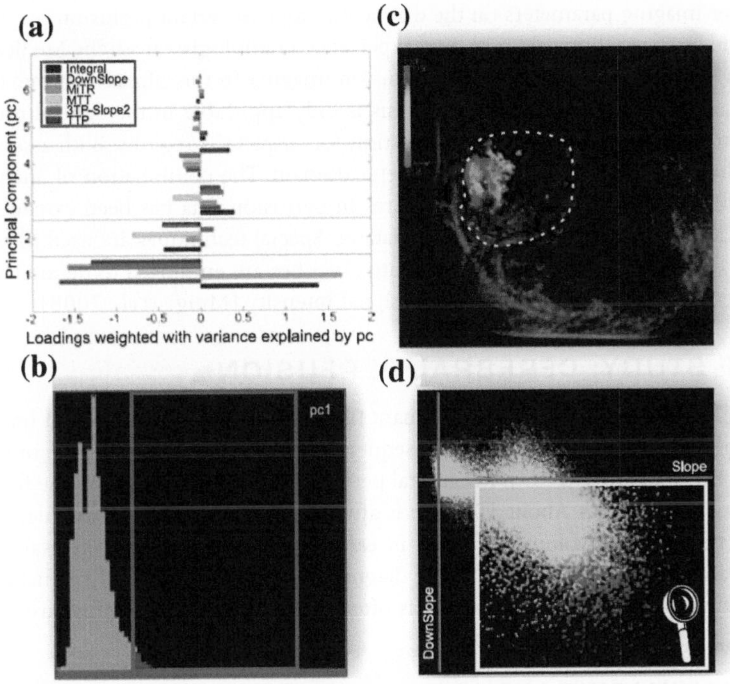

FIGURE e16.19 *Analysis of DCE-MRI mammography data. Examination of the trend represented by the first principal component (pc_1, lower bar chart in (a)). High scores in pc_1 have been brushed (b) and the selection is visualized within the context of the right mamma in (c). The selection has been color-coded according to Slope. Yellow and red regions indicate as fast wash-in. The boundary of the tumor has been delineated. The selection in (b) is transferred to a scatterplot (d) opposing Slope and Down-Slope. Zooming in on the plot reveals that regions exhibiting a fast wash-in as well as a fast wash-out have been detected (red dots).*

(PCs), a weighted combination of the attributes where each PC carries a loading that characterizes its importance. The efficient use of PCA is not straightforward: many aspects, such as normalization, have to be considered (see [Oeltze *et al.*, 2007] for an in-depth discussion of these issues related to perfusion data and derived parameters).

Inspired by Doleisch *et al.* [2003], the trends as well as the original perfusion parameters are displayed in 2D histograms and scatterplots and are used for (smooth) brushing of relevant subsets of the data (see Fig. e16.19). This strategy turned out to be useful to discriminate different tissues in cerebral perfusion data, tumor perfusion and myocardial perfusion data. In most cases, the PCA resulted in two major trends (the principal directions). One trend represents the amount of contrast enhancement (a combination of the parameters "Integral" and PE) and the second trend represents the speed of enhancement (a combination of TTP and MTT). Due to patient-specific differences, the correlations as well as the PCA results (weighting of perfusion parameters) may differ strongly, but a larger analysis in breast tumor perfusion showed that still the two most important principal directions are quite reliable to assess perfusion (although their exact meaning differs due to the PCA results).

Evaluation of Visual Analysis Techniques The overall analysis pipeline is probably too complex for routine diagnosis. However, it may be essential for researchers investigating the effects of CAs, magnetic field strength and other imaging parameters on the diagnostic value of certain perfusion parameter combinations. The pipeline has been discussed with two experienced radiologists from the Medical Faculty of the University of Magdeburg, both familiar with perfusion imaging in the clinical routine, though not in a research context. Both argued that the data analysis is only applicable in the clinical routine, if carried out in the background leading to an initial suggestion for suspicious regions. Both assessed brushing as valuable for exploring a non-standardized parameter domain. The combination of analysis techniques, linking and brushing for efficiently locating features in perfusion data has been extended with a dense visualization of TICs for all voxels of a perfusion dataset. Special techniques are used to reduce clutter in the visualization of a multitude of TICs and dedicated brushes are employed to define TIC target shapes, e.g., a sudden increase and a later decrease of the signal intensity [Muigg *et al.*, 2008].

16.6 CASE STUDY: CEREBRAL PERFUSION

In contrast to highly permeable vessels in malignant tumors, microvessels in normal brain tissue do not leak as a result of the blood brain barrier. Consequently, there is no enhancement in the extracellular volume which is essential for DSC-MRI. In cerebral perfusion imaging, we observe the first pass of the CA through the vessel components. About 10 seconds after the first pass of blood circulation, a broadened second pass can be seen. The volume of blood in each voxel is diagnostically relevant. It is measured by the integral parameter of the TIC. The major diagnostic task where cerebral perfusion is essential, is the cerebral ischemic stroke. Perfusion imaging is often used in addition to diffusion-weighted imaging which provides complementary information.

16.6.1 MEDICAL IMAGING AND PREPROCESSING

CT and MRI are primarily used to assess cerebral perfusion in clinical routine. MRI studies suffer from a lower spatial resolution compared to CT, but allow scanning of the entire brain, and are thus better suited to detect an infarction, if its location is not a priori known. Both CT and MRI are useful in diagnosing the acute ischemic stroke and in decision making for therapeutic interventions [Wintermark *et al.*, 2005]. For cerebral perfusion, Dynamic Susceptibility Contrast (DSC) imaging is employed, as we explained in § 16.2. With DSC-MRI, the contrast agent reaches the capillary bed after 5–10 seconds and the first passage through the capillary bed lasts approximately 18 seconds. Thus, a high temporal resolution is essential to record the signal intensity change. Typical imaging parameters in DSC-MRI are 128×128 matrix, 2 mm spatial resolution in the plane, and 7 mm slice thickness.

Preprocessing of cerebral perfusion data is relatively straightforward, since severe motion artifacts rarely occur. If visual inspection indicates a relevant motion artifact, the general techniques described in § 16.3.1 are usually sufficient [Oeltze *et al.*, 2009]. Further preprocessing may include brain segmentation and the conversion from signal intensities to changes in contrast agent concentration as well as noise reduction (§ 16.3).

16.6.2 DIAGNOSIS OF ISCHEMIC STROKE

Cerebral perfusion images are used for ischemic stroke diagnosis, in particular to discriminate cerebral hemorrhage and ischemic stroke. Both situations represent medical emergencies that require immediate actions. In case of an ischemic stroke, the existence and the extent of "tissue at risk" surrounding the core of the stroke has to be evaluated. While the core exhibits no significant perfusion (recall Fig. e16.1, p. e21), "tissue at risk" is characterized by a reduced and delayed perfusion. The perfusion characteristics of the "tissue at risk" is due to collateral blood flow that may for a certain time compensate for the blocked vasculature. Surgical and chemical interventions may salvage at least parts of the "tissue at risk." The most promising treatment is *thrombolysis* that resolves the blood klot by an intervention with a thrombolytic drug [den Boer and Folkers, 1997].

The value of combining cerebral perfusion and diffusion-weighted image data for predicting stroke evolution is discussed in [Rose *et al.*, 2001]. In both types of data, areas of ischemic brain tissue can be identified in acute stroke patients. The mismatch between these areas has been reported to present the "tissue at risk" [Warach *et al.*, 1995]. Sorensen *et al.* [1999] argue that MTT as well as two specific parameters for cerebral perfusion, namely regional cerebral blood volume (rCBV) as well as the regional cerebral blood flow (rCBF), are essential to assess stroke. rCBF (Eq. e16.2) and rCBV (Eq. e16.3) are quantitative perfusion parameter that require to transform TICs to concentration time curves and their normalization with the arterial input function (AIF), as discussed in § 16.3.2.

$$\mathrm{rCBF} = \frac{\mathrm{rCBV}}{\mathrm{rMTT}}[\mathrm{ml/min/100g}]. \tag{e16.2}$$

$$\mathrm{rCBV} = \frac{k_H}{\rho} * \frac{\int_0^\infty \mathrm{CTC}(t)dt}{\int_0^\infty \mathrm{AIF}(t)dt}[\mathrm{ml/100g}] \tag{e16.3}$$

The reliable determination of rCBF and rCBV is described in [Østergaard *et al.*, 1996]. Similar quantitative parameters (pulmonary CBF and pulmonary CBV) are determined to evaluate lung perfusion data [Kohlmann *et al.*, 2011].

The *regional cerebral blood flow* is the perfused vessel volume (in ml) of a vessel voxel divided by the tissue mass (in g) of this voxel. The *regional cerebral blood volume* is the amount of blood (in ml) that travels through the voxel. The theoretical basis of these computations is discussed, e.g., in [Meyer-Bäse *et al.*, 2007].

The symmetry of the brain is essential for a diagnostic evaluation of static and dynamic images. Whether or not a part of the brain appears to be pathological is judged by comparing it with the corresponding part of the other hemisphere. To support symmetry considerations, cerebral perfusion tools provide a feature to define a region of interest (ROI) in one hemisphere and let the system define the corresponding ROI in the other hemisphere. The simultaneous display of TICs relating to the both regions supports the evaluation of a correlation between them. In cerebral perfusion diagnosis, *synchronized lenses* may be used to exploit the symmetry of the brain in axial views [Wintermark *et al.*, 2005]. A lens is mirrored on a relocatable, vertical line of symmetry (see Fig. e16.20).

Visual Analytics Oeltze *et al.* [2009] described a visual analytics strategy to support the diagnosis of ischemic strokes. Using the general framework to analyze perfusion data (recall § 16.5), they applied PCA for dimension reduction and could show that the two major directions are suitable to select the relevant brain tissue (Fig. e16.21).

They presented the concentration time curves of the entire dataset in a curve view to enable the selection of interesting regions via brushing (see Fig. e16.22). To support the selection, dedicated brush types have been designed that characterize, e.g., regions with increasing signal intensity and regions without perfusion that might be selected to exclude them from further analysis. Thus, in Figure e16.22, the infarcted tissue and the "tissue at risk" could be selected. Oeltze *et al.* [2009] describe various brush shapes and combination facilities and explain how the diagnosis of cerebral perfusion data benefits from these exploration facilities. Although stroke diagnosis triggered these developments, they can be translated to other perfusion data and related diagnostic tasks.

Their system was evaluated by means of two patient data studies, relating to patients with an acute ischemic stroke in the parietal lobe after thrombosis of the middle cerebral artery. Data were acquired at three points in time, reflecting the development of the brain in the first hours after system onset.

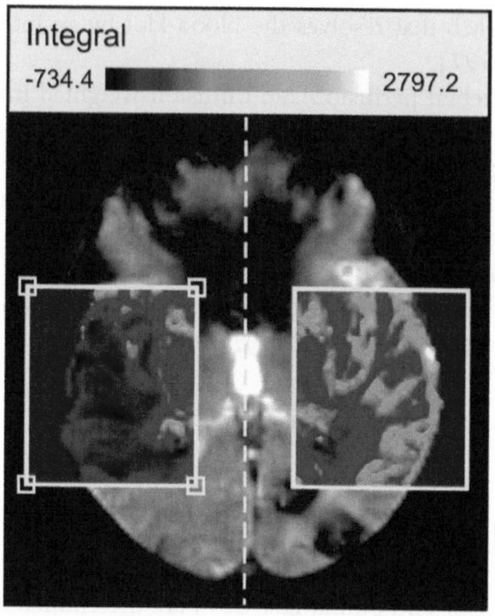

FIGURE e16.20 Synchronized lenses in both hemispheres of the brain support the comparison between the symmetric regions. The peak enhancement is the foreground parameter mapped to an optimized color scale and TTP is the background parameter. The core of the stroke in the right hemisphere becomes obvious by comparing the regions inside the synchronized lenses (From: [Oeltze, 2010]).

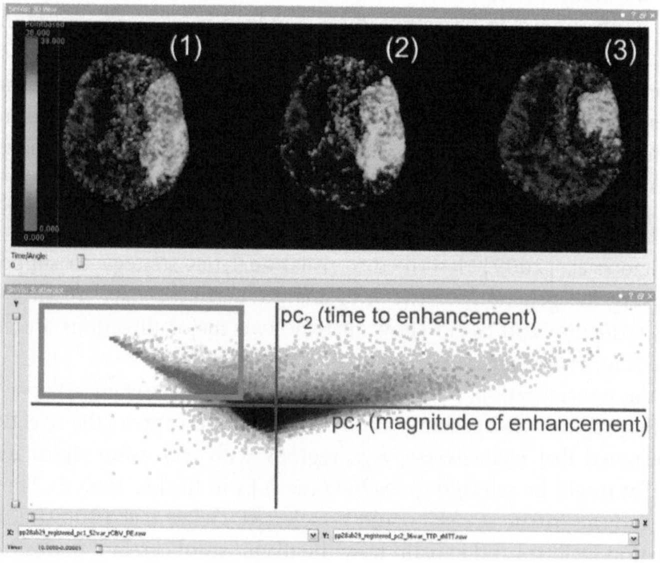

FIGURE e16.21 *A scatterplot indicates the distribution of voxels along the two major trends of the PCA. One dimension primarily represents the timing (slow or fast enhancement) and the second represents the amount of enhancement. With a brush, a certain interval is selected in both dimensions. The three views in the top row show the selected voxels in the longitudinal study. It turns out that brain perfusion has improved over time, since low and delayed enhancement are restricted to a smaller area in the last dataset (From: [Oeltze et al., 2009]).*

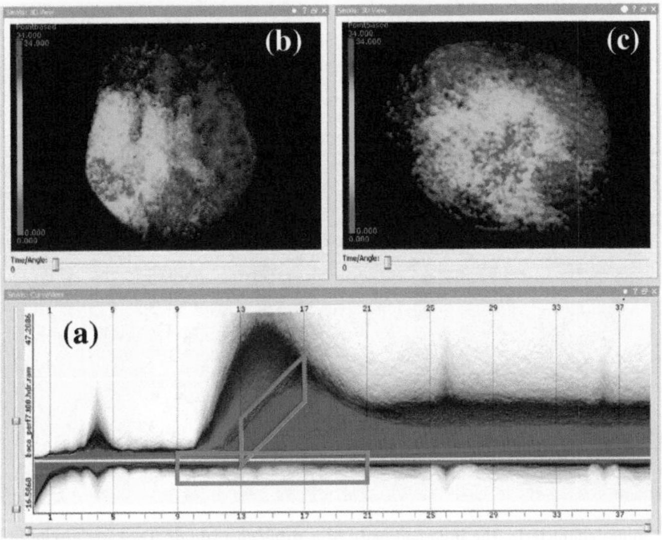

FIGURE e16.22 *Multiple coordinated view with a curve view and two 3D visualizations. In the curve view (a), two brushes are defined to select the tissue at risk (slanted brush) and the infarction core (horizontal brush). The selected curves and the corresponding voxels are emphasized in the 3D visualization. The color of the voxels represents the time to peak. Interaction in both views, e.g., clipping in the 3D views and transformation of brushes in the curve view support the analysis of cerebral perfusion data (From: [Oeltze et al., 2009]).*

16.6.3 BRAIN TUMOR DIAGNOSIS

Compared to ischemic stroke diagnosis, brain tumor diagnosis is a more recent and less widespread application of cerebral perfusion. MR perfusion imaging is employed to assess tumor neoangiogenesis and to better estimate the tumor grade and patient prognosis. Prognosis is essential in case of glioblastoma, a malignant brain cancer with poor prognosis, but with high variability in the survival time of patients. With respect to imaging, an intact blood-brain barrier cannot be assumed.

In a cooperation between the University of Bergen and the University of Magdeburg, seven brain tumor datasets were analyzed with a slightly modified version of the analysis pipeline described in § 16.5 (recall [Oeltze *et al.*, 2007]). Brain and tumor segmentation are major preprocessing steps. The quantitative parameters rCBF and rCBV were derived.

The correlation between these parameters seems to be higher for low-grade tumors than for high-grade tumors according to first experiments. A scatterplot with the dimensions rCBV and rCBF may be used for brushing and emphasizing brain regions with low rCBF and rCBV values. The correlation analysis may also be used to exclude tumor voxels with a low correlation between rCBF and rCBV. A detailed inspection of such voxels revealed that they primarily occur in border regions and that the low correlation probably relates to neoangiogenetic activity that occurs in more regions of a highly malignant high-grade tumor. By color-coding such voxels according to their cerebral blood flow this hypothesis was further confirmed, since indeed voxels with high perfusion are selected (Fig. e16.24).

Another technique to analyze and quantify inhomogeneity is to compute the local correlation coefficients (LCC) between rCBF and rCBV [Glaßer *et al.*, 2013]. Figure e16.23 displays the slices of a tumor color-coded with the LCC value. In this particular example, data from longitudinal studies are analyzed. Note that the timepoints here differ in years between the examinations. At each timepoint, a

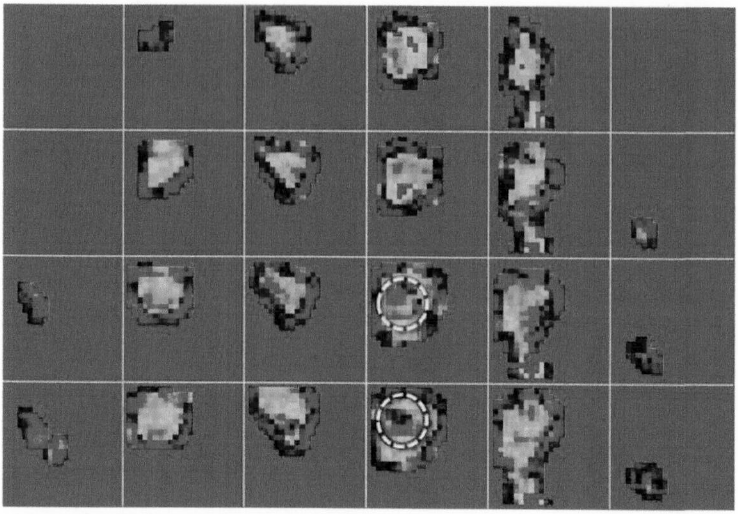

FIGURE e16.23 *LCC values characterize the inhomogeneity of a suspicious tumor. They are displayed here for all slices at four points in time. The tumor obviously grew and the LCC values exhibit stronger inhomogeneity over time (Courtesy of Sylvia Glaßer, University of Magdeburg).*

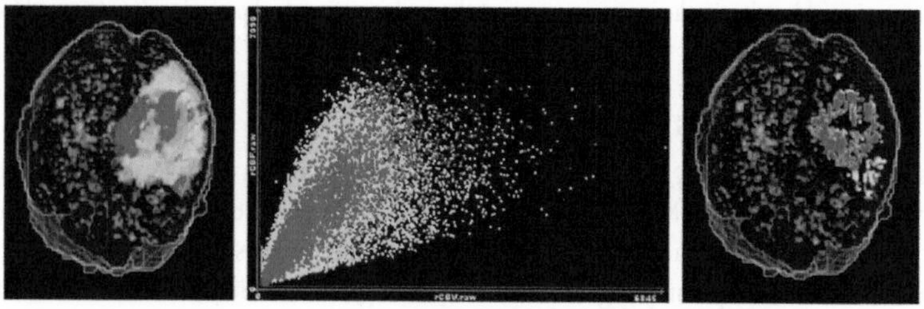

FIGURE e16.24 **Left:** *A segmented brain tumor is shown with tumor voxels color-coded according to the regional cerebral blood flow with red corresponding to the highest values(rCBV).* **Middle:** *The scatterplot indicates that rCBF and rCBV do not correlate well (red: tumor voxels, yellow: remaining brain voxels).* **Right:** *Negative brushing (correlating regions are selected to be excluded) reveals that low correlation occurs in a large boundary region. Color coding according to rCBV shows that the perfusion in this region is high, which is probably due to strong neoangiogenetic activity (Courtesy of Sylvia Glaßer, University of Magdeburg).*

perfusion study with the typical 40–80 timepoints is available. Thus, a matrix with slices and timepoints results.

We briefly mentioned this research, although it is at an early stage since it illustrates the potential power of a visual analytics approach.

16.7 CASE STUDY: BREAST TUMOR PERFUSION

Breast cancer is the most common cancer and cause of cancer-related death in women. Early detection of breast tumors and the assessment of their dignity (malignant or benign lesions) are crucial to treat patients successfully. Several image acquisition techniques have been employed for breast cancer diagnosis. X-ray mammography is still the most widely used technique. Dynamic contrast-enhanced magnetic resonance imaging (DCE-MRI) mammography has been introduced by Heywang *et al.* [1986]. However, only recently it gained widespread acceptance, which is partially due to effective computer support [Wood, 2005].

DCE-MRI is currently the most sensitive modality for the detection of invasive breast cancer. Thus, the number of malignant cancers, which are not detected (*false negatives*), is lower compared to other imaging modalities such as X-ray mammography. However, compared to X-ray mammography, DCE-MRI only exhibits a moderate specificity, i.e., a relative high rate of tumors is incorrectly classified as being malignant (*false positives*) [Kuhl, 2007]. In particular, smaller tumors and tumors in dense breasts of younger (pre-menopausal) women are detected more reliably with DCE-MRI. Thus, DCE-MRI is the modality of choice for screening younger women with a high risk for breast cancer due to a history of breast cancer in the family.

Although there is a significant difference in the enhancement pattern between malignant and (most) benign tumors, there is some overlap, e.g., with inflammative changes, (benign) fibroadenoma and breast cancer. A recent survey and meta analysis of ten publications reported an average sensitivity for experienced radiologists of 79% and a specificity of 56% that could slightly be increased with computer-aided detection to 83% and 62% [Dorrius *et al.*, 2011].

For the detection of wash-out curves, the ROI should be manually placed in the area of a tumor with the strongest enhancement. If the tumor is very heterogeneous, this part of the tumor cannot be determined easily. The average TIC is only expressive if the ROI is small and does not include necrotic tumor cells or surrounding tissue. The heterogeneity of tumor vascularization, the close neighborhood of necrotic and vital tumor tissue, and the subjectiveness of ROI placement harden the interpretation of the kinetics. If a possibly malignant tumor has been detected, core needle biopsy must be carried out to confirm or reject malignancy. Since core needle biopsy of a benign region close to a malignant tumor results in a false histopathological report, it is important to determine the most malignant part of the tumor and its precise localization [Glaßer *et al.*, 2010a].

16.7.1 MEDICAL IMAGING AND PREPROCESSING

In DCE-MRI mammography, T1-weighted images are employed. Contrast enhancement lasts considerably longer than in cerebral blood vessels. Therefore, longer acquisition times are employed. There are many different sequences and protocols, but commonly, DCE-MRI mammography data is characterized by a high spatial resolution and a low temporal resolution. Data processing, in particular motion correction, is challenging. The elastic registration method introduced by Rueckert *et al.* [1999] is the standard method correction. The low temporal resolution hampers the use of pharmacokinetic modeling. Typical parameters for DCE-MRI mammography data are: 512 × 512 matrix, 2 mm slice thickness, 60–80 slices, and 3–6 time points with a temporal resolution of 60–90 seconds.

3TP Method Degani *et al.* [1997] suggest to use only three points in time (3 TP method), which should be chosen such that wash-in can be assessed by subtracting image intensities at t_2 and t_1 and wash-out by considering t_3 and t_2. The quality of the MR scanner has a strong influence on the diagnostic quality. As an example, the survey of Dorrius *et al.* [2011] shows that the best diagnostic results in tumor perfusion studies were achieved with a modern 3 Tesla scanner. For more details on tumor perfusion, see [Degani *et al.*, 1997, Heywang-Köbrunner *et al.*, 1997, Kuhl, 2007].

Motion Correction is often accomplished with the non-rigid B-spline-based registration method developed by Rueckert *et al.* [1999]. A more recent approach refines this method in a two-step approach, where the method by Rueckert *et al.* [1999] serves as a first step. In particular, for the analysis of small enhancing lesions, a second local step is promising. Local corrections are based on assumptions that the movement (with respect to translation and rotation) is strongly limited [Schäfer *et al.*, 2010]. In this paper, three similarity metrics, including normalized mutual information, were compared. The method was validated by computing the fit of a pharmacokinetic model. This kind of validation is motivated by the fact that such models capture contrast agent dynamics in a tumor region well. Thus, in the absence of motion artifacts, a good fit should be possible. A review of motion correction in DCE-MRI mammography data was given in [Guo *et al.*, 2006].

16.7.2 VISUAL EXPLORATION OF DCE-MRI MAMMOGRAPHY DATA

In the following, selected visualization techniques for DCE-MRI mammography that go beyond the standard visual exploration (recall § 16.4.1) are described.

Color Coding Two parameters describing the diagnostically significant shape and amplitude of each voxel's TIC may be mapped to color [Kohle *et al.*, 2002]:

- the slope of the early CA enhancement to brightness and
- the slope of the late wash-out to the color value, encoding suspicious wash-out in red.

Using continuous color values creates a smooth transition between slowly enhancing and depleting regions.

Projection Methods For the integration of morphologic information and perfusion parameters, 3D visualization techniques are useful. To avoid visual clutter, the visualization of perfusion parameters should be restricted to those voxels, which exhibit a high dynamic (significant changes of signal intensities). Projection techniques, such as MIP and Closest Vessel Projection (CVP) [Napel *et al.*, 1993] (recall § 11.3.1), provide a direct link between pixels and the corresponding voxels with the related TIC. Thus, with a colorized projection image, morphological information can be visualized together with physiological parameters [Kohle *et al.*, 2002]. Projection methods are established for the visualization of small, enhanced regions embedded in a relatively transparent data volume, e.g., the distribution of filamentary vessels.

Kohle *et al.* [2002] introduced a colorized temporal MIP (maximum value along the temporal scale). With this approach, voxels characterized by a strong dynamics (either in the wash-in or wash-out phase) are represented by a color that incorporates the wash-in as well as the wash-out behavior by mapping these values to the hue-, saturation- and value-component of a color in a HSV color space. The most intense voxel along the projection ray is no longer selected; rather, the voxel that represents the first local maximum above a certain threshold is taken. The threshold has to be adjusted to display only the interesting structures. A threshold of 20% relative enhancement is appropriate for visualizing DCE-MRI mammography data. Figure e16.25 shows a colored CVP. Both MIP and CVP are offered as whole-volume visualization techniques and as slab rendering—restricted to a portion of the data characterized by two parallel clipping planes.

This particular example also illustrates the difficulties of the diagnosis of breast tumors. The roundish shape of the tumor without stellar components suggests a benign character. The wash-out behavior (see the yellow and red parts in Fig. e16.25) indicates malignancy. However, biopsy, histopathological report and follow-up confirm a fibroadenoma.

Volume Rendering and Information Visualization Techniques To speed up the analysis, volume rendering and information visualization techniques were developed to efficiently extract essential information. Coto *et al.* [2005] presented several investigation tools (e.g., scatterplots and volume rendering) for the classification

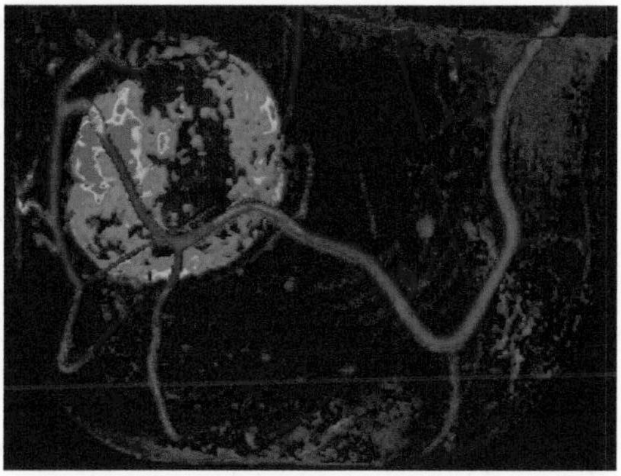

FIGURE e16.25 *A gray scale MIP of the subtraction volume of two early points in time is combined with a color-coded CVP of DCE-MRI mammography data. The color encodes the dynamical behavior: bright voxels show a strong enhancement for an early period, less intense voxels show less enhancement. A blue color indicates a continuous enhancement for a later period in time, and a green color indicates a plateau in the TIC. Yellow and red colors indicate a rapid wash-out (Courtesy of Sven Kohle, Fraunhofer MEVIS Bremen).*

and visualization of DCE-MRI mammography data. The approach combines *brushing* and *linking* interaction with effective visualization of the selected suspicious areas. The concept of *importance driven volume rendering* [Viola *et al.*, 2005] was used to show the suspicious region.

For the computation of the time-intensity curves, the pre-contrast scan (t_0) is subtracted from all post-contrast scans (t_i). This step emphasizes the gradient in the temporal dimension of the analyzed curve and highlights suspicious areas. An enhancement scatterplot (see Fig. e16.26, left) is calculated. It shows the relative enhancement of the pre-contrast step with respect to the post-contrast step t_i. In the interaction step, brushing is performed on one of the scatterplots, while the selected set is emphasized on all remaining

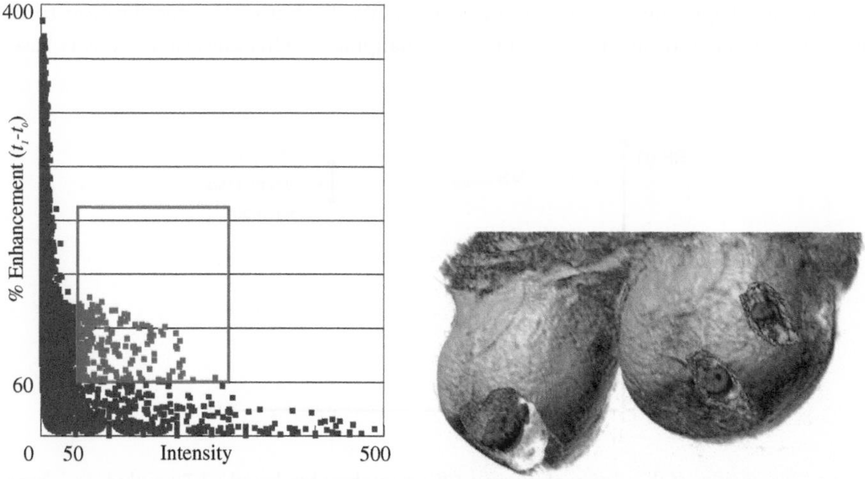

FIGURE e16.26 *Enhancement scatterplot with a selected region for time step* t_1 *(left) and importance-driven volume rendering of areas defined by brushing on a set of enhancement scatterplots (right) (Courtesy of Ernesto Coto, Central University of Venezuela).*

scatterplots. If the brushing is performed on multiple scatterplots, the result of the selection is calculated by a logical "and" operation. The selection set and the way of interaction with the scatterplots depends on the specific application. The result of the interaction can be displayed in a 2D view by highlighting the selected areas, or in a 3D view with importance driven volume rendering (see Fig. e16.26, right).

16.7.3 VISUAL ANALYSIS OF DCE-MRI MAMMOGRAPHY DATA

Visual analytics methods (recall § 16.5) to understand perfusion data are quite complex and currently not suitable for routine diagnosis. They may, however, be clearly useful for medical research in disease understanding and in improving imaging techniques. In the following, we describe the application of visual analytics techniques to a larger series of breast tumor datasets. These techniques are later employed to assess the *heterogeneity* of breast tumors, a parameter that is derived from the enhancement kinetics and turns out to be more specific than any established perfusion parameter [Preim *et al.*, 2012].

A visual analysis approach is useful to support the subjective and error-prone ROI placement as a prerequisite for TIC visualization. To quantify the relative enhancement (RE) of a tumor, the percentaged signal intensity increase is calculated. SI is the pre-contrast and SI_c is the post-contrast signal intensity. The RE can be plotted over time, yielding RE curves, which can be classified in

- *slow* enhancement (less than 50%),
- *normal* enhancement (between 50 and 100%), and
- *fast* enhancement (more than 100%)

after CA arrival. According to the behavior in later stages (see Fig. e16.27), it can be classified in:

- *steady curves* (continuously increasing signal intensity in the post-contrast phase, at least 10%),
- *plateau curves* (signal intensity change in the interval between −10 and +10%), and
- *wash-out* (descending signal intensity by at least 10%)

Since any of the three types of initial contrast shape may occur along with any of the three types of late post-contrast shape, nine classes of curves exist. We later use this classification to discuss the heterogeneity of tumors. A wash-out curve indicates malignancy. This kind of analysis is based on data

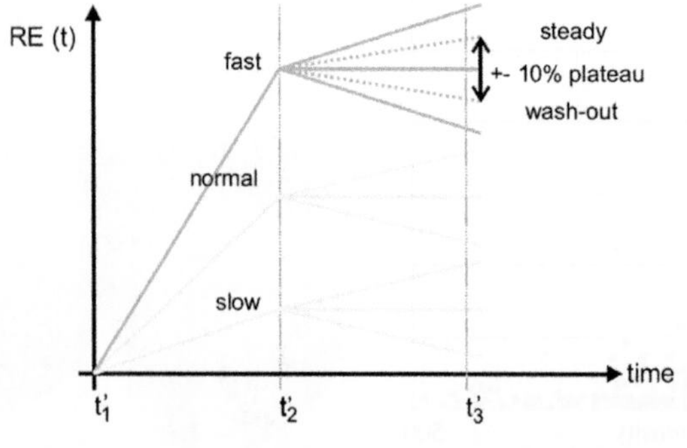

FIGURE e16.27 *Classification of the relative enhancement (RE) curve shape based on the 3 TP method. Each curve is classified based on the CA accumulation between* t_1 *and* t_2 *(slow, normal and fast) and the curve shape between* t_2 *and* t_3 *(steady, plateau and wash-out) yielding nine different classes.*

available immediately before the contrast agent arrives t_1, 2 minutes and 6 minutes after CA arrival (t_2 and t_3). Thus, it is inspired by the 3 TP method [Degani *et al.*, 1997]. Please note that the curves depicted in Figure e16.27 are idealized—in practice any kind of mixture of these curves occurs.

Glyph Display In § 16.4.2 we briefly explained the potential of glyphs to represent the multidimensional space of perfusion parameters. This general concept has been refined for tumor diagnosis [Glaßer *et al.*, 2010b]. For each voxel, the curve shape is analyzed with respect to the relative enhancement and the curve type. This information is mapped to color and texture according to the scheme in Figure e16.28. In Figure e16.29 these glyphs are employed to display voxels of a benign and a malignant tumor. Note that the blue voxels (low enhancement) are border voxels and likely represent portions where tumor and surrounding tissue are averaged (partial volume effect). With this mapping strategy, the curve shape may be directly inferred from each glyph. This type of visualization is not familiar to radiologists, but it supports the analysis of tumors with borderline enhancement characteristics, e.g., a rather slow to normal early enhancement followed by a wash-out.

Semi-automatic Region Selection Region selection for TIC analysis is a necessary and error-prone step of the analysis. Because of the heterogeneity of breast tumors, there is a considerable high inter- and intra-observer variability. To overcome subjectiveness, whole lesion analysis is recommended [Preim *et al.*, 2012]. According to recommendations of the American College of Radiology (ACR) regions should not be too small (at least three voxels) to compensate for noise [Kuhl, 2007]. If voxels with inhomogeneous contrast agent kinetics are summarized, the averaged TIC is misleading. Some authors suggest to display the standard deviation at each time step to convey at least the amount of inhomogeneity. However, it would be more appropriate to determine regions automatically. Glaßer *et al.* [2010b] suggest a rather simple, yet effective method and summarize voxels based on a four component feature vector comprising perfusion parameters. A Pearsson correlation of at least 99% was considered as similarity criterion for merging voxels. Figure e16.30 shows the decomposition and the related TICs.

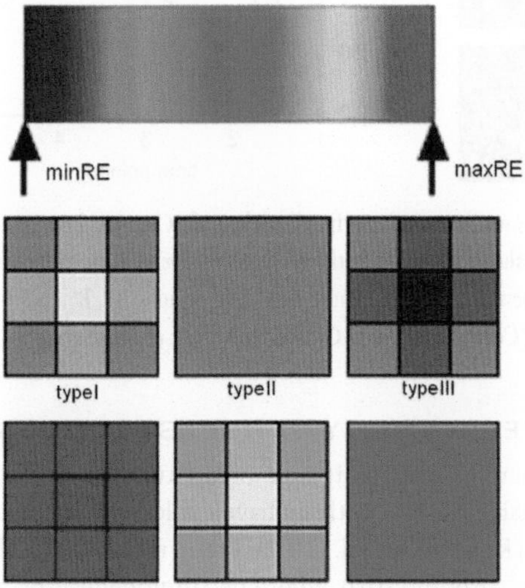

FIGURE e16.28 *The color of the glyph indicates the relative enhancement with red for (suspicious) high enhancement. The pattern represents whether the curve is steadily increasing (type 1), has a plateau shape (type 2) or wash-out-characteristics (type 3) (Courtesy of Sylvia Glaßer, University of Magdeburg. See also [Glaßer et al., 2010b]).*

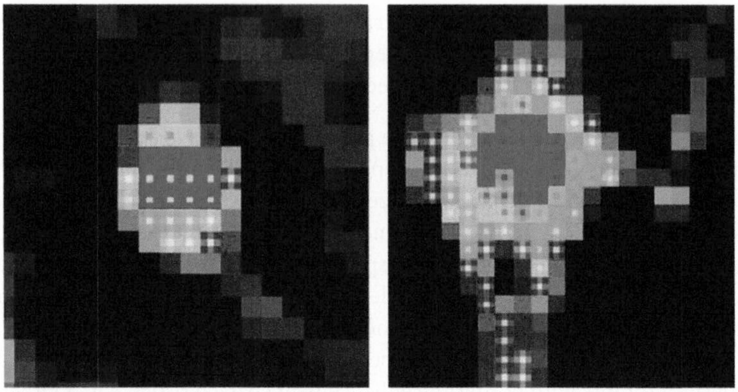

FIGURE e16.29 *Glyphs for a voxel-wise mapping of the RE curve shape in the intermediate and late post-contrast phase for each voxel.* **Left:** *A small benign tumor with high RE values (red colors) and mostly steady curves (see brighter centers of glyphs) is depicted. Since breast tumors are heterogeneous, there are also voxels with wash-out-curves (see top row of color-coded voxels).* **Right:** *A representative slice of a small malignant tumor is shown. The area in the center is characterized by a strong wash-in (red colors) and wash-out (glyphs with dark centers) (Courtesy of Sylvia Glaßer, University of Magdeburg).*

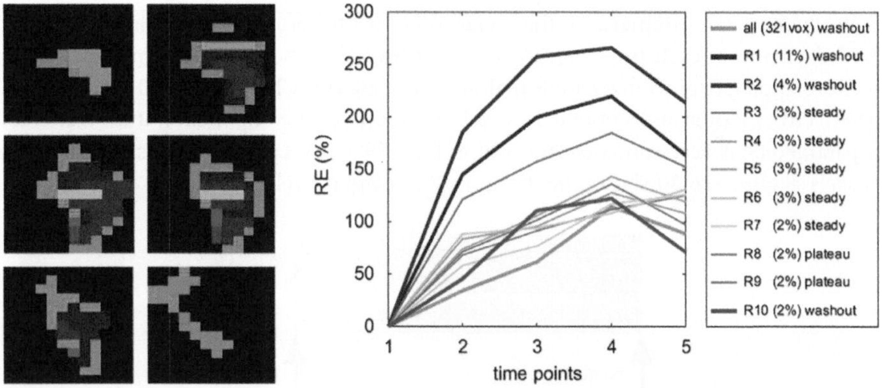

FIGURE e16.30 *Analysis of regions with similarly perfused voxels.* **Left:** *Computed regions in adjacent slices.* **Right:** *The RE curve diagram of the 10 biggest regions is shown along with the percentaged size and the curve class. The curve representing the average enhancement of the entire tumor is shown in gray. The most suspicious regions R_1, R_2 and R_{10} exhibit curves that are classified as wash-out curve (recall Fig. e16.27) (Courtesy of Sylvia Glaßer, University of Magdeburg).*

16.7.4 ASSESSING HETEROGENEITY OF BREAST TUMORS

Since the discrimination of benign and malignant breast tumors in DCE-MRI by means of perfusion parameters is still not very reliable, several authors have explored whether the *heterogeneity* of such tumors is a better diagnostic criterion [Karahaliou *et al.*, 2010, Preim *et al.*, 2012]. This is motivated by the fact that malignant cancer with necrotic parts and parts where neoangiogenesis occurs are rather inhomogeneous. This raises the question how heterogeneity may be quantified. The analysis of Karahaliou *et al.* [2010] was based on a selected slice and heterogeneity was assessed on the basis of three perfusion parameters. Preim *et al.* [2012] analyzed whole lesions and combined five perfusion parameters. A rather simple criterion is the number of regions in which a tumor is decomposed by applying a homogeneity criterion. This simple criterion does not account for the size of tumors (larger tumors are probably decomposed in more regions) and for the degree of variability between the regions.

Despite these limitations, Preim *et al.* [2012] could show that a higher number of regions indeed occurs significantly more often in malignant tumors than in benign ones. In a study with 68 small enhancing lesions from 50 patients, the 37 malignant lesions had on average 17 regions (determined with the method described in [Glaßer *et al.*, 2010b]), whereas the 31 benign lesions had eight regions. Benign and malignant lesions had no significant difference in size and patient age was very similar—thus, the comparison seems to be unbiased. Another significant result of their study was that malignant tumors had more different classes of relative enhancement curves (from the nine possible classes (recall Fig. e16.27) 6.2 occurred in malignant lesions and 5.3 in benign lesions. The ground truth for this study was a histopathological report that was available for 60 lesions and a longer follow-up that ensured a benign diagnosis in eight cases. The pathologists' report is rather reliable, however, it is of course also not correct in 100% of all cases. In particular in a tumor with mixed benign and malignant portions one biopsy of a small part may be misleading.

Discussion The sensitivity and specificity of the heterogeneity criterion is still rather low. The selection of small enhancing lesions with unclear findings in X-ray or ultrasound is very hard to diagnose reliably without biopsy (therefore 60 biopsies were taken). The region decomposition may reliably detect the most suspicious tumor regions—an information that is essential for biopsy planning.

The heterogeneity analysis described above was based on data where motion correction was performed with the method by Rueckert *et al.* [1999]. Better results might be possible with the refined motion correction developed by Schäfer *et al.* [2011] (recall § 16.7.1).

The study of [Preim *et al.*, 2012] is mentioned as an example for the use of visual analytics for medical research on perfusion data. Medical research usually involves larger series of patient data and a lot of statistics (only a few key results are mentioned here). A streamlined analysis of the data and a careful management of all relevant results is essential in addition to visual exploration techniques to enable such research. There are many more research questions around perfusion data and their use for specific diagnostic questions.

16.8 CASE STUDY: MYOCARDIAL PERFUSION

Cardiac perfusion data are acquired to detect and characterize the coronary heart disease (CHD). We have already dealt with this disease in § 11.7.2, where we discussed how volume rendering contributes to the assessment of calcified or vulnerable soft plaques. Perfusion imaging may add to this diagnosis, e.g., by detecting the disease at an earlier stage based on its effect on microcirculation. CHD is characterized by a perfusion deficit caused by stenosis in one of the major supplying arteries. Perfusion imaging helps to assess whether or not a stenosis is *hemodynamically relevant*—that is, whether blood supply of the myocardium is affected. Similar to ischemic stroke diagnosis CHD is treated with revascularization therapies, such as bypass surgery or percutaneous intervention.

16.8.1 MEDICAL IMAGING AND PREPROCESSING

Perfusion imaging in the heart is performed with nuclear medicine techniques (PET and SPECT) but increasingly more with MRI. PET is very specific in assessing the state of heart tissue, but it is expensive and the availability is limited. MR perfusion imaging is often part of a comprehensive MRI study that investigates various effects characterizing the myocardium in a non-invasive radiation-free manner. In the following, we focus on MRI perfusion, which is the recommended imaging modality of the American

Heart Association (AHA) and the American College of Cardiology for assessing hypoperfused tissue of the myocardium [Oeltze, 2010].

Rest and Stress Perfusion To investigate the perfusion of the myocardium, perfusion data is often acquired at rest and stress that is either induced by a pharmaceutical drug, e.g., adenosine or physical exercise. Stress leads to a higher demand of oxygen and as a consequence to vasodilation, a process that enables the coronary vessels to transport more blood. Thus, the *coronary flow reserve* is defined as the ability of the coronary arteries to increase blood flow under stress by vessel dilation. With perfusion imaging in rest and stress state the severity of CHD can be reliably assessed. Imaging is ECG-triggered to ensure that imaging is always at the same point in the heart cycle. Various techniques, including breath hold maneuvers, are employed to reduce the effects of respiratory motion. Similar to cerebral perfusion imaging, the analysis is usually restricted to the first pass. First pass cardiac MRI perfusion was introduced by Atkinson *et al.* [1990] and has since then become an established technique [Gerber *et al.*, 2008]. Typically, three to six slices are acquired. Thus, in contrast to cerebral and tumor perfusion, 3D visualizations are of limited value due to the low number of slices. The slices do not cover a myocardium region completely. Instead, there are gaps of approximately 1 cm (see Fig. e16.31). The in-plane resolution is approximately 2 mm with a matrix of 128 × 128 or 256 × 256. Data are acquired at end diastole over a sequence of 30–60 seconds.

To acquire rest and stress perfusion data such that both may be compared is technically challenging, since the heartbeat is strongly accelerated under stress. Thus, the timing of ECG-triggered acquisition is different. Sophisticated registration techniques have been developed to establish a correspondence between the slices in rest and stress perfusion data [Hennemuth *et al.*, 2008].

Preprocessing Noise reduction in cardiac MR perfusion data is often performed with anisotropic diffusion filtering [Oeltze, 2010]. Fitting the gamma variate or a Fermi function are also employed to compute perfusion parameters in a robust manner [Gerber *et al.*, 2008]. Segmentation is often employed to restrict the analysis of perfusion to the myocardium (Fig. e16.31). Segmentation also enables to characterize the location and extent of perfusion deficits.

Motion correction is essential due to the severe respiratory motion effects. A combination of rigid and elastic registration employing mutual information as the similarity metric, and a gradient descent method for optimization [Rueckert *et al.*, 1999] works reasonably well for most datasets [Oeltze *et al.*, 2006]. For parameter computation, the user applies the motion-corrected perfusion dataset and selects a ROI in

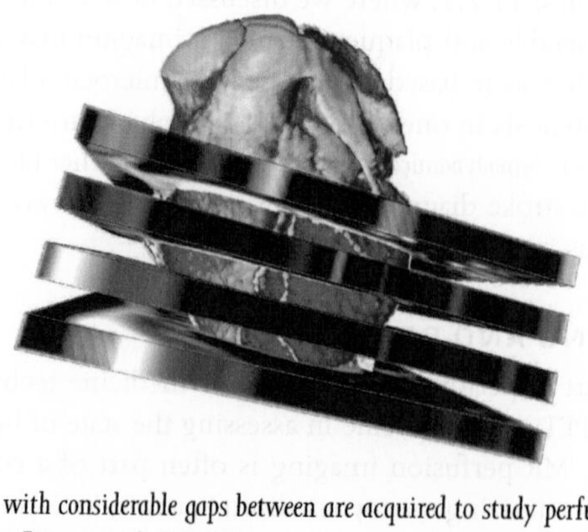

FIGURE e16.31 *Four thick slices with considerable gaps between are acquired to study perfusion. The slices are shown along with a volume rendering of CT data (From: [Hennemuth, 2012]).*

healthy myocardial tissue. Utilizing these data, the parameters are calculated for each voxel of the dataset. Since the diagnostic questions mostly relate to the myocardium of the left ventricle, the visualization of perfusion parameters is restricted to this structure.

Myocardial Segments The myocardium of the left ventricle is often divided into the 17 segments according to the recommendations of the AHA (recall Fig. e16.4, page e24). The 17 segments are defined based on four short axis slices and serve to communicate diagnostic results in a standardized manner. The location of these slices is selected such that the basal, mid-cavity, and apical part of the myocardium is represented. Besides perfusion information, also functional information on wall thickness and wall thickness changes are described by means of that model. The Bull's eye plot is a prominent example of a map-like display in medical visualization (recall Chap. e14). The number of segments (17) is a trade-off. On the one hand, the number is low enough to give a good overview on myocardial tissue state. On the other hand, the number is not too low to lose most interesting information due to averaging.

16.8.2 MULTIPARAMETER VISUALIZATIONS FOR CARDIAC PERFUSION ANALYSIS

In cardiac perfusion imaging, similar to the other application areas, descriptive and quantitative perfusion parameters are employed. Quantitative perfusion analysis requires again the normalization with the arterial input function that is derived from a blood pool region. The parameters PE, TTP, Up-Slope, and MTT have been evaluated as especially meaningful [Al-Saadi *et al.*, 2000]. In addition, the parameter MPRI (*myocardial perfusion reserve index*) is exploited to assess combined rest and stress perfusion. The MPRI characterizes the coronary flow reserve as the ratio between the Up-Slope at rest and under stress and thus facilitates a more reliable detection of ischemic areas. In healthy persons, the coronary flow is increased three to six times to normal flow, whereas in patients with a severe CHD it is often only about 1.5 times increased.

Multiparameter visualizations (recall § 16.4.2) are potentially useful for evaluating cardiac perfusion data (see Fig. e16.32). Among the useful multiparameter techniques are animated movements that show signal intensity changes over time averaged for the AHA segments. Breeuwer [2002] introduced the *Perfusogram* that is based on such animations.

Refined Bull's-eye Plot for Rest/Stress Comparison In a rest/stress comparison, (multi)parameter visualizations may be displayed side-by-side to identify areas where perfusion defects first appear or become worse with stress. In order to simplify a mental integration of rest and stress perfusion in one area, a refined Bull's eye plot (BEP) was introduced in [Oeltze *et al.*, 2006]. Each segment ring is bisected, thus, duplicating the number of segments. The resulting outer and inner rings represent the stress and the rest state, respectively (Fig. e16.33). This circular bisection ensures that neighboring segments in the plot are adjacent in the myocardium as well. Compared to the BEP from Oeltze *et al.* [2006], the segments are visually separated by means of a gap for better recognizability. The refined plot may also be used for comparing two different perfusion parameters.

The diagnosis of CHD benefits from a link to morphologic image data, in particular MR angiography data. Oeltze *et al.* [2006] provided a link between the Bull's-eye plot and the 3D view of the coronaries and picking facilities for both. A segment of the plot exhibiting a suspicious parameter value may be selected by pointing—resulting in an animated emphasis of the corresponding vessel branch in the 3D view (Fig. e16.34) and vice versa emphasizing the supplied segments.

In this section, we could only touch cardiac perfusion and its clinical application that involves a careful integration of perfusion data with other MR imaging modalities. For more information, we refer to [Hennemuth *et al.*, 2008, Oeltze, 2010, Termeer *et al.*, 2008, Termeer, 2009]. In particular, we recommend

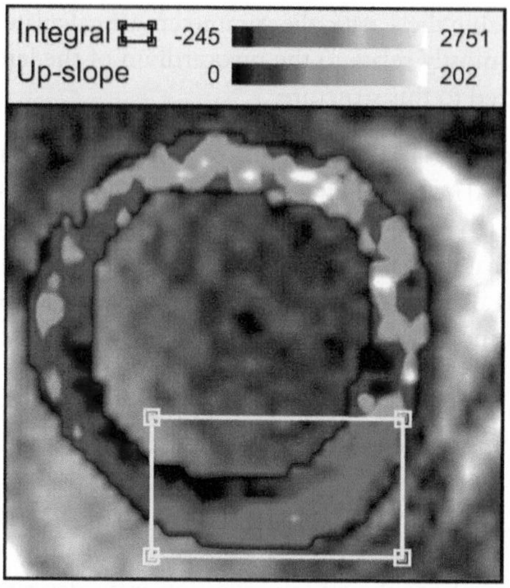

FIGURE e16.32 *Parameter "Up-slope" is displayed for the myocardium in the context of an original slice. Parameter "integral" is projected through a user-defined lens. Dark inferior and septal regions indicate a perfusion defect (From: [Oeltze, 2010]).*

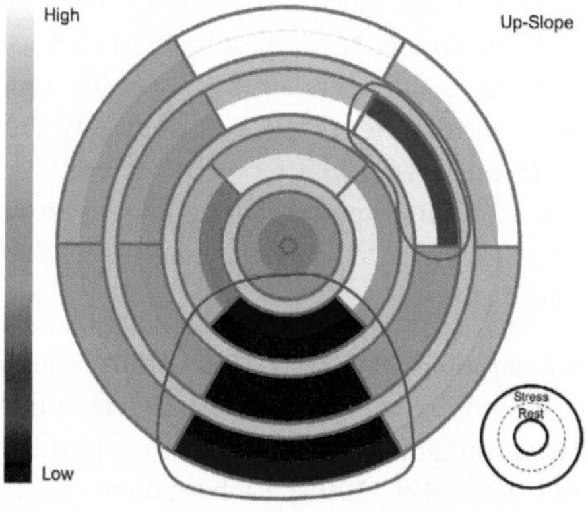

FIGURE e16.33 *Integrated visualization of the parameter PE for the rest and stress state in a refined Bull's-eye plot. An ischemic area is revealed in each slice (ring) from anterior to inferoseptal along the septum. Dark regions mark a diminished perfusion. Apically, the perfusion defect may remain unnoticed if perfusion is only examined at rest. Segment 17 is missing, since no slice has been acquired at the apex (Courtesy of Steffen Oeltze, University of Magdeburg).*

the recent PhD thesis [Hennemuth, 2012], where the underlying image analysis problems are carefully analyzed and a number of new techniques were presented.

16.9 FURTHER APPLICATION AREAS

Perfusion analysis bears a great potential in other diagnostic tasks as well. It has been shown that lung perfusion [Nikolaou *et al.*, 2004] enhances selected diagnostic processes, such as detecting disorders of

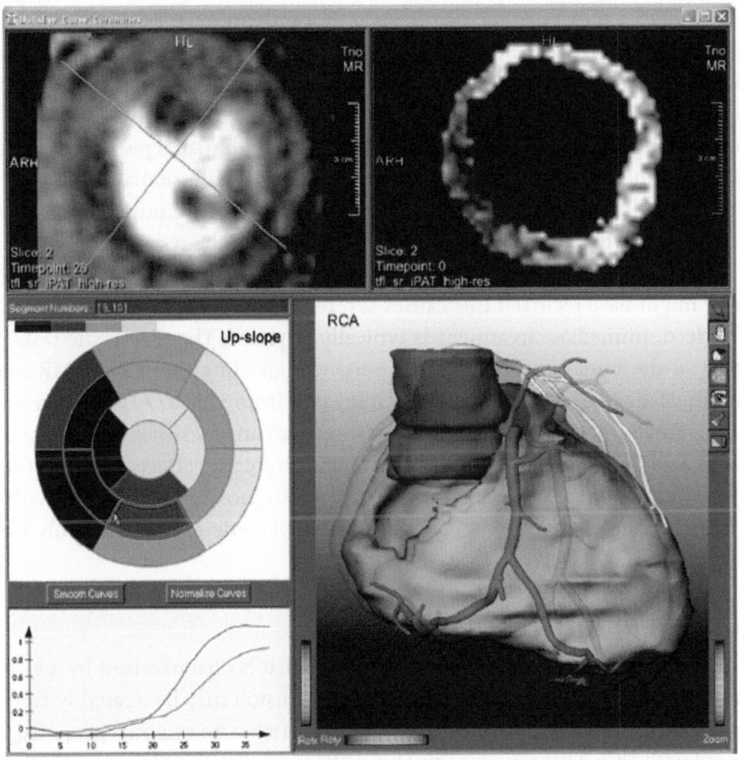

FIGURE e16.34 *Anatomy and myocardial perfusion of a patient suffering from atherosclerosis of the RCA and the LAD. Upper left: Apical slice of the original perfusion dataset and the AHA-based segmentation of the myocardium overlaid. Upper right: Apical slice of the parameter volume computed for Up-Slope. Middle left: Selection of two segments in the Bull's-eye plot, which color-codes the parameter Up-Slope. Segment 17 is missing since no slice has been acquired at the apex itself. Lower left: Time-intensity curves corresponding to the selected segments. Lower Right: Coronary branch (RCA) supplying the selected segments. The animated focusing is illustrated by a semi-transparent overlay of a previous point in time (Courtesy of Steffen Oeltze, University of Magdeburg).*

pulmonary vessels and acute pulmonary embolism. Also for the diagnosis and treatment monitoring of asthma and the chronic obstructive pulmonary disease (COPD), perfusion imaging may play an essential role [Kohlmann *et al.*, 2011], in particular to reliably discriminate these two diseases. In the following, we briefly discuss two application areas that gained a lot of attention in recent years: prostate cancer diagnosis and renal perfusion studies.

16.9.1 PROSTATE CANCER DIAGNOSIS

Similar to the prevalence of breast cancer in women, prostate cancer is the most common cancer in men and the second leading cause of cancer death in men [Franiel *et al.*, 2011]. MR imaging plays an essential role in diagnosis, tumor staging, and treatment planning. Prostate cancer is shown as low intensity signal in T2-weighted images. However, the low signal intensity is not specific to cancer. Other pathologies, such as prostatitis and fibrosis, lead to a similar intensity. Thus, a variety of functional MRI techniques are increasingly used to yield a more specific diagnosis. Among them is DCE-MRI. Similar to breast cancer, also prostate cancer exhibits early and strong enhancement [Franiel *et al.*, 2011]. The analysis of DCE-MRI with pharmacokinetic models was suggested and applied by several groups to enhance the diagnosis and reduce the need for biopsies.

Moreover, color-coding of pharmacokinetic parameters in a high spatial resolution supports *tumor staging* that involves the determination of infiltrated structures. Staging is an essential diagnostic procedure with direct consequences for the treatment, e.g., whether or not surgical removal is recommended. Among other applications where perfusion imaging was proven to improve the results is the detection of recurrent prostate cancer. A reliable detection of recurrent prostate cancer is essential: if patients are unnecessarily warned that cancer might have recurred this causes severe psychological problems. On the other hand, if cancer recurred indeed, immediate treatment is typically required. The diagnostic task is difficult, since radiation treatment of the initial cancer leads to signal changes in conventional MR that are similar to cancer. The sensitivity of diagnosis could be strongly increased from 38% to 72% (with a similar specificity) with DCE-MRI data. Finally, perfusion data also contributes to an assessment of tumor aggressiveness, a crucial parameter to avoid overly aggressive treatment with severe side effects [Franiel *et al.*, 2009]. Franiel *et al.*, [2011] give a comprehensive survey on prostate cancer diagnosis and treatment with DCE-MRI citing 100 studies. So far, in all these studies only simple pharmacokinetic models and only basic visualization techniques were employed.

16.9.2 RENAL PERFUSION STUDIES

Renal perfusion is essential to assess renal vascular diseases that is characterized by a loss of microvessels and may eventually lead to kidney failure. Reduced renal perfusion may be treated with drugs that induce neoangiogenesis. Besides renal perfusion, the *glomerular filtration rate* is an essential property of renal function that may be assessed with DCE-MRI renography. Due to its high spatial and temporal resolution DCE-MRI challenges nuclear medicine renography—the old gold standard of renal perfusion assessment [Zikic *et al.*, 2008]. Renal perfusion is assessed in two compartments of the kidney: in the *renal cortex* and the *renal medulla*. These compartments may be separated based on the properties of the related TICs (see Fig. e16.35).

Many aspects of data acquisition and data processing are similar to the applications we discussed before. A typical spatial resolution of DCE-MRI data is 3 × 3 mm in plane and 7 mm slice distance; the temporal resolution is 2.5 seconds with an acquisition time of at least 5 minutes [Cutajar *et al.*, 2010]. Medical research is focused on the effect of contrast agent administration and other scanning parameters. Gadolinium (Gd)-DPTA is employed in various concentrations. The acquisition takes several minutes and due to the location of the kidney strong motions are involved. Different acquisition and image processing techniques were explored to reduce motion artifacts, e.g., respiratory gating. Motion correction with registration is challenging due to the amount of motion and the strong changes of the image intensity due to the contrast bolus. Thus, without any constraints related to the kidney shape, a deformable non-rigid registration would lead to strong and anatomically implausible changes of the kidney shape.

Zikic *et al.* [2008] thus introduced a rigid registration scheme based on the observation that primarily translational movement in the coronary slices occurs. The user input is reduced to the selection of one coronary slice and a sketch of the kidney in that slice. As a quality measure, they consider that high-frequency changes in the perfusion are strongly reduced and in general smoother curves result. Song *et al.* [2006] solved a combined registration-segmentation problem where both processes are intertwined. To characterize renal perfusion quantitatively, again the arterial input function (AIF) is defined by placing a ROI in a large feeding artery and the specific position and extent of that ROI has a strong influence on the derived *renal blood flow* [Cutajar *et al.*, 2010] leading to research that automatizes ROI placement. Finally,

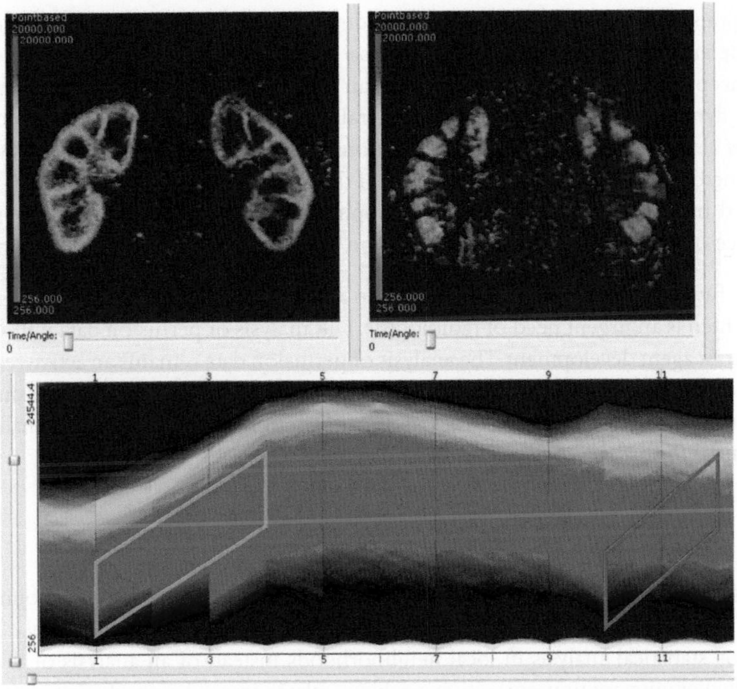

FIGURE e16.35 *The lower image depicts all TICs of a renal perfusion study. Gradient sum brushes are employed to select regions with similar perfusion characteristics. In the top left image, the renal cortex is shown based on the selection with left brush. The right image shows the renal medulla where contrast enhancement occurs later (Courtesy of Steffen Oeltze, University of Magdeburg).*

compartment models play an essential role in evaluating renal perfusion. A modified renal Tofts model is employed, for example by Cutajar *et al.* [2010]. Major perfusion parameters are MTT, TTP, PE, and Up-Slope [Michaely *et al.*, 2006]. Current research also focuses on arterial spin labeling (ASL), an MR acquisition technique to study perfusion without any contrast agent. Winter *et al.* [2011] and Wu *et al.* [2011a], for example, compare perfusion measures derived from ASL and DCE-MRI and found a good correspondence.

16.10 CONCLUDING REMARKS

Perfusion data have a great potential for diagnosis and treatment monitoring for a couple of severe and widespread diseases, such as coronary heart disease, various types of cancer and cerebral ischemic stroke. Perfusion data are analyzed by inspecting the original time-dependent data and by deriving perfusion parameters that have no dynamic character. Perfusion parameters characterize the shape of signal intensity change or, after normalization and other transformations, quantitative aspects, such as regional blood flow or regional blood volume. So far, the potential of perfusion imaging has not been fully realized, since image acquisition is insufficiently standardized.

We presented general techniques for analyzing and exploring perfusion data. Many aspects of the exploration of perfusion data are relevant for other dynamic medical volume data. As an example, the analysis of dSPECT (dynamic Single Photon Emission Computed Tomography) data is also based on the selection of regions and the investigation of curves depicting changes over time in these regions [Pohle *et al.*, 2004]. The analysis of functional MRI data also involves the analysis of time series [Friston *et al.*, 1995]. The concept of Profile Flags, which enable an integrated view of the time-intensity curves and the underlying dynamic image data, is also a general approach for exploring dynamic medical image data [Mlejnek *et al.*, 2006]. Glyph-based visualizations enable the simultaneous display of a couple of perfusion parameters. They are promising because of their large design space. However, users may easily be overwhelmed by either too complex glyph mappings or a too dense display of glyphs. We tried to provide guidance on how *intuitive* glyphs for perfusion data may be derived.

Outlook In the future, it might be expected that the acquisition of perfusion parameters will be better standardized, which is an urgent need of radiologists. The analysis of perfusion data will also benefit from research in contrast agent development. The analysis of perfusion data remains an active research topic. The integration of advanced clustering techniques and more elaborate techniques for assessing heterogeneity may help to streamline diagnostic procedures and make them more reproducible. Finally, in-depth user studies are essential to further advance perfusion diagnosis.

FURTHER READING

We have not discussed the rather new imaging modality of contrast-enhanced ultrasound perfusion. An inspiring paper on how these and related image data may be analyzed is [Angelelli *et al.*, 2011]. Their key idea is to employ statistical analysis in local neighborhoods instead of an analysis of the whole dataset. A particularly challenging motion correction problem relates to cardiac perfusion data, since complex movements occur and the target anatomy changes their shape due to the heart beat at the same time. The latter movement may *not* be corrected by motion compensation. Instead, a model of the heart movement needs to be incorporated. For a review on cardiac perfusion, we recommend [Gupta *et al.*, 2012]. Wintermark *et al.* [2005] give an overview on seven brain perfusion imaging techniques, including CT and MRI.

We discussed pharmacokinetic modeling to analyze perfusion data. Similar modeling problems occur in other types of dynamic medical image data, such as PET. The general problem of fitting model curves and estimating parameters in treated in Feng *et al.* [1996].

We could give only a brief overview of segmentation in perfusion data. Many more specific methods have been developed. In particular texture analysis is frequently employed to segment structures [Gon and Brady, 2008, Woods *et al.* 2007]. For breast cancer diagnosis, it is promising to combine the morphologic analysis of the shape of a lesion with the dynamic analysis of enhancement kinetics. A first attempt in this direction is described in Glaßer *et al.* [2011].

Part V

Treatment Planning, Guidance and Training

Part V "Treatment planning, guidance and training" covers surgical planning, intraoperative support and surgical training. In Chapter 17, we discuss general requirements and solution strategies for computer-assisted surgery.

Chapter 18 is dedicated to intraoperative visualization, image-guided surgery, and augmented reality in surgery. Here we will discuss how medical image data is integrated with an intervention itself. We discuss advanced techniques combining pre- and intraoperative imaging data similar to a car navigation system. The constraints of intraoperative use, interaction techniques appropriate in these settings and limitations with respect to setup times and accuracy will be carefully considered.

We go on and discuss the visual exploration of medical flow data, resulting from measurements or simulations (Chap. 19) with a focus on blood flow data, a very active research area in recent years that also is relevant for medical treatment planning, e.g., neurovascular intervention and surgery.

In Chapter 20, we discuss image analysis and visualization for ENT surgery planning (neck resection, endoscopic sinus surgery, insertion of implants in middle ear surgery). Task analysis and evaluation are carefully described to provide orientation for the development of similar systems. Image analysis (model-based segmentation), interactive visualization, measurements, and documentation support are crucial.

In Chapter 21, the use of medical visualization techniques for educational purposes, in particular for anatomy and surgery education is discussed. Besides describing application areas, this chapter introduces some new techniques, such as labeling and animation of medical volume data, collision detection, and soft tissue deformation for surgical simulation.

Visual Computing for Medicine, Second Edition. http://dx.doi.org/10.1016/B978-0-12-415873-3.00034-1

Chapter 17

Computer-Assisted Surgery

17.1 INTRODUCTION

Surgery generally refers to the act of cutting the tissue of a patient for the purpose of treatment or diagnosis. Surgical procedures can be minimally-invasive or open. In minimally-invasive surgery, instruments are inserted through a relatively small incision, for example in *laparoscopy*, where minimally-invasive procedures are performed in the abdomen or pelvis with the aid of a camera. In *interventional radiology*, minimally-invasive procedures are performed under image guidance, often involving the use of catheters. In *angioplasty* for example, a narrowed or obstructed blood vessel is repaired by inserting a balloon, using a catheter, and then inflating the balloon in the obstructed part of the vessel. During open surgery, the surgeon acquires direct access to the surgical site. Minimally-invasive and interventional procedures benefit most from careful preoperative planning and guidance, and have triggered a great deal of medical image analysis and visualization research.

Surgery can also be classified according to the organ or system that it targets, for example *neurosurgery* for the nervous system (§ 17.5.3), and *hepatic* surgery for the liver (§ 17.5.4). Other classifications include the technology that is used, the type of procedure and the purpose.

Computer-assisted surgery, or CAS, refers to the use of computer technology for the preoperative planning and for the intraoperative guidance of surgical interventions. Through the integration of computer technology, CAS aims to improve the surgical process and its long-term outcome by increasing accuracy and reducing the invasiveness, morbidity, duration, and costs that are associated with surgical procedures. In practice, existing computer-assisted surgery implementations adhere to the CAS pipeline shown in Figure 17.1. The pipeline starts with the acquisition of patient-specific data, which is often imaging-based, for example X-ray, CT, or MRI, but can also be of other types, for example measurements with a 3D optical tracking system. This data is then processed in order to extract higher level patient-specific information, generally through segmentation, and to prepare it for the visualization stage. In the visualization stage, the surgical planning is performed. The surgeon is able to study the patient anatomy and pathology based on the acquired data and processing results, can virtually perform the surgical procedure and in some cases examine the predicted surgical outcome.

The resultant surgical plan then has to be transferred to the operating room so that it can be applied to the surgical process. This can be achieved through the use of image-guided surgery, through mechanical guidance, through explicit documentation, or through the mental model that the surgeon builds up during the planning stage. The first two are examples of explicit guidance, while the second two are more implicit in nature. These guidance approaches are discussed in more detail in § 17.4.

Visualization plays an important role in computer-assisted surgery. In the planning phase, visualization techniques are used to display the acquired patient-specific data, the derived measurements and the predicted surgical outcome, and to enable the surgeon to interact with all the components in an efficient manner, for example to explore alternative approaches for a surgery. Also in image-guided surgery, the

---

This chapter was authored by Thomas Kroes, Charl Botha, and Bernhard Preim. The first two authors contributed equally.

Visual Computing for Medicine, Second Edition. http://dx.doi.org/10.1016/B978-0-12-415873-3.00017-1

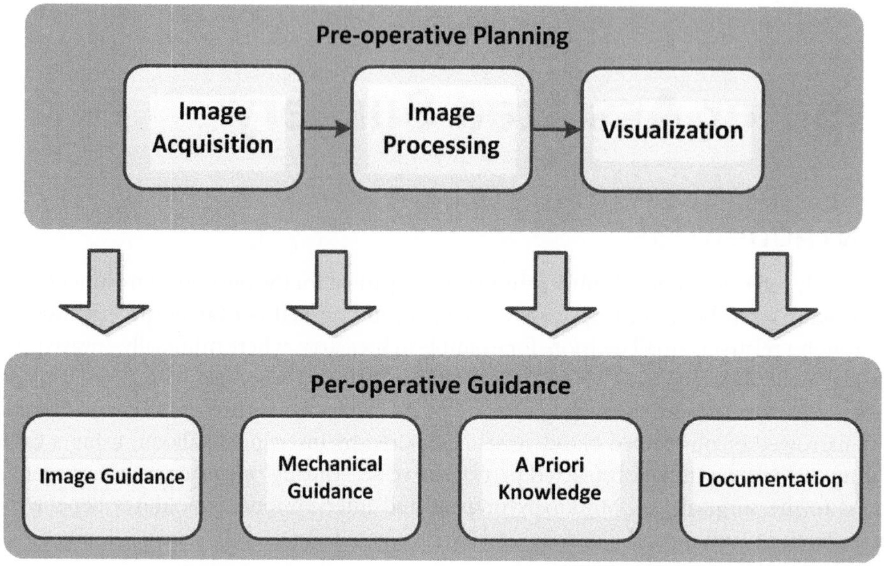

FIGURE 17.1 *The computer-assisted surgery pipeline.*

performed planning has to be displayed in the correct anatomical context and updated as well as possible to reflect the changing operative situation.

There are a number of surveys and overviews dealing with computer-assisted surgery in general, see § 17.6. In this chapter, we focus on computer-assisted surgery where visualization plays an important role.

Organization The rest of this chapter organized as follows. In § 17.2 we introduce a number of standard tasks that have to be performed during computer-assisted surgery, mostly during the planning stage. In § 17.3 discuss the basic visualization techniques that are employed in CAS systems, including visual representations, interaction and simulation techniques. In § 17.4 we introduce the four major ways of making available guidance during surgery. In § 17.5 we document the four major application areas of computer-assisted surgery, namely oral and maxillofacial surgery, orthopedic surgery, neurosurgery, and finally hepatic surgery.

17.2 GENERAL TASKS

Computer-assisted surgery systems all attempt to facilitate one or more of the following general tasks in surgical planning and guidance.

Spatial Understanding of Anatomy By exploring visualizations of the patient-specific data, the surgeon's existing knowledge of the anatomy in the target region is augmented by spatial understanding of the patient-specific anatomy. This is a basic and important task especially in the case of complex anatomy, for example in pelvic soft tissue surgery.

Spatial Understanding of Pathology The location, shape and embedding of any pathology, for example tumors and metastases, can be studied during the planning phase. This and the previous task play an important role in the general preoperative preparation and familiarization, but are also important for more specific subsequent tasks, such as access or resection planning. Studying the exact infiltration of anatomical structures by tumors falls under this task. Also see § 20.4.1 for the specific example of tumor infiltration in ENT surgery planning.

Access Planning In different types of surgery, a target point embedded somewhere within the anatomy has to be reached while minimizing damage to the surrounding structures. The planning of this trajectory is often based solely on the surgeon's experience and general knowledge of the anatomy, although there are an increasing number of examples of supporting this process with automatic [Navkar *et al.*, 2010, Shamir *et al.*, 2010] and visualization methods [Khlebnikov *et al.*, 2011, Rieder *et al.*, 2011]. The main goal is to determine one or more access paths to the target point that minimize risk to the surrounding tissue, or that shorten the time required. Access planning is usually also a part of resection, reconstruction and implant planning, the following three tasks.

Resection Planning In surgery, resection refers to the partial removal of an organ, gland, or tumor and surrounding tissue. This is mostly done to remove diseased or necrotic tissue. The main goal here is the removal of as much as possible at-risk tissue and as little as possible healthy tissue. Some risk structures, such as nerves and muscles, are particularly important, whereas others are even vital and need to be considered as hard constraints. A planning that takes into account as much as possible preoperative data and in many cases segmentations of the involved structures can increase the chances of a successful resection.

Reconstruction Planning In surgical reconstruction, anatomical structures that have been damaged through trauma, or are congenitally deformed, are repaired. These are complex procedures that require extensive planning. The main goal is a complete strategy for the cutting, relocation and reconstruction of anatomical structures that will result in an aesthetically and functionally suitable end result. Examples include orthognathic, oral, and maxillofacial surgery, discussed in § 17.5.1.

Implant Planning Implants refer to any foreign objects that are to be introduced into the human body, and include joint prostheses, screws for spinal fusion, and so forth. The main goal here depends on the type of implant, but it is generally speaking a surgical plan that helps to ensure that the implant can be installed with as little as possible damage to the anatomy and can perform its function for as long as possible. In the case of joint prostheses for example, an implant should generally have sufficient bone contact to help ensure long-term durability, and should result in acceptable postoperative patient range of motion [Krekel *et al.*, 2006]. The type and size of the prosthesis as well as the parameters of its implantation are important in this regard. In the case of thoracic pedicle screw insertion, the screws should be secure in the vertebra and should avoid the spinal cord at all costs [Rajasekaran *et al.*, 2007].

17.3 VISUALIZATION TECHNIQUES

In § 17.5 we will study examples of computer-assisted surgery from the perspective of its four major application areas: oral and maxillofacial, neurosurgery, orthopedic, and hepatic surgery. In this section, we discuss examples of the different types of visualization techniques that are employed in computer-assisted surgery.

We have identified three major types of visualization techniques in CAS, namely visual representation, interaction, and simulation. After discussing the three types, we explain the discuss how *quantitative visualization* techniques can be used to enrich CAS-related visualization with quantitative information.

17.3.1 VISUAL REPRESENTATION

Visual representation techniques in CAS aim to display all available data to the surgeon in order to facilitate pre and intraoperative decision-making. At the most basic level, visualization techniques are applied to medical images to show the patient's anatomy, the relevant pathology, and the embedding of the latter in the former. The next step is to add virtual surgical instruments and implants to the visualization, enabling the surgeon to study the interaction between these foreign objects and the existing anatomy and pathology. Finally, simulations of patient function as well as surgical interactions can be visually represented to further assist the decision-making process.

Anatomy and Pathology The primary concern of visual representation of anatomy and pathology is to faithfully and accurately communicate patient anatomy and pathology to the surgeon. CAS systems often rely on volume data, such as CT and MRI, in which case there are three basic visualization techniques that can be applied [Brodlie and Wood, 2001]: multiplanar reformation or slicing, surface rendering and direct volume rendering.

In multiplanar reformatting (MPR), or slicing, data is sampled along an arbitrarily positioned and oriented plane in the data. Oblique angles are possible with this type of visual representation, and they are used in some application areas such as spinal surgery (in which the cutting plane is aligned with the planned access path). However, surgeons, especially in orthopedics, are more attuned to the standard axial, sagittal, and coronal views which they were taught, possibly with an additional 3D view [Lattanzi *et al.*, 2002].

Curved Planar Reformation, or CPR, is a variation on this theme where data is sampled along a curved planar structure, usually determined by some anatomical structure, such as blood vessels. CPR is discussed in detail in Chapter 11. An example using CPR for maxillofacial surgery planning is discussed in § 17.5.1.

Surface rendering, discussed in Chapter 6, entails extracting surfaces, often represented as polygons, from the volume data, either by isosurfacing, or converting segmented objects to surfaces, and then displaying the extracted surfaces. In CAS literature, this is still used far more frequently than direct volume rendering. This is largely due to the fact that surface rendering has a longer history in medical applications, and that medical users have built up quite some experience with its use and interpretation.

With direct volume rendering, or DVR, volumetric data is displayed without an intermediate surface extraction step, instead either casting light rays through the data or projecting volume data points onto the display. DVR is discussed in detail in Chapters 7 and 8. In contrast to surface rendering, DVR is able to display more volumetric information at the same time, and offers great flexibility in specifying the appearance of the resulting renderings. In CAS solutions however, this flexibility is often seen as a disadvantage. Furthermore, surfaces still offer more possibilities in terms of structural simulation, and in the representation of anatomy and surgical instruments in motion.

Besides the three standard types of visual representation techniques, there are examples of techniques built for a specific purpose, such as the visual representation of vessels, see Chapter 11. This is used for example in hepatic surgery, see § 17.5.4. In an interesting example of intraoperative visualization, Hansen *et al.* [2010a] projected illustrative representations of liver anatomy and the embedded lesions onto the liver during surgery, in an augmented reality setup. Figure 17.2 shows an example of this.

Virtual Surgical Actions To be able to plan surgery, it should be possible to perform the procedure, or parts of it, virtually. This is also called *process simulation* and is discussed in detail in § 17.3.3, while the actual interaction techniques are briefly discussed in § 17.3.2.

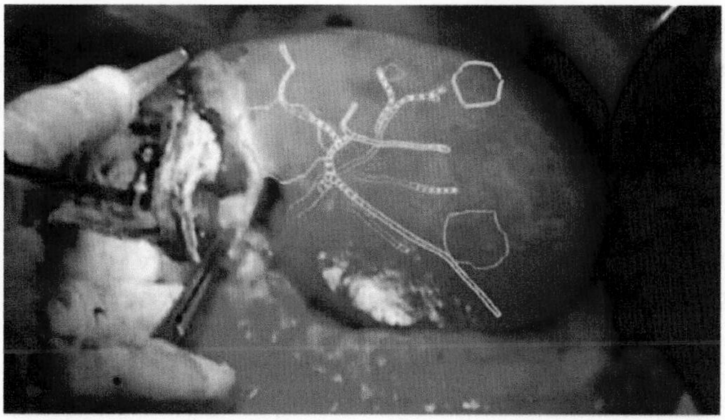

FIGURE 17.2 *Augmented video image in liver surgery. Illustrative representation of planning data is projected onto liver (From: [Hansen et al., 2010a]).*

The results of these virtual surgical actions need to be visually represented using a suitable metaphor. When a joint prosthesis or screw is virtually placed for example, this should be shown in such a way that the user can judge whether risk structures have been avoided and sufficient bone contact has been attained.

Predicted Outcome An overview of the different types of simulation techniques that are used in CAS will be given in § 17.3.3. Especially simulation techniques that try to predict the outcome of a procedure or action generate data that can also be used to enrich existing visualizations. Enhancing visualizations in this way can help operating surgeons to fine-tune their decision-making.

For example, Krekel *et al.* [2006] show the interactively calculated postoperative shoulder range of motion with motion envelopes that represent the maximum reach of the shoulder joint. In addition, the difference between two surgical options in terms of postoperative range of motion is explicitly visualized as green (improvement) and red (deterioration) polygons (Fig. 17.6).

Another example is that of Dick *et al.* [2009], shown in Figure 17.3, who interactively calculate stress in bones before and after an endoprosthesis is virtually placed.

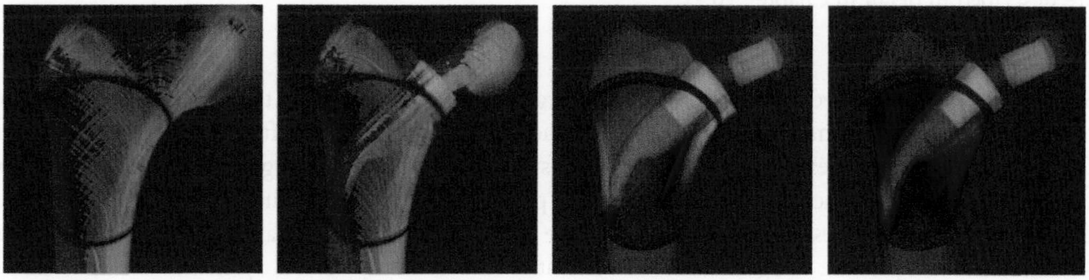

FIGURE 17.3 *Interactive visualizations of simulated stress tensor fields for a human femur under load. From left to right: 1. Stress directions and magnitudes in the physiological state (violet = tension, green = compression). 2. Principal stresses after a simulated implant surgery. 3. Change of normal stresses with respect to the principal stress directions of the physiological state (red = increase, yellow = decrease). 4. Change of shear stresses (From: Dick et al. [2009]).*

17.3.2 INTERACTION

Computer-assisted surgery systems incorporate the standard range of interaction possibilities afforded by visualization in general, recall Chapter 5. Examples are camera positioning, clipping, cutting, and per-object appearance. However, due to the underlying anatomical model, the specific task at hand and the time constraints imposed, a number of additional interaction techniques have been employed for computer-assisted surgery.

Automatic Viewpoint Determination makes it possible for the user to specify a point of interest, usually with a single click, and then have a suitable camera position and view direction be automatically calculated. Kohlmann *et al.* [2007] take into account occlusion, previous camera position, object pose preference, and so forth to calculate the best viewpoint for a given point of interest. Mühler *et al.* [2007] calculate viewpoints based on a complete structure of interest, also taking into account occlusion and structure importance. In their selection of viewpoints, they also consider whether it is suitable for local exploration.

In the operating room, the situation is even more constrained, with the surgeon often not even being able to come into contact with the computer equipment running the visualizations. In cardiovascular ablation procedures, for example, the operating cardiologist issues verbal commands to an assistant who then interacts with the guidance and visualization console.

In some types of surgery the surgeon loses the sensation of touch, either because surgery takes place through a very small incision, or the instruments are indirectly operated by the surgeon, through for instance operating robots like the da Vinci Surgical System. In virtual surgery, the sensation of touch is usually not there to begin with. In these cases, mechanical actuators are used to mimic the tactile feedback a surgeon normally experiences when touching instruments, and tissue. There are still a number of challenges to be solved in implementing haptic feedback for telesurgery, including force sensing at the surgical site, sensor/actuator asymmetry in the practical case where perfect force sensing is not available and the availability of both force and tactile sensing [Okamura, 2004].

Measurement is a also key component of CAS systems. Accurate spatial measurements are essential in establishing a good surgical plan. Common metrics are distances, angles, and volumes. Measurement functionality is often encapsulated by so-called widgets, virtual measurement devices which can be manipulated interactively (see § 10.3, for example). For instance hepatic surgery planning, which is discussed in § 17.5.4, relies on volume measurements. Computer-assisted oral and maxillofacial surgery uses underlying cephalometry to measure abnormalities in the facial region, see § 17.5.1. Orthopedic surgical planning often relies on angular measurements. Measurements in medical visualization in general are described in detail in Chapter 10.

17.3.3 SIMULATION

Simulation techniques used in computer-assisted surgery can be classified into two groups. *Process simulation* techniques attempt to mimic the surgery itself, including elements such as soft tissue cutting simulation. *Outcome simulation* techniques attempt to predict the results and impact of the surgery on the patient. State of the art CAS systems are increasingly equipped with patient-specific surgical simulation tools that predict the outcome of surgery, estimate risks and simulate "what if" scenarios. Because both types of surgical simulation techniques are integrated with visualization functionality in CAS systems, we discuss them here.

Process Simulation Process simulation techniques are used in surgical simulators, which create virtual environments in which a surgical procedure can be executed on a virtual patient, with the objective to measure surgical skills, educate, train, and rehearse surgical procedures. This can be done for needle insertion procedures [Chentanez *et al.*, 2009], different types of minimally-invasive surgery [Cotin *et al.*, 1999, Radetzky and Nürnberger, 2002, Lee *et al.*, 2010] and open surgery. The main goal is to establish a *user experience* that plausibly simulates real surgery, by accurately modeling soft tissue, tool tissue interaction such as cutting and suturing, haptic feedback, bleeding, and anatomical appearance.

Besides the compact discussion shown here, § 21.5 contains a detailed treatment of simulation techniques for surgery and interventional radiology, including the important concepts collision detection, force feedback, and soft tissue deformation.

Modeling of soft tissues and their interaction with medical instruments is an active area of research in surgical simulation. Soft tissue simulation aims to mimic the deformable and elastic nature of skin and other non-rigid structures in the human body. In surgical simulators, soft tissues are either simulated by *physically based mass-spring models* [Keeve *et al.*, 1996], see § 21.5.1, or by *Finite Element* (FE) models, first used for surgery simulation by Bro-Nielsen [1998]. Mass-spring models, discussed in more detail in § 21.5 and § 20.5.2, have the advantage of being computationally cheap, but at the expense of physical accuracy and stability. FE models, on the other hand, are more physically accurate, but require more computation. All state of the art soft tissue simulations have in common that certain assumptions are made with respect to the material being simulated, e.g., isotropy and homogeneity. This is acceptable for surgical simulation in the context of training, but not for patient-specific simulation in the context of surgical planning.

Especially in surgical simulators, there is a high demand for responsive user interfaces, which implies that soft tissue simulations should run at interactive speeds. The introduction of *General Purpose computation on Graphics Processing Units* (GPGPU) has contributed significantly to the possibilities in this regard. An increasing number of algorithms make use of the GPU for acceleration. Good examples include a GPU-accelerated mass-spring system for surgical simulation [Mosegaard *et al.*, 2005] and GPU-accelerated FE solvers [Taylor *et al.*, 2008, Comas *et al.*, 2008]. Sørensen and Mosegaard [2006] survey GPU-based techniques for both FE and spring-mass models for simulating deformable surfaces in surgical simulation. Cutting simulations are also important aspects of surgical simulators. Cutting simulations often deal with soft tissue [Jeřábková and Kuhlen, 2009] and often extend existing soft tissue models, but can also target bony structures [Pflesser *et al.*, 2002, Agus *et al.*, 2003, Morris *et al.*, 2006]. The fidelity of a surgical simulation can be further increased by, for example, adding haptic feedback and sound cues, as well as emulating the appearance of wet surfaces due to an irrigation device as shown in Figure 17.4 [Kerwin *et al.*, 2009].

Outcome Simulation While process simulation techniques model the surgical procedure itself, including for example tissue-tool interaction, outcome simulation techniques attempt to predict the results of virtually performed surgical actions so that *what-if* scenarios can be explored. In the literature, four main kinds of outcome simulation can be found:

- aesthetic,
- structural,
- motion, and
- blood flow.

Aesthetic outcome simulations are most common in plastic and in oral and maxillofacial surgery, where the cosmetic outcome of the surgery is important. Aesthetic outcome simulation attempts to predict the results of surgery on muscles, skin, and other soft tissue, often as a consequence of the changes made to the underlying bony structures. In oral and maxillofacial surgery, *orthognathic surgery*, or jaw correction through bone cutting, or *osteotomy* and repositioning, is an often-occurring procedure. Planning systems for osteotomy often employ the finite element method to predict soft tissue changes resulting from changes

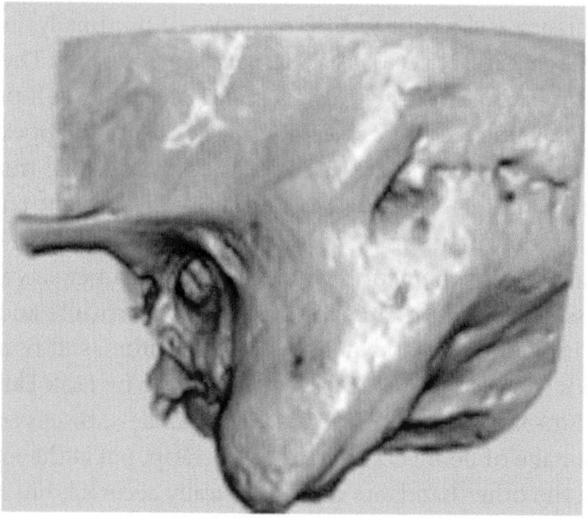

FIGURE 17.4 *Emulation of wet bone surfaces during temporal bone surgical simulation (From: [Kerwin et al., 2009]).*

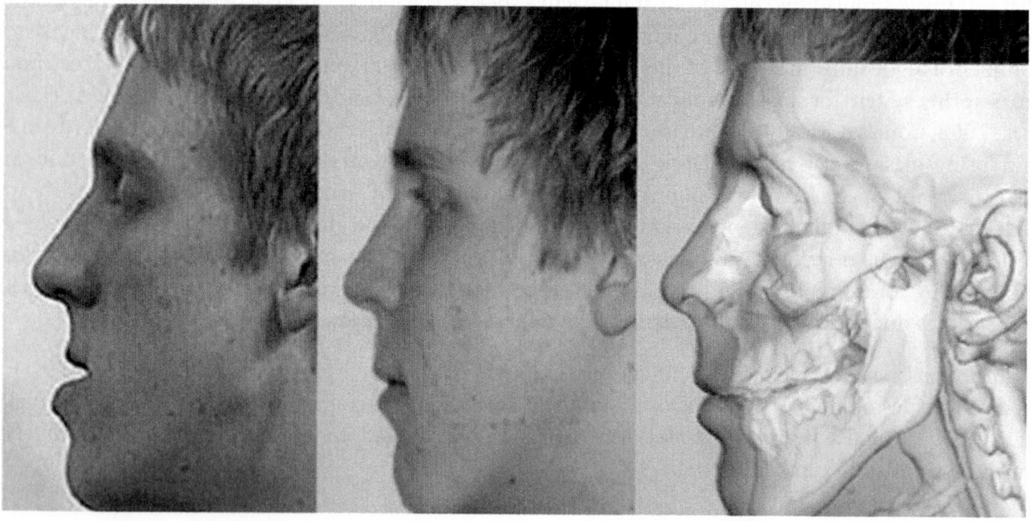

FIGURE 17.5 *The two images on the left depict the pre and postoperative situation respectively, while the third image shows an overlay of the postoperative photograph and the altered planning model with predicted facial soft tissue (From: [Zachow et al., 2006]).*

to the underlying bone, and hence the resultant facial appearance [Keeve *et al.*, 1996, Zachow *et al.*, 2001, Chabanas *et al.*, 2003, Westermark *et al.*, 2005]. Figure 17.5 shows examples from such a system. These models can also be used to predict the appearance of postoperatsystem. ive facial expressions, for example under different emotions [Gladilin *et al.*, 2004, Koch, 2001]. Other application areas include the simulation of the outcome of breast plastic surgery [Kim *et al.*, 2008] and of rhinoplasty, or nose surgery [Lee *et al.*, 2001].

Structural outcome simulation aims at predicting the structural integrity or durability of some surgical result. A number of examples can be found in *computer-assisted orthopedic surgery*, or CAOS, where the long-term bonding between a bone and an implant is an important success factor. The type, size, and placement of orthopedic implants have a profound effect on the durability of the implant [Iannotti *et al.*, 2005]. For this reason algorithms are being developed that simulate the structural integrity of an implant and its anatomical embedding, so that optimal placement parameters can be specified. Implant-bone bonding and durability can be modeled using finite element methods, for example in predicting loosening of glenoid components from the scapula [Couteau *et al.*, 2001]. In more recent work, forces and stresses in the implant and the surrounding bone could be simulated and visualized in real-time using the GPU [Dick *et al.*, 2009], enabling the surgeon to experiment interactively with different implant configurations. Having an adaptive resolution grid representation for the structure that is being simulated is just as important as the GPU in enabling interactive performance. Figure 19.44 shows an example stress distribution (see Fig. 17.5).

Motion outcome simulation techniques predict the postsurgical range of motion and possible impingement sites after an orthopedic implant has been virtually placed in the hip [Digioia *et al.*, 2000, Hu *et al.*, 2001], knee or the shoulder [Krekel *et al.*, 2006]. These are especially useful when they are applied dynamically during the virtual surgical session. As the surgeon is exploring different possibilities in terms of prosthesis type and placement, the planning system can give feedback about the expected range of motion and possible impingements in real-time, thus facilitating decision-making. Figure 17.6 shows an example of a shoulder range of motion visualization.

Blood Flow outcome simulations model and predict the postoperative outcome in terms of changed blood flow. One such example is that of virtual stenting [Cebral and Lohner, 2001, Xiong and Taylor, 2010], discussed in more detail in § 19.5.6, where the effect of a placed stent on the blood flow in and around an aneurysm is simulated. By predicting the effect a given stent and placement will have on for example the pressure and wall shear stress, the placement can be optimized to help guarantee a good outcome. Figure 17.7 shows an example of wall shear stress visualization before and after the virtual stenting.

Discussion Simulation techniques form an important component in computer-assisted surgery. Initially, they were primarily used to simulate the surgical process itself, in other words increasing the realism and plausibility of the virtual surgery. This type of simulation is called *process simulation*. *Outcome simulation* techniques attempt to model and predict the probable results of a certain surgical action, thereby contribution information that can be used during preoperative decision-making.

Justifying and even evaluating the need for the increased realism that *process simulation* can bring is complicated. Whereas in training scenarios increased realism is certainly important, its necessity in surgical planning is debatable. In contrast, validated *outcome simulation* techniques are useful in planning, especially in the case of complex surgical procedures. Convincing examples additional to those already mentioned above include blood flow simulation for arterial bypass grafts [Ku *et al.*, 2002, Taylor *et al.*, 1999] and blood circulation in the liver for hepatectomy [Saito *et al.*, 2005].

17.3.4 QUANTITATIVE VISUALIZATION

For precise planning of surgery or interventions, *quantitative information* needs to be added to all of the different visualization techniques discussed above. In Chapter 10 we discussed how measures, such as distances or angles between bones, may be integrated in 2D and 3D views to provide *explicit* quantitative information. Such integrated measures are explicitly associated with the points that they relate to, which

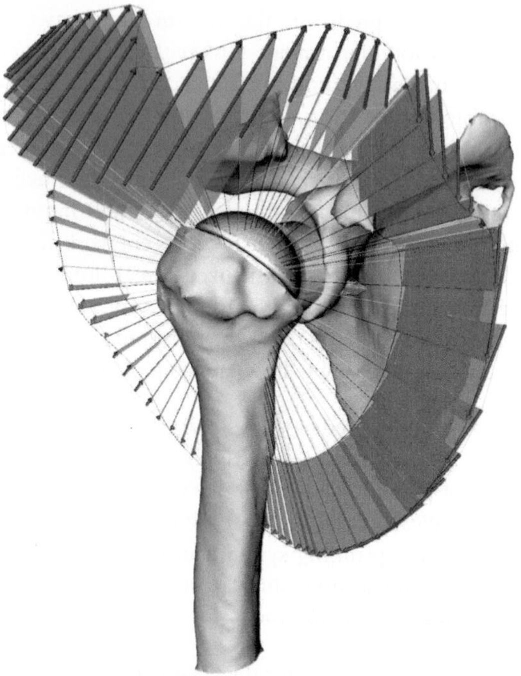

FIGURE 17.6 *Visualization of shoulder range of motion, or ROM, for a specific prosthesis and placement configuration. Green planes show improvement and red planes a decrease in ROM relative to a user-configured baseline. The ROM is computed and updated on-the-fly (From: [Krekel et al., 2006]).*

contributes to the clarity of the visualization. However, this can also be seen as a limitation when more quantitative information needs to be conveyed.

An alternative is to employ a visualization technique that maps an essential quantitative value to a 3D surface visualization. In particular, the distance of anatomical structures to a pathology might be crucial to assess whether the pathology may be completely removed or destroyed, with low risk to the adjacent structures [Hansen *et al.*, 2009]. Also, the thickness of the myocardial wall, the thickness of the cortex (gray matter) or the average diameter of a vascular structure are clinically relevant examples.

Quantitative visualizations are particularly valuable if they are continuously adapted to interactively steered treatment components. The position of a source of radiation, the position of an implant and the position and orientation of biopsy needles are examples of such treatment components. While the patients' anatomy is considered static, the devices are moved during planning and the consequences of the current position and orientation should be instantly visible.

17.3.4.1 Color-Coding and Isolines

Common mapping techniques include color-coding and isolines [Marai *et al.*, 2004, Süßmuth *et al.*, 2010, Rieder *et al.*, 2011]. As an example, Marai *et al.* [2004] employ both techniques to convey potential contact areas between bones. As a second example, see Figure 17.8, where color encodes the distances between cranial nerves and pathologic vessel structures that exhibit a contact to nerves causing the neurovascular

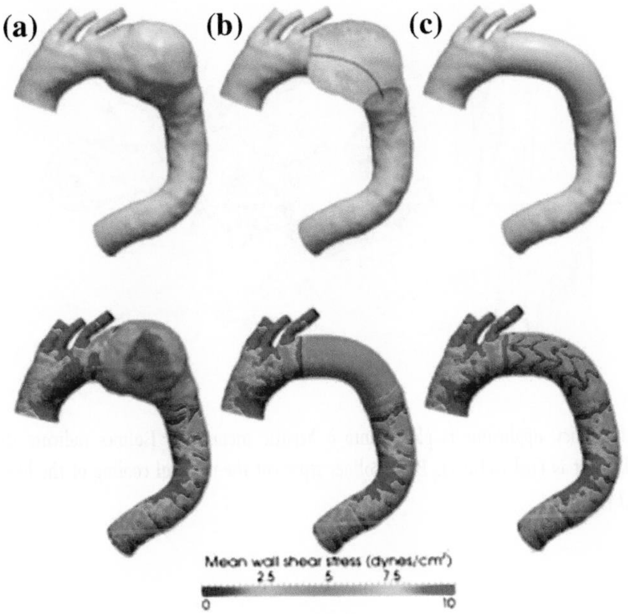

FIGURE 17.7 On the left, the situation before the stenting is shown, in the middle the model with aneurysm removed, and on the right the poststenting situation is shown. The surfaces in the bottom row have been color-coded with the simulated wall shear stress (From: [Xiong and Taylor, 2010]).

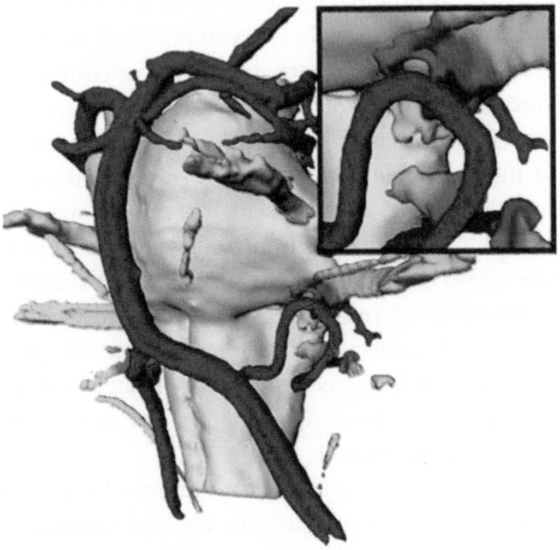

FIGURE 17.8 The neurovascular compression syndrome is characterized by contacts between nerves and vascular structures. For surgical planning it is essential to understand where these structures are too close. The yellow to red colors (see also the close up) represent distances (From: [Süßmuth et al., 2010]).

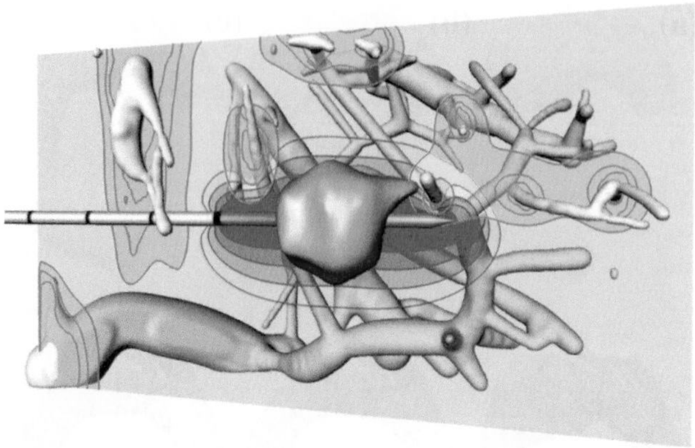

FIGURE 17.9 *A radio frequency applicator is placed into a hepatic metastasis. Isolines indicate the simulated ablation zone incorporating the heat-sink effect is (red isolines). Blue isolines represent the thermal cooling of the blood vessels around the lesion* (From: [Rieder et al., 2011]).

compression syndrome [Süßmuth *et al.*, 2010]. The combined use of colors and isolines is shown in Figure 17.9, where the simulated temperature around a radio frequency applicator is represented. These mapping techniques are not immediately intuitive. Thus, a legend must be provided to convey the semantics of differently colored regions or isolines.

Continuous Versus Discrete Color Scales Although continuous color scales that map distance or thickness of a certain interval to a continuous set of colors provide a maximum of information, discussions with surgeons and other medical doctors clearly reveal that discrete color scales or combinations of discrete color scales with isolines are preferred, provided that reasonable intervals are chosen to be represented by the same color. This preference can be explained since the treatment decisions are discrete, often even yes/no decisions. A few colors are a more suitable basis for such decisions. As an example, vascular structures below a certain diameter threshold (2 mm) are not essential in surgery since they may be easily coagulated and their influence on blood supply or drainage is limited. Beyond that threshold, vascular structures are essential and surgeons prepare a resection strategy that aims at saving such structures. However, if this is not feasible, there is another threshold (5 mm) that is used to decide whether a reconstruction of that vessel is necessary in case it needs to be resected. Thus, a mapping technique that represents to which of these three categories a vessel segment belongs, is ideal to support such planning considerations. Similarly, safety margins of about 5, 10, and 15 mm around a malignant tumor are often considered as essential to decide on the operability of a patient [Preim *et al.*, 2000].

Figure 17.10 indicates safety margins around malignant tumors. Surgical decisions may be supported further by computing for all possible safety margins, the affected vascular territories and thus the percentage of parenchyma that remains functional. The computations may be summarized in an interactive plot of safety margin vs. remnant. In that plot, surgeons may select a point on the curve representing a certain safety margin to see the resulting distribution of resected volume and remnant volume [Hansen *et al.*, 2009]. This interactive graph structure is called the *risk graph*.

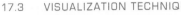

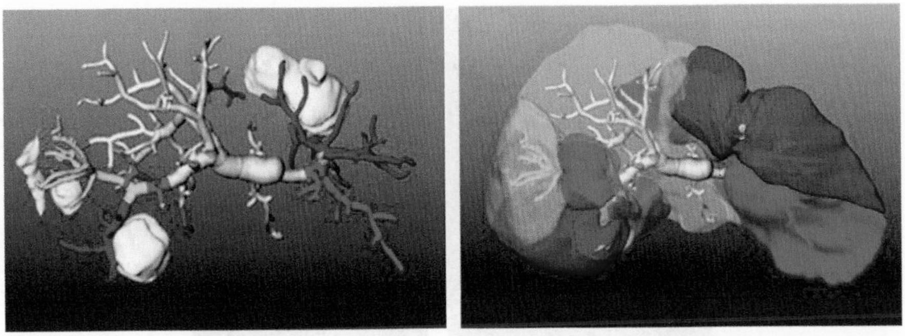

FIGURE 17.10 **Left:** *The visualization of vessels around a tumor in three discrete levels (safety margin of 5 mm (red), 10 mm (yellow), and 15 mm (green)).* **Right:** *Based on the analysis of vessels surrounding the tumors, the related territories for each safety margin are computed and shown in the same colors (Courtesy of Christian Hansen, Fraunhofer MEVIS. See also [Hansen et al., 2009]).*

17.3.4.2 Glyph-Based Quantitative Visualizations

While color-coding is certainly the most widely used technique for quantitative medical visualization, glyphs represent a powerful alternative [Dick *et al.*, 2011a]. We introduced and defined them in § 16.4.2 where glyphs were discussed to display perfusion parameters. Glyphs are placed at discrete positions and their density might be adapted to the underlying values, e.g., more glyphs might be placed in regions where the quantitative value changes strongly, whereas fewer glyphs convey the value in homogeneous regions. With an appropriate glyph design, the glyphs may also take a similar role to reference lines and indicate the direction of a distance line that represents the minimum distance between a point and a surface.

Directional glyphs serve as bridging structures between the moving object and the fixed reference objects [Dick *et al.*, 2011a]. Cylindrical glyphs, where the cylinder height represents the quantitative value, are an appropriate choice and may be placed on the surface of the moving object. There are two obvious choices for the direction. Glyphs may be placed

- in the direction of the computed minimum distance,[1] or
- orthogonally to the surface (pointing in the direction of the surface normal).

As Dick *et al.* [2011a] illustrated, the first approach leads to visual clutter, looks very unnatural, and cannot be recommended. Thus, they employed glyphs at the surface of an implant pointing in the direction of the local surface normal for 3D implant planning. The glyphs represent the minimum distances to the boundary of the bone to which the implant should be inserted (see Fig. 17.11).

The radius is the second parameter of a cylindrical glyph shape and may be adapted to distance as well. Dick *et al.* [2011a] suggest to reduce the radius with increasing distance. In interactive exploration of implant positions, the glyphs thus have a constant volume and appear squeezed if distance increases. This physically plausible behavior was rated as comprehensible by users. In addition, this glyph mapping strategy emphasizes regions with small (critically low) distances since the radius is increased. Finally, a threshold is recommended to restrict the distance visualization to relevant portions (see Fig. 17.12). Dick

1 Minimum distance computation was discussed in § 10.4.

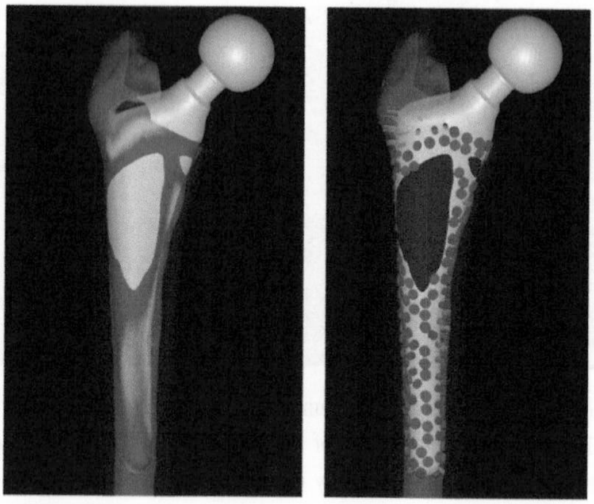

FIGURE 17.11 *Comparison of two quantitative visualization techniques to convey the minimum distances between points of an implant to the surface of a bone in which it should be embedded.* **Left:** *Continuous color-coding.* **Right:** *cylindrical glyphs (Courtesy of Christian Dick, Technical University of Munich).*

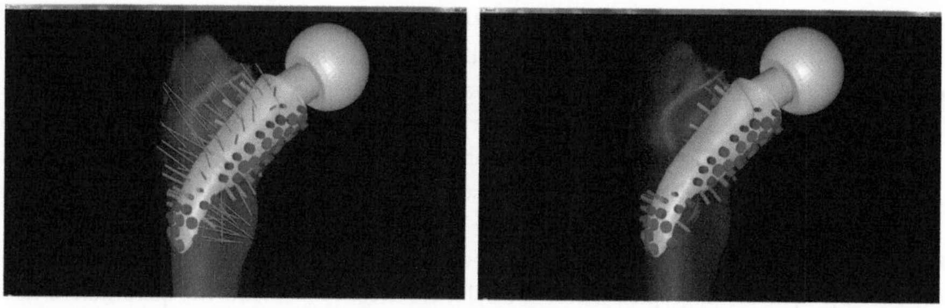

FIGURE 17.12 **Left:** *Distance color-coding without a limit.* **Right:** *A threshold avoids that large (and less relevant) distances are shown (Courtesy of Christian Dick, Technical University of Munich).*

et al. [2011a] discuss further options for quantitative visualizations, e.g., visualizations that integrate axial cross sections and use them to display further hints related to distances.

In addition to mapping distance to glyph height (and indirectly to the radius), distance is also mapped to color. This redundant mapping may be considered unnecessary at first glance. However, due to the limited depth cues of a (monoscopic) 3D visualization, color indeed improves the comprehensibility of the quantitative visualization.

When the implant is moved, the shape, size, color, and density of the glyphs need to be adapted. While the approach was developed for and evaluated within a specific application, namely hip replacement surgery planning, it is clearly broadly applicable to situations where one object is moved in relation to a fix object. The glyph-based visualization supports the *geometric* aspects of implant planning (the implant should fit in the inner zone of the bone and not hurt the outer shell of stiff cortical bones [Dick *et al.*, 2011a]. Another essential aspect of this planning procedure is the biomechanical stress distribution depending on the implant position. We will discuss this application in § 19.6.1. Of course, both aspects geometry and biomechanics are intertwined. Thus, a non-physiological stress distribution may be caused by an unfortunate geometric placement.

17.3.4.3 Computing Distance Fields

Quantitative visualizations rely on complex computations that can hardly be done in advance in a preprocessing step. Imagine a therapy planning system where the user may freely select anatomical structures and then gets a 3D visualization of the whole regional anatomy with the distance to the selected reference object color-coded. In this scenario, it would be necessary to compute a whole set of volumetric distance fields. With moving reference objects, such as implants, precomputation can be cumbersome and on-demand computation becomes interesting.

To be useful for fluent interactive exploration, this computation must be carried out in a very efficient manner. The principle of distance field computation is shown in Figure 17.13. Starting from a reference structure, adjacent voxels in orthogonal direction receive the distance and other neighboring voxels are assigned the corresponding Euclidean distances. The process is similar to a region growing segmentation and may be restricted to a certain maximum distance. Figure 17.14 illustrates this growing process and the result in one slice. The efficient computation of distance field relies on approximations (reducing the amount of floating point arithmetic) and on graphics hardware realization [Schneider *et al.*, 2009].

17.4 GUIDANCE APPROACHES

Guidance approaches refer to the methods that are applied *during* surgery to be able to apply the surgical planning. This can be done implicitly, for example when the surgeon relies on their experience and

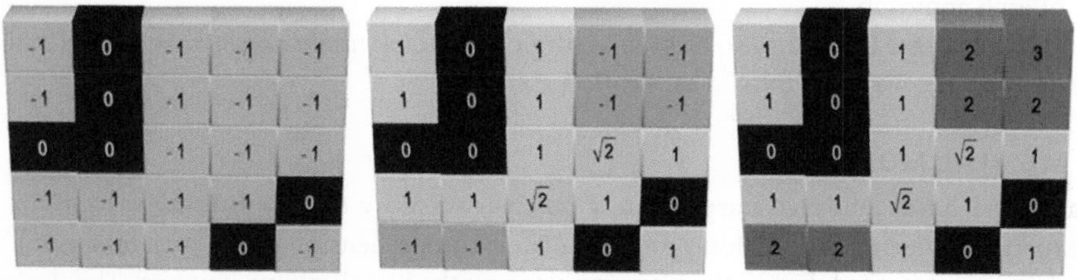

FIGURE 17.13 Principle of distance field computation. The distances relate to the structure represented by the black voxels (From: [Süßmuth et al., 2010]).

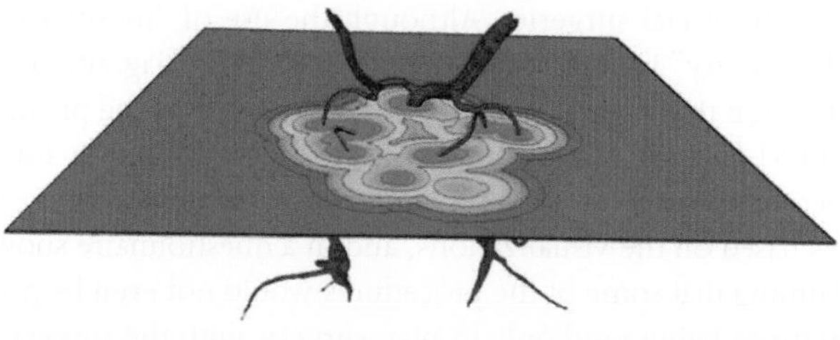

FIGURE 17.14 2D visualization of a distance field around vascular structures (From: [Süßmuth et al., 2010]).

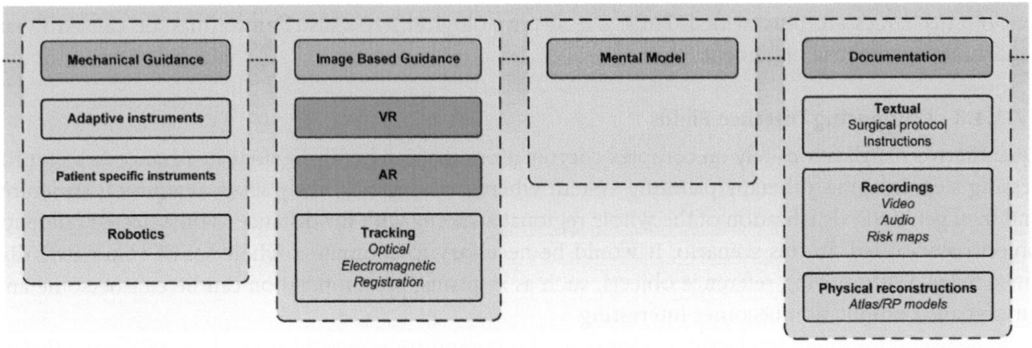

FIGURE 17.15 *Schematic overview of the four identified guidance approaches: Mechanical Guidance, Image-based Guidance, Mental Model, and Documentation.*

memory of the performed planning, or explicitly, for example when optical tracking of instruments and anatomy is used to follow the preoperative planning as closely as possible.

In this section, we will discuss the four different guidance approaches that we have identified: *Mental model-based*, where the surgeon relies on their experience and their memory of the planning; image-based, where 3D tracking systems and medical imaging are used; documentation-based, where specially prepared, usually static, documentation is consulted by the surgeon; and finally mechanical guidance-based, where physical instruments, in some cases patient-specific or adjustable, are used to perform the surgery according to plan. Figure 17.15 shows the four guidance approaches along with a number of subtypes of each approach.

These guidance approaches can also be seen as surgical planning *transfer modalities*, as they exist to transfer information from the planning into actual surgical actions.

17.4.1 MENTAL MODEL

In mental model-based guidance, surgeons rely on their memory of the planning session, in addition to their experience, during the surgical procedure. Their comprehension of the patient-specific anatomy and pathology is augmented during the planning stage by the visualizations involved. The decisions that they make also serve as a persistent result of the planning. There is no explicit guidance mechanism at play. However, this is the oldest and probably the most popular guidance approach, for surgical planning performed with or without a computer.

In one of the first examples, Vannier *et al.* [1983b] generated 3D surface visualizations from CT data for the planning of 200 craniofacial surgeries. Although the use of "industrial blueprint diagrams for application to craniofacial surgery" is mentioned, the sparsity of the diagrams and the complexity of the surgery leads to the conclusion that mental model-based guidance was the primary application path.

Hemminger *et al.* [2005] assessed the use of real-time 3D visualization for cardiothoracic surgery planning with three experienced surgeons on 23 complex cases. In this study, the surgeons changed their plans in 65% of the cases based on the visualizations, and in a questionnaire showed a strong preference for the visualizations, claiming that some of the procedures would not even be possible without. This is a clear example of visualizations being used only to plan surgery, with the surgery itself being performed purely based on the mental model of the surgeon built up during the planning stage.

Not implementing explicit surgical guidance is clearly the most straightforward guidance approach in CAS. It deviates the least from the traditional surgical pipeline, in fact only adding computer-based technology to the already existing planning phase, and for the surgery itself relying exclusively on the surgeon's expertise. Nonetheless, measuring the added value of such approaches is important.

17.4.2 DOCUMENTATION

In documentation-based guidance, the planning phase yields some form of document that contains guidelines and other information that can be used during surgery to apply the surgical plan. The surgeon relies for a large part on their mental model of the planned surgery, with the documentation serving to augment this model.

Resection Maps [Lamata *et al.*, 2008] and Risk Maps [Hansen *et al.*, 2010c, Hansen, 2012], simplified visual representations of and for liver resection planning, are good examples of how documentation can encapsulate surgical planning. These are discussed in more detail in § 14.5.2.

MeVis Distant Services, a surgical planning company, also employs this guidance approach to transfer a collection of liver resection proposals in the form of an interactive PDF, to its surgical clients. Figure 17.16 shows an example of such a report. The embedded 3D visualizations can be interacted with, both through rotation and through toggling the visibility of the displayed structures.

With rapid prototyping techniques, for example stereolithographic biomodelling, solid plastic replicas of patient anatomy can be manufactured on demand, based on three-dimensional image data [Petzold *et al.*, 1999]. These replicas can be used for surgical planning, and it has also been reported that the manufactured models can be sterilized and taken into the operating room to serve as a tactile guide during surgery [D'Urso *et al.*, 1999]. This is another interesting case of documentation-based surgical

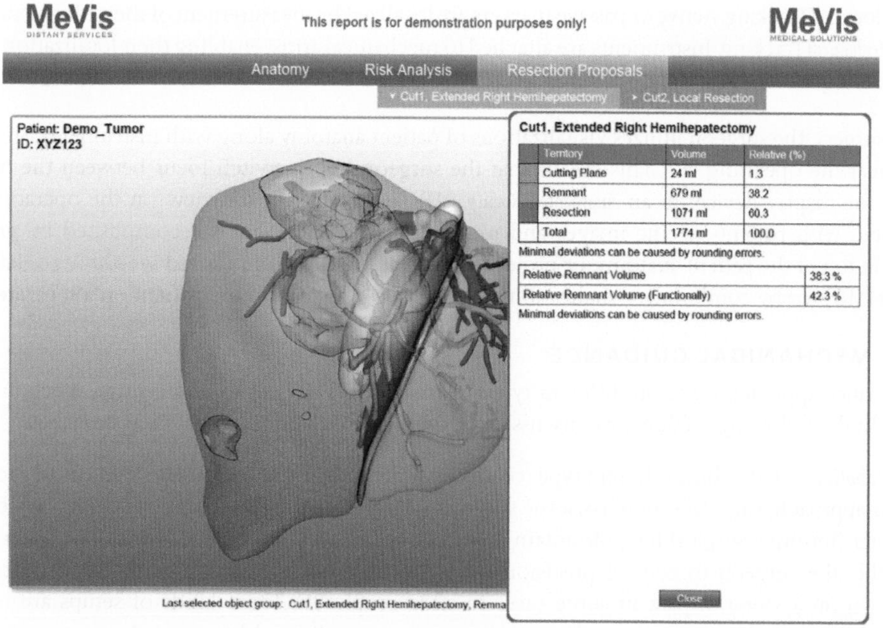

FIGURE 17.16 *Example of liver resection documentation prepared by MeVis Distant Services for its surgical clients.*

guidance, where the documentation takes the form of a three-dimensional replica of the surgical site. The manufacturing process has been significantly improved in recent years. It is cheaper, more versatile and supports a wide variety of materials. Rapid prototyping will play an increasingly important role in surgical guidance in the coming years.

17.4.3 IMAGE-BASED GUIDANCE

Image-guided Surgery, or IGS, refers to surgery where preoperative imaging is used together with intraoperative tracking, and in some cases intraoperative imaging, to guide the surgical procedure [Peters, 2006]. The preoperative image data is associated with, or *registered* to, the patient, so that tracked instruments and patient anatomy can be shown in the context of the preoperative image data and surgical plan. Intraoperative imaging is sometimes used to further improve the registration between patient and preoperative data.

IGS starts with acquisition of tomographic images from the patient, preferably as close to the time of operation as possible. At the start of surgery, preoperative imaging and medical instruments are associated with the patient. To this end, the surgeon either identifies corresponding anatomical landmarks on both the anatomy of the virtual and real patient, or obtains images during surgery and registers them to the preoperative images using techniques described in § 4.8. Once the virtual and real patient are aligned, medical instruments are tracked with respect to the patient by employing one or more of the four main tracking technologies [Hassfeld and Mühling, 2001]:

- *Optical* Tracking. Passive or active (light-emitting) markers are localized using video cameras, often in a stereo configuration.
- *Electromagnetic* Tracking. Active markers affect an imposed electromagnetic field, thus enabling their three-dimensional localization.
- *Ultrasound* Tracking. Active or passive markers are localized by measurement of their ultrasonic echoes.
- *Mechanical* Tracking. Instruments are attached to mechanical arms, enabling their localization through reading out the angles of the joints.

During surgery, the surgeon utilizes visualizations of patient anatomy along with instruments on a display device near the operating site. This means that the surgeon has to switch focus between the operating site and the display device. In an *Augmented Reality* (AR) environment, the view on the operating site is augmented with patient-specific images and medical instruments. This is accomplished by projecting images on top of the patient anatomy, or projecting images on a video-projected see-through *Head Mounted Display* (HMD), or by combining visualizations with a live video feed of the patient on a separate display.

17.4.4 MECHANICAL GUIDANCE

This guidance approach relies on different types of mechanical devices to guide surgical actions during surgery. In the following sections, we discuss three types of mechanical guidance approaches.

Medical Robotics Of the three different types of mechanical guidance, *Medical Robotics* is the most prominent. With this approach, surgical robots assist the surgeon with performing the planned surgery. Systems such as Da Vinci (Intuitive Surgical Inc., Mountain View, CA) and Zeus (Computer Motion Inc., Santa Barbara, CA) enable the surgeon to control precision robotic arms from a console, where the surgical site is also shown on a video display, in some cases in stereoscopic 3D. These kinds of setups are especially useful in minimally-invasive surgery. Their advantages over traditional laparoscopic surgery include the 3D visualization of the surgical site, something that in traditional laparoscopy is monoscopic, improved dexterity, more degrees of freedom, elimination of physiologic tremors, ability to scale motion from the surgeon's macroscopic input to microscopic actuating arms, possibility to perform surgery at a distance, and ergonomics Lanfranco *et al.* [2004].

Patient-specific Instruments Patient-specific instruments are guidance instruments, analogous to jigs in manufacturing, that are designed and manufactured for a specific patient anatomy and surgical planning. They are designed to fit uniquely on some part of the patient anatomy, usually the bony structures, after which they can act as a guide for drilling, sawing, and other surgical actions. Usually these instruments are designed based on medical imaging data of the patient along with the parameters of the surgical planning.

Radermacher *et al.* [1998] discussed the application of such guidance devices, manufactured with a computer-controlled milling device, in spine, hip, and knee surgery, and applied it clinically for pelvic repositioning osteotomies. Goffin *et al.* [2001] presented a patient-specific template with drill guides for inserting screws in the C2 vertebra. The template was manufactured using medical grade stereolithographic rapid prototyping techniques. It was evaluated on cadavers, and underwent preliminary clinical testing. Other examples include a patient-specific device for guide-wire positioning in hip surface replacement [Raaijmaakers *et al.*, 2010], shown in Figure 17.17, and templates for total knee replacement [Hafez *et al.*, 2006].

Adjustable Instruments Adjustable instruments are similar to patient-specific instruments in that they are supposed to fit uniquely on the patient anatomy in order to guide some surgical action according to the performed planning. They deviate, in that they can be adjusted if necessary, even during the surgery itself. The general idea is that the instrument can be adjusted, based on the surgical planning stage, to encapsulate information about both the planning and the patient anatomy. When the instrument is attached to the patient anatomy during surgery, it helps to guide surgical actions. If the planning is fine-tuned, the guidance instrument can be readjusted.

Steppacher *et al.* [2011] demonstrated this idea for total hip replacement with a device called the *HipSextant*. During planning, the surgeon specifies three anatomical points and the desired hip cup orientation based on 3D visualizations of the patient CT data, after which the planning software automatically calculates the adjustable parameters of the HipSextant. During surgery, the HipSextant fits on the bony anatomy of the patient. If for example the desired cup orientation is changed, the instrument can be adjusted to follow suit. Figure 17.18 shows the virtual and the real HipSextant device.

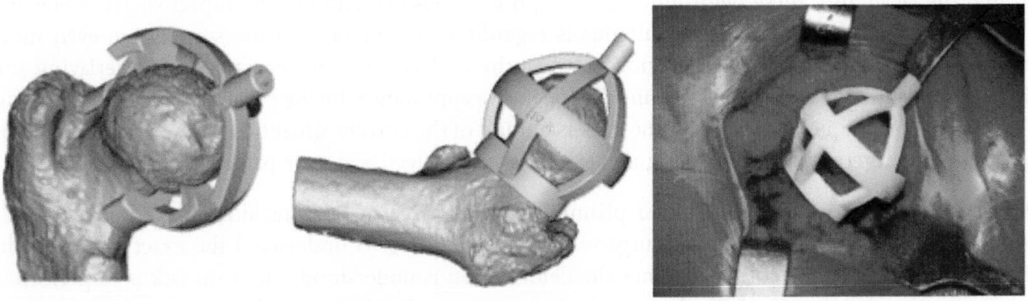

FIGURE 17.17 *Drill guide for hip resurfacing surgery (From: Raaijmaakers et al., [2010]).*

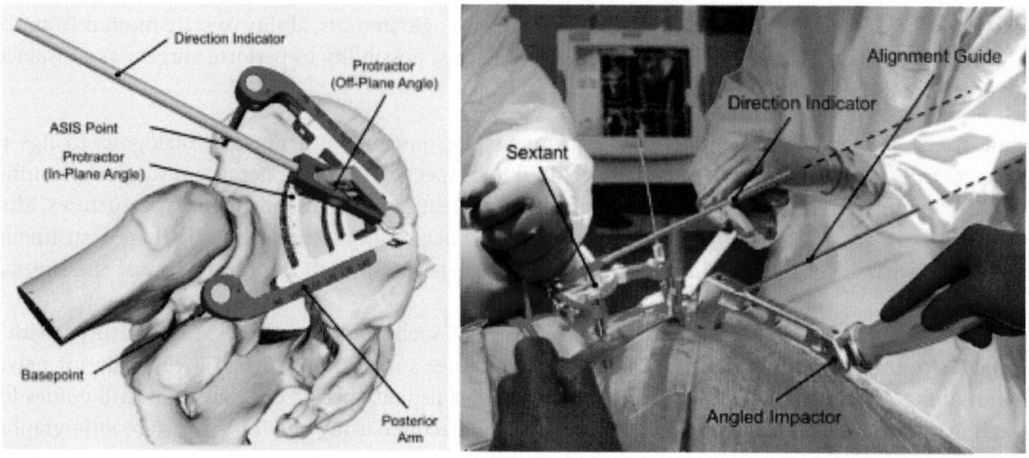

FIGURE 17.18 *Adaptive instruments for placement of artificial cup in hip surgery, in both pre and intraoperative phase* (From: Steppacher et al. [2011]).

17.5 APPLICATION AREAS

Computer-assisted surgery has been applied in several areas of surgery, of which oral and maxillofacial surgery, brain surgery, orthopedic surgery, and hepatic surgery are the most prominent ones, judging by the amount of literature. The following sections we discuss each of the application areas, focusing on the role of visualization.

17.5.1 ORAL AND MAXILLOFACIAL SURGERY

Oral and maxillofacial surgery (OMS) refers to surgery performed on the craniomaxillofacial complex, consisting of the skull, mouth, jaws, neck, face, and surrounding tissues, such as nerves and muscles. Severe facial trauma, tumors, congenital defects in the facial region, and aesthetics are the most important reasons for undergoing OMS. OMS deals primarily with the reconstruction, cutting, and relocation of bones in the facial area, also called orthognathic surgery, and treatment of soft tissues of the face in plastic and reconstructive surgery.

Motivation In OMS, the main goal is to repair deformities of the craniomaxillofacial complex. Being in and around the facial area, these deformities are exceptionally visible, and greatly impact social interaction [Mollemans et al., 2007]. Hence, requirements regarding the outcome of the surgery are even more stringent. Due to the complex interaction between the underlying bony structures and overlaying soft tissues such as muscle and skin, predicting postoperative appearance during planning can be challenging. Visualization techniques that facilitate the understanding of the current situation and the desired outcome augment the surgeon's planning ability, and can be used in effective doctor-patient communication.

Pipeline The general tasks (§ 17.2) for planning and guidance in OMS include spatial understanding of anatomy and pathology, with the surgeon's main goal being to understand the exact nature of the deformation that is to be corrected. Once the deformation is understood, the main task is to perform a reconstruction planning (§ 17.2), during which the surgeon decides exactly how to cut and reconstruct bony structures and soft tissues to reach the desired end result. However, OMS also includes tumor resection, hence in the relevant cases involving also access, resection, and implant planning [Hassfeld and Mühling, 2001].

Computer-assisted OMS was one of the earliest examples of computer-assisted surgery documented in the academic literature. Vannier *et al.* [1983b] presented a system for the extraction and CAD-based modeling of 3D surfaces of the skull and skin from preoperative CT, diagnosis, and surgical planning based on these surfaces, and finally postoperative CT-based evaluation. By the time of publication, their system had already been used in over two-hundred clinical cases.

Their work already embodied most of the standard pipeline for OMS. Preoperative imaging is used to generate suitable visualizations of the patient in which the anatomy and relevant pathology (deformation or tumor) can be studied. Based on this, a surgical plan including access, resection, reconstruction, and implants, as well as an outcome simulation (§ 17.3.3), can be made. In the case of OMS, it is even more important than usual to discuss the planning and the expected outcome with the patient, due to the visibility and impact of the results. During surgery, any one of the guidance approaches (§ 17.4) can be used. After surgery, postoperative imaging can be used to evaluate the results.

Image Acquisition In OMS, CT, MRI, and ultrasound are used. In order to be able to image all relevant structures, it is advantageous to be able to fuse the different modalities [Hassfeld and Mühling, 2001]. CT is used for imaging the osseous structures, but suffers from metal artifacts. MRI is not only used due to its zero-radiation nature and soft tissue imaging capabilities, but also due to its ability to image on arbitrary planes, and to its functional imaging possibilities. MRI can also suffer from motion and metal artifacts. Ultrasound is ubiquitous and can be used to measure functional parameters such as circulation and vascular support, but suffers from noise and geometrical distortions and cannot faithfully depict skeletal structures.

Image Processing In order to plan a reconstruction or a tumor resection, segmentations of the bony structures, the tumor if present, at-risk structures, such as vessels and nerves, the skin surface, and other soft tissues such as the muscles are required. These segmentations are required for the straightforward visualization of the anatomy and pathology, but also for the predictive outcome simulation described in the next paragraph. In practice, segmentation is still mostly done with semi-automatic thresholding and region growing [Marchetti *et al.*, 2011, Swennen *et al.*, 2009], although the use of more modern techniques such as the level set method have been reported [Mollemans *et al.*, 2007]. Swennen *et al.* [2009] presented a method based the image registration and processing of two scans (one low dosage) of the patient with different bits.

Visualization As explained previously, the predicted postoperative appearance is very important. This example of outcome simulation (§ 17.3.3) is used during the planning to check the effect of surgical actions, and in doctor-patient communication. In one of the earliest OMS examples, Altobelli *et al.* [1993] segmented anatomical structures from CT data, and then manually repositioned soft tissue fragments based on the bony surfaces under them, in certain cases taking into account bone-skin motion ratios from literature. With this, it was possible to visualize the possible outcome of a craniofacial procedure, also in terms of how the patient's skin surface geometry would change.

Currently, more advanced soft tissue simulation techniques are used, such as the finite element method (FEM) [Bro-Nielsen, 1998], the mass-spring model (MSM), and the mass tensor model (MTM) [Cotin *et al.*, 2000b]. These models need to combine *accurate enough* performance with *interactivity*, as it is important for the surgeon to be able to explore different possibilities during the planning. In a quantitative and qualitative comparison of linear and non-linear FEM, MSM, and MTM methods, Mollemans *et al.* [2007]

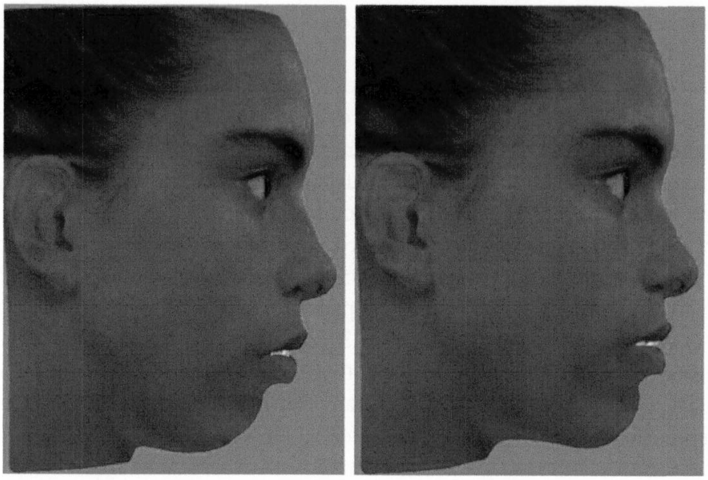

FIGURE 17.19 *On the left, visualization of the textured preoperative face of the patient and on the right, the predicted postoperative situation (From: [Mollemans et al., 2007]).*

found MTM and linear FEM to be the most accurate, with MTM being significantly faster than the other approaches. Figure 17.19 shows the visualizations used by Mollemans *et al.* [2007] for the qualitative evaluation of the outcome prediction. This gives an impression of the functionality of OMS planning tools. Note that photographic information of the patient is mapped onto the 3D skin surface. Soft tissue deformation is discussed in more detail in § 21.5.1.

Intraoperative Guidance As explained in § 17.4.3, image-based guidance of oral and maxillofacial surgery can employ mechanical, electromagnetic, ultrasound, or optical navigation. The accuracy of the registration between preoperative data and the intraoperative situation is crucial. In order to help ensure this, guidance often makes use of a stereotactic frame, or of anatomical, and artificial markers, such as screws or a dental splint.

By tracking surgical instruments and relating preoperative imaging and planning to the intraoperative situation, surgeons can successfully perform their planned actions.

17.5.2 ORTHOPEDIC SURGERY

Orthopedic surgery refers to the surgical treatment of musculo-skeletal trauma, degenerative diseases, infections, congenital disorders, and tumors in or near bones. *Computer-assisted orthopedic surgery* (CAOS) is the specialism of CAS that deals with orthopedic surgery.

In orthopedic surgery, examples of commonly performed procedures are the following:

- In joint replacement, or arthroplasty, damaged joints are replaced by artificial endoprostheses.
- Bone fractures are surgically repaired when conservative treatment has failed, or is associated with increased risk.
- Spinal fusion is used to treat deformities of the spine or pain due to abnormal motion. Two or more vertebrae are joined by fixating them with pedicle screws and other metal structures.
- Bone tumors are surgically removed.

Motivation The human skeleton is centrally important for human mobility. Orthopedic surgery can have a significant effect on short-term and long-term post-operative patient function. For example in shoulder replacement, the patient's ability to perform activities of daily living, such as eating, or self-care, should be maintained as well as possible. Furthermore, the long-term durability of the shoulder prosthesis should be maximized, in order to minimize the chances of high-risk revision surgery. By integrating preoperative data acquisition and computer technology in the surgical process, surgeons have more information to help guide their decision-making.

Pipeline As there are CAOS systems catering to a number of different orthopedic surgical procedures, all tasks in § 17.2 are relevant. Based on preoperative imaging and other measurements, CAOS systems enable surgeons to visualize and measure parameters of the surgical site, for example, to help decide on the size and type of an endoprosthesis. This stage can involve functionality for virtually performing the surgery so that different approaches can be experimented with, in some cases with outcome simulation (§ 17.3.3). Surgical guidance can take any of the forms discussed in § 17.4. Image-based guidance products are commercially available.

Image Acquisition In the planning of joint replacement, it is still common to employ template-over-X-ray planning. Transparencies of different endoprostheses are manually overlaid on X-rays of the joint that is to be replaced, and visually judged by the surgeon. In general, X-rays are commonly used for diagnosis and surgical planning in orthopedics.

CAOS systems often make use of CT datasets acquired preoperatively, as these offer high resolution 3D datasets with the best bone-soft tissue contrast. However, Langlotz and Nolte [2004] point out that this is not always the best option for all orthopedic procedures. Some procedures, such as lumbar pedicle screw placement, can be sufficiently accurately performed with fluoroscopy-based navigation (see § 2.9.2 for more information on fluoroscopy), in contrast to preoperative CT with image-based guidance. An interesting alternative is a procedure called *Surgeon Defined Anatomy* (SDA), where anatomical information is required by probing bone surfaces during surgery using a navigated instrument. This method can be further enhanced by deforming statistical shape models of the bones in question to fit the acquired surface landmarks [Fleute *et al.*, 1999, Stindel *et al.*, 2002].

Image Processing Bony structures have to be segmented from preoperative data. With CT, there is sufficient contrast between bony structures and the surrounding tissues to facilitate segmentation. However, by definition there is some pathology involved, and this can have a detrimental effect on the image quality which in turn complicates segmentation. Think of diseases affecting bone density and joint space, such as arthritis, the presence of endoprostheses causing metal artifacts, or bone trauma that results in many different fractures that need to be segmented.

Segmentation approaches often make use of region growing, followed by a number of corrective steps to close boundaries, fill holes, and refine boundary locations by use of image gradients and extracted surfaces [Kang *et al.*, 2003]. Joint separation is an often-occurring challenge due to its necessity for joint replacement planning, and its complication due to joint space narrowing. Techniques employ joint-specific heuristics [Zoroofi *et al.*, 2003] or iterative refinement and additional image features such as surface curvature [Krekel *et al.*, 2010].

The segmented structures are used for virtually performing surgical actions, such as implanting an endoprosthesis, resecting bone, or implanting a screw, and for simulation, both structural and kinematic.

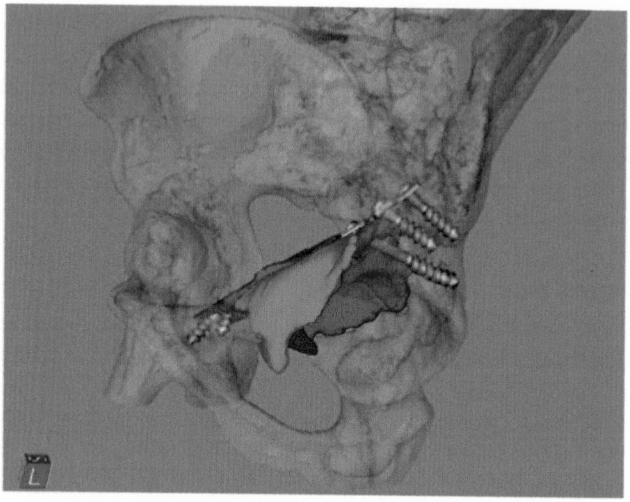

FIGURE 17.20 *Fixation of pelvic fragments for trauma surgery. Individual fragments are color-coded. By making the pelvis partially transparent, the direction and length of the fixation screws is visible* (From: [Cimerman and Kristan, 2007]).

Visualization During computer-assisted orthopedic surgery planning, three main tasks are performed. The first is examining virtual representations of the anatomy and pathology in order to build up familiarity with the intraoperative situation. The second is interacting with the visual representations by virtually performing surgical actions, such as placing a screw or implant, hereby exploring aspects such as prosthesis size, and bone-prosthesis fit. Finally, outcome simulations can be performed to predict the expected results of surgical actions in terms of structure and function, as discussed in § 17.3.3.

As discussed in § 17.3.1, there is a strong preference for basic MPR visualization, unless the complexity of the anatomy or the planned procedure calls for 3D representations. For example, Figure 17.20 shows a computerized planning of a multipart pelvic fracture repair.

Intraoperative Guidance Guidance during orthopedic surgery is similar to that performed in Oral and Maxillofacial Surgery, discussed in § 17.5.1. Figure 17.21 shows an example of a pedicle screw placement being navigated with an optical guidance system.

17.5.3 NEUROSURGERY

Neurosurgery, or neurological surgery, refers to surgery in the brain, the spinal cord, and other nerves. In neurosurgery, either affected tissue is removed or studied, or the function of the brain and nervous system is augmented or modulated with a neural prosthesis or implant. Examples of tissue removal and study include the resection of brain tumors, also called *gliomas*, the removal of epilepsy-triggering parts of the cortex, or tissue biopsies. Examples of neural prostheses include electrical spinal cord stimulators for pain treatment and deep brain stimulation devices for movement disorders. Some neurosurgical procedures are open, in which case a craniotomy, or temporary removal of a bone segment from the skull to access the brain, has to be performed, while other procedures, such as biopsies, are performed minimally-invasively.

Motivation The brain houses human consciousness and personality, and is also responsible for a great deal of our low level functionality. Damage to the brain carries with it a great deal of risk. Patients could lose

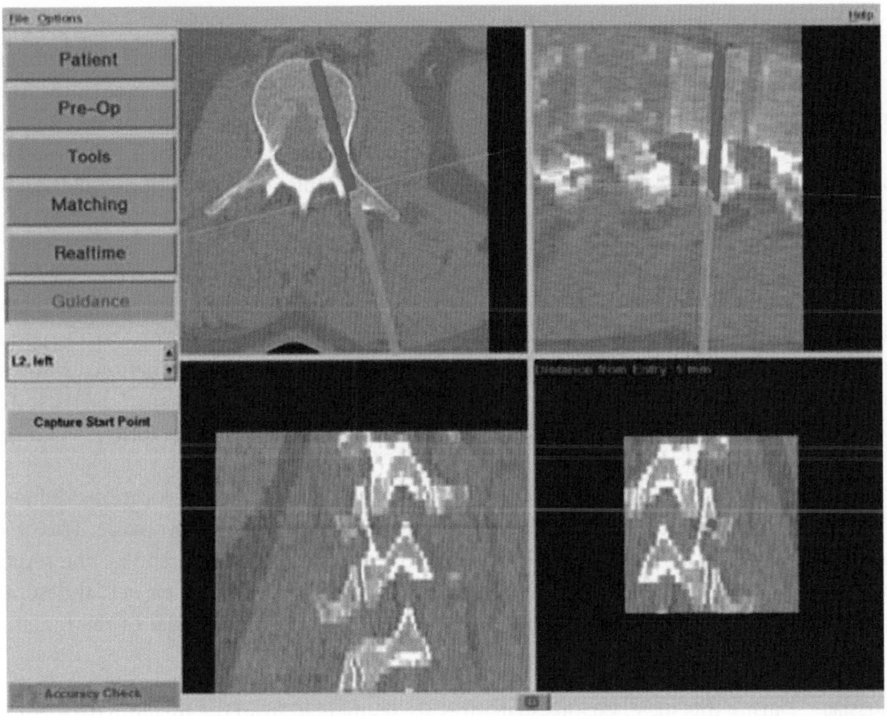

FIGURE 17.21 *CT-based navigation of pedicle screw placement in vertebra L2. The pre-operatively planned screw insertion is shown in red and the intraoperatively tracked screw placement instrument is shown in green (From: [Langlotz and Nolte, 2004]).*

important functionality, undergo personality changes or even lose their lives if the brain is damaged. It makes sense that every measure that has the potential of increasing the safety and probability of success of brain surgery is considered immensely important.

Computer-assisted surgery has proved to be just such a measure. Maciunas [2006] states: "Computer-assisted neurosurgery has become so successful that it is rapidly becoming indistinguishable from, quite simply, neurosurgery." The integration of modern medical imaging techniques with which both the structure and function of neural tissue can be studied, advanced visualization techniques and surgical guidance all contribute to better surgery on this critically important human organ.

Pipeline The general tasks for planning and guidance are spatial understanding of anatomy (§ 17.2) and pathology (§ 17.2). Understanding the embedding of the tissue that is to be removed within its vulnerable surroundings is important. Access planning (§ 17.2) is always relevant, as the surgical site has to be reached often via the skull and via healthy neural structures. Depending on the specific procedure, for example tumor resection, or stent placement, resection or implant planning is also performed.

Already in the late 1970s and early 1980s, work started on using three-dimensional graphics from preoperative CT to locate and display brain lesions preoperatively [Brown, 1979, Kelly and Alker, 1981]. This information was used to adjust a stereotactic frame intraoperatively in order to be able to access these lesions, either for biopsy or for resection. In neurosurgery, stereotactic frames are mechanical devices that are attached to the skull during surgery and can then be used as reference coordinate systems.

Computer-assisted neurosurgery still follows this general recipe. Some form of pre-operative imaging coupled with suitable image processing and visualization is employed in order to plan the surgical procedure. In the case of neurosurgery, there are more interesting than usual examples, such as the use of fMRI for the determination of important regions of neural activity, for example in the motor cortex. During surgery, either a stereotactic frame is used and the procedure is called *frame-based*, or it is not used, in which case it is called *frameless*. In both cases image-based guidance is employed. In the following paragraphs, we will discuss each of these stages in more detail.

Image Acquisition Neurosurgery makes use of CT as well as MRI and its variants, such as MRA, fMRI, and DTI. CT and MRI are used for imaging the general structure of anatomy and pathology. MRA, or Magnetic Resonance Angiography, emphasizes blood vessels. DTI, or diffusion tensor imaging, can be used to image the neural fiber bundles that should be spared during surgery, while fMRI, or functional MRI, is used to chart out important functional regions in the cortex of the brain that need to be spared. DTI and fMRI are discussed in more detail in Chapter 15. In some cases, positron emission tomography (PET), may also be used for the improved location of tumor tissue.

For certain procedures, such as the placement of electrical stimulators in locations defined by the electrophysiology of the brain, electrophysiological measurements have to be made. This is done by inserting a recording and/or stimulating electrode into the brain [Finnis *et al.*, 2003]. The responses are measured via electrodes, as well as the patient's physiological responses and their verbal descriptions of their experiences. Based on this information, the surgeon builds a mental model of the function of the relevant part of the brain.

Image Processing During this stage, various structures are segmented from the imaging data. For example, brain tumor segmentations are used to measure their shape and volume, while segmentations of the whole brain are used to improve intraoperative registration [Archip *et al.*, 2007], and used as mask for other data, for example DTI-derived parameters [Clark *et al.*, 2003]. In the case of fMRI and DTI, the acquired data is further processed to yield respectively regions of neural activation or fiber tractographies.

Registration is used extensively to fuse different modalities preoperatively, and to map patient-specific data to the available atlases of the brain so that anatomical structures can be identified.

Visualization During the visualization stage, the main goals of the neurosurgeon include general familiarization with the complex 3D anatomy and pathology, and especially the accurate localization of the target structures, for example the tumor, and risk structures, for example fiber bundles from DTI, important functional brain regions from fMRI and blood vessels. In most cases however, the overarching goal is specifying an access path to the pathology that minimizes damage to the risk structures [Gering *et al.*, 1999a, Beyer *et al.*, 2007, Rieder *et al.*, 2008].

Related to this, is answering the important question whether a lesion is operable or not. Tumors can either infiltrate or push aside functional tissue [Gering *et al.*, 1999a]. In the latter case they are operable, in the former case not. Gering *et al.* [1999a] give another example with a tumor in Broca's area on the left side of the brain, where speech processing normally takes place. Through the 3D visualization of fMRI data, it could be established that the speech activity had already migrated to the right side of the brain.

Systems include at least slice-based visualization of preoperative data. Examining stacks of slices and then mentally building up a 3D representation of the relevant structures can probably still be called the norm. More recent examples combine various different modalities to offer the best possible view of the anatomy, with a special focus on the risk structures, and the pathology. Beyer *et al.* [2007] combined CT, MRI, DSA, PET, and fMRI in interactive multimodal volume rendering for the planning of surgery

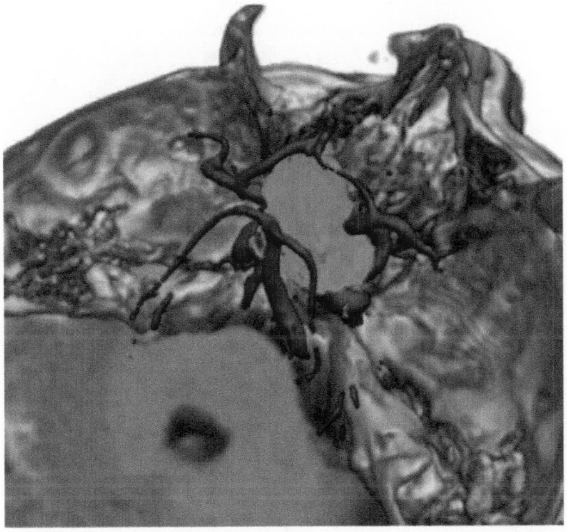

FIGURE 17.22 *Combined rendering of CT, MRI, and MRA for tumor resection planning (From: Beyer et al. [2007]).*

of deep-seated lesions in the brain. CT and MRI are suitable for imaging the tissues of the brain and the enclosing skull. DSA, or Digital Subtraction Angiography, shows vessels. PET, as mentioned above, highlights tumor metabolism. See Figure 17.22 for an example. Blaas *et al.* [2007a] demonstrated that MRI, fMRI, and DTI could be combined in a system supporting dynamic queries, for example showing all fiber bundles servicing selected neural regions of activity and within a certain distance of the tumor.

Rieder *et al.* [2008] introduced visualization techniques to facilitate the specification of an access path, for example highlighting risk structures close to the tumor and to the path, and explicitly showing the depth to the tumor when the view direction is head on. See Figure 17.23 for an example. Their system is also interesting insofar as they manage with only MRI, fMRI, and DTI, but no CT. Furthermore, they underline the importance of showing landmarks during planning that can be located also during surgery, for example the gyri and sulci on the cortex, and landmarks on the skull itself.

Virtual endoscopy techniques are also used for the planning of minimally-invasive neurosurgery. An example of this, the planning of minimally-invasive pituitary gland surgery is discussed in § 13.6.4.

In *deep brain stimulation*, or DBS, stimulating electrodes are implanted in deep brain structures, such as the *thalamus* or the *basal ganglia*. DBS is often used to treat Parkinson's disease, a debilitating disorder of the central nervous system, as well as other movement disorders. Before the electrodes can be implanted, trajectories from the surface of the head to the electrode target locations have to be determined. These trajectories have to avoid critical brain structures in order to minimize the risk of complications. This is a good example of surgical *access planning* as described in § 17.2.

Bériault *et al.* [2012] present a comprehensive approach to the planning of such procedures. By using different MRI protocols, their system calculates a whole collection of trajectories that satisfy a number of surgical criteria, such as the avoidance of critical brain structures like the venous and arterial vessels. Their approach is able to deal with a configurable set of both hard and soft constraints, and finally yields a safety-based ranking of the possible trajectories. The trajectories are visualized as a color-mapped surface on the 3D cortex, based on which the most suitable trajectory can be selected by the neurosurgeon. The approach was retrospectively evaluated on 14 DBS planning cases, on which it generally came up

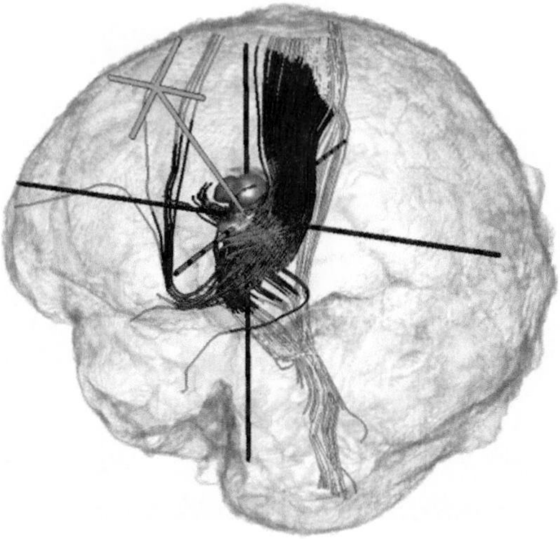

FIGURE 17.23 *Computerized access planning for brain tumor removal, consisting of an access path (cyan) lesion and functional data (Courtesy of Christian Rieder, Fraunhofer MEVIS. See also [Rieder et al., 2008]).*

with lower risk trajectories. The two participating neurosurgeons qualitatively evaluated all automatically computed trajectories as suitable for surgery, and in many cases equivalent or preferable to the trajectories that were actually used in surgery. Essert *et al.* [2012] detail a similar solution to the problem, but make use of a *geometric constraint solver* based on DBS planning rules that they had acquired from neurosurgeons, as well as on patient-specific and generic image data, to compute an optimal trajectory.

Intraoperative Guidance Neurosurgical guidance can take three main forms [Grunert *et al.*, 2003]. Anatomical landmarks, for example bony landmarks, cranial nerves and vessels, can be used by the surgeon to mentally match the current intraoperative situation to the preoperative planning. This guidance approach, an example of the *mental model* guidance approach (§ 17.4.1), is mature and is often preferred for microneurosurgery, that is neurosurgery done under a surgical microscope and with miniaturized instruments.

Alternatively, mechanical devices, such as a stereotactic frame, can be used for procedures requiring a straight access path. With these frame-based approaches, an instance of *mechanical guidance* (§ 17.4.4), a target position and straight trajectory to it, preoperatively determined often based on imaging, can be accurately guided during surgery. However, unlike anatomical guidance, this method does not allow for easy adaptation during surgery.

Finally, computer-based navigation, including the use of tracking equipment and intraoperative imaging, falls somewhere in between the previous two methods in terms of flexibility and accuracy. Following the general image-based guidance pipeline (§ 17.4.3), the neurosurgical procedure is planned based on pre-operative imaging. During surgery, the patient's anatomy is fixed or continuously tracked, and the preoperative imaging and plan are registered to it. Surgical instruments are also tracked so that they can be displayed relative to the tracked anatomy and the rich preoperative data. Anatomy and instrument tracking can take place via optical, electromagnetic, and ultrasound tracking systems or via intraoperative imaging.

Intraoperative imaging plays a further important role in neurosurgical guidance. A common problem with image-based guidance in neurological surgery is the occurrence of brain shift [Roberts *et al.*, 1998].

Between the time of image acquisition, diagnosis and actual surgery and during the surgery itself, brain tissue shape can change significantly. Brain shift occurs due to physiological motion, swelling, removal of tissue, displacement of cerebrospinal fluid, and so on. With intraoperative imaging, the preoperative data and planning can be updated to the possibly changed shape of the brain tissue [Gering *et al.*, 1999a].

Finally, as mentioned in the acquisition paragraph, various techniques are used intraoperatively to chart out functional regions of the brain by making use of general anatomical knowledge, cortical stimulation, transcranial magnetic stimulation, magnetic source imaging, MEG and fMRI. In some cases, the acquisition is done during surgery, and in others preoperative imaging is mapped to the surgical situation. Schulder *et al.* [1998] compared preoperative fMRI imaging data, registered to a frameless stereotactic system, with Somatosensory Evoked Potentials (SSEPs; currents sent via electrodes through skin to map out nerve pathways) and cortical stimulation intraoperatively. They showed that surgery on lesions in or around the sensorimotor cortex could be performed safely based only on preoperative fMRI.

17.5.4 HEPATIC SURGERY

The most common liver diseases are primary hepatic carcinoma, hepatitis C, and liver cirrhosis. Depending on the characteristics and the severity of the disease, surgical treatment might be necessary. Common strategies aim at removing the diseased parts of the liver, or at replacing them with a graft from a living donor (*Living Donor Liver Transplantation* or LDLT) or from donated specimens of the liver. When a liver tumor is not resectable, alternative treatment options are radio frequency ablation (RFA) or *interstitial laser coagulation* [Heisterkamp *et al.*, 1999] (ILC). Both are minimally-invasive techniques where tumor tissue is destroyed by introducing a thin probe into the tumor and heating it up with either radio frequency or optical energy.

Motivation Traditional liver surgery poses a number of challenges, in particular the resection of parts of the liver. Resection can have a profound impact on liver blood flow. Liver resection planning is usually based on the Couinaud classification, which divides the liver into eight autonomous segments or vascular territories. These territories mark regions of vascular structures that can be resected relatively safely without harming the blood flow of other territories. However, due to the varying shape and size of the liver from patient to patient, as well as the effect that pathology, such as a tumor can have on the segmentation, this scheme is not always reliable. The introduction of 3D medical imaging has made it possible to use patient-specific data as the basis for improved liver surgery planning. In the case of RFA or ILC treatment, a probe tip has to be positioned as accurately as possible within tumor tissue. Here it is also clear that the integration of 3D medical imaging and visualization can help to ensure successful outcome.

Pipeline In this case, the general tasks for planning and guidance are spatial understanding of anatomy (§ 17.2) and pathology (§ 17.2), as the location of the tumor relative to the liver vasculature heavily affects the resection strategy, and is also important in the case of ablation. Furthermore, this is a clear example of the access (§ 17.2) and resection planning tasks (§ 17.2).

Computer-assisted liver surgery systems generally offer an environment in which the liver and its vessels can be visualized along with the embedded pathology, based on CT or MRI data. In the case of resection planning, a straight or curved resection plan can be specified, maximizing the removal of the pathology while minimizing damage to the surroundings, and especially to the portal venous supply and venous drainage. In the case of ablation-based treatment, a suitable access path can be planned. During surgery, guidance can be given either via documentation of the resection plan, or via image guidance, for example with intraoperative ultrasound or an augmented reality projection. Reduction in tumor size can be postoperatively examined based on a new CT scan. In the following, we will discuss each of these pipeline stages in more detail.

Image Acquisition Usually contrast-enhanced CT images are used for liver surgery planning, although there are examples of MRI [Hashimoto *et al.*, 1991, Masutani *et al.*, 1995]. Regular CT images expose vascular structures poorly, due to minimal differences between the intensity levels of vessels and surrounding tissue. For this reason a contrast agent is injected in the blood stream during image acquisition.

Image Processing In order to better control the effect of surgery on the blood supply of the parts of the liver remaining after resection, it is important to segment and model the vessels of the liver, the vascular territories, and the pathology that is to be removed or treated. For general planning purposes, an accurate description of the liver boundary should also be available. A great number of approaches to these segmentation and modeling tasks have been proposed [Heimann *et al.*, 2009, Schenk *et al.*, 2000], varying from the manual, through the interactive to the fully automatic [Soler *et al.*, 2001]. For example, Zahlten *et al.* [1995] employed wavefront propagation, similar to region growing, within the vascular tree, with bifurcation recognition, and symbolic tree generation being performed contemporaneously. This algorithm resulted in a label mask of the vessels, with each label value pointing back to the accompanying symbolic tree representation storing higher-level information about the topology of the extracted tree. Alternative approaches first compute the mask of the vessel tree, and then simplify the voxel mask using skeletonization and smoothing techniques [Soler *et al.*, 2001]. Selle *et al.* [2002] presented a complete pipeline for the segmentation, analysis, and visualization of the hepatic vasculature. This pipeline was integrated in the HepaVision product, and had in this context already been used in 130 oncologic resections and 40 living-related liver transplants.

Visualization As mentioned above, liver surgery planning tools generally provide an environment within which the liver, its vessels, the vascular territories and the pathology can be visualized. Within this environment, the parameters of the liver resection can be determined, either by specifying a linear or deformable cutting plane, or by specifying the volume that needs to be removed, for example with slice-drawing [Konrad-Verse *et al.*, 2004]. Resection proposals have also been automatically computed [Bourquain *et al.*, 2002]. In the case of ablation or coagulation, a suitable probe entry position and direction can be determined.

Intraoperative Guidance Image-guided surgery techniques (§ 17.4.3) can be used for the guidance of liver surgery. By matching vessel centerlines extracted from intraoperative ultrasound (IOUS) to the pre-operative vessel centerlines and taking into account deformation, and then combining this with optical instrument tracking, surgical actions can be shown within the context of the high resolution pre-operative data and surgical plan [Lange *et al.*, 2004b]. Alternatively, laser range scanning technology can be used to match the liver surface, instead of IOUS with vessel centerlines [Cash *et al.*, 2007]. Feuerstein *et al.* [2008] have presented experimental results on using augmented reality for the guidance of minimally-invasive, i.e., laparoscopic, liver resection.

The resection plan can also be represented using a 2D Resection Map [Lamata *et al.*, 2010] or a simplified Risk Map [Hansen *et al.*, 2010c] for use as documentation-based guidance (§ 17.4.2) during surgery. In a similar vein, Tumor Maps have been proposed for the postoperative evaluation of tumor ablation results [Rieder *et al.*, 2008]. All three of these techniques are discussed in more detail in § 14.5.2.

17.6 CONCLUSIONS

In this chapter, we discussed computer-assisted surgery from a visualization standpoint. During our discussion, we introduced the CAS pipeline, describing the different stages that usually occur, namely image acquisition, image processing and visualization in the planning phase, and finally the guidance phase. We listed the general tasks that practitioners need to do using CAS systems. We then discussed the different visualization techniques employed in CAS, divided into three classes: Visual Representation, Interaction, and Simulation. We have not discussed measurement here, although it is essential in CAS. Measurements in medical visualization are treated in Chapter 10. We detailed the four different approaches that can be employed to guide surgical actions, usually based on some form of preoperative planning. Finally, we discussed in some detail the four main application areas of CAS, namely oral and maxillofacial surgery, orthopedic surgery, neurosurgery, and hepatic surgery. For each of these application areas, our discussion followed the stages of the CAS pipeline.

As you will have seen, computer-assisted surgery is really a textbook example of medical visualization, spanning the whole gamut of methods, all the way from image acquisition, image processing, visualization, interaction, simulation, image-based guidance and tracking, and finally evaluation. Analyzing or developing CAS systems requires broad expertise across the whole spectrum.

It is also clear that neurosurgery is the application area where CAS is considered the most to be a necessary and default part of surgery. The statement is even made that it is not possible anymore to distinguish between neurosurgery and computer-assisted neurosurgery. The extreme risk involved in neurosurgery, as well as the early acceptance of the stereotactic frame, has helped to incorporate CAS this deeply. In other disciplines, for example orthopedics, surgical guidance is often eschewed, even when suitable equipment is available. There is still much work to be done in terms of measuring and showing the added value of computer-assisted surgery.

That being said, the *potential* of computer-assisted surgery is universally recognized. The deep integration of interactive simulation, in order to add information concerning physiology and projected postsurgical outcome, is an important avenue of research that will add significant value to existing solutions.

FURTHER READING

Joskowicz and Taylor [2001] and Taylor and Joskowicz [2002] reviewed CAS from an engineering perspective. They classify CAS systems as either being a *surgical CAD/CAM system* or a *surgical assistant system*. They give an outlook and propose future developments. Stoyanov *et al.* [2003] discussed the state of the art with respect to minimally-invasive computer-assisted surgery (MICAS). Vidal *et al.* [2006] have written an extensive review on medical virtual environments. Their work covers a broad spectrum, from educational tools to telemedicine. Kersten-Oertel *et al.* [2010] introduced the DVV taxonomy, in which Image-guided Surgery (IGS) is decomposed into Data, Visualization Processing, and View. They showed how to apply the taxonomy based on 15 state-of-the-art IGS papers. The work of Holmes *et al.* [2008] discussed the role of visualization in IGS. Earlier reviews include Rhodes [1997], Cinquin *et al.* [1995], Taylor *et al.* [1996], Haubner *et al.* [1997], Rhodes [1997], and Satava [1999].

Chapter 21, *Computer-Assisted Medical Education*, details the use of visual computing techniques also in the context of surgical training. Both training and planning applications are heavily reliant on surgical simulation concepts.

Chapter 18

Image-Guided Surgery and Augmented Reality

18.1 INTRODUCTION

In the previous chapters, we primarily learned about image analysis, visualization, and interaction techniques for diagnosis and treatment planning. These techniques may provide valuable support for treatment decisions, such as the surgical strategy with a particular access path to the pathology. However, surgeons and interventional radiologists demand also *intraoperative guidance* to deliver the treatment precisely, as it was planned. The use of printouts from a planning system is often of limited value, since it is very hard to translate them to the intraoperative situation.

This chapter focuses on techniques that are used during an intervention. Hence, they are called *intraoperative* in contrast to the previous *preoperative* techniques. In intraoperative visualization, a lot of research is motivated by the challenges of minimally-invasive surgery and interventions, such as needle insertion, laparoscopic and endoscopic interventions. In particular, we introduce augmented reality (AR) techniques where relevant information from preoperative images is superimposed with live images from surgery. Metaphorically, many people refer to this technology as *x-ray vision*, i.e., the surgeon is able to see through the skin or an organ and observes the operative site before he or she actually arrives there. Such technologies were introduced in the 1990s in industrial applications, such as the assembly and maintenance of aircrafts and cars. Workers were supported by placing blueprints onto surfaces [Kockro *et al.*, 2009]. In the car industry, AR is also used to support the early design stage where a physical model of a basic design is produced and then enhanced by projecting various details with regard to interior design. Thus, instead of producing many (expensive) physical models, variants are discussed by means of AR technology [Menk *et al.*, 2011]. In a similar way, planned resection lines, surgical targets, or risk structures may be displayed along with organ surfaces, the skull or other anatomical structures.

Potential and Risks of Intraoperative Guidance Intraoperative visualization, in particular in navigated surgical interventions, bears a great potential, similar to GPS-based car navigation. Ideally, the target regions, e.g., a deep-seated tumor, may be reached faster with reduced risks of harming critical structures, and consequently preoperative surgical planning may be realized more accurately. Thus, implants in total knee replacement, hip or shoulder replacement may be fitted more accurately and, hopefully, the rate of revision surgery is reduced. In very difficult cases, e.g., a large deep-seated tumor close to vital structures, navigation and intraoperative visualization may even shift the border of operability. Major application areas are ENT and neurosurgery as well as orthopedics.

However, from the very beginning we also want to make the reader aware of potential and real drawbacks. Intraoperative imaging, navigation and visualization is currently expensive, difficult to integrate in the narrow space of operating rooms and leads to considerable setup times that usually increase the overall duration of surgery. The competent use of all this technology, designed to ease the surgeon's tasks, requires considerable training that is far beyond the effort of learning to use a car navigation system. Once surgeons are able to use the technology, they start to rely on it and may overtrust it. At the same time, they may loose

Visual Computing for Medicine, Second Edition. http://dx.doi.org/10.1016/B978-0-12-415873-3.00018-3

some competence, that is necessary if the technology does not work properly. Compared to car navigation, where some drivers loose geographic knowledge to quickly locate a route in a street map, surgeons may become less familiar with anatomical peculiarities and anatomical variants within a particular patient.

Relation to Previous Chapters The discussion in this chapter is based on intraoperative imaging in § 2.9, where the intraoperative use of CT, MRI, fluoroscopy and ultrasound as well as image-guided interventions, such as tumor ablation, were discussed.

As another prerequisite for learning about image-guided surgery, we discussed human-computer interaction and in particular constraints related to the situation in an operating room (§ 5.8). There, we also briefly looked into ergonomic problems, in particular of minimally-invasive operations, where the surgical workspace is not directly visible in the patient, but presented on a monitor leading the surgeon to often change his or her head. Remote control of such monitors, e.g., with gestures and vision-based techniques was also discussed there. Mobile devices (recall § 5.9) have a great potential to provide support in the limited space of an operating room. However, problems of sterility have to be carefully considered.

Image-guided Surgery Intraoperative techniques are used when the patient is lying on the operating room (OR) table. Intraoperative visualization requires an appropriate dataset of the patient, preprocessing, e.g., segmentations, a sufficiently accurate registration procedure that maps the patient's dataset to the patient himself. Once this registration is obtained and carefully validated, visual output from the dataset and surgical instruments can be mapped to the patient. These instruments need to be tracked by a *navigation system*. Thus, surgeons can locate instruments on the patient (with their eyes) and in the dataset (through the registration mapping). This setup with a direct correlation between the patient's dataset and the patient is referred to as *image-guided surgery* (IGS). Many IGS setups also involve intraoperative imaging, such as fluoroscopy and intraoperative ultrasound. The basic scheme of IGS systems is shown in Figure 18.1.

Organization § 18.2 will look into general constraints for intraoperative visualization techniques and the setup of image-guided surgery (IGS). An IGS system combined with an optical device, e.g., a surgical

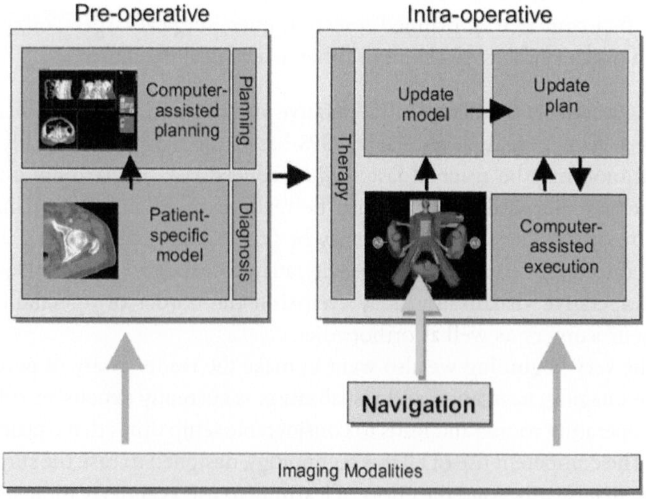

FIGURE 18.1 *Basic components of image-guided surgery systems (Courtesy of Michael Scheuering, SIEMENS Forchheim).*

microscope or endoscope enables *augmented reality* (AR) solutions where an overlay of patient data and the real patient in the OR is performed. This overlay requires to align the real patient data with the preoperative patient data, which is a typical registration problem to be discussed in § 18.3.

To guide physicians during surgery and interventions, instruments need to be localized or *tracked* with respect to patient data. In § 18.4, we describe such tracking techniques and discuss them with respect to accuracy and feasibility. For the usability and usefulness of medical AR, the *display mode* is essential. A special instance of intraoperative support by visualization and acoustic feedback is navigated control, discussed in § 18.5.

While the classical head-mounted display (HMD) has serious usability problems, more recently developed display modes, e.g., projection-based AR, video see-through devices, and more lightweight HMDs are more promising. These issues are discussed in § 18.6. Basic and advanced visualization techniques for medical AR are discussed in § 18.7. This includes illustrative rendering, such as feature lines and smart visibility techniques, e.g., ghostviews and virtual mirrors. Finally, we discuss selected applications in § 18.8.

18.2 IMAGE-GUIDED SURGERY

Interacting with data in an intraoperative setup requires an appropriate dataset that represents the specific target anatomy of the patient. The time between the acquisition of the dataset and the intervention should be as short as possible to avoid changes of the local anatomy of the patient. However, changes and movements are intrinsic to several body parts: The heart is beating and the lungs as well as the abdominal area are moved through breathing. Due to this movement, some body parts are extremely difficult to handle in intraoperative visualization. A display is needed that presents preoperative and navigation information. Preoperative information includes segmentation results and related 2D and 3D visualization, surgical targets, resection planes and safety margins, trajectories for needles and catheters, and related textual information, such as distance measures.

If the display in the OR is close to the patient in the sterile region, it also needs to be sterilized (see Fig. 18.2, left), which reduces the quality of displayed information considerably. As an alternative, the display may be placed further away, which increases the mental effort of looking forth and back (Fig. 18.2, right). Figure 18.3 presents a second example of a navigation system where the displayed information is more clearly seen.

18.2.1 OVERVIEW OF IGS APPLICATIONS

IGS is relevant in all situations where complex navigational requirements exist, e.g., in surgery of the middle ear (mastoidectomy). Beyond challenging open surgery, IGS is strongly motivated by the increasing use of minimally-invasive surgery and interventional radiology. Intraoperative imaging and guidance are particularly important when the operation site is only indirectly visible. IGS systems are in a very heterogenous state regarding their maturity and feasibility for actual clinical use. On the one hand, in ENT, neuro- and orthopedic surgery, IGS systems have been available and frequently used since at least a decade. In these areas, IGS systems enhance needle placement, e.g., in spine surgery, support endoscopic surgery, e.g., in the paranasal sinus as well as minimally-invasive neurosurgery. Also in dental implantology IGS is widespread. On the other hand, e.g., in abdominal surgery, where soft tissue deformation has to be taken into account, research prototypes dominate. Most of these systems are (only) tested on phantoms or in animal experiments. In this chapter, we intend to cover both established applications as well as experimental setups.

Typical IGS setups provide a view of the patient through the surgeon's eyes and to the patient's datasets through the screen of the navigation system. If a surgeon positions a navigated instrument, e.g., a scalpel on

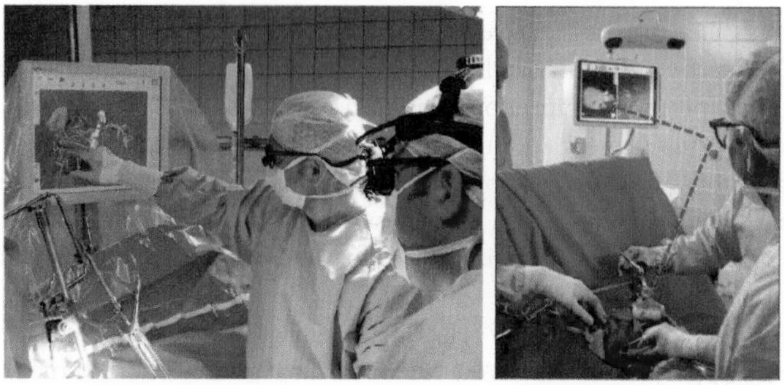

FIGURE 18.2 **Left:** *Surgeons discuss the surgical strategy intraoperatively by means of a sterilized display.* **Right:** *The display is placed outside the sterile area. The red arrows indicate how strong the viewing direction differs between looking at the patient and the display (Courtesy of Karl Oldhafer, General Hospital Celle).*

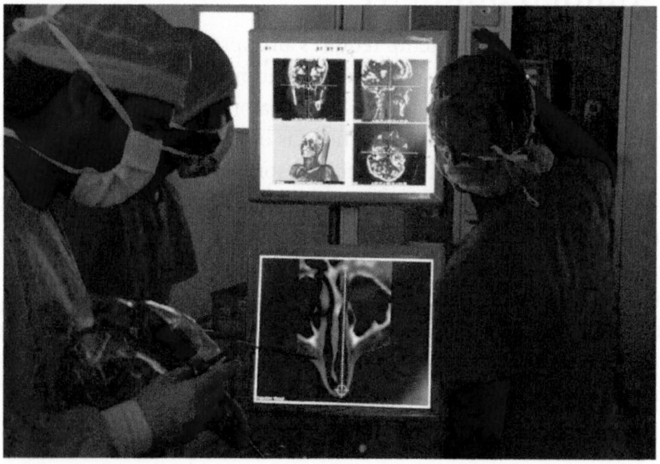

FIGURE 18.3 *The position of an instrument in relation to preoperative CT data is shown in the lower display along with the relation to the pathology in the paranasal sinus. The upper display provides additional 2D and 3D views for an overview (Courtesy of Cascination, Bern).*

the patient, an abstract representation of that instrument is displayed on the multiplanar reconstructions (see Fig. 18.4). The use of 2D slice views is typical also for intraoperative visualization. The simplicity of slice views, where no information is occluded, is an essential aspect here. Thus, the arrangement of the four views and a vertical panel with interface elements (recall Fig. 18.4) is the generic layout of IGS systems.

18.2.2 MEDICAL AUGMENTED REALITY

With conventional IGS systems, the patient is lying on the OR table and the patient's data is shown in a distant location on the screen of a navigation system. Hence, the surgeon must move the head away from the patient to look on the screen and back. The information presented at two different sites need to be mentally fused, which is distracting. To improve this cumbersome situation, virtual reality techniques are used to

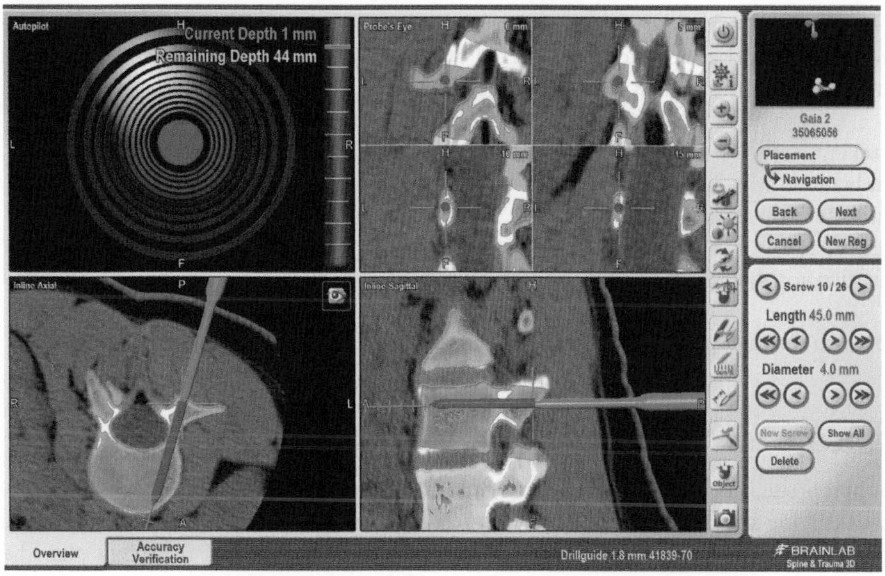

FIGURE 18.4 *The position of surgical instruments in spine tumor surgery is overlaid on the registered preoperative data. Orthogonal views and a 3D view provide complementary information to assess the instrument position (Courtesy of Brainlab, Feldkirchen).*

integrate reality and virtuality into an *augmented* or *mixed reality*.[1] This integrated visualization is the goal of medical AR. It is related to the fused visualization of different datasets, e.g., PET and CT data from the same patient and requires to cope with similar problems, e.g., to establish a correspondence between the datasets and to present the fused information without excessive visual clutter (recall § 4.8.5). To explain medical AR and the implications of providing this overlay of information, we need to mention virtual reality first.

Virtual reality, in general, is the simulation of a world consisting of virtual objects with which the user can interact. The results of the interaction are then presented back to the user, thus having a closed interaction/reaction loop. Traditionally, virtual reality describes only virtual objects along with interaction facilities, such as head tracking and grasping, that enable to be *immersed* in the virtual reality scene, e.g., a city model. According to Azuma [1997] we may define augmented reality as follows.

Definition 18.1. **Augmented reality** is an extension of virtual reality where a representation of the reality is combined with the representation of the virtual reality. Augmentation refers to the goal of this combination, namely to improve people's senses and abilities. To achieve these goals, the virtual and the real world need to be aligned (registered) with sufficient accuracy and the virtual representation needs to be interactive and should be updated in real time.

The position and orientation of the virtual objects are either fixed to the virtual space or they are fixed to marker objects [Sherman and Craig, 2003]. Marker objects are physical representations of the virtual objects.

In an IGS system, the virtual representation of the dataset is registered to the reality of the patient on the OR table or on intraoperative image data, such as video images or intraoperative ultrasound. Thus,

1 Actually, mixed reality is a more general term than augmented reality (AR) that covers also other types of combinations of the real and virtual world.

medical AR requires a complete alignment pipeline, where instruments are tracked, cameras need to be calibrated and patient data need to be registered, which may even be necessary several times in case of patient movements. A medical AR system has the following components:

- tracking,
- calibration,
- intraoperative registration,
- display, and
- visualization system.

In the next two sections we describe these components and the alignment pipeline in detail.

18.3 REGISTRATION

Once an appropriate dataset has been acquired, it is transferred to the OR computer system and mapped to the patient lying on the OR table. In addition to (segmented) patient data, other essential results of preoperative planning, e.g., implants, insertion points or other parts of treatment plans have to be registered with the intraoperative position and pose of the patient and the current position of surgical instruments, catheters or other tools [Sauer *et al.*, 2008].

This mapping is called *registration* (recall § 4.8) and requires the identification of specific features or *anatomical landmarks* in the dataset and on the patient. These features are often identified through *fiducials*, a type of marker that is glued to the skin of patients. These markers are clearly visible in MRI or CT datasets. Alternatively, some surgical disciplines use bolt heads that are screwed into the bone. While screwing of bolts into the bone sounds a bit terrifying, it inflicts only minor lesions, but provides superior accuracy. To register the patient to preoperative data, anatomical landmarks may also be used. Anatomical landmarks are clearly defined points, such as the center of a bifurcation of vascular structures. In particular, in neuroanatomy and orthopedics, e.g., the knee, a large variety of anatomical landmarks is defined in medical textbooks. To automatically and precisely identify such landmarks may be difficult, since the identification of a point landmark often first requires the identification of a plane or line along which the point landmark resides. An alternative way of defining the relationship between a dataset and the patient is a *stereotactic frame*, an apparatus that spans a coordinate system. The stereotactic frame is attached (drilled) to the head before scanning and is then registered to the patient. Surgical instruments can be attached to the frame and thus can be navigated during the intervention. An advantage of frame-based stereotactic surgery is the high navigation accuracy, while drawbacks are the more elaborated and cumbersome setup and the more invasive attachment of the frame to the head. With the advent of reliable fiducial-based navigation, frame-based stereotactic surgery became less common. Hence, in the following we will focus on fiducial-based navigation.

Peculiarities of Intraoperative Registration In § 4.8, we introduced registration and described its use for a couple of applications, e.g., multimodal registration of different datasets acquired preoperatively or registration of follow-up images to baseline data to support the evaluation of treatment progress. In these applications, it is usually acceptable if registration takes a while, e.g., a few minutes, if it yields a very precise overlay. In intraoperative registration, however, speed is crucial. There are a couple of strategies to accelerate registration. Rigid registration is significantly faster than non-rigid registration. Even non-rigid registration may be sufficiently fast if it is performed at a coarser level or if the criteria to terminate the optimization are chosen such that a certain level of inaccuracy is tolerated. Due to the consequences of misalignment, however, careful control of errors, both visually and computationally, is essential.

18.3.1 TISSUE DEFORMATION AND BRAIN SHIFT

In some areas, the relevant anatomy is rather fix and thus an initial rigid-body registration of patient data to the current patient is sufficient. As an example, in trauma surgery and many orthopedics interventions, a fix anatomy may be assumed. However, in other areas of the human body the anatomy is constantly deformed due to heart beat, breathing, or the surgery itself. In addition to *organ deformation*, there is also *organ motion*, e.g., abdominal organs are translated due to motion. Deformations and motions of the anatomy are challenges in intraoperative visualization, since the resulting changes of the anatomy are difficult to predict. A repositioning of the patient may change the anatomy, as well as a cut through the skin, the muscles, or the bones.

If the skull is opened for a neurosurgical procedure, the pressure situation within will change once the *dura*, the leather-like skin of the brain, is cut (see Fig. 18.5). Hence, the shape and the position of the brain will slightly change—this instance of organ deformation is known as *brain shift*. This phenomenon is carefully quantified in [Nimsky *et al.*, 2000] and [Hastreiter *et al.*, 2004], who also describe compensation strategies.

Moreover, the removal of tissue from the body (e.g., a tumor) represents a significant change. Fortunately, these changes may be limited to a local region, or can be compensated for by a variety of techniques. If a sufficient compensation is achieved, the preoperatively acquired dataset is still usable in areas away from the origin of change. In the other cases, the surgeon cannot rely on the preoperatively acquired datasets. Thus, intraoperative imaging may be performed (recall § 2.9). Intraoperative imaging may be used repeatedly, e.g., after every changing action of the surgeon. The downside is that the devices must be registered and accommodated in a typically already cramped OR.

18.3.2 FIDUCIAL-BASED REGISTRATION

The minimum number of markers for defining the transformation matrix for the registration (position and orientation) is three. In most cases, however, at least six markers are matched to allow for a minimization

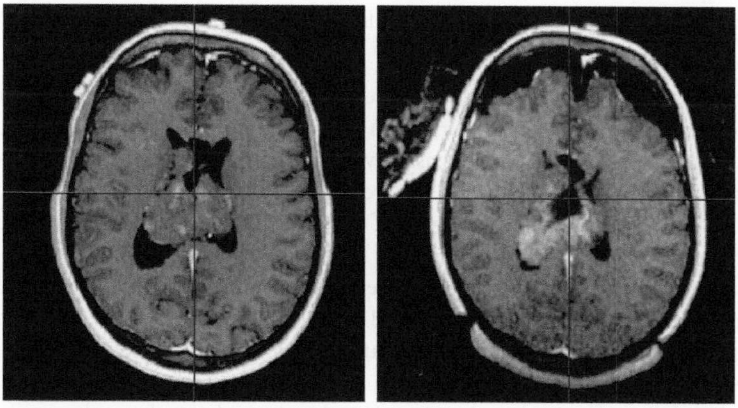

FIGURE 18.5 Tissue deformation due to brain shift. **Left:** Preoperative image of MR head scan. **Right:** Intraoperative image of MR head scan after opening of the skull. The brain has shifted due to the changes of pressure inside of the skull [Lürig et al., 1999] (Courtesy of Peter Hastreiter, University of Erlangen-Nürnberg).

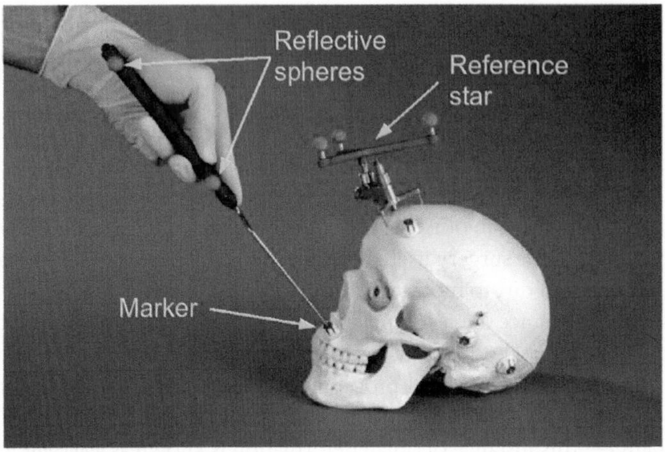

FIGURE 18.6 *Tracked pointer tool to identify fiducial positions and to enable registration with preoperative data. The pointer tool selects one marker on the maxilla of the skull. A reference star is connected to the forehead (Courtesy of Brainlab, Feldkirchen).*

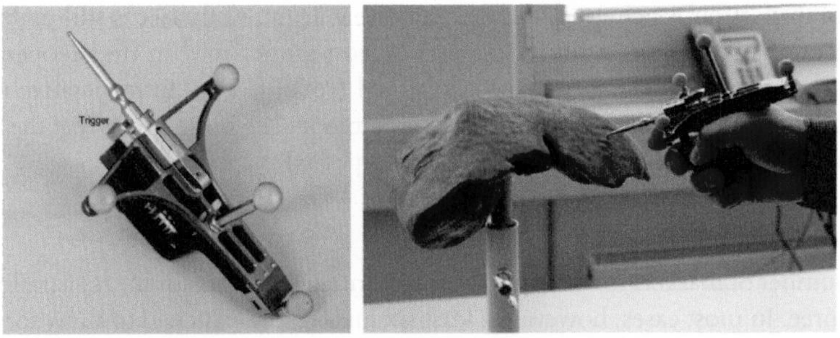

FIGURE 18.7 *An ergonomic pointing tool (AXIOS 3D) for landmark selection and the reference star for tracking. Its use is demonstrated by selecting points on the surface of a 3D print of a liver (Courtesy of Darko Ojdanic, Fraunhofer MEVIS Bremen).*

of registration errors. Once all markers are identified within the dataset and on the patient, the actual optimization process to compute the transformation between these points is started (recall § 4.8).

The quality of the registration, which is basically its accuracy in the workspace, depends largely on how the markers are arranged on the patient. The workspace is the area of the intervention in which the navigation system tracks the instruments. Outside of the workspace, the cameras of the navigation system do not see the instruments, or the accuracy is greatly reduced. For a good registration, the markers should span a space as large as possible around the respective body part. In case of the head, for example, markers are frequently positioned on the frontal, back, and lateral (sideways) parts of the head. Furthermore, markers are positioned on the upper and lower parts (see Fig. 18.6). If such a uniform arrangement cannot be achieved, the accuracy of the registration in the less covered areas will be significantly lower. The accuracy and usability of point-based registration also depends on the tool provided for landmark selection. In Figure 18.7, a recently introduced tool from AXIOS 3D[2] and its use are illustrated. It is also

2 http://www.axios3d.de/

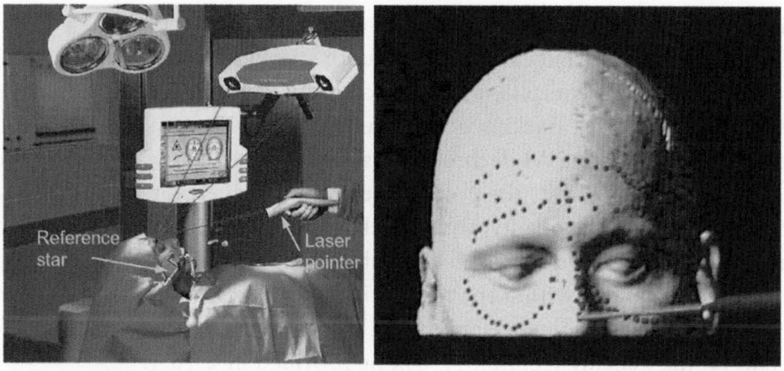

FIGURE 18.8 *ICP-based registration of a point cloud.* **Left:** *A laser pointer (Brainlab's z-touch®) is used to indicate points on the facial skin that is seen by the infrared light cameras of a navigation system (Brainlab's VectorVision®). The red lines indicate the path from the laser pointer to the skin, and the line-of-sights from the cameras to the position on the skin indicated by the laser.* **Right:** *Acquired point cloud on the facial skull. A pointer tool points to the tip of the nose (Left image is courtesy of Jürgen Hoffmann, University of Tübingen, right image is courtesy of Brainlab, Feldkirchen).*

intended to localize a set of predefined landmarks that are emphasized in preoperative data. Since the tool provides a number of buttons and a scroll wheel, it may also be used later during surgery for controlling the display of the navigation system [Ojdanic *et al.*, 2012].

18.3.3 POINT-BASED REGISTRATION

An alternative registration method, which employs the Iterative Closest Point (ICP) registration algorithm, acquires a point cloud on the skin of the patient, which is then matched with a surface representation of the patient's dataset [Besl and McKay, 1992]. This point cloud can be generated through a laser point projected on the skin, which in turn is measured through an already registered camera. Thus, the skin of the patient needs not to be touched. Brainlab's z-touch®, for example, is such a laser pointer, and is measured through an infrared camera of the navigation system (see Fig. 18.8, left and next section).

Registration by Means of Time-of-flight Cameras Time-of-flight (TOF) cameras are able to record a depth image that is a distribution of depth values along with a usual camera image. The intraoperative use of TOF cameras, in principle, enables to record a dense representation of depth values instead of single landmarks. Signals need to be postprocessed due to noise and other artifacts. There are a few promising attempts to use this technology for markerless registration of pre- and intraoperative image data [Haase *et al.*, 2012, Mersmann *et al.*, 2011].

Accuracy of Registrations The registration accuracy of the ICP-based method depends on the arrangement or localization of the data acquired for the registration (fiducial position, point cloud distribution). The larger the space included by the convex hull of the points, the better the registration accuracy will be. Unfortunately, the location of the points for this method is limited to the area that is visible to the cameras that measure them. This means that backfacing regions, e.g., the back of the head, or areas hidden by hair or other body parts, cannot be used. This is different from landmark- or fiducial-based registration, where only the relevant parts of the pointing device that are seen by the cameras (see Fig. 18.6) must be visible. For surgery around the head, the area of the forehead and around the orbits (eye sockets) is frequently used to acquire the point cloud, since they provide firmness and some spatial extent at the same time (see Fig. 18.8, right). Hoffmann *et al.* [2005] showed that the accuracy of the ICP-based registration is not as good as fiducial-based registration, but can be sufficient for specific interventions. The major advantage of this approach, however, lies in the contactless registration, which may be required if that region is injured.

The accuracy also depends on the tracking device used by the navigation system. These devices typically need a warm-up time of up to 1 hour. While these slow systems are still in use, modern systems have warm-up times of less than 10 minutes, e.g., the Polaris Spectra™. Furthermore, measurement interferences with the tracking device reduce the quality of the tracking. This can be scattered light (mostly day light) for optical tracking systems, or magnetic or metallic objects for electro-magnetic tracking systems.

The identification of landmarks within the patient is performed by a pointing device that consists of a calibrated long needle with a handle (see Fig. 18.6). This pointer must be localized through a tracking device. More details on the tracking technology will be provided in § 18.4.

18.4 CALIBRATION AND TRACKING

Tracking systems have the task of localizing (moving) objects in space in real-time. In IGS, surgical tools and instruments, in addition to imaging devices such as endoscopes, are tracked and registered to patient data. For intraoperative visualization, tracking is relevant, e.g., to display the current position of a navigated instrument, an endoscopic camera or an ultrasound probe.

Definition 18.2. **Tracking** is the process of measuring the positions and orientations (the poses) of objects with respect to a reference coordinate system.

It is essential that not only the position but also the orientation of instruments or endoscopes is known. Thus, the intraoperative visualization may represent, e.g., the data that is visible from the current endoscope or ultrasound probe. Thus, in total six degrees of freedom need to be determined. While there are many different tracking approaches in virtual reality, we will focus on *electro-magnetic* and *optical tracking*—the two widely used approaches in image-guided interventions. Later, we will also briefly look into vision-based tracking. Tracking in medical AR is, in general, easier than tracking in many other settings, since

- the working space is indoors (controlled light conditions),
- it is well-defined, and
- rather small [Sielhorst *et al.*, 2008].

For IGS, instruments need to be calibrated for their successful tracking. Instrument tracking is essential to locate the tip of an instrument in the patient anatomy. In an AR application, also the camera capturing reality must be tracked, and hence calibrated. First, We study instrument calibration, and then camera calibration.

18.4.1 CALIBRATING INSTRUMENTS

As mentioned in § 18.3, the patient's dataset is mapped to the patient through the registration step. Technically, the patient on the OR table is first located in the OR coordinate system, whose origin is typically located right on the OR table. However, before the OR table is recognized by the navigation system, it must also be tracked. Hence, infrared tracking sensors or infrared-reflecting markers must be fixed to the OR table. In the following, we assume an optical tracking technology that is the standard approach in most cases. The typical configuration consists of at least three markers arranged in a specific star-shaped pattern, hence a widespread tool from Brainlab® is the *reference star*.

In the registration step, the dataset is mapped to the OR coordinate system. Note that the patient must remain in a constant position on the OR table, and hence to the infrared tracking sensor. If the patient is moved on the OR table, the registration procedure must be repeated.

Similar to the OR table, every tracked (navigated) instrument is identified through a specific configuration of markers (often called a *reference array*) connected to the instrument by a *marker clamp*. Each instrument is uniquely identified by the configuration of markers (e.g., number of markers, distance and angles between markers).

Pivoting The physical distance and direction of the tip of the instrument to the markers is measured in a calibration step and stored afterwards (see Fig. 18.9). This process is referred to as *pivoting*. It requires a *pivot block* that is a substantial mass and should be designed such that it does not move unintentionally. The pivot block contains a small cavity, called *pivot* just large enough to accommodate the pilot tip. Pivot calibration is described, e.g., in [Maurer *et al.*, 1997] (see Fig. 18.10).

Please note that this kind of instrument calibration, is restricted to rigid instruments, such as pointers or ablation needles. For flexible catheters, the relation between the infrared tracking sensor and the instrument tip changes and requires other forms of tracking. A checkerboard pattern is often used for calibration due to its highly regular shape (see Fig. 18.11).

Each reflective marker is now seen by the two infrared cameras. Hence, the position of the markers can be computed by measuring the distance to the cameras through triangulation (see Fig. 18.12). If the configuration of markers is recognized, the orientation of the respective instrument is computed from the marker positions. Otherwise, the user will be requested to calibrate the new instrument. While for a full pose three markers are required, some instruments (e.g., the pointer tool in Fig. 18.6) are only tracked by two markers. In this case, the navigation system cannot compute the complete pose; a rotation around the axis of these two markers will not be recognized. Furthermore, the navigation system cannot determine if the tip or the distal end of the instrument points toward the patient. In most cases, the system will then make a reasonable assumption, which may nevertheless still be wrong.

Typical navigated instruments are

- the pointer to identify anatomical structures of the patient (see Fig. 18.6),
- electrodes for EEGs (electroencephalograms) to measure the electric activity of the brain,
- intraoperative image devices, such as ultrasound probes (see Fig. 18.13), and the C-arc,
- cavitron ultrasonic surgical aspirator (CUSA) for tumor aspiration and removal,

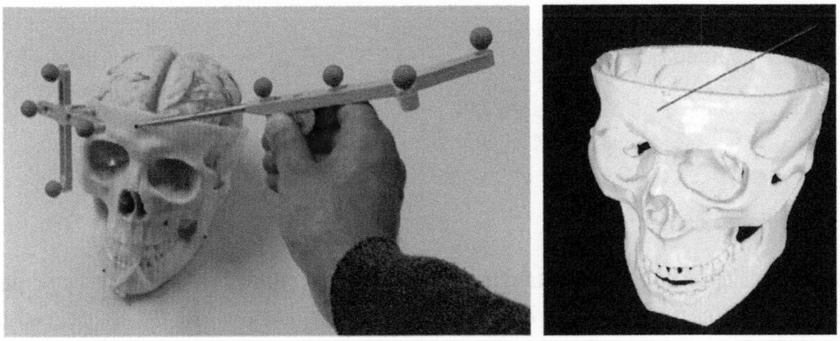

FIGURE 18.9 *An infrared tracking sensor on the left is used to identify the OR table (skull phantom). The 3D view on the right serves to verify the registration to the preoperatively acquired CT data (Courtesy of Zein Salah, University of Magdeburg).*

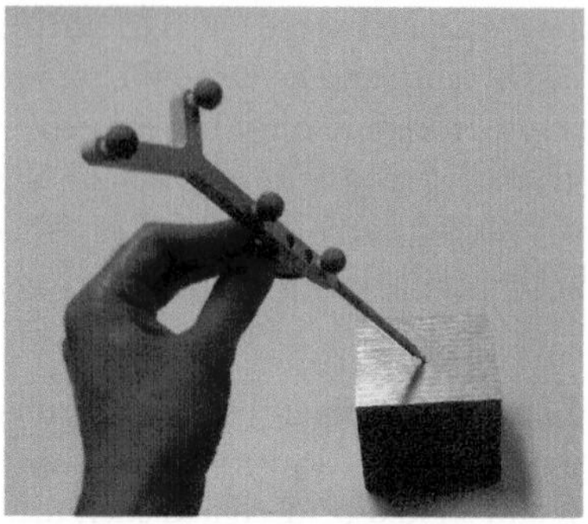

FIGURE 18.10 Before a tool is used, pivoting is performed by moving the tool tip in the small cavity on top of the pilot block (Courtesy of Zein Salah, University of Magdeburg).

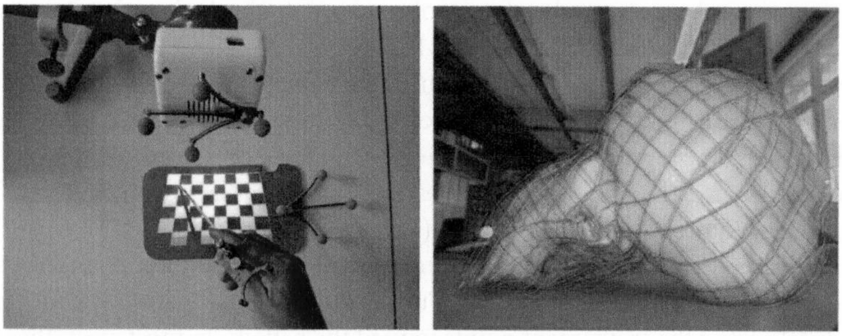

FIGURE 18.11 A checkerboard pattern is used for calibration (left). The right image shows that the pattern is correctly deformed to match the organ shape (Courtesy of Kate Gavaghan, University of Bern).

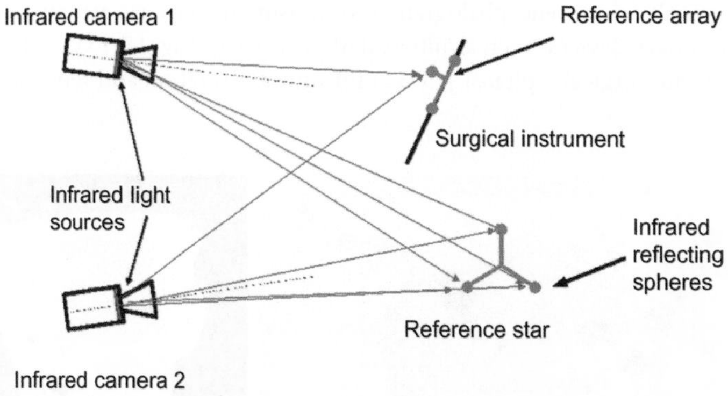

FIGURE 18.12 Marker triangulation for optical tracking: Infrared light is emitted from the light sources and is reflected by the reflecting spheres. The infrared cameras measure the direction of the reflection and compute the distance and then the position by triangulating the measured information. Note that all spheres are measured; only one measurement is shown for the reference array of the surgical instrument for clarity only (Courtesy of Markus Neff, Brainlab, Feldkirchen).

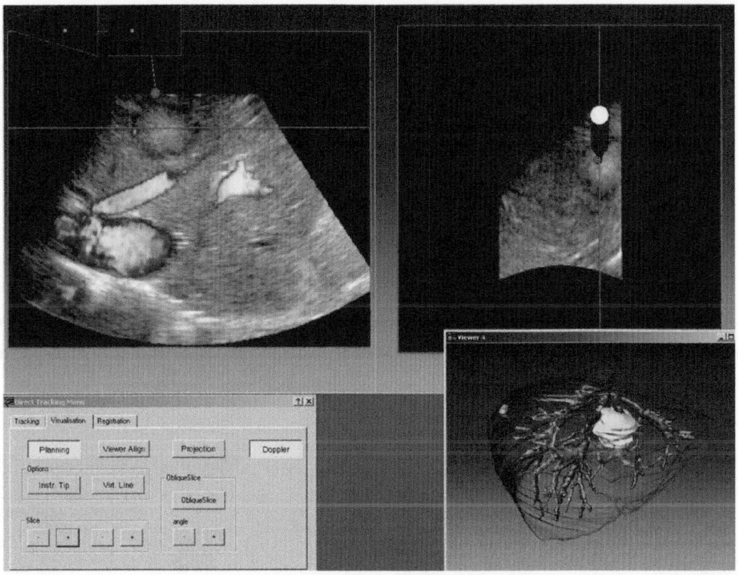

FIGURE 18.13 *Intraoperative imaging in the OR. Intraoperative 3D ultrasound data is acquired with a tracked ultrasound probe. The surgeon examines the liver with a tracked pointing tool to plan the resection of the liver (Courtesy of Thomas Lange, Clinic for Surgery and Surgical Oncology, Charité - Universitätsmedizin Berlin).*

- burrs for creating burr holes, or
- endoscopes.

For these instruments, the position of the calibrated instrument tip and the orientation of the instrument are indicated in the multiplanar reconstructions, and possibly in the 3D reconstruction. The pointer is a passive tool that is tracked by the navigation systems. Burrs and CUSA devices, on the other hand, are used as *active tracking devices*.

18.4.2 CAMERA CALIBRATION

Definition 18.3. Camera calibration is the process of determining the intrinsic camera parameters, namely the focal length and principal point.

If a camera, e.g., a microscope camera, with variable zoom and focus should be calibrated, the calibration has to be adapted to changing focal length. One possible strategy is to perform a manual calibration for selected zoom levels and employ an interpolation of hand-eye transforms and intrinsic camera parameters in between.

Calibration is usually performed with a pinhole camera model [Tsai, 1987]. For camera calibration several toolkits, e.g., the MATLAB and OPENCV are available. If we again assume passive optical tracking, a reference array of markers must be connected to the camera (see Fig. 18.14, left) and the geometric relationship between the camera image and the reference array must be determined. Once this is the case, the virtual information from the patient's dataset can be aligned with the camera image (see Fig. 18.15).

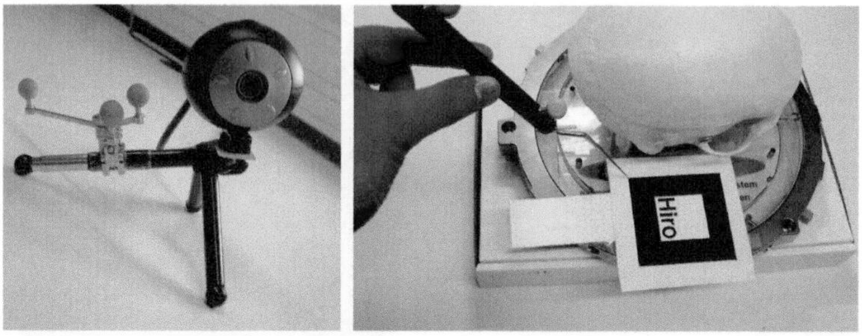

FIGURE 18.14 *Calibrating a camera.* **Left:** *A reference array is attached to a simple web camera.* **Right:** *The corners of the marker pattern (black frame with "Hiro" written in it) of the vision-based tracking system are referenced with a pointer tool (Courtesy of Jan Fischer, University of Tübingen).*

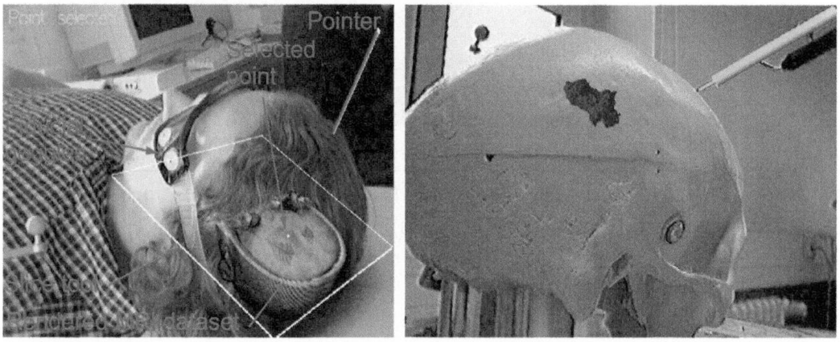

FIGURE 18.15 *Aligned virtual and real information.* **Left:** *Point selection in patient's dataset with pointer tool and oblique slice tool overlayed on camera image. The registration goggles are carrying the fiducials.* **Right:** *Overlayed segmented tumor (red) and tool (yellow) representation (Courtesy of Angel del Río and Jan Fischer, University of Tübingen).*

Establishing the relationship between camera image and reference array is not easy. If the tedious and unreliable measurement of the relationship with a ruler is to be avoided, a special calibration step must be devised. Fischer *et al.* [2004b] describe such a calibration step using the widespread ARToolkit [Kato and Billinghurst, 1999]. The ARToolkit is a vision-based tracking toolkit that searches for a specific pattern in an image, the camera image, to estimate the pose of the camera. In the approach by Fischer and colleagues, the camera is positioned over such a marker pattern (a video marker) and the pose of the camera relative to that marker is computed by the ARToolkit. At the same time, the camera and its reference array are located in the workspace of the navigation system. Hence, the navigation system "sees" the camera (its reference array actually). If the video marker (its corners) is also referenced with a tracked pointer tool to the navigation system (see Fig. 18.14, right), the transformation is completely determined.[3] This chain of transformations connects the camera image via the video marker and the reference array to the navigation system. Note that this is a one-time calibration procedure and must be repeated only if the reference array of the camera is moved afterwards [Fischer *et al.*, 2004b]. The same camera calibration scheme has been reused later by several other groups, see, e.g., [Salah *et al.*, 2011].

3 For the computation of the transformation, the information of the navigation system must be exchanged with the vision-based tracking system. This requires an interface between those components that may not always be available.

18.4.3 OPTICAL TRACKING

Among the two tracking technologies for medical AR, optical tracking meanwhile is the dominant technology and thus described first and in more detail before we discuss the major alternative, namely electromagnetic tracking. Optical tracking identifies the pose of a tracked object by measuring light that is either transmitted or reflected by this object. When this light is transmitted from the object—typically through LEDs—we refer to this as *active optical tracking*. In *passive optical tracking* light is reflected. Since active tracking requires cables running to the LEDs, it is used rarely only in the OR. Hence, we will focus on passive tracking. Passive tracking is achieved through specific markers connected to the surgical instruments. They are typically spherical and coated with an infrared light retroreflecting material. This light is transmitted from an infrared light source at the optical tracking system, reflected by the markers, and finally measured by two cameras that are positioned at a defined distance from each other. Most optical tracking systems use NDI's Polaris®, its successor Polaris Spectra™, or the smaller Polaris Vicra™ cameras (see Fig. 18.16). The integration of such cameras in a navigation system is depicted in Figure 18.17. Both NDI systems have a high tracking accuracy of 0.25 mm. The Polaris Vicra™ cameras are lightweight, but have a smaller measuring volume where tracking has a high accuracy compared to the Polaris Spectra™ camera. Both systems can track passive wireless tools, but only the Polaris Spectra™ can track active tools. Also the update rate differs: the Polaris Spectra™ achieves 60 Hz, which is excellent, whereas the Polaris Vicra™ only achieves an update rate of 20 Hz. This technology is widely used for ENT, neurosurgery and dental implantology with a base of more than 11.000 installations worldwide (October 2012, according to www.ndigital.com). But also prototypical AR systems for abdominal surgery, such as the system developed by Stefan Weber and colleagues in Bern, employ the Polaris Vicra™ [Gavaghan *et al.*, 2012].

Optical tracking provides a high measurement accuracy and is not influenced by any conducting or metallic objects nearby. However, passive optical tracking requires that the infrared light reflected by the markers is seen by the cameras. If this line-of-sight is blocked, that respective object cannot be localized. For surgical instruments, only parts outside of the human body can be tracked. The markers are located at the (visible) distal end of the instrument. The relation between tip and distal end of the instrument must be fixed (to be measured in a calibration step). Thus, flexible catheters or endoscopes can usually not be used in this setup. Some advanced systems enable even tracking of flexible endoscopes using sophisticated image analysis to compensate for the missing information. Thus, tracking of bronchoscopes was feasible [Mori *et al.*, 2005, Luó *et al.*, 2011]. However, since such algorithms are rather complex, they can usually not be performed in real time. Furthermore, any scattered infrared light from a different source, e.g., the sun, will disturb the optical tracking. Hence, care must be taken to block out such light sources.

Inside-out Tracking The optical tracking described before is referred to as outside-in tracking. In contrast, *inside-out tracking* with an HMD means that a camera is attached to the helmet and this camera tracks a

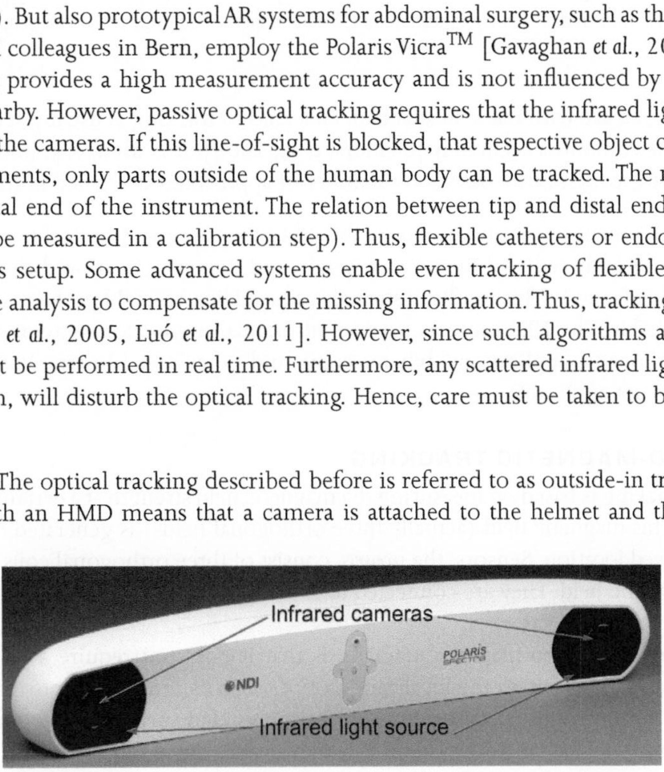

FIGURE 18.16 *Polaris Spectra™ optical infrared camera system (Courtesy of NDI).*

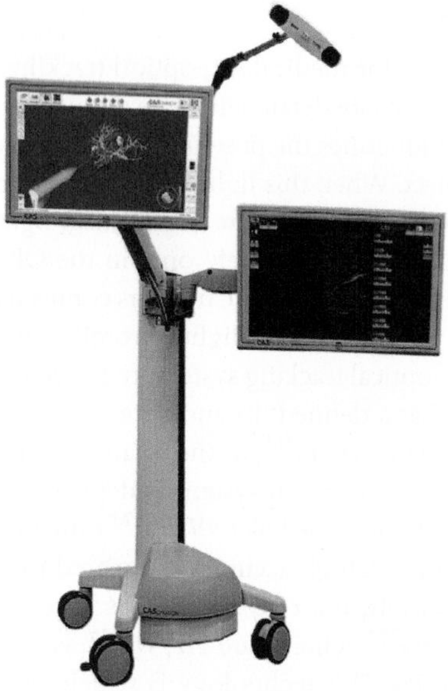

FIGURE 18.17 *A modern navigation system based on optical tracking with two displays for presenting planning information and intraoperative guidance. Here, the instrument tip in relation to CT data is shown (Courtesy of Cascination, Bern).*

reference frame, e.g., an arc with markers attached. This kind of tracking is usually very precise, since the head position can be computed accurately [Sielhorst *et al.*, 2008]. It is used, e.g., in the CAMPAR system [Sielhorst *et al.*, 2006], which is the basis for a number of approaches described in the following.

Summary The development in recent years contributed to the success of optical tracking. The necessary equipment was significantly reduced in size and weight and thus may be moved close to the workspace instead of being rather far away. This results in strongly reduced line-of-sight problems. Thus, the reference objects are better visible. The NDI cameras used in all Brainlab navigation systems are widely used. In particular, in all orthopedic applications, where screws and other metal instruments are used, electro-magnetic tracking is not applicable.

18.4.4 ELECTRO-MAGNETIC TRACKING

Electro-magnetic tracking is based on measuring the magnetic field strength at a certain location [Sherman and Craig, 2003]. This magnetic field (actually three orthogonal fields) is generated by a field generator, the *transmitter*, at a fixed location. Sensors, the *receivers*, consist of three orthogonal coils in which voltage is induced by the magnetic field. They are connected to moving objects, e.g., surgical instruments and thus measure the pose of these objects.

A major advantage of electro-magnetic tracking is that it does not require a line-of-sight between transmitter and receiver. This allows the localization of the sensors in instruments that are moved inside a body cavity, which is a very important feature for image-guided surgery. Unfortunately, these sensors need to be connected with the tracking systems through a cable. Since this cable runs through the sterile area of the intervention, it must be wrapped in sterile drapes and may annoy the surgeons at the OR table. Furthermore, electro-magnetic tracking suffers from two major causes of artifacts:

- If instruments or objects of conducting material are introduced to the magnetic field, eddies are generated in the field which disturb the magnetic field and hence the measurements. Moreover, if a magnetic field is generated nearby, e.g., by an intraoperative MR scanner, electro-magnetic tracking is difficult to use.
- Objects of ferromagnetic material will also disturb the measurements, and hence cannot be used.

Overall, electro-magnetic tracking provides reasonable accuracy, if the magnetic field is not disturbed by other magnetic fields, or by conducting and ferromagnetic materials. Since most surgical instruments are made from metal, this is a problem in the OR. However, electro-magnetic tracking in the OR has made progress and several companies provide solutions specifically for the OR. MEDTRONIC is a major company that provides navigation systems based on electro-magnetic tracking.

18.4.5 SUMMARY

In this section we got to know the major ingredients for navigation and visualization techniques that consider the current pose of instruments. Calibration, tracking and registration are the three major steps necessary for a correct alignment. All these steps introduce errors and these errors obviously sum up. While a large number of studies analyzed these errors for various setups, the major result is an upper limit for the error. For a surgical user it is very hard to estimate, at least roughly, the current error and thus to assess whether the displayed information is sufficiently reliable. Current research tackles this problem and aims at online error estimation, using models of tracking accuracy under various conditions. Sielhorst *et al.* [2008] present some concepts for error estimation using their work and those of other groups.

18.5 NAVIGATED CONTROL

While pointer-based navigation is widespread, it only provides a limited support. Instead of recalling the current position at discrete points, a continuous tracking of the instrument position is desirable. Moreover, it is desirable that the surgeon gets noticed and warned whenever he or she approaches critical structures. In practice, a sufficiently high update rate is needed to ensure timely warnings. A special variation of this approach, Navigated Control®, limits an active tool to a specific area of the dataset [Hein and Lueth, 1999]. This requires, however, to preoperatively define the admissible workspace and the critical structures to be protected. This is a rather complex interaction task. With the definition of a workspace, a navigated surgical drill, for example, stops drilling if its position and orientation does not satisfy specified conditions. Thus, the task of navigating a surgical instrument becomes a shared activity between the surgeon and a machine [Manzey *et al.*, 2011]. Navigated Control® has the potential to mitigate complications, and thus to increase patient safety and quality of intervention. This concept has gained a lot of attention in the last decade and has been clinically evaluated in functional endoscopic sinus surgery [Strauss *et al.*, 2005] and in temporal bone surgery [Strauss *et al.*, 2007]. In Figure 18.18, the principle of Navigated Control® is illustrated.

In a large interdisciplinary effort, this advanced support was evaluated with respect to its consequences for the mental workload of surgeons as well as for the results of surgery [Manzey *et al.*, 2011]. The risk structures to be protected include the dura mater, the auditory ossicles, and the nervus facialis—thus, focusing on relevant risk structures in real interventions.[4]

The authors recorded any injury of risk structures, the time needed for the operation, their situation awareness as well as the surgeon's workload. Subjective ratings as well as physiologic measurements, e.g., with ECG signals and respiration, were conducted. They found that Navigated Control® increased the

4 Temporal bone surgery, in particular for implanting hearing aids, is also discussed in § 20.3.

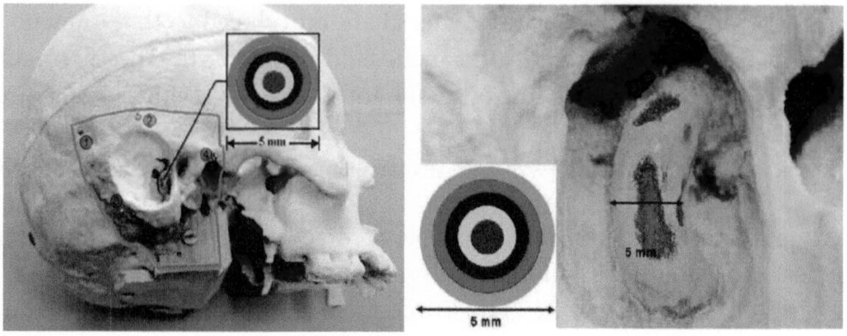

FIGURE 18.18 *Based on a pre-defined workspace (indicated in blue) the instrument position is monitored and visualized in different viewing directions (Courtesy of Mathias Hofer, University of Leipzig. See also [Hofer et al., 2010]).*

perceived and actual patient safety. Less experienced surgeons had a stronger benefit from the support. On the other hand, the time for surgery increased. Also the subjective workload increased. This gave rise to re-consider the specific implementation of Navigated Control®. Instead of completely stopping surgical devices if they leave the predefined workspace, users may be warned acoustically or the devices may be slowed down. Although a little less effective in preventing complications, these less invasive realizations would likely reduce the severity of interrupts caused by the system and thus also lead to less distractions. For a discussion of Navigated Control® as an automation tool and the consequences of that automation for surgeons, see [Manzey *et al.*, 2009]. The success of the whole system, of course, critically depends on registration accuracy and thus on the reliability of warnings or interrupts generated by the system. Registration techniques for Navigated Control® are discussed by [Hofer *et al.*, 2010].

18.6 DISPLAY MODES

The next two sections are dedicated to medical augmented reality. We start with discussing *display modes*, i.e., the hardware for the integrated display of real and virtual information in this section and then go on with discussing *visualization techniques*, i.e., the software aspect of the display. We do not restrict the discussion to technical possibilities but consider perceptual aspects that should also guide the selection of visualization techniques. The display systems for medical AR can be classified in the following groups [Sielhorst *et al.*, 2008]:

- *Optical see-through displays* project the virtual objects onto a view of the reality. This can be achieved either through a mirror that maps the virtual objects onto a semi-transparent view screen (e.g., most head-mounted displays), or through a semi-transparent display that allows to see the reality through the screen itself.
- *Video see-through devices* capture the reality through a camera and enrich the video stream with virtual objects by mixing both signals electronically. Also HMDs are available with video see-through displays.
- *Projection-based AR* systems project the virtual information directly on the patient.
- In *microscope augmentation* the virtual information is overlaid with the microscope's view, e.g., in neuro- or spine surgery.
- In *endoscope augmentation* the endoscope view is enhanced with virtual information.

Microscope and endoscope augmentation can be considered as special instances of optical see-through displays. We treat them as special categories here, since they are directly related to imaging techniques in surgery. Thus, augmentation of microscopes and endoscopes does not alter the intraoperative workflow strongly. Guided by Sielhorst *et al.* [2008], we start with a brief history that is used to introduce the essential concepts and set the stage for a more detailed discussion later.

18.6.1 BRIEF HISTORY OF MEDICAL AR

AR was envisioned early and already in the 1960s IVAN SUTHERLAND introduced a major innovation for virtual and augmented reality, namely a tracked head-mounted display (HMD) [Sutherland, 1968]. SUTHERLAND's "ultimate display" was an optical see-through HMD.

An HMD contains small displays, e.g., LCDs with semi-transparent mirrors. In AR applications, these displays contain mixed representations of the virtual and the real world. These visual representations may be generated separately for both eyes enabling stereo perception. Due to many technical problems and limited processing capabilities, it took almost twenty years after SUTHERLAND's invention until the first real-world applications appeared. Among them was a medical AR system that integrated CT data and the view of an operation microscope where microscope movement was tracked to update the initial registration [Roberts *et al.*, 1986]. A further milestone was the first video see-through display for augmenting ultra-sound images [Bajura *et al.*, 1992]. This system employed magnetic tracking to compute the position of the ultrasound probe. It was primarily used to show the ultrasound images of the fetus inside a pregnant woman's womb [Sauer *et al.*, 2008].

A comprehensive HMD-based medical AR framework was developed at Siemens Corporate Research in Princeton. Their RAMP system "Reality Augmentation for Medical Procedures" employed an additional camera on top of the HMD for inside-out tracking [Sauer *et al.*, 2000, 2008]. Later versions enabled also instrument tracking. The system was primarily targeted at neurosurgical interventions.

Projection-based Augmented Reality Projector technology has developed considerably in recent years. Modern projectors have a high spatial resolution, e.g., 1920 × 1200 pixels, a high refresh rate, e.g., 120 Hz, and a high brightness resolution, e.g., 7200 brightness values. Moreover, they support stereo projection. A leading example is the F35 AS3D projector from PROJECTIONDESIGN. Projection-based AR is a widespread variant also in industrial applications [Schwerdtfeger *et al.*, 2008, Menk *et al.*, 2011].

In medical AR, the body of the patient or an organ exposed during surgery is used as projection area and thus does not require that the surgeon has to move the head. Video or laser projection may be employed. Projection on such an irregular surface is challenging and requires a powerful projector. The surgeon must be tracked to adapt the projection of virtual information to his or her current viewing direction. A particular challenge is to visualize information that is below an organ surface, since parallax errors occur. Parallax errors may be compensated in principle by accurate head or eye tracking, but the procedures are tedious and often not accurate enough.

Augmented Microscopes and Binoculars These AR techniques are motivated by the frequent use of microscopes in ENT and neurosurgery. OR microscopes have experienced an enormous development in the last decades. They may be flexibly tilted and adjusted with respect to focus length and zoom to deliver excellent images of the situs. Furthermore, the ergonomic quality of modern OR microscopes is excellent and thus enables their use also for longer operations (see Fig. 18.19 for an example). The right image shows how this microscope was enhanced for providing OR views. Even co-observation for a second surgeon is supported by providing a second microscope view that is fitted with the same video signal provided via a beam splitter.

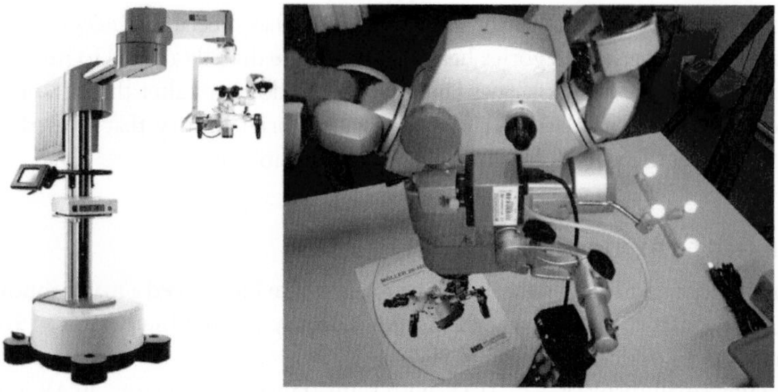

FIGURE 18.19 *A modern OR microscope (Möller 3-1000) from Möller-Wedel. The left image shows the whole instrument and the right image the main part that is moved close to the surgeons head. The panel in front, like a remote control unit of a TV, offers facilities to adjust zoom and focus level. The reference star, not being part of the default configuration, was attached for navigating the instrument (Courtesy of Zein Salah, University of Magdeburg).*

Thus, with the optional overlay of virtual information, the familiar workflow changes only slightly (after successful setup of the system).

Augmented Endoscopes Another line of development was augmentation of endoscopic images. In this area, pioneering work was done by Freysinger *et al.* [1997] in ENT surgery and by Shahidi *et al.* [1998] in neurosurgery. The system presented by Shahidi *et al.* [1998] employs optical tracking of the endoscope and presents the endoscopic view side-by-side with a corresponding virtual endoscopy view derived from preoperative CT or MRI data. Thus, here the relevant information is not integrated in one view but at least the views are close to each other avoiding that the surgeon has to move his head. We briefly mentioned TOF-cameras as an intraoperative imaging technique to record depth images for intraoperative registration. This technique is particularly attractive for augmenting endoscopy [Haase *et al.*, 2012].

Augmented Reality Windows Finally, we want to mention *augmented reality windows* as a further class of display modes. Here, instead of using a helmet, a semi-transparent mirror is placed between the user and the patient [Sielhorst *et al.*, 2008]. Virtual images are typically created with an autostereoscopic monitor, which involves a reduced spatial resolution. A crucial advantage is that no tracking of the user is required. However, accurate calibration of the mirror is necessary.

18.6.2 OPTICAL SEE-THROUGH DISPLAYS

Although HMDs were considered fascinating, the user experience, in particular if the HMD was used longer than a few minutes, was detrimental. To wear a (heavy) helmet and see virtual objects in only moderate spatial resolution and an update rate that was not sufficient to create the impression of smooth movements in a virtual environment literally causes headaches. Meanwhile, the user experience has strongly improved in all aspects. HMDs have a high spatial resolution (1280×1024 pixels is typical) and a sufficient update rate (60 Hz) [Bichlmeier *et al.*, 2009b]. For the user experience also an accurate pose estimation is essential to provide a correct overlay of real and virtual image date.

One serious problem with optical see-through displays remains: users tend to erroneously perceive virtual information overlaid as being *in front of* real information. While this is appropriate, e.g., for resection lines overlaid on top of an organ or bone, it represents a problem for internal structures. It is very difficult to convey that certain augmented information is located deep inside an organ [Kockro *et al.*, 2009].

18.6.3 VIDEO SEE-THROUGH DISPLAYS

In video see-through displays, the real view is not directly seen but electronically controlled and integrated with virtual information. Since this reduces the resolution and image quality, it is not immediately obvious why video see-through is a good AR display concept. However, there are a number of crucial advantages [Sielhorst *et al.*, 2008]:

- The virtual and real content can be very flexibly, in fact arbitrarily, combined. Thus, perceptual issues related to depth perception may be optimized.
- The display of the real view may be delayed, if necessary, to be perfectly synchronized with the virtual information. Thus, confusing and annoying delays may not occur.
- The real and the virtual data are displayed with similar constraints, e.g., with respect to contrast and color spectrum.
- Finally, the overlay does not depend on the viewer's position and it is completely known. Thus, the results can be used for a more objective validation.

Moreover, the integration of virtual and real information in one consistent view enables a correct depth perception. Thus, the most severe problem of optical see-through displays is overcome. However, current technology does not allow to display the information in the same resolution and contrast as the naked eye would perceive it.

Rolland and Fuchs [2000] discuss the advantages and disadvantages of optical and video see-through HMDs. For a recent and comprehensive review of head-worn display designs and technologies, we recommend [Rolland *et al.*, 2012]. As a general remark, despite all improvements of display technology, a HMD always hampers peripheral vision and the mobility of the surgeon—aspects that are quite important in actual clinical use.

18.6.4 AUGMENTED MICROSCOPE DISPLAYS

The key idea of augmenting microscope displays is the insertion of a semi-transparent mirror in the optics, actually a special instance of an optical see-through display. Thus, the advantages of video see-through discussed above do not hold for microscope augmentation. However, the acceptance of a display mode that is very close to the existing workflow is generally high.

The first augmented monoscopic operating microscope was presented by Roberts *et al.* [1986], followed by an augmented stereoscopic operating microscope introduced by Edwards *et al.* [1995]. However, infrared tracking limited the update rate considerably. Later, BIRKFELLNER and colleagues introduced the VARIOSCOPE AR, which used a very compact head-mounted display (HMD) and optical tracking to mimic a surgical microscope. Their system finally supported variable zoom, focus and eye distances [Figl *et al.* 2005]. Early video see-through systems suffered from low latency. Sauer *et al.* [2000] achieved a high update rate of 30 fps and also an accurate overlay of virtual and real data. Augmented microscopes have a precise optical axis aligned with the direction at which the eyes perceive the surgical site and the augmentation. The virtual information is presented at the same focal plane as the real image. This further enhances correct depth perception.

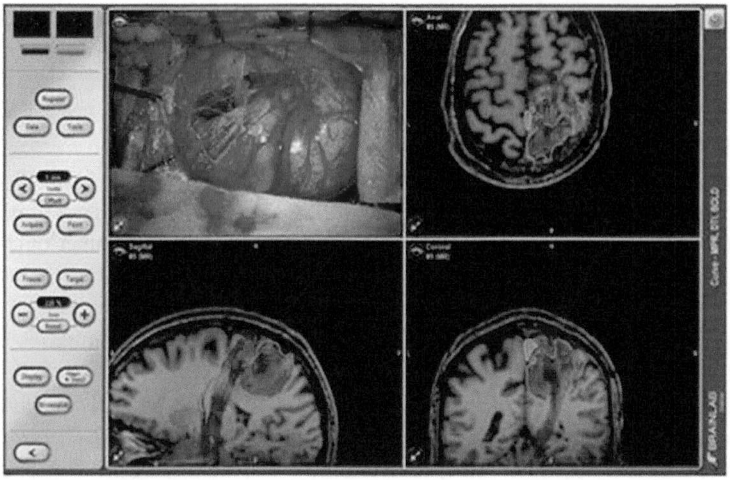

FIGURE 18.20 *The microscopic view enhanced with anatomical data and fiber tracts, determined with DTI (Courtesy of Brainlab Microscope Integration®).*

However, the user cannot change the viewing direction and thus cannot benefit from the parallax as a depth cue. Sauer *et al.* [2008] explain that a parallax shift occurs when the real surgical site is seen through a semi-transparent screen. The extent of that shift depends on the current position of the viewer. Thus, the screen and the viewer need to be tracked to compensate for the parallax shift. The VARIOSCOPE performed that correction.

The first augmented *stereo microscope* was introduced by Edwards *et al.* [1995] and was used for interventions in neurosurgery (see also [Edwards *et al.*, 1999]). The segmentation information was either presented as wireframe, or as a point cloud representing vertices of the mesh derived from the segmentation. These very simple display techniques were necessary at that time to cope with the performance limitations.

While the first systems suffered from a low update rate due to the constraints of infrared tracking at that time and a rather low accuracy, meanwhile submillimeter accuracy and sufficient display rates are possible.

By now, augmented microscope displays are also part of commercial products, such as the Brainlab® Cranial Navigation Software (see Fig. 18.20). In practice, such support is difficult to achieve, since it requires to adapt the software to each major microscope.

18.6.5 AUGMENTED REALITY WINDOWS

Among the first systems was the work presented by Blackwell *et al.* [1998] aiming at AR support in orthopedics, e.g., for joint replacement or arthroscopy. With this system, users wear tracked shutterglasses involving cables and power supply. A high resolution and update rate was achieved. However, the whole equipment was difficult to use with complex calibration procedures and long setup times [Gavaghan *et al.*, 2012]. Later, more compact setups without cables were developed, but usually either with a limited field of view or only monoscopic displays [Sielhorst *et al.*, 2008].

The AR is presented on one screen and hence the surgeon no longer needs to change the view direction to see the patient and the dataset. Consequently, the surgeon is not looking at the patient while interacting with the system. This is the typical scenario of endoscopic interventions where the surgeon follows the endoscopic images on a video screen. For non-endoscopic surgery, however, the surgeon typically prefers

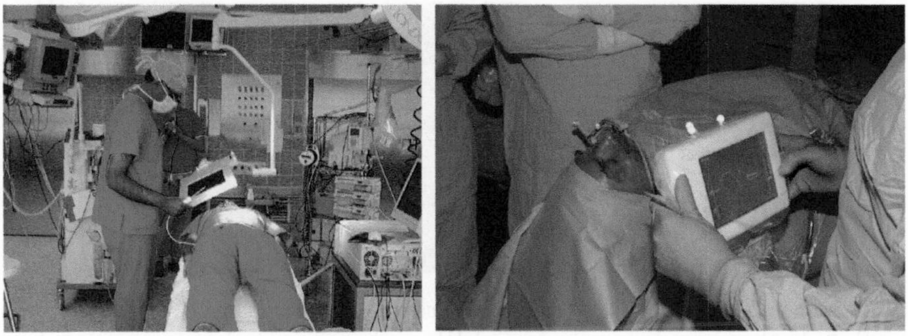

FIGURE 18.21 *Display options that direct the view at the patient.* ***Left:*** *Semi-transparent LCD mounted on a swivel arm.* ***Right:*** *Tracked LCD with a camera on the other side. Left image is courtesy of Bernd Schwald of the MEDARPA project, ZGDV Darmstadt. Right image is courtesy of Tim Lueth and Stefan Weber, MiMed, Technical University of Munich.*

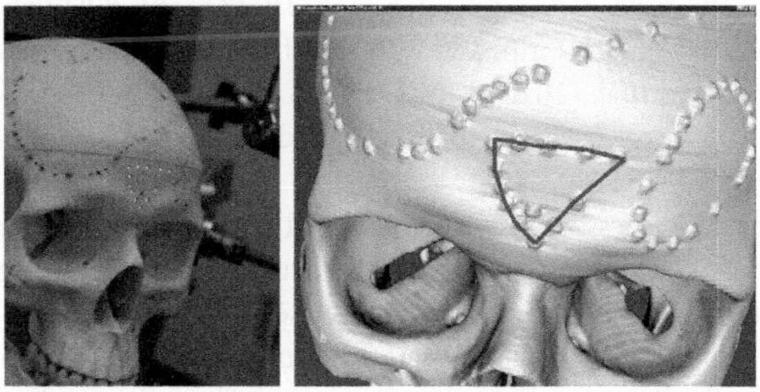

FIGURE 18.22 *A laser projection system is used to overlay the planned resection path on a (plastic) skull. Fiducials were injected for accurate registration (From: [Glossop et al., 2003]).*

to keep the view on the patient. For such situations, a tracked semi-transparent LCD screen mounted on a swivel arm was introduced by Schwald *et al.* [2002]. In an OR setting, this device is positioned between the surgeon and the patient such that the surgeon looks through that device (see Fig. 18.21). A somewhat similar device was introduced by Weber *et al.* [2003], which provides a tracked display with a camera on the patient-facing side to capture a video stream of the patient. In contrast to the mounted MEDARPA display, this display is held in the hands of a surgeon (see Fig. 18.21, right).

18.6.6 PROJECTION-BASED MEDICAL AUGMENTED REALITY

The basic concept of projection-based medical AR was introduced by [Hoppe *et al.*, 2003 and Glossop *et al.*, 2003]. Glossop *et al.* [2003] illustrated the use of their laser-based projection system for craniotomies where the path of the planned resection was displayed on the skull (see Fig. 18.22). Kahrs *et al.* [2006] describe preclinical experiences. For the practical use, details of the technical setup are essential, e.g., a proper placement of the projector in the narrow space of an OR.

Most systems using projection-based AR employ a static projector, e.g., mounted at the ceiling. In contrast, a group at the University of Bern developed a lightweight small handheld device with a special grip to be hold conveniently [Gavaghan *et al.*, 2011a]. This *image overlay projection device* (IOD) enables to project

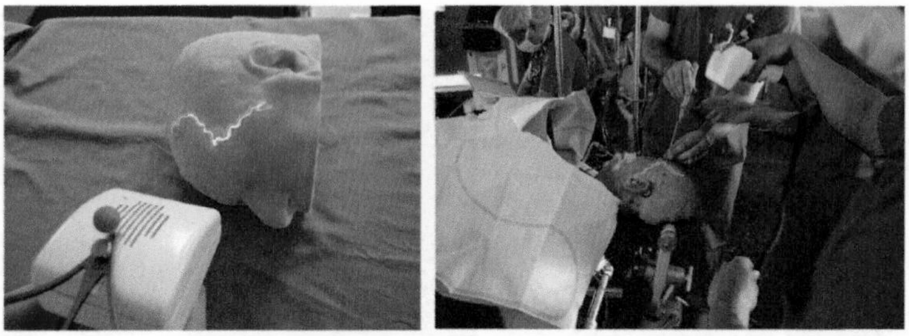

FIGURE 18.23 **Left:** *The principle of handheld projected AR is demonstrated with a phantom. The laser lines are wide enough to be easily recognizable.* **Right:** *The image overlay projection device is held by one physician to assist the operating surgeon performing a resection according to the preoperatively defined resection line that is overlaid on the skull (Courtesy of Kate Gavaghan, University of Bern).*

data with laser projection technology to a surface in front of the surgeon. The IOD with its retro-reflective spheres is tracked and can be used in any pose (see Fig. 18.23). The IOD delivers overlay information in good quality when held between 50 mm and 300 mm from the projection surface, which represents a reasonable interval [Gavaghan *et al.*, 2011b]. In § 18.8.3 we will discuss how this technology can be employed for navigated liver surgery. Projector-based medical AR with handheld devices gained more attention recently [Kobler *et al.*, 2012].

Projection-based medical AR is less intrusive than most other display modes and thus promising despite the parallax error involved in displaying deep-seated structures. In general, applications involving rigid and superficial structures benefit most from projection-based medical AR.

As Gavaghan *et al.* [2012] point out, projecting data on soft tissue, such as skin or an organ, is challenging, since local deformations in the line of sight lead to distortions. Thus, the display of deep-seated structures on soft tissue is the most problematic situation.

18.7 VISUALIZATION TECHNIQUES FOR MEDICAL AUGMENTED REALITY

The visual overlay of real and virtual information requires not only an appropriate display device but also appropriate visualization techniques. The fused visualization of real and virtual information is an instance of a multimodal visualization problem. We discussed other instances of that general problem in Chapter 4, where segmentation information should be presented along with the original data (§ 4.5.7), and in the registration section (§ 4.8.5), where multimodal data, e.g., from PET and CT data should be displayed simultaneously. Now we discuss the adaptation of similar techniques for AR. Before this discussion we explain a particular challenge in AR, namely the occlusion problem that needs to be addressed to enable proper depth perception.

18.7.1 THE OCCLUSION PROBLEM OF AUGMENTED REALITY

The main issue with AR is that only a small amount of information about the reality is captured in a 2D image (or video stream). Hence, the virtual information is simply drawn over the 2D image of the reality in many AR systems. This, however, will not generate a proper depth for both worlds—a problem first discussed by Bajura *et al.* [1992]. Due to the lack of depth information for reality, we cannot properly sort the virtual objects according to their depth position. Hence, they are drawn on top of real objects,

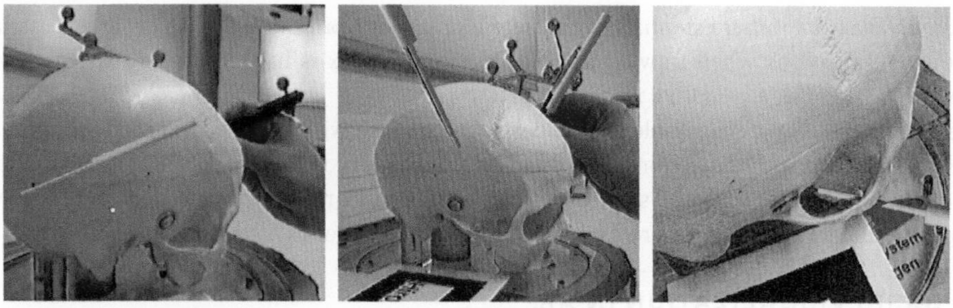

FIGURE 18.24 *Virtual occlusion of reality.* ***Left:*** *The pointer tool vanishes behind the skull model, but its virtual representation is rendered still in front of the skull.* ***Middle:*** *Virtual representation of the tool behind the skull is correctly occluded.* ***Right:*** *Detail of the cheek bone correctly occludes part of the tool (Courtesy of Jan Fischer, University of Tübingen).*

even if they should be located behind them (see Fig. 18.24, left). Thus, real objects can be hidden by virtual objects but not vice versa [Sauer *et al.*, 2001]. This can severely disturb the user's immersion and interpretation of the position of the objects in the scene [Fischer *et al.*, 2004a]. The occlusion problem may lead to erroneous assessments and to a confusing situation, where occlusion and other depth cues, e.g., from stereo vision, are conflicting.

To solve this problem, the 3D information, e.g., the depth values of all elements of the real world need to be integrated in computer graphic models. The resulting geometry is used to setup the depth buffer to provide the correct depth information for the rendering of the virtual objects. Since the modeling of a whole OR is too tedious, solely the patient is modeled using the patient's dataset. This information enables a proper depth representation (see Fig. 18.24, middle). The respective 3D information can be computed by reconstructing an isosurface representing the body part, thus creating a *shadow geometry* which is only rendered into the depth buffer but not into the framebuffer. Hence, it will be taken into account for the depth sorting, but it will not be displayed on the screen [Fischer *et al.*, 2004a].

An easier alternative is to avoid the display of virtual information in a way that substantially occludes real information. Rough wire frame representations or silhouettes are appropriate options. If surfaces should be displayed, it is better to render them transparently [Sauer *et al.*, 2008].

18.7.2 DEPTH CUES IN AUGMENTED REALITY

Drascic and Milgram [1996] provided a thorough analysis of perceptual problems related to AR. A more recent study of perceptual problems by Kruijff *et al.* [2010] indicates that many problems in older studies are solved in most modern systems by technological solutions, e.g., problems due to latency, low resolution or inaccurate calibration. Some problems—Kruijff *et al.* [2010] call them *hard* problems—however, remain, since they are deeply related to depth perception. Among them is to ensure a correct stereo perception, which is challenging, since it requires to estimate the individual intraocular distance (the distance between the eyes) exactly instead of relying on some kind of average value.

For medical AR, the occlusion problem is particularly important, since we strongly infer spatial relations by this depth cue. "Without occlusion handling, virtual objects will appear floating over real objects and any impression of depth will be lost" [Kutter *et al.*, 2008]. However, other depth cues are also relevant for correct depth perception (recall § 8.3). Stereo display modes, e.g., stereo microscopes, stereo endoscopes, or autostereoscopic displays are frequently used in order to benefit from stereo perception. Ponce and Born [2008] explain that 5–10% of the population cannot perceive stereoscopic depth cues.

Motion parallax is another essential depth cue which arises from the ability to observe a spatial object in continuous transitions when moving around. Motion parallax is hard to achieve when only a small field of view is available, e.g., with a microscope.

Some depth cues that are favorable in preoperative planning with 3D visualization, are not feasible in intraoperative AR. Shadow projections, semi-transparent shadow volumes, or advanced lightning effects are not applicable in the complex situation where virtual and real information is overlaid. However, occlusion and shape from shading are useful and viable depth cues in AR [Kutter *et al.*, 2008].

18.7.3 BASIC VISUALIZATION IN AR

In intraoperative visualization, the view to the patient, e.g., through a microscope, should be clear but enhanced with some essential information. A direct integration of the microscope view and virtual information derived from preoperative data is desirable, since neurosurgeons look through the microscope most of the time. The microscope, of course, needs to be tracked, usually with passive markers.

The overlay of intraoperative images with preoperative image data is a very similar visualization task like overlaying original image data with segmentation information. Consequently, basic solutions are also similar: the region of a crucial anatomical structure may be drawn semi-transparently or the boundary may be indicated by contours. In contrast to the overlay of segmentation information that is usually performed in slice views, we have a more complex 3D situation here. Thus, instead of presenting one contour, a stack of contours is essential and the contour corresponding to the focus layer of the microscope should be emphasized. These basic techniques are widely used. In [Salah *et al.*, 2010] they were fine-tuned for brain tumor surgery and discussed with neurosurgeons (see Fig. 18.25). As a second example we show the overlay of relevant information for minimally-invasive spine surgery. Here, the exact position of the vertebrae is essential to guide the needle insertion process. The phantom shown in Figure 18.26 is realistic, since in surgery also only the skin is visible. In addition to the segmentation information, it may be useful to display also original data, at least optionally (Fig. 18.26, right). As the discussions in these projects and research carried out in other groups clearly reveal, there is a demand for more advanced and perceptually motivated intraoperative visualization.

In Chapter 12 we discussed illustrative visualization techniques that adapt the visibility locally to the importance of structures and regions as well as low-level illustration techniques that emphasize prominent features, e.g., silhouettes. In recent years, such illustrative visualization techniques were adapted and refined for intraoperative use. In the following two subsections we describe such approaches.

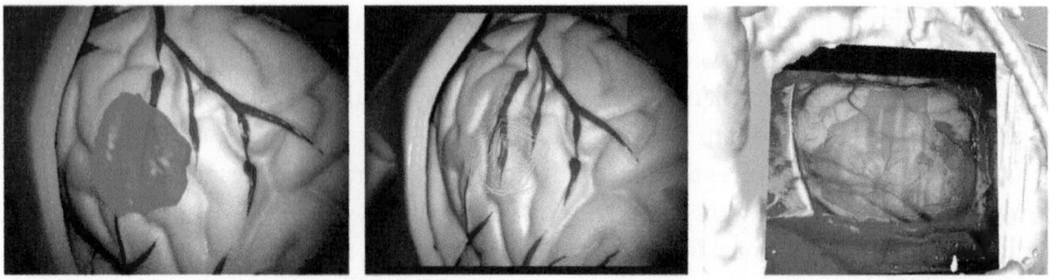

FIGURE 18.25 *The preoperatively acquired segmentation information of a brain tumor should be overlaid with the brain surface.* **Left:** *The tumor region is transparently overlaid on a phantom.* **Middle:** *The contours of the tumor are shown on top of a phantom.* **Right:** *Colored overlay on images of a real surgical microscope. The transparency level was carefully adjusted to enable a sufficiently clear view on the operating area (From: [Salah et al., 2010]).*

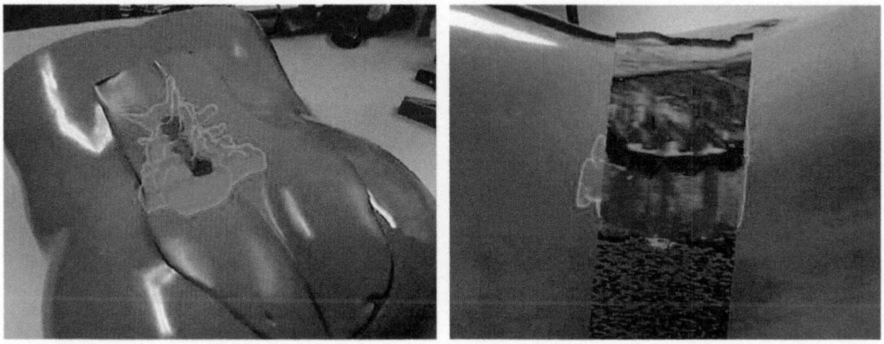

FIGURE 18.26 *Relevant information for minimally-invasive spine surgery is overlaid with data from the OR (here simulated with a phantom).* **Left:** *Only segmentation information related to vertebra (cyan), discs (green), and spinal canal (pink) is shown.* **Right:** *In addition, a portion of the underlying MRI data is presented (From: [Salah et al., 2011]).*

18.7.4 SMART VISIBILITY IN AR

In § 12.10 we got to know *smart visibility* techniques where the visibility of structures or regions was modified in order to support a certain communicative intent, e.g., to show a deep-seated tumor in the context of the enclosing organ. Focus-and-context (F+C) visualizations, cutaways, and ghosted views are widespread smart visibility techniques. In this section, we will get to know how such techniques may be used and refined for intraoperative visualization. To be really useful in medical AR, efficient GPU-based realizations are essential to provide the visual support in real time. We will also get to know one new concept, the *magic mirror* that is motivated by problems in surgery and thus introduced here.

Focus-and-context Visualizations in Medical AR The first dedicated F+C visualization for medical AR was introduced by Bichlmeier *et al.* [2007]. The video ghosting technique provided by them was promising, but rendering was restricted to static polygonal meshes. Later, Kutter *et al.* [2008] employed GPU raycasting and could provide a number of rendering modes, such as maximum intensity projection, with sufficient performance. Existing high-quality F+C visualizations, such as ClearView [Krüger *et al.*, 2006], support monoscopic visualization only. Kutter *et al.* [2008] refined that technique for stereo visualization and accelerated it to meet the high demands of an AR system (30 fps stereo rendering are essential to avoid annoying latency effects). Figure 18.27 presents example views of their system that are displayed in a HMD. Among the strategies to achieve this high performance is the consequent use of occlusion culling: real objects occlude a large portion of the volume data and derived surface models. These portions should be identified early and removed from further processing.

Magic Mirrors as Smart Visibility Paradigm for AR A virtual or *magic mirror* is a metaphor for providing useful information beyond rendering from a single viewpoint. The core association of that metaphor is that a different perspective is enabled (recall the discussion of metaphors in § 5.3). The use of virtual mirrors for AR applications in medicine is an innovative idea [Bichlmeier *et al.*, 2007, 2009a, Navab *et al.*, 2007a]. It is inspired by the use of mirrors in medicine, in particular the use of mirrors by dentists to explore otherwise hidden areas of the oral cavity. While access to hidden areas is the major motivation for integrating a virtual mirror, Bichlmeier *et al.* [2010] list a number of further application areas. Virtual mirrors can support navigation tasks, in particular in narrow or branching areas. In contrast to the real mirror, there are no physical

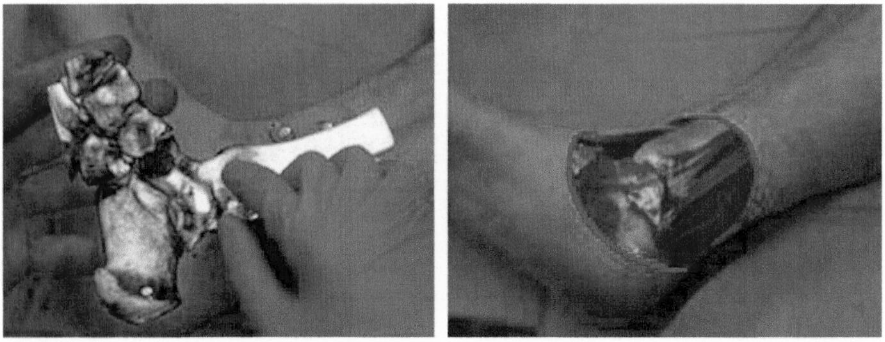

FIGURE 18.27 *AR view of bony structures aiming at supporting a trauma surgeon.* **Left:** *The drill entering the ankle is visible, and appears visually continuous with its virtual representation.* **Right:** *Focus-and-context rendering using shading as additional depth cue (Courtesy of Oliver Kutter, Technical University of Munich. See also [Kutter et al., 2008]).*

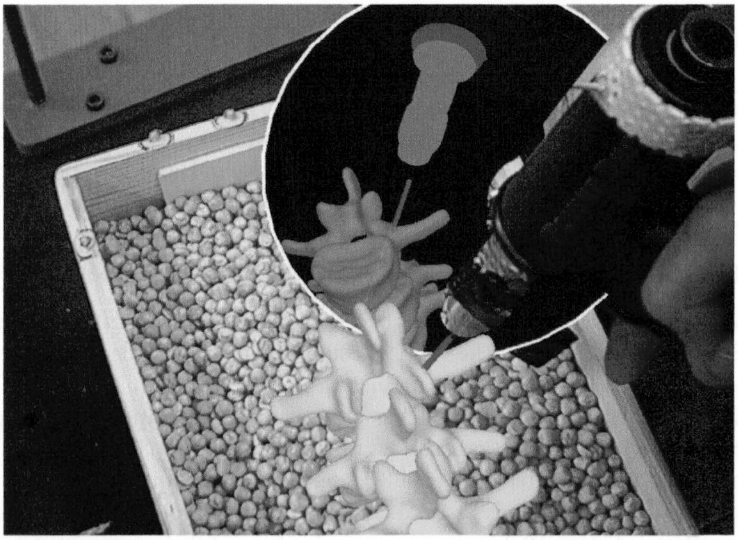

FIGURE 18.28 *The virtual mirror as navigation aid for spine surgery. In this intervention, pedicle screws are inserted to fixate a segment of the spine. The mirror may be rotated around the drilling device to reach different lateral views (Courtesy of Christoph Bichlmeier and Nassir Navab, CAMP, Technical University of Munich).*

limits to place a virtual mirror. A virtual mirror also enables a second perspective on a visible object. This additional perspective may strongly support the shape perception of an object with complex morphology.

Fixed and Movable Mirrors Like real mirrors, they may be fixed to a certain instrument or anatomical region or be interactively transformed. Fixed mirrors, such as those attached to a car, do not impose any navigation effort, but their flexibility is limited. Movable mirrors, like that of a dentist, enable a more active exploration of spatial relations. Figure 18.28 presents an example from minimally-invasive spine surgery.

Another essential example, described in [Wang *et al.* 2012] is the use of a mirror for angiography where X-ray images of an aneurysm are enhanced with 3D visualization displayed in the virtual mirror. Thus, 2D and 3D anatomical information can be presented simultaneously at *one* monitor instead of being displayed at separate monitors, as it is usually done. The virtual mirror is particularly useful for AR applications, since it somehow compensates for the lack of depth cues essential in interactive exploration of 3D models. In particular, the motion during interactive rotation provides such depth cues.

To be realized in AR, a flexible virtual mirror needs to be tracked and it should be controlled by a handheld device that acts as a remote control. As a series of publications from BICHLMEIER and colleagues shows, there are a number of applications, e.g., positioning of implants, osteotomy operations close to nerves or major vessels, control and positioning of screws and posing of drill canals. Bichlmeier *et al.* [2010] presented an evaluation where the virtual mirror is integrated in an AR system with video see-through HMD. The specific tasks resemble minimally-invasive surgery where surgeons only see small regions of the skin and penetrate trocars and other instruments. The virtual mirror was used as a navigation aid and the majority of 31 users performed navigation faster and more precise (with less collisions). It is not surprising that some users experienced problems with handling the virtual mirror in the beginning. Although a mirror is a familiar concept, the use of a virtual mirror in computer-assisted surgery is innovative and thus not familiar to users in the beginning. The virtual mirror as well as the previously described F+C visualizations are realized as components of the CAMPAR system [Sielhorst *et al.*, 2006].

18.7.5 ILLUSTRATIVE VISUALIZATION IN AR

In abdominal surgery, an AR visualization that overlays the real view of an organ with the virtual view of essential vascular structures and tumors may guide the surgeon. With conventional rendering techniques, the virtual objects are shaded and thus occlude a considerable portion of the real surgical view. Depth information related to the topology of vascular structures is hard to infer from conventional shading only. With feature lines, in particular with silhouettes, a sparse rendition of vascular structures is possible that enables a better view on the patient. On the other hand, explicit depth information may be included, e.g., a hatching style where the density of the lines encodes depth. Moreover, silhouettes may be enhanced with depth cues, e.g., the stroke thickness may be varied with depth.

Such a visualization is probably unfamiliar at first glance, but with some experience it provides more precise information. Figure 18.29 compares intraoperative AR views with conventional and illustrative rendering. While this example provides an anatomical overview, Figure 18.30 presents a detail view focused on the spatial relations around one tumor (both images are from clinical tests involving "real" patients). Similarly, also planned resection areas may be displayed and dedicated support for laparoscopic surgery is feasible [Hansen *et al.*, 2010b]. The user study with six surgical experts, of course, cannot provide a definitive answer to the clinical value of the illustrative visualization. However, the most essential initial result, namely that all surgeons could judge depth faster and more accurately, is promising. Suggestions from surgeons relate to a less abstract tumor visualization (Fig. 18.30, right) and to a less complex encoding of depth information along vessels. For more details on the illustrative visualization of vascular structures (recall § 12.9.3). Hansen [2012] performed a user study with these and other related illustrations to understand the effects on depth perception. When participants made wrong depth judgements, they were informed and discussed what caused that wrong assessment. One result of this discussion was that information need to be carefully reduced, otherwise the probability of wrong assessments increases (the two images in this chapter were correctly interpreted). The adaptation of line styles depending on the visibility is an effective approach, e.g., the line style of a vessel changes after a tumor.

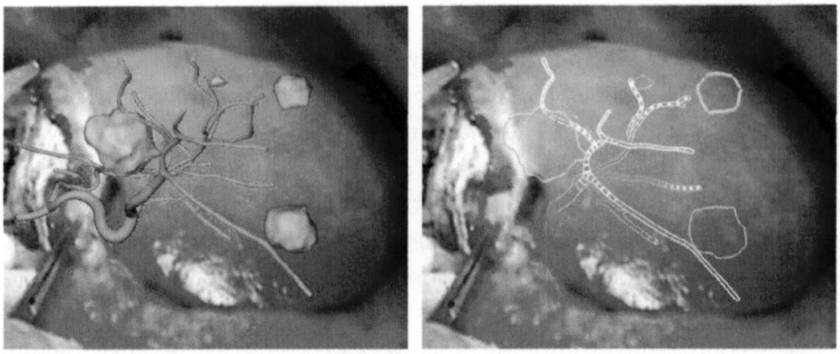

FIGURE 18.29 *Augmented reality overview visualization for liver surgery. The liver and its surrounding represent the surgical situation captured with a video camera. Virtual information related to the major portal vein branches and the tumors are overlaid with projector-based AR.* **Left:** *Conventional surface rendering occludes a relevant portion of the surgical reality.* **Right:** *Illustrative rendering with silhouettes and depth-encoding hatching lines (From: [Hansen et al., 2010b]).*

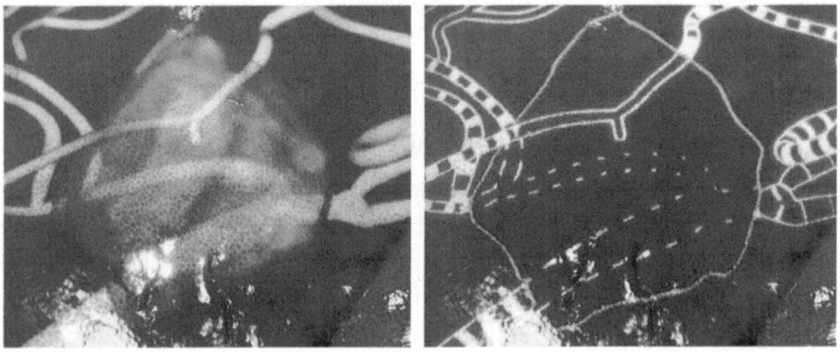

FIGURE 18.30 *Augmented reality detail view focused on the spatial relations around a tumor. The vascular branches, their branching pattern and spatial order should be conveyed.* **Left:** *Conventional surface rendering with a semi-transparent tumor to show also vessel segments behind.* **Right:** *The tumor is only outlined with a silhouette. This abstract representation makes it possible to display more detail related to the depth of vascular structures (From: [Hansen et al., 2010b]).*

18.7.6 INTERACTION IN THE OR

The simplest interaction task to be supported in the OR is to provide convenient access to preoperatively acquired data, derived segmentation information, and related 3D models.

Exploration of Preoperative Data Clipping, zooming, and rotating 3D models supports rehearsal of the anatomy for preparation immediately before surgery or in case of a challenging intraoperative situation. Even these simple tasks are challenging to realize in an ergonomic manner taking the context of surgery into account. The surgeon is focused on the intervention, eventually interrupting it. The required sterility further hampers intuitive, e.g., touch-based interaction. We briefly discussed this issue as a challenging HCI problem in medicine (recall § 5.8). Some kind of remote control is promising. Recent work employs gestures and vision techniques based on a camera such as the MICROSOFT KINECT or tracked devices, e.g., the pointing tool AXIOS 3D (recall Fig. 18.7).

Update of Preoperative Planning Usually, navigation and intraoperative visualization should ease the realization of a surgery as closely as possible to a preoperative plan. However, it turns out frequently, in particular in tumor surgery, that the actual pathology differs considerably in size and shape. A tumor is often larger than expected and additional metastases are frequently found. In this case, the surgeon has to decide whether a successful surgery is still feasible without a substantial risk for the patient. Moreover, in case surgery turns out to be feasible, the surgeon has to update the plan, e.g., with respect to nearby vascular structures and vascular territories. Interaction support is necessary for intraoperative planning. Of course, a system supporting this task must be easier to use than a complex preoperative planning tool and, again, the interaction should be designed to meet the sterility requirement in the OR.

Hansen *et al.* [2008] developed and evaluated such an intraoperative planning system. Although it is dedicated to liver surgery, the underlying concepts are more general. The user may modify an existing tumor or enter an additional tumor in a simplified manner by approximating it with a sphere. This is much faster and easier than to segment that tumor precisely. If additional tumors are found, they are directly defined in the 2D ultrasound image on the navigation system's display (see Fig. 18.31). With this information and using all the preoperatively analyzed structures, such as the liver, the vascular systems and their branching patterns, an updated analysis is possible. This analysis calculates which vessel segments are in the safety margin of the new or modified tumor, which vessel segments depend on the directly affected parts, and which portion of liver tissue would no longer be supplied with blood or is in risk of venous congestion.

Thus, with a rather simple input, the preoperatively analyzed data can be enhanced and reused to generate a new resection plan or to deduce that successful surgery is no longer possible. Hansen *et al.* [2008] also carefully discussed how the ultrasound plane can be shown simultaneously with planning data to integrate the intraoperative imaging with preoperative data.

Once camera alignment and occlusion of virtual objects are addressed, the system can be used in an OR setting. Typically, the display of the navigation system is operated via touchscreen or a draped pointing device [Ojdanic *et al.*, 2012]. Draping is necessary due to the sterility requirement. Since both options are not perfect, considerable research was performed in recent years to interact with wireless technology in a more convenient way.

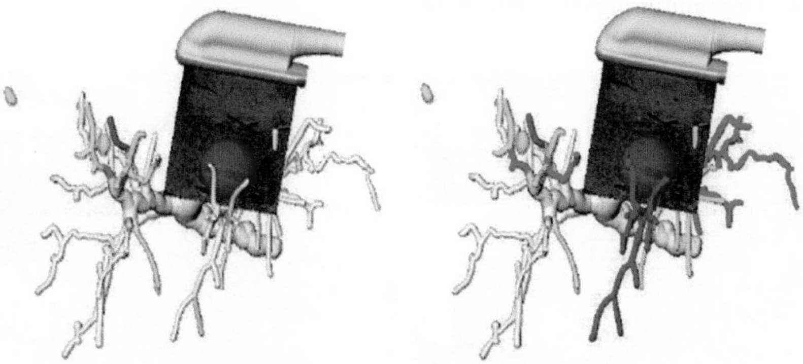

FIGURE 18.31 **Left:** *An additional tumor (red) was localized with intraoperative 2D ultrasound (see the abstracted display of the ultrasound probe).* **Right:** *The planning model is adapted accordingly with new vessel segments now at risk if this tumor is removed (Courtesy of Christian Hansen, Fraunhofer MEVIS. See also [Hansen et al., 2008]).*

A typical interaction in medical AR is the examination of the patient enriched with virtual information of target or risk structures, e.g., to navigate the surgical instruments to the target. However, these instruments can also be used to interact with the navigation system to modify parameters or to trigger specific operations, such as special rendering styles. Figure 18.15 (left), page 852 shows an example of a medical AR setup which used the pointer tool and a cutting plane tool to identify specific structures in the head to be used for a tissue classification [del Río *et al.*, 2005, 2006].

Interaction Stickers Fischer *et al.* [2005] introduced an interaction device, the *interaction sticker*, that is based on stickers that can be printed on sterilizable material and hence attached in the immediate proximity of the surgeon. This way, the surgeon can interact with the navigation system without directing personnel to modify the system parameters directly at the user interface of the navigation system. Typical tasks are

- the repositioning of the datasets,
- the application of clip planes, or
- the activation of a screen shot.

Also the drawing of an intervention plan directly on the representation of the patient (see Fig. 18.32) is possible. Currently, this is either only shown in the patient's dataset, or alternatively drawn with color markers directly on the target organ.

Before the interaction sticker can be used, it must be registered to the system by calibrating its respective activation fields with the pointing tool before the intervention. If a predefined interaction sticker is used, the calibration can be simplified by using video markers recognizable and differentiable by ARToolkit (see Fig. 18.33).

Measurements We discussed the role of measurements, such as distance and angular measurements, in Chapter 10. The focus there was on diagnostic and treatment planning applications. In particular, distance measurements are also important intraoperatively. As an example, the distance between a surgical instrument and the surgical target is an essential information that may be permanently presented [Kockro *et al.*, 2009]. Since other measures, such as those related to risk structures, may also be essential, some interaction facilities are necessary to define which measures should be displayed. To reduce the need for intraoperative interaction, measurement information for a particular kind of surgery may be specified once and re-used for similar surgical interventions.

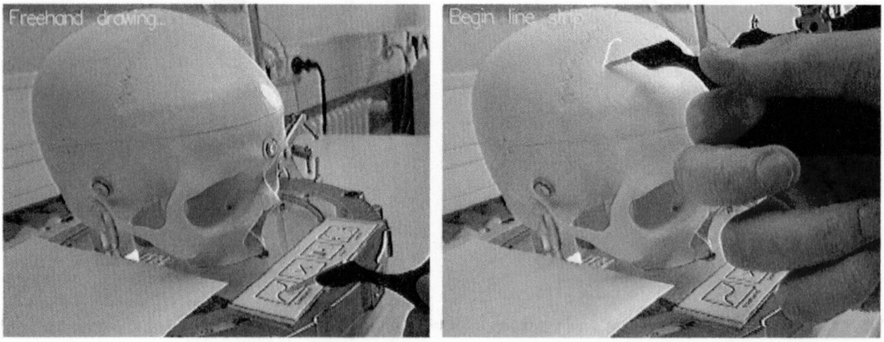

FIGURE 18.32 Intervention planning in the OR: An intervention plan is drawn virtually on a "patient." (Courtesy of Jan Fischer, University of Tübingen).

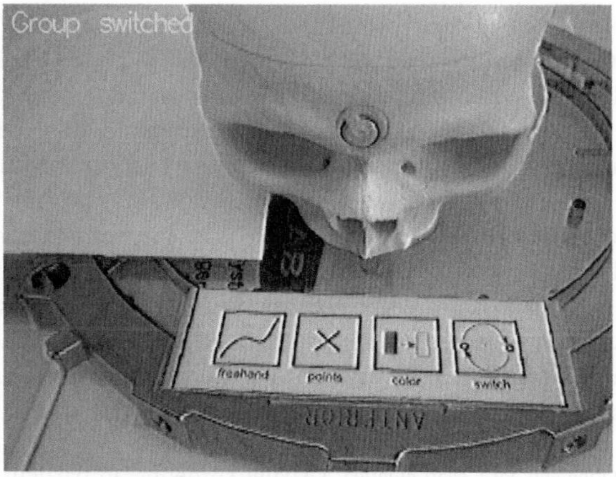

FIGURE 18.33 *Interaction sticker: Calibrated fields on a sterilizable sticker act as interaction buttons activated through the pointing device (Courtesy of Jan Fischer, University of Tübingen).*

18.7.7 CALIBRATED AUGMENTED REALITY ENDOSCOPE

As pointed out above, the setup where the surgeon sees patient and features from the patient's dataset on a screen resembles the setup of an endoscopic intervention. Hence, it is a natural step to combine a navigated conventional optical endoscope with a virtual endoscope (see Chap. 13). This scenario was already described in [Bartz *et al.*, 2003] for applications in neurosurgery and maxillo-facial surgery. However, to realize augmented reality endoscopes is very challenging due to the difficulties in the internal calibration. Endoscopes employ wide angle views, that is, strongly distorted images arise (see § 13.4). The information extracted from these images must be used for the calibration.

Once the optical endoscope is internally and externally calibrated as an instrument (through the optical infrared tracking system) and as a camera (through the vision-based tracking system), the virtual objects can be embedded into the endoscopic image. Note that we assume here that the video stream from the endoscopic camera is already digitized. While this is provided by a fully digital endoscope, it does require framegrabbing for standard analog endoscopes.

18.8 APPLICATIONS

In this section, we discuss clinical applications based on the technology presented in this chapter. While many research projects focused on selected technical challenges, rather few systems are motivated by clinical needs and carefully realized to solve them.

After general remarks on clinical applicability of medical AR (§ 18.8.1), we consider neurosurgery as a more established area where no severe deformations due to breathing and heart beat occur and where the skull provides a good reference frame (§ 18.8.2), as well as liver surgery which may be considered an emerging application area (§ 18.8.3).

18.8.1 WORKFLOW ANALYSIS FOR MEDICAL AUGMENTED REALITY

Before we discuss selected applications of medical AR, some general comments are necessary to understand the clinical practice and the success of advanced technology support. First of all, it is essential to deeply understand the current clinical workflow (recall our discussion of workflow analysis in § 5.2.3.1). To say it in the words of Nassir Navab who was extraordinarily successful in that area: "We can augment the reality only if we know what it is and *how* it needs to be augmented." [Navab *et al.*, 2007b]. This includes an understanding of the individual steps in surgery, their dependency and frequency, the kind of information that is required and the decisions to be taken. Surgeons grasp tissue, dissect it, use their optical aids, such as a microscope, and the amount of information necessary to support them is very different and specific for each of these actions. Medical AR should fit as seamlessly as possible in the current workflow. AR should rather enhance existing workflows and not require surgeons to completely change familiar procedures—they would consequently avoid such technology that invalidates their experience. To gain this in-depth understanding requires many careful observations in the OR as well as interviews to clarify the relevance of certain aspects. Many further parameters can be recorded using sensors, endoscopic cameras, and other technology already available in the OR. Despite the strong differences between the individual interventions, there are some general aspects clearly described by Navab *et al.* [2007b]:

- *Surgeons need augmentation only for a short duration.* Usually, surgeons, in particular experienced surgeons, benefit from an overlay of virtual information only in a limited time frame (compared to the overall duration of surgery).
- *Provide an initial in-situ visualization.* An in-situ visualization of virtual information is particularly relevant in the beginning of surgery. To see the patient on the OR table and to rehearse the anatomy based on preoperative data in the context of that patient, is a powerful mental support.
- *Adaptive information presentation.* Information needs differ from surgeon to surgeon as well as from situation to situation. Default visualization parameters for different stages in the surgical workflow, e.g., a "workflow-driven" presentation should be provided as well as settings to tailor the visualization to the current surgeon.

The latter aspect is particularly important. With AR there is a risk to overwhelm the user with too much information. Careful adaptation may enable a tailored and easy-to-comprehend information.

Consider the Whole Operative Workflow According to Kalkofen *et al.* [2006], visualization techniques applied during intraoperative imaging should be similar to those used in preoperative planning. We do not completely agree with Kalkofen *et al.* [2006] who state that the *same* techniques should be used, since this may not be appropriate due to the different context. But at least the differences should be restricted to a minimum, i.e., colors for objects usually should be the same. Finally, also follow-up image data is acquired to verify the outcome of surgery. Here again, similar techniques for segmentation, registration, and visualization should be used.

Software Strategy for Clinical Use of Medical AR The clinical application requires a reliable quality of registration, tracking, and calibration and software that is used without any confusion even under the severe pressure of a complex intervention. Kalkofen *et al.* [2006] further emphasize the need for an appropriate and integrated software strategy that strongly reuses components and libraries that are already tested and certified, e.g., Image-Guided Software Toolkit (IGSTK) [Gary *et al.*, 2006].[5]

Support for Documentation As we stated in § 3.6.6.3, *documentation* plays a crucial role in all stages of medical diagnosis and treatment. Every step needs to be fully documented for further treatment, exchange with colleagues, accounting with insurance companies and for legal reasons. In particular, surgical interventions—often the core of the whole diagnostic-therapeutic pipeline—need to be documented

5 http://www.igstk.org/

[Kalkofen *et al.*, 2006]. Software support for this unloved and tedious procedure is highly welcome and in fact needed.

18.8.2 NEUROSURGERY

We discussed neurosurgical planning in § 17.5.3. Here, we extend this discussion and explain intraoperative navigation support and visualization. "A neurosurgical operation is a challenge to spatial comprehension. Skin incision, craniotomy and tissue dissection are directly dependent on a comprehensive structural understanding of the surgical target, its surrounding structures, and the surgical corridor that leads to it" [Kockro *et al.*, 2009]. Thus, navigation support is desirable for interventions, such as tumor surgery, clipping of cerebral aneurysms and epilepsy surgery. Among the goals of using intraoperative visualization in neurosurgery is the reduction of the number of re-operations due to recurring brain tumors. In particular optimal resection control based on intraoperative imaging and navigation may improve the clinical outcome. The DEX-RAY system by Kockro *et al.* [2009] provides video-augmented reality. The surgeon employs a handheld probe, similar to the image overlay device (recall Fig. 18.34). The probe contains a small video camera that is directed to the surgical field. The video stream, obtained with that camera, is enhanced with preoperative data and related planning results. DEX-RAY is presented along with six detailed descriptions of the actual clinical use. The system provides useful information presented in a large window that is complemented by three orthogonal slice views. The system use is only limited in narrow cavities where simply not enough light is available to acquire video data in high quality.

There are also commercial products for intraoperative visualization in neurosurgery, such as the Brainsuite® iMRI from Brainlab. It integrates intraoperative MRI with surgical planning and a ceiling-mounted navigation system.[6] One challenge to be tackled in a commercial product is to achieve compatibility with OR tables from different manufacturers. Registration with preoperative data is performed automatically without the need to access anatomical landmarks.

18.8.3 LIVER SURGERY

Liver surgery is often accomplished to treat patients with hepatocellular carcinoma or metastasis, primarily from colorectal cancer. Navigation and AR support would be highly desirable, since often deep-seated tumors need to be treated close to adjacent risk structures, such as major vascular structures. On the other

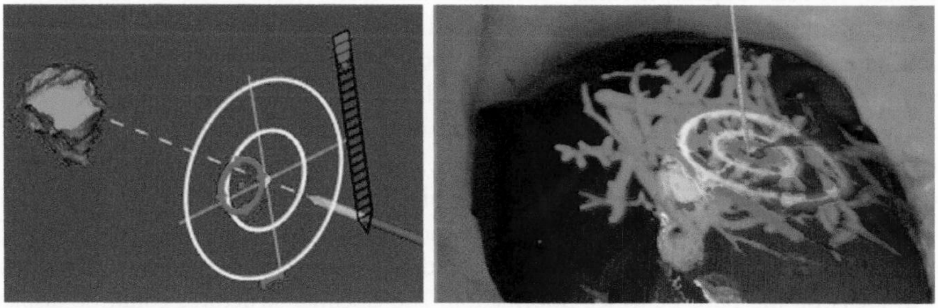

FIGURE 18.34 *Image guidance in RFA.* **Left:** *the guidance elements, the depth bar and the shooting target are shown schematically. Also the needle tip and the trajectory are displayed. Thus, several treatment strategies may be evaluated.* **Right:** *the guidance is actually overlaid to the liver surface along with preoperatively segmented vessels and tumors (From: [Gavaghan et al., 2011b]).*

6 www.brainlab.com

hand, navigation support for surgery of soft tissue structures is very difficult to provide. There are different treatment options in case of cancer in the liver. For AR support, surgery and interventional approaches are relevant. We mentioned already some concepts that were rather general but aiming particularly at liver surgery, e.g., the illustrative visualization and interaction techniques introduced by Hansen *et al.* [2008, 2010b] and Ojdanic *et al.* [2012]. Besides the conventional open surgery aiming at complete tumor removal with a sufficient security margin, there are (minimally-invasive) laparoscopic techniques and ablation therapies, most notably radio-frequency ablation (RFA), where the whole tumor should be destroyed by applying energy and heating the tissue. Increased accuracy leading to the complete destruction of a metastasis is known to have a positive effect on the tumor recurrence. Navigation support is easier for tumor ablation, since the movements during surgery are more restricted. However, respiratory motion still causes considerable problems and often limits support for larger targets that are easier to locate. We cannot go into the details of specific solutions for motion compensation here, but want to point the reader to a series of publications that studied possible solutions and the amount of errors in needle placement that cannot be avoided [Maier-Hein *et al.*, 2008a,b,c].

Augmented Reality for Laparoscopic Surgery Laparoscopic surgery is motivated by the fact that only a small number of patients is eligible to open surgery, e.g., due to a bad general condition, and due to the rather low long-term survival rate after ablation. At least some patients can better tolerate laparoscopic liver surgery than open surgery and might benefit from a better long-term result compared to ablation. A major challenge in laparoscopic surgery is to define and realize an appropriate access to the pathology. Three to five ports are placed on the patient and used to maneuver the instruments and the laparoscope to the right region. The system developed by Feuerstein *et al.* [2008] is focused on supporting this task. Fiducials at the patient's skin are employed as landmarks for the registration. The registration allows the user to simulate a camera flight along the laparoscope's axes, and thus to assess potential port positions. In laparoscopic surgery, carbon dioxide is insufflated to achieve optimal visibility of internal structures. This, however, causes deformations of soft tissue organs, such as the liver. Feuerstein *et al.* [2008] employ a mobile C-arm for intraoperative imaging to employ current imaging data. The most severe problem that may occur in laparoscopic surgery is bleeding of a major vessel, which requires to transform the minimally-invasive surgery to an open surgery. The intraoperative guidance may help to reduce the rate of such unfortunate transformations. This, however, has to be demonstrated in a clinical study.

Augmented Reality for Radio-frequency Ablation RFA, like other interventions where a catheter or needle is placed in a pathology, requires to determine an entry point and a target point. The preoperatively planned target point, often centrally located in a tumor, is difficult to locate precisely during the intervention. With their image overlay device (recall § 18.6.6) Gavaghan *et al.* [2011a] can provide dedicated support for this demanding task (see Fig. 18.34). For this purpose, the IOD is combined with a navigation system designed and developed for liver surgery [Peterhans *et al.*, 2011]. Often a patient has several metastases to be treated. The metastasis closest to the trajectory of the ablation tool is chosen as current target. Gavaghan *et al.* [2011b] evaluated their system in animal experiments (porcine liver, see Fig. 18.34, right). While in Figure 18.34 (right) a lot of information is presented, the visualization of vascular structures may be displayed to focus on the pure guidance information. The essential structures could be displayed in a comprehensible manner and depth perception was supported well. Only structures inside the liver are affected by parallax error and thus their perceived location is slightly displaced—an issue that still needs to be better handled.

A comprehensive system for supporting liver punctures with medical AR has also been developed in a cooperation between the French institutes IRCAD and INRIA [Nicolau *et al.*, 2005].

The navigation system presented by Peterhans *et al.* [2011] was also used to support open liver surgery where again the spatial relation of a tumor to the surrounding vasculature is essential. In addition, injuries of nearby biliary ducts need to be prevented. The additional challenge here is to quickly detect and analyze changes of the liver shape. With a sophisticated deformation model, Peterhans *et al.* [2011] solved that problem sufficiently well for actual use in surgery. As a major effect, the anatomical orientation of surgeons aiming at a tumor they do not see, is improved. On the downside, the additional setup time was about 16 minutes (for experienced users).

AR in liver surgery relies on fast and accurate tracking of the involved soft tissue structures. This highly demanding problem is still not completely solved, but recent progress indicates that accurate tracking might be possible in the foreseeable future [Markert *et al.*, 2010, Peterhans *et al.*, 2011].

18.8.4 VALIDATION AND CLINICAL EVALUATION

Validation, i.e., a systematic analysis of the accuracy of information provided in navigated surgery is an essential prerequisite for clinical use. Widespread clinical use beyond research projects and pilot studies also requires systematic clinical evaluation, i.e., an analysis of risks in surgery, clinical outcome, and costs, e.g., related to the equipment and OR use. Finally, such studies are an essential prerequisite to analyze the cost justification.

Validation Intraoperative visualization in navigated surgery strongly relies on accurate tracking, registration, and calibration. Since navigated surgery systems to be used during surgery are high-risk medical products, the accuracy of individual steps and the overall system accuracy need to be carefully analyzed under realistic conditions. While this aspect of validation may be largely accomplished with phantom data or in animal experiments, use in real surgery is necessary to analyze the accuracy of the intervention, e.g., in case of implant placement or pedicle screw insertion. Without going into detail, it is obviously a challenging organizational task to prepare, conduct, analyze, and interpret such validation studies. Among others, such studies raise ethical concerns and require ethical board approval and, due to the often considerable setup and training effort, such studies are also expensive.

Clinical Evaluation While technical accuracy is a necessary prerequisite for improved clinical results, it cannot guarantee them. Clinical evaluation studies focus on the outcome of navigated surgery also in comparison to surgery without this support. Often, the outcome, e.g., the longevity of implants can only be judged after many years including a number of follow-up examinations. Hence, comprehensive evaluation studies lack far behind the current technical development. On the other hand, care providers often wait for such studies to decide in which cases the additional costs of navigated surgery should be recompensated. Issues of validation and clinical evaluation of augmented reality in surgery are discussed in [Janin and Korb, 2008].

18.9 SUMMARY

In this chapter we discussed how the results of preoperative planning can be applied in the intraoperative setting. Major prerequisites for an intraoperative application are appropriate dataset acquisition, registration of the patient and the respective datasets as well as calibration and tracking. We briefly introduced image-guided surgery as an established technology to provide navigation support in surgery. Tracking of position and pose of surgical instruments to display them along with the patient anatomy is a major component of surgical navigation. Medical augmented reality is an advanced variant of IGS where the relevant preoperative data and navigation information are presented along with the patient's body and instead of at a separate monitor.

With medical AR systems, previously hidden targets (e.g., lesions and tumors) or risk structures (nerves or blood vessels) can be seen while interacting with the patient. Although this integration of all relevant information has obvious advantages, it comes at a price of additional calibration and tracking that increases setup times and introduces further potential sources of error. The integration of real and virtual information also causes notable perceptual problems and a lot of current research aims at solving these problems. The increased use of intraoperative navigation, including Navigated Control® and the emerging use of medical AR, allows not only to perform conventional surgery more precisely but is likely to enable new kinds of surgery with smaller surgical targets.

In the beginning of medical AR development, also real-time rendering was a serious problem and medical AR was used primarily in systems with expensive high-end graphics computers. Meanwhile, performance problems are largely solved and all necessary equipment is available off-the-shelf at a reasonable price. Thus, many AR setups use standard virtual reality components, in particular standard tracking technology. However, the use of such technology in a medical setting, in particular an OR, requires special certification of all components. Therefore, the strategy from several research groups is to integrate AR in already certified medical navigation systems.

Furthermore, ORs are typically small rooms that do not easily accommodate the extra equipment. In addition, extra equipment often requires tedious setup procedures. Section 18.4.2 described an IGS configuration that employs an already certified navigation system, minor additional components, and a simplified setup, thus removing most of the issues that obstructed AR from being a successful application in the OR. The seamless integration of AR in existing workflows and navigation systems is crucial for their widespread clinical acceptance.

While navigated surgery is widespread for complex interventions since at least a decade, AR and related advanced intraoperative visualization techniques are still often in the prototyping stage. Navab *et al.* [2012] state that "The development of AR systems for use in the medical field still faces three major challenges: the correct perception of virtual data in the real world, integrating AR into complex medical workflows, and implementing the required change in culture." The most promising strategies with respect to clinical application are those that may be seamlessly integrated in current workflows, e.g., in microscopy and endoscopy. Besides rigorous workflow support and development according to legal constraints, there is also a need for further research. In particular, more in-depth AR perception studies are required, as already pointed out by Sauer *et al.* [2008]. Among the few existing studies, Johnson *et al.* [2004] gained considerable attention. Their study measured over- and underestimation of depth values in stereo AR systems depending on various parameters. Later, Bichlmeier *et al.* [2007] compared seven different rendering modes for medical AR in spine surgery and assessed depth perception.

Outlook Like in other areas where AR solutions are developed and refined, new display devices are promising. In particular, the development of trackable eyeglasses has a lot of momentum. Current devices are lightweight, provide an adjustable intraocular distance and the most advanced are combined with precise head tracking. Being developed for the mass market of entertainment they are rather low-cost devices compared to the very special and expensive AR equipment developed earlier.

FURTHER READING

An ideal addition to this chapter is the book "Image-Guided Interventions" [Peters and Cleary, 2008]. In particular, the chapter by Sauer *et al.* [2008] has a similar scope like this chapter and is written by experts who developed a number of AR systems, highlighting challenges and practical solutions. Cleary and Peters [2010] give a historical overview over two decades of development based on advances in medical imaging. It includes both components of IGS and applications, including evolving new minimally-invasive procedures. Kersten-Oertel *et al.* [2012] provided a very systematic survey containing a taxonomy of visualization techniques in image-guided surgery using the data, the visualization processing and the view as major criteria to describe and classify 17 systems.

Scheuering *et al.* [2003] introduced an AR system for liver surgery, which they combined with video sequences. More information on this system is provided in [Scheuering, 2003]. Another AR system for liver surgery planning was described by Bornik *et al.* [2003].

Olbrich *et al.* [2005] proposed a partial and periodic combination of virtual and video-endoscopic images for endoscopic liver surgery. Related techniques were also used for robot-assisted port placement for heart surgery [Feuerstein *et al.*, 2005]. The CAMP group in Munich was particularly successful in designing and evaluating AR technology for the OR. In addition to many papers that we cited throughout the chapter, we recommend the PhD theses [Bichlmeier, 2010, Sielhorst, 2008, Feuerstein, 2008] that are available online. The PhD thesis of Jan Fischer describes rendering methods for medical AR [Fischer, 2008].

We briefly discussed the promising area of using illustrative techniques for medical augmented reality. It might be interesting to look beyond medical applications to understand illustrative concepts used for example in industrial applications of AR [Kalkofen *et al.*, 2007, Fischer *et al.*, 2008].

Various solutions have been proposed for the occlusion problem of AR. Breen *et al.* [1996] proposed a model-based approach for static occlusion, which was later extended by Fuhrmann *et al.* [1999] for the user's body. A variation of the latter approach for marker occlusion of the user's hand was presented by Malik *et al.* [2002]. Dynamic occlusion with static backgrounds on the basis of textures for the background objects was addressed by Fischer *et al.* [2003]. Finally, Berger [1997] and Lepetit and Berger [2000] examined occlusion in stored video sequences.

As mentioned above, the ARToolKit [Kato and Billinghurst, 1999] is the standard, but not the only vision-based tracking solution. ARTag Fiala [2004] is more reliable and provides a more robust vision-based tracking solution. However, it is—in contrast to the ARToolKit—not available in source code, and hence, its integration may be difficult or even not possible.

One solution to tissue deformation is the intraoperative acquisition of new image data intraoperatively. A popular approach is to integrate data from tracked ultrasound scanner [Sauer *et al.*, 2001, Vogt *et al.*, 2003] and register it to preoperatively acquired CT or MRI datasets [Lange *et al.*, 2002,2004a]. Alternatively, calibrated and tracked intraoperative X-ray systems are an option proposed by Navab *et al.* [1999]. Another alternative for intraoperative imaging is MRI with an open low-field MRI scanner [Kettenbach *et al.*, 2000] or with a full-field MRI scanner [Nimsky *et al.*, 2006b].

Chapter 19

Visual Exploration of Simulated and Measured Flow Data

19.1 INTRODUCTION

In recent years, the acquisition and generation of flow data played an essential role in medical research and partially also in treatment planning. A particularly important example is the measurement and simulation of blood flow. This is motivated by increasing evidence that blood flow changes in a characteristic way as a consequence of vascular diseases, such as aneurysms [Cebral *et al.*, 2011], aortic dissection, or cardiovascular diseases, such as atherosclerosis [Wischgoll *et al.*, 2009b]. All these diseases primarily occur in regions with complex (sometimes even turbulent) and instable flow that changes strongly over time. Blood flow may be measured, e.g., with Doppler ultrasound or special MRI sequences. As an alternative, blood flow may be simulated with computational fluid dynamics (CFD). Simulations not only represent the current physiological situation but also enable to predict the effect of treatment, e.g., of stenting or coiling an aneurysm.

In a similar way, biomechanical simulations enable to predict the stress distribution depending on the choice and placement of an implant. Biophysical simulations are also accomplished to investigate the electrophysiology of the heart, and thus to better understand arrhythmia, and to simulate the temperature distribution caused by heat-inducing tumor therapies, such as radio-frequency ablation. These different kinds of simulations have many commonalities. Medical image data needs to be processed to generate surface meshes of the relevant anatomy. These surface meshes are transformed in volume grids representing also a mesh of the internal structures. Finally, simulations, in most cases finite volume simulations, are performed. As a result, multivalued and multidimensional, time-dependent flow data needs to be explored and analyzed. These flow data represent the regional distribution of attributes, such as flow speed, flow direction, pressure, and further related attributes such as velocity or pressure gradient.

The generation of simulation models and the exploration of the related results are promising, but relatively new in medicine. However, these techniques are extensively used in engineering and some natural sciences, such as for simulations of air flow around cars, planes, and ships and analysis (aerodynamics), and studies of weather phenomena (hydrodynamics) and of electro-magnetic fields, e.g., in welding processes are widespread. Modeling and measurements of flow phenomena are performed in order to better understand the underlying processes and to optimize them, e.g., by a modification of the geometry of engine components. For these widespread applications, sophisticated software support is available. However, it is not tailored to the filigree human anatomy and special treatment questions in medicine. Thus, we primarily describe research prototypes tailored to these questions.

In real life, most flow phenomena are time-dependent, i.e., flow patterns change over time. Thus, time-dependent (*unsteady*) simulations are more realistic than simplified steady simulations. However, steady simulations are much faster to compute, the results require much less storage and are easier to explore. As a consequence, both steady and unsteady simulations have a role in medical flow investigations.

Visual Computing for Medicine, Second Edition. http://dx.doi.org/10.1016/B978-0-12-415873-3.00019-5

Organization We first explain basic techniques for visualization and exploration of flow (§ 19.2). In § 19.3, we explain how surface meshes, suitable for simulation, are generated from medical image data. These surface meshes are used as input to generate a volume grid as a basis for actual simulations. In this section, we build on and extend the discussion of surface mesh extraction for visualization purposes (Chap. 6). We go on and describe two case studies in more detail: the visual exploration of cardiac blood flow related to diagnosis of cardiac diseases (§ 19.4). and the exploration of simulated blood flow for treatment planning in cerebral aneurysms (§ 19.5). In this context, we briefly introduce computational fluid dynamics (CFD). This is a very large field. Thus, we can only give the reader an idea of basic concepts. Finally, in § 19.6 we give a brief overview of other biophysical simulations that pose interesting visualization and interaction problems.

19.2 BASIC FLOW VISUALIZATION TECHNIQUES

Flow data may be acquired in 2D, e.g., at a plane, in 2 1/2 D, i.e., at a (curved) surface and in 3D. While all flow data are essential in medical applications, 3D data has the greatest potential situation, and is thus the focus of this section. The following introduction is based on survey articles from [McLoughlin *et al.*, 2010] and [Peng and Laramee, 2009, Salzbrunn *et al.*, 2008]. According to them, basic flow visualization techniques may be classified in:

- direct,
- feature-based,
- texture-based,
- geometry-based, and
- partition-based.

The following subsections introduce these different approaches and discuss their application. Besides these direct flow visualization techniques, the visualization of scalar quantities, such as pressure or velocity magnitude (speed), is essential for evaluating flow data. Isosurfaces or contour plots in cross-sectional areas are among the frequently used techniques. Since we discussed scalar visualization techniques in other chapters, we focus here on flow visualization.

19.2.1 DIRECT FLOW VISUALIZATION TECHNIQUES

Direct techniques map all elements of a vector field to a graphics primitive (glyph) or color. An early example for a direct technique was the ray-casting approach from Frühauf [1996] that applies direct volume rendering to vector fields. Arrow glyphs that represent the flow direction are often color-coded according to the magnitude of the local vector that typically represents flow speed. If only the magnitude of the flow is essential, colorcoding is the most widespread technique. Direct techniques are not particularly suited for 3D data, since occlusion and visual clutter are serious problems, even with interaction techniques such as clipping.

Even in 2D, direct techniques have substantial disadvantages. In a regular grid, the grid structure is disturbing, leading to the idea of *jittered* placement, where the glyph positions are slightly perturbed. A large number of glyphs is hard to interpret and glyph visualizations of flow are not coherent—users have to mentally integrate adjacent glyphs to understand the flow at a higher level. This problem might be slightly reduced again by a small perturbation of glyph positions with the goal that one glyph G_1 starts close to an adjacent glyph G_2 in the direction of G_1 (see Fig. 19.1). However, for a larger vector field it remains difficult to see the "big picture" with a direct visualization technique.

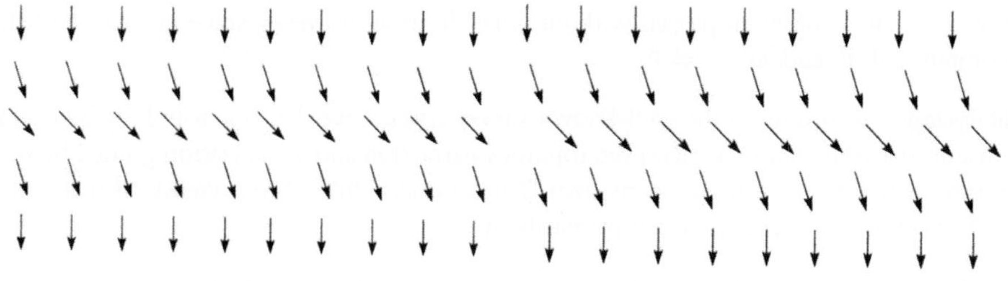

FIGURE 19.1 *The regular placement of glyphs (left) is optimized with small translations for better perception (right) (Courtesy of Colin Ware).*

19.2.2 FEATURE-BASED FLOW VISUALIZATION TECHNIQUES

Instead of rendering the entire dataset, feature-based techniques filter the data and render only relevant portions. Features may be direct attribute values, such as magnitude of the flow velocity, but also derived properties, such as pressure gradient. There are a couple of typical characteristics of flow fields known from fluid mechanics, vector field analysis and topology.

Since simulated and measured flow data is available at discrete grids, the necessary derivatives have to be numerically approximated as differences between vectors in the neighborhood. In the following, we characterize some essential properties from a vector field, denoted as $\vec{v}$. $\vec{v}$ might be steady $\vec{v}(x)$ or unsteady $\vec{v}(x, t)$.

The *divergence* is a vector operator that characterizes the change of a little volumetric element of the flow. The computation of the divergence (also called density of the fluid) in a continuously differentiable vector field in the (x, y, z) Cartesian coordinate system is carried out according to Equation 19.1. The divergence is a signed scalar value. In incompressible media, such as blood, it is always zero, but in compressible media, such as gas, it is an interesting property that changes locally. The divergence represents the density of the net outward flux of a vector field from a given point.

$$div\,\vec{v} = \vec{\nabla} \cdot \vec{v} = u_x + v_y + w_z = \frac{\partial u}{\partial x} + \frac{\partial v}{\partial y} + \frac{\partial w}{\partial z} \tag{19.1}$$

The *vorticity*, an attribute often used to characterize cardiac and cerebral blood flow, characterizes the local swirling behavior of flow and is computed according to Equation 19.2:

$$\vec{\omega} = rot\,\vec{v} = \vec{\nabla} \times \vec{v} = \left(\frac{\partial v_z}{\partial y} - \frac{\partial v_y}{\partial z}, \frac{\partial v_x}{\partial z} - \frac{\partial v_z}{\partial x}, \frac{\partial v_y}{\partial x} - \frac{\partial v_x}{\partial y}\right)^T \tag{19.2}$$

The term "rotation" indicates that vorticity is a measure for local circulation. $\partial\vec{v}_x$, $\partial\vec{v}_y$, and $\partial\vec{v}_z$ represent the partial derivatives of the flow field $\vec{v}$. In contrast to divergence, vorticity is a vector characterizing the double rotation velocity in x, y, and z direction. As a final example, we define *helicity* according to Levy *et al.* [1990], since this feature is often discussed in relation to blood flow. The *normalized helicity* H_n is defined in a flow field everywhere except at critical points according to Equation 19.3:

$$H_n = \frac{\vec{v} \cdot \vec{\omega}}{|\vec{v}| \cdot |\vec{\omega}|} \tag{19.3}$$

In this definition, H_n is the cosine of the angle between velocity $\vec{v}$ and vorticity $\vec{\omega}$ [Jiang *et al.*, 2005].[1] Helicity may be employed to assess vortex core regions, since the angle between $\vec{v}$ and $\vec{\omega}$ is small in

1 We discriminate between velocity as a vector with a certain direction and a magnitude and speed as a scalar value representing the magnitude of the velocity vector.

such regions. Helicity is often employed without normalization, however, since normalized helicity can only be computed if $\vec{v}$ and $\vec{\omega}$ are $\neq 0$.

Vector Field Topology According to the well-known survey articles, we describe topology here as a special aspect of feature-based techniques. However, topology extraction and visualization guided by such topological features active research topic on its own [Theisel *et al.*, 2003, 2005, Weinkauf *et al.*, 2005]. The topology of a vector field is characterized primarily by:

- *critical points*, i.e., points where the local vector is zero (in all components),
- critical points characteristics, and
- critical points connections.

A critical point may be

- a *sink*, also called *attracting node* where all vectors converge,
- a *source*, a diverging point of a vector field, also called *repelling node*,
- an *attracting focus*, where the flow is attracted in a spiral pattern,
- a *repelling focus*, where the flow is repelled in a spiral pattern,
- a *saddle point*, or
- a *center point* that is embedded by (circular) flow around (see Fig. 19.2).

A *laminar flow*, e.g., in a healthy straight branch of the vascular system, where the flow is roughly parallel, does not exhibit critical points. However, flows in curved areas, at bifurcations, after obstacles and narrowings tend to exhibit *turbulent behavior*[2]—these areas tend to contain critical points that may change their position and character very fast. Critical points may also occur in the transition zone between laminar and turbulent flows.

In the human vascular system, narrowings may result from a stenosis after plaque formation. Flow data provides complementary information to the geometry that allows to better assess the relevance of a stenosis. Both the flow patterns and quantitative values, such as the speed, are relevant for diagnosis. While in laminar flow it is straightforward to predict where a massless particle will arrive if injected in the flow, in turbulent flow adjacent particles may end up at completely different points.

Critical points need to be determined by means of interpolation, since usually no single value is exactly zero. Critical points may only occur in cells, where the sign of all components is different for the vertices

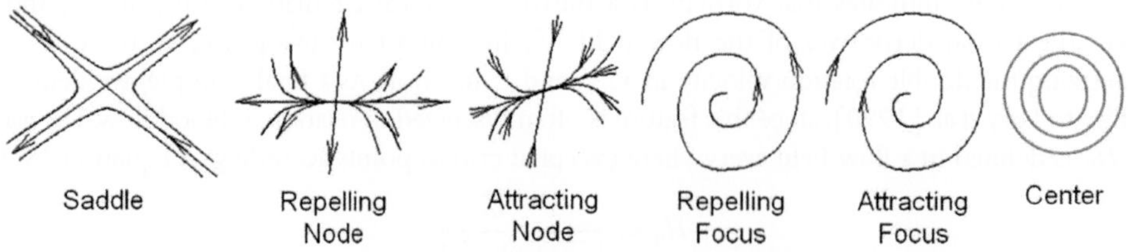

FIGURE 19.2 *Vector field topology is characterized by critical points. Six different types of critical points may occur in a 2D vector field.*

2 Turbulent behavior not only depends on the geometry but also on the viscosity of the liquid and the velocity. More precisely, with these numbers the Reynolds number is determined. If this number is below a threshold, the flow is considered to be laminar, otherwise turbulent.

of that cell. In a regular 3D grid, a cell consists of eight vectors $\vec{v}_1, \ldots, \vec{v}_8$ and when positive and negative x, y, and z values occur in these eight vectors, a subdivision in eight subvolumina reveals if a critical point is inside. This point can be determined with trilinear interpolation.

Local Analysis with the Jacobian While humans can easily recognize the different types of critical points in Figure 19.2, it would be interesting to determine their type automatically. This is possible by an analysis of the surrounding vector field. The Jacobian matrix of the (numerically approximated) partial derivatives in the neighborhood is used for an eigenanalysis. In the 2D case, the characteristic quadratic polynomial has two complex nulls with a real and an imaginary component. The sign of these four components (R_1, I_1 from the first and R_2, I_2 from the second null) indicates which type of critical point occurs (recall Fig. 19.2). Thinking carefully about the possible outcomes, of the eigenanalysis reveals that the list of six cases is not exhaustive, e.g., if R_1 or R_2 equal zero, other configurations occur.

As a general remark, the extraction of features to guide the visualization of flow is a powerful concept. However, a substantial and compute-intensive analysis of the whole field might be necessary, e.g., to determine and classify all critical points.

Using Features for Visualization A rather recent but essential trend is to combine flow visualization with *information visualization* techniques. We introduced information visualization techniques in § 16.5.1 in the context of perfusion data. Flow data, as they arise from biophysical simulations, are also high-dimensional data where information visualization and *visual analytics* techniques, such as clustering and dimension reduction, might help to focus on relevant attributes.

With feature-based techniques, users may select region in attribute views, such as histograms (for a scalar feature, such as speed) or scatterplots (for a combination of two features). Feature-based techniques are not restricted to binary decisions whether or not to render a certain portion of the vector field. Instead, fuzzy or smooth selections are possible, similar to *smooth brushing* (recall § 16.5.1). As an example, the flow speed may be used as criterion to filter the flow, guided by a transfer function that maps speed to opacity. This technique can be used in combination with arrow glyphs, but also with the texture-based and geometric techniques described below. In their pioneering work, Doleisch and Hauser [2002] presented the SimVis system to analyze data resulting from typical engineering simulations with information visualization techniques (see Fig. 19.3).

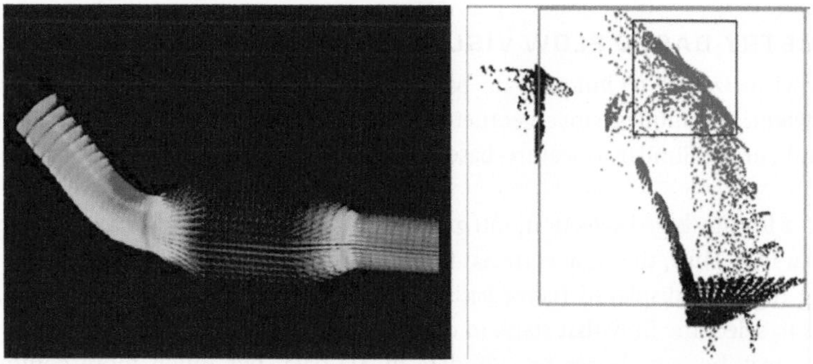

FIGURE 19.3 *Simulated flow in an exhaust pipe of a catalyzer is displayed. Smooth brushing in the scatterplot view (right) determines the visibility and opacity of flow-related information. Thus, features may be flexibly specified (Courtesy of Helmut Doleisch, SimVis Vienna).*

For a survey on features that might be derived from flow data, in particular from pathlines, the reader is referred to [Shi *et al.*, 2007]. As an example, they compute the differences between pathlines and streamlines at the same location in unsteady flow fields. Moreover, the Euclidean distance between start and end point of pathlines and streamlines characterizes whether the flow is primarily *laminar* or *swirling*. However, this distance measure is not perfectly reliable, since helical flow may be perfectly laminar—leading to almost constant distances.

The *winding angle*, the sum of all angles between subsequent points, is a further relevant feature. More recently, Lez *et al.* [2011] provided a system to support flow exploration based on pathline attributes in a carefully defined multiple-coordinated view framework. Pathline attributes were computed at different scales: the computation at a higher level is used to decide whether it is worthwhile to refine the analysis at a finer level.

19.2.3 TEXTURE-BASED FLOW VISUALIZATION

Texture-based methods use an input texture and modify it according to the local properties of the flow field. In contrast to geometric representations of the flow, a dense representation of the vector field arises, which is in principle better suited for 2D flow fields. The classical texture-based method is the line integral convolution (LIC), where a convolution filter is employed to modify a noise texture [Cabral and Leedom, 1993]. Given a streamline σ, LIC computes the image intensity I at pixel x_0 according to Equation 19.4, where T represents the noise texture and k the filter kernel. L represents the length of the streamline that is centered around s_0.

$$I(x_o) = \int_{s_0-L}^{s_0+L} k \cdot (s - s_0) T(\sigma(s)) ds \qquad (19.4)$$

Similar to the volume rendering integral (recall § 7.1), it is not solved analytically but instead approximated as a sum of elementary components. The numerical integration is performed with either Euler- or Runge-Kutta methods. A good trade-off between accuracy and speed is usually achieved with 4th-order Runge-Kutta methods.

Many improvements of the original technique were suggested, e.g., to integrate directional information (oriented LIC) [Wegenkittl and Gröller, 1997], to make the images independent from the resolution of the input texture and to accelerate the computation [Stalling and Hege, 1995]. Since these methods play a minor role in the following, we point the reader to the overview articles [Peng and Laramee, 2009] and [McLoughlin *et al.*, 2010] for further information.

19.2.4 GEOMETRY-BASED FLOW VISUALIZATION METHODS

Geometric flow visualization techniques are based on an integration along the vector field. They are referred to as *geometric* techniques, since geometric primitives, such as lines, ribbons, or tubes, are fitted along the integral curves. Similar to feature-based methods, usually of the whole data contributes to the visualization.

In contrast to a feature-based selection, integral curves are either started in a certain region of interest (ROI) or end in a ROI. Thus, the flow is traced from a certain interesting region or the flow that arrives in an interesting region is displayed (*inverse tracing*). It is also possible, but less common, to specify two regions in order to select the flow that starts in one region and ends in the second.

These regions may be, e.g., boxes or cylinders in 3D data, but much more common—at least in medical applications—are planes, as we will see later. Oblique planes in medical image data are referred to as *multiplanar reformatting* or MPR. Instead of a complete plane intersecting the whole dataset, usually a smaller plane is employed that intersects, for example, a vessel segment or a heart chamber.

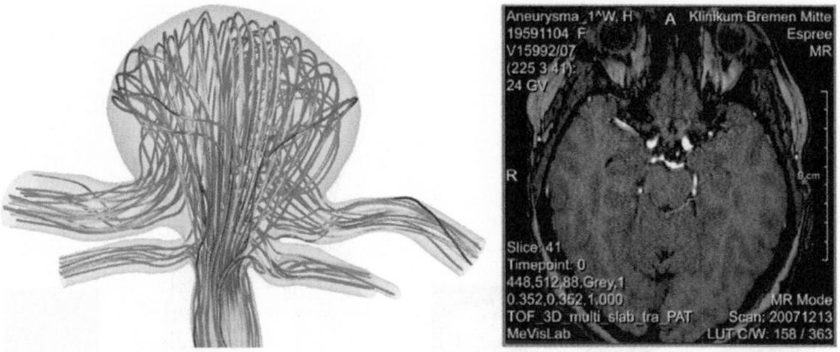

FIGURE 19.4 **Left:** *Color-coded streamlines in a vascular pathology as a standard output option of a widespread finite volume modeling tool. Here, the color encodes the particle ID and not a scalar attribute, such as speed (ANSYS Fluent).* **Right:** *For medical doctors, the relation to the underlying MRI dataset on the right is hard to infer (Courtesy of Gabor Janiga, University of Magdeburg).*

Generation of Integral Curves A common way to depict flow is using *integral curves*. There are two main approaches depending on whether the flow data is steady or time-dependent: *streamlines* and *pathlines*. Streamlines are related to steady flow, whereas pathlines convey the movement of massless particles in unsteady flow fields. While streamlines do not intersect, pathlines may intersect. Pathlines are often considered the "most intuitive methods to convey unsteady flow" [Lez *et al.*, 2011].

In measured flow data where the temporal resolution is low, the error is accumulated at each integration step of the pathlines, and therefore the reliability of pathlines decreases rapidly [Vilanova *et al.*, 2012]. In these cases, streamlines representing an average of a certain portion, e.g., systolic or diastolic blood flow, is a viable option. Figure 19.4 (left) contains streamlines to display blood flow. Without support, however, it is not obvious how the flow relates to the image data (see Fig. 19.4, right). We later show how such basic flow visualization techniques may be enhanced to better represent the flow and the related anatomy.

Probing and Seeding *Probing* relates to the selection of a subset of a large dataset and serves to inquire detailed information in that region. We discussed probing, e.g., in perfusion imaging, where voxels or circular regions were selected to inquire the detailed time-intensity curvestime-intensity curve in these regions. *Probing* is essential in flow data, since it enables a local flow analysis and defines which regions are displayed [de Leeuw and van Wijk, 1993].

Seed points for streamline, pathline or particle generation are usually determined in a user-selected ROI or a plane (see Figs. 19.5 and 19.6). Simple seeding strategies employ regular or random samples, leading to roughly equal distances of the streamlines in the seed region. As the seminal paper of Turk and Banks [1996] illustrates, further away from the seed region originally adjacent streamlines may become even closer, leading to an overrepresentation of a certain part of the vector field, or diverge strongly. The latter situation is worse, since interesting aspects, e.g., critical points, may be unrecognizable. Turk and Banks [1996] introduced an algorithm that enhanced streamline placement in 2D in an iterative process, where initially small streamlines were connected or deleted and new streamlines started.

In particular for branching elongated structures, such as vessels, the flow diverges at bifurcations leading to gaps. Sobel *et al.* [2004] presented a sweep line algorithm that detects such gaps and initiates further seeding to ensure that the distance between all represented flow features is below a defined threshold. Figure 19.6 illustrates this seeding strategy. A more recent approach, introduced by Rosanwo *et al.* [2009], ensures uniform seeding and good domain coverage in vascular geometries, such as cerebral aneurysms.

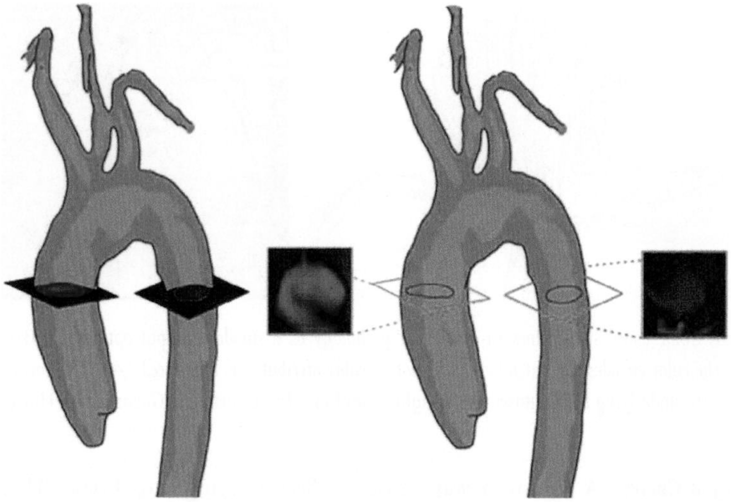

FIGURE 19.5 *In the aorta, the user specified two seeding planes (**left**). The **right** image illustrates how the flow through these planes may be presented in an undistorted manner. It is sufficient to slightly indicate the positions of these planes. The flow speed is color-coded in the slices with a color scheme known from Doppler sonography (From: [van Pelt et al., 2010]).*

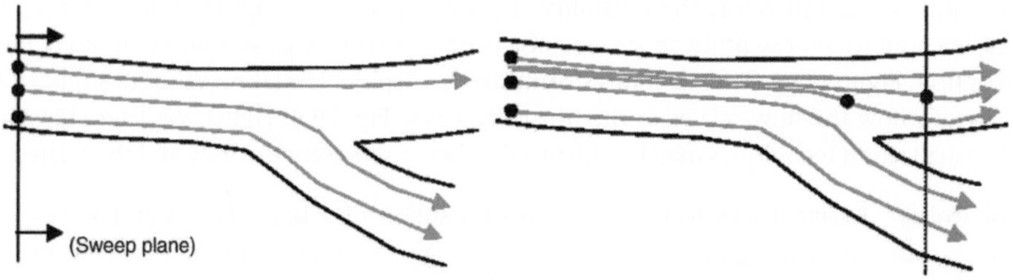

FIGURE 19.6 **Left:** *In the probing plane, three streamlines are initiated to capture the flow with a desired sampling distance.* **Right:** *A plane is swept from the probing plane, representing the inflow, to the outflow. At two places (see the disks) gaps were noticed and further streamlines were initiated (From: [Sobel et al., 2004]).*

Alternatively, seeding may be applied such that certain regions are preferred, e.g., the flow near boundaries or the flow in central portions of the seed region. Flow near the enclosing surfaces is often particularly interesting, since the flow interacts with the surface in these regions, leading to deposits or corrosion in technical applications and potentially to plaques and other lesions in vessel walls. van Pelt et al. [2010] therefore suggested *seeding templates* (see Fig. 19.7, for various seeding distributions).

Parameters of Integral Curves Integral curves have a number of parameters:

- integration length (boundary of the integration interval), leading to either long or small streamlines,
- the stepsize for the numerical integration, often referred to as h or in case of unsteady fields: Δt. Small steps lead to an improved accuracy at the expense of the computational effort,
- color, and

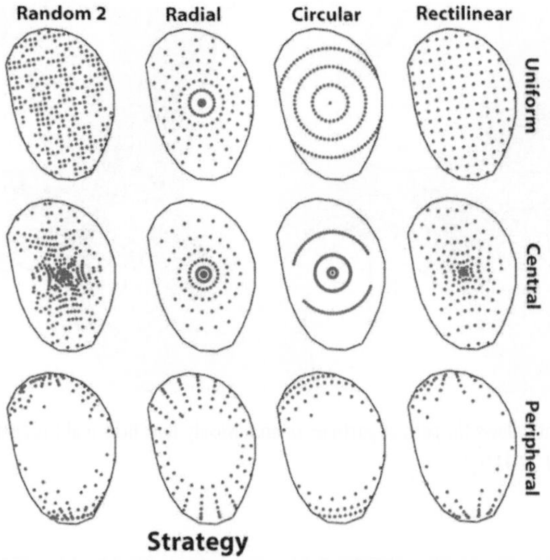

FIGURE 19.7 *A selection of seeding templates for investigating measured blood flow* (From: [*van Pelt et al.*, 2010]).

- other rendering attributes, e.g., illumination and depth attenuation that might improve depth perception.

Among the essential additions to the original streamlines is the integration of (Phong-like) illumination leading to valuable depth cues to better convey 3D flow [Zöckler *et al.*, 1996].

Particle Tracing In particular for evaluating unsteady vector fields, it is common to display the movement of massless *particles* emitted in the region of interest. Similar to streamline generation, seeding positions are essential parameters. Particle tracing is a computationally demanding process. It may be realized with GPU support [Kondratieva *et al.*, 2005]. A perceptual effective technique is animated local highlighting, where the highlighted region moves over time focusing on the particle trajectory. This technique can be applied to both particles and pathline (see Fig. 19.8) [van Pelt *et al.*, 2010].

19.2.5 PARTITION-BASED FLOW VISUALIZATION TECHNIQUES

Flow exploration should be supported at different levels to provide a more holistic view of the data. Partition-based techniques, usually involving some kind of clustering, aim at this holistic view [Salzbrunn *et al.*, 2008]. Goals and techniques in partition-based flow visualization are similar to cartography where different layers with more and more abstract representations are used to support the exploration at different levels.

An active research area is *flow clustering* [Telea and van Wijk, 1999], where individual vectors or more high-level primitives, such as streamlines and pathlines, are analyzed with respect to their similarity and eventually summarized to a cluster.

Clustering may be performed hierarchically, leading to more and more aggregated information toward the top of the cluster tree (bottom-up clustering). Similarity in case of streamlines is a weighted combination of several attributes, including curvature and bending energy. Garcke *et al.* [2001] suggested to employ the clustered flow to draw one arrow glyph representing the average flow in that cluster on top of

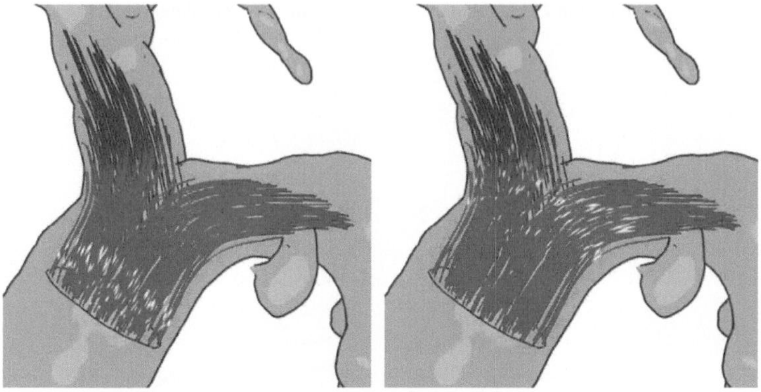

FIGURE 19.8 *A local highlight follows the path of particles in an unsteady flow field, and thus emphasizes the major characteristics of the flow* (From: [van Pelt et al., 2010]).

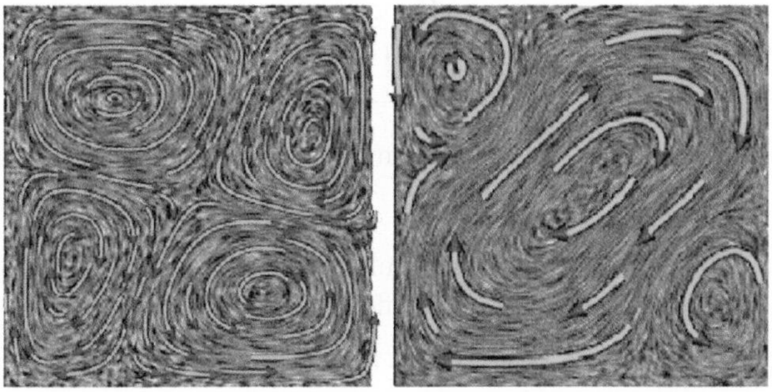

FIGURE 19.9 *A dense texture-based flow representation is complemented by arrow glyphs that represent the flow at coarser levels. At the right, only a few glyphs represent flow at the highest level* (Courtesy of Tobias Preusser, University of Bonn).

a dense texture-based flow visualization (see Fig. 19.9). Many different clustering algorithms have been employed for flow field clustering, e.g., techniques that employ a fixed number of clusters or those that may generate an arbitrary number (see the survey from Salzbrunn *et al.* [2008].

Flow clustering may be combined with lens-based exploration, where a visual representation with a high spatial resolution is shown inside the lens region only. Flow clustering is related to *flow segmentation*, where the flow domain is decomposed in regions with similar flow properties, e.g., vortex regions [Lez *et al.*, 2011]. In contrast to segmentation, clustering is usually hierarchical. van Pelt *et al.* [2012b] employed clustering to analyze flow in the coronary arteries.

19.2.6 EVALUATION OF FLOW VISUALIZATION TECHNIQUES

Since there is a large number of flow visualization techniques available, evaluation has become a crucial issue. It is necessary to compare existing methods and their parameters with respect to their ability to efficiently convey flow features relevant for particular application areas. The pioneering study was performed by Laidlaw *et al.* [2001] and later refined by Laidlaw *et al.* [2005]. The basic strategy of LAIDLAW and colleagues was to compare the methods based on their suitability to convey critical points and their classification. Thus, users had to encircle regions where they believed that a critical point occurs and classified it by means of a popup-menu containing the types of critical points shown in Figure 19.2. This is a very general study goal, and needs to be followed by more specific evaluations, related to biophysical simulations or measurements of blood flow data and related treatment planning tasks. However, many aspects of the experiment design may serve as orientation. Forsberg *et al.* [2009] extended the evaluation for 3D vector fields.

In another experiment from the same group Feliz *et al.* [2008] employ visualization experts and their criticism to compare flow visualization techniques. That is similar to the concept of expert evaluation in human-computer interaction, where usability experts critique a design based on a prediction of whether (real) users would be able to efficiently use an interactive system.

19.3 FROM MEDICAL IMAGE DATA TO SIMULATION MODELS

Simulation models are based on medical image data that depict the target anatomy in a good quality w.r.t. resolution, contrast, and signal-to-noise ratio (SNR). Usually, CT or MRI image data are employed (not ultrasound data). There are several steps necessary to generate simulation models from medical imaging data. This process is often summarized as a *reconstruction pipeline* and serves to simulate biophysical aspects in a patient-specific manner. Many aspects of this reconstruction process were already summarized by [Cebral and Löhner, 1999]. The major aspects of this transformation are:

- the segmentation of the target anatomy,
- the transformation of the segmentation result into a smooth and optimized triangle mesh, and
- the transformation of this mesh in a volume grid.

We discuss specific segmentation problems related to the use for simulation, discuss requirements for surface meshing and methods to fulfill these requirements. Trade-offs between accuracy, smoothness, triangle number, and triangle quality are at the heart of the surface mesh generation and optimization process.

Since numerical simulations are very compute-intensive, the underlying geometry should be as small as possible. Clipping of the triangle meshes (with subsequent remeshing of the clipping planes) is an essential aspect of model generation. This model reduction should be performed such that accuracy is not strongly affected.

This, however, is difficult to achieve, since the influence of a certain part of the geometry on the flow in other parts depends on many parameters and is difficult to predict. As a general rule, structures should be clipped in larger straight regions such that the inflow profile can develop appropriately. For special application problems, dedicated investigations were accomplished to study which inflow and outflow regions need to be considered to obtain reliable results.

Finally, volume grids consisting of tetrahedra or prisms are created from the triangle meshes. The overall process is not only complex but also challenging, since substantial knowledge in medical image processing and computational geometry is required.

19.3.1 SEGMENTATION AND MESHING FOR SIMULATION

We already discussed preprocessing of medical image data in general (Chap. 4.2), and the enhancement of vascular structures and segmentation techniques to delineate them (recall § 11.4.1). For simulation purposes, often a (rather small) subset of the image data is relevant. Thus, cropping is a first step. For

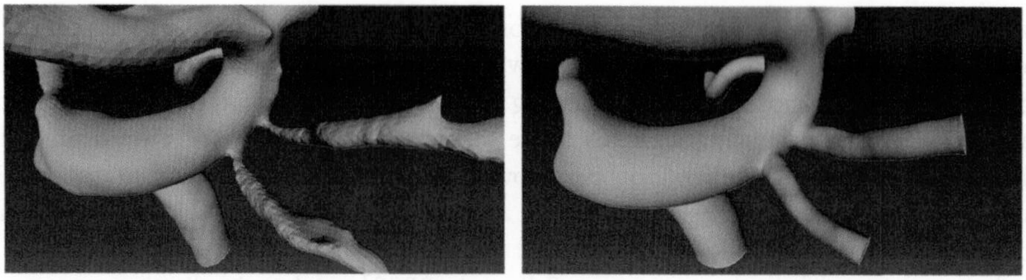

FIGURE 19.10 *Small side vessels, segmented from CT data, are suppressed close to the larger parent vessel. This is due to a typical attenuation artifact, where the contrast agent in a large vessel overshadows its surrounding. The local diameter needs to be corrected to prevent strong inaccuracies in the simulation (Courtesy of Mathias Neugebauer, University of Magdeburg).*

the generation of simulation models, it is essential that a segmentation method is used that enables the transformation to a smooth surface mesh. Binary segmentation results from manual segmentation, for example, are not appropriate, since the low coherency between adjacent slices and the results of jittered manual drawing within a slice lead to surfaces with strong artifacts.

In the following, we discuss some specific problems related to vascular structures. However, similar problems might be essential for the generation of simulation models of other anatomical structures. Some vessel segmentation problems are almost unnoticeable for visualization but lead to severe problems in simulation:

- attenuation of small side vessels with a reduced diameter, and
- existence of small stubs.

The first problem occurs primarily in CT data, where small vessels bifurcating from large parent vessels are attenuated at the branching, and thus appear smaller than they actually are. In a simulation, this would lead to a very fast flow in that narrowed region. Thus, this erroneous geometry needs to be corrected (see Fig. 19.10). These artifacts and their correction are discussed in more detail in [Mönch *et al.*, 2011b].

The second problem appears if an intensity-based or region growing algorithm detects the beginning of a small side vessel, but due to the partial volume effect its intensity is too low to be fully recognized. In these cases, small bumps occur on the parent vessel. These have only a small effect on the resulting visualization but the simulation would be strongly affected. Therefore, these bumps need to be removed. They might be avoided with a sophisticated model-based segmentation or later corrected with polygon modeling tools. The use of such tools is often necessary to fine-tune surface meshes, also for example to integrate stents, catheters or implants in biomedical simulations. Cebral and Löhner [1999] mention further situations where polygon modeling is essential, e.g., when two separate segmentation results need to be combined in one triangle mesh or vice versa, if they are erroneously connected and need to be separated. In case of vascular structures, these erroneous connections are known as *kissing vessel artifacts*.

19.3.2 REQUIREMENTS FOR SURFACE MESHES

We already discussed the transformation from segmented volume data to surface meshes in Chapter 6. There, we were interested in *smooth* and *accurate* surface meshes for a perceptually effective visualization of the target anatomy, e.g., as a basis for preoperative decisions. For the generation of simulation models, smoothness is again essential, because surface details may have a huge impact on numerical simulation and may even hamper convergence. Non-shrinking approaches, such as TAUBIN's low-pass-filter, should be also used for simulation purposes [Cebral and Löhner, 1999] (recall the discussion of smoothing algorithms in § 6.6).

Accuracy is crucial, since simulation produces quantitative results, such as velocities and pressure, and such numbers are misleading if they are based on coarse representations of the anatomy. The accuracy of the simulation of blood flow, for example, depends on many factors, such as the correct representation of dynamics, vessel wall elasticity and other parameters. However, the accurate representation of the geometry is the most essential parameters. Fortunately, it is also easier to represent the geometry faithfully than to incorporate advanced effects in the simulation [Janiga *et al.*, 2013]. For simulation, three further requirements to surface meshes are essential:

1 a high triangle quality,
2 an appropriate number of triangles to represent surface features, and
3 a gradual change in triangle size.

In general, elements, e.g., triangles, tetrahedra, quadrilaterals, that are almost isotropic have a high quality, whereas strongly deformed highly anisotropic elements have a low quality. Thus, an equilateral triangle has the maximum quality. Triangles with very low and very large angles, however, have a low quality. For simulation, it is essential that *all* triangles have at least a minimum quality, since otherwise the internal volume grid—derived from the surface mesh—also yields a low quality and the numerical simulation might not converge. There are basically two measures for triangle quality:

- *equi-angle skewness* (EAS), and
- the ratio between incircle and outcircle.

The EAS for triangles is computed according to Equation 19.5. $\theta_{\min}$ and $\theta_{\max}$ are the minimum and maximum angle with a triangle T. For quadrilaterals, the 60 and 120° components need to be replaced by 90°. EAS values are in the interval [0,1], with 0 representing the best quality.[3] The ratio between the incircle (the maximum circle completely inside a triangle) and the outcircle (the smallest circle that comprises a triangle completely) is 0.5 for an equilateral triangle. Thus, 0.5 represents the optimum quality and 0 a very low quality (the interval is [0, 0.5]).

$$Q_{EAS} = \max\left\{\frac{\theta_{\max} - 60^\circ}{120^\circ}, \frac{60^\circ - \theta_{\min}}{60^\circ}\right\} \tag{19.5}$$

Trade-off Between Accuracy and Simulation Times A low *triangle number* is in principle also desirable for visualization, since it reduces the computational power required for rendering. With modern graphics hardware this problem is, however, not urgent for typical surface meshes derived from CT or MRI data. For simulation purposes, however, a large triangle mesh leads to an internal volume grid with a much larger size, and the element number defines the systems of equations to be solved. To avoid overly long simulation times, it is still essential to limit the element number.

Gradual Change in Triangle Size The third requirement states that abrupt changes between small and large triangles need to be avoided. It is not necessary that the element size is globally constant. However, changes of the element size in a neighborhood should be only slightly.

3 Unfortunately, in some systems, EAS is computed differently and values of 1 represent the best quality there.

In the next subsection, we discuss how these requirements may be fulfilled. For readers with specific interest in mesh generation, we recommend Alliez *et al.* [2005a,b].

19.3.3 GENERATION OF SURFACE MESHES

Meshes should faithfully represent surface details and more global features, whereas the smaller local features require a higher density of the mesh. Without a local adaptation of mesh density, very large meshes with a uniform resolution would be necessary, since the smallest features that should be represented define the density for the whole mesh. This can be well illustrated with vascular trees, where vessel segments with strongly different diameters are included and a high resolution is (only) necessary for the finest branches.

Scale-Independent Meshes In § 11.5.2 we discussed a vessel surface generation technique that is guided by approximated curvature [Wu *et al.*, 2010]. In a similar vein, for simulation meshes Kuprat and Einstein [2009] introduced the *gradient limited feature size* measure that directly is defined on a triangle mesh and was also employed by Wischgoll *et al.* [2009b] for generating vascular simulation models. With that measure, approximately the same number of layers is employed for vascular branches of all different sizes, and thus a very good trade-off between element number and accuracy is achieved.[4]

Clipping the Surface Mesh In many cases, the simulation domain might be smaller than previously segmented objects. Thus, the surface meshes may be clipped to reduce the domain and thus the element number. In blood flow simulations, for example, a pathology usually represents the focus area and the parent vessel with a certain inflow and outflow region represent the contextual vasculature. This region is probably much smaller than the whole vascular tree. This clipping process is an advanced interaction. It might be supplied, e.g., by restricting the movement of clipping planes such that they are always perpendicular to centerlines. Figure 19.11 shows a pipeline of processing steps to derive a surface mesh that fulfills the requirements for simulation, discussed in § 19.3.2.

Mesh Simplification and Refinement For most biophysical simulation models, the resolution of the surface meshes from segmentation results is larger than it is necessary to derive a sufficiently accurate simulation model. These algorithms iteratively summarize adjacent vertices and control the resulting error (recall § 6.7.1). The powerful and widely used algorithm from Garland and Heckbert [1997] employs a quadratic

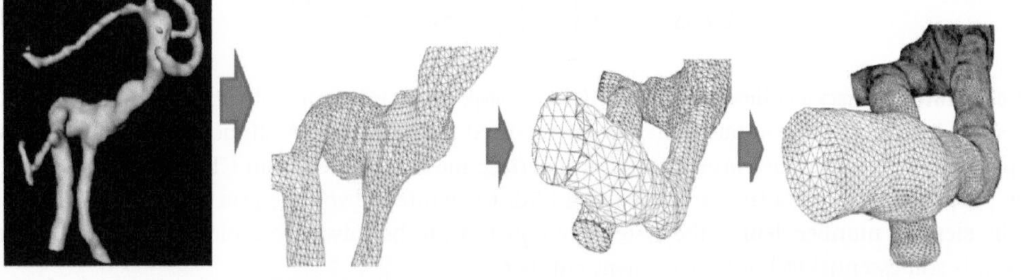

(a) Shaded surface (b) Wireframe (c) Clipped (d) Remeshed

FIGURE 19.11 *Meshes are generated from the segmentation (a, b), clipped at the in- and outflow region (c) and then remeshed (d) to yield a good triangle quality (Courtesy of Mathias Neugebauer, University of Magdeburg).*

4 It is realized within the LaGriT-PNNL tool (https://lagrit.lanl.gov/).

error metric. With appropriate error control, details are well preserved, and the triangle size reflects the curvature.

If the initial triangle meshes from anatomical reconstructions do not have a sufficient resolution, e.g., because a particularly high accuracy is desired, the mesh needs to be refined. This process is usually guided by a background grid with a certain desired element size [Cebral and Löhner, 1999].

Generation of Triangle Meshes with High Quality The triangle meshes produced by algorithms, such as Marching Cubes and its refinements, do *not* ensure high quality. Very thin, degenerated triangles (called slivers) may occur. Thus, these triangle meshes need to be remeshed. In this process, edges between triangles are swapped to avoid long edges (see Fig. 19.12, top row). It might also be necessary to insert new vertices, and thus to increase the local element number to guarantee a minimum quality. This process is performed for the two triangles forming a quadrilateral and it is called *diagonal swapping*. Diagonal swapping is not always possible, e.g., in case of concave quadrilaterals intersecting or overlapping triangles occur [Cebral and Löhner, 1999]. Small edges are removed and the resulting mesh is triangulated again, a process called *edge collapse*, see Figure 19.12, bottom row. The operations that improve the triangle quality also induce an error, similar to mesh smoothing and mesh simplification. This error needs to be controlled to ensure that no relevant features are removed. Frequently, edge collapse and diagonal swapping is only enabled if the dihedral angle between the adjacent faces is below a threshold, e.g., 10°. Remeshing algorithms have further parameters, such as a threshold for the desired maximum equi-angle skewness, the minimum or maximum triangle surface area or the maximum edge length. Figure 19.13 illustrates how these modifications affect the triangle quality. Element quality is typically color-coded with red representing low quality and green representing excellent quality.

Element Size As we have discussed in § 19.3.2, element sizes should not change abruptly. Such abrupt changes may occur when relevant details are represented in high density while other regions, such as almost flat regions, are simplified and represented with large elements. In this case, a remeshing step is necessary to ensure gradual transitions in the element size at the expense of enlarging the element number (Fig. 19.14).

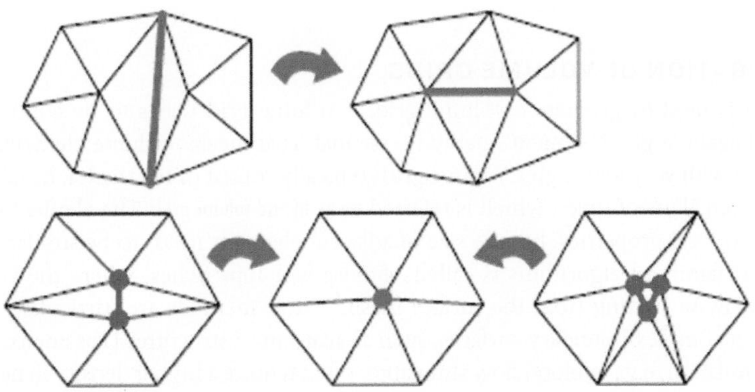

FIGURE 19.12 **Top row:** Long edges are flipped to improve the triangle quality (diagonal swapping). **Bottom row:** Small edges (left) and small triangles (right) are reduced to one vertex (edge collapse) (Courtesy of Ragnar Bade, University of Magdeburg).

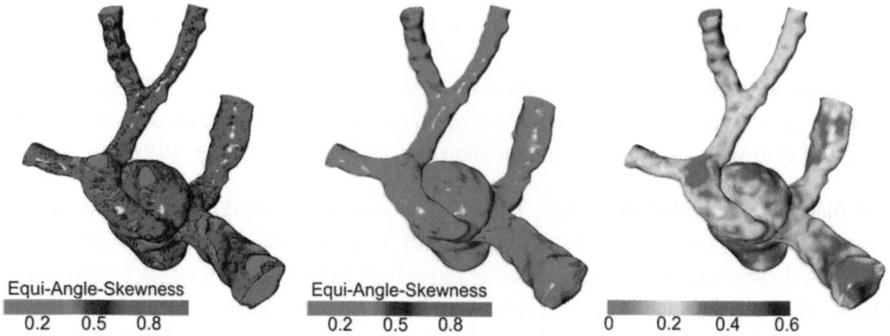

FIGURE 19.13 *A vascular surface mesh before (left) and after remeshing (middle, right) with the operations illustrated in Figure 19.12. A sufficient equi-angle skewness for all triangles is achieved, indicated by the green color. In the right image, color encodes triangle size and no abrupt changes occur (Courtesy of Mathias Neugebauer, University of Magdeburg).*

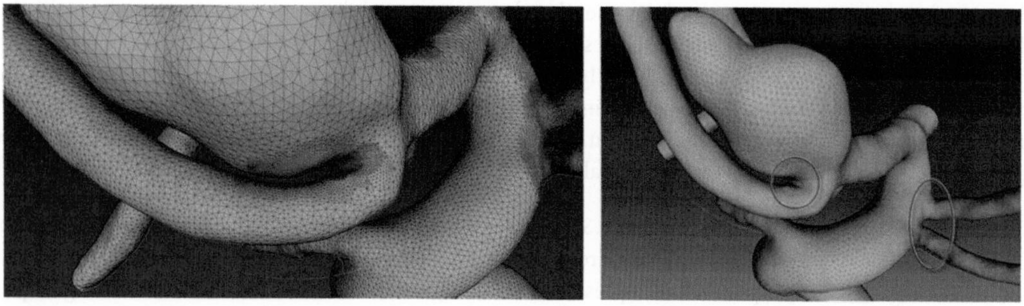

FIGURE 19.14 *A vascular surface mesh was modified to compensate for image reconstruction artifacts. The locally decreased element size, e.g., at the two bifurcations on the right, requires a remeshing to ensure gradual changes of element size. Regions where remeshing lead to prominent changes are encircled in the right image (Screenshot of Sculptris, Courtesy of Mathias Neugebauer, University of Magdeburg).*

19.3.4 GENERATION OF VOLUME GRIDS

The surface grid is used to generate a volume grid. A volume grid needs to be continuous and non-overlapping and again, a good element quality is essential. That means, volume elements should not be strongly distorted with very low angles. Volume grids typically consist of tetrahedra, hexahedra (wedges), or a mixture of both element types, which is referred to as *hybrid volume grids*. The element size may vary to represent adjust to local properties, but the size of adjacent elements needs to be similar.

A widely used family of algorithms is called *Advancing front* approaches, where the volume elements are generated stepwise starting from the surface mesh.[5] These methods are particularly suited for grid generation within complex boundary surfaces, such as anatomical structures [Rassineux, 1998]. Volume grids for CFD simulation, e.g., in blood flow simulation often require a higher density in near-wall regions, whereas a relatively coarse grid close to the center, i.e., the vessel centerline is sufficient.

5 The term advancing front algorithm is also used for remeshing surface meshes to improve their triangle quality.

Hybrid Volume Grids In recent years, hybrid volume grids consisting of *prisms* and *tetrahedra* were used for blood flow simulation. Three outer layers of prisms and internal tetrahedra represent a good configuration to enable more detailed analysis in the near-wall portions (see Fig. 19.15). The prisms have a thickness of 0.01–0.02 mm, whereas the average element size of the tetrahedra is around 0.250 mm [Berg *et al.*, 2013]. This increased spatial resolution enables a better representation of wall-near flow patterns. Also in other areas of biophysical simulation, hybrid grids are common (see Fig. 19.16). A general strategy to guide the local density of surface and volume grids is the use of *density fields* representing a locally different target resolution.

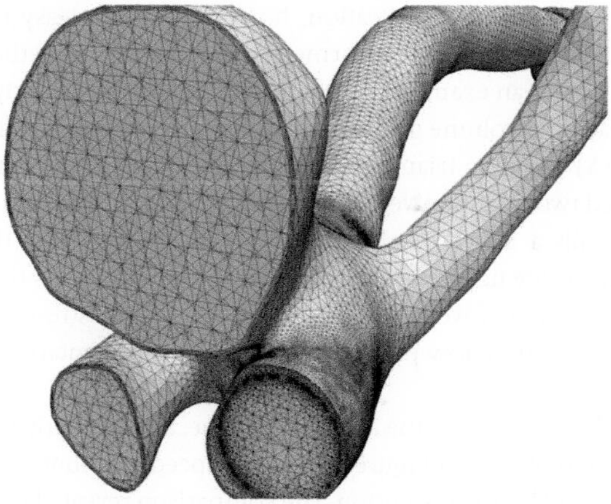

FIGURE 19.15 *A hybrid volume grid for blood flow simulation with an appropriate trade-off between accuracy and low element number. The fine mesh represents the near-wall region and stent struts (Courtesy of Gabor Janiga, University Magdeburg).*

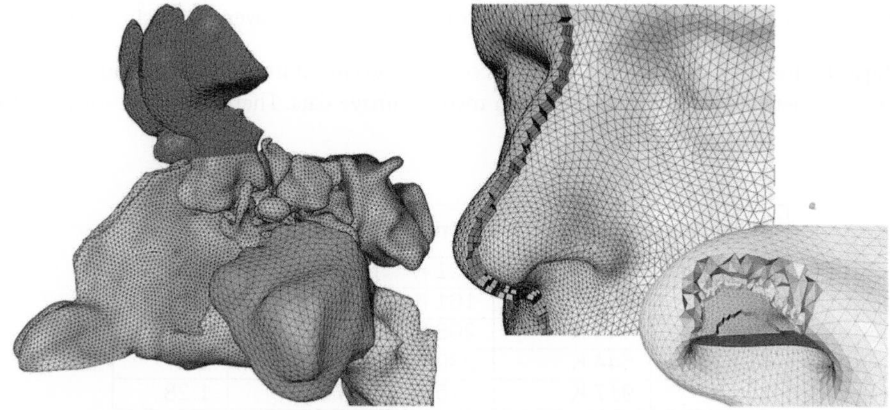

FIGURE 19.16 ***Left:*** *Geometric model of the nasal anatomy.* ***Right:*** *Hybrid volume grid with prisms and tetrahedra derived from the surface mesh (Courtesy of Stefan Zachow, Zuse-Institute Berlin).*

Generation of Hexahedral Grids As an alternative to tetrahedral or hybrid meshes, also pure hexahedral meshes are employed for biomedical simulations. They are based on a quadrilateral surface representation. In case of elongated or branching structures, often *sweeping* methods are employed, where a single-surface mesh is projected along a specified trajectory until the whole structure is represented [Blacker, 1996, Cook and Oakes, 1982]. Along this trajectory, templates are fitted to cross sections of the target anatomy.

In case of branching structures, there is no 1:1-correspondence between the start and end cross section. In case of such topological differences, more advanced one-many, or many-many modeling techniques are used [Lai *et al.*, 1996, Shepherd *et al.*, 2000]. These are also sweeping-based techniques. For vascular structures, including event trifurcations and other complex branchings, NURBS modeling is also feasible [Zhang *et al.*, 2006b].

Grid Independence Analysis For a specific application, however, it is not easy to decide on the necessary accuracy. Therefore, *grid independence analysis* is performed in order to examine the effect of different resolutions on the simulation results. As an example, Neugebauer *et al.* [2008] investigated the effect of different resolutions of vascular surface and volume grids (§ 19.3.4) on blood flow simulation. They created hybrid volume grids (see Fig. 19.15) based on triangle meshes in five different resolutions. To assess the effect of the resolution, they analyzed two quantitative parameters (*wall shear stress* and *maximum speed*, see Table 19.1). The wall shear stress is actually a 3D vector. However, in almost all settings the direction of that vector and the individual components are not important. The relevant parameter is the magnitude of that vector. As a simplification, like many others, we employ the term wall shear stress to denote the magnitude of this vector. Moreover, they compared flow patterns by means of representative visualizations [Janiga *et al.*, 2013].

In Figure 19.17, the wall shear stress in the aneurysm dome, a particularly important simulation result, is shown for two different resolutions. In Figure 19.18, the speed distribution in a plane is compared for simulations with the highest and lowest resolution. The comparison revealed that a rather coarse resolution with 31 K triangles, 240 K tetrahedra and 121 K prisms is sufficient for "normal" configurations with one average size aneurysm and a normal inflow and outflow region. The configuration in Figure 19.18 is rather complex with two outflow vessels that bifurcate close to the aneurysm. As a consequence, four outflow vessel segments have to be considered. These results are similar to those reported by Ford *et al.* [2008], where tetrahedral volume grids of different cerebral aneurysms were created. The size of the models was between 373 K and 470 K elements, corresponding to an average spacing of 0.25 mm.

Software Support In this section, we described a couple of advanced image analysis and mesh processing techniques to generate simulation models from medical image data. There are many software tools that

#Triangles	#Tetrahedra	#Prisms	WSS (max)	V (max)
31 K	240 K	121 K	161	1.21
41 K	338 K	161 K	171	1.23
52 K	444 K	208 K	172	1.25
61 K	544 K	239 K	172	1.27
106 K	917 K	415 K	171	1.28

TABLE 19.1 *Different resolutions of a grid for blood flow simulation and the resulting simulation parameters: wall shear stress and maximum speed.*

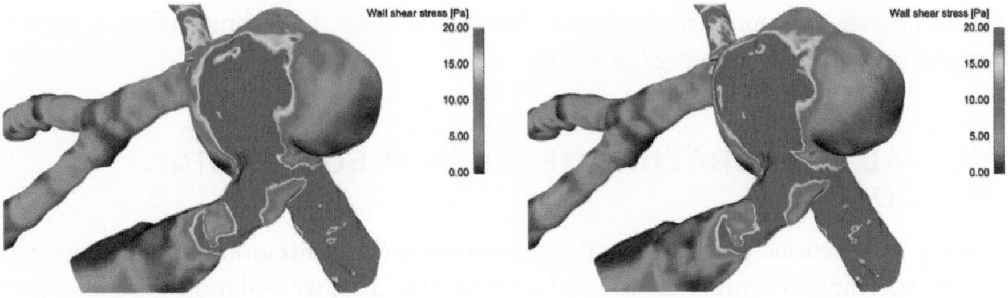

FIGURE 19.17 *The blood flow in a cerebral aneurysm is simulated based on a volume grid with 240 K tetrahedra and 121 K prisms (left) and with 544 K tetrahedra and 239 K prisms (right). The wall shear stress, an essential scalar flow quantity, is color-coded and the similarity of the results indicates that the lower resolution is sufficient (Courtesy of Mathias Neugebauer, University of Magdeburg).*

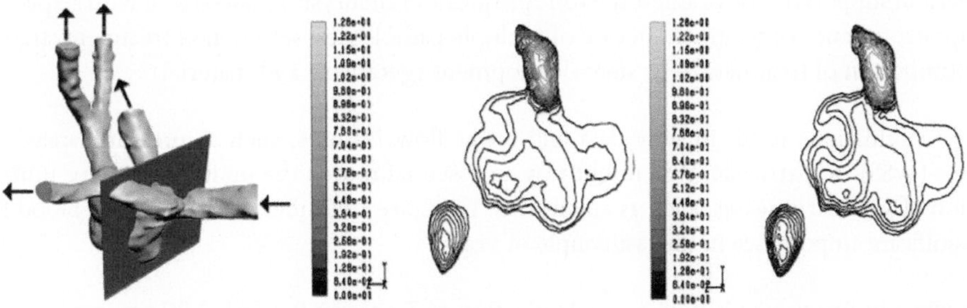

FIGURE 19.18 **Left:** *Speed distribution in a representative plane through an aneurysm.* **Middle:** *Speed distribution from the simulation with 240 K tetrahedra and 121 K prisms.* **Right:** *results obtained with the highest resolution consisting of 917 K tetrahedra and 415 K prisms (Courtesy of Mathias Neugebauer, University of Magdeburg).*

support parts of this process, e.g., segmentation and centerline extraction, or surface mesh processing, or generation of volume grids. Sculptris is a powerful modeling tool with advanced support for polygon modeling, remeshing and mesh smoothing.[6] Also, the open source software MeshLab provides many useful functions to adjust and postprocess unstructured 3D triangular meshes.[7] For the generation of volume grids, the open source software NetGen is a viable option. It is an automatic 3D tetrahedral mesh generator and enables mesh optimization and mesh refinement [Schöberl, 1997]. [8]

Amira was used, for example, for the preprocessing for the simulation of nasal airflow, but also for preprocessing for soft-tissue simulation. It comprises powerful and flexible modules for all necessary steps to generate simulation grids [Stalling *et al.*, 2005]. In particular for vascular modeling, the Vascular Modeling toolkit (VMTK) is highly recommended [Antiga *et al.*, 2008, Piccinelli *et al.*, 2009] (see http://www.vmtk.org/). It is focused on all aspects of generating grids for blood flow simulation with specialized functions, e.g., for cardiac blood flow. It is available as separate package but also integrated with other packages, including the 3D slicer (www.slicer.org).

6 http://sculptris.en.softonic.com/.
7 Meshlab was developed at the Visual Computing Lab of ISTI-CNR, Pisa and is available at: http://meshlab.sourceforge.net/.
8 http://www.hpfem.jku.at/netgen/.

Few systems provide a comprehensive support. Among them are the commercial tools ANSYS IcemCFD and the free tool GMSH (http://geuz.org/gmsh/).

19.4 VISUAL EXPLORATION OF MEASURED CARDIAC BLOOD FLOW

In the following two sections we deal with the generation and visualization of blood flow data. Before we dive into the specific problems of cardiac and cerebral flow data, we will motivate and explain the use of blood flow data, representing the hemodynamics, in a broader sense. Blood flow data are acquired to achieve:

- a better understanding of vascular diseases (formation and progress) as a fundamental research problem,
- decision support for treatment planning, e.g., in case of valve defects and congenital heart disease,
- decision support in case of atherosclerotic plaques and aneurysms (assessment with respect to risk of rupture, urgency of treatment in case of multiple pathologies, selection of treatment strategy), and
- optimization of treatment, e.g., stent development (geometry and material).

Blood flow simulations result in flow data and scalar flow features, such as pressure, speed and wall shear stress (WSS). In particular, WSS might play an essential role in the understanding of initiation and progression of vascular diseases, such as aneurysms. There are a number of reasons why blood flow data gained significant importance in the last couple of years:

- progress in image acquisition, e.g., introduction of 7 or even 9.4 Tesla MRI scanners,
- advances in imaging protocols and sequences (substantial results from medical physics research),
- progress in processing blood flow data,
- clinical availability of postprocessing software,
- principally, clinical value has been demonstrated in many pilot studies. However, substantial further research and development is required.

In the following, we introduce measured flow data and describe their use for the diagnosis of cardiovascular diseases.

19.4.1 MEDICAL BACKGROUND

Flow data is essential to improve understanding of a number of heart diseases, such as defects of the mitral and aortic valve, Marfan syndrome, and congenital heart failures. Congenital heart failures are characterized by complex malformations leading to strong abnormalities in the hemodynamics. In adult patients, the aortic dissection caused by a tear in the aortic wall is an essential problem that gives rise to an analysis of the blood flow behavior [van Pelt *et al.*, 2011]. Flow data is used in preclinical research for diagnosis, risk assessment and prognosis. The following discussion is based on a research prototypes that are not commercially available yet.

Medical doctors want to analyze the efficiency of the circulation, correlations between blood flow patterns, morphology and pathogenesis. More specifically, they are interested, e.g., in the venous filling during diastole and the systolic arterial outflow. As an example, they are interested in regions with strong and helical flow, in regions with sudden flow deceleration and in regions with complex multidirectional flow that changes over the heart cycle [Markl *et al.*, 2011]. Measurements through planes intersecting great arteries may reveal shunt flow or regurgitation [Gatehouse *et al.*, 2010].

Flow Patterns and Cardiovascular Diseases Recently, there was a number of medical publications related to the impact of flow patterns on cardiovascular diseases. The impact of different flow patterns on the bicuspid aortic valve is discussed in [Hope *et al.*, 2012]. Francois *et al.* [2012] analyzed flow patterns in patients with a Fallot tetralogy. Geiger *et al.* [2011] investigated the flow patterns that are typical in Marfan syndrome. One of the oldest studies is from Bogren *et al.* [2004] and it is related to atherosclerosis. They investigated healthy persons and patients with a wide age spectrum. It turns out that there are characteristic changes of blood flow related to age. Thus, as with many other diseases, it is difficult to reliably discriminate natural age-related changes from pathologies that require treatment. As a general remark, in healthy and younger persons flow is primarily laminar. Vortex cores exist primarily in case of pathologies. While in the publications described above flow patterns were subjectively determined, in future work a more reliable objective and quantitative analysis of the flow behavior might be possible.

19.4.2 IMAGE ACQUISITION

Cardiac blood flow may be analyzed with catheter-based examinations—an invasive method that is still considered the gold standard [Hennemuth *et al.*, 2011]. The measurements, however, are very local and difficult to put into context. A cheap and non-invasive alternative is Doppler ultrasound. This real-time modality requires a skilled operator to *probe* the flow at the most interesting regions. However, the images are noisy and difficult to interpret. In particular, most quantitative evaluations require a more reproducible approach, which is described in the following. Two aspects of Doppler ultrasound are also relevant for other imaging modalities:

- The flow direction in x, y, and z direction is mapped to RGB color space. Since at least some users are familiar with this color scheme, it is widely used to encode directional information.
- The ultrasound probe has the shape of a tapered cylinder and is used to locally analyze the flow in the corresponding region.

Blood Flow Imaging with PC-MRI Blood flow may be measured directly with a special MR sequence, referred to as *Phase-Contrast MR imaging*. This is a non-invasive acquisition technique that does not require a contrast agent. Gradients induce different field strengths in different positions leading to a flow-induced phase shift. This phase shift is proportional to the flow speed and thus enables a *quantitative flow measurement*. Typically, MRI acquisition was prone to flow artifacts. By clever adjustments of the sequences, the acquisition has become sensitive to flow. Due to the relatively long acquisition times, flow is usually measured in planes interactively defined in anatomical images. Flow may be measured *within* a predefined plane or *through* that plane. In the resulting images, speed is encoded as gray value, with black and white representing maximum speed in opposite directions. In 4D the spatial resolution is lower. However, the acquisition times are improving probably leading to a wider acquisition of the flow data in the whole volume.

Velocity Eencoding An essential acquisition parameter of PC-MRI is *velocity encoding* (VENC). This term is a bit confusing, since it is related to speed, not to velocity. It specifies the largest speed that can be measured unambiguously. The VENC is employed to transform phase angles in the interval $[-\pi, \pi]$ to speed. The specification of that parameter considers known physiologic measures in healthy patients, e.g., in the aorta a VENC of 150 cm/s. However, in case of severe pathologies, much larger speeds may occur. If the VENC parameter is chosen too low, aliasing and phase wraps occur. If, however, a too large value is selected,

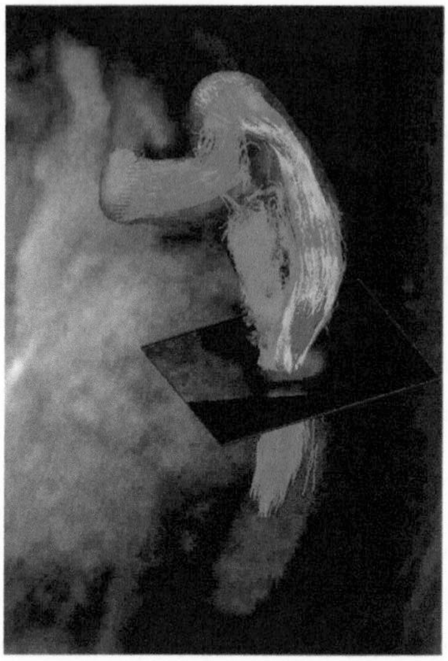

FIGURE 19.19 *4D cardiac flow visualization with path lines seeded in a plane orthogonal to the aorta. The patient suffers from an aortic isthmus stenosis and already has a bypass. Data are acquired for treatment monitoring with a temporal resolution of 25 ms. The VENC in all three directions was 250 cm/s and the total scanning time was 12 minutes (Screenshot of SIEMENS 4D flow, Courtesy of Uta Preim, Herzzentrum Leipzig).*

flow with lower speeds cannot be faithfully recorded and the stroke volume of the heart is underestimated. Figure 19.19 represents an example where the choice of the VENC did not lead to artifacts. Thus, ideally, the VENC closely approximates the true maximum speed of the patient [Greil *et al.*, 2002].

4D Flow Measurements The acquisition of cardiac flow results in seven datasets with an equal number of images. One anatomical dataset (with a rather low blood-to-myocard contrast), three modulus datasets and three flow datasets, each representing the velocity in one direction (anterior-posterior, foot-head, right-left). Figure 19.20 shows an example with a spatial resolution of $2.5 \times 2.5 \times 2.5$ mm. Also higher spatial resolutions, similar to static MRI data, such as $0.8 \times 0.8 \times 1.4$ mm, are possible [Schwenke *et al.*, 2011].

Image acquisition of cardiac flow is still an area of active research, where sequences are further optimized with respect to reducing scanning times as well as reducing motion and other artifacts with techniques, such as respiratory self-gating.

Comparison: 2D and 4D Flow 4D flow measurements take a rather long time, about 20 minutes. 4D flow acquisition does not require to specify planes, thus image acquisition is simplified. Moreover, 4D flow delivers more information that is useful for assessing pathophysiological states. Essential parameters, such as the WSS, may be computed in a postprocessing step, albeit with limited accuracy.

However, there are still drawbacks that hamper the widespread clinical use of 4D flow measurements. Image quality is rather low, in particular in case of irregular breathing. Despite ECG and respiratory gating, artifacts may occur and the specification of the VENC parameter is error-prone. The spatial resolution may be too coarse for small vessels and small inflow jets. In general, postprocessing is time-consuming.

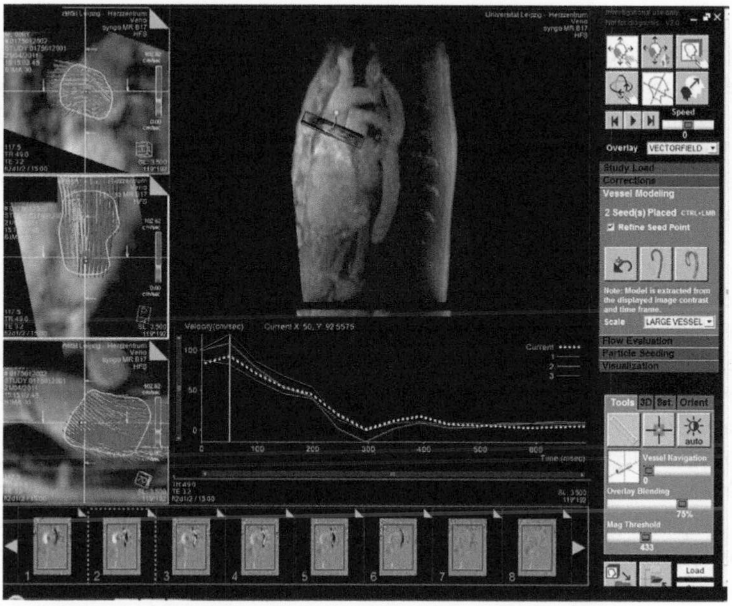

FIGURE 19.20 *Acquisition and evaluation of cardiac flow. A plane is adjusted in the overview image to guide the further analysis. On the left, a transversal, coronal and sagittal view are arranged in a column. The average speed over time is plotted for the selected region (Screenshot of SIEMENS 4D flow, Courtesy of Uta Preim, Herzzentrum Leipzig).*

19.4.3 PREPROCESSING CARDIAC BLOOD FLOW DATA

In the following, we briefly discuss how cardiac PC-MRI data may be preprocessed to reduce artifacts and to identify the vascular structures to enable a sufficiently accurate quantitative analysis and a visual exploration of cardiac flow.

Reduction of Artifacts in Cardiac PC-MRI Data In addition to typical image noise and inhomogeneities in MRI data, two artifacts deserve special attention:

- artifacts due to eddy currents,
- phase wraps, and
- artifacts due to aliasing.

Eddy currents cause spatially and temporally slowly varying image gradients that lead to a positive or negative offset in the phase images representing flow velocities. Although these offsets amount only to 1 or 2 cm/s, they seriously hamper quantitative evaluation [Gatehouse *et al.*, 2010]. The amount and character of these artifacts is noticeable in stationary voxels, that is in voxels where the intensity changes only slightly (due to noise). The intensity values of these static voxels tend to increase in more distant parts. Thus, the phase offsets, caused by eddy current artifacts, may be corrected by fitting polynomial planes to the velocities of static regions and subtracting these values [Lankhaar *et al.*, 2005, Hennemuth *et al.*, 2011].

Phase wraps occur if the speed at a particular voxel supersedes the *velocity encoding* speed (VENC). In this case, 2π phase jumps occur due to the use of the mathematical arctangent function. Phase unwrapping is an active research area, since it is relevant for many image acquisition techniques (even outside of medicine). It is based on certain assumptions to compensate for the missing information that cannot be guaranteed. Local and global methods exist and are typically very time-consuming. The method to detect and correct phase wraps, described in [Diaz and Altamirano-Robles, 2004] is employed in several toolboxes, e.g., in the MEVIS Flow toolbox [Hennemuth *et al.*, 2011].

Segmentation Segmentation of vascular structures in PC-MRI data facilitates flow analysis and exploration. This segmentation task has similarities with vessel segmentation in static image data (recall § 11.4.1), but the flow data pose specific problems. Simple techniques combine thresholding and morphologic postprocessing operations on temporal maximum intensity projections (MIP). These temporal MIP data contain the most intensive voxel over time. Segmentation with temporal MIP data is based on the assumption that vessels are characterized by regions where the signal intensity is increased due to the flow speed. More advanced methods consider the actual vector information and employ more advanced model assumptions [Solem *et al.*, 2004]. Despite the progress being achieved, segmentation is rarely used in practice, since it works notoriously bad in case of severe pathologies, where model assumptions do not hold. Thus, considerable effort is spent on designing visual exploration solutions that do not require segmentation but focus instead of advanced probing[van Pelt *et al.*, 2011].

19.4.4 QUANTITATIVE ANALYSIS

For diagnostic purposes, visual exploration and quantitative analysis are essential. Quantitative values obtained for a particular patient are compared with known average values from scientific literature to classify a pathology and assess its severity. Essential quantitative values are:

- the mean speed in a region of interest,
- the maximum speed $s_{\max}$,
- the antegrade and retrograde volume flow rate, and
- the stroke volume.

The *volume flow rate* in a particular plane is the product from the cross-sectional area and the mean velocity. If there is a reverse (retrograde) flow, it is essential to assess the (regular) antegrade flow, the retrograde flow and the relation between both, the so-called regurgitation fraction. These values have a clinical relevance in assessing possible defects of the mitral valve and the aortic valve. Grading schemes classify the aortic and mitral valve insufficiency by regurgitation fraction. To quantify arteriovenous shunts, the stroke volume of the pulmonal artery Q_p is divided by the stroke volume of aorta Q_a. In healthy patients, this quotient is roughly 1. If Q_p is significantly larger than Q_a, the patient has a left-right-shunt and if Q_a is significantly larger, a right-left shunt is diagnosed.

The maximum speed $s_{\max}$ is employed to compute the pressure gradient Δp according to the Bernoulli equation assuming an incompressible flow, where friction by viscosity may be neglected. This pressure gradient is used to assess the severity of an aortic stenosis, for example $\Delta p < 40$ mm Hg relates to an aortic stenosis of degree 1, whereas $\Delta p > 65$ mm Hg relates to a stenosis of degree 3. However, care is necessary to evaluate these measures: the maximum speed might be missed because it occurs in another plane or time frame. Furthermore, turbulent flow causes artifacts. Thus, echocardiography leads to more reliable stenosis grading.

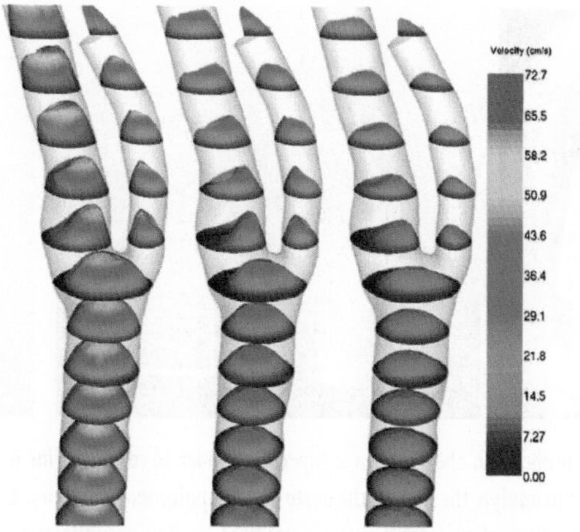

FIGURE 19.21 *The speed profile in a model of the carotid bifurcation is indicated at three points in time. In addition, it is useful to indicate when the time points are in relation to the blood cycle (systole, diastole) (From: [Antiga, 2002]).*

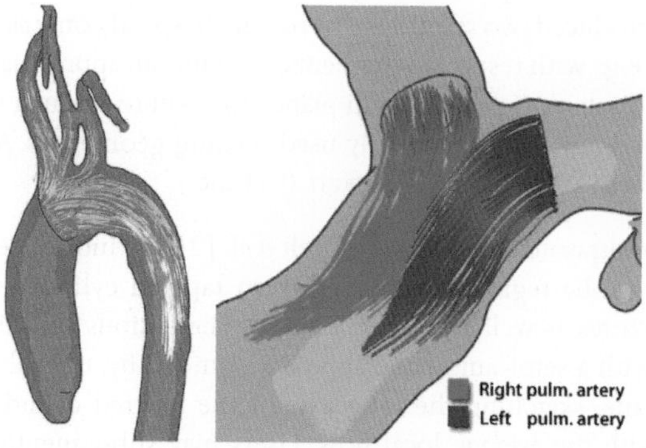

FIGURE 19.22 **Left:** *A plane through the aorta is used for seeding streamlines. Color encodes speed in the range of 0–2 m/s.* **Right:** *Two planes in the left and right pulmonary artery were defined for reverse tracing. The flow in both planes is laminar and in general very similar (From: [van Pelt et al., 2010]).*

19.4.5 VISUAL EXPLORATION

Standard techniques, in particular streamlines, pathlines, and particle tracing (recall § 19.2), are widely used in the exploration of cardiac blood flow. These geometry-based techniques are usually controlled by local cross-sectional planes. It is possible to combine several planes and to observe the flow starting from both regions. Colorcoding is applied to convey speed [van Pelt *et al.*, 2010]. For encoding speed, the rainbow color scale is the defacto standard. van Pelt *et al.* [2010] quantized and perceptually weighted the rainbow coding (see Fig. 19.22, left). Direction is mapped to RGB color space. In case of several seeding planes, color may also be used to discriminate the flow from both planes (see Fig. 19.22, right). This is essential, e.g., to clearly separate aortic and pulmonary flow [Barker *et al.*, 2010].

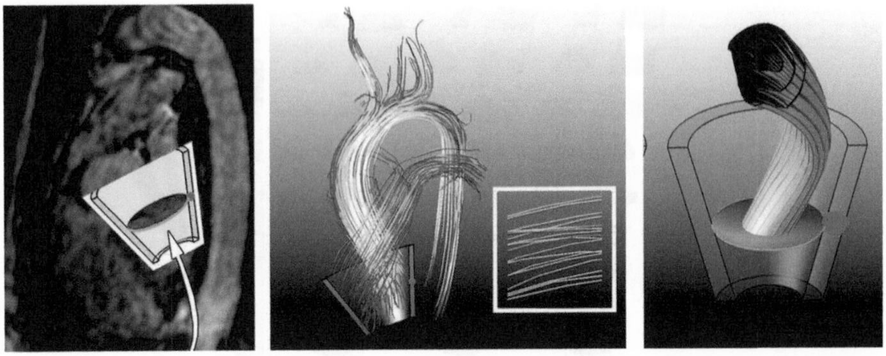

FIGURE 19.23 **Left:** *A virtual probe with the shape of a tapered cylinder is employed for local flow analysis.* **Middle:** *The virtual probe is placed in the heart chamber to analyze the flow in the aorta and the pulmonary arteries. Long illuminated pathlines are employed for flow visualization.* **Right:** *As an alternative, stream surfaces are used for flow visualization* (From: [van Pelt et al., 2011]).

Seeding based on a plane requires considerable interaction. In regions, such as the heart chamber, no clear centerline is available. Thus, simplified and guided interaction is essential. van Pelt *et al.* [2010] and Hennemuth *et al.* [2011] introduced two solutions that require to specify only *one* point. In both systems, the neighborhood is analyzed, e.g., with respect to gradients, to define an appropriate region. In addition, profile views are useful that indicate flow properties in planes adjacent to vascular structures (see Fig. 19.21).

Besides planes, there are some more frequently used seeding geometries. Among them are cylinders, boxes, and splines. All of these are available in ENSIGHT (CEI Inc.).

Virtual Probing Inspired by ultrasound probing, van Pelt *et al.* [2011] introduced *virtual probing* as a seeding strategy. The shape of the probe region is chosen to be a tapered cylinder, since this shape may well approximate vascular structures as well as heart chambers. The tedious and difficult manual positioning is significantly enhanced with a semi-automatic approach, guided by an analysis of the local flow. Thus, it is sufficient to draw a line, sketching the long axis of the tapered cylinder. The precise orientation is automatically aligned with the average local flow. Users may subsequently modify the position and orientation of the probe. Figure 19.23 illustrates the probe and its alignment.

Integration of Flow Features Visual exploration benefits from an extraction of flow features, such as strong helicity or swirlicity [Heiberg *et al.*, 2003]. With appropriate parameters for these flow features, the visualization may be restricted to regions that exhibit these features.

19.4.6 ILLUSTRATIVE VISUALIZATION TECHNIQUES

Since blood flow data is complex, illustrative visualization techniques are considered to convey essential information more clearly.

A couple of illustrative techniques (recall Chap. 12) were developed for cardiac blood flow measurements and refined in evaluations. Inspired from comics, van Pelt *et al.* [2011] employ elliptical glyphs derived from spheres by deformation for particle tracing. Strong deformation, leading to elongated glyphs, represent high speed. A further comic-inspired technique is the use of speedlines where the speed is mapped to linewidth (fast particles have thin speedlines, see Fig. 19.24). The speedlines indicate the direction of the particle's movement. Particles may be injected interactively, resembling a bolus of a

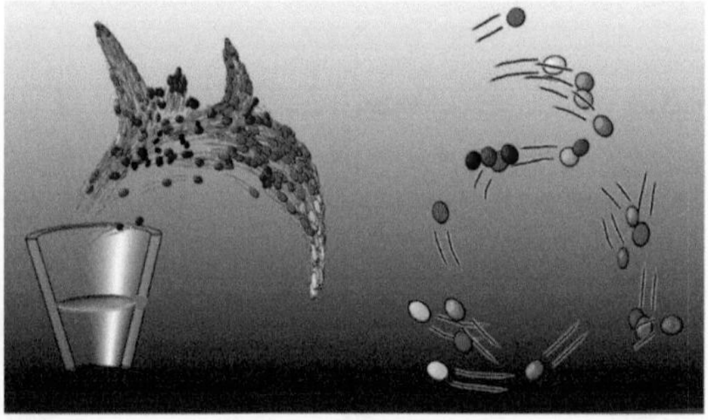

FIGURE 19.24 *Illustrative particles: elliptical glyphs with speedlines (right) indicate speed of the flow emitted in a virtual probe. Thus, color may be used for further blood flow attributes, such as residence time and vorticity (From: [van Pelt et al., 2011]).*

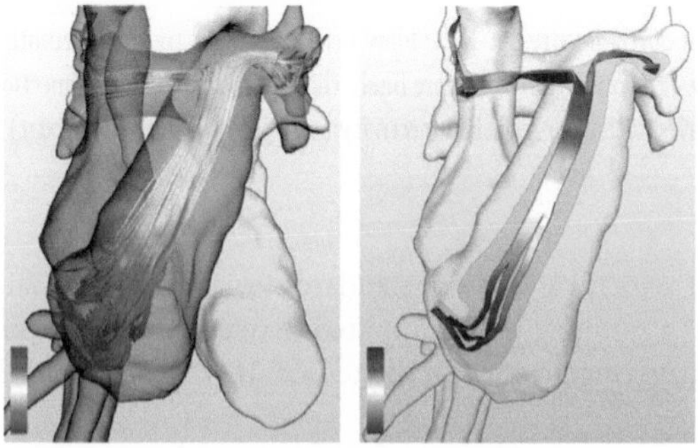

FIGURE 19.25 *The systolic blood flow is displayed with a color scale indicating speed.* ***Left:*** *The highest speed occurs between the ventricle and the left and right pulmonary arteries (LPA and RPA).* ***Right:*** *3D flow arrows emphasize the basic flow direction clearly (From: [Born et al., 2013]).*

contrast agent. For interactive use, it is crucial that particle tracing is realized with GPU support. Ellipsoids are rendered via geometry shaders as quadrilateral imposters aligned with the current viewport [van Pelt *et al.*, 2011]. Halos applied to speedlines further support depth perception.

Born *et al.* [2013] employed the concept of *line predicates* to create "abstract depictions of line bundles" and render them as 3D arrows. Moreover, tube-like structures with hatching textures are added to convey vortex information (see Fig. 19.25).

19.4.7 UNCERTAINTY VISUALIZATION

Like every medical image acquisition, flow measurements involve a certain degree of uncertainty that can be modeled by a Gaussian distribution. For PC-MRI data, the standard deviation σ is proportional to the VENC parameter. With a VENC of 150 cm/s and a signal-to-noise ratio of 10, which is typical within vessels, σ amounts to 7 cm/s [Schwenke *et al.*, 2011]. This uncertainty may have a strong effect on long pathlines, since it accumulates. This amount of uncertainty is locally different and may be estimated by anisotropic fast marching methods that compute minimal paths from a seeding point. Intuitively, the faster the flow, the more reliable is its direction. A metric tensor is computed according to Equation 19.6,

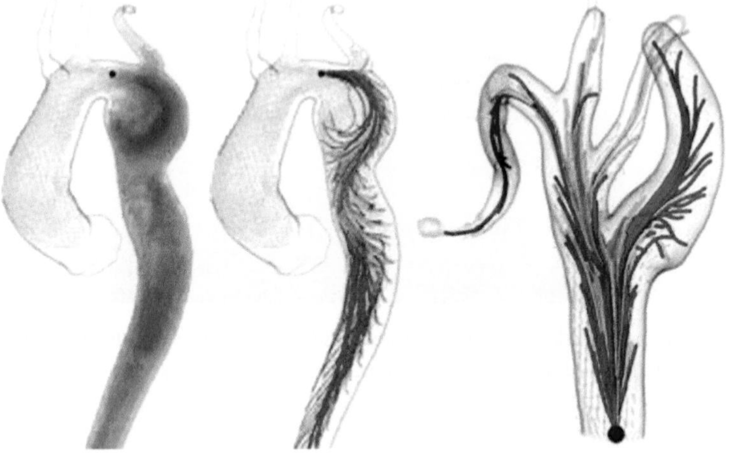

FIGURE 19.26 Blood flow in an aortic aneurysm. **Left:** Flow field and connectivity information. **Middle:** Blood flow trajectories with color representing connectivity. Red connections are more likely than green and yellow connections (seed point in the upper image). **Right:** A second example of trajectories with color-coded connectivity (seed point in the bottom part) (From: [Schwenke et al., 2011]).

where $\vec{v}$ denotes the local velocity and σ the standard deviation of the Gaussian distribution used for modeling the uncertainty. If a minimal path computed between a seeding point a and a potential target b corresponds well to the major eigenvector of the tensor M, this path is likely.

$$M^{-1} = \vec{v} \cdot \vec{v}^T + \sigma \cdot I \tag{19.6}$$

This uncertainty analysis is related to probabilistic fiber tracking (recall § 15.3.3.4). It may be used to display the most likely trajectories only, or to encode the connectedness and thus the likelihood of a connection (see Fig. 19.26). Further research is necessary to determine optimum visualizations of uncertainty information. Probably, the additional (possible) pathlines should be displayed only locally. Thus, a relocateable lens for displaying uncertainty information might be inspiring—an idea first described by Lundström *et al.* [2007] for medical volume rendering.

19.5 EXPLORATION OF SIMULATED CEREBRAL BLOOD FLOW

In § 11.7.1, we discussed the visualization of cerebral vasculature for the diagnosis of aneurysms and arteriovenous malformations. There, we also discussed the medical background. Here, we add that WSS likely plays an essential role. However, due to the large variability in the wall thickness, the risk of rupture cannot be directly inferred from the WSS value [Kadasi *et al.*, 2012].

Later, we considered virtual angioscopy (recall § 13.6.3) as an example for virtual endoscopy and briefly mentioned that the assessment of cerebral aneurysms before and after treatment is an essential application [Colpan *et al.*, 2007, Orbach *et al.*, 2006]. Also, in § 14.5.4, we introduced techniques to represent scalar flow features, such as the WSS [Neugebauer *et al.*, 2009a]. In this section, we restrict to the exploration of the flow data itself which is essential to better assess the risk of rupture and the specific choice of a stent to hamper inflow and induce thrombosis.

Computational Hemodynamics In the following, we explain how computational fluid dynamics (CFD) simulations of blood flow further enhance diagnosis and treatment decisions. They are employed to better understand the formation of vascular diseases and to optimize their treatment. This particular application of CFD is widely known as *computational hemodynamics*. In biophysical simulations, an *initialization stage* needs to be considered, where the behavior is notably different from the periodic stable behavior in later stages. In blood flow simulations, for example, Berg *et al.* [2013] employ the simulation results related to the 3rd cardiac cycle only and ignore the first to cycles.

Treatment Decisions Aneurysms occur at some typical locations with a rather high likelihood, and they may occur simultaneously at different positions. This situation occurs in about 20% of all cases and thus represents a serious treatment challenge. For discussing flow in aneurysms, it is essential to note that technical progress in stent design and stent deployment as well as improved navigation even in case of strongly bended vascular structures enables endovascular treatment in more complex situations. Covering the neck of an aneurysm with a stent that acts as a *flow diverter* may alter the hemodynamics and induce thrombosis within the aneurysm. Thrombosis would effectively stop further growth and prevent rupture [Seshadhri *et al.*, 2011]. Research questions relate to a better understanding of stenting effects. In particular, sometimes the flow is altered strongly and thrombosis occurs soon, whereas in other cases the flow basically remains unchanged [Janiga *et al.*, 2009].

The major questions in treating these patients are the risk of aneurysm rupture and the treatment options, including interventional procedures, such as *stenting* and *coiling*, and neurosurgical operation (*clipping* of aneurysms). With respect to the risk of rupture, most investigations consider a single aneurysm only. Recently, Berg *et al.* [2013] also considered the effects of multiple aneurysms, which is essential, since they occur in 15% to 33% of the cases.

Proper visualization clearly reveals the location of the aneurysm and the in- and outflow, which is essential for access planning and for deciding whether intervention or surgery is more promising. Focus-and-context renderings using segmented vascular structures as focus turned out to be useful for such tasks [Neugebauer *et al.*, 2009b], but need to be complemented by visual exploration of blood flow.

19.5.1 BLOOD FLOW SIMULATIONS

There are different approaches how blood flow may be simulated based on the extracted vascular anatomy and further assumptions, e.g., regarding inflow, outflow, and viscosity:

- Lattice Boltzmann simulation,
- Finite volume simulation,

Lattice Boltzmann simulations consider particles, representing different components of blood, and simulate their behavior, including collisions. The term is due to the discrete Boltzmann equation that has to be solved. Lattice Boltzmann simulation is a relatively recent simulation technique for fluid dynamics. It originates from molecular dynamics where it was used to simulate the complex interactions between molecules. In general, Lattice Boltzmann simulations are less sensitive to complex geometric shapes and they can be easily parallelized leading to fast implementations on GPUs.

In contrast, finite volume simulation is based on the Navier-Stokes equation and considers *macroscopic properties* of the blood flow, that is, blood is considered as one homogeneous fluid instead of a mixture of red and white blood cells as well as other constituents that have different properties. We focus in the following on finite volume simulation which is currently the more widespread technology.

Readers who are interested in lattice Boltzmann simulations are referred to the seminal paper [Chen and Doolen, 1998], to general textbooks [Succi, 2001, Sukop and Thorne, 2007] and the highly informative wikipedia entry[9] that includes links to open source and other software as well as many citations. The specific use of lattice Boltzmann simulation for blood flow is described, e.g., in [Wang and Bernsdorf, 2009] for blood flow in a stenotic region as well as in [Sun and Munn, 2008, Liu, 2012].

Finite Volume Simulation Blood flow simulation is a special instance of biomedical simulations. These simulations are based on a couple of input parameters that are used as *boundary conditions*. In all applications that are discussed in this chapter, boundary conditions include the relevant and patient-specific anatomy. In the case of blood flow, it includes also the inflow- and outflow speed. At least for diagnosis and treatment planning, *physically correct* simulations are aimed at. The behavior of tissue is represented by partial differential equations (PDE). The boundary conditions are necessary to come up with an unambiguous solution of the PDEs. The standard tools for such simulations are the finite volume methods (FVM). FEM and FVM solvers are specialized on solving large systems of coupled PDEs, representing the physical behavior at all cells of an appropriate volume grid. Such grids are usually unstructured. Widespread commercial FVM solvers are ANSYS FLUENT[10] and ANSYS CFX. OPENFOAM is an open source CFD package, frequently used for blood flow simulations.[11]

The density of the grid may be adapted to represent particularly interesting regions in more detail. Appropriate adaptive refinement and multigrid strategies are an area of active research [Altrogge *et al.*, 2007]. In general, a higher spatial resolution is desirable in regions with high curvature, or close to a pathology [Berg *et al.*, 2013].

Similar to adaptive spatial resolution, also the time-step might be adapted to consider the varying dynamics in different stages of the simulated process [Preusser and Peitgen, 2010]. If the underlying phenomena are modeled with sufficient accuracy, and if both the spatial resolution, characterized by the volume grid, and the temporal resolution is high, the simulation converges against the true solution. Inaccuracy results in particular from an uncertainty of input parameters, that may often only be roughly estimated, e.g., the inflow speed in a particular blood vessel.

Since the number of such equations is often large—in biomedical applications where a few million cells are typical—numerically efficient techniques are employed that take advantage of the sparse nature of the coefficient matrix (most elements are zero). Despite this, performance problems may arise and trigger efficient implementation strategies, e.g., on the GPU [Georgii and Westermann, 2006].

Computational Fluid Dynamics (CFD) CFD simulations approximate the hemodynamics in vascular segments based on Navier-Stokes equations. These PDEs consider fluids as incompressible media (in contrast to gas). The basis for these equations are the laws of conservation: energy, impulse, and mass. The tools that actually solve the equation systems are referred to as *CFD solvers*.

Simple blood flow simulations are based on a constant viscosity μ—this assumption is called *Newtonian behavior*. A density of $\rho = 1.094$ g/cm^3 and a viscosity μ of 0,003–000.4 Poise (kg/ms) are often used [Cebral *et al.*, 2005]. More realistically, blood is considered as non-Newtonian fluid where the viscosity is larger in wall near regions. CASSON's model, for example, considers this non-Newtonian behavior [Perktold *et al.*, 1991]. However, more realism comes at the expense of increased computation times. This gives rise to comparisons to better understand whether the additional computation effort is justified.

9 http://en.wikipedia.org/wiki/Lattice_Boltzmann_methods.
10 http://www.ansys.com/Products/Simulation+Technology/Fluid+Dynamics/ANSYS+Fluent.
11 http://www.openfoam.com/.

Boyd and Buick [2007] found that the differences are low and if not the highest accuracy is necessary, Newtonian behavior is a reasonable simplification.

There are further parameters that influence both realism and computational effort.

- geometry of the vessels,
- speed profile at the inflow,
- regional distribution of the speed at the inflow plane,
- elasticity of the vessel wall (Poisson number), and
- thickness of the vessel wall.

A simplified simulation considers the inflow velocity as constant over the whole cross section, whereas a more advanced simulation considers a speed profile, e.g., the Womersly profile. Another essential parameter is the time dependency. Steady-state simulations consider an average inflow speed, whereas unsteady simulations consider pulsatile blood flow with its strong difference between the speed in systolic and diastolic phase. Perhaps surprisingly, even the influence of the pulsatile behavior is rather low—at least qualitative results may be obtained with steady simulations. To obtain reliable WSS values in this near-wall region, hybrid grids with at least three prism layers are used (recall Fig. 19.15).

If the elasticity of the vessel wall should be incorporated, a coupled simulation problem arises: the flow simulation needs to be coupled with a (simultaneous) biomechanical simulation of the movements of the vessel wall. This is not only a challenging problem, but also leads to a very high computational effort. Moreover, the individual parameters of the patient (elasticity and vessel wall thickness) may not be determined in-vivo. Thus, this additional complexity is usually avoided and the vessel wall is instead assumed to be a rigid tube not affected by the flow. Theoretical analysis indicates that the error induced by this simplification is rather low in the cerebral arteries [Kim *et al.*, 2007b, Seshadhri *et al.*, 2011]. Moreover, the relevant material properties could only be estimated with high inaccuracy and thus, elasticity of the wall is neglected. Major results of blood flow simulations are direction and speed of the flow, the WSS and the oscillatory shear index (OSI).

Blood flow simulations in larger vessels, in particular in the coronary vessels, where heart muscle contraction and heart valve movement exert a stronger influence on the vessel wall and the uncertainty involved in neglecting this influence is considerable (see Fig. 19.27).

Spatial and Temporal Resolution These parameters affect the computational effort and the accuracy significantly. A temporal resolution of 0.025 s (40 Hz) and a spatial resolution of 0.5 mm were often considered appropriate [Hassan, 2004] (recall Fig. 19.15 for an example of a volume grid). With an average duration of 0.75 s of a cardiac cycle, this represents 30 measurements per cardiac cycle. More recent publications employ a significantly higher temporal resolution, e.g., 9600 per cardiac cycle [Ford *et al.*, 2008]. Ford *et al.* [2008] explain that in cerebral aneurysms high frequency fluctuations of the inflow jet, i.e., velocity magnitude and pressure occur likely. Thus, with a too low temporal resolution, the flow is erroneously considered as laminar. They observed such high frequency changes at approximately 110 Hz which gives rise to a temporal resolution that is at least twice as high.

19.5.2 EXTRACTION OF LANDMARKS

The exploration of vascular structures and the embedded flow strongly benefits from landmarks (*geometric descriptors*) that characterize important points, lines, and planes and enable a *guided* interaction. Such geometric descriptors may also be used to decompose the relevant anatomy in meaningful subregions to ease the exploration of complex flow data. Landmarks may be used for labeling and, even more important,

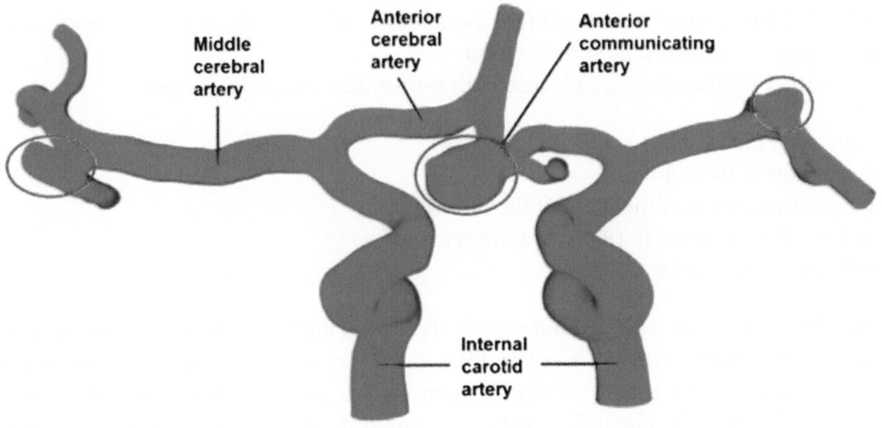

FIGURE 19.27 *Cerebral aneurysms may occur simultaneously at several places. In this example, three aneurysms are encircled. A major treatment decision relates to the question of which aneurysm should be treated with priority (Courtesy of Philipp Berg, University of Magdeburg).*

for guiding movements in the complex 3D anatomy. This guided exploration may lead to a more efficient and more reproducible interaction [Hanson and Wernert, 1997].

The choice of such landmarks is, of course, very specific for a particular anatomical region. We describe and illustrate this principle for the specific example of cerebral aneurysms.

Skeletonization A widely used geometric descriptor is the *vessel centerline*, determined by some kind of skeletonization algorithm (recall § 11.4.2). The vessel centerline is often used in order to move a cross-sectional plane that is always aligned perpendicular to the centerline, presenting the maximum-sized area. In vessel analysis packages, the cross-sectional view displays the intensity values from the original image data, e.g., the CT Hounsfield values. In case of blood flow data, this strategy may be used to present any scalar value derived from the flow or the flow data itself, e.g., by using some glyph mapping.

Further Anatomical Landmarks To understand *which* landmarks are actually important to characterize the local vessel anatomy, Neugebauer *et al.* [2010] asked a couple of neuroradiologists to draw cerebral aneurysms and extracted characteristic points commonly used by them. As a result, it turns out that

- the dome point of an aneurysm,
- the (curved) ostium plane, where the blood enters the aneurysm, and
- a so-called central aneurysm axis (the closest connection between the parent vessel's centerline and the dome point)

are essential (see Fig. 19.28). These landmarks may be employed for constrained navigation, e.g., to move a plane along the central aneurysm axis or to employ the ostium plane as the seeding region where streamline integration starts. The robust and precise detection is challenging due to the large variety of pathological situations [Neugebauer *et al.*, 2010]. Landmark extraction is probably significant for other anatomical regions, since it provides a familiar reference frame for medical doctors.

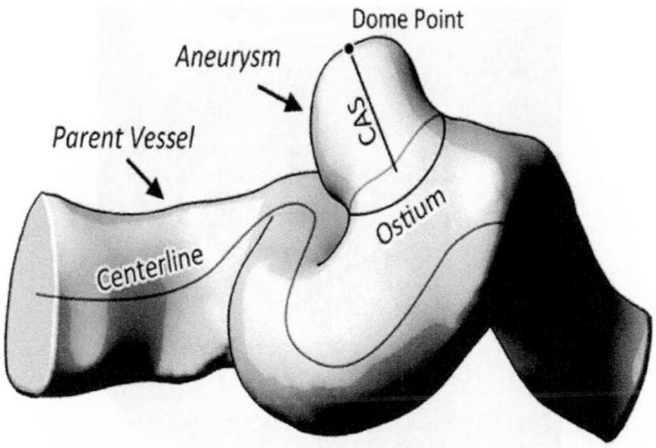

FIGURE 19.28 *Landmarks for characterizing cerebral aneurysms (From: [Neugebauer et al., 2010]).*

19.5.3 ANATOMY-GUIDED FLOW EXPLORATION

The flow exploration should employ familiar techniques, such as color-coded (illuminated) streamlines. However, these techniques should be adjusted such that the relevant features are effectively visualized. In particular, the geometric descriptors described above enable a streamlined visual exploration.

Flow Through the Ostium Plane The most essential aspect of streamline use is the seeding strategy (recall § 19.2.4). The usual strategy of selecting a ROI without any guidance is not effective, since neuroradiologists are particularly interested in the inflow and outflow of an aneurysm. Thus, the ostium plane is the optimal seeding geometry. Therefore, Neugebauer *et al.* [2011] provide a smoothed and remeshed ostium surface for seeding (see Fig. 19.29). It is also crucial to clearly see the inflow and outflow part of the ostium, since treatment targets specifically the inflow region. In Figure 19.30, this separation is emphasized.

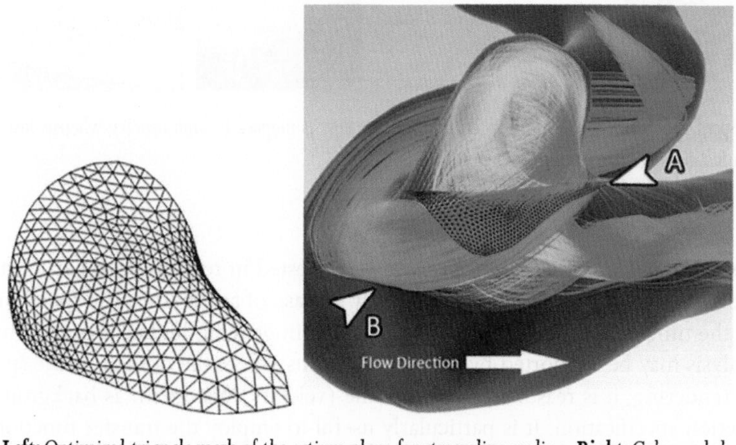

FIGURE 19.29 **Left:** *Optimized triangle mesh of the ostium plane for streamline seeding.* **Right:** *Color-coded streamlines seeded at the vertices of the ostium mesh provide an overview of the flow in the aneurysm (From: [Neugebauer et al., 2011]).*

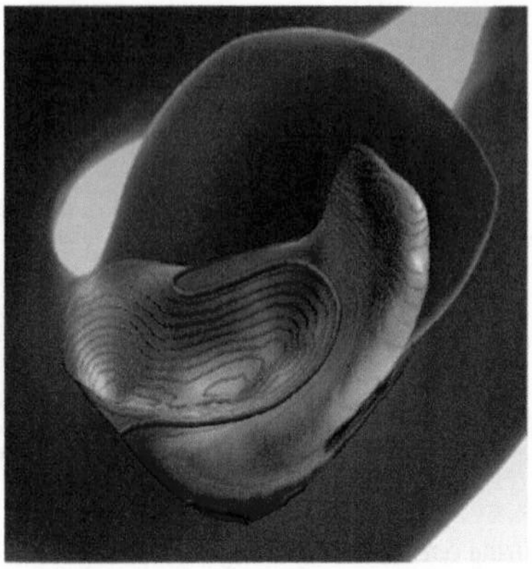

FIGURE 19.30 *Color encodes speed and isolines encode the volumetric flow rate. The red tube separates the inflow from the outflow in the ostium plane. The deformation of the ostium plane, a kind of height field, encodes the signed volume flow (From: [Neugebauer et al., 2011]).*

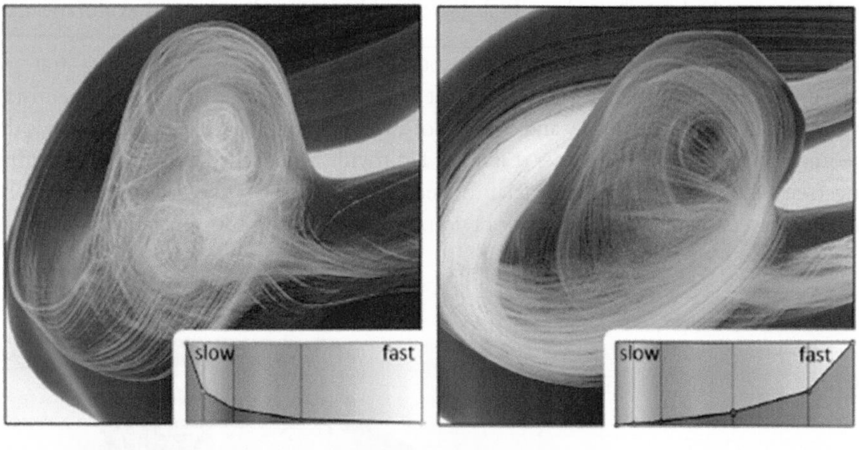

FIGURE 19.31 *Speed is mapped to color and opacity.* ***Left:*** *Slow flow is mapped to high opacity, whereas fast flow is transparent.* ***Right:*** *Emphasis on fast flow (From: [Neugebauer et al., 2011]).*

Filtering Flow Based on Speed Medical doctors are also interested in regions with particularly slow or fast flow, or in regions, where the speed changes abruptly. In case of aneurysms, the speed indirectly reveals the *turnover time*, the time the blood stays in the aneurysm (in general, higher turnover times are better). This kind of analysis may be supported by transfer functions where the domain is the speed of the flow. Like in volume rendering, it is reasonable to show the (velocity) histogram as background information for transfer function specification. It is particularly useful to employ the transfer function to map speed to opacity, thus effectively hiding flow that is not relevant (see Fig. 19.31).

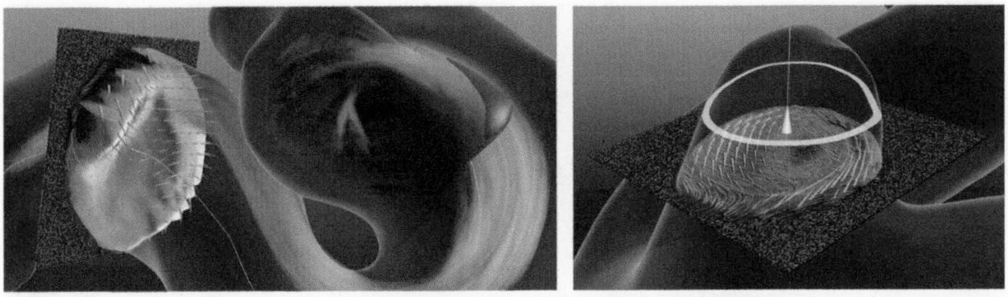

FIGURE 19.32 *Widgets to explore the cross-sectional flow are moved along the parent vessel's centerline (left) and along the central aneurysm axis (right) (From: [Neugebauer et al., 2011]).*

Since the sign of the flow indicates inflow and outflow, the transfer function may be adjusted to emphasize the distinction between both flow directions.

Guided Exploration The landmarks for the exploration might also be used to restrict the movement of a cross-sectional plane in the aneurysm. Neugebauer *et al.* [2011] introduced a *parent vessel widget* and *central axis widget* that may be moved along these path landmarks (see Fig. 19.32). The flow attributes to be displayed along these planes may be flexibly adjusted. The volumetric flow rate and the speed are the most essential parameters.

Guided exploration does not necessarily mean that it is impossible to deviate from a predefined path. There are many variants to combine a preference direction with free exploration where the user is attracted to the predefined path, but may deviate. A particularly successful example is a potential field approach employed for virtual colonoscopy (see Hong *et al.* [1997]). For a more general discussion of guided exploration, see, e.g., Hanson and Wernert [1997] and Elmqvist *et al.* [2008].

Visual Exploration of the Inflow Jet As a further support based on the extraction of the ostium plane, the *inflow jet* may be analyzed and displayed. The inflow jet and the resulting *impingement zone*, where the jet touches the aneurysm wall, are essential to characterize the risk of an aneurysm [Cebral *et al.*, 2011]. Based on this large-scale analysis (272 patients), the authors consider the following parameters as essential to assess the risk associated with a cerebral aneurysm:

- flow complexity,
- flow stability,
- inflow jet concentration, and
- size of the impingement zone.

The study indicated that the majority of ruptured aneurysms were associated with complex and unstable flow (about 70%), and with a concentrated inflow jet hitting a small impingement zone (about 65% of the cases).

The inflow jet may be characterized as the flow seeded in the ostium plane that is roughly parallel and very fast. It occurs in most but not all aneurysms. The surface area (as absolute value and relative to the overall size) is essential. Figure 19.33 illustrates the inflow jet and the impingement zone. Gasteiger *et al.* [2012] described an automatic approach to identify, characterize and visualize the inflow jet and the impingement zone.

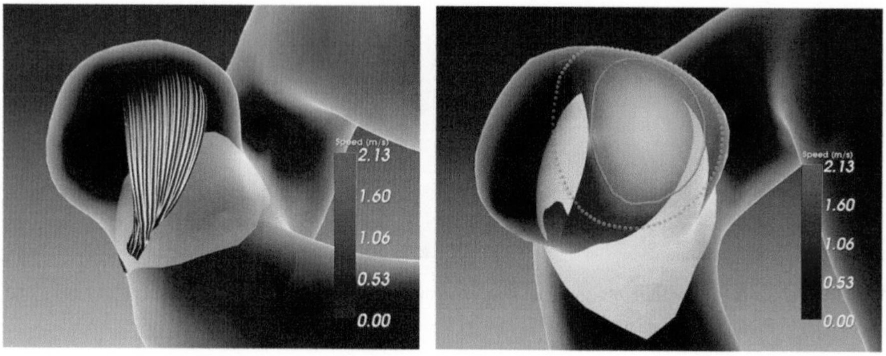

FIGURE 19.33 **Left:** *inflow jet boundary surface enhanced with stripes to convey surface shape.* **Right:** *The shape of the inflow jet and the impingement zone (see the outline) is emphasized (Courtesy of Rocco Gasteiger, University of Magdeburg).*

19.5.4 LENS-BASED INTERACTION

Focus-and-context visualizations are commonly used to avoid cluttering. Gasteiger *et al.* [2011] propose the FlowLens, which is a user-defined 2D magic lens [Bier *et al.*, 1993].[12] This lens allows the combination of different flow attributes by showing a different attribute and visualization within and outside the lens. Additionally, they incorporate a 2.5D lens to enable probing and slicing through the flow. To simplify the interface, they provide *anatomical scopes* which are task-based. Each scope consists of pairs of focus-and-context attributes. A visualization template is proposed to represent each pair (see Fig. 19.34).

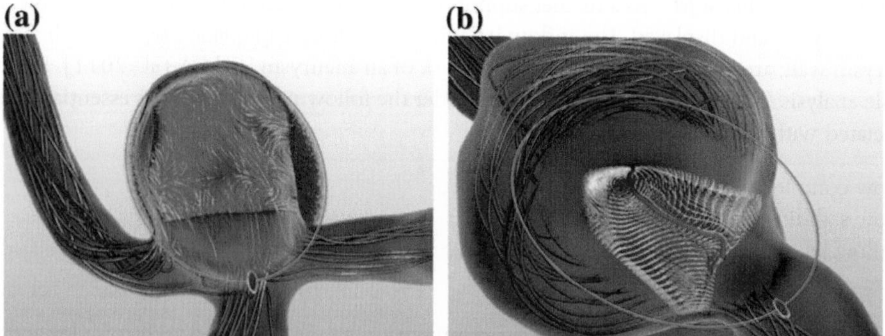

FIGURE 19.34 *Two examples of the FlowLens which is depicted with a red contour line and two handles. Outside the lens the flow is visualized with illustrative and color-coded streamlines. Inside the lens, a view-aligned probe plane with a LIC visualization for the investigation of the degree of vorticity (a) as well as the flow pressure at the ostium as isosurfaces (b) are embedded. Additionally, the ostium surface is shown within the lens of the LIC visualization as anatomical landmark (From: [Gasteiger et al., 2011]).*

12 We discussed lens-based interaction also in § 16.4.2 to explore multidimensional data.

19.5.5 VISUALIZATION OF VASCULATURE AND EMBEDDED FLOW

We extend the discussion of illustrative techniques for visualizing flow data (recall § 19.4.6) and explain how these techniques enable a better depiction of vasculature and embedded flow.

The flow strongly depends on local variations of the enclosing vascular structures. Strong changes in flow velocity occur at stenotic regions, and high speed flow occurs primarily at bifurcations or strongly curved areas. Thus, it is important to investigate the morphology of vascular structures and the internal flow simultaneously. In case of simulated flow, such an integrated analysis may reveal that a significant flow feature is due to a small variation of the surface which actually results from an inaccuracy in the previous segmentation. The simplest idea to display flow and vascular anatomy at the same time is to render the vascular surface transparently. However, depending on the transparency level, either the vascular anatomy is hardly recognizable, or the internal flow is strongly obscured by the vessel wall. Interrante *et al.* [1997] showed that opacity mapping a kind of texture mapping, where opacity is modulated, leads to a better visualization of embedded structures. This technique has been used for blood flow visualization by Sobel *et al.* [2004]. Although an improvement, the more recently developed smart visibility techniques are more promising, since they enable to adjust the local transparency to the content.

Ghosted Views Smart visibility techniques [Viola *et al.*, 2005] modify the transparency locally to make an important internal object visible. Thus, the flow may be considered as important object and the vessel wall's transparency is (only) modified to reveal streamlines where they actually should be displayed. The effect of this adaptation is obvious at the vessel boundaries where no internal flow lines need to be considered. This very idea has been realized by Gasteiger *et al.* [2010]. The specific solution employs a Fresnel reflection model [Schlick, 1993], where the reflection term was replaced by opacity (see Figs. 19.35 and 19.36 for a comparison of that technique with conventional semi-transparent rendering).

They refined their technique by an additional boundary enhancement and by an integration of the previously described landmarks that were used to emphasize these features with line rendering. Also depth attenuation are provided to improve depth perception. As a variant, it is possible to hide partially obscured flow lines to further reduce visual clutter (see Fig. 19.36).

Perceptual Study The perceptual effectiveness of these flow visualization techniques was analyzed in a study, where the users' performance with different techniques was recorded. Users should, for example,

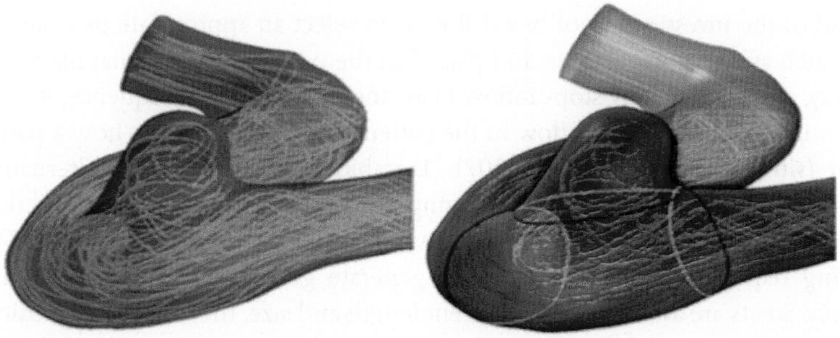

FIGURE 19.35 *In the left image, the vascular anatomy is rendered semi-transparently and the flow is shown with streamlines. In the right image, a ghosted view technique is used to better depict the internal flow. The lines indicate the ostium plane and the immediate in- and outflow (From: [Gasteiger et al., 2010]).*

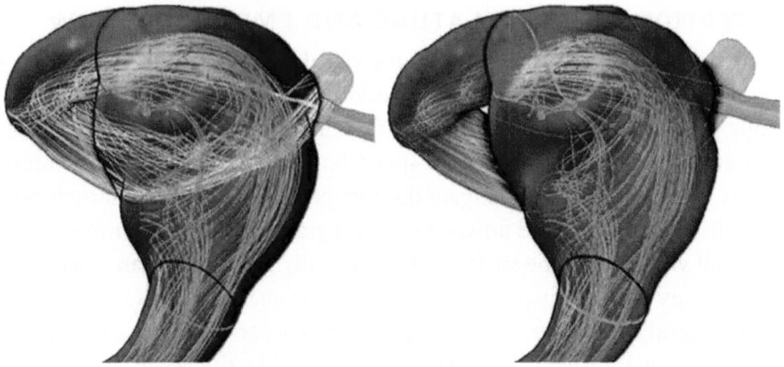

FIGURE 19.36 *A ghosted view technique is used to show the internal flow. While all streamlines are displayed in the left image, the right image contains only streamline portions that are not obscured by more frontal streamlines (From: [Gasteiger et al., 2010]).*

answer which one of two vessel segments is closer and place a gauge figure to estimate the local surface normal. They could rotate the 3D visualization in certain limits in order to realistically perceive the spatial relations. The ghosting techniques indeed lead to better performance [Baer *et al.*, 2011]. van Pelt *et al.* [2011] performed a user study that discussed the usefulness of the features they developed for cardiac blood flow. As an example, they could show that illustrative particles reveal recirculation very well. However, this study is more an informal evaluation, being part of a more general paper, and not a rigorous perception-based study.

Illustrative Visualization Another family of visualization techniques useful for depicting anatomical context and embedded flow is *illustrative visualization* (recall § 12.4). Illustrative visualization provides a couple of feature lines that may convey shape features sparsely. In particular, silhouettes and occluding contours are relevant to display the vascular anatomy [Gasteiger *et al.*, 2010, van Pelt *et al.*, 2010]. Occluding contours may be shown temporarily when the user navigates to support camera control.

19.5.6 VIRTUAL STENTING

The ultimate goal of the investigation of blood flow is to select an appropriate treatment for the patient. Thus, implants, such as stents, are chosen and placed in the patient in a way that likely changes the flow in the desired way, e.g., significantly stops inflow in an aneurysm. As a consequence, it should be possible to simulate not only the current blood flow in the patient, but also to predict how a particular stent will change the flow (*virtual stenting* [Kim *et al.*, 2007b, Larrabide *et al.*, 2008]). The alternative endovascular treatment is *coiling*. Virtual coiling is more challenging due to the complex geometry of the coils [Morales *et al.*, 2011]. The most recent and substantial work was described by Morales *et al.* [2013].

Virtual stenting requires, on the one hand, to generate geometric models of the implants with a sufficient accuracy. Stents are available with different length and size, they differ in porosity and flexibility. Flexible stents are required in curved vessel segments. Due to this variety, the optimal choice is challenging even for an experienced neuroradiologist. The realistic simulation of the stents' influence on flow requires considerable geometric detail. As an example, the simulation of a stented model for the VISC Challenge 2009 consisted of 4.590 K elements [Janiga *et al.*, 2009].

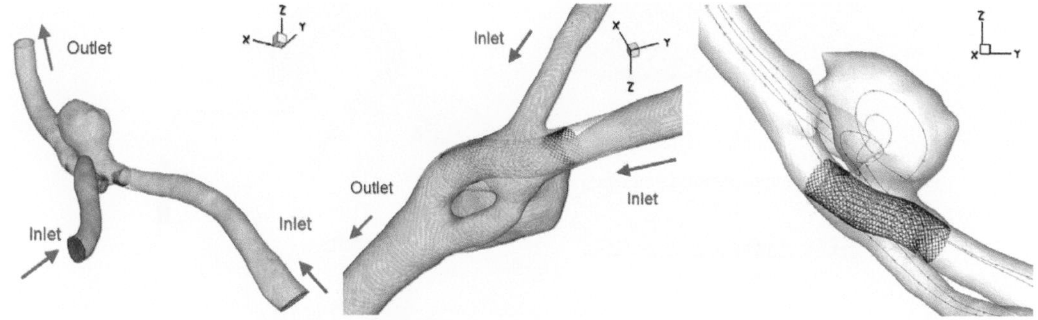

FIGURE 19.37 **Left:** *Patient model provided for the VISC Challenge 2009.* **Middle:** *Modified geometry with a stent.* **Right:** *Streamlines convey the results of the simulation (From: [Janiga et al., 2009]).*

VISC To stimulate research in virtual stenting, the virtual intracranial stenting challenge (VISC) was created and has been carried out annually since 2007.[13] The organizers provide patient data and a stent geometry, and engineering teams come up with vascular reconstructions, stent deployment, and hemodynamics simulations. Janiga *et al.* [2013] provide an in-depth discussion of virtual stenting for the VISC 2010 dataset with a basilary tip aneurysm. With their system different configurations of stents were analyzed, e.g., with respect to the residence time. Wall-tight stent deployment is achieved with a new free-form deformation.

Vascular Modeling for Virtual Stenting The geometry of the vasculature changes as a consequence of an inserted implant, e.g., it is widened. To adapt the surface models of vascular structures appropriately is challenging and currently only feasible in a tedious manual process. Mesh editing tools, such as SCULPTRIS and MESHLAB, are employed to adapt the geometry and then remesh in order to achieve (again) an appropriate triangle number with a good triangle quality. Figure 19.37 illustrates the use of such tools for *virtual stenting*. The process is described in detail in [Mönch *et al.*, 2011b].

Multiple Stents The effects of stents on turnover time, WSS and further relevant attributes may likely be enhanced if two stents (stent in stent) or even three stents are employed. However, care must be taken not to occlude small side vessels. Kim *et al.* [2007b] give an overview on virtual stenting with up to three stents and discuss a particular case, a wide-neck basilar aneurysm that is difficult to treat.

Virtual Stenting with Phantom Data Besides patient data, as they are used in the VISC contests, simple phantoms are essential to understand the influence of stent parameters on the resulting flow. Seshadhri *et al.* [2011] simulated 72 stent configurations in a simple phantom with a saccular aneurysm to compare their efficiency depending on wire density and thickness. The intra-aneurysmal flow velocity, WSS, mean speed, and vortex topology can be strongly modified by a suitable implant. Intra-aneurysmal turnover time increased rapidly with decreasing stent porosity. Figure 19.38 shows some of the stent models and different simulation results from that study. They found, for example, that for small aneurysms with a large neck stents were highly effective, whereas for large aneurysms with a small neck-to-dome ratio no stent was effective.

13 VISC 2011: http://www.cistib.upf.edu/visc11/.

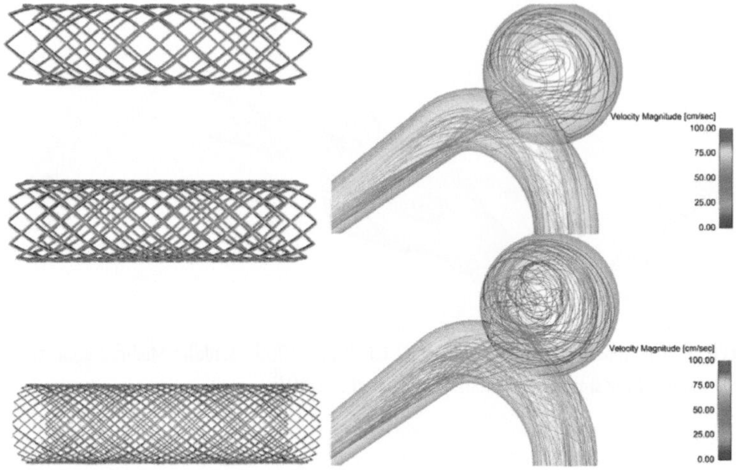

FIGURE 19.38 *Top row: Different stent configurations for virtual stenting of a bifurcation aneurysm. Bottom row: Corresponding simulation results (streamlines encode the velocity magnitude) (Courtesy of Philip Berg, University of Magdeburg. See also [Seshadhri et al., 2011]).*

19.5.7 SOFTWARE ASSISTANT

Neugebauer *et al.* [2013] describe the integration of the different exploration techniques in a software assistant, called AmniVis. The target audience are biomedical researchers exploring special instances, such as multiple aneurysms (see Figure 19.27) and datasets, acquired shortly before rupture. A key feature required by these users is support in the selection of relevant regions, in particular those where blobs or daughter aneurysms occur. Circular regions which exhibit this characteristic are semi-automatically detected and used for seeding (see Fig. 19.39). The Willmore energy, a curvature-based metric, is employed for detecting such regions [Neugebauer *et al.*, 2013].

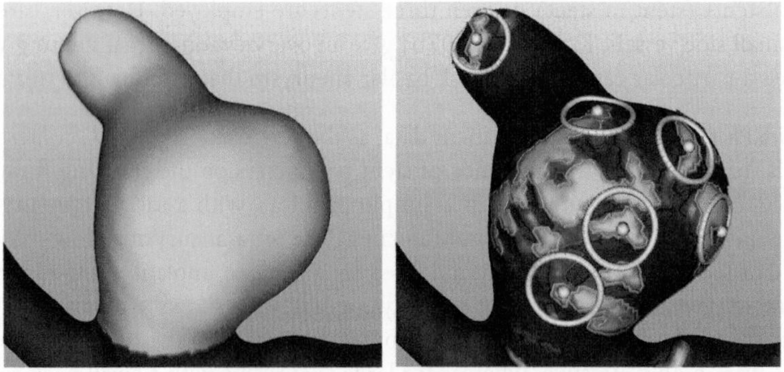

FIGURE 19.39 **Left:** *An aneurysm with daughter aneurysm.* **Right:** *After applying a curvature-based energy measure, the connected components with high curvature are determined and a circular seeding is defined for each large connected component (From: [Neugebauer et al., 2013]).*

To explore the flow, small planar views with the streamlines in the selected regions are displayed. In these views, the user may select the point in time manually, or cycle through the points in time (see Fig. 19.40). The overview 3D visualization is combined with such planar views in an automatically defined layout (see Fig. 19.41). The presented system was the result after multiple iterations of in-depth discussions concerning all aspects of the visualization and interaction. The chosen visualization techniques favor spatial exploration over temporal exploration, since the target users considered the spatial aspects more important (the analysis is often focused on one point in time, often the end-diastolic stage or on two points in time). An essential feature, even for experienced users, is the automatic computation of a viewpoint for the 3D view that is appropriate to show the corresponding flow features. Strategies for computing good and *stable* viewpoints, that is viewpoints that show a target structure also after slight rotations, were presented by Tao *et al.* [2013]. These techniques consider application-specific knowledge, e.g., preferred global viewing directions that are typical in medicine. Viewpoints for emphasizing essential flow features were introduced by Mühler *et al.* [2007]. These ingredients are useful for a software assistant that aids in the exploration of blood flow.

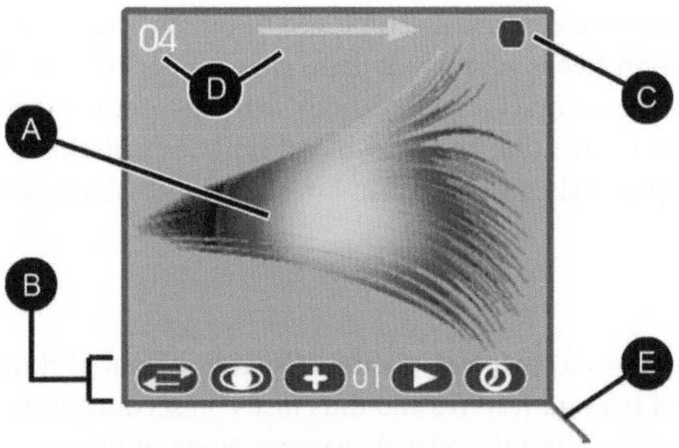

FIGURE 19.40 *For each region, a small 2D view with associated widgets is created. It allows to classify the aneurysm (B), to determine an appropriate viewpoint automatically, to select a time step (From: [Neugebauer et al., 2013]).*

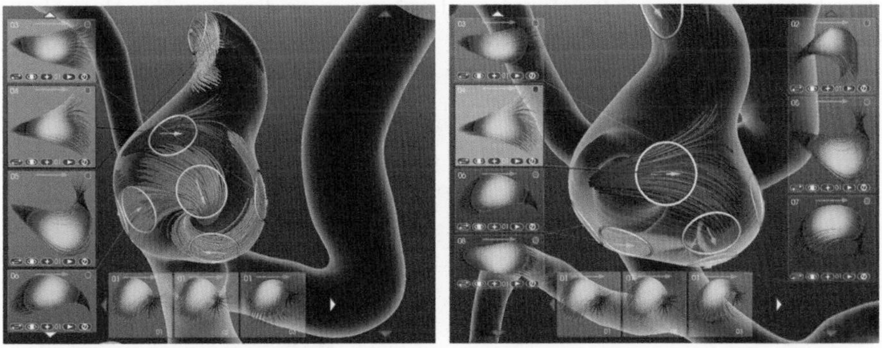

FIGURE 19.41 **Left:** *The AmniVis Explorer integrates a 3D view with circular seeding regions and 2D view summarizing the flow in these regions.* **Right:** *The user has selected one region and the 3D view highlights the corresponding flow (From: [Neugebauer et al., 2013]).*

19.5.8 VALIDATION

We can only briefly touch validation issues here. Clearly, validation is essential to understand under which circumstances results of CFD simulations are trustworthy. The construction of realistic phantoms representing the vascular surface geometry, the implementation of realistic flow conditions resembling the cardiac cycle using a pump, the realization of a liquid that resembles blood, and the reliable measurement of flow properties such as speed are crucial to verify the predictions of CFD against experimental measurements [Ford *et al.*, 2008].

Phantoms should be anatomically realistic and represent a variety of aneurysm shapes ideally constructed from patient-specific data with rapid prototyping. Usually, geometric models need some postprocessing, e.g., to prevent too small structures or structures very close to each other, since such structures cannot be physically constructed (see [Mönch *et al.*, 2011b]). There are different techniques to experimentally validate flow simulations. Among them are Laser Doppler Velocimetry (LDV), Particle Image Velocimetry (PIV), and Particle Tracking Velocimetry (PTV) [Bordás *et al.*, 2012]. While for CFD simulation, a single blood cycle is sufficient, experimental validation requires more cycles (at least three) to compensate for measurement uncertainty. Simple averaging of the measures is usually performed [Ford *et al.*, 2008]. Figure 19.42 gives an impression of the validation.

Since biophysical simulations are primarily employed to predict treatment effects and thus to support treatment decisions, validation needs to address these predictions as well. As an example, Imbesi and Kerber [2001] investigated the accuracy of simulations, with respect to stenting and coiling of cerebral aneurysms. Finally, we want to mention that also blood flow measurements with 4D PC-MRI—due to their inherent artifacts—require validation by phantom studies [Tateshima *et al.*, 2001].

19.5.9 DISCUSSION

A variety of advanced techniques for exploring simulated and measured flow were presented. They aim at an effective exploration of relevant features and thus focus on seeding and probing strategies as well as on integrated presentation of flow and the related anatomy. None of these systems, however, is in regular clinical use. Even the SIEMENS tool is a research prototype, not a commercial product. For routine use, a streamlined workflow, predefined views and carefully selected default values are essential to simplify the interaction considerably. With respect to more basic research questions, there is only limited experience so far regarding the actually important flow features and their automatic detection. The value of feature-based methods needs to be investigated in the future.

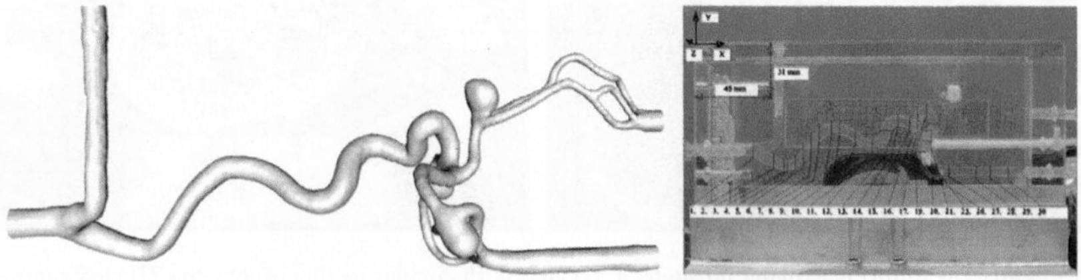

FIGURE 19.42 **Left:** *A silicon phantom used for validating blood flow simulations.* **Right:** *The Laser Doppler Velocimetry facility to experimentally validate flow simulations (Courtesy of Gabor Janiga, University of Magdeburg).*

19.6 BIOMEDICAL SIMULATION AND MODELING

In the following, we describe two further applications, where the visual exploration of simulation results is promising for treatment planning. We start with orthopedics, and in particular with total hip replacement, where implant selection and placement may be improved by considering biomechanical simulation of the load distribution (§ 19.6.1) and we continue with the simulation of temperature distribution after radio-frequency ablation (RFA), a rather new treatment option that is already widely used as tumor therapy (§ 19.6.2). Similar to the visual exploration of blood flow, simulation results need to be displayed along with the relevant anatomy and implants (in case of total hip replacement) and radio-frequency applicators (in case of RFA treatment). While stress tensors are the major simulation result in biomechanics, temperature simulations primarily yield a map of the (temporarily) changing temperature distribution.

19.6.1 BIOMECHANICAL SIMULATION IN ORTHOPEDICS

Biomechanical simulations play an essential role in a couple of orthopedic interventions [Bessho *et al.*, 2007]. They enable the surgeons to select proper implants, to place and angulate them in a favorable way. In conventional treatment planning, e.g., by CT or X-ray data, these preoperative decisions consider geometric factors only. Thus, planning aims at a good fit of the plant in the anatomy of a particular joint. However, to ensure long-term stability of implants in hips, knees, and shoulder, functional aspects must not be neglected. In particular, the biomechanical stress situation in the remaining bones should be considered. Bones consist of living tissue that constantly adapts to the mechanical load situation by bone formation or resorption [Simoes and Vaz, 2002]. The goal of preoperative planning is to create a situation where the stress distribution in the remaining bones remains as close as possible to its original state. Stress shielding by a large implant should be avoided, since it leads to bone remodeling and loss [Dick *et al.*, 2009].

A favorable physiological situation can be achieved by incorporating biomechanical simulations based on patient-specific data. Thus, the whole pipeline of segmenting CT data, extracting surface models, and remeshing them as a basis for volume grid generation and finite element simulation (recall § 19.3) has to be performed. Similar to virtual stenting (recall § 19.5.6), the geometry of the potential implants has to be considered as well.

Total Hip Replacement As an example, we consider total hip replacement. Simulation is based on material properties, in particular on *elasticity* characterized by the Young modulus and the Poisson number. These values differ locally, since the femur consists of compact cortical bone and spongious trabecular bone. Fortunately, the elasticity parameters can be reliably estimated from the CT density values. Forces applied to an elastic material lead to *tension* and *compression*.

We will not describe the simulation process and its underlying assumptions, but briefly discuss the visualization of the results for the specific example of total hip joint replacement, where the femoral head is replaced—a kind of surgery that affects a large and still growing number of primarily elder patients (see Fig. 19.43).

Strain-stress Tensors as Major Simulation Result The major simulation results are strain-stress tensors. A tensor is a symmetric 3×3 matrix, thus it is more complex than the vector-valued data we have considered so far. We will learn more about tensor visualization in Chapter 15. Here, it might be sufficient to state that an eigenanalysis of the tensor delivers three eigenvectors $\vec{e_1}$, $\vec{e_2}$, and $\vec{e_3}$, and three eigenvalues λ_1, λ_2, and λ_3 and the visualization of the vector corresponding to the largest eigenvalue λ_1 is an essential information often used for visualizing tensor data. Similar to streamlines and pathlines, the information

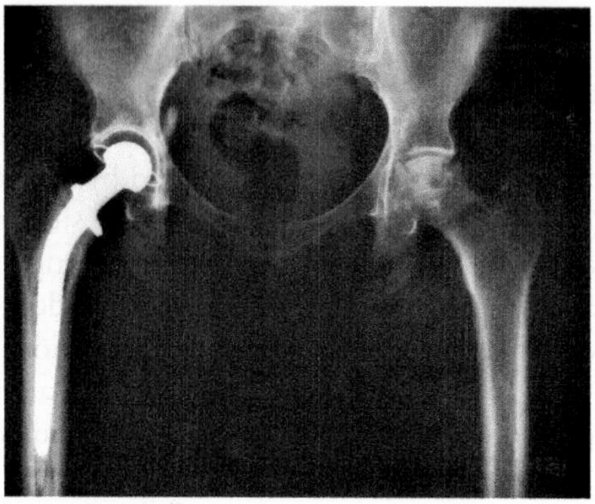

FIGURE 19.43 *In total hip replacement, a bonding cement is used to fix the metal prostheses into the shaft of the femur and the plastic cup to the acetabulum. Cement-free implants are also possible. Various designs and materials are available leading to different effects on the remaining bone (Courtesy of Wikipedia).*

is tracked over a larger region. If none of the three eigenvalues is significantly larger than the others, the direction is ambiguous and tracking is stopped. In this particular example of stress tensors, the resulting lines are referred to as *stress lines*. Moreover, scalar values are often derived from tensor data.

Visual Exploration of Simulation Results Visual exploration is guided by requirements that are very similar to blood flow visualization: the simulation results need to be analyzed both at a global and on a more local level. Moreover, the simulation results need to be analyzed along with the skeletal anatomy and the implant geometry. DICK and colleagues tackled this problem and described their solutions in a couple of publications [Dick *et al.*, 2008, 2009].

They visualized the stress tensor by classifying whether tension or compression occurs and by assigning different colors accordingly. The absolute stress magnitude is mapped to opacity, thus focusing on regions with higher stress values. To provide the spatial context, the opacity of the bone surface and the implant in the focus region is improved (Fig. 19.44).

In particular, they presented a focus-context visualization that enables a detailed analysis of the simulation results in a focus region (Fig. 19.44), similar to the FLOWLENS concept developed later [Gasteiger *et al.*, 2011]. A particular challenge, again similar to virtual stenting, is the comparative visualization of the current stress distribution versus the predicted distribution after implant placement. In contrast to vascular implants, ideally, simulation results are almost unchanged. Thus, regions where the stress distribution changes strongly are most interesting and critical.

Computational Steering A great advantage of this particular system is that the simulations are performed extremely fast, enabling interactive steering. That is, the user may change the implant position and angulation and can immediately assess how these changes affect the biomechanical situation. This was possible by a GPU implementation of the finite element solver [Georgii and Westermann, 2006]. More recently, they developed a CUDA-based framework for even better performance [Dick *et al.*, 2011b].

For further details, in particular the comparative visualization, the selection of simulated implants and the feedback from users, we refer to the paper [Dick *et al.*, 2009]. In this project, also new ideas for visualizing distances arose that were discussed in § 17.3.4.

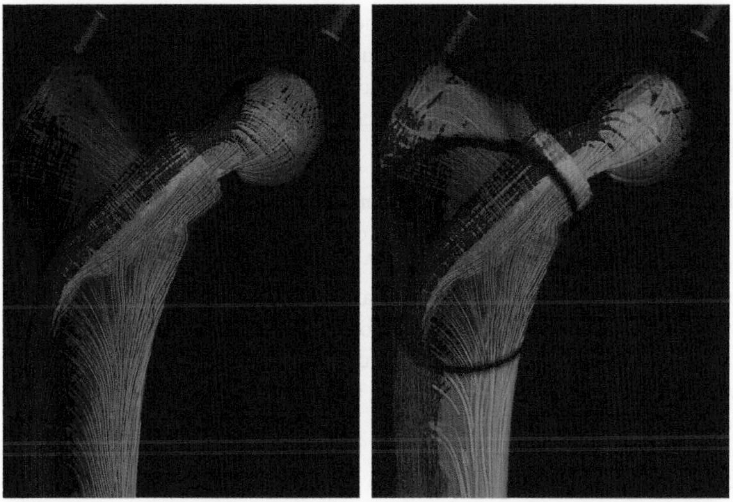

FIGURE 19.44 *Biomechanical simulations for total hip replacement.* ***Left:*** *The simulated stress distribution is visualized with green and violet tensor lines, representing regions with compression and tension.* ***Right:*** *A focus-context visualization enables a better depiction of the implant geometry and a local analysis in the surrounding bone (From: [Dick et al., 2009]).*

19.6.2 SIMULATION AND VISUALIZATION FOR PLANNING RADIO-FREQUENCY ABLATION

Medical Background Hepatic cancer and liver metastases are frequent and serious medical problems. Surgical removal of all tumors with a sufficient security margin is still the most promising treatment with five year survival rates of some 30%. However, often the location and size of tumors or the overall medical conditions of the patient do not allow surgery. Among the treatment options in such cases, *thermoablation* gained an enormous interest within the last 10–15 years. These interventions are primarily performed by radiologists putting a catheter in the tumor center to heat the tissue and thus to destroy the tumor cells. There are various options using different physical effects to produce the desired temperature in the target region, e.g., Laser-induced interstitial thermotherapy (LITT) and radiofrequency ablation (RFA). These therapies are popular among patients, since they can be performed with regional anesthesia and the hospitalization time is very short. RFA is widely considered as a safe, effective and easily applicable treatment option [Weihusen *et al.*, 2010].

Since RFA is by far the most widespread therapy, we focus the following discussion on this treatment. RFA is performed with a needle-shaped mono- or bipolar applicator, connected to an electric generator. The *active zone* of the applicator is placed in the malignant tissue and the electric current leads to heating to temperatures of 60 °C and more. At such temperatures, proteins denaturate irreversibly and the cells die. RFA is feasible if tumors are not too large (<3 cm), since the extent of the thermolesion that can be produced is limited. If tumors are slightly above this limit, they might be treated with two RFA applicators. The long-term effect depends on whether the tumor was indeed destroyed completely. In contrast to surgery, where the pathologist analyzes the removed tissue to state whether the tumor was removed completely, such a pathological workup is not feasible in RFA treatment. Moreover, intraoperative imaging only yields "a shadow of the lesion leaving an unknown amount of uncertainty" [Preusser and Peitgen, 2010].

Thus, it is essential to be able to predict whether complete tumor ablation may be achieved. This prediction is not easy, since it has to consider various effects, e.g., the cooling effect of adjacent vascular structures that depends on their diameter and the corresponding flow rate. Moreover, it is essential to predict where the applicators should be placed to achieve an optimum effect and to decide about power setup and ablation time [Altrogge *et al.*, 2007].

Simulation of Temperature Distribution After Radio-frequency Ablation Similar to the other application areas, patient-specific simulation requires a segmentation of the target structures, in particular of the liver, the hepatic vasculature and the tumors. Simulation of RFA temperature distribution is an active research field. The approaches differ in complexity, realism, and computational effort. Electric and thermal tissue parameters as well as biochemical properties of proteins are essential input parameters [Altrogge *et al.*, 2006]. Similar to other biomedical simulations, such parameters are notoriously difficult to define for an individual patient. Without going into detail, we want to mention at least the major elements of such simulations (according to [Altrogge *et al.*, 2007]):

- Electric current heats the tissue according to its electrical resistance. This effect is represented in the *electrostatic equation* that considers electric potential ϕ and electric conductivity σ as input.
- The *bioheat transfer equation* models how heat is diffused in the surrounding tissue. A special term represents the dissipation of heat due to blood circulation. Tissue density, thermal conductivity, and heat capacity are the parameters of this equation.
- The cell proteins denaturate irreversibly at a certain temperature, depending on a couple of further parameters. This process is modeled by the ARRHENIUS formalism.

The three processes are coupled and further increase the complexity of the solution. The use of these simulation results for access planning, requires to display them along with the hepatic anatomy and skeletal structures that effectively limit access options. To come up with efficient solutions, the spatial resolution of the volume grids is carefully adapted. It needs to be increased close to the active zones of the applicator and close to the (cooling) vessels (see Fig. 19.45).

Uncertainty analysis plays an essential role in RFA simulation. It is related to inaccuracy in image acquisition and segmentation, but primarily to the biological variability of tissue properties, like electric

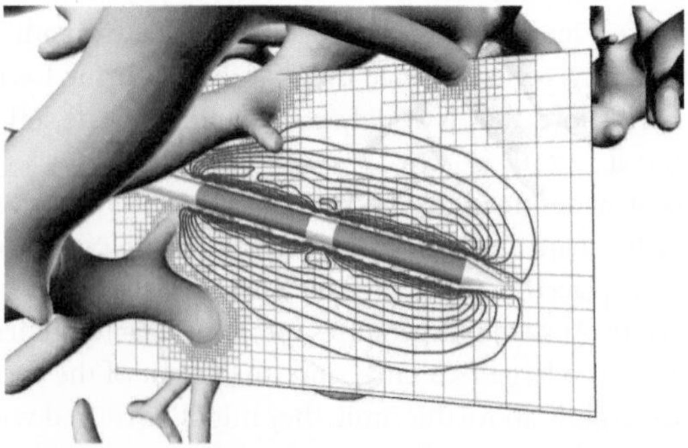

FIGURE 19.45 *Simulation of the temperature distribution for RFA planning. The vascular structures and a bipolar applicator (two active zones) is shown along with isolines representing the temperature. The adaptive hexahedral grid is overlaid. Please note the high resolution close to vascular structures (Courtesy of Christian Rieder, Fraunhofer MEVIS).*

and thermal conductivity [Preusser and Peitgen, 2010]. To understand uncertainty, values are considered as specific instances of a *distribution* with certain stochastic parameters, similar to our discussion of blood flow uncertainty (recall [Schwenke *et al.*, 2011]).

Visual Exploration The simulation produces unsteady data representing the ablation zone over time. The ablation zone is defined as the surface, where the simulated temperature is above 60°. Due to the uncertainty in the input parameters one might think of a visualization that considers the reliability of the result, but arguably, the visualization would become more complex. The ablation zone should be visualized in 2D slice data and it is useful if the temporal development is also indicated. A 3D visualization acts as an overview: it should display the ablation zone, the tumor and the local vasculature simultaneously (Fig. 19.46). The cooling effect of vascular structures prevents a simple ellipsoidal shape of the ablation zone. It is interesting to visualize this difference, in particular if several larger vessels are close to the tumor (Fig. 19.47). The visual exploration of radio-frequency ablation has been carefully studied by RIEDER and

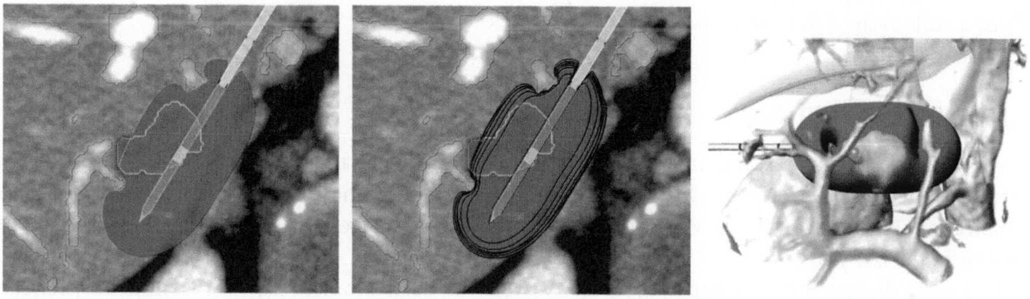

FIGURE 19.46 *Visualization for RFA planning. The simulated ablation zone (isosurface corresponding to a temperature of 60 °C) and the relevant anatomy are shown simultaneously.* ***Left:*** *The ablation zone and the RF applicator shown as overlay on a 2D slice view with the segmented tumor contoured.* ***Middle:*** *The lines represent the ablation zone at different points in time.* ***Right:*** *The ablation surface is rendered as transparent object with shading, silhouette and boundary enhancement to support depth perception (From: [Rieder et al., 2011]).*

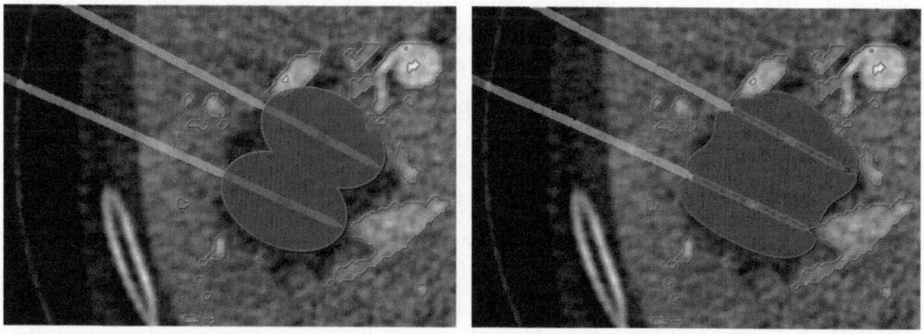

FIGURE 19.47 *CT slices with ablation zones for two applicators overlaid.* ***Left:*** *Without considering blood circulation, the ablation zone is the intersection of two ellipsoids.* ***Right:*** *The ablation zone is significantly altered based on the cooling effect of adjacent vascular structures (From: [Rieder et al., 2011]).*

colleagues. The most essential publication on this issue is [Rieder *et al.*, 2011]. Besides visual exploration, they also described a fast GPU-based approximation of the finite element simulation. Thus, similar to Dick *et al.* [2009], they are able to steer applicator placement and the simulation is performed immediately, enabling the user to try different configurations.

19.7 CONCLUDING REMARKS

In this chapter, we got to know flow visualization techniques and learned about their applications in exploring simulated and measured flow data. While many visualization techniques, discussed in this book, were primarily developed for medical image data, flow visualization techniques were primarily developed for applications in engineering and natural sciences, where simulations are widely used. It is still inspiring to look at these applications to understand flow visualization techniques, their parameterization and combination for real-world applications. The use of simulation for treatment planning and the related visualization challenges represent major research fields. For more regular use, the individual techniques need to be carefully combined, integrated in appropriate software assistants that provide *guidance* instead of just a collection of flexible tools.

FURTHER READING

There is a lot of ongoing research in flow visualization, that is potentially useful for medical visualization. Instead of picking a few papers, we want to point the reader to the major conferences, such as IEEE Visualization, EuroVis, and Pacific Vis. Each of these annual conferences had substantial flow visualization sessions in the last years.

We briefly discussed RFA simulation. As an overview on such simulations, we recommend [Berjano, 2006]. A couple of investigations particularly relate to the cooling effect of blood circulation, see, e.g., [Frericks *et al.*, 2008]. A more recent effort on approximating cooling effects is described in [Kröger *et al.*, 2010]. A bit related to RFA, regional hyperthermia is a tumor treatment, where tumors should be destroyed by applying heat. Antenna placement and energy setup are among the parameters to optimize in this treatment. Simulation and visualization of the anatomy along with the simulation results was investigated, e.g., in [Gellermann *et al.*, 2000, Ranneberg *et al.*, 2010, Weiser, 2009]. The visual exploration of measured cardiac blood flow remains an active research area, as recent papers indicate [Born *et al.*, 2012] and [van Pelt *et al.*, 2012a]. Also for understanding flow in cardiac vessels, simulations are performed. Borkin *et al.* [2011] describe the visualization of the simulation results with 2D (planar projections) and 3D visualizations. In particular, they investigated different color maps for presenting scalar flow features expressively. The 2D visualization represents the branching hierarchy well (see Fig. 19.49).

There are many more examples of substantial progress due to biomedical simulations and the visual analysis of their results. As an example, Pernod *et al.* [2011] introduced a model of cardiac electrophysiology to simulate radio-frequency ablation in the heart. Also Dössel *et al.* [2007] provide a model of electrophysiology useful for treatment planning. Frank Sachse's book discusses the simulation of cardiac electrophysiology and cardiac mechanics [Sachse, 2004]. A very inspiring paper from Zachow *et al.* [2009] is dedicated to the visual exploration of nasal airflow, based on CFD simulations. This research is motivated by the need for a better understanding of nasal breathing, resulting temperature and gradient distributions as a prerequisite for better drug delivery. Visual analytics techniques are employed for feature selection, and advanced visualization, including boundary enhancement for displaying anatomy and simulated flow, are used (see Fig. 19.48).

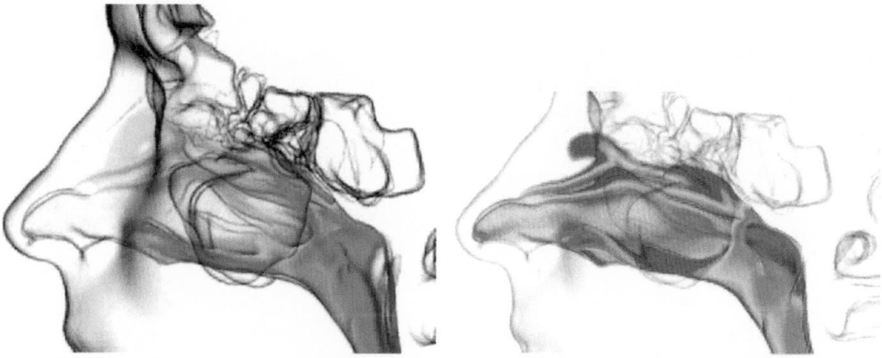

FIGURE 19.48 *Visual exploration of nasal airflow.* **Left:** *Nasal airflow is displayed along with the anatomy extracted from CT data. Silhouettes improve the perception of the anatomy without obstructing the flow data.* **Right:** *With information visualization techniques the intersection of regions with slow flow and high temperatures is selected. Color represents flow speed (From: [Zachow et al., 2009]).*

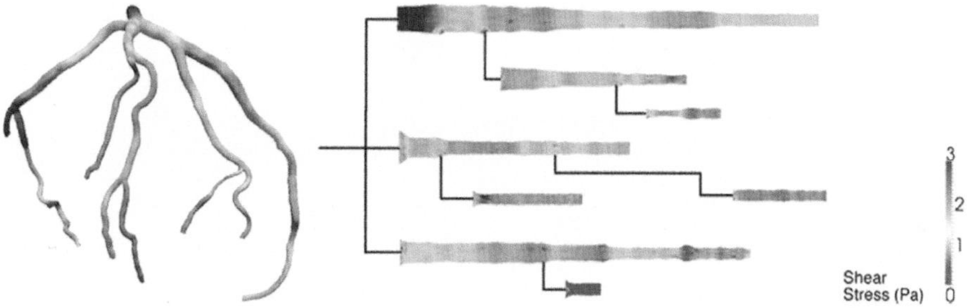

FIGURE 19.49 *Scalar flow features are determined along a cardiac tree. The 3D visualization (left) is transformed in a planar 2D visualization that represents the branching hierarchy (From: [Borkin et al., 2011]).*

With respect to simulation methods, we focused on finite volume simulations for CFD and finite element simulation for other biomedical problems. There are alternative methods, that are faster but less accurate. Examples are mass-spring models, chain-mail algorithms and meshless techniques, in particular particle-based simulation [Mueller *et al.*, 2004, Müller *et al.*, 2004]. Such methods are essential in surgery simulation.

Outlook Significant further research is necessary to better understand relations between blood flow features and pathologies. This would be a prerequisite for building systems that emphasize relevant features and feature combinations and thus guide users through a flow exploration session instead of confronting them with complex user interfaces and completely free interaction. The largest portion of this chapter was devoted to the exploration of simulation results. Simulation results have a rather high degree of uncertainty that is locally varying and depends on very specific characteristics of a particular patient. The analysis of this uncertainty and its visualization is essential for future work, in particular to fulfill regulatory requirements and to achieve routine clinical use.

Chapter e20

Visual Computing for ENT Surgery Planning

20.1 INTRODUCTION

In this chapter, we will explain how general strategies for computer-assisted surgery are adapted, implemented, and employed to meet the needs of ENT surgery (ear, nose, throat). This special surgical discipline is characterized by a high level of technical support. The very first computer-assisted surgical assistance systems were developed in this area [Klimek *et al.*, 1993]. Also, advanced early surgical simulators were realized for ENT surgery [Edmond *et al.*, 1997, Weghorst *et al.*, 1998].

The high density of crucial anatomical structures in the ear, nose, and throat makes surgery highly demanding. Accuracy is often essential, e.g., in implanting hearing aids, and esthetic considerations are often relevant. On the other hand, anatomical structures are relatively fixed and do not exhibit large displacements of tissue in surgery. This makes ENT surgery an ideal goal for computer-assistance. In ENT surgery, computer-assistance was focused for a long time on intraoperative navigation [Koele *et al.*, 2002]. In this chapter, we focus instead on 3D visualizations used for surgical planning and interdisciplinary treatment discussions in ENT surgery. First attempts were made in the 1990s [Moharir *et al.*, 1998], but only recently systems were developed that go beyond the prototype stage.

Organization We start with virtual endoscopy solutions for planning and training functional endoscopic sinus surgery (§ 20.2). This intervention is performed in the nasal region if patients suffer from sinusitis. Although this type of surgery is often a rather simple procedure that does not require advanced planning, it becomes risky in case of extended sinusitis when surgery needs to be performed close to the skull base or close to the optical nerve. In § 20.3, we discuss surgery in the filigrane ear region where implants and hearing aids are inserted in order to improve hearing. Implant selection and placement are essential aspects of this kind of surgery. The largest part of the chapter is devoted to the removal of tumors in the neck region, e.g., neck dissections where surgeons are interested in a detailed inspection of the spatial relations around primary tumors and metastases. We introduce neck dissection in § 20.4 and go on with discussing image analysis and interactive visualization for neck surgery planning (§ 20.5 and 20.6). The computer support in all three areas is primarily based on high resolution CT data. In addition, color images and palpatory findings from fiber endoscopy are employed.

Although we discuss specific problems and possible solutions, the reader is encouraged to think about transferring these experiences to other surgical disciplines. Virtual endoscopy of the sinus region is representative for intervention support in other anatomical regions. Likewise, neck surgery planning has many similarities in both requirements and viable solutions with other kinds of tumor surgery.

Visual Computing for Medicine, Second Edition. http://dx.doi.org/10.1016/B978-0-12-415873-3.00020-1

20.2 PLANNING AND TRAINING ENDOSCOPIC SINUS SURGERY

20.2.1 MEDICAL BACKGROUND

Sinus surgery is applied if patients suffer from chronic sinusitis—mucosal swellings that hamper ventilation. Figure e20.1 illustrates the target anatomy. Mucosal swellings may occur in all four paranasal sinuses, in severe cases even simultaneously. This state is called *pansinusitis* and obviously requires a comprehensive surgery. Since the 1980s, surgery is performed via an endoscope and with special instruments suitable for the small space. This procedure is called *functional endoscopic sinus surgery* (FESS) [Lloyd, 1989].

The ethmoid air cells and the sinus ostia are opened to restore the ventilation. This minimally-invasive approach does not only lead to faster recovery but is also clearly preferred over open surgery from an esthetical point of view. Minimally-invasive procedures, however, are challenging for the surgeon, since the direct visual access to the situs is missing. Instead, the situs is displayed at an endoscopic monitor. The surgeon uses a couple of anatomical landmarks, such as the middle turbinate and the uncinate process, for orientation. These landmarks, however, are missing when the disease comes back and relapse surgery is required. In these cases, the orientation is particularly difficult. In case of younger patients (12–14 years), the question arises whether the meatus (the airways) are large enough to move the endoscope through. If mucosal swellings close to the orbita, the optical nerve, or the skull base need to be removed, the operation is risky and intraoperative navigation support is desirable (§ 18.5). The most challenging situation occurs in case of malignant tumors where complete removal is essential (in case of benign mucosal swellings, a small remaining portion is acceptable if a severe risk to other structures can thus be avoided).

Preoperatively, a virtual endoscopy through the sinus may help to make the surgeon familiar with the patient's individual anatomy and to preview the actual surgery. Thus, virtual endoscopy may be part of the planning procedure but can also be considered as a training tool. The value of virtual endoscopy is determined by the amount of realism and by the insights it provides, e.g., the ability to see hidden structures along with obscuring structures. Color, texture, and wetness effects are essential ingredients of visual realism. For training purposes, where residents train the use of the endoscope and learn instrument-tissue interactions, realistic haptic feedback is essential as well [Pössneck *et al.*, 2005].

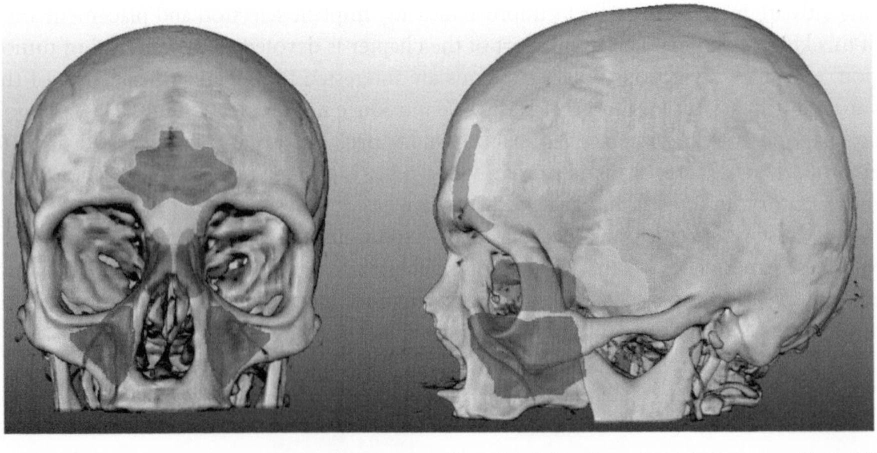

FIGURE e20.1 *Relevant anatomical structure of the sinuses (frontal and lateral view). Red: Sinus maxillaris, Yellow: Sinus sphenoidalis, Blue: Sinus frontalis, Green: Sinus ethmoidalis (From: [Krüger et al., 2008]).*

20.2.2 VIRTUAL ENDOSCOPY FOR SINUS SURGERY

Virtual endoscopy (recall Chap. 13) requires CT data with high spatial resolution. Similar to other application areas, virtual endoscopy in the nasal cavity became viable with the advent of spiral and multislice CT data [Han *et al.*, 2000]. The first virtual endoscopy system for the sinus anatomy was presented by DeNicola *et al.* [1997] using the ADVANTAGE NAVIGATOR from GE Medical Systems. The target anatomy must be segmented and a path for a fly-through must be computed and should be used as a basis for guided navigation (recall Chap. 13, where these steps were discussed in detail). Virtual endoscopy may be considered as:

- a *diagnostic tool* and thus as an alternative to fiber endoscopy,
- a *planning tool* for surgeons to evaluate risks and the feasibility of surgery in case of obstructed or stenotic nasal meatus,
- a *training tool* for residents to enable them to practice with virtual models, and
- a tool for *patient consult*, before endoscopic sinus surgery to explain them the procedure and the associated risk in a descriptive way.

As a diagnostic tool, virtual endoscopy is useful and has the advantage that it can be performed as a postprocessing step without the patient and without local anesthesia. Septum deviation and perforation and meatal obstruction are clearly seen. However, as Han *et al.* [2000] already pointed out, mucosal surface and secretions are hardly visible. On the other hand, virtual endoscopy might deliver additional information compared to fiber endoscopy in case of a very narrow nasal meatus.

Virtual endoscopy is useful as a planning tool if it is able to present the anatomy of the patient precisely and realistically, thus simulating the actual intervention. This requires to consider similar projection, e.g., a 45° or a 70° wide angle projection is frequently used. It is also desirable that the appearance of anatomical structures is similar to their appearance in the real world. Thus, colors and textures indicating a wetness effect for mucosa, for example, should be employed.

The use of virtual endoscopy for training and patient consult raises similar requirements: realism and simple interaction are essential. For training, haptic feedback and tissue deformation are essential additions not necessary for planning. On the other hand, training does not require patient-specific data.

20.2.3 THE SINUS ENDOSCOPY SYSTEM

In the following, we focus on the planning scenario and describe the development and evaluation of a the SINUS ENDOSCOPY that is focused on the requirements of FESS system [Krüger *et al.*, 2008, Strauß *et al.*, 2009]. The system employs high resolution spiral CT data (slice distance: 1.0 mm) to enable a faithful presentation of the anatomy. This results in 100–250 slices and with an in-plane resolution of 512 × 512 pixels to an overall data volume of 50–125 MByte. Pathologies include mucosal swellings, tumor, and polyps of different sizes. We discuss the requirements, the visualization options, the user interface, and a few planning components that are beyond pure visualization of the target anatomy.

Requirements Virtual endoscopy will be employed to assess anatomical variants and pathologies. The nasal sinuses comprise both large hollow shapes and fine labyrinths—both should be accessed with virtual endoscopy. Even small passages due to swollen or pathological structures should be accessible. A high accuracy of the visual representation is essential. Discussions with ENT surgeons lead to the following requirements:

- The preparation time should be less than 2 minutes.
- The system should be flexible to adjust to different hardware setups.

- Planning components, such as drawing on top of the anatomy and measurements, should be included.
- Virtual endoscopy should support archiving.

The first requirement clearly excludes any solutions that require the segmentation of the target anatomy. Instead, volume rendering with appropriate transfer functions is the only viable solution. The second requirement means that the system should be developed and tested with different hardware setups and the rendering quality should adapt to the performance of the underlying hardware—leading to fast update times even at slower computers. The third requirement states that the system should not only provide high-quality and fast rendering of the target anatomy. In addition, specific treatment planning questions should be directly supported. The most essential aspect is to enable surgeons to draw on the anatomy in an intuitive way to specify where to cut. This information should also be stored and thus be useful for documentation or discussion with a colleague according to the final requirement. In addition, there should be support for creating and storing snapshots and animations.

Visual realism and performance The size of clinical datasets ($\leq$ 125 MBytes) enables to load them completely onto modern graphic cards for rather less complex models. The raycasting system consequently uses the graphics hardware. Semi-transparent volume rendering is provided, since the binary decision related to isosurface rendering seems not appropriate. Also, the filigrane anatomy of the nasal labyrinth would require a very large triangle mesh to represent the anatomy faithfully. Illumination, depth attenuation (fog effects), and other depth cues via texturing of the tissue surrounding the sinuses are provided, since they clearly enhance the shape recognition. Textures are based on digital photos and should resemble human skin. Other shading effects, such as wetness and the secretion level inside the nose, are provided to display the target anatomy in a familiar way by simulating the appearance from real endoscopy. An added lens distortion is also included to exploit the familiarity with fiber endoscopy.[1] They are incorporated as default settings, if a powerful graphics card is available. Otherwise, as default value they are disabled to avoid slow performance. Figure e20.2 illustrates the different appearance depending on the available graphics hardware. Better rendering quality on low-end systems is feasible in case the camera is not moved. Thus, in this situation the lowresolution image is automatically replaced by an image in better quality. First pass rendering and empty space skipping are used (recall § 13.4). Aliasing artifacts are avoided with interleaved sampling (the GPU realization of Scharsach *et al.* [2006] was employed).

Segmentation, and thus the integration of polygonal meshes representing segmented objects was not considered essential due to the inherent time constraints. However, a component to fuse volume data with polygonal meshes was integrated in the virtual endoscopy renderer for selected cases where additional preparation may be justified. The "Look behind the wall" effect when, e.g., segmented pathologies are visible behind walls, is the major benefit that is only possible with appropriate segmentation.

User Interface The virtual endoscopy system has two user interface components:

- the graphical user interface (GUI) that enables to adjust various parameters of the rendering, the layout of different viewing components and further options, and
- the control of the virtual camera.

GUI Components The GUI was designed to limit the necessary space and to leave the largest part of the screen for virtual endoscopy and related views. Moreover, the GUI components should not be spread over the screen, but be visually focused. Thus, they were integrated in one vertical column to be placed on the

1 Users employed 45° and 0° fiber endoscopy.

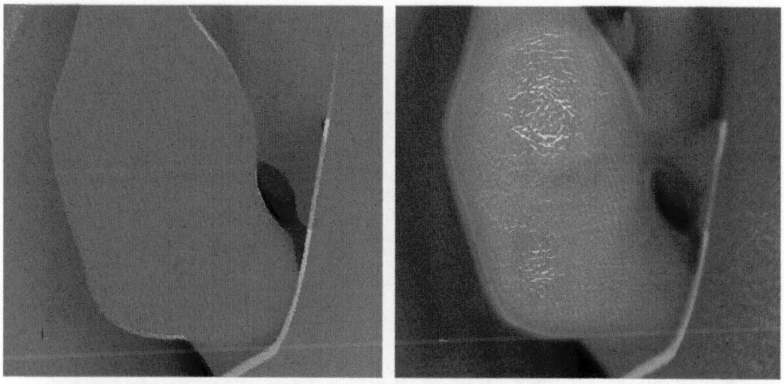

FIGURE e20.2 **Left:** *The viewport resolution is reduced, illumination and wetness effects are disabled to provide a fast rendering on cheap early graphics cards.* **Right:** *Rendering in full resolution with high quality on more recent and powerful graphics cards* (From: [*Krüger et al.*, 2008]).

left. The user interface for viewing fiber endoscopy at an appropriate monitor served as orientation—it has a moderate complexity and consists primarily of sliders, e.g., for contrast and brightness. Sliders enable fast numerical input with moderate accuracy.

The initial GUI incorporated all widgets necessary for a fine-grained control of rendering parameters. While this design was useful for development and testing, it was too complex for regular use. Thus, the most essential development in the GUI was reduction of functions by either omitting some functions or summarizing them at a higher level. The most notable example was the number of sliders for the control of rendering options that could be reduced from 13 to 5.

Camera Control The camera is moved manually and can be placed with a pointing device or be incrementally moved with appropriate buttons. Zooming and panning are essential features that are integrated as well. The current camera position is indicated as a crosshair in axial slice views—a standard technique to enable that the user relates the endoscopic view to the underlying slice images (see Fig. e20.3).

While realistic tissue deformation is not essential, collision detection was provided, since the user looses orientation if he or she moves through the walls. Approximate computations leading to fast but conservative results should be preferred instead of slow accurate distance measurements (recall § 10.4, where distance computation was discussed).

Integration of Planning Components The user can draw on the tissue surface, e.g., to mark where he has to cut in surgery or to discuss with colleagues or residents. Two tools are provided for painting: a small pen for marking outlines and a brush for roughly defining regions that appear as hatching. The painting on the 2D viewport plane has to be projected on the (closest) anatomical structure and has to be stored along with it (Fig. e20.4). In addition, distance measurements are supported, since they enable to estimate whether nasal airways are wide enough to insert a fiber endoscope.

20.2.4 EVALUATION AND CLINICAL USE

Informal Evaluations During the development, several informal evaluations and interviews were performed. As an example, we observed an ENT surgeon using the system for planning an actual intervention. He appreciated the similarity to intraoperative views and the usability. The surgeon optimized visualization parameters like transfer function setting, texturing attributes, and the visibility of secretion. The

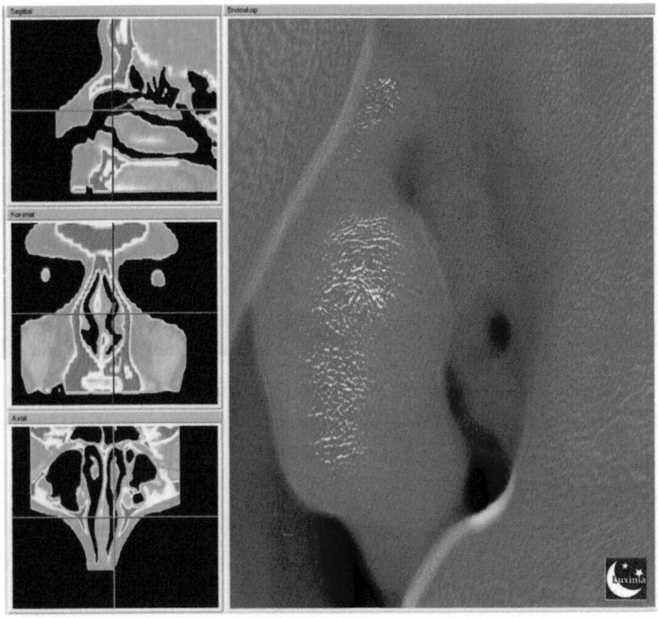

FIGURE e20.3 *Three orthogonal slice views and the endoscopic 3D view are combined in the Sinus Endoscopy system. The crosshair cursor in the slice views indicates the camera position (From: [Krüger et al., 2008]).*

Sinus Endoscopy system was also demonstrated at a workshop with European ENT surgeons. There, it was employed with cadaver datasets. The cadavers could also be operated and investigated parallel with real endoscopes and instruments. The surgeons considered the clear visualization of the Rec. frontalis or the Concha nasalis medialis as essential. Such informal and formative evaluations were useful to detect minor problems. However, for assessing the usefulness of the whole system, a more comprehensive and larger study was conducted.

Systematic Evaluation The large scale evaluation of the Sinus Endoscopy system was performed between 2007 and 2008 at two hospitals in Leipzig. In total, virtual endoscopy was performed in 125 patients in addition to fiber endoscopy. The system was employed by five experienced ENT surgeons. The Sinus Endoscopy system was used for both surgical planning and patient consult. Eighty nine questionnaires from surgeons and 114 from patients were filled (see [Strauß et al., 2009] for more details).

Feedback from Surgeons Surgeons reported a better understanding of the patient individual anatomy and of the planned intervention compared to the traditional planning with 2D slices. The investigation of the Rec. frontalis benefits from the system due to the highly individual anatomy of this structure. The similarity between the preoperative virtual endoscopy and the real anatomy in the intervention was assessed on a 5-point Likert scale (1 represents identical visualizations and 5 no correspondence between them). An average score of 2.21 confirms a good correspondence. However, the ability to adjust the transfer function was considered as both an advantage and a limitation. On the one hand, the visualization could thus be adapted to the dataset. On the other hand, the actual appearance was considered somehow arbitrary, since the extent of visible swellings could thus be manipulated.

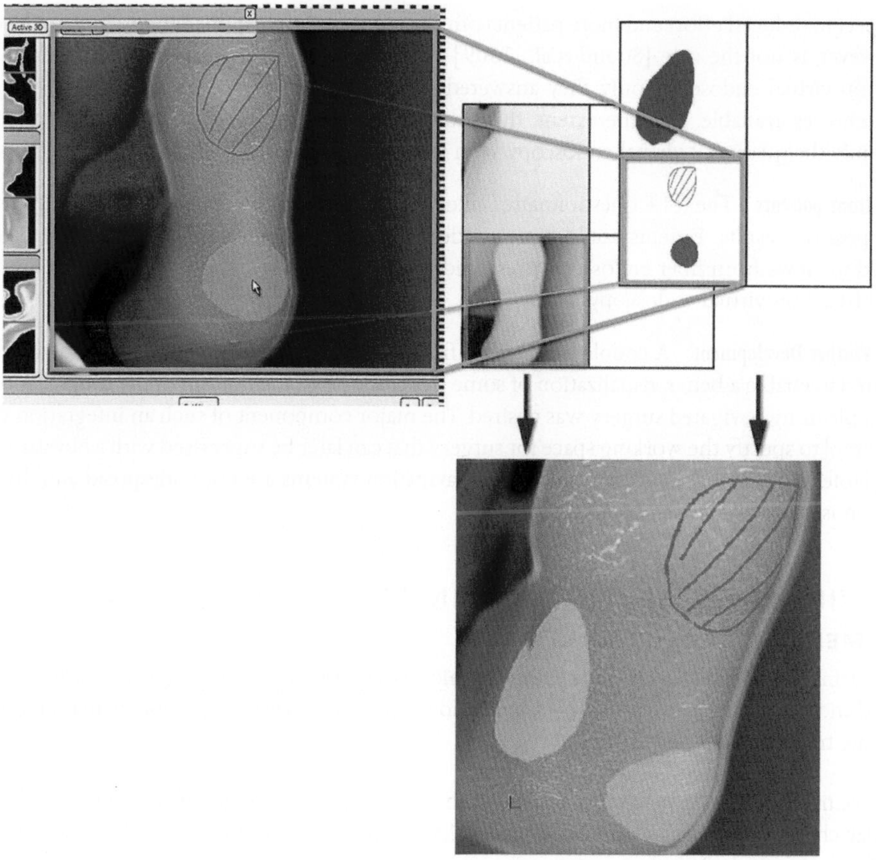

FIGURE e20.4 *A snapshot of the drawn image is stored into a projection atlas texture, along with the tissue depth. By transforming the tissue position with the snapshot's view-projection matrix, texture coordinates are generated for the lookup* (From: [Krüger et al., 2008]).

The surgeons welcomed the real-time behavior of the system combined with an extraordinary visual quality. On the other hand, they questioned the texturing, since it is globally applied, thus also to structures that look different in nature. This raises a fundamental concern: high visual quality including realistic texturing is essential. On the other hand, CT data as the only input does not provide sufficient information for discriminating structures and differentiating textures appropriately.

ENT surgeons also welcomed the functionality provided to maneuver through the nasal sinuses and considered them superior compared to fiber endoscopy. At the same time, and probably based on these powerful functions, they sometimes felt lost and—without proper points to reset—they started the whole navigation again from the very beginning. This clearly shows that users need simple functions to save and name views (camera position, orientation, and optionally lens distortion) in order to reuse these points later.

With respect to regular clinical use, not only the quality of virtual endoscopy as a planning tool is essential but also whether virtual endoscopy may replace fiber endoscopy as a diagnostic tool. A clear advantage with respect to reduced effort and more patient comfort is only possible if fiber endoscopy can be omitted. This, however, is not the case [Strauß *et al.*, 2009]. Asked, whether they can renounce fiber endoscopy and rely on virtual endoscopy only, they answered "I disagree" or even "I strongly disagree"—the two negative choices available. To some extent, this subjective statement may be a matter of familiarization, but certainly the quality of virtual endoscopy with respect to diagnosis needs to be increased.

Feedback from patients The 114 questionnaires filled by patients reported almost exclusively encouraging and positive results. Patients could better understand the anatomical situation and the pathologies compared to views from fiber endoscopy presented to them. They also felt that the surgeons were better prepared based on virtual endoscopy.

Hints for Further Development A couple of ideas for future developments were uttered. Tissue deformation was desired to enable a better visualization of some structures, e.g., the bottom of the tongue. A combination with planning navigated surgery was desired. The major component of such an integration would be a flexible tool to specify the working space for surgery that can later be supervised with a NAVIGATED CONTROL system [Hofer *et al.*, 2006]. However, since such navigation systems are not widespread and diverse, this connection is not a major "selling argument."

20.3 VISUAL COMPUTING FOR INNER AND MIDDLE EAR SURGERY

20.3.1 MEDICAL BACKGROUND

Severe hearing impairment is an important chronic disease and since hearing loss is often age-related more and more people are affected. There are various kinds of hearing impairments that determine the appropriate treatment [Gerber, 2013]:

- *conductive hearing loss*. Sound does not reach the inner ear, e.g., due to an interruption of the ossicular chain. Often malfunction of cochlear hair cells cause malfunction of the cochlear amplifier [Dammann *et al.*, 2001].
- *sensorineural hearing loss*. The information transmission through the auditory nerve to the brain is impaired, e.g., due to infection or trauma.
- *combined hearing loss*. Conductive and sensorineural hearing loss occur simultaneously.

In addition to the patient's anatomy, the residual hearing ability has to be considered and maintained leading to a complex planning process.

Diagnostic Imaging Due to the fine anatomy, imaging with a high spatial resolution is accomplished. CT data that cover a small area but deliver submillimeter accuracy is used for diagnosis and treatment planning. A resolution of $0.1 \times 0.1 \times 0.1$ mm is currently feasible and widely used. This special kind of CT data is referred to as HR (High Resolution)-CT data. Figure e20.5 gives an overview of the relevant anatomy.

20.3.2 ACTIVE AND PASSIVE IMPLANTS

In severe cases, conventional (non-implantable) hearing aids are not able to sufficiently compensate for hearing loss. In particular, conductive hearing loss often require ***implantable hearing aids*** and thus a complex surgical intervention where a sufficiently large cavity in the temporal bone needs to be generated. Advanced surgical planning and intraoperative guidance primarily aims at reducing the need for such a large cavity.

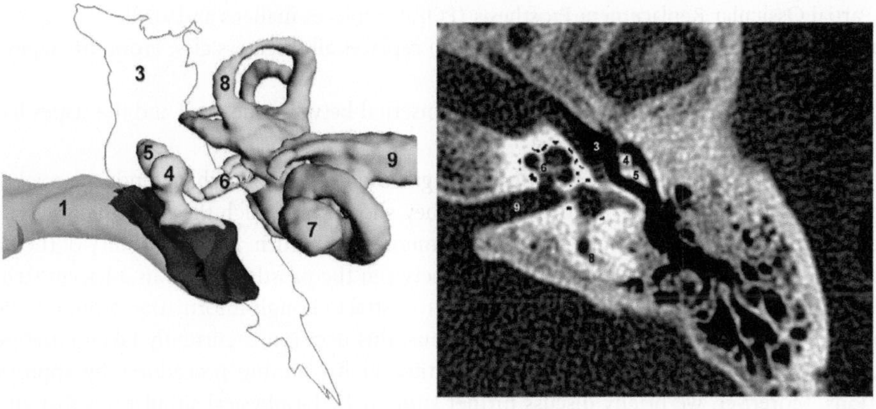

FIGURE e20.5 *Anatomy of the ear and its representation in HRCT data of the petrous bone region. (1) Auditory canal, (2) tympanic membrane, (3) tympanic cavity, (4) malleus, (5) anvil, (6) stapes, (7) cochlea, (8) arcade, and (9) auditory nerve (From: [Dornheim et al., 2008a]).*

Implants may be *passive*, that is they just bridge over a gap in the ossicle chain or *active* meaning that they consist of multiple components, i.e., a microphone, a sound processing unit amplifier and a battery [Gerber, 2013]. The most important *active implant* is the *cochlear implant* that is implanted in the inner ear. Some active implants are placed in the skull base, e.g., the *bone bridge*. The bone bridge consists of an external audio processor, that is worn under the hair and an implant placed under the skin [Achena *et al.*, 2012].

For treating hearing impairment in the middle ear, there are active and passive implants that bypass the outer ear and stimulate the ossicle chain directly. We will later show examples, where total ossicular replacement prosthesis (TORP) and partial ossicular replacement prosthesis (PORP) implants are used.

20.3.3 PREOPERATIVE PLANNING

The inner and middle ear represent the most complex and finest anatomy in the ENT domain. It is also strongly variable and fitting of hearing aids has to be carefully prepared for the patient-specific anatomy. Surgery in this area is accomplished to preserve or restore the sense of balance and hearing capabilities. Accurate preoperative planning may improve preoperative decisions and enable precise realization of surgery, e.g., supported by navigation systems or even robots [Bell *et al.*, 2012]. Simple 3D visualizations, such as threshold-based isosurfaces and direct volume rendering are not appropriate to represent and explore the fine anatomy faithfully. Nevertheless they improve anatomic understanding compared to 2D slices only. Tomandl *et al.* [2000] and Yoo *et al.* [2000] discussed how volume rendering can be fine-tuned to explore the ear anatomy. A "clear and realistic depiction of the anatomical structures and medical devices is required." [Dammann *et al.*, 2001]. This requirement can only be met based on an explicit segmentation of the target structures, as will be discussed in the following.

Surgery in the inner and middle ear, similar to sinus surgery, often occurs close to the N. facialis and, similar to neck surgery, close to the A. carotis. Middle ear surgery serves to implant hearing aids in case the ossicle chain exhibits a gap or unfunctional parts that need replacement. Access planning and implant placement are major tasks and thus similar to, e.g., some orthopedic interventions. Surgery is performed with an operation microscope. Three types of implants are currently used:

- A Partial Ossicular Replacement Prosthesis (PORP) replaces malleus and anvil.
- Total Ossicular Replacement Prosthesis (TORP) replaces all three ossicles. From the stapes only the elliptical base plate is preserved.
- Stapes prostheses replace the stapes. They are inserted between the anvil and the stapes base plate.

These kinds of prostheses are available in different length and geometry. All three kinds of prostheses need to transmit oscillations. Thus, after being inserted, they should not touch the tympanic cavity. They are fixed at both ends but should not hurt the tympanic membrane in turn. For the stability of the prosthesis and an unaltered transmission of sound, the angle between the prostheses and its adjacent structures is also essential [Bance *et al.*, 2004]. It is very difficult to extract enough information from CT slice views to preoperatively select implants of a proper size. Thus, this decision is currently taken intraoperatively. In the following, we describe concepts for supporting such planning procedures by appropriate 3D visualizations. Moreover, we briefly discuss further support by biophysical simulations that attempts to predict the hearing ability.

20.3.4 VISUAL EXPLORATION OF THE INNER AND MIDDLE EAR ANATOMY

Visual Exploration of the Inner Ear Anatomy The inner ear anatomy is crucial for a variety of hearing-aids implants. It should be displayed along with the geometric models of the necessary medical devices, e.g., transducer, microphone, and other implantable parts. Geometric surface models of the temporal bone, including the mastoid cavity and the implant should be presented along with interaction facilities that enable an interactive fitting. Such a tool was pioneered by Dammann *et al.* [2001] where rather simple but robust segmentation techniques from a commercial tool were employed and used to generate surface visualizations of implants and anatomical structures. Later, the same group came up with a more streamlined surface model generation [Salah *et al.*, 2006].

Visual Exploration of the Middle Ear Anatomy The middle ear anatomy is essential for middle ear surgery as well as access for neurosurgery. The complex anatomy is very hard to understand from pure cross-sectional images, in particular in case of severe pathologies [Rodt *et al.*, 2002]. A careful combination of 3D visualizations with 2D slice views, e.g., where some slices are incorporated as reference in a 3D visualization may support the mental reconstruction of the patient anatomy.

While for neurosurgical planning, transfer function-based volume rendering is appropriate, the small anatomical details of the ossicle chain cannot be presented in sufficient detail for implant planning. This is due to the notorious partial volume effects in small structures. Thus, Seemann *et al.* [1999] suggested hybrid rendering where volume rendering of the anatomical context is complemented by surface rendering of the segmented target anatomy. Segmentation of the skeletal structures is possible, in principal, with thresholding. Dornheim *et al.* [2008a] used a rough initial contour and applied a threshold of 700 HU to identify skeletal structures. Substantial post-processing is necessary to separate the individual bones and to represent surface details precisely enough. The cochlea inside the inner ear can also be segmented based on a threshold (−800 HU). The tympanic membrane is difficult to segment. In [Dornheim *et al.*, 2008a] this step was performed manually. The auditory canal, however, can be segmented reliably with region growing. Figure e20.6 illustrates some visualizations based on these segmentations. Such visualizations form the basis for a geometry-oriented planning process that considers the access and size of the tympanic cavity. In Figure e20.7 the middle ear anatomy along with PORP and TORP is shown. For a real planning system, advanced support for this virtual placement is required (recall § 5.6.3).

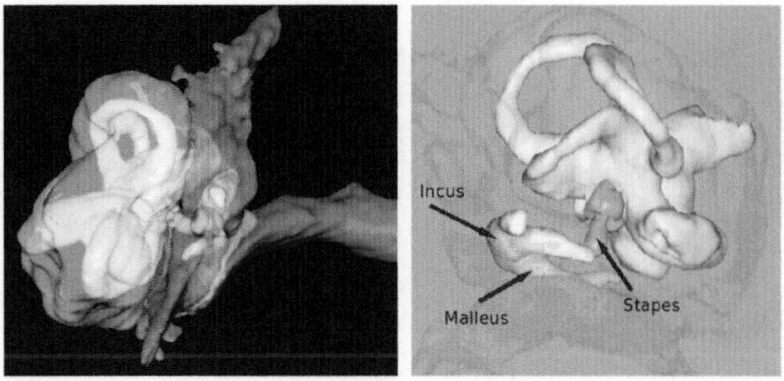

FIGURE e20.6 *3D visualizations of the middle ear anatomy. The tympanic cavity is rendered semitransparently as context for the skeletal structures of the inner ear. The inner ear anatomy (stapes, malleus, incus) are shown as opaque surface rendering* (From: [Dornheim et al., 2008a]).

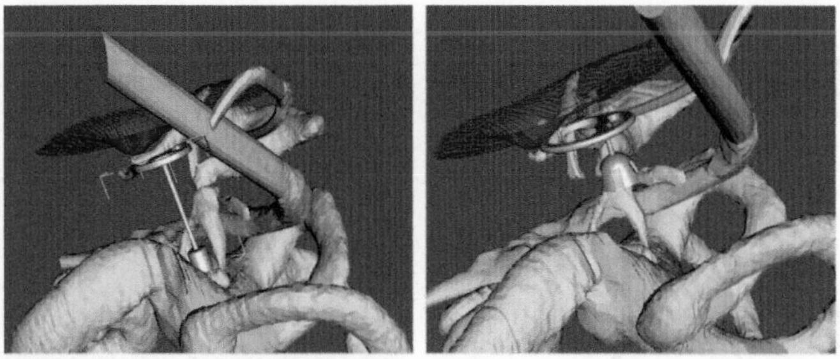

FIGURE e20.7 *Visualization of the middle ear anatomy along with a TORP (left) and a PORP (right)* (From: [Dornheim et al., 2008a]).

20.3.5 IMPLANTING A DIRECT ACOUSTIC COCHLEA STIMULATOR

Gerber *et al.* [2012] described the planning process for the implantation of the *Direct Acoustic Cochlea Stimulator*, a hearing aid that requires direct access to the middle ear. The drilling of the mastoid bone cavity (diameter 2–3 cm) needs to be planned and the risk, e.g., with respect to the distance to the facial nerve has to be considered (see Fig. e20.8). The mastoid bone is roughly segmented with a combination of thresholding and selection of an ROI. The facial nerve is roughly marked in the slices to define a curved planar reformation that is a suitable basis for a more elaborate segmentation. However, due to the small size of that nerve, it is not clearly recognizable in all slices and the segmentation thus exhibits some uncertainty.

Later, he used this planning system and extended it toward intraoperative guidance. With a strongly improved patient-to-image registration, their system is able to provide guidance information with the high accuracy and reliability that is essential for clinical use [Gerber, 2013]. It is interesting that the author found an increased need for preoperative planning based on the availability of improved intraoperative guidance.

20.3.6 VIRTUAL OTOSCOPY

In addition to interactive 3D visualization from an outside point of view, endoscopic viewing was considered useful to better assess abnormalities of the ossicle chain [Himi *et al.*, 2000, Kikinis *et al.*, 1996b]. Middle ear surgery poses a variety of requirements which are similar to sinus surgery. Again, a complex

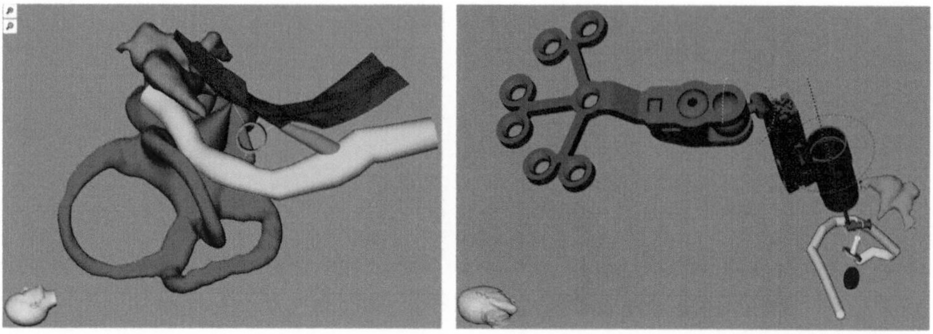

FIGURE e20.8 **Left:** *The drilling trajectory is planned along with the ear anatomy. It is also quantitatively analyzed, e.g., with respect to distances to the facial nerve and the external auditory canal.* **Right:** *The whole implant geometry is shown and may be interactively changed, e.g., prosthesis length and orientation (Courtesy of Nikolas Gerber, University of Bern).*

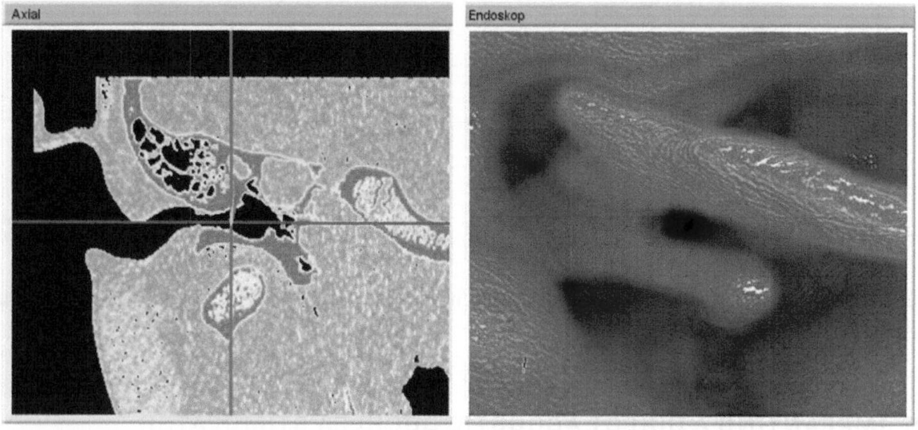

FIGURE e20.9 *Virtual endoscopy of the inner ear that is not accessible with a real fiberendoscope. The combination of a slice view and the endoscopic 3D view provides useful information (From: [Krüger et al., 2008]).*

bony anatomy has to be represented. Wetness of tissue and secretion are again essential aspects. The special kind of endoscopy that deals with the investigation of the middle ear is referred to as *virtual otoscopy*. This term is related to *otoscopy*—the investigation of the middle ear with a microscope. As Rodt *et al.* [2004] pointed out, virtual otoscopy is also valuable to assess postoperative success, evaluating, e.g., the course of electrodes and the correct placement of a hearing aid.

During a workshop with ENT surgeons, virtual endoscopy of the ear with an adapted version of the SINUS ENDOSCOPY system was presented. In order to evaluate whether SINUS ENDOSCOPY is also applicable for this application area, we generated virtual endoscopy views for two cases. Therefore, the two HRCT datasets were loaded, and besides the reduction of the secretion value nearly to zero, no parameter adjustments had to be performed (see Fig. e20.9). The feedback of the surgeons was also positive with respect to the recognizability of structures. With real endoscopy it would not be possible to prepare an operation, due to the invasive nature of this task.

Standardized Endoscopic Views Rodt *et al.* [2002] discussed not only thresholds for generating endoscopic fly throughs but also a set of six viewpoints based on anatomical landmarks that should be employed to explore endoscopic views in a reproducible manner. These six viewpoints serve to systematically search for pathologies and to compare pathological situations with normal ones. Moreover, such a standardization facilitates a structured report of an endoscopic examination.

20.3.7 BIOPHYSICAL SIMULATION

For implant planning and placement it is desirable to predict the hearing ability and to compare various options to come up with an optimal strategy. Hearing abilities are characterized by a audibility curve that depicts the hearing level (in decibel) over the frequency (20–20,000 Hz). The hearing loss is often not uniform but varies significantly over the frequency range and the output of simulations is an audible curve and not just one average hearing level.

Therefore, biophysical simulations were carried out [Beer *et al.*, 1999] and experimentally validated. As has been discussed in Chapter 19, simulations require accurate and smooth models with a good triangle quality. For performance reasons, the polygonal meshes should be carefully reduced. For an FEM simulation, the tympanic cavity as well as its transitions to adjacent structures, such as ligaments, muscles and tendons, and the internal structures need to be described as a set of volume elements, e.g., a set of tetrahedra. These volume elements are derived from an appropriate surface representation, e.g., a triangle mesh with good triangle quality. Figure e20.10 presents such surface models. The remeshing step to improve the triangle quality increased the minimum inner angle from 0.18° to 18.17° and thus the triangle quality from 0.11% to 28.41%. Biophysical simulation require also mechanical parameters like the elasticity of all the components and the thickness of the tympanic membrane [Decraemer *et al.*, 2003].

20.4 NECK SURGERY PLANNING

The treatment of patients with head and neck cancer is challenging, since there is a growing number of treatment options, including various chemotherapies, radiation treatment and surgical removal (*neck dissection*). These treatment options may also be combined, e.g., a chemotherapy is applied to first downsize the tumor to make it resectable at all or to enable a more gentle strategy.

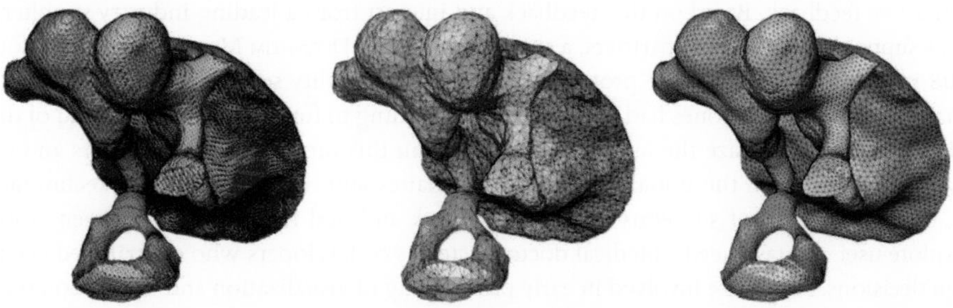

FIGURE e20.10 *A surface model of the relevant anatomy (left, 110 K triangles) was simplified with error control (16 K triangles) and subsequent remeshing to improve the triangle quality (23 K triangles) (Courtesy of Stefan Zachow, Zuse Institute Berlin).*

Neck dissection is a demanding procedure, where enlarged and potentially malignant lymph nodes have to be removed. The difficulty of the procedure is due to the complex anatomical relations in the neck region: muscles, nerves and various crucial vascular structures are very close to each other. Preoperatively, surgeons have to decide if a surgical intervention is adequate and whether or not a gentle strategy, preserving most anatomical structures, is feasible. Computer support for this intervention has to consider the following questions:

- Are there critically enlarged lymph nodes?
- Where are they located in relation to risk structures, e.g., major blood vessels?
- Do they even infiltrate these structures?

To answer these questions, all relevant anatomical structures, e.g., vascular structures, nerves, and muscles, have to be selectively visualized. Due to the sometimes low contrast to surrounding tissues, this is only feasible, if they are explicitly segmented. The segmentation information is also used for a quantitative analysis. Moreover, dedicated visualization techniques are necessary to analyze the spatial relations around selected lymph nodes.

Project Background To develop image analysis and visualization algorithms and to integrate them into a dedicated software assistant for the above-mentioned and related questions was the goal of two sequential national research projects starting in 2004 and lasting 5 years in total.[2] Research was focused on automatic segmentation of relevant structures, e.g., lymph nodes [Dornheim *et al.*, 2006b] and blood vessels [Dornheim *et al.*, 2008b] and advanced visualization of these structures, e.g., by cutaway views for emphasizing lymph nodes [Krüger *et al.*, 2005] and careful combinations of slice-based and 3D visualizations [Tietjen *et al.*, 2006]. In visualization, we first attempted to display as many anatomical structures as possible simultaneously, using, e.g., silhouettes and opacity mapping to support shape and depth perception. Later, it became obvious that the resulting visualizations are too complex. Intraoperative visualization was not tackled, since, in general, open surgery has lower demands for intraoperative guidance compared to endoscopic and interventional procedures. In contrast to abdominal, neuro, or heart surgery, the target anatomy in the neck is rather close to the skin. Thus, localization of tumors and relevant risk structures is fairly easy.

Two research prototypes for segmentation and for interactive exploration and documentation were developed and used in clinical practice since 2006. Initial refinements were targeted at improved segmentation (more automatic segmentation methods), modifications of the graphical user interface and a direct support for the surgical workflow. First, the clinical partners started to present these systems internally, e.g., at the tumor board, and later at their workshops, and conferences, leading to additional and constructive feedback. Based on this feedback and interest from a leading industry supplier, and the continuous support of the clinical partners, a spin-off company, Dornheim Medical Images, was founded in early 2008 in order to transform the prototypes into product quality software. Even in this (late) stage, new demands arose while old ones had to be rethought, leading to further research. Instead of discussing technical details, we emphasize the lessons learned. Within this project, medical doctors and computer scientists collaborated from the initial stages. Questionnaires and other task analysis techniques (recall § 5.2.1), e.g., observation of surgeons during their work and oral interviews, have been employed to deeply explore user and task needs. Medical doctors acted as codevelopers who contributed essentially to any design decisions. They were involved in early prototyping of visualization and interaction techniques, primarily in informal discussions where different options were presented and compared. Later, similar to

2 The project background description is based on [Preim *et al.*, 2010].

the virtual sinus endoscopy project, the medical doctors performed evaluations at a larger scale leading to increased visibility among ENT surgeons and further insights for the development team. We start with a discussion of the medical background (neck anatomy and surgical strategies) in § 20.4.1 and derive requirements for computer support (§ 20.4.2).

20.4.1 MEDICAL BACKGROUND

Patients with a malignant tumor in the mouth and neck region are likely to develop lymph node metastases in the neck region where a large number of lymph nodes is concentrated. Up to 50% of such local metastases were observed [Fischer *et al.*, 2009b]. For the long-term survival of the patients, it is essential that not only the primary cancer but also all metastases are early and completely removed—this intervention is called *neck dissection*.

Medical Imaging Neck dissection planning is based on high resolution medical image data. In routine diagnosis, CT as well as MRI data are employed. A very good soft tissue contrast is the major argument for using MRI. The soft tissue contrast enables, e.g., a good discrimination between inflammation and tumor. Skeletal and cartilaginous structures, however, are better visible in CT data. The higher resolution of multislice CT data (slice distance of 1 mm) is preferable to detect and characterize lymph nodes. Shape, size, infiltration, and vascularization are indicators for malignancy. Metastases are likely to exhibit a spherical shape, are larger and tend to infiltrate surrounding structures—these attributes can be well determined in CT data. Also, a central necrosis, a safe sign for malignancy, is obvious in CT data. Strong vascularization is an essential indicator for a malignant cancer. However, these vascular structures are too small to be visible in CT and MRI data. Only color Doppler sonography is able to represent the flow induced by smaller vascular structures (Fig. e20.11). Thus, sonography has a place in diagnostics and surgical planning, but is only employed by highly specialized medical doctors.

In some hospitals, radiologists present the cases to the surgeons and answer questions; actually leading to a joint discussion of surgical strategies. In other hospitals, basically the surgeons themselves interpret

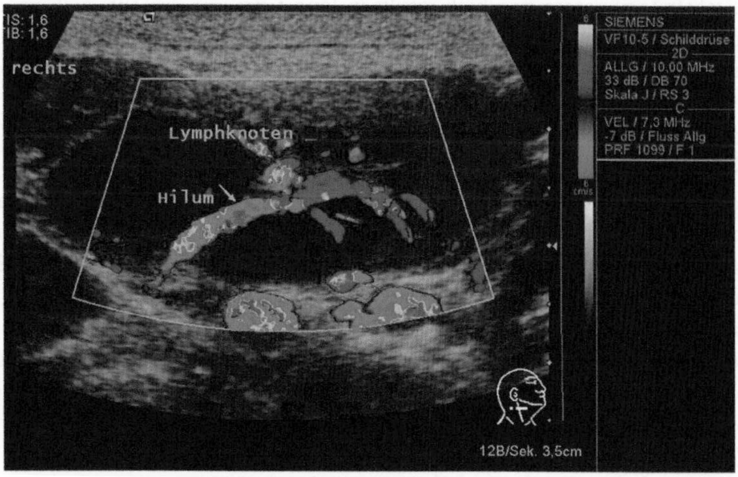

FIGURE e20.11 *Colored Doppler sonography delivers information in high spatial resolution and in addition particularly indicates the vascularization of a lymph node—an essential indicator for malignancy* (Courtesy of Christoph Arens, University of Magdeburg).

the image data to come to their own decisions. CT data are much easier to interpret and therefore preferred by surgeons. While MRI provides a large space of choices for enhancing and suppressing structures, the correct interpretation of these images is a matter for experienced radiologists. A typical MRI study involves at least three scanning sequences, the images of which have to be mentally integrated. CT provides standardized Hounsfield values and only one CT neck dataset has to be analyzed instead of a series of MRI data. The decision on an imaging modality in case of (older) cancer patients is not influenced by the X-ray exposure of CT data.

Even better diagnosis and therapy planning may be performed with combined PET/CT data. This combination increases the sensitivity of the detection of metastases. However, it is still an expensive modality with limited availability. Thus, we focus on pure CT data and additional endoscopic intervention.

Surgical Strategies The choice of surgical strategies depends primarily on the existence and location of enlarged lymph nodes. If a patient with a known cancer in the mouth or neck region exhibits lymph nodes with a diameter beyond 1 cm, this lymph node is suspicious to be a metastasis. Judging the size of a lymph node, is difficult. Since lymph nodes exhibit low contrast to surrounding structures, they may be even difficult to recognize. Moreover, due to the limited resolution of the data, each measurement exhibits an inherent uncertainty of at least the spacing of a voxel (this value equals 0.5–2 mm in our datasets).

Lymph Node Levels The location of lymph nodes is described with respect to five *lymph node levels*. This characterization is important, since usually all lymph nodes in one level are removed if one of them is affected. Lymph node levels are a typical example for a classification that is employed to discuss the location of pathologies in a standardized manner. The liver segments defined by Couinaud, as well as lung segments are other examples with widespread use in oncology. Anatomical classifications provide a common frame of reference for cooperation between medical doctors, e.g., between radiologists and surgeons.

In particular, the infiltration of a large muscle (M. sternocleidomastoideus), a nerve (N. facialis), the larynx or blood vessels determine the surgical strategy. If the Arteria carotis interna is strongly infiltrated (infiltration of a large portion of the circumference), the pathology is regarded as not resectable, since this structure is life-critical. The infiltration of other structures, such as muscles and nerves, is not prohibitive, but makes a radical strategy necessary which results in long-term impairment, such as paralysis if the N. facialis is resected or loss of voice if the larynx has to be completely removed. Figure e20.12 gives an overview on the neck anatomy. The identification and analysis of lymph nodes with respect to size, shape, and distance to vital anatomical structures is crucial for the surgeon's decision.

20.4.2 TASK ANALYSIS

As a major prerequisite for re-developing a research prototype into a practical tool for real world use, we entered again in a stage of in-depth task analysis (this process was first described in [Preim *et al.*, 2010]). While a trade-off between scientifically interesting questions and real needs was required in the research project, a rigorous analysis of tasks, preferences, and priorities was necessary for the actual clinical use. This analysis was accomplished as a larger set of interviews at the ENT department in Leipzig as well as through observations of clinical processes including surgery. In principle, the same techniques have been used within the research project, but in a significantly lower scale. This analysis was focused on an understanding of:

1 individual surgical planning, particularly preoperative decisions,
2 integration of information derived from radiology data and other examinations,
3 collaborative treatment planning, in particular tumor board discussions,

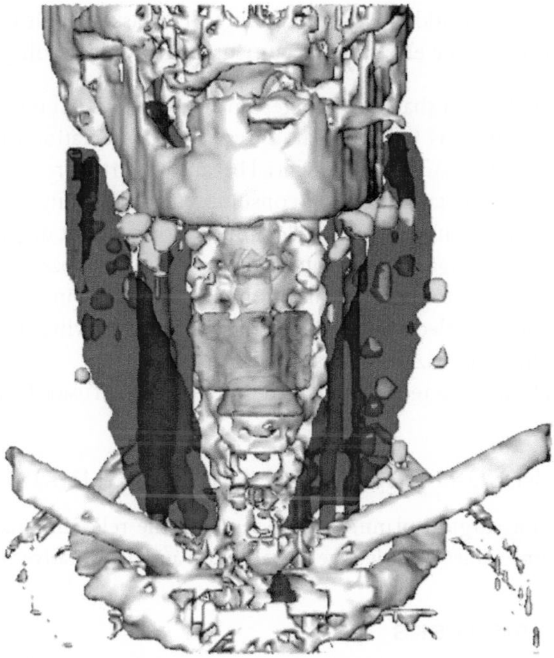

FIGURE e20.12 *3D visualization of the neck anatomy based on CT data of a patient. Bones are displayed in white, muscles are brown, lymph nodes yellow. The elongated red and blue structures depict the two major vascular structures: Aorta carotis interna and Vena jugularis (Courtesy of Christian Tietjen, University of Magdeburg).*

4 patient consultation, and
5 documentation.

To represent the results, informal scenario descriptions have been created, discussed, refined, and verified by discussing them with the clinical experts [Cordes *et al.*, 2009] (recall § 5.2.3.2). These scenarios describe different clinical cases, all examinations which are accomplished to come to a diagnosis, the planning process and the postoperative situation. Special care was necessary to cover a representative set of different diseases (different with respect to number and size of metastases, location of metastases, infiltration of risk structures). A few examples, related to selected issues of the list above, might highlight this process.

Infiltrations Potential infiltrations of anatomical structures by a tumor are investigated in detail with respect to the likelihood of an infiltration, the extent of an infiltration (*Which portion of a vessel cross section is affected by an infiltration? What is the longitudinal extent of this infiltration?*). Thus, dedicated visualizations are desired which contain just the risk structure, the tumor and the possible infiltration area. Radiologists often conclude that infiltration is likely even if not directly visible in case of a distorted outline of an adjacent anatomical structure.

Integration of Panendoscopic Findings Besides CT or MRI data, endoscopic interventions are the most important source of information. With an endoscope, the surgeon investigates possible tumors using optical information and touch sense. Laryngoscopy is an endoscopic examination that serves to evaluate possible larynx infiltration in detail. This information is represented in special sheets of paper, where schematic drawings of the neck anatomy are added with the findings. The task analysis clearly revealed a need for integrating this information with the electronic documentation and the findings from CT data.

Documentation is an essential aspect that was underestimated in the initial research project. For medical doctors in general, and for surgeons in particular, a careful documentation of diagnostic information, treatment decisions, and patient consultation is essential because of juristic reasons and of the account with social insurance. Such bureaucratic tasks are time-consuming and annoying for the surgeons. Therefore, it turned out that any support which shortens the documentation without degrading its quality is highly welcome. Thus, we carefully investigated, e.g., automatic tumor staging, based on measurements applied to all metastases and generated automatic visualizations for direct use in the documentation to reveal all relevant findings. This includes electronic versions of schematic drawings that are frequently used by medical doctors to represent tumor size and location.

In § 20.6.5 we discuss how these requirements are fulfilled in the TUMOR THERAPY MANAGER.

20.5 IMAGE ANALYSIS FOR NECK SURGERY PLANNING

The essential prerequisite for surgical planning is to segment the relevant anatomical and pathological structures. The segmentation enables the selective visualization and quantitative analysis of the patient data.

20.5.1 IMAGE ANALYSIS TASKS

Based on many discussions with various clinicians and an analysis of medical publications the following target structures were identified as being the most relevant for preoperative planning:

- Vascular structures (V. jugularis, A. carotis),
- Muscles (M. sternocleidomastoideus),
- Skeletal structures (mandible and clavicle),
- Pharynx,
- N. accessorius, N. vagus (if they can be delineated),
- Larynx,
- Primary tumor, and
- Lymph nodes.

In selected cases, specific requirements for computer-supported planning arise, e.g., the segmentation of additional structures or certain measurements. These requirements are indicated by medical doctors by filling a structured form [Cordes *et al.*, 2006]. In the basic version of our dedicated image analysis software, livewire combined with shape-based interpolation [Schenk *et al.*, 2000], interactive marker-based watershed [Hahn and Peitgen, 2003] and basic region growing methods have been employed [Cordes *et al.*, 2006].

While the vascular structures, muscles, and the glands could be segmented with these semi-automatic methods, the relevant nerves could often not be identified due to their size in relation to the image resolution. In CT data with low slice distance, the N. accessorius and N. vagus could be identified manually in a few slices only. As only the approximate path of these nerves is essential for surgeons, the nerves are partially segmented and used for an *approximate visualization* (§ 20.6.1). Primary tumors were segmented manually as well. They exhibited low contrasts and could only be distinguished by exploiting considerable anatomical knowledge. The average effort for the segmentation of all target structures is about 90 minutes (see [Cordes *et al.*, 2006] for an evaluation with ten users and two datasets). The average length of the most time-consuming segmentation subtasks was:

- lymph node: 19 minutes,
- vascular structures: 19 minutes, and
- M. sternocleidomastoideus: 17 minutes.

In extreme cases, overall lymph node segmentation may take up to 90 minutes. Since this is significantly more than can be afforded in routine clinical work, an acceleration of image analysis was aimed at and is described in the following subsections.

20.5.2 MODEL-BASED SEGMENTATION FROM CT NECK DATA

The necessary speed-up of the overall segmentation can only be achieved with model-based segmentation (recall § 4.5). Such model-based approaches are difficult to develop and very specific for a certain anatomical structure. The structures that lead to the longest segmentation times were tackled with high priority. There are various options, e.g., Statistical Shape Models (SSMs) or Active Contours.

Mass-spring Models We employed instead mass-spring models where geometric objects are defined by:

- a set of *masses*, characterizing the basic shape, and
- a set of *springs* with a certain elasticity that define to which extent the model may be locally stretched or compressed to adapt to particular image data.

A mass-spring model is derived from one template segmentation and thus the segmentation process is related to template-based segmentation (recall [Montagnat and Delingette, 1997]). Obviously, it is reasonable to employ one framework to segment *all* relevant target structures. An individual adaption to each individual structure is necessary, but by using one framework experiences gained in the adaptation to a single structure may be employed for other structures.

The development of appropriate segmentation models takes considerable time and requires a lot of experience, since many parameters are involved and the relation between initialization and model adaptation is complex. However, alternative approaches also require considerable experience, and, in addition, often a large set of trained examples. A major advantage of mass-spring models (MSM) is that they do not require such a training set and indeed the basic shape of the models is often derived by just one example referred to as *prototype*. This example, of course, is carefully chosen to be a typical representative of that shape.

Initialization in model-based segmentation is often performed by a rough specification of location, size, and orientation of the target structure. As an example, an average model might be projected over the image data and is dragged, scaled, and rotated to roughly fit to the image data. In contrast, with MSM the user selects a few *landmarks* that serve as hints for the model placement. Our experience indicates that this initialization leads to better results (see, e.g., [Dornheim *et al.*, 2006a] for a quantitative analysis) and, depending on the number of landmarks to specify, tends to be faster. The higher accuracy is due to the fact, that landmark-based initialization leads to a non-linear, elastic fitting process, whereas affine transformations can only represent a global rigid transformation. Obviously, anatomical shapes from patient to patient do not only differ in size, orientation, and position, but instead many local changes occur.

Sensors in Mass-spring Models Mass-spring models are heavily used in soft tissue simulation and in surgery simulation where the response to forces exerted by the user are thus reflected. To use this concept in segmentation, *sensors* are employed to capture certain image information, such as intensity values and gradients. In segmentation, however, no physical process is simulated. Model assumptions include expected intensity values, gradient magnitude, gradient direction, and curvature-related measures. The expected shape is represented by the initial configuration of masses. These model assumptions guide a simulation process where the positions of masses are iteratively adapted to the actual image information.

Thus, the process is similar to *active contours* where *internal* and *external forces* guide an optimization process to adapt a *deformable model* to image features. Internal forces represent assumptions related to the object shape. External forces represent user input, e.g., the initial placement of the model, and sensor information. The simulation stops when the internal and external forces are at equilibrium state. In practice, a stopping criteria is employed that terminates the simulation when all changes of positions are below a certain threshold. The choice of that threshold is a trade-off between speed and accuracy, that is usually carried out by the developers and hidden from the users.

Intensity and Gradient Sensors A sensor dragging their associated mass to voxels of a given gray value range is referred to as *intensity sensor*. A direction-weighted sensor steering toward voxels at gradients of high magnitude and expected direction is referred to as *gradient sensor*. Thus, in CT data, intensity sensors reflect that target structures exhibit a certain range of Hounsfield values, and gradient-related information is employed to attract the model to edges (large gradient magnitude) and to favor smooth shapes (slight changes of the gradient direction only) [Dornheim *et al.*, 2007].

Stable Mass-spring Models with Torsion Forces A notorious problem of using MSMs for segmentation in 3D data is stability—the models tend to collapse easily, since the image information is weak and the springs do not sufficiently stabilize such models. Thus, the major idea introduced by Dornheim and Toennies is to use a stabilized version, referred to as *stable mass-spring models* (SMSM) [Dornheim *et al.*, 2005b]. In an SMSM, the angles between adjacent springs are limited. Thus, not only the rest length of a spring is captured, but also its relative rest direction. Every change to that direction initiates a *torsion force* that try to compensate for that change and actually leads to stable directions.

Simulation Parameters SMSMs simulate a physical adaptation process that is steered by a couple of parameters. The choice of these parameters primarily determines whether the optimization process converges at all and how fast it converges. A *damping factor* (<1) ensures that the model actually converges. The stopping criterion is a combination of a maximum number of simulation steps, e.g., 1000 and a small ε-threshold that represents the minimum amount of change necessary to continue the simulation. Numerical simulation always requires a step size Δt that also needs to be selected carefully to provide accurate results (low Δt) and reasonable simulation time (avoid too low Δt). As a preprocessing step, all datasets were isotropically resampled to compute gradients in a normalized way [Dornheim *et al.*, 2005b].

The use of SMSMs, however, is also not straightforward, since the models must be designed to be still flexible enough to adapt to the actual image information. In the following, we briefly describe specific instances of SMSMs used for segmentation of anatomical structures from CT neck data. We omit almost all details and thus the user might consider this method to be rather straightforward to use. Actually, the three segmentation tasks were developed in the framework of three Master theses—thus, it took half a year for very good and carefully supervised students to develop a segmentation method for one type of anatomical structure. While the development of the models is challenging, the use is often straightforward.

20.5.3 MODEL-BASED SEGMENTATION OF NECK VASCULATURE

For planning neck dissections, the carotid artery and the jugular vein are particularly important. Vessel segmentation is an active research area (recall § 11.4.1). However, existing methods, such as the vessel crawler [McIntosh and Hamarneh, 2006], do not consider the specific properties of the two major vessels in the neck region. The main vessels and the first bifurcations are essential, whereas other branches due to their small diameter are less relevant. Dornheim *et al.* [2008b] presented another instance of stable mass-spring models to segment these structures based on a few points selected by the user. They exploit the following properties of these vessels:

- Most blood vessels in the neck are roughly parallel to the body axis and thus exhibit roughly circular cross sections.
- The carotid artery and the jugular vein have few bifurcations, often just one major bifurcation.
- The outline represents a strong gradient. However, adjacent high-intensity structures may interrupt that high gradient.
- The interior intensity values are rather homogenous but may change gradually due to contrast agent inhomogeneity.

For the segmentation of neck blood vessels, the coherency across the slices is exploited. Thus, information from neighboring slices are taken into account to robustly determine the contour in a particular slice.

Initialization The mass-spring models are started at the center lines of the two target vessels. These center lines have to be specified as roughly as possible by the user. At least one start and end point as well as one point after a bifurcation need to be selected. In regions with higher curvature, further points should be selected. Before the SMSMs start their growing process, the centerline is estimated using cubic splines fitted to the points selected by the user. Since a cylindrical model bounded by four adjacent slices is used, one central axis point per slice is determined by sampling the spline (Fig. e20.13).

Model Adaptation The centerline voxels, determined in the initialization stage, are used to create a cylindrical SMSM that is designed to segment a vessel segment composed of four planes. Centerline voxels are located exactly in the slices of the underlying data reflecting its spatial resolution. The planes are cross sections along the vessel that are perpendicular to the vessel centerline. Thus, the planes are oblique and their orientation usually does not correspond to slices in the original data. The number of adjacent planes reflected in one model is a trade-off. With four planes, sufficient information from the surrounding slices are considered to exploit coherency without generating a too complex model that leads to long computation times. The overall segmentation result is just a composition of these segments. The circular model within one plane consists of two concentric rings (see Fig. e20.14), similar to the lymph node model (described in § 20.5.5). The outer ring, where gradient sensors are placed, serves to detect the edges represented by a strong gradient magnitude. The inner ring (a slightly scaled-down version of the outer ring) represents the homogeneous inner region of a vessel. Here, intensity sensors are employed to assess intensity values and homogeneity of these values. This inner layer is essential to stop the growing process before the model gets distracted by adjacent structures exhibiting a high gradient to the surrounding.

The local vessel radius and gray values are derived from a ray casting, starting from the centerline points (see [Dornheim *et al.*, 2008b] for the specific homogeneity criteria and thresholds). The assumption of a circular cross section is incorporated by a filtering step that removes outliers at the contour. Figure e20.14 illustrates the growing process in 2D planes and in 3D. It is valuable to actually display this process and

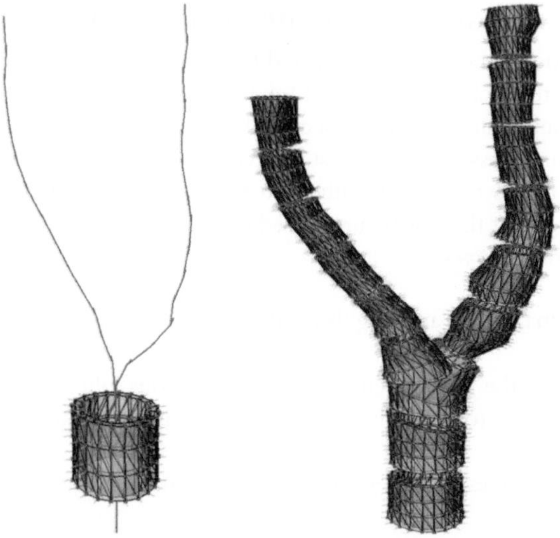

FIGURE e20.13 ***Left:*** *the centerline and one cylindrical segment of the overall segmentation model.* ***Right:*** *The overall vessel segmentation is composed by the individual segments representing two branches (From: [Dornheim et al., 2008b]).*

the intermediate results, since it "explains" how the results are determined. If the actual process takes too long (more than a few seconds), a sequence of a few intermediate steps may be recorded and displayed when the user invokes these segmentation results for the first time.

Examples for resulting segmentations of the A. carotis are shown in Figure e20.15. As we have discussed in Chapter 11, easy-to-interpret vessel visualizations require either dedicated methods or aggressive smoothing with the drawback that accuracy may suffer. With SMSMs, segmentation results are determined at the subvoxel level. Thus, without any advanced visualization techniques it is sufficient to display just the resulting triangle mesh (Fig. e20.15).

Evaluation The segmentation method has been evaluated using 14 CT datasets with varying image quality, in particular with varying slice distance (0.7–5 mm). Thirty vessels were segmented from these datasets. The model-based segmentation was compared with one expert segmentation. The resulting deviations were compared with the differences between two (further) expert segmentations. It was hypothesized that the accuracy of the model-based segmentation was in the same order of magnitude than the expert accuracy reflected by the intra-observer variability. The usual accuracy measures mean surface distance, Hausdorff distance as higher bound for local inaccuracy, and volume overlap were determined. Mean surface distance was 0.78 mm ($\sigma = 0.47$ mm) compared to intra-observer variability of 0.62 mm (σ 0.83 mm). The Hausdorff distance was 7.00 mm ($\sigma = 6.04$ mm) indicating that stronger deviations may occur and thus quality control using slices is necessary. However, intra-observer variability 8.57 mm ($\sigma = 6.95$ mm) was even higher. Volumetric segmentation error was only 0.25% ($\sigma = 0.10\%$) and thus similar to intra-observer variability 0.21% ($\sigma = 0.07\%$). The segmentation interaction time is low: Users set 6–12 points within 15 seconds. The computation time for the system was 4 minutes per vessel (in 2008). However, the implementation was not optimized, e.g., using multiple cores.

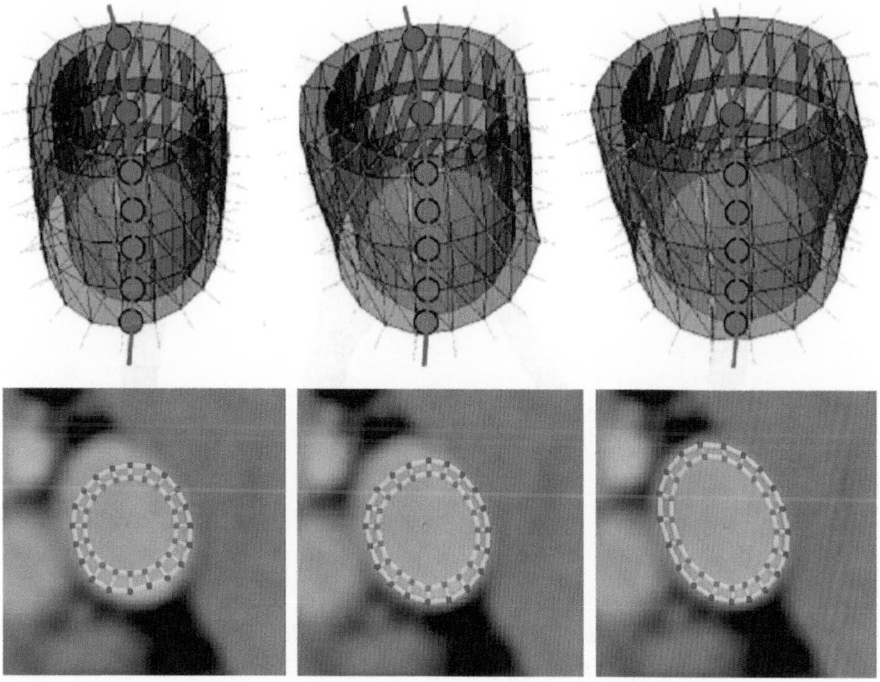

FIGURE e20.14 *Cylindrical models are employed for vessel segmentation. An outer layer of gradient sensors and an inner layer of intensity sensors are used to guide the growing process. 2D and 3D view of the model adaptation process that proceeds from left to right (From: [Dornheim et al., 2008b]).*

20.5.4 MODEL-BASED SEGMENTATION OF THE THYROID CARTILAGE

We briefly discuss the segmentation of the thyroid cartilage (a part of the larynx) that plays an essential role in neck surgery [Dornheim *et al.*, 2006a]. The potential infiltration of this structure determines whether a surgical strategy is possible that preserves the patients' voice. A model-based approach is essential, since strong intensity variations occur and any simple segmentation approach is not promising. The model creation process is the most complex of all segmentation models described in that section. It is based on a sample segmentation, a *prototype*, that is converted in a surface model with the Marching Cubes algorithm. The resulting model is significantly smoothed and simplified to reduce its complexity. This postprocessing is performed with error control to limit the resulting inaccuracy. Simplification was performed with a target number of 50–200 vertices. The resulting vertices are employed as masses for the segmentation model and the edges as spring forces.

Initialization Due to the complex shape of the thyroid cartilage the initialization is rather complex. In total, six anatomical landmarks have to be selected by the user (in a predefined order). However, these landmarks are quite obvious and a user with sufficient anatomical background, e.g., a radiology assistant can easily select these points. The landmarks specified by the user serve as hints for an initial adaptation process. The transformation of the prototype to the landmarks is a non-linear (elastic) transformation.

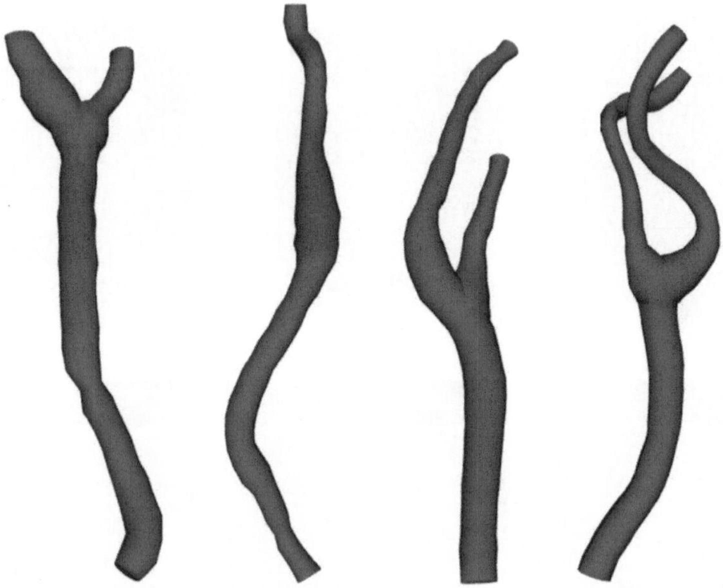

FIGURE e20.15 *Four examples of the segmentation of the A. carotis. Note that the smooth appearance is a direct result from the segmentation process and not due to subsequent smoothing (From: [Dornheim et al., 2008b]).*

Model Adaptation The actual adaptation is performed very similar to the initialization. The landmarks set by the user are still considered as hard constraints. However, in this stage the sensor input is used to guide the adaptation, whereas in the initialization the sensor input was disabled and only the spring and torsion forces influenced the model. The spring length and directions from the initial stage are used as rest length and rest direction for the second stage.

Evaluation Again, two expert segmentations (from eleven CT datasets) were employed to assess intra-observer variability and one expert segmentation was employed to compare model-based segmentation with the current gold standard. The average surface distance (1.06 mm) is acceptable. The Hausdorff distance of 9.84 mm, however, is considerable and almost twice as high as intra-observer variability (5.23 mm). More severe deviations primarily occur in the lower part of the larynx (below the Adam's shape) where the hyoid bone may distract the larynx segmentation. Due to the complex shape of the thyroid cartilage, corrections of the segmentation in a few slices were often necessary. A set of postprocessing tools for intuitive correction of such results was later developed (recall § 4.6.2) [Proksch *et al.*, 2010]. Although motivated by problems in this specific segmentation task, they are broadly applicable. The computation time was 0.5–1.5 min for the initialization and 2–4 minutes for the model adaptation (in 2006).

In the clinical application we noticed that there are sometimes severe problems with the accuracy and interaction effort. The affected cases had one important similarity: they all relate to female patients. The reason is quite obvious: the model was derived from the thyroid cartilage of a male person and the anatomical differences between man and woman in that structure are often too large. Thus, two models are needed and the DICOM header should be analyzed to judge whether the current case relates to a woman or not to select the "right" segmentation model.

20.5.5 MODEL-BASED SEGMENTATION OF LYMPH NODES

The efficient segmentation of lymph nodes requires the use of model knowledge. Simple semi-automatic procedures may segment isolated lymph nodes but are unable to cover the variety of lymph nodes (Fig. e20.16). The variety of anatomical situations is larger than in the vicinity of lung nodules in CT thorax data. Thus, approaches developed for the segmentation of these lymph nodes [Kuhnigk *et al.*, 2004] are not applicable to neck lymph nodes. Model knowledge related to expected intensity values, shape, size, and gradients is required [Dornheim *et al.*, 2007, Honea and Snyder, 1999]. On the other hand, the shape of lymph nodes is rather simple. Thus, SMSMs based on a sample segmentation are suitable. As basic model shape, two spheres are employed with an outer sphere using gradient sensors and an inner sphere using intensity sensors. The outer sensors search for edges, whereas the inner sensors try to preserve the object shape. Thus, the inner sensors avoid that the model outbreaks to nearby strong gradients. The model has 100 masses and 338 springs.

Initialization The model is initiated either with one click that is interpreted as a click inside the target lymph node, or with two clicks that are considered as selection of an insight and outside point. The optional second click may be useful in case of weak gradients to discriminate the lymph node from a surrounding structure.

Model Adaptation Based on a proper initialization the model adapts to the image information. It is essential that all model assumptions are employed. The intensity values may be similar for adjacent vascular structures, but these differ in shape. Assumptions with respect to shape and size (interval [1 cm, . . . , 3 cm]) are also essential to prevent that adjacent lymph nodes are considered as one object. The lower size boundary is based on the observation that smaller lymph nodes are irrelevant for neck dissection planning. The upper size boundary was defined such that giant lymph nodes are excluded. Such lymph nodes likely exhibit atypical changes in shape and intensity—thus, they cannot be reliably segmented with that model.

Evaluation The segmentation model was evaluated with 40 lymph nodes from five CT datasets. The same evaluation scheme as for vascular structures was employed. The average surface distance to an expert segmentation was 0.46 mm (compared to the intra-observer variability of 0.37 mm) and the Hausdorff distance was 2.74 mm (compared to 2.48 mm variability between the two experts). Figure e20.17 illustrates the comparison—the expert used the mouse as input device, leading to jagged contours. The computer-generated contour is smooth and likely to be more accurate in most regions. The computation

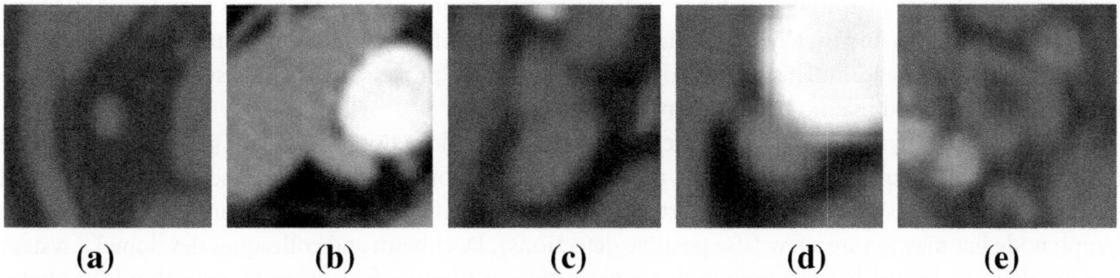

FIGURE e20.16 *Neck lymph nodes in CT data: (a) isolated neck lymph node, (b) neck lymph node adjacent to M. sternocleidomastoideus, (c) two adjacent lymph nodes, (d) lymph node touching high-contrast structure (blood vessel), and (e) lymph node with a central (dark) necrosis. (b), (c), and (d) exhibit partially weak gradients (From: [Dornheim et al., 2007]).*

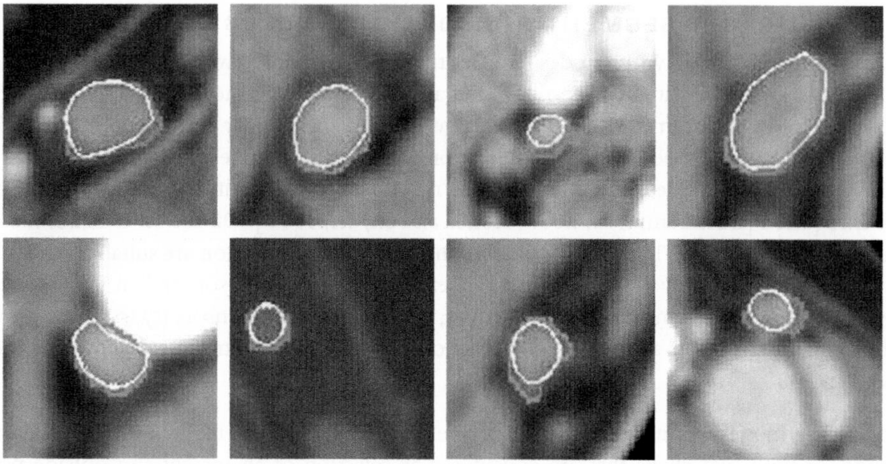

FIGURE e20.17 *Comparison of expert segmentations with model-based segmentation. The rough expert contours result from jitter in mouse input (From: [Dornheim et al., 2006b]).*

time was 2–30 seconds per lymph node (smaller lymph nodes are segmented faster). The evaluation indicated the necessity of *all* model assumptions. The segmentation quality strongly degraded if one of these assumptions, e.g., the roughly circular shape was not considered. Thus, it is likely that no simpler model would be sufficient for lymph node segmentation.

Pathological Lymph Nodes The model-based segmentation described above reliably detects "normal" lymph nodes of a certain size (that may be healthy or malignant). It was not trained to detect lymph nodes with central necrosis (appears as dark spot inside), or strongly deformed lymph nodes, or lymph nodes that exhibit a boundary that is very weak for a large portion. The segmentation approach was later adapted and refined to pathological lymph nodes [Dornheim *et al.*, 2010b]. Actually, a new segmentation model was required, since pathological lymph nodes differ too strongly from "normal" ones to be covered by the same segmentation model.

20.5.6 DETECTION OF LYMPH NODES

Neck surgery planning strongly benefits from the automatic segmentation of (most) lymph nodes. However, users still have to find each lymph node to initiate the model adaptation. It is desirable if lymph nodes are also *detected* automatically. This would not only accelerate the process, but as ENT surgeons clearly state increase the likelihood that no relevant lymph node is missed.

The detection of lymph nodes is a typical computer-aided detection task (recall § 3.6.4). Due to the large variety in particular of pathological lymph nodes this can only be done with a certain sensitivity and specificity. A high sensitivity is more important than a high specificity (users should not miss an important lymph node but may ignore a few false positive detections). Dornheim and colleagues developed a system that employs the model-based lymph node segmentation techniques for automatic detection [Dornheim *et al.*, 2010a].

The basic idea to accomplish detection with an SMSM is straightforward: model instances are placed in the whole dataset and the growing process is performed at all these positions. At some places, the model may be adapted with a good *quality of fit*, whereas in most places, the quality of fit is poor, since no lymph node occurs there.

Performance Issues This basic idea has some obvious problems. The first is run-time and performance. In a large CT dataset, the whole volume needs to be sampled with a rather high density not to miss any lymph node and the complex model adaptation process is started several thousand times. The second problem is closely related to the experience with the model-based segmentation of lymph nodes: the variability of (pathological) lymph nodes is too large to cover all types of lymph nodes in one model. As a consequence, aggravating the performance problem, different models need to be started at any sampling position.

Using Expectation Maps to Reduce Search Space Fortunately, there are some strategies to cope with the performance problem. Lymph nodes occur primarily rather close to certain anatomical structures, such as vascular structures and muscles. Thus, if these other structures are already segmented, an *expectation map* may be generated around these structures to restrict the search for lymph nodes to these areas. The overall process, that may be transferred to many other object detection tasks, is illustrated in Figure e20.18. The actual dataset, the model information for a specific structure and additional information to restrict the search are used as input. The segmentation model is placed at various places and a couple of segmentations occurs at all places where the quality of fit reached a certain level. A final model selection process further restricts the results based on further model knowledge leading to a few segmented target structures.

Application and Results The detection scheme was evaluated using five CT datasets where an experienced radiologist has segmented the lymph nodes. The lymph nodes cover a wide range of shapes, sizes, and gradient magnitude. The lymph nodes were searched in four regions: around the left and right mandible and around the left and right V. jugularis. Expectation maps were created by combining two sorts of information: proximity to the four anatomical structures and thresholds for lower and higher intensity values. With this combination, the search space could be reduced by more than 90%.

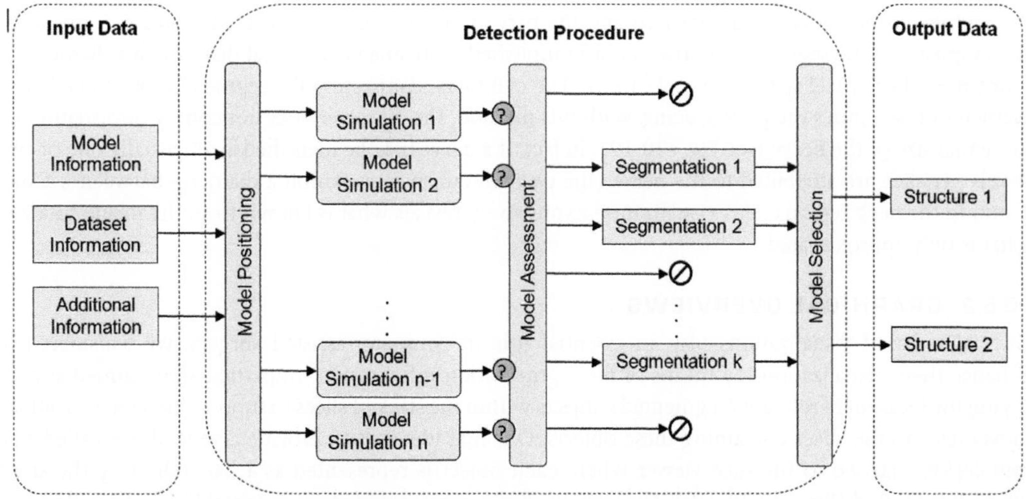

FIGURE e20.18 *General object detection scheme. At many places, objects are searched and the search results are filtered in the "Model Assessment" and "Model Selection" stage (From: [Dornheim et al., 2010a]).*

In one dataset, 29 lymph nodes were present and all could be detected. The algorithm checked 13.500 positions, actually started 958 models and delivered 38 lymph nodes (29% false positives). This was achieved in exactly 2 minutes with a setup where four CPU cores worked in parallel. Misclassification primarily occurs when contrast-enhanced vascular structures exhibit similar intensity values and shape [Dornheim *et al.*, 2010a]. Image quality and the detection rate are correlated: a high spatial resolution is required for a high sensitivity.

20.5.7 DISCUSSION

Image analysis, in particular efficient and reliable segmentation, is a core part of computer support for neck surgery planning. Similar to other highly specific applications, there are no simple and easy-to-adapt solutions. Instead, image analysis is a major research and development task. Without model-based techniques that make the segmentation as robust, reproducible, and efficient as possible, the interactive visualization described in the following would not be possible in routine clinical practice. From a software development perspective, it is difficult to develop and later maintain completely different segmentation approaches. The family of segmentation methods described here was realized within a coherent software library providing substantial support for developing new or refining existing segmentation models.

20.6 INTERACTIVE VISUALIZATION FOR NECK SURGERY PLANNING

In the following, we describe selected examples of advanced visualization techniques that were inspired by the specific needs in neck surgery planning. They are selected based on their broad applicability.

20.6.1 APPROXIMATE VISUALIZATIONS OF NERVES

As has been discussed in § 20.5.1, nerves can only be identified in selected slices. Nerves usually proceed almost linearly and do not deviate strongly from the straight connection between positions found in some slices. Since it is important to prevent the injury of nerves, *approximate visualizations* were generated where the segmented portions are emphasized and the part in between is reconstructed as linear connection. The emphasis of the segmented portions is accomplished with small cylindrical disks, with a diameter of four times of the pixel spacing, e.g., 2–3 mm. The cylinders, connecting the segmented portions, have a diameter of two times the pixel spacing. With this method, the diameter does not convey information on the actual size of the nerve (see Fig. e20.19). In fact, if a nerve may be identified at all, usually one or two voxels per slice are attributed to the nerve (the two relevant nerves exhibit a diameter between 0.5 and 1 mm in the neck region). This visualization expressively reveals what is known from the image data and what is only approximated.

20.6.2 GRAPHICAL OVERVIEWS

Since slice-based visualizations play an essential role in computer-assisted surgery, we considered to enhance these visualizations by means of the segmentation information. In particular, we aimed at conveying the location of relevant (segmented) objects within the stack of slices to support directed (scrollbar) movements to the slices containing these objects. Our first idea was to provide a vertical bar, called a *lift chart display*, attached to the slice viewer where each object is represented as a bar indicating the slices where it is located (Fig. e20.20, left). The current slice is represented as a horizontal line to provide a link between the overview and the currently selected slice [Tietjen *et al.*, 2006]. While such a visualization may indeed be helpful for surgical planning tasks, it is too complex in our specific example, as the feedback

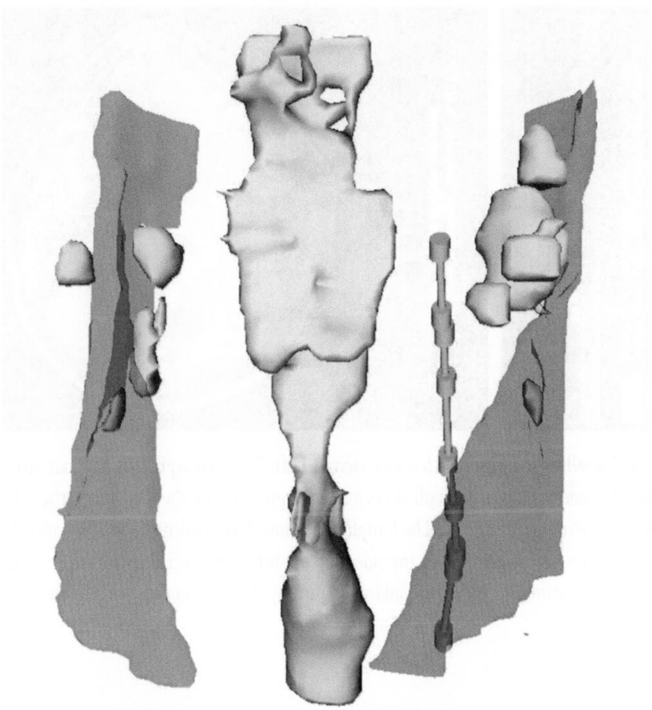

FIGURE e20.19 *Approximate visualization of N. facialis for neck dissection planning. The orange disks indicate the segmented portions. The connection between the disks is accomplished by means of cylinders—thus, the space between the segmented portions is linearly interpolated. The yellow structures represent the lymph nodes and the brown structures represent the M. sternocleidomastoideus. The vertically aligned structures in the central part show the larynx and the pharynx (Courtesy of Arno Krüger, University of Magdeburg).*

from medical doctors clearly revealed. A variety of modifications turned out to be necessary to make it a useful tool (Fig. e20.20, right). The original name is not very expressive: in human-computer interaction, similar concepts were developed [Byrd, 1999] and are known as *enhanced scrollbar*, a name that clearly relates to a scrollbar widget.

Most of the modifications are aimed at a faster localization of enlarged lymph nodes. In general, in the head and neck region, the symmetry should be employed to distinguish objects in the left and right half. If there is a large number of such lymph nodes, it is not important which lymph node is represented in a particular slice. Instead, it should be clearly visible, in which slices enlarged lymph nodes occur at all. Therefore, we condense the information related to all lymph nodes, instead of indicating individual lymph nodes. Another refinement is the ability to add certain landmarks in the visualization as labels.

20.6.3 SMART VISIBILITY AND ILLUSTRATIVE RENDERING TECHNIQUES

Silhouette Rendering Silhouettes play an essential role for enhancing object recognition, in particular in case of dense object representations, as they occur in the neck region. Convexities, concavities, or inflections of contours in the retinal image allow the observer to draw reliable inferences about local surface geometry

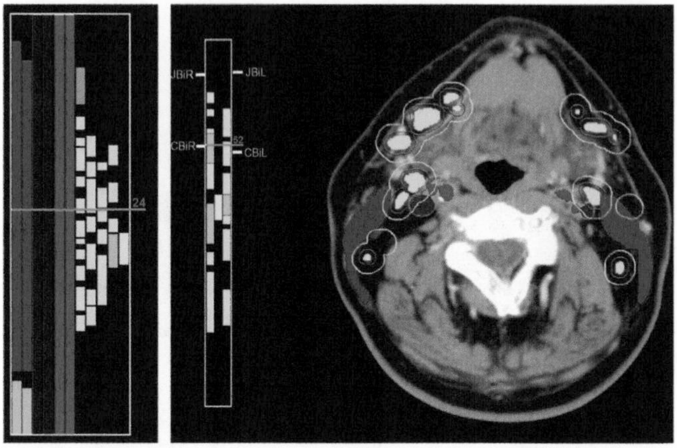

FIGURE e20.20 *Enhanced scrollbar to be used with a slice viewer.* **Left:** *Each bar represents one anatomical structure. The A. carotis interna and the V. jugularis (left and right) occur in all slices and are represented by the four long vertical bars (colored blue and red).* **Right:** *Only lymph nodes and the tumor are shown. The lymph nodes have been condensed (yellow bars). The horizontal arrangement is based on the symmetry: structures are represented at the side they are belonging to. Labels related to crucial anatomical landmarks, such as bifurcations of the vascular structures, have been added.* (Courtesy of Christian Tietjen, University of Magdeburg)

(recall § 12.5.1). However, due to the simplified depiction, the perceived information on the surface is not complete. Therefore, it is primarily used to indicate the context objects, such as bones (Fig. e20.21).

In addition, silhouettes may be used to discriminate two classes of objects; those which exhibit a certain feature are rendered with silhouettes enabled, whereas the remaining objects are drawn without silhouettes. A reasonable use of this strategy is to enable silhouettes for objects, which are more "interesting," since silhouettes direct the user's attention. In neck surgery planning, many lymph nodes have to be explored by the user. In particular, lymph nodes which are enlarged and touch a critical structure are essential. In Figure e20.22, the lines where enlarged lymph nodes and a muscle intersect are rendered with silhouettes. ENT surgeons regard this as substantial help, since it is otherwise not recognizable, whether the lymph node is only approaching a critical structure or touches it. However, if a lymph node touches another structure, it is usually not clear whether the lymph node (only) displaces this structure or actually penetrates it (infiltration).

Smart Visibility Rendering The exploration of volume data can benefit from cutaway views and ghosting [Viola *et al.*, 2005] (recall § 12.10). Inspired by their work, we use cutaways in neck surgery planning to emphasize lymph nodes and their neighborhood. For visualizing lymph nodes, we generate cylindrical cutting volumes with the cylinders aligned orthogonal to the viewing plane. The cylinder is scaled such that the target lymph node is completely visible with an additional and adjustable safety margin. To clearly indicate the chosen illustration technique, we display a thin bright silhouette at the border of the cutaway region. The lymph node is also visually enhanced by increasing the saturation of color.

The process of efficiently computing these cutaway views based on convex hulls, OpenGL 2.0 and the fragment shader functionality from modern GPUs is described in [Krüger *et al.*, 2005]. A more powerful solution for cutaway rendering with better performance and more visual realism, e.g., illumination was

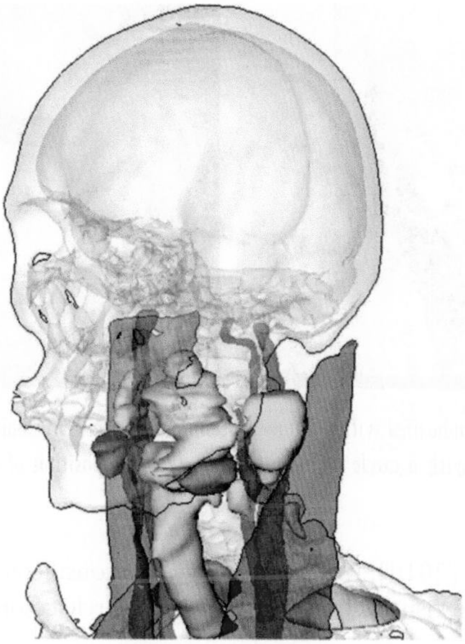

FIGURE e20.21 Silhouettes are generated for the bones and muscles which serve as anatomical context (Courtesy of Christian Tietjen, University of Magdeburg).

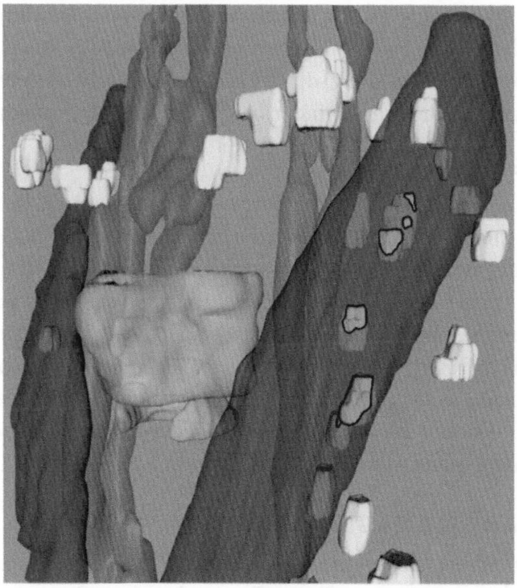

FIGURE e20.22 Silhouette rendering reveals lymph nodes which touch and potentially infiltrate a critical structure. The brown muscle is rendered with semitransparent fibers (Courtesy of Arno Krüger, University of Magdeburg).

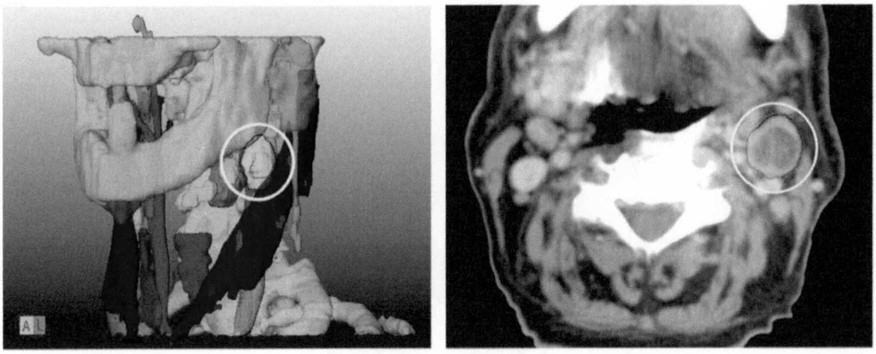

FIGURE e20.23 *The lymph node emphasized with a cutaway technique in the 3D visualization (see the circle) is simultaneously emphasized in the original slices also with a circle to indicate the extent and position of the cutaway (Courtesy of Arno Krüger, University of Magdeburg).*

later described by Kubisch *et al.* [2010]. The cutaway region is considered as a conventional object which is superimposed on the 2D slice visualization—resulting in a circle colored in the same way as in the 3D visualization (see Fig. e20.23).

Discussion Cutaway views support the localization very well. However, the infiltration of adjacent anatomical structures cannot be assessed, since these are removed. For assessing infiltration, ghostviews are better suited. The use of both, cutaways and ghostviews, is useful to expose emphasized structures. Emphasis and spatial understanding can be achieved in a visualization with constant camera position or by applying minor rotations. However, large scale rotations in ghostviews or cutaway views are confusing, in particular when the cylindrical region is large in the z-direction. Therefore, the removal of anatomical structures should be restricted to situations when the cylinder height required to expose the target structure is small.

20.6.4 COLLECTIONS

A special concept, originally developed for neck surgery planning might be useful for a wide range of applications, even beyond surgery planning. In order to accelerate the planning process, we allow to summarize a subset of anatomical or pathological structures together with their appearance, e.g., color, transparency, and the current viewing direction. We refer to such a subset as a *collection*. Collections may be stored, named, and later reused. Collections are presented as a list with a label and a representative snapshot. On the one hand, collections represent a flexible concept, since the additional collections may be added (see Fig. e20.24). On the other hand, collections contribute to a standardized process dedicated to the surgical decisions. They might also be used for a guided step-by-step planning process, where the individual collections are displayed in a sequential manner. This concept was introduced by Mühler *et al.* [2010].

20.6.5 TUMOR THERAPY MANAGER

In this subsection, we discuss how the requirements stated in § 20.4.2 are actually fulfilled in a comprehensive software assistant, that we refer to as TUMOR THERAPY MANAGER. Compared to earlier versions of that tool, the name suggests that primarily general functions for tumor surgery planning and documentation are included, not only highly specific functions for neck surgery.

Infiltrations Tumor segmentation involves a large amount of uncertainty, thus, the overlap between a tumor and an adjacent structure might strongly underestimate the actual infiltration. Thus, it is valuable

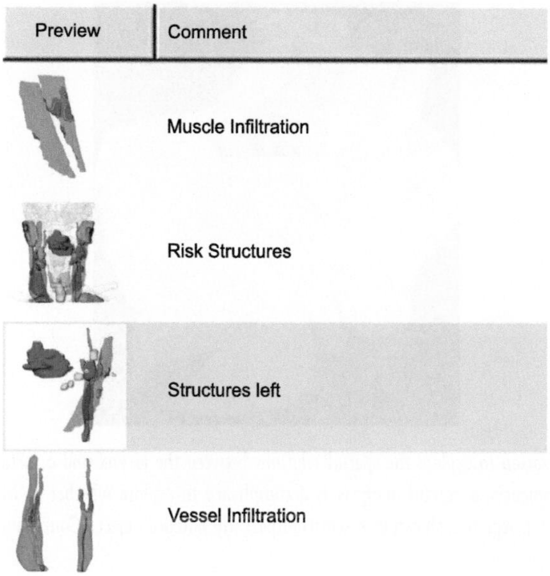

FIGURE e20.24 *Collections for neck surgery planning represented as icons and related verbal description. By selecting a collection, the related subset of objects is displayed at once (Courtesy of Konrad Mühler, University of Magdeburg).*

if the potential infiltration area is explicitly indicated by a radiologist and shown along with the anatomy. Since the infiltration area is not an anatomical region that may be identified with an automatic approach, manual effort is necessary. However, since this region is rather small and needs to be defined only roughly, a few minutes are sufficient for this task. Infiltration areas should be displayed strikingly different from anatomical surfaces and thereby indicate the *vague character*. One possibility is the display as a hatched semitransparent object. A design study that illustrates this concept is shown in Figures e20.25 and e20.26. Infiltration areas should also be displayed in 2D slices. Display parameters, such as color, transparency and texture, should be chosen such that the relation to the 3D display is clearly recognizable (Fig. e20.26).

Infiltrations of muscles, nerves, blood vessels, and the larynx are crucial in neck dissection planning. The larynx is the most complex of these anatomical structures. Thus, a 3D model including just the larynx, the potential infiltration area and a tumor is more appropriate to investigate whether it may be conserved to preserve the voice of the patient.

Figures e20.25 and e20.26 illustrate how visualizations support the assessment of (possible) infiltrations. Such visualizations are part of a step-by-step planning approach where a series of simple visualizations is generated to understand how surgical procedures may affect anatomical structures.

Besides 2D and 3D overview visualizations, virtual endoscopy views are essential to support the assessment of infiltrations. Figure e20.27 presents an example where a potential infiltration is displayed in a 3D overview and a virtual endoscopy view simultaneously.

Integration of Panendoscopic Findings Endoscopy is performed as a diagnostic procedure after the acquisition of CT data. The complementary information from endoscopy needs to be integrated with the information from CT data. The ideal solution, as ENT surgeons explained us, is to register endoscopy information with CT data to provide one *coherent 3D model* and thus also to document the endoscopic intervention. At

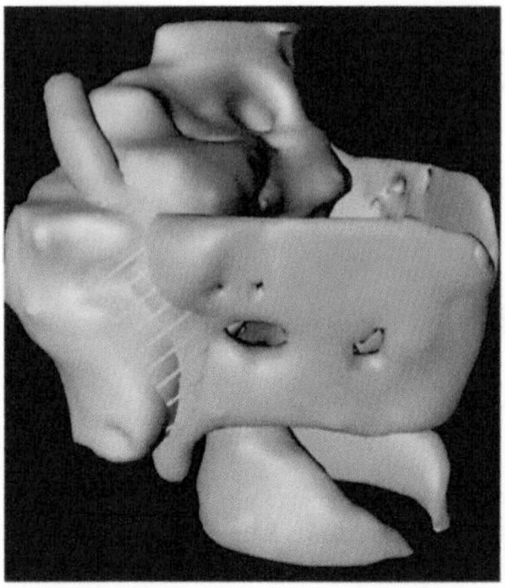

FIGURE e20.25 *3D visualization to explore the spatial relations between the larynx and a metastasis. Since the removal of the larynx would have severe consequences, a careful analysis is accomplished to explore whether at least parts of the larynx may be conserved. The potential infiltration region is shown as a semitransparently hatched object (Courtesy of Dornheim Medical Images).*

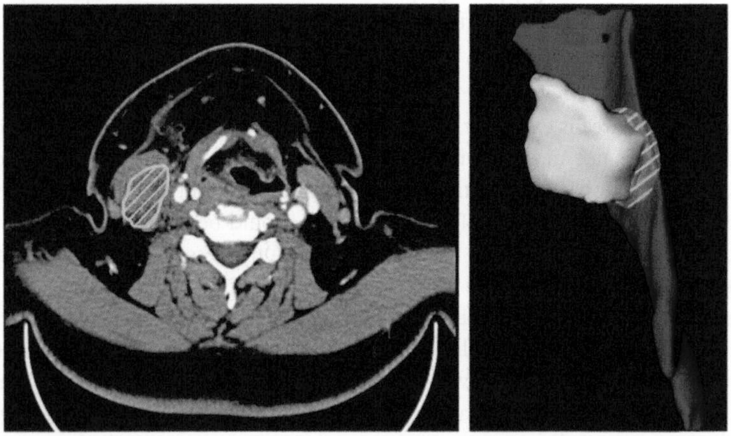

FIGURE e20.26 *2D and 3D visualization of a large muscle, an enlarged lymph, node and the potential infiltration area (Courtesy of Dornheim Medical Images).*

the time of writing, this is attempted in a research project, but since this is an ambitious goal it is not clear whether it could be done in a sufficiently reliable manner. A less ambitious but also useful goal is to enable the user to manually cross-reference snapshots from endoscopy with CT data (Fig. e20.28). In a similar way, it is desirable to integrate biopsy results at the location where the biopsy was taken in order to further integrate the relevant diagnostic information.

Another useful function for integrating panendoscopic and palpatory findings is an easy-to-use editing tool that enables a modification of shapes [Boehm *et al.*, 2009]. Thus, shapes determined from segmenting CT data may be adapted to the impression from endoscopy and palpatory examination—a function that

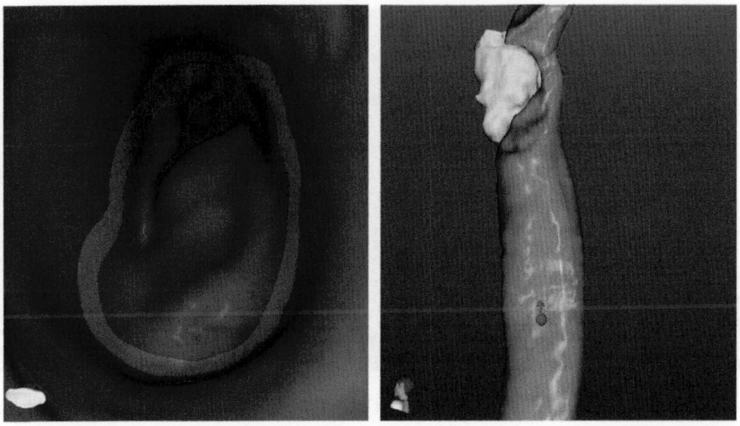

FIGURE e20.27 *Virtual endoscopy and 3D context in side-by-side view.* ***Left:*** *Safety distance colorization of inner pharynx surface reveals outside contact areas.* ***Right:*** *Red glyph indicates view position and direction. A glass-like effect provides better visual perception than simple transparency. The small red arrow indicated the viewing direction of the camera in the left endoscopic view (Courtesy of Dornheim Medical Images).*

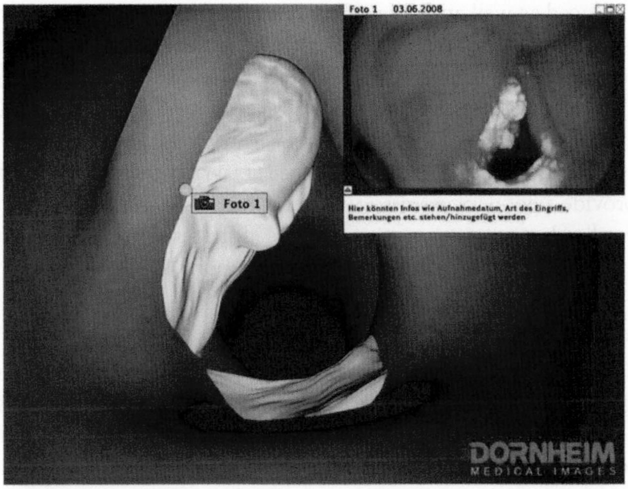

FIGURE e20.28 *In a virtual endoscopy derived from CT data, a photo of the corresponding real intervention is added at the corresponding position (Courtesy of Dornheim Medical Images).*

is primarily motivated by the tumor appearance that might be significantly different. These differences are crucial if infiltration of risk structures occurs (see Fig. e20.29).

Documentation is the last step in a workflow-oriented planning process. Currently, this step is the least supported step and is carried out manually. For documentation, a typical sheet of paper is reproduced as an electronic sheet. If possible, all entries are automatically filled in by results from the analysis and

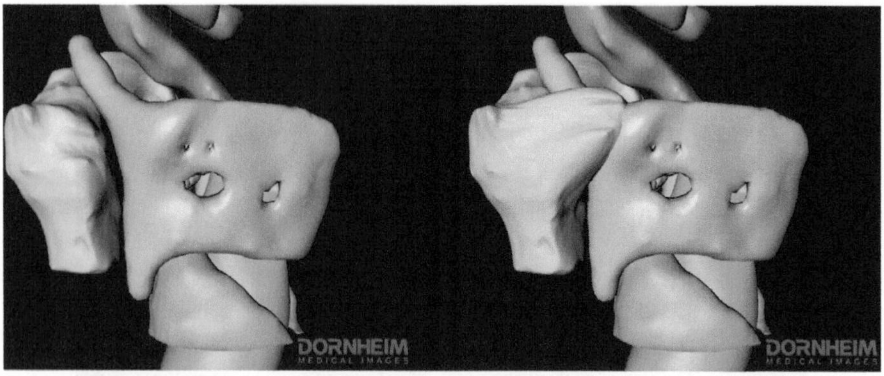

FIGURE e20.29 *The tumor model derived from CT data (left) is modified according to the endoscopy findings. The user simply outlines regions of the larynx that are likely infiltrated and the tumor shape is fitted to that region effectively enlarging the tumor shape (right). Thus, the integrated information may be employed for planning surgery (Courtesy of Dornheim Medical Images).*

the planning process. In addition to verbal comments, in many hospitals schematic drawings are used to integrate sketches that depict tumor size and location (see Fig. e20.30). These schematic drawings are electronically reproduced as well and are used to enter additional information by drawing. Thus, the whole documentation can be realized in an electronic manner. The documentation is further enhanced with automatically generated screenshots. As an example Figure e20.31 shows the location of a tumor and its automatically derived measures. In Chapter 10, we employed further examples from neck surgery planning to illustrate the importance of measurements.

Figure e20.32 illustrates the GUI design of the TUMOR THERAPY MANAGER. It is designed to provide a good usability but also to provide a good *user experience* with an attractive layout, comprised of carefully designed visual components. Feedback at various occasions clearly indicates that perceived attractiveness is indeed important to gain acceptance for a new kind of software support.

20.6.6 CLINICAL USE AND DISCUSSION

The TUMOR THERAPY MANAGER has been used for planning more than 100 neck surgery interventions (in early 2011 according to [Rössling *et al.*, 2011]).[3] Eight surgeons (all at the University Hospital Leipzig) used the system. The datasets acquired for neck dissection planning contained a tumor in the head and neck region and were suspected of containing lymph node metastases as well. Datasets stem from three different radiology departments, thus representing a typical spectrum of clinical datasets. The quality of the datasets was diverse with respect to the signal-to-noise ratio, motion artifacts as well as the slice distance (0.7–3 mm).

In most cases, only a subset of functions was used to segment, quantify, and visualize the tumors. In some 40 cases, the full set of functions—including the virtual endoscopy and the documentation functions—was used. The computer-assisted planning process was initially performed in addition to the conventional planning process based on CT slices. This is not necessary but serves to compare the different workflows [Preim *et al.*, 2010]. More recently, the software partially replaced the conventional planning

3 The following discussion of the clinical use is primarily based on an initial report in [Preim *et al.*, 2010]. Aspects that are based on a more recent study [Rössling *et al.*, 2011] are explicitly marked.

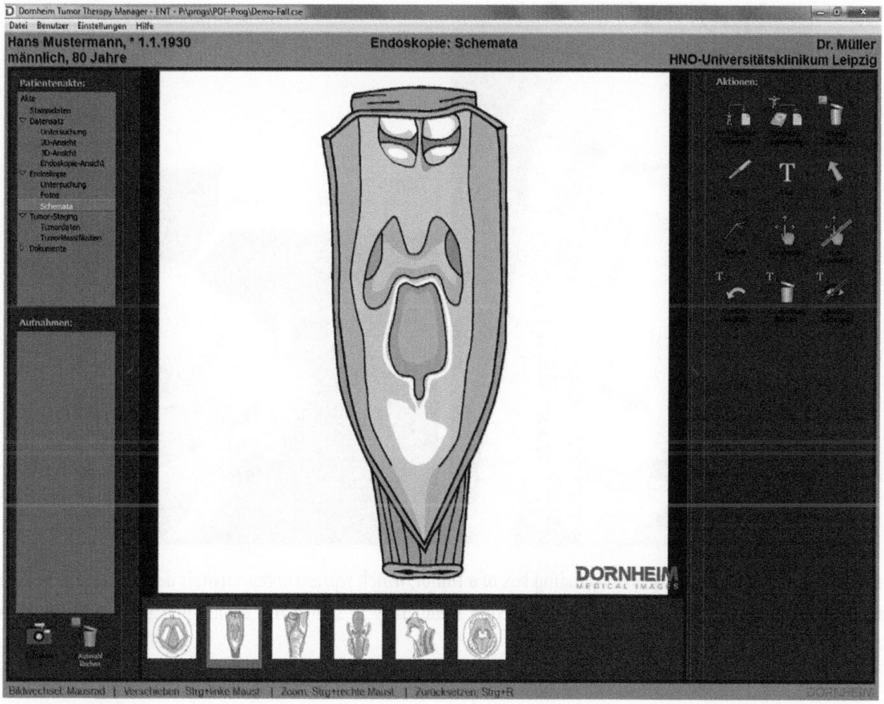

FIGURE e20.30 *Schematic drawings of the neck anatomy are provided in electronic form (bottom thumbnail images) in order to annotate them with findings from endoscopy. The currently selected drawing (large central image) may be modified with the tools on the right (Courtesy of Dornheim Medical Images).*

[Rössling *et al.*, 2011], which was possible due to better support of the software and more experience and trust of the users.

In approximately 10 cases, the 3D visualizations were employed in the tumor board for interdisciplinary discussions. In general, the surgeon feels safer with the computer-assisted planning and better prepared for surgery. Only in rare cases, however, he changes the surgical strategy with respect to radicality and access.

The computer-assisted planning process is accomplished in difficult cases where the tumor disease is at a later stage and therefore treatment is particularly challenging (roughly 70% of the patients in the study exhibit a tumor in the late stages III and IV, and 10% exhibit metastases). The system is used in one hospital, although care was taken in the task analysis stage that it is not overly specialized for this specific setting.

The TUMOR THERAPY MANAGER is considered particularly useful for planning treatment of surgical interventions at the larynx. This is because all relevant target structures (cricoid cartilage, thyroid cartilage) can be segmented and discriminated well. With respect to tumors in the oropharynx, not all relevant structures can be separated and thus the 3D visualization is less helpful. Primarily one surgeon describes that he particularly appreciates the precise documentation function. This allows for the first time to communicate precisely the findings of the panendoscopy, in particular the estimated depth-infiltration of vascular structures and other tissue. He reports that with these functions he is more careful in the endoscopy, since more findings can be reported.

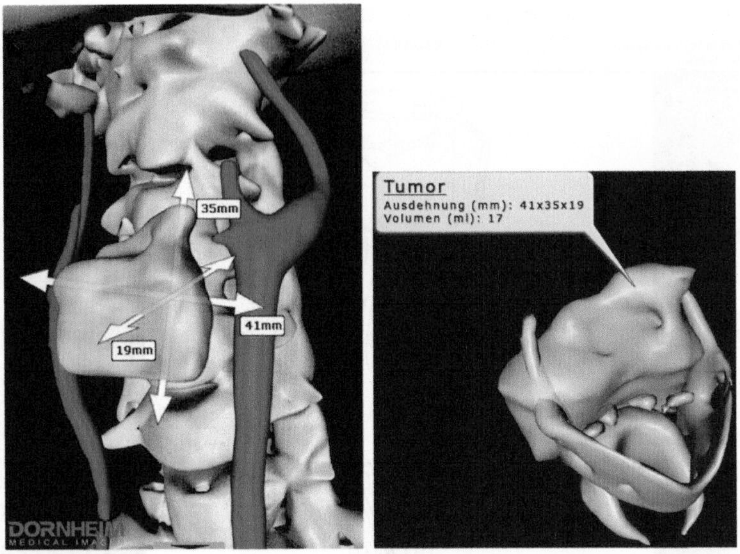

FIGURE e20.31 **Left:** The object-oriented bounding box of a tumor, which represents its extent, is determined and visualized as part of the documentation. **Right:** As an alternative, the extent of a tumor may be shown like a tooltip (Courtesy of Dornheim Medical Images).

Rössling *et al.* [2011] discuss the experiences of the clinical use in more detail, including measurement, annotation and PACS integration. They also report that the average time for computer-assisted planning (provided that all segmentation results are provided) only increases by 2 minutes which is likely to be an acceptable effort.

Discussion Despite the long-term effort described here, still not all clinical needs are fulfilled in an optimal way. In some hospitals, ultrasound or MRI are primarily used for diagnosis and treatment planning. Thus, it is desirable to adapt visual computing solutions to the peculiarities of such data. Multimodal visualization, including information derived from different image data, is at least in some hospitals a useful extension. In particular, if radiation treatment or chemotherapy are part of the overall treatment plan, treatment response has to be carefully evaluated, which gives raise to comparative visualization solutions highlighting how the shape and size of tumors have changed over time.

20.7 CONCLUDING REMARKS

Segmentation is essential to enable selective visualization and quantitative analysis of anatomical structures in the head and neck region. We described model-based approaches that are highly specific for certain structures, thus they are not broadly applicable. However, this high level of adaptation to data and anatomic structures was required to meet the demands of clinical practice. Virtual endoscopy is essential in all three areas we have discussed here: middle ear, neck and sinus surgery. It provides information in an intuitive way and supports planning and patient consult. However, the amount of additional information derived from virtual endoscopy does not justify a lengthy preparation. Thus, we also described a method that does not incorporate prior segmentation.

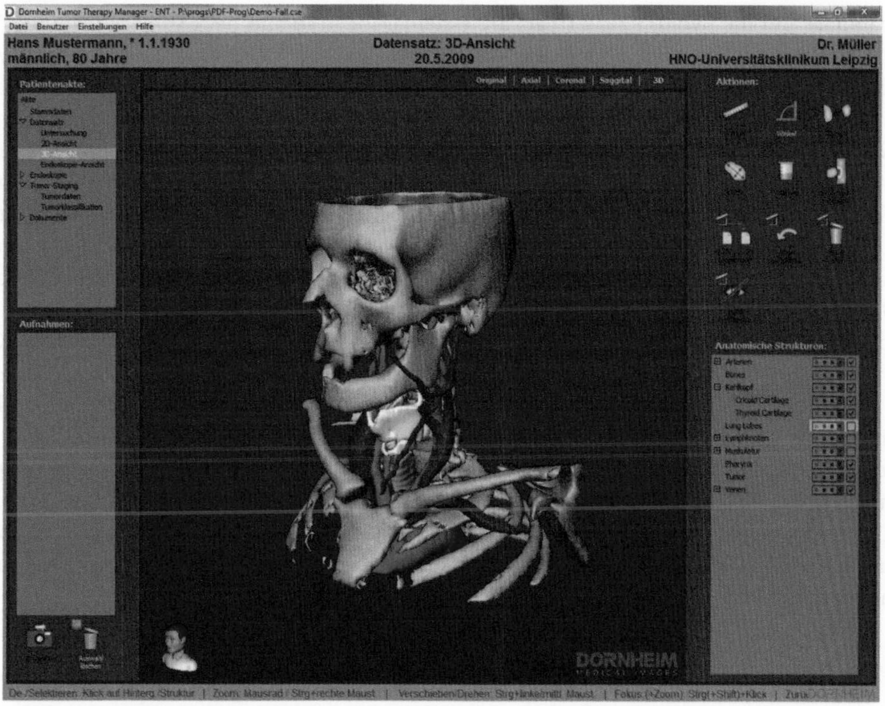

FIGURE e20.32 *User interface of the tumor therapy manager. Most of the available space is used for the visualization area, where 2D or 3D visualizations may be displayed. Major tasks, such as tumor staging, are available via the icons on the left side, whereas detailed interactions relating to the visualization are provided in a toolbar (right) (Courtesy of Dornheim Medical Images).*

We discussed two issues of uncertain information and its visualization: incomplete segmentation results, e.g., nerve segmentation, and potential infiltration areas. In particular, the optimal visualization of infiltration areas is an open issue. The approach presented in this chapter (hatched semitransparent surface) should be seen as a starting point to design and develop alternatives and use them for a rigorous user study.

Throughout the chapter we discussed examples, where medical doctors demanded and used drawing facilities to record their findings, either in relation to schematic drawings or in relation to 3D visualizations, such as virtual sinus endoscopy. To support convenient drawing, also with modern input devices, is thus an essential aspect of surgical planning systems.

FURTHER READING

We discussed segmentation of CT neck data in considerable detail using mass-spring models. In recent years, several alternative approaches were described. Teng *et al.* [2010] combine thresholding with 3D active contours for lymph node delineation. They target primarily at radiation treatment planning where the target region is larger than the actual tumor. Atlas-based approaches were developed and clinically evaluated [Lee and Rosowski, 2009, Stapleford *et al.*, 2010]. An automatic classification for lymph nodes according to the lymph node levels is highly desirable. Som *et al.* [1999] introduced such a system. Moreover, Teng *et al.* [2006] introduced a system that supports the segmentation of a couple of further structures, such as the mandible and the hyoid. PET/CT data are essential for head and neck surgery planning. Wu *et al.* [2012a] describe a method to locate and delineate nasopharyngeal carcinoma automatically. They analyze the CT data to automatically locate the (thin) neck region and search for relevant structures also guided by the uptake values in corresponding regions from PET data.

The following hints are focused on ear surgery, since we discussed that portion of ENT surgery rather briefly. Anatomical reconstructions of the middle ear with HR-CT are discussed in [Decraemer *et al.*, 2003]. Semi-automatic segmentation of the mastoid bone—an essential step for ear surgery planning—is described by Salah *et al.* [2006]. Virtual otoscopy was developed early and refined carefully. In addition to the papers already mentioned [Rodt *et al.*, 2002, 2004], the work of Klingenbiel *et al.* [2000] and Neri *et al.* [2001] is outstanding. With respect to surgical training for FESS, we refer to [Pössneck *et al.*, 2005].

The determination of boundary conditions for biophysical ear simulations is discussed by Gea *et al.* [2010] using a combination of animal experiments and measurements in humans. For understanding hearing disabilities and planning surgery, the middle ear pressure and its local distribution along the tympanic membrane is essential. Among the methods used to determine that pressure is Laser Doppler Velocimetry, [Lee and Rosowski, 2001]. The largest series of virtual otoscopy examinations (213 patients) based on CT and MRI data is documented in Rodt *et al.* [2004]. A careful analysis of 33 patients with conductive deafness let Pandey *et al.* [2009] conclude "that virtual otoscopy improves evaluation of the ossicular chain particularly that of smaller structures such as the stapes superstructure which may influence decisions regarding planning of ossiculoplasty."

Chapter e21

Computer-Assisted Medical Education

21.1 INTRODUCTION

This chapter is dedicated to educational applications of medical visualization techniques. Interactive 3D visualizations have great potential for anatomy education as well as for surgery education, with users ranging from high school students and physiotherapists to medical doctors who want to rehearse therapeutical interventions. Computer-assisted training systems enhance surgical manuals, surgical courses, and cadaver studies by providing up-to-date multimedia content. In particular case-based systems with self-assessment tools support problem-oriented learning and thus potentially improve problem-solving capabilities.

Recent advances include web-based systems that enable personalized access with an individual profile and a list of favorite entries, as well as possibilities to upload content and discuss with colleagues. Among the potential users, case-based e-learning and interactive use of 3D models have also gained reasonable acceptance. In a recent survey, the majority of 176 German medical students answered that they like using such systems for educational purposes and for preparing exams [Birr *et al.*, 2013]. In the same survey, it turned out that most multimedia systems based on canned drawings are criticized because of their low level of interactivity. However, the actual experience of medical students with interactive 3D visualizations is low. Thus, carefully designed and easy-to-use systems are required to stimulate the proliferation of educational systems based on interactive 3D visualizations.

The Role of Visualization Techniques While advanced visualization techniques currently play only a minor role, they have the potential to enhance the display of complex interventions. Among the few systems having adopted advanced visualization techniques at an early stage is the VoxelMan, an anatomy education system that even gave rise to the development of new visualization techniques, such as high-quality rendering at subvoxel accuracy and advanced vessel visualization.

Surgical Simulators The most complex systems targeting on medical education are surgical simulators that aim at providing a realistic virtual environment for practicing complex surgical interventions.

Many challenging tasks have to be solved to provide a convincing environment: Force feedback when tissue is touched or penetrated, collision detection, soft tissue deformation, cutting, and the simulation of various complications. We discuss these problems and focus on the interactive visualization techniques used in these settings. In addition, we discuss the design of such systems, the selection and structure of the underlying content and aspects of validation. In particular, the assessment of skills acquired with a training system, and the relevance of the acquired skills for clinical practice, have gained much attention in recent years.

Increasingly, simulators are also employed for catheter-based interventions, where assistant doctors have to learn the selection of catheters and their deployment for complex vascular interventions. These interventions have many advantages for the patient, including reduced trauma and postoperative pain, but they exhibit inherent problems and pitfalls for the surgeon due to the small size of the incision through which all actions have to be performed. These problems include the lack of dexterity due to the loss of two degrees of freedom (instruments can only be moved forward or backward), the lack of fine-manipulation, and the degradation of force feedback in the interaction with human tissue which is

Visual Computing for Medicine, Second Edition. http://dx.doi.org/10.1016/B978-0-12-415873-3.00021-3

essential for the palpation of the patient [Tavakoli *et al.*, 2006]. We describe some of the general problems, such as modeling elastic tissue properties, collision detection, simulating soft tissue deformation, and adequate force feedback.

We primarily discuss applications in anatomy, interventional radiology, and different surgical disciplines. This is motivated by the benefit of interactive rendering of volume data and derived 3D models in these areas. Computer support may enhance education in selected medical disciplines. However, traditional forms of learning, such as lectures, and dissections of cadavers or physical models, as well as giving assistance during surgical interventions, shall not be replaced by any software solution.

Training with Physical Models Another recent trend is the use of physical models derived from medical image data and produced with rapid prototyping technology. Segmentation and surface extraction are two essential steps related to the topic of this book. Due to progress in manufacturing technology, physical models are becoming much more affordable and at the same increasingly flexible with respect to the materials used. The great potential of physical models is that they may represent a variety of pathologies and enable the use of real surgical instruments. The emerging use of physical models is primarily motivated by the shortage of cadavers available for surgical training.

Organization As a basis for the discussion of case studies, we introduce general concepts of computer-based training (§ 21.2) and metaphors for educational systems. Case studies in anatomy education (§ 21.3) and surgery education (§ 21.4) follow. The second part of the chapter is dedicated to systems that *train* procedures, instead of only presenting interactive multimedia content. This part starts with a discussion of the underlying techniques (§ 21.5), including haptics, collision detection, and soft tissue simulation. Case studies (simulation systems) in interventional radiology (§ 21.6) and surgery (§ 21.7) follow. We introduce simulation technology that employs rapid prototyping to enable training with physical models (§ 21.8). Finally, we discuss *skills assessment*, that is, concepts and systems that assess what was learned using a computer-assisted training system (§ 21.9).

21.2 e-LEARNING IN MEDICINE

e-learning systems in medicine have been used for almost 50 years [Owen *et al.*, 1965]. Due to the widespread availability of suitable computers and enhanced use of the multimedia presentation capabilities, the interest and popularity of e-learning has grown in recent years. Many experiments showed that the combination of presenting knowledge simultaneously with audio and video materials increases the retention of knowledge considerably [Mehrabi *et al.*, 2000].

Although the initial costs of e-learning development are considerable, these systems can be updated more flexibly compared to traditional media. Also, the mode of presentation used in state-of-the-art e-learning systems is considered to be superior. It turns out that the large majority considered e-learning as useful, as a substantial help in self-study and exam preparation. In recent years, this also lead to broad acceptance of such education systems.

Constructivism and Situated Learning Chittaro and Ranon [2007] further elaborate on the pedagogical motivation, in particular of interactive 3D visualization. *Constructivism* is a fundamental pedagogical theory according to which learning primarily occurs if trainees are "engaged in meaningful tasks." According to this theory, when we interact with an environment (a real or simulated environment), this enables direct, even unconscious experience and thus an increased *depth of experience* compared to, e.g., learning from listening to a teacher or reading a textbook. In essence, we *construct* the knowledge as learners ourselves. Among the medical education system explicitly mentioning constructivism as guiding theory is the anatomy teaching system ZYGOTE BODY [Kelc, 2012].

Another relevant concept of pedagogic theory is *situated learning*—a concept where learning experiences are provided in a context that is very similar to situations where this knowledge should be applied. Thus, surgery simulation or surgery training with physical models and real surgical instruments represents a setting where situated learning is possible. For education in medicine, an advantage of e-learning is that clinical pictures are represented graphically.

Learning Objectives General concepts and rules of thumb for e-learning systems should be considered in the design and evaluation of educational systems for anatomy and surgery. e-learning systems should be based on a clear understanding of *learning objectives* and the *target user group*. The processes to acquire this understanding are known as *task analysis* and *audience analysis* [Lee and Owens, 2000] (recall Chap. 5). The design of e-learning systems is a special aspect of interactive system design. Therefore, textbooks on this topic, such as [Shneiderman and Plaisant, 2009] are relevant here. In particular, the scenario-based approach to user interface design, advocated by Rosson and Carroll [2003], is highly recommended and has been proven successful in e-learning projects, such as the SPINESURGERYTRAINER [Kellermann *et al.*, 2011] and the LIVERSURGERYTRAINER [Mönch *et al.*, 2013]. The core idea of this approach is that developers and users agree on essential scenarios, sequences of user input and system output described informally in natural language. These scenarios should guide the analysis stage, the prototyping activities, user evaluations as well as the documentation of interactive systems (recall § 5.2.3.2).

e-learning systems should provide a *self-steered* and *directed* method of learning. With e-learning systems, users can "pick an individual learning pace" [Mehrabi *et al.*, 2000]. A path to the learning environment that can be followed, left and re-entered freely, is necessary. It is essential that users can explore the material, for example by interrogating graphical representations, by answering multiple-choice questions or by solving tasks which involve a manipulation of graphical objects.

Examples for learning objectives in anatomy are the following. Students should be able

- to locate certain structures,
- to know the functional relation between certain structures, and
- to recognize typical variations of certain structures.

Learning objectives should be explicitly specified, and they should guide the design and development of e-learning systems. The analysis and understanding of learning objectives may serve as a basis to guide the user and provide an appropriate learning experience.

Success Criteria In summary, to enable successful learning, e-learning systems should:

- provide realistic and *appealing examples*,
- support *active participation* where users not only observe prepared sequences of images, textual description, and animation, but have to make decisions and to solve tasks,
- provide *adequate feedback*, in particular when the user solved a task,
- provide *self-assessment tools*, such as quizzes or multiple-choice questions,
- allow the user a *flexible exploration* of tasks and material with navigation aids telling the user what has been done and what could be done next.

Finally, the success of e-learning systems also depends on the motivation of learners. If the use of an e-learning system is perceived as diligent work only, few users will fully exploit its capabilities. The study of techniques from the area of computer games may help to get inspirations for combining learning with an entertainment experience.

e-learning in Anatomy and Surgery In medicine cognitive and motor skills are important. *Cognitive skills* comprise factual knowledge, e.g., names of anatomical structures, and knowledge of procedures, e.g., the selection of a basic treatment, the steps to be performed, complications, follow-up and postoperative management. *Motor skills* comprise psychomotor skills to actually perform a procedure, e.g., to apply the right amount of pressure to insert a catheter in a vascular tree or to perform suturing and knot tying in laparoscopic surgery. Cognitive skills may be verified with a quiz or multiple-choice questionnaires [Oropesa *et al.*, 2010]. The training of motor skills requires training systems which enable to practice the actual procedure. The assessment of motor skills is largely performed by observations from experts and by some automatic measures, related to dexterity. The assessment of motor skills is far less standardized compared to cognitive skills assessment [Oropesa *et al.*, 2010].

e-learning systems for anatomy and surgery education focus on the acquisition of cognitive skills. They require appropriate image data and segmentation results. Based on these data, high-quality renderings can be generated and interactively explored as an essential component of such e-learning systems. Thus, in addition to the above-mentioned general requirements for e-learning systems in medicine, there are some further requirements for systems related to image data, e.g., in radiology and surgery. These systems should:

- provide 2D visualizations with overlays representing segmentation results,
- provide high-quality 3D models and related visualizations to explore spatial relations, e.g., margins and vascular supply areas,
- provide *integrated* 2D and 3D visualization with synchronization, e.g., when objects are selected,
- provide easy-to-use interaction facilities, such as incremental rotation.

While clinical applications require fast segmentation and visualization, educational systems require primarily high-quality results. By the way, the accuracy of visualizations is less important. Smooth surfaces without distracting features are preferred.

21.2.1 DATASETS FOR MEDICAL EDUCATION

Datasets play a key role in medical education. High resolution datasets with a good signal-to-ratio and only few artifacts enable the detailed exploration of anatomical structures. The acquisition of such datasets requires considerable experience, appropriate infrastructure and thus is expensive. Fortunately, the best datasets are publicly available and triggered a boost of educational systems.

Visible Human The most widely used data sources for anatomy education are the Visible Human datasets. These 3D datasets originate from two bodies that were given to science, frozen, and digitized into horizontally spaced slices. A total number of 1871 cryosection slices were generated for the Visible Man (1 mm slice distance) and even more for the Visible Woman (0.33 mm slice distance). Besides photographic cryosectional images, fresh and frozen CT data, as well as MR images, were acquired. The project was carried out at the University of Colorado (Head: Dr. Victor Spitzer) under contract of the National Library of Medicine, Bethesda, Maryland [Spitzer *et al.*, 1996, Spitzer and Ackerman, 2008].

The Visible Human datasets have a high quality that was unprecedented at that time (1994). For example, CT data were acquired with high radiation—resulting in an excellent signal- to-noise-ratio—and without breathing and other motion artifacts. However, the quality of the data is not perfect: The frozen body was cut in four blocks prior to image acquisition leaving some noticeable gaps in the data.

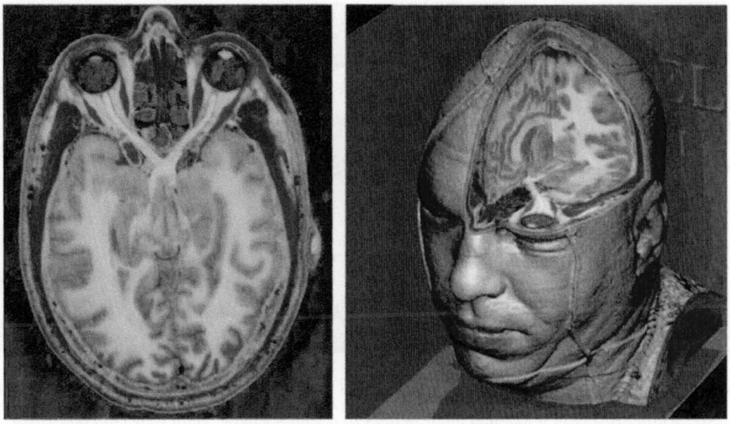

FIGURE e21.1 *Photographic data from the Visible Human Male dataset.* **Left:** *a slice view.* **Right:** *a volume rendering with clipping enabled (From: [Tiede et al., 1996]).*

The Visible Human datasets are employed for a variety of educational systems, e.g., the VoxelMan for anatomy education [Höhne *et al.*, 2003] and many training systems for interventional radiology and surgery. Figure e21.1 shows examples of the Visible Human cryosections.

Visible Korean and Chinese Visible Human Datasets from people of other regions in the world were also needed for medical education. In the "Visible Korean Human" project, a dataset of a 65-year-old patient was provided [Park *et al.*, 2006]. The Chinese Visible Human avoided some problems of the original Visible Human project [Zhang *et al.*, 2006a]. In particular, the image acquisition was performed with a very large milling machine that did not require to cut the body. Thus, the section loss, which occurred in the Visible Human project as a result from cutting the body, could be avoided. Also smaller details were better preserved and did not fall from the milling machine. In contrast to the Visible Korean Human, the Chinese dataset contains normal female and male adults. The Chinese Visible Human also exhibits a superior spatial resolution (in-plane resolution 170 μm). The raw data (photographs, CT and MRI data) is not sufficient for medical education systems. The precise segmentation of the target structures is another essential prerequisite. In a long-term effort, 869 segmented structures of the male dataset and 860 of the female dataset were provided [Wu *et al.*, 2012b].

Further Anatomical Data and Outlook The University of Colorado, Center for Human Simulation, where the Visible Human datasets were acquired, continued its efforts to acquire anatomical data at a very high quality. Spitzer and Ackerman [2008] provide a survey on datasets acquired between 2003 and 2008. The dataset with the highest quality represents the foot and ankle region with 5000 visible light photographs acquired in 2007, see Figure e21.2. This increased resolution resembles high magnification images from arthroscopy and indeed is used for an arthroscopy simulator showing ligaments and tendons in an excellent quality. Other datasets represent the prostate and pelvis region, the wrist and hand as well as the thorax and heart region.

Still, the number and quality of such datasets does not fulfill all requirements for medical education. A larger diversity of datasets representing various pathologies is desirable. For some applications, data are needed in a special configuration, e.g., some diagnostic and treatment procedures require flexing the neck

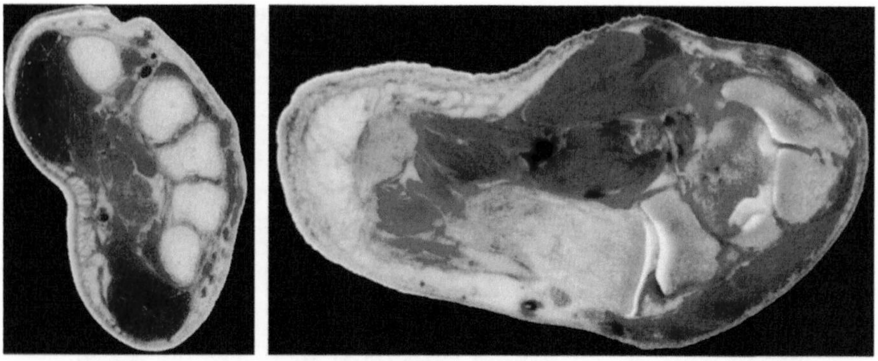

FIGURE e21.2 *Two cross-sectional views of datasets with improved resolution compared to the Visible Human datasets.* **Left:** *Cross section of a wrist dataset.* **Right:** *A slice of a foot and ankle dataset of a young female. Data were cut every 0.05 mm (From: [Spitzer and Ackerman, 2008]).*

as much as possible. Spitzer and Ackerman [2008] report on ongoing work to simulate the movement of ligaments and spinal nerves depending on the movement of the vertebrae.

Clinical Data An alternative source of data are high-quality clinical data which represent the variety of anatomical structures and pathologies. As an example, the first versions of the VoxelMan were based on a cerebral MRI dataset [Höhne *et al.*, 1992]. For anatomy education, some care is necessary to use data from a healthy person with normal anatomical relations. If anatomical differences should be compared, the selection of cases should be representative with respect to typical variants.

The segmentation of these datasets can be accomplished with general segmentation techniques (recall § 4.3). A special aspect is the segmentation of photographic datasets of the different Visible Human projects. These datasets represent colored voxels (24 Bit per voxel, representing a red, green, and blue component). The segmentation of colored data in RGB space is described by Schiemann *et al.* [1997].

For anatomy education, in principle all anatomical structures which can be derived from the image data are relevant. The VoxelMan, for example, is based on the segmentation of 650 objects (clinical applications often require the segmentation of fewer than 10 objects). The identification and delineation of functional areas in the brain requires considerable expert knowledge, since these areas are not represented as recognizable objects in the image data.

Geometric Modeling Segmented medical image data are the basis for 3D visualizations, but a dedicated effort is required to obtain high-quality 3D models. A simple surface extraction leads to aliasing effects. Therefore, smoothing, e.g., by subdividing and simplifying polygonal meshes is desirable [Brenton *et al.*, 2007]. High-end systems even add realistic textures, e.g., to convey the structure of muscles. Specialized modeling tools are employed for these purposes. The most comprehensive tools were developed for the film-making industry, where realistic appearance and behavior of virtual characters is essential. Maya is among such tools and used for example by Brenton *et al.* [2007] to create high-quality models (see Fig. e21.3).

Applications The Visible Human datasets have been employed for numerous medical education systems. Prominent examples are the VoxelMan [Pommert *et al.*, 2001], the VoxelMan Temporal Bone Simulator [Zirkle *et al.*, 2007] and an arthroscopy simulator to train endoscopic examinations of the knee

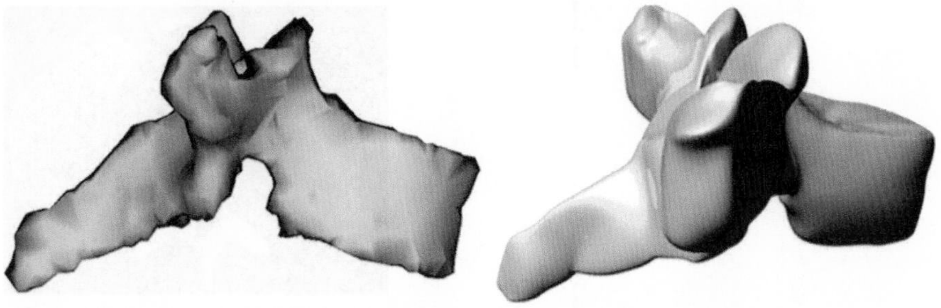

FIGURE e21.3 **Left:** *Surface extraction from the Visible Human dataset leads to a noisy surface of vertebrae.* **Right:** *After subdivision with Maya a smooth appearance results that is more appropriate for anatomy education* (From: [Brenton et al., 2007]).

[Heng *et al.*, 2004a]. The training system for lumbar punctures, developed at the University of Lübeck [Färber *et al.*, 2009, Fortmeier *et al.*, 2013b], employs both the Visible Human and the Visible Korean dataset. Also a variety of other needle-based interventions were trained by means of these datasets. Even a whole journal, the Visible Human Journal of Endoscopy,[1] was founded, presenting papers where findings are correlated with Visible Human images, particularly with endoscopic views.

Spitzer and Ackerman [2008] give an overview of 15 years of using the Visible Human datasets, emphasizing how strongly 3D stereo visualizations of the data have been used for anatomy education at many sites in the US. They summarize the impact of the Visible Human datasets as follows: "The assignment of physical properties, the development of algorithms for interaction of surgical tools with this virtual anatomy and the availability of high-fidelity haptic interfaces provide the basis for fully immersive surgical training and certification." In the course of this chapter, we shall get to know many of these applications.

21.2.2 KNOWLEDGE REPRESENTATION

Although interactive visualizations are the primary components of medical education systems, they are not sufficient to effectively support learning processes. The mental integration of visual elements and related symbolic knowledge is an essential learning goal. Symbolic knowledge relates to concepts, names, and functions of anatomical objects and to various relations between them, for example, which area is supplied by a certain vascular structure. Knowledge representation schemes employ segmentation information and allow for the addition of various relations between individual objects. Before we actually discuss knowledge representations, it should be noted that anatomy is studied according to its different subdivisions. Important subdivisions of anatomy are (cf. http://www.webanatomy.com/, accessed: April 30, 2013):

- *clinical anatomy*: the study of anatomy that is most relevant to the practice of medicine.
- *comparative anatomy*: the study of the anatomies of different organisms, drawing contrasts and similarities between the structure and function of the anatomies.
- *cross-sectional anatomy*: anatomy viewed in the transverse plane of the body.
- *radiographic anatomy*: the study of anatomy as observed with imaging techniques such as conventional X-ray, MRI, CT, and ultrasonography. Images which relate to cross-sectional and radiographic anatomy are shown in Figure e21.4.
- *regional anatomy*: the study of anatomy by regional parts of the body, e.g., thorax, heart, and abdomen. In regional anatomy, all biological systems, e.g., skeletal, and circulatory, are studied with an emphasis on the interrelation of the systems and their regional function.

1 http://www.vhjoe.org/.

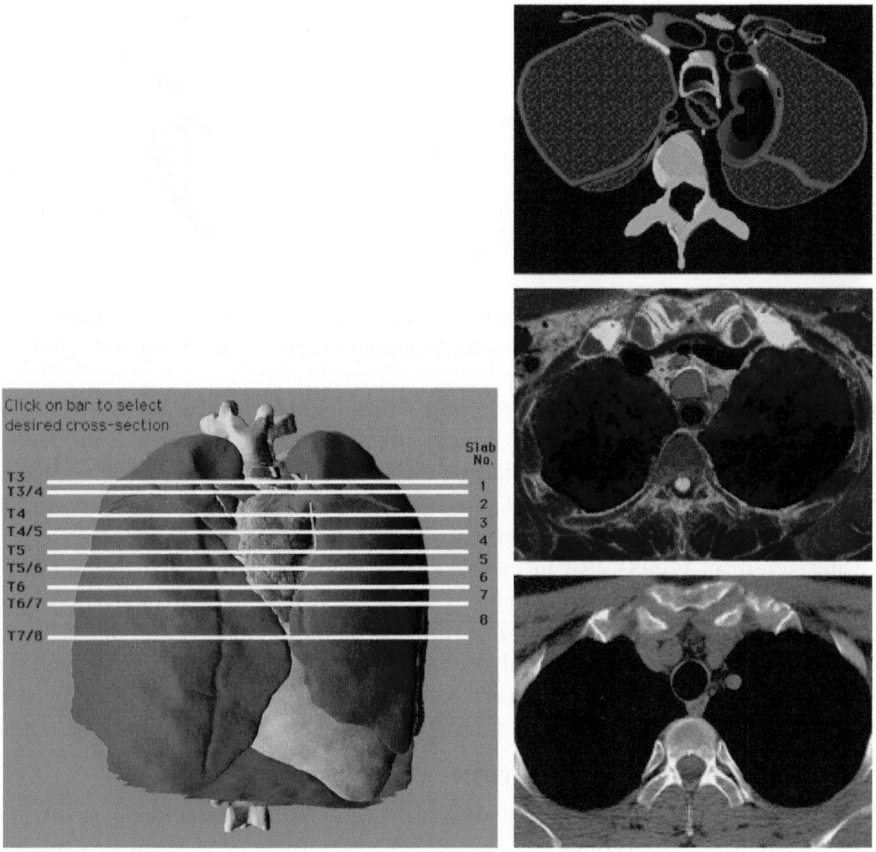

FIGURE e21.4 *A 3D overview (left) is used to show different levels for which cross-sectional and radiographic images are provided. The images on the right relate to the T1 level in the left image (Screenshot of the Digital Anatomist).*

- *systemic anatomy*: the study of anatomy by biological systems, e.g., skeletal, muscular, and circulatory system. In systemic anatomy, a single biological system is studied concurrently across all body regions.
- *macroscopic anatomy*: the study of anatomy with the unaided eye, essentially visual observation. Typically, macroscopic anatomy is explored using dissected cadavers.
- *microscopic anatomy*: the study of anatomy with the aid of the light microscope and with electron microscopes that provide subcellular observations. Microscopic anatomy is based on very high resolution images, and provides insight at a level which is not possible with tomographic image data or with dissecting cadavers.

These different aspects of anatomy form different "views" on the anatomy. For example, the kidney is part of the abdominal viscera in the *regional anatomy* and part of urogenital system in the *systemic anatomy* [Pommert *et al.*, 2001].

Ideally, e-learning systems for anatomy comprise and integrate all aspects, for example by smoothly blending in data in different resolutions. There is some progress toward this vision in recent years, e.g., in some surgical simulators that blend microCT and CT data, but the technical problems with respect to data size and handling are still challenging. Clinical anatomy and radiographic anatomy can be explored with medical volume data and derived information. As an example of combining different aspects of anatomy, the DIGITAL ANATOMIST [Brinkley *et al.*, 1999] provides 3D overviews where the positions of certain slabs are marked (Fig. e21.4). For each slab, the related information is shown as CT slice, as photographic data and as clipped 3D visualization. Users may zoom, rotate, and label anatomical structures. Also 15 neurological pathways (recall Chap. 15) and 18 histologic dissections are illustrated.

e-learning for the study of *comparative anatomy* requires a variety of different datasets (along with segmentation results) that represent at least the typical anatomical variants. As an example, hepatic vasculature may exhibit variants, such as an (additional) accessory hepatic vein, a trifurcation of the portal vein main branch or inferior veins [Birr *et al.*, 2013]. Most e-learning systems do not support this important aspect of anatomy.

Many anatomy education systems focus on *regional anatomy* and represent the relation between labels and segmentation results. Some systems provide textual labels and related textual explanations with facilities to explore them along with the graphical representation [Preim *et al.*, 1997]. A sophisticated representation of symbolic anatomical knowledge however goes far beyond this and effectively builds an ontology composed of different views, e.g., different kinds of relations between anatomical objects. The first advanced (digital) knowledge representation for anatomy has been developed by Schubert *et al.* [1993]. Among others, they represent:

- *part-of relations* (one object belongs to a larger object, for example a functional brain area),
- *is-a relations* which group anatomical objects to categories,
- *supplied by relations*, which characterize the blood supply.

This knowledge is integrated in a *semantic net*—a flexible knowledge representation (see Fig. e21.5). The relation between variably labeled volumes and the symbolic knowledge is referred to as *intelligent voxel*. This relation provides the basis to interactively interrogate parts of graphical representations. Similar concepts for knowledge representation have been used later for the DIGITAL ANATOMIST [Brinkley *et al.*, 1999] and the ANATOMYBROWSER [Kikinis *et al.*, 1996a] (see § 21.3). Smit *et al.* [2012] have recently extended these concepts to support completely free-form relations between arbitrarily represented, i.e., not necessarily voxel-based, anatomical structures.

While such knowledge representations are primarily discussed for anatomy, they are also relevant for operative medicine. Knowledge representations supporting operative disciplines may incorporate instruments, typical resection areas, and puncture points in their relation to anatomical structures.

Primal Pictures PRIMAL PICTURES contains a comprehensive set of anatomy-related and physiology-related educational systems. Primal Pictures is based on geometric models with an excellent quality that can only be achieved with substantial anatomical illustration know-how, e.g., with respect to the use of colors. The interactive handling of these 3D models was performed by means of VRML. The first generation of web-based 3D visualization systems was based on specialized formats and plugins, most notably VRML (virtual reality markup language). VRML was also used for medical education, e.g., in Primal Pictures. According to the different subdivisions of anatomy that we have described in § 21.2.2, Primal Pictures is focused on regional, systemic, and cross-sectional anatomy. As an example for *systemic anatomy*, modules are provided that convey the dynamics of moving muscles, ligaments and their influence on skeletal structures. Dedicate modules are available, e.g., for illustrating the knee and its dynamics, the hand and the hip. Interactive 3D visualizations are provided along with textual labels and explanations.

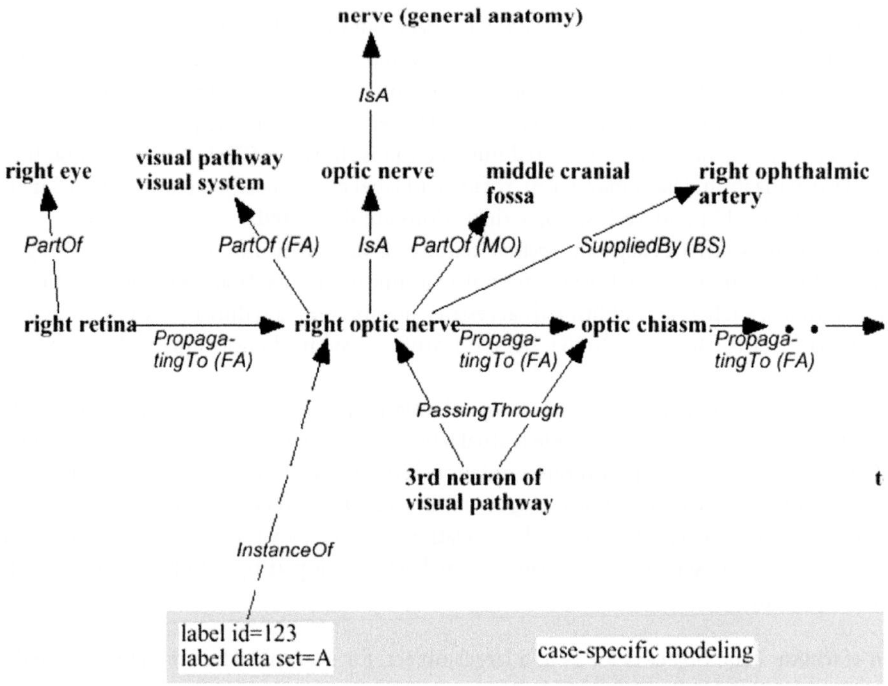

FIGURE e21.5 *A semantic net describes anatomical knowledge and serves as a basis for interactive interrogation (Inspired by [Schubert et al., 1993]).*

21.2.3 WEB-BASED MEDICAL EDUCATION SYSTEMS

The full potential of computer-assisted education systems may only be exploited with web-based systems. The access to such systems is not limited to any location or to a specific device. In particular, advanced anatomy and surgery training systems, such as surgical simulators, were developed with proprietary tools and relied on very specific hardware limiting access to very small groups of people. We discuss web technology and open standards here, since systems based on such technology tend to provide "easier reuse, easier integration with existing content and lower price" [Chittaro and Ranon, 2007].

Web-based learning is often classified into (cf. [Chittaro and Ranon, 2007]):

- tutorials,
- online discussion groups, and
- virtual patients.

Tutorials relate to content provided by an expert, usually including different media and links, e.g., to further information, such as publications. Discussion groups emphasize joint activities facilitated by web-based systems, including discussions between teachers and trainees. In the medical education terminology, *virtual patient* is a term that includes the visualization and interaction of patient data including all kinds of simulations and animations, e.g., to show the effect of treatment.

21.2.3.1 Potential and Limitations

The potential of web-based learning in general and in medicine in particular has often been discussed: Rich content may be provided and even adapted to the individual learner and thus provide an engaging learning experience. There are some further advantages, e.g., learning experiences may be documented automatically.

However, as Cook [2007] discusses based on substantial experiences with many web-based learning systems, this potential is very difficult to exploit fully; there are clear limitations and disadvantages. Online discussion cannot fully replace the social interaction that occurs in face-to-face meetings, for example, and subtle technical problems are difficult to avoid and may disturb significantly.

In particular, the promise of an individualized and *adaptive learning experience* that compensates for differences in baseline knowledge, learning and cognitive styles is very difficult to realize in practice, despite a large body of research on such adaptation processes (see e.g., [Brusilovsky, 2003]). Cook [2007] argues that a teacher is usually better able to adapt the presentation in small groups to such differences.

21.2.3.2 Essential Design Aspects

In addition to all general aspects on good user interface design discussed in Chapter 5, there are a number of specific aspects in designing web-based learning. They are described concisely in a step-by-step approach by Cook and Dupras [2004]. We want to highlight one aspect because of its great importance for designing learning systems: *Active learning* should be encouraged. This includes the provision of mechanisms to *apply knowledge*, and the support of *problem-based learning* instead of abstract principles and self-assessment. They present a detailed explanation, citing many successful examples to realize this principle, and conclude with "The degree of success in this area will in large part determine the effectiveness of the educational website." Later, we discuss at various stages how this principle is realized in practical systems.

21.2.3.3 Web Technology

VRML The potential of web technology for providing unlimited access to interactive 3D visualizations led to the definition of VRML in 1994. VRML, the virtual reality markup language, later became an official ISO standard in 1997. Based on the OPEN INVENTOR specification, VRML employs a scene graph description of a 3D model, that is a direct acyclic graph that represents the geometry, material properties, e.g., colors and transparency, textures, 2D and 3D text, transformations, light sources, and the virtual camera. A polygonal surface, for example extracted with the Marching Cubes algorithm, is represented as an "IndexedFaceSet" node. This memory-efficient scheme comprises the coordinates of vertices and the association of these vertices to faces avoiding any redundancy. All major visualization toolkits enable VRML export of the results.

In addition to the geometry, also the behavior is represented in nodes of the scene graph, e.g.,

- with sensors that observe certain properties and may trigger a reaction,
- with manipulators that may control clipping planes or other widgets, and
- with nodes that enable collision detection, e.g., to detect whether a surgical instrument touches an anatomical structure.

An essential aspect for creating feature-rich medical education applications is the combination of Java and VRML.

VRML was also widely used for developing medical education systems. John [2007] provides an overview categorizing systems in general tools for medical education, educational tools for diagnosis and procedure training as well as collaboration support. As an example, Brodlie *et al.* [2000] presented VRML-based prototypes for vascular surgery and neurosurgery. However, the low bandwidth in the 1990s and the requirement to install a VRML browser at the client side hampered widespread use. In addition, 3D interaction and navigation was often very difficult. Thus, trainees easily became lost in the 3D environments or were confronted with an overwhelming number of options.

X3D and WebGL X3D (extensible 3D), like VRML, is an open ISO standard defined by the W3 consortium and thus it is independent of any specific platform. It is largely backwards-compatible with VRML. Thus, VRML files need only minor adaptation to be used as X3D files [Chittaro and Ranon, 2007]. The development of X3D was triggered by progress in graphics hardware, in particular improved programming capabilities and multitexturing. Thus, it provides a number of new nodes and capabilities. In addition, X3D files may also be encoded in XML and thus easily mixed with other content that is available in XML. Often, it is advantageous that also a memory-efficient binary encoding of X3D data is provided.

HTML5 references X3D for declarative 3D content but does not define the actual integration. X3DOM[2] was developed to integrate X3D in web applications directly [Behr *et al.*, 2009]. The mapping of live DOM elements to a X3D scene model is very similar to the integration of interactive 2D vector graphics via SVG [Behr *et al.*, 2009]. Such a direct integration not only provides advantages for the users, namely that no plugin needs to be installed. Also developers benefit because synchronization problems between DOM content and plugin-based manipulations are avoided and of course also because developers do not need to focus on the peculiarities of just one plugin. Behr *et al.* [2009] described the X3DOM architecture in detail and compares it with various other approaches of integrating interactive 3D graphics with web browsers. Implementation strategies for X3DOM are explained in [Behr *et al.*, 2010]. More recently, Behr *et al.* [2011] introduced a multitude of advanced mechanisms for supporting dynamics (animations) and 3D interactions with appropriate events and update mechanisms. Finally, Behr *et al.* [2012] introduced a separation of the large and unstructured geometry data from the structured (and much smaller) scene information to improve handling and performance.

The "Medical Working Group" has defined MedX3D that adds advanced volume rendering and transfer function specification to X3D. This extension is essential, e.g., for surgical simulators, where tasks, such as drilling, require voxel representations [John *et al.*, 2008, Jung *et al.*, 2008]. The "long-term goal of the working group is to enable the creation of interoperable medical training and simulation systems using open standards" [John, 2007]. Currently the working group is engaged with the DICOM Working Groups and are proposing X3D as the DICOM 3D Graphics standard.[3]

In 2012, after demonstrating that the extensions fulfill the needs of key applications in medical diagnosis, treatment and education, this extension was officially integrated in the ISO standard X3D as "Volume Rendering Component." This extension is comprehensive and supports a large variety of rendering and illumination styles, such as cartoon rendering. Like the core of X3D, the volume rendering is specified as a scene graph, containing *scene graph nodes* that define the geometry and appearance of individual components, such as subvolumes or surgical instruments.

With the introduction of WebGL as part of HTML 5, advanced 3D visualization in the web browser, without the need to install a plugin, has become possible. WebGL is a low-level graphics API based on OpenGL ES 2.0 and enables hardware-accelerated rendering of 3D graphics. It supports mobile rendering and efficient shader programming. Frameworks such as X3DOM can utilize WebGL to perform 3D rendering.

---

2 http://www.x3dom.org/.

3 Nigel John, personal communication.

21.2.4 WEB 2.0 IN SURGICAL EDUCATION

Web 2.0 represents an enhanced use of the web. Instead of a few authors providing content and many receivers using that content in the intended way, users may annotate, comment, and link the content as well as provide content themselves. Prominent examples are social networks, such as FACEBOOK and LINKEDIN, but also video platforms, such as YOUTUBE. Professional networks, such as LINKEDIN, may serve as orientation with respect to attributing capabilities and experiences to users.

For medical education these concepts are attractive as well. However, medical doctors as target user group and patient data as content represent a very special situation that demands dedicated solutions. A web-based educational environment enables the distribution of carefully prepared content, such as segmented medical data and related 3D visualizations. Informed consent by patients and strict anonymization are, of course, mandatory. User-generated content is more difficult to manage—the system evolves in a way that is hard to predict. At least certain categories should be prepared. In addition keywords are necessary to enable efficient search.

At the time of writing, a German research project aiming at exploiting Web 2.0 technology for surgery education is being concluded, hopefully followed by a stage where the platform is extensively used. The design of the platform, called SURGERYNET, is guided by general functionalities for social platforms [Richter and Koch, 2008]. Thus, a social platform should provide rich features for

- exchanging information,
- identity management (decisions related to the visibility of information),
- contact management, including contacts to leading experts, and
- context awareness, making individual users aware of their peers and the common goals and activities.

Franken and Jeners [2012] explain how this basic functionality is realized for web-based surgery education. SURGERYNET also provides a conference calendar, hints to live operations that may be observed, but also contributions from industrial suppliers, e.g., related to the use of new surgical instruments.[4] Users may create comprehensive profiles, link to other users, create lists with contributions relevant to them and create bookmarks within the text. They may create exchange folders, invite colleagues to view and edit material and thus cooperate in a flexible and powerful manner. Figure e21.6 presents an example.

In contrast to most other platforms, SURGERYNET has no strong editorial board that acts as filter for new content but instead encourages a more spontaneous upload of content by users. Probably high-quality contributions are viewed more often, better assessed and then displayed more prominently leading to an *implicit quality control* that is more consistent with the general Web 2.0 philosophy. With this philosophy, the content is not that strictly categorized (although categories and keyword lists for tagging are suggested), and a larger variety of content may be provided.

An annotation tool is integrated with SURGERYNET in order to define and emphasize anatomical structures as well as to label them (see Fig. e21.7). This web-based annotation tool is intended to author a contribution, e.g., an interactive 3D visualization, but also to support the exchange of annotated data.

Virtual Liver The VIRTUAL LIVER introduced by Crossingham *et al.* [2009] illustrates liver anatomy and typical variants of liver resection. This system provides simple interactions suitable for web-based solutions. As an example, simple labeling techniques are integrated in order to convey anatomical names. A 3D model

4 www.surgerynet.de.

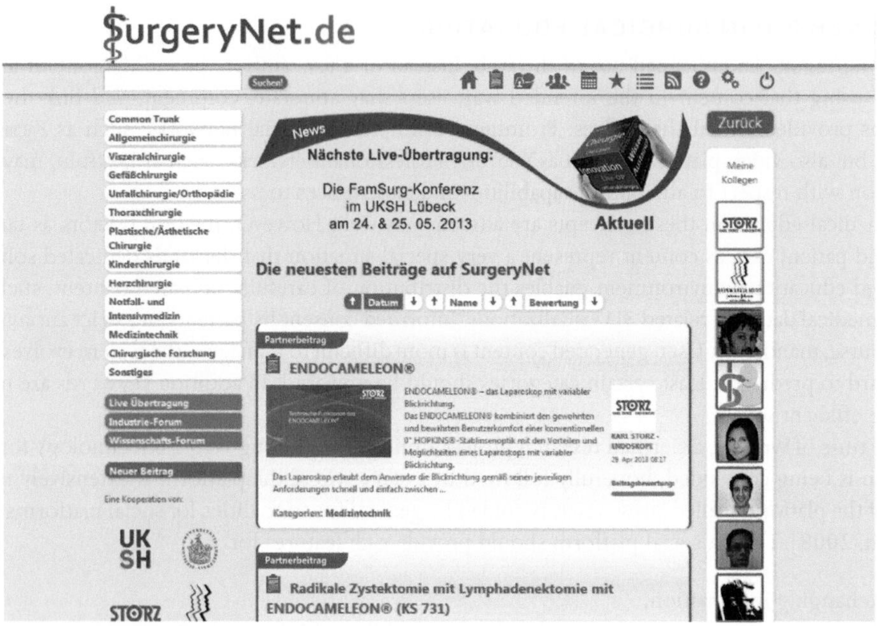

FIGURE e21.6 The SurgeryNet platform provides entries to educational material for all surgical disciplines. Also links, e.g., related to congresses, live demos and talks are integrated. Like a typical social network, the icons on the right represent the list of professional colleagues.

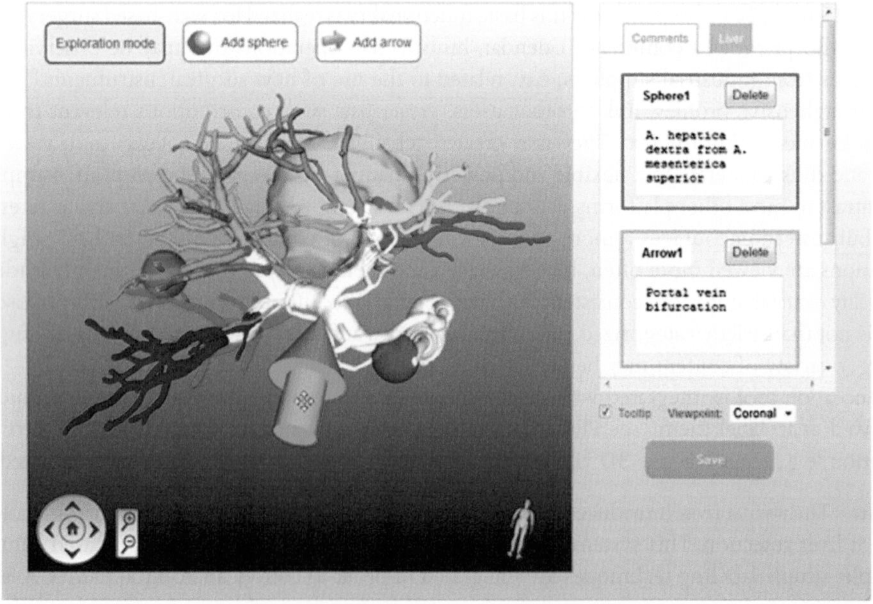

FIGURE e21.7 In the authoring mode of SurgeryNet, 3D visualizations may be enriched with arrows and spheres to annotate structures (Courtesy of Steven Birr, University of Magdeburg).

may be rotated in fix steps around fix axes. This constrained and simplified interaction is appropriate in these settings. In general, the whole interaction seems to be very well adapted to the target user group.

However, only one dataset, representing a healthy liver, is provided. Thus, all learning objectives that involve an assessment of the variety of vascular anatomy and spatial relations cannot be achieved. The major web technology used in this system is ADOBE FLASH.

Webop Webop is a comprehensive system that supports a wide range of learning objectives.[5] It is focused on OR videos using the medium film intensively to convey maneuvers to be carried out during interventions. A large set of such videos is provided representing not only the variability of anatomical situations but also possible differences in operation techniques and tactics including complication management. These videos are annotated and substantial quality control was provided. However, the interactivity is rather limited. Users select videos, may interrupt the presentation and move forward and backward. In contrast, with interactive 3D visualization they could control the camera position and orientation.

A crucial advantage is that videos are integrated in textual chapters that incorporate links to scientific publications and ongoing clinical trials. Moreover, Webop can be used as e-book on a mobile device with the typical multitouch interaction, e.g., to zoom into images or control the videos integrated in the e-book. Webop is described and discussed in detail by Pape-Koehler *et al.* [2010, 2013].

SurgyTec SurgyTec is another comprehensive web-based platform for surgery education providing a large number of videos that document surgical procedures, but also slide shows, full courses and events.[6] Theoretical background knowledge, expert opinions and many case reports are included. Members may also upload content, e.g., inform the community of upcoming events.

WeBSurg WeBSurg refers to itself as the "World Virtual University." It provides a large set of slide shows and streamed presentations related to all aspects of surgery. An editorial team lead by the famous French surgeon JACQUES MARESCAUX and with other experts from IRCAD (Institut de recherche contre les cancers de l'appareil digestif) Strasbourg cares for the high quality of the contributions. According to the pioneering role of IRACD in minimally-invasive surgery and using virtual reality in surgery, the use of new technology is a focus of WeBSurg [Mutter *et al.*, 2011]. Figure e21.8 gives an impression about the organization and content of WeBSurg. Even a collection of whole datasets and derived 3D models is available for download and exploration with a 3D rendering system (Fig. e21.9). Currently, WeBSurg has probably the largest and most diverse community of users. According to [Mutter *et al.*, 2011], the users originate from more than 200 countries.

Discussion There are a number of similarities in the described systems. Pape-Koehler *et al.* [2010] provides a comparison, however, due to the rapid development in this area, not all statements are still valid. Most of the platforms have an editorial board that ensure high-quality contributions but prevents fast updates. These editorial boards act similar to those of journals: they try to acquire contributions contacting opinion leaders and recognized experts for a particular intervention and evaluate the content they provide. A notable difference is the importance of high-quality video material. Thus, most of the platforms described above provide technical assistance to support the acquisition of high-quality videos and the editing process to cut and annotate the raw material.

A common aspect is also that new surgical methods, which are not currently broadly accepted, are slightly overrepresented in these platforms. This is reasonable, since web-based platforms enable faster

5 http://www.webop.de/.

6 http://www.surgytec.com/.

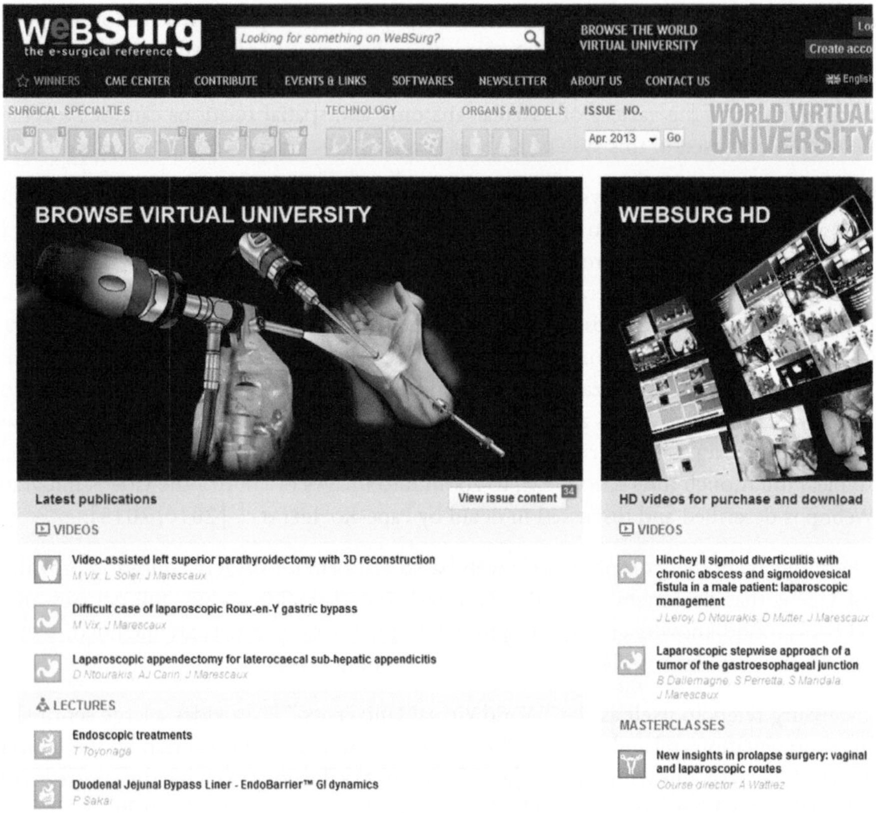

FIGURE e21.8 *A large variety of material is provided by WeBSurg organized according to surgical disciplines, organs, and technologies (Screenshot of WeBSurg).*

distribution of knowledge and thus have an advantage over traditional learning media with their long update periods.

All platforms grow significantly with respect to the content. Thus, the concern raised by Pape-Koehler *et al.* [2010] that web-based platforms are far from providing complete textbook knowledge is probably no longer true. However, it gets more complex to quickly find relevant contributions.

On the other hand, the facilities provided to edit, structure, annotate, and upload the content for such platforms are still complex and difficult to use or too simple in their functionality. Moreover, patient data needs to be very carefully and completely anonymized—this essential process is rarely supported by the platforms. Thus, in contrast to social networks, where many users not only "consume" content, but participate by sharing content, web-based medical education platforms provide content that only a small number of providers have contributed. Thus, there is clear need to improve the tools to provide high-quality content, in particular for anonymization and video editing.

Validation and skills assessment is crucial for all kinds of medical education technology. The most substantial effort so far to assess the effect of using a web-based surgical education site on the skills and relevant knowledge of surgeons is described in Pape-Koehler *et al.* [2013]. They performed a randomized trial that compared multimedia-based training (with WEBOP), with practical training and combined multimedia and

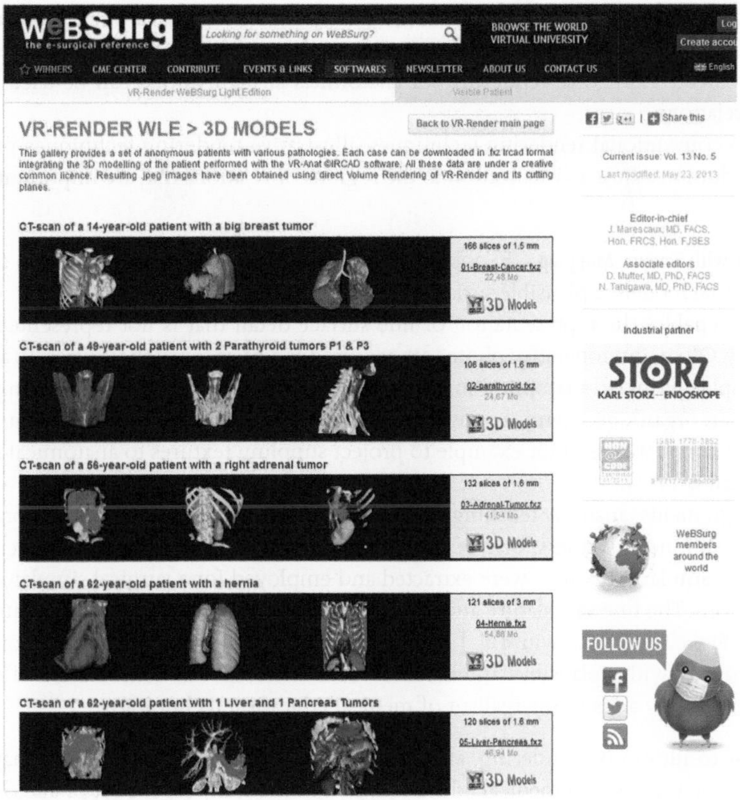

FIGURE e21.9 *Datasets, segmentation information and 3D models are provided for interactive exploration (Screenshot of WeBSurg).*

practical training with respect to laparoscopic cholecystectomy—a frequent minimally-invasive procedure. They could demonstrate a strong effect of multimedia training (compared to no training) evaluating the pre- and post-tests related to 12 relevant aspects of that intervention. The effect on surgical novices was even larger than that of practical training.

All these systems do not focus on image analysis, visualization and interactive exploration of medical image data—the major topics of this book. They are mentioned here, because such web-based platforms represent an essential context for developments in visual computing. Thus, advanced medical visualization may acquire significant influence if properly integrated in these platforms. Of course, these platforms are to support physicians (primarily surgeons). Therefore, only contributions prepared together with medical experts can reasonably be shared with the community.

21.2.5 VISUALIZATION TECHNIQUES FOR MEDICAL EDUCATION

In this chapter, we do not focus on new visualization or image analysis techniques. However, a variety of the techniques presented in the previous chapters are relevant for medical education. Some of them were introduced primarily motivated by use cases from education and training.

Illustrative Rendering In Chapter 12 we learned about low-level and high-level illustration techniques. Low-level illustration techniques enable to emphasize boundaries and other salient features of complex anatomical shapes. High-level illustration techniques adapt the visibility of objects and regions, e.g., by rendering portions of an object transparent or removing it completely. Such illustrative techniques are clearly useful to create expressive renderings of anatomical structures that can be used to *explain* spatial and functional relations.

In contrast to conventional rendering techniques, illustrative rendering techniques provide a significantly more freedom to adjust a visualization to the regions or relations that are important for a particular learning goal.

Enhanced Realism with Texture Mapping To achieve a high degree of realism, and thus to increase trust in training with virtual models, a plausible surface appearance, similar to that of real organs, is advantageous. Texture mapping enables the representation of fine surface detail that is not represented in the explicit surface geometry. Often, intraoperative photos are acquired as a basis for such textures. To actually project a texture on a complex wrinkled anatomical surface without confusing distortions is challenging. Techniques that decompose an organ's geometry, e.g., with polycubes [Tarini *et al.*, 2004], represent a viable option. In a modified version it was used for example to project stippling textures to anatomical structures [Baer *et al.*, 2007] (recall § 12.7).

With these ingredients, anatomy teaching or surgery simulation systems may incorporate surface visualizations where shininess, wetness, or fiber directions of anatomical structures are accurately reflected (see Fig. e21.10). Similarly, textures were extracted and employed for a surgical simulator to train endoscopic interventions. The fine vasculature and the effect of bleeding is represented in a simplified manner by textures (see Fig. e21.11). Kerwin *et al.* [2009] described how a surgery simulator for temporal bone surgery was enhanced with a plausible simulation of wetness effects. The combination of realistic textures and shading significantly adds to the realism of medical education technology.

Labeling Similar to illustrative rendering, also the labeling techniques described in Chapter 10 are primarily motivated by use cases in medical education. To automatically label a set of anatomical structures in 2D or 3D visualizations is essential to get familiar with anatomical names and to relate them to the

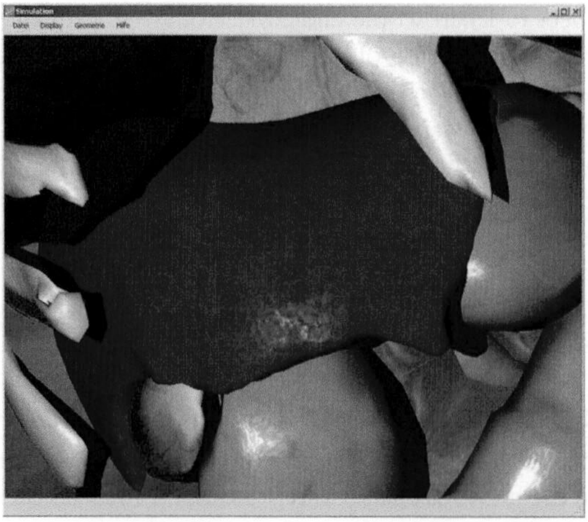

FIGURE e21.10 *The liver is textured based on a digital photo during a laparotomy. Trilinear interpolation is employed to map the texture on the curved liver surface. These models are used for a surgical simulation system (Courtesy of Simon Adler, Fraunhofer IFF Magdeburg).*

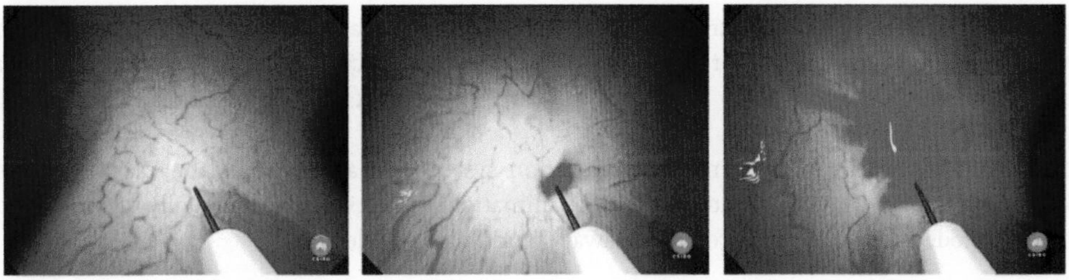

FIGURE e21.11 *Incorporating realistic textures in a endoscopic surgery simulation system* (Courtesy of Christoph Russ, Australian E-Health Research Centre, CSIRO).

corresponding shapes. While in radiology reports often only a single structure is annotated and labeled, for educational purposes it is often necessary to present a number of labels simultaneously. This gives rise to more advanced algorithms to place internal or external labels that avoid intersecting lines and obscuring relevant image regions.

Animating Medical Visualizations As a final family of visualization techniques relevant for educational systems we briefly discuss *animation*, a topic that was not introduced in any of the previous chapters.

Animations may effectively convey complex spatial relations between anatomical objects. As an example, a large series of educational animations was generated in the DIGITAL ANATOMIST project (see § 21.3). Animations may also be used to convey

- different stages of development, e.g., growth processes,
- functional information, such as the range of motion of joints, and
- transportation, e.g., of cells that react on an attack to the immune system.

Thus, animations can convey the dynamics of pathological and physiological processes. A clear time frame is useful in these use cases [Brenton *et al.*, 2007].

Compared to static illustrations, animations offer additional degrees of freedom to emphasize objects and to clarify their spatial configuration by performing gradual frame-to-frame changes. The observation of gradual changes between visualizations is mentally easier compared to the interpretation of two static images. The space of meaningful animation techniques depends on the data and derived information. Most anatomy education as well as surgical education systems are based on medical volume data and derived segmentation information. Typical animation techniques include the rotation of the whole dataset, zooming toward relevant structures, the movement of clipping planes, the movement of the camera along a certain path, for example through tubular structures, and gradual changes of the transparencies of objects. The design of animations that are successful in educational settings should consider findings from perceptual psychology. As an example, the number of movements that take place simultaneously should be limited [Tversky *et al.*, 2002].

These drawbacks gave rise to the development of script-based specification methods for animation design. These animation systems employ *decomposition rules*, which define the mapping of high-level specifications to low-level commands. A first attempt to generate dedicated animations of medical volume data is described in [Mühler *et al.*, 2006]. This scripting language supports slice-based visualizations and movements of clipping planes. It can be tailored to clinical tasks, such as evaluating the infiltration of a risk structure by a tumor or evaluating the resectability of a tumor patient. Default techniques to emphasize different categories of anatomical structures are employed. As an example, a camera movement along an object's centerline is appropriate for elongated objects, such as vascular structures. Later, the animation authoring was further enhanced by incorporating components that support the *re-use* of animations for similar datasets [Mühler and Preim, 2010].

Animations are widely used in medical education systems. As an example, the DIGITALANATOMIST (§ 21.3.2) provides a large set of animations. In these animations, objects are incrementally included, rotated, zoomed, exploded (outer objects are moved away), and finally labeled.

21.3 ANATOMY EDUCATION

In the following, we briefly describe computer support for anatomy education. We emphasized the importance of a careful user and task analysis for developing medical education systems. With respect to anatomy education, Brenton *et al.* [2007] and Jastrow and Hollinderbäumer [2004] discuss that the mental ability to understand anatomical structures as 3D objects is very important and hardly supported by other modes of education. Therefore, we restrict the discussion to systems which employ 3D models instead of scanned drawings. Keyword searches and high-quality images were also mentioned as important features desired by medical students.

Our discussion is focused on middle- and long-term projects systems carried out at research institutions since these are documented well in the literature. We start this section with the VOXELMAN—the pioneering 3D anatomy teaching system.

21.3.1 VOXELMAN

The first version of the VOXELMAN was based on a labeled MRI head dataset [Höhne *et al.*, 1992]. The system supports a flexible exploration of the data, labeling of anatomical structures as well as the inquiry of a sophisticated knowledge base (recall § 21.2.2). The knowledge base is employed to "interrogate" the graphical representation using context-sensitive pop-up menus. Direct volume rendering was employed for 3D visualization, which was unusual at that time due to the high demands for system performance.

The second generation of the VOXELMAN supports regional, systematic, and radiographic anatomy based on the Visible Human dataset and segmentation information as well as an advanced knowledge base. 650 anatomical constituents as well as 2000 relations between them are represented in the knowledge base [Pommert *et al.*, 2001]. The VOXELMAN provides many interaction facilities to explore the Visible Human data and the correspondence between the different datasets. Clipping and cutting facilities are included to virtually dissect the patient. For example, a clipping plane may be moved through a 3D volume-rendered image and simultaneously corresponding slices of CT and photographic data are shown. X-ray images may be simulated (as an average projection of the CT data, Fig. e21.12, left) and cross sections of CT data can be integrated with 3D surface renderings (Fig. e21.12, right).

21.3.2 DIGITALANATOMIST

The DIGITALANATOMIST is a long-term project, carried out at the Structural Informatics Group of the Department of Biological Structure at the University of Washington. The knowledge base underlying the system is huge. Already in 1999, 26,000 anatomical concepts and 28,000 semantic links were represented [Brinkley *et al.*, 1999]. The links are explored with a hypertext functionality; the represented relations are very similar to those used in the VOXELMAN (recall Fig. e21.5 and § 21.3.1). Labeled histologic image data based on tissue samples are available.

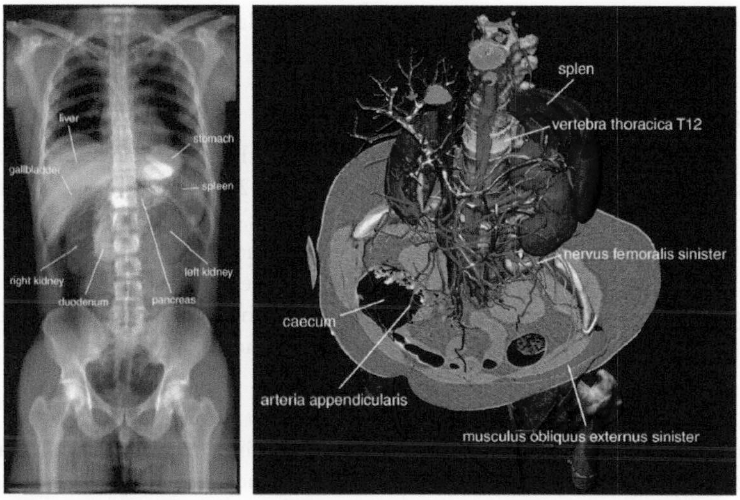

FIGURE e21.12 *Different viewing modes used in the* VOXELMAN. **Left:** *simulated X-ray.* **Right:** *CT slices combined with surface rendering of selected objects (From: [Pommert et al., 2001]).*

The DIGITALANATOMIST contains a quiz where people can select objects and enter their names, as a simple kind of self-assessment. In some animations, vascular structures grow along a path. Often, structures are clipped to reveal the insights. All drawings can be modified by adding outlines and labels. The system may be used in different modes, for examples as a tutorial or in a question-and-answer mode. The interaction facilities to explore the 3D models, however, are limited.

The DIGITALANATOMIST is available as web platform.[7] The project was finished in 2008 and thus does not make use of any recent web technology.

21.3.3 ANATOMYBROWSER

The ANATOMYBROWSER, developed at the Brigham and Womens Hospital in Boston, is also a comprehensive system representing a wealth of anatomical relations [Kikinis *et al.*, 1996a]. It was probably the first system available on standard PCs and later as web-service based on Java. The focus of the ANATOMYBROWSER is also on neuroanatomy. Labeled MRI data have been used as major data source for the system. Since a variety of datasets, in particular of the brain, is included, comparative anatomy can be explored. The comprehensive knowledge base enables a flexible exploration. The ANATOMYBROWSER project was finished in 2003, but the system is still available.[8]

21.3.4 PRIMAL PICTURES

In addition to the systems and concepts discussed in the scientific literature, also a commercial entity should be mentioned: PRIMAL PICTURES[9] presents a well-known suite of anatomy education tools. The next generation of anatomy education tools will likely incorporate realistic movements and functional information, for example with respect to blood flow and metabolism. Anatomy education tools may also be extended to

7 http://www9.biostr.washington.edu/da.html.

8 http://www.spl.harvard.edu/archive/spl-pre2007/pages/papers/AnatomyBrowser/current/.

9 see http://www.primalpictures.com/.

provide case studies of pathologies. Primal pictures also provide large sets of interactive 3D visualizations which present important sports injuries.

21.3.5 ZYGOTE BODY

This recently introduced tool is based on a substantial analysis of the current situation in anatomy teaching and the potential and necessity for computer support [Kelc, 2012]. It employs recent Web3D technology and received very good feedback in a user study with 73 users. An interesting aspect of the evaluation relates to the question which anatomical structures users found most interesting. It turned out that muscles were considered primarily interesting, because they have a complex structure that is not easy to understand and they are represented well in the 3D models. Structures of the central or peripheral nervous system, on the other hand, are very small and difficult to fully understand.

21.3.6 BIODIGITAL HUMAN

BioDigital Human is another recent development that already gained considerable acceptance. It provides intuitive interaction with 3D visualizations of the anatomy, but moreover conveys a number of animations revealing physiology. Thus, users may watch the beating heart and dissect it virtually. A model of atrial fibrillation is included and devices, such as implants, may be integrated. Thus, BioDigital Human actually provides more than anatomy knowledge. The system is described in [Qualter *et al.*, 2012], but it is recommended to watch the set of videos available at YouTube to fully appreciate the interactive technology.

21.3.7 LiverAnatomyExplorer

In contrast to the previously described systems, the LiverAnatomyExplorer was developed recently and employs rather new web-based technology [Birr *et al.*, 2013]. It has a clear focus on liver anatomy, in particular the variability of vascular supply and drainage should be conveyed. Thus, the LiverAnatomyExplorer employs case data that was extracted from contrast-enhanced abdominal CT data. Important variants of the vascular anatomy were identified primarily because their occurrence determines surgical decisions (§ 21.4.2). In addition to the learning module, there is a prototypic authoring component where tasks and solutions may be assigned to individual cases. This authoring component is carefully designed: users are strictly guided by a wizard in the process of uploading, structuring, and editing the material.

The requirement analysis among 176 students and 13 physicians revealed enthusiasm about web-based teaching, also among the physicians from which most were engaged in teaching activities. However, very few students and only a minority of physicians consider themselves as familiar with interactive 3D visualization. Thus, to avoid navigation problems in 3D content and to enable intuitive interaction has high priority.

Technical Concept All geometric models are derived from medical image data (high resolution CT angiography). A variety of segmentation techniques was used to create binary segmentation masks of all relevant structures. The raw surfaces representing the segmentation results were simplified and smoothed (reducing in a file size that was an order of magnitude smaller than before this step). The files were converted to X3D and used in a X3DOM wrapper application (Fig. e21.13).

For a web-based educational system, the performance is a crucial issue and more important than a very high accuracy. Thus, after segmentation, results may be represented in a lossy jpeg compression. Segmentation results are presented as overlays that are stored as SVG files (see Fig. e21.13). SVG, scalable vector graphics, is appropriate, since the amount of data is reduced and the visual quality, e.g., after scaling the viewer, is better than in a pixel-oriented file format. More precisely, the Raphael SVG framework

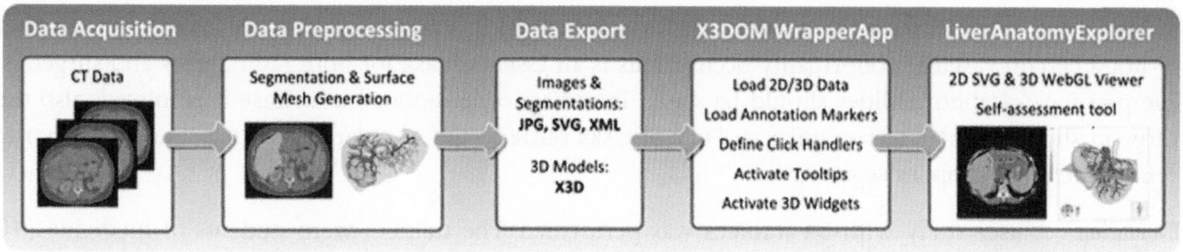

FIGURE e21.13 *Data processing for a web-based educational system includes image segmentation and transformation to formats that are suitable for web-based viewing. The actual educational system is built on top of a wrapper application based on WebGL and X3DOM* (From: [Birr et al., 2013]).

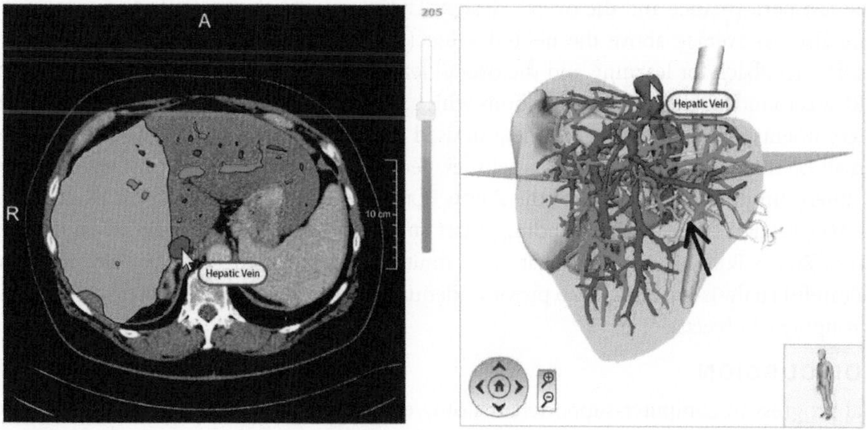

FIGURE e21.14 **Left:** *In the 2D slice view, segmentation information is presented as colored overlay. The hepatic vein is temporarily labeled after the trainee moved the cursor of its region.* **Right:** *Also in the 3D view the hepatic vein is labeled. Rotation and zooming is performed by means of the widgets placed on top of the viewer. A mannequin is integrated as orientation widget to convey the current viewing direction* (From: [Birr et al., 2013]).

along with JavaScript is employed to realize a plugin-free 2D slice viewer (Fig. e21.14, left). A very useful function is to enhance selected objects and to present labels temporarily.

XML is used to represent and label the various segmentation results. As a prerequisite for interactive 3D viewing, geometric 3D models are stored as X3D files. The X3D files have a size of 5–10 Mbytes and can be rendered in real-time (20–25 fps) with a modern graphics card.

Although the content and the specific didactic concept is focused on liver anatomy, the whole technical concept can be re-used for any other type of educational system based on medical volume data.

User Interface Design The cases are presented in 2D and 3D viewers developed on the basis of WebGL and X3D. Users can interrogate the visualizations by moving the cursor over an interesting region and getting context-sensitive information in a tooltip. Interactive 3D viewing is possible and synchronized with the 2D view, e.g., in case of selections (Fig. e21.14). A 3D widget, inspired by GOOGLE MAPS, was developed to enable stepwise rotation (30° per step) and zooming. The transitions are realized continuously by interpolating between the viewpoints to avoid sudden and confusing changes.

The LiverAnatomyExplorer also enables self-assessment. In this mode, trainees are asked, e.g., whether or not a certain vascular abnormality occurs. This is an essential task for both radiologists and surgeons. The presence of abnormalities should be stated in a diagnostic report, but in case it is missed, also the surgeon should be able to recognize it. Further tasks relate to the vascular supply, e.g., "select the portal vein branch that supplies segment five."

Evaluation A user study with 54 trainees was performed. The trainees were students of medicine (40 females, average age 24 years). After a tutorial, students used the system to explore the data and to answer quiz-like questions, which was mandatory to get further cases. After the test, a questionnaire with 14 questions was filled on a 5-point Likert scale and verbal comments were also collected. Eight questions related to user interface issues and six to the perceived learning effort. The answers to all user interface questions were—with one exception—above average with the highest values for the self-explanatory nature, the fast performance and the overall design. The answers with respect to the perceived learning effect were also on average above the neutral value (3), but lower than for the user interface-related questions. The feedback for learning and the overall learning success were assessed with 3.5. The lowest value (2.8) was found for the learning questions which turned out to be partially too difficult for students.

Verbal comments revealed that the mannequin used as orientation cue was highly welcome. The selection of small or thin structures, that is sometimes necessary to answer questions, was considered as a problem. Interestingly, the evaluation of the Zygote Body revealed the same problem [Kelc, 2012]. More advanced 3D selection techniques, including smart snapping strategies, were discussed in § 5.6.1. The evaluation of Zygote Body also revealed that often multiple 3D objects need to be selected or deselected and that a careful analysis is necessary to provide adequate support in all these situations, e.g., by enabling flexible grouping of objects.

21.3.8 DISCUSSION

Substantial progress in computer-supported anatomy education was achieved in recent years due to the availability of high resolution data, strongly improved (graphics) hardware, standards for web-based viewing as well as increasing awareness of essential didactic concepts. The complex systems described by Brenton *et al.* [2007] in highly interdisciplinary cooperations are showcase examples indicating the potential of computer support.

However, significant further development is necessary. Conceptually, this relates to a better integration into curricula, comprehensive studies and their documentation to assess learning effort and acceptance. Among few systems that not only provide substantial features to learn various aspects of anatomy, but also to support in-depth evaluation, belongs the work of Temkin *et al.* [2006].

Technologically, in particular user interface issues are essential to significantly reduce the need for cadaver dissection. For this purpose, students should be able to "feel" the anatomy. Force feedback and more intuitive 3D input should replace simple mouse-based interaction. We later discuss haptics for surgery simulation where this is used more extensively. More dynamics, e.g., visualizations of contractions and articulations of muscles are also essential features for future systems. Finally, collaboration should be better supported, e.g., with modern tabletop systems.

21.4 SURGERY EDUCATION

The design of e-learning systems for surgery has to consider the different constituents of surgery education [Mehrabi *et al.*, 2000].

- *Surgical theory* relates to factual knowledge as a basis for decision-making processes.

- *Clinical surgery* is based on surgical theory and comprises pathological variations, differential diagnosis, and therapeutic alternatives. In clinical surgery, students should critically reflect on the solution of surgical problems.
- The study of *operative techniques* is based on knowledge in the former areas and aims at skills development.

While Mehrabi *et al.* [2000] focused on surgery, a very similar discrimination is relevant for interventional radiology, where, e.g., a clot in a vascular structure is removed with a catheter. This intervention also requires similar theoretical knowledge and finally skills with respect to maneuvering a flexible catheter in vascular structures.

A related, but somewhat different classification is presented by Waxberg *et al.* [2004]. They regard the acquisition of surgical skills as a special instance of the general process of the acquisition of motor skills. This process consists of three stages:

- *a cognitive phase* where a novice becomes familiar with the process to be performed and learns how to attempt first trials,
- *the associative phase* where the subject learns to perform the skill and which teaches subtle adjustments, and
- *the autonomous phase* which begins after several months of practice and relates to the time when the skill can be performed largely automatically.

In § 21.4.2, we briefly review systems for studying surgical theory and clinical surgery and discuss one of them, dedicated to liver surgery, in more detail.

Most research on surgery education and simulation was carried out with respect to the study of operative techniques. Surgery simulators have been developed, e.g., to simulate the behavior of soft tissue or the drilling of skeletal structures, the interaction of surgical devices with soft tissue as well as different surgical techniques, secondary effects and complications. A brief review of these systems and the challenging tasks that have to be solved is given in § 21.7. With respect to the stages described above, such systems support the *associative phase*, often without supporting the cognitive phase.

e-learning Systems for Studying Clinical Surgery The potential and necessity of e-learning systems for surgery education was recognized early [Klar and Bayer, 1990]. e-learning systems for clinical surgery are necessary in order to cope with the rapid growth of relevant knowledge in the surgical disciplines [Mehrabi *et al.*, 2000]. Meanwhile, in many countries surgery simulation is also discussed as a means toward more effective and more standardized education. Due to the shortage of experienced surgeons, these experts do not have sufficient time for educational activities.

In the following, we describe two exemplary systems where the interaction with medical image data plays an essential role. The conceptual design of both systems is based on the *four-component-instructional-design model* [van Merriënboer *et al.*, 2002]. This model was selected, since it is focused on the transfer of procedural knowledge. Thus, problem-solving strategies should be improved instead of acquiring factual knowledge.

The model suggests the emphasis of subtasks that may be critical (due to the involved risk). Moreover, the arrangement of training cases into simple, moderately difficult and difficult cases is suggested. The amount of information and guidance provided by an educational system should be adapted to these different levels of difficulty. Finally, supportive information should be presented just in time (that is, when they are actually needed).

21.4.1 COGNITIVE TASK ANALYSIS FOR SURGERY AND INTERVENTIONAL TRAINING SYSTEMS

The task analysis that is necessary as a basis for designing training systems is challenging and needs to include a deep understanding of the relevant procedures. Classical techniques, such as observation of a few procedures, recording the sequence of actions and eventually supported by short interviews to prepare a *workflow description*, are a basis, but not sufficient. Experienced surgeons and interventional radiologists perform procedures with a very high level of automation, like an experienced piano player. They are not aware of most of their decisions, since they are carried out unconsciously. When asked about their approach, they can usually not fully explain why they chose a particular instrument, a particular access strategy, or why they avoided alternatives.

Cognitive task analysis is an in-depth task analysis that is usually performed by psychologists that made themselves familiar with the task to the extent of a trainee. In surgery this means, that he or she knows the basic approach, the role of all team members, the essential instruments and their importance in surgery as well as the basic workflow. Cognitive task analysis is based on several observations followed by in-depth interviews with multiple experts to discuss observations to reveal this hidden or implicit knowledge. Video recordings in order to repeatedly observe and analyze the handling are essential.

An inspiring and substantial effort has been made by Johnson *et al.* [2006] to perform a cognitive task analysis for interventional radiology. It was focused on five frequent procedures, such as arterial palpation and ultrasound-guided biopsy. As an example, arterial needle puncture is characterized as a process with 101 steps and 24 decision points, summarized in a 20 page document. These and similar descriptions are available at the website of CRaiVe (Collaborator in Radiological Interventional Virtual Environments).[10] Cognitive task analysis has also been used for informing the design of surgical training, see e.g., [Campbell *et al.*, 2011].

21.4.2 LiverSurgeryTrainer

The LiverSurgeryTrainer contains cases of patients with liver tumors that are presented with a wealth of information comprising the anamnesis and initial diagnosis, radiologic diagnosis, and image analysis results. Therapeutic decisions, such as resectability and resection strategy, can be trained. Expert opinions are integrated and used to provide feedback to the learning surgeon. The system uses planning functionalities, e.g., virtual resection (see Fig. e21.15). In particular intraoperative video sequences are employed to show how the planned resection was actually performed. In cooperation with experienced surgeons, learning objectives and more elementary goals are determined. Based on this discussion, the LiverSurgeryTrainer provides a *workflow*, starting from the anamnesis and diagnosis. Operability (based on clinical parameters) and resectability (based on the individual liver anatomy) should be evaluated based on the patient's anatomy. Figure e21.16 shows the start screen that gives an overview of the available steps.

A comprehensive overview of the LiverSurgeryTrainer is given in [Mönch *et al.*, 2013].

Medical Background We briefly explained the vascular anatomy of the liver in § 21.3.7. Thus, here we focus on tumor surgery and living donor liver transplants.

Living donor liver transplants (LDLT) are motivated by the shortage of donor organs for patients with severe and progressive liver disease. The liver of a healthy volunteer donor is split in a way that the donor can live with the remaining portion and the receiver with the resected part. LDLT is possible since the liver regenerates, that is, after surgery it grows until it reaches almost its original size after a few month. LDLT surgery is very demanding, since the whole liver needs to be split and the vascular supply and drainage

10 http://www.hpv.cs.bangor.ac.uk/CRaIVE/projects.php.

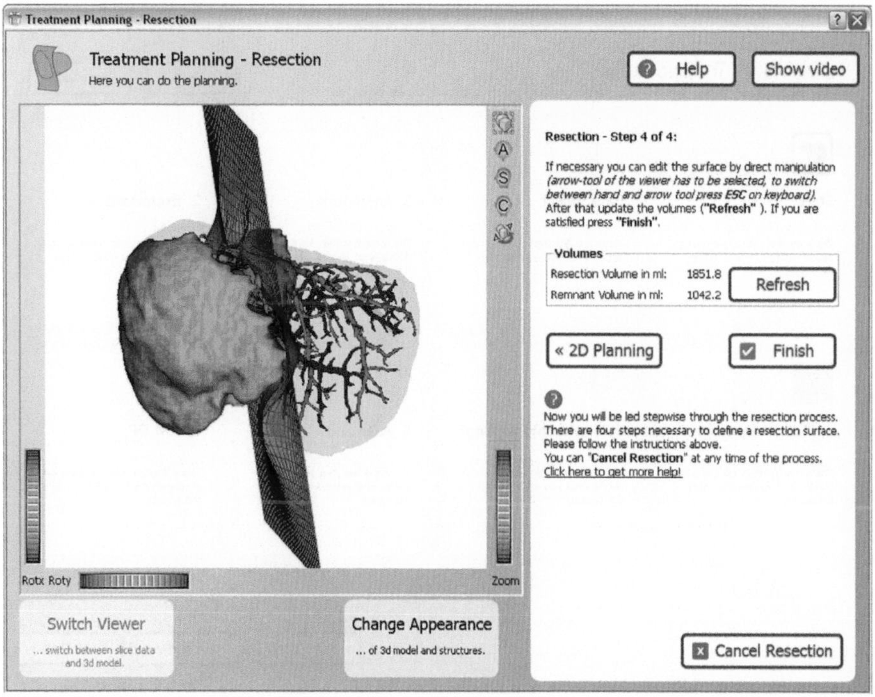

FIGURE e21.15 *The* LiverSurgeryTrainer *provides support for therapy decisions in oncologic liver surgery. A predefined workflow guides the trainee through the environment. In the current step, the resection should be planned. Later, the user can observe several sequences of an annotated intraoperative video* (Courtesy of Konrad Mühler, University of Magdeburg).

as well as the bile duct supply needs to be ensured for both the donor and the receiver. An understanding of vascular abnormalities is of paramount importance to understand whether or not a potential donor is indeed suitable.

In case of hepatic carcinoma or hepatic metastasis from colorectal cancer, surgical removal of all tumors has the best prognosis. However, this good prognosis requires that all tumors are removed with a sufficient safety margin. Thus, patients with further metastasis in other organs do not benefit, since in this systemic stage no local treatment can significantly improve survival rates. Complete surgical removal is only possible

- if the patient's general state allows a complex surgery,
- if the liver function is not severely hampered, e.g., by a late-stage cirrhosis, and
- if sufficient functional liver volume remains after surgery.

There are various typical resections that differ in their extent:

1. a *hemihepatectomy* (removal of right or left lobe of the liver),
2. an *extended hemihepatectomy* (removal of right or left lobe of the liver and additional segments), and
3. a *central resection* (removal of central/middle segments)

In addition, there are so-called non-anatomical resections, e.g., a wedge resection where a peripheral tumor with a safety margin is removed without further consideration of vascular supply areas. As in

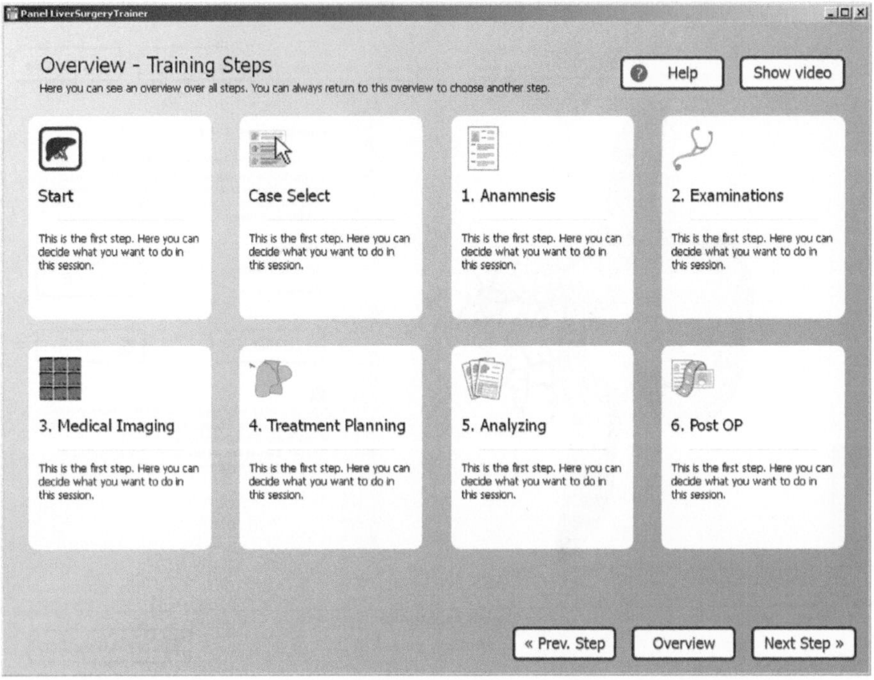

FIGURE e21.16 *The graphically oriented overview of the LiverSurgeryTrainer (Courtesy of Konrad Mühler, University of Magdeburg).*

clinical practice, training is based on bi- or triphasic contrast-enhanced CT data and derived segmentation information. In addition, clinical information is provided, e.g., to assess the severity of a cirrhosis.

Learning Objectives At a high level, the learning objectives may be specified as follows. Assistant doctors should be able to

- assess the resectability of a patient,
- determine the extent of a resection,
- plan the resection in detail, e.g., with respect to the portal vein, the hepatic artery and the veins.

These rather high-level goals require that assistant doctors know the decomposition of the liver in functional units, the so-called liver segments, the vascular structures (portal vein, hepatic vein, hepatic artery, and bile ducts) as well as their typical variants (recall § 21.3.7).

The role of the safety margin in tumor surgery is discussed in [Pawlik *et al.*, 2005]. Fischer *et al.* [2007] have shown that computer-assisted planning enhances surgical outcomes. The classification of different degrees of difficulty is also based on research in surgery, e.g., the work of Beller *et al.* [2009]. The training of LDLT cases is based on experiences in LDLT planning and donor evaluation [Radtke *et al.*, 2007].

Case Database The selection of cases and the enrichment of the image data with segmentation, planning information, such as safety margins and tumor volume, textual annotation, and expert suggestions is essential. The LiverSurgeryTrainer provides 16 cases, two of them for training decisions related to living donor liver transplants and 14 for tumor surgery. Surgical experts classified these 14 cases in three levels of difficulty (2 difficult, 7 moderately difficult, 5 easy cases). The classification of cases also considers vascular abnormalities (recall § 21.3.7). Cases with central tumor, metastases in both liver lobes and with associated severe cirrhosis are classified as more difficult, whereas easy cases contain smaller tumors in peripheral regions. The level of difficulty is the most important attribute presented to the trainees for the selection of a training case. Other essential information, such as age, gender, and major diagnosis, is also provided. A weakness of the case database is that all cases are actually resectable. Thus, the LiverSurgeryTrainer cannot illustrate why certain patients are not eligible to surgery.

According to the defined workflow, trainees should select a case, deal with the diagnostic results and perform resection planning before their result is analyzed (see Fig. e21.17).

In addition to all relevant information that is provided preoperatively, selected intraoperative views and videos are provided (Fig. e21.18). Moreover, the documented resected tissue (Fig. e21.19) is also shown to illustrate whether surgical removal was possible as intended.

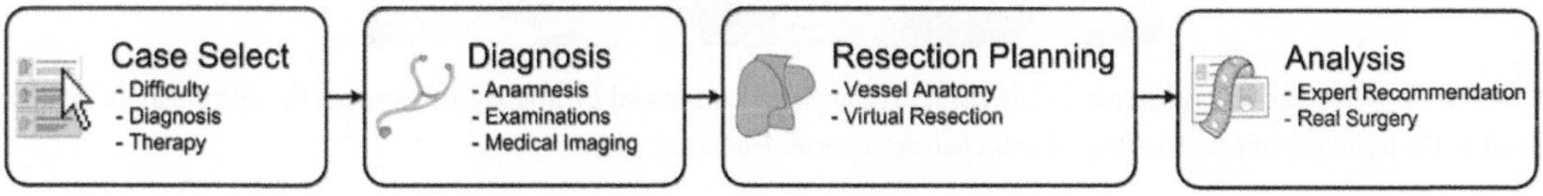

FIGURE e21.17 *Workflow supported by the LiverSurgeryTrainer. Resection planning is the core component with a number of subcomponents including 2D and 3D visualizations (Courtesy of Konrad Mühler, University of Magdeburg).*

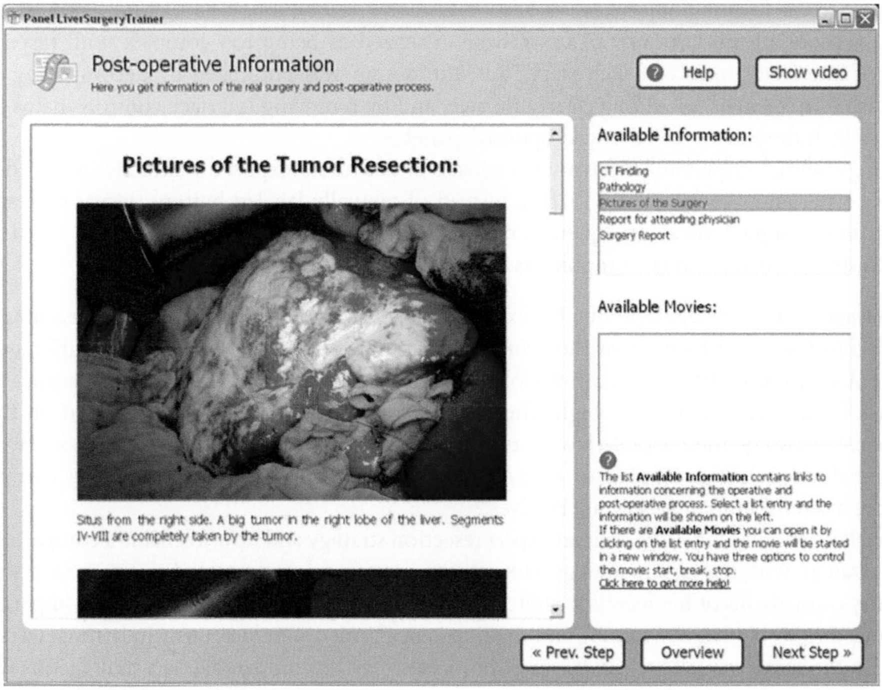

FIGURE e21.18 *Intraoperative views are provided in order to assess how the planned intervention was actually performed (Courtesy of Karl Oldhafer, General Hospital Celle).*

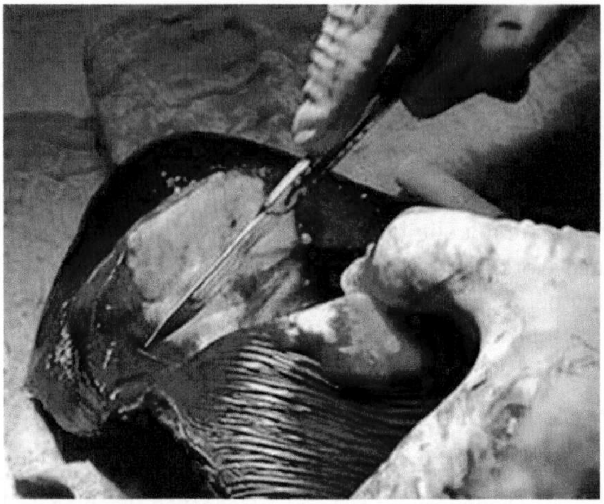

FIGURE e21.19 *The removed tumor (white tissue) is completely surrounded by liver tissue. However, the safety margin is rather small at the top of the tumor (Courtesy of Karl Oldhafer, General Hospital Celle).*

User Interface Design The whole design process was guided by a discussion of scenarios (recall § 5.2.3.2) and in later stages by feedback during evaluations of the system. Scenarios in particular helped to determine which cases are essential and how these cases should be used to enable trainees to get relevant experience with respect to the learning objectives.

Initial versions of the LiverSurgeryTrainer were criticized as being too complex with respect to the number of interface controls in each step. Thus, the design was optimized by decomposing complex actions into simpler steps, providing clear guidance, and by removing interface controls that were rarely needed, or by hiding them in "advanced options" panels.

Another essential impression from user feedback is that users expect an attractive visual design—a good user experience (recall § 5.5.3). Thus, instead of textually labeled buttons, visual representations were carefully designed. As a consequence, most panels contain a few large, primarily visual interface controls instead of many textual components (see Fig. e21.20 for examples).

Expert Feedback Adequate and reproducible expert feedback is a crucial component of e-learning systems in general. In the case of operative medicine, there is not *one* correct solution, but different feasible strategies. A solution is criticized when it violates essential guidelines, e.g., the safety margin is too low or the risk for a vital structure too high. The strategies actually used by experts depend on their own experience, but also on their *surgical school*. To reflect this aspect, two resection proposals from two experts are presented for each case. Of course, there are more viable strategies in most cases, but two proposals also invoke a careful thinking about alternatives.

A crucial question is how to present an expert resection strategy and how to enable a comparison of the trainee's strategy with the expert strategy. The resection strategy is represented in a resection shape. The trainee may compare his or her resection strategy with that of an expert as a side-by-side comparison with synchronized viewers (that is, zooming and rotation is performed simultaneously in both viewers, see Fig. e21.21). In the same way, also the two expert proposals may be compared. The simultaneous display of all three resections was considered inappropriate, since resections are rather complex and there is neither enough space at a typical screen, nor it is convenient to compare three complex shapes simultaneously.

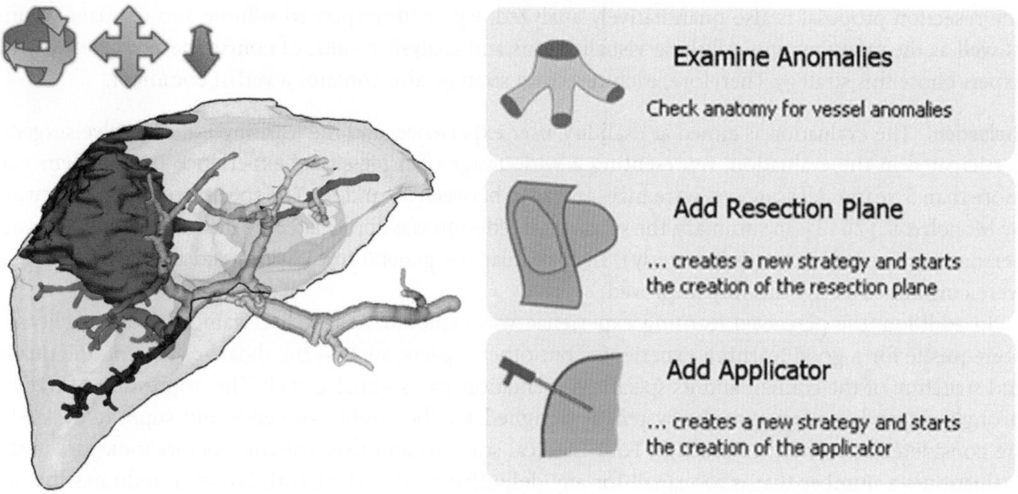

FIGURE e21.20 **Left:** Incremental 3D interaction with appropriate buttons is less flexible but easier to control and better suited for the target user group. **Right:** For all steps, a carefully designed icon is provided (Courtesy of Konrad Mühler, University of Magdeburg).

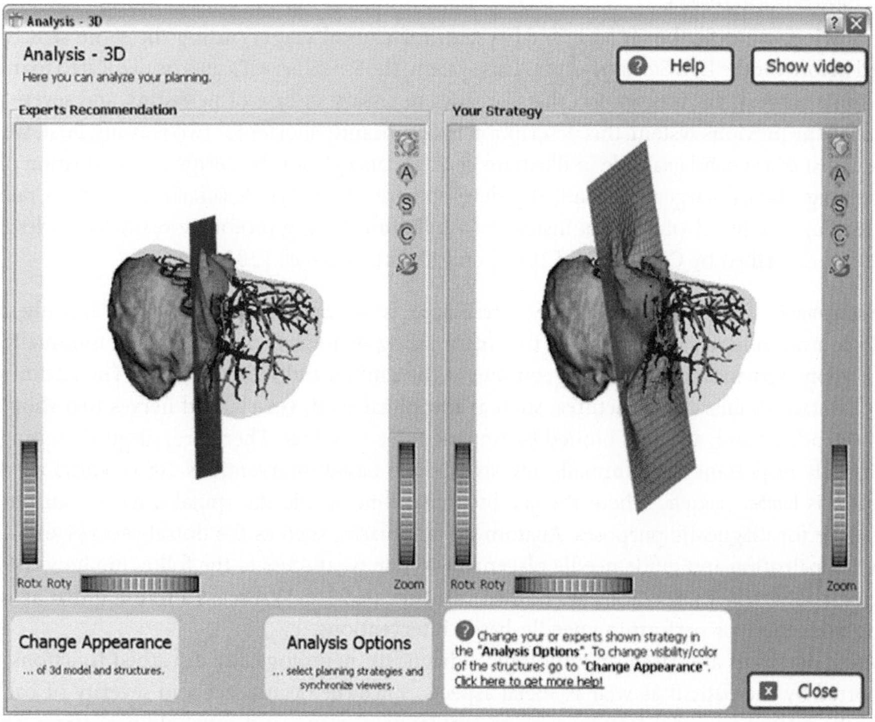

FIGURE e21.21 The resection proposal performed by an expert and by a trainee are compared in synchronized 3D viewers (Courtesy of Konrad Mühler, University of Magdeburg).

The resection proposal is also quantitatively analyzed, e.g., with respect to volume and remnant volume as well as the safety margin. All these visualizations and analysis results, of course, do not reveal *why* the expert chose this strategy. Therefore, each resection strategy also contains a verbal comment.

Evaluation The evaluation is aimed at usability, user experience, and the learning effect. Twelve surgeons participated in the evaluation, representing a wide range of professional experience (six of them with more than 5 years). All surgeons were male and aged between 27 and 63. The specific results are discussed by Mönch *et al.* [2013]. In summary, the substantial redesign was appreciated by the test persons (the same persons participated in an earlier study). In particular the general impression, and the ease of learning were considered as significantly improved.

In addition, the perceived learning experience was explored. At least a certain level of usability is a prerequisite for a good learning experience, but other aspects, such as the didactic concept, the quality and structure of the content and its specific presentation are essential as well. The impression of trainees strongly depends on whether the system is designed for the "right" audience and supports tasks that are considered as relevant in practice. Four medical students and two assistant doctors took part in that evaluation—a number that is too small for any definitive results. The trend, however, indicates that test persons improved their understanding of the planning workflow, the abilities to explore the 3D models and to virtually resect patients [Mönch *et al.*, 2013]. Thus, they will likely be able to use complex planning tools. It remains to be evaluated how such a training improves other skills relevant for clinical practice.

21.4.3 SPINESURGERYTRAINER

In the following, we describe an additional system for clinical surgery using the same structure as we employed before for the LIVERSURGERYTRAINER. This system, the SPINESURGERYTRAINER, is dedicated to minimally-invasive spine surgery, an intervention that becomes necessary in case of persisting and severe prolapse. Compared to the previous system, this description is significantly shorter for two reasons. First, we describe this system just as a second example to illustrate general concepts for the design and evaluation of systems for supporting clinical surgery. Second, the development of the SPINESURGERYTRAINER was a rather small project, leading to a proof-of-concept instead of a fully functioning prototype ready for widespread use. The system is described by Cordes *et al.* [2008] and Kellermann *et al.* [2011].

Medical Background The focus of the SPINESURGERYTRAINER is orthopedic spine surgery [Oppenheimer *et al.*, 2009]. In contrast to open surgery where the surrounding anatomy is directly visible, minimally-invasive surgery is more demanding for the surgeon due to the limited and indirect vision. The anatomy around the spine contains vulnerable structures, such as the spinal cord, vessels, and nerves that should not be hurt. On the other hand, access is limited by impenetrable vertebrae. Therefore, surgical training systems are particularly important for minimally-invasive needle-based interventions. An essential needle-based intervention is **lumbar puncture**, where the cerebrospinal fluid inside the spinal canal is extracted with a biopsy needle for diagnostic purposes. Anatomical landmarks, such as the dorsal process and iliac crest, are found by palpation and guide needle placement. While we discuss in the following how the anatomy is displayed and treatment decisions are trained, we later (§ 21.6.3) discuss a training that also involves the dexterity needed for performing needle-based interventions.

Treatment decisions are based on radiological diagnosis, neurologically disturbed functions, discomforts reported by the patient as well as social aspects, since the occurrence and severity of back pain is known to be related to social factors, such as employment status and psychological stress. The spatial relation between nerval and spinal structures as well as the location of the spine in relation to surrounding muscles and vascular structures has to be considered [Cordes *et al.*, 2008]. While access from the back

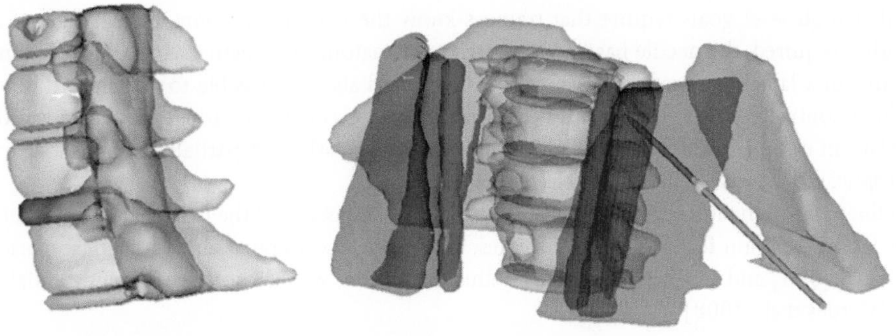

FIGURE e21.22 **Left:** *The anatomy of the spine.* **Right:** *The spine and its surrounding anatomy where a needle needs to be carefully maneuvered to avoid damage to crucial structures* (Courtesy of Kathrin Hintz, University of Magdeburg).

is by far easier, since only very few structures are encountered, it may be impossible due to the specific location of the pathology. Figure e21.22 illustrates the relation between the needle and crucial anatomical structures. In particular, herniated disks in the cervical region often require frontal access (along a variety of essential structures in the neck). But even in this region, sometimes the (easier) access from the back is possible and should be chosen in these cases.

Learning Objectives Using the SpineSurgeryTrainer, trainees should reinforce their relevant anatomical knowledge (on top of the assumed basic knowledge). In addition, they should learn how

- to decide on an effective therapy,
- to access the pathology (see Fig. e21.23),
- small variations of the position and orientation of the affected vertebral influence the decision with respect to the access.

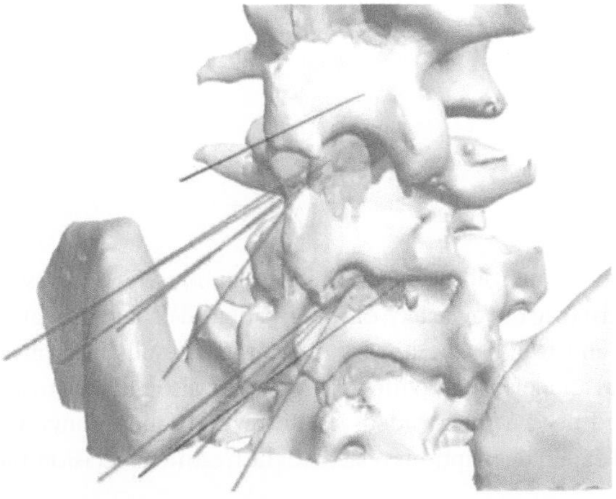

FIGURE e21.23 *Possible (green) and impossible (red) needle placement in the cervical spine. To get an intuitive understanding of possible needle angulation and placement is an essential learning goal in spine surgery training* (Courtesy of Mathias Färber, University of Lübeck).

These rather high-level goals require that trainees know the relevant anatomy. In particular if a ventral access path is required, the needle has to pass a variety of anatomical structures and some of them should not be hurt. In a later stage, as an additional goal it should also be possible to understand how exactly the needle is controlled. This goal requires that the different elasticity of tissue types is conveyed, that is, haptics plays an essential role. With this addition, the SPINESURGERYTRAINER partially belongs to a system for studying *operation techniques* [Kellermann *et al.*, 2011].

The refinement of the learning objectives as well as the discussion of the case database and the specific user interface were again focused on user stories, and derived conceptual and concrete scenarios (recall Benyon *et al.* [2005] and § 5.2.3.2). To convey this discussion, we cite portions of an essential concrete scenario [Cordes *et al.*, 2008]:

> *"During the planning of the injection the assistant doctor has to pay attention to follow the right injection path to avoid lesions of important structures and to place the needle to the target point* [Comment 1]. *To understand how to place the injection, he clicks on the help button in the menu and reads the help texts for this step. After that, he chooses the therapy by clicking the button "Injection" and starts the planning. With a left mouse click he defines one marker for the penetration point and one for the target point of the needle in the 2D view. Therefore, he has to navigate through the slices by using a slider next to the viewer. The needle takes up its position. In an animation (started by pressing the button "Show animation") the user can observe the injection of the needle to his defined position. He can also manually move the needle forwards and backwards, using a slider, to get a better impression of the injection path and the penetrated structures."* [Comment 1: *A warning should be presented, if a collision with important structures occurs.*]

The comment is just one example of feedback from experienced medical doctors. The learning objectives are not comprehensive, e.g., the insertion of an artificial spinal disk, the resection of a spinal disk or other related treatment steps cannot be trained.

Case Database The surgical intervention differs strongly depending on the specific vertebra involved. Thus, ideally the case database should contain cases from the cervical, thoracic, and lumbar spine. For each case, CT and MRI data are relevant and should be provided along with the segmentation information, e.g., the spinal canal. The image data, e.g., the selection of MR sequences is guided by the recognizability of the following structures:

- the vertebral bodies,
- the spinal disks,
- the dura, and
- the nerve roots.

As anatomical context also the thyroid gland, trachea, gullet, muscles and vessels should be delineated.

In addition to image data, again, a variety of other patient data is essential to support treatment decisions. These include age and weight, the history of pain, the results of a physical examination and the assessment of professional and leisure activities. The latter are also relevant to assess which limitations are crucial for the patient and need to be avoided. Again, revised (and anonymized) reports from surgery, videos, photographs, and expert descriptions related to the treatment decision and postoperative follow-up are provided.

In order to support decision-making, we deliberately integrated very similar cases where the "right" treatment decisions differ. To find such very similar cases in real patient data might be very difficult, since they might be rare. However, with enough medical knowledge, the data of one case may be slightly changed, e.g., by a small rotation of a prolapse or another minor shift in the anatomy to "create" the new case. Of course, care is necessary to avoid situations that are not plausible or even obviously impossible.

User Interface Design The concrete user interface design is guided by scenario-related specifications and a decomposition according to the components of the *four-component-instructional-design model* (recall van Merriënboer *et al.* [2002]). As an example, one subtask is to familiarize with 3D interaction (picking, zooming, rotation). This subtask is relevant for some trainees and is supported by a 3D viewer with a simple 3D model and step-by-step instruction. Any supportive information, e.g., help texts, are displayed along with a dialog or as balloon help.

Similar to the LiverSurgeryTrainer, a workflow is suggested and presented in the left column of the overall layout (see Fig. e21.24).

The user is directed through that workflow and offered information for each step. This information does not only relate to handling the system but also to expert comments describing and explaining their choices. In the *analysis step* the trainee can compare his or her therapy strategy visually and textually with those of two experts.

The visualization in this system is not optimized with respect to perceptual aspects. With an adaptive use of transparency, enhanced contrasts or an emphasis of the needle, the system's impression may certainly

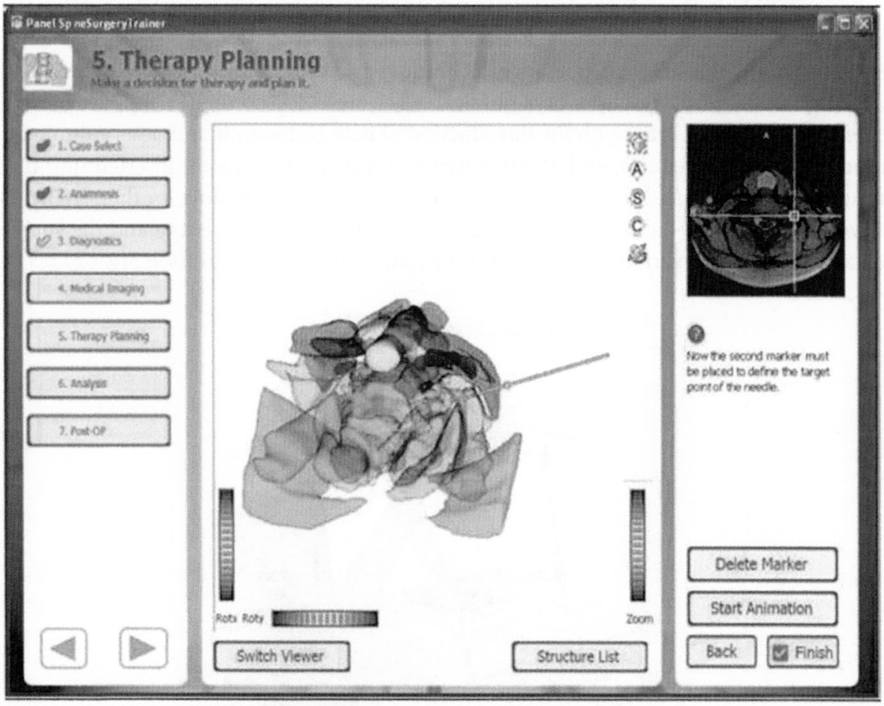

FIGURE e21.24 Basic layout of the SpineSurgeryTrainer that follows the workflow represented by the steps in the left column. In the current step, the trainee can practice needle placement. The 3D model of the cervical spine region includes vertebrae, spinal disks, nerve roots, and surrounding structures. After defining the penetration and target point of the needle in a slice view, the trainee checks the position of the needle in the 3D model and observes an animation of the needle placement (Courtesy of Kathrin Hintz, University of Magdeburg).

be improved. Needle insertion in a complex anatomical setting is also a use case where stereoscopic rendering is likely to be helpful.

The most essential task is to define the path of a needle. Since the needle is not elastic, it follows a linear path and thus the user has to define two distinct points:

- the *penetration point* (sometimes called *puncture point*), and
- the *target point* of the virtual needle.

2D and 3D visualizations are provided to define and eventually adjust these points. To convey the effects of a virtual needle insertion, the affected anatomical structures are emphasized. We also discussed to move them apart by virtual spread tools. An even better support would be achieved if a realistic soft tissue deformation would be integrated.

Evaluation An essential aspect in the informal evaluation was that trainees indeed understood *transitions* in the treatment decision due to small changes of the patient status. This is probably the most general finding of this development: Systems for training clinical surgery should be based on an analysis of such transitions and deliberately integrate them in the training process.

21.5 SIMULATION FOR SURGERY AND INTERVENTIONAL RADIOLOGY

Computer support for the study of operative techniques is motivated by the desire to avoid damage to patients early in the learning curve of a physician. The need for computer support in this area has strongly increased in the last years with the introduction of new endoscopic and other minimally-invasive interventions. In these procedures, endoscopic instruments and a camera are inserted into the patient's body through natural or artificial orifices. These procedures reduce the trauma for the patient and lead to faster recovery. For the surgeon, the direct view to the operating situs is missing and the surgeon has to learn the handling of new instruments developed for minimally-invasive use (see Fig. e21.25).

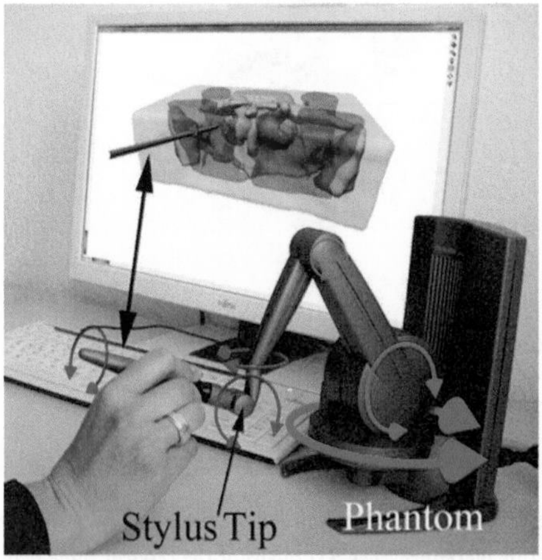

FIGURE e21.25 *In an extended version, needle placement is enhanced with force feedback. However, the tissue is still considered as static and thus, the realism of the training is limited (Courtesy of Kerstin Kellermann, University of Magdeburg).*

Even experienced surgeons have to obtain new skills, in particular with respect to the *eye-hand coordination*. It is documented for many interventions that the rate of complications is strongly related to the experience of the operator with this particular intervention. Therefore, a risk-free learning environment as well as the training of a wide range of clinical cases is required [Sierra *et al.*, 2003].

Without computer support, surgeons either use dedicated mechanical systems (referred to as "endo trainers" or "box trainers"), animals, or cadaveric material. The same elongated instruments as used in minimally-invasive interventions are used in these settings. Some mechanical systems are restricted to the manipulation of plastic objects which do not provide the elasticity of living tissue. The use of animals and cadaveric material is more realistic, but also not as realistic as desired—in particular the perfusion of living tissue makes a strong difference. Moreover, the use of animals poses ethical problems and is expensive. These drawbacks are the primary motivation for the development of surgery simulators [Delingette and Ayache, 2005].

Computer support for studying *operation techniques* requires surgery simulators that provide a look and feel close to real interventions at the living patient. Correct (visually realistic) organ models and textures are an important prerequisite. This requirement, however, also yields for anatomy education and relates to models and datasets (recall § 21.2.1).

The degree of realism that is actually required in training systems is an aspect of ongoing debate. The hypotheses that increased realism leads to faster or improved skills assessment have not really been supported by user studies. It is even discussed whether a certain amount of abstraction leads to optimal training effects in capabilities such as hand-eye coordination.

Oropesa *et al.* [2010] suggest that some of the distracting factors in a real operating situation should be avoided in virtual reality-based training. There is no definitive answer on how important an accurate visualization of bleedings, coagulation and fume actually is for the training effectiveness. However, for the acceptance of training among both trainees and experts, a high degree of realism is likely essential, even beyond the degree that improves efficiency.

Even the importance of force feedback for minimally-invasive training is questioned according to some study results. It may be sufficient to visually indicate closeness of an instrument to certain tissues. In the survey of Oropesa *et al.* [2010], three out of five surgical simulation systems provide force feedback only on an optional basis and one does not provide it at all. Figure e21.26 gives an example where the distance of a surgical instrument (trocar) to the spleen and pancreas is color-coded, instead of making use of force feedback.

A general decision in the design of surgical simulators is whether surface or volume representations should be used. Speed of rendering and collision detection are advantages of surface models [Brodlie *et al.*, 2000]. More accurate physical simulation is in general achieved with volume representations.

One essential aspect of realism in surgery simulators is the ability to perform arbitrary free-form cuts. This particular aspect was discussed in § 9.9, since it is also essential for surgery planning. However, we did not consider soft tissue deformation of the manipulated tissue that will be discussed in the following, along with other requirements essential for surgery simulation:

- *Soft tissue deformation*. Soft tissue should behave naturally when forces are applied and when the tissue is teared or cut.
- *Variable training scenarios*. Effective training requires variable scenarios with respect to anatomical variants, as well as to pathological variations, complications that need to be handled, etc.
- *Haptic interaction*. Realistic training with haptic devices is essential, in particular to support eye-hand coordination. Appropriate force-feedback devices are required and a fast update is necessary, since the tactile sense has a very high temporal resolution.

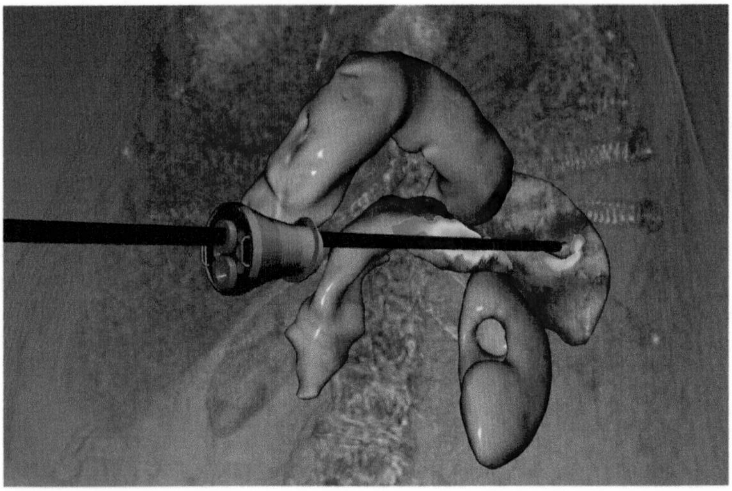

FIGURE e21.26 *When an instrument approaches an organ closer than a threshold, this distance is color-coded on the organ surface. The instrument is below the stomach and above the left kidney (Courtesy of Simon Adler, Fraunhofer IFF Magdeburg).*

- *Collision detection.* If surgical instruments touch anatomical structures (or other instruments), these collisions need to be detected very fast to initiate a physically plausible response.
- *Realization of surgical devices, procedures, and effects.* In surgical interventions, various devices, e.g., drill tools and scalpels, are employed in a well-defined manner. These devices need to be modeled with respect to geometry and behavior. The resulting effects, e.g., bleeding if vasculature is hurt, irrigation, and coagulation smoke, must be modeled in a plausible (not necessarily realistically) manner.

Figure e21.27 summarizes the components of a virtual reality surgical simulator, that we discuss in the following. In an implementation, the control flow may differ and may be more flexible than using a "central component" for all interactions between the components.

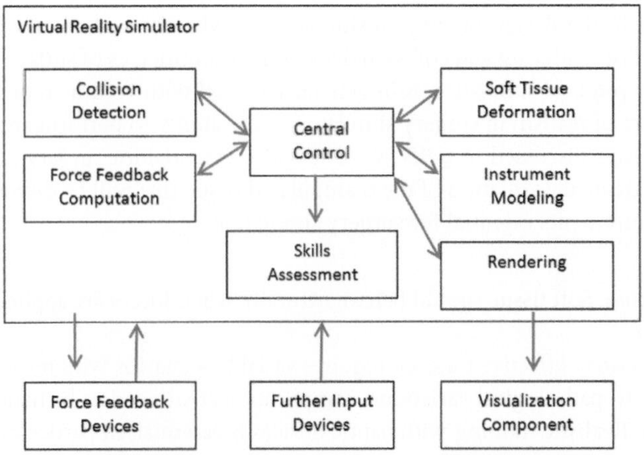

FIGURE e21.27 *Basic components of a virtual reality simulator and related input and output components as well as their interaction.*

Force feedback is realized with either one or two devices (*dual force feedback*), e.g., to practice needle placement while holding an ultrasound probe. The "visualization component" may be a conventional screen. However, to provide the desired level of immersion and engagement for procedural training, stereo rendering or even more immersive VR workbenches are useful (see, e.g., the work of Ullrich *et al.* [2010]). At least binocular goggles should be provided.

21.5.1 SOFT TISSUE DEFORMATION

Real-time and precise simulation of soft tissue deformation is still a major challenge. Different methods are used to accomplish the simulation, resulting in a different speed and accuracy. A realistic estimation of stiffness parameters (Young's modulus, shear modulus, bulk modulus, viscosity) is required as basis for the simulation models. The reliable approximation of these input parameters is difficult. Ex vivo measurements are not reliable, since the degree of perfusion of an organ has a strong influence on its elastic properties [Delingette and Ayache, 2005]. Non-invasive invivo measures may be accomplished by employing the fact that the elasticity of a sample is related to the velocity of sound waves which can be measured with ultrasound.

Soft tissue deformation in surgery simulators is in general based on the theory of continuum mechanics (more precisely *elasticity theory*) which has been used for a long time to analyze and predict deformations of elastic bodies. Human tissue is characterized by a non-linear relation between forces and resulting deformations. Also, hysteresis effects occur [Maurel *et al.*, 1998].

The method of reference to computationally handle elasticity theory is the Finite Element Method (FEM), which was briefly described in Chapter 19 in the context of CFD (computational fluid dynamics).

The specific resistance of tissue for a deformation is either derived directly from the image data or it is assigned to a specific tissue type. With CT data structures of high density, such as bones, have a high resistance, whereas structures with moderate or low intensity have a rather low resistance. More precise modeling is possible, if all relevant areas are segmented and assigned to a certain tissue type, such as skin, or muscle, and stiffness properties for these tissues are employed.

Finite Element Modeling Similar to blood flow, also the behavior of soft tissue can be described by the Navier-Stokes equations, systems of non-linear partial differential equations [Ciarlet, 1988]. FEM, based on an appropriate discretization of the spatial domain is employed to numerically approximate the solution of these equations. Similar to blood flow simulations, the discretization of the domain is often realized as a tetrahedral grid that is constructed based on a triangle surface mesh and completely fills the anatomical structure. As a difference, in soft tissue simulation it is usually not necessary to represent the wall-near structures with a higher accuracy (and different grid type).

Besides the grid type and the actual volume mesh, boundary conditions which restrict the deformation and the selection of appropriate time steps for the numerical solution influence the stability, the speed, and the accuracy of the solution. To prevent instabilities in the simulation, thin and elongated tetrahedra should be avoided. An overview on 3D mesh generation is given by Bern and Plassmann [1999].

FEM allows a precise modeling of soft tissue deformation. The deformations resulting from manipulations, such as poking, tearing, pulling, and cutting might be represented realistically. FEM has been used for surgery simulation for almost two decades (first described by Bro-Nielsen and Gramkow [1996]). In general, precise FEM simulations are very slow. This gave rise to a number of variations and completely different simulation methods.

For cutting, the affected tetrahedra need to be subdivided [Bielsen *et al.*, 1999]. This, however, may also introduce an increased stiffness of the system due to the increased element number. As an alternative, the nodes can be repositioned in order to prevent the complexity of the grid from increasing considerably [Nienhuys and van der Stappen, 2001]. A simplified version of FEM solutions (considering only linear elasticity) was presented by Nienhuys and van der Stappen [2001]. For small deformations (less than 10% of the organ size), *linear elasticity* is considered a valid approximation [Delingette and Ayache, 2005]. For a more recent overview on soft tissue deformation derived from continuum mechanics, see Famaey and VanderSloten [2008].

Simulation with Mass-spring Models Mass-spring models are based on a mesh consisting of masses (nodes) and springs which connect the masses (recall § 20.5.2, where we discussed the use of mass-spring models for model-based segmentation). Strut springs are often added to keep the mass-spring surfaces maintain their shape. Deformations are realized applying Hooke's law that performs a linear elasticity approximation (that is reasonable for small deformations).

The topology of the mesh and the spring parameters determine the behavior of a mass-spring model in a simulation. In order to simulate the dynamics of a mass-spring system, the relation between position, velocity, and acceleration for the mass m_i at point p_i at time t can be described as [Waters and Terzopoulos, 1990]:

$$F_i^{ext}(t) = m_i \frac{d^2 p_i(t)}{dt^2} + \gamma \frac{dp_i(t)}{dt} + F_i^{int}(t) \quad \text{(e21.1)}$$

γ denotes a damping factor, $F_i^{int}(t)$ denotes the internal elastic force caused by strains of adjacent springs of p_i. $F_i^{ext}(t)$ is the sum of all external forces. The dynamics is thus described by a system of second-order ordinary differential equations. For an efficient numerical solution, Equation e21.1 is typically reduced to two coupled first-order differential equations. Either Euler's method or a higher order Runge-Kutta method is employed to solve the equation system (recall [Waters and Terzopoulos, 1990]). Figure e21.28 illustrates the use of mass-spring models for simulating deformations and cutting procedures. Bro-Nielsen *et al.* [1998] used mass-spring models for an abdominal trauma surgery simulator.

To enable fast simulations, the propagation of forces in the mass-spring model may be restricted. Choi *et al.* [2003] suggest a layer model and estimate—depending on the depth of the penetration—which layers need to be considered in the force propagation. Obviously, based on the damping factors, more distant nodes in a mass-spring model are affected less. To avoid lengthy computations of small effects, the propagation may be stopped.

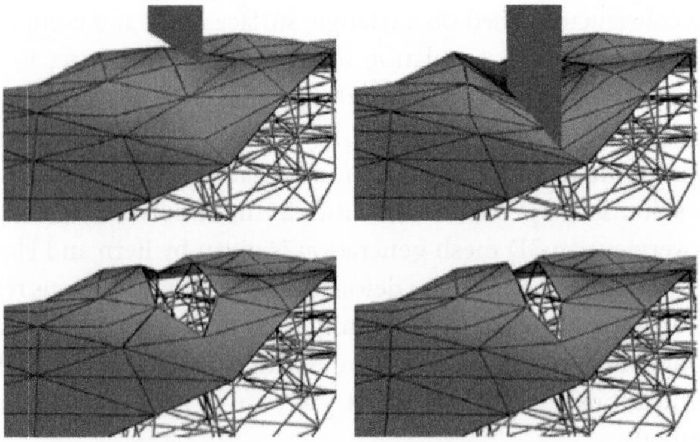

FIGURE e21.28 *Simulating soft tissue deformation with a surgical instrument using mass-spring models (images above). Also cutting procedures may be simulated in a plausible manner with mass-spring models (images below) (From: [Teschner et al., 2000]).*

Simulations based on mass-spring models are generally faster than simulations based on FEMs at the expense of accuracy. In general, it is difficult to derive spring constants such that a realistic behavior results.

21.5.2 VARIABLE TRAINING SCENARIOS

The need for variable training scenarios is described by Sierra *et al.* [2004]. They compare surgical training with flight training and argue that flight training with an invariable landscape and constant weather conditions would not be effective. Similar, repeated surgical training with the same organ "obscures training since the user adapts to this special anatomy." Three strategies are possible to develop variable training scenarios:

- A large number of individual patient data is selected and analyzed to represent the variety of anatomical and pathological variations.
- The data are generated with dedicated modeling tools instead of reconstructing models from clinical data.
- Based on a clinical datasets, *parameterizable models* of the anatomy and pathology are developed to generate individual cases flexibly. The problems of reconstructing, simplifying and smoothing surface models have to be solved within this strategy.

All three strategies have their merits and pitfalls. The first, more conventional strategy, requires to analyze a large variety of medical volume data, which involves laborious segmentation tasks. Even a larger selection might be considered as too restrictive by surgical users. The advantage of this method is that all examples are realistic with respect to the morphology of the relevant objects and the spatial relations between them. The second strategy requires an enormous modeling effort to provide sufficiently realistic models. Freeform modeling with variants of B-spline and Bézier patches is not only time-consuming, but requires considerable experience. An advantage of this strategy is that the problems of correcting and smoothing reconstructed models may be avoided.

The alternative is to employ either one or only a few models and adjust parameters to vary anatomical shapes and pathological variations. This strategy requires to study and represent the variability of anatomical structures as well as an understanding of the growth process of pathological variations. Care is necessary to avoid the generation of unrealistic models.

Parameterizable Models The use of parameterizable models for surgical training has been suggested by Sierra *et al.* [2004]. They use active shape models (ASM), often employed for model-based image segmentation (recall § 4.5.3 and Cootes *et al.* [1994]) to represent anatomical variations. By adjusting the major modes of variation, they can thus generate an arbitrary number of different instances of an organ. For pathological variations, statistical models are not feasible, since the range of pathological cases varies too strongly. Instead, they attempt to model the growth processes and came up with a model of tumor growth. Cellular automatons are based on a simple set of rules which allows to simulate a large variety of growing phenomena, including aspects of tumor growth. Such simulations should also consider that a pathology arises in a certain organ and is adapted to it and other surrounding structures [Sierra *et al.*, 2003].

Later, the tumor growth model was significantly enhanced [Lloyd *et al.*, 2007]. With the enhanced model, the growth of the tumor is coupled with angiogenic sprouting. Thus, the later stages of a tumor disease with significant neoangiogenesis are modeled and oxygen and blood support is integrated. Such a model is very useful for surgery simulation, but of course enables also more basic science experiments related to an *understanding* of tumor diseases.

Toward Automatic Mesh Generation The use of variable training scenarios also has consequences for other aspects of surgery simulation. It is no longer feasible to generate the meshes for soft tissue simulation with a large amount of manual work. Instead, the meshes have to be generated in a fully automatic fashion, which represents a serious difficulty, since the meshes have to fulfill a variety of requirements to allow an efficient and numerically stable simulation (recall § 19.3.2).

21.5.3 COLLISION DETECTION

Collision detection is the general term for algorithms that detect objects touching or penetrating each other. This information is essential, e.g., to provide realistic force feedback. But even without force feedback, collision detection provides increased realism. Otherwise, tools are just moved through bones and other anatomical structures leading to a very unrealistic experience.

Collision detection algorithms compute the

- pair of involved objects,
- the area of contact,
- the depth of a penetration, and
- the angle of penetration.

Training systems for surgery and interventional radiology require real-time feedback, which is difficult to achieve due to the typically large geometric complexity of anatomical structures. With this requirement, *penalty-based methods* are favored that apply a force that depends on the penetration depth of a rigid object in a deformable object [Raghupathi *et al.*, 2004].

There are different categories of collision detection problems and consequently different algorithms and data structures to perform the necessary computations fast and precise enough. In the training of surgery and interventional procedures, there are three fundamentally different situations:

- procedures applied to non-deformable objects, such as drilling a bone with a bone burr, and
- procedures, where soft tissue deformations occur, such as penetrating skin with a needle,
- procedures, where both the tool and the affected tissue are deformable objects, e.g., when a guide wire is inserted in a vascular structure.

Obviously, the second situation is more challenging than the first, since constant updates of a large geometry representation against which collisions are checked, is required. The third type of situation primarily occurs interventional radiology. It is even more demanding and viable solutions emerged only recently (and will be discussed later).

A comprehensive and up-to-date review of collision detection is given by Teschner *et al.* [2005]. In general, a discrimination is made between *rigid body* and *deformable object* collision detection. Self occlusions may occur when deformable objects are considered. Unfortunately, simulating soft tissue in surgery simulators falls into the latter class of collision detection problems. Volumetric as well as surface models are employed for surgical simulation and collision detection. With both kinds of models, a general strategy is to adapt the resolution of the surface or volume mesh by re-tessellating around the region of the cut.

Modeling of Surgical Tools Collision detection in surgical simulators usually considers surgical tools as non-deformable objects. The simplest (and fastest) representation of a surgical tool considers only *one* contact point at the tip of an instrument to be checked for collisions. For some instruments, e.g., a sphere-shaped burr for drilling bones, this would be a very coarse simplification (in § 21.7.2, we discuss the training of bone drilling).

In other systems, e.g., that presented by Basdogan *et al.* [2004], collision detection is applied to a straight line, greatly simplifying any device that is more complex than a needle. A cylinder representation is more accurate to reflect the volumetric nature of most tools.

Algorithms for collision detection fall into two categories:

- *deterministic algorithms*, which precisely compute collisions and related information, and
- *stochastic algorithms* that employ probabilistic assumptions and approximate the required information.

We do not consider stochastic algorithms here, although they are potentially useful for surgery simulation, since they allow to balance real-time requirements with accuracy. The interested reader is referred to Klein and Zachmann [2003].

Hierarchical Data Structures for Collision Detection To efficiently detect collisions, space partitioning schemes are employed (recall § 10.4 where such data structure for distance computations were discussed). Axis-aligned bounding boxes (AABB), oriented bounding boxes (OBB), k-dimensional discrete orientation polytops (k-DOPs), and bounding spheres are among the widely used data structures for efficient collision detection. With such data structures, the necessary tests and computations can be restricted to a subset of leafs of a hierarchy. However, the use of hierarchical data structures requires additional setup time to construct the hierarchy and additional time to update and adapt the hierarchy as a consequence of motions and collisions.

For the non-rigid soft tissue objects considered in surgery simulation, the update process is considerably more complex than for rigid objects. Teschner *et al.* [2005] argue that for this task AABBs are the most appropriate data structure. Here, the structure of an AABB tree can be kept, but the extent of the nodes has to be corrected. Other structures, e.g., k-DOPs and OBBs, enclose the geometry more tightly (see also vanDenBergen [1997]). Spillmann *et al.* [2007] employed bounding spheres hierarchies and combined collision detection with an efficient *collision response*, using the again the hierarchy for efficiency.

An efficient collision handling scheme was introduced by García-Pérez *et al.* [2009]. They applied a fuzzy logic scheme to infer parameters of the collision response. With this system, the interpenetration of several vertices, affected by a collision, may be avoided. The system aims particularly at laparoscopic surgery simulators.

Collision Detection for Simulating Intravascular Interventions While general solutions for efficient collision detections are available and mature, there is still a demand for refined and advanced algorithms to cope with special challenges. As an example, the collisions of instruments moved inside vascular structures with the vessel wall, are very expensive to compute with the methods described above. This is due to the fact that the instruments are so close to the complex vascular anatomy that the computation does not benefit strongly from the object hierarchy. Li *et al.* [2012] present a solution to reduce the search space for collisions using a search tree that represents the vessel centerline and its bifurcations. Such support is indeed necessary to achieve real-time performance in training systems for intravascular interventions (see § 21.6.5).

21.5.4 FORCE AND TACTILE FEEDBACK

We briefly discussed force feedback in § 5.7.2. Due to its particular importance for training interventional radiology and surgery we extend this discussion here.

The tactile sense plays an essential role for any task where objects should be grasped in virtual reality. Movement times are reduced and the perceived level of difficulty decreases simultaneously. These aspects are in particular relevant in many surgical tasks. Force feedback adds to the effect of collision detection—both features improve the exploration of a complex target anatomy and make it faster [Kellermann *et al.*, 2011]. Three main categories of haptics are essential for surgery and interventional procedures [Coles *et al.*, 2011]:

- *tactile feedback*,
- *force feedback*, and
- *torque feedback*.

Tactile Feedback represents our sensations when deliberately touching a surface. Tactile includes a sensation of the roughness, stiffness, and texture, as well as the sensation of wetness and temperature. In medicine it is essential for palpation, e.g., palpation of the pulse, or a surface-near tumor.

Force Feedback represents the resistance of obstacle. Thus, force feedback is crucial for needle placement tasks where the resistance of different tissue types when being penetrated needs to be perceived. Blunt dissection is another important surgical task where force feedback leads to lower error rates and reduced task completion times [Wagner *et al.*, 2002].

Torque Feedback is perceived when an instrument is rotated. It is closely related to force feedback, since it also represents a sense of resistance. Catheters and guide wires are strongly sensitive for torque movements, since almost no twisting occurs.

All these components of haptic feedback are based on computing forces representing the interaction between surgical devices or other instruments and the patient's anatomy. Ideally, all three components are computed. Force feedback depends on the position and orientation of the applied force, i.e., an accurate force feedback needs to be computed for six degrees of freedom (DOF).

This computation must be very efficient, since a high update rate is necessary to be perceived as realistic. The magic number, cited very often, is that a frequency of 1 kHZ is the minimum. Coles *et al.* [2011] discuss a number of precise investigations that indicate that the necessary frequency is overestimated with 1 kHz. The credible study performed by Booth *et al.* [2003] leads to a minimum frequency of 550–600 Hz and considers that this number also depends on the specific kind of contact. Stiff contacts require a slightly higher frequency of feedback than softer contacts. In essence, the necessary update rate is significantly higher than that for visual feedback (30 Hz), which gives rise to different geometric representations. Thus, while rendering is performed with an accurate geometric representation, the necessary computations for providing force and tactile feedback are performed based on representations with a lower resolution.

21.5.4.1 Force Feedback and Tactile Devices

Force Feedback Devices were announced in the 1960s by the computer graphics pioneer Ivan Sutherland and realized for the first time in the famous project Grope a decade later [Batter and Brooks, 1971].

Meanwhile, there is a variety of tactile input devices available. Due to high demands on accuracy low cost devices primarily developed for computer games are currently not appropriate for surgery simulation. However, these devices are in fast development and it may be possible that similar to the effect of GPUs for visualization also in haptics rendering, devices from the game industry get broadly accepted. Tactile input devices provide a *grasp*, e.g., a stylus. Two different kind of grasps are *precision grasps* and *power grasps*, suitable for different applications.

Most surgery simulators are based on the PHANTOM devices from SensAble Technologies. There are devices providing three degrees of freedom (3-DOF) representing translations in the *x*-, *y*-, and *z*-direction (PHANTOM Omni) and advanced devices providing 6-DOF haptics (PHANTOM Premium). These advanced and more expensive devices allow to transform objects in three translational and three rotational directions. 3-DOF devices are adequate to represent point-based interactions between surgical devices and the anatomy (the surgical device or more general the manipulator is represented as a point). If more advanced interactions, such as line-surface interactions, should be represented, 6-DOF devices are required. The PHANTOM devices exhibit a pen-based end-effector, often called a *stylus*.

In general, there are three categories of haptic input devices:

- *general haptic devices*, e.g., joysticks developed for the gaming market,
- *modified haptic devices* that resemble the actual instruments, e.g., syringe and needle, and
- *dedicated haptic devices* for training surgery and intervention.

The obvious advantage of general devices is that they are widespread, carefully tested and rather cheap. They often have end effectors that are shaped as pens or balls [Coles *et al.*, 2011]. The second option is often a good trade-off, since it avoids most of the challenges of developing a completely new device. Primarily, the grips are modified to provide a greater degree of realism (see Fig. e21.29 for an example). Among the widely available devices, only those that provide 6-DOF force feedback and torque feedback are able to simulate the full spectrum of movements in interventions.

Tactile Devices While force feedback is rather simple and well understood, tactile feedback depends on many aspects involving various receptors. Coles *et al.* [2011] mention 13 different technologies and devices based on this variety. Most of them are heavy, non-portable solutions. While tactile devices play a role in master-slave robots, such as the DAVINCI system, they currently have a very limited role in training

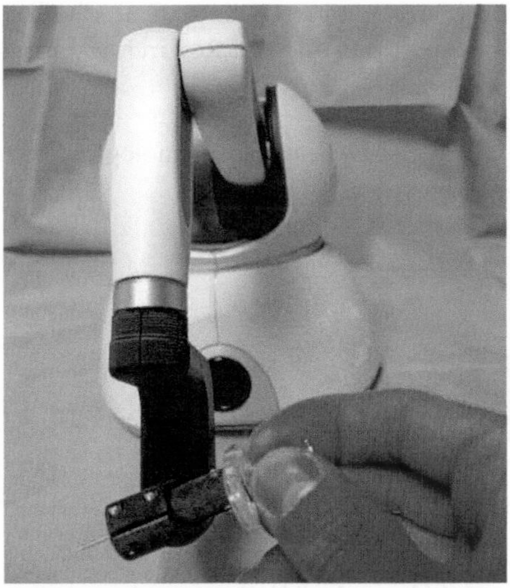

FIGURE e21.29 *A Sensable Phantom Omni device modified to mount the actual needle used during a procedure* (Courtesy of Nigel John, Bangor University).

systems. One aspect, however is that, the *vibrotactile sensation* is easier to simulate and may be used for medical education systems. Many users are aware of vibrations produced by a mobile phone that is silent to alert the user when a message or call comes in. Vibration does not provide the rich high-dimensional information of sensing a surface but it may provide useful feedback, e.g., when a bone burr is simulated, since the real process is also characterized by substantial vibrations.

21.5.4.2 Haptic Rendering

Haptic rendering is the process of calculating a reaction force (the *collision response*) for a specified position of the haptic input device. Usually, this position is represented as a point indicating the endpoint of the haptic device [Laycock and Day, 2003]. Haptic rendering becomes more complex (and more realistic) when the computation is not restricted to a single point representing the tip of an instrument.

The first step of a haptic rendering algorithm is collision detection discussed above. For haptic rendering, the instruments and tools are usually reduced to a few representative points. The second step involves the determination of the intersected area of the manipulated object and the determination of the penetration depth. Based on this information, a force is computed and applied to the arm of the tactile input device.

Efficient Solutions Based on Multimodal Representations Due to the high performance requirements of collision detection and haptic rendering, often models of different type and spatial resolution are employed for visualization, soft tissue deformation and collision detection/force feedback (*multimodal representation*). The highest resolution is employed for the visualization model and this model needs to represent the surface only. For soft tissue deformation a tetrahedral mesh of moderate resolution is a typical choice. Collision detection, as mentioned above, benefits from hierarchical data structures, such as a bounding sphere hierarchy (see Fig. e21.30). Of course, these representations have to be synchronized with each other: When the liver tissue moves, both the visual representation and the collision detection representation have to be adapted accordingly.

Software Support To actually provide an application with tactile feedback not only requires an appropriate input device, but also software to control the device. Research work in surgery simulation is typically based on one of the following solutions:

- the GHOST library that is provided by SensAble Technologies to control the PHANTOM devices,
- the OPEN HAPTICS toolkit also provided by SensAble,
- the REACHIN API,

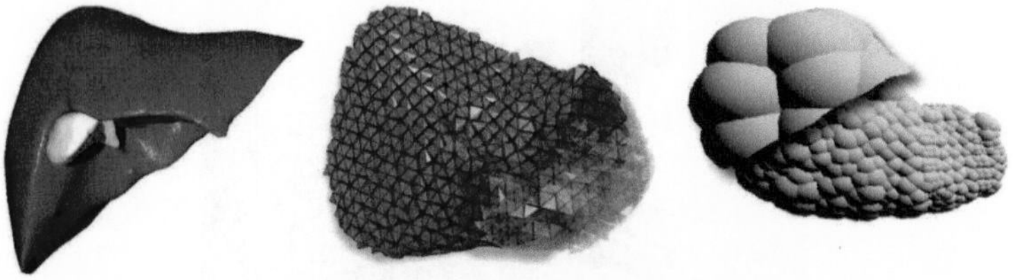

FIGURE e21.30 **Left:** *The visualization (of liver and gall bladder) is based on a high resolution triangle mesh representing the surface only.* **Middle:** *The tetrahedra representation is appropriate for soft tissue deformation.* **Right:** *The bounding sphere hierarchy is used for fast collision detection (Courtesy of Simon Adler, Fraunhofer IFF Magdeburg).*

- the HaptX engine, developed for gaming
- the open source Chai3D software,[11] as well as
- systems based on hardware from Immersion Medical, Xitact, and Force Dimension.

The ReachIn API as well as HaptX are provided by ReachIn. Open Haptics, although being commercial, is free for academic use [Coles *et al.*, 2011]. Chai3D is a rather comprehensive system with many examples and careful documentation supporting various platforms. However, at the time of writing, the latest available version is more than three years old. Thus, the development may have a low level of activity. Coles *et al.* [2011] describe these (and a few more) systems in more detail.

Discussion Haptic rendering is still not as mature as visual display technology. In particular tactile feedback is very difficult to provide accurately, since the biological processes that occur are only partially understood [Coles *et al.*, 2011]. Due to the significant computational effort and the necessary high update rate, most haptic rendering systems are still restricted. As discussed for collision detection, surgical instruments are usually considered as rigid-body objects. However, there are surgical interventions where the flexibility of the tool is crucial. As example serves root canal surgery in dentistry. A first prototype for the simulation of deformable tools is presented in [Laycock and Day, 2003].

Moreover, soft tissue deformation and haptic rendering is usually restricted to a single organ. In reality, deformations of one organ affect neighboring organs and the deformation of one organ depends on the neighboring organs.

Most systems provide force feedback only for anatomical structures that have been segmented and assigned properties, such as the Young modulus and stiffness. This restriction can be overcome with *haptic volume rendering* [Lundin *et al.*, 2005]. Haptic volume rendering resembles gray level gradient shading [Höhne and Bernstein, 1986]. Instead of using surface normals for shading, local intensity differences are analyzed and a gradient direction is determined on the voxel level. The image intensity, in case of CT data the Hounsfield value, is also considered to influence the amount of force feedback. The haptic forces differ along the needle.

21.5.5 SOFTWARE FOR SURGERY SIMULATION

The simulation of interventional procedures and surgery made substantial progress in recent years also because of the availability of powerful toolkits. We briefly describe three widespread frameworks in chronological order of introduction.

Spring The Spring framework includes soft tissue simulation, cutting, haptics and collision detection [Montgomery *et al.*, 2002]. It was extended by the authors of the toolkit to incorporate various special effects that are essential for realistic surgery simulation. At the time of writing, the website is no longer available.

GiPSi The GiPSi framework (General interactive Physical Simulation interface)[12] provides comprehensive support for the simulation, including linear and non-linear FEM based on solvers for differential equations. Different models for visualization and simulation are supported, including their synchronization [Cavusoglu *et al.*, 2006, Goktekin *et al.*, 2004]. The showcase example motivating the development was heart simulation. Haptic device handling and collision detection are not supported.

11 http://www.chai3d.org.
12 http://gipsi.case.edu/.

SOFA Finally, the SOFA framework (Simulation Open Framework Architecture)[13] should be mentioned. It is the most comprehensive framework based on a large development team.

It provides three distinct models: a collision model, a visual model and a behavioral model (for soft tissue deformation) and thus support efficient multimodal representations as shown in Figure e21.30. These models differ in resolution and thus are separated. Different tasks operating on these are also performed in different threads. Synchronization is also supported. Powerful solvers for differential equations and linear equation systems are provided. Parameters of the simulation, e.g., collision algorithms, constraints, and solvers, are described in XML files, which enables simple editing. Complex models may be created with a scene graph description. The whole design targets at optimal reuse.

SOFA was introduced by Allard *et al.* [2007] and became widespread after a series of presentations at MICCAI, SIGGRAPH, and VCBM in 2010. A number of additional features were integrated meanwhile and further investigations were performed. Marchal *et al.* [2008] discuss the validation and verification of the soft tissue deformation provided by SOFA, including the numerical approximation and the assessment of the realism of the physical behavior. They emphasize that open source software, such as SoFa enables a comparison of algorithms and metrics. Saupin *et al.* [2008] described precise methods for contact modeling to improve haptic realism in surgical simulators. Various simulation techniques, including mass-spring and FE models.

SOFA is available on the Linux, MacOS, and Windows platforms. The comprehensive system consisted of 450,000 lines of code in October 2012.

Both GiPSi and SOFA are active developments at the time of writing.

21.6 SIMULATION FOR TRAINING INTERVENTIONAL PROCEDURES

The training of interventions and the training of surgery have many common aspects but also distinctive features that warrant to treat them in separate sections. Interventions are performed by interventional (neuro)radiologists or cardiologists under control of imaging and thus have different target audience than surgery training systems. While open surgery usually does not require frequent intraoperative imaging (with some exceptions, e.g., in neurosurgery), minimally-invasive procedures raise similar challenges like interventions, namely a difficult hand-eye coordination and tissue handling. In contrast to interventions, live full-color high resolution images from a camera are displayed in minimally-invasive surgery instead of a rather low-resolution gray scale image, e.g., from fluoroscopy. Among the similarities is the general approach for computer-assisted training that involves a pretest, the actual training stage and a posttest for skills assessment. Tissue handling is also a common problem. In open surgery, special skills, such as accurately drilling bones, are essential.

21.6.1 NEEDLE-BASED INTERVENTIONS

Before we describe specific examples, we discuss some general aspects of needle-based interventions. Needle-based interventions are frequently applied, e.g., to obtain tissue samples (*biopsy*), to inject fluids, e.g., in regional anesthesia, or as a prerequisite for more advanced procedures, e.g., in vascular interventions. Before needles are actually inserted, the presence of anatomical features is verified, primarily by palpation, thus involving subtle tactile sensations [Coles and John, 2010]. While biopsy needles may be considered to be straight linear rods, guide wires and catheters used to treat vascular diseases are flexible

13 http://www.sofa-framework.org/.

and adapt to some extent to the surrounding anatomy. Needles may penetrate skin and soft tissue, but are not able to penetrate skeletal structures. Haptic forces that are simulated for training needle placement must consider at least two different components:

- *friction* that occurs when the needle is moved tangential to a surface, and
- *penetration* when the needle is moved in the orthogonal direction and thus enters a structure.

Of course, the gliding movement that causes friction requires considerably lower forces than the penetration. Moreover, in a penetration situation, suddenly the necessary force drops significantly. In general, needles deform anatomical surfaces only locally. Thus, the computation of deformation forces should be restricted to a small region around the needle tip in order to provide a fast response. However, even these local changes may require to remesh the surface models because at least some tetrahedra may degenerate.

Currently, most needle insertion training systems are trained with modified force feedback devices (recall Fig. e21.29).

21.6.2 HAPTIC DEVICES FOR NEEDLE-BASED INTERVENTIONS

Physicians need to carefully control the orientation of needles, their depth by advancing or pulling the needle. In § 21.5.4, we introduced general, modified, and dedicate haptic input devices.

Although 6-DOF devices are desirable, also systems using haptic devices with 3-DOF were employed, to provide cheap solutions. An example is the CathSim Accu-Touch system.

To acquire the necessary motor skills for needle-based interventions, a special haptic device is highly beneficial. Luboz *et al.* [2009] introduce such a device based on the optical sensors of a 2D mouse. The shell of the mouse was removed to provide access to the roller ball. A 3 mm hole was drilled in the roller ball to accommodate a catheter. The depth is measured with a potentiometer with this design, the needle may be rotated by around 45° which is sufficient for simulating needle punctures. The optical sensors of a mouse, however, are not very accurate: They enable an angular resolution of 3°, which is sufficient for determining whether the vessel was indeed punctured, but an improved accuracy was considered desirable [Luboz *et al.*, 2009]. For an in-depth discussion of haptic devices and their suitability for training needle-based interventions, see Coles *et al.* [2011]. They compare the Falcon device from Novint, the devices produced by SensAble technologies and those by Force Dimensions. In the comparison,

- the price,
- the degrees of freedom for force feedback,
- the supported workspace,
- the availability of torque feedback as well as
- the frequency of use in interventional training

are considered.

21.6.3 SIMULATION OF LUMBAR PUNCTURES

We have already introduced the medical background of lumbar punctures in § 21.4.3. In this diagnostic procedure a biopsy needle is moved in the spinal canal to extract cerebrospinal fluid. The procedure is easier in case of slim patients and more difficult in case of obese patients. Lumbar punctures can be trained with dolls to some extent, but the complex anatomy cannot be understood from such training [Färber *et al.*, 2009]. A more realistic training involves soft tissue deformation and force feedback and preferably involves cases that differ in their degree of difficulty.

Early attempts at such simulators, e.g., [Singh *et al.*, 1994], provide force feedback only in three dimensions. That means that only the needle position may be transformed but not the needle orientation. More recent systems, e.g., the training system presented by Färber *et al.* [2009], Kellermann *et al.* [2011] provide 6-DOF force feedback. The virtual penetration of the skin with force feedback benefits from modeling friction. A moderate friction value (0.5 in a 0–1 range) supports in gliding along the skin and was reported to be more efficient than free-hand control [Kellermann *et al.*, 2011].

To support learning, it is sometimes better to deviate from realistic behavior. The discussions with surgeons, underlying the design of the SpineSurgeryTrainer, revealed that they want to touch and clearly feel vulnerable structures, such as nerves and vascular structures. Thus, in contrast to their real-world behavior, they were assigned high stiffness values in order to support this tactile experience [Kellermann *et al.*, 2011]. To support early stages of learning, even the needle insertion was performed differently than in reality. Users first chose a target point and then determined the orientation, whereas in reality, of course, a needle first has to penetrate the skin (Fig. e21.31).

Färber *et al.* [2009] suggest to compute the forces for the needle tip as well as for 15 positions along the needle. The trainee uses a setup with a virtual reality workbench and stereo glasses to have an immersive experiences (see Fig. e21.32). 2D and 3D visualizations are provided to fully understand the needle position and orientation in the anatomical context.

In the following, we describe some more aspects of lumbar puncture training system developed at the University of Lübeck in a long-term project [Färber *et al.*, 2009, Fortmeier *et al.*, 2012, 2013a]

Case Database and Didactic Concept The training system employs the Visible Human and Visible Korean datasets making available also the colored slice visualizations. In addition, three patient data datasets, representing different degrees of difficulty, are employed. The system can be operated in three different modes aiming at beginners, advanced users, and experts. The visualization options and guidance by the system are adjusted according to this selection. Figure e21.33 illustrates the visualization options.

Evaluation The evaluation of the system was based on a questionnaire representing the assessment of the trainees and based on objective data gathered during the training session. Prior to the actual test, trainees were made familiar with force feedback using a very simple and artificial scene. In the questionnaire, a number of statements were made and the trainees commented how strongly they agree or disagree (a six point Likert scale with 1 representing strong agreement and 6 strong disagreement). With 42 users, the results are rather stable.

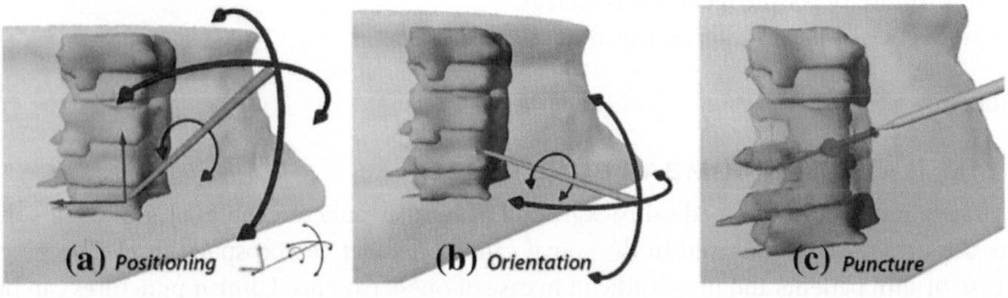

FIGURE e21.31 Training workflow in the enhanced SpineSurgeryTrainer. **Left:** The target point in the spine region is defined first and then the needle tip is locked. **Middle:** After gliding along the skin, orientation of the biopsy needle is determined. **Right:** The needle is advanced until the right penetration depth is achieved (Courtesy of Kerstin Kellermann, University of Magdeburg).

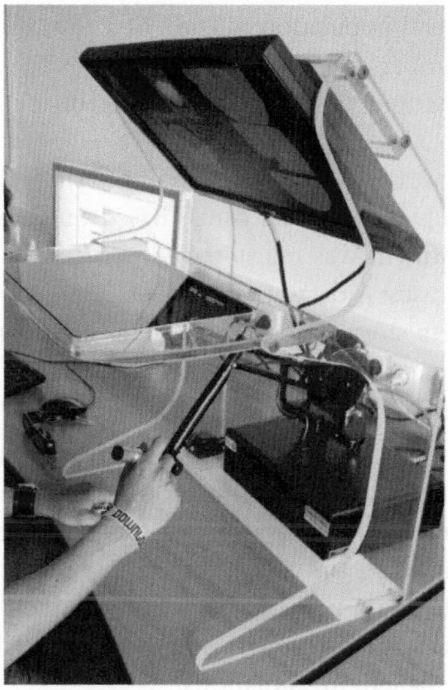

FIGURE e21.32 *Setup of the system for training lumbar punctures with a tactile input device and a VR workbench (Courtesy of Mathias Färber, University of Lübeck).*

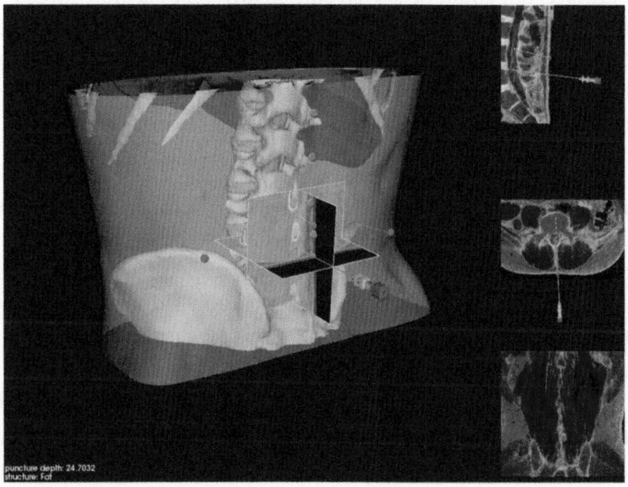

FIGURE e21.33 *Needle insertion based on the Visible Human dataset (see colored slice views on the right). A 3D overview visualization and a close-up primarily provide visual feedback (Courtesy of Mathias Färber, University of Lübeck).*

Users clearly felt different tissue as a consequence of haptic feedback (average 1.5). They also assessed the different visualization options as helpful for understanding the spine anatomy (1.6) and thus considered the overall training as useful (1.5). The display of patients was regarded as realistic, although with lower agreement (2.0). From the literature on human computer interaction it is known that test persons tend to be more positive than the general population outside of a test, in particular if they cannot compare alternatives. Thus, the absolute numbers need to be interpreted with care. However, the differences, e.g., between the usefulness of stereoscopic viewing and force feedback likely transfer to the larger target group.

On the objective side it was assessed whether the trainees successfully completed needle insertion, that is, whether they actually reached the spinal canal. Based on various components, an overall score representing the efficiency of treatment was registered. A particularly interesting detail is how strongly the results differed between two cases: A dataset of an obese patient and the Visible Korean dataset. Test persons have a much higher success rate and score with the Visible Korean dataset.

21.6.4 ULTRASOUND-GUIDED BIOPSY SIMULATION

To remove tissue samples based on ultrasound guidance is a frequent task in clinical routine, e.g., in the abdominal region. It is also a prerequisite for other interventional procedures, such as draining bile from the liver. An ultrasound probe is moved to the target region and provides a life image of the target anatomy. Biopsies need to be performed with care, since even thin biopsy needles may cause bleedings. To actually localize the pathology may be difficult, in particular, if it is small, hard to discriminate from surrounding tissue, deep-seated or difficult to access due to adjacent structures at risks or impenetrable bones. Training systems should incorporate such challenging situations.

Ni and colleagues developed a system that supports this navigation task [Ni *et al.*, 2008, 2011]. It is based on ultrasound data that was acquired at different time steps and later composed to a panoramic view (note that the field of view of ultrasound is limited). This composition is difficult for ultrasound data with its inherent artifacts but could be solved sufficiently. Very accurate force profiles for the relevant tissue types, e.g., muscles and skin are incorporated to provide the necessary haptic realism. They are based on earlier work by Brett *et al.* [1997b]. Force and torque feedback is provided. An enhanced degree of realism was achieved by Vidal *et al.* [2008], where the grip of the force feedback device was modified to resemble an ultrasound probe. In this system, a second force feedback device was used to simulate the needle.

Respiratory Motion An essential problem for biopsies in the abdominal region is the respiratory motion that complicates the localization of small targets. Thus, it needs to be incorporated in a realistic training system as well. Respiratory motion can be very different with respect to the extent of motion and temporal patterns. For training, a rather simple periodic pattern is probably sufficient. An elliptical area of influence was modeled as a reasonable tradeoff between accuracy and performance.

21.6.5 SIMULATION OF CATHETERS AND GUIDE WIRE INSERTION

Increasingly more pathologies are treated by means of catheters inserted to a vascular structure, e.g., to re-open a strongly calcified vessel. Such *endovascular* procedures are performed to treat cerebral vasculature, e.g., in case of a stroke, coronary vasculature, e.g., in case of coronary artery diseases, or peripheral vasculature.

21.6.5.1 Medical Background

Catheters and guide wires are inserted in the vasculature to treat these diseases with a minimum of patient discomfort compared to open vascular surgery. Angioplasty, stenting and coil embolization are examples for intravascular interventions.

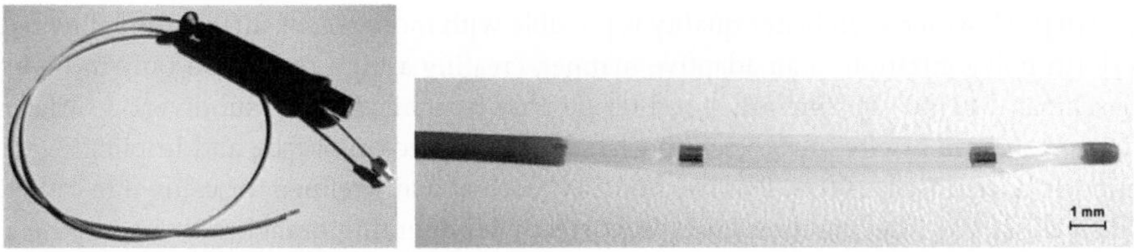

FIGURE e21.34 **Left:** *A flexible catheter with control unit.* **Right:** *A balloon catheter that expands to treat stenosis* (Courtesy of *Axel Böse, University of Magdeburg*).

Catheters are thin long, often flexible tools and their shape and material is refined for special interventional procedures. Figure e21.34 displays two catheters that may be employed for treating vascular diseases. The insertion of a catheter is referred to as *catheterization*.

Guide wires and catheters may be very long: 1 or even 1.7 m are possible which needs to be reflected in the training. When the guide wire is in a sufficiently advanced position, the puncture needle is removed and the guide wire is used as a conduit for the catheter. The combination of guide wire and catheter is translated (pushed and pulled) and rotated by the physician, using the grasp at the proximal end for steering.

Not all vascular diseases can actually be treated in this minimally-invasive manner. In particular, when sufficient access is required for open vascular surgery, e.g., bypass surgery is still necessary. In the case of an interventional procedure, the "right" catheter needs to be selected, e.g., with respect to length, thickness, shape, and elasticity. Although decision support for the choice of treatment is also desirable, we focus on training systems to actually perform the intravascular procedure. Readers interested in the medical procedures are referred to Schneider [2003].

21.6.5.2 Vascular Modeling

An essential prerequisite for the simulation is an appropriate surface mesh representing the relevant part of a vascular system.

Requirements The vascular surface mesh representation should be smooth and accurate and should not contain any internal structures that would hamper the movement of a catheter. These requirements are the same as those for virtual angioscopy an endoscopic procedure to move a camera through vasculature (recall § 13.6.3).

Moreover, it should be appropriate for a fast and numerically stable simulation, that is, the triangle quality needs to be high (degenerated triangles with very small angles need to be avoided) and the geometric complexity should be low. These additional requirements are very similar to those of blood flow simulation where the surface mesh also serves as input for volume mesh generation (§ 19.3.2).

Selection of a Modeling Technique In Chapter 11, we introduced a number of vascular surface modeling techniques. Here, we discuss which of them fulfills the set of requirements stated above. Even the best explicit surface reconstruction, e.g., based on truncated cones, cannot avoid internal polygons and exhibits discontinuities at branchings [Hahn *et al.*, 2001].

Convolution surfaces [Oeltze and Preim, 2005] avoid these problems but require a remeshing step to ensure a sufficient triangle quality. Other implicit surface representations are more accurate and exhibit a better triangle quality, e.g., the modified MPU implicits (recall § 11.6.2 and Schumann *et al.* [2008],

Wu *et al.* [2010]). However, even better quality is possible with more recent surface modeling techniques, which perform polygonization in an adaptive manner, creating a high resolution only in highly curved areas [Kretschmar *et al.*, 2012]. Similarly good results may be achieved with subdivision surfaces.

One method that we briefly introduced in Chapter 11 is based on *sweeping* and implicitly reconstructs vascular models [Li and Tian, 2009]. This method has been explicitly refined for using it in catheterization training [Li *et al.*, 2012]. They put emphasis on correctly representing branches and compose a vascular tree of tubular segments and a branching model that are smoothly blended. Bezier surfaces and sweeping are the basic methods and ensure that the surface normal changes continuously.

21.6.5.3 Catheter and Guide Wire Modeling

A training system for learning intravascular procedures requires to simulate the elastic behavior of the associated instruments, in particular of *guide wires* and *catheters*.

Physical Effects Catheters and guide wires are elastic and inextensible. There are various further effects to be considered, e.g., the guide wire is influenced by friction against the vessel wall. The catheter is restricted by the vessel wall (unless excessive power against it is applied). The catheter tends toward a state of minimum potential energy after the input of the physician stops. The potential energy E equals the sum of its bending, twisting and stretching energy (the three terms in Eq. e21.2) [Huang *et al.*, 2011].

$$E = 1/2 \int \mu\kappa^2 ds + 1/2 \int \beta m^2 ds + 1/2 \sum_{0}^{n-1} k(\overline{e}_j - e_j)^2 \qquad \text{(e21.2)}$$

In this equation, s represents the arc-length parameterized centerline, μ the stiffness tensor, k the 2D curvature vector along the centerline, m the material twist, $\overline{e}_j$ and e_j represent the initial and current edge length.

An essential property of most guide wires and catheters is that they are highly resistant against twist. Thus, the physician has excellent torque control and some authors, e.g., Li *et al.* [2012] neglect the twist in modeling the dynamics. Since these devices are inextensible, a length-constraint should be included in the simulation [Huang *et al.*, 2011]. The flexibility of the tip of the catheter differs strongly from the remaining part. Thus, this property is relevant and incorporated in recent training simulators [Tang *et al.*, 2012]. Guide wires and catheters are modeled as sets of (straight) linear rods.

The deformation of the vessel wall and the deformation of guide wires and catheters are two tightly connected processes and need to be simulated as a coupled process to achieve a high degree of realism.

Modeling Technology Since catheters and guide wires are very long structures, they are in most systems modeled as 1D objects. Thus, the whole volume is adapted as a consequence of moving node positions arranged at a 1D chain.

The material parameters of guide wires and catheters are known. Thus, finite element modeling enables to accurately simulate the effects. However, the underlying effects are non-linear, leading to a very high computational effort when typical solvers, such as Lagrangian multipliers [Li *et al.*, 2012, Spillmann and Harders, 2010], are employed. Fortunately, the necessary computations can also be performed efficiently on the GPU [Taylor *et al.*, 2008].

An advanced system for guide wire simulation was developed at the Image Sciences Institute in Rotterdam [Alderliesten *et al.*, 2007]. It employs *Cosserat models* for a higher-order finite element simulation. Cosserat models are based on the elasticity theory provided by the French mathematician EUGÈNE COSSERAT. According to this theory, a local rotation of points as well as the translation is considered. In addition to classic elasticity, which only considers one kind of stress, both a couple stress (a torque per unit area) and a force stress (force per unit area) are modeled. Cosserat models were heavily used in biomechanics, e.g., to predict the response of bone to forces [Park and Lakes, 1986]. They have also been used in surgical simulation, see for example Spillmann and Teschner [2009]. With the Cosserat model, a guide wire is composed of a set of straight non-bendable beams. This model enables very good torque control [Luboz *et al.*, 2009]. The models consider two types of energy:

- bending energy, and
- external contact.

This non-linear modeling scheme enables accurate, however time-consuming solutions. While the system introduced by Alderliesten *et al.* [2007] could not achieve real-time behavior, more recent catheterization training systems accelerated the computation to enable real-time behavior [Tang *et al.*, 2012].

Catheters may also be simulated with mass-spring models. An early system was described by Basdogan *et al.* [2001]. Masses were defined as particles distributed around the centerline of the catheter. The careful definition of damping elements and torsion control enables reasonably realistic results with less computational effort. Luboz *et al.* [2009] present a comprehensive and advanced system based on a complete environment including a haptic device—developed for interventional radiology. The simulator contains a *pulse simulator* to train the location of the femoral artery of a patient model.

To provide the necessary performance, the simulator for training the Seldinger technique [Luboz *et al.*, 2009] is realized as a mass-spring model with appropriate distribution of particles (representing masses). Up to 700 particles are employed, resulting in a resolution of 2 mm for a 1.4 m catheter (from the femoral arteries to the neck vessels). The different structures may collide with each other—in these cases the needle has top priority, that is, other instruments strictly follow the needle.

Multigrid Solvers Without presenting any detail, we want to mention the recently introduced iterative multigrid strategy for catheter simulation [Li *et al.*, 2012]. The final solution is achieved by performing several steps of the simulation using a hierarchy of representations—a strategy that is useful for a variety of medical image computing problems, e.g., for registration. For the sake of brevity, we cannot discuss the validation of these and related procedures: the basic idea is to use physical phantoms and to compare the behavior of real catheters with virtual catheters. Li *et al.* [2012] reported an average error of only 10–15% of the local vessel diameter, which is a very good result.

21.6.5.4 Simulation of the Seldinger Technique

All intravascular interventions described above require an initial maneuver to access an appropriate segment of the vascular tree. The standard approach to get this access is referred to as the *Seldinger technique* [Seldinger, 1953]. With this technique, physicians feel the pulsation of an artery and perform an initial needle puncture. Then, a guide wire is inserted, which requires careful tactile sensations and dexterity [Luboz *et al.*, 2009].

Luboz *et al.* [2009] present a simulation system that enables training of this key procedure of interventional radiology along with guide wire and catheter simulation. This special training system is motivated by the high level of motor skills required to perform the procedure safely.

Database In the phase documented by Luboz *et al.* [2009], already 23 cases were included, representing vascular pathologies such as aortic aneurysms, aortic dissection, arterial stenosis and renal aneurysms.

Evaluation Trainees should virtually treat the vascular pathologies by choosing an entry point, inserting the guide wire and various instruments. All these actions are tracked and monitored for later analysis. Besides subjective feedback from the trainees, the accuracy was analyzed by means of a silicone phantom filled with a viscous fluid. In summary, a combined model of guide wire, catheter and needle as well as vessel deformations with a special haptic device provide substantial support for training vascular interventions.

21.7 SYSTEMS FOR TRAINING OPERATIVE TECHNIQUES

The design and development of e-learning systems to train surgical procedures is a complex endeavor. A careful user and task analysis including an understanding of the context of use is required as input in the early design process (recall § 21.4.1). The simulation to train operative techniques needs to be "part of a wider training course for an end to end training curriculum" [Coles and John, 2010]. In the following, we briefly describe some prominent and long-term efforts in surgical simulator development starting with minimally-invasive surgery (endoscopic surgery, laparoscopic surgery) and later discuss one example of open surgery, namely temporal bone surgery where a bone burr is employed to drill bones, e.g., to create a cavity for a hearing implant.

21.7.1 LAPAROSCOPIC SURGERY

In laparoscopic surgery, only small incisions in the skin are performed. They are employed to insert long and thin tools (a camera to display the situs and surgical instruments). Essential tasks in laparoscopic surgery are:

- port placement,
- suturing,
- knot tying,
- tissue manipulation, and
- camera navigation.

Eye-hand coordination is challenging, since movements of the tool to the left lead to translations on the right and vice versa. Thus, even a surgeon with considerable experience in open surgery needs a lot of training to perform the same surgery in this minimally-invasive manner. Based on these challenges Coles *et al.* [2011] state: "There are more simulators available in laparoscopy than for any other medical speciality." The importance of substantial training is recognized also because of reports of serious complications [Grantcharov *et al.*, 2004].

KISMET A long-term effort on laparoscopic surgery simulation has been carried out at the Research Center of Karlsruhe. Many aspects of real laparoscopic interventions have been carefully modeled in their KISMET (Kinematic Simulation, Monitoring and Off-Line Programming Environment for Telerobotics) system [Kühnapfel *et al.*, 2000]. Anatomical objects are represented as surface models and soft tissue deformation is realized with mass-spring models. Many effects, such as bleeding and coagulation, are faithfully simulated in their system. A special modeling system was developed to generate the underlying geometric and kinematic models. The system has been refined and force feedback was added [Maass *et al.*, 2003]. The system reached a mature state that enabled clinical tests and a significant learning effect could be demonstrated [Lehmann *et al.*, 2005].

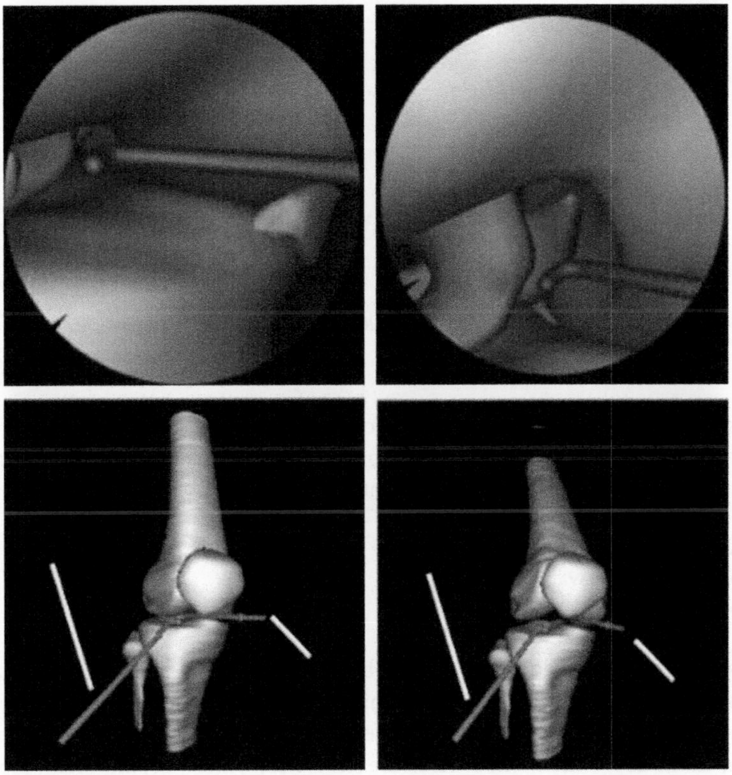

FIGURE e21.35 *Internal (top row) and external (bottom row) views to train arthroscopy (From: [Heng et al., 2004a]).*

Arthroscopic Surgery A special and important example of endoscopic surgery is arthroscopic surgery, i.e., surgical interventions at the knee. There have been a number of dedicate systems for arthroscopy. As an essential example, we describe the system introduced by Heng *et al.* [2004a]. The knee compartments were modeled precisely. Internal and external views are provided to support the understanding of the spatial relations (see Fig. e21.35). Before the actual surgery, an *inspection* is performed and trainees need to learn the navigation in that narrow area.

The knee anatomy contains non-deformable bones and deformable muscles and ligaments. The soft tissue deformation of the deformable objects is constrained by the non-deformable objects that may not be penetrated. The specific FE model is a hybrid combination of an *operational region* and a *non-operational region*. The operational region is the local environment of the pathology where more detail is needed, whereas the more distant non-operational region is modeled in lower detail. Also, topological changes and non-linear deformations are only considered in the operational region.

21.7.2 TEMPORAL BONE SURGERY SIMULATION

Temporal bone surgery (or middle ear surgery) is accomplished primarily in order to attach Cochlea implants as hearing aids and to remove tumors (mastoidectomy) [John *et al.*, 2001]. For this purpose, it is necessary to drill through the mastoid bone (see Fig. e21.36) without hurting relevant structures nearby. Petrous bone surgery involves a surgical site with complex anatomy. Key anatomical features—derived by

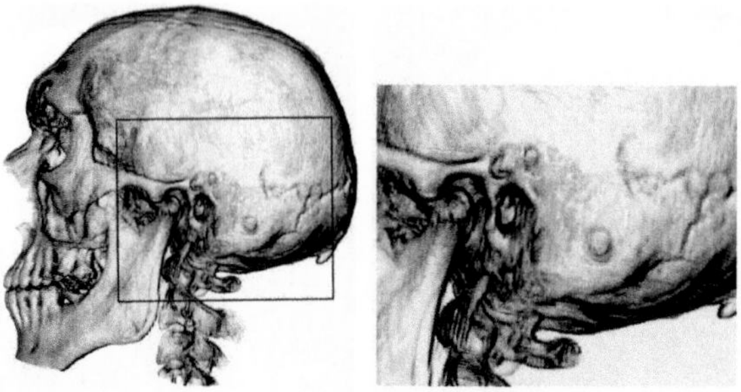

FIGURE e21.36 *Overview of the skull and a closeup view of the mastoid region* (From: [*Agus et al.*, 2003]).

the task analysis—are for example the facial nerve, other neural features, and the jugular bump. The task analysis also provides information related to the most important instruments and materials, as well as to the preferred display type. Three types of instruments are primarily used:

- a *burr* reducing tracebular bone in fine dust,
- an *irrigator* to introduce water, and
- a *sucker* which removes bone dust and water.

Temporal bone surgery is performed by the surgeon holding a high-speed burr in one and a suction device in the other hand. The latter is used to remove the mixing of bone dust with water [John *et al.*, 2001]. The primary learning objectives are to train access to the middle ear and to train the drilling process itself. It is important that all the above-mentioned effects are simulated. Otherwise, important aspects such as the need for regular irrigation and suction are not perceived [Agus *et al.*, 2003].

Learning this type of surgery with conventional training is very expensive, since advanced microsurgical skills need to be acquired. Wiet *et al.* [2011] estimate that a five year period with annual costs of 80.000 is required to gain proficiency.

Virtual temporal bone surgery has attracted much research in the last years. The IERAPS (Integrated Environment for the Rehearsal And Planning of Surgical Intervention) project represents the second large-scale effort to virtual petrous bone surgery [John *et al.*, 2001].

The OHIO VIRTUAL TEMPORAL BONE SIMULATOR was already introduced in [Wiet and Bryan, 2000] and focused on bone removal. Meanwhile it experienced a long development and continuous improvement [Wiet *et al.*, 2011, 2012]. The latest development was based on different data sources. Besides standard CT data, also microCT and ultraCT data were employed with a spatial resolution of 0.06 mm and 0.006 mm, respectively. In particular the display of neural structures benefits from this very high resolution. However, data handling is challenging with the high amount of data involved (500 Gbytes). The Ohio Virtual Temporal Bone simulator was disseminated to eight research institutions, enabling a large validation study with 66 trainees [Wiet *et al.*, 2012]. Besides visual and haptic feedback, also acoustic feedback is provided to convey the sound of the drill (this technique was also used in the VOXEL-MAN temporal bone simulator presented by Zirkle *et al.* [2007]).

Bone removal is accomplished by extending virtual resection techniques described in Chapter 9. Multiresolution approaches such as octrees are essential to effectively localize the voxels which are affected by the movement of the virtual tool. Voxels that are removed become transparent, whereas voxels affected by local bleeding become reddish. While in virtual resection the removal of voxels is just a Boolean operation, in surgery simulation it is necessary to provide adequate force feedback. A physically motivated simulation of the burr/bone interaction is feasible but rather complex, since secondary effects caused by the irrigator and the sucker need to be considered [Agus *et al.*, 2003].

A long-term effort on simulating petrous bone surgery has also been accomplished at the University hospital Hamburg-Eppendorf [Petersik *et al.*, 2002, Pflesser *et al.*, 2002] by the same group that pioneered anatomy education with voxel-based models (recall § 21.3). Among others, they focused on a high-quality visual representation of all relevant anatomical structures. The system employs high-quality volume visualization at subvoxel accuracy and haptic rendering based on a volume representation. The spatial accuracy of the data as well as of the rendering supports the tactile sense of small anatomical structures (e.g., nerves), which is essential for the trainee's learning process. The drill is represented as a sphere-shaped tool, where 26 positions at the sphere's surface are sampled to detect collisions. Soft tissue deformation is not considered, since drilling the temporal bone does not cause significant elastic deformations.

The trainee may choose different kinds of drills or perform drilling while watching the scene displayed in stereoscopic mode. Much effort was spent on mimicking the real situation, in particular with respect to the patient's orientation, the surgeon's viewing direction and hand orientation. The trainees use the stylus of the force feedback device (PHANTOM 1.0 from SENSABLE TECHNOLOGIES), which mimics the drill. They thus get the haptic feeling of the real procedure. Even drilling vibrations and sounds have been faithfully simulated.

21.7.3 WEB-BASED SURGICAL SIMULATORS

As discussed in § 21.2.3, web-based systems strongly improve the accessability and enable widespread use. Of course, a full-fledged surgical simulator cannot be operated just by a mouse and a web browser [John, 2007]. However, low fidelity simulation with simplified geometric models is possible. Even soft tissue deformation may be enabled if a "cheap" solution, such as the ChainMail algorithm, is used [Li and Brodlie, 2003]. Dodd *et al.* [2002] introduced lumbar puncture training with a combination of Java applets and VRML. Even some kind of force feedback is provided by extending VRML with special haptic nodes. The REACHIN interface was employed for this purpose.[14] In the absence of force feedback, collision detection may be used to prevent interpenetration of objects and convey collisions with visual or audio feedback.

21.7.4 COMMERCIAL SURGICAL SIMULATORS

In the following, we give a brief overview on commercial systems to encourage readers to look for more and up-to-date information. The focus of commercial products is minimally-invasive surgery, primarily laparoscopic surgery. The following list of vendors and products is a selective list, that is by no means comprehensive.

SIMBIONIX[15] is a leading provider that offers simulator-based training for minimally-invasive surgery (LAP Mentor for, ARTHRO Mentor for arthroscopy with a knee and shoulder module). The LAP Mentor supports 60 basic tasks and procedures in laparoscopy including suturing and anastomosis exercises and cholecystectomy training. The ARTHRO Mentor supports both diagnostic and therapeutic procedures. As a third example, we mention the ANGIO Mentor that enables the training of endovascular surgery, e.g., for treating diseases of the cerebral vasculature. For all products, several validation studies are documented.

MENTICE[16] is another company that offers several simulation-based training systems. The VIST Lab supports the training of endovascular procedures, including a wide range of interventions, e.g., aortic valve

---

14 http://www.reachin.se/products/reachinapi/.

15 http://simbionix.com/.

16 http://www.mentice.com/.

implantation, coronary angiography, and renal interventions. Again, the development was added by substantial validation studies. Also a portable variant, VIST-C, is available that may be used for training courses.

SurgicalScience[17] provides basic laparoscopy training with their LapSim system. The basic tasks and procedures are similar to the LAP Mentor. EndoSim, the second major product, provides colonoscopy and bronchoscopy training.

Finally, we mention to the products of Simendo.[18] They offer support for various endoscopic and laparoscopic training procedures and handling special devices for endoscopy.

In general, these high-end systems meanwhile do not rely on general haptic devices but employ modified or completely custom-made instruments to provide a high degree of realism.

21.8 TRAINING SYSTEMS BASED ON PHYSICAL MODELS

All training systems described so far do not operate with real instruments, such as microscopes, ultrasound probes, guide wires, and needles. Even if force feedback is provided, force feedback devices are only loosely related to real instruments. Even the most advanced systems that employ modified haptic devices cannot fully convey the impression of real instruments.

To integrate real instruments and other devices is *one* major motivation for training based on physical models. Another major motivation for training with physical models comes from the shortcomings of training with cadavers. Not only that reports from many countries indicate that there is severe shortage of cadavers [Wiet *et al.*, 2012], but cadavers do not represent the full spectrum of pathologies. As an example, for learning temporal bone surgery, pathologies around the inner and middle ear are crucial. Cadavers rarely exhibit such pathologies. The large-scale use of animals for training has also severe problems, among them ethical problems.

Finally, touching, moving and rotating a geometric model of anatomical and pathological structures is just perceived as more realistic and supports a collaborative discussion between two trainees. Abdel-Sayed and von Segesser [2011] summarize the potential of rapid prototyping for procedural training in cardiovascular surgery as follows:

1 better identification of structural abnormalities, e.g., complex congenital heart failures,
2 more reliable identification of the best surgical strategy, and
3 improved surgical skills by a realistic training setting.

These statements—despite being related to cardiovascular surgery—can be largely generalized to many interventional and surgical procedures.

Although procedural training is the most essential application for physical models, Thomas *et al.* [2010] convincingly demonstrated that it may also be used for anatomy education when virtual information is overlaid with physical information (recall Chap. 18 where we discussed such *augmented reality* solutions primarily for surgery).

In the following, we describe the generation of physical models from medical image data and present selected examples of the use of such systems for training. Furthermore, we describe the basic technology and two selected applications in surgery training.

17 http://www.surgical-science.com/.
18 http://www.simendo.eu/.

21.8.1 GEOMETRIC MODELING AND RAPID PROTOTYPING

The potential of rapid prototyping for surgical training was recognized early. Begall and Vorwerk [1998] suggested to use physical models for the training of temporal bone surgery. Widespread use, however, was not possible at that time. In recent years, rapid prototyping technology developed at a rapid pace and now allows to create larger models, models with different materials and colors, even with semi-transparent materials. Last but not least, the acquisition of rapid prototyping technology and the price to use it decreased considerably. The term "rapid" is somewhat debatable—the process lasts a couple of hours. Knox *et al.* [2005] comment this ironically: "The word rapid ...uses an industrial rather than a medical timescale." While this is a serious argument for the use in clinical routine, for medical training the duration of fabrication is no serious counter-argument.

Thus, instead of using cadavers, physical models may be created with rapid prototyping (also referred to as stereolithography). These physical models may be easily replicated ensuring reproducibility of the training experience and supporting skills assessment. As an example, Figure e21.37 shows a physical model of the skull attached with various microcontrollers that are employed to detect injuries during surgical training, e.g., drill procedures at the lateral skull. Besides various advantages of the training with physical models, a common problem is that *physiology* can hardly be realized [Coles *et al.*, 2011].

Rapid Prototyping Technology The actual rapid prototyping process is also challenging and involves the choice of the technology, device and materials. There are different rapid prototyping technologies, such as stereolithography and laser sintering. Silicone is a frequently used material. Abdel-Sayed and von Segesser [2011] give an overview on techniques and materials. There are various vendors of rapid prototyping machines, e.g., Z CORPORATION with the series of ZPrinter 150–850.[19] In particular, with cheaper 3D printers it might be necessary to smoothen the result slightly. Choi *et al.* [2002] describe artifacts from rapid prototyping. Basically, the physical objects are created by milling away unwanted parts of a solid block by or building up the model in an accretion process.

Creating Vascular Models Knox *et al.* [2005] describe the use of rapid prototyping for creating vascular models for teaching. They created accurate models of a carotid stenosis and of a basilar tip aneurysm. Lermusiaux *et al.* [2001] also discussed the fabrication of vascular surface models. In their particular case, aortic aneurysms were created in their original size. Smaller problems occur in the reproduction

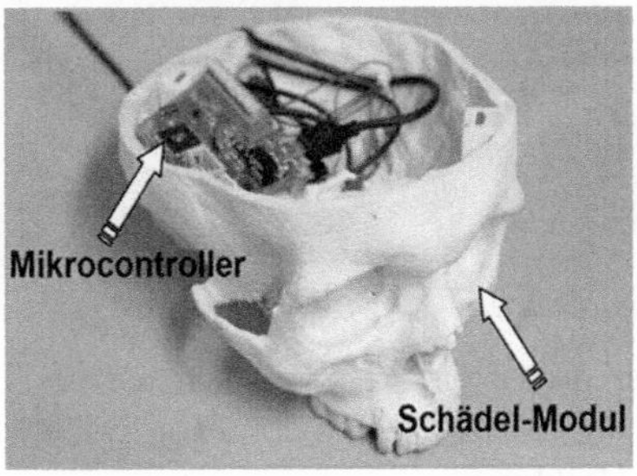

FIGURE e21.37 Physical models attached with electronic devices enable reliable assessment of trainees' performance in a training session (Courtesy of Werner Korb, University of Applied Sciences, Leipzig).

19 http://www.zcorp.com.

of complex anatomical structures, such as vasculature. Knox *et al.* [2005] discuss that upper surfaces of vascular structures are more faithfully represented than lower surfaces. Choi *et al.* [2002] discuss limitations of accuracy in creating physical models of anatomical structures. However, in summary, rapid prototyping has developed into a feasible method that produces accurate models, and with an advanced 3D printer also a substantial flexibility is available.

Geometric Modeling Why are physical models relevant in a chapter on computer-assisted medical education? The physical models are based on geometric models that are primarily created from patient data, such as CT and MRI. Thus, image segmentation and surface extraction are crucial.

Even for the use of geometric models in a virtual environment, surface models are often carefully post-processed, e.g., with smoothing or remeshing (recall). For rapid prototyping, *modeling* plays an even more important role. Very thin structures cannot be physically built. Structures that are too close to each other, are merged in a physical model, an occurrence that should be avoided by an appropriate modification.

Also BLENDER[20] and 3DS MAX[21] possess 3D modeling functionality, enabling the deformation of a model, in order to remove bulges and perform other modifications. However, as professional tools they exhibit quite complex user interfaces. Often, the necessary processing steps can also be performed with SCULPTRIS,[22] a much simpler tool that enables dilation, extrusion, and smoothing. Such operations are performed intuitively by moving corresponding tools over the surface. Often, before but also after such modifications, some kind of *mesh repair* is necessary, e.g., to remove holes or to ensure a good triangle quality. An advanced tool to support these tasks is MESHLAB.[23] Users have fine-grained control over the vertices and faces to which such operations are performed. To illustrate the modeling tasks, Figure e21.38 shows how a vascular model is adapted, e.g., for use in a simulator of vascular interventions.

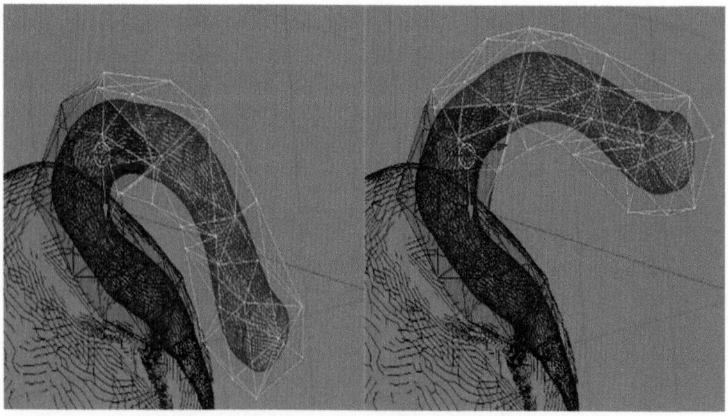

FIGURE e21.38 *Blender is employed to deform a branch of a vascular structure that is too close to another one. The deformation is performed by means of the visual hull (left) and the transformation is propagated to all vertices and edges in the relevant region (Courtesy of Tobias Mönch, University of Magdeburg).*

20 http://www.blender.org/.
21 http://usa.autodesk.com/3ds-max/.
22 http://www.sculptris.com/.
23 http://meshlab.sourceforge.net/.

An alternative to polygon modeling tools are those that operate at the voxel level, such as FreeForm. Geomagic FreeForm[24] is operated with a haptic input device to provide intuitive modeling. While most training systems based on rapid prototyping do not provide self-assessment tools and tools to analyze the trainees' performance, the following two subsections present advanced systems that were equipped with opto-electrical cables and sensors to provide this kind of feedback.

21.8.2 TEMPORAL BONE SURGERY

As we have discussed in § 21.7.2, temporal bone surgery is a particularly challenging surgical task due to the high density of small but crucial anatomical structures. Therefore, a high demand for simulation but also for training with physical models exists, motivating also the pioneering work of Begall and Vorwerk [1998].

Later different attempts have been made to provide a feasible training system based on rapid prototyping technology, e.g., [Suzuki *et al.*, 2004]. We describe the comprehensive training system introduced by Straušs *et al.* [2009]. Its design is based on substantial didactic considerations. These relate to different aspects of dexterity in temporal bone surgery, the complementary mental models of spatial relations as well as to typical learning curves that are characterized by two stages with rapid progress. The initial steep learning curve should be accomplished without access to patients. After a later plateau, there is a second significant increase in performance and avoidance of complications that requires real surgery. Based on these considerations, a list of requirements was defined. Besides some obvious requirements related to ease-of-use, cost effectiveness, and realism of the following requirements are crucial:

- The results of training need to be assessed quantitatively to provide feedback and in order to judge whether this training stage can be finished.
- The training should trigger a moderate level of stress, a so-called *positive stress.* It is expected that this stress level is only achieved if trainees perceive that they control the training effectively.

System Design The training system introduced by Straušs *et al.* [2009] is based on physical models, incorporating the skeletal structures, but also essential risk structures, such as the Nervus facialis, the internal carotid artery and the ossicle chain (see Fig. e21.39, left). Gypsum powder and a bonding agent are used to create the physical model where the risk structures are represented as canals. After initial feedback, the physical models were refined with respect to the use of colors, the representation of some anatomical details and the hardness degree of the canal for the N. facialis. The target anatomy is embedded in a complete model of the skull (see Fig. e21.39, right) to provide a realistic context and enable better handling (the whole target anatomy is rather small). Of course, after a training session the skull model may be reused and only the temporal bone needs to be generated again. In a very similar way, Abdel-Sayed and von Segesser [2011] describe how a model of the heart is inserted in a much larger thorax model.

Trainees used an OR microscope, aspirators and milling machines like in real surgery. The structures at risk are equipped with detectors and fiberoptic cables to detect injuries and assess their severity.

System Evaluation The training system was used by eight experienced surgeons and eight novices and the results were compared with a second group of trainees that employed human cadavers. The evaluation was based on log files and automatically determined injuries, questionnaires completed by the trainees and an assessment of the surgery by an expert with respect to completeness of surgery and injuries. Selected results of this evaluation are:

24 http://geomagic.com/en/products/freeform/overview.

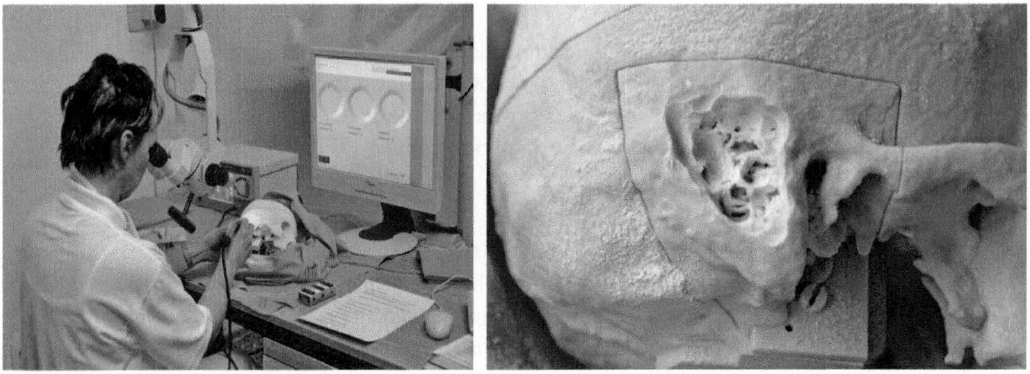

FIGURE e21.39 **Left:** *With an OR microscope realistic surgery training may be performed with a physical model of the temporal bone.* **Right:** *The temporal bone model that is consumed in the training activity is embedded in a reusable skull model (Courtesy of Gero Strauß, IRDC Leipzig).*

- The visual and haptic realism of training with physical models was assessed as very high (1.8 on a scale from −2 to 2, with 2 representing the highest degree of realism). This is an even a better assessment of this group than the assessment related to the training with cadavers, probably because the soft tissue structures in cadavers strongly differ from living tissue.
- Also the injuries happening during training were considered as very realistic (1.6 at the same scale).
- Experts caused less injuries and in particular injuries of lower severity, e.g., injuries of the N. facialis.

Based on the prototype described in Strauss *et al.* [2009], a commercial product was created and regularly used for training courses. Similar model creation processes were designed to support sinus and skull base surgery.[25]

21.8.3 TRAINING OF SPINE SURGERY

Korb *et al.* [2011] describe an advanced mechatronic system based on physical models for training spine surgery in the lumbar spine segments. They carefully investigated a large variety of materials in order to select a combination that provides very good haptical realism. Synthetic and organic materials, e.g., polyurethane and variants of gelatin) were assessed systematically by anatomists and neurosurgeons. A manufacturing process was designed and refined to produce all necessary materials reliably and efficiently. The modeling tasks were performed with FreeForm. The system design was based on many visits to the OR with a focus on neurosurgical interventions on the spine.

Figure e21.40 shows an example of a physical model used for spine surgery training. The system also contains an artificial blood pump. The liquid used for this pump resembles blood in its appearance as well as in major biomechanical properties, e.g., viscosity. Thus, when the trainee damages certain anatomical structures in the model, a realistic bleeding is simulated.

The whole system was evaluated by eleven surgeons primarily with respect to optical and haptic realism. Vertebra and prolapse as well as the dura were considered as realistic by the majority of the test persons.

25 www.phacon-leipzig.de/.

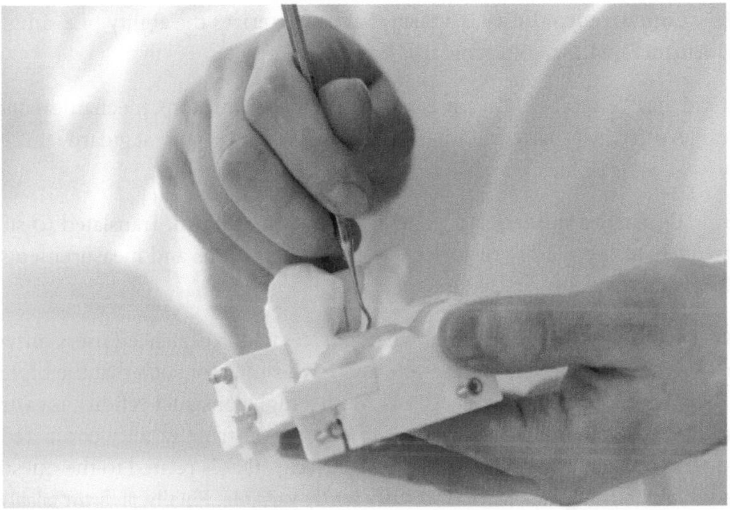

FIGURE e21.40 *A physical model of a vertebra with various materials representing different levels of stiffness and elasticity was created with rapid prototyping (Courtesy of Werner Korb, University of Applied Sciences, Leipzig).*

21.9 SKILLS ASSESSMENT

Once surgical simulators are designed, developed, and refined after gathering initial feedback from the first users, skills assessment becomes an important issue. Surgical simulators should enable

- a substantial learning effect, and
- a learning effect that can be transferred to real surgery.

In particular commercial systems put emphasis on skills assessment, since a proven benefit is essential for marketing. While this is not our motivation here, skills assessment is primarily important to ensure that surgical and interventional training finds its way in clinical routine and actually improves clinical care. An essential question is which tasks should be used to assess and certify the acquired skills. This selection benefits from a careful cognitive task analysis, including decision points (recall § 21.4.1 and [Johnson *et al.*, 2006].

21.9.1 IMPORTANT TERMS

There are some frequently used terms discussed in the validation of surgical simulators that will be defined in the following:

Definition 21.1. **Face validity** is a general term that summarizes *subjective assessments* whether a test or simulation seems to actually measure what it is supposed to measure.

If the face validity of a simulator is low, users do not take the corresponding training seriously. As an example, force feedback devices with a syringe-shaped end effector tend to have a higher face validity than general force feedback devices when used for training needle-based interventions. Thus, trainees and experts *believe* that the training is realistic and that the acquired skills may be transferred to clinical practice. Face validity is verified with expert reviews and questionnaires.

Definition 21.2. Concurrent validity is a term that characterizes the ability of a simulator to compare the trainees' performances with a gold standard.

The gold standard may be another (already carefully assessed simulator), mechanical or cadaver training. If the training results of trainees have a similar tendency like in the gold standard, this further increases trust in a simulator.

Definition 21.3. Construct validity is a general psychological term. Translated to surgery simulator, construct validity refers to the validity of inferences that observations and measurements derived from a simulator actually characterize surgical skills.

A high construct validity is usually assumed when novices and experienced users differ significantly in their results (error rates, task completion times, ...) within a simulator such that the higher experience of experts leads to better results [Oropesa *et al.*, 2010]. With a high construct validity, measures are expected to be reliable and reproducible. It is more difficult to ensure construct validity compared to face validity.

A widely used term in skills assessment is also *content validity*, that is related to the question whether the material provided in the training is realistic and sufficiently variable. Finally, *predictive validity* is the term that characterizes the degree to which success in a training simulator can be transferred to clinical practice. Thus, a high predictive validity is the ultimate goal of a training system.

Frameworks for Skill Assessment have been developed that are relevant and inspiring for surgery simulation [Oropesa *et al.*, 2010]. The *Objective Structured Clinical Examination* (OSCE) was introduced in the 1970s to assess the trainees' performance at various clinical stations manually but in a reproducible manner (using standardized checklists). The OSCE also incorporates technical skills assessment but only as a minor aspect. This lead to the introduction of the *Objective Structured Assessment of Technical Skills* (OSATS) in the 1990s focusing on procedural knowledge. Minimally-invasive surgery has a number of unique aspects not reflected in OSATS. Again a refined assessment framework was developed: the *Global Assessment of Laparoscopic Skills* (GOALS). This assessment framework is not bound to any particular kind of training (cadaver, mechanical, virtual reality), which enables to use it to compare the efficiency of different training systems. For more details on the application of these frameworks, see Fried and Feldman [2008].

For other kinds of surgery, e.g., in otolaryngology, but also for interventional radiology, there is no such reliable, practical, and standardized skills assessment [Wiet *et al.*, 2012].

21.9.2 AUTOMATIC SKILLS ASSESSMENT

When the trainees' actions are consequently monitored, an automatic skills assessment is possible. This is highly desirable due to the large effort and subjective variability of manual skills assessment by experts.

A relevant parameter is the time required to solve tasks with the simulator assuming that experts make less erroneous or unnecessary movements and are faster. For some procedures, it is questionable that trainees should aim for speed, e.g., in complex intervascular procedures, where slow and careful working might be more desirable compared to fast working with high risk. However, almost all automatic skills assessment tools consider time an essential parameter.

Most other parameters are either related to hand movement or to tool-tissue interactions. Hand movement may be assessed with respect to smoothness and other parameters derived from a speed profile. Tool-tissue interactions may be characterized by the forces that are applied to the tissue [Oropesa *et al.*, 2010]. The opto-electronic devices attached to a physical model shown in Figure e21.41 are used to

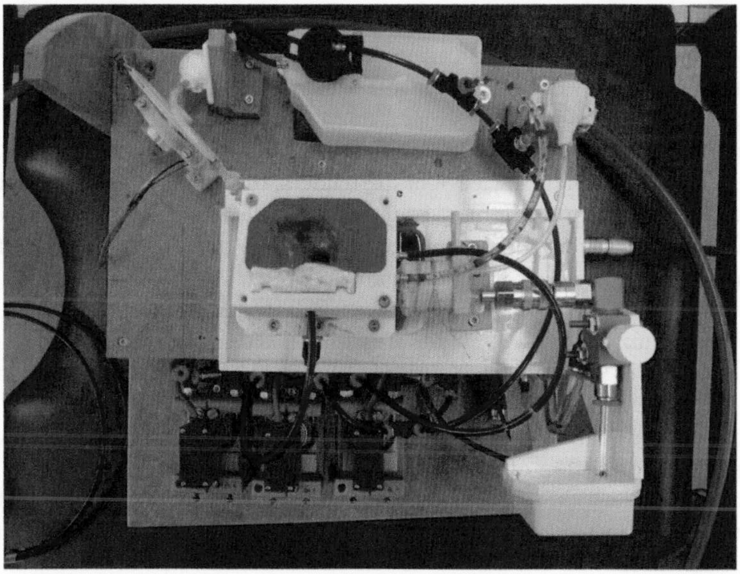

FIGURE e21.41 *A complex setup with physical model, blood pump and various sensors enables realistic training of spine surgery with automatic skills assessment (Courtesy of Werner Korb, University of Applied Sciences, Leipzig).*

determine such measures. Tissue damage, dangerous movements, economy of movements may also be detected and are frequently employed for automatic skills assessment [Wiet *et al.*, 2012].

The specific role of one particular force- or movement-related parameter to a relevant surgical skill is only partially understood so far. Thus, more research is necessary to ensure construct and predictive validity of such measures.

In the following, we briefly describe selected studies to give examples for viable and reliable methods of validation.

21.9.3 SKILLS ASSESSMENT STUDIES

One of the earliest validation studies relates to the minimally-invasive VR simulator for laparoscopic surgery (MIST VR) [Taffinder *et al.*, 1998]. They defined a score for various aspects of psychomotor skill and conducted two studies related to the simulator: the first study assesses surgeons of different surgical experience to validate the scoring system and the second study investigates the effect of a standard laparoscopic surgery training course. Experienced surgeons (more than 100 laparoscopic cholecystectomies) were significantly more efficient, made less correctional submovements and completed the tasks faster than trainee surgeons. Thus, the *construct validity* was high. The training course caused an improvement in efficiency and a reduction in errors for trainee surgeons.

Another study also related to the MIST VR simulator was presented by Grantcharov *et al.* [2004]. This randomized clinical trial is recognized as a high-quality study [Oropesa *et al.*, 2010], since rigorous statistical analysis was performed and confounding variables likely to cause bias carefully avoided. In a randomized manner, ten trainees were assigned to a virtual reality training group and ten received no training. Training consisted of ten repetitions of six basic tasks relevant in laparoscopic surgery. A final cholecystectomy of all 20 trainees was analyzed by two independent observers. Training improved operation time, economy of movement and error rate in a significant manner.

Sutherland *et al.* [2006] provided a comprehensive analysis of randomized controlled trials to assess the acquired skills with various forms of surgical training available at that time. These studies lead to contradictory results even for similar procedures. The survey indicates how difficult it is to perform and compare studies. The background knowledge of the trainees, the time of training and the specific tasks are among the confounding factors that make comparisons challenging. In essence, the studies showed a significant training effect by simulator training (compared to no training), but no significant advantage of either mechanical or virtual reality-based training.

Oropesa *et al.* [2010] give an overview on more recent skills assessment and validation studies applied to commercial surgical simulators. Some 30 studies are mentioned that were focused on either face, content, construct, concurrent, or predictive validity. Basically all commercial simulators, mentioned in § 21.7.4, were subject to such studies.

The Ohio Temporal Bone Simulator was also subject to a validation study. In a multiinstitutional study with 66 trainees a significant effect of the simulator training could be demonstrated [Wiet *et al.*, 2012]. Compared to cadaver training, the effect of simulator training was not significantly different, which is a good result at second glance due to the shortage of cadavers and the automatic skill assessment only possible with the simulator.

Discussion Despite the efforts to create and refine advanced surgery simulators, these are rarely integrated into the medical curriculum. The integration with other modes of learning is essential for a widespread use of surgery simulators. There are some encouraging examples. The minimally-invasive virtual reality simulator (MIST VR) was used for a *competency-based training curriculum*—a structured virtual reality training program aimed at achieving previously defined competency levels [Aggarwal *et al.*, 2006].

21.10 SUMMARY

In this chapter, we described educational systems and the visualization techniques and strategies which characterize them. Educational systems are based on high-quality datasets, reliable segmentation results, and symbolic knowledge bases carefully linked to the corresponding portions of medical volume data. Although many technical problems have been solved, computer support still plays a minor role in medical education. It is necessary to fine-tune educational systems to the relevant learning objectives, to create stimulating experiences using these systems and to increase the awareness of instructors. Training systems still need to be better integrated into traditional courses and curricula.

Outlook Despite the success of anatomy education systems much work lies ahead. Educational systems in general are based on only one level of spatial resolution—usually the resolution of medical image data. The incorporation of higher resolution medical image data (MicroCT and microscopic data), the development of interaction facilities to explore data at different levels are two of the remaining challenges.

Advanced visual support and computer-assisted training in operative disciplines still often focus on low-level technical problems primarily related to haptic and visual realism. A particular limitation is the focus on single organs. Whole body parts are not considered due to the associated complexity of modeling systems of organs.

Moreover, real surgery is a team effort, involving several physicians (including anesthesia specialists) and support staff. Collaborative training, e.g., in order to handle critical incidents, is a challenge for future training systems. Finally, surgery simulators today do not consider functional aspects. In the future, physiologic modeling of organic systems, such as cardiovascular and digestive systems, will be included in surgery simulation.

A promising area for future work aiming at improved acceptance is the use of game technology and concepts, such as structuring training in appropriate levels, computing scores, providing bonus points, etc. As an example Qin *et al.* [2010] present a system where orthopedic surgery training is enhanced by such concepts. The particular learning goal is to improve blood management—an essential aspect since severe blood loss is a major complication of orthopedic surgery. Also Chan *et al.* [2010] employ gaming concepts for improving biopsy needle placement. From a practical point of view, computer-assisted training systems, in particular the high-end simulators, are just very expensive. Among others, more efficient content generation is necessary to develop solutions at more affordable prices.

FURTHER READING

A simulator for hepatic surgery was developed at INRIA, primarily to train laparoscopic interventions [Cotin *et al.*, 2000a, Delingette and Ayache, 2005]. We have not carefully discussed tool-tissue interactions in surgery simulation. For an overview, see Misra *et al.* [2008]. A valuable source of information concerning biomechanical properties of human tissue is the book [Humphrey, 2004].

Surgery simulation in a simplified manner may also be performed with the ChainMail algorithm [Gibson, 1997, Li and Brodlie, 2003].

With respect to the surgical simulation, we want to point to the MISTELS system (McGill Inanimate System for Training and evaluation of Laparoscopic Skills). A series of publications describes its development, its use and its validation with respect to the ability to assess surgical skills reliably [Derossis *et al.*, 1998, Dauster *et al.*, 2005, Feldman *et al.*, 2004].

Our discussion of training systems for needle-based interventions is by far not complete. Other notable developments were carried out at the National University of Singapore for percutaneous vertebroplasty (using a glove from Cyber Grasp and a Delta haptic device [Chui *et al.*, 2006] and at the Centre for Advanced Studies, Italy, where a trainer for catheter insertion was accomplished). This trainer used a head-tracked stereoscopic viewing system [Zorcolo *et al.*, 1999]. A system for training Chinese acupuncture was presented by Heng *et al.* [2004b]. Later Heng *et al.* [2006] also described specific visco-elastic models for muscles and adipose tissue to simulate needle penetration. Tavakoli *et al.* [2006] provide an in-depth discussion of haptic interaction issues for endoscopic surgery training. As a more general hint for thinking about haptics, the work of Formaglio *et al.* [2008] is recommended. They discuss ergonomic problems, particularly fatigue effects, of current force feedback devices and discuss research attempts toward a device that may be released and remain at their previous position, similar to the mouse at the desktop.

Due to its high importance, we discussed spine surgery training at various stages of the chapter. Readers interested in this area are also directed to Ra *et al.* [2002].

References

G. Abdoulaev, S. Cadeddu, G. Delussu et al. ViVa: The Virtual Vascular Project. *IEEE Transactions on Information Technology in Biomedicine*, 22(4):268–274, 1998.

A. Abildgaard, A. K. Witwit, J. S. Karlsen, E. A. Jacobsen, B. Tennöe, G. Ringstad, and P. Due-Tönnessen. An autostereoscopic 3D display can improve visualization of 3D models from intracranial MR angiography. *International Journal of Computer Assisted Radiology and Surgery*, 5(5):549–554, 2010.

F. Achena, C. Montaldo, and A.L. Nucaro. The down-up bone bridge approach for cochlear and middle ear implants: Our experience in 34 patients. *Clinical Otolaryngology*, 37(2):158–161, 2012.

S. Achenbach, W. Moshage, D. Ropers, and K. Bachmann. Curved multiplanar reconstruction for the evaluation of contrast-enhanced electron beam CT of the coronary arteries. *American Journal of Radiology*, 170(4):895–899, 1998.

R. Adams and L. Bischof. Seeded Region Growing. *IEEE Transactions on Pattern Analysis and Machine Intelligence*, 16(6):641–647, 1994.

A. S. Agatson, W. R. Janowitz, F. Hildner, N. R. Zusner, M. J. Viamonte, and R. Detrano. Quantification of coronary artery calcium using ultrafast computed tomography. *Journal of American College of Cardiology*, 15(4):827–832, 1990.

R. Aggarwal, T. Grantcharov, K. Moorthy, J. Hance, and A. Darzi. A competency-based virtual reality training curriculum for the acquisition of laparoscopic psychomotor skill. *American Journal of Surgery*, 191(1):128–133, 2006.

M. Agus, A. Giachetti, E. Gobbetti, G. Zanetti, and A. Zorcolo. Real-time Haptic and Visual Simulation of Bone Dissection. *Presence: Teleoperators and Virtual Environments*, 12(1):110–122, 2003.

M. Agus, F. Bettio, A. Giachetti, E. Gobbetti, J. A. I. Guitián, F. Marton, J. Nilsson, and G. Pintore. An interactive 3D medical visualization system based on a light field display. *The Visual Computer*, 25(9):883–893, 2009.

N. Al-Saadi, E. Nagel, M. Gross, A. Bornstedt, B. Schnackenburg, C. Klein, W. Klimek, H. Oswald, and E. Fleck. Noninvasive detection of myocardial ischemia from perfusion reserve based on cardiovascular magnetic resonance. *Circulation*, 101(12):1379–1383, Mar 2000.

T. Alderliesten, M. K. Konings, and W. J. Niessen. Modeling friction, intrinsic curvature, and rotation of guide wires for simulation of minimally invasive vascular interventions. *IEEE Transactions on Biomedical Engineering*, 54(1):29–38, 2007.

B. Alfano, A. Brunetti, M. Arpaia et al. Multiparametric display of spin-echo data from MR studies of brain. *Journal of Magnetic Resonance Imaging*, 5:217–225, 1995.

K. Ali, K. Hartmann, and T. Strothotte. Label layout for interactive 3D illustrations. *WSCG*, 13(1):1–8, 2005.

F. Allamandri, P. Cignoni, C. Montani, and R. Scopigno. Adaptively Adjusting Marching Cubes Output to Fit A Trilinear Reconstruction Filter. In *Proc. of Eurographics Workshop on Visualization in Scientific Computing*, pages 25–34, 1998.

J. Allard, S. Cotin, F. Faure, P.-J. Bensoussan, F. Poyer, C. Duriez, H. Delingette, and L. Grisoni. SOFA an Open Source Framework for Medical Simulation. In *Proc. of Medicine Meets Virtual Reality (MMVR)*, February 2007.

P. Alliez, D. Cohen-Steiner, M. Yvinec, and M. Desbrun. Variational tetrahedral meshing. *ACM Transactions on Graphics*, 24(3):617–625, 2005a.

P. Alliez, É. Colin de Verdière, O. Devillers, and M. Isenburg. Centroidal voronoi diagrams for isotropic surface remeshing. *Graphical Models*, 67(3):204–231, 2005b.

D. E. Altobelli, R. Kikinis, J. B. Mulliken, H. Cline, W. Lorensen, and F. Jolesz. Computer-assisted three-dimensional planning in craniofacial surgery. *Plastic and Reconstructive Surgery*, 92(4):576–585; discussion 586–587, 1993.

I. Altrogge, T. Kröger, T. Preusser, C. Büskens, P. L. Pereira, D. Schmidt, A. Weihusen, and H.-O. Peitgen. Towards optimization of probe placement for radiofrequency ablation. In *Proc. of Medical Image Computing and Computer-Assisted Intervention (MICCAI)*, pages 486–493, 2006.

I. Altrogge, T. Preusser, T. Kröger, C. Büskens, P. L. Pereira, D. Schmidt, and H. O. Peitgen. Multiscale optimization of the probe placement for radiofrequency ablation. *Academic Radiology*, 14(11):1310–1324, 2007.

Visual Computing for Medicine, Second Edition. http://dx.doi.org/10.1016/B978-0-12-415873-3.00035-3

P. Angelelli and H. Hauser. Straightening Tubular Flow for Side-by-Side Visualization. *IEEE Transactions on Visualization and Computer Graphics*, 17(12):2063–2070, 2011.

P. Angelelli, K. Nylund, O. H. Gilja, and H. Hauser. Interactive Visual Analysis of Contrast-enhanced Ultrasound Data based on Small Neighborhood Statistics. *Computers & Graphics - Special Issue on Visual Computing in Biology and Medicine*, 35(2):218–226, 2011.

M. Ankerst, M. M. Breunig, H.-P. Kriegel, and J. Sander. Optics: ordering points to identify the clustering structure. In *Proc. of the 1999 ACM SIGMOD international conference on Management of data*, SIGMOD '99, pages 49–60, 1999.

L. Antiga. Geometric reconstruction for computational mesh generation of arterial bifurcations from ct angiography. *Computerized Medical Imaging and Graphics*, 26(11):227–235, 2002.

L. Antiga, M. Piccinelli, L. Botti, B. Ene-Iordache, A. Remuzzi, and D. A. Steinman. An image-based modeling framework for patient-specific computational hemodynamics. *Med. Biol. Engineering and Computing*, 46(11):1097–1112, 2008.

D. Apelt, H. Strasburger, R. Rascher-Friesenhausen, J. Klein, and B. Preim. Generalizing the Evaluation of Medical Image Processing Tools by Use of Gabor Patterns. *Methods Inf. Med.*, 48(4):331–335, 2009.

D. Apelt, H. Strasburger, J. Klein, and B. Preim. Impact of Adaptation Time on Contrast Sensitivity. In *Proc. of SPIE Medical Imaging*, volume 7627, 2010.

N. Archip, O. Clatz, S. Whalen, D. Kacher, A. Fedorov, A. Kot, N. Chrisochoides, F. Jolesz, A. Golby, P. M. Black, and S. K. Warfield. Non-rigid alignment of pre-operative MRI, fMRI, and DT-MRI with intra-operative MRI for enhanced visualization and navigation in image-guided neurosurgery. *NeuroImage*, 35(2):609–624, 2007.

S. G. Armato, G. McLennan, M. F. McNitt-Gray, C. R. Meyer, D. Yankelevitz, D. R. Aberle et al. Lung Image Database Consortium: Developing a Resource for the Medical Imaging Research Community. *Radiology*, 232(3):739–748, 2004.

S. G. Armato, G. McLennan, L. Bidaut et al. The Lung Image Database Consortium (LIDC) and Image Database Resource Initiative (IDRI): A completed reference database of lung nodules on CT scans. *Medical Physics*, 38:915–931, 2011.

A. Armillotta, P. Bonhoeffer, G. Dubini, S. Ferragina, F. Migliavacca, G. Sala, and S. Schievano. Use of rapid prototyping models in the planning of percutaneous pulmonary valved stent implantation. *Proc. of the Institution of Mechanical Engineers Part H-Journal of Engineering in Medicine*, 221(4):407–416, 2007.

D. Arthur and S. Vassilvitskii. k-means++: the advantages of careful seeding. In *Proc. of ACM-SIAM symposium on Discrete algorithms (SODA)*, pages 1027–1035, 2007.

I. Ascencio-Lopez, O. Meruvia-Pastor, and H. Hidalgo-Silva. Adaptive Incremental Stippling using the Poisson-Disk Distribution. *Journal of graphics, gpu, and game tools*, 15(1):29–47, 2010.

D. J. Atkinson, D. Burstein, and R. R. Edelman. First-pass cardiac perfusion: Evaluation with ultrafast MR imaging. *Radiology*, 174(3):757–762, 1990.

O. Kin-Chung Au, C.-L. Tai, H.-K. Chu, D. Cohen-Or, and T.-Y. Lee. Skeleton extraction by mesh contraction. *ACM Transactions on Graphics*, 27(3):44:1–44:10, 2008.

L. M. Auer, D. Auer, and J. F. Knoplioch. Virtual endoscopy for planning and simulation of minimally invasive neurosurgery. In *Proc. of CVRMed*, volume 1205 of *Lecture Notes in Computer Science*, pages 315–318. Springer, 1997.

B. B. Avants and J. P. Williams. An Adaptive Minimal Path Generation Technique for Vessel Tracking in CTA/CE-MRA Volume Images. In *Proc. of Medical Image Computing and Computer-Assisted Intervention (MICCAI)*, volume 1935 of *Lecture Notes in Computer Science*, pages 707–716. Springer, 2000.

R. Avila and L. M. Sobierajski. A Haptic Interaction Method for Volume Visualization. In *Proc. of IEEE Visualization*, pages 197–204, 1996.

L. Axel. Cerebral blood flow determination by rapid-sequence computed tomography: theoretical analysis. *Radiology*, 137:679–686, 1980.

S.R. Aylward and E. Bullitt. Initialization, Noise, Singularities, and Scale in Height-Ridge Traversal for Tubular Object Centerline Extraction. *IEEE Transactions on Medical Imaging*, 21(2):61–75, 2002.

F. S. Azar, D. N. Metaxas, and M. D. Schnall. Methods for modeling and predicting mechanical deformations of the breast under external perturbations. *Medical Image Analysis*, 6:1–27, 2002.

R. Azuma. A Survey of Augmented Reality. *Presence: Teleoperators and Virtual Environments*, 6(4):355–385, 1997.

R. Bade, F. Ritter, and B. Preim. Usability Comparison of Mouse-Based Interaction Techniques for Predictable 3D Rotation. In *Proc. of Smart Graphics*, pages 138–150, 2005.

R. Bade, J. Haase, and B. Preim. Comparison of Fundamental Mesh Smoothing Algorithms for Medical Surface Models. In *Proc. of Simulation and Visualization*, pages 289–304, 2006.

R. Bade, Olaf Konrad, and Bernhard Preim. Reducing Artifacts in Surface Meshes Extracted from Binary Volumes. *Journal of WSCG*, 15(1–3):67–74, 2007.

A. Baer, C. Tietjen, R. Bade, and B. Preim. Hardware-Accelerated Stippling of Surfaces Derived from Medical Volume Data. In *Data Visualization (Proc. of Eurographics/IEEE Symposium on Visualization)*, pages 235–242, 2007.

A. Baer, R. Gasteiger, D. W. Cunningham, and B. Preim. Perceptual Evaluation of Ghosted View Techniques for the Exploration of Vascular Structures and Embedded Flow. *Computer Graphics Forum*, 30(3):811–820, 2011.

M. Baiker, J. Milles, J. Dijkstra, T. D. Henning, A. W. Weber, I. Que, E. L. Kaijzel, C.W.G.M. Löwik, J. H. C. Reiber, and B.P.F. Lelieveldt. Atlas-based whole-body segmentation of mice from low-contrast Micro-CT data. *Medical Image Analysis*, 14(6):723–737, 2010.

S. Baillet, J. C. Mosher, and R. M. Leahy. Electromagnetic brain mapping. *IEEE Signal Processing Magazine*, 18(6):14–30, 2001.

C. L. Bajaj, V. Pacucci, and D. R. Schikore. The Contour Spectrum. In *Proc. of IEEE Visualization*, pages 167–173, 1997.

M. Bajura, H. Fuchs, and R. Ohbuchi. Merging Virtual Objects with the Real World: Seeing Ultrasound Imaginery within the Patient. In *Proc. of ACM SIGGRAPH*, pages 203–210, 1992.

D. H. Ballard. Generalizing the Hough Transform to Detect Arbitrary Shapes. *Pattern Recognition*, 13(2):111–122, 1981.

M. Balzer, T. Schlömer, and O. Deussen. Capacity-constrained point distributions: a variant of lloyd's method. *ACM Transactions on Graphics*, 28(3), 2009.

M. Bance, D. P. Morris, R. G. Vanwijhe, M. L. Kifte, and R. J. Funnell. Comparison of the Mechanical Performance of Ossiculoplasty Using a Prosthetic Malleus-to-Stapes Head with a Tympanic Membrane-to-Stapes Head Assembly in a Human Cadaveric Middle Ear Model. *Otology & Neurotology*, 25(6):903–909, 2004.

A. Barker, J. Bock, R. Lorenz, and M. Markl. 4D Flow MR Imaging. *MAGNETOM Flash*, 44(2):46–52, 2010.

A. H. Barr. Superquadrics and Angle-Preserving Transformations. IEEE Computer Graphics and Applications, 1(1):16–23, 1981.

J.F. Barrett and N. Keat. Artifacts in ct: Recognition and avoidance. *Radiographics*, 24(6):1679–1691, 2004.

W. A. Barrett and E. N. Mortensen. Interactive Live-wire Boundary Extraction. *Medical Image Analysis*, 1(4):331–341, 1997.

D. Bartz and M. Skalej. VIVENDI - A Virtual Ventricle Endoscopy System for Virtual Medicine. In *Data Visualization (Proc. of Eurographics/IEEE Symposium on Visualization)*, 1999.

D. Bartz, M. Meißner, and T. Hüttner. Opengl-assisted occlusion culling for large polygonal models. *Computers & Graphics*, 23(5):667–679, 1999a.

D. Bartz, W. Straßer, M. Skalej, and D. Welte. Interactive Exploration of Extra- and Intracranial Blood Vessels. In *Proc. of IEEE Visualization*, pages 389–392, 1999b.

D. Bartz, Ö. Gürvit, M. Lanzendörfer, A. Kopp, A. Küttner, and W. Straßer. Virtual Endoscopy for Cardio Vascular Exploration. In *Proc. of Computer Assisted Radiology and Surgery*, pages 960–964, 2001.

D. Bartz, D. Mayer, J. Fischer, S. Ley, Á. del Río, S. Thust, C. P. Heussel, H.-U. Kauczor, and W. Straßer. Hybrid segmentation and exploration of the human lungs. In *Proc. of IEEE Visualization*, pages 177–184, 2003.

C. Basdogan, C. Ho, and M. A. Srinivasan. Virtual Environments for Medical Training: Graphical and Haptic Simulation of Laparoscopic Common Bile Duct Exploration. *IEEE/ASME Transactions on Mechatronics*, 6(3):267–285, 2001.

C. Basdogan, S. De, J. Kim, M. Muniyandi, H. Kim, and M. A. Srinivasan. Haptics in Minimally Invasive Surgical Simulation and Training. *IEEE Computer Graphics and Applications*, 24(2):56–64, 2004.

P. J. Basser and D.K. Jones. Diffusion-tensor MRI: theory, experimental design and data analysis - a technical review. *NMR in Biomedicine*, 15:456–467, 2002.

J. J. Batter and F. P. Brooks. GROPE-I: A computer display to the sense of feel. In *Proc. of IFIP Congress on Information Processing*, pages 759–763, 1971.

B. G. Baumgart. A polyhedron representation for computer vision. In *Proc. of the national computer conference and exposition*, AFIPS '75, pages 589–596, 1975.

K. M. Beason, J. Grant, D. C. Banks, B. Futch, and M. Y. Hussaini. Pre-computed Illumination for Isosurfaces. In *Proc. of Conference on Visualization and Data Analysis*, pages 1–11, 2006.

S. Beckhaus, F. Ritter, and T. Strothotte. CubicalPath - Dynamic Potential Fields for Guided Exploration in Virtual Environments. In *Proc. of Pacific Conference on Computer Graphics and Applications*, pages 387–396, 2000.

K. Been, E. Daiches, and C. Yap. Dynamic map labeling. *IEEE Transactions on Visualization and Computer Graphics*, 12:773–780, 2006.

H. J. Beer, M. Bornitz, and H. J. Hardke et al. Modelling of Components of the Human Middle Ear and Simulation of Their Dynamic Behaviour. *Audiology & Neuro-Otology*, 4(3-4):156–162, 1999.

K. Begall and U. Vorwerk. Artificial petrous bone produced by stereolithography for microsurgical dissecting exercises. *ORL J. Otorhinolaryngol Relat. Spec.*, 60(5):241–245, 1998.

P. Begemann. *CT- and MR-Guided Interventions*, chapter CT-Guided Interventions: Indications, Techniques, Pitfalls, pages 11–20. Springer, 2008.

J. Behr, P. Eschler, Y. Jung, and M. Zöllner. X3DOM: a DOM-based HTML5/X3D integration model. In *Proc. of Web 3D Technology*, Web3D, pages 127–135, 2009.

J. Behr, Y. Jung, J. Keil, T. Drevensek, M. Zöllner, P. Eschler, and D. Fellner. A scalable architecture for the HTML5/X3D integration model X3DOM. In *Proc. of Web 3D Technology*, Web3D, pages 185–194, 2010.

J. Behr, Y. Jung, T. Drevensek, and A. Aderhold. Dynamic and interactive aspects of x3dom. In *Proc. of Web 3D Technology*, Web3D, pages 81–87, 2011.

J. Behr, Y. Jung, T. Franke, and T. Sturm. Using images and explicit binary container for efficient and incremental delivery of declarative 3D scenes on the web. In *Proc. of Web 3D Technology*, Web3D, pages 17–25, 2012.

S. Behrens, H. Laue, M. Althaus, T. Böhler, B. Kuemmerlen, H.K. Hahn, and H.-O. Peitgen. Computer assistance for MR based diagnosis of breast cancer: Present and future challenges. *Computerized Medical Imaging and Graphics*, 31(4-5):236–247, 2007.

U. Behrens and R. Ratering. Adding Shadows to a Texture-Based Volume Renderer. In *Proc. of IEEE/ACM Symposium on Volume Visualization*, pages 39–46, 1998.

U. Behrens, J. Teubner, C.J.G. Evertsz, M. Walz, H. Jürgens, and H.-O. Peitgen. Computer-Assisted Dynamic Evaluation of Contrast-Enhanced-MRI. In *Proc. of Computer Assisted Radiology*, pages 362–367. Elsevier, 1996.

M.A. Bekos, M. Kaufmann, M. Nöllenburg, and A. Symvonis. Boundary labeling with octilinear leaders. *Algorithmica*, 57(3):436–461, 2010.

B. Bell, M. Caversaccio, N. Gerber, V. Hamacher, M. Kompis, C. Nauer, L. Nolte, C. Stieger, A. Arnold, and S. Weber. A self-developed and constructed robot for minimally invasive cochlear implantation. *Acta oto-laryngologica*, 132(4):355–360, 2012.

S. Beller, S. Eulenstein, T. Lange, M. Niederstrasser, M. Hünerbein, and P.M. Schlag. A new measure to assess the difficulty of liver resection. *European Journal of Surgical Oncology*, 35(1):59–64, 2009.

W. Benger, H. Bartsch, H.-C. Hege, H. Kitzler, A. Shumilina, and A. Werner. Visualizing neuronal structures in the human brain via diffusion tensor MRI. *International Journal of Neuroscience*, 116(4):461–514, 2006.

D. Benyon, P. Turner, and S. Turner. *Designing Interactive Systems*. Pearson Education, 2005.

P. Berg, G. Janiga, O. Beuing, M. Neugebauer, and D. Thévenin. Hemodynamics in Multiple Intracranial Aneurysms: The Role of Shear Related to Rupture. 3(3):177–181, 2013.

M. Berger. Resolving Occlusion in Augmented Reality: A Contour Based Approach without 3D Reconstruction. In *Proc. of the IEEE Conference on Computer Vision and Pattern Recognition*, pages 91–96, 1997.

L. D. Bergmann, B. E. Rogowitz, and L. A. Treinish. A Rule-Based Tool for Assisting Colormap Selection. In *Proc. of IEEE Visualization*, pages 118–125, 1995.

S. Bériault, F.A. Subaie, D.L. Collins, A.F. Sadikot, and G.B. Pike. A multi-modal approach to computer-assisted deep brain stimulation trajectory planning. *International Journal of Computer Assisted Radiology Surgery*, 7(5):687–704, 2012.

E. J. Berjano. Theoretical modeling for radiofrequency ablation: state-of-the-art and challenges for the future. *BioMedical Engineering OnLine*, 5:24, 2006.

M. Bern and P. Plassmann. *Handbook of Computational Geometry*, chapter Mesh Generation. Elsevier Science, 1999.

P. Besl and N. McKay. A Method for Registration of 3-D Shapes. *IEEE Transactions on Pattern Analysis and Machine Intelligence*, 14(2):239–256, 1992.

M. Bessho, I. Ohnishi, J. Matsuyama, T. Matsumoto, K. Imai, and K. Nakamura. Prediction of strength and strain of the proximal femur by a CT-based finite element method. *Journal of Biomechanics*, 40(8):1745–1753, 2007.

J. Beyer, M. Hadwiger, S. Wolfsberger, and K. Buhler. High-Quality Multimodal Volume Rendering for Preoperative Planning of Neurosurgical Interventions. *IEEE Transactions on Visualization and Computer Graphics*, 13(6):1696–1703, 2007.

J. Beyer, M. Hadwiger, W. Jeong, H. Pfister, and J. Lichtman. Demand-driven volume rendering of terascale EM data. In *SIGGRAPH Talks*, page 57, 2011.

C. Bichlmeier, T. Sielhorst, S. M. Heining, and N. Navab. Improving Depth Perception in Medical AR. In *Proc. of Workshop Bildverarbeitung für die Medizin*, pages 217–221, 2007.

C. Bichlmeier, S. M. Heining, M. Feuerstein, and N. Navab. The Virtual Mirror: A New Interaction Paradigm for Augmented Reality Environments. *IEEE Transactions on Medical Imaging*, 28(9):1498–1510, 2009a.

C. Bichlmeier, M. Kipot, S. Holdstock, S. M. Heining, E. Euler, and N. Navab. A Practical Approach for Intraoperative Contextual In-Situ Visualization. In *International Workshop on Augmented environments for Medical Imaging including Augmented Reality in Computer-aided Surgery (AMI-ARCS 2009)*. MICCAI Society, 2009b.

C. Bichlmeier, E. Euler, T. Blum, and N. Navab. Evaluation of the Virtual Mirror as a Navigational Aid for Augmented Reality Driven Minimally Invasive Procedures. In *Proc. of the International Symposium on Mixed and Augmented Reality (ISMAR)*, 2010.

D. Bielsen, V. A. Maiwald, and M.H. Gross. Interactive Cuts through 3-Dimensional Soft Tissue. *Computer Graphics Forum*, 18(3):31–38, 1999. Proc. of Eurographics.

E.A. Bier. Snap-dragging in three dimensions. In *Proc. of the ACM symposium on Interactive 3D graphics*, pages 193–204, 1990.

E.A. Bier, M. Stone, K. Pier, W. Buxton, and T. DeRose. Toolglass and magic lenses: the see-through interface. In *Proc. of ACM SIGGRAPH*, pages 73–80, 1993.

Å. Birkeland, V. Soltészová, D. Hönigmann, O. H. Gilja, S. Brekke, T. Ropinski, and I. Viola. The Ultrasound Visualization Pipeline - A Survey. *CoRR*, abs/1206.3975, 2012.

S. Birr, R. Dachselt, and B. Preim. Mobile Interactive Displays for Medical Visualization. In *Proc. of Workshop on Data Exploration for Interactive Surfaces at ITS'11*, 2011a.

S. Birr, V. Dicken, B. Geisler, K. Mühler, B. Preim, and C. Stöcker. Interaktive Reports für die Planung von Lungentumoren. In *Mensch & Computer*, pages 131–140, 2011b.

J. Blaas, C. P. Botha, B. Peters, F. M. Vos, and F. H. Post. Fast and reproducible fiber bundle selection in DTI visualization. In *Proc. of IEEE Visualization*, pages 59–64, 2005.

J. Blaas, C. P. Botha, C. Majoie, A. Nederveen, F. M. Vos, and F. H. Post. Interactive Visualization of Fused fMRI and DTI for Planning Brain Tumor Resections. In *Proc. of SPIE Medical Imaging*, volume 6509, 2007a.

J. Blaas, C. P. Botha, and F. H. Post. Interactive Visualization of Multi-Field Medical Data Using Linked Physical and Feature-Space Views. In *Data Visualization (Proc. of Eurographics/IEEE Symposium on Visualization)*, pages 123–130, 2007b.

D. Black, C. Hansen, J. Loviscach, and H.-O. Peitgen. Auditory support for image-guided liver surgery. In *Proc. of Computer Assisted Radiology and Surgery (CARS)*, pages 187–188, 2010.

T. Blacker. The cooper tool. In *Proc. of International Meshing Roundtable (IMR)*, pages 13–29, 1996.

M. H. Blackmon, M. Kitajima, and P. G. Polson. Repairing usability problems identified by the cognitive walkthrough for the web. In *Proc. of the ACM conference on Human Factors in Computing Systems*, pages 497–504, 2003.

A. F. Blackwell. The reification of metaphor as a design tool. *ACM Trans. on Computer-Human Interaction*, 13(4):490–530, 2006.

M. Blackwell, C. Nikou, A. M. DiGioia, and T. Kanade. An Image Overlay System for Medical Data Visualization. In *Proc. of Medical Image Computing and Computer-Assisted Intervention (MICCAI)*, pages 232–240, 1998.

A. Blake and M. Isard. *Active Contours*. Springer, 1998.

J. Blinn. Light Reflection Functions for Simulation of Clouds and Dusty Surfaces. In *Proc. of ACM SIGGRAPH*, pages 21–29, 1982a.

J. F. Blinn. Models of Light Reflection for Computer Synthesized Pictures. *Proc. of ACM SIGGRAPH*, 11:192–198, 1977.

J.F. Blinn. A Generalization of Algebraic Surface Drawing. *ACM Transactions on Graphics*, 1(3):235–256, 1982b.

J. Bloomenthal. An Implicit Surface Polygonizer. In *Graphics Gems IV*, pages 324–349. Academic Press, Boston, 1994.

J. Bloomenthal and K. Shoemake. Convolution Surfaces. *Proc. of ACM SIGGRAPH*, 25(4):251–256, 1991.

J. Bloomenthal, C. Bajaj, J. Blinn, M.-P. Cani, A. Rockwood, B. Wyvill, and G. Wyvill, editors. *Introduction to Implicit Surfaces*. Morgan Kaufman, 1997.

T. Blum, H. Feußner, and N. Navab. Modeling and Segmentation of Surgical Workflow from Laparoscopic Video. In *Proc. of Medical Image Computing and Computer-Assisted Intervention (MICCAI)*, pages 400–407, 2010.

J. E. Bobrow. A direct minimization approach for obtaining the distance between convex polyhedra. *International Journal of Robotic Research*, 8(3):65–76, 1989.

S. Bock, C. Kühnel, T. Boskamp, and H.-O. Peitgen. Robust vessel segmentation. In *Proc. of the SPIE*, volume 6915S, pages 391–399, 2008.

A. Boehm, J. Dornheim, M. Fischer, G. Strauß, A. Dietz, and B. Preim. 3D-Panendoscopy. *International Journal of Computer Assisted Radiology and Surgery*, 4 (Supplement 1):222–223, 2009.

J. Bogaert, S. Dymarkowski, and A. M. Taylor, editors. *Clinical Cardiac MRI:With Interactive CD-ROM*. Springer, 2005.

H. G. Bogren, M. H. Buonocore, and R. J. Valente. Four-dimensional magnetic resonance velocity mapping of blood flow patterns in the aorta in patients with atherosclerotic coronary artery disease compared to age-matched normal subjects. *Journal of Magnetic Resonance Imaging*, 19(4):417–427, 2004.

P. M. Boiselle, K. F. Reynolds, and A. Ernst. Multiplanar and three-dimensional imaging of the central airways with multidetector CT. *AJR Am. J. Roentgenol.*, 179(2):301–308, 2002.

S. A. Bolliger, M. J. Thali, S. Ross, U. Buck, S. Naether, and P. Vock. Virtual autopsy using imaging: bridging radiologic and forensic sciences. A review of the Virtopsy and similar projects. *European Radiology*, 18:273–282, 2008.

S. Booth, F. De Angelis, and T. Schmidt-Tjarksen. The influence of changing haptic refresh-rate on subjective user experiences - lessons for effective touch-based applications. In *Proc. of EuroHaptics*, pages 374–383, 2003.

R. Bordás, S. Seshadhri, G. Janiga, M. Skalej, and D. Thévenin. Experimental validation of numerical simulations on a cerebral aneurysm phantom model. *Interventional Medicine and Applied Science*, 4(4):193–205, 2012.

M. Borkin, K. Gajos, A. Peters, D. Mitsouras, S. Melchionna, F. J. Rybicki, C. L. Feldman, and H. Pfister. Evaluation of Artery Visualizations for Heart Disease Diagnosis. *IEEE Transactions on Visualization and Computer Graphics*, 17(12):2479–2488, 2011.

D. Borland and R.M. Taylor. Rainbow color map (still) considered harmful. *IEEE Computer Graphics and Applications*, 27(2):14–17, 2007.

S. Born, W. M. Jainek, M. Hlawitschka, G. Scheuermann, C. Trantakis, J. Meixensberger, and D. Bartz. Multimodal Visualization of DTI and fMRI Data Using Illustrative Methods. In *Proc. of Workshop Bildverarbeitung für die Medizin*, pages 6–10, 2009.

S. Born, M. Pfeifle, M. Markl, and G. Scheuermann. Visual 4D MRI Blood Flow Analysis with Line Predicates. In *Proc. of IEEE PacificVis*, pages 105–112, 2012.

S. Born, M. Markle, M. Markl, and G. Scheuermann. Illustrative Visualization of Cardiac and Aortic Blood Flow from 4D MRI Data. In *Proc. of IEEE PacificVis*, 2013.

L. Bornemann, V. Dicken, J.-M. Kuhnigk, D. Wormanns, H.-O. Shin, H.-C. Bauknecht, V. Diehl, M. Fabel, S. Meier, O. Kress, S. Krass, and H.-O. Peitgen. Oncotreat: a software assistant for cancer therapy monitoring. *International Journal of Computer Assisted Radiology and Surgery*, 1:231–242, 2007.

A. Bornik, R. Beichel, B. Reitinger, G. Gotschuli, E. Sorantin, F. Leberl, and M. Sonka. Computer Aided Liver Surgery Planning Based on Augmented Reality Techniques. In *Proc. of Workshop Bildverarbeitung für die Medizin*, pages 249–253, 2003.

A. Bornik, R. Beichel, and D. Schmalstieg. Interactive editing of segmented volumetric datasets in a hybrid 2D/3D virtual environment. In *VRST*, pages 197–206, 2006.

T. Boskamp, D. Rinck, F. Link, B. Kümmerlen, G. Stamm, and P. Mildenberger. New Vessel Analysis Tool for Morphometric Quantification and Visualization of Vessels in CT and MR Imaging Data Sets. *RadioGraphics*, 24(1):287–297, 2004.

A. Boss, S. Bisdas, A. Kolb, M. Hofmann, U. Ernemann, C. D. Claussen, C. Pfannenberg, B.J. Pichler, M. Reimold, and L. Stegger. Hybrid PET/MRI of Intracranial Masses: Initial Experiences and Comparison to PET/CT. *The Journal of Nuclear Medicine*, 51(8):1198–1205, 2010.

C. P. Botha and F. H. Post. Hybrid scheduling in the DeVIDE dataflow visualisation environment. In H. Hauser, S. Strassburger, and H. Theisel, editors, *Proc. of Simulation and Visualization*, pages 309–322. SCS Publishing House Erlangen, 2008.

M. Botsch, S. Steinberg, S. Bischoff, and L. Kobbelt. OpenMesh: A generic and efficient polygon mesh data structure. In *Proc. of OpenSG Symposium*, 2002.

M. Botsch, L. Kobbelt, M. Pauly, P. Alliez, and B. Levy. *Polygon Mesh Processing*. CRC Press, 2010.

J. Böttger, D. S. Margulies, P. Horn, U. W. Thomale, I. Podlipsky, I. Shapira-Lichter, S. J. Chaudhry, C. Szkudlarek, K. Mueller, G. Lohmann, T. Hendler, G. Bohner, J. B. Fiebach, A. Villringer, P. Vajkoczy, and A. Abbushi. A software tool for interactive exploration of intrinsic functional connectivity opens new perspectives for brain surgery. *Acta Neurochirurgica*, 153(8):1561–1572, 2011.

J. Böttger, A. Schäfer, G. Lohmann, A. Villringer, and D. Margulies. Force-directed edge-bundling for the visualization of functional connectivity. In *Proc. Organization for Human Brain Mapping*, 2012.

H. Bourquain, A. Schenk, F. Link, B. Preim, G. Prause, and H. O. Peitgen. HepaVision2: a software assistant for preoperative planning in living-related liver transplantation and oncologic liver surgery. *Computer Assisted Radiology and Surgery (CARS 2002)*, pages 341–346, 2002.

D.A. Bowman, E. Kruiff, J. la Viola, and I. Papyrev. *3D User Interfaces: Theory and Practice*. Addison Wesley, 2004.

J. Boyd and J.M. Buick. Comparison of newtonian and non-newtonian flows in a two-dimensional carotid artery model using the lattice boltzmann method. *Physics in Medicine and Biology*, 52(20):6215–6228, 2007.

Y. Boykov and M.-P. Jolly. Interactive Organ Segmentation Using Graph Cuts. In *Proc. of Medical Image Computing and Computer-Assisted Intervention (MICCAI)*, volume 1935 of *Lecture Notes in Computer Science*, pages 276–286. Springer, 2000.

Y. Boykov and M.-P. Jolly. Interactive graph cuts for optimal boundary and region segmentation of objects in N-D images. In *International Conference on Computer Vision*, volume 1, pages 105–112, 2001.

Y. Boykov and O. Veksler. *The Handbook of Mathematical Models in Computer Vision*, chapter Graph Cuts in Vision and Graphics: Theories and Applications. Springer, 2006.

Y. Boykov, V. S. Lee, H. Rusinek, and R. Bansal. Segmentation of Dynamic N-D Data Sets via Graph Cuts Using Markov Models. In *Proc. of Medical Image Computing and Computer-Assisted Intervention (MICCAI)*, pages 1058–1066, 2001.

I. Braude, J. Marker, K. Museth, J. Nissanov, and D. E. Breen. Contour-based surface reconstruction using mpu implicit models. *Graphical Models*, 69(2):139–157, 2007.

C. Brechbuehler, G. Gerig, and O. Kübler. Parameterization of closed surfaces for 3D Shape. *Computer Vision and Image Understanding*, 62(2):154–170, 1995.

R. Brecheisen, A. Vilanova, B. Platel, and B. ter Haar Romeny. Parameter Sensitivity Visualization for DTI Fiber Tracking. *IEEE Transactions on Visualization and Computer Graphics*, 15(6):1441–1448, 2009.

R. Brecheisen, B. Platel, B. M. ter Haar Romeny, and A. Vilanova. Illustrative uncertainty visualization of DTI fiber pathways. *The Visual Computer*, 29(5):297–309, 2013.

D. Breen, R. Whitaker, E. Rose, and M. Tuceryan. Interactive Occlusion and Automatic Object Placement for Augmented Reality. *Computer Graphics Forum*, 15(3):11–22, 1996.

M. Breeuwer. Comprehensive visualization of first-pass myocardial perfusion: The uptake movie and the perfusogram. In *International Society for Magnetic Resonance in Medicine (ISMRM)*, 2002.

H. Brenton, J. Hernandez, F. Bello, P. Strutton, S. Purkayastha, T. Firth, and A. Darzi. Using multimedia and Web3D to enhance anatomy teaching. *Computers & Education*, 49(1):32–53, 2007.

A. D. Brett, M. F. Wilkins, and C. J. Taylor. A User Interface for 3D Statistical Model Building of Anatomical Structures. In *Proc. of Computer Assisted Radiology and Surgery*, pages 246–251. Elsevier, 1997a.

P. N. Brett, T. J. Parker, A. J. Harrison, T. A. Thomas, and A. Carr. Simulation of resistance forces acting on surgical needles. *Journal of English Medicine*, 211(4):335–347, 1997b.

J. F. Brinkley, B. Wong, K. P. Hinshaw, and C. Rosse. Design of an Anatomy Information System. *IEEE Computer Graphics and Applications*, 19(3):38–48, 1999.

M. H. Briscoe. *Preparing Scientific Illustrations: A Guide to Better Posters, Presentations, and Publications*. Springer, 1996.

G. Brix, W. Semmler, R. Port, L. R. Schad, G. Layer, and W. J. Lorenz. Pharmacokinetic parameters in CNS Gd-DTPA enhanced MR imaging. *J. Comput. Assist. Tomogr.*, 15(4):621–628, 1991.

M. Bro-Nielsen. Finite element modeling in surgery simulation. *Proc. of the IEEE*, 86(3):490–503, 1998.

M. Bro-Nielsen and C. Gramkow. Fast Fluid Registration of Medial Images. In *Proc. of Visualization in Biomedical Computing*, volume 1131 of *LNCS*, page 267–276. Springer, 1996.

M. Bro-Nielsen, D. Helfrick, B. Glass, X. Zeng, and H. Connacher. VR simulation of abdominal trauma surgery. In *Proc. of Medicine Meets Virtual Reality*, pages 117–123. IOS Press, 1998.

K. Brodlie and J. Wood. Recent Advances in Volume Visualization. *Computer Graphics Forum*, 20(2):125–148, June 2001.

K. Brodlie, N. El-Khalili, and Y. Li. Using web-based computer graphics to teach surgery. *Computers & Graphics*, 24:157–161, 2000.

M. A. Brown and R. C. Semelka. *MRI: Basic Principles and Applications*. Wiley-Blackwell, 4th edition, 2010.

R.A. Brown. A computerized tomography-computer graphics approach to stereotaxic localization. *Journal of Neurosurgery*, 50(6):715–720, 1979.

S. Bruckner and E. Gröller. VolumeShop: An Interactive System for Direct Volume Illustration. In *Proc. of IEEE Visualization*, pages 671–678, 2005.

S. Bruckner and E. Gröller. Style Transfer Functions for Illustrative Volume Rendering. *Computer Graphics Forum*, 26(3):715–724, 2007a.

S. Bruckner and E. Gröller. Enhancing Depth-Perception with Flexible Volumetric Halos. *IEEE Transactions on Visualization and Computer Graphics*, 13(6):1344–1351, 2007b.

S. Bruckner and E. Gröller. Instant Volume Visualization using Maximum Intensity Difference Accumulation. *Computer Graphics Forum*, 28(3):775–782, 2009.

S. Bruckner, S. Grimm, A. Kanitsar, and E. Gröller. Illustrative Context Preserving Volume Rendering. In *Data Visualization (Proc. of Eurographics/IEEE Symposium on Visualization)*, pages 69–76, 2005.

S. Bruckner, S. Grimm, A. Kanitsar, and E. Gröller. Illustrative Context-Preserving Exploration of Volume Data. *IEEE Transactions on Visualization and Computer Graphics*, 12:1559–1569, 2006.

S. Bruckner, E. Gröller, K. Mueller, B. Preim, and D. Silver. Illustrative Focus+Context Approaches in Interactive Volume Visualization. In *Scientific Visualization: Advanced Concepts*, pages 136–162, 2010.

A. Brun, H. J. Park, H. Knutsson, and C. F. Westin. Coloring of DT-MRI fiber traces using laplacian eigenmaps. In *EUROCAST*, pages 518–529. Springer, 2003.

A. Brun, H. Knutsson, H.-J. Park, M. E. Shenton, and C.-F. Westin. Clustering fiber traces using normalized cuts. In *Proc. of Medical Image Computing and Computer-Assisted Intervention (MICCAI)*, pages 368–375. 2004.

N. Bruno and J. E. Cutting. Minimodularity and the perception of layout. *Journal of Experimental Psychology: General*, pages 161–170, 1988.

P. Brusilovsky. Adaptive navigation support in educational hypermedia: the role of student knowledge level and the case for meta-adaptation. *British Journal of Educational Technology*, 34(4):487–497, 2003.

C. Bruyns, S. Senger, A. Menon, K. Montgomery, S. Wildermuth, and R. Boyle. A survey of interactive mesh-cutting techniques and a new method for implementing generalized interactive mesh cutting using virtual tools. *The Journal of Visualization and Computer Animation*, 13:21–42, 2002.

K. Bucci, A. Bevan, and M. Roach. Advances in radiation therapy: Conventional to 3D, to IMRT, to 4D, and beyond. *A Cancer Journal for Clinicians*, 55:117–134, 2005.

J. Buchanan and M. Sousa. The edge buffer: A data structure for easy silhouette rendering. In *Proc. of Symposium on Non-Photorealistic Animation and Rendering (NPAR)*, pages 39–42. ACM Press, 2000.

M. J. Budoff. *Cardiac CT Imaging: Diagnosis of Cardiovascular Disease*. Springer, 2010.

R.W. Bukowski and C.W. Séquin. Object associations: a simple and practical approach to virtual 3D manipulation. In *Proc. of the ACM symposium on Interactive 3D graphics*, pages 131–138, 1995.

E. Bullitt, S.R. Aylward, E.J. Jr. Bernard, and G. Gerig. Computer-assisted visualization of arteriovenous malformations on the home personal computer. *Neurosurgery*, 48(3):576–582, 2001.

O. Burgert and J. Luszcz. Multi-Dimensional Presentation State - Towards a DICOM Mechanism for Consistent Presentation of Higher Dimensional Medical Imaging Data. In *Proc. of Medicine Meets Virtual Reality*, 2012.

M. Burns, J. Klawe, S. Rusinkiewicz, A. Finkelstein, and D. DeCarlo. Line drawings from volume data. *ACM Transactions on Graphics*, 24(3):512–518, 2005.

M. Burns, M. Haidacher, W. Wein, I. Viola, and M.E. Gröller. Feature emphasis and contextual cutaways for multimodal medical visualization. *Focus*, pages 275–282, 2007.

S. Busking, A. Vilanova, and J.J. van Wijk. Particle-based non-photorealistic volume visualization. *The Visual Computer*, 24(5):335–346, 2008.

C. R. Butson, G. Tamm, S. Jain, T. Fogal, and J. Krueger. Evaluation of Interactive Visualization on Mobile Computing Platforms for Selection of Deep Brain Stimulation Parameters. *IEEE Transactions on Visualization and Computer Graphics*, 19(1):108–117, 2013.

B. Buxton. *Sketching the User Experience: Getting the Design Right and the Right Design*. Morgan Kaufman, 2007.

T. Buzug. *Introduction to Computed Tomography: From Photon Statistics to Modern Cone-beam CT*. Springer, 2008.

D. Byrd. A scrollbar-based visualization for document navigation. In *Proc. of the ACM conference on Digital libraries (DL)*, pages 122–129. ACM, 1999.

D. B. Karron C. M. Wegner. Surgical navigation using audio feedback. *Studies In Health Technology And Informatics*, 39:450–458, 2010.

J. Caban and P. Rheingans. Texture-based Transfer Functions for Direct Volume Rendering. *IEEE Transactions on Visualization and Computer Graphics*, 14(6):1364–1371, 2008.

B. Cabral and L. C. Leedom. Imaging vector fields using line integral convolution. In *Proc. of ACM SIGGRAPH*, pages 263–270, 1993.

B. Cabral, N. Cam, and J. Foran. Accelerated Volume Rendering and Tomographic Reconstruction Using Texture Mapping Hardware. In *Proc. of IEEE/ACM Symposium on Volume Visualization*, pages 91–98, 1994.

W. Cai and H. Yoshida. Electronic cleansing in CT colonography: past, present, and future. In *Proc. of Virtual Colonoscopy and Abdominal Imaging: computational challenges and clinical opportunities*, MICCAI'10, pages 1–8, 2011.

J. Campbell, L. Tirapelle, K. Yates, R. Clark, K. Inaba, D. Green, D. Plurad, L. Lam, A. Tang, R. Cestero, and M. Sullivan. The effectiveness of a cognitive task analysis informed curriculum to increase self-efficacy and improve performance for an open cricothyrotomy. *Journal Surgery Education*, 68(5):403–407, 2011.

H. Carr, J. Snoeyink, and U. Axen. Computing contour trees in all dimensions. In *Proc. of the ACM-SIAM symposium on Discrete algorithms*, SODA '00, pages 918–926, 2000.

J.M. Carroll, R.L. Mack, and W.A. Kellogg. *Handbook of Human-Computer Interaction*, chapter Interface Metaphors and User Interface Design, pages 67–85. North-Holland: Elsevier Science Publishers, 1990.

V. Caselles, R. Kimmel, and G. Sapiro. Geodesic Active Contours. *International Journal of Computer Vision*, 22(1):61–79, 1997.

D. Cash, M. Miga, S. Glasgow, B. Dawant, L. Clements, Z. Cao, R. Galloway, and W. Chapman. Concepts and Preliminary Data Toward the Realization of Image-guided Liver Surgery. *Journal of Gastrointestinal Surgery*, 11(7):844–859, 2007.

M. Cenk Cavusoglu, T. Goktekin, and F. Tendick. GiPSi: A Framework for Open Source/Open Architecture Software Development for Organ-Level Surgical Simulation. *IEEE Transactions on Information Technology in Biomedicine*, 10(2):312–322, 2006.

J. R. Cebral and R. Löhner. From Medical Images to CFD Meshes. In *Proc. of International Meshing Roundtable (IMR)*, pages 321–331, 1999.

J. R. Cebral and R. Lohner. From Medical Images to Anatomically Accurate Finite Element Grids. *International Journal of Numerical Methdos in Engineering*, 51:985–1008, 2001.

J. R. Cebral, M. A. Castro, S. Appanaboyina, C. M. Putman, D. Millan, and A. F. Frangi. Efficient pipeline for image-based patient-specific analysis of cerebral aneurysm hemodynamics: technique and sensitivity. *IEEE Transactions on Medical Imaging*, 24(4):457–467, 2005.

J. R. Cebral, F. Mut, J. Weir, and C. M. Putman. Association of Hemodynamic Characteristics and Cerebral Aneurysm Rupture. *American Journal of Neuroradiology*, 31:264–270, 2011.

M. D. Cerqueira, N. J. Weissman, V. Dilsizian, A. K. Jacobs, S. Kaul, W. K. Laskey, D. J. Pennell, J. A. Rumberger, T. Ryan, and M. S. Verani. Standardized Myocardial Segmentation and Nomenclature for Tomographic Imaging of the Heart. *Circulation*, 105(4):539–542, 2002a.

M.D. Cerqueira, N.J. Weissman, V. Dilsizian, A.K. Jacobs, S. Kaul, W.K. Laskey, D.J. Pennell, J.A. Rumberger, T. Ryan, and M.S. Verani. Standardized myocardial segmentation and nomenclature for tomographic imaging of the heart: a statement for healthcare professionals from the Cardiac Imaging Committee of the Council on Clinical Cardiology of the American Heart Association. *Circulation*, 105(4):539–542, 2002b.

M. Chabanas, V. Luboz, and Y. Payan. Patient specific finite element model of the face soft tissues for computer-assisted maxillofacial surgery. *Medical Image Analysis*, 7(2):131–151, 2003.

W.-Y. Chan, D. Ni, W.-M. Pang, J. Qin, Y.-P. Chui, S. Chun-Ho Yu, and P.-A. Heng. Learning Ultrasound-Guided Needle Insertion Skills through an Edutainment Game. *Transactions of Edutainment*, 4:200–214, 2010.

Y. L. Chang and X. Li. Adaptive image region-growing. *IEEE Transactions on Image Processing*, 3(6):868–872, 1994.

D. Chen, Z. Liang, M. Wax, L. Li, B. Li, and A. Kaufman. A Novel Approach to Extract Colon Lumen from CT Images for Virtual Colonoscopy. *IEEE Transactions on Medical Imaging*, 19(12):1220–1226, 2000.

M. Chen, S. Mountford, S. Joy, and A. Sellen. A study in interactive 3-D rotation using 2-D control devices. In *Proc. of ACM SIGGRAPH*, pages 121–129, 1988.

M. Chen, C. D. Correa, S. Islam, M. W. Jones, P.-Y. Shen, D. Silver, S. J. Walton, and P. J. Willis. Manipulating, Deforming and Animating Sampled Object Representations. *Computer Graphics Forum*, 26(4):824–852, 2007.

S. Chen and G.D. Doolen. Lattice boltzmann method for fluid flows. *Annu. Rev. Fluid Mech.*, 30:329–364, 1998.

S. J.-S. Chen, M. Kersten-Oertel, S. Drouin, and D. L. Collins. Visualizing the path of blood flow in static vessel images for image guided surgery of cerebral arteriovenous malformations. pages 831630–831630–10, 2012.

W. Chen, M. L. Giger, U. Bick, and G. M. Newstead. Automatic identification and classification of characteristic kinetic curves of breast lesions on DCE-MRI. *Medical Physics*, 33(8):2878–2887, 2006.

Y. Chen, W. Guo, Q. Zeng, X. Yan, F. Huang, H. Zhang, G. He, B. C. Vemuri, and Y. Liu. Estimation, smoothing, and characterization of apparent diffusion coefficient profiles from high angular resolution DWI. In *Proc. of Computer Vision and Pattern Recognition (CVPR)*, volume 1, page I–588, 2004.

N. Chentanez, R. Alterovitz, D. Ritchie, L. Cho, K. K. Hauser, K. Goldberg, J. R. Shewchuk, and J. F. O'Brien. Interactive simulation of surgical needle insertion and steering. *ACM Transactions on Graphics*, 28(3):88:1–88:10, 2009.

L. H. Cheong, T. S. Koh, and Z. Hou. An automatic approach for estimating bolus arrival time in dynamic contrast MRI using piecewise continuous regression models. *Physics in Medicine and Biology*, 48(5), 2003.

L. Chittaro. Visualizing information on mobile devices. *Computer*, 39:40–45, March 2006.

L. Chittaro. Designing visual user interfaces for mobile applications. In *Proc. of the ACM SIGCHI symposium on Engineering interactive computing systems (EICS)*, pages 231–232, 2011.

L. Chittaro and R. Ranon. Web3D technologies in learning, education and training: motivations, issues, opportunities. *Computers & Education*, 49(1):3–18, 2007.

Z. Cho, J. Jones, and M. Singh. *Foundations of Medical Imaging*. Wiley, New York, NY, 1993.

J. Y. Choi, J. H. Choi, N. K. Kim, Y. Kim, J. K. Lee, M. K. Kim, J. H. Lee, and M. J. Kim. Analysis of errors in medical rapid prototyping models. *International Journal of Oral Maxillofacial Surgery*, 31(1):23–32, 2002.

K.-S. Choi, H. Sun, and P.-A. Heng. Interactive deformation of soft tissues with haptic feedback for medical learning. *IEEE Transactions on Information Technology in Biomedicine*, 7(4):358–363, 2003.

P. Chojecki and U. Leiner. Berührungslose Gestik-Interaktion im Operationssaal Touchless Gesture-Interaction in the Operating Room. *i-com*, 9(1):13–20, 2009.

P. L. Choyke, A. J. Dwyer, and M. V. Knopp. Functional Tumor Imaging with Dynamic Contrast-Enhanced Magnetic Resonance Imaging. *Journal of Magnetic Resonance Imaging*, 17:509–520, 2003.

G. E. Christensen. Consistent Linear-Elastic Transformations for Image Matching. In *Information Processing in Medical Imaging*, volume 1613 of *Lecture Notes in Computer Science*, pages 224–237. Springer, 1999.

G. E. Christensen. Consistent Nonlinear Elastic Image Registration. In *IEEE Proceedings of Mathematical Methods in Biomedical Image Analysis*, pages 37–43, Kauai, Hawai, 2001.

J. Christensen, J. Marks, and S. Shieber. An empirical study of algorithms for point-feature label placement. *ACM Transactions on Graphics*, 14:203–232, 1995.

A. Chu, W.-Y. Chan, J. Guo, W.-M. Pang, and P.-A. Heng. Perception-aware depth cueing for illustrative vascular visualization. In *Proc. of International Conference on BioMedical Engineering and Informatics*, pages 341–346, 2008.

C. K. Chui, J. Teo, Z. Wang, J. Ong, J. Zhang, K. M. Si-Hoe, S. H. Ong, C. H. Yan, S. C. Wang, H. K. Wong, J. H. Anderson, and S. H. Teoh. Integrative haptic and visual interaction for simulation of PMMA injection during vertebroplasty. *Studies in Health Technologies and Informatics*, 119:96–98, 2006.

P. Cignoni, C. Montani, and R. Scopigno. A comparison of mesh simplification algorithms. *Computers & Graphics*, 22(1):37–54, 1998.

P. Cignoni, F. Ganovelli, C. Montani, and R. Scopigno. Reconstruction of Topologically Correct and Adaptive Trilinear Surfaces. *Computers & Graphics*, 24(3):399–418, 2000.

M. Cimerman and A. Kristan. Preoperative planning in pelvic and acetabular surgery: the value of advanced computerised planning modules. *Injury*, 38(4):442–449, 2007.

P. Cinquin, E. Bainville, C. Barbe, E. Bittar, V. Bouchard, L. Bricault, G. Champleboux, M. Chenin, L. Chevalier, Y. Delnondedieu, L. Desbat, V. Dessenne, A. Hamadeh, D. Henry, N. Laieb, S. Lavallee, J.M. Lefebvre, F. Leitner, Y. Menguy, F. Padieu, O. Peria, A. Poyet, M. Promayon, S. Rouault, P. Sautot, J. Troccaz, and P. Vassal. Computer assisted medical interventions. *IEEE Engineering in Medicine and Biology Magazine*, 14(3):254 –263, 1995.

G. Cipriano and M. Gleicher. Text scaffolds for effective surface labeling. *IEEE Transactions on Visualization and Computer Graphics*, 14(6):1675–1682, 2008.

C. A Clark, T. R. Barrick, M. M. Murphy, and B. A. Bell. White matter fiber tracking in patients with space-occupying lesions of the brain: a new technique for neurosurgical planning? *NeuroImage*, 20(3):1601–1608, 2003.

K. Cleary and T. M. Peters. Image-guided interventions: technology review and clinical applications. *Annu. Rev. Biomed. Engineering*, 15(12):119–142, 2010.

L. Cmolík and J. Bittner. Layout-aware optimization for interactive labeling of 3D models. *Computers & Graphics*, 34(4):378–387, 2010.

A. Cockburn and S. Brewster. Multimodal feedback for the acquisition of small targets. *Ergonomics*, 48(9):1129–1150, 2005.

D. Cohen-Or, Y. Chrysanthou, C. T. Silva, and F. Durand. A survey of visibility for walkthrough applications. *IEEE Transactions on Visualization and Computer Graphics*, 9(3):412–431, 2003.

F. Cole, K. Sanik, D. DeCarlo, A. Finkelstein, T. Funkhouser, S. Rusinkiewicz, and M. Singh. How well do line drawings depict shape? *ACM Transactions on Graphics*, 28:28:1–28:9, 2009.

T. R. Coles and N. W. John. The Effectiveness of Commercial Haptic Devices for Use in Virtual Needle Insertion Training Simulations. In *Proc. of Advances in Computer-Human Interactions*, pages 148–153, 2010.

T. R. Coles, D. Meglan, and N. W. John. The Role of Haptics in Medical Training Simulators: A Survey of the State of the Art. *IEEE Transactions on Haptics*, 4(1):51–66, 2011.

D. Collins, A. Zijdenbos, V. Kollokian, J. Sled, N. Kabani, C. Holmes, and A. Evans. Design and Construction of a Realistic Digital Brain Phantom. *IEEE Transactions on Medical Imaging*, 17(3):463–468, 1998.

M. E. Colpan, Z. Sekerci, E. Cakmakci, T. Donmez, N. Oral, and D. J. Mogul. Virtual endoscope-assisted intracranial aneurysm surgery: evaluation of fifty-eight surgical cases. *Minimally Invasive Neurosurgery*, 50(1):27–32, 2007.

O. Comas, Z. A. Taylor, J. Allard, S. Ourselin, S. Cotin, and J. Passenger. Efficient Nonlinear FEM for soft tissue modelling and its GPU implementation within the open source framework SOFA. In *Proc. of the 4th international symposium on Biomedical Simulation*, ISBMS '08, pages 28–39, 2008.

D. A. Cook. Web-based learning: pros, cons and controversies. *Clinical Medicine*, 7(1):37–42, 2007.

D. A. Cook and D. M. Dupras. A Practical Guide To Developing Effective Web-based Learning. *Journal of General Internal Medicine*, 19(6):698–707, 2004.

R. L. Cook. Stochastic sampling in computer graphics. *ACM Transactions on Graphics*, 5(1):51–72, 1986.

W. A. Cook and W. R. Oakes. Mapping methods for generating three-dimensional meshes. *Computers in Mechanical Engineering*, pages 67–72, 1982.

A. Cooper. *The inmates are running the asylum*. Macmillan, 1999.

T. F. Cootes, A. Hill, C. J. Taylor, and J. Haslam. The Use of Active Shape Models for Locating Structures in Medical Images. *Image and Vision Computing*, 12(6):355–366, 1994.

T. F. Cootes, G.J. Edwards, and Chris J. Taylor. Active Appearance Models. *IEEE Transactions on Pattern Analysis and Machine Intelligence*, 23(6):681–685, 2001.

T. F. Cootes, G. J. Edwards, and Chris J. Taylor. A Comparative Evaluation of Active Appearance Model Algorithms. In *British Machine Vision Conference*, volume 2, pages 680–689, 1998.

J. Cordes, J. Dornheim, B. Preim, I. Hertel, and G. Strauß. Preoperative Segmentation of Neck CT Datasets for the Planning of Neck Dissections. In *Proc. of SPIE Medical Imaging*. Spie Press, 2006.

J. Cordes, K. Hintz, J. Franke, C. Bochwitz, and B. Preim. Conceptual design and prototyping implementation of a case-based training system for spine surgery. In S. Hambach, A. Martens, and B. Urban, editors, *Proc. of the eLBa Science Conference (e-Learning Baltics)*, pages 169–178, 2008.

J. Cordes, J. Dornheim, and B. Preim. Szenariobasierte Entwicklung von Systemen für Training und Planung in der Chirurgie. *i-com*, 9(1):5–12, 2009.

N.D. Cornea, D. Silver, and P. Min. Curve-skeleton properties, applications, and algorithms. *IEEE Transactions on Visualization and Computer Graphics*, 13:530–548, 2007.

I. Corouge, S. Gouttard, and G. Gerig. A Statistical Shape Model of Individual Fiber Tracts Extracted from Diffusion Tensor MRI. In *Proc. of Medical Image Computing and Computer-Assisted Intervention (MICCAI)*, number 3217 in LNCS, pages 671–679. Springer, 2004a.

I. Corouge, S. Gouttard, and G. Gerig. Towards a shape model of white matter fiber bundles using diffusion tensor MRI. In *Proc. of International Symposium on Biomedical Imaging (ISBI)*, pages 344–347, 2004b.

C. D. Correa and K.-L. Ma. Size-based Transfer Functions: A New Volume Exploration Technique. *IEEE Transactions on Visualization and Computer Graphics*, 14(6):1380–1387, 2008.

C. D. Correa and K.-L. Ma. Visibility-driven transfer functions. In *Proc. of IEEE Pacific Vis.*, pages 177–184, 2009.

C. D. Correa and K.-L. Ma. Visibility Histograms and Visibility-Driven Transfer Functions. *IEEE Transactions on Visualization and Computer Graphics*, 17(2):192–204, 2011.

C. D. Correa and D. Silver. Dataset Traversal with Motion-Controlled Transfer Functions. In *Proc. of IEEE Visualization*, pages 359–366, 2005.

C. D. Correa, D. Silver, and M. Chen. Discontinuous Displacement Mapping for Volume Graphics. In *Proc. of Volume Graphics*, pages 9–16, 2006a.

C. D. Correa, D. Silver, and M. Chen. Feature aligned volume manipulation for illustration and visualization. *IEEE Transactions on Visualization and Computer Graphics*, 12(5):1069–1076, 2006b.

S. Cotin, H. Delingette, and N. Ayache. Real-time elastic deformations of soft tissues for surgery simulation. *IEEE Transactions on Visualization and Computer Graphics*, 5(1):62–73, 1999.

S. Cotin, H. Delingette, and N. Ayache. A Hybrid Elastic Model allowing Real-Time Cutting, Deformations and Force-Feedback for Surgery Training and Simulation. *The Visual Computer*, 16(8):437–452, 2000a.

S. Cotin, H. Delingette, and N. Ayache. A hybrid elastic model for real-time cutting, deformations, and force feedback for surgery training and simulation. *The Visual Computer*, 16(8):437–452, 2000b.

E. Coto, S. Grimm, S. Bruckner, E. Gröller, A. Kanitsar, and O. Rodriguez. MammoExplorer: An Advanced CAD Application for Breast DCE-MRI. In *Proc. of Vision, Modeling, and Visualization*, pages 91–98, 2005.

B. Couteau, P. Mansat, É. Estivalèzes, R. Darmana, M. Mansat, and J. Egan. Finite element analysis of the mechanical behavior of a scapula implanted with a glenoid prosthesis. *Clinical Biomechanics*, 16(7):566–575, 2001.

J.R. Cox, V.W. Gerth, and W.F. Holmes. The programmed console: An aid to the radiologist in treatment planning. In *Proc. First International Conference on the Use of Computers in Therapeutic Radiology*, pages 12–14, 1966.

R. W. Cox. AFNI: what a long strange trip it's been. *NeuroImage*, 2011.

C. Crassin, F. Neyret, S. Lefebvre, and E. Eisemann. Gigavoxels: Ray-guided streaming for efficient and detailed voxel rendering. In *Proc. of Symposium on Interactive 3D graphics and games*, pages 15–22, 2009.

B. Crespin, C. Blanc, and C. Schlick. Implicit Sweep Objects. *Computer Graphics Forum*, 15(3):165–174, 1996.

J. L. Crossingham, J. Jenkinson, N. Woolridge et al. Interpreting three-dimensional structures from two-dimensional images: a web-based interactive 3D teaching model of surgical liver anatomy. *HPB*, 11(6):523–528, 2009.

B. Csébfalvi, L. Mroz, H. Hauser, A. König, and E. Gröller. Fast Visualization of Object Contours by Non-Photorealistic Volume Rendering. *Computer Graphics Forum*, 21(3):452–460, 2001. Proc. of Eurographics, Manchester, Great Britain.

D. W. Cunningham and C. Wallraven. *Experimental Design: From user studies to psychophysics*. A.K. Peters, 2011.

R. A. Curry and B. B. Tempkin. *Sonography: Introduction to Normal Structure and Function*. W.B. Saunders, 2004.

M. Cutajar, I. A. Mendichovszky, P. S. Tofts, and I. Gordon. The importance of aif roi selection in dce-mri renography: reproducibility and variability of renal perfusion and filtration. *European Journal of Radiology*, 74(3):e154–60, 2010.

F. Dachille, K. Kreeger, M. Wax, A. Kaufman, and Z. Liang. Interactive Navigation for PC-based Virtual Colonoscopy. In *Proc. of SPIE Medical Imaging*, volume 4321, 2001.

F. Dammann, A. Bode, E. Schwaderer, M. Schaich, M. Heuschmid, and M. M. Maassen. Computer-aided surgical planning for implantation of hearing aids based on CT data in a VR environment. *Radiographics*, 21(1):183–191, 2001.

B. Dauster, A. P. Steinberg, and M. C. Vassiliou et al. Validity of the MISTELS Simulator for Laparoscopy Training in Urology. *Journal of Endourology*, 19:541–545, 2005.

M. de Bruijne, B. Ginneken, J. B. A. Maintz, W. J. Niessen, and M. A. Viergever. Active shape model based segmentation of abdominal aortic aneurysms in CTA images. In *Proc. of SPIE Medical Imaging*, volume 4684, pages 463–474, Bellingham WA, 2002. SPIE Press.

M. de Bruijne, B. van Ginneken, M.A. Viergever, and W.J. Niessen. Interactive segmentation of abdominal aortic aneurysms in CTA images. *Medical Image Analysis*, 8(2):127–138, 2004.

P. de Feyter, editor. *Computed Tomography of the Coronary Arteries*. Taylor & Francis, 2004.

W. L. de Graaf, J. J. M. Zwanenburg, F. Visser, M. P. Wattjes, P. J. W. Pouwels, J. J. G. Geurts, C. H. Polman, F. Barkhof, P. R. Luijten, and J. A. Castelijns. Lesion detection at seven Tesla in multiple sclerosis using magnetisation prepared 3D-FLAIR and 3D-DIR. *European Radiology*, 22:221–231, 2012.

Commission Internationale de l'Eclairage (CIE). Cie recommendations on uniform color spaces–color difference equations psychometric color terms. *CIE Publication*, 15(E-1.3.1), 1978.

W. C. de Leeuw and J. J. van Wijk. A Probe for Local Flow Field Visualization. In *Proc. of IEEE Visualization*, pages 39–45, 1993.

D. DeCarlo and S. Rusinkiewicz. Highlight lines for conveying shape. In *Proc. of Non-photorealistic animation and rendering, NPAR*, pages 63–70, 2007.

D. DeCarlo, A. Finkelstein, S. Rusinkiewicz, and A. Santella. Suggestive Contours for Conveying Shape. In *Proc. of ACM SIGGRAPH*, pages 848–855, 2003.

D. DeCarlo, A. Finkelstein, and S. Rusinkiewicz. Interactive Rendering of Suggestive Contours with Temporal Coherence. In *Proc. of Symposium on Non-Photorealistic Animation and Rendering (NPAR)*, pages 15–24. ACM Press, 2004.

W. F. Decraemer, J. J. Dirckx, and W. R. Funnell. Three-dimensional modelling of the middle-ear ossicular chain using a commercial high-resolution X-ray CT scanner. *Journal of the Association of Research in Otolaryngology*, 4(2):250–263, 2003.

H. Degani, V. Gusis, D. Weinstein, S. Fields, and S. Strano. Mapping pathophysiological features of breast tumors by MRI at high spatial resolution. *Nature in Medicine*, 2:780–782, 1997.

A. del Río, J. Fischer, M. Köbele, D. Bartz, and W. Straßer. Augmented Reality Interaction for Semiautomatic Volume Classification. In *Proc. of Eurographics Symposium on Virtual Environments*, pages 113–120, 2005.

A. del Río, J. Fischer, M. Köbele, J. Hoffmann, F. Duffner, M. Tatagiba, W. Straßer, and D. Bartz. Intuitive Volume Classification in Medical AR. *GMS Journal on Current Topics in Computer and Robot Assisted Surgery*, 1(1), 2006.

H. Delingette and N. Ayache. Hepatic Surgery Simulation. *Communications of the ACM*, 48(2):31–36, 2005.

H. Delingette, G. Subsol, S. Cotin, and J. Pignon. A Craniofacial Surgery Simulation Testbed. In *Proc. of Visualization in Biomedical Computing*, volume 2359, pages 607–618. SPIE Press, 1994.

T. Delmarcelle and L. Hesselink. Visualization of second order tensor fields and matrix data. In *Proc. of IEEE Visualization*, pages 316–323, 1992.

T. Delmarcelle and L. Hesselink. Visualizing second-order tensor fields with hyper-streamlines. *IEEE Computer Graphics and Applications*, 13(4):25–33, 1993.

J. A. den Boer and P. J. M. Folkers. MR perfusion and diffusion imaging in ischaemic brain disease. *Medica Mundi*, 41(2):20–35, 1997.

J. E. Dennis and R. B. Schnabel. *Numerical Methods for Unconstrained Optimization and Nonlinear Equations*. Prentice Hall, 1983.

V. J. Dercksen, M. Oberlaender, B. Sakmann, and H.-C. Hege. Interactive Visualization–a Key Prerequisite for Reconstruction and Analysis of Anatomically Realistic Neural Networks. *Visualization in Medicine and Life Sciences II*, pages 27–44, 2012.

T. DeRose, M. Kass, and T. Truong. Subdivision surfaces in character animation. In *Proc. of ACM SIGGRAPH*, pages 85–94. ACM Press, 1998.

A. M. Derossis, G. M. Fried, and M. Abrahamowicz et al. Development of a model for training and evaluation of laparoscopic skills. *American Journal of Surgery*, 175:482–487, 1998.

M. Desbrun, M. Meyer, P. Schröder, and A. Barr. Implicit Fairing of Irregular Meshes Using Diffusion and Curvature Flow. In *Proc. of ACM SIGGRAPH*, pages 317–324, 1999.

M. Desbrun, E. Kanso, and Y. Tong. Discrete differential forms for computational modeling. ACM SIGGRAPH Courses, 2006.

M. Descoteaux, E. Angelino, S. Fitzgibbons, and R. Deriche. Apparent diffusion coefficients from high angular resolution diffusion imaging: Estimation and applications. *Magnetic Resonance in Medicine*, 56(2):395–410, 2006.

M. Descoteaux, R. Deriche, T. R. Knosche, and A. Anwander. Deterministic and probabilistic tractography based on complex fibre orientation distributions. *IEEE Transactions on Medical Imaging*, 28(2):269–286, 2009.

O. Deussen, J. Hamel, A. Raab, S. Schlechtweg, and T. Strothotte. An Illustration Technique Using Hardware-Based Intersections. In *Proc. of Graphics Interface*, pages 175–182, 1999.

O. Deussen, S. Hiller, C. van Overfeld, and T. Strothotte. Floating Points: A Method for Computing Stipple Drawings. *Computer Graphics Forum*, 19(3):40–51, 2000.

M. Dewey, E. Zimmermann, M. Laule, W. Rutsch, and B. Hamm. Three-vessel coronary artery disease examined with 320-slice computed tomography coronary angiography. *European Society of Cardiology*, 29(13):1669, 2008.

A. Dhawan. *Medical Image Analysis*. Wiley-IEEE Press, 2003.

C. Diaz and L. Altamirano-Robles. Fast Noncontinuous Path Phase-Unwrapping Algorithm Based on Gradients and Mask. In *Proc. of Progress in Pattern Recognition, Image Analysis and Applications*, volume 3287 of *Lecture Notes in Computer Science*, pages 116–123. Springer, 2004.

J. Díaz, H. Yela, and P.-P. Vázquez. Vicinity Occlusion Maps - Enhanced depth perception of volumetric models. In *Proc. of Computer Graphics International*, pages 56–63, 2008.

J. Díaz, P.-P. Vázquez, I. Navazo, and F. Duguet. Real-Time Ambient Occlusion and Halos with Summed Area Tables. *Computers & Graphics*, 34:337–350, 2010.

J. Díaz, E. Monclús, I. Navazo, and P.-P. Vázquez. Adaptive Cross-sections of Anatomical Models. *Computer Graphics Forum*, 31(7-2):2155–2164, 2012.

C. Dick, J. Georgii, R. Burgkart, and R. Westermann. Computational Steering for Patient-Specific Implant Planning in Orthopedics. In *Proc. of Eurographics Workshop on Visual Computing in Biology and Medicine (VCBM)*, pages 83–92, 2008.

C. Dick, J. Georgii, R. Burgkart, and R. Westermann. Stress Tensor Field Visualization for Implant Planning in Orthopedics. *IEEE Transactions on Visualization and Computer Graphics*, 15(6):1399–1406, 2009.

C. Dick, R. Burgkart, and R. Westermann. Distance Visualization for Interactive 3D Implant Planning. *IEEE Transactions on Visualization and Computer Graphics*, 17(12):2173–2182, 2011a.

C. Dick, J. Georgii, and R. Westermann. A real-time multigrid finite hexahedra method for elasticity simulation using CUDA. *Simulation Modelling Practice and Theory*, 19(2):801–816, 2011b.

V. Dicken, B. Wein, H. Schubert, J.-M. Kuhnigk, S. Kraß, and H.-O. Peitgen. Novel Projection Views for Simplified Reading of Thorax CT Scans with Multiple Pulmonary Nodules. In *Proc. of Computer Assisted Radiology and Surgery*, pages 59–64. Springer, 2003.

J. Diepstraten, D. Weiskopf, and T. Ertl. Interactive Cutaway Illustrations. *Computer Graphics Forum*, 22(3):523–532, 2003.

H. Digabel and C. Lantuejoul. Iterative Algorithms. In *Proc. of 2nd European Symposium on Quantitative Analysis of Microstructures in Material Science*, pages 85–99, Stuttgart, 1978. Riederer.

A. M. Digioia, B. Jaramaz, C. Nikou, R. S. Labarca, J. E. Moody, and B. D. Colgan. Surgical navigation for total hip replacement with the use of hipnav. *Operative Techniques in Orthopaedics*, 10(1):3–8, 2000.

E. W. Dijkstra. A note on two problems in connection with graphs. *Numerische Mathematik*, 1:269–271, 1959.

Z. Ding, J. C. Gore, and A. W. Anderson. Classification and quantification of neuronal fiber pathways using diffusion tensor MRI. *Magnetic resonance in medicine*, 49(4):716–721, 2003.

E. Dodd, M. Riding, and N. John. Building Realistic Virtual Environments using Java and VRML. In *Proc. of Irish Workshop on Computer Graphics*, pages 53–61, 2002.

S. Doddi, M. V. Marathe, A. Mirzaian, B. M. E. Moret, and B. Zhu. Map labeling and its generalizations. In *Proc. of the ACM-SIAM symposium on Discrete algorithms*, SODA '97, pages 148–157, 1997.

K. Doi. Computer-aided diagnosis in medical imaging: Historical review, current status and future potential. *Computerized Medical Imaging and Graphics*, 31:198–211, 2007.

H. Doleisch and H. Hauser. Smooth brushing for focus+context visualization of simulation data in 3D. *Proc. of Winter School of Computer Graphics (WSCG)*, 10(1):147–154, 2002.

H. Doleisch, M. Gasser, and H. Hauser. Interactive feature specification for focus+context visualization of complex simulation data. In *Data Visualization (Proc. of Eurographics/IEEE Symposium on Visualization)*, pages 239–248, 2003.

F. Dong and G. J.Clapworthy. Volumetric texture synthesis for non-photorealistic volume rendering of medical data. *The Visual Computer*, 21(7):463–473, 2005.

F. Dong, G. J. Clapworthy, H. Lin, and M. A. Krokos. Volume Rendering of Fine Details Within Medical Data. In *Proc. of IEEE Visualization*, pages 387–394, 2001.

F. Dong, G. J. Clapworthy, H. Lin, and M. A. Krokos. Non-Photorealistic Rendering of Medical Volume Data. *IEEE Computer Graphics and Applications*, 23(4):44–52, 2003.

D. Dooley and M. Cohen. Automatic Illustration of 3D Geometric Models: Lines. In *Proc. Symposium on Interactive 3D Graphics*, pages 77–82, 1990.

J. Dornheim, L. Dornheim, B. Preim, I. Hertel, and G. Strauß. Generation and Initialization of Stable 3D Mass-Spring Models. In *Proc. of DAGM (Deutsche Arbeitsgemeinschaft für Mustererkennung)*, pages 162–171, 2006a.

J. Dornheim, H. Seim, B. Preim, I. Hertel, and G. Strauß. Segmentation of Neck Lymph Nodes in CT Datasets with Stable 3D Mass-Spring Models. In *Proc. of Medical Image Computing and Computer-Assisted Intervention (MICCAI)*, Lecture Notes in Computer Science, pages 478–485. Springer, 2006b.

J. Dornheim, H. Seim, B. Preim, I. Hertel, and G. Strauß. Segmentation of Neck Lymph Nodes in CT Datasets with Stable 3D Mass-Spring Models. *Academic Radiology*, 14(11):1389–1399, 2007.

J. Dornheim, S. Born, S. Zachow, M. Gessat, D. Wellein, G. Strauß, B. Preim, and D. Bartz. Bildanalyse, Visualisierung und Modellerstellung für die Implantatplanung im Mittelohr. In *Proc. of Simulation and Visualization*, pages 139–154, 2008a.

J. Dornheim, D. Lehmann, L. Dornheim, B. Preim, and G. Strauß. Reconstruction of Blood Vessels from Neck CT Datasets using Stable 3D Mass-Spring Models. In *Proc. of Eurographics Workshop on Visual Computing in Biology and Medicine (VCBM)*, pages 77–82, 2008b.

L. Dornheim, K. D. Tönnies, and K. Dixon. Automatic Segmentation of the Left Ventricle in 3D SPECT Data by Registration with a Dynamic Anatomic Model. In *Proc. of Medical Image Computing and Computer-Assisted Intervention (MICCAI)*, volume 3749 of *Lecture Notes in Computer Science*, pages 335–342. Springer, 2005a.

L. Dornheim, K. D. Tönnies, and J. Dornheim. Stable Dynamic 3D Shape Models. In *Proc. of IEEE International Conference on Image Processing (ICIP)*, 2005b.

L. Dornheim, J. Dornheim, and I. Rössling. Complete fully automatic model-based segmentation of normal and pathological lymph nodes in CT data. *International Journal of Computer-Assisted Radiology and Surgery*, 5(5), 2010a.

L. Dornheim, J. Dornheim, I. Rössling, and T. Mönch. Model-based Segmentation of Pathological Lymph Nodes in CT Data. In *Proc. of SPIE Medical Imaging*, number 7623 in Proc. of SPIE, 2010b.

B. A. Dosher, G. Sperling, and S. A. Wurst. Tradeoffs between stereopsis and proximity luminance covariance as determinants of perceived 3d structure. *Vision Research*, 26(3):973–990, 1986.

O. Dössel, D. Farina, M. Mohr, M. Reumann, and G. Seemann. Modelling and imaging electrophysiology and contraction of the heart. In *Proc. of Advances in Medical Engineering*, pages 3–16, 2007.

R. A. Drebin, L. Carpenter, and P. Hanrahan. Volume rendering. *SIGGRAPH Comput. Graph.*, 22(4):65–74, June 1988.

R. O. Duda, P. E. Hart, and D. G. Stork, editors. *Pattern Classification*. Wiley Interscience, 2 edition, 2001.

F. Duffner, W. Dauber, M. Skalej, and E. Grote. A New Endoscopic Tool for the CRW Stereotactic System. In *Stereotactic and Functional Neurosurgery*, volume 67(3-4), pages 213–217, 1994.

Paul S. D'Urso, Timothy M. Barker, W. John Earwaker, Lain J. Bruce, R. Leigh Atkinson, Michael W. Lanigan, John F. Arvier, and David J. Effeney. Stereolithographic biomodelling in cranio-maxillofacial surgery: a prospective trial. *Journal of Cranio-Maxillofacial Surgery*, 27(1):30–37, 1999.

M. Dürst. Letters: Additional References to Marching Cubes. *Computers & Graphics*, 22(2):72–73, 1988.

C. Dyken, G. Ziegler, C. Theobalt, and H.-P. Seidel. High-speed Marching Cubes using HistoPyramids. *Computer Graphics Forum*, 27(8):2028–2039, 2008.

D. Ebert and P. Rheingans. Volume illustration: non-photorealistic rendering of volume models. In *Proc. of IEEE* Visualization, pages 195–202, 2000.

R. R. Edelman. Contrast-enhanced MR imaging of the heart: overview of the literature. *Radiology*, 232(3):653–668, Sep 2004.

C. Edmond, D. Heskamp, and D. Sluis et al. ENT Endoscopic Surgical Training Simulator. In *Proc. of Medicine Meets VR*, pages 518–528, 1997.

P. J. Edwards, D. L. G. Hill, D. J. Hawkes, R. Spink, A. C. F. Colchester, A. J. Strong, and M. J. Gleeson. Neurosurgical Guidance Using the Stereo Microscope. In *Proc. of Computer Vision, Virtual Reality and Robotics in Medicine (CVRMed)*, pages 555–564, 1995.

P. J. Edwards, A. P. King, C. R. Maurer, D. A. de Cunha, D. J. Hawkes, and D. L. G. Hill et al. Design and Evaluation of a System for Microscope-Assisted Guided Interventions (MAGI). In *Proc. of Medical Image Computing and Computer-Assisted Intervention (MICCAI)*, Lecture Notes in Computer Science, pages 842–851, 1999.

A. Ehlert, Z. Salah, and D. Bartz. Data reconstruction and visualization techniques for forensic pathology. In *Data Visualization (Proc. of Eurographics/IEEE Symposium on Visualization)*, pages 323–330, 2006.

J. Ehrhardt, R. Werner, A. Schmidt-Richberg, B. Schulz, and H. Handels. Generation of a Mean Motion Model of the Lung Using 4D-CT Image Data. In *Proc. of Eurographics Workshop on Visual Computing in Biology and Medicine (VCBM)*, pages 69–76, 2008.

J. Ehrhardt, R. Werner, A. Schmidt-Richberg, and H. Handels. Statistical Modeling of 4D Respiratory Lung Motion Using Diffeomorphic Image Registration. *IEEE Transactions on Medical Imaging*, 30(2):251–265, 2011.

A. Einstein and R. Fürth. Investigations on the theory of the Brownian movement. *Ann. der Physik*, 1905.

A. Eklund, O. Friman, M. Andersson, and H. Knutsson. A GPU accelerated interactive interface for exploratory functional connectivity analysis of fMRI data. In *Proc. of IEEE International Conference on Image Processing (ICIP)*, pages 1589–1592, 2011.

N. Elmqvist, M.E. Tudoreanu, and P. Tsigas. Evaluating motion constraints for 3D wayfinding in immersive and desktop virtual environments. In *Proc. of the ACM SIGCHI conference on Human factors in computing systems*, CHI '08, pages 1769–1778, 2008.

F. Enders, N. Sauber, D. Merhof, P. Hastreiter, C. Nimsky, and M. Stamminger. Visualization of white matter tracts with wrapped streamlines. In *Proc. of IEEE Visualization*, pages 51–58, 2005.

K. Engel, M. Kraus, and T. Ertl. High-Quality Pre-Integrated Volume Rendering Using Hardware-Accelerated Pixel Shading. In *Proc. of Symposium on Graphics Hardware*, pages 9–16, 2001.

K. Engel, M. Hadwiger, J. Kniss, C. Rezk-Salama, and D. Weiskopf. *Real-Time Volume Graphics*. A.K. Peters Ltd., 2006.

K. H. Englmeier, G. Hellwig G, J. Griebel, S. Delorme, M. Siebert, and G. Brix. Morpho-functional visualization of dynamic mr-mammography. *Stud. Health Technol. Inform.*, 107:838–841, 2004.

B. J. Erickson, E. A. Krupinski, and K. P. Andriole. A multicenter observer performance study of 3D JPEG2000 compression of thin-slice CT. *Journal of Digital Imaging*, pages 639–643, 2010.

L. Ertöz, M. Steinbach, and V. Kumar. Finding clusters of different sizes, shapes, and densities in noisy, high dimensional data. In *Proc. of SIAM international conference on data mining*, volume 47, 2003.

C. Essert, C. Haegelen, F. Lalys, A. Abadie, and P. Jannin. Automatic computation of electrode trajectories for deep brain stimulation: a hybrid symbolic and numerical approach. *International Journal of Computer Assisted Radiology Surgery*, 7(4):517–532, 2012.

M. Ester, H.-P. Kriegel, J. Sander, and X. Xu. A Density-Based Algorithm for Discovering Clusters in Large Spatial Databases with Noise. In *Proc. of Knowledge Discovery and Data Mining (KDD)*, pages 226–231, 1996.

M. H. Everts, H. Bekker, J. B. T. M. Roerdink, and T. Isenberg. Depth-Dependent Halos: Illustrative Rendering of Dense Line Data. *IEEE Transactions on Visualization and Computer Graphics*, 15(6):1299–1306, 2009.

M. Fabel, H. von Tengg-Kobligk, F. Giesel, L. Bornemann, V. Dicken, A. Kopp-Schneider, C. Moser, S. Delorme, and H.-U. Kauczor. Semi-automated volumetric analysis of lymph node metastases in patients with malignant melanoma stage iii/iv-a feasibility study. *European Radiology*, 18:1114–1122, 2008.

A. X. Falcao and J. K. Udupa. Segmentation of 3D Objects using Live Wire. In *Proc. of SPIE Medical Imaging*, volume 3034(1), pages 228–239, 1997.

A. X. Falcao, J. K. Udupa, S. Samarasekera, S. Sharma, B. E. Hirsch, and R. de Alencar Lofufo. User-steered image segmentation paradigms: Live-wire and live-lane. *Graphics Models and Image Processing*, 60(4):223–260, 1998.

A. X. Falcao, K. Jayaram, J. K. Udupa, and F. K. Miyazawa. An ultra-fast usersteered image segmentation paradigm: Live-wire-on-the fly. *Proc. of SPIE Medical Imaging*, 3661:184–191, 1999.

N. Famaey and J. VanderSloten. Soft tissue modelling for applications in virtual surgery and surgical robotics. *Comput. Methods Biomech. Biomed. Engin.*, 11(54):351–366, 2008.

X. Fan, P.-L. Bazin, and J. L. Prince. A multi-compartment segmentation framework with homeomorphic level sets. In *Proc. of IEEE Conference on Computer Vision and Pattern Recognition (CVPR)*, 2008.

L. Fang, Y. Wang, B. Qiu, and Y. Qian. Fast maximum intensity projection algorithm using shear warp factorization and reduced resampling. *Magnetic Resonance in Medicine*, 47(4):696–700, 2002.

M. Färber, F. Hummel, C. Gerloff, and H. Handels. Virtual reality simulator for the training of lumbar punctures. *Methods of information in medicine*, 48:493–501, 2009.

G. Fauconnier and M. Turner. *Cambridge Handbook of Metaphor and Thought*, chapter Rethinking Metaphor. New York: Cambridge University Press, 2008.

J.-D. Fekete and C. Plaisant. Excentric labeling: dynamic neighborhood labeling for data visualization. In *Proc. of the ACM SIGCHI conference on Human factors in computing systems*, CHI '99, pages 512–519, New York, NY, USA, 1999. ACM.

L. Feldkamp, L. Davis, and J. Kress. Practical Cone-Beam Algorithm. *Journal of the Optical Society of America A*, 1(6):612–619, 1984.

L. S. Feldman, V. Sherman, and G. M. Fried. Using simulators to assess laparoscopic competence: ready for widespread use? *Surgery*, 135:28–42, 2004.

D. A. Feliz, C. D. Jackson, F. Drury, and D. H. Laidlaw. Using Visual Design Experts in Critique-Based Evaluation of 2D Vector Visualization Methods. *IEEE Transactions on Visualization and Computer Graphics*, 14(4):877–884, 2008.

P. Felkl, A.-L. Fuhrman, A. Kanitsar, and R. Wegenkittl. Surface Reconstruction of the Branching Vessels for Augmented Reality Aided Surgery. *BIOSIGNAL 2002*, 16:252–254, 2002.

P. Felkl, R. Wegenkittl, and K. Bühler. Surface Models of Tube Trees. In *Proc. of Computer Graphics International*, pages 70–77, 2004.

D. Feng, S.-C. Huang, Z. Wang, and D. Ho. An unbiased parametric imaging algorithm for nonuniformly sampled biomedical system parameter estimation. *IEEE Transactions on Medical Imaging*, 15(4):512–518, 1996.

H. Fenlon, D. Nunes, P. Schroy, M. Barish, P. Clarke, and J. Ferrucci. A Comparison of Virtual and Conventional Colonoscopy for the Detection of Colorectal Polyps. *New England Journal of Medicine*, 341(20):1496–1503, 1999.

J. S. Ferguson and G. McLennan. Virtual bronchoscopy. *Proc. American Thoracic Society*, 2(6):486–491, 2005.

M. Ferrant, A. Nabavi, B. Macq, F. A. Jolesz, R. Kikinis, and S. K. Warfield. Registration of 3D Intraoperative MR Images of the Brain Using a Finite Elment Biomechanical Model. *IEEE Transactions on Medical Imaging*, 20(12):1384–1397, 2001.

M. Feuerstein, S. M. Wildhirt, R. Bauernschmitt, and N. Navab. Automatic Patient Registration for Port Placement in Minimally Invasixe Endoscopic Surgery. In *Proc. of Medical Image Computing and Computer-Assisted Intervention (MICCAI)*, Lecture Notes in Computer Science, pages 287–294, 2005.

M. Feuerstein, T. Mussack, S. M. Heining, and N. Navab. Intraoperative Laparoscope Augmentation for Port Placement and Resection Planning in Minimally Invasive Liver Resection. *IEEE Transactions on Medical Imaging*, 27(3):355–369, 2008.

H. Feussner. The Operating Room of the Future: A View from Europe. *Seminars in Laparoscopic Surgery*, 10(3):149–156, 2003.

M. Fiebich, C. M. Straus, V. Sehgal, B. C. Renger, K. Doi, and K. R. Hoffmann. Automatic bone segmentation technique for CT angiographic studies. *Journal of Computer Assisted Tomography*, 23(1):155–161, 1999.

M. Figl, C. Ede, J. Hummel, F. Wanschitz, R. Ewers, H. Bergmann, and W. Birkfellner. A fully automated calibration method for an optical see-through head-mounted operating microscope with variable zoom and focus. *IEEE Transactions on Medical Imaging*, 24(11):1492–1499, 2005.

D. Filip, O. Yadid-Pecht, C. N. Andrews, and M. P. Mintchev. Self-stabilizing colonic capsule endoscopy: pilot study of acute canine models. *IEEE Transactions on Medical Imaging*, 30(12):2115–2125, 2011.

P. Fillard, C. Poupon, and J.-F. Mangin. A novel global tractography algorithm based on an adaptive spin glass model. In *Proc. of Medical Image Computing and Computer-Assisted Intervention (MICCAI)*, pages 927–934, 2009.

M. Finke, B. Stender, R. Bruder, A. Schläfer, and A. Schweikhard. An Experimental Comparison of Control Devices for Automatic Movements of a Surgical Microscope. In *Proc. of Computer Assisted Radiology and Surgery*, pages 311–312, 2010.

K. W. Finnis, Y.P. Starreveld, A.G. Parrent, A.F. Sadikot, and T.M. Peters. Three-dimensional database of subcortical electrophysiology for image-guided stereotactic functional neurosurgery. *IEEE Transactions on Medical Imaging*, 22(1):93–104, 2003.

B. J. Fisch and R. Spehlmann. *Fisch and Spehlmann's EEG Primer: Basic Principles of Digital and Analog EEG*. Elsevier Health Sciences, 1999.

J. Fischer, H. Regenbrecht, and G. Baratoff. Detecting Dynamic Occlusion in front of Static Backgrounds for AR Scenes. In *Proc. of Eurographics Symposium on Virtual Environments*, pages 153–161, 2003.

J. Fischer, D. Bartz, and W. Straßer. Occlusion Handling for Medical Augmented Reality Using a Volumetric Phantom Model. In *Proc. of ACM Symposium on Virtual Reality Software and Technology*, pages 174–177, 2004a.

J. Fischer, M. Neff, D. Bartz, and D. Freudenstein. Medical Augmented Reality based on Commercial Image Guided Surgery. In *Proc. of Eurographics Symposium on Virtual Environments*, pages 83–86, 2004b.

J. Fischer, D. Bartz, and W. Straßer. Intuitive and Lightweight User Interaction for Medical Augmented Reality. In *Proc. of Vision, Modeling, and Visualization*, pages 375–382, 2005.

J. Fischer, M. Haller, and B. Thomas. Stylized Depiction in Mixed Reality. *International Journal of Virtual Reality*, 7(4):71–79, 2008.

L. Fischer, K. Hoffmann, J. O. Neumann, M. Schöbinger, L. Grenacher, and B. Radeleff. Impact of Virtual Operation Planning on Liver Surgery. *Imaging Decision*, 1:39–44, 2007.

M. Fischer, G. Strauss, and S. Gahr. Three-dimensional visualization for preoperative planning and evaluation in head and neck surgery. *Laryngorhinootologie*, 88(4):229–233, 2009a.

M. Fischer, G. Strauß, S. Gahr, I. Richter, S. Müller, O. Burgert, J. Dornheim, B. Preim, A. Dietz, and A. Boehm. Three-dimensional Visualization for Preoperative Planning and Evaluation in Head and Neck Surgery. *Laryngo-Rhino-Otologie*, 88:229–233, 2009b.

B. Fischl, M. I. Sereno, and A. M. Dale. Cortical Surface-Based analysis: II: inflation, flattening, and a Surface-Based coordinate system. *NeuroImage*, 9(2):195–207, 1999.

A. E. Flanders, R. H. Wiggins III, and M. E. Gozum. Handheld Computers in Radiology. *Radiographics*, 23:1035–1047, 2003.

M. Fleute, S. Lavallée, and R. Julliard. Incorporating a statistically based shape model into a system for computer-assisted anterior cruciate ligament surgery. *Medical Image Analysis*, 3(3):209–222, 1999.

T.G. Flohr, C.H. McCollough, H. Bruder, M. Petersilka, K. Gruber, and C. Suss. First performance evaluation of a dual-source ct (DSCT) system. *European Journal of Radiology*, 16(2):256–268, 2006.

O. Fluck, C. Vetter, W. Wein, A. Kamen, B. Preim, and R. Westermann. A Survey of Medical Image Registration on Graphics Hardware. *Computer Methods and Programs in Biomedicine*, 104(3):45–57, 2011.

M.D. Ford, H.N. Nikolov, J. S. Milner, S. P. Lownie, E. M. Demont, W. Kalata, F. Loth, D.W. Holdsworth, and D. A. Steinman. PIV-measured versus CFD-predicted flow dynamics in anatomically realistic cerebral aneurysm models. *Journal of Biomechanical Engineering*, 130(2):021015(9 pages), 2008.

A. Formaglio, M. Fei, S. Mulatto, M. de Pascale, and D. Prattichizzo. Autocalibrated Gravity Compensation for 3DoF Impedance Haptic Devices. In *EuroHaptics*, pages 43–52, 2008.

B. D. Fornage, N. Sneige, M. J. Faroux, and E. Andry. Sonographic appearance and ultrasound guided fine-needle aspiration biopsy of breast carcinomas smaller than 1 cm. *Journal of Ultrasound in Medicine*, 9:559–568, 1990.

A. S. Forsberg, J. Chen, and D. H. Laidlaw. Comparing 3D Vector Field Visualization Methods: A User Study. *IEEE Transactions on Visualization and Computer Graphics*, 15(6):1219–1226, 2009.

D. Forsberg, C. Lundström, M. T. Andersson, and H. Knutsson. Model-Based Transfer Functions for Efficient Visualization of Medical Image Volumes. In *SCIA*, pages 592–603, 2011.

D. Fortmeier, A. Mastmeyer, and H. Handels. GPU-Based Visualization of Deformable Volumetric Soft-Tissue for Real-Time Simulation of Haptic Needle Insertion. In *Proc. of Workshop Bildverarbeitung für die Medizin*, pages 117–122, 2012.

D. Fortmeier, A. Mastmeyer, and H. Handels. Image-Based Palpation Simulation With Soft Tissue Deformations Using Chainmail on the GPU. In *Proc. of Workshop Bildverarbeitung für die Medizin*, pages 140–145, 2013a.

D. Fortmeier, A. Mastmeyer, and H. Handels. Optimized image-based soft tissue deformation algorithms for visualization of haptic needle insertion. *Studies in Health Technologies and Informatics*, 184:136–140, 2013b.

R. S. J. Frackowiak, K. J. Friston, C. D. Frith, R. J. Dolan, and J. C. Mazziotta, editors. *Human Brain Function*. Academic Press USA, 1997.

C. Francois, S. Srinivasan, M. Schiebler, S. Reeder, E. Niespodzany, O. Wieben B. Landgraf, and A. Frydrychowicz. 4D cardiovascular magnetic resonance velocity mapping of alterations of right heart flow patterns and main pulmonary artery hemodynamics in tetralogy of Fallot. *Journal of Cardiovascular Magnetic Resonance (JCMR)*, 14(1):16, 2012.

A. F. Frangi, W. J. Niessen, K. L. Vincken, and M. A. Viergever. Multiscale vessel enhancement filtering. In *Proc. of Medical Image Computing and Computer-Assisted Intervention (MICCAI)*, volume 1496 of *Lecture Notes in Computer Science*, pages 130–137. Springer, 1998.

A. F. Frangi, W. J. Niessen, and M. A. Viergever. Three-dimensional modeling for functional analysis of cardiac images: a review. *IEEE Transactions on Medical Imaging*, 20(1):21–25, 2001.

A.F. Frangi, W.J. Niessen, R.M. Hoogeveen, T. van Walsum, and M.A. Viergever. Model-based quantitation of 3D magnetic resonance angiographic images. *IEEE Transactions on Medical Imaging*, 18:946–956, 1999.

T. Franiel, L. Lüdemann, M. Taupitz, J. Rost, P. Asbach, and D. Beyersdorff. Pharmakokinetische MRT der Prostata: Parameter zur Unterscheidung von Low-grade- und High-grade-Prostatakarzinomen. *Fortschr Röntgenstr*, 181:536–542, 2009.

T. Franiel, L. Lüdemann, M. Taupitz, J. Rost, P. Asbach, and D. Beyersdorff. Dynamic contrast-enhanced magnetic resonance imaging and pharmacokinetic models in prostate cancer. *European Journal of Radiology*, 21:616–626, 2011.

L. R. Frank. Anisotropy in high angular resolution diffusion-weighted MRI. *Magnetic Resonance in Medicine*, 45(6):935–939, 2001.

L. R. Frank. Characterization of anisotropy in high angular resolution diffusion-weighted MRI. *Magnetic Resonance in Medicine*, 47(6):1083–1099, 2002.

S. Franken and N. Jeners. SurgeryNet - Eine Kooperationsplattform zur individuellen Aus- und Weiterbildung in der Chrirurgie. In *Proc. of Computer-and Robot Assisted Surgery (CURAC)*, pages 140–145, 2012.

J. Freixenet, X. Munoz, D. Raba, J. Marti, and X. Cufi. Yet Another Survey on Image Segmentation: Region and Boundary Information Integration. In *European Conference on Computer Vision*, volume III, pages 408–422, 2002.

B. B. Frericks, J. P. Ritz, T. Albrecht, S. Valdeig, A. Schenk, K. J. Wolf, and K. Lehmann. Influence of intrahepatic vessels on volume and shape of percutaneous thermal ablation zones: in vivo evaluation in a porcine model. *Invest Radiology*, 43(2):211–218, 2008.

D. Freudenstein, D. Bartz, M. Skalej, and F. Duffner. A New Virtual System for Planning of Neuroendoscopic Interventions. *Computer Aided Surgery*, 6(2):77–84, 2001.

W. Freysinger, A. R Gunkel, and W. F. Thumfart. Image-guided endoscopic ENT surgery. *European archives of oto-rhino-laryngology*, 254(7):343–346, 1997.

G. M. Fried and L. S. Feldman. Objective assessment of technical performance. *World Journal of Surgery*, 32(2):156–160, 2008.

O. Friman, M. Hindennach, C. Kühnel, and H.-O. Peitgen. Multiple hypothesis template tracking of small 3d vessel structures. *Medical Image Analysis*, 14(2):160–171, 2010.

K. J. Friston. Functional and effective connectivity in neuroimaging: A synthesis. *Human Brain Mapping*, 2(1-2):56–78, January 1994.

K. J. Friston, C. Frith, P. F. Liddle, R. Dolan, A. A. Lammertsma, and R. S. J. Frackowiak. The relationship between global and local changes in PET scans. *Journal of Cerebral Blood Flow and Metabolism*, 10:458–466, 1990.

K. J. Friston, C. Frith, P. F. Liddle, and R. S. J. Frackowiak. Comparing functional (PET) images: The assessment of significant change. *Journal of Cerebral Blood Flow and Metabolism*, 11:690–699, 1991.

K. J. Friston, P. Jezzard, and R. Turner. Analysis of functional MRI time-series. *Human Brain Mapping*, 1:153–171, 1994.

K. J. Friston, A. P. Holmes, J.-B. Poline, P. J. Grasby, S. C. R. Williams, R. S. J. Frackowiak, and R. Turner. Analysis of fMRI time series revisited. *NeuroImage*, 2:45–53, 1995.

B. Fröhlich and J. Plate. The cubic mouse: a new device for three-dimensional input. In *Proc. of the ACM SIGCHI conference on Human factors in computing systems (CHI)*, pages 526–531, 2000.

T. Frühauf. Raycasting vector fields. In *Proc. of IEEE Visualization*, pages 115–121, 1996.

H. Fuchs, Z. Kedmen, and S. Uselton. Optimal Surface Resconstruction from Planar Contours. *Communications of the ACM*, 20(10):693–702, 1977.

A. Fuhrmann, G. Hesina, F. Faure, and M. Gervautz. Occlusion in Collaborative Augmented Environments. *Computers & Graphics*, 23(6):809–819, 1999.

E. Furman-Haran, D. Grobgeld, and H. Degani. Dynamic Contrast-Enhanced Imaging and Analysis at High Spatial Resolution of MCF7 Human Breast Tumors. *Journal of Magnetic Resonance Imaging*, 128:161–171, 1997.

W. Galitz. *The Essential Guide to User Interface Design: An Introduction to GUI Design Principles and Techniques, Third edition*. Wiley, 2007.

V. García-Pérez, E. Muñoz-Moreno, S. Aja-Fernández, and C. Alberola-López. A 3-D Collision Handling Algorithm for Surgery Simulation Based on Feedback Fuzzy Logic. *IEEE Transactions on Information Technology in Biomedicine*, 13(4):451–457, 2009.

H. Garcke, T. Preußer, M. Rumpf, A. Telea, U. Weikard, and J. J. van Wijk. A Phase Field Model for Continuous Clustering on Vector Fields. *IEEE Transactions on Visualization and Computer Graphics*, 7(3):230–241, 2001.

M. Garland. Multiresolution Modeling: Survey and Future Opportunities. In *Eurographics STAR report 2*, 1999.

M. Garland and P. S. Heckbert. Surface simplification using quadric error metrics. In *Proc. of ACM SIGGRAPH*, pages 209–216, 1997.

K. Gary, L. Ibáñez, S. R. Aylward, D. Gobbi, M. B. Blake, and K. Cleary. IGSTK: An Open Source Software Toolkit for Image-Guided Surgery. *IEEE Computer*, 39(4):46–53, 2006.

R. Gasteiger, C. Tietjen, A. Baer, and B. Preim. Curvature- and Model-Based Surface Hatching of Anatomical Structures Derived from Clinical Volume Datasets. In *Proc. of International Symposium on Smart Graphics*, pages 255–262. Springer, 2008.

R. Gasteiger, M. Neugebauer, C. Kubisch, and B. Preim. Adapted Surface Visualization of Cerebral Aneurysms with Embedded Blood Flow Information. In *Proc. of Eurographics Workshop on Visual Computing in Biology and Medicine (VCBM)*, pages 25–32, 2010.

R. Gasteiger, M. Neugebauer, O. Beuing, and B. Preim. The FLOWLENS: A Focus-and-Context Visualization Approach for Exploration of Blood Flow in Cerebral Aneurysms. *IEEE Transactions on Visualization and Computer Graphics*, 17(12):2183–2192, 2011.

R. Gasteiger, D. J. Lehmann, R. van Pelt, G. Janiga, O. Beuing, A. Vilanova, H. Theisel, and B. Preim. Automatic Detection and Visualization of Qualitative Hemodynamic Characteristics in Cerebral Aneurysms. *IEEE Transactions on Visualization and Computer Graphics*, 18(12):2178–2187, 2012.

P. D. Gatehouse, M. P. Rolf, M. J. Graves, M. B. Hofman, J. Totman, B. Werner et al. Flow measurement by cardiovascular MR: a multi-centre multi-vendor study of background phase offset errors that can compromise the accuracy of derived regurgitant or shunt flow measurements. *J. Cardiovasc. Magn. Reson.*, 14(12):5–12, 2010.

K. Gavaghan, M. Peterhans, T. Oliveira-Santos, and S. Weber. A Portable Image Overlay Projection Device for Computer-Aided Open Liver Surgery. *IEEE Transactions on Biomedical Engineering*, 58(6):1855–1864, 2011a.

K. Gavaghan, T. Oliveira-Santos, Peterhans M, M. Reyes, H. Kim, S. Anderegg, and S. Weber. A Portable Image Overlay Projection Device for Computer-Aided Open Liver Surgery. *International Journal of Computer Assisted Radiology Surgery*, 7(4):547–556, 2012.

K. A. Gavaghan, S. Anderegg, M. Peterhans, T. Oliveira-Santos, and S. Weber. Augmented Reality Image Overlay Projection for Image Guided Open Liver Ablation of Metastatic Liver Cancer. In *Proc. of Workshop on Augmented Environments for Computer-Assisted Interventions: AE-CAI*, 2011b.

S. L. Gea, W. F. Decraemer, W. R. Funnell, J. J. Dirckx, and H. Maier. Tympanic membrane boundary deformations derived from static displacements observed with computerized tomography in human and gerbil. *Journal of the Association of Research in Otolaryngology*, 11(1):1–17, 2010.

B. Geiger and R. Kikinis. Simulation of endoscopy. In *Proc. of Computer Vision, Virtual Reality and Robotics in Medicine (CVRMed)*, pages 277–281. Springer, 1995.

J. Geiger, M. Markl, L. Herzer, D. Hirtler, F. Loeffelbein, B. Stiller, M. Langer, and R. Arnold. Aortic flow patterns in patients with Marfan syndrome assessed by flow-sensitive four-dimensional MRI. *Journal of Magnetic Resonance Imaging*, 3(3):594–600, 2011.

J. Gellermann, P. Wust, D. Stalling, M. Seebass, J. Nadobny, R. Beck, J. Beier, H. C. Hege, P. Deuflhard, and R. Felix. Clinical evaluation and verification of the hyperthermia treatment planning system hyperplan. *International Journal of Radiation Oncology Biology Physics*, 47(4):1145–1156, 2000.

H. K. Genant and D. G. Boyd. Quantitative bone mineral analysis using dual energy computed tomography. *Invest. Radiol.*, 12(6):545–551, 1977.

J. Georgii and R. Westermann. A multigrid framework for real-time simulation of deformable bodies. *Computers & Graphics*, 30(3):408–415, 2006.

B. L. Gerber, S. V. Raman, K. Nayak, F. H. Epstein, P. Ferreira, L. Axel, and D. L. Kraitchman. Myocardial first-pass perfusion cardiovascular Magnetic Resonance: History, theory, and current state of the art. *Journal of Cardiovascular Magnetic Resonance*, 10(1):18, 2008.

N. Gerber, B. Bell, M. Kompis, C. Stieger, M. Caversaccio, and S. Weber. A software tool for preoperative planning of implantable hearing devices. *International Journal of Computer Assisted Radiology and Surgery*, 7(Supplement 1):134–135, 2012.

A. Gerhards, P. Raab, S. Herber, K.F. Kreitner, T. Boskamp, and P. Mildenberger. Software-assisted CT-postprocessing of the Carotid Arteries. *Fortschritte auf dem Gebiet der Röntgenstrahlen und der bildgebenden Verfahren*, 176(6):570–577, 2004.

G. Gerig, R. Kikinis, O. Kübler, and F. A. Jolesz. Nonlinear Anisotropic Filtering of MRI Data. *IEEE Transactions on Medical Imaging*, 11(2):221–232, 1992.

G. Gerig, T. Koller, G. Székely, C. Brechbühler, and O. Kübler. Symbolic Description of 3D structures applied to cerebral vessel tree obtained from MR angiography volume data. In *Proc. of Information Processing in Medical Imaging*, volume 687 of *Lecture Notes in Computer Science*, pages 94–111. Springer, 1993.

G. Gerig, G. Kindlmann, R. Whitaker, R. Machiraju, T. Möller, and T. S. Yoo. Image Processing for Volume Graphics. ACM SIGGRAPH Coursenotes, Course 50, 2002.

G. Gerig, S. Gouttard, and I. Corouge. Analysis of brain white matter via fiber tract modeling. *Proc. of IEEE Engineering in Medicine and Biology Society*, 6:4421–4424, 2004.

D. T. Gering, A. Nabavi, R. Kikinis, W. E. L. Grimson, N. Hata, P. Everett, F. A. Jolesz, and W. M. Wells III. An integrated visualization system for surgical planning and guidance using image fusion and interventional imaging. In *Proc. of Medical Image Computing and Computer-Assisted Intervention (MICCAI)*, pages 809–819, 1999b.

O. Gerovichev, P. Marayong, and A. M. Okamura. The Effect of Visual and Haptic Feedback on Manual and Teleoperated Needle Insertion. In *Proc. of Medical Image Computing and Computer-Assisted Intervention (MICCAI)*, pages 147–154, 2002.

T. Gerstner and M. Rumpf. Multiresolutional Parallel Isosurface Extraction based on Tetrahedral Bisection. In *Proc. of the VolVis '99 Workshop*. Springer, pages 267–278, 1999.

A. Giachetti and G. Zanetti. AQUATICS Reconstruction Software: The Design of a Diagnostic Tool Based on Computer Vision Algorithms. In *Proc. of ECCV Workshops CVAMIA and MMBIA*, pages 48–63, 2004.

S. F. F. Gibson. Constrained Elastic Surface Nets: generating smooth surfaces from binary segmented data. In Wells William M. et al., editors, *Proc. of Medical Image Computing and Computer-Assisted Intervention (MICCAI)*, volume 1496 of LNCS. Springer, pages 888–898, 1998.

S. F. F. Gibson. 3D Chainmail: A Fast Algorithm for Deforming Volumetric Objects. In *Proc. of the ASymposium on Interactive 3D Graphics (SI3D)*, pages 149–154, 1997.

E. Gladilin, S. Zachow, P. Deuflhard, and H. Hege. Anatomy- and physics-based facial animation for craniofacial surgery simulations. *Medical and Biological Engineering and Computing*, 42(2):167–170, 2004.

S. Glaßer, S. Oeltze, A. Hennemuth, C. Kubisch, A. Mahnken, S. Wilhelmsen, and B. Preim. Automatic Transfer Function Specification for Visual Emphasis of Coronary Artery Plaque. *Computer Graphics Forum*, 29(1):191–201, 2010a.

S. Glaßer, U. Preim, K. D. Tönnies, and B. Preim. A visual analytics approach to diagnosis of breast DCE-MRI data. *Computer and Graphics*, 34(5):602–611, 2010b.

S. Glaßer, K. Scheil, U. Preim, and B. Preim. The File-Card-Browser View for Breast DCE-MRI Data. In *Proc. of Workshop Bildverarbeitung für die Medizin*, pages 314–318, 2011.

S. Glaßer, S. Oeltze, U. Preim, A. Bjornerud, H. Hauser, and B. Preim. Visual analysis of longitudinal brain tumor perfusion. In *Proc. of SPIE Medical Imaging*, 2013.

A. Glassner. *Principles of Digital Image Synthesis - Volume One*. Morgan Kaufmann Publishers, Inc., San Francisco, USA, 1995.

N. D. Glossop, C. Wedlake, J. Moore, T. M. Peters, and Z. Wang. Laser Projection Augmented Reality System for Computer Assisted Surgery. In *Proc. of Medical Image Computing and Computer-Assisted Intervention (MICCAI)*, pages 239–246, 2003.

E. Gobbetti, P. Pili, A. Zorcolo, and M. Tuveri. Interactive virtual angioscopy. In *Proc. of IEEE Visualization*, pages 435–438, 1998.

E. Gobbetti, F. Marton, and J. A. I. Guitián. A single-pass GPU ray casting framework for interactive out-of-core rendering of massive volumetric datasets. *The Visual Computer*, 24(7):797–806, 2008.

J. Goffin, K. Van Brussel, K. Martens, J. Vander Sloten, R. Van Audekercke, and M. H. Smet. Three-dimensional computed tomography-based, personalized drill guide for posterior cervical stabilization at C1-C2. *Spine*, 26(12):1343–1347, 2001.

T. Goktekin, M. C. Cavusoglu, F. Tendick, and S. Sastry. GiPSi: An Open Source/Open Architecture Software Development Framework for Surgical Simulation. In *Proc. of International Symposium on Medical Simulation (ISMS)*, pages 240–248, 2004.

J. Goldfeather and V. Interrante. A novel cubic-order algorithm for approximating principal direction vectors. *ACM Transactions on Graphics*, 23(1):45–63, 2004.

B. Goldstein. *Sensation and Perception*. Wadsworth Publishing, Pacific Grove, CA, 7th edition, 2006.

Y. C. Gon and M. Brady. Texture-based simultaneous registration and segmentation of breast DCE-MRI. In *Proc. of International Workshop on Digital Mammography (IWDM)*, pages 174–180, 2008.

R. C. Gonzales and R. E. Woods. *Digital Image Processing*. Prentice Hall, 2nd edition, 1998.

A. A. Gooch and B. Gooch. *Non-Photorealistic Rendering*. AK Peters, Ltd., 2001.

B. Gooch, P. P. J. Sloan, A. Gooch, P. Shirley, and R. F. Riesenfeld. Interactive technical illustration. In *Proc. of ACM Symposium on Interactive 3D graphics*, pages 31–38, 1999.

B. Gooch, A. A. Gooch, and M. C. Sousa. *Illustrative Visualization*. A.K. Peters Ltd. Publishers, 2002.

G. Gorla, V. Interrante, and G. Sapiro. Texture synthesis for 3D shape representation. *IEEE Transactions on Visualization and Computer Graphics*, 9(4):512–524, 2003.

A. Van Gossum and M. Ibrahim. Video capsule endoscopy: what is the future? *Gastroenterol Clin North Am*, 39(4):807–826, 2010.

S. Gottschalk, M. C. Lin, and D. Manocha. Obbtree: A hierarchical structure for rapid interference detection. In *Proc. of ACM SIGGRAPH*, pages 171–180, 1996.

T. Götzelmann, K. Ali, K. Hartmann, and T. Strothotte. Form follows function: Aesthetic interactive labels. In *Computational Aesthetics*, pages 193–200, 2005.

T. Götzelmann, K. Hartmann, and Th. Strothotte. Contextual Grouping of Labels. In *Proc. of Simulation and Visualization*, pages 245–258. SCS, 2006.

L. Grady. Random Walks for Image Segmentation. *IEEE Transactions on Pattern Analysis and Machine Intelligence*, 28(11): 1768–1783, 2006.

L. Grady and G. Funka-Lea. An Energy Minimization Approach to the Data Driven Editing of Presegmented Images/Volumes. In *MICCAI (2)*, pages 888–895, 2006.

T. P. Grantcharov, V. B. Kristiansen, J. Bendix, L. Bardram, J. Rosenberg, and P. Funch-Jensen. Randomized clinical trial of virtual reality simulation for laparoscopic skills training. *British Journal of Surgery*, 91(2):146–150, 2004.

P. Gravel, G. Beaudoin, and J. A. de Guise. A method for modeling noise in medical images. *IEEE Transactions on Medical Imaging*, 23(10):1221–1232, 2004.

G. Greil, T. Geva, S. E. Maier, and A. J. Powell. Effect of acquisition parameters on the accuracy of velocity encoded cine magnetic resonance imaging blood flow measurements. *Magnetic Resonance in Medicine*, 15(1):47–54, 2002.

U. Grenander and M. I. Miller. Computational anatomy: An Emerging Discipline. *Quart. App. Math.*, 56:617–694, 1998.

P. Grunert, K. Darabi, J. Espinosa, and R. Filippi. Computer-aided navigation in neurosurgery. *Neurosurgical Review*, 26(2):73–99, 2003.

A. Grzesik, J. Bernarding, J. Braun, H.-C. Koennecke, K. J. Wolf, and T. Tolxdorff. Characterization of Stroke Lesions Using a Histogram-Based Data Analysis Including Diffusion- and Perfusion-Weighted Imaging. In *Proc. of SPIE Medical Imaging: Physiology and Function from Multidimensional Images*, volume 3978, 2000.

H. Gumprecht, G. K. Ebel, D. P. Auer, and C. B. Lumenta. Neuronavigation and functional MRI for surgery in patients with lesion in eloquent brain areas. *Minimally Invasive Neurosurgery*, 45(3):151–153, 2002.

Y. Guo, R. Sivaramakrishna, C.C. Lu, J.S. Suri, and S. Laxminarayan. Breast image registration techniques: a survey. *Medical and Biological Engineering and Computing*, 44(1):15–26, 2006.

R. Gupta, A. C. Cheung, S. H. Bartling, J. Lisauskas, M. Grasruck, C. Leidecker, B. Schmidt, T. Flohr, and T. J. Brady. Flat-panel volume CT: fundamental principles, technology, and applications. *Radiographics*, 28(7):2009–2022, 2008.

V. Gupta, H. A. Kirisli, E. A. Hendriks, R. J. van der Geest, M. van de Giessen, W. J. Niessen, J. H. C. Reiber, and B. P. F. Lelieveldt. Cardiac MR perfusion image processing techniques: A survey. *Medical Image Analysis*, 16(4):767–785, 2012.

D. Gur and J. H. Sumkin. CAD in screening mammography. *AJR Am. J. Roentgenology*, 187(6):1474, 2006.

M. Guye, G. Bettus, F. Bartolomei, and P. Cozzone. Graph theoretical analysis of structural and functional connectivity MRI in normal and pathological brain networks. *Magnetic Resonance Materials in Physics, Biology and Medicine*, 23(5):409–421, 2010.

S. Haase, C. Forman, T. Kilgus, R. Bammer, L. Maier-Hein, and J. Hornegger. ToF/RGB Sensor Fusion for Augmented 3D Endoscopy using a Fully Automatic Calibration Scheme. In *Proc. of Bildverarbeitung für die Medizin*, pages 111–116, 2012.

E. Haber and J. Modersitzki. Volume Preserving Image Registration. In *Proc. of Medical Image Computing and Computer-Assisted Intervention (MICCAI)*, volume 3216 of *Lecture Notes in Computer Science*, pages 591–598. Springer, 2004.

E. Haber and J. Modersitzki. Beyond Mutual Information: A simple and robust alternative. In *Proc. of Workshop Bildverarbeitung für die Medizin*, pages 1–5. Springer, 2005.

M. Hadwiger, A. Kratz, C. Sigg, and K. Bühler. GPU-Accelerated Deep Shadow Maps for Direct Volume Rendering. In *ACM SIGGRAPH/EG Conference on Graphics Hardware*, pages 27–28, 2006.

M. Hadwiger, L. Fritz, C. Rezk-Salama, T. Höllt, G. Geier, and T. Pabel. Interactive Volume Exploration for Feature Detection and Quantification in Industrial CT Data. *IEEE Transactions on Visualization and Computer Graphics*, 14(6):1507–1514, 2008.

M. A. Hafez, K. L. Chelule, B. B. Seedhom, and K. P. Sherman. Computer-assisted Total Knee Arthroplasty Using Patient-specific Templating. *Clinical Orthopaedics and Related Research*, 443(&NA;):184–192, 2006.

S.M. Hafner. *Intercultural Software User Interfaces: Basics, concepts and methods*. VDM Verlag Dr. Müller, 2011.

P. Hagmann, L. Jonasson, P. Maeder, J.-P. Thiran, V. J. Wedeen, and R. Meuli. Understanding diffusion MR imaging techniques: from scalar diffusion-weighted imaging to diffusion tensor imaging and beyond. *Radiographics: A Review Publication of the Radiological Society of North America, Inc.*, 26 Suppl 1:205–223, 2006.

H. K. Hahn and H.-O. Peitgen. The Skull Stripping Problem in MRI Solved by a Single 3D Watershed Transform. In *Proc. of Medical Image Computing and Computer-Assisted Intervention (MICCAI)*, pages 134–143, 2000.

H. K. Hahn and H.-O. Peitgen. IWT-Interactive Watershed Transform: A hierarchical method for efficient interactive and automated segmentation of multidimensional grayscale images. In *Proc. of SPIE Medical Imaging*, volume 5032, pages 643–653. SPIE, 2003.

H.K. Hahn, B. Preim, D. Selle, and H.-O. Peitgen. Visualization and Interaction Techniques for the Exploration of Vascular Structures. In *Proc. of IEEE Visualization*, pages 395–402, 2001.

M. Haidacher, D. Patel, S. Bruckner, A. Kanitsar, and E. Gröller. Volume visualization based on statistical transfer-function spaces. In *Proc. of PacificVis*, pages 17–24, 2010.

J. V. Hajnal, D. L. G. Hill, and D. J. Hawkes. *Medical Image Registration*. CRC Press, 2001.

S. Haker, S. Angenent, A. Tannenbaurn, and R. Kikinis. Nondistorting flattening maps and the 3-D visualization of colon CT images. *IEEE Transactions on Medical Imaging*, 19(7):665–670, 2000.

L. Hallpike and D. J. Hawkes. Medical image registration: an overview. *Imaging*, 14:455–463, 2002.

E. Halpern. *Clinical Cardiac CT: Anatomy and Function*. Springer, 2011.

P. Han, W. Pirsig, F. Ilgen, J. Gorich, and R. Sokiranski. Virtual Endoscopy of the Nasal Cavity in Comparison with Fiberoptic Endoscopy. *Europ. Archives of Oto-Rhino-Laryngology*, 257(10):578–583, 2000.

G.B. Hanna, S.M. Shimi, and A. Cuschieri. Task Performance in Endoscopic Surgery Is Influenced by Location of the Image Display. *Annals of Surgery*, 227(4):481–484, 1998.

C. Hansen and C. Johnson. *The Visualization Handbook*. Elsevier, 2004.

C. Hansen, A. Köhn, S. Schlichting, F. Weiler, S. Zidowitz, M. Kleemann, and H.-O. Peitgen. Intraoperative modification of resection plans for liver surgery. *Int. J. Computer Assisted Radiology and Surgery*, 3(3-4):291–297, 2008.

C. Hansen, S. Zidowitz, M. Hindennach, A. Schenk, H. Hahn, and H.-O. Peitgen. Interactive determination of robust safety margins for oncologic liver surgery. *International Journal of Computer Assisted Radiology and Surgery*, 4(5):469–474, 2009.

C. Hansen, F. Ritter, J. Wieferich, H. Hahn, and H.-O. Peitgen. Illustration of Vascular Structures for Augmented Reality in Liver Surgery. In *Proc. of World Congress on Medical Physics and Biomedical Engineering*, volume 25/4, pages 2113–2116, 2010a.

C. Hansen, J. Wieferich, F. Ritter, C. Rieder, and H.-O. Peitgen. Illustrative visualization of 3D planning models for augmented reality in liver surgery. *International Journal of Computer Assisted Radiology and Surgery*, 5(2):133–141, 2010b.

C. Hansen, S. Zidowitz, A. Schenk, K.-J. Oldhafer, H. Lang, and H.-O. Peitgen. Risk maps for navigation in liver surgery. In *Proc. of SPIE Medical Imaging*, pages 762528–762528–8, 2010c.

A.J. Hanson and E. Wernert. Constrained 3D Navigation with 2D Controllers. In *Proc. of Dagstuhl Seminar on Scientific Visualization*, pages 175–182, 1997.

W. Hao, W. Che, X. Zhang, and Y. Wang. 3D model feature line stylization using mesh sharpening. In *Proc. of the ACM SIGGRAPH Conference on Virtual-Reality Continuum and its Applications in Industry*, VRCAI '10, pages 249–256, 2010.

A. K. Hara, R. G. Paden, A. C. Silva, J. L. Kujak, H. J. Lawder, and W. Pavlicek. Iterative reconstruction technique for reducing body radiation dose at ct: feasibility study. *AJR Am. J. Roentgenol.*, 193(3):764–771, 2009.

M. Harders and G. Székely. Enhancing human-computer interaction in medical segmentation. In *Proc. of the IEEE*, volume 91, pages 1430–1442, 2003.

M. Harrower. Tips for designing effective animated maps. *Cartographic Perspectives*, 44:63–65, 2003.

M. Harrower and B. Sheesley. Utterly Lost: Methods for Reducing Disorientation in 3-D Fly-Over Maps. *Cartography and Geographic Information Science*, 34(1):17–27, 2007.

J. A. Hartigan and M. A. Wong. A K-means clustering algorithm. *Applied Statistics*, 28:100–108, 1979.

F. Hartmann and A. Schläfer. Touch-less control of operating room lights. In *Proc. of CARS*, pages 208–209, 2012.

K. Hartmann, K. Ali, and T. Strothotte. Floating labels: Applying dynamic potential fields for label layout. In *Smart Graphics*, pages 101–113, 2004.

R. H. Hashemi, W. G. Bradley, and C. J. Lisanti. *MRI: The Basics*. Lippincott Williams & Wilkins, 3rd edition, 2011.

D. Hashimoto, T. Dohi, M. Tsuzuki, T. Horiuchi, Y. Ohta, K. Chinzei, M. Suzuki, and Y. Idezuki. Development of a computer-aided surgery system: three-dimensional graphic reconstruction for treatment of liver cancer. *Surgery*, 109(5):589–596, 1991.

T. Hassan. Computational Replicas: Anatomic Reconstruction of Cerebral Vessels as Volume Numerical Grids at Three-Dimensional Angiography. *American Journal of Neuroradiology*, 25:1356–1365, 2004.

S. Hassfeld and J. Mühling. Computer assisted oral and maxillofacial surgery – a review and an assessment of technology. *International Journal of Oral and Maxillofacial Surgery*, 30(1):2–13, 2001.

P. Hastreiter and T. Ertl. Integrated Registration and Visualization of Medical Image Data. In *Proc. of Computer Graphics International*, pages 78–85, 1998.

P. Hastreiter, C. Rezk-Salama, B. Tomandl, K. Eberhardt, and T. Ertl. Fast Analysis of Intracranial Aneurysms Based on Interactive Direct Volume Rendering and CTA. In *Proc. of Medical Image Computing and Computer-Assisted Intervention (MICCAI)*, pages 660–669, 1998.

P. Hastreiter, C. Rezk-Salama, G. Soza, M. Bauer, G. Greiner, R. Fahlbusch, O. Ganslandt, and C. Nimsky. Strategies for brain shift evaluation. *Medical Image Analysis*, 8(4):447–464, 2004.

M. Haubner, C. Krapichler, A. Losch, K.-H. Englmeier, and W. Van Eimeren. Virtual reality in medicine-computer graphics and interaction techniques. *IEEE Transactions on Information Technology in Biomedicine*, 1(1):61–72, 1997.

M. D. Hayhurst, W. MacNee, and D. C. Flenley. Diagnosis of pulmonary emphysema by computerized tomography. *Lancet*, 2:320–322, 1984.

T. He and L. Hong. Reliable Navigation for Virtual Endoscopy. In *Proc. of IEEE Medical Imaging*, 1999.

T. He, L. Hong, A. Kaufman, and H. P. Pfister. Generation of transfer functions with stochastic search techniques. In *Proc. of IEEE Visualization*, pages 227–234, 1996.

M. Heath, K. Bowyer, D. Kopans, R. Moore, and W. P. Kegelmeyer. The digital database for screening mammography. In *Proc. of the Workshop on Digital Mammography*, pages 212–218, 2001.

F. Heckel, O. Konrad, H. K. Hahn, and H.-O. Peitgen. Interactive 3D medical image segmentation with energy-minimizing implicit functions. *Computers & Graphics*, 35(2):275–287, 2011.

F. Heckel, S. Braunewell, G. Soza, C. Tietjen, and H. K. Hahn. Sketch-based Image-independent Editing of 3D Tumor Segmentations using Variational Interpolation. In *Proc. of Eurographics Workshop on Visual Computing in Biology and Medicine (VCBM)*, pages 73–80, 2012.

H. C. Hege and D. Stalling. LIC: acceleration, animation, and zoom. In *ACM SIGGRAPH Course 8*, pages 17–49, 1997.

E. Heiberg, T. Ebbers, L. Wigström, and M. Karlsson. Three-Dimensional Flow Characterization Using Vector Pattern Matching. *IEEE Transactions on Visualization and Computer Graphics*, 9(3):313–319, 2003.

T. Heimann, I. Wolf, and H.-P. Meinzer. Active Shape Models for a Fully Automated 3D Segmentation of the Liver - An Evaluation on Clinical Data. In *Proc. of Medical Image Computing and Computer-Assisted Intervention (MICCAI)*, pages 41–48, 2006.

T. Heimann, B. van Ginneken, M.A. Styner, Y. Arzhaeva, V. Aurich, C. Bauer, A. Beck, C. Becker, R. Beichel, G. Bekes, F. Bello, G. Binnig, H. Bischof, A. Bornik, P. Cashman, Ying Chi, A. Cordova, B.M. Dawant, M. Fidrich, J.D. Furst, D. Furukawa, L. Grenacher, J. Hornegger, D. Kainmuller, R.I. Kitney, H. Kobatake, H. Lamecker, T. Lange, Jeongjin Lee, B. Lennon, Rui Li, Senhu Li, H.-P. Meinzer, G. Nemeth, D.S. Raicu, A.-M. Rau, E.M. van Rikxoort, M. Rousson, L. Rusko, K.A. Saddi, G. Schmidt, D. Seghers, A. Shimizu, P. Slagmolen, E. Sorantin, G. Soza, R. Susomboon, J.M. Waite, A. Wimmer, and I. Wolf. Comparison and Evaluation of Methods for Liver Segmentation From CT Datasets. *IEEE Transactions on Medical Imaging*, 28(8):1251–1265, 2009.

A. Hein and T. Lueth. Image-Based Control of Interactive Robotics Systems. In *Proc. of Medical Image Computing and Computer-Assisted Intervention (MICCAI)*, volume 1679 of *Lecture Notes in Computer Science*, pages 1125–1132, 1999.

J. Heisterkamp, R. van Hillegersberg, and J. N. M. IJzermans. Interstitial laser coagulation for hepatic tumours. *British Journal of Surgery*, 86(3):293–304, 1999.

B. Hemminger, P. Molina, T. Egan, F. Detterbeck, K. Muller, C. Coffey, and J. Lee. Assessment of Real-Time 3D Visualization for Cardiothoracic Diagnostic Evaluation and Surgery Planning. *Journal of Digital Imaging*, 18(2):145–153, 2005.

W. R. Hendee and C. J. Morgan. Magnetic resonance imaging part I—Physical principles. *Western Journal of Medicine*, 141(4):491–500, 1984.

P. A. Heng, P. F. Fung, T. T. Wong, Y. H. Siu, and H. Sun. Interactive navigation and bronchial tube tracking in virtual bronchoscopy. *Stud. Health Technol. Inform.*, 62:130–133, 1999.

P. A. Heng, Chun-Yiu Cheng, Tien-Tsin Wong, Yangsheng Xu, Yim-Pan Chui, Kai-Ming Chan, and Shiu-Kit Tso. A virtual-reality training system for knee arthroscopic surgery. *IEEE Transactions on Information Technology in Biomedicine*, 8(2):217–227, 2004a.

P. A. Heng, T.-T. Wong, K.-M. Leung, Y.-P. Chui, and H. Sun. A haptic needle manipulation simulator for chinese acupuncture learning and training. In *Proc. of ACM SIGGRAPH Virtual Reality continuum and its applications in industry*, VRCAI, pages 57–64, 2004b.

P.-A. Heng, T.-T. Wong, K.-M. Leung, Y.-P. Chui, and H. Sun. A Haptic Needle Manipulation Simulator for Chinese Acupuncture Learning and Training. *International Journal of Image Graphics*, 6(2):205–230, 2006.

A. Hennemuth, T. Boskamp, D. Fritz, C. Kühnel, S. Bocka, D. Rinck, M. Scheuering, and H.-O. Peitgen. One-click coronary tree segmentation in CT angiographic images. In *Proc. of Computer Assisted Radiology and Surgery*, pages 317–321. Elsevier, 2005.

A. Hennemuth, A. Seeger, O. Friman, S. Miller, B. Klumpp, S. Oeltze, and H.-O. Peitgen. A comprehensive approach to the analysis of contrast enhanced cardiac MR images. *IEEE Transactions on Medical Imaging*, 27(11):1592–1610, 2008.

A. Hennemuth, O. Friman, C. Schumann, J. Bock, J. Drexl, and M. Markl et al. Fast Interactive Exploration of 4D MRI Flow Data. In *Proc. of SPIE Medical Imaging*, pages 489–492, 2011.

J. Hennig. The Historical Documentation of Scientific Developments: Scientists Should Participate (editorial). *Journal of Magnetic Resonance Imaging*, 19:521–522, 2003.

J. Hennig and O. Speck. *High-Field MR Imaging*. Springer, 2011.

K. Henriksen, J. Sporring, and K. Hornbæk. Virtual trackballs revisited. *IEEE Transactions on Visualization and Computer Graphics*, 10(2):206–216, 2004.

M. Hernandez-Hoyos, M. Orkisz, P. Puech, C. Mansard-Desbleds, P. Douek, and I.E. Magnin. Computer-assisted analysis of three-dimensional MR angiograms. *Radiographics*, 22:421–436, 2002.

F. Hernell, P. Ljung, and A. Ynnerman. Efficient Ambient and Emissive Tissue Illumination using Local Occlusion in Multiresolution Volume Rendering. In *Proc. of Volume Graphics*, pages 1–8, 2007.

F. Hernell, P. Ljung, and A. Ynnerman. Interactive Global Light Propagation in Direct Volume Rendering using Local Piecewise Integration. In *IEEE/EG Int. Symp. on Volume and Point-Based Graphics*, pages 105–112, 2008.

F. Hernell, P. Ljung, and A. Ynnerman. Local Ambient Occlusion in Direct Volume Rendering. *IEEE Transactions on Visualization and Computer Graphics*, 15(2):548–559, 2009.

A. Hertzmann and D. Zorin. Illustrating Smooth Surfaces. In *Proc. of ACM SIGGRAPH*, pages 517–526, 2000.

S.H. Heywang, D. Hahn, H. Schmidt, I. Krischke, W. Eiermann, R. Bassermann, and J. Lissner. MR imaging of the breast using Gd-DTPA. *Journal of Computer Assisted Tomography*, 10(2):199–204, 1986.

S.H. Heywang-Köbrunner, P. Viehweg, A. Heinig, and C. Kuchler. Contrast-enhanced MRI of the breast: accuracy, value, controversies, solutions. *European Journal of Radiology*, 24:94–108, 1997.

S. Hiller, H. Hellwig, and O. Deussen. Beyond Stippling - Methods for Distributing Objects on the Plane. *Computer Graphics Forum*, 22(3):515–522, 2003.

T. Himi, M. Sakata, T. Shintani, H. Mitsuzawa, M. Kamagate, J. Satoh, and H. Sugimoto. Middle Ear Imaging Using Virtual Endoscopy and its Application in Patients with Ossicular Chain Anomaly. *Oto-Rhino-Laryngology and its related specialities*, 62(6):216–320, 2000.

K. Hinckley. *Handbook of Human-Computer Interaction*, chapter Input Technologies and Techniques. Lawrence Erlbaum & Associates, Washington, DC, 2007.

K. Hinckley, J. Tullio, R. Pausch, D. Proffitt, and N. Kassell. Usability analysis of 3d rotation techniques. In *Proc. of the ACM symposium on User interface software and technology (UIST)*, pages 1–10, 1997.

K. Hinckley, R. Pausch, D. Profitt, and N.F. Kassel. Two-handed virtual manipulation. *ACM Transactions on Human Computer Interaction*, 5(3):260–302, 1998.

J. Hladuvka, A. König, and E. Gröller. Curvature-based transfer functions for direct volume rendering. In *Spring Conference on Computer Graphics*, pages 58–65, 2000.

M. Hlawitschka and G. Scheuermann. HOT-lines: tracking lines in higher order tensor fields. In *Proc. of IEEE Visualization*, pages 27–34, 2005.

E. R. S. Hodges. *The Guild Handbook of Scientific Illustration*. Van Nostrand Reinhold, 1989.

E. R. S. Hodges, editor. *The Guild Handbook of Scientific Illustration*. John Wiley & Sons, 2nd edition, 2003.

K. H. Hoehne, M. Riemer, and U. Tiede. Viewing Operations for 3D-Tomographic Gray Level Data. In *Proc. of Computer Assisted Radiology*, pages 599–609, 1987.

K. H. Hoehne, M. Bomans, M. Riemer, R. Schubert, U. Tiede, and W. Lierse. Interactive 3D Segmentation of MRI and CT Volumes Using Morphological Operations. *Journal of Computer Assisted Tomography*, 16:285–294, 1992.

K.H. Hoehne, U. Obermoeller, and M. Boehm. X-Ray Functional Imaging - Evaluation of the Properties of Different Parameters. In *Proc. Conference on Digital Radiography*, pages 224–228, 1981.

M. Hofer, G. Strauß, K. Koulechov, M. Fischer, T. Neumuth, C. Trantakis, W. Korb, A. Dietz, and T. Lueth. First clinical trial of the navigated controlled shaver in functional endoscopic sinus surgery. *International Journal of Computer Assisted Radiology and Surgery*, 1(1):318–320, 2006.

M. Hofer, E. Dittrich, C. Baumberger, M. Strauss, A. Dietz, T. Lueth, and G. Strauss. The influence of various registration procedures upon surgical accuracy during navigated controlled petrous bone surgery. *Otolaryngology–head and neck surgery*, 143(2):258–262, 2010.

J. Hoffmann, C. Westendorff, C. Leitner, D. Bartz, and S. Reinert. Validation of 3D-Laser Surface Registration for Image-Guided Craniomaxillofacial Surgery. *Journal for Cranio-Maxillofacial Surgery*, 33(1):13–18, 2005.

K. H.öhne and R. Bernstein. Shading 3D-images from ct using gray-level gradients. In *IEEE Transactions on Medical Imaging*, volume MI-5, pages 45–47, 1986.

K. H. Höhne, M. Bomans, M. Riemer, R. Schubert, U. Tiede, and W. Lierse. A 3D Anatomical Atlas Based on a Volume Model. *IEEE Computer Graphics and Applications*, 12:72–78, 1992.

K. H. Höhne, A. Pommert, M. Riemer, T. Schiemann, R. Schubert, U. Tiede, and W. Lierse. Anatomical atlases based on volume visualization. In *Proc. of IEEE Visualization*, pages 115–123, 1992.

K.-H. Höhne, B. Pflesser, A. Pommert, K. Priesmeyer, M. Riemer, T. Schiemann, R. Schubert, U. Tiede, H. Frederking, S. Gehrmann, S. Noster, and U. Schumacher. *VOXEL-MAN 3D Navigator: Inner Organs. Regional, Systemic and Radiological Anatomy*. Springer Electronic Media, Heidelberg, 2003.

D. Holmes, M. Rettmann, and R. Robb. *Image-Guided Interventions*, chapter Visualization in Image-Guided Interventions, pages 45–80. Springer, 2008.

W. F. Holmes. External beam treatment-planning with the programmed console. *Radiology*, 94(2):391–400, 1970.

D. Holten. Hierarchical edge bundles: Visualization of adjacency relations in hierarchical data. *IEEE Transactions on Visualization and Computer Graphics*, 12(5):741–748, 2006.

K. Holtzblatt. *The Human Computer Interaction Handbook*, chapter Contextual Design, pages 941–963. Lawrence Erlbaum, 2003.

D. Honea and W. E. Snyder. Three-dimensional active surface approach to lymph node segmentation. In *Proc. of SPIE Medical Imaging*, volume 3361, pages 1003–1011. SPIE, 1999.

L. Hong, A. Kaufman, Y.-C. Wei, A. Viswambharan, M. Wax, and Z. Liang. 3D Virtual Colonoscopy. In *Proc. of IEEE Symposium on Frontier in Biomedical Visualization*, pages 26–32, 1995.

L. Hong, S. Muraki, A. Kaufman, D. Bartz, and T. He. Virtual Voyage: Interactive Navigation in the Human Colon. In *Proc. of ACM SIGGRAPH*, pages 27–34, 1997.

Q. Hong, Q. Li, and J. Tian. Virtual Angioscopy Based on Implicit Vasculatures. In *Proc. of Computational Science and Its Applications (ICCSA)*, volume 6785 of *LNCS*, pages 592–603. Springer, 2011.

Q. Hong, Q. Li, and J. Tian. Implicit Reconstruction of Vasculatures Using Bivariate Piecewise Algebraic Splines. *IEEE Transactions on Medical Imaging*, 31(3):543–553, 2012.

W. Hong, X. Gu, F. Qiu, M. Jin, and A. Kaufman. Conformal virtual colon flattening. In *Proc. of ACM Symposium on Solid and Physical Modeling*, pages 85–93. ACM, 2006.

D. Hönigmann, J. Ruisz, and C. Haider. Adaptive Design of a Global Opacity Transfer Function for Direct Volume Rendering of Ultrasound Data. In *Proc. of IEEE Visualization*, pages 489–496, 2003.

M. D. Hope, J. Wrenn, M. Sigovan, E. Foster, E. E. Tseng, and D. Saloner. Imaging Biomarkers of Aortic Disease - Increased Growth Rates With Eccentric Systolic Flow. *Journal of the American College of Cardiology (JACC)*, 60(4):356–357, 2012.

K. Hopf, P. Chojecki, F. Neumann, and D. Przewozny. Novel autostereoscopic single-user display with user interaction. In *Proc. of SPIE*, volume 6392, pages 27–34, 2006.

H. Hoppe. Progressive Meshes. In *Proc. of ACM SIGGRAPH*, pages 99–108, 1996.

H. Hoppe, T. DeRose, T. Dachamp, J. McDonald, and W. Stützle. Mesh Optimization. In *Proc. of ACM SIGGRAPH*, pages 19–26, 1993.

H. Hoppe, G. Eggers, T. Heurich, J. Raczkowsky, R. Marmulla, H. Wörn, S. Hassfeld, and J. L. Moctezuma. Projector Based Visualization for Intraoperative Navigation: First Clinical Results. In *Proc. of Computer Assisted Radiology and Surgery*, pages 771–776, 2003.

H. Hoppe, H. P. Dinkel, B. Walder, G. von Allmen, M. Gugger, and P. Vock. Grading airway stenosis down to the segmental level using virtual bronchoscopy. *Chest*, 125(2):704–711, 2004.

S. Hornus, A. Angelidis, and M.-P. Cani. Implicit Modeling using Subdivision Curves. *The Visual Computer*, 19(2-3):94–104, 2003.

K. M. Horton, M. R. Horton, and E. K. Fishman. Advanced visualization of airways with 64-MDCT: 3D mapping and virtual bronchoscopy. *American Journal of Roentgenology*, 189(6):1387–1396, 2007.

G. N. Hounsfield. Computerised transverse axial scanning (tomography) I. Description of system. *British Journal of Radiology*, 46:1016–1022, 1973.

G. N. Hounsfield. Computed medical imaging: Nobel lecture. *Journal of Computer Assisted Tomography*, 4(5):665–674, 1980.

E. M. Hsiao, F. J. Rybicki, and M. Steigner. CT Coronary Angiography: 256-Slice and 320-Detector Row Scanners. *Curr. Cardiol Rep.*, 12(1):68–75, 2010.

Q. Hu, U. Langlotz, J. Lawrence, F. Langlotz, and L.-P. Nolte. A fast impingement detection algorithm for computer-aided orthopedic surgery. *Computer Aided Surgery*, 6(2):104–110, 2001.

Y. Hu and R. A. Malthaner. The feasibility of three-dimensional displays of the thorax for preoperative planning in the surgical treatment of lung cancer. *European Journal of Cardiothoracic Surgery*, 31(3):506–511, 2007.

D. Huang, W. Tang, T. Ruan Wan, N. W. John, D. Gould, Y. Ding, and Y. Chen. A new approach to haptic rendering of guidewires for use in minimally invasive surgical simulation. *Journal of Visualization and Computer Animation*, 22(2-3):261–268, 2011.

J. D. Humphrey, editor. *An Introduction to Biomechanics: Solids and Fluids, Analysis and Design*. Springer, 2004.

Z. Huo, M. L. Giger, C. J. Vyborny, D. E. Wolverton, R. A. Schmidt, and K. Doi. Automated computerized classification of malignant and benign masses on digitized mammograms. *Academic Radiology*, 5(3):155–168, 1998.

R. Hussein, U. Engelmann, A. Schroeter, and H. P. Meinzer. DICOM structured reporting: Part 1. Overview and characteristics. *Radiographics*, 24(3):891–896, 2007a.

R. Hussein, U. Engelmann, A. Schroeter, and H. P. Meinzer. DICOM structured reporting: Part 2. Problems and challenges in implementation for PACS workstations. *Radiographics*, 24(3):897–909, 2007b.

J. P. Iannotti, E. E. Spencer, U. Winter, D. Deffenbaugh, and G. Williams. Prosthetic positioning in total shoulder arthroplasty. *Journal of Shoulder and Elbow Surgery*, 14(1, Supplement):S111–S121, 2005.

L. Ibanez and W. Schroeder. *The ITK Software Guide 2.4*. Kitware, 2005.

S. G. Imbesi and C. W. Kerber. Analysis of slipstream flow in a wide-necked basilar artery aneurysm: evaluation of potential treatment regimens. *American Journal of Neuroradiology*, 22(4):721–724, 2001.

E. Imhof. Positioning names on maps. *The American Cartographer*, 2(2):128–144, 2008.

M. Ingrisch, O. Dietrich, U.I. Attenberger, K. Nikolaou, S. Sourbron, M.F. Reiser, and C. Fink. Quantitative pulmonary perfusion magnetic resonance imaging: influence of temporal resolution and signal-to-noise ratio. *Invest. Radiol.*, 45(1):7–14, 2010.

V. Interrante, H. Fuchs, and S. M. Pizer. Enhancing Transparent Skin Surfaces with Ridge and Valley Lines. In *Proc. of IEEE Visualization*, pages 52–59, 1995.

V. Interrante, H. Fuchs, and S. M. Pizer. Conveying the 3D Shape of Smoothly Curving Transparent Surfaces via Texture. *IEEE Transactions on Visualization and Computer Graphics*, 3(2):98–117, 1997.

A. Irimia, M. C. Chambers, C. M. Torgerson, and J. D. Van Horn. Circular representation of human cortical networks for subject and population-level connectomic visualization. *NeuroImage*, 60(2):1340–1351, 2012.

T. Isenberg, B. Freudenberg, N. Halper, S. Schlechtweg, and T. Strothotte. A Developer's Guide to Silhouette Algorithms for Polygonal Models. *IEEE Computer Graphics and Applications*, 23(4):28–37, 2003.

M. Jackowski, A. A. Goshtasby, and M. Satter. Interactive Tools for Image Segmentation. In *Proc. of SPIE Medical Imaging*, 1999.

H. Jadvar and J. Anthony Parker. *Clinical PET and PET/CT*. Springer, 2005.

W. M. Jainek, S. Born, D. Bartz, W. Straßer, and J. Fischer. Illustrative Hybrid Visualization and Exploration of Anatomical and Functional Brain Data. *Computer Graphics Forum*, 27(3):855–862, 2008.

G. Janiga, O. Beuing, S. Seshadhri, M. Neugebauer, R. Gasteiger, B. Preim, G. Rose, M. Skalej, and D. Thévenin. Virtual stenting using real patient data. In *Proc. of Conference on Fluid Flow Technologies* (CMFF'09), pages 871–878, 2009.

G. Janiga, C. Rössl, M. Skalej, and D. Thévenin. Realistic virtual intracranial stenting and computational fluid dynamics for treatment analysis. *Journal of Biomechanics*, 46(1):7–12, 2013.

P. Janin and W. Korb. *Image-Guided Interventions*, chapter Assessment of Image-Guided Interventions, pages 531–546. Springer, 2008.

P. Jannin, M. Raimbault, X. Morandi, L. Riffaud, and B. Gibaud. Model of surgical procedures for multimodal image-guided neurosurgery. *Comput. Aided Surgery*, 8(2):98–106, 2003.

H. Jastrow and A. Hollinderbäumer. On the use and value of new media and how medical students assess their effectiveness in learning anatomy. *Anatomical Record Part B*, 280B(1):20–29, 2004.

L. Jeřábková and T. Kuhlen. Stable Cutting of Deformable Objects in Virtual Environments Using XFEM. *IEEE Computer Graphics and Applications*, 29(2):61–71, 2009.

M. Jiang, R. Machiraju, and D. Thompson. *The Visualization Handbook*, chapter Detection and Visualization of Vortices. Elsevier Academic Press, 2005.

Y. Jiang, R.M. Nishikawa, R.A. Schmidt, C.E. Metz, M.L. Giger, and K. Doi. Improving breast cancer diagnosis with computer-aided diagnosis. *Academic Radiology*, 6(1):22–33, 1999.

R. Jianu, C. Demiralp, and D. H Laidlaw. Exploring 3D DTI fiber tracts with linked 2D representations. *IEEE Transactions on Visualization and Computer Graphics*, 15(6):1449–1456, 2009.

X. Jin, C.-L. Tai, J. Feng, and Q. Peng. Convolution surfaces for line skeletons with polynomial weight distributions. *Journal of Graphical Tools*, 6(3):17–28, 2001a.

Y. Jin, L. Fayad, and A. Laine. Contrast Enhancement by Multi-scale Adaptive Histogram Equalization. In *Proc. of SPIE Wavelets: Applications in Signal and Image Processing*, volume 4478, pages 206–213, 2001b.

B. Jobard and W. Lefer. Creating evenly-spaced streamlines of arbitrary density. *Visualization in scientific computing*, 97:43–55, 1997.

N. W. John. The impact of Web3D technologies on medical education and training. *Computers & Education*, 49(1):43–51, 2007.

N. W. John, N. Thacker, M. Pokric, A. Jackson, G. Zanetti, E. Gobbetti, A. Giachetti, R. J. Stone, J. Campos, A. Emmen, A. Schwerdtner, E. Neri, S. S. Franceschini, and F. Rubio. An integrated simulator for surgery of the petrous bone. *Studies Health Technology Information*, 81:218–224, 2001.

N. W. John, M. Aratow, J. Couch, D. Evestedt, A. D. Hudson, N. Polys, R. F. Puk, A. Ray, K. Victor, and Q. Wang. Medx3D: standards enabled desktop medical 3D. *Studies in health technology and informatics*, 132:189–194, 2008.

H. J. Johnson and G. E. Christensen. Consistent Landmark and Intersity-Based Image Registration. *IEEE Transactions on Medical Imaging*, 21(5):450–461, 2002.

J. P. Johnson, E. A. Krupinski, M. Yan, H. Roehrig, A. R. Graham, and R. S. Weinstein. Using a Visual Discrimination Model for the Detection of Compression Artifacts in Virtual Pathology Images. *IEEE Transactions on Medical Imaging*, 30(2):306–314, 2011.

L. G. Johnson, P. J. Edwards, L. D. Griffin, and D. J. Hawkes. Depth perception of stereo overlays in image-guided surgery. In *Proc. of SPIE Medical Imaging 2004: Image Perception, Observer Performance, and Technology Assessment*, pages 263–272, 2004.

S. Johnson, A. Healey, J. Evans, M. Murphy, M. Crawshaw, and D. Gould. Physical and cognitive task analysis in interventional radiology. *Clinical Radiology*, 61(1):97–103, 2006.

T. R. Johnson, B. Krauss, M. Sedlmair, M. Grasruck, H. Bruder, D. Morhard, C. Fink, S. Weckbach, M. Lenhard, B. Schmidt, T. Flohr, M. F. Reiser, and C. R. Becker. Material differentiation by dual energy CT: initial experience. *Eur Radiol.*, 17(6):1510–1517, 2007.

I. T. Jolliffe. *Principal Component Analysis*. Springer, New-York, 1986.

M.-P. Jolly and L. Grady. 3D general lesion segmentation in CT. In *Proc. of IEEE International Symposium on Biomedical Imaging* (ISBI), pages 796–799, 2008.

A. Jones, I. McDowall, H. Yamada, M. T. Bolas, and P. E. Debevec. Rendering for an interactive 360 degree light field display. *ACM Transactions on Graphics*, 26(3):40, 2007.

C. M. Jones, T. Athanasiou, S. Nair, O. Aziz, S. Purkayastha, V. Konstantinos, P. Paraskeva, R. Casula, B. Glenville, and A. Darzi. Do technical parameters affect the diagnostic accuracy of virtual bronchoscopy in patients with suspected airways stenosis? *American Journal of Roentgenology*, 55(3):445–451, 2005.

D. K. Jones. Challenges and limitations of quantifying brain connectivity in vivo with diffusion MRI. *Imaging in Medicine*, 2(3):341–355, 2010.

A. Joshi, X. Qian, D. P. Dione, K. R. Bulsara, C. K. Breuer, A. J. Sinusas, and X. Papademetris. Effective visualization of complex vascular structures using a non-parametric vessel detection method. *IEEE Transactions on Visualization and Computer Graphics*, 14(6):1603–1610, 2008.

S. C. Joshi, S. M. Pizer, P. T. Fletcher, P. A. Yushkevich, A. Thall, and J. S. Marron. Multi-scale Deformable Model Segmentation and Statistical Shape Analysis Using Medial Descriptions. *IEEE Transactions on Medical Imaging*, 21(5):538–550, 2002.

L. Joskowicz and R.H. Taylor. Computers in imaging and guided surgery. *Computing in Science Engineering*, 3(5):65–72, 2001.

E. Jovanov, K. Wegner, V. Radivojevic, D. Starcevic, M. S. Quinn, and D. B. Karron. Tactical audio and acoustic rendering in biomedical applications. *IEEE Transactions on Information Technology in Biomedicine*, 3(2):109–118, 1999.

L. Ju, M. K. Hurdal, J. Stern, K. Rehm, K. Schaper, and D. Rottenberg. Quantitative evaluation of three cortical surface flattening methods. *NeuroImage*, 28(4):869–880, 2005.

T. Judd, F. Durand, and E. H. Adelson. Apparent ridges for line drawing. *ACM Transactions on Graphics*, 26(3):19, 2007.

Y. Jung, R. Recker, M. Olbrich, and U. Bockholt. Using X3D for medical training simulations. In *Proc. of Web3D*, pages 43–51, 2008.

L. M. Kadasi, W. C. Dent, and A. M. Malek. Cerebral aneurysm wall thickness analysis using intraoperative microscopy: effect of size and gender on thin translucent regions. *Journal of Neurointerventional Surgery*, 5(3):201–206, 2013.

L. A. Kahrs, H. Hoppe, M. Riechmann, J. Raczkowsky, and H. Wörn. Preclinical experiments for locating surgical structures below organ surfaces using projection-based augmented reality. In *Proc. of Computer Assisted Radiology and Surgery*, 2006.

D. Kainmueller, T. Lange, and H. Lamecker. Shape constrained automatic segmentation of the liver based on a heuristic intensity model. In B. van Ginneken T. Heimann M. Styner, editor, *Proc. of MICCAI Workshop 3D Segmentation in the Clinic: A Grand Challenge*, pages 109–116, 2007.

J. Kajiya. The Rendering Equation. In *Proc. of ACM SIGGRAPH*, pages 143–150, 1986.

J. Kajiya and B. Herzen. Ray Tracing Volume Densities. In *Proc. of ACM SIGGRAPH*, pages 165–174, 1984.

W. Kalender. *Computer Tomography*. PUBLICIS MCD Verlag, München, Germany, 2000.

W. A. Kalender, R. Hebel, and J. Ebersberger. Reduction of CT artifacts caused by metallic implants. *Radiology*, 164:576–577, 1987.

W. A. Kalender, D. Felsenberg, O. Louis, P. Lopez, E. Klotz, M. Osteaux, and J. Fraga. Reference values for trabecular and cortical vertebral bone density in single and dual-energy quantitative computed tomography. *European Journal of Radiology*, 18(2):75–80, 1989.

D. Kalkofen, B. Reitinger, P. Risholm, A. Bornik, R. Beichel, D. Schmalstieg, and E. Samset. Integrated Medical Workflow for Augmented Reality Applications. In *Proc. of International Workshop on Augmented environments for Medical Imaging and Computer-aided Surgery (AMI-ARCS)*, pages 113–120, 2006.

D. Kalkofen, E. Méndez, and D. Schmalstieg. Interactive Focus and Context Visualization for Augmented Reality. In *ISMAR*, pages 191–201, 2007.

M.K. Kalra. *Mdct: From Protocols to Practice*. Springer, 2008.

W. C. Kan, W. S. Lee, W. H. Cheung, V. P. Wallace, and E. Pickwell-Macpherson. Terahertz pulsed imaging of knee cartilage. *Biomed. Opt. Express*, 20:967–974, 2010.

K. Kanda, S. Mizuta, and T. Matsuda. Volume visualization using relative distance among voxels. In *Proc. of Medical Imaging 2002: Visualization, Image-Guided Procedures, and Display*, pages 641–648, 2002.

B. Kane and S. Luz. A study of the impact of collaborative tools on the effectiveness of clinical pathology conferences. In *Proc. of APCHI '04*, volume 3101 of *Lecture Notes in Computer Science*, pages 656–660. Springer, 2004.

B. Kane and S. Luz. Multidisciplinary medical team meetings: An analysis of collaborative working with special attention to timing and teleconferencing. *Comput. Supported Coop. Work*, 15:501–535, 2006.

B. Kane and S. Luz. Achieving diagnosis by consensus. *Comput. Supported Coop. Work*, 18:357–392, 2009.

B. Kane, S. Luz, and S. Jing. Capturing multimodal interaction at medical meetings in a hospital setting: Opportunities and challenges. In *Proc. of Multimodal Corpora: Advances in Capturing, Coding and Analyzing Multimodality*, pages 140–145, 2010.

Y. Kang, K. Engelke, and W. A. Kalender. A new accurate and precise 3-D segmentation method for skeletal structures in volumetric CT data. *IEEE Transactions on Medical Imaging*, 22(5):586–598, 2003.

Y. Kang, K. Engelke, and W. A. Kalender. Interactive 3D editing tools for image segmentation. *Medical Image Analysis*, 8(1):35–46, 2004.

A. Kanitsar, D. Fleischmann, R. Wegenkittl, P. Felkel, and E. Gröller. CPR: curved planar reformation. In *Proc. of IEEE Visualization*, pages 37–44, 2002.

A. Kanitsar, R. Wegenkittl, D. Fleischmann, and E. Gröller. Advanced curved planar reformation: Flattening of vascular structures. In *Proc. of IEEE Visualization*, pages 43–50, 2003.

A. Kanitsar, D. Fleischmann, R. Wegenkittl, and E. Gröller. *Scientific Visualization: The Visual Extraction of Knowledge from Data*, chapter Diagnostic Relevant Visualization of Vascular Structures, pages 207–228. Springer, 2005.

S. R. Kannan, R. Devi, S. Ramathilagam, and K. Takezawa. Effective FCM noise clustering algorithms in medical images. *Comp. in Bio. and Med.*, 43(2):73–83, 2013.

Y.-H. Kao, M. M.-H. Teng, K.-C. Liu, I.-P. Lam, and Y.-C. Lin. Hemodynamic segmentation of MR perfusion images in patients with unilateral carotid stenosis using independent component analysis. *Journal of Magnetic Resonance Imaging*, 28(5):1125–1132, 2008.

A. Karahaliou, K Vassiou, and Arikidis N. S. Assessing heterogeneity of lesion enhancement kinetics in dynamic contrast-enhanced mri for breast cancer diagnosis. *The British Journal of Radiology*, 83:296–306, 2010.

M. Kass, A. Witkin, and D. Terzopoulos. Snakes: active contour models. *International Journal of Computer Vision*, 1(4):321–331, 1988.

K. Kassil and A. J. Stewart. Evaluation of a tool-mounted guidance display for computer-assisted surgery. In *Proc. of ACM Human factors in computing systems*, CHI '09, pages 1275–1278, 2009.

H. Kato and M. Billinghurst. Marker Tracking and HMD Calibration for a video-based Augmented Reality Conferencing System. In *Proc. of IEEE and ACM International Workshop on Augmented Reality*, pages 85–94, 1999.

D. Kay and D. Greenberg. Transparency for Computer Synthesized Images. In *Proc. of ACM SIGGRAPH*, pages 158–164, 1979.

E. Keeve, S. Girod, P. Pfeifle, and B. Girod. Anatomy-based facial tissue modeling using the finite element method. In *Proc. of IEEE Visualization*, pages 21–28, 1996.

S. Keil, F. Behrendt, S. Stanzel, M. Sühling, A. Koch, J. Bubenzer, G. Mühlenbruch, A. Mahnken, R. Günther, and M. Das. Semi-automated measurement of hyperdense, hypodense and heterogeneous hepatic metastasis on standard MDCT slices. Comparison of semi-automated and manual measurement of RECIST and WHO criteria. *European Radiology*, 18:2456–2465, 2008.

R. Kelc. Zygote Body: A New Interactive 3-Dimensional Didactical Tool for Teaching Anatomy. *WebmedCentral ANATOMY*, 3(1), 2012.

K. Kellermann, M. Neugebauer, and B. Preim. A 6DOF Interaction Method for the Virtual Training of Minimally Invasive Access to the Spine. In *Proc. of CURAC*, pages 143–148, 2011.

P. J. Kelly and G. J. Alker. A stereotactic approach to deep-seated central nervous system neoplasms using the carbon dioxide laser. *Surgical Neurology*, 15(5):331–334, 1981.

E. Keppel. Approximating Complex Surfaces by Triangulation of Contour Lines. *IBM Journal of Research and Development*, 19(1):2–11, 1975.

M. Kersten-Oertel, P. Jannin, and D. Collins. DVV: Towards a Taxonomy for Mixed Reality Visualization in Image Guided Surgery. In *Medical Imaging and Augmented Reality*, volume 6326 of *LNCS*, pages 334–343, 2010.

M. Kersten-Oertel, P. Jannin, and D. Louis Collins. DVV: A Taxonomy for Mixed Reality Visualization in Image Guided Surgery. *IEEE Transactions on Visualization and Computer Graphics*, 18(2):332–352, 2012.

T. Kerwin, H.-W. Shen, and D. Stredney. Enhancing Realism of Wet Surfaces in Temporal Bone Surgical Simulation. *IEEE Transactions on Visualization and Computer Graphics*, 15(5):747–758, 2009.

T. Kerwin, B. Hittle, H.-W. Shen, D. Stredney, and G. J. Wiet. Anatomical Volume Visualization with Weighted Distance Fields. In *Proc. of Eurographics Workshop on Visual Computing in Biology and Medicine (VCBM)*, pages 117–124, 2010.

J. Kettenbach, D. Kacher, S. Koskinen, S. Silverman, A. Nabavi, D. Gering, C. Tempany, R. Schwartz, R. Kikinis, P. Black, and F. Jolesz. Interventional and Intraoperative Magnetic Resonance Imaging. *Annual Review of Biomedical Engineering*, 2(August):661–690, 2000.

R. Khlebnikov, B. Kainz, J. Muehl, and D. Schmalstieg. Crepuscular Rays for Tumor Accessibility Planning. *IEEE Transactions on Visualization and Computer Graphics*, 17(12):2163–2172, 2011.

Y. Kho and M. Garland. Sketching mesh deformations. *ACM Transactions on Graphics*, 24(3):934, 2005.

R. Kikinis, M. E. Shenton, D. V. Iosifescu, R. W. McCarley, P. Saiviroonporn, H. H. Hokama et al. A Digital Brain Atlas for Surgical Planning, model driven segmentation and teaching. *IEEE Transactions on Visualization and Computer Graphics*, 2(3):232–241, 1996a.

R. Kikinis, C. Umanns, S. Jones, W. Lorensen, and F. Jolesz. Virtual otoscopy. In *Proc. of IMAGE Society Conference and Exhibition*, pages 192–196, 1996b.

D. H. Kim, P. J. Pickhardt, A. J. Taylor, W. K. Leung, T. C. Winter, J. L. Hinshaw, D. V. Gopal, M. Reichelderfer, R. H. Hsu, and P. R. Pfau. CT Colonography versus Colonoscopy for the Detection of Advanced Neoplasia. *New England Journal of Medicine*, 357(14):1403–1412, 2007a.

M. Kim, E. Levy, H. Meng, and L. N. Hopkins. Quantification of Hemodynamic Changes Induced by Virtual Placement of Multiple Stents. *Neurosurgery*, 61:1305–1313, 2007b.

S. Kim, H. Hagh-Shenas, and V. Interrante. Showing Shape with Texture: two directions seem better than one. In *Human Vision and Electronic Imaging VIII, SPIE*, pages 339–332, 2003.

T.-Y. Kim and U. Neumann. Opacity Shadow Maps. In *Proc. of the Eurographics Workshop on Rendering Techniques*, pages 177–182, 2001.

Y. Kim and S. C. Horli. *Handbook of Medical Imaging: Display and PACS*, volume 3. SPIE Press, 2000.

Y. Kim, K. Lee, and W. Kim. 3D virtual simulator for breast plastic surgery. *Computer Animation and Virtual Worlds*, 19(3-4):515–526, 2008.

G. Kindlmann. Superquadric tensor glyphs. In *Data Visualization (Proc. of Eurographics/IEEE Symposium on Visualization)*, pages 147–154, 2004a.

G. Kindlmann and J. W. Durkin. Semi-automatic generation of transfer functions for direct volume rendering. In *Proc. of IEEE/ACM Symposium on Volume Visualization*, pages 79–86, 1998.

G. Kindlmann, D. Weinstein, and D. Hart. Strategies for direct volume rendering of diffusion tensor fields. *IEEE Transactions on Visualization and Computer Graphics*, 6(2):124–138, 2000.

G. L. Kindlmann, R. T. Whitaker, T. Tasdizen, and T. Möller. Curvature-Based Transfer Functions for Direct Volume Rendering: Methods and Applications. In *Proc. of IEEE Visualization*, pages 513–520, 2003.

P. Kipfer and R. Westermann. GPU Construction and Transparent Rendering of Iso-Surfaces. In *Proc. of Vision, Modeling, and Visualization*, pages 241–248, 2005.

A. P. Kiraly, S. Qing, and H. Shen. A novel visualization method for the ribs within chest volume data. In *Proc. of SPIE Medical Imaging*, pages 51–58, 2006.

C. Kirbas and F. Quek. A Review of Vessel Extraction Techniques and Algorithms. *ACM Computing Surveys*, 36(2):81–121, 2004.

R. Klar and U. Bayer. Computer-asssisted teaching and learning in medicine. *International Journal of Biomedical Computing*, pages 7–27, 1990.

J. Klein and G. Zachmann. Time-Critical Collision Detection Using an Average-Case Approach. In *Proc. of ACM Symposium on Virtual Reality Software and Technology*, 2003.

J. Klein, P. Bittihn, P. Ledochowitsch, H. K. Hahn, O. Konrad, J. Rexilius, and H.-O. Peitgen. Grid-based spectral fiber clustering. In *spiemi*, pages 65091–65091E, 2007.

L. Klimek, M. Wenzel, and R. Mösges. Computer-Assisted Orbital Surgery. *Ophtalmic Surgery*, 24(6):411–417, 1993.

R. Klingenbiel, H.C. Bauknecht, R. Lehmann, P. Rogalla, M. Werbs, H. Behrbohm, and O. Kaschke. Virtual otoscopy: technique indications and initial experience with multi-slice spiral. *Fortschr Roentgenstr*, 172(9):872–878, 2000.

F. Klumb, V. Duboise-Ferriere, N. Roduit, C. Barea, T. Strgar, K. Ahmed, M. Assal, and P. Hoffmeyer. Virtual manipulation of medical images with hand gestures in the operating room. In *Proc. of CARS*, pages 206–207, 2012.

C. Knapheide. Smart UI: Mit dem iPad auf Visite. *inside: health IT SPECIAL*, (4):16–19, 2011.

J. Kniss, G. Kindlmann, and C. Hansen. Multi-Dimensional Transfer Functions for Interactive Volume Rendering. *IEEE Transactions on Visualization and Computer Graphics*, 8(3):270–285, 2002a.

J. Kniss, S. Premoze, C. Hansen, and D. Ebert. Interactive Translucent Volume Rendering and Procedural Modeling. In *Proc. of IEEE Visualization*, pages 109–116, 2002b.

J. Kniss, S. Premoze, C. Hansen, P. Shirley, and A. McPherson. A Model for Volume Lighting and Modeling. *IEEE Transactions on Visualization and Computer Graphics*, 9(2):150–162, 2003a.

J. M. Kniss, S. Premoze, M. Ikits, A. E. Lefohn, C. D. Hansen, and E. Praun. Gaussian Transfer Functions for Multi-Field Volume Visualization. In *Proc. of IEEE Visualization*, pages 497–504, 2003b.

M.V. Knopp, E. Weiss, H.P. Sinn, J. Mattern, H. Junkermann, J. Radelaff, A. Magener, G. Brix, S. Delorme, I. Zuna, and G. van Kaick. Pathopysiologic basis of contrast enhancement in breast tumors. *Journal of Magnetic Resonance Imaging*, 10:260–266, 1999.

K. Knox, C. W. Kerber, S. Singel, M. Bailey, and S. Imbesi. Rapid prototyping to create vascular replicas from CT scan data: Making tools to teach, rehearse, and choose treatment strategies. *Catheterization and Cardiovascular Interventions*, 65(1):47–53, 2005.

J.M. Ko, M.J. Nicholas, J.B. Mendel, and P.J. Slanetz. Prospective assessment of computer-aided detection in interpretation of screening mammography. *AJR Am. J. Roentgenol.*, 187(6):1483–1491, 2006.

L. Kobbelt, M. Botsch, U. Schwanecke, and H.-P. Seidel. Feature sensitive surface extraction from volume data. In *Proc. of ACM SIGGRAPH*, pages 57–66, 2001.

J.-P. Kobler, M. Kuhlemann, and T. Ortmaier. A Laser Projector Augmented Drill for Surgical Applications: Design and Feasibility Study. In *Proc. of Computer Assisted Radiology and Surgery (CARS)*, 2012.

M. A. Koch, D. G. Norris, and M. Hund-Georgiadis. An investigation of functional and anatomical connectivity using magnetic resonance imaging. *Neuroimage*, 16(1):241–250, 2002.

R. A. Kockro, Y. T. Tsai, P. Hwang, C. Zhu, K. Agusanto, L. X. Hong, and L. Serra. Dex-Ray: Augmented Reality Neurosurgical Navigation with a Handheld Probe. *Neurosurgery*, 65(4):795–808, 2009.

A. Koechl, A. Kanitsar, F. Lomoschitz, E. Groeller, and D. Fleischmann. Comprehensive Assessment of Peripheral Arteries using Multi-path Curved Planar Reformation of CTA Datasets. *Europ. Rad.*, 13:268–269, 2003.

W. Koele, H. Stammberger, A. Lackner, and P. Reittner. Image guided surgery of paranasal sinuses and anterior skull base–five years experience with the InstaTrak-System. *Rhinology*, 40(1):1–9, 2002.

J. J. Koenderink. *Solid shape*. MIT Press, Cambridge, Massachusetts, London, England, 1990.

S. Kohle, B. Preim, J. Wiener, and H.-O. Peitgen. Exploration of Time-varying Data for Medical Diagnosis. In *Proc. of Vision, Modeling, and Visualization*, pages 31–38. Aka, 2002.

P. Kohlmann, S. Bruckner, M. Eduard Groller, and A. Kanitsar. LiveSync: Deformed Viewing Spheres for Knowledge-Based Navigation. *IEEE Transactions on Visualization and Computer Graphics*, 13(6):1544–1551, 2007.

P. Kohlmann, S. Bruckner, A. Kanitsar, and E. Gröller. LiveSync++: enhancements of an interaction metaphor. In *Proc. of Graphics Interface*, pages 81–88, 2008.

P. Kohlmann, S. Bruckner, A. Kanitsar, and E. Gröller. Contextual picking of volumetric structures. In *Proc. of IEEE PacificVis*, pages 185–192, 2009.

P. Kohlmann, H. Laue, S. Krass, and H.-O. Peitgen. Fully-Automatic Determination of the Arterial Input Function for Dynamic Contrast-Enhanced Pulmonary MR Imaging. In *Proc. of Medical Image Understanding and Analysis*, pages 281–285, 2011.

A. Köhn, J. Drexl, F. Ritter, M. König, and H.-O. Peitgen. GPU Accelerated Image Registration in Two and Three Dimensions. In *Proc. of Bildverarbeitung für die Medizin*, pages 261–265, 2006.

P. Kok, M. Baiker, E. A. Hendriks, F. H. Post, J. Dijkstra, C. W.G.M. Löwik, B. P.F. Lelieveldt, and C. P. Botha. Articulated Planar Reformation for Change Visualization in Small Animal Imaging. *IEEE Transactions on Visualization and Computer Graphics*, 16(6):1396–1404, 2010.

K. Kollia, S. Maderwald, N. Putzki, M. Schlamann, J. M. Theysohn, O. Kraff, M. E. Ladd, M. Forsting, and I. Wanke. First clinical study on ultra-high-field MR imaging in patients with multiple sclerosis: comparison of 1.5T and 7T. *American Journal of Neuroradiology*, 30(4), 2009.

E. Kollorz, J. Penne, J. Hornegger, and A. Barke. Gesture recognition with a Time-Of-Flight camera. *International Journal of Intelligent Systems Technologies and Applications*, 5(3/4):334–343, 2008.

P. Kondratieva, J. Krüger, and R. Westermann. The Application of GPU Particle Tracing to Diffusion Tensor Field Visualization. In *Proc. of IEEE Visualization*, pages 10–17, 2005.

A. H. König and E. Gröller. Mastering Transfer Function Specification by using VolumePro Technology. In *Proc. of Spring Conference on Computer Graphics*, volume 17, pages 279–286, 2001.

M. König and H.-O. Peitgen. Visualization of local correlation in image registration. In *Proc. of Simulation and Visualization*, pages 165–174. SCS, 2005.

M. König, E. Klotz, and L. Heuser. Perfusion CT in Acute Stroke: Characterization of Cerebral Ischemia using Parameter Images of Cerebral Blood Flow and their Therapeutic Relevance. *Electromedica*, 66(2):61–67, 1998.

M. König, M. Kraus, C. Theek, E. Klotz, W. Gehlen, and L. Heuser. Quantitative Assesment of the Ischemic Brain by Means of Perfusion-Related Parameters Derived from Perfusion CT. *Stroke*, 32:431–437, 2001.

O. Konrad-Verse, B. Preim, and A. Littmann. Virtual Resection with a Deformable Cutting Plane. In *Proc. of Simulation and Visualization*, pages 203–214. SCS, 2004.

J. Kopf, D. Cohen-Or, O. Deussen, and D. Lischinski. Recursive Wang tiles for real-time blue noise. *ACM Transactions on Graphics*, 25(3):509–518, 2006.

R. Koppe, E. Klotz, J. Op De Beek, and H. Aerts. 3D Vessel Reconstruction Based on Rotational Angiography. In *Proc. of CAR*, pages 101–107, 1995.

W. Korb, M. Sturm, B. Andrack, G. Bausch, N. Geissler, J. Handwerk, M. Müller, A. Seifert, H. Steinke, and J. Meixensberger. Development and Validation of a Prototype for Training of Discectomy. *International Journal of Computer Assisted Radiology and Surgery*, 6(1):121–122, 2011.

R. Kosara, S. Miksch, and H. Hauser. Semantic Depth of Field. In *Proc. of the IEEE Symposium on Information Visualization (INFOVIS)*, pages 97–104, 2001.

R. Kosara, C.G. Healey, V. Interrante, D.H. Laidlaw, and C. Ware. User Studies: Why, How, and When? *IEEE Computer Graphics and Applications*, 23:20–25, 2003.

N. Kotava, A. Knoll, M. Schott, C. Garth, X. Tricoche, C. Kessler, E. Cohen, C. D. Hansen, M. E. Papka, and H. Hagen. Volume rendering with multidimensional peak finding. In *Proc. of PacificVis*, pages 161–168, 2012.

P. R. Krekel, C. P. Botha, E. R. Valstar, P. W. de Bruin, P. M. Rozing, and F. H. Post. Interactive simulation and comparative visualisation of the bone-determined range of motion of the human shoulder. In *Proc. of Simulation and Visualization*, pages 275–288, 2006.

P. R. Krekel, E. R. Valstar, F. H. Post, P. M. Rozing, and C. P. Botha. Combined Surface and Volume Processing for Fused Joint Segmentation. *The International Journal for Computer Assisted Radiology and Surgery*, 5(3):263–273, 2010.

F. W. Kremkau. *Diagnostic Ultrasound*. W.B. Saunders, 6 edition, 2002.

J. Kretschmar, T. Beck, C. Tietjen, B. Preim, and M. Stamminger. Reliable Adaptive Modelling of Vascular Structures with Non-Circular Cross-Sections. *Computer Graphics Forum*, 31(3):1055–1064, 2012.

K. Krissian. Flux-based anisotropic diffusion applied to enhancement of 3-D angiogram. *IEEE Transactions on Medical Imaging*, 21(11):1440–1442, 2002.

K. Krissian, X. Wu, and V. Luboz. Smooth Vasculature Reconstruction with Circular and Elliptic Cross Sections. *Stud. Health Technol. Inform.*, 119:273–278, 2006.

T. Kröger, T. Pätz, I. Altrogge, A. Schenk, K.S. Lehmann, B.B. Frericks, J.-P. Ritz, H.-O. Peitgen, and T. Preusser. Fast Estimation of the Vascular Cooling in RFA Based on Numerical Simulation. *The Open Biomedical Engineering Journal*, 4:16–26, 2010.

J. Kronander, D. Jönsson, J. Löw, P. Ljung, A. Ynnerman, and J. Unger. Efficient Visibility Encoding for Dynamic Illumination in Direct Volume Rendering. *IEEE Transactions on Visualization and Computer Graphics*, 18(3):447–462, 2012.

A. Krüger, C. Tietjen, J. Hintze, B. Preim, I. Hertel, and G. Strauß. Interactive Visualization for Neck-Dissection Planning. In *Data Visualization (Proc. of Eurographics/IEEE Symposium on Visualization)*, pages 295–302, 2005.

A. Krüger, C. Kubisch, G. Strauß, and B. Preim. Sinus endoscopy - application of advanced gpu volume rendering for virtual endoscopy. *IEEE Transactions on Visualization and Computer Graphics*, 14(6):1491–1498, 2008.

A. Krüger, K. Stampe, S. Irrgang, I. Richter, G. Strauß, and B. Preim. Eingabegeräte und Interaktionstechniken für die virtuelle Endoskopie. In *Mensch & Computer 2008*, pages 237–246. Oldenbourg Verlag, 2008.

J. Krüger and R. Westermann. Linear algebra operators for GPU implementation of numerical algorithms. *ACM Transactions on Graphics*, 22(3):908–916, 2003.

J. Krüger and R. Westermann. Acceleration Techniques for GPU-based Volume Rendering. In *Proc. of IEEE Visualization*, pages 287–292, 2003.

J. Krüger, J. Schneider, and R. Westermann. ClearView: An Interactive Context Preserving Hotspot Visualization Technique. *IEEE Transactions on Visualization and Computer Graphics*, 12(5):941–948, 2006.

W. Krüger. The Applicaton of Transport Theory to Visualization of 3-D Scalar Data Fields. In *Proc. of IEEE Visualization*, pages 273–280, 1990a.

W. Krüger. Volume Rendering and Data Feature Enhancement. In *Proc. of IEEE/ACM Symposium on Volume Visualization*, pages 21–26, 1990b.

E. Kruijff, J. E. Swan II, and S. Feiner. Perceptual issues in augmented reality revisited. In *Proc. of IEEE International Symposium on Mixed and Augmented Reality (ISMAR)*, pages 3–12, 2010.

E. A. Krupinski. Technology and perception in the 21st-century reading room. *Journal of American College of Radiology*, pages 433–440, 2006.

E. A. Krupinski. Optimizing the pathology workstation "cockpit": Challenges and solutions. *J. Pathol. Inform.*, 1:1–19, 2010.

E. A. Krupinski, J. Johnson, H. Roehrig, J. Nafziger, J. Fan, and J. Lubin. Use of a human visual system model to predict observer performance with crt vs lcd display of images. *Journal of Digital Imaging*, 17(4):258–263, 2004.

E. A. Krupinski, K. S. Berbaum, R. T. Caldwell, K. M. Schartz, M. T. Madsen, and D. J. Kramer. Do long radiology workdays affect nodule detection in dynamic CT interpretation? *J. Am. Coll. Radiol.*, 9(3):191–198, 2012a.

E. A. Krupinski, L. D. Silverstein, S. F. Hashmi, A. R. Graham, R. S. Weinstein, and H. Roehrig. Observer Performance Using Virtual Pathology Slides: Impact of LCD Color Reproduction Accuracy. *Journal of Digital Imaging*, 25(6):738–743, 2012b.

K. J. Kruszynski, R. van Liere, and J. A. Kaandorp. An Interactive Visualization System for Quantifying Coral Structures. In *Data Visualization (Proc. of Eurographics/IEEE Symposium on Visualization)*, pages 283–290, 2006.

J. P. Ku, M. T. Draney, F. R. Arko, W. A. Lee, F. P. Chan, N. J. Pelc, C. K. Zarins, and C. A. Taylor. In vivo validation of numerical prediction of blood flow in arterial bypass grafts. *Annals of Biomedical Engineering*, 30(6):743–752, 2002.

C. Kubisch, C. Tietjen, and B. Preim. GPU-based Smart Visibility Techniques for Tumor Surgery Planning. *International Journal of Computer Assisted Radiology and Surgery*, pages 667–678, 2010.

C. Kubisch, S. Glaßer, M. Neugebauer, and B. Preim. *Visualization in Medicine and Life Sciences*, chapter Vessel Visualization with Volume Rendering, pages 109–134. Springer, 2012.

C. K. Kuhl. The current status of breast MR imaging. *Radiology*, 244(2):356–378, 2007.

W. Kuhn. 7+/− Questions and Answers about Metaphors for GIS User Interfaces. In W. Kuhn, editor, *Cognitive Aspects of Human-Computer Interaction for Geographic Information Systems*, number 83 in D, pages 113–122, 1995.

U. G. Kühnapfel, H. K. Çakmak, and H. Maaß. Endoscopic surgery training using virtual reality and deformable tissue simulation. *Computers & Graphics*, 24(5):671–682, 2000.

J. M. Kuhnigk, H. K. Hahn, M. Hindennach, V. Dicken, S. Krass, and H.-O. Peitgen. Lung lobe segmentation be anatomy-guided 3D watershed transform. In *Proc. of SPIE Medical Imaging*, volume 5032, pages 1482–1490. SPIE Press, 2003.

J.-M. Kuhnigk, V. Dicken, L. Bornemann, D. Wormanns, S. Krass, and H.-O. Peitgen. Fast Automated Segmentation and Reproducible Volumetry of Pulmonary Metastases in CT-Scans for Therapy Monitoring. In *Proc. of Medical Image Computing and Computer-Assisted Intervention (MICCAI)*, pages 933–941, 2004.

J.-M. Kuhnigk, V. Dicken, L. Bornemann, A. Bakai, D. Wormanns, S. Krass, and H.-O. Peitgen. Morphological segmentation and partial volume analysis for volumetry of solid pulmonary lesions in thoracic CT scans. *IEEE Transactions on Medical Imaging*, 25(4):417–434, 2006.

S. Kundu, M. Itkin, D.A. Gervais, V.N. Krishnamurthy, M.J. Wallace, J.F. Cardella, D. L. Rubin, and C.P. Langlotz. Prospective assessment of computer-aided detection in interpretation of screening mammography. *Journal of Vascular and Interventional Radiology*, 20(7 Suppl):275–277, 2009.

A. P. Kuprat and D. R. Einstein. An anisotropic scale-invariant unstructured mesh generator suitable for volumetric imaging data. *J. Comput. Phys.*, 228:619–640, 2009.

Y. Kurzion and R. Yagel. Interactive Space Deformation with Hardware-Assisted Rendering. *IEEE Computer Graphics and Applications*, 17(5):66–77, 1997.

O. Kutter, A. Aichert, C. Bichlmeier, S. M. Heining, B. Ockert, E. Euler, and N. Navab. Real-time Volume Rendering for High Quality Visualization in Augmented Reality. In *Proc. of Augmented environments for Medical Imaging including Augmented Reality in Computer-aided Surgery (AMI-ARCS)*, 2008.

H. Kye and D. Jeong. Accelerated MIP based on GPU using block clipping and occlusion query. *Computers & Graphics*, 32:283–292, 2008.

P. Lacroute and M. Levoy. Fast Volume Rendering Using a Shear-Warp Factorization of the Viewing Transformation. In *Proc. of ACM SIGGRAPH*, pages 451–458, 1994.

S. C: Ladd. Whole-body MRI as a screening tool? *European Journal of Radiology*, 70(3):452–462, 2009.

S. C. Ladd and M. E. Ladd. Perspectives for preventive screening with total body MRI. *European Radiology*, 17(11):2889–2897, 2007.

M. Lai, S. Benzley, G. Sjaardema, and T. Tautges. A Multiple Source and Target Sweeping Method for Generating All Hexahedral Finite Element Meshes. In *Proc. of International Meshing Roundtable (IMR)*, pages 217–225, 1996.

D. H. Laidlaw, E. T. Ahrens, D. Kremers, M. J. Avalos, R. E. Jacobs, and C. Readhead. Visualizing diffusion tensor images of the mouse spinal cord. In *Proc. of IEEE Visualization*, pages 127 –134, October 1998.

D. H. Laidlaw, R. M. Kirby, J. Scott Davidson, T. S. Miller, M. da Silva, W. H. Warren, and M. J. Tarr. Quantitative Comparative Evaluation of 2D Vector Field Visualization Methods. In *Proc. of IEEE Visualization*, pages 143–150, 2001.

D. H. Laidlaw, R. M. Kirby, C. D. Jackson, J. S. Davidson, T. S. Miller, M. da Silva, W. H. Warren, and M. J. Tarr. Comparing 2D Vector Field Visualization Methods: A User Study. *IEEE Transactions on Visualization and Computer Graphics*, 11(1):59–70, 2005.

S. Lakare and A. Kaufman. Anti-Aliased volume extraction. In *Data Visualization (Proc. of Eurographics/IEEE Symposium on Visualization)*, pages 113–122, 2003.

S. Lakare, M. Wan, M. Sato, and A. Kaufman. 3D Digital Cleansing Using Segmentation Rays. In *Proc. of IEEE Visualization*, pages 37–44, 2000.

R. C. Lalouche, D. Bickmore, F. Tessler, H. K. Mankovich, and H. Kangaraloo. Three-dimensional reconstruction of ultrasound images. In *Proc. of SPIE Medical Imaging*, pages 59–66, 1989.

W. Lamadé, G. Glombitza, and L. Fischer. The impact of 3-dimensional reconstructions on operation planning in liver surgery. *Archives of Surgery*, 135(11):1256–1261, 2000.

E. LaMar, B. Hamann, and K. Joy. Multiresolution Techniques for Interactive Texture-Based Volume Visualization. In *Proc. of IEEE Visualization*, pages 355–361, 1999.

E. LaMar, B. Hamann, and K. I. Joy. A magnification lens for interactive volume visualization. In *Proc. of the Pacific Conference on Computer Graphics and Applications*, pages 223–230, 2001.

P. Lamata, A. Jalote-Parmar, F. Lamata, and J. Declerck. The resection map, a proposal for intraoperative hepatectomy guidance. *International Journal of Computer Assisted Radiology and Surgery*, 3(3):299–306, 2008.

P. Lamata, F. Lamata, V. Sojar, P. Makowski, L. Massoptier, S. Casciaro, W. Ali, T. Stüdeli, J. Declerck, O. Elle, and B. Edwin. Use of the resection map system as guidance during hepatectomy. *Surgical Endoscopy*, 24(9):2327–2337, 2010.

H. Lamecker, T. Lange, and M. Seebass. A Statistical Shape Model for the Liver. In *Proc. of Medical Image Computing and Computer-Assisted Intervention (MICCAI)*, volume 2488 of *Lecture Notes in Computer Science*, pages 422–427. Springer, 2002.

H. Lamecker, M. Seebass, H.-C. Hege, and P. Deuflhard. A 3D Statistical Shape Model of the Pelvic Bone for Segmentation. In *Proc. of SPIE Medical Imaging*, volume 5370, pages 1341–1351. SPIE, 2004.

J. Lander. Under the Shade of the Rendering Tree. *Graphics Developer Magazine*, 7(2):17–21, 2000.

A. R. Lanfranco, A. E. Castellanos, J. P. Desai, and W. C. Meyers. Robotic surgery. *Annals of Surgery*, 239(1):14–21, 2004.

T. Lange, S. Eulenstein, M. Hünerbein, and P.-M. Schlag. Vessel-Based Non-Rigid Registration of MR/CT and 3D Ultrasound for Navigation in Liver Surgery. *Computer Aided Surgery*, 8(5):228–240, 2002.

T. Lange, S. Eulenstein, M. Hünerbein, H. Lamecker, and P.-M. Schlag. Augmenting Intraoperative 3D Ultrasound with Preoperative Models for Navigation in Liver Surgery. In *Proc. of Medical Image Computing and Computer-Assisted Intervention (MICCAI)*, volume 3217 of *Lecture Notes in Computer Science*, pages 534–541, 2004a.

T. Lange, S. Eulenstein, M. Hünerbein, H. Lamecker, and P.-M. Schlag. Augmenting Intraoperative 3D Ultrasound with Preoperative Models for Navigation in Liver Surgery. In *Proc. of Medical Image Computing and Computer-Assisted Intervention (MICCAI)*, volume 3217 of *LNCS*, pages 534–541, 2004b.

M. S. Langer and H. H. Bülthoff. Depth discrimination from shading under diffuse lighting. *Perception*, 29(6):649–660, 2000.

E. Langetepe and G. Zachmann. *Geometric Data Structures for Computer Graphics*. A K Peters, 2006.

F. Langlotz and Lutz-P. Nolte. Technical Approaches to Computer-Assisted Orthopedic Surgery. *European Journal of Trauma*, 30(1):1–11, 2004.

J. W. Lankhaar, M. B. Hofman, J. T. Marcus, J. J. Zwanenburg, T. J. Faes, and A. Vonk-Noordegraaf. Correction of phase offset errors in main pulmonary artery flow quantification. *Journal of Magnetic Resonance Imaging*, 22(1):73–79, 2005.

I. Larrabide, A. Radaelli, and A. F. Frangi. Fast Virtual Stenting with Deformable Meshes: Application to Intracranial Aneurysms. In *Proc. of Medical Image Computing and Computer-Assisted Intervention (MICCAI)*, pages 790–797, 2008.

G. Läthen, S. Lindholm, R. Lenz, A. Persson, and M. Borga. Automatic Tuning of Spatially Varying Transfer Functions for Blood Vessel Visualization. *IEEE Transactions on Visualization and Computer Graphics*, 5:2345–2352, 2012.

R. Lattanzi, M. Viceconti, M. Petrone, P. Quadrani, and C. Zannoni. Applications of 3D medical imaging in orthopaedic surgery:introducing the hip-op system. In *Proc. International Symposium on 3D Data Processing Visualization and Transmission*, pages 808–811, 2002.

P. C. Lauterbur. Image formation by induced local interactions: examples employing nuclear magnetic resonance. *Nature*, 242:190–191, 1973.

K. Lawonn, R. Gasteiger, and B. Preim. Qualitative Evaluation of Feature Lines on Anatomical Surfaces. In *Proc. of Workshop Bildverarbeitung für die Medizin*, pages 187–192, 2013a.

K. Lawonn, T. Mönch, and B. Preim. Streamlines for Illustrative Real-time Rendering. *Computer Graphics Forum*, 33(3):321–330, 2013b. Proc. of Eurovis.

S. D. Laycock and A. M. Day. The Haptic Rendering of Polygonal Models involving Deformable Tools. In I. Oakley, S. O'Modhrain, and F. Newell, editors, *Proc. of EuroHaptics*, pages 176–192, 2003.

D. Le Bihan, J.-F. Mangin, C. Poupon, C. A. Clark, S. Pappata, N. Molko, and H. Chabriat. Diffusion tensor imaging: Concepts and applications. *Journal of Magnetic Resonance Imaging*, 13(4):534–546, 2001.

C. Y. Lee and J. J. Rosowski. Effects of middle-ear static pressure on pars tensa and pars flaccida of gerbil ears. *Hearing Research*, 153(1-2):146–163, 2001.

C.Y. Lee and J. J. Rosowski. Effects of middle-ear static pressure on pars tensa and pars flaccida of gerbil ears. *Radiother. Oncol.*, 93(3):474–478, 2009.

J.-S. Lee. Digital image smoothing and the sigma filter. *Computer Vision, Graphics, and Image Processing*, 24:255–269, 1983.

S.-L. Lee, M. Lerotic, V. Vitiello, S. Giannarou, K.-W. Kwok, M. Visentini-Scarzanella, and G.-Z. Yang. From medical images to minimally invasive intervention: Computer assistance for robotic surgery. *Computerized Medical Imaging and Graphics*, 34(1):33–45, 2010.

S. W. Lee, H. Shinohara, M. Matsuki, J. Okuda, E. Nomura, H. Mabuchi et al. Preoperative simulation of vascular anatomy by three-dimensional computed tomography imaging in laparoscopic gastric cancer surgery. *Journal of the American College of Surgeons*, 197(6):927–936, 2003.

T.-Y. Lee, C.-H. Lin, and H.-Y. Lin. Computer-aided prototype system for nose surgery. *IEEE Transactions on Information Technology in Biomedicine*, 5(4):271–278, 2001.

W. W. Lee and D. L. Owens. *Multimedia-Based Instructional Design: Computer-Based Training, Web-Based Training, and Distance Learning*. Jossey-Bass/Pfeiffer, A Wiley Company, 2000.

K. S. Lehmann, J. P. Ritz, H. Maass, H. K. Cakmak, U. G. Kuehnapfel, C. T. Germer, G. Bretthauer, and H. J. Buhr. A prospective randomized study to test the transfer of basic psychomotor skills from virtual reality to physical reality in a comparable training setting. *Annals of Surgery*, 241(3):442–449, 2005.

T. M. Lehmann, W. Oberschelp, E. Pelikan, and R. Repges. *Bildverarbeitung für die Medizin*. Springer, 1997.

T. M. Lehmann, J. Bredno, and K. Spitzer. On the Design of Active Contours for Medical Image Segmentation: A Scheme for Classification and Construction. *Methods of Information in Medicine*, 1:89–98, 2003.

B. Lelieveldt, A. Frangi, S. Mitchell, H. van Assen, S. Ordas, J. Reiber, and M. Sonka. *The Handbook of Mathematical Models in Computer Vision*, chapter 3D Active Shape and Appearance Models in Cardiac Image Analysis. Springer, 2006.

V. Lepetit and M. Berger. A Semi-Automatic Method for Resolving Occlusion in Augmented Reality. In *Proc. of the IEEE Conference on Computer Vision and Pattern Recognition*, pages 225–230, 2000.

P. Lermusiaux, C. Leroux, J. C. Tasse, L. Castellani, and R. Martinez. Aortic aneurysm: Construction of a life-size model by rapid prototyping. *Annals of Vascular Surgery*, 15(2):131–135, 2001.

D. Lesage, E. D. Angelini, I. Bloch, and G. Funka-Lea. A review of 3D vessel lumen segmentation techniques: Models, features and extraction schemes. *Medical Image Analysis*, 13(6):819–845, 2009.

H. Levkowitz. Color icons: merging color and texture perception for integrated visualization of multiple parameters. In *Proc. of IEEE Visualization*, pages 164–170, 1991.

H. Levkowitz. *Color Theory and Modeling for Computer Graphics, Visualization, and Multimedia Applications*. Kluwer Academic Publishers, 1997.

H. Levkowitz and G.T. Herman. The design and evaluation of color scales for image data. *IEEE Computer Graphics and Applications*, 12(1):72–80, 1992.

M. Levoy. Display of Surfaces from Volume Data. *IEEE Computer Graphics and Applications*, 8(3):29–37, 1988.

M. Levoy. Efficient Ray Tracing of Volume Data. *ACM Transactions on Graphics*, 9(3):245–261, 1990.

Y. Levy, D. Degani, and A. Seginer. Graphical visualization of vortical flows by means of helicity. *AIAA Journal*, 10(2):1347–1352, 1990.

A. Lez, A. Zajic, K. Matkovic, A. Pobitzer, M. Mayer, and H. Hauser. Interactive Exploration and Analysis of Pathlines in Flow Data. In *Proc. of International Conference in Central Europe on Computer Graphics, Visualization and Computer Vision* (WSCG 2011), pages 17–24, 2011.

F. Li, J. A. Leighton, and V. K. Sharma. Capsule endoscopy: a comprehensive review. *Minerva Gastroenterol Dietol.*, 53(3):257–272, 2007.

Q. Li and J. Tian. 2d piecewise algebraic splines for implicit modeling. *ACM Transactions on Graphics*, 28(2), 2009.

S. Li and K. Mueller. Accelerated, High-Quality Refraction Computations for Volume Graphics. In *Proc. of Volume Graphics*, pages 73–81, 2005.

S. Li, J. Guo, Q. Wang, Q. Meng, Y.-P. Chui, J. Qin, and P. A. Heng. A Catheterization-Training Simulator Based on a Fast Multigrid Solver. *IEEE Computer Graphics and Applications*, 32(6):56–70, 2012.

X. Li, J. Tian, X. Wang E. Li, J. Dai, and L. Ai. Adaptive total linear least square method for quantification of mean transit time in brain perfusion MRI. *Magnetic Resonance Imaging*, 21(5):503–510, 2003.

Y. Li and K. Brodlie. Soft Object Modelling with Generalised ChainMail - Extending the Boundaries of Web-based Graphics. *Computer Graphics Forum*, 22(4):717–728, 2003.

M. C. Lin and J. F. Canny. A Fast Algorithm for Incremental Distance Calculation. In *Proc. of IEEE International Conference on Robotics and Automation (ICRA)*, volume 2, pages 1008–1014, 1991.

W. C. Lin and S. Y. Chen. A new surface interpolation technique for reconstructing 3D objects from serial cross-sections. *Computer Vision, Graphics, and Image Processing*, 48:124–143, 1989.

F. Lindemann and T. Ropinski. Advanced Light Material Interaction for Direct Volume Rendering. In *Proc. of Volume Graphics*, pages 101–108, 2010.

F. Lindemann and T. Ropinski. About the Influence of Illumination Models on Image Comprehension in Direct Volume Rendering. *IEEE Transactions on Visualization and Computer Graphics*, 17(12):1922–1931, 2011.

S. Lindholm, P. Ljung, C. Lundström, A. Persson, and A. Ynnerman. Spatial conditioning of transfer functions using local material distributions. *IEEE Transactions on Visualization and Computer Graphics*, 16(6):1301–1310, 2010.

D. Lindner, C. Renner, C. Trantakis, C. Chalopin, D. Fritzsch, R. Haase, and J. Meixensberger. Intraoperative contrast enhanced ultrasound angiography (tusa) - a new method in neurosurgery. *International Journal of Computer Assisted Radiology and Surgery (CARS)*, 3:72–73, 2008.

C. Lindstroem, P. Ljung, and A. Ynnerman. Extending and Simplifying Transfer Function Design in Medical Volume Rendering Using Local Histograms. In *Data Visualization (Proc. of Eurographics/IEEE Symposium on Visualization)*, pages 263–270, 2005.

P. Lindstrom and G. Turk. Fast and memory efficient polygonal simplification. In *Proc. of IEEE Visualization*, pages 279–286, 1998.

F. Link, M. Koenig, and H.-O. Peitgen. Multi-Resolution Volume Rendering with per Object Shading. In *Proc. of Vision, Modeling, and Visualization*, pages 185–191, 2006.

Y. Lipman, O. Sorkine, M. Alexa, D. Cohen-Or, D. Levin, C. Rössl, and H.-P. Seidel. Laplacian Framework for Interactive Mesh Editing. *International Journal of Shape Modeling*, 11(1):43–62, 2005.

Yanhong Liu. A lattice boltzmann model for blood flows. *Applied Mathematical Modelling*, 36(7):2890–2899, 2012.

Y. Livnat, H.-W. Shen, and C. R. Johnson. A Near Optimal Isosurface Extraction Algorithm Using the Span Space. *IEEE Transactions on Visualization and Computer Graphics*, 2:73–84, 1996.

P. Ljung, C. Lundström, and A. Ynnerman. Multiresolution Interblock Interpolation in Direct Volume Rendering. In *Data Visualization (Proc. of Eurographics/IEEE Symposium on Visualization)*, pages 259–266, 2006.

B. A. Lloyd, D. Szczerba, and G. Székely. A coupled finite element model of tumor growth and vascularization. In *Proc. of Medical Image Computing and Computer-Assisted Intervention (MICCAI)*, pages 874–881, 2007.

G. A. S. Lloyd. Diagnostic Imaging of the Nose and Paranasal Sinuses. *The Journal of Laryngology and Otology*, 103:453–460, 1989.

G. Lohmann. *Volumetric Image Analysis*. Wiley & Teubner, 1998.

T. Lokovic and E. Veach. Deep shadow maps. In *Proc. of ACM SIGGRAPH*, pages 385–392, 2000.

W. E. Lorensen. The exploration of cross-sectional data with a virtual endoscope. In *Interactive technology and the new paradigm for healthcare*, pages 221–230, 1995.

W. E. Lorensen and H. E. Cline. Marching Cubes: A High Resolution 3D Surface Construction Algorithm. In *Proc. of ACM SIGGRAPH*, pages 163–169, 1987.

W. E. Lorenson. Geometric Clipping Using Boolean Textures. In *Proc. of IEEE Visualization*, pages 268–274, 1993.

C. Lorenz and N. Krahnstöver. 3D Statistical Shape Models for Medical Image Segmentation. In *Second International Conference on 3-D Imaging and Modeling*, pages 414–423, 1999.

C. Lorenz, T. C. Carlssen, T. M. Buzug, C. Fassnacht, and J. Weese. Multi-scale line segmentation with automatic estimation of width, contrast, and tangential direction in 2D/3D medical images. In *Proc. of CVRMed/MRCAS*, volume 1205 of *Lecture Notes in Computer Science*, pages 233–242. Springer, 1997.

O. Louis, R. Luypaert, W. Kalender, and M. Osteaux. Reproducibility of CT bone densitometry: operator versus automated ROI definition. *European Journal of Radiology*, 8(2):82–84, 1988.

A. Lu, J. Taylor, M. Hartner, D. S. Ebert, and C. D. Hansen. Hardware Accelerated Interactive Stipple Drawing of Polygonal Objects. In *VMV*, pages 61–68, 2002.

A. Lu, C. J. Morris, J. Taylor, D. S. Ebert, C. D. Hansen, P. Rheingans, and M. Hartner. Illustrative Interactive Stipple Rendering. *IEEE Transactions on Visualization and Computer Graphics*, 9(2):127–138, 2003.

V. Luboz, X. Wu, K. Krissian, C.-F. Westin, R. Kikinis, S. Cotin, and S. Dawson. A Segmentation and Reconstruction Technique for 3D Vascular Structures. In *Proc. of Medical Image Computing and Computer-Assisted Intervention (MICCAI)*, pages 43–50, 2005.

V. Luboz, C. Hughes, D. Gould, N. W. John, and F. Bello. Real-time Seldinger technique simulation in complex vascular models. *International Journal of Computer Assisted Radiology and Surgery*, 4(6):589–596, 2009.

B. Lucas, G.D. Abram, N.S. Collins, D.A. Epstein, D.L. Gresh, and K.P. McAuliffe. An architecture for a scientific visualization system. In *Proc. of IEEE Visualization*, pages 107–114, 1992.

R. E. A. Lucht, M. V. Knopp, and G. Brix. Classification of signal-time curves from dynamic MR mammography by neural networks. *Magnetic Resonance Imaging*, 19(1):51–57, 2001.

R. E. A. Lucht, S. Delorme, and G. Brix. Neural network-based segmentation of dynamic MR mammographic images. *Magnetic Resonance Imaging*, 20(1):147–154, 2002.

D. Luebcke, M. Reddy, J. Cohen, A. Varshney, B. Watson, and R. Huebner. *Level of Detail for 3D Graphics*. Morgan Kaufmann Publishers, San Francisco, CA, 2004.

T. Luft, C. Colditz, and O. Deussen. Image enhancement by unsharp masking the depth buffer. *ACM Transactions on Graphics*, 25(3):1206–1213, 2006.

E. B. Lum and K.-L. Ma. Lighting transfer functions using gradient aligned sampling. In *Proc. of IEEE Visualization*, pages 289–296, 2004.

K. Lundin, B. Gudmundsson, and A. Ynnerman. General Proxy-Based Haptics for Volume Visualization. In *Proc. of World Haptics Conference (WHC)*, pages 557–560. IEEE, 2005.

C. Lundstrom, P. Ljung, and A. Ynnerman. Local Histograms for Design of Transfer Functions in Direct Volume Rendering. *IEEE Transactions on Visualization and Computer Graphics*, 12(6):1570–1579, November 2006.

C. Lundström, P. Ljung, A. Persson, and A. Ynnerman. Uncertainty Visualization in Medical Volume Rendering Using Probabilistic Animation. *IEEE Transactions on Visualization and Computer Graphics*, 13(6):1648–1655, 2007.

C. Lundström, T. Rydell, C. Forsell, A. Persson, and A. Ynnerman. Multi-touch table system for medical visualization: Application to orthopedic surgery planning. *IEEE Transactions on Visualization and Computer Graphics*, 17(12):1775–1784, 2011.

X. Luó, T. Kitasaka, and K. Mori. Bronchoscopy Navigation beyond Electromagnetic Tracking Systems: A Novel Bronchoscope Tracking Prototype. In *Proc. of Medical Image Computing and Computer-Assisted Intervention (MICCAI)*, pages 194–202, 2011.

C. Lürig, P. Hastreiter, C. Nimsky, and T. Ertl. Analysis and Visualization of the Brain Shift Phenomenon in Neurosurgery. In *Data Visualization (Proc. of Eurographics/IEEE Symposium on Visualization)*, pages 285–289, 1999.

J. T. Lurito, M. J. Lowe, C. Sartorius, and V. P. Matthews. Comparison of fMRI and Intraoperative Direct Cortical Stimulation in Localization of Receptive Language Areas. *Journal of Computer Assisted Tomography*, 24(1):99–105, 2000.

M. Lysaker, A. Lundervold, and X.C. Tai. Noise Removal Using Fourth-Order Partial Differential Equation with Applications to Medical Magnetic Resonance Images in Space and Time. *IEEE Transactions on Image Processing*, 12(12): 1579–1590, 2003.

M. DeNicola, L. Salvolini, and U. Salvolini. Virtual endoscopy of nasal cavity and paranasal sinuses. *European Journal of Radiology*, 24(3):175–180, 1997.

H. Maass, B. Chantier, H. K. Çakmak, and U. Kühnapfel. How to Add Force Feedback to a Surgery Simulator. In *International Symposium on Surgery Simulation and Soft Tissue Modeling*, volume 2673 of *Lecture Notes in Computer Science*, pages 165–174. Springer, 2003.

R. Maciejewski, I. Woo, W. Chen, and D. S. Ebert. Structuring Feature Space: A Non-Parametric Method for Volumetric Transfer Function Generation. *IEEE Transactions on Visualization and Computer Graphics*, 15(6):1473–1480, 2009.

R. Maciejewski, Y. Jang, I. Woo, H. Jänicke, K. P. Gaither, and D. S. Ebert. Abstracting Attribute Space for Transfer Function Exploration and Design. *IEEE Transactions on Visualization and Computer Graphics*, 19(1):94–107, 2013.

R. J. Maciunas. Computer-assisted neurosurgery. *Clinical neurosurgery*, 53:267, 2006.

A. Macovski. Noise in MRI. *Magnetic Resonance Medicine*, 36(3):494–497, 1996.

M. Maddah, K. H. Zou, W. M. Wells, R. Kikinis, and S. K. Warfield. Automatic Optimization of Segmentation Algorithms Through Simultaneous Truth and Performance Level Estimation (staple). In *Proc. of Medical Image Computing and Computer-Assisted Intervention (MICCAI)*, volume 3216 of *Lecture Notes in Computer Science*, pages 274–282. Springer, 2004.

M. Maddah, W. E. L. Crimson, and S. K. Warfield. Statistical modeling and EM clustering of white matter fiber tracts. In *Proc. of International Symposium on Biomedical Imaging (ISBI)*, pages 53–56, 2006.

M. Maddah, W. E. L. Grimson, S. K. Warfield, and W. M. Wells. A unified framework for clustering and quantitative analysis of white matter fiber tracts. *Medical Image Analysis*, 12(2):191–202, 2008.

F. Maes, A. Collignon, D. Vandermeulen, G. Marechal, and P. Suetens. Multimodality Image Registration by Maximization of Mutual Information. *IEEE Transactions on Medical Imaging*, 16(2):187–198, 1997a.

F. Maes, D. Vandermeulen, G. Marchal, and P. Suetens. Fast multimodality image registration using multiresolution gradient-based maximization of mutual information. In *Proc. of image registration workshop*, pages 191–200, Greenbelt, Maryland, USA, 1997b.

A. Mahnken and J. Ricke, editors. *CT- and MR-Guided Interventions*. Springer, 2008.

L. Maier-Hein, F. Pianka, S. A. Müller, U. Rietdorf, A. Seitel, A. M. Franz, I. Wolf, B. M. Schmied, and H.-P. Meinzer. Respiratory liver motion simulator for validating image-guided systems ex-vivo. *International Journal of Computer Assisted Radiology and Surgery*, 2(5):287–292, 2008a.

L. Maier-Hein, A. Tekbas, A. M. Franz, R. Teztlaff, S. A. Müller, F. Pianka, I. Wolf, H. U. Kauczor, B. M. Schmied, and H.-P. Meinzer. Respiratory motion compensation for CT-guided interventions in the liver. *Comput. Aided Surgery*, 13(3):125–138, 2008b.

L. Maier-Hein, A. Tekbas, A: Seitel, F. Pianka, S. Mueller, and S. Satzl et al. In vivo accuracy assessment of a needle-based navigation system for CT-guided radiofrequency ablation of the liver. *Medical Physics*, 35(12):5385–5396, 2008c.

J. Maintz and M. Viergever. A survey of medical image registration. *Medical Image Analysis*, 2(1):1–36, 1998.

M. M. Malik, T. Möller, and E. Gröller. Feature peeling. In *Proc. of Graphics Interface*, pages 273–280, 2007.

S. Malik, C. McDonald, and G. Roth. Hand Tracking for Interactive Pattern-based Augmented Reality. In *Proc. of IEEE and ACM International Symposium on Mixed and Augmented Reality*, 2002.

R. Malladi, J. A. Sethian, and B. C. Vemuri. Shape Modeling with Front Propagation: A Level Set Approach. *IEEE Transactions on Pattern Analysis and Machine Intelligence*, 17(2):158–175, 1995.

F. Malmberg, E. Vidholm, and I. Nyström. A 3D live-wire segmentation method for volume images using haptic interaction. In *Proc. of Discrete Geometry for Computer Imager*, pages 663–673, 2006.

P. Mansfield. Multi-planar image formation using NMR spin echos. *J Physics C: Solid State*, 10:55–58, 1977.

D. Manzey, S. Roettger, J. Elin Bahner-Heyne, D. Schulze-Kissing, A. Dietz, J. Meixensberger, and G. Strauss. Image-guided navigation: the surgeon's perspective on performance consequences and human factors issues. *The international journal of medical robotics + computer assisted surgery*, 5(3):297–308, 2009.

D. Manzey, M. Luz, S. Mueller, A. Dietz, J. Meixensberger, and G Strauss. Automation in Surgery: The Impact of Navigated-Control Assistance on Performance, Workload, Situation Awareness, and Acquisition of Surgical Skills. *Human Factors*, 53:584–599, 2011.

G. E. Marai, D. H. Laidlaw, S. Andrews, C. M. Grimm, and J. J. Crisco. Estimating joint contact areas and ligament lengths from bone kinematics and surfaces. *IEEE Transactions on Biomedical Engineering*, 51:790–799, 2004.

M. Marchal, J. Allard, C. Duriez, and S. Cotin. Towards a Framework for Assessing Deformable Models in Medical Simulation. In *Proc. of International Symposium on Biomedical Simulation (ISBMS)*, pages 176–184, 2008.

C. Marchetti, A. Bianchi, L. Muyldermans, M. Di Martino, L. Lancellotti, and A. Sarti. Validation of new soft tissue software in orthognathic surgery planning. *International Journal of Oral and Maxillofacial Surgery*, 40(1):26–32, 2011.

J. Marino, W. Zeng, X. Gu, and A. Kaufman. Context preserving maps of tubular structures. *IEEE Transactions on Visualization and Computer Graphics*, 17(12):1997–2004, 2011.

M. Markert, A. Koschany, and T. Lüth. Tracking of the liver for navigation in open surgery. *International Journal of Computer Assisted Radiology and Surgery*, 5(3):229–235, 2010.

M. Markl, J. Geiger, R. Arnold, A. Stroh, D. Damjanovic, D. Föll, and F. Beyersdorf. Comprehensive 4-Dimensional Magnetic Resonance Flow Analysis After Successful Heart Transplantation Resolves Controversial Intraoperative Findings and Reveals Complex Hemodynamic Alterations. *Circulation*, 123:e381–e383, 2011.

L. Markosian, M. A. Kowalski, D. Goldstein, S. J. Trychin, J. F. Hughes, and L. D. Bourdev. Real-time nonphotorealistic rendering. In *Proc. of ACM SIGGRAPH*, pages 415–420, 1997.

J. Marks, B. Andalman, P.A. Beardsley, W. Freeman, S. Gibson, J. Hodgins, T. Kang, B. Mirtich, H. Pfister, W. Ruml, K. Ryall, J. Seims, and S. Shieber. Design galleries: a general approach to setting parameters for computer graphics and animation. In *Proc. of ACM SIGGRAPH*, pages 389–400. ACM Press, 1997.

D. Marr. Early processing of visual information. *Philosophical Transactions of the Royal Society of London*, 275:483–524, 1976.

D. Martín, G. Arroyo, M. V. Luzón, and T. Isenberg. Scale-dependent and example-based grayscale stippling. *Computers & Graphics*, 35(1):160–174, 2011.

N. A. Martin, R. Khanna, C. Doberstein, and Bentson J. Therapeutic embolization of arteriovenous malformations: the case for and against. *Clin. Neurosurgery*, 46:295–318, 2000.

Y. Masutani, Y. Yamauchi, M. Suzuki, Y. Ohta, T. Dohi, M. Tsuzuki, and D. Hashimoto. Development of interactive vessel modelling system for hepatic vasculature from MR images. *Medical and Biological Engineering and Computing*, 33(1):97–101, 1995.

Y. Masutani, K. Masamune, and T. Dohi. Region-Growing-Based Feature Extraction Algorithm for Tree-Like Objects. In *Proc. of Visualization in Biomedical Computing*, volume 1131 of *LNCS*, pages 161–171. Springer, 1996.

W. Maurel, Y. Wu, N. Thalmann, and D. Thalmann. *Biomechanical Models for Soft Tissue Simulation*. Esprit Series. Springer, 1998.

C. R. Maurer, J. Michael Fitzpatrick, M. Y. Wang, R. L. Galloway Jr., R. J. Maciunas, and G. S. Allen. Registration of Head Volume Images Using Implantable Fiducial Markers. *IEEE Transactions on Medical Imaging*, 16(4):447–462, 1997.

N. Max. Optical Models for Direct Volume Rendering. *IEEE Transactions on Visualization and Computer Graphics*, 1(2):99–108, 1995.

N. Max and M. Chen. Local and Global Illumination in the Volume Rendering Integral. In *Scientific Visualization: Advanced Concepts*, pages 259–274, 2010.

D. Mayhew. *The Usability Engineering Lifecycle: A Practitioner's Handbook for User Interface Design*. Morgan Kaufman, 1999.

B. H. McCormick, T. A. DeFanti, and M. D. Brown. Visualization in Scientific Computing. *Computer Graphics*, 21(6), 1987.

E. G. McFarland, B. Levin, D. A. Lieberman, P. J. Pickhardt, C. Daniel Johnson, S. N. Glick, D. Brooks, and R. A. Smith. Revised Colorectal Screening Guidelines: Joint Effort of the American Cancer Society, U.S. Multisociety Task Force on Colorectal Cancer, and American College of Radiology. *Radiology*, 248:717–720, 2008.

T. McGraw and M. Nadar. Stochastic DT-MRI Connectivity Mapping on the GPU. *IEEE Transactions on Visualization and Computer Graphics*, 13(6):1504–1511, 2007.

K. McGuinness and N. E. O'Connor. A comparative evaluation of interactive segmentation algorithms. *Pattern Recognition*, 43:434–444, 2010.

T. McInerney and D. Terzopoulos. Deformable Models in Medical Image Analysis: A Survey. *Medical Image Analysis*, 1(2):91–108, 1996.

C. McIntosh and G. Hamarneh. Vessel Crawlers: 3D Physically-based Deformable Organisms for Vasculature Segmentation and Analysis. In *Proc. of the IEEE Computer Society Conference on Computer Vision and Pattern Recognition*, pages 1084–1091, 2006.

T. McLoughlin, R. S. Laramee, R. Peikert, F. H. Post, and M. Chen. Over Two Decades of Integration-Based, Geometric Flow Visualization. *Computer Graphics Forum*, 29(6):1807–1829, 2010.

T. McLoughlin, M. W. Jones, R. S. Laramee, R. Malki, I. Masters, and C. D. Hansen. Similarity Measures for Enhancing Interactive Streamline Seeding. *IEEE Transactions on Visualization and Computer Graphics*, 19(8):1342–1353, 2013.

D. L. McShan, A. Silverman, D. M. Lanza, L. E. Reinstein, and A. S. Glicksman. A computerized three-dimensional treatment planning system utilizing interactive colour graphics. *The British Journal of Radiology*, 52(618):478–481, 1979.

E. R. McVeigh and M. J. Bronskill. Noise and filtration in MR imaging. *Medical Physics*, 12(5):586–591, 1985.

A. Mehrabi, C. Glückstein, A. Benner, B. Hashemi, C. Herfarth, and F. Kalinowski. A new way for surgical education-development and evaluation of a computer-based training module. *Computers in Biology and Medicine*, 30:97–109, 2000.

H. Meire, D. Cosgrove, K. Dewbury, and P. Wilde, editors. *Clinical Ultrasound: A Comprehensive Text*, volume 1. Churchill Livingstone, Edinburgh, 2 edition, 1993.

M. Meißner, J. Huang, D. Bartz, K. Mueller, and R. Crawfis. A Practical Evaluation of Four Popular Volume Rendering Algorithms. In *Proc. of IEEE/ACM Symposium on Volume Visualization and Graphics*, pages 81–90, 2000.

C. Men, H. E. Romeijn, Z. C. Taskin, and J. F. Dempsey. An exact approach to direct aperture optimization in imrt treatment planning. *Physics in Medicine and Biology*, 52:7333–7352, 2007.

C. Menk, E. Jundt, and R. Koch. Visualisation Techniques for Using Spatial Augmented Reality in the Design Process of a Car. *Computer Graphics Forum*, 30(8):2354–2366, 2011.

J. Mensmann, T. Ropinski, and K. Hinrichs. Interactive Cutting Operations for Generating Anatomical Illustrations from Volumetric Data Sets. *Journal of WSCG*, 16(1–3):89–96, 2008.

D. Merhof, F. Enders, F. Vega, P. Hastreiter, C. Nimsky, and M. Stamminger. Integrated visualization of diffusion tensor fiber tracts and anatomical data. In *Proc. of Simulation and Visualization*, pages 153–164, 2005a.

D. Merhof, M. Sonntag, F. Enders, P. Hastreiter, R. Fahlbusch, C. Nimsky, and G. Greiner. Visualization of diffusion tensor data using evenly spaced streamlines. In *Proc. of Vision, Modelling and Visualization (VMV)*, pages 79–86. Bibliothek der Universität Konstanz, 2005b.

D. Merhof, M. Sonntag, F. Enders, C. Nimsky, P. Hastreiter, and G. Greiner. Hybrid Visualization for White Matter Tracts using Triangle Strips and Point Sprites. *IEEE Transactions on Visualization and Computer Graphics*, 12(5), 2006a.

D. Merhof, M. Sonntag, F. Enders, C. Nimsky, P. Hastreiter, and G. Greiner. Hybrid Visualization for White Matter Tracts using Triangle Strips and Point Sprites. *IEEE Transactions on Visualization and Computer Graphics*, 12(5):1181–1188, 2006b.

S. Mersmann, M. Müller, A. Seitel, F. Arnegger, R. Tetzlaff, M. Baumhauer, B. M. Schmied, H.-P. Meinzer, and L. Maier-Hein. Time-of-Flight Kameratechnik für Augmented Reality in der computergestützten Chirurgie. In *Proc. of Bildverarbeitung für die Medizin*, pages 219–223, 2011.

O. E. Meruvia-Pastor and T. Strothotte. Frame-Coherent Stippling. In *Proc. of Eurographics Conference - short paper*, 2002.

C. Mess and T. Ropinski. Efficient Acquisition and Clustering of Local Histograms for Representing Voxel Neighborhoods. In *Proc. of Volume Graphics*, pages 117–124, 2010.

C. Metz, M. Schaap, A. van der Giessen, T. van Walsum, and W. Niessen. Semi-automatic coronary artery centerline extraction in computed tomography angiography data. In *Proc. of IEEE Symposium on Biomedical Imaging: From Nano to Macro*, pages 856–859, 2007.

M. Meyer, M. Desbrun, P. Schröder, and A. Barr. Discrete differential-geometry operators for triangulated 2-manifolds. In *International Workshop on Visualization and Mathematics*, pages 35–57, 2002.

M. Meyer, M. Desbrun, P. Schroeder, and A. H. Barr. *Visualization and Mathematics*, chapter Discrete Differential-Geometry Operators for Triangulated 2-Manifolds. Springer, 2003.

S. Meyer, M. Müller-Schimpfle, H. Jürgens, and H.O. Peitgen. MT-DYNA: Computer Assistance for the Evaluation of Dynamic MR and CT Data in a Clinical Environment. In *Proc. of Computer Assisted Radiology and Surgery*, pages 331–334. Elsevier, 1999.

A. Meyer-Bäse, O. Lange, A. Wismüller, and M. K. Hurdal. Analysis of Dynamic Susceptibility Contrast MRI Time Series Based on Unsupervised Clustering Methods. *IEEE Transactions on Information Technology in Biomedicine*, 11(5):563–573, 2007.

J. Meyer-Spradow, T. Ropinski, J. Mensmann, and K. Hinrichs. Voreen: A Rapid-Prototyping Environment for Ray-Casting-Based Volume Visualizations. *IEEE Computer Graphics and Applications*, 29(6):6–13, 2009.

D. Meyers, S. Skinner, and K. Sloan. Surfaces from contours. *ACM Transactions on Graphics*, 11(3):228–258, 1992.

H.J. Michaely, K. Nael, S.O. Schoenberg, J.P. Finn, N. Oesingmann, K.P. Lodemann, M.F. Reiser, and S.G. Ruehm. Renal perfusion: comparison of saturation-recovery turboflash measurements at 1.5t with saturation-recovery turboflash and time-resolved echo-shared angiographic technique (treat) at 3.0t. *Journal of Magnetic Resonance Imaging*, 24(6):1413–1419, 2006.

M. I. Miller. Computational anatomy: Shape, growth, and atrophy comparison via diffeomorphisms. *NeuroImage*, 23:19–33, 2004.

G. S. Mintz, S. E. Nissen, W. D. Anderson, S. R. Bailey, R. Erbel, and P. J. Fitzgerald et al. American College of Cardiology Clinical Expert Consensus Document on Standards for Acquisition, Measurement and Reporting of Intravascular Ultrasound Studies (IVUS). A report of the American College of Cardiology Task Force on Clinical Expert Consensus Documents. *Journal of American College of Cardiology*, 37:1478–1492, 2001.

S. Misra, K. T. Ramesh, and A. M. Okamura. Modeling of Tool-Tissue Interactions for Computer-Based Surgical Simulation: A Literature Review. *Preseence*, 17(5):463–491, 2008.

G. Mistelbauer, A. Morar, A. Varchola, R. Schernthaner, I. Baclija, A. Köchl, A. Kanitsar, S. Bruckner, and E. Gröller. Vessel Visualization using Curvicircular Feature Aggregation. *Computer Graphics Forum*, 33(3):231–240, 2013. Proc. of Eurovis.

S. C. Mitchell, J. G. Bosch, J. H. C. Reiber, B. P. F. Lelieveldt, R. J. van der Geest, and M. Sonka. 3-D active appearance models: segmentation of cardiac MR and ultrasound images. *IEEE Transactions on Medical Imaging*, 21(9):1167–1178, 2002.

M. Mlejnek, P. Ermes, A. Vilanova, R. van der Rijt, H. van den Bosch, E. Gröller, and F. Gerritsen. Profile flags: a novel metaphor for probing of t2 maps. In *Proc. of IEEE Visualization*, pages 599–606, 2005.

M. Mlejnek, P. Ermes, A. Vilanova, R. van der Rijt, H. van den Bosch, E. Gröller, and F. Gerritsen. Application-oriented extensions of profile flags. In *Data Visualization (Proc. of Eurographics/IEEE Symposium on Visualization)*, pages 339–346, 2006.

B. Moberts, A. Vilanova, and J. J. van Wijk. Evaluation of fiber clustering methods for diffusion tensor imaging. In *Proc. of IEEE Visualization*, pages 65–72, 2005.

J. Modersitzki. *Numerical Methods for Image Registration*. Oxford University Press, 2004.

D. S. Modha and R. Singh. Network architecture of the long-distance pathways in the macaque brain. *Proc. of the National Academy of Sciences*, 107(30):13485–13490, July 2010.

K. Mogalle, C. Tietjen, G. Soza, and B. Preim. Constrained Labeling of 2D Slice Data for Reading Images in Radiology. In *Proc. of Eurographics Workshop on Visual Computing in Biology and Medicine (VCBM)*, pages 131–138, 2012.

V. Moharir, M. P. Fried, D. M. Vernick, I. P. Janecka, J. Zahajsky, L. Hsu, W. E. Lorensen, M. Anderson, W. M. Wells, P. Morrison, and R. Kikinis. Computer-Assisted Three-Dimensional Reconstruction of Head and Neck Tumors. *Laryngoscope*, 108(11):1592–1598, 1998.

W. Mollemans, F. Schutyser, N. Nadjmi, F. Maes, and P. Suetens. Predicting soft tissue deformations for a maxillofacial surgery planning system: From computational strategies to a complete clinical validation. *Medical Image Analysis*, 11(3):282–301, 2007.

T. Möller, R. Machiraju, K. Mueller, and R. Yagel. A Comparison of Normal Estimation Schemes. In *Proc. of IEEE Visualization*, pages 19–26, 1997.

J. H. Moltz, L. Bornemann, J.-M. Kuhnigk, V. Dicken, E. Peitgen, S. Meier, H. Bolte, M. Fabel, H.-C. Bauknecht, M. Hittinger, A. Kiessling, M. Pusken, and H.-O. Peitgen. Advanced segmentation techniques for lung nodules, liver metastases, and enlarged lymph nodes in ct scans. *IEEE Journal of Selected Topics in Signal Processing*, 3(1):122–134, 2009a.

J. H. Moltz, M. Schwier, and H.-O. Peitgen. A General Framework for Automatic Detection of Matching Lesions in Follow-Up CT. In *Proc. of IEEE International Symposium on Biomedical Imaging (ISBI)*, pages 843–846, 2009b.

A. Momose and J. Fukuda. Phase-contrast radiographs of nonstained rat cerebellar specimen. *Medical Physics*, 22(4):375–379, 1995.

A. Momose, T. Takeda, and Y. Itai. Blood vessels: Depiction at phase-contrast x-ray imaging without contrast agents in the mouse and rat—feasibility study. *Radiology*, 263(2):593–596, 2000.

J. Mönch, K. Mühler, C. Hansen, K.-J. Oldhafer, G. Stavrou, C. Hillert, C. Logge, and B. Preim. The LiverSurgeryTrainer: training of computer-based planning in liver resection surgery. *International Journal of Computer Assisted Radiology and Surgery*, Januar: Epub ahead of print, 2013.

T. Mönch, S. Adler, P. Hahn, I. Rössling, and B. Preim. Distance-aware smoothing of surface meshes for surgical planning. In *Proc. of International Workshop on Digital Engineering (IWDE)*, pages 45–51, 2010a.

T. Mönch, S. Adler, and B. Preim. Staircase-Aware Smoothing of Medical Surface Meshes. In *Proc. of Eurographics Workshop on Visual Computing in Biology and Medicine (VCBM)*, pages 83–90, 2010b.

T. Mönch, R. Gasteiger, G. Janiga, H. Theisel, and B. Preim. Context-aware mesh smoothing for biomedical applications. *Computers & Graphics*, 35(4):755–767, 2011a.

T. Mönch, M. Neugebauer, and B. Preim. Optimization of Vascular Surface Models for Computational Fluid Dynamics and Rapid Prototyping. In *Proc. of International Workshop on Digital Engineering (IWDE)*, pages 16–23, 2011b.

T. Mönch, C. Kubisch, K. Lawonn, R. Westermann, and B. Preim. Visually Guided Mesh Smoothing for Medical Applications. In *Proc. of Eurographics Workshop on Visual Computing in Biology and Medicine (VCBM)*, pages 91–98, 2012.

T. Mondor and H. Finley. The perceived urgency of auditory warning alarms used in the hospital operating room is inappropriate. *Canadian Journal of Anesthesia*, 50(3):209–214, 2003.

E. Moniz. *Die zerebrale Arteriographie und Phlebographie*. Springer, Berlin, 1940.

J. Montagnat and H. Delingette. A Hybrid Framework for Surface Registration and Deformable Models. In *Proc. of Computer Vision and Pattern Recognition (CVPR)*, pages 1041–1046, 1997.

K. Montgomery, C. Bruyns, J. Brown, S. Sorkin, F. Mazzella, G. Thonier, A. Tellier, B. Lerman, and A. Menon. Spring: A General Framework for Collaborative, Real-time Surgical Simulation. In *Medicine Meets Virtual Reality (MMVR)*, pages 23–26, 2002.

H. G. Morales, I. Larrabide, A. J. Geers, L. San Roman, J. Blasco, J. M. Macho, and A. F. Frangi. A virtual coiling technique for image-based aneurysm models by dynamic path planning. *IEEE Transactions Medical Imaging*, 32(1):119–129, 2013.

H. G. Morales, I. Larrabide, M. Kim, M.-C. Villa-Uriol, J. M. Macho, J. Blasco, L. San Roman, and A. F. Frangi. Virtual Coiling of Intracranial Aneurysms Based on Dynamic Path Planning. In *Proc. of Medical Image Computing and Computer-Assisted Intervention (MICCAI)*, Vol. (1), pages 355–362, 2011.

K. Mori, D. Deguchi, K. Akiyama, T. Kitasaka, C. R. Maurer, Y. Suenaga, H. Takabatake, M. Mori, and H. Natori. Hybrid Bronchoscope Tracking Using a Magnetic Tracking Sensor and Image Registration. In *Proc. of Medical Image Computing and Computer-Assisted Intervention (MICCAI)*, Vol. (2), pages 543–550, 2005.

K. Mori, Z. Jiang, Y. Nimura, T. Kitasaka, K. Misawa, and M. Fujiwara. Anatomical name annotation on blood vessels rendered by volume rendering and its application to virtual laparoscopy. In *Proc. of MICCAI 2011 Workshop: Augmented Environments for Computer Assisted Interventions*, pages 277–284, 2011.

S. Mori and P. B. Barker. Diffusion magnetic resonance imaging: its principle and applications. *The Anatomical Record*, 257(3):102–109, 1999.

C. Morosi, G. Ballardini, and P. Pisani. Diagnostic Accuracy of the Double-Contrast Enema for Colonic Polyps in Patients with or without Diverticular Disease. *Gastrointestinal Radiology*, 16:346–347, 1991.

D. Morris, C. Sewell, F. Barbagli, K. Salisbury, N.H. Blevins, and S. Girod. Visuohaptic Simulation of Bone Surgery for Training and Evaluation. *IEEE Computer Graphics and Applications*, 26(6):48–57, 2006.

D. F. Morrison. *Multivariate Statistical Methods*. Thomson Brooks/Cole, 4th edition, 2005.

E. N. Mortensen, B. S. Morse, W. A. Barrett, and J. K. Upuda. Adaptive Boundary Detection Using Live-wire Two-dimensional Dynamic Programming. *IEEE Computers in Cardiology*, pages 635–638, 1992.

J. Mosegaard, P. Herborg, and T.S. Sorensen. A GPU accelerated spring mass system for surgical simulation. *Studies in health technology and informatics*, 111:342–348, 2005.

M. Moser and D. Weiskopf. Interactive direct volume rendering on mobile devices. In *Proc. of Vision, Modeling, and Visualization*, pages 217–226, 2008.

K. Mouridsen, S. Christensen, L. Gyldensted, and L. Ostergaard. Automatic selection of arterial input function using cluster analysis. *Magnetic Resonance in Medicine*, 55(3):524–531, 2006.

L. Mroz, A. König, and E. Gröller. Real-Time Maximum Intensity Projection. In *Proc. of Data Visualization*, pages 135–144. Springer, 1999.

L. Mroz, H. Hauser, and E. Gröller. Interactive high-quality maximum intensity projection. In *Computer Graphics Forum*, pages 341–350, 2000.

K. Mueller, T. Möller, and R. Crawfis. Splatting Without the Blur. In *Proc. of IEEE Visualization*, pages 363–371, 1999.

M. Mueller, S. Schirm, and M. Teschner. Interactive Blood Simulation for Virtual Surgery Based on Smoothed Particle Hydrodynamics. *Technology and Health Care*, 12:25–31, 2004.

K. Mühler and B. Preim. Automatic textual annotation for surgical planning. In *Proc. of Vision, Modeling, and Visualization*, pages 277–284, 2009a.

K. Mühler and B. Preim. Automatische Annotation medizinischer 2D- und 3D-Visualisierungen. In *Proc. of Bildverarbeitung für die Medizin (BVM)*, pages 11–15. Springer, 2009b.

K. Mühler and B. Preim. Reusable Visualizations and Animations for Surgery Planning. In *Computer Graphics Forum*, pages 1103–1112, 2010.

K. Mühler, R. Bade, and B. Preim. Adaptive Script-Based Design of Animations for Medical Education and Therapy Planning. In *Proc. of Medical Image Computing and Computer-Assisted Intervention (MICCAI)*. Springer, 2006.

K. Mühler, M. Neugebauer, C. Tietjen, and B. Preim. Viewpoint selection for intervention planning. In *Proc. of EuroVis*, pages 267–274, 2007.

K. Mühler, C. Tietjen, F. Ritter, and B. Preim. The medical exploration toolkit: An efficient support for visual computing in surgical planning and training. *IEEE Transactions on Visualization and Computer Graphics*, 16(1):133–146, 2010.

P. Muigg, J. Kehrer, S. Oeltze, H. Piringer, H. Doleisch, B. Preim, and H. Hauser. A four-level focus+context approach to interactive visual analysis of temporal features in large scientific data. *Computer Graphics Forum*, 27(3):775–782, 2008.

T. H. Mulkens, P. Bellinck, M. Baeyaert, D. Ghysen, X. Van Dijck, E. Mussen, C. Venstermans, and J. L. Termote. Use of an automatic exposure control mechanism for dose optimization in multi-detector row CT examinations: clinical evaluation. *Radiology*, 237(1):213–223, 2005.

D. Müller and A. Mäder. Robust semi-automated path extraction for visualising stenosis of the coronary arteries. *Computerized Medical Imaging and Graphics*, 32(6):463–475, 2008.

M. Müller, S. Schirm, M. Teschner, B. Heidelberger, and M. H. Gross. Interaction of fluids with deformable solids. *Journal of Visualization and Computer Animation*, 15(3-4):159–171, 2004.

D. Mumford and J. Shah. Optimal approximations by piecewise smooth functions and variational problems. *Communication on Pure and Applied Mathematics*, 42(5):577–685, 1989.

A. Müns, J. Meixensberger, S. Arnold, A. Schmitgen, F. Arlt, C. Chalopin, and D. Lindner. Integration of a 3D ultrasound probe into neuronavigation. *Acta Neurochir.*, 153(7):1529–1533, 2011.

J. Murre and D. Sturdy. The connectivity of the brain: multi-level quantitative analysis. *Biological Cybernetics*, 73(6):529–545, 1995.

A. Mussetto, O. Triossi, S. Gasperoni, and T. Casetti. Colon capsule endoscopy may represent an effective tool for colorectal cancer screening: a single-centre series. *Digestive and Liver Disease*, 44(4):357–358, 2012.

D. Mutter, M. Vix, B. Dallemagne, S. Perretta, J. Leroy, and J. Marescaux. WeBSurg: An innovative educational Web site in minimally invasive surgery–principles and results. *Surgical Innovation*, 18(1):8–14, 2011.

A. Nabavi, P. Black, D. Gering, C. Westin, V. Mehta, R. Pergolizzi Jr., M. Ferrant, S. Warfield, N. Hata, R. Schwartz, W. Wells, R. Kikinis, and F. Jolesz. Serial Intraoperative Magnetic Resonance Imaging of Brain Shift. *Neurosurgery*, 48(4):787–797, 2001.

M. Näf, G. Székely, R. Kikinis, M. Shenton, and O. Kübler. 3D Voronoi Skeletons and their Usage for the Characterization and Recognition of 3D Organ Shape. *Computer Vision and Image Understanding*, 66:147–161, 1997.

Z. Nagy and R. Klein. High-Quality Silhouette Illustration for Texture-Based Volume Rendering. In *Proc. of Winter School in Computer Graphics (WSCG)*, pages 301–308, 2004.

S. Napel, G.D. Rubin, and R. B. Jeffrey. STS-MIP: A New Reconstruction Technique for CT of the Chest. *Journal of Computer Assisted Tomography*, 17(5):832–838, 1993.

J. Näppi and H. Yoshida. Adaptive correction of the pseudo-enhancement of ct attenuation for fecal-tagging CT colonography. *Medical Image Analysis*, 12(4):413–426, 2008.

T. W. Nattkemper and A. Wismuller. Tumor feature visualization with unsupervised learning. *Medical Image Analysis*, 9(4):344–351, 2005.

N. Navab, A. Bani-Hashemi, and M. Mitschke. Merging Visible and Invisible: Two Camera-augmented Mobile C-arm (CAMC) Applications. In *Proc. of IEEE and ACM International Workshop on Augmented Reality*, pages 134–141, 1999.

N. Navab, M. Feuerstein, and C. Bichlmeier. Laparoscopic Virtual Mirror: New Interaction Paradigms for Monitor Based Augmented Reality. In *Proc. of IEEE Virtual Reality*, pages 43–50, 2007a.

N. Navab, J. Traub, T. Sielhorst, M. Feuerstein, and C. Bichlmeier. Action- and Workflow-Driven Augmented Reality for Computer-Aided Medical Procedures. *IEEE Computer Graphics and Applications*, 27(5):10–14, 2007b.

N. Navab, T. Blum, L. Wang, A. Okur, and T. Wendler. First Deployments of Augmented Reality in Operating Rooms. *IEEE Computer*, 45(7):48–55, 2012.

N. Navkar, N. Tsekos, J. Stafford, J. Weinberg, and Z. Deng. Visualization and Planning of Neurosurgical Interventions with Straight Access. In *Proc. of Information Processing in Computer-Assisted Interventions (IPCAI)*, volume 6135 of LNCS, pages 1–11, 2010.

M. Negahdar, A. Ahmadian, N. Navab, and K. Firouznia. Path Planning for Virtual Bronchoscopy. In *Proc. of IEEE Engineering in Medicine & Biology*, pages 156–159, 2006.

T. R. Nelson and T. T. Elvins. Visualization of 3D ultrasound data. *IEEE Computer Graphics and Applications*, 13(6):50–57, 1993.

E. Neri, D. Caramella, M. Panconi, S. Berrettini, S. Sellari Franceschini, F. Forli, and C. Bartolozzi. Virtual endoscopy of the middle ear. *European Radiology*, 11(1):41–49, 2001.

A. Neubauer and S. Wolfsberger. Virtual Endoscopy in Neurosurgery: A Review. *Neurosurgery*, 72(1):A97–A106, 2013.

A. Neubauer, M.-T. Forster, R. Wegenkittl, L. Mroz, and K. Bühler. Efficient Display of Background Objects for Virtual Endoscopy using Flexible First-Hit Ray Casting. In *VisSym*, pages 301–310, 2004a.

A. Neubauer, S. Wolfsberger, M. Forster, L. Mroz, R. Wegenkittl, and K. Bühler. STEPS - An Application for Simulation of Transsphenoidal Endonasal Pituitary Surgery. In *Proc. of IEEE Visualization*, pages 513–520, 2004b.

A. Neubauer, S. Wolfsberger, M.-T. Forster, L. Mroz, R. Wegenkittl, and K. Bühler. Advanced Virtual Endoscopic Pituitary Surgery. *IEEE Transactions on Visualization and Computer Graphics*, 11(5):497–507, 2005.

M. Neugebauer, G. Janiga, S. Zachow, M. Skalej, and B. Preim. Generierung qualitativ hochwertiger Modelle für die Simulation von Bluttfluss in zerebralen Aneurysmen. In *Proc. of Simulation and Visualization*, pages 221–236, 2008.

M. Neugebauer, R. Gasteiger, O. Beuing, V. Diehl, M. Skalej, and B. Preim. Map Displays for the Analysis of Scalar Data on Cerebral Aneurysm Surfaces. *Computer Graphics Forum*, 28(3):895–902, 2009a.

M. Neugebauer, R. Gasteiger, V. Diehl, O. Beuing, and B. Preim. Automatic generation of context visualizations for cerebral aneurysms from MRA datasets. *International Journal of Computer Assisted Radiology and Surgery (CARS)*, 4(Supplement 1):112–113, 2009b.

M. Neugebauer, V. Diehl, M. Skalej, and B. Preim. Geometric Reconstruction of the Ostium of Cerebral Aneurysms. In *Proc. of Vision, Modeling, and Visualization*, pages 307–314, 2010.

M. Neugebauer, G. Janiga, O. Beuing, M. Skalej, and B. Preim. Anatomy-Guided Multi-Level Exploration of Blood Flow in Cerebral Aneurysms. *Computer Graphics Forum*, 30(3):1041–1050, 2011.

M. Neugebauer, K. Lawonn, O. Beuing, P. Berg, G. Janiga, and B. Preim. AmniVis - A System for Qualitative Exploration of Near-Wall Hemodynamics in Cerebral Aneurysms. *Computer Graphics Forum*, 33(3):251–260, 2013. Proc. of Eurovis.

L. Neumann, B. Csabfalvi, A. König, and E. Gröller. Gradient Estimation in Volume Data using 4D Linear Regression. In *Proc. of Eurographics*, pages 351–357, 2000.

T. Neumuth. Tutorial on surgical process modeling and surgical workflows. In *Proc. of CURAC*, 2011.

T. Neumuth, N. Durstewitz, M. Fischer, G. Strauß, A. Dietz, J. Meixensberger, P. Jannin, K. Cleary, H. U. Lemke, and O. Burgert. Structured recording of intraoperative surgical workflows. In *SPIE Medical Imaging 2006 - PACS and Imaging Informatics: Progress in Biomedical Optics and Imaging*. SPIE: Bellingham, 2006.

T. Neumuth, P. Jannin, J. Schlomberg, J. Meixensberger, P. Wiedemann, and O. Burgert. Validation of knowledge acquisition for surgical process models. *J. Am. Med. Inform. Assoc.*, 16(1):72–80, 2009.

T. Neumuth, P. Jannin, J. Schlomberg, J. Meixensberger, P. Wiedemann, and O. Burgert. Analysis of surgical intervention populations using generic surgical process models. *International Journal of Computer Assisted Radiology and Surgery*, 6(1):59–71, 2011.

T. K. Nguyen, A. Eklund, H. Ohlsson, F. Hernell, P. Ljung, C. Forsell, M. T. Andersson, H. Knutsson, and A. Ynnerman. Concurrent Volume Visualization of Real-Time fMRI. In *Proc. of Volume Graphics*, pages 53–60, 2010.

D. Ni, W.-Y. Chan, J. Qin, Y. Qu, Y.-P. Chui, S. S. Ho, and P. A. Heng. An Ultrasound-Guided Organ Biopsy Simulation with 6DOF Haptic Feedback. In *Proc. of Medical Image Computing and Computer-Assisted Intervention* (MICCAI), pages 551–559. Springer, 2008.

D. Ni, W. Y. Chan, J. Qin, Y.-P. Chui, I. Qu, S. S. Ho, and P. A. Heng. A Virtual Reality Simulator for Ultrasound-Guided Biopsy Training. *IEEE Computer Graphics and Applications*, 31(2):36–48, 2011.

K. Nicolaides. *The Natural Way to Draw*. Houghton Mifflin, 1941.

S. Nicolau, A. Garcia, X. Pennec, L. Soler, and N. Ayache. An augmented reality system to guide radio-frequency tumour ablation. *Journal of Visualization and Computer Animation*, 16(1):1–10, 2005.

J. Nielsen. *Usability Engineering*. Morgan Kaufman, 1993.

J. Nielsen and R. Mack. *Usability Inspection Methods*. Wiley, New York, 1994.

G. Nielson and B. Hamann. The Asymptotic Decider: Removing the Ambiguity in Marching Cubes. In *Proc. of IEEE Visualization*, pages 83–91, 1991.

H.-W. Nienhuys and A. F. van der Stappen. A Surgery Simulation Supporting Cuts and Finite Element Deformation. In *Proc. of Medical Image Computing and Computer-Assisted Intervention (MICCAI)*, pages 145–152, 2001.

K. Nikolaou, S.O. Schoenberg, G. Brix, J.P. Goldman, U. Attenberger, B. Kuehn, O. Dietrich, and M.F. Reiser. Quantification of pulmonary blood flow and volume in healthy volunteers by dynamic contrast-enhanced magnetic resonance imaging using a parallel imaging technique. *Invest. Radiol.*, 39(9):537–545, 2004.

C. Nimsky, O. Ganslandt, S. Cerny, P. Hastreiter, G. Greiner, and R. Fahlbusch. Quantification of, visualization of, and compensation for brain shift using intraoperative magnetic resonance imaging. *Neurosurgery*, 47(5):1070–1079, 2000.

C. Nimsky, O. Ganslandt, B. von Keller, and R. Fahlbusch. Preliminary Experience in Glioma Surgery With Intraoperative High-Field MRI. *Acta Neurochirurgica*, 88:21–29, 2003.

C. Nimsky, O. Ganslandt, P. Hastreiter, R. Wang, T. Benner, A. G. Sorensen, and R. Fahlbusch. Preoperative and intraoperative diffusion tensor imaging-based fiber tracking in glioma surgery. *Neurosurgery*, 56(1):130–137; discussion 138, 2005.

C. Nimsky, O. Ganslandt, F. Enders, D. Merhof, T. Hammen, and M. Buchfelder. Visualization Strategies for Major White Matter Tracts for Intraoperative Use. *International Journal of Computer Assisted Radiology and Surgery*, 1(1):13–22, 2006a.

C. Nimsky, B. von Keller, O. Ganslandt, and R. Fahlbusch. Intraoperative high-field magnetic resonance imaging in transsphenoidal surgery of hormonally inactive pituitary macroadenomas. *Neurosurgery*, 59(1):105–114, 2006b.

W. L. Nowinski, G. Qian, K. N. Prakash, I. Volkau, W. K. Leong, S. Huang, A. Ananthasubramaniam, J. Liu, T. T. Ng, and V. Gupta. Stroke Suite: Cad systems for acute ischemic stroke, hemorrhagic stroke, and stroke in ER. In *Proc. of Medical Imaging and Informatics, Revised Selected Papers*, pages 377–386, 2008.

M. Nulkar and K. Mueller. Splatting with Shadows. In *Proc. of Volume Graphics*, pages 35–50, 2001.

H. Nyquist. Certain Factors Affecting Telegraph Speed. *Bell System Technical Journal*, 3(3):324–346, 1924.

N. M. O'Connell, R. J. Toomey, M. McEntee, J. Ryan, J. Stowe, A. Adams, and P. C. Brennan. Optimization of region of interest luminances may enhance radiologists' light adaptation. *Academic Radiology*, 15(4):488–493, 2008.

L. J. O'Donnell and C.-F. Westin. Automatic tractography segmentation using a high-dimensional white matter atlas. *IEEE Transactions on Medical Imaging*, 26(11):1562–1575, 2007.

L. J. O'Donnell, C.-F. Westin, and A. J. Golby. Tract-Based Morphometry for White Matter Group Analysis. *NeuroImage*, 45(3):832–844, 2009.

S. Oeltze and B. Preim. Visualization of Vascular Structures with Convolution Surfaces. In *Data Visualization (Proc. of Eurographics/IEEE Symposium on Visualization)*, pages 311–320, 2004.

S. Oeltze and B. Preim. Visualization of Vascular Structures with Convolution Surfaces: Method, Validation and Evaluation. *IEEE Transactions on Medical Imaging*, 25(4):540–549, 2005.

S. Oeltze, F. Grothues, A. Hennemuth, A. Kuŝs, and B. Preim. Integrated Visualization of Morphologic and Perfusion Data for the Analysis of Coronary Artery Disease. In *Data Visualization (Proc. of Eurographics/IEEE Symposium on Visualization)*, pages 131–138, 2006.

S. Oeltze, H. Doleisch, H. Hauser, P. Muigg, and B. Preim. Interactive visual analysis of perfusion data. *IEEE Transactions on Visualization and Computer Graphics*, 13(6):1392–1399, 2007.

S. Oeltze, A. Malyszczyk, and B. Preim. Intuitive Mapping of Perfusion Parameters to Glyph Shape. In *Proc. of Workshop Bildverarbeitung für die Medizin*, pages 262–266, 2008.

S. Oeltze, H. Hauser, J. Rorvik, A. Lundervold, and B. Preim. Visual Analysis of Cerebral Perfusion Data – Four Interactive Approaches and a Comparison. In *Proc. of the Symposium on Image and Signal Processing and Analysis (ISPA)*, pages 588–595, 2009.

S. Ogawa, T. M. Lee, A. R. Kay, and D. W. Tank. Brain magnetic resonance imaging with contrast dependent on blood oxygenation. *Proc. of the National Academy of Sciences*, 87(24):9868–9872, 1990.

S. Ogawa, D. W. Tank, R. Menon, J. M. Ellermann, S. G. Kim, H. Merkle, and K. Ugurbil. Intrinsic signal changes accompanying sensory stimulation: functional brain mapping with magnetic resonance imaging. *Proc. of the National Academy of Sciences of the United States of America*, 89(13):5951–5955, 1992.

R. Ohbuchi, D. Chen, and H. Fuchs. Incremental Volume Reconstruction and Rendering for 3D Ultrasound Imaging. In *Proc. of Visualization in Biomedical Computing*, pages 312–323, 1992.

Y. Ohtake, A. Belyaev, M. Alexa, G. Turk, and H.-P. Seidel. Multilevel Partition of Unity Implicits. *ACM Transactions on Graphics*, 22(3):463–470, 2003.

Y. Ohtake, A. G. Belyaev, and H.-P. Seidel. Ridge-valley lines on meshes via implicit surface fitting. *ACM Transactions on Graphics*, 23(3):609–612, 2004.

D. Ojdanic, L. Chen, and H. O. Peitgen. Improving interaction in navigated surgery by combining pan-tilt mounted laser and a pointer with triggering. In *Proc. of SPIE Medical Imaging*, 2012.

A.M. Okamura. Methods for haptic feedback in teleoperated robot-assisted surgery. *Industrial Robot: An International Journal*, 31(6):499–508, 2004.

S. D. Olabarriaga and A. W. M. Smeulders. Interaction in the segmentation of medical images: a survey. *Medical Image Analysis*, 5(2):127–142, 2001.

B. Olbrich, J. Traub, S. Wiesner, A. Wichert, H. Feußner, and N. Navab. Respiratory Motion Analysis: Towards Gated Augmentation of the Liver. In *Proc. of Computer Assisted Radiology and Surgery*, pages 248–253, 2005.

A. Olwal, O. Frykholm, K. Groth, and J. Moll. Design and Evaluation of Interaction Technology for Medical Team Meetings. In *Proc. of INTERACT (1)*, pages 505–522, 2011.

D. Onceanu and A. J. Stewart. Direct surgeon control of the computer in the operating room. In *Proc. of Medical Image Computing and Computer-Assisted Intervention (MICCAI)*, pages 121–128, 2011.

A. Opalach and S.C. Maddock. Implicit Surfaces: Appearance, Blending and Consistency. In *Proc. of European Workshop on Computer Animation*, pages 233–245, 1993.

H. Oppenheimer, I. DeCastro, and D.E. McDonnell. Minimally invasive spine technology and minimally invasive spine surgery: a historical review. *Neurosurgery Focus*, 27:E9.1–E9.15, 2009.

D. B. Orbach, B. K. Pramanik, J. Lee, T. S. Maldonado, T. Riles, and R. I. Grossman. Carotid artery stent implantation: evaluation with multi-detector row CT angiography and virtual angioscopy: initial experience. *Radiology*, 238(1):309–320, 2006.

I. Oropesa, P. Lamata, P. Sanchez-González, J. B. Pagador, M. E. Garcia, F. M. Sánchez-Margallo, and Enrique J. Gómez. *Virtual Reality*, chapter Virtual reality simulators for objective evaluation on laparoscopic surgery: Current trends and benefits. InTech, 2010.

A. Osborn. *Diagnostic Cerebral Angiography*. Lippincott Williams and Wilkins, A Wolters Kluwer Company, second edition, 1999.

S. Osher and J. A. Sethian. Fronts Propagating with Curvature Dependent Speed: Algorithms Based on Hamilton-Jacobi Formulations. *Journal of Computational Physics*, 79(1):12–49, 1988.

N. A. Otsu. A Threshold Selection Method from Gray-Level Histograms. *IEEE Transactions on Systems, Man, and Cybernetics*, 9(1):62–66, 1979.

M. Otte. Elastic Registration of fMRI Data Using Bezier-Spline Transformations. *IEEE Transactions on Medical Imaging*, 20(2):193–206, 2001.

S. G. Owen, R. Hall, J. Anderson, and G. A. Smart. A comparison of programmed instruction with conventional lectures in the teaching of electrocardiography to final-year medical students. *Journal of Medical Education*, 40(11):1058–1062, 1965.

J. D. Owens, D. Luebke, N. Govindaraju, M. Harris, J. Krüger, A. E. Lefohn, and T. J. Purcell. A Survey of General-Purpose Computation on Graphics Hardware. *Computer Graphics Forum*, 26(1):80–113, 2007.

E. Özarslan and T. H. Mareci. Generalized diffusion tensor imaging and analytical relationships between diffusion tensor imaging and high angular resolution diffusion imaging. *Magnetic Resonance in Medicine*, 50(5):955–965, 2003.

E. Özarslan, B. C. Vemuri, and T. H. Mareci. Generalized scalar measures for diffusion MRI using trace, variance, and entropy. *Magnetic Resonance in Medicine*, 53(4):866–876, 2005.

N. Padoy, T. Blum, A. Ahmadi, H. Feussner, M.-O. Berger, and N. Navab. Statistical modeling and recognition of surgical workflow. *Medical Image Analysis*, 16(3):632–641, 2010.

T. Paek, M. Agrawala, S. Basu, S. Drucker, T. Kristjansson, R. Logan, K. Toyama, and A. Wilson. Toward universal mobile interaction for shared displays. In *Proc. of the ACM conference on Computer supported cooperative work (CSCW)*, pages 266–269, 2004.

V. Paelke, C. Reimann, and W. Rosenbach. A visualization design repository for mobile devices. In *Proc. of Afrigraph*, pages 57–62, 2003.

D. S. Paik, C. F. Beaulieu, R. B. Jeffrey, G. D. Rubin, and S. Napel. Automated flight path planning for virtual endoscopy. *Medical Physics*, 25(5):629–637, 1998.

D S Paik, C F Beaulieu, Jr Jeffrey, R B, C A Karadi, and S Napel. Visualization modes for CT colonography using cylindrical and planar map projections. *Journal of Computer Assisted Tomography*, 24(2):179–188, 2000.

S. Pajevic and C. Pierpaoli. Color schemes to represent the orientation of anisotropic tissues from diffusion tensor data: application to white matter fiber tract mapping in the human brain. *Magnetic Resonance in Medicine*, 42(3):526–540, 1999.

T. Pakkanen and R. Raisamo. Appropriateness of foot interaction for non-accurate spatial tasks. In *CHI EA: Extended abstracts on Human factors in computing systems (ACM CHI '04)*, pages 1123–1126, 2004.

A. K. Pandey, J. R. Bapuraj, A. K. Gupta, and N. Khandelwal. Is there a role for virtual otoscopy in the preoperative assessment of the ossicular chain in chronic suppurative otitis media? Comparison of HRCT and virtual otoscopy with surgical findings. *European Radiology*, 19(6):1408–1416, 2009.

C. Pape-Koehler, C. Chmelik, and A. M. Aslund M. Heiss. Elektronische operationslehren und blogs. *Zentralblatt Chirurgie*, 135(5):467–471, 2010.

C. Pape-Koehler, M. Immenroth, S. Sauerland, R. Lefering, C. Lindlohr, J. Toaspern, and M. Heiss. Multimedia-based training on internet platforms improves surgical performance: a randomized controlled trial. *Surgical Endoscopy*, 27(5):1737–1747, 2013.

H. C. Park and R. S. Lakes. Cosserat micromechanics of human bone: strain redistribution by a hydration-sensitive constituent. *J. Biomechanics*, 19(2):385–397, 1986.

J. S. Park, M. S. Chung, S. B. Hwang, B. S. Shin, and H. S. Park. Visible Korean Human: its techniques and applications. *Clinical Anatomy*, 19(3):216–224, 2006.

K.J. Park, C.J. Bergin, and J.L. Clausen. Diagnosis of pulmonary emphysema by computerized tomography. *Lancet*, 211(2):541–547, 1999.

V. Pascucci. Isosurface Computation Made Simple. In *Data Visualization (Proc. of Eurographics/IEEE Symposium on Visualization)*, pages 293–300, 2004.

D. Patel, M. Haidacher, J.-P. Balabanian, and E. Gröller. Moment Curves. In *Proc. of the IEEE Pacific Visualization Symposium*, pages 201–208, 2009.

T. M. Pawlik, C. R. Scoggins, D. Zorzi, A. Andrea, C. Eng, S. A. Curley et al. Effect of surgical margin status on survival and site of recurrence after hepatic resection for colorectal metastases. *Annals of Surgery*, 241:715–722, 2005.

G. Pearson and M. Weiser. Of moles and men: the design of foot controls for workstations. *SIGCHI Bulletin*, 17(4):333–339, 1986.

T. H. J. M Peeters, V. Prckovska, M. van Almsick, A. Vilanova, and B. M. ter Haar Romeny. Fast and sleek glyph rendering for interactive HARDI data exploration. In *Proc. of IEEE Pacific Visualization*, pages 153–160, 2009.

Z. Peng and R. S. Laramee. Higher Dimensional Vector Field Visualization: A Survey. In *Proc. of EG UK Theory and Practice of Computer Graphics (TPCG)*, pages 149–163, 2009.

E. Penner and R. Mitchell. Isosurface Ambient Occlusion and Soft Shadows with Filterable Occlusion Maps. In *IEEE/EG Int. Symp. on Volume and Point-Based Graphics*, pages 57–64, 2008.

K. Perktold, M. Resch, and H. Florian. Pulsatile non-Newtonian flow characteristics in a three-dimensional human carotid bifurcation model. *Journal of Biomechanical Engineering*, 113(8):464, 1991.

A. Perlich, B. Preim, M. de La Simone, C. Gomes, E. Stindel, and A. Presedo. Computer-Aided Surgery Planning for Lower Limb Osteotomy. In *Proc. of Bildverarbeitung für die Medizin (BVM)*, pages 194–198, 2011.

E. Pernod, M. Sermesant, E. Konukoglu, J. Relan, H. Delingette, and N. Ayache. A multi-front eikonal model of cardiac electrophysiology for interactive simulation of radio-frequency ablation. *Computers & Graphics*, 35(2):431–440, 2011.

P. Perona and J. Malik. Scale-space and edge detection using anisotropic diffusion. *IEEE Transactions on Pattern Analysis and Machine Intelligence*, 12(7):629–639, 1990.

A. Persson, T. Brismar, C. Lundström, N. Dahlström, F. Othberg, and Ö. Smedby. Standardized Volume Rendering for MR Angiography Measurements in the Abdominal Aorta. *Acta Radiologica*, 47(2):172–178, 2006.

A. Persson, M. Lindblom, and C. Jackowski. A state-of-the-art pipeline for postmortem CT and MRI visualization: from data acquisition to interactive image interpretation at autopsy. *Acta Radiology*, 52(5):522–536, 2011.

M. Peterhans, A. vom Berg, B. Dagon, D. Inderbitzin, C. Baur, D. Candinas, and Weber S. A navigation system for open liver surgery: design, workflow and first clinical applications. *Int. J. Med. Robot.*, 7(1):7–16, 2011.

T. M. Peters. Image-guidance for surgical procedures. *Physics in Medicine and Biology*, 51(14):R505–R540, 2006.

T. M. Peters and K. Cleary. *Image-Guided Interventions: Technology and Applications*. Springer, 2008.

A. Petersik, B. Pflesser, U. Tiede, and K.-H. Höhne. Realistic haptic volume interaction for petrous bone surgery simulation. In *Proc. of Computer Assisted Radiology and Surgery*, pages 252–257. Springer, 2002.

I. Petzold and G. Gröger. Fast Screen Map Labeling: Data Structures and Algorithms. In *Proc. of International Cartographic Conference*, pages 288–298, 2003.

R. Petzold, H.-F. Zeilhofer, and W. A. Kalender. Rapid prototyping technology in medicine—basics and applications. *Computerized Medical Imaging and Graphics*, 23(5):277–284, 1999.

H.-P. Pfister, J. Hardenbergh, J. Knittel, H. Lauer, and L. Seiler. The VolumePro Real-Time Ray-casting System. In *Proc. of ACM SIGGRAPH*, pages 251–260, 1999.

H.-P. Pfister, B. Lorensen, C. Bajaj, G. Kindlmann, W. Schroeder, L. Avila, K. Martin, R. Machiraju, and J. Lee. The transfer function bake-off. *IEEE Computer Graphics and Applications*, 21(3):16–22, 2001.

B. Pflesser, A. Petersik, U. Tiede, K. H. Höhne, and R. Leuwer. Volume Cutting for Virtual Petrous Bone Surgery. *Computer Aided Surgery*, 7(2):74–83, 2002.

B. T. Phong. Illumination for computer generated pictures. *Communications of the ACM*, 18(6):311–317, 1975.

M. Piccinelli, A. Veneziani, D. A. Steinman, A. Remuzzi, and L. Antiga. A Framework for Geometric Analysis of Vascular Structures: Application to Cerebral Aneurysms. *IEEE Transactions on Medical Imaging*, 28(8):1141–1155, 2009.

P. Pickhardt. Three-Dimensional Endoluminal CT Colonoscopy (Virtual Colonoscopy): Comparison of Three Commercially Available Systems. *American Journal of Roentgenology*, 181(6):1599–1606, 2003.

P. Pickhardt, J. Choi, I. Hwang, J. Butler, M. Puckett, H. Hildebrandt, R. Wong, P. Nugent, P. Mysliwiec, and W. Schindler. Computed Tomographic Virtual Colonoscopy to Screen for Colorectal Neoplasia in Asymptomatic Adults. *New England Journal of Medicine*, 349(23):2191–2200, 2003.

P. Pili, A. Zorcolo, E. Gobbetti, and M. Tuveri. Interactive 3D visualization of carotid arteries. *International Angiology*, 16(3):153, 1997.

U. Pinkall and K. Polthier. Computing discrete minimal surfaces and their conjugates. *Experimental Mathematics*, 2(1):15–36, 1993.

S. M. Pizer, E. P. Amburn, J. D. Austin et al. Adaptive histogram equalization and its variations. *Computer Vision, Graphics, and Image Processing*, 39:355–368, 1987.

S. M. Pizer, P. T. Fletcher, Y. Fridman, D. S. Fritsch, A. G. Gash, and J. M. Glotzer et al. Deformable M-Reps for 3D Medical Image Segmentation. *International Journal of Computer Vision*, 55(2-3):85–106, 2003.

K. Pohl and C. Rupp. *Basiswissen Requirements Engineering*. Dpunkt.Verlag, 2009.

R. Pohle and K. D. Toennies. Self-lerning model-based segmentation of medical images. *Image Processing and Communication*, 7(3-4):97–113, 2002.

R. Pohle, M. Wegner, K. Rink, K. D. Tönnies, A. Celler, and S. Blinder. Segmentation of the left ventricle in 4d-dSPECT data using free form deformation of super quadrics. In Milan Sonka and J. Michael Fitzpatrick, editors, *Proc. of SPIE Medical Imaging*, volume 5370 of *Proc. of SPIE*, pages 1388–1394, February 2004.

P. G. Polson, C. H. Lewis, J. Rieman, and C. Wharton. Cognitive Walkthroughs: A Method for Theory-Based Evaluation of User Interfaces. *International Journal of Man-Machine Studies*, 36(5):741–773, 1992.

A. Pommert and K. Höhne. Evaluation of Image Quality in Medical Volume Visualization: The State of the Art. In *Proc. of Medical Image Computing and Computer-Assisted Intervention (MICCAI)*, volume 2489 of *Lecture Notes in Computer Science*, pages 598–605. Springer, 2002.

A. Pommert, K.H. Höhne, B. Pflesser, E. Richter, M. Riemer, T. Schiemann, R. Schubert, U. Schumacher, and U. Tiede. Creating a high-resolution spatial/symbolic model of the inner organs based on the visible human. *Medical Image Analysis*, 5(3):221–228, 2001.

C. R. Ponce and R.T. Born. Stereopsis. *Current Biology*, 18(18):845–850, 2008.

K. Popuri, D. Cobzas, A. Murtha, and M. Jägersand. 3D variational brain tumor segmentation using Dirichlet priors on a clustered feature set. *International Journal of Computer Assisted Radiology and Surgery*, 7(4):493–506, 2012.

T. Porter and T. Duff. Compositing Digital Images. In *Proc. of ACM SIGGRAPH*, pages 253–259, 1984.

A. Pössneck, E. Nowatius, C. Trantakis, H. Cakmak, H. Maaß, U. Kühnapfel, A., and G. Strauß. A virtual reality training system in endoscopic sinus surgery. In *Proc. of Computer Assisted Radiology and Surgery*, pages 527–530, 2005.

K. Potter, A. Gooch, B. Gooch, P. Willemsen, J. M. Kniss, R. F. Riesenfeld, and P. Shirley. Resolution Independent NPR-Style 3D Line Textures. *Computer Graphics Forum*, 28(1):56–66, 2009.

S. R. Prasad, K. S. Jhaveri, S. Saini, P. F. Hahn, E. F. Halpern, and J. E. Sumner. CT Tumor Measurement for Therapeutic Response Assessment: Comparison of Unidimensional, Bidimensional, and Volumetric Techniques; Initial Observations. *Radiology*, 225:416–419, 2002.

J.-S. Praßni, T. Ropinski, and K. Hinrichs. Efficient boundary detection and transfer function generation in direct volume rendering. In *Proc. of Vision, Modeling, and Visualization*, pages 285–294, 2009.

J.-S. Praßni, T. Ropinski, J. Mensmann, and K. Hinrichs. Shape-based transfer functions for volume visualization. In *Proc. of IEEE PacificVis*, pages 9–16, 2010.

V. Prčkovska, T. H.J.M Peeters, M. van Almsick, B. ter Haar Romeny, and A. Vilanova i Bartroli. Fused DTI/HARDI visualization. *IEEE Transactions on Visualization and Computer Graphics*, 17(10):1407–1419, 2011.

B. Preim. Human-Computer Interaction in medical visualization. In *Proc. Dagstuhl Workshop Scientific Visualization 2010*, pages 292–310, 2011.

B. Preim, A. Raab, and T. Strothotte. Coherent Zooming of Illustrations with 3D-Graphics and Text. In *Proc. of Graphics Interface*, pages 105–113, 1997.

B. Preim, D. Selle, W. Spindler, K. J. Oldhafer, and H.-O. Peitgen. Interaction Techniques and Vessel Analysis for Preoperative Planning in Liver Surgery. In *Proc. of Medical Image Computing and Computer-Assisted Intervention (MICCAI)*, pages 608–617, 2000.

B. Preim, C. Tietjen, W. Spindler, and H.-O. Peitgen. Integration of Measurement Tools in Medical Visualizations. In *Proc. of IEEE Visualization*, pages 21–28, 2002.

B. Preim, S. Oeltze, M. Mlejnek, E. Gröller, A. Hennemuth, and S. Behrens. Survey of the Visual Exploration and Analysis of Perfusion Data. *IEEE Transactions on Visualization and Computer Graphics*, 15(2):205–220, 2009.

B. Preim, J. Dornheim, L. Dornheim, and A. Boehm. Clinical impact of the tumor therapy manager. In *Proc. of Conference Compendium of IEEE VisWeek—Discovery Exhibition*, 2010.

U. Preim, S. Glaßer, B. Preim, F. Fischbach, and J. Ricke. Computer-Aided Diagnosis in Breast DCE-MRI - Quantification of the Heterogeneity of Breast Lesions. *European Journal of Radiology*, 81(7):1532–1538, 2012.

T. Preusser and H.-O. Peitgen. Patient-Specific Planning for Radio-Frequency Ablation of Tumors in the Presence of Uncertainty. *it - Information Technology*, 52(5):265–271, 2010.

D. Proksch, J. Dornheim, and B. Preim. Interaktionstechniken zur Korrektur medizinischer 3D-Segmentierungen. In *Proc. of Bildverarbeitung für die Medizin (BVM)*, pages 420–424, 2010.

S. Prothmann, S. Puccini, B. Dalitz, A. Kühn, L. Röedel, C. Zimmer, and T. Kahn. Präoperatives Mapping der Sprachareale mittels fMRI bei Patienten mit Hirntumoren: ein Methodenvergleich. *Fortschritte auf dem Gebiet der Röntgenstrahlen und bildgebenden Verfahren*, 177(11):1522–1531, 2005.

J. Pruitt and J. Grudin. Personas: practice and theory. In *Proc. of Designing for user experiences*, pages 1–15. ACM, 2003.

A. Puig, D. Tost, and I. Navazo. An interactive cerebral blood vessel exploration system. In *Proc. of IEEE Visualization*, pages 443–446, 1997.

Z. Qian, X. Huang, D. Metaxas, and L. Axel. Robust Segmentation of 4D Cardiac MRI-tagged Images via Spatio-temporal Propagation. In *Proc. of SPIE Medical Imaging*, Proc. of SPIE, February 2005.

J. Qin, Y.-P. Chui, W.-M. Pang, K.-S. Choi, and P.-A. Heng. Learning Blood Management in Orthopedic Surgery through Gameplay. *IEEE Computer Graphics and Applications*, 30(2):45–57, 2010.

F. Qiu, F. Xu, Z. Fan, N. Neophytos, A. Kaufman, and K. Mueller. Lattice-Based Volumetric Global Illumination. *IEEE Transactions on Visualization and Computer Graphics*, 13:1576–1583, 2007.

J. Qualter, F. Sculli, A. Oliker, Z. Napier, S. Lee, J. Garcia, S. Frenkel, V. Harnik, and M. Triola. The BioDigital Human: A Web-based 3D Platform for Medical Visualization and Education. *Studies in health technology and informatics*, 173:359–361, 2012.

S. Quinlan. Efficient Distance Computation Between Non-Convex Objects. In *Proc. of IEEE International Conference on Robotics and Automation (ICRA)*, pages 3324–3329, 1994.

J. B. Ra, S. M. Kwon, J. K. Kim, J. Yi, K. H. Kim et al. Spine Needle Biopsy Simulator Using Visual and Force Feedback. *Computer Aided Surgery*, 7(6):353–363, 2002.

M. Raaijmaakers, F. Gelaude, K. D. Smedt, T. Clijmans, J. Dille, and M. Mulier. A custom-made guide-wire positioning device for Hip Surface Replacement Arthroplasty: description and first results. *BMC Musculoskeletal Disorders*, 11(1):161, 2010.

K. Radermacher, F. Portheine, M. Anton, A. Zimolong, G. Kaspers, G. Rau, and H. W. Staudte. Computer assisted orthopaedic surgery with image based individual templates. *Clinical Orthopaedics and Related Research*, 354:28–38, 1998.

A. Radetzky and A. Nürnberger. Visualization and simulation techniques for surgical simulators using actual patient's data. *Artificial Intelligence in Medicine*, 26(3):255–279, 2002.

A. Radjenovic, B. J. Dall, J. P. Ridgway, and M. A. Smith. Measurement of pharmacokinetic parameters in histologically graded invasive breast tumours using dynamic contrast-enhanced MRI. *British Journal of Radiology*, 81(962):120–128, February 2008.

A. Radtke, S. Nadalin, G. C. Sotiropoulos, E. P. Molmenti, T. Schroeder, C. Valentin-Gamazo, H. Lang, M. Bockhorn, H. O. Peitgen, C. E. Broelsch, and M. Malago. Computer-Assisted Operative Planning in Adult Living Donor Liver Transplantation: A New Way to Resolve the Dilemma of the Middle Hepatic Vein. *World Journal of Surgery*, 31(1):179–185, 2007.

L. Raghupathi, L. Grisoni, F. Faure, D. Marchal, M.-P. Cani, and C. Chaillou. An Intestinal Surgery Simulator: Real-Time Collision Processing and Visualization. *IEEE Transactions on Visualization and Computer Graphics*, 10(6):708–718, 2004.

S. Rajasekaran, S. Vidyadhara, P. Ramesh, and A. P. Shetty. Randomized clinical study to compare the accuracy of navigated and non-navigated thoracic pedicle screws in deformity correction surgeries. *Spine*, 32(2):56–64, 2007.

B. Raman, R. Raman, L. Raman, and C. F. Beaulieu. Radiology on handheld devices: Image display, manipulation, and pacs integration issues. *RadioGraphics*, 24:299–310, 2004.

B. Raman, R. Raman, G. D. Rubin, and S. Napel. Improved speed of bone removal in computed tomographic angiography using automated targeted morphological separation: method and evaluation in computed tomographic angiography of lower extremity occlusive disease. *Journal of Computer-Assisted Tomography*, 32(3):485–491, 2008a.

B. Raman, R. Raman, G. D. Rubin, and S. Napel. Semiautomated quantification of the mass and distribution of vascular calcification with multidetector CT: method and evaluation. *Radiology*, 247(1):241–250, 2008b.

B. Raman, R. Raman, G. D. Rubin, and S. Napel. Automated Tracing of the Adventitial Contour of Aortoiliac and Peripheral Arterial Walls in CT Angiography (CTA) to Allow Calculation of Non-calcified Plaque Burden. *J. Digit. Imaging*, 2011.

M. Ranneberg, M. Weiser, M. Weihrauch, V. Budach, J. Gellermann, and P. Wust. Regularized Antenna Profile Adaptation in Online Hyperthermia Treatment. *Medical Physics*, 37:5382–5394, 2010.

R. Raskar and M. F. Cohen. Image precision silhouette edges. In *Proc. of Symposium on Interactive 3D Graphics (SI3D)*, pages 135–140, 1999.

A. Rassineux. Generation and optimization of tetrahedral meshes by advancing front techniques. *International Journal of Numerical Methods in Engineering*, 41:651–674, 1998.

O. Ratib, J. M. McCoy, D. Ric McGill, M. Li, and A. Brown. Use of Personal Digital Assistants for Retrieval of Medical Images and Data on High-Resolution Flat Panel Displays. *RadioGraphics*, 23:267–272, 2003.

R. Rau, D. Weiskopf, and H. Ruder. Special Relativity in Virtual Reality. In *Proc. of Mathematical Visualization*, pages 269–279, 1998.

P. Rautek, S. Bruckner, and E. Gröller. Semantic layers for illustrative volume rendering. *IEEE Transactions on Visualization and Computer Graphics*, 13(6):1336–1343, 2007.

P. Rautek, S. Bruckner, E. Gröller, and I. Viola. Illustrative visualization: new technology or useless tautology? *SIGGRAPH Comput. Graph.*, 42(3):4:1–4:8, 2008.

S. Ray, R. Hagge, M. Gillen, M. Cerejo, S. Shakeri, L. A. Beckett, T. Greasby, and R. D. Badawi. Comparison of 2D and 3D iterative watershed segmentation methods in hepatic tumor volumetrics. *Medical Physics*, 35(12):5869–5881, 2008.

S. Raya and J. Udupa. Shape-based Interpolation of Multidimensional Objects. *Journal of WSCG*, 9(1):33–42, 1990.

A. Razdan and M. Bae. Curvature Estimation Scheme for Triangle Meshes Using Biquadratic Bezier Patches. *Computer Aided Design*, pages 1481–1491, 2005.

G. Reina, K. Bidmon, F. Enders, P. Hastreiter, and T. Ertl. GPU-based hyperstreamlines for diffusion tensor imaging. In *Data Visualization (Proc. of Eurographics/IEEE Symposium on Visualization)*, pages 35–42, 2006.

F. Reinders, M. Jacobson, and F. Post. Skeleton graph generation for feature shape description. In *Data Visualization (Proc. of Eurographics/IEEE Symposium on Visualization)*, pages 73–82, 2000.

M. Reisert, I. Mader, C. Anastasopoulos, M. Weigel, S. Schnell, and V. Kiselev. Global fiber reconstruction becomes practical. *NeuroImage*, 54(2):955–962, 2011.

B. Reitinger, A. Bornik, R. Beichel, and D. Schmalstieg. Liver Surgery Planning Using Virtual Reality. *IEEE Computer Graphics and Applications*, 26(6):36–47, 2006a.

B. Reitinger, D. Schmalstieg, A. Bornik, and R. Beichel. Spatial Analysis Tools for Medical Virtual Reality. In *Proc. of IEEE Symposium on 3D User Interface (3DUI)*, pages 29–36, 2006b.

M. Remy-Jardin, J. Remy, M. Artaud, D. Fribourg, and A. Naili. Tracheobronchial tree: Assessment with volume rendering-technical aspects. *Radiology*, 208:393–398, 1998.

C. Rezk-Salama. GPU-Based Monte-Carlo Volume Raycasting. In *Proc. of Pacific Graphics*, pages 411–414, 2007.

C. Rezk-Salama, P. Hastreiter, J. Scherer, and G. Greiner. Automatic adjustment of transfer functions for direct volume rendering. In *Proc. of Vision, Modeling, and Visualization*, pages 357–364, 2000a.

C. Rezk-Salama, M. Scheuering, G. Soza, and G. Greiner. Fast Volumetric Deformation on General Purpose Hardware. In *Proc. of the ACM SIGGRAPH/EUROGRAPHICS Workshop on Graphics Hardware*, pages 17–24, 2001.

C. Rezk-Salama, M. Keller, and P. Kohlmann. High-Level User Interfaces for Transfer Function Design with Semantics. *IEEE Transactions on Visualization and Computer Graphics*, 12(5):1021–1028, 2006.

C. Rezk Salama, M. Hadwiger, T. Ropinski, and P. Ljung. Advanced Illumination Techniques for GPU Volume Raycasting. In *ACM SIGGRAPH Courses Program*, 2009.

P. Rheingans. Color, change, and control for quantitative data display. In *Proc. of IEEE Visualization*, pages 252–259, 1992.

M.L. Rhodes. Computer graphics and medicine: a complex partnership. *IEEE Computer Graphics and Applications*, 17 (1):22–28, 1997.

A. Richter and M. Koch. Functions of Social Networkung Services. In *Proc. of International Conference on the Design of Cooperative Systems (COOP)*, pages 87–98, 2008.

M. Richtscheid, M. Grimm, and G. Sakas. Freehand 3D/4D ultrasound acquisition, processing and visualisation. In *Proc. of the Fourth Germany-Korea Joint Conference Advanced Medical Image Processing*, 1999.

C. Rieder, F. Ritter, M. Raspe, and H.-O. Peitgen. Interactive Visualization of Multimodal Volume Data for Neurosurgical Tumor Treatment. *Computer Graphics Forum*, 27(3):1055–1062, 2008.

C. Rieder, A. Weihusen, C. Schumann, S. Zidowitz, and H.-O. Peitgen. Visual support for interactive Post-Interventional assessment of radiofrequency ablation therapy. *Computer Graphics Forum*, 29(3):1093–1102, 2010.

C. Rieder, T. Kroeger, C. Schumann, and H. K. Hahn. GPU-based Real-Time Approximation of the Ablation Zone for Radiofrequency Ablation. *IEEE Transactions on Visualization and Computer Graphics*, 17(12):1812–1821, 2011.

H. Ringl, R. E. Schernthaner, and C. Kulinna-Cosentini et al. Lossy three-dimensional jpeg2000 compression of abdominal ct images: assessment of the visually lossless threshold and effect of compression ratio on image quality. *Radiology*, pages 467–474, 2007.

K. Rink and K. D. Toennies. Distance-based Speed Functions for Level Set Methods in Image Segmentation. In *Proc. of British Machine Vision Conference (BVMC)*, pages 283–292, 2008.

T. Ritschel. Fast GPU-based Visibility Computation for Natural Illumination of Volume Data Sets. In *Proc. of Eurographics Short Paper Proceedings*, pages 17–20, 2007.

F. Ritter, B. Preim, O. Deussen, and T. Strothotte. Using a 3D Puzzle as a Metaphor for Learning Spatial Relations. In *Proc. of Graphics Interface*, pages 171–178. Morgan Kaufmann Publishers, 2000.

F. Ritter, C. Hansen, B. Preim, V. Dicken, O. Konrad-Verse, and H.-O. Peitgen. Real-Time Illustration of Vascular Structures for Surgery. *IEEE Transactions on Visualization and Computer Graphics*, 12(5):877–884, 2006.

F. Ritter, C. Hansen, K. Wilkens, A. Köhn, and H.-O. Peitgen. User interfaces for direct interaction with 3D planning data in the operating room. *i-com*, 9(1):24–31, 2009.

F. Ritter, T. Boskamp, A. Homeyer, H. Laue, M. Schwier, F. Link, and Peitgen H.-O. Medical Image Analysis: A visual approach. *IEEE Pulse*, 2(6):60–70, 2011.

D. W. Roberts, J.W. Strohbehn, J.F. Hatch, W. Murray, and H. Kettenberger. A frameless stereotactic integration of computerized tomographic imaging and the operating microscope. *Journal of Neurosurgery*, 65:545–549, 1986.

D. W. Roberts, A. Hartov, F. E. Kennedy, M. I. Miga, K. D. Paulsen, R. J. Maciunas, P. J. Kelly, R. a. E. Bakay, and G. H. Barnett. Intraoperative brain shift and deformation : A quantitative analysis of cortical displacement in 28 cases. Commentaries. *Neurosurgery*, 43(4):749–760, 1998.

P. K. Robertson and J. F. O'Callaghan. The Generation of Color Sequences for Univariate and Bivariate Mapping. *IEEE Computer Graphics and Applications*, 6(2):24–32, 1986.

A. Roche, G. Malandain, N. Ayache, and S. Prima. Towards a better Comprehension of Similarity Measures Used in Medical Image Registration. In *Proc. of Medical Image Computing and Computer-Assisted Intervention (MICCAI)*, volume 1679 of *Lecture Notes in Computer Science*, pages 555–566. Springer, 1999.

D. Rodgman and M. Chen. Refraction in Volume Graphics. *Graphical Models*, 68:432–450, 2006.

T. Rodt, P. Ratiu, H. Becker, S. Bartling, D. Kacher, M. Anderson, B. Jolesz, and R. Kikinis. 3D visualisation of the middle ear and adjacent structures using reconstructed multi-slice CT datasets, correlating 3D images and virtual endoscopy to the 2D cross-sectional images. *Neuroradiology*, 24(9):783–790, 2002.

T. Rodt, H. P. Burmeister, S. Bartling, J. Kaminsky, B. Schwab, R. Kikinis, and H. Becker. 3D-Visualisation of the middle ear by computer-assisted post-processing of helical multi-slice CT data. *Laryngorhinootologie*, 12(7):1684–1692, 2004.

B. Rogowitz and A.D. Kalvin. The "which blair project": a quick visual method for evaluating perceptual color maps. In *Proc. of IEEE Visualization*, pages 183–190, 2001.

B. Rogowitz, L. Treinish, and S. Bryson. How not to lie with visualization. *Computers in Physics*, 10(3):268–274, 1996.

T. Rohlfing, C. R. Maurer Jr., D. A. Bluemke, and M. A. Jacobs. Volume-Preserving Non-Rigid Registration of MR Breast Images Using Free-Form Deformation with an Incompressibility Constraint. *IEEE Transactions on Medical Imaging*, 22(6):730–741, 2003.

K. Rohr. *Landmark-Based Image Analysis*. Kluwer Academic Publishers, 2001.

K. Rohr, H. S. Stiehl, R. Sprengel, T. M. Buzug, J. Weese, and M. H. Kuhn. Landmark-Based Elastic Registration Using Approximating Thin-Plate Splines. *IEEE Transactions on Medical Imaging*, 20(6):526–534, 2001.

J. P. Rolland and H. Fuchs. Optical Versus Video See-Through Head-Mounted Displays in Medical Visualization. *Presence*, 9(3):287–309, 2000.

J. P. Rolland, K. P. Thompson, H. Urey, and M. Thomas. See-through head worn display (hwd) architectures. In J. Chen, W. Cranton, and M. Fihn, editors, *Handbook of Visual Display Technology*, pages 2145–2170. Springer, 2012.

W. Röntgen. Über eine neue Art von Strahlen (Vorläufige Mittheilung). *Sitzungsberichte der physikalisch-medizinischen Gesellschaft zu Würzburg*, pages 132–141, 1895.

J. Roos, D. Fleischmann, A. Koechl, T. Rakshe, M. Straka, A. Napoli, A. Kanitsar, M. Sramek, and E. Gröller. Multipath Curved Planar Reformation of the Peripheral Arterial Tree in CT Angiography. *Radiology*, 244:281–290, 2007.

J. E. Roos, T. Rakshe, D. N. Tran, J. Rosenberg, M. Straka, T. El-Helw, M. C. Sofilos, S. Napel, and D. Fleischmann. Lower extremity CT angiography (CTA): initial evaluation of a knowledge-based centerline estimation algorithm for femoro-popliteal artery (FPA) occlusions. *Academic Radiology*, 16(6):646–653, 2009.

T. Ropinski, F. Steinicke, and K. Hinrichs. Interactive Importance-Driven Visualization Techniques for Medical Volume Data. In *Proc. of Vision, Modeling, and Visualization*, pages 273–280, 2005.

T. Ropinski, F. Steinicke, and K. Hinrichs. Visually Supporting Depth Perception in Angiography Imaging. In *Proc. of International Symposium on Smart Graphics*, pages 93–104, 2006.

T. Ropinski, J.-S. Praßni, J. Roters, and K. Hinrichs. Internal Labels as Shape Cues for Medical Illustration. In *Proc. of Vision, Modeling, and Visualization*, pages 203–212, 2007.

T. Ropinski, J. Kasten, and K. H. Hinrichs. Efficient Shadows for GPU-based Volume Raycasting. In *Int. Conference in Central Europe on Computer Graphics, Visualization and Computer Vision*, pages 17–24, 2008a.

T. Ropinski, J. Meyer-Spradow, S. Diepenbrock, J. Mensmann, and K. H. Hinrichs. Interactive Volume Rendering with Dynamic Ambient Occlusion and Color Bleeding. *Computer Graphics Forum*, 27(2):567–576, 2008b.

T. Ropinski, J. Praßni, F. Steinicke, and K. Hinrichs. Stroke-Based Transfer Function Design. In *Proc. of Volume Graphics*, pages 41–48, 2008c.

T. Ropinski, S. Hermann, R. Reich, M. Schafers, and K. Hinrichs. Multimodal Vessel Visualization of Mouse Aorta PET/CT Scans. *IEEE Transactions on Visualization and Computer Graphics*, 15:1515–1522, 2009.

T. Ropinski, C. Döring, and C. Rezk-Salama. Interactive Volumetric Lighting Simulating Scattering and Shadowing. In *Proc. of IEEE Pacific Visualization*, pages 169–176, 2010a.

T. Ropinski, C. Döring, and C. Rezk Salama. Advanced Volume Illumination with Unconstrained Light Source Positioning. *IEEE Computer Graphics and Applications*, 30(6):29–41, 2010b.

O. Rosanwo, C. Petz, S. Prohaska, H.-C. Hege, and I. Hotz. Dual streamline seeding. In *Proc. of IEEE PacificVis.*, pages 9–16, 2009.

S. E. Rose, J. B. Chalk, M. P. Griffin, A. L. Janke, F. Chen, G. J. McLachan, D. Peel, F. O. Zelaya, H. S. Markus, D. K. Jones, A. Simmons, M. O'Sullivan, J. M. Jarosz, W. Strugnell, D.M. Doddrell, and J. Semple. MRI Based Diffusion and Perfusion Predictive Model to estimate stroke evolution. *Magnetic Resonance Imaging*, 19(8):1043–1053, 2001.

B. R. Rosen, J. W. Belliveau, J. M. Vevea, and T. J. Brady. Perfusion imaging with NMR contrast agents. *Magnetic Resonance in Medicine*, 14(2):249–65, 1990.

C. Rössl, L. Kobbelt, and H.-P. Seidel. Line Art Rendering of Triangulated Surfaces Using Discrete Lines of Curvatures. In *Proc. of Winter School in Computer Graphics (WSCG)*, pages 168–175, 2000.

I. Rössling, C. Cyrus, L. Dornheim, P. Hahn, B. Preim, and A. Boehm. Interaktive Visualisierung von Abständen und Ausdehnungen anatomischer Strukturen für die Interventionsplanung. In *Proc. of Bildverarbeitung für die Medizin (BVM)*, pages 381–385, 2009.

I. Rössling, C. Cyrus, L. Dornheim, A. Boehm, and B. Preim. Fast and flexible distance measures for treatment planning. *International Journal of Computer Assisted Radiology and Surgery*, pages 633–646, 2010.

I. Rössling, J. Dornheim, L. Dornheim, A. Boehm, and B. Preim. The Tumor Therapy Manager - Design, Refinement and Clinical Use of a Software Product for ENT Surgery Planning and Documentation. In *Proc. of Information Processing in Computer-Assisted Interventions (IPCAI)*, pages 1–12, 2011.

M.B. Rosson and J.M. Carroll. *Scenario-based design*. L. Erlbaum Associates Inc., Hillsdale, NJ, USA, 2003.

D. Röttger, S. Müller, and D. Merhof. The BundleExplorer: a focus and context rendering framework for complex fiber distributions. In *Proc. Eurographics Workshop on Visual Computing for Biology and Medicine*, pages 1–8, 2012.

S. Röttger, M. Bauer, and M. Stamminger. Spatialized Transfer Functions. In *Data Visualization (Proc. of Eurographics/IEEE Symposium on Visualization)*, pages 271–278. Eurographics Association, 2005.

F. Roux, D. Ibarrola, M. Tremoulet, Y. Lazorthes, P. Henry, J. Sol, and I. Berry. Methodological and Technical Issues for Integrating Functional Magnetic Resonance Imaging Data in a Neuronavigational System. *Neurosurgery*, 49(5):1145–1156, 2001.

S. Roy, A. Carass, P.-L. Bazin, S. M. Resnick, and J. L. Prince. Consistent segmentation using a Rician classifier. *Medical Image Analysis*, 16(2):524–535, 2012.

G. D. Rubin and S. Napel. Helical CT angiography of renal artery stenosis. *American Journal of Roentgenology*, 168(4):1109–1111, 1997.

G. D. Rubin, M. D. Dake, S. Napel, R. B. Jeffrey Jr, C. H. McDonnell, F. G. Sommer, L. Wexler, and D. M. Williams. Spiral CT of renal artery stenosis: comparison of three-dimensional rendering techniques. *Radiology*, 190(1):181–189, 1994.

D. Rueckert, L.I. Sonoda, C. Hayes, D.L.G. Hill, M.O. Leach, and D.J. Hawkes. Nonrigid registration using free-form deformations: application to breast MR images. *IEEE Transactions on Medical Imaging*, 18(8):712–721, 1999.

J. Ruiz-Alzola, C. F. Westin, S. K. Warfield, C. Alberola, S. Maier, and R. Kikinis. Nonrigid registration of 3D tensor medical data. In *Medical Image Analysis*, 6(2):143–161, 2002.

E. J. Rummeny, P. Reimer, and W. Heindel, editors. *Ganzkörper MR-Tomographie*. Thieme, 2002.

S. Rusinkiewicz. Estimating Curvatures and Their Derivatives on Triangle Meshes. In *Proc. of International Symposium on 3D Data Processing, Visualization and Transmission*, pages 486–493, 2004.

S. Rusinkiewicz, M. Burns, and D. DeCarlo. Exaggerated shading for depicting shape and detail. *ACM Transactions on Graphics*, 25(3):1199–1205, 2006.

C. Russ, C. Kubisch, F. Qiu, W. Hong, and P. Ljung. Real-time Surface Analysis and Tagged Material Cleansing for Virtual Colonoscopy. In *Proc. of Volume Graphics*, pages 29–36, 2010.

G. J. M. Rutten, N. F. Ramsey, P. C. Van Rijen, H. J. Noordmans, and C. W. M. Van Veelen. Development of a functional magnetic resonance imaging protocol for intraoperative localization of critical temporoparietal language areas. *Annals of Neurology*, 51(3):350–360, 2002.

P. Sabella. A Rendering Algorithm for Visualizing 3D Scalar Fields. In *Proc. of ACM SIGGRAPH*, pages 51–58, 1988.

I. Sabo-Napadensky and O. Amir. Reduction of scattering artifact in multislice CT. In *Proc. of SPIE Medical Imaging: Physics of Medical Imaging*. SPIE, 2005.

F. B. Sachse. *Computational Cardiology: Modeling of Anatomy, Electrophysiology, and Mechanics*, volume 2966 of *Lecture Notes in Computer Science*. Springer, 2004.

S. Saito, J. Yamanaka, K. Miura, N. Nakao, T. Nagao, T. Sugimoto, T. Hirano, N. Kuroda, Y. Iimuro, and J. Fujimoto. A novel 3D hepatectomy simulation based on liver circulation: Application to liver resection and transplantation. *Hepatology*, 41(6):1297–1304, 2005.

T. Saito and T. Takahashi. Comprehensible rendering of 3-D shapes. In *Proc. of ACM SIGGRAPH*, pages 197–206, 1990.

F. Sakai, G. Gamsu, J.G. Im, and C.S. Ray. Pulmonary function abnormalities in patients with ct-determined emphysema. *Journal of Computer Assisted Tomography*, 11:963–968, 1987.

G. Sakas and S. Walter. Extracting surfaces from fuzzy 3D-ultrasound data. In *Proc. of ACM SIGGRAPH*, pages 465–474, 1995.

Z. Salah, D. Bartz, E. Schwaderer, F. Dammann, and W. Straßer. A Segmentation Pipeline for Robot-Assisted ENT-Surgery. Technical Report WSI-2003-7, Dept. of Computer Science (WSI), University of Tübingen, September 2003.

Z. Salah, M. Kastner, F. Dammann, E. Schwaderer, M. Maassen, D. Bartz, and W. Straßer. Preoperative planning of a complete mastoidectomy: semiautomatic segmentation and evaluation. *International Journal of Computer Assisted Radiology and Surgery*, 1(4):213–222, 2006.

Z. Salah, B. Preim, A. Samii, R. Fahlbusch, and G. Rose. Enhanced Interoperative Visualization for Brain Surgery: A Prototypic Simulation Scenario. In *Proc. of CURAC*, pages 125–130, 2010.

Z. Salah, B. Preim, E. Elolf, J. Franke, and G. Rose. Improved Navigated Spine Surgery Utilizing Augmented Reality Visualization. In *Proc. of Workshop Bildverarbeitung für die Medizin*, pages 319–323, 2011.

Z. Salah, D. Weise, B. Preim, J. Classen, and G. Rose. Navigation-Supported Diagnosis of the Substantia Nigra by Matching Midbrain Sonography and MRI. In *Proc. of SPIE Medical Imaging*, 2012.

J. J. Saleem and A. L. Russ. Current challenges and opportunities for better integration of human factors research with development of clinical information systems. *Yearbook of medical informatics*, 1(4):48–58, 2009.

M. Salisbury, S. E. Anderson, R. Barzel, and D. Salesin. Interactive pen-and-ink illustration. In *Proc. of ACM SIGGRAPH*, pages 101–108, 1994.

M. Salisbury, C. R. Anderson, D. Lischinski, and D. Salesin. Scale-Dependent Reproduction of Pen-and-Ink Illustrations. In *Proc. of ACM SIGGRAPH*, pages 461–468, 1996.

R. Salvador, J. Suckling, M. R. Coleman, J. D. Pickard, D. Menon, and E. Bullmore. Neurophysiological Architecture of Functional Magnetic Resonance Images of Human Brain. *Cerebral Cortex*, 15(9):1332 –1342, 2005.

T. Salzbrunn, H. Jänicke, T. Wischgoll, and G. Scheuermann. The State of the Art in Flow Visualization: Partition-Based Techniques. In *Proc. of SimVis*, pages 75–92, 2008.

P. Saraiya, C. North, and K. Duca. An Insight-Based Methodology for Evaluating Bioinformatics Visualizations. *IEEE Transactions on Visualization and Computer Graphics*, 11(4):443–456, 2005.

L. Saroul, S. Gerlach, and R. D. Hersch. Exploring curved anatomic structures with surface sections. In *Proc. of IEEE Visualization*, 2003.

L. Saroul, O. Figueiredo, and R. D. Hersch. Distance preserving flattening of surface sections. *IEEE Transactions on Visualization and Computer Graphics*, 12(1):26–35, 2006.

R. Satava. The Operating Room of the Future: Observations and Commentary. *Seminars in Laparoscopic Surgery*, 10(3):99–105, 2003.

R. M. Satava. Emerging technologies for surgery in the 21st century. *Archives of surgery (Chicago, Ill.: 1960)*, 134(11):1197–1202, 1999.

F. Sauer, F. Wenzel, S. Vogt, Y. Tao, Y. Genc, and A. Bani-Hashemi. Augmented Workspace: Designing an AR Testbed. In *Proc. of IEEE and ACM Int. Symp. On Augmented Reality (ISAR)*, pages 47–53, 2000.

F. Sauer, A. Khamene, B. Bascle, L. Schimmang, F. Wenzel, and S. Vogt. Augmented Reality Visualization of Ultrasound Images: System Description, Calibration, and Feature. In *Proc. of IEEE and ACM International Workshop on Augmented Reality*, page 30, 2001.

G. Saupin, C. Duriez, and S. Cotin. Contact Model for Haptic Medical Simulations. In *Proc. of International Symposium on Biomedical Simulation (ISBMS)*, pages 157–165, 2008.

M. Schaap, A. M. R. Schilham, K. J. Zuiderveld, M. Prokop, E.-J. Vonken, and W. J. Niessen. Fast Noise Reduction in Computed Tomography for Improved 3-D Visualization. *IEEE Transactions on Medical Imaging*, 27(8):1120–1129, 2008.

M. Schaap, C. T. Metz, T. van Walsum, A. G. van der Giessen, A. C. Weustink, N. R. A. Mollet et al. Standardized Evaluation Methodology and Reference Database for Evaluating Coronary Artery Centerline Extraction Algorithms. *Medical Image Analysis*, 13(5):701–714, 2009.

M. Schaap, T. van Walsum, L. Neefjes, C. Metz, E. Capuano, M. de Bruijne, and W. J. Niessen. Robust Shape Regression for Supervised Vessel Segmentation and its Application to Coronary Segmentation in CTA. *IEEE Transactions on Medical Imaging*, 30(11):1974–1986, 2011.

S. Schäfer, C. M. Hentschke, and K. D. Tönnies. Local similarity measures for ROI-based registration of DCE-MRI of the breast. In *Medical Image Understanding and Analysis (MIUA)*, pages 159–163, 2010.

S. Schäfer, U. Preim, S. Glaßer, B. Preim, and K. D. Tönnies. Local similarity measures for lesion registration in dce-mri of the breast. *Annals of the BMVA*, 3:1–13, Dec 2011.

H. Scharsach, M. Hadwiger, A. Neubauer, S. Wolfsberger, and K. Bühler. Perspective isosurface and direct volume rendering for virtual endoscopy applications. In *Data Visualization (Proc. of Eurographics/IEEE Symposium on Visualization)*, pages 315–322, 2006.

P. R. Schauer, W. H. Schwesinger, C. P. Page, R. M. Stewart, B. A. Levine, and K. R. Sirinek. Complications of surgical endoscopy. A decade of experience from a surgical residency training program. *Surgical Endoscopy*, 11(1):8–11, 1997.

A. Schenk, G. Prause, and H.-O. Peitgen. Efficient Semi-Automatic Segmentation of 3D Objects in Medical Images. In *Proc. of Medical Image Computing and Computer-Assisted Intervention (MICCAI)*, volume 1935 of *Lecture Notes in Computer Science*, pages 134–143. Springer, 2000.

A. Schenk, G. P. M. Prause, and H.-O. Peitgen. Local cost Computation for Efficient Segmentation of 3D Objects with Live Wire. In *Proc. of SPIE Medical Imaging*, volume 4322, pages 1357–1364. SPIE, 2001.

M. Scheuering, A. Schenk, A. Schneider, B. Preim, and G. Greiner. Intra-operative Augmented Reality for Minimally Invasive Liver Interventions. In *Proc. of SPIE Medical Imaging*, pages 407–417, 2003.

T. Schiemann, U. Tiede, and K. H. Höhne. Segmentation of the Visible Human for High Quality Volume Based Visualization. *Medical Image Analysis*, 1:263–271, 1997.

C. Schiers, U. Tiede, and K. H. Hoehne:. Interactive 3D-registration of image volumes from different sources. In *Proc. of Computer-Assisted Radiology (CAR)*, volume 6, pages 666–670, 1989.

S. Schlechtweg, T. Germer, and T. Strothotte. RenderBots-Multi-Agent Systems for Direct Image Generation. *Computer Graphics Forum*, 24(2):137–148, 2005.

P. Schlegel, M. Makhinya, and R. Pajarola. Extinction-based Shading and Illumination in GPU Volume Ray-Casting. *IEEE Transactions on Visualization and Computer Graphics*, 17(12):1795–1802, 2011.

H. P. Schlemmer, B. J. Pichler, M. Schmand, Z. Burbar, C. Michel, R. Ladebeck, K. Jattke, D. Townsend, C. Nahmias, P.K. Jacob, W.D. Heiss, and C.D. Claussen. Simultaneous MR/PET imaging of the human brain: feasibility study. *Radiology*, 248(3):1028–1035, 2008.

C. Schlick. A Customizable Reflectance Model for Everyday Rendering. In *Eurographics Workshop on Rendering*, 1993.

T. Schlömer, D. Heck, and O. Deussen. Farthest-Point Optimized Point Sets with Maximized Minimum Distance. In *High Performance Graphics*, pages 135–142, 2011.

T. Schlossbauer, G. Leinsinger, A. Wismuller, O. Lange, M. Scherr, A. Meyer-Baese, and M. Reiser. Classification of small contrast enhancing breast lesions in dynamic MRI using a combination of morphological criteria and dynamic analysis based on unsupervised vector-quantization. *Investigative Radiology*, 43(1):56–64, 2008.

M. Schlüter, B. Stieltjes, J. Rexilius, H. K. Hahn, and H.-O. Peitgen. Unique planar color coding of fiber bundles and its application to fiber integrity quantification. In *Proc. of IEEE International Symposium on Biomedical Imaging (ISBI): Nano to Macro*, pages 900–903, 2004.

M. Schlüter, O. Konrad-Verse, H. K. Hahn, B. Stieltjes, J. Rexilius, and H.-O. Peitgen. White matter lesion phantom for diffusion tensor data and its application to the assessment of fiber tracking. In *Proc. of SPIE Medical Imaging: Physiology, Function and Structure from Medical Images*, pages 835–844, 2005.

M. Schlüter, B. Stieltjes, H. K. Hahn, J. Rexilius, O. Konrad-Verse, and H.-O. Peitgen. Detection of tumour infiltration in axonal fibre bundles using diffusion tensor imaging. *The International Journal of Medical Robotics and Computer Assisted Surgery*, 1(3):80–86, 2005.

D. Schmauss, C. Schmitz, A. K. Bigdeli, S. Weber, N. Gerber, A. Beiras-Fernandez et al. Three-dimensional printing of models for preoperative planning and simulation of transcatheter valve replacement. *The annals of thoracic surgery*, 93(2):e31–e33, 2012.

G. P. Schmidt, M. F. Reiser, and A. Baur-Melnyk. Whole-body imaging of the musculoskeletal system: the value of MR imaging. *Skeletal Radiology*, 36(12):1109–1119, 2007.

G. P. Schmidt, M. F. Reiser, and A. Baur-Melnyk. A state-of-the-art pipeline for postmortem CT and MRI visualization: from data acquisition to interactive image interpretation at autopsy. *European Journal of Radiology*, 70(3):393–400, 2009.

K. Schmierer, H.G. Parkes, P.-W. So, S.F. An, S. Brandner, R.J. Ordidge, T.A. Yousry, and D.H. Miller. High field (9.4 tesla) magnetic resonance imaging of cortical grey matter lesions in multiple sclerosis. *BRAIN - A Journal of Neurology*, 133:858–867, 2010.

J. Schneider, M. Kraus, and R. Westermann. GPU-based Real-time Discrete Euclidean Distance Transforms with Precise Error Bounds. In *Proc. of Computer Vision Theory and Applications VISAPP*, pages 435–442, 2009.

P. Schneider. *Endovascular Skills: Guidewire and catheter skills for Endovascular Surgery*. Marcel Dekker, 2003.

J. Schöberl. NETGEN - an advancing front 2D/3D-mesh generator based on abstract rules. *Computing in Visualization and Science*, 1:41–52, 1997.

J.-M. Schoffelen and J. Gross. Source connectivity analysis with MEG and EEG. *Human Brain Mapping*, 30(6):1857–1865, 2009.

J. Schöning, F. Daiber, A. Krüger, and M. Rohs. Using hands and feet to navigate and manipulate spatial data. In CHI *EA: Extended abstracts on Human factors in computing systems (ACM CHI '09)*, pages 4663–4668, 2009.

M. Schott, V. Pegoraro, C. D. Hansen, K. Boulanger, and K. Bouatouch. A Directional Occlusion Shading Model for Interactive Direct Volume Rendering. *Computer Graphics Forum*, 28(3):855–862, 2009.

M. Schott, A.V. Grosset, T. Martin, V. Pegoraro, S. T. Smith, and C. D. Hansen. Depth of Field Effects for Interactive Direct Volume Rendering. *Computer Graphics Forum*, 30(3):941–950, 2011.

M. Schott, T. Martin, A.V.P. Grosset, and C. Brownlee. Combined Surface and Volumetric Occlusion Shading. In *Proc. of IEEE Pacific Visualization*, 2012.

W. Schroeder, K. Martin, and B. Lorensen. *The Visualisation Toolkit*. Kitware, third edition, 2001.

R. Schubert, K. H. Hoehne, A. Pommert, M. Riemer, T. Schiemann, and U. Tiede. Spatial Knowledge Representation for Visualization of Human Anatomy and Function. In *Proc. of Information Processing in Medical Imaging*, volume 687 of *Lecture Notes in Computer Science*, pages 168–181. Springer, 1993.

M. Schulder, J. A Maldjian, W. C Liu, A. I Holodny, A. T Kalnin, I. K Mun, and P. W Carmel. Functional image-guided surgery of intracranial tumors located in or near the sensorimotor cortex. *Journal of neurosurgery*, 89(3):412–418, 1998.

T. Schultz and G. Kindlmann. A Maximum Enhancing Higher-Order Tensor Glyph. *Computer Graphics Forum*, 29(3):1143–1152, 2010.

T. Schultz, J. Weickert, and H.-P. Seidel. A Higher-Order Structure Tensor. In D. Laidlaw and J. Weickert, editors, *Visualization and Processing of Tensor Fields*, Mathematics and Visualization, pages 263–279. Springer Berlin Heidelberg, 2009.

F. Schulze, K. Bühler, and M. Hadwiger. Interactive Deformation and Visualization of Large Volume Datasets. In *Proc. of Computer Graphics Theory and Applications (GRAPP)*, pages 39–46, 2007.

F. Schulze, K. Bühler, A. Neubauer, A. Kanitsar, L. Holton, and S. Wolfsberger. Intra-operative virtual endoscopy for image guided endonasal transsphenoidal pituitary surgery. *International Journal of Computer Assisted Radiology and Surgery*, 5(2):143–154, 2010.

J. P. Schulze and A. Rice. Real-Time Volume Rendering of Four Channel Data Sets. In *Proc. of IEEE Visualization*, pages 598.34, 2004.

J. Schulze-Döbold, U. Wössner, S. P. Walz, and U. Lang. Volume rendering in a virtual environment. In *Proc. of the 7th Eurographics conference on Virtual Environments & 5th Immersive Projection Technology*, EGVE'01, pages 187–198, 2001.

C. Schumann, S. Oeltze, R. Bade, B. Preim, and H.-O. Peitgen. Model-free Surface Visualization of Vascular Trees. In *Data Visualization (Proc. of Eurographics/IEEE Symposium on Visualization)*, pages 283–290, 2007.

C. Schumann, M. Neugebauer, R. Bade, B. Preim, and H.-O. Peitgen. Implicit Vessel Surface Reconstruction for Visualization and Simulation. In *International Journal of Computer Assisted Radiology and Surgery*, volume 2(5), pages 275–286, 2008.

B. Schwald, H. Seibert, and T. Weller. A Flexible Tracking Concept Applied to Medical Scenarios Using an AR Window. In *Proc. of IEEE and ACM International Symposium on Mixed and Augmented Reality*, pages 261–262, 2002.

T. Schwarz, T. Heimann, R. Tetzlaff, A.-M. Rau, I. Wolf, and H.-P. Meinzer. Interactive surface correction for 3D shape based segmentation. In *Proc. of SPIE Medical Imaging*, volume 6914, 2008.

M. Schwenke, A. Hennemuth, B. Fischer, and O. Friman. Blood Flow Computation in Phase-Contrast MRI by Minimal Paths in Anisotropic Media. In *Proc. of Medical Image Computing and Computer-Assisted Intervention (MICCAI)*, pages 436–443, 2011.

N. F. Schwenzera, L. Stegger, S. Bisdas, C. Schraml, A. Kolb, A. Boss, M. Müller, M. Reimold, U. Ernemann, C. D. Claussen, C. Pfannenberg, and H. Schmidt. Simultaneous PET/MR imaging in a human brain PET/MR system in 50 patients: Current state of image quality. *European Journal of Radiology*, 81(11):3472–3478, 2012.

B. Schwerdtfeger, D. Pustka, A. Hofhauser, and G. Klinker. Using laser projectors for augmented reality. In *Proceedings of the 2008 ACM symposium on Virtual reality software and technology*, VRST '08, pages 134–137, 2008.

M. Schwier, J. H. Moltz, and H.-O. Peitgen. Object-based analysis of CT images for automatic detection and segmentation of hypodense liver lesions. *International Journal of Computer Assisted Radiology and Surgery*, 6(6):737–747, 2011.

A. Secord. Weighted Voronoi stippling. In *Proc. of Symposium on Non-Photorealistic Animation and Rendering (NPAR)*, pages 37–43, 2002.

M. Seemann, O. Seemann, H. Bonel, M. Suckfüll, K. Englmeier, A. Naumann, C. Allen, and M.F. Reiser. Evaluation of the middle and inner ear structures: comparison of hybrid rendering, virtual endoscopy and axial 2D source images. *European Radiology*, 9(9):1432–1458, 1999.

H. Seim, D. Kainmueller, M. Heller, H. Lamecker, S. Zachow, and H.-C. Hege. Automatic Segmentation of the Pelvic Bones from CT Data Based on a Statistical Shape Model. In *Proc. of Eurographics Workshop on Visual Computing in Biology and Medicine (VCBM)*, pages 93–100, 2008.

H. Seim, D. Kainmueller, M. Heller, S. Zachow, and H.-C. Hege. Automatic Extraction of Anatomical Landmarks from Medical Image Data: An Evaluation of Different Methods. In *Proc. of ISBI*, pages 538–541, 2009.

H. Seim, D. Kainmueller, H. Lamecker, M. Bindernagel, J. Malinowski, and S. Zachow. Model-based Auto-Segmentation of Knee Bones and Cartilage in MRI Data. In *Proc. of MICCAI Workshop Medical Image Analysis for the Clinic: A Grand Challenge*, pages 215–223, 2010.

S. I. Seldinger. Catheter replacement of the needle in percutaneous arteriography; a new technique. *Acta Radiologica*, 39(5):368–376, 1953.

D. Selle, W. Spindler, B. Preim, and H.-O. Peitgen. *Mathematics Unlimited: Springers Special Book for the World Mathematical Year 2000*, chapter Mathematical Methods in Medical Image Processing: Vessel analysis for Preoperative Planning in Liver Surgery, pages 1039–1059. Springer, 2000.

D. Selle, B. Preim, A. Schenk, and H.-O. Peitgen. Analysis of Vasculature for Liver Surgery Planning. *IEEE Transactions on Medical Imaging*, 21(11):1344–1357, 2002.

K.-S. Seo. Automatic Hepatic Tumor Segmentation Using Composite Hypotheses. In *Proc. of International Conference on Image Analysis and Recognition (ICIAR)*, LNCS, pages 922–929. Springer, 2005.

Y. Seppenwoolde, H. Shirato, K. Kitamura, S. Shimizu, M. van Herk, J.V. Lebesque, and K. Miyasaka. Precise and real-time measurement of 3D tumor motion in lung due to breathing and heartbeat, measured during radiotherapy. *Journal of Computer Assisted Tomography*, 53(4):822–834, 2002.

P. Sereda, A. Vilanova Bartrolí, I. Serlie, and F. A. Gerritsen. Visualization of Boundaries in Volumetric Data Sets Using LH Histograms. *IEEE Transactions on Visualization and Computer Graphics*, 12(2):208–218, 2006a.

P. Sereda, A. Vilanova, and F. A. Gerritsen. Mirrored LH Histograms for the Visualization of Material Boundaries. In *Proc. of Vision, Modeling, and Visualization*, pages 237–244, 2006b.

I. Serlie, F. Vos, R. van Gelder, J. Stoker, R. Truyen, F. Gerritsen, Y. Nio, and F. Post. Improved visualization in virtual colonoscopy using image-based rendering. In *Data Visualization (Proc. of Eurographics/IEEE Symposium on Visualization)*, pages 137–146, 2001.

I. Serlie, R. Truyen, J. Florie, F. H. Post, L. J. van Vliet, and F. Vos. Computed Cleansing for Virtual Colonoscopy Using a Three-Material Transition Model. In *Proc. of Medical Image Computing and Computer-Assisted Intervention (MICCAI)*, Volume 2, pages 175–183, 2003.

J. Serra. *Image Analysis and Mathematical Morphology*. Academic Press, London, 1982.

S. Seshadhri, G. Janiga, O. Beuing, M. Skalej, and D. Thévenin. Impact of Stents and Flow Diverters on Hemodynamics in Idealized Aneurysm Models. *Journal of Biomechanical Engineering*, 133(7):071005/1–9, 2011.

J. A. Sethian. *Level Set Methods and Fast Marching Methods*. Cambridge University Press, Cambridge, 1999.

R. Shahidi, B. Wang, M. Epitaux, R. P. Grzeszczuk, and J. R. Adler Jr. Volumetric Image Guidance via a Stereotactic Endoscope. In *Proc. of Medical Image Computing and Computer-Assisted Intervention (MICCAI)*, pages 241–252, 1998.

R. Shamir, I. Tamir, E. Dabool, L. Joskowicz, and Y. Shoshan. A Method for Planning Safe Trajectories in Image-Guided Keyhole Neurosurgery. In *Proc. of Medical Image Computing and Computer-Assisted Intervention (MICCAI)*, volume 6363 of LNCS, pages 457–464, 2010.

R. Shen, P. Boulanger, and M. Noga. MedVis: A Real-Time Immersive Visualization Environment for the Exploration of Medical Volumetric Data. In *Proc. of BioMedical Visualization (MEDIVIS '08)*, pages 63–68, 2008.

W. Shen and A. Pang. Anisotropy based seeding for hyperstreamline. *IASTED Computer Graphics and Imaging (CGIM)*, 2004.

Y. Shen, H. K. Kang, Y. Y. Jeong, S. H. Heo, S. M. Han, K. Chen, and Y. Liu. Evaluation of early gastric cancer at multidetector CT with multiplanar reformation and virtual endoscopy. *Radiographics*, 31(1):189–199, 2011.

D. M. Shepard, M. C. Ferris, G. Olivera, and T. R. Mackie. Optimizing the delivery of radiation to cancer patients. *SIAM Review*, 41:721–744, 1999.

J. F. Shepherd, S. A. Mitchell, P. M. Knupp, and D. R. White. Methods for Multisweep Automation. In *Proc. of International Meshing Roundtable (IMR)*, pages 77–87, 2000.

L. Shepp and B. Logan. The Fourier Reconstruction of a Head Section. *IEEE Transactions on Nuclear Science*, 21:21–43, 1974.

A. Sherbondy, D. Akers, R. Mackenzie, R. Dougherty, and B. Wandell. Exploring connectivity of the brain's white matter with dynamic queries. *IEEE Transactions on Visualization and Computer Graphics*, 11(4):419–430, 2005a.

A. J. Sherbondy, D. Holml, G.D. Rubin, P. K. Schraedley, T. Winograd, and S. Napel. Alternative input devices for efficient navigation of large CT angiography data sets. *J. Am. Med. Inform. Assoc.*, 234(2):391–398, 2005b.

W. Sherman and A. Craig. *Understanding Virtual Reality*. Morgan Kaufmann Publishers, San Francisco, 2003.

J. Shi and J. Malik. Normalized cuts and image segmentation. *IEEE Transactions on Pattern Analysis and Machine Intelligence*, 22(8):888–905, 2000.

K. Shi, H. Theisel, H. Hauser, T. Weinkauf, K. Matkovic, H.-C. Hege, and H.-P. Seidel. Path Line Attributes - an Information Visualization Approach to Analyzing the Dynamic Behavior of 3D Time-Dependent Flow Fields. In *Proc. Topo-In-Vis 2007*, 2007.

J. S. Shimony, D. Zhang, J. M. Johnston, M. D. Fox, A. Roy, and E. C. Leuthardt. Resting State Spontaneous Fluctuations in Brain Activity: A New Paradigm for Presurgical Planning using fMRI. *Academic Radiology*, 16(5):578, 2009.

H. Shin, B. King, M. Galanski, and H. K. Matthies. Development of an intuitive graphical user interface for volume rendering of multidetector CT data. In *Proc. of Computer Assisted Radiology and Surgery*, volume 1256 of *International Congress Series*, pages 264–269. Elsevier, 2003.

M. Shiozawa, N. Sata, K. Endo, M. Koizumi, Y. Yasuda, H. Nagai, and H. Takakusaki. Preoperative virtual simulation of adrenal tumors. *Abdominal Imaging*, 34(1):113–120, 2009.

P. Shirley and A. Tuchman. A polygonal approximation to direct scalar volume rendering. In *Proc. of the workshop on Volume visualization*, pages 63–70, 1990.

B. Shneiderman. *Designing the User Interface*. Addison Wesley, 3 edition, 1997.

B. Shneiderman. *Designing the User Interface: Strategies for Effective Human-Computer Interaction, 4th Edition*. Addison Wesley, 2004.

B. Shneiderman and B. Bederson. *The Craft of Information Visualization*. Morgan Kaufmann, 2003.

B. Shneiderman and C. Plaisant. *Designing the User Interface: Strategies for Effective Human Computer Interaction*. Addison Wesley, 5th edition, 2009.

D. Sibbing, H.-C. Ebke, K. I. Esser, and L. Kobbelt. Topology Aware Quad Dominant Meshing for Vascular Structures. In *Proc. of Mesh Processing in Medical Image Analysis (MeshMed)*, pages 147–158, 2012.

J. Siebert, T. Rosenbaum, and J. Pernicone. Automated Segmentation and Presentation Algorithms for 3D MR Angiography (Poster Abstract). In *Proc. of 10th Annual Meeting of the Society of Magnetic Resonance in Medicine*, page Poster 758, 1991.

D. Sieger and M. Botsch. Design, Implementation, and Evaluation of the Surface mesh Data Structure. In *Proc. of International Meshing Roundtable*, pages 533–550, 2011.

T. Sielhorst, M. Feuerstein, J. Traub, O. Kutter, and N. Navab. Campar: A software framework guaranteeing quality for medical augmented reality. *International Journal of Computer Assisted Radiology and Surgery*, 1(Supplement 1):29–30, 2006.

T. Sielhorst, M. Feuerstein, and N. Navab. Advanced Medical Displays: A Literature Review of Augmented Reality. *IEEE/OSA Journal of Display Technology; Special Issue on Medical Displays*, 4(4):451–467, 2008.

R. Sierra, M. Bajka, and G. Székely. Evaluation of Different Pathology Generation Strategies for Surgical Training Simulators. In *Proc. of Computer Assisted Radiology and Surgery*, pages 376–381, 2003.

R. Sierra, M. Bajka, C.Karadogan, G. Székely, and M.Harders. Coherent Scene Generation for Surgical Simulators. In *Proc. of Medical Simulation Symposium*, 3078, pages 221–229, June 2004.

S. S. Silva, B. S. Santos, J. Madeira, A. Silva, and A. Silva. A 3D tool for left ventricle segmentation editing. In *Proc. of International Conference on Image Analysis and Recognition Image Analysis and Recognition (ICIAR)*, pages 79–88, 2010.

M. Silvestri, M. Simi, C. Cavallotti, M. Vatteroni, V. Ferrari, C. Freschi, P. Valdastri, A. Menciassi, and P. Dario. Autostereoscopic three-dimensional viewer evaluation through comparison with conventional interfaces in laparoscopic surgery. *Surg. Innov.*, 18(3):223–230, 2011.

J. A. Simoes and M. A. Vaz. 4D Flow MR Imaging. *Journal of Engineering in Medicine*, 216(5):341–346, 2002.

A. Singh, D. Goldgof, and D. Terzopoulos. *Deformable Models in Medical Image Analysis*. IEEE Computer Society, 1999.

S. K. Singh, M. Bostrom, D. O. Popa, and C. W. Wiley. Design of an Interactive Lumbar Puncture Simulator with Tactile Feedback. In *Proc. of International Conference on Robotics and Automation (ICRA)*, pages 1734–1739, 1994.

J. G. Sled, A. P. Zijdenbos, and A. C. Evans. A nonparametric method for automatic correction of intensity nonuniformity in MRI data. *IEEE Transactions on Medical Imaging*, 17(1):87–97, 1998.

P. P. Sloan, J. Kautz, and J. Snyder. Precomputed Radiance Transfer for Real-Time Rendering in Dynamic, Low-Frequency Lighting Environments. In *Proc. of ACM SIGGRAPH*, pages 527–536, 2002.

M. Smelyanskiy, D. Holmes, J. Chhugani, A. Larson, D. M. Carmean, D. Hanson, P. Dubey, K. Augustine, D. Kim, A. Kyker, V. W. Lee, A. D. Nguyen, L. Seiler, and R. Robb. Mapping High-Fidelity Volume Rendering for Medical Imaging to CPU, GPU and Many-Core Architectures. *IEEE Transactions on Visualization and Computer Graphics*, 15:1563–1570, 2009.

N. N. Smit, A. C. Kraima, D. Jansma, M. C. de Ruiter, and C. P. Botha. A unified representation for the model-based visualization of heterogeneous anatomy data. In *Proc. of EuroVis Short Papers*, pages 85–89, 2012.

J. S. Sobel, A. S. Forsberg, D. H. Laidlaw, R. C. Zeleznik, D. F. Keefe, I. Pivkin, G. E. Karniadakis, P. Richardson, and S. Swartz. Particle Flurries: Synoptic 3D Pulsatile Flow Visualization. *IEEE Computer Graphics and Applications*, 24(2):76–85, 2004.

P. Soille and H. Talbot. Directional morpholgical filtering. *IEEE Transactions on Pattern Analysis and Machine Intelligence*, 23(11):1313–1329, 2001.

J. E. Solem, M. Persson, and A. Heyden. Velocity Based Segmentation in Phase Contrast MRI Images. In *Proc. of Medical Image Computing and Computer-Assisted Intervention (MICCAI) (1)*, pages 459–466, 2004.

L. Soler, H. Delingette, G. Malandain, J. Montagnat, N. Ayache, C. Koehl, O. Dourthe, B. Malassagne, M. Smith, D. Mutter, and J. Marescaux. Fully automatic anatomical, pathological, and functional segmentation from CT scans for hepatic surgery. *Computer Aided Surgery*, 6(3):131–142, 2001.

P. M. Som, H. D. Curtin, and A. A. Mancuso. An imaging-based classification for the cervical nodes designed as an adjunct to recent clinically based nodal classifications. *Arch. Otolaryngol. Head Neck Surg.*, 125(4):388–396, 1999.

T. Song, V. Lee, H. Rusinek, S. Wong, and A. Laine. Integrated four dimensional registration and segmentation of dynamic renal MR images. In *Proc. of Medical Image Computing and Computer-Assisted Intervention (MICCAI)*, volume 4191, pages 758–765. Springer, 2006.

M. Sonka and J. M. Fitzpatrick. *Handbook of Medical Imaging*, volume 2. SPIE Press, Bellingham, Washington, USA, 2000.

M. Sonka, V. Hlavac, and R. Boyle. *Image Processing, Analysis, and Machine Vision*. Brooks-Cole, 2 edition, 1999.

H. Sonnet, S. Carpendale, and T. Strothotte. Integrating expanding annotations with a 3D explosion probe. In *Proc. of Advanced visual interfaces (AVI)*, pages 63–70, 2004.

A.G. Sorensen, W.A. Copen, L. Ostergaard, F.S. Buonanno, R.G. Gonzalez, G. Rordorf, B.R. Rosen, L.H. Schwamm, R.M. Weisskoff, and W.J. Koroshetz. Hyperacute Stroke: Simultaneous Measurement of Relative Cerebral Blood Volume, Relative Cerebral Blood Flow, and Mean Tissue Transit Time. *Radiology*, 210(2):519–527, 1999.

T. Sørensen and J. Mosegaard. An Introduction to GPU Accelerated Surgical Simulation. In *Biomedical Simulation*, volume 4072 of LNCS, pages 93–104, 2006.

M. C. Sousa, D. S. Ebert, D. Stredney, and N. A. Svakhine. Illustrative Visualization for Medical Training. In *Computational Aesthetics*, pages 201–208, 2005.

G. Soza, M. Bauer, P. Hastreiter, C. Nimsky, and G. Greiner. Non-rigid Registration with Use of Hardware-Based 3D Bézier Functions Source. In *Proc. of Medical Image Computing and Computer-Assisted Intervention (MICCAI)*, volume 2489 (1) of *Lecture Notes in Computer Science*, pages 549–556. Springer, 2002.

G. Sparacia, F. Bencivinni, A. Banco, C. Sarno, T. V. Bartolotta, and R. Lagalla R. Imaging processing for CT angiography of the cervicocranial arteries: evaluation of reformatting technique. *Radiol. Med.*, 112(2):224–238, 2007.

J. Spillmann and M. Harders. Inextensible elastic rods with torsional friction based on Lagrange multipliers. *Journal of Visualization and Computer Animation*, 21(6):561–572, 2010.

J. Spillmann and M. Teschner. Cosserat Nets. *IEEE Transactions on Visualization and Computer Graphics*, 15(2):325–338, 2009.

J. Spillmann, M. Becker, and M. Teschner. Efficient updates of bounding sphere hierarchies for geometrically deformable models. *Journal of Visual Communication and Image Representation*, 18(2):101–108, 2007.

V. M. Spitzer and M. J. Ackerman. The visible human at the university of colorado 15 years later. *Virtual Reality*, 12(4):191–200, 2008.

V. M. Spitzer, M. J. Ackerman, A. L. Scherzinger, and D. Whitlock. The visible human male: A technical report. *J. Am. Med. Inform. Assoc.*, 3(2):118–130, 1996.

O. Sporns, D. R. Chialvo, M. Kaiser, and C. C. Hilgetag. Organization, development and function of complex brain networks. *Trends in Cognitive Sciences*, 8(9):418–425, 2004.

O. Sporns, G. Tononi, and R. Kötter. The human connectome: A structural description of the human brain. *PLoS Comput. Biol.*, 1(4):e42, 2005.

D. Stalling and H.-C. Hege. Fast and resolution independent line integral convolution. In *Proc. of ACM SIGGRAPH*, pages 249–256, 1995.

D. Stalling, M. Seebass, and S. Zachow. Mehrschichtige Oberflächenmodelle zur computergestützten Planung in der Chirurgie. In *Proc. of Workshop Bildverarbeitung für die Medizin*, pages 203–207, 1999.

D. Stalling, M. Westerhoff, and H.-C. Hege. *The Visualization Handbook*, chapter Amira: A highly interactive system for visual data analysis, pages 749–767. Elsevier Academic Press, 2005.

D. Staneker, D. Bartz, and M. Meißner. Improving Occlusion Query Efficiency with Occupancy Maps. In *Proc. of IEEE Symposium on Parallel and Large Data Visualization and Graphics*, pages 111–118, 2003.

D. Staneker, D. Bartz, and W. Straßer. Occlusion Culling in OpenSG PLUS. *Computers & Graphics*, 28(1):87–92, 2004.

D. Staneker, D. Bartz, and W. Straßer. Occlusion-driven scene sorting for efficient culling. In *Proc. of Computer graphics, virtual reality, visualisation and interaction in Africa*, pages 99–106, 2006.

L.J. Stapleford, J.D. Lawson, C. Perkins, S. Edelman, L. Davis, M.W. McDonald, A. Waller, Schreibmann E., and Fox T. Effects of middle-ear static pressure on pars tensa and pars flaccida of gerbil ears. *Int. J. Radiat. Oncol. Biol. Phys.*, 77(3):959–966, 2010.

R. Steenblik. The chromostereoscopic process: A novel single image stereoscopic process. In *Proc. of SPIE - True 3D Imaging Techniques and Display Technologies*, 1987.

S. Stegmaier, M. Magallïoen, and T. Ertl. A Generic Solution for Hardware-Accelerated Remote Visualization. In *Data Visualization (Proc. of Eurographics/IEEE Symposium on Visualization)*, pages 87–94, 2002.

S. Stegmaier, M. Strengert, T. Klein, and T. Ertl. A simple and flexible Volume Rendering Framework for Graphics-Hardware-Based Raycasting. *Proc. of Volume Graphics*, pages 187–195, 2005.

M. B. Stegmann, R. Fisker, B. K. Ersboll, H. H. Thodberg, and L. Hyldstrup. Active appearance models: Theory and Cases. In *Proc. of 9th Danish Conference on Pattern Recognition and Image Analysis*, volume 1, pages 49–57, 2000.

T. Stein and X. Décoret. Dynamic label placement for improved interactive exploration. In *Proc. of Non-photorealistic animation and rendering*, NPAR '08, pages 15–21, 2008.

S. Steppacher, J. Kowal, and S. Murphy. Improving Cup Positioning Using a Mechanical Navigation Instrument. *Clinical Orthopaedics and Related Research®*, 469(2):423–428, 2011.

L. Østergaard, R. M. Weisskoff, D. A Chesler, C. Gyldensted, and B. R. Rosen. High resolution measurement of cerebral blood flow using intravascular tracer bolus passages. part i: mathematical approach and statistical analysis. *Magnetic Resonance in Medicine*, 36:715–725, 1996.

A. J. Stewart. Vicinity Shading for Enhanced Perception of Volumetric Data. In *Proc. of IEEE Visualization*, pages 355–362, 2003.

T. Stewart and D. Trevis. *The Human Computer Interaction Handbook*, chapter Guidelines, Standards and Styleguides, pages 991–1005. Lawrence Erlbaum, 2003.

E. Stindel, J. L. Briard, P. Merloz, S. Plaweski, F. Dubrana, C. Lefevre, and J. Troccaz. Bone morphing: 3D morphological data for total knee arthroplasty. *Computer Aided Surgery*, 7(3):156–168, 2002.

R. Stokking, K. Zuiderveld, and M. A Viergever. Integrated volume visualization of functional image data and anatomical surfaces using normal fusion. *Human Brain Mapping*, 12(4):203–218, 2001.

R. Stokking, I. G. Zubal, and M. A Viergever. Display of fused images: methods, interpretation, and diagnostic improvements. *Seminars in Nuclear Medicine*, 33(3):219–227, 2003.

C. Stoll, S. Gumhold, and H.-P. Seidel. Visualization with stylized line primitives. In *Proc. of IEEE Visualization*, pages 88–95, 2005.

D. Stoyanov, M. ElHelw, B. P. Lo, A. Chung, F. Bello, and G.-Z. Yang. Current Issues of Photorealistic Rendering for Virtual and Augmented Reality in Minimally Invasive Surgery. In *Proc. of Information Visualization*, pages 350–358, 2003.

R. Stramare, G. Scattolin, V. Beltrame, M. Gerardi, M. Sommavilla, C. Gatto, P. Mosca, L. Rubaltelli, C. R. Rossi, and C. Saccavini. Structured reporting using a shared indexed multilingual radiology lexicon. *International Journal of Computer Assisted Radiology and Surgery*, 7(4):621–633, 2012.

G. Strauss, K. Koulechov, R. Richter, A. Dietz, C. Trantakis, and T. Lüth. Navigated control in functional endoscopic sinus surgery. *International Journal of Medical Robotics and Computer Assisted Surgery*, 1(3):31–41, 2005.

G. Strauss, K. Koulechov, M. Hofer, E. Dittrich, R. Grunert, H. Moeckel et al. The navigation-controlled drill in temporal bone surgery: a feasibility study. *Laryngoscope*, 117(3):434–441, 2007.

G. Strauß, N. Bahrami, A. Pössneck, M. Strauß, A. Dietz, W. Korb et al. Evaluation eines trainingssystems für die felsenbeinchirurgie mit opto-elektrischer detektion. *HNO*, 57:999–1009, 2009.

G. Strauß, E. Limpert, M. Fischer, M. Hofer, C. Kubisch, A. Krüger, A. Dietz, J. Meixensberger, C. Trantakis, M. Strauß, and B. Preim. Virtual endoscopy of the nose and paranasal sinuses in real-time. Surgical planning system - Sinus endoscopy. HNO, 57(8):789–796, 2009.

T. Strothotte and S. Schlechtweg. *Non-Photorealistic Computer Graphics: Modeling, Rendering, and Animation*. Morgan Kaufmann, San Francisco, 2002.

R. Strzodka and A. Telea. Generalized Distance Transforms and Skeletons in Graphics Hardware. In *Data Visualization (Proc. of Eurographics/IEEE Symposium on Visualization)*, pages 221–230. Eurographics Association, 2004.

R. Strzodka, M. Droske, and M. Rumpf. Image registration by a regularized gradient flow - a streaming implementation in dx9 graphics hardware. *Computing*, 73(4):373–389, 2004.

M. Styner, G. Gerig, C. Brechbühler, and G. Székely. Parametric estimate of intensity inhomogeneities applied to MRI. *IEEE Transactions on Medical Imaging*, 19(3):153–165, 1998.

S. Succi. *The Lattice Boltzmann Equation for Fluid Dynamics and Beyond*. Oxford University Press, 2001.

P. Suetens. *Foundations of Medical Imaging*. Cambridge University Press, Cambridge, UK, 2002.

M. C. Sukop and D. T. Thorne. *Lattice Boltzmann Modeling: An Introduction for Geoscientists and Engineers*. Springer, 2007.

C. Sun and L. L. Munn. Lattice Boltzmann simulation of blood flow in digitized vessel networks. *Comput. Math. Appl.*, 55(7):1594–1600, 2008.

Y. Sun, M. Y. Sy, Y. X. Wang, A.T. Ahuja, Y.T. Zhang, and E. Pickwell-Macpherson. A promising diagnostic method: Terahertz pulsed imaging and spectroscopy. *World J. Radiol.*, 28:55–65, 2011.

Z. Sun and K.-H. Ng. Coronary computed tomography angiography in coronary artery disease. *World Journal of Cardiology*, 3(9):303–310, 2011.

Z. Sun, S. A. Al Dosari, C. Ng, A. al Muntashari, and S. Almaliky. Multislice CT Virtual Intravascular Endoscopy for Assessing Pulmonary Embolisms: a Pictorial Review. *Korean Journal of Radiology*, 11:222–230, 2010.

E. Sundén, A. Ynnerman, and T. Ropinski. Image Plane Sweep Volume Illumination. *IEEE Transactions on Visualization and Computer Graphics*, 17(12):2125–2134, 2011.

A. Sunguroff and D. Greenberg. Computer generated images for medical applications. *SIGGRAPH Comput. Graph.*, 12(3):196–202, 1978.

J. Süßmuth, W.-D. Protogerakis, A. Piazza, F. Enders, R. Naraghi, G. Greiner, and P. Hastreiter. Color-encoded distance visualization of cranial nerve-vessel contacts. *International Journal of Computer Assisted Radiology and Surgery*, pages 647–654, 2010.

I. E. Sutherland. A head-mounted three dimensional display. In *Proc. of the fall joint computer conference, part I*, AFIPS, pages 757–764, 1968.

L. M. Sutherland, P. F. Middleton, A. Anthony, J. Hamdorf, P. Cregan, D. Scott, and G. J. Maddern. Surgical simulation: a systematic review. *Annals of Surgery*, 243(3):291–300, 2006.

M. Suzuki, Y. Ogawa, A. Kawano, A. Hagiwara, H. Yamaguchi, and H. Ono. Rapid prototyping of temporal bone for surgical training and medical education. *Acta Otolaryngology*, 124(4):400–402, 2004.

N.A. Svakhine, D.S. Ebert, and W.M. Andrews. Illustration-Inspired Depth Enhanced Volumetric Medical Visualization. *IEEE Transactions on Visualization and Computer Graphics*, 15(1):77–86, 2009.

G. R. J. Swennen, W. Mollemans, C. De Clercq, J. Abeloos, P. Lamoral, F. Lippens, N. Neyt, J. Casselman, and F. Schutyser. A Cone-Beam Computed Tomography Triple Scan Procedure to Obtain a Three-Dimensional Augmented Virtual Skull Model Appropriate for Orthognathic Surgery Planning. *Journal of Craniofacial Surgery*, 20(2):297–307, 2009.

N. Taffinder, C. Sutton, and R. J. Fishwick et al. Validation of virtual reality to teach and assess psychomotor skills in laparoscopic surgery: results from randomised controlled studies using the MIST VR laparoscopic simulator. *Stud. Health Technol. Inform.*, 50:124–130, 1998.

T. Takeda, A. Momose, J. Wu, Q. Yu, T. Zeniya, T. T. Lwin, A. Yoneyama, and Y. Itai. Vessel Imaging by Interferometric Phase-Contrast X-Ray Technique. *Circulation*, 105:1708–1712, 2002.

W. Tang, T. R. Wan, D. A. Gould, T. How, and N. W. John. A Stable and Real-Time Nonlinear Elastic Approach to Simulating Guidewire and Catheter Insertions Based on Cosserat Rod. *IEEE Transactions on Biomedical Engineering*, 59(8):2211–2218, 2012.

J. Tao, J. Ma, C. Wang, and C.-K. Shene. A Unified Approach to Streamline Selection and Viewpoint Selection for 3D Flow Visualization. *IEEE Transactions on Visualization and Computer Graphics*, 19(3):393–406, 2013.

A. Tappenbeck, B. Preim, and V. Dicken. Distance-Based Transfer Function Design: Specification Methods and Applications. In *Proc. of Simulation and Visualization*, pages 259–274. SCS, 2006.

M. Tarini, K. Hormann, P. Cignoni, and C. Montani. Polycube-maps. *ACM Transactions on Graphics*, 23(3):853–860, 2004.

T. Tasdizen, R. T. Whitaker, P. Burchard, and S. Osher. Geometric Surface Smoothing via Anisotropic Diffusion of Normals. In *Proc. of IEEE Visualization*, pages 125–132, 2002.

S. Tateshima, Y. Murayama, J. P. Villablanca, T. Morino, H. Takahashi, T. Yamauchi, K. Tanishita, and F. Vinuela. Intraaneurysmal flow dynamics study featuring an acrylic aneurysm model manufactured using a computerized tomography angiogram as a mold. *Journal of Neurosurg*, 95:1020–1027, 2001.

G. Taubin. A signal processing approach to fair surface design. In *Proc. of ACM SIGGRAPH*, pages 351–358, 1995a.

G. Taubin. Estimating the tensor of curvature of a surface from a polyhedral approximation. In *Proc. of the International Conference on Computer Vision (ICCV)*, pages 902–907, 1995b.

M. Tavakoli, R. V. Patel, and M. Moallem. A haptic interface for computer-integrated endoscopic surgery and training. *Virtual Reality*, 9(2):160–176, 2006.

C. A. Taylor, M. T. Draney, J. P. Ku, D. Parker, B. N. Steele, K. Wang, and C. K. Zarins. Predictive medicine: computational techniques in therapeutic decision-making. *Computer Aided Surgery*, 4(5):231–247, 1999.

R. H. Taylor and L. Joskowicz. Computer-integrated surgery and medical robotics. *Standard Handbook of Biomedical Engineering and Design*, pages 325–353, 2002.

R. H. Taylor, J. Funda, L. Joskowicz, A. D. Kalvin, S. H. Gomory, A. P. Gueziec, and L. M. G. Brown. An overview of computer-integrated surgery at the IBM Thomas J. Watson Research Center. *IBM Journal of Research and Development*, 40(2):163–183, 1996.

Z.A. Taylor, M. Cheng, and S. Ourselin. High-Speed Nonlinear Finite Element Analysis for Surgical Simulation Using Graphics Processing Units. *IEEE Transactions on Medical Imaging*, 27(5):650–663, 2008.

R.J. Teather and W. Stuerzlinger. Guidelines for 3D positioning techniques. In *Proc. of Futureplay*, pages 61–68, 2007.

A. Telea and J. J. van Wijk. Simplified Representation of Vector Fields. In *Proc. of IEEE Visualization*, pages 35–42, 1999.

A. Telea and J. J. van Wijk. An augmented Fast Marching Method for computing skeletons and centerlines. In *Data Visualization (Proc. of Eurographics/IEEE Symposium on Visualization)*, pages 251–259. Eurographics Association, 2002.

B. Temkin, E. Acosta, A. Malvankar, and S. Vaidyanath. An interactive three-dimensional virtual body structures system for anatomical training over the internet. *Clinical Anatomy*, 19(3):267–274, 2006.

M. ten Caat, N. M. Maurits, and J. B. T. M. Roerdink. Functional unit maps for data-driven visualization of high-density EEG coherence. In *Data Visualization (Proc. of Eurographics/IEEE Symposium on Visualization)*, pages 259–266, 2007.

D. Tenbrinck, X. Jiang, A. Sawatzky, M. Burger, W. Haffner, P. Willems, M. Paul, and J. Stypmann. Impact of Physical Noise Modeling on Image Segmentation in Echocardiography. In *Proc. of Eurographics Workshop on Visual Computing in Biology and Medicine (VCBM)*, pages 33–40, 2012.

C.-C. Teng, L. G. Shapiro, and I. J Kalet. Automatic segmentation of neck CT images. In *Proc. of the IEEE Symposium on Computer-Based Medical Systems (CBMS)*, pages 442–445, 2006.

C.-C. Teng, L. G. Shapiro, and I. J Kalet. Head and neck lymph node region delineation with image registration. *BioMedical Engineering OnLine*, 9:30, 2010.

B. ter Haar Romeney, editor. *Geometry Driven Diffusion*. Kluwer Academic Publishers, Dordecht, 1994.

M. Termeer, J. O. Bescos, M. Breeuwer, A. Vilanova, F. Gerritsen, and E Gröller. CoViCAD: comprehensive visualization of coronary artery disease. *IEEE Transactions on Visualization and Computer Graphics*, 13(6):1632–1639, 2007.

M. Termeer, J. O. Bescós, M. Breeuwer, A. Vilanova, F. Gerritsen, E. Gröller, and E. Nagel. Visualization of myocardial perfusion derived from coronary anatomy. *IEEE Transactions on Visualization and Computer Graphics*, 14(6):1595–1602, 2008.

D. Terzopoulos, A. Witkin, and M. Kass. Constraints on deformable models: Recovering 3D shape and nonrigid motion. *Artificial Intelligence*, 36(1):91–123, 1988.

M. Teschner, S. Girod, and B. Girod. Direct Computation of Nonlinear Soft-Tissue Deformation. In *Proc. of Vision, Modeling, and Visualization*, pages 383–390, 2000.

M. Teschner, S. Kimmerle, B. Heidelberger, G. Zachmann, L. Raghupathi, and A. Fuhrmann. Collision Detection for Deformable Objects. *Computer Graphics Forum*, 24(1):61–81, 2005.

M. J. Thali, K. Yen, W. Schweitzer, P. Vock, C. Boesch, C. Ozdoba, G. Schroth, M. Ith, M. Sonnenschein, T. Doernhoefer, E. Scheurer, T. Plattner, and R. Dirnhofer. Virtopsy, a new imaging horizon in forensic pathology: virtual autopsy by postmortem multislice computed tomography (MSCT) and magnetic resonance imaging (MRI)–a feasibility study. *Journal of Forensic Science*, 48(2):386–403, 2003.

H. Theisel. Exact Isosurfaces for Marching Cubes. *Computer Graphics Forum*, 21(1):19–31, 2002.

H. Theisel, T. Weinkauf, H.-C. Hege, and H.-P. Seidel. Saddle Connectors - An Approach to Visualizing the Topological Skeleton of Complex 3D Vector Fields. In *Proc. of IEEE Visualization*, pages 225–232, 2003.

H. Theisel, J. Sahner, T. Weinkauf, H.-C. Hege, and H.-P. Seidel. Extraction of Parallel Vector Surfaces in 3D Time-Dependent Fields and Application to Vortex Core Line Tracking. In *Proc. of IEEE Visualization*, pages 80–87, 2005.

P. Thévenaz, T. Blu, and M. Unser. *Handbook of Medical Imaging, Processing and Analysis (Editor I. N. Bankman)*, chapter Image Interpolation and Resampling, pages 393–420. Academic Press, San Diego CA, USA, 2000.

J.-P. Thirion and A. Gourdon. The 3D Marching Lines Algorithm. *CVGIP: Graphical Model and Image Processing*, 58(6):503–509, 1996.

J. J. Thomas and K. A. Cook. *Illuminating the Path: The Research and Development Agenda for Visual Analytics*. IEEE Press, 2005.

R. G. Thomas, N. W. John, and J. M. Delieu. Augmented reality for anatomical education. *Journal of Visual Commununication in Medicine*, 33(1):6–15, 2010.

P. Thompson, K. May, and R. Stone. Chromostereopsis: a multi-component depth effect. *Displays*, 14:227–234, 1993.

U. Tiede, M. Bomans, and K. H. Höhne. A computerized three-dimensional atlas of the human skull and brain. *American Journal of Neuroradiology*, 14(3):551–559, 1993.

U. Tiede, T. Schiemann, and K. H. Höhne. Visualizing the Visible Human. *IEEE Computer Graphics and Applications*, 16(1):7–9, 1996.

U. Tiede, T. Schiemann, and K. H. Höhne. High quality rendering of attributed volume data. In *Proc. of IEEE Visualization*, pages 255–262, 1998.

U. Tiede, N. von Sternberg-Gospos, P. Steiner, and K. H. Höhne. Virtual Endoscopy Using Cubic QuickTime-VR Panorama Views. In *Proc. of Medical Image Computing and Computer-Assisted Intervention (MICCAI)*, pages 186–192, 2002.

C. Tietjen, T. Isenberg, and B. Preim. Combining Silhouettes, Surface, and Volume Rendering for Surgery Education and Planning. In *Data Visualization (Proc. of Eurographics/IEEE Symposium on Visualization)*, pages 303–310, 2005.

C. Tietjen, B. Meyer, S. Schlechtweg, B. Preim, I. Hertel, and G. Strauß. Enhancing Slice-based Visualizations of Medical Volume Data. In *Data Visualization (Proc. of Eurographics/IEEE Symposium on Visualization)*, pages 123–130, 2006.

C. Tietjen, R. Pfisterer, A. Baer, R. Gasteiger, and B. Preim. Hardware-Acceelerated Illustrative Medical Surface Visualization with Extended Shading Maps. In *Proc. of International Symposium on Smart Graphics*, pages 166–177. Springer, 2008.

H. Timinger, V. Pekar, J. von Berg, K. C. J. Dietmayer, and M. Kaus. Integration of Interactive Corrections to Model-Based Segmentation Algorithms. In *Proc. of Bildverarbeitung für die Medizin*, pages 171–175, 2003.

K.-D. Toennies. *Guide to Medical Image Analysis - Methods and Algorithms*. Springer, 2012.

P. Tofts and A. Kermode. Simultaneous MRI measurement of Blood Flow, Blood Volume, and Capillary Permeability in Mamma Tumors using Two Different Contrast Agents. *Journal of Magnetic Resonance Imaging*, 12(6):991–1003, 1991.

B. F. Tomandl, P. Hastreiter, K. E. Eberhardt, C. Rezk-Salama, R. Naraghi, H. Greess, U. Nissen, and W. J. Huk. Virtual labyrinthoscopy: visualization of the inner ear with interactive direct volume rendering. *Radiographics*, 20(2):547–558, 2000.

B. F. Tomandl, T. Hammen, E. Klotz, H. Ditt, B. Stemper, and M. Lell. Bone-subtraction CT angiography for the evaluation of intracranial aneurysms. *Am J Neuroradiol.*, 27(1):55–59, 2006.

C. Tominski, G. Fuchs, and H. Schumann. Task-Driven Color Coding. In *Proc. of the International Conference Information Visualisation*, IV '08, pages 373–380, 2008.

S. Treavett and M. Chen. Pen-and-Ink Rendering in Volume Visualization. In *Proc. of IEEE Visualization*, pages 203–210, 2000.

T. Treichel, M. Gessat, T. Prietzel, and O. Burgert. DICOM for Implantations-Overview and Application. *Journal of Digital Imaging*, 25(3):352–358, 2011.

A. Treisman. Preattentive processing in vision. *Computer Vision, Graphics, and Image Processing*, 31(2):156–177, 1985.

R. Tsai. A versatile camera calibration technique for high-accuracy 3D machine vision metrology using off-the-shelf TV cameras and lenses. *IEEE Journal of Robotics and Automation*, 3(4):323–344, 1987.

J. Tschirren, K. Palagyi, J. M. Reinhardt, E. A. Homan, and M. Sonka. Segmentation, Skeletonization, and Branchpoint Matching - A Fully Automated Quantitative Evaluation of Human Intrathoracic Airway Trees. In *Proc. of Medical Image Computing and Computer-Assisted Intervention (MICCAI)*, volume 2489 of *Lecture Notes in Computer Science*, pages 12–19. Springer, 2002.

D. S. Tuch. Q-ball imaging. *Magnetic Resonance in Medicine*, 52(6):1358–1372, 2004.

D. S. Tuch, R. M. Weisskoff, J. W Belliveau, and V. J. Wedeen. High angular resolution diffusion imaging of the human brain. In *Proc. of the 7th Annual Meeting of ISMRM*, page 321, 1999.

D. S Tuch, T. G. Reese, M. R. Wiegell, N. Makris, J. W Belliveau, and V. J. Wedeen. High angular resolution diffusion imaging reveals intravoxel white matter fiber heterogeneity. *Magnetic Resonance in Medicine*, 48(4):577–582, 2002.

G. Turk and D. Banks. Image-guided streamline placement. In *Proc. of ACM SIGGRAPH*, pages 453–460, 1996.

B. Tversky, J. Morrison, and M. Betrancourt. Animation: can it facilitate? *International Journal of Human-Computer Studies*, 57:247–262, 2002.

T. Twellmann, O. Lichte, and T. W. Nattkemper. An adaptive tissue characterization network for model-free visualization of dynamic contrast-enhanced magnetic resonance image data. *IEEE Transactions on Medical Imaging*, 24(10):1256–1266, 2005.

R. Tyler. Visualization of multiple fields on the same surface. *IEEE Computer Graphics and Applications*, 22(3):6–10, October 2002.

F.-Y. Tzeng, E. B. Lum, and K.-L. Ma. A Novel Interface for Higher-Dimensional Classification of Volume Data. In *Proc. of IEEE Visualization*, pages 505–512, 2003.

J. K. Udupa. *Handbook of Medical Imaging*, volume 3, chapter Three-Dimensional Visualization: Principles and Approaches, pages 5–66. SPIE, 2000.

J. K. Udupa and G. T. Herman. *3D Imaging in Medicine*. CRC Press, 2000.

J. K. Udupa and S. Samarasekera. Fuzzy Connectedness and Object Definition: Theory, Algorithms and Applications in Image Segmentation. *Graphics Models and Image Processing*, 58(3):246–261, 1996.

J. K. Udupa, S. Samarasekera, and W. A. Barrett. Boundary detection via dynamic programming. In *Proc. of Visualization in Biomedical Computing*, volume 1808, pages 33–39. SPIE, 1992.

J. K. Udupa, L. Wei, S. Samarasekera, Y. Miki, M. A. van Buchem, and R. I. Grossman. Multiple Sclerosis Lesion Quantification Using Fuzzy Connectedness Principles. *IEEE Transactions on Medical Imaging*, 16(5):598–609, 1997.

S. Ullrich, O. Grottke, R. Rossaint, M. Staat, T. M. Deserno, and T. Kuhlen. Virtual needle simulation with haptics for regional anaesthesia. In *Proc. of the IEEE Virtual Reality 2010 Workshop on Medical Virtual Envirnoments*, 2010.

C. Upson and M. Keeler. VBUFFER: Visible Volume Rendering. In *Proc. of ACM SIGGRAPH*, pages 59–64, 1988.

C. van Bemmel, L. Spreeuwers, M. Viergever, and W. Niessen. Level-Set Based Carotid Artery Segmentation for Stenosis Grading. In *Proc. of Medical Image Computing and Computer-Assisted Intervention (MICCAI)*, volume 2489 of *Lecture Notes in Computer Science*, pages 36–43. Springer, 2002.

C. M. van Bemmel, L. J. Spreeuwers, M. A. Viergever, and W. J. Niessen. Level-Set Based Artery-Vein Separation in Blood Pool Agent CE-MR Angiograms. *IEEE Transactions on Medical Imaging*, 22(10):1224–1234, 2003.

A. Van Dixhoorn, B. Vissers, L. Ferrarini, J. Milles, and C. P. Botha. Visual analysis of integrated resting state functional brain connectivity and anatomy. In *Proc. of Eurographics Workshop on Visual Computing in Biology and Medicine (VCBM)*, pages 57–64, 2010.

A. F. van Dixhoorn, J. Milles, B. van Lew, and C. P. Botha. BrainCove: a tool for voxel-wise fMRI brain connectivity visualization. In *Proc. of Eurographics Workshop on Visual Computing in Biology and Medicine (VCBM)*, pages 99–106, 2012.

A. van Gelder and K. Kim. Direct Volume Rendering with Shading via Three-dimensional Textures. In *Proc. of IEEE/ACM Symposium on Volume Visualization*, pages 23–30, 1996.

B. van Ginneken, A. F. Frangi, J. Staal, B. M. ter Haar Romeny, and M. A. Viergever. Active shape model segmentation with optimal features. *IEEE Transactions on Medical Imaging*, 21(8):924–933, 2002.

J. J. G. van Merriënboer, R. E. Clark, and M. B. M. de Croock. Blueprints for Complex Learning: The 4C/ID-Model. *Educational Technology Research & Development*, 50(2):39–64, 2002.

P. M. A. van Ooijen, M. Oudkerk, R.J. van Geuns, B.J. Rensing, and P.J. de Feyter. Coronary artery fly-through using electron beam computed tomography. *European Radiology*, 102(1):E6–E10, 2000.

P. M. A. van Ooijen, G. de Jonge, and M. Oudkerk. Coronary fly-through or virtual angioscopy using dual-source MDCT data. *European Radiology*, 17(11):2852–2859, 2007.

R. van Pelt, A. Vilanova, and H. M. M. van de Wetering. GPU-based particle systems for illustrative volume rendering. In *Proc. of Volume Graphics*, pages 89–96, 2008.

R. van Pelt, J. O. Bescós, M. Breeuwer, R. E. Clough, E. Gröller, B. M. ter Haar Romeny, and A. Vilanova. Exploration of 4D MRI Blood Flow using Stylistic Visualization. *IEEE Transactions on Visualization and Computer Graphics*, 16(6):1339–1347, 2010.

R. van Pelt, J. O. Bescós, M. Breeuwer, R. E. Clough, E. Gröller, B. M. ter Haar Romenij, and A. Vilanova. Interactive Virtual Probing of 4D MRI Blood-Flow. *IEEE Transactions on Visualization and Computer Graphics*, 17(12):2153–2162, 2011.

R. van Pelt, A. Fuster, R. Fick, G. Claassen, B. ter Haar Romeny, H. van Assen, and L. Florack. 3D Saddle Point Detection and Applications in Cardiac Imaging. In *Proc. of ISBI*, 2012a.

R. van Pelt, S. Jacobs, B. M. ter Haar Romenij, and A. Vilanova. Visualization of 4D Blood-Flow Fields by Spatiotemporal Hierarchical Clustering. *Computer Graphics Forum*, 31(3):1065–1074, 2012b.

J. C. van Rijn, J. B. Reitsma, J. Stoker, P. M. Bossuyt, S. J. van Deventer, and E. Dekker. Polyp miss rate determined by tandem colonoscopy: a systematic review. *Am J Gastroenterol*, 101(2):343–350, 2006.

B. van Schooten, E. van Dijk, A. Suinesiaputra, and J. Reiber. Interactive navigation of segmented MR angiograms using simultaneous curved planar and volume visualizations. *International Journal of Computer Assisted Radiology and Surgery*, pages 1–9, 2010.

G. vanDenBergen. Efficient collision detection of complex deformable models using AABB trees. *Journal of Graphical Tools*, 2(4):1–14, 1997.

M. W. Vannier, J. L. Marsh, and J. O. Warren. Three Dimensional Computer Graphics for Craniofacial Surgical Planning and Evaluation. In *Proc. of ACM SIGGRAPH*, pages 263–273, 1983a.

M. W. Vannier, G. C. Conroy, J. L. Marsh, and R. H. Knapp. Three-Dimensional Cranial Surface Reconstructions Using High-Resolution Computed Tomography. *American Journal of Physical Anthropology*, 67:299–311, 1985.

Michael W. Vannier, Jeffrey L. Marsh, and James O. Warren. Three dimensional computer graphics for craniofacial surgical planning and evaluation. *SIGGRAPH Comput. Graph.*, 17(3):263–273, 1983b.

L. P. Vardoulakis, A. K. Karlson, D. Morris, G. Smith, J. Gatewood, and D. S. Tan. Using mobile phones to present medical information to hospital patients. In *Proc. of the ACM SIGCHI conference on Human factors in computing systems (CHI)*, pages 1411–1420, 2012.

F. Vega, N. Sauber, B. Tomandl, C. Nimsky, G. Greiner, and P. Hastreiter. Enhanced 3D-Visualization of Intracranial Aneurysms Involving the Skull Base. In *Proc. of Medical Image Computing and Computer-Assisted Intervention (MICCAI)*, volume 2879 of *LNCS*, pages 256–263. Springer, 2003.

F. Vega, N. Sauber, B. Tomandl, C. Nimsky, G. Greiner, and P. Hastreiter. Automatic Adjustment of Bidimensional Transfer Functions for Direct Volume Visualization of Intracranial Aneurysms. In *Proc. of SPIE Medical Imaging*, volume 5367 of *LNCS*, pages 275–284. SPIE Press, 2004.

M. Viceconti. Ct-based surgical planning software improves the accuracy of total hip replacement preoperative planning. *Medical Engineering & Physics*, 25(5):371–377, 2003.

F. P. Vidal, F. Bello, K. W. Brodlie, N. W. John, D. Gould, R. Phillips, and N. J. Avis. Principles and Applications of Computer Graphics in Medicine. *Computer Graphics Forum*, 25(1):113–137, 2006.

F. P. Vidal, N. W. John, A. E. Healey, and D. A. Gould. Simulation of ultrasound guided needle puncture using patient specific data with 3D textures and volume haptics. *Journal of Visualization and Computer Animation*, 19(2):111–127, 2008.

E. Vidholm, S. Nilsson, and I. Nyström. Fast and robust semi-automatic liver segmentation with haptic interaction. In *Proc. of Medical Image Computing and Computer-Assisted Intervention (MICCAI)*, volume 4191 of *LNCS*, pages 774–781. Springer, 2006.

A. Vilanova, A. König, and E. Gröller. VirEn: Virtual Endoscopy System. *Machine Graphics & Vision*, 8(3):469–487, 1999.

A. Vilanova, R. Wegenkittl, A. König, and E. Gröller. Nonlinear virtual colon unfolding. In *Proc. of IEEE Visualization*, Proc. of IEEE Visualization, pages 411–420, 2001.

A. Vilanova, G. Berenschot, and C. van Pul. DTI visualization with streamsurfaces and evenly-spaced volume seeding. In *Data Visualization (Proc. of Eurographics/IEEE Symposium on Visualization)*, pages 173–182, 2004.

A. Vilanova, S. Zhang, G. Kindlmann, and D. Laidlaw. An introduction to visualization of diffusion tensor imaging and its applications. In J. Weickert and H. Hagen, editors, *Visualization and Processing of Tensor Fields*, pages 121–153. Springer Berlin Heidelberg, 2006.

A. Vilanova, B. Preim, R. van Pelt, R. Gasteiger, M. Neugebauer, and T. Wischgoll. Visual Exploration of Simulated and Measured Blood Flow. *Computing Research Repository (CoRR)*, abs/1209.0999, 2012.

G. Vincent, I. Scott C. Wolstenholme, and M. Bowes. Fully Automatic Segmentation of the Knee Joint using Active Appearance Models. In *Proc. of Medical Image Analysis for the Clinic: A Grand Challenge*, pages 224–230, 2010.

L. Vincent and P. Soille. Watersheds in Digital Spaces: an Efficient Algorithm Based on Immersion Simulations. *IEEE Transactions on Pattern Analysis and Machine Intelligence*, 13(6):583–598, 1991.

D. J. Vining, R. Y. Shifrin, E. F. Haponik, K. Liu, and R. H. Choplin. Virtual bronchoscopy. *Radiology, Suppl. P*, 193:261, 1994a.

D. J. Vining, R. Y. Shifrin, E. F. Haponik, K. Liu, and R. H. Choplin. Virtual reality imaging of the airways. *Radiology, Suppl. P*, 193:422, 1994b.

D. J. Vining, K. Liu, R.H. Choplin, and E. F. Haponik. Relationships of virtual reality endobronchial simulations to actual bronchoscopic findings (preliminary report). *Chest*, 109(2):549–553, 1996.

I. Viola and E. Gröller. Smart visibility in visualization. *Proc. of EG Workshop on Computational Aesthetics in Graphics, Visualization and Imaging*, pages 209–216, 2005.

I. Viola, A. Kanitsar, and E. Gröller. Importance-driven volume rendering. In *Proc. of IEEE Visualization*, pages 139–146, 2004.

I. Viola, A. Kanitsar, and E. Gröller. Importance-driven feature enhancement in volume visualization. *IEEE Transactions on Visualization and Computer Graphics*, 11(4):408–418, 2005.

I. Viola, M. Feixas, M. Sbert, and E. Gröller. Importance-driven focus of attention. *IEEE Transactions on Visualization and Computer Graphics*, 12(5):933–940, 2006.

S. Vogt, A. Khamene, F. Sauer, A. Keil, and H. Niemann. A High Performance AR System for Medical Applications. In *Proc. of IEEE and ACM International Symposium on Mixed and Augmented Reality*, pages 270–271, 2003.

J. Vollmer, R. Mencel, and H. Mueller. Improved laplacian smoothing of noisy surface meshes. In *Proc. of Eurographics*, pages 131–138, 1999.

F. Volonte, J. H. Roberta, O. Ratib, and F. Triponeza. A lung segmentectomy performed with 3D reconstruction images available on the operating table with an iPad. *Interactive CardioVascular and Thoracic Surgery*, 12:1066–1070, 2011.

U. von Luxburg. A Tutorial on Spectral Clustering. *Statistics and Computing*, 17(4):395–416, 2007.

F. M. Vos, R. E. van Gelder, I. W. O. Serlie, J. Florie, C. Y. Nio, A. S. Glas, F. H. Post, R. Truyen, F. A Gerritsen, and J. Stoker. Three-dimensional Display Modes for CT colonography: Conventional 3D virtual colonoscopy versus unfolded cube projection1. *Radiology*, 228(3):878–885, 2003.

T. Vrtovec, B. Likar, and F. Pernus. Automated curved planar reformation of 3D spine images. *Physics in medicine and biology*, 50(19):4527–4540, 2005.

V. Šoltészová, D. Patel, S. Bruckner, and I. Viola. A Multidirectional Occlusion Shading Model for Direct Volume Rendering. *Computer Graphics Forum*, 29(3):883–891, 2010.

V. Šoltészová, D. Patel, and I. Viola. Chromatic Shadows for Improved Perception. In *Proc. of Non-Photorealistic Animation and Rendering (NPAR)*, pages 105–115, 2011.

V. Šoltészová, L. Emilie Sævil Helljesen, W. Wein, O. H. Gilja, and I. Viola. Lowest-Variance Streamlines for Filtering of 3D Ultrasound. In *Proc. of Eurographics Workshop on Visual Computing in Biology and Medicine (VCBM)*, pages 41–48, 2012.

E. Vuçini, D. Patel, and E. Gröller. Enhancing Visualization with Real-Time Frequency-based Transfer Functions. In *Proc. of IS&T/SPIE Conference on Visualization and Data Analysis*, 7868, pages 78680L–1–78680L–12, 2011.

C Wagner, N Stylopoulos, and R Howe. Force feedback in surgery: analysis of blunt dissection. In *Proc. of the 10th symposium on haptic interfaces for virtual environment and teleoperator systems*, pages 68–74, 2002.

F. Wagner and A. Wolff. Map labeling heuristics: provably good and practically useful. In *Proc. of the symposium on Computational geometry*, SCG '95, pages 109–118, 1995.

J. Wagner, S. Huot, and W. E. Mackay. BiTouch and BiPad: designing bimanual interaction for hand-held tablets. In *Proc. of the ACM SIGCHI conference on Human factors in computing systems*, pages 2317–2326, 2012.

M. Wan, Z. Liang, Q. Ke, L. Hong, I. Bitter, and A. E. Kaufman. Automatic centerline extraction for virtual colonoscopy. *IEEE Transactions on Medical Imaging*, 21(11):1450–1460, 2002.

D. Wang and J. Bernsdorf. Lattice Boltzmann simulation of steady non-Newtonian blood flow in a 3D generic stenosis case. *Comput. Math. Appl.*, 58(5):1030–1034, 2009.

G. Wang and M. W. Vannier. GI tract unraveling by spiral CT. *Proc. of SPIE Medical Imaging*, 2434(1):307–315, 1995.

G. Wang, G. McFarland, B. P Brown, and M. W. Vannier. GI tract unraveling with curved cross sections. *IEEE Transactions on Medical Imaging*, 17(2):318–322, 1998.

J. Wang, P. Fallavollita, L. Wang, M. Kreiser, and N. Navab. Augmented Reality during Angiography: Integration of a Virtual Mirror for Improved 2D/3D Visualization. In *Proc. of the International Symposium on Mixed and Augmented Reality (ISMAR)*, 2012.

L. Wang, Y. Zhao, K. Müller, and A. Kaufman. The Magic Volume Lens: An Interactive Focus+Context Technique for Volume Rendering. In *Proc. of IEEE Visualization*, pages 367–374, 2005a.

M. Wang, A. Radjenovic, T. W. Stapleton, R. Venkatesh, S. Williams, E. Ingham, J. Fisher, and Z. Jin. A novel and non-destructive method to examine meniscus architecture using 9.4 Tesla MRI. *Osteoarthritis and Cartilage*, 18:1417–1420, 2010.

X. H. Wang, J. E. Durick, A. Lu, D. L. Herbert, S. K. Golla, K. Foley, C. S. Piracha, D. D. Shinde, B. E. Shindel, C. R. Fuhrman, C. A. Britton, D. C. Strollo, S. S. Shang, J. M. Lacomis, and W. F. Good. Characterization of radiologists' search strategies for lung nodule detection: slice-based versus volumetric displays. *Journal of Digital Imaging*, 21(1):39–49, 2008.

Y.-S. Wang and T.-Y. Lee. Curve-Skeleton Extraction Using Iterative Least Squares Optimization. *IEEE Transactions on Visualization and Computer Graphics*, 14(4):926–936, 2008.

Z. Wang, B. Li, and Z. Liang. Feature-based Texture Display for Detection of Colonic Polyps on Flattened Colon Volume. In *Proc. of IEEE Engineering in Medicine and Biology*, 2005b.

L. C. Wanger. The effect of shadow quality on the perception of spatial relationships in computer generated imagery. In *Proc. of Symposium on Interactive 3D graphics*, pages 39–42, 1992.

S. Warach, J. Gaa, B. Siewert, P. Wielopolski, and R. Edelman. Acute human stroke studied by whole brain echo planar diffusion-weighted magnetic resonance imaging. *Ann. Neurol.*, 37(2):231–241, 1995.

C. Ware. Designing with a 2 1/2-D attitude. *Information Design Journal*, 10(3):258–265, 2001.

S. K. Warfield, K. H. Zou, and W. M. Wells. Validation of Image Segmentation and Expert Quality with an Expectation-Maximization Algorithm. In *Proc. of Medical Image Computing and Computer-Assisted Intervention (MICCAI)*, volume 1 of *Lecture Notes in Computer Science*, pages 298–306. Springer, 2002.

D. Wassermann, L. Bloy, E. Kanterakis, R. Verma, and R. Deriche. Unsupervised White Matter Fiber Clustering and Tract Probability Map Generation: Applications of a Gaussian Process framework for white matter fibers. *NeuroImage*, 51(1):228–241, 2010.

K. Waters and D. Terzopoulos. A Physical Model of Facial Tissue and Muscle Articulation. In *Proc. of Visualization in Biomedical Computing*, pages 77–82, 1990.

O. Watzke and W. A. Kalender. A pragmatic approach to metal artefact reduction in CT: merging of metal artefact reduced images. *European Radiology*, 14:849–856, 2004.

S. L. Waxberg, K. H. Goodell, D. V. Avgerinos, S. D. Schwaitzberg, and C. G. L. Cao. Evaluation of physcial versus virtual surgical training simulators. In *Proc. of the Human Factors and Ergonomics Society*, pages 1675–1679, 2004.

S. Weber, M. Klein, A. Hein, T. Krueger, T. Lüth, and J. Bier. The Navigated Image Viewer - Evaluation in Maxillofacial Surgery. In *Proc. of Medical Image Computing and Computer-Assisted Intervention (MICCAI)*, volume 2878 of *Lecture Notes in Computer Science*, pages 762–769, 2003.

V. J. Wedeen, R. P. Wang, J. D. Schmahmann, T. Benner, W. Y. I. Tseng, G. Dai, D. N. Pandya, P. Hagmann, H. D'Arceuil, and A. J. de Crespigny. Diffusion spectrum magnetic resonance imaging (DSI) tractography of crossing fibers. *NeuroImage*, 41(4):1267–1277, 2008.

J. Weese, M. Kaus, C. Lorenz, S. Lobregt, R. Truyen, and V. Pekar. Shape Constrained Deformable Models for 3D Medical Image Segmentation. In *Proc. of Information Processing in Medical Imaging (IPMI)*, pages 380–387, 2001.

R. Wegenkittl and E. Gröller. Fast oriented line integral convolution for vector field visualization via the Internet. In *Proc. of IEEE Visualization*, pages 309–316, 1997.

S. Weghorst, C. Airola, P. Oppenheimer, C. V. Edmond, T. Patience, D. Heskamp, and J. Miller. Validation of the Madigan ESS Simulator. In *Proc. of Medicine Meets VR - Art, Science, Technology: Healthcare (R)Evolution*, pages 399–405, 1998.

J. Weickert. A Review of Nonlinear Diffusion Filtering. In *Scale-Space Theory in Computer Vision*, volume 1252 of *Lecture Notes in Computer Science*, pages 3–28. Springer, 1997.

A. Weihusen, L. Hinrichsen, T. Carus, R. Dammer, R. Rascher-Friesenhausen, T. Kröger, H.-O. Peitgen, and T. Preusser. Towards a Verified Simulation Model for Radiofrequency Ablations. In *Proc. of Information Processing in Computer-Assisted Interventions (IPCAI)*, pages 179–189, 2010.

F. Weiler, C. Rieder, C. A. David, C. Wald, and H. K. Hahn. AVM-Explorer: Multi-Volume Visualization of Vascular Structures for Planning of Cerebral AVM Surgery. In K. Bühler and A. Vilanova, editors, *Proc. of Eurographics 2011 - Dirk Bartz Prize*, pages 9–12. Eurographics Association, 2011.

F. Weiler, C. Rieder, C. A. David, C. Wald, and H. K. Hahn. On the Value of Multi-Volume Visualization for Preoperative Planning of Cerebral AVM Surgery. In *Proc. of Eurographics Workshop on Visual Computing in Biology and Medicine (VCBM)*, pages 49–56. Eurographics Association, 2012.

T. Weinkauf, H. Theisel, K. Shi, H.-C. Hege, and H.-P. Seidel. Extracting Higher Order Critical Points and Topological Simplification of 3D Vector Fields. In *Proc. of IEEE Visualization*, pages 71–78, 2005.

D. Weinstein, G. Kindlmann, and E. Lundberg. Tensorlines: Advection-diffusion based propagation through diffusion tensor fields. In *Proc. of IEEE Visualization*, pages 249–253, 1999.

M. Weiser. Optimization and Identification in Regional Hyperthermia. *International Journal of Applied Electromagnetics and Mechanics*, 30: 265–275, 2009.

D. Weiskopf, U. Kraus, and H. Ruder. Searchlight and Doppler Effects in the Visualization of Special Relativity: A Corrected Derivation of the Transformation of Radiance. *ACM Transactions on Graphics*, 18(3):278–292, 1999.

K. L. Weiss, S. O. Stiving, E. E. Herderick, J.F. Cornhill, and D.W. Chakeres. Hybrid color MR imaging display. *American Journal of Roentgenology*, 149(4):825–829, 1987.

W. M. Wells-III, P. Viola, H. Atsumi, S. Nakajima, and R. Kikinis. Multi-modal volume registration by maximization of mutual information. *Medical Image Analysis*, 1:35–51, 1996.

T. Wendler, A. Hartl, T. Lasser, J. Traub, F. Daghighian, S. I. Ziegler, and N. Navab. Towards Intra-operative 3D Nuclear Imaging: Reconstruction of 3D Radioactive Distributions Using Tracked Gamma Probes. In *Proc. of Medical Image Computing and Computer-Assisted Intervention (MICCAI)*, pages 909–917, 2007.

R. Werner, J. Ehrhardt, A. Schmidt-Richberg, A. Heiß, and H. Handels. Estimation of motion fields by non-linear registration for local lung motion analysis in 4d ct image data. *International Journal of Computer Assisted Radiology and Surgery*, 5(6):595–605, 2010.

S. Wesarg, M. F. Khan, and E. Firle. Localizing Calcifications in Cardiac CT Data Sets Using a New Vessel Segmentation Approach. *Journal of Digital Imaging*, 19(3):249–257, 2006.

S. Wesarg, M. Kirschner, and M. Fawad Khan. 2D Histogram based volume visualization: combining intensity and size of anatomical structures. *International Journal of Computer Assisted Radiology and Surgery*, 5(6):655–666, 2010.

A. Westermark, S. Zachow, and B. L. Eppley. Three-dimensional osteotomy planning in maxillofacial surgery including soft tissue prediction. *The Journal of Craniofacial Surgery*, 16(1):100–104, 2005.

C. Westin, S. Maier, B. Khidhir, P. Everett, F. Jolesz, and R. Kikinis. Image Processing for Diffusion Tensor Magnetic Resonance Imaging. In *Proc. of Medical Image Computing and Computer-Assisted Intervention (MICCAI)*, volume 1679 of LNCS, pages 441–452. Springer Berlin/Heidelberg, 1999.

C. F. Westin, S. E. Maier, H. Mamata, A. Nabavi, F. A. Jolesz, and R. Kikinis. Processing and visualization for diffusion tensor MRI. *Medical image analysis*, 6(2):93–108, 2002.

L. Westover. Interactive Volume Rendering. In *Proc. of Chapel Hill Workshop on Volume Visualization*, pages 9–16, 1989.

W. De Wever, V. Vandecaveye, and S. Lanciotti J. A. Verschakelen. Multidetector CT-generated virtual bronchoscopy: an illustrated review of the potential clinical indications. *European Respiratory Journal*, 23(5):776–782, 2004.

A. Wiebel, F. M. Vos, D. Foerster, and H.-C. Hege. WYSIWYP: What You See Is What You Pick. *IEEE Transactions on Visualization and Computer Graphics*, 18(12):2236–2244, 2012.

J. I. Wiener, K. J. Schilling, C. Adami, and N. A. Obuchowski. Assessment of suspected breast cancer by MRI: A prospective clinical trial using a combined kinetic and morphologic analysis. *American Journal of Roentgenology*, 184(3):878–886, 2005.

G. Wiet, D. Stredney, and D. Wan. Training and simulation in otolaryngology. *Otolaryngol. Clin. North Am.*, 44(6): 1333–1350, 2011.

G. Wiet, D. Stredney, , T. Kerwin, B. Hittle, S. A. Fernandez, M. Abdel-Rasoul, and B. Welling. Virtual Temporal Bone Dissection System: Development and Testing. *Laryngoscope*, 122(Suppl. 1):S1–S12, 2012.

G. J. Wiet and J. Bryan. Virtual temporal bone dissection. In *Proc. of Medicine Meets Virtual Reality*, pages 378–384, 2000.

J. Wilhelms and A. van Gelder. Octrees for Faster Isosurface Generation. *ACM Transactions on Graphics*, 11(3):201–227, 1992.

A. Wimmer, G. Soza, and J. Hornegger. A generic probabilistic active shape model for organ segmentation. In *Proc. of Medical Image Computing and Computer-Assisted Intervention (MICCAI)*, pages 26–33, 2009.

O. Wink, W. J. Niessen, and M. A. Viergever. Fast delineation and visualization of vessels in 3-D angiographic images. *IEEE Transactions on Medical Imaging*, 19(4):337–346, 2000.

G. Winkenbach and D. Salesin. Computer-generated pen-and-ink illustration. In *Proc. of ACM SIGGRAPH*, pages 91–100, 1994.

G. Winkenbach and D. Salesin. Rendering parametric surfaces in pen and ink. In *Proc. of ACM SIGGRAPH*, pages 469–476, 1996.

J.D. Winter, K.S. St.Lawrence, and H. L. Cheng. Quantification of renal perfusion: comparison of arterial spin labeling and dynamic contrast-enhanced MRI. *Journal of Magnetic Resonance Imaging*, 34(3):608–615, 2011.

M. Wintermark, M. Sesay, and E. Barbier et al. Estimating Kinetic Parameters From Dynamic Contrast-Enhanced T1-Weighted MRI of a Diffusable Tracer: Standardized Quantities and Symbols. *Stroke*, 36(9):83–99, 2005.

R. Wirestam and F. Stahlberg. Wavelet-based noise reduction for improved deconvolution of time-series data in dynamic susceptibility-contrast MRI. *MAGMA*, 18(3):113–118, 2005.

T. Wischgoll, E. Moritz, and J. Meyer. Navigational Aspects of an Interactive 3D Exploration System for Cardiovascular Structures. In *Proc. of IASTED Int. Conference on Visualization, Imaging, and Image Processing*, pages 721–726, 2005.

T. Wischgoll, J. Meyer, B. Kaimovitz, Y. Lanir, and G. S. Kassab. A Novel Method for Visualization of Entire Coronary Arterial Tree. *Annals of Biomedical Engineering*, 35(5):694–710, 2007.

T. Wischgoll, J. S. Choy, and G. S. Kassab. Extraction of Morphometry and Branching Angles of Porcine Coronary Arterial Tree from CT-Images. *American Journal of Physiology - Heart & Circulatory Physiology*, 297(5):1949–1955, 2009a.

T. Wischgoll, D. R. Einstein, A. P. Kuprat, X. Jiao, and G. S. Kassab. *Computational Cardiovascular Mechanics - Modeling and Applications in Heart Failure*, chapter Vascular Geometry Reconstruction and Grid Generation, pages 103–119. Springer, 2009b.

A. Wismüller, A. Meyer-Baese, O. Lange, M. F. Reiser, and G. Leinsinger. Cluster analysis of dynamic cerebral contrast-enhanced perfusion MRI time-series. *IEEE Transactions on Medical Imaging*, 25(1):62–73, 2006.

C. Wittenbrink, T. Malzbender, and M. Goss. Opacity-weighted Color Interpolation for Volume Sampling. In *Proc. of IEEE/ACM Symposium on Volume Visualization*, pages 135–142, 1998.

A. Wolff, L. Knipping, M. van Kreveld, T. Strijk, K. Pankaj, and A. Agarwal. *Innovations in GIS VII: GeoComputation*, chapter Simple and Efficient Algorithm for High-Quality Line Labelling, pages 11–20. Taylor and Francis, 2000.

S. Wolfsberger and A. Neubauer. *Endoscopic Pituitary Surgery: Endocrine, Neuro-Ophthalmologic and Surgical Management*, chapter Virtual Endoscopy in Endoscopic Pituitary Surgery, pages 183–196. New York, NY: Thieme, 2011.

S. Wolfsberger, M. T. Forster, M. Donat M., A. Neubauer, K. Bühhler, R. Wegenkittl, T. Czech, J. A. Hainfellner, and E. Knosp. Virtual endoscopy is a useful device for training and preoperative planning of transsphenoidal endoscopic pituitary surgery. *Minimally Invasive Neurosurgery*, 47(4):214–220, 2004.

S. Wolfsberger, A. Neubauer, K. Bühhler, R. Wegenkittl, T. Czech, S. Gentzsch, H. G. Böhcher-Schwarz, and E. Knosp. Advanced virtual endoscopy for endoscopic transsphenoidal pituitary surgery. *Neurosurgery*, 59(5):1001–1009, 2006.

J. H. Won, G. D. Rubin, and S. Napel. Flattening the abdominal aortic tree for effective visualization. In *Proc. IEEE Eng. Med. Biol. Soc.*, pages 3345–3348, 2006.

J.-H. Won, Y. Jeon, J. Rosenberg, S. Yoon, G. D. Rubin, and S. Napel. Uncluttered Single-Image Visualization of Vascular Structures Using GPU and Integer Programming. *IEEE Transactions on Visualization and Computer Graphics*, 18(1):81–93, 2013.

P. C. Wong and R. D. Bergeron. 30 years of multidimensional multivariate visualization. In *Scientific Visualization*, pages 3–33. IEEE Computer Society, 1997.

C. Wood. Computer Aided Detection (CAD) for breast MRI. *Technology in Cancer Research & Treatment*, 4(1):49–53, 2005.

Z. J. Wood, H. Hoppe, M. Desbrun, and P. Schröder. Removing excess topology from isosurfaces. *ACM Transactions on Graphics*, 23(2):190–208, 2004.

B. J. Woods, B. D. Clymer, T. Kurc, J. T. Heverhagen, R. Stevens, A. Orsdemir, O. Bulan, and M. V. Knopp. Malignant-lesion segmentation using 4D co-occurrence texture analysis applied to dynamic contrast-enhanced magnetic resonance breast image data. *Journal of Magnetic Resonance Imaging*, 25(3):495–501, 2007.

R. B. Workman and R. E. Coleman. *PET/CT essentials for clinical practice*. Springer, 2006.

K. J. Worsley, J.-I. Chen, J. Lerch, and A. C. Evans. Comparing functional connectivity via thresholding correlations and singular value decomposition. *Philosophical Transactions of the Royal Society B: Biological Sciences*, 360(1457):913 –920, May 2005.

B. Wu, P.-L. Khong, and T. Chan. Automatic detection and classification of nasopharyngeal carcinoma on pet/ct with support vector machine. *International Journal of Computer Assisted Radiology and Surgery*, 7(4):635–646, 2012a.

J. Wu, M. Wei, Y. Li, X. Ma, F. Jia, and Q. Hu. Scale-adaptive surface modeling of vascular structures. *BioMedical Engineering OnLine*, 9, 2010.

M. T. Wu, H. B. Pan, A. A. Chiang, H. K. Hsu, H. C. Chang, N. J. Peng, P. H. Lai, H. L. Liang, and C. F. Yang. Prediction of postoperative lung function in patients with lung cancer: comparison of quantitative CT with perfusion scintigraphy. *American Journal of Roentgenology*, 178(3):667–672, 2002.

W. C. Wu, M. Y. Su, C. C. Chang, W. Y. Tseng, and K. L. Liu. Quantification of renal perfusion: comparison of arterial spin labeling and dynamic contrast-enhanced MRI. *Radiology*, 261(3):845–853, 2011a.

X. Wu, V. Luboz, K. Krissian, S. Cotin, and S. Dawson. Segmentation and reconstruction of vascular structures for 3d real-time simulation. *Medical Image Analysis*, 15(1):22–34, 2011b.

Y. Wu and H. Qu. Interactive Transfer Function Design Based on Editing Direct Volume Rendered Images. *IEEE Transactions on Visualization and Computer Graphics*, 13(5):1027–1040, 2007.

Y. Wu, L.-W. Tan, Y. Li, B.-J. Fang, B. Xie, T.-N. Wu et al. Creation of a female and male segmentation dataset based on Chinese Visible Human (CVH). *Computerized Medical Imaging and Graphics*, 36(4):336–342, 2012b.

Z. Wu and J. M. Sullivan. Multiple material marching cubes algorithm. *Int. J. Numer. Meth. Engng*, 58:189–207, 2003.

C. Wyman, S. Parker, P. Shirley, and C. Hansen. Interactive Display of Isosurfaces with Global Illumination. *IEEE Transactions on Visualization and Computer Graphics*, 12:186–196, 2006.

G. Wyvill, C. McPheeters, and B. Wyvill. Animating Soft Objects. *The Visual Computer*, 2(4):235–242, 1986.

X. Xie, Y. He, F. Tian, H.-S. Seah, X. Gu, and H. Qin. An Effective Illustrative Visualization Framework Based on Photic Extremum Lines (PELs). *IEEE Transactions on Visualization and Computer Graphics*, 13:1328–1335, 2007.

Y. Xie and Q. Ji. A new efficient ellipse detection method. In *International Conference on Pattern Recognition*, pages II: 957–960. IEEE, 2002.

Z. Xie and G. E. Farin. Image Registration Using Hierarchical B-Splines. *IEEE Transactions on Visualization and Computer Graphics*, 10(1):85–94, 2004.

G. Xiong and C. Taylor. Virtual Stent Grafting in Personalized Surgical Planning for Treatment of Aortic Aneurysms Using Image-Based Computational Fluid Dynamics. In *Proc. of Medical Image Computing and Computer-Assisted Intervention (MICCAI)*, volume 6363 of *LNCS*, pages 375–382, 2010.

K. Xu, Y. Xiong, Y. Wang, K. Tan, and G. Guo. A simple and stable feature-preserving smoothing method for contours-based reconstructed meshes. In *Proc. of Computer Graphics and Interactive Techniques in Australasia and Southeast Asia (GRAPHITE)*, pages 391–398, 2006.

R. Yagel, D. Stredney, G. J. Wiet, P. Schmalbrock, L. B. Rosenberg, D. Sessanna, and Y. Kurzion. Building a virtual environment for endoscopic sinus surgery simulation. *Computers & Graphics*, 20(6):813–823, 1996.

H. Yagou, A. G. Belyaev, and D. Weiz. Mesh Median Filter for Smoothing 3-D Polygonal Surfaces. In *Proc. of Symposium on Cyber Worlds (CW)*, pages 488–498, 2002a.

H. Yagou, Y. Ohtake, and A. G. Belyaev. Mesh Smoothing via Mean and Median Filtering Applied to Face Normals. In *Proc. of Geometric Modeling and Processing (GMP)*, pages 124–131, 2002b.

J. Yan and T. Zhuang. Applying improved fast marching method to endocardial boundary detection in echocardiographic images. *Pattern Recognition Letters*, 24(15):2777–2784, 2003.

X. Yang, L.-Y. Gai, P. Li, Y.-D. Chen, T. Li, and L. Yang. Diagnostic accuracy of dual-source CT angiography and coronary risk stratification. *Vascular Health and Risk Management*, 6:935–941, 2010.

T. Yasuda, Y. Hashimoto, S. Yokoi, and J. I. Toriwaki. Computer system for craniofacial surgery planning based on CT data. *IEEE Transactions on Medical Imaging*, 9(3):270–280, March 1990.

M. Yazdi and L. Beaulieu. Artifacts in Spiral X-ray CT Scanners: Problems and Solutions. *International Journal of Biological and Life Sciences*, 4(3):135–139, 2008.

P. J. Yim and D. J. Foran. Volumetry of hepatic metastases in computed tomography using the watershed and active contour algorithms. In *Proc. of the IEEE conference on Computer-based medical systems (CBMS)*, pages 329–335, 2003.

K. S. Yoo, G. Wang, J. T. Rubinstein, and M. W. Vannier. Semiautomatic segmentation of the cochlea using real-time volume rendering and regional adaptive snake modeling. *Journal of Digital Imaging*, 14(4):173–181, 2000.

T. S. Yoo. *Insight into Images Principles and Practice for Segmentation, Registration and Image Analysis*. AK Peters, 2004.

H. Yoshida and J. Näppi. Three-Dimensional Computer-Aided Diagnosis Scheme for Detection of Colonic Polyps. *IEEE Transactions on Medical Imaging*, 20(12):1261–1274, 2001.

H. Yoshida, Y. Masutani, P. Mac Eneaney, D. T. Rubin, and A. H. Dachman. Computerized Detection of Colonic Polyps at CT Colonography on the Basis of Volumetric Features: Pilot Study. *Radiology*, 222(2):327–336, 2002.

H. Young, R. Baum, U. Cremerius, K. Herholz, O. Hoekstra, A.A. Lammertsma, J. Pruim, and P. Price. Measurement of clinical and subclinical tumour response using [18F]-fluorodeoxyglucose and positron emission tomography: review and 1999 EORTC recommendations. *European Journal of Cancer*, 35(13):1773–1782, 1999.

I. R. Young. Significant Events in the Development of MRI (editorial). *Journal of Magnetic Resonance Imaging*, 19:523–526, 2003.

M. J. Young, M. S. Landy, and L. T. Maloney. A perturbation analysis of depth perception from combinations of texture and motion cues. *Vision Research*, 33(18):2685–2696, 1993.

H. Yu, C. Wang, C.-K. Shene, and J. H. Chen. Hierarchical Streamline Bundles. *IEEE Transactions on Visualization and Computer Graphics*, 18(8):1353–1367, 2012.

S. Zachow, E. Gladilin, H.-F. Zeilhofer, and R. Sader. Improved 3D Osteotomy Planning in Cranio-maxillofacial Surgery. In *Proc. of Medical Image Computing and Computer-Assisted Intervention (MICCAI)*, volume 2208 of LNCS, pages 473–481, 2001.

S. Zachow, E. Gladilin, R. Sader, and H.-F. Zeilhofer. Draw and Cut: Intuitive 3D osteotomy planning on polygonal bone models. In *Proc. of Computer Assisted Radiology and Surgery*, pages 362–369. Springer, 2003.

S. Zachow, H.-C. Hege, and P. Deuflhard. Computer assisted planning in cranio-maxillofacial surgery. *Journal of Computing and Information Technology*, 14(1):53–64, 2006.

S. Zachow, T. Hierl, and B. Erdmann. On the predictability of tissue changes for osteotomy planning in maxillofacial surgery: a comparison with postoperative results. In *Proc. of Computer Assisted Radiology and Surgery*, pages 648–653, 2004.

S. Zachow, P. Muigg, T. Hildebrandt, H. Doleisch, and H.-C. Hege. Visual Exploration of Nasal Airflow. *IEEE Transactions on Visualization and Computer Graphics*, 15(6):1407–1414, 2009.

C. Zahlten, H. Jürgens, C.J.G. Evertsz, R. Leppek, H.-O. Peitgen, and K.J. Klose. Portal vein reconstruction based on topology. *European Journal of Radiology*, 19(2):96–100, 1995.

W. Zbijewski and F. J. Beekman. Efficient Monte Carlo Based Scatter Artifact Reduction in Cone-Beam Micro-CT. *IEEE Transactions on Medical Imaging*, 25(7):817–827, 2006.

X. Zeng, L. Staib, R. Schultz, and J. Duncan. Survey: Interpolation methods in medical image processing. *IEEE Transactions on Medical Imaging*, 18(10):100–111, 1999.

C. Zhang and R. Crawfis. Volumetric Shadows Using Splatting. In *Proc. of IEEE Visualization*, pages 85–92, 2002.

C. Zhang and R. Crawfis. Shadows and Soft Shadows with Participating Media Using Splatting. *IEEE Transactions on Visualization and Computer Graphics*, 9(2):139–149, 2003.

C. Zhang, D. Xue, and R. Crawfis. Light Propagation for mixed Polygonal and Volumetric Data. In *Proc. of Computer Graphics International*, pages 249–256, 2005.

L. Zhang, Y. He, X. Xie, and W. Chen. Laplacian lines for real-time shape illustration. In *Proc. of the Symposium on Interactive 3D graphics and games*, pages 129–136, 2009.

L. Zhang, Y. He, and H.-S. Seah. Real-time computation of photic extremum lines (PELs). *Visual Computer*, 26(6-8):399–407, 2010a.

L. J. Zhang, S. Y. Wu, J. B. Niu, Z. L. Zhang, H. Z. Wang, Y. E. Zhao, X. Chai, C. S. Zhou, and G. M. Lu. Dual-energy CT angiography in the evaluation of intracranial aneurysms: image quality, radiation dose, and comparison with 3D rotational digital subtraction angiography. *American Journal of Roentgenology*, 194(1):23–30, 2010b.

S. Zhang and D. H. Laidlaw. DTI fiber clustering in the whole brain. In *Proc. of IEEE Visualization Poster Compendium*, 2004.

S. Zhang, C. Demiralp, and D. H. Laidlaw. Visualizing diffusion tensor MR images using streamtubes and streamsurfaces. *IEEE Transactions on Visualization and Computer Graphics*, 9(4):454–462, 2003.

S.-X. Zhang, P.-A. Heng, and Z.-J. Liu. Chinese visible human project. *Clinical Anatomy*, 19(3):204–215, 2006a.

Y Zhang. A survey of evaluation methods for image segmentation. *Pattern Recognition*, 29:1335–1346, 1996.

Y. Zhang, Y. Bazilevs, S. Goswami, C. L. Bajaj, and T. J. R. Hughes. Patient-specific vascular nurbs modeling for isogeometric analysis of blood flow. In *Proc. of International Meshing Roundtable (IMR)*, pages 73–92, 2006b.

L. Zhao, C. P. Botha, J. O. Bescos, R. Truyen, F. M. Vos, and F. H. Post. Lines of Curvature for Polyp Detection in Virtual Colonoscopy. *IEEE Transactions on Visualization and Computer Graphics*, 12(5):885–892, 2006.

L. Zheng, D. Maksimov, and T. Stutzmann. Reconstruction of Branching Blood Vessels from CT Data. In *Proc. of Computer Vision for Intravascular and Intracardiac Imaging*, pages 120–127, 2008.

J. Zhou, A. Döring, and K. D. Tönnies. Distance Based Enhancement for Focal Region Based Volume Rendering. In *Proc. of Workshop Bildverarbeitung für die Medizin*, pages 199–203, 2004.

J.-Y. Zhou, D. W. K. Wong, F. Ding, S. K. Venkatesh, Q. Tian, Y.-Y. Qi, W. Xiong, J. J. Liu, and W. K. Leow. Liver tumour segmentation using contrast-enhanced multi-detector CT data: performance benchmarking of three semiautomated methods. *European Radiology*, 20(10):1738–1748, 2010.

Y. Zhou and A. W. Toga. Efficient skeletonization of volumetric objects. *IEEE Transactions on Visualization and Computer Graphics*, 5(3):196–209, 1999.

L. Zhu, S. Haker, and A. Tannenbaum. Flattening maps for the visualization of multibranched vessels. *IEEE Transactions on Medical Imaging*, 24(2):191–198, 2005.

L. Zhukov and A. H. Barr. Oriented tensor reconstruction: tracing neural pathways from diffusion tensor MRI. In *Proc. of IEEE Visualization*, pages 387–394, 2002.

S. Zhukov, A. Iones, and G. Kronin. An ambient light illumination model. In *Proc. of the Eurographics Workshop on Rendering*, pages 45–55, 1998.

D. Zikic, S. Sourbron, X. Feng, H. J. Michaely, A. Khamene, and N. Navab. Automatic Alignment of Renal DCE-MRI Image Series for Improvement of Quantitative Tracer Kinetic Studies. In *Proc. of SPIE Medical Imaging*, 2008.

K. Zilles, E. Armstrong, A. Schleicher, and H.-J. Kretschmann. The human pattern of gyrification in the cerebral cortex. *Anatomy and Embryology*, 179(2):173–179, 1988.

M. Zirkle, D.W. Roberson, R. Leuwer, and A. Dubrowski. Using a virtual reality temporal bone simulator to assess otolaryngology trainees. *Laryngoscope*, 117(2):258–263, 2007.

B. Zitova and J. Flusser. Image Registration Methods: A Survey. *Image and Vision Computing*, 21:977–1000, 2003.

M. Zöckler, D. Stalling, and H.-C. Hege. Interactive visualiztion of 3D-vector fields using illuminated streamlines. In *Proc. of IEEE Visualization*, pages 107–113, 1996.

A. Zorcolo, E. Gobbetti, P. Pili, and M. Tuveri. Catheter insertion simulation with combined visual and haptic feedback. In *Proc. of First Phantom Users Research Symposium*, 1999.

R.A. Zoroofi, Y. Sato, T. Sasama, T. Nishii, N. Sugano, K. Yonenobu, H. Yoshikawa, T. Ochi, and S. Tamura. Automated segmentation of acetabulum and femoral head from 3-d CT images. *IEEE Transactions on Information Technology in Biomedicine*, 7(4):329–343, 2003.

E. V. Zudilova-Seinstra, P. J. H. de Koning, A. Suinesiaputra, B. W. van Schooten, R. J. van der Geest, J. H. C. Reiber, and P. M. A. Sloot. Evaluation of 2D and 3D glove input applied to medical image analysis. *Int. J. Hum.-Comput. Stud.*, 68(6):355–369, 2010.

S. Zwick, G. Brix, P. S. Tofts, R. Strecker, A. Kopp-Schneider, H. Laue, W. Semmler, and F. Kiessling. Simulation-based comparison of two approaches frequently used for dynamic contrast-enhanced MRI. *European Journal of Radiology*, 20:432–442, 2010.

Index

D

H

I

J

K

L

Q

R

S

W

X

Z